Hitler

BRENDAN SIMMS

Hitler

Only the World Was Enough

ALLEN LANE
an imprint of
PENGUIN BOOKS

ALLEN LANE

UK | USA | Canada | Ireland | Australia
India | New Zealand | South Africa

Allen Lane is part of the Penguin Random House group of companies
whose addresses can be found at global.penguinrandomhouse.com

First published 2019

001

Copyright © Brendan Simms, 2019

The moral right of the author has been asserted

Set in 10.2/13.5 pt Sabon LT Std
Typeset by Jouve (UK), Milton Keynes
Printed and bound in Great Britain by Clays Ltd, Elcograf S.p.A.

A CIP catalogue record for this book is available from the British Library

ISBN: 978-1-846-14247-5

For Katherine

'*In the end man takes his livelihood from the earth, and the earth is the trophy which destiny gives to those peoples who fight for it.*'
Adolf Hitler, 1943, quoted in Helmut Krausnick,
'Zu Hitler's Ostpolitik im Sommer 1943',
Vierteljahrshefte für Zeitgeschichte, 2 (1954), pp. 311–12

Contents

Abbreviations

In order to reduce the already very large number of references, documents from these collections, which are easily available, have been cited in shortened form.

ADAP   *Akten zur Deutschen Auswärtigen Politik 1918–1945. Aus dem Archiv des Auswärtigen Amtes.* Series C. (1933–7), Series D (1937–41) and Series E: (1941–5) (Göttingen, 1950–81)
BAK   Bundesarchiv Koblenz
BayHSTA   Bayerisches Hauptstaatsarchiv, Abt. IV, Kriegsarchiv
BT   Klaus Gerbet (ed.), *Generalfeldmarschall Fedor von Bock. Zwischen Pflicht und Verweigerung. Das Kriegstagebuch* (Munich and Berlin, 1995)
DVW   Hans-Adolf Jacobsen (ed.), *Dokumente zur Vorgeschichte des Westfeldzuges, 1939–1940* (Göttingen, Berlin and Frankfurt, 1956)
DW   Hans-Adolf Jacobsen (ed.), *Dokumente zum Westfeldzug, 1940* (Berlin, Göttingen and Frankfurt, 1960)
ES   Hildegard von Kotze and Helmut Krausnick (eds.), *'Es spricht der Führer'. 7 exemplarische Hitler-Reden* (Gütersloh, 1966)
ET   Hildegard von Kotze (ed.), *Heeresadjutant bei Hitler, 1938–1943. Aufzeichnungen des Majors Engel* (Stuttgart, 1974)
FE   Martin Moll (ed.), *Führer-Erlasse, 1939–1945* (Stuttgart, 1997)
FK   Willi A. Bölcke (ed.), *Deutschlands Rüstung im Zweiten Weltkrieg. Hitlers Konferenzen mit Albert Speer, 1942–1945* (Frankfurt, 1969)
GT   *Die Tagebücher von Joseph Goebbels im Auftrag des Instituts für Zeitgeschichte und mit Unterstützung des Staatlichen Archivdienstes Russlands,* ed. Elke Fröhlich, 24 vols. (Munich, 1993–2006)
HB   Wolf Rüdiger Hess (ed.), *Hess Briefe, 1908–1933* (Munich, 1987)
HP   Lothar Gruchmann and Reinhard Weber (eds.), *Der Hitler-Prozess 1924. Wortlaut der Hauptverhandlung vor dem Volksgericht München I,* 4 vols. (Munich, 1997–9)

HT   Hans-Adolf Jacobsen (ed.), *Franz Halder. Kriegstagebuch. Tägliche Aufzeichnungen des Chefs des Generalstabes des Heeres 1939–1942*, 3 vols. (Stuttgart, 1962–4)

HW   Walther Hubatsch (ed.), *Hitlers Weisungen für die Kriegsführung, 1939–1945* (Frankfurt, 1962)

IMT   *Der Prozess gegen die Hauptskriegverbrechen vor dem Internationalen Militärgerichtshof* (Nuremberg, 1949)

KB   Martin Vogt (ed.), *Herbst 1941 im Führerhauptquartier. Berichte Werner Koeppens an seinen Minister Alfred Rosenberg* (Koblenz, 2002)

KP   Willi A. Boelcke (ed.), *Kriegspropaganda 1939–1941. Geheime Ministerkonferenzen im Reichspropagandaministerium* (Stuttgart, 1966)

KTB, OKW   Helmuth Greiner and Percy Ernst Schramm (eds.), *Kriegstagebuch des Oberkommandos der Wehrmacht*, 4 vols. (in 7 parts) (Frankfurt, 1961–5).

LB   Helmut Heiber (eds.), *Hitlers Lagebesprechungen. Die Protokollfragmente seiner militärischen Konferenzen, 1942–1945* (Stuttgart, 1962)

LOC   Library of Congress

LV   Gerhard Wagner (ed.), *Lagevorträge des Oberbefehlshabers der Kriegsmarine vor Hitler 1939–1945* (Munich, 1972)

MK   Christian Hartmann, Thomas Vordermayer, Othmar Plöckinger and Roman Töppel (eds.), *Hitler. Mein Kampf. Eine kritische Edition* (Munich and Berlin, 2016).

RH   Friedrich Hartmannsgruber (ed.), *Regierung Hitler. Akten der Reichskanzlei*, 7 vols. (Berlin and Munich, 1983–2015)

RSA   Institut für Zeitgeschichte (ed.), *Adolf Hitler, Reden, Schriften und Anordnungen. Februar 1925 bis Januar 1933*, 17 vols. (Munich, 1992–2003)

RT   Jürgen Matthäus and Frank Bajohr (eds.), *Alfred Rosenberg. Die Tagebücher von 1934 bis 1944* (Frankfurt, 2015)

SA   Eberhard Jäckel with Axel Kuhn (eds.), *Adolf Hitler. Sämtliche Aufzeichnungen, 1905–1924* (Stuttgart, 1980)

SD   Andreas Hillgruber (ed.), *Staatsmänner und Diplomaten bei Hitler. Vertrauliche Aufzeichnungen über Unterredungen mit Vertretern des Auslandes 1939–1941*, 2 vols. (Frankfurt, 1967–70)

WA   Henry Ashby Turner (ed.), *Otto Wagener. Hitler aus nächster Nähe. Aufzeichnungen eines Vertrauten 1929–1932* (Frankfurt, 1978)

Acknowledgements

My greatest debt is to my wife, Anita Bunyan, for all her support over more than thirty years and for help on this project. I also thank Christopher Andrew, Mark Austin, Maximilian Becker, Ilya Berkovich, Tim Blanning, James Boyd, Christopher Clark, Norman Domeier, Alan Donahue, Andreas Fahrmeir, Bill Foster, Eric Frazier, Allegra Fryxell, Bernhard Fulda, Claire Gantet, Manfred Görtemaker, Christian Goeschel, Bobby Grampp, Tom Grant, Neil Gregor, Henning Grunwald, Christian Hartmann, Daniel Hedinger, Winfried Heinemann, Lukas Helfinger, Dorothy Hochstetter, Luisa Hulsroj, Nora Kalinskij, Gerhard Keiper, Jennifer Jenkins, Klaus Lankheit, Charlotte Lee, Clara Maier, Heinrich Meier, Mary-Ann Middlekoop, David Motadel, Marlene Mueller-Rytlewski, William Mulligan, Fred Nielsen, Mikael Nilsson, Jeremy Noakes, Wolfram Pyta, Phillips O'Brien, Darren O'Byrne, William O'Reilly, James Carleton Paget, Nathalie Price, Helen Roche, Gabriel Rolfes, Ulrich Schlie, Klaus Schmider, K. D. Schmidt, Klaus Schwabe, Constance Simms, Daniel Simms, Maja Spanu, Alan Steinweis, Benedict Stuchtey, Hans Ulrich Thamer, Liz Wake, Thomas Weber, Steffen Werther, Jo Whaley, Samuel Garrett Zeitlin and Rainer Zitelmann. I dedicate this book to my youngest daughter, Katherine.

Prologue

By July 1918, the First World War had raged for nearly four years. Private First Class Adolf Hitler of the 16th Bavarian Reserve Infantry Regiment had served in it almost from the very beginning. He had seen the German Reich defy the mighty coalition consisting of the Entente empires Britain, France and Russia as well as a number of smaller powers. Towards the end of the previous year, one of them – the Tsarist Empire – had been brought to its knees by a combination of military defeat and revolution. In the meantime, however, the Reich had provoked the antagonism of another and even more formidable power: the United States.

Germany was now in a race to smash France and drive Britain back across the Channel before American troops could arrive in force. At first, her efforts were crowned with success. German armies surged forward along the western front. Adolf Hitler marched with them, only to witness the moment at which the tide began to turn during the Second Battle of the Marne.

Fresh, numerous and driven by an enthusiasm which compensated for their lack of experience, the Americans burst among the exhausted Bavarian reservists. They had a shattering effect on the morale of Hitler's comrades and left an enduring impression on the man himself. He encountered at least two of these new enemies directly. On 17 July 1918, the brigade adjutant, Fritz Wiedemann, wrote that 'Private First Class Hitler dropped off two American prisoners (taken by R[eserve Regiment] 16) at the headquarters of 12 Royal Bavarian Infantry Brigade.'[1]

Who these men were and what Hitler made of the incident at the time are not recorded. We do know, however, how he later interpreted what became a seminal moment in his life and thus in the history of the twentieth century.

Hitler was convinced that these 'doughboys' were the descendants of German emigrants, lost to the Fatherland for lack of 'living space' to feed them, who had returned as avengers in the ranks of an unstoppable enemy army. In subsequent speeches, he repeatedly came back to the moment 'in the mid-summer of 1918, when the first American soldiers appeared on the battlefields of France, well-grown men, men of our own blood, whom we had deported for centuries, who were now ready to grind the motherland itself into the mud'.[2]

This, then, is where it all began: the preoccupation with Germany's demographic weakness, for which *Lebensraum* in the east was ultimately to become the only remedy; the respect for and fear of the 'Anglo-Saxon' powers with their apparently infinite spatial, demographic, natural and economic resources; and the determination to avoid another racial civil war between Anglo-Saxon and Teuton – incited by 'world Jewry' – if possible or to survive it should a renewed contest prove unavoidable.

Introduction

Just over twenty years ago, a German reviewer counted more than 120,000 books and articles on Hitler and the Third Reich,[1] a figure which has increased substantially since. The best of the biographies have reflected their times and scholarly trends. Alan Bullock's pioneering *Hitler: A Study in Tyranny*, written just nine years after 1945 and at the height of the Cold War, saw him as an exemplar of the 'Age of Unenlightened Despotism', but also as an 'opportunist entirely without principle'.[2] Intentionally or not, this interpretation chimed with the wider intellectual context of totalitarianism theory, and the more local propensity of his colleague A. J. P. Taylor to privilege happenstance and contingency over deeper patterns of explanation. Two decades later, Joachim Fest wrote a celebrated biography which was more literary than scholarly, but admired by many professional historians. It was the first large-scale imaginative attempt to explain how a man like Hitler could gain and keep power in an economically advanced and culturally sophisticated country such as Germany.[3] This was a milestone in the history of the Federal Republic, and the culmination of thirty years of research and soul-searching. Fest's biography was thus as much a book about Germans as it was about Hitler.

It took another twenty years for the next 'classic' biography to appear. The two volumes by Ian Kershaw, which remain the standard work, reflected the considerable quantity of research done on the Nazi dictatorship over the previous decades, especially the 'turn' towards social history, and the long debate between 'intentionalists', who drew a more or less straight line from pragmatic statements in the 1920s to the end of Hitler's career, and 'structuralists', who emphasized institutional rivalries and dynamics.[4] Fest had been criticized for abstracting Hitler too much from his surroundings.[5] Kershaw's Hitler, by contrast, was highly contextualized. He undertook to 'focus not upon the personality of Hitler', but on the 'character of his power', which required him to 'look in the first instance to others, not to Hitler himself'.[6] Kershaw's biography also took account of the 'voluntarist' turn, by which historians increasingly stressed the active collaboration of the population in Nazi initiatives. The enduring power of institutions and groupings was recognized, and individual agency was restored to historical actors, both great and small.[7] The 'myth' surrounding the Führer was shown to be as much constructed by others as his own confection.[8]

Kershaw's Hitler did not control everything, because he did not need to: the principal players 'worked towards the Führer' on their own initiative.[9] His power rested not so much on his own demonic energy, as on the cooperation of the German elites and the population at large. Hitler was cut down to size, though he still remained highly visible.

Since then, there have been further biographies and specialist studies.[10] Volker Ullrich particularly emphasizes Hitler's personality.[11] Shortly afterwards, Peter Longerich has crowned a long engagement with the history of the Third Reich with his own interpretation, which took into account many of the detailed studies that have appeared since the appearance of Kershaw's two volumes.[12] He showed Hitler to be much more than a mere 'catalyser' of pre-existing forces in German society and a much more dominant figure than the 'structuralist' view had allowed. At around the same time, Wolfram Pyta's book, though not strictly speaking a biography, showed how the 'cultural' turn in historical studies could provide new insights into Hitler's self-fashioning as a 'genius' and the 'performative' nature of his rule.[13] Most recently, Hans-Ulrich Thamer's short biography has reminded us once again of the importance of violence and seduction in Hitler's relationship with the German people.[14]

There are many respects in which the author's own offering cannot compete with this field. It can obviously never be the first major work on its subject, nor will it be the last word. It does not aspire to the literary flair of Joachim Fest, the scale and depth of Ian Kershaw, Peter Longerich's profound understanding of the Nazi domestic system, the theoretical sophistication of Wolfram Pyta, or the psychological penetration of Volker Ullrich. Nor does this biography try to reinvent the wheel. It takes account of but does not attempt to synthesize the vast recent specialized research on the Third Reich more generally.[15] It cannot explain the profound connection that Hitler had with the German people.[16] Instead, this is a book not about the Hitler they voted for, but the Hitler they got. It is not about what he 'achieved', but about what he intended. Finally, Hitler's personality and private life remain elusive throughout, though facets of them – some unexpected – will emerge. That said, while the author cannot provide the 'whole' Hitler himself, he hopes to show that our picture of him has hitherto been seriously incomplete.

This biography makes three big and interrelated new claims. First, that Hitler's principal preoccupation throughout his career was Anglo-America and global capitalism, rather than the Soviet Union and Bolshevism. Secondly, that Hitler's view of the German *Volk* – even when purged of Jews and other 'undesirables' – was highly ambivalent, reflecting a sense of inferiority by comparison with the 'Anglo-Saxons'. Thirdly, that we have – for very understandable reasons – focused too much on Hitler's murderous 'negative eugenics' against the Jews and other 'undesirables' and not enough on what he regarded as his 'positive eugenics', which were designed to 'elevate' the German people to the level of their British and American rivals.[17] All this means that we have missed the extent to which Hitler was locked in a worldwide struggle not just with 'world Jewry' but with the 'Anglo-Saxons'. The author's ambition here is not merely 'additive', the provision of a new dimension to an existing framework. Rather, he wishes his work to be understood as 'substitutive'. If the claims therein are sustainable, then Hitler's biography, and perhaps the history of the Third Reich more generally, need to be fundamentally rethought.

This biography therefore breaks with much of the prevailing view, or views, on Hitler. He did not place the German people on a racial pedestal, but was consumed throughout by fear of their enduring fragility. Hitler did not believe that the United States had been crippled by the Wall Street Crash, and it remained a central factor in his thinking from the early 1920s onwards. The book also rebuts the tenacious belief that the principal driver of Hitler's world view, and source of his virulent anti-Semitism, was fear of the Soviet Union or Bolshevism. It consequently does not accept the centrality, for him, of the eastern front in the Second World War. The book does not see a meaningful 'conceptual pluralism' in any area of Nazi domestic or foreign policy which really mattered to Hitler. Hitler was not a prisoner of any force in German society, of competing power centres. If German government was often in a state of 'polycratic chaos', this was certainly not the result of any conscious attempt on the dictator's part to 'divide and rule'. That said, none of the works cited are totally without either value or error, and this book inevitably concurs with scholars of the Third Reich on some issues and parts company on others. This is reflected in the notes, where the literature is generally cited when in explicit agreement, while errors are usually corrected only by implication.

The author, in fact, draws heavily on the work of others. He has been inspired by some recent general historiographical trends. First, the 'transnational' turn has provided a new framework for German history, in which events there are understood as part of broader European and even global processes.[18] The subfield of *Histoire Croisée* offered a particularly valuable stimulus for understanding the enduring German–American entanglement which shaped so much of Hitler's thinking and career.[19] Secondly, 'globalization': the Hitler of this biography was, for all his specificity, a product of global forces.[20] He fits well into recent work on world capitalism.[21] Thirdly, the 'environmental turn' enables us to see Hitler as primarily a Malthusian, a politician of scarcity.[22] Fourthly, recent studies of global governance, especially the Anglo-American cartel which emerged in the early twentieth century, sharpened the author's perception of Hitler's revolt against this order.[23]

Fifthly, historical studies of migration and race, especially those on Anglo-American settler colonialism, and research into the international politics of race, in particular the stress on the 'Anglo-Saxon hegemons', have provided a context for thinking about Hitler's world view.[24] In this sense, Germany can be seen, and was seen by contemporary Germans – including Hitler – as both colonizing and colonized; it was not clear to which side of the 'global colour line' it really belonged. The Reich was the 'replenisher', not the 'replenished',[25] the 'fertilizer' – to use Hitler's own phrase – not the fertilized. Conversely, as Aimé Césaire pointed out back in the mid-1950s, Hitler's imperial project in Europe inverted the traditional racial order by reducing many white men to an inferior status usually reserved for people of colour.[26] Sixthly, the 'spatial turn' in the historical literature helps us to understand how Germany, having transitioned from the traditional *Reich* into a nation, was now reconceived once again as an empire on a global scale.[27] Finally, the 'temporal turn' in historical studies prompted the author to pay particular attention to time, timing and – especially – timelines in Hitler's thinking.[28] The expansion and contraction of time in his mind will emerge as a crucial variable.

More specifically, it will be clear from the text that the author is greatly indebted to the many works on Nazi Germany that have appeared over the past twenty years.[29] Mark Mazower has provided a framework for understanding the Third Reich as a European empire in Europe.[30] Tim Snyder has stressed the 'environmental' dimension to Hitler's thinking. Adam Tooze has shown the extent to which the United States needs to be understood as the principal reference point for the Third Reich from the start, but especially after the wartime battle for production commenced.[31] The American dimension to twentieth-century German history more generally has been well described by Mary Nolan, Philipp Gassert, and Stefan Kühl.[32] Johann Chapoutot has reminded us of the enduring importance of ideas in the Nazi project,[33] and Lars Lüdicke has recalled to mind the astonishing consistency of thought on key issues over twenty-five years.[34]

This biography has also benefited from the numerous new studies on particular periods or aspects of Hitler's life. Dirk Bavendamm put Hitler's youth under the microscope; Brigitte Hamann re-examined Hitler's time in Vienna, showing that there was no evidence for any anti-Semitic sentiment on his part during those years.[35] Instead, as Anton Joachimsthaler demonstrated, Hitler's 'path' really began in Munich.[36] Thomas Weber has illuminated Hitler's experiences during the First World War. Othmar

Plöckinger and Thomas Weber took a much closer look at Hitler's crucial years in Munich immediately after the war. Plöckinger also wrote a detailed analysis of the gestation and legacy of *Mein Kampf*.[37] Despina Stratigakos examined Hitler's domestic architectural preferences and activities, a hitherto neglected subject.[38] Anna Maria Sigmund was the first to examine the complicated *ménage à trois* between Hitler, his niece Geli Raubal and his chauffeur Emil Maurice.[39] Heike Görtemaker wrote the first satisfactory account of his relationship with Eva Braun.[40] Timothy Ryback provided an insight into Hitler's reading habits, while Bill Niven examined his cinematic preferences.[41] Fritz Redlich subjected Hitler to serious psychiatric analysis,[42] Johannes Hürter examined Hitler's relationship wth his senior military commanders,[43] and Stephen Fritz has made a strong case that Hitler was no military amateur.[44]

There have also been several important studies on Hitler's role in the Third Reich. Christian Goeschel has traced the evolution of his 'fascist alliance' with Mussolini.[45] Kurt Bauer showed that he was centrally involved in the failed Austrian coup of 1934.[46] Andreas Krämer's study of the May crisis of 1938 and its aftermath showed a dictator reacting to outside events, but completely in control of the German national security apparatus.[47] Angela Hermann's study of the Munich crisis and its consequences showed that the 'conceptual pluralism' in Nazi foreign policy only existed at the level below the dictator himself.[48] Rolf-Dieter Müller has persuasively argued that Hitler's plan in 1938–9 was to attack the Soviet Union, and that he was only deflected by the Polish refusal to cooperate.[49] The centrality of the American dimension in 1940–41 has been emphasized in Ian Kershaw's study of Hitler's fateful decisions.[50] Edward Westermann and Carroll Kakel have compared Hitler's war in Russia with the conquest of the American West.[51] The volumes of *Das Deutsche Reich und der Zweite Weltkrieg*, in effect the official German history of the war, have shown Hitler's centrality to the course of the conflict.[52] Finally, Hitler's central role in the murder of six million Jews has been proven beyond all doubt by Richard Evans, Peter Longerich and others involved in the rebuttal of David Irving's claims to the contrary.[53] Magnus Brechtken and Maximilian Becker of the Institute for Contemporary History in Munich are currently preparing a scholarly edition of Hitler's speeches as chancellor.[54]

The arguments made in this book are based on plentiful, if uneven, source materials. Many of these are well known, others have been surprisingly neglected and some are, to the best of the author's knowledge, completely new. The principal source for the first thirty years or so of Hitler's life is the complete edition of his correspondence, writings and remarks (some of them reported at second hand) until 1924; the known forgeries therein have been discounted.[55] This collection is reasonably full for the years from 1919, but sketchy before then; for example, we have no records whatsoever for a full year between August 1908 and August 1909.[56] From the mid-1920s onwards, this biography relies mainly on the critical editions of *Mein Kampf*,[57] the Second Book and the voluminous edition of his speeches and writings between 1925 and 1933.[58]

As one would expect, there is an exponential increase in the number of records for the period after Hitler took power in 1933. An important source for the Third Reich itself is the pioneering collection by Max Domarus, which mostly consists of speeches; it is incomplete and the editorial standards leave a lot to be desired.[59] There is also a much smaller, but rather better edition of seven of the most important Hitler speeches by Hildegard von Kotze and Helmut Krausnick.[60] The documents of Hitler's cabinets give us a valuable insight into his practice of government, and the Documents on German Foreign Policy also contain many statements by him.[61] For the war years, we have Martin Moll's edition of Hitler's 'decrees', Walther Hubatsch's collection of Hitler's 'Directives', Willi Boelcke's edition of his conferences with Albert Speer on war production, and the *Lagebesprechungen*, the surviving protocols of Hitler's military briefings.[62] These serial sources are supplemented by memoirs, diaries, the recent extremely valuable 'Itinerary' compiled by Harald Sandner and other printed sources.[63] While most of the material cited in this book has been in the public domain for some time, the importance of some of it has not been recognized, with a number of key statements lying hiding in plain sight for decades.

As with all historical sources, those for Hitler, particularly the diaries and memoirs, must be treated with caution. Joseph Goebbels, for example, intended most of his diaries for publication and the biographer must beware of his aggrandisements from beyond the grave.[64] Albert Speer, for his part, not merely engaged in blatant distortion and apologetics, but also tended to exaggerate his special bond with Hitler.[65] Some apparently contemporaneous sources, such as Otto Wagener's *Aufzeichnungen* and Gerhard Engel's diary, were in fact written up many years after the events they describe, but cross-checking shows them to be almost without exception a reliable guide.[66] We also need to be careful with the records of Hitler's wartime 'Table Talk', which, though generally accurate on his sentiments, contains some demonstrable distortions and should not be taken as a verbatim record of what he actually said.[67] None of his supposed utterances there have been cited as direct speech. With suitable caveats, all these records have been used where appropriate.

By contrast, this biography has discounted a number of 'classic' sources altogether. With regard to Hitler's early life, which has been distorted by *Mein Kampf* and subsequent 'memories' of his contemporaries, the author has taken the rather drastic step of relying only on material generated at the time. This ruled out, for example, the memoirs of his childhood friend Kubizek.[68] No reliance was placed on anything said or quoted by Werner Maser.[69] Sources like the 'Breiting conversations' and the recollections of Hermann Rauschning, which have long been treated with suspicion but still crop up in some reputable accounts, were not used.[70] Finally, with considerable reluctance, the author has entirely disregarded Hitler's alleged 'Testament' from early 1945. The sentiments therein clearly chime with those of Hitler, and indeed with the argument of this book, but a recent forensic examination shows its provenance to be too dubious to place any reliance on its content.[71]

The new sources used for this biography fall into two categories. Some simply gloss or elaborate well-known aspects of Hitler's career. Others, however, support the central arguments of the book. The Bavarian Kriegsarchiv yielded new material on Hitler's First World War experience, including his seminal encounter with American soldiers and the struggle of his regiment with their new adversaries more generally. Other Munich depositories confirmed the depth of Hitler's concern about Bavarian separatism. The records of the Foreign Office contained valuable material on returning German emigrants and the plan to 'exchange' them for departing German Jews. So far as the author is aware, none of these particular documents have been used by other biographers of Hitler, and it is unlikely that they were aware of them.

In order to marshal all this material into a coherent argument, the author has adopted a 'funnel' approach. At the outset, where the sources are sparse, he has sought to be as all-encompassing as possible. As the book progresses, as the main lines of interpretation become clearer, and the source material more copious, the focus narrows. This also reflects the fact that Hitler was remarkably open about his thinking in his early years and became progressively more cautious. In general, the author has attempted to show rather than tell. This involves extensive exegesis and direct quotation from Hitler himself. Unlike some works, therefore, this biography is 'context-light' and 'Hitler-centric'.[72] We will not lose him from sight for more than a paragraph or two at a time. This is not to suggest, of course, that Hitler was an entirely *sui generis* thinker – it is well known that he drew extensively on others – merely that we shall be focusing on what he believed, rather than where he got it from. Following Richard Evans's injunction, we will privilege 'analysis, argument and interpretation' over 'the language of the court prosecutor and the sermonizing moralist'.[73] No attempt has been made to contradict Hitler systematically, as to do so would have burst the bounds of the book and resulted in a very different work. Unless they have reason to believe otherwise, readers – to borrow a phrase – would be well advised to regard everything he said as a lie, including the 'and' and the 'the'. One way or the other, the 'truth content' of Hitler's writings and speeches is of less importance to this biography than their meaning and intention. Here, the author has tried throughout to get into Hitler's mind, without letting him get into his.

The three central contentions of the book are supported by a number of sub-arguments. Many of these will be familiar even to the lay reader, and most will be well known to specialists in the field. Others may have been briefly noted before, but their true significance has been missed. There are also some very central strands in the argument which are – to the author's best knowledge – completely new. If Hitler's preoccupation with Britain is no secret, and the extent of his engagement with the United States has been a staple of more recent studies, previous historians have not recognized his demographic obsession with German emigration and its centrality to his world view. While the connection between Hitler's anti-Semitism and his anti-capitalism is often noted, and has been the subject of some individual studies, its centrality to his world view, and the extent to which he was fighting a war against 'international high finance' and 'plutocracy' from start to finish, has not been understood at all. The extent of Hitler's anxiety about the racial coherence of the German people, which he attributed to centuries of political and cultural fragmentation, has not been well understood either. For this reason, the salience of the Bavarian separatist threat, the challenge of European integration, the spectre of a Habsburg restoration and the 'black' (clerical) menace at various points in Hitler's career require considerable amplification.

The argument will unfold in six parts. The first deals with Hitler's early life until the end of the world war, during which he showed increasing signs of political consciousness after a very slow start, but no sign at all of any political vocation or leadership potential. The war plunged Hitler into a traumatic encounter with the might of Anglo-America, whose military, economic, financial and demographic strength crushed the Reich and smashed his universe. In 1919–22, the first contours of his world view become visible: the fear of Anglo-America, the associated hostility to global capitalism and international Jewry and anxiety that internal weaknesses such as socialism, Bolshevism, mass emigration and especially Bavarian separatism were rendering the Reich helpless in the face of external enemies. During this period, Hitler seems to have been operating on the assumption that the regeneration of Germany would require many years, perhaps generations. In Part II, which covers the years 1923–7, we see how time initially speeded up for Hitler in order both to pre-empt the danger of an apparently separatist putsch and to take advantage of an apparently favourable domestic and international constellation. After the failure of his own coup, Hitler reverted to a much longer timeline and began to conceive his *Lebensraum* concept as the answer to Germany's racial degeneration, especially the haemorrhage of so many healthy emigrants to America. This was perforce a long-term project, so that time slowed down again for Hitler.

In Part III, which deals with the period 1928–32, we see Hitler elaborate a modernizing project designed to strengthen the Reich against the American challenge, especially the loss of the 'best' elements of German society through emigration to the New World, and to provide an alternative to the widely popular idea of European integration. Taking advantage of the economic distress caused by the Depression, he also devised a strategy for the seizure of power rather sooner than he had previously expected. Part IV, which covers the years 1933–6, examines Hitler's social, economic and racial transformation project, which was designed to eliminate 'negative' elements in German society, such as Jews and the disabled, and to facilitate the development of more 'positive' racial strands. If the 'racial' clock was, by its very nature, set to a much longer timeline, Hitler's diplomatic and military policies followed a much more immediate agenda. There was no plan for world domination on his part, merely a determination to secure for Germany the territorial enlargement he believed necessary to survive in a world of global powers.

In Part V, dealing with the period 1937–40, time speeded up once more as Hitler reacted to the hostility of Anglo-America. We will see how the Führer, who did not originally set out to achieve global domination, or even to occupy so much of mainland Europe, was driven by the logic of war and expansion into broadening the conflict ever more. Finally, in Part VI, which covers the years 1941–5, Hitler's career reached its culmination in the confrontation with Roosevelt's America, with the resulting scramble for *Lebensraum* and the destruction of European Jewry. As the 'Anglo-Saxon' powers coalesced against him, Hitler became convinced that only a truly global policy would be enough to secure the Reich against its enemies. German armies now stood on two continents and menaced a third. Hitler also had plans to strike the western hemisphere, at least from the air. For a brief moment it seemed as if the whole world was in his grasp, but the trophy remained beyond his reach, and soon after the inevitable descent began, culminating in the Reich's second and even more destructive defeat at the hands, as Hitler saw it, of the 'Anglo-Saxons', the Jews and their allies.

PART ONE

Humiliation

The first three decades of Hitler's life were characterized by obscurity and deprivation of one sort or another. Not long after his birth in the far west of the Habsburg Empire into modest but not impoverished circumstances, Adolf Hitler's situation rapidly deteriorated. His father and mother both died, the latter after a traumatic illness, and he squandered his small inheritance. His artistic talents were not recognized in Vienna. Hitler stumbled, and suffered severe hardship, before rallying and moving to Munich, then the second city of the German Empire. There he just about got by. Beyond this explicit rejection of the Habsburg Empire, Hitler showed no overt signs of politicization before reaching the age of twenty-five. The war proved to be both a liberating and a dislocating experience. During the four years of his military service, Hitler was wounded, subjected to shattering bombardments, decorated, blinded and defeated, along with so many other Germans. He ended the conflict as he began it, as a rather lonely figure on the margins of German and world history.

I

Sketch of the Dictator as a Young Man

Adolf Hitler was born an Austrian by historical accident on 20 April 1889. His birthplace, Braunau am Inn, had been part of the Duchy of Bavaria for hundreds of years before being ceded to the Habsburg monarchy at the Treaty of Teschen which concluded the War of the Bavarian Succession in 1779. It changed hands several times during the tumults of the Revolutionary and Napoleonic Wars, returning to Austria for good in 1815. Culturally and ethnographically, the border along the River Inn between Germany and what became the Austro-Hungarian Empire marked a distinction without a difference, at least in Braunau and environs. The German dialect and traditional customs differed little on both sides of the river. Even though Hitler soon moved further east, residing in a number of other places, he remained within Upper Austria and thus the 'Central Bavarian' dialect area.[1] Hitler later frequently referred to himself as a Bavarian.[2]

Politically, however, the gulf was enormous. For about a thousand years, Braunauers had been part of the Holy Roman Empire, a political commonwealth which embraced most Germans until its collapse in 1806. Their German orientation was maintained through membership of the German Confederation after 1815. In 1866–71, however, the Prussian chief minister, Otto von Bismarck, extruded Austria and crushed France in order to enable the 'small German' unification of the Second Reich. The Habsburgs responded by looking south and east, and by seeking a compromise with the unruly Magyars. Thanks to the new status of the Hungarian crown, Braunauers were now 'Imperial and Royal' subjects of a multinational empire, rather than of an expressly German polity. The border with the German Empire ran only 300 metres away at Simbach on the other side of the Inn. The Hitlers must have seen it every day. His father Alois's sympathies are said to have been pan-German, coupled to a liberal or at least free-thinking outlook sceptical of the Roman Catholic Church;[3] there is no reliable evidence that Alois was either disloyal to the Habsburgs, anti-Semitic, drunken or violent towards his children.

Adolf was a younger child in a sprawling family.[4] He had an older half-brother, Alois Jnr, and half-sister, Angela, from his father's first marriage to Franziska Matzelsberger. After her death, Alois had married his cousin, Klara Pölzl, with whom he had six children, of whom only two survived, Adolf himself and his younger sister Paula. Two of Hitlers' four siblings died before he was born and one when Hitler was hardly ten years of age. Klara's sister Johanna, nicknamed 'Hanitante', was a major figure in their lives. Alois's work soon took the family from their home in the Salzburger Vorstadt street to nearby Hafeld, Lambach. He also worked for a while in the German border town of Passau. Alois eventually retired to Leonding,[5] where he collapsed and died over a morning glass of wine in a local hostelry on 3 January 1903.

The widowed Klara moved the family first to Linz and then Urfahr on the other side of the Danube. Hitler's education at the Staats Realschule Linz continued.[6] The school at Linz was known for its German nationalist and anti-Habsburg sympathies. After doing well in his first years at school, Adolf became an indifferent pupil, with frequent absences, securing high marks only in drawing and sport, and only a 'satisfactory' for effort.[7] Although Hitler joined various cultural organizations while in Linz and Urfahr, such as the Linzer Musealverein, the Oberösterreichischer Musikalverein and the Oberösterreichischer Volksbildungsverein,[8] there is no contemporary evidence for any political engagement. There is nothing to suggest, either, that Hitler knew his fellow pupil Ludwig Wittgenstein, later a famous philosopher. One way or the other, Hitler was a poor student, who was forced to repeat a year, before finally leaving school aged sixteen.

What effect this drumbeat of death and change had on the young Adolf is not known. His experiences were in no sense remarkable: such emotional and financial insecurities were common at the time, and perhaps to all times. It is true that both father and son (as it later turned out) formed attachments to their female cousins, but this was not unusual in rural areas, then and since. He seems to have enjoyed normal friendships, especially with his fellow Wagnerian August Kubizek, whom he first encountered at a performance and who shared his artistic interests. There was therefore nothing in Hitler's early childhood, about which very little is known for sure, to suggest what was to come later.

Hitler's main preoccupations after leaving school were his financial security, his emotional life, pursuing a career as an artist and the health of his mother. The first known letter by Hitler was penned in February 1906, together with his sister Paula, asking the Finanzdirektion Linz for payment of his orphan's pension.[9] He visited Vienna on a number of occasions and soon moved to the imperial capital. There he pursued an interest in the operas of Richard Wagner. In the summer of 1906, Hitler saw *Tristan and Isolde* as well as *The Flying Dutchman*. He also attended the Stadttheater. He was engrossed by not only the music but especially the architecture of opera. A postcard of the Court Opera House Vienna recorded that he was impressed by the 'majesty' of its exterior, but had reservations about an interior 'cluttered' with velvet and gold.[10]

In early 1907, Hitler's mother was diagnosed with cancer and operated on without success. She had no medical insurance, but bills were kept low by the kindness of her Jewish doctor, Eduard Bloch. Hitler helped to look after his mother during her illness and he seems to have been devastated by her death in late December 1907. He did, however, take time out to travel to Vienna during the treatment and even took a room there in the early autumn.[11] It is certain, in any case, that Hitler neither blamed Bloch for his mother's death nor became an anti-Semite in consequence. On the contrary, he remained in friendly contact with Bloch for some time after and even sent him a hand-painted card wishing him a happy new year.[12] Much later, Hitler enabled Bloch to escape from Austria on terms far more favourable than those granted to his unfortunate fellow Jews.

Hitler's artistic ambitions, meanwhile, suffered a severe setback. In early September 1907, he joined 111 other applicants to the Viennese Akademie für Bildende Künste. About a third were weeded out at the first stage, but Hitler was allowed to continue to the next round a month later. This time, however, he was less fortunate: his drawings were rated 'unsatisfactory', so that he was not among the twenty-eight candidates eventually admitted.[13] Hitler decided to move to Vienna permanently regardless in February 1908. He borrowed a large sum of money from his 'Hanitante' in the course of 1908 to finance himself, and for the rest got by with his orphan's pension.[14] A family friend, Magdalena Hanisch, tried to ease his path in the capital by enlisting the support of Alfred Roller, a highly influential professor at the Kunstgewerbeschule, whose stagings of Wagner operas were hugely admired by Hitler; he dubbed Roller the 'great master of stage illustration'. Her letter to her friend Johanna Motloch, who acted as the conduit, is the only contemporary description of Hitler that we possess. 'I would like to help this young man,' she wrote, 'he has nobody who can put in a good word for him or help him with advice and deed. He came alone to Vienna and had to go everywhere alone, without guidance to gain admission.'[15] All that was keeping Hitler in Linz, she added, was the question of his orphan's pension. Röller agreed to see Hitler, who in turn thanked Johanna Motloch profusely. No meeting, however, took place.

Hitler's first place of residence in Vienna was a room in the Stumper-gasse. His landlady, Maria Zakreys, was Czech and by Hitler's account spoke imperfect German. Hitler's interests at this time were primarily musical and architectural. In mid February 1908, he announced his inten-tion to buy a piano, and when two months later his friend Kubizek promised to bring a viola the young Adolf playfully threatened to buy two crowns' worth of cotton wool for his ears. By the middle of the summer, however, Hitler had lost some of his exuberance. He confessed to living the life of a 'hermit', persecuted by bed bugs, made worse by the fact that there was nobody to wake him up: Frau Zakreys was away. Nevertheless, Hitler developed an interest in city-planning, especially the layout and architecture of Linz.[16] A month later, Hitler's spirits had not lifted: he apologized to Kubizek for his long silence, adding that 'I couldn't think of anything to tell you.' He occupied himself by reading newspapers – there was reference to a subscription – and writing, apparently about city planning and architecture: 'I am now writing quite a lot, normally in the afternoons and evenings.'[17] Hitler's malaise may have been at least partly financial in origin. He certainly seems to have experienced a period of poverty, telling Kubizek subsequently that 'you don't have to bring me cheese and butter any more, but I thank you for the thought'. He was not too poor, however, to miss a performance of Wagner's *Lohengrin*.[18]

Shortly afterwards, Hitler left the Stumpergasse and was swallowed up by the city for more than a year. He lodged with Helene Riedl in the Fel-berstrasse until August 1909. His only known activity during this period was a second and equally unsuccessful application to the Academy. Hitler then lived for about a month as a tenant of Antonia Oberlerchner in the Sechshauserstrasse, leaving in mid September 1909. Even less is known about what came next. He certainly underwent some sort of economic and perhaps psychological crisis, leading to a descent from respectability. A few years later, well before he was famous, Hitler told the Linz authori-ties that the autumn of 1909 had been a 'bitter time' for him.[19] According to a statement he gave to the Viennese police in early August 1910, he spent time in a sanctuary for the homeless at Meidling. How Hitler extri-cated himself is not known, but he was able to pay for a bed at the more respectable men's hostel in the Meldemannstrasse in Vienna-Brigittenau from February 1910.[20] There he started to paint postcards and pictures which his crony and 'business' partner Reinhold Hanisch would sell to dealers; this relationship soured when he reported Hanisch to the authori-ties for allegedly embezzling some of the money.[21]

Hitler was now once more submerged by the city. We have extensive descriptions of what he did and thought during this time from his pen and from some of his contemporaries, but all of these accounts stem from after the time when Hitler became a public figure and was actively seeking to shape his own biographical narrative, especially in *Mein Kampf*. All we know for sure is that Hitler had to mark time in the Austro-Hungarian Empire until he was twenty-four so as to keep collecting his orphan's pension. It did not help that he fell out with his half-sister Angela Raubal over their inheritance, and was forced to give way after a court appearance in Vienna in early March 1911.[22] It is possible that Hitler heard Karl May, the best-selling author of western novels, in late March 1912.[23] In the spring of 1913, Hitler collected the last instalment of his pension. There was now nothing to keep him in Vienna.

When Hitler went to Munich in May 1913 his worldly possessions filled a small suitcase. His known mental baggage was even smaller.[24] It consisted mainly of negatives. He showed no sign of any anti-Semitism in his dealings with Eduard Bloch in Linz, quite the contrary. Later, Hitler had friendly business dealings with at least two Jews to whom he hawked his paintings in Vienna: the Moravian Jew Siegfried Löffner, who was questioned by police in connection with the alleged Hanisch fraud, and the Hungarian Jew Samuel Morgenstern, who kept a careful record of these purchases.[25] Nor do we have any contemporary evidence that Hitler reacted badly to the multinational character of the Austro-Hungarian capital. He lived happily for nearly a year under the roof of a Czech spinster, Maria Zakreys, and betrayed no irritation at her limited command of German. His documented interests were architecture, town planning and music, particularly the connections between them. There was surely much more going on inside his head, but we cannot be certain what it was.

Hitler's self-description varied, but the common denominator was creativity. He registered himself as an 'artist' in the Stumpergasse in mid February 1908, as a 'student' in the Felberstrasse in mid November 1908, as a 'writer' in the Sechshauserstrasse in late August 1909, and as a 'painter' at the Meldemannstrasse in early February 1910 and again in late June 1910.[26] At this time, the constant changes of address cannot have been primarily designed to evade military service, as he always registered his arrivals and departures. They are in any case entirely typical for someone of Hitler's background and interests. Drifting in and out of solvency, leaving a mark only where they tangled with the law or registered with the city authorities was the fate of millions in pre-1914 Europe.

When Hitler arrived in Munich in late May 1913, he engaged in his first documented political act. He and his new companion Rudolf Häusler took a room with the tailor Josef Popp in the Schleissheimerstrasse. He registered himself as 'stateless', which is a clear statement of hostility towards his native Austria-Hungary. It may also have been intended to throw the imperial authorities off the scent as they tried to call him up for the military service for which Hitler had been liable, like the rest of his cohort in the empire, since turning twenty years of age in April 1909. By August 1913, the Magistracy at Linz was indeed looking for him on suspicion of desertion, and were told in October by Hitler's relatives that he had moved to Vienna. He had given the bureaucracy there no forwarding address, but enquiries at the hostel in Brigittenau soon established that he had moved to Munich. It took the Austro-Hungarian authorities until January 1914 to track him down to the Schleissheimerstrasse in Munich.[27] Soon after, Hitler was ordered to appear before the Magistracy in Linz. This provoked a long apologia from him, pleading poverty, claiming that he had already reported for duty in Vienna in February 1910. He was eventually mustered in Salzburg by the Austrian authorities, in early February 1914, and found to be physically unfit to serve.[28] In the meantime, Hitler continued to make his living by selling pictures, just as he had in Vienna.[29]

All this makes our picture of the young Hitler closer to a sketch than a full portrait. To be sure, he was already more than a mere cipher: his artistic interests were already well established; his hostility to the Habsburg Empire, though not the reasons for it, was a matter of record. There was no sign whatever, though, of the ideas and ambitions to come.[30] How could it have been otherwise? What Hitler experienced in Linz and Vienna may well have shaped his later views on domestic politics, on race and on culture. But he had not yet seen anything, and – so far as we know – not taken in much of what was going on outside of the Habsburg Empire and its German ally. There is no surviving contemporary evidence that he was much aware either of France or the Russian Empire or the Anglo-World of the British Empire and the United States. That was about to change. If the Hitler of 1914 had as yet left almost no mark on the world, the world was about to make its mark on him.

2

Against a 'World of Enemies'

Hitler appears to have responded to the outbreak of the First World War with enthusiasm. A contemporary photograph – taken before they had met by his later associate and propagandist Heinrich Hoffmann – seems to show Hitler among the cheering crowd on the Odeonsplatz in Munich on 2 August 1914.[1] He volunteered to fight in the Bavarian army,[2] and was recruited two weeks later into the 16th Bavarian Reserve Infantry Regiment, known as the List Regiment after the name of its commander. This unit was not a 'volunteer' regiment as such, but consisted of a cross-section of mainly south Bavarian society, some of whom had volunteered, such as Hitler, others of whom were conscripted. It spent the next few weeks training, mainly in Munich itself, but also at Lechfeld camp south of Augsburg. He was taught to use the standard-issue rifle, before being sent to support the German advance through Belgium and northern France.[3]

Hitler did not, in other words, react to the outbreak of war by disappearing. Instead, he immediately volunteered for the German (technically, the Bavarian) army, an unusual choice. In August 1914, therefore, Hitler definitively turned his back not just on Austria-Hungary, but opted decisively *for* Germany. It was his first major documented political statement.

The main enemy, Hitler now believed, lay across the Channel. His very first surviving letter after he joined up, to his former landlady Anna Popp in Munich, announces his hope that he 'would get to England', presumably as part of an invading force.[4] Strikingly, Hitler did not target the Tsarist Empire to the east, even though it was at this point menacing East Prussia; throughout the war, indeed, he made only a single (surviving) reference to the eastern front.[5] Nor did he single out the French hereditary enemy. In focusing on Britain, Hitler may have been echoing the contemporary discourse of 'England Hatred' in Germany generally, and his unit in particular,[6] or he may even have been ahead of it. A week later, when the List Regiment had arrived in Lille, northern France, they were assembled in the Place de Concert to hear an 'Order by the Bavarian Crown

Prince against the Englishman'. 'We have now the fortune,' they heard, 'to have the Englishmen on our front, the troops of that people whose antagonism has been at work for so many years in order to surround us with a ring of enemies and strangle us.'[7] One way or the other, Hitler's expressed desire to get to grips with the British – long before he reached the front and at a time when the British Expeditionary Force only represented a small fraction of the allied troops facing Germany in the west – represents his second major political statement, and one which points to the future development of his world view, based in large part on respect for and fear of British power.

Not long after, the List Regiment duly encountered the British at Gheluvelt, and then at Wytschaete and Messines in Belgian Flanders.[8] The story of the BEF in 1914 is traditionally seen as an unequal struggle with the German juggernaut. This is true enough in the broad sense, but it is important to remember that at the tactical level the picture was much more differentiated. The List Regiment's clash with men from the Yorkshire Regiment, the legendary Coldstream Guards, Black Watch, Grenadier Guards and Gordon Highlanders was a battle between amateurs and professionals. Some of the Listers, among them Hitler himself, had had no military background at all prior to the war. With the exception of some of the officers, none were regulars. The BEF, by contrast, were experienced soldiers, many of whom had seen action before, and most of them were better and quicker shots than their German adversaries. Gheluvelt was thus a profoundly unequal battle.

In the circumstances, the List Regiment acquitted itself well, but it suffered horrendous casualties. Hitler himself participated in several frontal attacks, three if his own account is to be believed. He spoke of 'heaviest battles' in the ranks, but said that eventually 'the English [*sic*] were beaten'. The 'defeat' inflicted on the British proved to be shortlived, however, as the Bavarians were ejected from Gheluvelt soon after by the Worcesters. Hitler was promoted *Gefreiter* – private first class – and assigned as an orderly – dispatch runner – to the regimental staff. Since then, he claimed, 'I can say that I risked my life daily and looked death in the eye', probably not an exaggeration for this period of his military service. On 2 December, Hitler was rewarded for his service with the Iron Cross Second Class. 'It was,' he wrote, 'the happiest day of my life.' He asked his landlord to keep the newspaper recording his decoration as a memento 'if the Lord our God lets me live'.[9]

At the end of a lengthy letter describing his experiences at the front, Hitler reflected in early February 1915 on the domestic and strategic situation of Germany.[10] He lamented the loss of life in a struggle against an 'international world of enemies', and expressed the hope not only that 'Germany's external enemy' would be crushed but also that her 'inner internationalism' would disintegrate. It is possible that the latter phrase was inspired by anti-Semitism, or it may have been a swipe against the transnational loyalties of German Catholics and Social Democrats. Hitler also prophesied that 'Austria will suffer the fate I have always predicted', by which he presumably meant its ultimate collapse.[11] His surviving letters tell us virtually nothing about the eastern front, and nothing at all about how he reacted to the sinking of the *Lusitania*, the allied propaganda campaign and many other important aspects of the war.

Hitler served out the rest of the conflict as a regimental dispatch runner, rather than in the front line, strictly speaking. It was still a pretty hazardous posting. For example, Hitler's next letter, in mid February 1915, described the impact of a shell on his position, from which he was 'rescued as by a miracle', but conceded that he was being 'made nervous by the constant artillery fire'. He also welcomed the fact that Germany was 'at last mobilizing opinion against England', further evidence of his preoccupation with Britain.[12] Eight days later, Hitler wrote of another 'terrible cannonade', and further battles with the British. Indeed, the List Regiment was forced on the defensive as more and more British troops arrived on the western front. Hitler's next major battle, in March 1915 at Neuve Chapelle, was preceded by even more massive British artillery bombardments. This was followed by the first encounter with imperial troops, men from the Indian army. A month later, at Fromelles and Aubers Ridge, Hitler faced more units from the Empire, especially Canadians. In time, the variety of exotic headgear in the enemy trenches – including 'turbans [and] peaky-pointed hats'[13] – gave the men of the List Regiment a depressing sense of the world arrayed in arms against them.

This impression was reinforced the following year. After a long quiet spell in regimental headquarters at Fournes – during which he seemed to spend a lot of time painting, sketching and reading – Hitler was back in action at Fromelles in French Flanders in May–June 1916. This time, the List Regiment was confronted with Australians and New Zealanders, many of them hardened veterans of Gallipoli. The Bavarians were once again discouraged to find themselves grappling with men who had travelled from the far side of the world to fight them in Flanders. Worse still, as Hitler's comrade Adolf Meyer recalled, some of the Australians were of German descent. One of his captives 'not only spoke excellent German, but bore my own name of Meyer into the bargain. Understandably: His father was a German, who had immigrated to Australia as a child with his parents and had later married an English woman there.'[14] What Hitler himself made at the time of his regiment's encounters with British imperial troops is not recorded.

Not long after, the List Regiment was sucked into the later stages of the Battle of the Somme, during which many German soldiers developed a healthy respect for British fighting qualities.[15] Hitler was lucky enough not to be right in the front line, exposed to machine-gun and small arms fire, but he was well within the range of enemy guns.[16] His dugout was soon hit by a British artillery round, injuring him in the left upper thigh. The wound was not life-threatening, but sufficiently serious for him to be evacuated. Hitler was sent to the army hospital in Beelitz, south-west of Berlin, to recuperate. Here he would have been confronted for the first time with the debilitating results of the allied blockade, which was the subject of an impassioned discourse in Germany. This alleged a British desire to 'exterminate' Germans, condemned the blockade's devastating effect on children and thus on the racial health of the nation, and stressed the need to preserve 'the next generation'.[17] Again, there is no surviving evidence of what Hitler made of these developments as they unfolded.

Subsequently, he was detailed to the Replacement Battalion of the List Regiment in Munich. There he fretted about his inability to rejoin his unit. 'A transport left a few days ago for the regiment,' he wrote to his fellow dispatch runner Balthasar Brandmayer in late December 1916, '[but] unfortunately I can't join it. They are only taking old babblers.'[18] In January 1917, Hitler wrote to the adjutant of the List Regiment, Fritz Wiedemann, that 'I am combat ready once again' and expressed his 'urgent wish . . . to return to [his] old regiment and old comrades'.[19] Max Unold, who served with him in the Replacement Battalion headquarters in the Luisenschule in Munich in early 1917, later confirmed that Hitler 'reported back [for duty] in the field'.[20] Unold was unusual company for Hitler, in that he was an expressionist painter and a founder of the *Münchener Neue Secession* in 1913.

In March 1917, Hitler was back with his unit in regimental headquarters. Shortly after, the Listers witnessed, though they were not directly involved in, the stupendous Canadian assault on Vimy Ridge. Before long, however, they were faced by ferocious British attacks during the Battle of Arras. Then, in the late summer of 1917, the List Regiment was back around Gheluvelt at the Third Battle of Ypres, during which it was brutally hammered by British artillery for more than a week. A combination of high explosive, shrapnel and gas caused fearful casualties. Hitler was directly caught up in the fighting, as the regimental headquarters was in the line of the British advance on the Ypres salient.[21] What he made of these experiences at the time is not known, as no contemporary records survive. When the shattered

List Regiment was finally pulled out of the line, it was dispatched to near Mulhouse in Alsace to recuperate. It was there that, after nearly three years of primarily battling British, Indian, Canadian, Australian and New Zealand troops, Hitler first faced a mainly French foe.

In the meantime, the United States had entered the war on the Allied side in early April 1917, albeit as an 'associated' rather than an Entente power. The move was seen by many on both sides of the Atlantic as an act of Anglo-Saxon solidarity with Britain directed against the 'Teutons'.[22] Millions of Americans, many of them foreign-born, prepared to cross the Atlantic.[23] A very substantial number of them were of German descent. The German-American community, which was already under pressure after the sinking of the *Lusitania*, was now plunged into crisis. In what was in many ways a dry-run for the later 'red scare', it was comprehensively 'othered' by American propaganda and civil society. Part of the animus underlying the campaign for the prohibition of alcohol was anti-German. In order to escape the stigma of being 'hyphenated Americans', many people of German descent embraced the hegemonic 'Anglo-Saxon' culture.[24] Once again, there is no surviving contemporary evidence of how Hitler reacted to these events, though he would have a lot to say about them later.

After its relatively uneventful posting in Alsace, the List Regiment was deployed in support of the great German spring offensive of 1918.[25] Moving up behind the assault troops, they encountered French colonial troops, Algerian Zouaves, in late March.[26] Then, in mid July 1918, the List Regiment ran into their first Americans at the Second Battle of the Marne, near Rheims. They were forced to beat a hasty retreat,[27] but not before taking some prisoners. Two of them were dropped off by Hitler at Brigade Headquarters.[28] The men of List Regiment were certainly under no doubt about the qualities of the Americans, and indeed Germany's other adversaries. A report of the II Battalion on the Second Battle of the Marne written a month later noted that 'The enemy (French, British, American) showed themselves tough in defence, [and] brave in attack.'[29] Colin Ross, who would later advise Hitler on the United States, and who was then serving on the western front, remembers not only the courage of the American soldiers, but also their frequent calling out to each other in German and the large number of German-speaking prisoners.[30]

By now, the Allied blockade, control of the skies and numerical superiority were beginning irreversibly to wear down Hitler's regiment. '[The] health and morale of the men,' the commander of the Third Battalion RIR 16 wrote that same month, 'suffers from the continuing lack of provisions'; similar sentiments were recorded in the other battalions. The war diary of the Second Battalion lamented the 'pressure from the far superior enemy

who constantly deploys new troops (English)'.[31] All this was of a piece with
the general picture along the line, which was of the offensive running out
of steam in the face of a crushing allied superiority in men, material and
sheer energy. General Ludendorff famously spoke of these times as the
'black day[s] of the German army'. Again, we do not know what Hitler
made of these developments at the time. The only established fact is that
he was once again decorated in early August 1918, this time with the Iron
Cross First Class. It was awarded on the recommendation of his Jewish
commanding officer, Lieutenant Hugo Gutmann from Nuremberg, even if
he was not the man who actually pinned the decoration on Hitler's chest.[32]

At this moment, the height of the Allied counter-offensive, Hitler was
sent for a week's training to Nuremberg in signalling, followed by a fortnight's leave in Berlin. While he was away, the Allies advanced relentlessly.[33]
The Listers faced a variety of enemies, sometimes the French but more
usually the British. As in many German formations, morale plummeted
under the weight of heavy Allied artillery bombardment and air attack. One
report bewailed that 'enemy aircraft completely control the skies'. Another
noted with alarm that 'The desire for rest increases among the officers and
men after each engagement. Only at least 4 weeks of quiet in good quarters
with proper nourishment could revitalize the physically and morally
exhausted ['used up'] fighters. The unit is currently at best suited for static
warfare on a quiet sector of the front.' By the end of the month, there was
no holding the British. 'Everybody has bolted,' one company commander
lamented, 'we are hanging in the air.'[34] He could not even send back men
to fetch ammunition, for fear they would not return. The rising flood of
Americans arriving at the front in the course of September 1918 aggravated
the widespread sense of depression.[35]

By early October 1918, the gloom in the unit had deepened still further.
Fridolin Solleder, an officer with the List Regiment, remembered an 'unequal struggle'. 'One man always fights against three or four. For how
long?' He lamented that 'since October 1918 more than one and a half
million fresh and aggressive Americans are in action on the other side of
the lines. Africa, Australia, India and Canada still send their youthful
cohorts to Europe.' 'Munitions, material, opinions [sic] and masses of men
face the German frontline soldier. The size of his struggle becomes hopeless.'[36] The prevailing sense of being at war with the whole world, of being
outnumbered, outgunned and 'out-opinioned', could not have been more
clearly expressed. After more than four years of war, the List Regiment,
like most of the German army, had had enough.

The returning Hitler was pitched into this crisis. In mid October, he
was injured in a gas attack by a British shell. Hitler was first treated in the

nearby Bavarian field casualty station at Oudenarde, site of the Duke of Marlborough's famous victory over the French more than two hundred years earlier. A week later, he was sent to convalesce in the Prussian Reserve Hospital at Pasewalk north-east of Berlin. There Hitler heard of the conclusion of the Armistice, and the German surrender, on 11 November 1918. It seems to have induced some sort of hysterical seizure. Most of the German army kept fighting to the last, and only stopped when ordered to do so,[37] but of the fact that it had been morally and militarily beaten in open battle there could be no doubt.

Thus ended Hitler's slightly more than four years of war. His record was in some senses unusual. After an intense spell in the front line at the beginning, he spent the rest of the conflict at Regimental Headquarters, some distance behind. This was unquestionably a safer posting than that of an ordinary infantryman or even of a battalion or company runner.[38] It was certainly more comfortable, giving him some time for reading and drawing; so far as we know, he mainly consulted books on architectural rather than political subjects.[39] Some Listers later claimed to regard him with suspicion on that account, and it is likely that Hitler's chances of being decorated were higher than average due to the fact that he was a familiar face among the officers making and deciding upon the recommendations.[40] It may be that Hitler refused promotion in order to remain with the regimental staff. There is no doubt, in any case, that Hitler exaggerated and embellished his account of the war, and was careful to conceal the fact that he was not actually in the front line for most of the war.[41]

That said, Hitler's record is less distinctive than it might seem. It was not uncommon for private soldiers to refuse commissions in order to remain with their friends. Moreover, though Hitler by all accounts completed his missions efficiently, he showed none of the initiative expected of a potential officer. It is also worth stressing that Hitler saw combat, death and destruction on numerous occasions. He was injured twice, not in accidents but by enemy fire. The regimental HQ was thus not really a 'rear area' in any meaningful sense. In short, there can be no doubt – even if later embellishments are stripped away – that Hitler was a courageous and effective,[42] if somewhat limited, soldier during his first war.

The impact of the war on Hitler's personality is unclear. For example, there is no evidence of any homosexual preferences,[43] or indeed of sexual activity of any kind. Nor did he seem to form any very close personal connections to his comrades similar to the homo-social bonds with, say, Goebbels and Speer in later life, though in both cases we should remember that the evidence comes largely from the two attention-seekers themselves, rather than from Hitler. He was the marginal figure in the surviving group photographs, making a somewhat semi-detached impression.[44] That said, the surviving letters and postcards do not suggest anything other than normal comradely relations with a range of fellow soldiers, such as congratulations on decorations and complaints about food. One way or the other, what is striking – and has often been remarked on – is that during the four years of Germany's greatest peril, the subsequent Führer showed no sign whatever of any leadership qualities.

As we shall see, the impact of the war on Hitler's world view over the long term was considerable.[45] That said, his claim that the news of the Armistice in November 1918 prompted him to 'become a politician' there and then needs to be taken with a large pinch of salt; there is no contemporary evidence for it. His political formation was not open, however. His hostility to the Habsburg Empire and allegiance to Germany were by now well established. He was conscious of the importance of propaganda, and the need to 'mobilize opinion' against the British. He saw the war as a struggle against not merely the external enemy, but also the 'inner' internationalism of German society, by which he might have meant socialist (the most probable target), clericalist, particularist or capitalist tendencies or a combination of all four. Above all, Hitler had come away from the war with a keen sense of the power of the Entente, especially the British, in his eyes the most formidable of the 'world of enemies' against which he had battled in vain those four years. France, the country in which he had been stationed for so long, had made much less of an impression.[46] Due to his injury, Hitler had missed the final collapse in late October and early November, but he witnessed the series of catastrophes from early August to the middle of October 1918, so he cannot have been in any doubt that the German army had ultimately succumbed to a massively superior enemy.

The main contours of his political thinking were not yet visible, however. There was as yet no engagement with the major forces of the age: Anglo-American capitalist democracy and Soviet Bolshevism. Most importantly, despite his later assertions in *Mein Kampf* and elsewhere, there was no sign whatever of anti-Semitism. There were nearly sixty identifiable Jews in his regiment, a higher number than their proportion of the population would have warranted, and some of them, such as Georg Dehn, were decorated.[47] There is no contemporary evidence of any clashes between these men and Hitler. More to the point, his subsequent ('relatively') benevolent treatment of Bloch and the Jews he had served with in the war – including Gutmann himself, once he was aware of the situation – suggests a lack of personal animus against them.[48] Indeed, his erstwhile superior officer, Major Fritz Wiedemann, who later became Hitler's adjutant, wrote shortly after the start of the Second World War that he had 'with agreement of the Führer helped some Jewish frontline fighters of the Bavarian Infantry Regiment 16 and enabled their emigration'.[49] In short, by the end of the war, Hitler had the 'world of enemies' firmly in his sights. The struggle against the Jews, in their capitalist or communist guises, had not yet begun, however, and nor had he explicitly targeted the United States.

3

The 'Colonization' of Germany

The immediate post-war years were a period of national disgrace for Germany. Its monarchy banished, shorn of large tracts of territory by the Versailles settlement and saddled with a huge reparations bill, the Reich was plunged into profound economic, political and psychological dislocation. Foreign soldiers, some of them men of colour, occupied substantial parts of the country. Germany had fought the world and lost; now many felt she was a colony of the global system. The very biological substance of the German people seemed to be at stake, as they grappled with the continuing blockade and then the prospect of long-term immiseration. Hitler experienced these travails both personally and politically. His own situation was even more marginal than most. He found his way through the turbulent aftermath of war with difficulty. Hitler was also even more exercised than most Germans about the state of the Reich. He looked for answers, and he soon found them. Hitler identified the root cause of Germany's humiliation as the power of Anglo-American and Jewish international capitalism, which used various instruments, in particular revolutionary communism, to keep the Reich in subjection. With the help of others, but essentially under his own steam, Hitler began to develop an ideology to make sense of the world around him. By the end of this period, Hitler had undertaken a comprehensive diagnosis of the Reich's ills, though he had yet to suggest a cure. Given the depths to which Germany had fallen, Hitler expected that national revival would take generations.

Shortly after the war ended, Hitler was discharged from hospital. He returned to the Bavarian capital, not as a matter of individual choice, but because he was ordered to do so. He would in any case have had to return to the city for the formal disbandment of his unit. Unlike most German soldiers, Hitler did not seek early demobilization.[1] Instead, he was assigned to the Replacement Battalion of the Second Bavarian Infantry Regiment in Munich. Hitler later referred to his *six* years in uniform,[2] rather than *four* years at war, suggesting that he regarded his continued struggle after November 1918 as part of his military service. Like many of those still in uniform, and many in civilian life, Hitler was still psychologically on a war footing. This was unsurprising given the continuing Allied blockade and the possibility of a return to war should the peace terms prove too onerous.[3] Significantly, he did not join either a paramilitary *Freikorps* or one of the border-guard formations battling Germany's neighbours to the east, the usual havens for those of a robustly 'national' disposition.[4] Hitler made no attempt to resist the short-lived radical left-wing Council government of Kurt Eisner in April–May 1919, and may even have been sympathetic to it.[5]

Three formative events then supervened. First, Hitler was selected by his officers to serve in the section of the army devoted to propaganda and 'enlightenment' under the direction of Captain Karl Mayr.[6] This indicates an understanding on their part of his aptitude for such work. He spent part of the summer of 1919 taking a Reichswehr training course for his new posting, which included a spell auditing a series of lectures at the University of Munich.[7] This 'education' involved warnings about the perils of Bolshevism, lamentations about Germany's fall from great power status, which was partly blamed on the machinations of the Jews, but also classes by Gottfried Feder on the need to break 'debt serfdom', and attacks on finance capitalism. Others lectured on the economic strangulation of Germany by the west.[8] The historian Karl Alexander von Müller spoke on the overwhelming power of Anglo-America, and the dangers of 'Anglo-Saxon world domination'.[9] That said, Hitler was not simply the passive recipient of a Reichswehr message, if only because the lecturers often contradicted each other.[10] As we shall see, his emerging ideology differed from it in important respects, notably in the even greater emphasis on anti-capitalism and his distinctive foreign policy views.

Secondly, Hitler was elected by the enlisted men as a *Vertrauensmann* – a soldier's representative (literally 'person of confidence' or 'trusted person') – a post created by the High Command to improve communications and relations with the rank and file.[11] This shows that he must already have commanded the support of a substantial body of his peers.

The third development was the news of the final humiliating terms of the Treaty of Versailles in late June 1919; their general outlines had been known since early May.[12] One of Hitler's former comrades later recalled seeing him study the treaty as soon as it became public.[13] The details were crucial for until that point the dire territorial and financial consequences of the war were not yet apparent. Moreover, even after the terms became known, many believed them so onerous that the Reich government would resume the war rather than submit to them.[14] It was on this basis, as an act of war, rather than out of pique, that the commander of the fleet interned at Scapa Flow in the Orkneys decided to scuttle his fleet rather than let it be used to coerce Germany. The National Assembly only accepted the treaty after a furious debate in July 1919. Massive public order problems followed in many German cities, including Munich.

On 20 August 1919, Hitler made his first contribution to a discussion in his Reichswehr unit; three days later, he delivered a whole speech on 'Peace Terms and Reconstruction'. This is the first known major political statement by Hitler. The text, unfortunately, has not survived, although its likely gist can be derived from remarks made not long after; for this, see more below. A day later, Hitler is recorded as speaking on the issue of 'Emigration'.[15] Two days later, a Reichswehr report describes him as having given 'a very good, clear and spirited lecture . . . on capitalism, during which he touched, indeed he had to touch, on the Jewish question'.[16] This was Hitler's first recorded reference to the Jews, and it was made very clearly in the context of capitalism,[17] rather than Bolshevism or the German Revolution. That this was no coincidence is shown by the now-famous letter he wrote to Adolf Gemlich three weeks later, on 16 September 1919.

The 'Gemlich letter', which is the first surviving longer political text by Hitler,[18] defined the Jewish 'problem' partly as a medical issue. Hitler dubbed the Jews the 'racial tuberculosis of the peoples'. Partly, the 'problem' was defined in political terms, with the Jews cast as the 'driving forces of the revolution', which had laid Germany low. Here he was referring not to the events of 1917 in Petrograd, but to the workers' and soldiers' councils of 1918 in Germany. But Hitler's primary emphasis was another aspect of the 'problem' entirely. His initial anti-Semitism was profoundly anti-capitalistic, rather than anti-communist in origin.[19] He spoke of the 'dance around the golden calf', the privileging of 'money', the 'majesty of money', the 'power of money' and so on. Hitler emphasized the transnational affinity between German Jews and those of Poland and the United States. The Jew, he claimed, did not describe himself as a Jewish German, Jewish Pole or Jewish American but 'always as a German, Polish or American Jew'. As yet, two years after the Russian Revolution, he seems to have nothing to say about communism, Bolshevism and the Soviet Union.[20] Hitler, in other words, became an enemy of the Jews before he avowedly became an enemy of Russian Bolshevism.

None of this is particularly surprising. Anti-Semitism in general, and anti-capitalist anti-Semitism in particular, had been a staple of German politics and political thought since the later nineteenth century.[21] It had an established presence in German right-wing parties and organizations such as the Deutsch-Nationale Volkspartei (DNVP), the Thule Society and the Pan-German League. Some groups, such as the Kampfbund gegen Zinsknechtschaft (League for the Breaking of Debt-slavery) and the Völkische Gewerkschaften (People's Trade Unions), were specifically directed against 'Jewish' capitalism.[22] More to the point, hostility to international capitalism, the force to which Germany's defeat was attributed, dominated the message which Hitler was subjected to by the Reichswehr indoctrinators. One way or the other, in Germany, and perhaps in Europe more generally, anti-Semitism and anti- (international) capitalism have historically been joined at the hip. With Hitler there is little point in talking about the one without the other.

Between his opening lectures to the *Aufklärungskommando* and his letter to Gemlich, Hitler had also made his first intervention in a quasi-public debate at the Sterneckerbräu in Munich. On 12 September 1919 he was sent to observe a meeting of the fringe 'German Workers' Party' (DAP). When one of the audience, Professor Adalbert Baumann, argued in favour of the Bavarian-led separation of southern Germany from the Reich,[23] Hitler attacked him vigorously and effectively drove his antagonist out of the room. The chairman of the Munich chapter of the DAP, Anton Drexler, subsequently remarked with admiration, 'Goodness, he's got a gob. We could use him.'[24] The encounter was significant in two ways. Firstly, it led to the entry of Hitler into the party towards the end of the month, possibly at Mayr's behest,[25] but more likely his own independent decision.[26] He quickly became one of its most important speakers, though at the beginning he was overshadowed by Dietrich Eckart and Gottfried Feder. Secondly, the exchange with Baumann was the first in what would become an increasingly bitter confrontation between Hitler and Bavarian separatists and particularists outraged at the reduced rights accorded by the Weimar Constitution to what had been the constituent states of Imperial Germany.[27]

From mid November 1919, Hitler mounted a series of full-scale attacks in public speeches on the main enemy – 'absolute enemies England and America'. It was Britain which had been determined to prevent Germany's rise to world power, in order not to jeopardize their 'world monopoly'. 'That was also the reason,' Hitler claimed, 'to make war on us. And now America. As a money country it had to intervene in the war in order not to lose the money they had lent.'[28] Here he explicitly made the link between his anti-capitalist critique and the hostile behaviour of the western coalition. This was closely connected to Hitler's anti-Semitism. 'The Americans put business above all else. Money is money even if it is soaked in blood. The wallet is the holiest thing for the Jew,' he claimed, adding: 'America would have struck with or without U-Boats.'[29] What is remarkable here is that the terms 'the Americans' and 'the Jews' were used almost interchangeably.

If Hitler's profound hostility to the Anglo-Saxon powers was shaped by his anti-Semitism, it was also distinct and, crucially, anterior to it. He had, after all, spent almost the entire war fighting the 'English', and latterly the United States. Hitler became an enemy of the British – and also of the Americans – before he became an enemy of the Jews.[30] Indeed, he became an enemy of the Jews largely *because* of his hostility to the Anglo-American capitalist powers. Hitler could not have been clearer: 'We struggle against the Jew,' he announced at a public meeting in early January 1920, 'because he prevents the struggle against capitalism.'[31]

The rest of Germany's adversaries, by contrast, fell into a second and milder category. The Russians and the French, so the argument ran, had become hostile 'as a result of their unfortunate situation or some other circumstances'.[32] Hitler was by no means blind to the extent of French antagonism, but it is striking that he discoursed at much greater length about the financial terms of the treaty, and the blockade, than the territorial losses to Germany's immediate neighbours. This focus on Anglo-American, and increasingly on US, strength, with or without anti-Semitism, was by no means unusual in Germany, or even Europe generally. It reflected a much broader post-war preoccupation with the immense global power of the United States.[33] As we shall see, Hitler's entire thinking, and the policies of the Third Reich after 1933, were in essence a reaction to it.

Hitler put the inquest into the defeat at the heart of his world view. The alleged fractures in German society played an important role here, the 'inner internationalism' to which he had referred during the war itself. By this Hitler primarily meant the Social Democrats and Independent Socialists (USPD), who allegedly put loyalty to their class comrades over that to the nation; it was their internationalism, not their socialism, that he objected to. It was the same anxiety as over capitalism, which Hitler rejected in its global, but, as we shall see, not necessarily in its local 'national' form. He also took aim at German particularism, especially in Bavaria, which threatened the integrity of the Reich. The principal internal enemy, however, was the Jews, who had 'stabbed Germany in the back', although Hitler rarely used this precise phrase.[34] All this has given the impression that Hitler, like so many other Germans, sought to blame the defeat primarily on internal scapegoats rather than facing up to the strength of the Entente. In fact, Hitler never subscribed to a monocausal domestic explanation for the disaster and much of his thinking, especially the later quest for *Lebensraum*, would be inexplicable if he had. Eliminating the

Jews and healing the domestic rifts inside Germany were necessary conditions for the revival of the Reich, but not sufficient ones.

Hitler was well aware of the industrial strength of the British Empire and the United States, but in his view the struggle against the Anglo-Americans during the First World War was not decided solely by material factors. His vision of international politics was essentially human-centred. On Hitler's reading, the late nineteenth and early twentieth centuries had been an epic demographic contest which the German Empire had spectacularly lost. She had failed to provide an outlet for her excess population either through economic or through territorial expansion, with the result that millions of Germans had emigrated. Meanwhile, her enemies built up huge empires which they could parlay into strength on the European battlefield. Hitler lamented 'that the Entente sent alien auxiliary peoples to bleed to death on European battlefields'.[35] He had personal experience of this, having confronted (British) Indian troops in 1915 and (French) Algerian Zouaves in 1918. Hitler's anxiety deepened on beholding the Africans and Moroccans who formed part of the French occupation forces in the 1920s. He accused France of 'only waiting for the warm season to throw an army of 800–900,000 blacks into [our] country to complete the work of the total subjugation and violation of Germany'.[36] Hitler's concern was thus not only racial, but strategic: that France would use the human reserves of Africa to oppress Germany, a weapon no longer available to Germany as she had lost her much smaller overseas empire as a result of the war.

The main threat posed by the European empires, however, was not the deployment of men from the 'subject races', but from the white settler colonies. Some of the most formidable British troops on the western front had come from Canada, Australia and New Zealand. They were numerous, well fed, fit, highly motivated, and often extremely violent.[37] Worse still was the fact that the Germans whom the Reich had exported in the nineteenth century for want of land to feed them had come back to fight against her as American soldiers during the war. In later speeches, as we shall see, Hitler repeatedly came back to the moment he had encountered his first American prisoners. The emigration question was the subject of his second known major speech in September 1919, and it also underlay his next disquisition, which was on the internal colonization of Germany. His thoughts on that subject so impressed his sponsor Captain Mayr that he announced his intention 'to launch this official report abridged or in full in the press in a suitable manner'.[38] Emigration was part of daily life in post-war Germany, so much so that a whole newspaper in Munich, *Der Auswanderer* ('The Emigrant'), was devoted to the topic.[39]

That said, although contemporary concern with the emigration issue went well beyond Hitler, it does not seem to have enjoyed a particular salience in the broader inquest into the war. It thus represents his distinctive contribution to the debate on German revival and one of the most important lessons he drew from the war. Henceforth the emigration question, and the associated American problem, lay at the very heart of Hitler's thinking.

Strikingly absent from Hitler's thinking immediately following the war, and indeed for some time thereafter, was any serious anxiety about Russian power or the Soviet Union.[40] This is not surprising, given that Germany's main enemy had been the western allies, and the fact that Russia had been defeated by 1917. Hitler was not even worried about communism as an external threat. The impact of the Baltic émigré and ferocious anti-Bolshevik Alfred Rosenberg during this period was not significant and, in any case, the two men did not even meet until a few months later.[41] Like many Germans,[42] Hitler saw Bolshevism as a disease, which had knocked Russia out of the war, and then undermined German resistance a year later. He did not fear a Soviet invasion, not even after the victory of the Reds in the Civil War. Instead, Hitler fretted that communism would destroy the last vestiges of German sovereignty in the face of the Entente. 'The threatened Bolshevik flood is not so much to be feared as the result of Bolshevik victories on the battlefields,' he warned, 'as rather as a result of a planned subversion of our own people', which would deliver them up to international high finance.[43] Significantly, Hitler wasted no words on the Soviet Union in his early statements from 1919 save to predict that it was set to become a 'colony of the Entente'. This means that capitalism and communism were not simply two equal sides of the anti-Semitic coin for Hitler. Bolshevism was clearly a subordinate force. Its function in the Anglo-American plutocratic system was to undermine the national economies of independent states and make them ripe for takeover by the forces of international capitalism.

By contrast, Hitler was profoundly concerned about German separatism, especially in Bavaria. In January 1920, in one of his earliest major speeches, Hitler hammered not merely separatism but Bavarian 'particularism', that is, more moderate federal aspirations. These, he argued, could only benefit those who wished to 'demolish' the Reich in Munich, Berlin, Paris and London; they were part of a policy of 'encirclement'. Hitler condemned anti-Prussian feeling, which was widespread across the political spectrum in Bavaria. Moreover, he saw the differentiation between separatism and federalism, much insisted on by many in Bavaria, as a distinction without a difference. The *Rosenheimer Tagblatt* complained that 'Hitler made an outrageous attempt to distract the audience by declaring federalism to be more or less synonymous with separatism.'

Rhetorically, Hitler rejected the alternative of a 'unitary or federal state' in favour of a 'state united against the outside world' to protect the Fatherland from being swamped by racial enemies. In the same spirit, he condemned the idea of a 'Danubian Confederation' which he claimed would make Bavaria dependent on Czech and French coal. 'Better a Bolshevik Greater Germany,' Hitler thundered at a party meeting, 'than south Germany dependent on the French and Czechs.'[44] It was a revealing statement, which showed that he regarded Bavarian particularism as a much greater – or at least more immediate – threat than communism. Hitler was clearly a supporter of a unitary state. His absolute rejection of federalism distinguished the NSDAP from not only much of the more moderate right, but also many who were close to National Socialism in almost every other respect. In a letter to the Austrian National Socialist, but opponent of *Anschluss*, Dr Walter Riehl, he set out his position in some detail. Unlike other parties, Hitler placed 'greatest emphasis on the complete unification of all German tribes without consideration for the previous citizenship'. Only this, Hitler claimed, would give 'the German people the status in the world which their numbers and culture warranted'. This required, Hitler continued, 'an agreed central point of the entire organization and administration of the state'.[45]

Also largely absent from Hitler's thinking at this time was any serious Slavophobia, at least in his contemporary recorded remarks.[46] To be sure, he shared the patriotic outrage against the claims of the new Polish state.[47] He condemned the Polish nationalist leader Korfanty as a 'robber chief, Polish cutthroat and eyegouger' and his followers as 'Polish bandit scum'.[48] 'The entire Polish policy of the Bethmann-Hollwegs,' he claimed with reference to the pre-1918 approach, 'was impaled on its failure to understand Polish national hatred. The establishment of the Polish state was the greatest crime against the German people.'[49] Hitler's remarks in that connection were based on national not racial considerations, just as his alleged concern about Czechs in Vienna – based purely on his own subsequent claims in *Mein Kampf* – were couched in national rather than racial terms. Interestingly, he refused to allow NSDAP members to join the anti-Polish uprisings in Upper Silesia,[50] which he evidently regarded as a distraction. For now, Hitler regarded the Slavs as the victims of Jewish capitalism, a fate they shared with the Germans, and hoped for the restoration of the 'true' Russian spirit in the Soviet Union. There was no sign yet of any territorial ambitions in the east. Pity, not hostility, was Hitler's main sentiment towards Russians at this point.

At the end of March 1920, Hitler took off his army uniform for good. By then, some of the main outlines of his world view, expressed consistently in private correspondence, public meetings and newspapers articles alike, were clearly visible: fear of the western allies, especially Britain, a profound demographic anxiety about the United States, a violent hostility to international capitalism, a sense of the subversive effects of socialism and communism, and, of course, a virulent anti-Semitism. None of these sentiments were visible before 1914. Fear of Britain and the 'world of enemies' was first expressed at the start of the conflict. The rest were a response not to defeat as such, or even to the revolution, but to the consequences of defeat. It was the Versailles settlement which brought home the meaning of November 1918. This was the subject of his first known political speech and its consequences dominated his later thinking. Unlike for most nationalists, territorial losses were the least of Hitler's concerns: as we have seen, he was far more worried about the long-term impact of perpetual debt bondage, the continued blockade and a resulting surge in emigration. In other words, it was not the war that made Hitler, or even the revolution, but the peace.

By early 1920, Hitler had found two new homes. On leaving the army, he found lodgings as a sub-tenant of Ernst and Maria Reichert in Thierschstrasse no. 41, in the inner Munich suburb of Lehel. It was a very modest berth in a working- and lower-middle-class neighbourhood. Hitler was an easy-going resident, who never locked his doors and allowed the Reicherts to use his gramophone and books during his frequent absences. We do not know what exactly he read, but the best-thumbed surviving volumes from his collection relate to history and art, whereas those on race and the occult gave the impression of being unread.[51] Hitler took his baths in the nearby Müllersches Volksbad. One of his neighbours was Hugo Erlanger, a Jewish First World War veteran, who ran a men's clothing and sports shop on the ground floor. He bought the entire house eighteen months later, effectively becoming Hitler's landlord.[52] The two men ran into each other frequently and exchanged polite greetings; Erlanger – who was later expropriated by the Third Reich – subsequently could not recall any hostility on Hitler's part. This casts an interesting light on Hitler's politics and his personality. There was clearly something abstract about his visceral anti-Semitism, which did not prevent him from having cordial personal relations with individual Jews, not an uncommon phenomenon among anti-Semites then and since, of course.

His new professional and political home was the DAP, which was renamed the 'National Socialist German Workers' Party' (NSDAP) in the course of 1920. Hitler was by now a recognized quantity on the local right-wing scene. In mid March 1920, while still technically in army service, Hitler flew at May's behest to Berlin at the height of the Kapp Putsch, where he was introduced by Dietrich Eckart to Erich Ludendorff, the legendary World War One general. There is no evidence that Hitler planned to take over the party at this stage, or that he saw it as a vehicle for the seizure of power. The growth of the NSDAP after he joined it was noteworthy, to be sure, and its social composition was remarkably heterogeneous,[53] but the overall figures were still modest. Regional expansion was slow: the first party presence outside Munich was established in Rosenheim in April 1920 and then four months later (August 1920) at Starnberg. There were only 195 members at the end of 1919. In July 1920, there were 1,100 and more than 2,000 at the end of the year. This was not nearly enough to have made any electoral impact, and in any case, Hitler abjured any attempt to enter parliament for 'moral and financial reasons'.[54]

Hitler believed political organization without propaganda was pointless.[55] His main concern at this point was to use the party as a platform to disseminate and elaborate his ideas. He was involved in the drafting of the twenty-five-point NSDAP (technically DAP) programme in February 1920, though it is unclear whether he can claim sole authorship.[56] The first four related to national integrity, foreign policy and territorial expansion; the next four concerned race, mostly strictures against the Jews. Hitler turned Wilson's idea of 'self-determination' back on the Allies with his call for 'the unification of all Germans in a Greater Germany on the basis of the right of peoples to self-determination'.[57] More than that, he demanded 'Land and soil (colonies) to feed our people and to settle our surplus population', the first unambiguous documented articulation of what subsequently became the *Lebensraum* concept. The geographic location of these future 'colonies' was not specified but at this time Hitler seems to have had overseas territories in mind. Later points attacked 'debt slavery', called for the breaking up and nationalization of large, cartelized industries, the expansion of old age welfare payments, land reform including expropriation for the public good and a strong central power for the Reich, with unlimited power for the Reichstag to legislate for all the regions. Internally, the main target of the programme was the Jews, capitalism and German separatism, rather than communism per se. Externally, the programme took aim not so much at the Soviet Union, as at the western powers, with its demand for living space, not in the east, but in overseas colonies, from which Germany was now shut out.

Hitler paid close attention to the iconography underpinning the message. A black swastika of his design on a white circle with red background was first flown as the official party emblem at a meeting in Salzburg in August 1920.[58] In one of his very few excursions into the occult, Hitler praised the swastika – as a 'symbol of the sun' which sustained a 'cult' of light among a 'community based on Aryan culture', not only in Europe, but in India and Japan as well. The use of the old imperial black, white and red colours was a calculated affront to the black, red and gold of the Weimar flag. 'The red is social,' he later explained, 'the white is national, and the swastika is anti-Semitic.'[59] By mounting the symbol diagonally, Hitler cleverly conveyed a sense of dynamism and movement.[60] Four months later, he oversaw the purchase of the *Völkischer Beobachter* newspaper and the Franz Eher Verlag, financed in part by a loan from a Reichswehr slush fund guaranteed by Dietrich Eckart, which gave the party a media platform with a print run of 8,000–17,000 appearing three times a week; after many ups and downs, the *Völkischer Beobachter* became a daily on 8 February 1923.[61] As the main organ of the NSDAP, the paper carried news of party activities, but it was also the main direct vehicle of communication between Hitler and the rank and file, which he could use to rehearse and enforce his ideological message.[62] The party also promoted Hitler as a 'charismatic' leader, who was destined to lead Germany out of its subjection.[63]

Over the next fifteen months, Hitler engaged in an intense programme of speeches in the major Munich beer halls; he practised his poses in front of a mirror. By the end of the year, he had made twenty-seven appearances in Munich, and twelve outside, including Bad Tölz, Rosenheim and even Stuttgart. The audiences ranged in number from 800 to about 2,000. During late September and the beginning of October 1920, Hitler made repeated trips to Austria and to support the National Socialist Party in neighbouring Württemberg in their election campaign. In early 1921, a speech on Versailles at the Zirkus Krone was heard by about 5,600 people. One eyewitness, his first biographer Konrad Heiden, recalled that the secret of the success of his speeches was that the audience became 'participants' rather than 'listeners'.[64]

There were some missteps. Hitler's opportunistic attempt to address a Munich crowd of 20,000 or so uninvited at a general rally outside the Feldherrnhalle in February 1921 was drowned out by the massed bands who struck up as he began to speak.[65] It is also worth remembering that many members had never seen or heard Hitler in person.[66] In general, though, his profile grew steadily, and he began to overtake the best-known orators, such as Gottfried Feder and Dietrich Eckart, as the public face of the party. Despite his somewhat mysterious aura – Hitler refused to allow any photograph of him to be taken – he had become a recognizable 'name' in Bavarian politics. His relationship with the Reichswehr in Bavaria, which had effectively incubated him, remained good even after he had left the ranks. In mid May 1921, Hitler met with the prime minister, Gustav von Kahr, marking his political recognition by 'official' Bavaria.[67] He had 'made it'.

Hitler had joined an existing party, not established a new one. This meant that he had to work with others and within structures which he did not as yet control, or even dominate. The collegial basis of the party was laid down by Hitler himself, who had drafted the Standing Orders in December 1919. 'The aims of the party are so extensive,' he wrote, 'that they are only to be achieved through an organization which is as tight as it is flexible.'[68] He argued that the governing committee could only hope to work effectively if it had the confidence of the mass of the membership, and the trust of each other. 'The first,' he said, 'requires the election of all members of the committee, including its chairman, by the membership in open assembly.' 'The second,' Hitler continued, 'excludes for all any form of control through a superior or parallel government, be it as a circle or a lodge.' In other words: discipline yes, dictatorship, no. The early organizational form of the party was thus quasi-democratic, not least because the law of associations which regulated the governance of all such associations in Germany gave Hitler and his colleagues no choice in the matter.

During this period Hitler collaborated with a range of figures, not all of whom were party members, in an informal and often non-hierarchical way. His closest associate was Rudolf Hess, a First World War veteran who had grown up in Egypt; the date of their first encounter (which was probably in May 1920) is disputed, but we know for a fact that he joined the NSDAP in July 1920.[69] A key interlocutor was the Reichswehr officer Ernst Röhm, whose meetings are documented from early 1920, though the first contacts may have taken place a lot earlier.[70] Hitler had frequent dealings with the staff of the *Völkischer Beobachter*, especially its executive editor, the playwright Dietrich Eckart, and his deputy Alfred Rosenberg, a Baltic German refugee from the Russian Revolution, who would influence Hitler's view of the Soviet Union;[71] the editor was his old regimental comrade Hermann Esser. In a rare gesture, Hitler explicitly acknowledged his debt to Eckart for his help with the *Völkischer Beobachter*, and to Rosenberg for his 'theoretical deepening of the party programme'.[72] In late 1920, Hitler met Max Erwin von Scheubner-Richter,[73] who had witnessed and been appalled by the massacre of the Armenians as a German consul in the East Anatolian town of Erzurum during the First World War. It was probably from him that Hitler got his determination that the Germans should not become a 'people like the Armenians', that is, the butt of foreign oppressors.[74] At around the same time, Hitler first encountered Gregor

Strasser, an apothecary from Landshut. The only significant dispute was with Karl Harrer, one of the original leaders of the DAP, who wanted the party to remain a sect, unlike Hitler and Drexler, who wanted to create a mass movement. In early 1920 Harrer was sidelined, and he was completely excluded by the end of the following year.

If Hitler was by now probably the best-known member of the party, there was no sign yet that he aspired to lead it. This may be because of the lengthy timetable he envisaged for the seizure of power in Germany, the revival of national dignity and strength, and then the reassertion of the Reich's authority on the international stage. Given the abject condition of the country immediately after Versailles, recovery would be a slow process. The pressing need of the moment, therefore, was not for political organization but for fundraising and propagandistic work, developing and disseminating the message as widely as possible. This, rather than any attempt to force the party to accept his unfettered leadership, is probably the reason why, in December 1920, he declared his 'permanent resignation from the [governing] committee of the party' and (less obviously) from its 'Press Committee'.[75] Hitler said he was prepared to continue speaking on behalf of the party wherever required. The idea that he might take over absolute control of the party seems to have come from others rather than himself. Drexler, for example, wrote in mid February 1921 that 'every revolutionary movement must have a dictatorial head and for that reason I consider especially our Hitler the most suitable candidate for our movement'.[76] So for the first eighteen months or so of his political career, Hitler's position was rather indeterminate. He became the party's principal speaker and fundraiser, and its public face, but he was not its chief and some of the time he was not even a member of its ruling committee.

It was the threat to the ideas and programme of the party, rather than his personal position, which drove Hitler to seize the leadership of the movement.[77] Anton Drexler and many others believed that the best way forward in the crowded radical nationalist milieu of the time was to merge with like-minded groups. Hitler opposed all such attempts, mainly because they threatened to compromise what he regarded as the party's greatest asset: its ideological coherence. The *casus belli* was Drexler's desire to join forces with the Deutsch-Sozialistische Partei (DSP), whose geographical centre of gravity lay far to the north, and which would theoretically give the NSDAP a much greater reach within Germany. Drexler discussed the modalities with the DSP at their party congress in Zeitz in Thuringia in late March 1921, and a few months later with the leader of the Franconian DSP, Julius Streicher. He also entered into negotiations with the radical nationalist ideologue Otto Dickel, head of the 'Deutsche Werkgemeinschaft',

NSDAP member and occasional party speaker, who was trying to fuse all the anti-Semitic and radical nationalist associations.[78] Hitler violently objected, not least because the DSP had turned him down for membership two years earlier,[79] and after his attempts to head off the merger failed, he resigned from the party altogether on 11 July 1921, setting out his reasons at some length a few days later.[80]

The NSDAP, he claimed, had been established on 'the basis of an extreme racial outlook and rejects any form of parliamentarism', including its present-day incarnation. It was intended to be quite different from all other 'so-called national movements', and so constructed that it would best serve to wage 'the battle for the crushing of the Jewish-international domination of our people'. The NSDAP was also a 'social or rather a socialist party', whose statutes laid down 'that the seat of its leadership was Munich and must remain Munich, now and for ever'. This programme, Hitler continued, had been agreed as 'immutable and inviolable in front of an audience of a thousand people, and invoked as a granite foundation in more than a hundred mass meetings'.[81] Now, Hitler claimed, these principles had been violated by plans to merge with another party, by the agreement at Zeitz to move the headquarters to Berlin and by the prospect that they would be abjured in favour of the programme of Otto Dickel, which he condemned as a 'meaningless, spongy [and] stretchable entity'. Specifically, Hitler objected to Dickel's belief that Britain was emerging from under the thumb of the Jews and to his admiration for the Jew Walther Rathenau. He was interested in propaganda, not organization, and the power of ideas, not bureaucratic power.

Hitler made his return strictly conditional on the fulfilment of his terms. First of all, he demanded the 'immediate summoning of an extra-ordinary general meeting of the membership' within eight days whose purpose was the replacement of the existing committee by a newly elected one chaired by himself. What is more, Hitler requested 'dictatorial powers for the immediate establishment of a working group tasked with the ruth-less purge of the party of the foreign elements' that had 'infiltrated' it. Secondly, he demanded 'the immutable acceptance of the principle that the seat of the movement was and would remain in Munich', and that the local Ortsgruppe Munich would be the headquarters until a national organiza-tion could be established. Thirdly, Hitler insisted that there should be no further 'change of the programme or the name', at least not for six years; those who agitated for this should be expelled. Fourthly, he said that the NSDAP and the DSP should not join forces. Indeed, he determined that there should never be mergers with any group but only 'takeover' without any form of 'concessions' on the side of the NSDAP. Fifthly, Hitler laid down that any such negotiations be subject to his veto and that he chose those representing the party. Hitler averred that he made these demands 'not because I crave power' but because he was convinced that 'without an iron leadership' the party would soon degenerate from a National Socialist Workers Party into a mere 'Occidental League'. Hitler had originally wanted to control the message rather than the party, but he now realized that he could not do the former without ensuring the latter.

It is not quite clear whether Hitler resigned with the intent of forcing the leadership's hand, or whether he left in despair and decided to lay down the law only after attempts to win him back showed the underlying strength of his position. Even then, his demands were more modest than they sounded, being subject (as the law required) to membership vote. The 'dictatorial powers' were not requested for the running of the party in general but limited to the sphere that Hitler was primarily concerned about, namely the re-establishment and maintenance of ideological coherence. This is what underlay his demand to purge deviators, to oversee the absorption of other groups and the retention of Munich as an ideological 'Rome' or 'Mecca'. The outcome, in any case, was the same. Hitler triumphed all along the line. Drexler caved in. The merger with the DSP was off, and nobody dared to suggest any fresh fusions on an equal basis. Munich remained the capital of the movement. Hitler joined the governing committee of the NSDAP as its chairman and conducted a thorough purge. Otto Dickel was expelled. Drexler was marginalized.[82] No party speaker ever again had a good word to say about a Jew, or attempted to suggest that the western powers were not controlled by the Jews.

Hitler's struggle with Drexler is common to most emerging political movements: the clash between the need for growth and the maintenance of ideological purity, which was the side which he took with such vigour. In July 1921, Hitler won his first political battle. He had become a politician. Whether Hitler had sought leadership or had leadership thrust upon him, it was clear that he now was increasingly not merely the de facto but the formal chief of the NSDAP. If he had once seen himself as a mere 'drummer' of the movement for the new Germany, he now aspired to be its leader.

Hitler now moved to reorganize and expand the NSDAP.[83] By the end of 1921, membership stood at about 6,000.[84] The party moved from Sterneckerbräu to larger premises at Corneliusstrasse 12. Local groups were founded in Hanover, Zwickau and Dortmund. Hitler tightened his control over the party, including the cells outside Germany. In the spring of 1922 the Austrian and Bohemian NSDAP accepted Hitler's authority.[85] Collegial decision-making was abolished. Sub-committees were now appointed by Hitler. Despite these moves, Hitler tried to keep out of day-to-day decision-making, and he saw his involvement in these matters simply as preparatory to resuming his propagandistic drive. Ideological purity rather than control for its own sake seems to have been his main concern. The only formal limitation was that imposed by the Weimar associational law, which meant that he could in theory at least still be held to account by the membership.[86]

In August 1921, Hitler established a formal party paramilitary formation, which was named the SA or Sturmabteilung on 5 October 1921, with headquarters in 39 Schellingstrasse, Munich. The first commander was Emil Maurice, who had already distinguished himself in brawling at Hitler's side, or on his behalf. The main task of this new force was to protect NSDAP meetings and disrupt those of the other side. Cyclist, motorized and mounted sections were established, with weapons and training being provided by the Reichswehr. The latter hoped to draw on the SA, as on other right-wing groupings, in the event of civil unrest or a French invasion. The initial growth of the Sturmabteilung was modest, reaching about 700–800 men in twelve months, and about 1,000 at the beginning of the following year. Meanwhile, where Hitler could not establish complete authority over regional party organizations, he compromised. The most significant of these accommodations was with Julius Streicher in Nuremberg, who by 1922 had acknowledged Hitler's supreme authority in return for more or less total domination of the NSDAP in Franconia.[87] Even in Bavaria, therefore, the party remained diverse and Hitler's level of direct control varied.[88]

In some ways, Bavaria was a congenial habitat. It considered itself a 'centre of order' in the Weimar chaos, an arcadia of conservative and patriotic values.[89] Hitler was protected and supported by the Bavarian Reichswehr, which only loosely acknowledged the precedence of the national authority at this time, and whose loyalties lay firmly in Munich rather than Berlin.[90] The president of the Munich Police, Ernst Pöhner, and the Chief of the Political Police, Wilhelm Frick, were NSDAP supporters. Hitler was also in constant contact with the numerous right-wing nationalist groupings which flourished in the city, and congregated around General Ludendorff, a patriotic icon from the war.[91] Hitler began to build up a cadre of leaders and advisers who were gathering around the NSDAP and often him personally. Gregor Strasser joined the party in October 1922. That same month, Hitler first met Hermann Göring, a charismatic and well-connected fighter ace, who opened many doors to business and high society.

In other ways, Hitler and the NSDAP sat uneasily in the Munich mainstream, which was dominated by Catholicism and the Bavarian People's Party (BVP).[92] The BVP had complete command of the local parliamentary political scene. All of the sixty-five BVP Landtag deputies were Catholic, six of them clerics; all but one of its twenty Reichstag members were Catholic, two of them clerics.[93] While the party was confessionally homogeneous, it was socially diverse, representing Bavarians from all classes, and was determined not to break away from the Reich but also to resist the Weimar Republic's vision of a more centralized state. Despite his Austrian – essentially south German – roots Hitler found it very difficult to break into this constituency. It was for this reason he attempted to reach out to the churches through his concept of 'positive Christianity'. Hitler claimed that Jesus had been 'slandered' by the same people who were scourging Germany today – the Jews.[94] 'We should follow the example of this man,' Hitler argued on another occasion, 'who was born poor in a cabin, who pursued high ideals and whom for this reason the Jews later crucified.'[95] 'The Christian religion is the only possible ethical basis of the German people,' he said soon after, adding that it was important to avoid any 'tension between the confessions', because 'religious divisions' had been one of 'the worst things to happen to the German people'.[96] Though Hitler made some headway with Bavarian Catholics in the early 1920s,[97] it was a demographic with which he struggled to connect until the end of his life.

Munich was thus an ambivalent habitat for the young NSDAP. It was stony ground for the Nazis not only politically and culturally, but also physically. The authorities began to take an ever dimmer view of Hitler's activities, especially when these disturbed public order. He spent two stretches in prison. He lost an important ally with the resignation of Ernst Pöhner as president of the Munich Police in September 1921. A month later, Hitler was summoned to police headquarters for a serious caution following a series of street brawls and beer-hall battles.[98] The *Völkischer Beobachter* was repeatedly banned for publishing inflammatory articles.[99] In March 1922, after his conviction for a breach of the peace, the Bavarian minister of the interior, Dr Franz Schweyer, seriously considered deporting Hitler to Austria, and the minister president, Count Lerchenfeld, made it clear to Hitler that he was in Bavaria on sufferance.[100] The police watched Hitler closely.

Hitler remained determined to establish himself in Munich, but only as a beacon to inspire the rest of Germany and as a base from which to take over the Reich as a whole. 'Munich must become a model,' he wrote in January 1922, 'the school but also the granite pedestal' of the movement.[101] 'We do not have a Bavarian mission today,' Hitler announced six months later, 'rather Bavaria has the most important mission of its entire existence.' Bavaria, on this reading, was not separate but rather 'the most German state in the German Reich'. Munich was a sanctuary and a bulwark, certainly, but above all it was a sally-port. The special role Hitler envisaged for Bavaria in Germany was thus not as a separate or autonomous entity, as the federalists and particularists wanted, but as the vanguard of national renewal. 'Not "away from Berlin",' Hitler intoned when discussing the relationship between Bavaria and the Reich, 'but rather "towards Berlin"' in order to 'liberate it from the seducers of the German people'.[102] It would soon become clear that was a very different agenda to that of the generally monarchist and particularist Bavarian military and political elites.

At this time, the party had very limited success with big business. To be sure, the former Siemens director Emil Gansser invited Hitler to speak at the 'National Klub of 1919' in Berlin. One attendee, the industrialist Ernst von Borsig, was so impressed by Hitler's apparent ability to bridge the gulf between the national cause and the working class that he invited him back for a second appearance. Hermann Aust, executive of a malt-coffee trading company in the capital, asked him to appear at the Bavarian League of Industrialists in Munich, then at the Herrenklub, and thereafter at the Merchants' Guild. None of these events led anywhere in financial terms. The reason for Hitler's lack of success is not hard to find. The NSDAP programme – for example point 13 with its attack on 'trusts' – was ferociously anti-capitalist and so, as we have seen, was much of Hitler's rhetoric. Despite Hitler's willingness to moderate his message to business audiences, emphasizing his anti-French and anti-Bolshevik themes, business was not reassured. Paul Reusch, a major Ruhr baron, noting the Nazi nationalization plan, remarked that 'we have no reason to support our own gravediggers'. The party remained dependent on donations from the Bavarian Reichswehr, either in cash or in kind in the form of weapons or vehicles, and from a motley group of smaller donors, mainly traders, retailers and small businessmen.[103]

Given the shortage of funds, the growth of the party and especially its propagandistic reach was impressive. There were significant gains in membership: 4,300 by the end of 1921, and more than 20,000 a year later.[104] The party organization was also an important source of funding through membership dues, entry charges for meetings, collections and interest-free loans from members. The party apparat grew, albeit modestly. In 1922, Hitler acquired a private secretary in the shape of Fritz Laubök, the son of a Nazi in Rosenheim. Attendance at party events also increased, and the message reached a much wider audience. There was a real quantum leap in early 1922, when Hitler regularly spoke to between 2,000 and 6,000 listeners in the larger beer halls. A high point was the *Deutsche Tag* in Coburg in October, which culminated in a massive brawl with hostile demonstrators.[105]

Not everyone was persuaded. The records of Hitler's speeches note many catcalls and interruptions. One of those who went to hear him speak in a beer hall on the Theresienstarsse was Franz Halder, his later chief of the general staff, who does not seem to have understood what Hitler was saying.[106] Hitler often had several engagements per night; 30 November and 13 December 1922 were records with ten simultaneous events. It no doubt helped that the party paid Hitler speaker fees for his appearances, which were for a long time his only income after being discharged from the army.

The purpose of all this activity was not the creation of a party organization capable of winning elections, still less that of a force capable of mounting an armed challenge to the Weimar Republic. Instead, Hitler's main aim remained the establishment of ideological coherence in the movement. 'The final strength of a movement,' he claimed in mid February 1922, lay 'not in the number of its local groupings but in its internal cohesion'. The constant reiteration of agreed positions generated loyalty and fervour. For example, when the authorities expressed doubts that the 'Gymnastics Section' of the SA was just engaged in physical exercise, Hitler responded by saying that party members as a whole also exercised 'if only with [their] mouths'. He remained adamantly opposed to contesting elections. Hitler claimed that 'there was no fruitful work to be done in parliament', and that 'individual National Socialists would be corrupted by the swamp of parliamentarism'.[107]

Throughout the early 1920s, therefore, Hitler used his speeches to rehearse and develop his ideology. During this period his words – which were, of course, acts in themselves – were more important than his deeds. The recent defeat and its causes remained the central preoccupation. Hitler repeated his conviction that the war had been caused by an Anglo-American capitalist conspiracy. Sometimes, he attributed the 'original sin' to Britain, whose commercial and colonial 'envy' of the Reich had driven a 'policy of encirclement' against Germany, and whose press had vilified her before and during the war as a nation of Huns and barbarians. On other occasions, he targeted the United States. 'Not least because the social welfare and the cultural development [of the German Empire] was a thorn in the eyes of the American trust-system,' he thundered in March 1921, 'we had to disappear from view.' Hitler repeatedly contrasted 'Germany's social culture' with American capitalism. He reserved particular scorn for US president Woodrow Wilson as the 'agent of international high finance'.[108]

The collapse of 1918 was explained in part through enemy strength, in part through enemy guile, and in part through German weakness or stupidity. Hitler was under no illusion about the 'superior leadership of the enemy', which nearly crushed the Reich in 1915–1916, when 'an enemy who was twice or three times as strong in terms of numbers and equipment' assaulted 'a practically reserve-less' German front line. Fighting France, and especially the British Empire, was bad enough, but what had ultimately tipped the scales was US intervention. This, Hitler was convinced, would have taken place with or without the U-boat war. Having previously been a 'passive' supporter of the Entente through the supply of armaments, the Americans intervened when Britain and France were on the verge of defeat in order not to lose the 'billions' which it was owed by the Allies. 'America was called in,' he claimed, 'and the power of international big capital thereby became openly involved.' Not only did the Entente have massive demographic and industrial resources at its disposal, Hitler argued, but it had also 'tortured' Germany through a 'hunger blockade' against the civilian population.[109]

All this was made much worse, in Hitler's view, by mistaken German strategy and the internal weakness of the Reich. The principal diplomatic error, he argued, was 'Germany's loyalty for better and for worse towards the scruffy Habsburg state' and the resulting failure to achieve a compromise peace with Russia. There was also an increasing sense of the baleful role played by Marxism, a 'poisonous' doctrine which had first paralysed and then corrupted the German people to the marrow. The German will to resist had been further undermined by calculated Allied deception. Once again, it was Wilson who was singled out for the most obloquy, as the man whose broken promises of fair treatment under the Fourteen Points had caused the Reich to give up when further resistance was not only possible but essential. Wilson, he said simply, was the 'cause of the collapse', the man who had brought the overwhelming power of the United States to bear on the Reich, and the Pied Piper who had convinced the Germans to lay down their arms on the basis of a fair peace.[110]

What linked all these explanations in Hitler's mind was the power and the malevolence of the Jews, the main controllers of an 'international capitalism' that needed 'ever more objects of exploitation'. It was they who under their Jewish ringleader Lord Northcliffe (who was in fact not only not Jewish but a fervent anti-Semite) had whipped up the British press into a frenzy against Germany before 1914. It was the 'international Jewish newspaper corporations', Hitler claimed, who had prevented a Russo-German rapprochement. It was they who owned the large American companies supplying the Allied war effort and who tricked the 'peaceful' American people into war with Germany against their better natures and best interests. It was the Jews who tried to manipulate Germany's food supply and who 'precipitated the revolution through hunger'. All this happened because the 'New York Stock Exchange' – the

'Headquarters of World Jewry' – was determined to crush Germany, the last remaining *Nationalstaat* which was 'not yet completely ruled by stock exchanges'.[111] In short, Hitler remained firmly wedded to the idea of a deadly synthesis between world Jewry, international capitalism and Anglo-America as Germany's nemesis.

Moreover, in Hitler's view the war was by no means over. Germany was still the victim of international capitalism, whose continuing power he repeatedly attacked. He spoke of 'international stock exchange and loan capital' as the main 'beneficiaries' of the peace treaty. Ever since the 'collapse of the Reich', Hitler claimed, the country had fallen under 'the rule of international, fatherlandless capital, independent of person, place and Nation'. International conferences – such as Genoa in April 1922 – were simply condemned as 'stock exchange conferences'. Hitler saw Jewish international capitalism and western democracy as linked. 'International Jewish stock exchange capital,' he believed, 'was the driving force of these western-democratic states.' He set up the 'equation' of 'democracy-capitalism-Jew'. For all these reasons, he argued, National Socialism was a 'new force whose aim could always only be anti-capitalist'.[112]

Hitler was not completely opposed to all forms of capitalism, though he sometimes gave that impression. He contrasted the blanket hostility of Social Democrats and Marxists to capitalism in general with his own distinction between allegedly pernicious and largely Jewish 'international loan capitalism' and nationally oriented 'productive industrial capitalism'. 'Factories and industrial capital,' he told an audience of SA, 'is national' and 'the capital of every country remains national'. For clarity, he stressed that National Socialism 'struggled against every form of big capital, irrespective of whether it is German or Jewish, if it is grounded not in productive work, but in the principle of interest, of income without work or toil'. Moreover, Hitler added, the NSDAP 'battled the Jew not only as the sole bearer of this [form of] capital', but also because he 'prevented' the 'systematic struggle' against it. In Hitler's view it was the determination of international capitalism to subjugate independent national economies which had led to the world war and the brutal peace settlement. This was the context in which he interpreted Allied attempts to control the Reichsbahn, the German national railways. Hitler accused the Jews of trying to 'grab' them, as part of a policy whose 'final aim was the destruction of our national economy and the enslavement of our workforce'.[113]

The Allied determination to annihilate Germany, Hitler believed, was demonstrated by their continuation of the blockade after the end of hostilities. 'One wants to destroy us completely,' he claimed, 'one wants to make our children sick and to allow them to waste away.' He saw in the demands for reparations in kind by German agriculture a plan to reduce her population through 'hunger' in accordance with Clemenceau's alleged policy to get rid of the '20 million excess' Germans. The main culprit, however, was Britain, which Hitler regarded as the 'master of the destruction of the health of peoples', with the Germans only the latest victims of a much broader global hunger strategy. The Treaty of Versailles was thus merely the continuation of the wartime blockade by other means.[114] In Hitler's rhetoric, the alleged campaign to undermine the 'substance' of the German *Volk* as a whole weighed much more heavily than the territorial losses.

The main purpose of this strategy, Hitler claimed, was to reduce Germany's population, partly through starvation but mainly through emigration. 'The loss of [our] entire merchant fleet,' he claimed, complements 'the destruction of our industry, and that means cutting through the main artery of our whole economic life.' 'We no longer have any world trade,' Hitler continued, 'so that we have currently lost the possibility of feeding around 20 million people.'[115] 'The Entente,' he lamented, 'advises us to emigrate in order to feed ourselves, and to make way for the Eastern Jews.'[116] Hitler, in other words, feared that Germany would become the victim of what is today called 'population replacement'. He frequently urged his audience to think of the 'thousands of German emigrants'.[117] This was the great trauma underlying Hitler's whole world view: the continued haemorrhaging of the best elements of the Reich who had left the Fatherland in order to enlarge the population of Germany's rivals, with the fatal results that had been seen in the Great War. Worse still, he argued, these best elements were being replaced by the Jewish dregs of central and eastern Europe in a kind of negative selection, designed to further undermine the racial coherence of the German people.[118]

International capital and the victor powers – the two were indistinguishable in Hitler's mind – had thus reduced Germany to the status of a 'colony'. The purpose of Versailles, he argued, was 'to make Germany ripe' for its fate as 'a colony of international capital', to 'soften up our people' in order to make them 'international slave workers'. He lamented that Germany was a 'wage slave of international capital'. Germany was no more than a 'colony of the international Jewish finance syndicate', Hitler argued, thus making the German people 'the slave of the outside world'. In April 1922, he fumed that 'we practically no longer have an independent German Reich, but really just a colony of the world outside'. The reparations payments ordained by Versailles, he said, constituted the brutal theft of German labour. 'Thus we have become the plaything of our enemies,' Hitler concluded, 'a slave people, of whom 10 million are working for the world outside for free.'[119]

All this was embedded in a broader, though idiosyncratic, critique of European imperialism. On the one hand, Hitler was bitterly critical of the British Empire. 'Where was the law,' he asked, 'when England flooded China and India with opium and North America with spirits in order to undermine these people the better to dominate them?' He also charged that Britain had 'reduced the Irish people from 8.5 to 4.5 million [through the potato famine]', and had 'cynically allowed' some 29,000 Boer women to die a miserable death in the 'concentration camps of South Africa'. He paid black people the back-handed compliment that he would rather have '100 Negroes in the hall than one Jew'.[120] On the other hand, Hitler objected not so much to colonialism as to what he would later call the 'negrification' of the Germans.[121] 'You don't really need a pair of trousers,' he had the Allies say, 'the Negro doesn't have one either.' Germany itself, he complained, had become 'the plantation of the interest of foreign capital'. It had fallen lower even than the 'Negro Republic Liberia', which at least enjoyed self-determination. Indeed, he lamented that 'today any Hottentot state is able to dispose over Germany', perhaps a reference to the fact that both Haiti and Liberia were signatories of the Versailles Treaty on the strength of their membership of the allied coalition. He feared, in short, that Germany would 'soon be relegated to a position similar to that of India, Ireland or Egypt'. Germany, Hitler concluded, was completely enslaved, it was considered as 'less than a Nigger [sic] state'.[122]

The notion that Germany was being enslaved and reduced to the status of an African colony was widespread at the time, not just in far right circles. Viktor Klemperer, a Jewish veteran of the same division in which Hitler had served, who was later a victim of Nazism, wrote that as 'The way the Entente powers talk of and to Germany makes me as bitter as if I personally were being treated like a negro';[123] on another occasion he compared the situation of the Reich with that of the Congo. Many Germans experienced occupation, reparations and the presence of enemy colonial troops as a form not only of subjugation but of emasculation,[124] a sentiment which extended from the far right to the SPD and even women's rights groups concerned about sexual violence.[125] The Weimar Germany in which Hitler operated was thus both colonized and post-colonial in an era of continuing western imperialism.[126] Defeat by the western powers had turned the international racial order upside down.

There had in fact been long-standing Anglo-Saxon doubts about the whiteness of Germans. As far back as 1751, in his *Observations concerning the increase of Mankind, peopling of countries etc.*, Benjamin Franklin had included them along with the Spaniards, Italians, French, Russians and Swedes as a people of 'swarthy complexion'. He 'excepted' only the

'Saxons' – probably meaning the Lower-Saxons, whose ancestors had set-tled England. These, Franklin said, 'with the English, make the principal body of White People on the face of the earth'. More recently, in 1916, the prominent American theorist Madison Grant published his lament for *The Passing of the Great Race*,[127] which also identified Germans and Scandi-navians as of clearly lower racial value than the Anglo-Celts, though preferable to eastern Europeans, Jews or blacks; of this, more later.

The sense of racial outrage at the treatment of Germany turned some National Socialists into anti-imperialists and sympathizers with the wretched of the earth, but not Hitler. In late 1922, British Intelligence reported that he attended a meeting of Egyptian, Turkish, Indian and Irish revolutionaries in Munich.[128] He probably did so at the suggestion of Ernst Count Reventlow, an early Nazi who seems to have had some genuine regard for these movements as common victims of British imperialism. Karl Haushofer also supported the aspirations of Indian nationalists. Hitler, for his part, remained not only contemptuous of the rights of non-European peoples, but also sceptical of their political value in the contest against the might of Anglo-America.

Worse still than the old European imperialism of western powers, according to Hitler, was the Jewish aspiration to world domination, of which the Germans were the principal victims. Drawing on the *Protocols of the Elders of Zion*, he claimed to see a grand plan to control the world. The ultimate aim of policy towards Germany and other independent states, Hitler stated at the beginning 1921, was the creation of a 'Jewish world state'. He came back to this theme repeatedly over the next two years, when he spoke of the 'Jewish-imperialist plans for world domina-tion', the 'Jewish world dictatorship' and the 'final aim [of the Jews]: world domination [and] the destruction of the national states'. In his notes for one speech, Hitler made the connections absolutely clear in point form: 'World domination with a Jewish capital – Zion – that means world enslavement: world stock exchange – world press – world culture. World language. All for slaves under one master.'[129] In this way, Hitler closed the circle of western imperialist, Jewish and capitalist enemies of the Reich.

Germany was by no means the only victim. Russia was in an even less enviable situation. The 'international money powers', he claimed, were after 'Russia's natural resources'. Bolshevism was integral to this aim, as it was in the German case. It was part of the 'intention of Jewish big capital, to destroy Russia completely in order to maximize profits'. This is further evidence of Hitler's attitude to communism, which he regarded as a disease rather than a military threat in its own right. Bolshevism had 'destroyed' Russia, by establishing the twelve-hour day, imposing 'the Jewish *knout*' and conducting a 'mass murder of the intelligentsia'. Russia was thus 'completely abandoned to hunger and poverty'. 'In Russia,' Hitler warned with reference to the famine there, '30 million so-called "proletarians" are cast down and have to scrabble in the grass for roots' to eat. When the Soviet foreign minister, Chicherin, announced at the Genoa conference that western governments could invest in Russia, Hitler remarked that 'international world capital was receiving permission to exploit and plunder these areas', reducing the 'ordinary Russian to nothing more than a job number'. 'The whole of Russia today', he concluded, 'is nothing more than a destroyed culture and a colony ripe for exploitation by foreign capital.'[130]

It is in this context that Hitler's evolving attitude to communism and the Soviet Union should be seen. At times, he suggested that Bolshevism and international capitalism were working together. He spoke of the way in which Jewish capitalism allegedly used Chinese 'cultural guardians' in Moscow, and black 'hangmen's assistants' on the Rhine, while the Soviets in Genoa 'walked arm in arm with big bankers'. The Jews, Hitler claimed, 'had their apostles in both camps' and thus agents on both the 'right' and the 'left'.[131] From time to time, Hitler claimed that communism was the main threat.[132] It is also true that after the Bolshevik victory in the Russian Civil War, the threat of international communism loomed larger in his mind than it had in 1919.[133] Hitler now called for 'the overcoming and extermination of the Marxist world view'. 'Developments in Russia must be watched closely,' he warned, because once the communists had 'consolidated their power' they would 'probably turn it against us'.[134]

Despite all this, Hitler still did not regard capitalism and communism simply as two equal sides of the same Jewish coin. He continued to see Bolshevism not so much as a threat in its own right as as an instrument of international Jewish capitalism to undermine the working of national economies and render them ripe for takeover by international finance capital (both Jewish and non-Jewish). Even after the end of the civil war, once Soviet power in Russia had been securely established, he saw Bolshevism primarily as a weapon in the armoury of international capitalism. 'The north [of Germany],' Hitler warned, was being assigned to 'Bolshevism', while the south was designated a 'French Protectorate'. The purpose of the exercise, he claimed, was the 'final subjection' of 70 million Germans in order to turn them into the 'worker for the whole world!' 'This,' Hitler suggested, 'is the final aim of the supranational stock exchange power.'[135] More generally, his rhetoric and attention were still overwhelmingly directed towards the threat posed by the western powers and international finance capitalism.

For this reason, Hitler was bitterly opposed to any form of internationalism, not just because he despised it in principle, but because he considered it humbug. In part, this hostility was directed towards the German left, whose blind faith in universal principles, Hitler argued, had left Germany defenceless during the world war and its aftermath. For this reason, he argued, '[we should] free ourselves of the illusion of the [Socialist] International and [the idea of] the Fraternity of Peoples'. Hitler's main objection to internationalism, however, was that it simply served the interests of the western imperial powers. Where was international law, he asked, when Louis XIV had plundered Germany in the late seventeenth century, when the British had bombarded neutral Copenhagen in 1807 and starved and oppressed the Irish, or when the Americans had displaced the native Indians. It had not escaped Hitler's attention that 'in the home of the inventor of the League of Nations [Wilson's America] one rejects the League as a utopia, a madness'. There was not even a racial solidarity among whites, Hitler lamented, because France had sent 'comrades from Africa in solidarity to enserf and muzzle the population on the Rhine'. For this reason, Hitler rejected the whole notion of international governance, claiming that 'The League of Nations is only a holding company of the Entente which wants to secure its ill-gotten gains.'[136]

As if all this was not bad enough, Germany was also plagued by continuing internal weakness. Hitler condemned the 'so-called battle against Berlin' – which was a staple of Bavarian rhetoric across the parties and classes – as a 'cover for the aim of catapulting Germany back into its former impotence and fragmentation through the elimination of the imperial capital', and to cause her to 'bleed to death' through the creation of 'two equally large rival individual states' doomed to a condition of 'perpetual fraternal strife'.[137] Nor was this hostility merely rhetorical. Hitler's first appearance in a Munich court was the result of a physical confrontation with the Bavarian particularist Otto Ballerstedt. In a two-hour peroration, he condemned Ballerstedt's press agitation and accused him of aiming for the dissolution and destruction of the Reich. The Bavarian League (Bayernbund), Hitler argued, claimed 'only to want the federal development of the German Reich', but 'in reality', Ballerstedt was striking at Germany itself and was thus 'pursuing the same aim that France had done for three hundred years'.[138]

Significantly, the first mission of his new paramilitary formation, undertaken even before it was christened the SA, was an attack not on the Jews, communists or Social Democrats, but on a meeting of Ballerstedt's Bayernbund in the Löwenbräukeller in the summer of 1921 under the banner 'we will not betray Bavaria'.[139] Hitler led an assault in which Ballerstedt was manhandled and the police were eventually called to break up the fight. His violent behaviour earned him a short jail sentence.[140] By contrast, it is not documented that Hitler ever personally laid hands on an individual Jew, either then or subsequently. Hitler's campaign against Bavarian federalism in general and his vendetta against Ballerstedt in particular continued throughout the 1920s and remained a preoccupation until he had him killed during the 'Night of the Long Knives'.

Hitler's view of foreign policy was, as we have seen, strongly ideological. That said, he was also beginning to develop a keen sense of geopolitics. In part, this followed the prevailing discourse of Germany's central location in Europe and her consequent vulnerability to 'encirclement'. He spoke of 'the position of our fatherland, which was geographically one of the most unfortunate in Europe'. Hitler inveighed repeatedly against the 'encirclement attempts of the Entente against Germany'. Where Hitler went much further than the nationalist mainstream was over the growing question of space, the *Raumfrage*, references to which increased exponentially during the early 1920s. In mid April 1920, Hitler lamented that 'the world was so unjustly distributed'. Four months later, he noted that Germany suffered from a crippling lack of space by comparison with Britain, which controlled about one-quarter of the entire globe. By March 1921, Hitler decried the injustice that Britain, with a smaller population, controlled 'three-quarters of the entire world', while more populous Germany had to make do with considerably less space. This sense of connection between Germany's 'disadvantageous military location' and the 'impossibility of securing the food supply in Europe'[141] stayed with Hitler to the end.

The cause of this unequal distribution, he believed, was global capitalism and its associated system of world governance. 'The international exploitation of capitalism must be combated', Hitler demanded, as well as that of 'international loan capital'. 'We want to turn world slaves into world citizens,' he announced. This required 'the liberation of our German people from the fetters of its international world enslavement'. This in turn meant that Germany would have to regain its military freedom of action. 'The German is either a free soldier,' Hitler argued, 'or a white slave.'[142] He therefore called upon the German people to relearn the old adage that 'whoever does not want to be a hammer must be an anvil', adding that 'we are an anvil today, and were being beaten until the anvil became a hammer', that is a 'German sword'. The idea that Germany must become a 'hammer' to avoid remaining an 'anvil' was a common trope at the time and one to which Hitler returned on a number of occasions.[143]

In short, Hitler saw the root of Germany's evils in her external subjection. 'Without liberating Germany from the chains of the peace treaties,' he claimed, 'there could be no chance of economic development for the nation.' 'The liberation of Germany,' Hitler continued, was 'only possible through national political cohesion at home and abroad.'[144] To that extent he was an exponent of the traditional primacy of foreign policy, and his emphasis on Germany's geopolitical exposure and her lack of 'space' was a commonplace of the time. It is also clear that he saw the enslavement of the Reich as the product not merely of enemy strength but of German weakness. This dictated a different sort of primacy of foreign policy, this time directed towards the mobilization of all the nation's domestic resources against the external enemy, another familiar theme in Prusso-German political thinking.[145] Any prospect of a vigorous German foreign policy, Hitler claimed, 'is predicated on a radical domestic political change'.[146]

In this context, the defeat of 1918 could be put to good use. Just as the catastrophe of 1806 had led to the Wars of Liberation in 1813, Hitler hoped that defeat in 1918 and the humiliation of Versailles would be followed by a national revival; 'fall', 'purification' and 'rebirth' were common tropes in Weimar Germany.[147] Hitler's rhetoric consciously mimicked that of the great patriotic martyr Palm, a Nuremberg bookseller who was executed by Napoleon in Hitler's hometown of Braunau for penning the rousing tract 'Germany in its deepest humiliation'. It was probably in this context that Hitler was first exposed to Carl von Clausewitz's notion that the failure to put up a strong resistance to the foreigner would make subsequent revival more difficult. He strongly believed that Germany's capitulation in 1918 had been premature, that her leaders should have mobilized a last-ditch French-style *levée en masse* which would have inspired later generations to resist. This belief was to remain with Hitler throughout his career, and became relevant again as military defeat beckoned once more in 1944–5.[148]

Hitler rejected the standard solutions to Germany's predicament. He wondered whether Zionism might be a solution to the 'Jewish Question', but quickly came down against the idea. Hitler saw in Jewish aspirations for statehood proof of their sense of national identity, despite all their international rhetoric. 'The Jews,' he wrote, were 'one people', who 'identified themselves as a people (Zionists)'. The 'proof' of this, Hitler continued, was 'Palestine'. Hitler was deeply sceptical, though, that the Zionist project could succeed, because it was completely inimical to the nature of Jewry. The 'Aryan' concept of the state, he claimed, was 'territorial', while the parasitic Jews could only feed off existing states, not establish one of their own. The Jew 'cannot build a state', he argued, because he was 'incapable of building a state'. Moreover, even if such a state could be erected, Hitler believed that it would merely increase the Jewish threat. 'The planned Zionist state "Jerusalem",' he argued, should not be regarded as an area of Jewish national settlement, but rather as 'the headquarters for Jewish world power plans for exploitation and nefarious activity'. For the rest of his life, in fact, Hitler stuck to the view that the establishment of a Jewish state, in Palestine or anywhere else, would simply create another focal point for world Jewry.[149]

He was also deeply critical of the plans of past imperial and present Weimar governments to grow or trade their way out of Germany's predicament. In the 1890s, Chancellor Caprivi had famously said that Germany must export goods if it were not to export people. In the 1920s, Stresemann and other leaders urged Germans to seek fulfilment through economic activity, and argued in favour of what we would today call a more geo-economic strategy to defend the national interest. Hitler rejected the 'purely economic way of looking at things', which he called the 'greatest mistake of German policy in the past decades'. 'The hoped-for peaceful seizure of [world] power through our economy,' he continued, 'has been a failure.' 'Industrialization [and] the peaceful capture of the world,' Hitler claimed, were doomed to fail, because one 'did not consider that there can be no economic policy without the sword [and] no industrialization without power'. 'The economy,' he explained, 'is only of secondary importance.' 'The main thing,' Hitler stressed, 'is national pride, [and] love of country.'[150] The primacy of politics in Hitler's thinking could not have been more clearly expressed.

Nor did Hitler want a restoration of the Second Empire. He was strongly critical of the failure of the traditional right to reach out to the alienated German working class and re-integrate them into the national fold. 'Why did one not give the people universal franchise', he asked with reference to the restrictive pre-1918 Prussian 'Three Class' electoral law, which advantaged the propertied elite, given that one was asking them to sacrifice their lives on the battlefield. The key question, Hitler stated, was not the state form itself, but what arrangement served the German people best in its quest to escape external subjection. Here there was remarkably little shift in his views throughout the early 1920s. The issue was not, he argued in April 1920, whether Germany should be 'a monarchy or a Republic', but rather 'which state form was best for the people'. 'We need a dictator of pure genius if we want to rise again.' 'We do not fetishize forms of government,' he explained in November 1921, 'the only thing that is decisive is the spirit which sustains it. The only consideration must be the welfare of the entire German people. In July 1922 he called for 'a German Reich, a Germanic state, and for all we care a German Republic'. In 1923, as Germany was racked by internal unrest, separatist movements, and renewed foreign occupation, he said that 'the form of the state took second place to the necessity of the fatherland'.[151] Hitler's constitutional thinking was not indebted to the glories of the imperial past, but focused on the needs of the present and the future.

Germany's salvation, he claimed, must begin with a profound inner transformation. 'First the internal enemy must be destroyed', he claimed, 'then it will be easy to crush the external enemy.' Hitler's domestic economic policy was vague at this stage, almost skeletal, but its general drift was unmistakable. He called for the nationalization of the entire banking and financial system, and thus the 'breaking of interest slavery', a term he had borrowed from Gottfried Feder.[152] His aim here was not so much public ownership in the Marxist sense, as national control over the levers of international financial manipulation. Hitler had not yet called for the physical destruction of world Jewry, but the elimination of German Jewry was already implicit, at least in the context of a future war, in case they might once again act as fifth columnists.[153] In the Gemlich letter of September 1919, he had already called for the 'complete removal of the Jews',[154] and in a letter of August 1920, one correspondent reports that Hitler believed that 'the bacillus' must be 'exterminated' in order to ensure the survival of the German people.[155] One way or the other, his domestic policy was essentially foreign policy.

Hitler was much more detailed on the need to rebuild the inner unity of Germany, especially relations between the classes. The reconciliation of the German worker to the nation after his exclusion in the Second Empire was at the heart of this project. Hitler defended the workers against standard conservative charges that they were 'knaves without a fatherland' who had shirked in the war. There should 'finally' be a struggle, he called, against the destructive spirit which Germany absorbed in the course of the century, which was 'the spirit of class interest and pride of rank'. For this reason, Hitler was a strong supporter of Bismarck's pioneering social legislation, though he felt it had not gone far enough. One listener reported how Hitler 'blamed the old state' for having 'treated its advanced social legislation as a matter of charity rather than entitlement', and for having 'failed to bridge the gap between mental and physical workers', and instead made itself the 'advocate of the established order'. As a result, the Kaiser's Germany had failed to protect the people from the corruption of 'Jewish mammonism'.[156]

Hitler therefore espoused 'socialism', but not as the Social Democrats, the Independent Socialists or the communists knew it. 'National' and 'social', he argued, were 'two identical terms'. 'True socialism teaches the most extreme performance of one's duties,' Hitler explained, 'real socialism in the highest form of the *Volk*.' 'Marxism is not socialism,' he claimed, 'I shall take socialism away from the socialists.' This was what the words 'worker' and 'socialist' in the party's name meant. There was 'no room', Hitler said, for 'class-conscious proletarians' in the party, just as there was no place either for a 'class-conscious bourgeois'.[157] He repeatedly reached out to workers.[158] All this explains Hitler's ambivalence towards communists, whom he regarded not only as good men led astray, but as temperamentally more congenial than the lukewarm bourgeois who clove to the safe middle path. 'I would rather be strung up in a Bolshevik Germany,' he averred, 'than be made blissful in a French southern Germany.' One observer noted that Hitler 'was courting the communists', saying that 'the two extremes, communists and students, should be brought together'. The centre ground, he claimed, was full of useless 'lickspittles' (*Schleimsieder*), whereas 'the communists had fought for their ideal with weapons and only been led astray'. They only need to be led towards the 'national cause'.[159] With German communists, Hitler hated the sin, but loved the sinner.

If Hitler saw Germany's salvation in a domestic revival, this did not make him blind towards foreign models. Indeed, the international context within which all his thinking was embedded made him particularly interested in the strength of rival powers. Hitler's principal model here was Britain. 'The British,' he admitted, 'are entitled to feel proud as a people.' Britain's vitality was based on the 'extraordinary brilliance' of her population. They had the 'British national sentiment which our people lacks so much' and they had maintained 'racial purity in the colonies', by which he meant the general absence of intermarriage between settlers and colonial administrators and the native population. Unlike the belated German national state after 1871, Britain enjoyed 'a centuries-long political-diplomatic tradition'. Unlike Germany, she had grasped the true connection between politics and economics. 'England has recognized the first principle of state health and existence,' Hitler argued, 'and has acted for centuries according to the principle that economic power must be converted into political power' and 'that political power must be used to protect economic life'. 'There are things that permit the British to exercise world domination,' he explained: 'a highly developed sense of national identity, clear racial unity, and finally the ability to convert economic power into political power, and political power into economic power'.[160]

There were, however, two profound contradictions in Hitler's thinking about Britain. First of all, he dubbed the country a 'second Jewry',[161] which sat ill with his otherwise respectful attitude. Hitler regarded British Jews as primarily urban, and so well integrated 'that they appeared to be British', which prevented the growth of anti-Semitism there. If true, then this might – in Hitler's reasoning – account for British hostility to the Reich, but he did not explain why this uniquely high level of Jewish penetration did not render her even weaker than Germany. This paradox at the heart of Hitler's view of the United Kingdom was never resolved. Secondly, there was the apparent contradiction that Britain had risen to greatness under the parliamentary system he so despised. There are grounds for believing, however, that he believed representative government suitable for the British but not for the Germans. 'If all Germans belonged to the tribe of the Lower Saxons [that is the tribe from which the English trace much of their descent – and the only one which Benjamin Franklin had considered fully white]', he remarked, 'the republican state form might be the most suited' to enabling the state 'to weather all storms and to draw on the best elements for running the country'. 'Because that is not the case [in Germany],' Hitler continued, 'the German people will always need an idol in the shape of a monarch.'[162] It was an early indication of Hitler's profound anxiety about German racial fragmentation in the face not so much of Jewry, as of the globally dominant Anglo-Saxons.

Hitler was also increasingly interested in the United States, which he came to regard as the repository of (in his view) all the best European racial elements, including the supposedly better sort of Germans. He remarked that, unlike Germany, which admitted swarms of eastern Jews, 'yellow people are not allowed to settle in America'.[163] In August 1922 he was introduced to Kurt Lüdecke, who had spent some time on business in the United States and whom Hitler would later send as an emissary across the Atlantic.[164] In the middle of that month, Rudolf Hess wrote on Hitler's behalf to the legendary automobile manufacturer, and fervent anti-Semite, Henry Ford for support.[165] Moreover, Anglo-America was also becoming interested in Hitler. He had appeared on the radar of the British Foreign Office as early as 1920, and by later 1922 he was firmly established in their minds as a figure to be reckoned with, but there was no attempt to make contact with him.[166]

By contrast, the United States embassy, probably influenced by Mussolini's coup in Italy, decided to take a closer look at this rising politician. In November 1922, the US assistant military attaché to Germany, Captain Truman Smith, came down from Berlin and met with Hitler on 20 November. Hitler argued that he was America's best chance of keeping the Bolsheviks out of Germany, condemned monarchy as 'an absurdity', claimed that 'dictatorship' was the only answer, denied any plans for a war against France and railed against 'the present abuse of capital'.[167] To be sure, these were all things that the American wanted to hear – apart from the remarks on capitalism – but they also represented Hitler's genuine views. One way or the other, the two men – both Wagnerians – seem to have hit it off. A 'marvelous demagogue', Smith wrote a few days later. 'I have rarely listened to such a logical and fanatical man. His powers over the mob must be immense.'[168]

It was Smith who put Hitler in touch with Ernst 'Putzi' Hanfstaengl immediately after their meeting. Hanfstaengl epitomized the relationship between Germany and the United States, which was to play such a central role in Hitler's thinking and policy over the next twenty years or so. Hanfstaengl's maternal grandfather, Wilhelm Heine, had emigrated to America as a liberal refugee from the failed 1848 revolution. He reached the rank of brigadier-general in the Union Army and served as a pallbearer at Lincoln's funeral.[169] Hanfstaengl's father owned a large art business in Munich. Hanfstaengl himself was partly brought up in the United States, where he attended Harvard University and was personally acquainted with the young Franklin Delano Roosevelt. From 1912, he had run the New York branch of his father's business. Hanfstaengl spent the war – which killed a brother fighting on the German side – in America. The business was ruined by the American entry into the conflict and the associated 'Trading with the Enemy Act'. Hanfstaengl became an enemy alien: the insider had become an outsider.

Over the next year, Hanfstaengl and Hitler were in almost daily contact. Hanfstaengl impressed upon Hitler not only the immense industrial and demographic power of the United States, but the fact that every German had a close relative there or in some other part of the world, something of which Hitler was already well aware. He argued that the party needed to reach out to the world through a coordinated foreign press policy.[170] Hanfstaengl now became effectively the NSDAP's external media liaison officer. He also entertained Hitler with his piano, playing from a repertoire which included not only Wagner but Harvard football marches. Captain Mayr later recalled the 'American methods of salesmanship' used to push out the Nazi message.[171] The United States thus increasingly became a model as well as a rival. Of course, as with Great Britain, Hitler's simultaneous insistence on the power of Jewry *in* the United States and the underlying racial power *of* the United States contradicted his own theories.[172] Once again, this paradox was never resolved, though it is the key to understanding both the origins of his whole world view and the events twenty years later which led to his downfall.

More immediately relevant to Germany's predicament were the dramatic recent examples of national revival, where peoples had bounced back from decline or catastrophic defeat. Perhaps surprisingly, Hitler was open to inspiration from France. 'The French Revolution was national and constructive,' he argued, 'whereas the German one wanted to be international and to destroy everything.' Hitler took a similarly positive view of later French radicalism. 'When France collapsed at Sedan,' he wrote, 'one made a revolution to rescue the sinking tricolour!' 'The war was waged with new energy,' he continued, and 'the will to defend the state created the French Republic in 1870', thus restoring 'French national honour'. This shows that Hitler's fundamental objection was not to the 'ideas of 1789', which he hardly ever mentioned. His real trauma – to which we will return later – was the fragmentation of Germany beginning with the Treaty of Westphalia in 1648.[173]

Hitler's most immediate outside inspirations, though, were the two countries which had undergone a fundamental domestic transformation since the end of the war. The first of these was Kemal Atatürk's Turkey, which came back from the brink of partition to see off the Greeks in 1922.[174] Germany had sunk so low, Hitler remarked in mid September 1922, scarcely ten days after Atatürk had recaptured Smyrna, that 'one must say today that the simplest Turk is more of a human being than we are'. Secondly, he enthused about Italy, where Mussolini and his fascists seized power in late October 1922 through his iconic 'March on Rome'. Shortly after, Hitler remarked coyly: 'one calls us German fascists', adding that he did not want to go into 'whether his comparison is true'. He was soon more forthright, demanding 'the establishment of a national government in Germany on the fascist model'. A year later, he told an interviewer from the *Daily Mail* that 'If a German Mussolini is given to Germany, people would fall down on their knees and worship him more than Mussolini has ever been worshipped.'[175]

Hitler now broke with the mainstream nationalist and revisionist consensus, which demanded that Italy surrender German-speaking South Tyrol. He argued that any new 'national government' would only be able to establish itself if it secured some major victories. These would be hard to achieve on the economic front, Hitler believed, and so the best bet was the incorporation (*Anschluss*) of Austria. This would require not only British but Italian approval. Moreover, Germany should align itself more generally with Mussolini's Italy, 'which has experienced its national rebirth and has a great future'. For both of these reasons, he condemned the 'palaver' about South Tyrol of the other nationalists in the strongest terms, emphasizing that 'there are no sentiments in politics, only the cool calculation of interest'.[176] Significantly, Hitler's support for an Italian alliance was primarily driven by geopolitics, not ideological affinity, because his first remarks to that effect were made not only well before the fascist takeover but also before his first mention of Mussolini.[177]

Hitler sometimes liked to say that the hard part was reviving Germany domestically; thereafter, dealing with her foreign enemies would be easy. In reality, he was under no illusions. A nationalist revival would make Germany 'capable of making an alliance' again, but this was only a necessary, not a sufficient condition to secure her position in the world. That would require actual allies. Temperamentally, Hitler was not averse to a Russian alliance, preferably without the communists, but if necessary with them. 'We must try to connect to the national [and] anti-Semitic Russia,' he demanded, 'not to the Soviets.' That said, in August 1920, nineteen years before the Hitler–Stalin Pact, he remarked that he would 'ally not only with Bolshevism but even with the devil in order to move against France and Britain'.[178] He feared, however, that this attempt to break free through a Russo-German pact would simply be crushed by the British and French. A British alliance was far more desirable, if that country could be kept out of the hands of the Jews.

Instead, Hitler looked further afield, at least conceptually. He hoped that he could confront the forces of international financial capitalism with the united front of the 'International of the productive', to mobilize 'voices for the defence of the rights of the productive peoples'. Germany would spearhead this effort, by purifying itself first. Hitler demanded no less than a pan-Aryan international anti-Semitic front. Inverting the *Communist Manifesto*'s famous slogan, he announced: 'not proletarians of all countries unite, but anti-Semites of all countries unite!' 'Aryans and anti-Semites of all peoples,' he elaborated, 'unite to fight against the Jewish race of exploiters and oppressors of all peoples.'[179] He repeated these injunctions in various forms on many occasions throughout the early 1920s,[180] and indeed beyond. Though Hitler never suggested that Nazism was 'for export', he was clear from the beginning that his programme required a high degree of international cooperation among international anti-Semites to compensate for Germany's weakness.

In the long run he believed that none of this would make any difference unless Germany solved the question of 'space'. At first, Hitler put his faith in colonial expansion, or restoration, as the way in which to solve the question of food supply and emigration.[181] 'Thanks to the loss of colonies,' he lamented, 'our industry is on the verge of collapse.' Germany had been punching well below its weight before 1914, he argued, because it had missed out on overseas expansion. There was an important shift in Hitler's spatial thinking around 1922, however. He came to see eastward expansion as the solution. 'In terms of foreign policy,' Hitler said in December 1922, 'Germany should prepare for a purely continental policy' and 'avoid violating British interests'. 'One should try to destroy Russia with the help of Britain,' he continued. 'Russia,' Hitler went on, 'would provide sufficient soil for German settlers and a wide area of activity for German industry.'[182] Though he had not yet alighted on the phrase *Lebensraum*, a further major plank of Hitler's thinking, the need for territorial enlargement to the east in order to secure the food supply of the German people and staunch the haemorrhage of emigration, was now in place. This was a policy primarily driven by fear and emulation of Anglo-America rather than anxiety about eastern communism or a desire to eliminate the Jews living there.

During the early 1920s, the broad outline of Hitler's domestic and foreign policy became increasingly clear, and most of it remained fixed until the end of his life. His hatred of the Jews was unmistakable, so was his fear of the western powers, which had evolved from rank hatred into something like awe. His admiration for the British and – as yet less markedly – the North Americans was evident. Hitler's elective affinity with Mussolini and others was freely avowed. There were, however, some surprising absences. For a man of strong subsequent opinions on the subject, he had said remarkably little so far – beyond a few swipes at Jewish Cubism, Futurism and 'kitsch' generally – about the role of culture in Germany's revival. Hitler had said much less than one might expect about the Soviet Union, and his fear of communism was dwarfed by that of capitalism. Even more remarkably, though there were some routine scatter-gun imprecations against the Poles in specific contexts to do with disputed territories in the east,[183] he had shown no signs of a blanket hostility towards Slavs in general or the Russian people in particular. What later became the *Lebensraum* conception was visible, but only in outline. His intellectual formation was not yet complete.

His authority in the party, by contrast, was now well established. The 'Führer principle' commanded widespread acceptance, even if his writ did not run equally in every part of his fiefdom. 'The Führer,' he said in late July 1922, 'must be an idealist, not least because he is leading those against whom everything has apparently conspired.' 'Nobody, great or small, needs to be ashamed of obedience,' he argued in mid November 1922 with regard to the SA, because 'they can elect their own leaders,' and those who are not worthy can be 'cast out'. 'Hitler took the view,' one witness to a speech given a few days later noted 'that only the leader was responsible to the mass. Commissions, committees' and other entities would 'slow down' not 'encourage the movement'. Occasionally, he reverted to the rhetoric of the 'drummer', for example when he lamented that Germany had not had a 'drum' like Lloyd George during the war.[184]

For the first eighteen months or so after his political emergence in 1919, Hitler seems to have conceived of the revival of Germany as a long-term process, in which he would play a supporting role, and which he might not live to witness himself. Even after his shift from *Trommler* to *Führer* in mid

1921, he advocated a steady process of ideological transformation rather than an insurrectionary takeover. During this period Hitler was an attentist, waiting for his propaganda and the march of events to turn the German population in his direction. 'People are still far too well off,' he remarked to Hanfstaengl, 'only when things are really bad will they flock to us.'[185]

In the second half of 1922, however, in the first of many temporal shifts in Hitler's career, he began to envisage a much shorter timeline. A new urgency crept into his rhetoric and actions; evolutionary languor gave way to revolutionary fervour. Germany, he argued, needed a 'dictator', that is, 'a man who if necessary can go over blood and corpses'. His regime 'could then be replaced by a form of government similar to that of the Lord Protector', which in turn could be followed by a monarchy.[186] This recourse to English history, which gives a sense of Hitler's range of historical reference, was a clever pitch for conservative backing for a coup which would give him dictatorial power, but held out the prospect of an evolution via a German Cromwell and a General Monk to the restoration of the monarchy. Driving this process was Hitler's growing conviction not only that he alone could save the country, but that a perfect storm of domestic challenges and external threats made it imperative that he do so soon. Time was speeding up. Germany was out of joint, and Hitler was more and more convinced that only he could put things right.

PART TWO

Fragmentation

In 1923–7, Hitler grappled with the forces of disintegration in Germany. The most immediately threatening of these remained German particularism, which was largely indistinguishable in his mind from separatism. Hitler was also deeply exercised by the supposed racial fragmentation of the German people. This he attributed partly to deep political divisions, aggravated by foreign and Jewish support for parliamentarism, and partly to the historical legacy of confessional strife. Hitler attempted to head off these dangers through a putsch in Munich. In his subsequent speeches and writing, Hitler contrasted this miserable vista with the natural coherence of the Anglo-American world, which now dominated Germany more than ever, not just militarily, but economically and culturally as well. Last but not least, during his prison term at Landsberg and after his release, Hitler fought the threatened fragmentation of the NSDAP. It was only with difficulty that Hitler re-established his authority over the ideological direction of the movement and the party apparatus, a process that was not yet complete by the late 1920s.

4

The Struggle for Bavaria

Weimar Germany faced many challenges in its early years, but the most existential was the threat of territorial disintegration. In the Rhineland and the Palatinate, the French authorities made sustained efforts to encourage groups which favoured regional autonomy, or even independence, at the expense of the Reich as a whole.[1] In Hanover and other parts of Germany there was a revival of traditional monarchist and anti-Prussian sentiment directed against Berlin. The main threat to the authority of the central state, however, came from Bavaria. This was partly a question of ideology and culture, pitting the Catholic, traditional and more conservative Bavarians against the often more Protestant or progressive areas of Germany. The main point at issue, though, was constitutional. In the Second Reich established by Bismarck in 1871, Munich had secured extensive reserved rights, many of which were lost to the Weimar Republic in 1919. The Bavarian People's Party, the principal political force in the region, was committed by its 'Bamberg Programme' of 1920 to a revision of the constitution in favour of greater powers for the constituent states, in effect a return to the status quo ante. Much of the early history of the Weimar Republic, in fact, was dominated by the question of the relations between Bavaria and the Reich, a conflict in which the threat of armed force was always implicit and sometimes overt.

These tensions were aggravated by a whole raft of other problems, which escalated throughout 1923. In January, the French occupied the Rhineland in retaliation for Germany's failure to keep up with her reparations payments. The Reich government proclaimed 'passive resistance'. There was intense social unrest, partly driven by galloping inflation, which wiped out middle-class savings and ruined pensions, and partly by the German Communist Party. A workers' revolt or a nationalist coup, or both, seemed likely. To make matters worse, there was widespread fear that the French would seek to occupy other parts of the country, ostensibly to enforce the peace terms, but actually to keep Germany in permanent subjection. For all their dreams of returning to the offensive, the government and the military leadership were profoundly conscious of the Reich's military weakness; the disarmament clauses at Versailles had left Germany defenceless.[2] This forced them to rely on paramilitary formations, both to suppress internal unrest and to provide some sort of credible resistance to a French invasion. Chancellor Cuno and General von Seeckt drew up a plan for a secret mobilization, in which the Reichswehr stored weapons and supported the paramilitaries. Hitler, like many other leaders, agreed to place his SA under army command in the event of a French attack. To that extent, the NSDAP was already part of the national establishment.[3]

Hitler's position at this time was complicated. He was still virtually unknown in most of Germany. The main Berlin newspapers ignored him and his party. They didn't even report on the riotous *Deutscher Tag* at Coburg, whose resonance was confined to south Germany.[4] Hitler had very few funders outside of Bavaria, with the notable exception of the Ruhr industrial baron Fritz Thyssen, who contributed substantially in the course of 1923.[5] That said, within the non-particularist Bavarian right-wing nationalist milieu, Hitler now enjoyed a commanding position. He was well known in Munich, which Thomas Mann described in a 1923 letter to the American journal *The Dial* as 'the city of Hitler'. His speeches drew large and ecstatic crowds. Karl Alexander von Müller, who heard him speak for the first time at the Löwenbräukeller in late January 1923, describes the 'burning core of hypnotic mass excitement'[6] created by the flags, the relentless marching music and the short warm-up speeches by lesser party figures before the man himself appeared amid a flurry of salutes. Hitler would then be interrupted at almost every sentence by tempestuous applause, before departing for his next engagement.

Over the next few months, the tempo of Nazi events and activities increased. There were in excess of 20,000 NSDAP members at the start of 1923, and that figure more than doubled over the next ten months to 55,000;[7] the SA nearly quadrupled from around 1,000 men to almost 4,000 during the same period.[8] Hitler himself was so prominent that the NSDAP was widely known as the 'Hitler-Movement', the term under which his activities were now recorded by the Bavarian police. He had become a cult figure. The *Völkischer Beobachter* became a daily paper in February 1923, giving preferential treatment to the printing of Hitler's speeches. Two months later, it began marking the Führer's birthday, an honour not accorded any other Nazi leader.[9] He had long given up the humble role of drummer.[10] Hitler spoke once again of the need for a dictator. The German people, he claimed, 'are waiting today for the man who calls out to them: Germany, rise up [and] march'.[11] There was no doubt from the context and rhetoric that he planned to play that role himself. His followers styled him not merely the leader of the national movement but Germany's saviour and future leader. The Oberführer of the SA, Hermann Göring, acclaimed him at his birthday rally on 20 April 1923 as the 'beloved Führer of the German freedom movement'. Alfred Rosenberg described him simply as 'Germany's leader [Führer]'.[12]

Conscious of his tenuous position within the Catholic Bavarian mainstream, Hitler continued to try to build bridges to the Church, or at least to its adherents. 'We want,' Hitler pledged, 'to see a state based on true Christianity. To be a Christian does not mean a cowardly turning of the cheek, but to be a struggler for justice and a fighter against all forms of injustice.'[13] The NSDAP did succeed in making some inroads among Catholic students at the university and the peasantry and in winning over quite a few clerics, including for a while Cardinal Faulhaber, but for the most part Hitler made little headway.[14] He also struggled to connect with the Bavarian aristocracy, which remained firmly focused on the Wittelsbach dynasty, especially Crown Prince Rupprecht, a credible figure on account of his role as a commander in the war.[15]

The French occupation of the Rhineland, the dire economic situation which escalated into a hyperinflation by the middle of the year, and the resulting rise in communist and other extreme left-wing agitation made Hitler's breeze blow stronger. Albert Leo Schlageter, executed in late May 1923, the great martyr of the nationalist resistance against the French occupiers in the Ruhr, was appropriated by the Nazis, even though it is unclear whether he was ever a member of the party.[16] That said, Hitler refused to join the cross-party non-violent *Ruhrkampf* against France. He argued that the real culprits lay in Berlin, not Paris. Shortly after the French struck, Hitler called on his audience in the Zirkus Krone to pursue 'a general settling of accounts with the domestic political enemies'; the slogan should be 'not down with France, but down with the November criminals'. 'No battle abroad,' he elaborated on another occasion, 'until victory has been secured at home.' Moreover, Hitler interpreted the French move within his established framework of an international capitalist plot against the Reich. France, he claimed, was 'in cahoots with international high finance' to subjugate Germany and seize her lands. Rejecting the call for national solidarity, Hitler was playing on a much larger stage. 'Down with the other parties, down with the unity front,' he demanded, 'that is the slogan, and the growth of anti-Semitism in England and France is more important than the struggle for the Ruhr.'[17]

In this perfervid atmosphere, Hitler deepened his links with the various paramilitary organizations in Bavaria, and the Reichswehr command in Munich. Under the patronage of Ernst Röhm, in whose Reichswehr office they met, the SA, the Bund Oberland, the Organisation Niederbayern, the Reichsflagge and Organisation Lenz formed a 'working group' in mid March 1923. The military command was entrusted to Hermann Kriebel, but the political direction largely devolved to Hitler. The Reichswehr Commander in Munich, General Otto von Lossow, introduced Hitler to the army chief of staff, Hans von Seeckt, in the Bavarian capital on 11 March 1923. The meeting was not a success. Hitler made a wild speech offering his support for an immediate military coup against the Reich government.[18] At Röhm's request, he produced a memorandum on the political situation five weeks later.[19] This warned that 'time' was running out: France would soon have Bolshevized Germany and thus completed its subjection. Now, Hitler argued, was the moment to 'seize power' and 'brutally cleanse' the country of its domestic enemies. The move from attentism to revolutionary activism, which had begun towards the end of the previous year, was now very evident.

During this period, Hitler continued to elaborate and develop his strategic thinking. Throughout 1923, he lambasted international capitalism – Jewish and non-Jewish – as the source of Germany's ills. Hitler provided a brief foreword to Gottfried Feder's book on the subject describing it as a 'catechism' of National Socialism.[20] The salience of anti-capitalism, fears of expropriation and exploitation and enslavement by foreign masters is very clear in the party's 'work of the committee for food security of the National Socialist movement', which Hitler blessed in the summer of 1923. It defined the 'internal enemy' as 'profiteering in the system of the national economy', the 'idea of class conflict' and 'immoral tendencies in government and law-making'. It lamented the crucifixion of the German middle class by the 'massive fraud' of 'our money economy', the general 'spirit of speculation' and the 'terror of the capitalist idea'. The document made no direct mention of Bolshevism or the Soviet Union. It recommended – with Hitler's approval – that the state protect the 'basic assets of the nation', namely 'foodstuffs and manpower' through 'an anti-capitalist legislation in the fields of land and settlement, housing, but also in the first instance in the field of the supply of necessities'. This would require the 'exclusion of foreign capital from German land and soil, businesses and cultural assets'.[21]

Like the Ludendorff circle, Hitler was much less worried about the fate of German minorities and the peripheral lands of the Reich than about the fate of the core area, which he believed to be threatened with subjection and even extinction.[22] Hitler was also beginning to look at long-term solutions to Germany's predicament. He rejected the common notion of an 'internal' colonization of sparsely populated German lands in favour of territorial expansion. 'The [re-]distribution of land alone,' he warned in the spring of 1923, 'cannot bring relief. The living conditions of a nation can at the end of the day only be improved through the political will to expand.'[23] The concept of *Lebensraum* is already clearly visible here, though the term itself was not used.

Throughout the spring and summer of 1923, Hitler steadily became more aggressive. In early March 1923 there was a meeting of paramilitary formations in Munich at which Hermann Esser suggested that if the French advanced across the Rhine, the Entente should be informed that all Jews would be interned and shot if they did not withdraw.[24] It is not clear whether this thought originally came from Hitler, but if it did it would be the first example of his subsequent strategy of using the Jews as hostages for the good behaviour of the western powers. In mid April 1923, a massive joint paramilitary exercise was held at the Fröttmaninger Heide near Freimann, followed by a march to the government quarter in Munich. A fortnight later, on May Day, there was a serious confrontation with organized labour at the Oberwiesenfeld. Hitler encouraged this escalation. He personally ordered the *Sturmabteilungen* not merely to defend their own assemblies, by beating up hecklers, but also to disrupt those of their enemies. Hitler further instructed them to abuse Jews on the streets and in cafés.[25] Rumours abounded that the NSDAP and the nationalist organizations would 'march on Berlin', clean out the stables there and establish a government capable of facing down the Entente.

Hitler also worked to expand his international links. These were partly designed to secure funding. One of the figures of whom Hitler had high hopes was the American automobile tycoon and Democratic Party Congressional candidate Henry Ford, who not only symbolized the kind of national productive capitalism he so admired but was an active anti-Semite into the bargain. His book, translated as *Der internationale Jude* (1921), had been a great success in Germany.[26] It was well known at the time that Hitler kept a portrait of Ford in his office, and there was talk of inviting the American to speak.[27] His overtures to Ford were a failure. According to Robert D. Murphy, US vice consul in Munich, who met Hitler in early March 1923, 'Mr Ford's organization had so far made no money contributions to the party' and 'his funds were principally contributed by patriotic Germans living abroad'.[28] Press reports spoke of Nazi hopes for 'America' and a joint struggle against Jews and capitalism.[29] At the end of August 1923, Hitler travelled to Switzerland in search of financial backing. 'Hitler is very engaging,' one of the ladies of the house of a wealthy Swiss supporter noted in her diary, 'his whole body trembles when he speaks,' which he did 'wonderfully'. Hitler told the Swiss general Wille: 'I will strike in the autumn.'[30]

Hitler's other motivation was to persuade the great powers to tolerate the rise of the NSDAP and to accept the outcome of any revolutionary action. His main targets here were the Americans and Italy. In April 1923, he told the prominent German-American journalist Karl von Wiegand that he rejected the claims of 'Bolshevik' Berlin 'just as the American colonists of Washington's times refused to appear before the courtly tribunal of George III'.[31] In June 1923, the *Völkischer Beobachter* formally announced that the NSDAP would not insist on the return of South Tyrol by Italy. In August 1923, Hitler sent Lüdecke to Italy to make contact with the fascist regime, but without success.[32] Hitler tried to win over the Americans through a series of interviews. In mid August 1923 he gave a fire-breathing interview to the New York *World* promising a 'fascist dictatorship' and demanding that 'officialdom must be reduced to a minimum', perhaps a sop to the 'small government' preferences of his American readers.[33]

These overtures suggest that Hitler's overwhelmingly negative image of Anglo-America had given way to a more positive attitude. This was partly tactically motivated, because he realized that his domestic aims could only be achieved with the support or at least the toleration of London and Washington. It was also partly driven by a shift in his strategic conception, which saw Britain less and less as the 'absolute enemy' of 1919–20 and more as a potential ally. A large part of Hitler's shift, however, seems to have been driven by a much broader engagement with the American 'way of life', probably the result of prolonged exposure to Hanfstaengl, with whom he was in almost daily contact at this time. This was reflected in the new large 'American' format given to the *Völkischer Beobachter* on 29 August 1923, which was much remarked upon at the time. Not everybody was happy with this trend or Hanfstaengl's associated swagger and American 'slang'. Friedrich Plumer, an early Nazi who later broke with Hitler, accused Hanfstaengl of 'Americanizing' the movement.[34]

Despite these strides, Hitler was now under severe pressure. Relations with the Munich authorities were extremely poor. He had already been imprisoned twice, and at the start of the year he was hauled in before the police to explain his behaviour at Coburg.[35] The Bavarian interior minister Schweyer attempted to ban the NSDAP party congress in Munich a fortnight later, and though he failed he did ensure that they were unable to meet in the open air, thus reducing the number of attendees.[36] Schweyer had another go at charging Hitler over the Oberwiesenfeld brawls, forcing the latter to write a memorandum to the Bavarian legal authorities in his own defence.[37]

Hitler could continue to play grandmother's footsteps with the authorities, by promising betterment and then going back on his commitments, but for how long? A mass rally at the Zirkus Krone in mid July 1923 was so full that he had to shut the doors half an hour before it started. The police commander on the night warned Hitler that he would not be allowed to unfurl the party banners inside the building.[38] The subsequent march to the main station in Munich led to a clash with the police; Hitler, on foot, confronted rubber-truncheon-wielding mounted officers. At the same time, Hitler was being criticized by the SA. Not for the last time in his career, their rank and file were straining at the leash, and could not understand why Hitler was not leading them to Berlin, or at least to the City Hall in Munich. Keeping large numbers of armed men in a state of semi-permanent revolution was not possible. If something was not undertaken soon, there was a real danger that the pot would either go off the boil, or boil over prematurely.

Hitler was thus at a strategic crossroads. On the one hand, he was calling for a long-term propagandistic effort to prepare the German people for a return to great power status. This implied a kind of revolutionary attentism, not unlike that of the pre-war Social Democrats,[39] in which the NSDAP would simply reap the fruits of its work further down the line. Hitler suggested as much at the start of the year, when he announced that 'one day the day will come at which we will launch a putsch, no not a putsch,' he added with contempt, 'but a puff of air and then this rock will disappear.'[40] When the time came, in other words, the NSDAP would simply huff and puff and blow the house down. On the other hand, the internal and external situation was constantly changing, presenting him with new opportunities but also new threats. He had long argued that there was no quick fix to Germany's ills. Could it be, however, that history could be speeded up, that destiny might be embraced rather than awaited?

The examples of Turkey and Italy seemed to suggest that it could. In the autumn of 1923, he let it be known that what Atatürk had done 'is what we will have to do in the future as well in order to liberate ourselves'.[41] Hitler subsequently cited him as a model for his 'beer hall' putsch. Hitler also acclaimed Mussolini as a model; he used Roman-style standards for the SA in explicit homage.[42] Though there is no evidence that Mussolini supported Hitler's plans for a coup, there is equally no doubt that he served as an important inspiration.[43]

In the late summer and autumn, the situation escalated still further. The French-backed separatist Hans Adam Dorten proclaimed a 'Rhenish Republic' in July 1923;[44] his supporters occupied government buildings in Aachen. On 26 September 1923, the Stresemann government announced the end of passive resistance against the French, its objectives unmet. The resulting sense of humiliation fuelled a widespread belief that a coup to establish a new 'national' government in Berlin was imminent. At around the same time, the communists were making substantial inroads in central Germany, especially Thuringia. In Bavaria, right-wing militias, including the SA, enjoying the full cooperation of the local Reichswehr, prepared to repel both communists and the French if necessary. They met repeatedly at rallies – 'German days' – across the province, first in Nuremberg, then at Hof, where Hitler gave one of the speeches, and finally in Bayreuth. The Generalstaatskommissar for Bavaria, and its de facto ruler, Gustav von Kahr, was known to be pondering his next move.

Hitler was not too worried about the communists, who had been crushed by the end of October. The real danger lay on the right. First, that the leaders of the national opposition in Bavaria would fluff the task of marching on Berlin. Hitler relentlessly pushed for action: 'either Berlin marches and ends in Munich,' he warned, 'or Munich marches and ends in Berlin'.[45] Secondly, there was the possibility that the NSDAP would be coopted as footsoldiers in support of an alien agenda, especially that of social conservatism. Thirdly, and most importantly, Hitler was worried about the ultimate intentions of the Bavarian government and many of the organizations which provided its political and military muscle. He feared that they wanted not to renationalize Germany through capturing Berlin but a separate conservative Bavaria instead. Whether this was their main aim or might simply be the default option in the face of determined republican and left-wing resistance in the rest of the Reich did not greatly matter to him. Nor, as we have seen, did Hitler distinguish between full-blown separatism and the claims of the Bavarian particularists to be returning to the old federal arrangements of the Second Empire. The result, in his view, would be the same: the fragmentation of the Reich in the face of extreme internal and external danger.

The Bavarian government and many of the groups associated with it were indeed planning to recalibrate the federal relationship with Berlin; they made no secret of it. Otto Pittinger, the leader of the 'Bund Bayern und Reich', was open about his desire to re-establish the Wittelsbach monarchy in Bavaria, and to return to the looser federal bonds of Bismarck's time. Kahr himself had repeatedly spoken at meetings in favour of the restoration of the Bavarian monarchy.[46]

Hitler responded to this existential challenge with a nuanced strategy. On the one hand, he relentlessly attacked the conservative monarchists. 'One should not imagine,' he pronounced in his speech to the *Deutscher Tag* in Hof in mid September 1923, 'that nationalism expresses itself' by demanding 'that the old flags should fly again, that the old authoritarian state should be resurrected and that the old conditions should be restored'. 'That,' he claimed, 'is not nationalism.'[47] On the other hand, Hitler sought to create a common front with conservatives and monarchists against the external enemy. On 25 September 1923, Scheubner-Richter was tasked with bringing about a meeting between Hitler and Crown Prince Rupprecht of Bavaria; the hope was that he could be persuaded to support a march on Berlin.[48] Party members were instructed, on pain of expulsion, to resign from all paramilitary formations not under the political leadership of the Kampfbund, that is, his own.[49] A drumbeat of mass meetings was planned.[50]

Hitler flanked this rhetoric with a carefully calibrated propagandistic effort. He gave a speech at Bayreuth – Wagner's city – in mid September 1923, and returned about a fortnight later to speak again. On that occasion, taking up the invitation of Winifred Wagner, the English-born wife of Wagner's son Siegfried, he went to the Wagner shrine at Wahnfried. There Hitler spoke to the composer's son-in-law, the racist political philosopher Houston Stewart Chamberlain, author of the best-selling *Foundations of the Nineteenth Century*, upon whom he made a very favourable impression.[51] Hitler paid homage at Wagner's grave. He also published an autobiographical text and a selection of his speeches under the title of *Adolf Hitler: His Life and His Speeches*.[52] The name on the front page was that of his associate Victor von Koerber, but the real author was Hitler. He rehearsed his political positions, including his attacks on 'Bolshevism' and 'international Jewish mammonism', but pointedly deleted all negative references to the United States, most likely in order to encourage US toleration of a successful coup. The principal purpose of the book was to cast Hitler as the saviour of Germany. Koerber-Hitler spoke of him no longer as a 'drummer' but as 'an architect who is building the mighty German cathedral'. No doubt drawing on his overtures to Bavarian Catholics, Hitler had himself styled as a messianic figure, whose political awakening was compared to the resurrection of Christ, and whose writings were a kind of holy writ.

On 26 September, on the same day as the end of passive resistance in the Ruhr, the Bavarian government announced a state of emergency. Kahr was made commissary general.[53] That same day, too, Hitler signed a proclamation in support of a 'Battle League to Break Interest Slavery'; pointedly, the main enemy was defined as international capitalism and the victor powers rather than the German left. In an accompanying 'open letter to the Bavarian government' in the *Völkischer Beobachter*, which he co-authored with – among others – Drexler and Gottfried Feder, Hitler criticized the planned handover of German national assets to support a new imposed Allied settlement.[54] What had previously been a straightforward clash between Berlin and right-wing Munich was now about to become a triangular contest pitting Kahr, the Reich government and the Munich nationalist scene, most prominently Hitler, against each other.

The following day, Hitler's intended series of mass meetings was banned. Nazi suspicions of Kahr's intentions grew.[55] Hitler condemned the measure as directed against the '*Völkisch* freedom movement'.[56] He warned Kahr and federalists generally against 'limiting' the 'historical mission of Bavaria purely to the jealous preservation of purely Bavarian concerns inside the white-blue Bavarian boundary posts' and of 'privileging' the 'justified demands for the recapture of Bavarian statehood within the framework of the Reich' at the expense of the 'necessary liberation of greater Germany'. This choice of words was already quite a concession to local sensitivities, but Hitler was quick to stress that he saw Bavaria's mission as 'coming to the aid of our threatened brothers in central and northern Germany'. 'Not only the future of Bavaria,' he added, 'but the future of Germany will be decided in Bavaria today.'[57] The chief of police, Seisser, later recalled that Hitler dismissed anybody who did not support him as 'either a nightwatchman or a separatist, Danube-monarchist, papal or French in sentiment'.[58]

Tension rose steadily throughout October. On 20 October, the Reich government in Berlin sacked Lossow, the army commander in Munich. Secure in Kahr's backing, he refused to move. Otto Pittinger's paramilitary Bund Bayern und Reich stood by to support them. The rest of the Reichswehr looked set to move against the 'mutineers'. Armed groups assembled on the Bavarian-Thurinigian border. Germany seemed on the verge of falling apart. Once again, Hitler inveighed against the federalists, this time with an even greater sense of urgency. 'The narrow-minded, purely Bavarian-oriented policy of the forces behind the Bavarian dictatorship,' he told an assembly of SA leaders, meant that across Germany Bavaria was now seen as a 'separatist' state trying to exit the Reich, abandoned by all its allies. This situation, Hitler fulminated, suited only Poincaré's France. The answer was 'tackling the German question in the last minute from Bavaria', culminating in the planting of the swastika on the Reichstag in Berlin. This was the Bavarian 'mission'.[59]

Despite the local demands on his time, Hitler made serious efforts to square international opinion. He gave an interview to the American United Press at Bayreuth in which he said that the Bavarian 'masses' would back him over Kahr and announced that he was 'no monarchist and would battle against all monarchic adventures, because the Hohenzollern and Wittelsbachers would merely encourage separatist divisions'.[60] Hitler also gave an interview to the distinguished German-American journalist George Sylvester Viereck, in which he claimed to be the only bulwark against 'Bolshevism' and revealed his territorial ambitions. 'We must regain our colonies and we must expand eastward,' he argued. 'There was a time when we could have shared the world with England. Now, we can stretch our cramped limbs only to the east. The Baltic is merely a German lake.'[61] At around the same time, he told an American newspaper of his plans for a 'Monroe Doctrine for Germany',[62] the first time he articulated a theme which was to run through his entire strategy. In mid October 1923, he made a public statement in *Corriere Italiano* once again renouncing any German claim to South Tyrol, as a gesture to Mussolini.[63] He was convinced that France would support a separatist coup, but seems to have believed that Britain and the United States would at least tolerate his own *Putsch*.[64]

Right at the end of October 1923, the *Völkisch* and paramilitary leaders assembled in Röhm's Reichswehr office in Munich and began preparations for armed action.[65] Their concern was at least as much to head off any separatist tendencies in the Bavarian leadership as it was to support them in joint action against Berlin. It was expected that Kahr would announce his plans for a coup against the Berlin government at a meeting scheduled for 8 November at the Bürgerbräukeller. If Hitler and his co-conspirators were going to forestall Kahr, and his suspected separatist agenda, or co-opt him for their own plans, this would be an excellent opportunity to catch all the major protagonists in one place.[66]

Hitler struck in an evening of high drama. He burst into the Bürgerbräukeller, fired his pistol into the ceiling and announced to general applause that the Bavarian government of Knilling and the Reich government in Berlin were deposed. Hitler 'suggested' Kahr as regent for Bavaria and Pöhner as minister president thereof. He promised that a 'German national government' would be announced in Munich that same evening. He 'recommended' that he himself should take over the 'leadership' until accounts had been settled with the 'criminals' in Berlin. Ludendorff was to be commander of a new national army; Lossow Reichswehr minister, and Seisser German minister of police. Attempting to marry Bavarian local pride and the pan-German mission, Hitler said that it was the task of the provisional government to march on the 'den of iniquity in Berlin'. In a considerable concession to Bavarian sensibilities he vowed 'to build up a cooperative federal state in which Bavaria gets what it deserves'.[67] Kahr, Lossow and Seisser were held captive and prevailed upon to support the coup.

The putschists now swung into action. Their 'Proclamation to all Germans' announced that the nation would no longer be treated like a 'Negro tribe'.[68] Hanfstaengl was detailed to inform and influence the foreign press; he tipped off Larry Rue of the *Chicago Tribune* that the coup was about to begin and appeared in the Bürgerbräukeller with a group of journalists from other countries.[69] The offices of the pro-SPD *Münchener Post* were smashed up by the SA, but there was no 'white terror' on the streets of Munich; Hitler's main anxiety was the Bavarian right, not the left. One of the few detentions was that of Count Soden-Fraunhofen, a staunch Wittelsbach loyalist who was accused of being a 'hireling of the Vatican'.[70] Winifred and Siegfried Wagner, who were almost certainly aware of the plot in advance, were due at the Odeon Theatre immediately after the coup, where Siegfried was to direct a Wagner concert, intended perhaps as a celebration.[71] Hitler announced melodramatically that 'the morning will see either a national government in Germany or our own deaths'.[72]

The morning brought the sobering realization that the putschists were on their own. There was no general national rising across the Reich. Kahr, Lossow and Seisser, who had given their 'word of honour' under duress to support the coup, slipped away and began to mobilize forces to restore order. Hitler's worst fears were confirmed: he was now fighting not merely red Berlin, but reactionary separatist forces in Munich. A bitter Nazi pamphlet rushed out that day announced that 'today the [November revolution] was to have been extinguished from Munich and the honour of the fatherland restored'. 'This,' the pamphlet added, invoking Hitler's rhetoric, 'would have been the Bavarian mission.' Kahr, Lossow and Seisser, alas, had betrayed the cause. Behind them, the pamphlet continued, stood 'the same trust of separatists and Jews' who had been responsible for the treasonous Armistice in 1918, the 'slave treaty of Versailles and the despicable stock-exchange speculation' and all other miseries.[73] It concluded with a call to make one last effort to save the situation. What was striking about this document was the far greater stress laid on the separatist-clerical and capitalist danger than on the threat of Bolshevism.

Hitler and his co-conspirators set out mid morning 9 November for central Munich in a column numbering about 2,000 men, many of them armed. Strasser, who had turned up from Nuremberg with a contingent of followers, was particularly belligerent. Their plan was unclear, but it seems to have been to wrest the initiative back from Kahr; Hitler may also have intended to go down fighting as he had vowed the night before. Outside the Feldherrenhalle at the Odeonsplatz, they encountered a police cordon. Hitler linked arms with Scheubner-Richter and the column marched straight at the police lines, weapons at the ready. It is not clear whether he was seeking death as a blood sacrifice to inspire future generations or whether he was trying to imitate Napoleon's famous confrontation with Marshal Ney, when the emperor marched slowly towards his old comrades, who refused to shoot. Shots were exchanged, leading to fatalities on both sides. Hitler himself escaped death only narrowly, injured his arm and fled the scene. Before the day was out, Kahr issued a proclamation announcing the failure of the 'Hitler-Putsch'.[74] The great drama had ended in complete fiasco.

A pamphlet published immediately after the failed coup, penned by either Hitler himself or someone briefed by him, traced the collapse of relations between Munich and Berlin throughout October 1923. It quoted from a conversation which allegedly took place between Hitler and Lossow, in which the latter 'repeatedly spoke of an Ankara-government', on the lines of the Turkish national revival under Atatürk, which would take on Berlin. The pamphlet went on to attack Kahr, who was allegedly 'completely dependent on the Roman Jesuits'. 'Because Hitler knew,' it continued, 'that the "black [i.e. clerical] danger" in Bavaria was even bigger than the red one', Hitler had been compelled to pre-empt the machinations of the Jesuits, the Wittelsbach dynasty, the French, the papacy and the Habsburgs.[75] The main lines of Hitler's rather contradictory interpretation of the Putsch were thus clear: it had been carried out both with the collusion of the Bavarian conservatives and in order to forestall their plans for a clerical, monarchist and separatist coup at the expense of the Reich as a whole.

On 11 November, Hitler was arrested at the home of Hanfstaengl at Uffing am Staffelsee, south of Munich. Just before his capture, Hitler managed to get off a short message to Alfred Rosenberg, asking him to lead the movement in his absence. He was imprisoned at Landsberg, awaiting trial.[76] Hitler seems at first to have undergone some kind of personal crisis, appearing depressed and even suicidal. Hess, not yet in Landsberg, spoke of him being 'emotionally very down'.[77] Following stormy interrogations, Hitler went on a ten-day hunger strike.[78] According to the recollection of the resident psychologist, Alois Maria Ott, Hitler was distraught at the death of his comrades and announced that 'I have had enough, I am done, if I had a revolver I would take it.' Ott succeeded in calming Hitler and persuaded him to call off his protest; the planned forcible feeding proved unnecessary.[79] In early December 1923, Winifred Wagner sent him blankets, books and other items to cheer him up; she also wrote frequently.[80] Hitler's spirits revived, and within a fortnight he was beginning to prepare his defence.

In mid December 1923, Hitler was questioned at Landsberg by the state prosecutor, Dr Hans Ehard. Still struggling with his injured arm, Hitler vowed 'to play his best trump-cards in the court room itself', and wondered aloud whether 'certain gentlemen' would have the courage to perjure themselves under oath in court. This was clearly directed at Kahr, Lossow and Seisser. Ehard reported that Hitler, having initially steadfastly refused to make any sort of statements on the record, to avoid 'having words put into his mouth', soon began to hold 'interminable political lectures'. He explained that he had struck because the men of the *Kampfbund* had been impatient for action, and could not be held back any longer. Ehard, probably acting on instructions from superiors who feared dirty linen being washed in public, asked Hitler directly whether he planned 'to bring the question of the alleged Bavarian separatist plans into [his] defence strategy'. Hitler pointedly declined to answer, but he soon launched into a lengthy attack on 'well-known, influential, one-sidedly religiously inclined circles, which pursued solely separatist aims and to this end pushed forward Kahr as a straw man'. 'These circles,' he added, 'sought the restoration of the monarchy.' In the context of what he called 'French plans to break up', these tendencies would lead to 'the separation of Bavaria' and the 'disintegration of the Reich'.[81] It is striking that Hitler again spent far more time on these dangers to the Reich than those from the left.

Hitler soon made himself comfortable in Landsberg.[82] Conditions were remarkably good, as both the warders and the other prisoners treated him as a celebrity, even after his sentencing. The terms of his incarceration did not involve compulsory labour, a regimented diet, prison clothes or restrictions on visitors. His main companions behind bars were his chauffeur and bodyguard Emil Maurice and Rudolf Hess; his authority was unquestioned. The young Nazi Hermann Fobke related that it was not so much a question of 'presenting to the boss' as being 'lectured to by the boss'.[83] Admirers brought him books, food and flowers and news. Helene Bechstein provided cheese. In all, more than 500 people, including Elsa Bruckmann, visited him in the first few months alone. Hanfstaengl later remarked that the cell looked like a 'delicatessen'. For all that, Hitler found captivity irksome, as he was kept cooped up and powerless to intervene in outside affairs. His surroundings were far from luxurious – Landsberg remained a prison, not a hotel. Music and hatred kept him going. 'I let out my annoyance in my apologia,' he wrote in January 1924, 'whose first part, at least, I hope will survive the court case and me. For the rest I am dreaming of Tristan and similar matters.'[84]

The NSDAP, meanwhile, was in disarray.[85] President Ebert announced that Hitler's followers would be prosecuted for treason. The party itself was declared illegal and went underground; its press was banned, including the *Völkischer Beobachter* and Streicher's newspaper *Der Stürmer*. The party premises were raided, with seven bags of potatoes being carried off by police along with all records and valuables. In Hesse and Württemberg the authorities moved quickly to stamp out any threatened copycat attempts. The Nazi leadership was now largely on the run, hiding among sympathizers in and around Munich. Hitler's choice of Rosenberg to head the party in his absence took everybody by surprise and caused general consternation. Rosenberg was aloof and cerebral and had no personal following in the movement. By contrast, the three deputies also appointed by Hitler – Julius Streicher, Max Amann and Hermann Esser – were powerful in their own right. Hitler did not explain his decision. It is possible that he saw Rosenberg as a straw man who would simply keep the seat warm for him for his release, but it may also be that he saw the main priority in his absence as the maintenance not of organizational coherence, but of ideological purity,[86] and for that Rosenberg was the perfect fit.

The world did not stand still while Hitler was in Landsberg. Rosenberg was confronted not simply with the practical question of how to pay for salaries, publications and other expenses, but also had to take a view on crucial political questions. The most pressing was whether the party should contest elections. Hitler was sceptical, but allowed Rosenberg to go ahead. Temporarily renamed the Grossdeutsche Volksgemeinschaft (GVG), because the party was banned under its old name, the Nazis joined a raft of other parties to contest the Bavarian Landtag elections under the banner of the Völkischer Block (VB); in Thuringia, they joined with Albrecht von Gräfe's Deutsch-Völkische Freiheitspartei (DVFP), a breakaway from the DNVP. Hitler tried to put a strict time limit on all agreements – for example that with the DVFP in late February 1924 – probably in order to leave his hands free after his release. One way or the other, the movement was still completely oriented towards Hitler, even while he languished in Landsberg. As the Munich leadership announced in mid March 1924, 'It is our responsibility to place in his hands not an unserviceable but a living instrument.'[87]

In late February 1924, Hitler was brought to stand trial before the *Volksgericht* in Munich in the old Infantry School on the Blutenburgstrasse. He was allowed to appear in a suit rather than prison clothes and sporting his Iron Cross. Security was strict, and the press interest, including from abroad, was intense. Hitler would no doubt have been pleased to know that 'one heard particularly many English voices'.[88] The Reich government had wanted the trial to be held in Leipzig, but the authorities in Munich were determined to keep it local, almost certainly because they feared what might otherwise emerge about their complicity in the various plots.[89] Berlin gave way in the context of a broader rapprochement with Bavaria. In mid February 1924, about a week before the trial began, the Bavarian Reichswehr submitted once again to command from Berlin, thus reversing Kahr and Lossow's position in November 1923; Kahr resigned.

Hitler famously used the courtroom as a platform from which to expound his world view, to refine his biography[90] and to slander his many enemies. What is much less well understood is that his main target throughout was Bavarian separatism, the charge which more than any other he levelled at Kahr, Lossow and Seisser. Picking up his pre-Putsch rhetoric, Hitler explained to the court on the very first day of proceedings that it was 'very difficult' to distinguish between 'disguised federalism' and a force which was 'publicly' espousing a course of action with 'separatist effects'. He reminded his listeners that the BVP 'Bamberg Programme contains the sentence that every [German federal] state has the right in future to conclude treaties with other [that is foreign] states – a sentence whose logical conclusion means the dissolution of the Reich'. His concern, he claimed, was that Kahr would either fail to march on Berlin, or do so without success, and then take the separatist option, probably with 'foreign help', that is, from France. More generally, Hitler was unhappy with the pervasive idea 'that one dresses up the struggle in the defence of purely Bavarian rights', a stance which would alienate the rest of Germany.[91] This rhetoric enabled him to outflank the triumvirate on the right, and to embarrass them on the wider German stage, as separatism was a clear violation of the Weimar constitution. It was no doubt for this reason that the Munich authorities were keen to hold the trial in Bavaria, and why they gave Hitler such an easy ride. He in turn colluded, reserving his most specific charges for the closed sessions, with the implicit threat that he could let rip in public if he wanted to.

The trial lasted just over a month, from 26 February to 27 March 1924. Hitler was not at the centre of proceedings at all times, and was a spectator for long stretches when his co-conspirators were in the dock. It did not matter. Hitler succeeded in asserting the leadership of the political struggle against the Weimar Republic, putting such luminaries as General Ludendorff in the shade. 'The political struggle,' he announced unambiguously, 'that is the confrontation and the settlement of accounts with the November criminals' is 'led by me and will remain my preserve.'[92] He did not deny the substance of the charges, but argued that he had acted at all times in the greater interest of Germany. His apparently forthright performance was favourably compared to the evident shiftiness of the 'triumvirate', who vigorously disputed any separatist intent and, even more implausibly, any conspiracy against the Reich government in Berlin. Even the chief state prosecutor Ludwig Stenglein attested to 'the purity of [Hitler's] convictions and his unselfish devotion to his life work'.[93] The credibility of Kahr, Lossow and Seisser, by contrast, was completely shredded under cross-examination, and by the testimony of the defendants and witnesses. Sometimes Kahr appeared so overwhelmed that his voice dropped to a whisper as the courtroom audience strained to hear him. The rampant Hitler, by contrast, was repeatedly told to lower his voice by the trial judge.[94]

Hitler's final speech was a triumphant reiteration of his beliefs and sense of mission. If he was a traitor, then so were Bismarck, Atatürk and Mussolini, whose treason had been ratified by success. Hitler decried that there was 'self-determination for every Negro tribe', but that 'Germany did not belong to the Negro tribes but stood under them'. The root of the German predicament, he continued, lay in Germany's exposed geopolitical position in Europe. 'The German people', Hitler argued, 'has perhaps the worst location of all nations in military-political terms. It is geographically extraordinarily badly located, surrounded by many rivals'. It was menaced by France's determination to 'Balkanize' Germany and to reduce her population. In this context he referred to 'Clemenceau's [alleged] aim to exterminate 20 million Germans in Europe, to break up Germany into individual states and to prevent the emergence of another united large Reich'. It was also threatened by Britain's supposed much broader policy of Balkanizing Europe as a whole in order to maintain the balance of power. There was no economic solution to this predicament, Hitler stressed, but only a powerful foreign policy based on the highest level of internal mobilization. Germany would need to get rid of 'international Jewry', which was coordinating the global forces against her. She would also need to pursue the related struggle against international capitalism. 'The battle against international stock exchange enslavement' and against the 'trustification' of the 'entire economy', Hitler demanded, must be taken up.[95]

These were all familiar themes from Hitler's previous statements, but this time he had the eyes of the German and even some of the international press upon him. His closing speech concluded with a resounding statement that though the court might secure a conviction, posterity would surely acquit him. In an obviously choreographed sequence, the other accused said they had nothing to add, with the result that Hitler's resonant last words were left ringing throughout the courtroom and shaped the story of the trial. He turned the defeat and humiliation of 9 November 1923 into a victorious narrative. If the attempted coup had actually had many fathers, it was now the 'Hitler-Putsch', a phrase with which Kahr had originally sought to scapegoat the Nazis but which had in fact propelled Hitler to the front of a crowded field of German 'saviours'. The sentences reinforced this impression. Ludendorff was acquitted, lenient treatment which tended to accentuate Hitler's role. Hitler himself was convicted of 'high treason' against the state and sentenced to five years' imprisonment – technically 'incarceration in a fortress' – with the opportunity of parole after six months and a fine of 200 goldmarks.

Hitler was now a hero not merely to the Bavarian right, but to many nationalists throughout Germany. What had begun in the public mind as the 'Ludendorff Trial' ended as the 'Hitler Trial'. 'I am occupying myself with

Hitler and the National Socialist movement,' the Rhenish student Joseph
Goebbels wrote in his diary in early March 1923, almost certainly following
press reports of the trial, 'and I suppose I shall have to do so for some time.'
He wished that every town would have its Adolf Hitler, 'who burns through
his holy fire everything that is tepid and dull'. Goebbels's conversion was a
slow one, however. Partly this was a question of style. As an intellectual,
Goebbels objected to the 'simplistic' nature of much of Hitler's rhetoric. It
was also a matter of policy. Goebbels, then an avowed Slavophile with more
than a sneaking regard for the Russian Revolution, was unhappy with
Hitler's view of the Soviet Union in particular and what he considered the
reactionary nature of his Munich entourage more generally.[96]

On his return to Landsberg to serve the rest of his sentence, Hitler was
confronted with some serious strategic questions. The paramilitary formations at his command during the Putsch had been scattered by the
authorities. Armed with a proclamation from Hitler naming him the
'military leader' of the *Kampfbund*,[97] Ernst Röhm began to revive the SA,
under the cover of a front organization, and went to confer with Hitler at
the very end of May 1924. Perhaps anxious not to provoke the authorities,
and mindful of his inability to seize power by force, the Führer insisted
that the SA keep a lower profile. Hitler also struck a more conciliatory
note towards the BVP, no doubt partly for tactical reasons but probably
also because the threat of Bavarian separatism had receded. That said, he
let it be known in May 1924 that he would continue to oppose the party
if it persisted with 'purely reactionary and particularist' policies.[98]

The next issue was elections, which Hitler had grudgingly allowed
Rosenberg to participate in. The central issue in German politics, Hitler
believed like many others, was the recommendations of the Reparations
Committee chaired by the American banker Charles Dawes, which the
government and the Weimar Coalition accepted. One of the most controversial proposals was to place the Reichsbahn under international
administration in order to secure its revenues for the payment of reparations.[99] It was, Hitler claimed, one of the 'primary aim of the *Völkisch*
movement' to fight this planned 'national crime'. Handing over the Reichsbahn, he continued, would cut the 'subtle and vitally necessary railway
network which ran across the area of the German people'.[100] Hitler was
violently opposed to the loss of a national asset to an internationally man-
dated austerity plan.

The Reichstag election of May 1924 was thus essentially a referendum
on the Dawes Plan. Throughout the campaign, Nazi propaganda and
iconography systematically, and more or less exclusively, targeted the
'Jewish capitalist'.[101] In this respect, its iconography differed little from that

of the communists and indeed of the cartoons by the leftist artist Georg Grosz.[102] The communist vote leaped from half a million in 1920 to 3.7 million. Right-wing parties walked off with an even larger share: 7.5 million votes. Of these only a small proportion went to the NSDAP's place-holder parties.[103] The north German Nazis, who opposed any involvement in the electoral process on principle and were generally to the left, were unimpressed, and so were their *Völkisch* allies. The south German party, who had done a lot better, and were less 'socialist', inclined more to repeating the experiment, and to continuing the relationship with the DVFP.

This brought the thorny question of the Nazi Party's relationship to other parties and groups back to the fore. There were vigorous discussions about which of the various groups in the alphabet soup of right-wing organizations the Nazis should align or unite with, and on what terms. Gregor Strasser and General Ludendorff strongly supported amalgamation with the DVFP to create a new National Socialist Freedom Party (NSFP). Hitler reluctantly agreed in broad terms but insisted that the main base and focus of the party remain in Munich. Tensions boiled over at the congress of the north German NSDAP in Hamburg in early June 1924, when delegates rejected the merger with the DVFP 'parliamentarism' and the 'party spirit' in general. They decided to break with Munich and set up a North German Directory.[104] The Frankfurt Nazis were so disgusted with the idea of a merger that they split to become the Deutsche Partei, pledging loyalty only to Hitler. These differences meant that Hitler was plagued by an interminable stream of people visiting Landsberg to brief him, to complain or to try to persuade him to support one faction or the other.[105]

Hitler responded by announcing his withdrawal from active politics in mid June 1924. 'From now on,' he wrote, 'no one has the right to act in my name.'[106] Gottfried Feder remarked after visiting him that Hitler was 'depressed [and] wants to withdraw completely from the movement' in order to 'work', that is, 'write' to earn money.[107] Over the next two months, Hitler repeated his message publicly on a number of occasions.[108] He was acting partly because he was disenchanted with the way in which the various mergers and collaborations were turning the party into a purely bourgeois organization, and partly because he had no real power to turn things around from prison.[109] One young Nazi responded that all Nazis were merely 'place-holders' awaiting the Führer's release; another said that 'Our programme is summarized in two words: "Adolf Hitler".'[110] Hitler's 'withdrawal' thus turned out to be an inspired move, not just because it relieved him of the responsibility of taking sides. It greatly reduced fissiparous tendencies because nobody could claim his backing, and there was no point in attempting to take over the party in his absence as his release was expected to be imminent. Clearly, the charisma which Hitler had taken to Landsberg remained with him for the duration of his sentence.

One reason why Hitler wanted to lie low was fear of having his release delayed, or of being deported to Austria. The Bavarian authorities had long hoped to do the latter, and in early May 1924, the Polizeidirektion in Munich told the Bavarian Ministry of the Interior that 'Hitler constitutes a permanent threat to the internal and external security of the state'.[111] In late April 1924, the Austrians agreed to accept him in principle.[112] Hitler managed to avoid deportation, but after being refused probation he failed to get out by 1 October as he originally hoped. On 16 October he made a statement that he should be allowed to stay, 'because I never felt myself to be an Austrian citizen but only a German'. 'My affection for my Austrian homeland is great,' Hitler continued, 'but so is hostility of the Austrian state', in which – like the 'earlier Habsburg state' – he could only see 'an obstacle for the unification of the German people'.[113] He asserted his right to German citizenship on the basis of his 'four-year commitment of my blood and life'. In the following month, he let it be known that he was 'the child of an Austrian territory which belonged to Bavaria a hundred years ago. His home town is Braunau.' 'For this reason,' he continued, 'he has an understanding for the stupidity of that border, which wants to divide Germans of the same tradition and language into two nations [sic].'[114]

5

Anglo-American Power and German Impotence

The main reason why Hitler withdrew from party management was his plan to write a 'large book', which he stated clearly in the declaration announcing his decision.[1] This project began as a quasi-legal defence of his actions for the court. It soon developed into the idea of producing, as Hitler told Siegfried Wagner in early May 1924, a 'comprehensive settlement of accounts with those gentlemen who cheered on 9 November', in other words Kahr, Lossow and Seisser. No doubt hopeful of signing a sensational book with high sales, various publishers offered their services to Hitler, either in person or by letter.[2] In time, however, the emphasis of the work changed again, probably in part thanks to some sort of explicit or implicit bargain with the Bavarian state to let sleeping dogs lie in return for a mild sentence. There were also positive reasons, however, for the new approach. Hitler wanted to use the relative peace of Landsberg to write a much broader manifesto elaborating the principles of National Socialism, charting a path to power for the movement and showing how Germany could regain her independence and great power status.[3] The first volume of *Mein Kampf*, most of which was written or compiled in Landsberg, seems to have been largely a solo effort, with relatively little input from others. Julius Schaub, another inmate who later became his personal adjutant, recalled that Hitler wrote *Mein Kampf* 'alone and without direct input from anyone', not even Hess, who had joined him in Landsberg.[4] Hitler typed the book himself, reading out or summarizing large sections to his fellow prisoners, who constituted an appreciative or at any rate a captive audience.[5] Sometimes, he was moved to tears by his own words.[6]

Incarceration gave Hitler a chance to read more widely and gather his thoughts.[7] One of his main preoccupations in Landsberg was the United States, which he was coming to regard as the model state and society, perhaps even more so than the British Empire. 'He 'devoured' the memoirs of a returned German emigrant to the United States.[8] 'One should take America as a model,' he proclaimed.[9] Hess wrote that Hitler was captivated by Henry Ford's methods of production which made automobiles available to the 'broad mass' of the people.[10] This appears to have been the genesis of the Volkswagen. Hitler envisaged that the automobile would further serve as 'the small man's means of transport into nature – as in America'.[11] He also planned to apply methods of mass production to housing, and experimented with designs for a *Volkshaus* for families with three to five children which would have five rooms and a bathroom with a garage in large terraced settlements. He was equally determined not be outdone in the construction of 'skyscrapers', and looked forward to the consternation of the '*Deutsch-Völkisch*' elements by putting the party headquarters into such an edifice. Quite apart from showing that Hitler had an interest in vernacular architecture, and not just in monumental public buildings, these plans prove that he was thinking of elevating the condition of the German working class through American-style suburban and metropolitan modernity.[12] This was the model of an ideal society against which he wrote *Mein Kampf*.

Modernity was not an end in itself, but a means by which the German people, especially the German working class and German women, could be mobilized in support of the project of national revival. Hitler exalted technological development – aeroplanes, typewriters, telephones and suspension bridges, and even domestic appliances. These would free German women from drudgery and enable them to be better wives producing more children. 'How little our poor women benefit from progress,' he lamented, 'there is so much one can do to make [a woman's life] easier with the help of technology! But most people still think today that a woman is only a good housewife if she is constantly dirty and working from early until late.' 'And then,' Hitler continued, 'one is surprised when the woman is not intellectual enough for the man, when he cannot find stimulation and recuperation.' Worse still, he went on, this was 'bad for the race' because it was 'obvious that his overtired wife will not have as healthy children as one who is well rested, can read good books and so on'.[13] The link between what Hitler would later call the racial 'elevation' of Germany, technological progress and maintaining the standard of living is already evident here.

Part and parcel of this programme of racial improvement was Hitler's support for what we would today call 'alternative' technology. 'Every farm,' he demanded, 'which does not possess any alternative source of energy' should set up a 'wind motor with dynamo and rechargeable batteries'. This might not be possible in the current economic climate, Hitler continued, but it would be a viable long-term investment. He rejected the idea that technological change took the romance out of farming. 'I couldn't care less about a romanticism,' he exclaimed, 'which puts people behind frosted windows in the twilight, [and] which lets women age prematurely through hard work'. Hitler therefore sneered at the city folk who went into the country for a day, enthused about the scenery and then returned to their modern and efficient homes in the city. Hitler claimed to support 'the preservation of nature', but in his view it should take the form of national parks in the mountains. 'Here too,' Hitler concluded, 'the Americans have made the right choice with their Yellowstone Park.'

In Landsberg, Hitler did not abate his ferocious hostility to international finance capitalism. He did, however, qualify some of his earlier ideas about 'national' economies. Significantly, he rejected the demands of the German automobile manufacturers to be protected against competition from Henry Ford through higher tariff barriers. 'Our industry needs to exert itself and achieve the same performance,' Hitler remarked. Once again, the United States was the explicit model.[14]

Hitler was also taking on board the concept of *Lebensraum*.[15] This was one of the key ideas of Hess's teacher and patron Karl Haushofer, the doyen of German *Geopolitik*. He visited Hess in prison, bringing him copies of Clausewitz and Friedrich Ratzel's 'Political Geography', one of the seminal geopolitical texts.[16] While there is no hard evidence that Haushofer met Hitler on those occasions it is highly likely he did so, or at any rate that his ideas found their way to him. In mid July, there was a debate about *Lebensraum* at Landsberg, which began with some good-natured joshing in the garden and ended with Hitler's 'marvelling' inner circle being provided with a lengthy definition of the term by Hess.[17] Its essence was simple: every people required a certain 'living space' to feed and accommodate its growing population. The idea seemed to provide the answer to the main challenge facing the Reich, which was the emigration of its demographic surplus to the United States. This was part of an important shift in Hitler's thinking, away from a potential Russo-German alliance and the prevention of emigration through the restitution of German colonies, towards the capture of *Lebensraum* in the east, contiguous to an expanded German Reich.[18] It had less to do with hatred of Bolshevism and eastern European Jewry, and more to do with the need to prepare the Reich for a confrontation or equal coexistence with an Anglo-America whose dynamism mesmerized Hitler more than ever.

The centrality of the British Empire and the United States in the gestation of *Mein Kampf* is evident from the early outlines he sketched in June 1924.[19] These were focused on foreign policy in general, and the Anglo-Americans in particular. Hitler criticized not only the failure to secure an alliance with Britain, but also the failure to make Germany strong in

Europe rather than pursue colonial, naval and commercial expansion, as the imperial government had done. This, he argued, was 'important especially in relation to the development of the American continent into the first world power'. The basis of the European great powers, Hitler continued, was too narrow. He compared them to inverted pyramids, whose base was overseas and whose apex was in Europe. By contrast, the United States had its 'base in America and its peaks in the rest of the world'. This made it a better model than Britain, which, however, benefited from its kinship with the United States. His outline referred explicitly to 'Great Britain and the Anglo-Saxon world' and the 'importance' of the United States as 'an Anglo-Saxon state' for Britain itself. The contours of Hitler's greatest preoccupation, the colossal strength of the 'Anglo-Saxon' world powers, were thus clearly visible.

While Hitler tried to reduce his exposure to petty party disputes in prison, it is striking that he tried to maintain engagement with the wider world, especially potential ideological sympathizers and funders in Italy and the United States. Despite the fact that he allowed Göring to find sanctuary in Italy after the Putsch, Mussolini was careful to keep the Nazis at arm's length.[20] That left America. In early January 1924, not long after the start of his incarceration at Landsberg, Hitler penned a letter of accreditation for his envoy Kurt Lüdecke. He asked Lüdecke 'to promote the interests of the German freedom movement in the United States and especially to collect money for them'.[21] At the end of January, Lüdecke set off with Winifred and Siegfried Wagner to Detroit. Despite Lüdecke's invocation of the 'solidarity of white men', and his offer to promote the kind of international anti-Semitism demanded by the *Dearborn Independent*, he was unable to persuade Ford at their meetings to provide any funding for the movement.[22] Lüdecke repeatedly visited Hitler in Landsberg in May and June 1924.[23] In 1924, a National Socialist *Ortsgruppe* was founded in the German quarter of Chicago, and there also appears to have been some sort of presence in New York City; a year later, Hitler personally thanked one of his activists in America for sending back money for the movement.[24] In general, however, the attempt to reach out to the United States was a failure.

Hitler was under no illusions about the timescale for the national and racial regeneration of Germany. The failure of the coup had cured him of any vanguardism. He was now thinking in terms not of years, or even decades, but of centuries. In late June 1924, he made a public announcement that 'the re-establishment of the German people is by no means a matter of the acquisition of technical weapons, but rather a question of the regeneration of our character'. 'Spiritual renewals,' Hitler continued, 'require, if they are to be more than just a passing phenomenon, *many centuries* [emphasis in the original]' to be 'successful'.[25] Five months later, Hess recorded that Hitler 'is under no illusions about the extent to which the "idea" can be implemented by him'. 'The ripening of ideas, the adapting of reality to the idea and the idea to reality,' he continued, 'will probably require many generations.' Hitler, Hess went on, saw his own role as merely 'setting up a new marker in the distance', 'loosening the soil' around the existing pole, which 'represented a major era in the development of mankind'. The task of 'ripping out' the pole and advancing it some way towards the goal, by contrast, would be the task 'of another, a greater man yet to come'.[26] In other words, after the certainty of 1923, Hitler was once again unsure whether he was the messiah himself rather than just John the Baptist, the 'drummer' of 1919–20.

In the second half of 1924, the internal disputes rumbled on.[27] In late July, there was a particularly acrimonious meeting at Weimar. Esser and Streicher undermined Rosenberg at every turn. Feder, Strasser, Gräfe and Ludendorff ganged up on him as well. Ludendorff eventually flounced out. Hitler did not send a deputy. The NSDAP and the DVFP went ahead with a shaky merger in the late summer to form the National-Sozialistische Freiheitsbewegung (NSFB). The North German Directory formed the National-Sozialistische Arbeitsgemeinschaft (NSAG), whose distinctly socialist leanings were anathema to Esser and Streicher in Bavaria. Throughout all this Hitler maintained a pointed silence in prison. One despairing member wrote to Hess 'Where do you belong now that the movement is splintered', receiving the reply 'To Hitler. To Hitler, who stands above it all.'[28] It was clear that the movement was in suspended animation, a Hamlet without a prince.

Hitler was released on probation on 20 December 1924. The iconic photograph by Heinrich Hoffmann of him beside a car in driving gear was not taken, as Hitler had wanted, just outside the prison itself, because the authorities objected, but in front of the historic city gate.[29] It was intended to convey a message of determination and dynamism, though Hitler himself could not drive and indeed never learned.

Despite the bravado, Hitler trod very carefully. Shortly after his release, Hitler had two meetings with the Bavarian minister president, Heinrich Held, at which he assured him that he would not attempt another putsch. He toned down some of the rhetoric in *Mein Kampf*, the second volume of which he was writing in the calm of his mountain retreat at Berchtesgaden, the use of which had been given to him by a well-wisher.[30] Hitler also moved to sort out his national status, which acquired renewed importance after the speaking ban. In early April 1925, he wrote to the authorities in

Linz requesting his 'release from Austrian citizenship'. Hitler also had a long discussion with the Austrian consul in Munich and expressed his desire to surrender his nationality.[31] On 30 April 1925, the Austrian authorities finally stripped him of the citizenship he had never accepted. This did not mean that Hitler had established his right to stay in Germany beyond all doubt – he was now formally 'stateless' – but he had at least ensured that it would be more difficult to deport him somewhere else. The threat of removal, however, remained, and the Bavarian authorities reminded him of it from time to time.[32]

Hitler's next moves were also closely watched by his followers, who waited impatiently for his lead. The divisions of the previous year did not end with Hitler's return from Landsberg but rather erupted with new ferocity as every faction, hiding behind a bewildering jungle of movements and acronyms, sought to win over the Führer. Hitler avoided confrontation, partly in order to concentrate on the completion of *Mein Kampf*.[33] 'Not a word from Hitler,' Goebbels noted right at the end of 1924, 'Oh this sly fox with the political instinct.' A fortnight later, he asked anxiously, 'What will Hitler do? That is the anxious question every day. Hopefully he will not go over to the camp of reaction.'[34] Hitler's reticence annoyed some of the rank and file, who complained that it would be better for him to sort out the 'problems' in the movement than to work on a 'high political work'. The Bavarian police, which kept a close eye on Hitler after his release, also reported that he seemed to be absorbed by *Mein Kampf*, which was concerned 'exclusively with Marxism and Jewry'.[35] This was, as we shall see, by no means a completely accurate summary, but it must have been read with relief by many in Munich because it suggested that Hitler was not intending to pursue his vendetta against Kahr, Lossow and Seisser.

In part, the disputes within the NSDAP were based on personal antipathy, or a struggle for access to Hitler, a theme which would grow in prominence as Hitler's own power grew. 'If one could have two hours alone with Hitler,' Goebbels exclaimed in exasperation, 'then everything could be sorted out, but he is surrounded like an old monarch.'[36] Relations within the Munich party were particularly bad, where infighting between Rosenberg, Hanfstaengl and Esser culminated in law suits. The divide was also cultural in nature, pitting northern and western Germans against southerners. Hitler did not encourage these disputes in order to strengthen his own authority, but regarded them as a threat to the coherence of the movement. In early April 1925, he sent a long letter to Rosenberg pleading with him to drop his law suits for the good of the party.[37] Henceforth disagreements were to be sorted out internally by the 'Investigative and Mediatory Committee', known as the USCHLA after its German acronym.[38]

More important to Hitler than anything else, however, were the ideological fissures in the movement, which had widened in his absence. These sometimes mirrored the other divisions and sometimes cut across them. Nazis disagreed violently about participation in elections, which found more favour in the south than the north, and the armed struggle against the 'system'. Conservative *Völkisch* elements faced off against those of a more 'socialist' disposition, principally in the north and west.

Above all, there were profound differences over foreign policy. The northerners tended towards internationalism. 'Is National Socialism a German matter or a world problem,' Goebbels asked rhetorically, adding that 'for me it goes well beyond Germany. What does Hitler think? The question needs to be answered.'[39] They called for an alliance with Russia (which also appealed to more socially conservative elements, such as Reventlow). Territorially, they demanded only the return of the German colonies and the restoration of the borders of 1914. Relations between the Arbeitsgemeinschaft and the party in the south under Esser, Streicher and Amann were poisonous. Critics advanced the classic early-modern critique of a clique of 'evil advisers' who were monopolizing Hitler, keeping the truth from him and steering the movement in a reactionary direction.

There were relatively few, such as Albrecht von Graefe, who wanted Hitler to return to the role of 'drummer' for the true nationalist messiah, Ludendorff.[40] A much greater problem was the fact that many of his followers knew him only by reputation, having never met him in person or heard him speak.[41] Hitler thus would have to move carefully in re-establishing his authority within the party. He had very few instruments at his disposal. He had next to no funds; he could only persuade and not command. One approach was to rely on his charisma communicated through speeches and personal contacts. Hitler gave thirty-eight speeches in 1925, and fifty-two in the following year.[42] This gave him limited traction, however, partly because the numbers attending were substantially lower than during his heyday in 1923, and partly because he was still banned from appearing in public in much of Germany. Hitler was thus forced to speak to closed party meetings, in salons,[43] or at private events. Nor could he put too much reliance on his personal magnetism. To be sure, individual doubters could be awed into line by his presence; they could convince themselves that he was interested in them, as they were in him. 'Hitler has arrived,' Goebbels wrote during one visit, 'my joy is great. He greets me like an old friend [and] coddles me.' 'How I love him, what a guy,' Goebbels went on. 'I would like Hitler to be my friend.'[44] Very often, however, doubts returned as soon as Hitler had left, particularly if he reneged on what had been agreed.

Charisma and leadership had to be complemented by organization. In late February 1925 Hitler officially relaunched the NSDAP. In his 'Basic guidelines for the re-establishment of the NSDAP',[45] Hitler laid down that existing members would have to reapply. He explicitly refused to take sides in the disputes of the past eighteen months and laid out his vision for the future. In a barnstorming first speech in Munich since his release, Hitler proclaimed all internal disputes 'over'.[46] Reconciliation was not so much negotiated as decreed. Hitler was realistic, even in public, about the difficulties of working with the very diverse group of individuals within the party. 'I don't regard it as the job of a political leader,' he remarked, 'to attempt to improve or even standardize the human material before him.'[47] He could not hope to compensate for the differences in 'temperament, character and capability'. Improving and harmonizing those, Hitler explained, would take centuries and required 'changes of the basic racial elements'. All the leader could do was 'to attempt through long engagement to find the "complementary" sides to each person' which could be combined to form a 'unity'. In other words, Hitler would have to work with the people he had rather than the people he would like to have had.

Hitler knew that the party needed to transcend his own person. Personal loyalty was not enough; he needed party cadres to obey not just him but their immediate superiors. The Führer principle was thus extended beyond the Führer himself. More talented and trained speakers were needed, so that the entire strain of communicating the message did not fall on him and a few others. 'We need speaker schools,' he announced in March 1925, 'because to this day this mass movement has only 10–12 good speakers.'[48] In other words, Hitler was learning not to hog his charisma, but to spread it around. His speeches and instructions increasingly referred not just to the Führer in the singular, but to the plural Führers upon whom the leadership of the movement depended.

Central to this was the establishment of a proper party bureaucracy.[49] Here the Social Democrats explicitly served as a model.[50] Hitler spoke grudgingly of the SPD as a party 'organized like the SA'.[51] Despite shortage of funds, the NSDAP moved to new premises in the Schellingstrasse in Munich in the summer of 1925, and Hitler signalled his plan to build a dedicated 'Party Headquarters' in Munich paid for by the membership; whether he still envisaged this as a skyscraper is not clear. Hitler also established the *Gau* structure, a 'shiring' of the whole country into administrative areas, which in turn were divided into *Bezirke* and *Ortsgruppen*.[52] He encouraged the local membership to use their initiative and if possible settle disputes without reference to Headquarters. This was partly an acknowledgement of the fact that his direct control was limited, partly a desire to reduce the incessant squabbling, but mainly a reflection of his belief in bureaucratic Darwinism. 'More than one committee can be set up in every area,' he wrote in connection with the presidential campaign, 'they can compete with each other, with the best committee being the one that has done most work.'[53] This was one of the first examples of the tendency towards 'polycracy' which Hitler would later have occasion to regret.

In March 1925, Hitler dispatched Gregor Strasser to restructure the party in north Germany. Strasser, though from Landshut in Bavaria, was temperamentally and ideologically much closer to the northerners. In September 1925, with Hitler's approval, he helped to establish a working group at Hagen in Westphalia. Goebbels – now a major figure in the north-western NSDAP – was tasked with editing a publication called *Nationalsozialistische Briefe*. There was a danger in all this, as Hitler himself observed, which was that the resulting room for manoeuvre would lead to 'the individual leader pursuing his own ideas', rather than those of the supreme Führer himself.[54] Hitler was also obliged by German associational law to hold an annual general meeting of the party in Munich, at which there should be elections and an opportunity to bring forward motions for discussion. None of this made the NSDAP a 'bottom-up' party. Hitler made no bones about the fact that the annual general meeting was just a charade to satisfy the rules of association.[55] Debate was strongly discouraged and motions were strictly controlled.

Hitler also resurrected the *Sturmabteilungen*, not as a paramilitary formation, as it had developed in the months preceding the Putsch, but as an organization dedicated to 'strengthening of the bodies of our youth, bringing them up on discipline and dedication to the common great ideal [and] training in the marshalling and reconnaissance service of the movement'. There should be no weapons, either carried openly or stored in depots. Anybody who violated that rule was to be expelled.[56] Hitler's concern here was to avoid being dragged into illegality by armed hotheads. The immediate effect of this ruling was to precipitate a breach with Röhm, for whom the paramilitary aspects of the SA remained central. He resigned and eventually emigrated to South America.[57] That same month Hitler created the 'Protective Squadron' soon known simply as the SS, a personal protection squad whose first leader, Josef Berchtold, placed particular stress on ideological purity.[58] In a critical assertion of authority, Hitler had established a monopoly of violence within the movement.

*

The principal method through which Hitler sought to re-establish control over the party was through ideological purity and coherence. He did this the hard way, seeking to achieve uniformity across a range of highly contentious issues. Hitler could not simply impose his views: he had to cajole and persuade. This was done through speeches, declarations, debates and, from the end of 1925, through the publication in succession of the two volumes of *Mein Kampf*.[59] These were only partly written from scratch at Landsberg and after his release, the rest being cobbled together from various articles and instructions, and even from drafts dating back to before the Putsch. Much of *Mein Kampf* originated as a direct response to the political events of 1925–6,[60] and Hitler used the text to lay down the law, at least implicitly, not just to the membership but also to his internal critics. For this reason the book needs to be seen in the context of the many contemporaneous statements he made before and after publication.

Contrary to his earlier threats, *Mein Kampf* was not a settling of accounts with his erstwhile conservative Bavarian allies, though he waited until the final pages of the second volume to abjure any thought of such a 'reckoning'.[61] Instead, the autobiographical sections, which are mostly fictional, should be seen as a *Bildungsroman*,[62] charting the political awakening of the hero. The chapter heading 'Viennese year of learning and suffering' was surely intended to echo Goethe's famous novel *The Sorrows of Young Werther*. The main – doctrinal – sections were designed to orient the party in its post-Landsberg struggles and to communicate his final judgements on policy.[63] With some important exceptions *Mein Kampf* proved a remarkably stable text, which changed little over nearly twenty years of reprinting.[64] Though the book was highly unreliable as a biographical source, it did summarize the direction of Hitler's thinking by the mid 1920s, key facets of which remained unchanged thereafter.

Much of what Hitler said in *Mein Kampf* and his various speeches rehearsed familiar themes from the time before the Putsch. There was the same focus on the forces of domestic fragmentation. Hitler inveighed once more against the 'mendacity of these so-called federalist circles' who were only promoting their 'dirty' party interest.[65] He continued to fulminate about the disintegrative effect of Marxism, and to lament the alienation of German workers. Hitler rose to new heights of invective against the German middle class, whom he dismissed as 'philistines', 'bourgeois boobies', who were so befuddled by the 'fug of associational meetings' that they were unable to transcend the 'usual jingoism of our bourgeois world of today'. He contrasted the robustness of the SA, who knew that 'terror can only be broken by terror', with 'bourgeois wimpishness'. Hitler also trenchantly restated his objections to parliamentarism and electoral politics, and western democracy in general, concluding that the 'majority principle' amounted to 'the demolition of the Führer idea as such'.[66]

The main danger of Germany's internal weakness was that it made her vulnerable to external attack, especially from the enemies that Hitler feared most: international capitalism, Anglo-America and the associated forces of world Jewry. Hitler critiqued the economics of inequality and exploitation, the 'jarring juxtaposition of poor and rich so close to each other', the 'role of money', in which 'money [became] God' and 'the false God of Mammon was offered incense'. He became increasingly convinced that 'the heaviest battle to be fought was no longer against enemy peoples but against international capital'.[67] Here Hitler insisted more than ever on his earlier distinction between national capital, which the state could control, and pernicious international capital, which controlled states or sought to do so.[68] One of its principal instruments of subjugation was revolutionary Marxism, which undermined national economies, societies and governments.[69] Others were economic immiseration and racial contamination, both of which also reduced the capacity of nations to resist international takeover. For Hitler, maintaining an independent national economy was therefore absolutely central to the defence of national identity, sovereignty and racial purity.

Hitler violently objected to international capitalism even when it was not Jewish, but he assigned the Jews a particularly malevolent role within the global capitalist system; this remained the principal root of his anti-Semitism. In *Mein Kampf*, as in his earlier rhetoric, Jews were inseparably linked with money and the whole capitalist system as 'traders', as 'middlemen', who levied an 'extortionate rate of interest' for their 'financial deals'. Jewry, he claimed, aimed at nothing less that the 'financial domination of the entire economy'. Yet because 'a Bolshevized world can only survive if it encompasses everything', a 'single independent state' – such as a revived Germany – could bring the whole juggernaut to a standstill.[70]

There was also, however, an open acknowledgement of the tactical nature of the anti-Semitic theme.[71] The focus on a 'single aim', that is on the Jews, Hitler explained, was 'practically' motivated. The masses, Hitler explained, were in fact very differentiated. Many might sign up to the fight against the Jews and Marxism, but the minute one added further goals, people would start peeling off, until the mass had fragmented. It was therefore essential to stick to a single, simple aim. Moreover, unlike the more confident British, Hitler argued, the German people was particularly prone to an 'objectivity hang-up' and might be tempted by the sheer number of enemies into thinking that they were themselves in the wrong. For this reason, he concluded, it was 'essential with a people like the Germans to point to one enemy and to march against one enemy', because 'one can if necessary mean many with one enemy'. Hitler returned to this theme in *Mein Kampf*, when he said that 'for purely emotional reasons one should not show the masses two or more enemies, because this would otherwise lead to a complete fragmentation of their striking power'.[72] The tactical use of anti-Semitism was also evident in another respect. When it was likely to put off potential backers, such as the well-to-do audience at the Nationalklub of 1919 in Hamburg, it was quietly dropped.[73]

Be that as it may, anti-Semitism remained at the core of Hitler's world view. He claimed the Jews brought the full weight of diplomatic, press, revolutionary and racial pressures to bear on national states that refused to submit. They began with domestic torments, such as parliamentarism, the press and the trade unions, which Hitler regarded as 'instruments' of the Jews, and 'Marxism', their 'assault column' and 'principal weapon', whose 'final aim remains the destruction of the non-Jewish national states'. Here Hitler was reprising his earlier argument that communism was simply an instrument of international capitalism, speaking of 'Marxism as a weapon for the demolition of the national economy and the erection of the rule of loan capitalism'. Hence his hostility to the trade unions, which Marxism had turned into an instrument to 'smash the economic basis of the free and independent national states, in order to destroy their national industry and their national trade as part of the enslavement of free peoples in the service of a supranational world finance Jewry'.[74] Hitler's rhetoric was thus far more anti-capitalist than anti-communist: references to Dawes in his speeches dwarfed those to Lenin at this time.[75] He continued to fear Bolshevism, not in the form of the Red Army, but principally as a virus which would render Germany ripe for takeover by the forces of international capitalism.

Worse still, Hitler claimed, international capitalism sought to destroy the German bloodline by 'contamination through Negro blood on the Rhine' (an allusion to colonial soldiers in the French forces of occupation) in order to 'begin the bastardization of the European continent from its central point'. Contamination of the blood, he warned, could only be removed in the course of 'centuries, if at all'. In this narrative, German mass emigration took on a particular importance. Hitler saw it as part of a concerted plan to destroy the biological substance of German people going back centuries. 'The German people had to send out their sons,' Hitler lamented, with the result that for some three hundred years, Germans had served as 'beasts of burden for other nations' and had moved to 'Australia, Central America and South America'.[76] He would return to this theme over and over in the years to come.

The main great power enemies of the Reich, according to Hitler, were not the Soviet Union, France or any other continental European state, but the British Empire and what he generally referred to as the 'American Union'. This enmity was complex, and it would not be exaggerated to speak of a love-hate relationship. Hitler deeply admired Anglo-America. He did not believe, though he sometimes affected to, that Germany had been defeated solely as a result of domestic dissensions. On the contrary, he frequently paid tribute to the strength and bravery of the enemy he had faced during the war.[77] One of his criticisms of German propaganda during the contest had been its portrayal of the British as a nation of cowardly shopkeepers. Hitler lambasted the 'newspapers and satirical magazines' for their 'high degree of self-deception because this nonsense gradually infected everything else, and the result was an under-estimation' of the British. The Germans, he lamented, came to believe that they were facing an 'unbelievably cowardly businessman'. Reality was very different. 'I still remember well,' Hitler continued, 'the surprised faces of my comrades when we met face to face with the Tommies in Flanders', when they found the British soldier to be a much more formidable proposition than they had expected. If the individual Briton was tough and courageous, collectively they were formidable. The British Empire, in Hitler's judgement, which was widely shared at the time, was simply the 'greatest power on earth'. 'How difficult it is,' he elaborated, 'to beat the British, we Germans know only too well.'[78]

It was therefore hardly surprising that *Mein Kampf* and Hitler's speeches were concerned with examining the basis for Britain's superiority. Partly, it was a question of will. Hitler praised the 'brutality' – a compliment in his lexicon – of Lloyd George in the war. He admired Britain's willingness to continue the struggle, despite the U-boat threat, 'whatever it costs'. Partly, it was a matter of clever propaganda. Hitler spoke of the 'psychological superiority of the Briton', who had defined the war as one for 'freedom' against German despotism. Partly, it was a question of careful strategy, a husbanding of resources. Hitler noted approvingly that the British invested their blood wisely and sparingly, pushing others to the front first. It would be, however, 'a stupidity to believe that the Briton will never be ready to sacrifice his own'. 'He will commit his blood,' he claimed, 'when it becomes necessary to do so.' Partly, it was a matter of superior national coherence. 'When the fur begins to fly,' he noted, 'the British unite as a race'; not so the Germans. Hitler lauded British social legislation as pioneering because it 'preserved the British people for the British state'. The success of this policy, he argued, had been seen during the war when British workers had been largely patriotic. Partly, it was the ability of

Britain to secure a huge global empire and to turn it to her political and military advantage in Europe. Here Hitler spoke of the 'characteristic of British statecraft to turn political power into economic gain, and to convert every economic gain immediately back into political power'.[79]

Hitler was well aware of the centrality of parliament to British history and her strength in the world. He spoke of 'England, the land of classical "democracy"', as the 'model of this [sort of] entity'. Hitler claimed that as a young man, his extensive newspaper reading had given him, 'a certain enduring admiration for the British parliament'. That admiration was still clearly visible in the mid 1920s. Hitler had at least a passing acquaintance with the layout and decor of the Palace of Westminster, which he found aesthetically more pleasing than the Austro-Hungarian assembly. 'When Barry first let his parliamentary palace rise out of the waters of the Thames,' he wrote, 'he reached into the history of the British Empire' to find inspiration for the '1,200 niches, corbels and pillars'. 'In this way,' he continued, Westminster 'became a temple to the glory of the nation.'[80] Paradoxically, Hitler regarded 'parliamentarism' as ruinous to German unity, but central to British power. The apparent contradiction is resolved by the fact that he believed the more coherent British were ready for democracy in ways that the Germans were not.

Hitler's admiration for Britain and its empire was matched, and in many ways exceeded, by his admiration for the United States. This did not stem from any Karl-May-style 'wild-west' romanticism on Hitler's part, but rather expressed his belief in the modernity and vast industrial potential of the New World.[81] Reflecting his growing preoccupation with 'space', Hitler was mesmerized by the sheer scale of America. The future of the world belonged to the 'giant states' and first among them was the US.[82] In one speech he contrasted 'how ridiculously small the area of current German settlement was, which one could traverse north to south by car in eighteen hours, while the express trains of the United States required six days in order to get from one ocean to the other'. In Mein Kampf he referred to the 'incredible internal power' of the 'American Union', and the 'gigantic colossus of the American state with its huge treasures of virgin soil'. Here Hitler was referring not so much to minerals as to food security. 'In North America,' he argued, 'which has gigantic grain-producing areas, it is not like with us.' There you found 'the best soil for growing grain, which does not need to be fertilized, earth which one farmed with the best machinery'.[83]

The principal reason for the strength of the United States, Hitler believed, was demographic. It was peopled by the allegedly racially sound descendants of British emigrants, and the best elements of continental

Europe. In *Mein Kampf,* Hitler spoke of the 'opening up of the American continent' by 'Aryans'. Foremost among these, at least numerically, were the Germans forced out by lack of living space at home in the eighteenth and nineteenth centuries and the oppressions of international capitalism in the twentieth century. 'Over centuries,' he wrote, 'the German emigrated to the other world [a shorthand for the Anglo-Saxon capitalist world] as the fertilizer for other peoples, as the cultural fertilizer for other nations.' 'This migration to America,' he told an audience on the subject of German emigration, 'made that country great.' Moreover, it had been the best who left. 'Endless droves of German farmers' sons went across the great water, across the Ocean to America,' Hitler claimed, 'this flow lasted for centuries and it involved the best elements which our people possessed.' Hitler's belief in the German contribution to the growth of the United States was so great that, repeating a tenacious canard in contemporary discourse, he claimed German had nearly become the language of the young Republic.[84]

Hitler was well aware, of course, that the establishment of the United States had only been possible through the expropriation, deportation and murder of the native American Indians. 'Three hundred years ago,' he argued, 'New York was a fishing village' when 'more and more people moved west and took possession of a new world'. 'This did not happen through peaceful discussion,' Hitler continued, but through the use of 'firearms and not least of firewater [meaning alcohol] until the red nation [Native Americans] succumbed'. 'Then one criss-crossed the area with a system of roads and railways,' Hitler went on, 'and there followed the founding of gigantic cities, until finally the white race controlled the entire continent, which today represents a cornerstone of the white race.' He accused the pacifists, socialists and liberals who had fled Germany for America of 'forgetting' that it was a country which had not been presented to the 'white man' by a 'host of angels', but rather taken from the 'redskins' with 'powder and shot', and brandy.[85] Hitler, in short, believed that American power rested on the violent seizure of land originally belonging to another people.

The price of demographic purity was eternal racial vigilance.[86] Here again, Hitler saw the United States as paradigmatic. Claiming that 'the result of every mixture of blood of the Aryan with lower peoples was the end of that culture', he contrasted 'North America, whose population consists largely of Germanic elements, which only mixed very little with lower coloured races', with Central and South America, where the mainly Latin immigrants had allegedly engaged in a much more profound mixing with the original population. He therefore concluded that 'the racially pure and unadulterated Germanic [inhabitant] rose to be master of the American [and] will remain master so long as he did not fall victim to contamination (*Blutschande*)'. Her immigration legislation, he noted approvingly, specifically discriminated against Asians, coloured and especially east European migrants. This was by no means enough, Hitler averred, but far better than the German situation. 'Because the American Union refuses entry to medically poor elements,' he wrote, and 'simply excludes certain races from citizenship, she is already taking the idea of a *Völkisch* state in embryonic form.' Hitler therefore saw the United States as the best example of the 'survival instinct' of the 'white man' and the most effective bulwark against the 'negrification' of the world.[87]

If racial degeneracy could generally be traced to some sort of miscegenation, Hitler also believed that it could also result from behavioural flaws. High on his list of vices was alcohol, which he regarded as an agent of corruption. 'Alcohol,' he claimed, 'is harmful to humanity' and had 'already destroyed' many more valuable Germans over the century than had been lost on the battlefield in the same period. 'Alcohol,' Hitler continued, 'is one of the worst causes of degeneration,' and he referred once again to the 'gruesome examples of the history of various colonial peoples'.[88] For this reason, Hitler was deeply impressed by the introduction of Prohibition in the United States in 1920, following a series of state-level bans in preceding decades. This set him apart not only from the beer- and wine-drinking German mainstream, but also from German-America, for whom the resulting loss of the beer-garden culture was particularly traumatic.[89] The Americans, he argued, took better care of the development of their race. 'A whole continent has declared war on alcohol poisoning,' Hitler wrote, 'in order to release a people from the devastating grip of this vice.' He warned that 'if the European states did not soon solve the alcohol question in the American sense, then America will completely rule the world in 100 years'.[90]

Hitler was also deeply impressed by what he regarded as the American socio-economic model, whose merits he had already acknowledged in Landsberg. Unlike hidebound Germany, it provided the opportunity for the development of talents across the social spectrum. 'If in the last decades the number of important inventions has increased especially in North America,' he argued, then this was not least due to the fact that 'many more talents from the lower classes enjoyed the chance of higher education than was the case in Europe.' American modernity was evident particularly in the rapid motorization of the continent: here Hitler claimed that 'there was one car per inhabitant in North America'. Unlike many contemporary critics of technological change, Hitler saw it as an unalloyed good. To those who claimed 'that new technology led to ever more unemployed' he countered that 'these inventions in turn created new jobs'. In particular, he celebrated Henry Ford, whose employees were able to afford their own car and home. This made them immune to the revolutionary virus. The American worker had thus been 'nationalized',[91] an achievement which Hitler hoped to replicate in Germany.

Hitler not only admired and feared Britain and the United States individually, he also regarded them as fundamentally akin. They enjoyed, though he himself did not quite put it that way, a 'special relationship'. Hitler did speak specifically of the 'sense of linguistic and cultural community' between Britain and the 'American Union'. Hitler described them collectively as 'Anglo-Saxons' and spoke of 'the past drive of the Anglo-Saxon to establish world domination'. His main concern, therefore, was the power of Anglo-America: how it could be imitated, reconciled, appeased, deterred, contained or at the very least delayed. He attributed Germany's defeat in 1918 to a combination of British skill in marshalling a global coalition before the conflict, her courage and 'brutality' during the war and her ability to undermine Germany from within, supported by American economic intervention from the start. He also claimed that shortly after the outbreak of war in 1914 'American shrapnel' exploded over the heads of the German columns.[92]

The main threat posed by Anglo-America was not industrial, however, but demographic. The descendants of the Germans whom the Reich had exported in the nineteenth century for want of land to feed them were now on the Anglo-American side. 'Whether it is 9 or 10 million Germans live in the North American Union is hard to say,' he claimed, 'but these Germans were lost to Germany from the start.' Hitler made a list of all the Germans living overseas. He claimed that the shells which had detonated over his head in the autumn of 1914 were 'produced in American factories with German workers at the machines'.[93] The topic of 'German engineers' working for the American war economy was one to which he would return much later in his career.

More importantly, Hitler believed that Germany's demographic surplus had recrossed the Atlantic to fight against the Reich as American soldiers during the final stages of the war. In the mid and late 1920s, Hitler repeatedly came back to the moment 'in the midsummer of 1918, when the first American soldiers appeared on the battlefields of France, well-grown men, men of our own blood, whom we had deported for centuries, who were now ready to grind the motherland itself into the mud.'[94] 'These lads, blond and blue-eyed, who are they really?' he asked on another occasion, making the racial connection explicit. 'They are all former German farmers' sons. Now they are our enemies.'[95] Moreover, the Germans who had left were always 'the best' ('*das Beste*'), the most dynamic elements. 'That all added up,' he argued, 'and gave a new continent a particular high-value character. We encountered it 1918 on the western front.'[96] The world war, one might say, had effectively been a German civil war. It was the ur-trauma which drove so much of his subsequent policy and programme.

The racial struggle which Germany had just lost, and she desperately needed to win the next time around, was therefore not primarily that between German and Slav or Jew, but the conflict between the Germans and an Anglo-America enriched by the most racially valuable elements of German society. It was, although Hitler did not quite put it that way, the confrontation between Teuton and Anglo-Saxon.

This is what Hitler was referring to in *Mein Kampf* when he spoke of the future 'general war struggle of the peoples'. He meant the final show-down not with the Jews, but rather with the other so-called Aryan or Nordic powers, namely Britain and the United States. 'If two peoples which are [racially] similarly inclined [i.e. both are Aryan] compete with each other,' he wrote, 'then victory will go to the one whose leadership has drawn on the best talents available,' whereas defeat awaited the people 'whose leadership was no more than a giant feeding trough for particular estates and classes', without consideration for the ability of its individual member.' If possible, however, such a confrontation should be avoided and he warned of 'hatred against Aryans, from whom we might be divided on almost every issue', and yet with whom Germans were 'connected by shared blood' and a 'common culture'.[97] Here it was the deadly narcissism of small racial difference that Hitler feared, especially as he believed Anglo-America to be the stronger of the two sides, both quantitatively and qualitatively.

It is in this context of Hitler's overarching preoccupation with Britain and the United States that Hitler's anti-Semitism should primarily be understood. He associated Jews not only with Anglo-American international capitalism, but also with the rise of racial false consciousness in the British Empire and the United States. In *Mein Kampf*, Hitler spoke of 'a Manchester liberalism of Jewish mindset'. He further claimed that 'Jews are the regents of the stock exchange forces of the American Union', who became with every passing year increasingly the 'controllers of the working power of a people of 120 million'. It was this power, Hitler argued, that enabled them to turn the immense force of Anglo-America against their fellow Aryans in the Reich. The ultimate aim, he claimed, drawing explicitly on the old conspiracy theory of the *Protocols of the Elders of Zion*, was the implementation of an 'action programme' for their plans for 'world conquest' based on 'the extermination of peoples'.[98] Worse still, as we have seen, the Jews allegedly undermined Germany at home, politically, culturally and racially, reducing her resistance to outside domination. Even on its own terms, of course, this theory suffered from some obvious internal contradictions. If the Jews were so inherently parasitical and disintegrative, why had they not also enfeebled Anglo-America? Conversely, if Anglo-America was as strong as he made out, then why had it not rid itself of the Jews? Be that as it may, Hitler's belief in the Anglo-American-Jewish symbiosis was sincerely held.

Much of this merely repeated what Hitler had been saying for some time, even if at greater length and with some important elaborations. The dangers of emigration and the power of Anglo-America had been among his earliest themes in 1919–20, and if they had been somewhat obscured by the dramas of 1921–3, they re-emerged with new vigour in the mid 1920s. Hatred of the Jews, the distinction between national and international capitalism, the need for territorial expansion to balance the great world empires and unions, the inadequacy of a purely economic or colonial response to the threats facing Germany, warnings about the dangers of domestic division, attacks on federalism and separatism, hostility to the Habsburgs, the primacy of foreign policy, the sense of Germany's national enslavement by the Entente and international capitalism, fear of encirclement, the need for an Italian alliance, the importance of propaganda, and the Führer concept were hardy perennials.[99] So were his rejection of alliances with the other global 'have-nots', parliamentarism and elections, the restoration of the monarchy and aristocracy, the League of Nations or global governance generally, Zionism, and the nostrums offered by the mainstream conservative nationalist right. These themes remained part of Hitler's repertoire, to varying degrees, right down to the end in 1945.

That said, there were important shifts evident in Hitler's thinking. Some topics were receding. There was less emphasis on the racial danger posed by French colonial forces of occupation, and indeed on the threat of French domination more generally; this peaked in 1921–3. German separatism, especially the Bavarian variety, remained a concern, but it never reached the fever pitch consuming Hitler just before and after the Munich Putsch. Some important new themes were also visible. In part, these reflected the changed political and geopolitical situation, or were made possible by them. If Hitler had once expected a nationalist restoration of the old Russia, and an end to 'Judaeo-Bolshevik' domination in the interests of international capital, he was now convinced that the Russian Revolution was there to stay. He stepped up his anti-communist broadsides, and while he never changed his view that Bolshevism was essentially an instrument of international capitalism, a superstructural phenomenon, Hitler did assign it a greater relative autonomy from then on. He spoke of the 'world plague of Bolshevism', the need for an 'ideo-logical war of destruction against Marxism and its puppeteers' and proclaimed the NSDAP the 'fanatical mortal foe of Marxism'.[100]

Crucially, Hitler was referring here to the threat of global communism, which in his view was directed from London and New York, in the interests of international capitalism, or the threat of a communist takeover in Germany, either electorally or by force of arms. Hitler still did not identify the Soviet Union itself as a serious military challenge, however, and – at this time at any rate – he spoke generally of 'Marxism' rather than of the more specifi-cally Russian 'Bolshevism'. The main purpose of his anti-communist rhetoric, therefore, was not so much to appeal to the German bourgeoisie as to dem-onstrate to the various party factions that the situation in eastern Europe had changed, and that Nazi grand strategy must change with it. An alliance with Russia, a stock demand not only of the Conservative right, but also of the more left-wing party element such as Goebbels and the Strassers, was ruled out as pointless and even pernicious; here Hitler explicitly rejected the Bis-marckian tradition.[101] More importantly, the continuing weakness of Russia now provided an opportunity to address Germany's crucial geopolitical weakness, the lack of space to accommodate her alleged demographic surplus.

The solution, Hitler argued, lay in overcoming the mismatch between space and population growth in Germany. 'We find ourselves today in a world of emerging great powers [he meant something close to the concept of 'superpowers'],' he wrote, 'in which our own Reich is declining ever more into irrelevance' because of its small size. 'Only a sufficiently large space on this earth secures a people's freedom of existence' in the context of its geopolitical exposure. For this reason, he claimed, 'the National Socialist movement must try to eliminate the discrepancy between our population and the size of our territory,' both from the perspective of 'food supply' and from the strategic point of view. He had already rejected the Caprivian idea of exporting goods rather than people, and the return of colonies. Both solutions, Hitler argued, were vulnerable to naval and commercial coercion by Anglo-America. He also dismissed the standard nationalist demand for a restoration of the borders of 1914, which would do no more than simply restore the unsatisfactory geopolitical constella-tion under which the Reich had lost the war.[102]

Instead, he called for territorial expansion – 'living space'[103] – within Europe, contiguous or nearly so with the German Reich, to wit in 'Russia and her vassal states'. He summarized all this in a concluding passage which subsequently became notorious. 'With this,' he concluded, 'we Germans consciously draw a line beneath the foreign policy of the pre-war period.' 'We start,' he continued, 'where one stopped six hundred years ago. We will end the eternal march of the Germans to the south and west of Europe and turn our eyes to the land in the east.' 'We will finally end the trade and colonial policy of the pre-war period,' Hitler went on, 'and go over to the territorial policy of the future.' Here he had in mind 'in the first instance only Russia and the neighbouring states subject to it'.[104]

Here Hitler meant neither Poland nor Czechoslovakia, but the Soviet Union. It was singled out not because it was the chief Jewish enemy, but for the entirely opposite reason that Jewish subversion there had rendered the territory ripe for takeover by Germany. The Soviet Union was to be attacked because it was weak, not because it was a threat. To be sure, Hitler, who had hitherto shown no hostility towards Slavs as such, now expressed a racial antagonism against them, albeit much milder than that which he showed towards the Jews. In *Mein Kampf* he attributed the historic strength of the Russian state to the 'state effectiveness of the [mainly Baltic] Germanic element in an inferior race',[105] which had been 'completely exterminated and extinguished' by the Revolution. It is also true that he preached the need to extirpate world communism, but here he had a more global threat in mind (more virulent in the democratic and capitalist west) than a specifically Soviet one. The crucial point is that Hitler did not primarily justify the quest for *Lebensraum* with the inherent inferiority of the Slav population there, as an ideological war against Bolshevism, or even as a first step towards the annihilation of the Jews in Europe. His main motive was that Germany, weak herself, would in his view have to colonize her even weaker neighbour before she was herself completely enslaved. Hitler targeted the Soviet Union not so much for what it was (ideologically), as for where it lay (geographically). There was, so to speak, nothing personal about it.

His aim throughout was not world domination, but simple national survival. There was, Hitler averred, no room for half-measures. Germany would have to be a world power, or she would go completely under. The half-measures and restraint of Bismarck's times, he argued, were outdated in a world of global empires. 'Germany will either be a world power or nothing,' Hitler wrote, 'but to be a world power one needs the necessary size.' This meant, he concluded, that 'the German people will only be able to guarantee their future through world power'.[106] Hitler may have spoken privately of his hopes for world hegemony, but this was probably bluster.[107] It is more likely that, at least at this stage, Hitler did not envisage 'world domination' by Germany, as opposed to the 'world power' status necessary for her very survival.

To sum up: the driving force behind Hitler's strategy in the mid 1920s, as in the period immediately after the First World War, remained fear and admiration of Anglo-America. *Lebensraum* in the east would kill two birds with one stone. First, it would provide Germany with the critical territorial mass necessary to balance the American Union and the British Empire, and to some extent that of France as well. Secondly, eastward expansion would secure the raw materials and especially the farmland necessary to feed the German demographic surplus. Eastern colonization was the answer to pernicious transatlantic and antipodean migration. Hitler was proposing to strike east, but he was really looking west.

Hitler's geopolitical shift towards *Lebensraum* in the mid 1920s was matched by an equally important transformation, or at least elaboration, in his thinking about domestic politics. This was his increasingly evident racial pessimism about the German people. He lamented 'our own fragmentation of the blood' as the result of 'centuries of racial decay'. Germany's internal divisions since the Reformation, Hitler argued, and the resulting external interference, had subverted the Aryan character of her people. 'With the Thirty Years War,' he claimed, 'a slow decline of our national power began.' The Reich was torn apart by confessional, class, political and regional differences. Worse still, Germany's exposed geopolitical position left her vulnerable to constant racial contamination. 'The geographically disadvantageous location of Germany,' he argued, 'facilitates a continuous influx which naturally results in hundreds of thousands of bastards.' Moreover, in his view the weakness of Germany meant that there was no effective immigration control. 'Everybody,' he complained, 'is indiscriminately admitted into Germany.'[108]

As if all this were not bad enough, the German people was further weakened by mass emigration because it was always the best and brightest who left. 'Hundreds and thousands of the best elements,' he lamented, 'were lost to our people for all time and with it we perhaps lost the most valuable [and] most energetic blood.' In *Mein Kampf* he wrote that 'experience has shown' that it was usually the 'healthiest and most energetic' who emigrated. The result, Hitler argued, was that 'our German people are no longer based on a unitary racial core', so that the basic racial elements were diffused not only territorially, but also within territories. In Germany, he went on, 'we find Slavic next to Nordic, Dinaric next to Slavic, western next to both of these and [various] mixtures interspersed'. [109] The German *Volk* was thus not co-terminous with the Nordic race. On the contrary, it was in his view locked into a downward racial spiral, in which the path dependency of uninterrupted racial decline rendered the Reich incapable of preventing further contamination and emigration.

Hitler's preoccupation with Anglo-America only sharpened this sense of

German racial inadequacy. He admired the 'racial instincts in foreign countries' by which the people rallied in 'critical moments' by 'thinking the same thing and coming to the same decisions', because in the end 'the language of blood will out'. Here he had in mind particularly those who could look back on a long, unbroken national history. 'That is not the case in Germany,' he claimed, 'that is the case in Britain,' which had risen continuously over the past 300 years. 'In this way,' Hitler continued, 'the British nation could fuse into a unity whose granite-like ability to resist could no longer be shaken.' Unlike the Germans, it was 'belief and pride' which united the British.[110] Hitler, in other words, was in no doubt that the British, and their descendants in North America, enjoyed a substantially higher average racial value than the German people.

This sense of hierarchy was confirmed by his engagement with American racial theorists. Hitler was familiar with Madison Grant, whose sensational *Passing of the Great Race* was translated into German and widely discussed in 1925, though it seems that the racial chapters of *Mein Kampf* were already complete by then.[111] Grant's book is usually taken as a contribution to anti-black racism in America, but its most remarkable feature was the author's clear stratification of the white races, and his unflattering view of the quality of German immigrants. According to him, only about 9 or 10 million Germans out of a total of some 70 million in 1914 were truly Nordic. This categorization gave considerable offence in 1920s Germany, especially on the right, but Hitler accepted the analysis. 'On the strength of the work of an American scholar [Grant] who proves that Germany hardly contains 9 to 10 million really Nordic-Aryan people,' Hitler argued, 'the American Union has established the immigration quotas. It privileges those from the Scandinavian countries, from Britain and only in third place those from Germany because it is already racially inferior.' He noted with approval that, unlike Germany, the United States 'does not allow every Polish Jew to immigrate' but 'puts a limit on numbers'.[112] There was no contradiction between this view and Hitler's despair about emigration. The Germans who went to the United States might be inferior to the resident Anglo-Saxons, but they were the best of a bad lot, he thought.

There was, in his view, a silver lining to this dark racial cloud. There had at least not been a 'crossbreeding' at the level of the lowest common denominator, creating a 'general racial mish-mash'. The 'blessing' of this absence of 'complete [racial] mixing' was that we 'today still have in the body of the German people large quantities of unadulterated Nordic-German people who constitute our most important treasure for the future'. Once Hitler came to power, the mining of that treasure was to be as important as the removal of what he considered racial dross. For now, the uneasy co-existence of various so-called unassimilated elements in the German people meant that 'at least part of our best blood remained pure and escaped racial decline'. This left open the possibility of selecting and multiplying the best strains in the existing German *Volk*. Hitler therefore defined the 'truly supreme mission' of the National Socialist state as putting the German people on a racially sound basis. 'The German Reich,' he wrote, should be a state 'encompassing all Germans with the task not only of collecting and maintaining the most valuable original racial elements but also of slowly and surely raising these to a dominant position.'[113] In other words, for Hitler, eliminating the Jews and other 'undesirable' elements was a necessary but not a sufficient condition for racial salvation. It was the perceived racial fragility of the German people itself, especially when contrasted to the vitality of Anglo-America, which was his greatest concern.

From now on, Hitler's racial thought and later racial policy would have two linked but separate planks. His 'negative eugenics' sought to eliminate the allegedly negative through the removal of 'inferior' elements deemed 'harmful' to the racial body politic, especially Jews, but also gypsies, the disabled and the insane.[114] His 'positive eugenics' sought to accentuate the positive, by elevating the allegedly 'superior' elements. Hitler started from his crucial distinction between the German *Volk* – which in his view was made up of many different racial strands – and the Nordic or Aryan race – which only constituted a minority within it. One way or the other, he warned in the penultimate paragraph of *Mein Kampf*, 'a state which devotes itself to the care of its best racial elements in an age of [general] racial contamination will one day became the lord of the world'.[115] This was a role which Hitler would have very much liked to claim for Germany, but his fear was that it would go to the United States.

Hitler's solution to all this was not based on any sort of Germanic, esoteric or supernatural faddery; these theories helped Germans to transcend their 'subaltern' European status after 1918.[116] Unlike many contemporary '*Völkisch*' activists, and some later prominent National Socialists, especially the subsequent SS leader Heinrich Himmler, Hitler had little time for abstruse Aryan theories or the celebration of the ancient Germanic tribes. In *Mein Kampf*, Hitler made fun of these enthusiasts. 'If anything is "*unvölkisch*",' he wrote, 'then it is this throwing around of particularly old Germanic expressions.' He lampooned the 'German-*Völkisch* wandering scholars' and the '*Völkisch* Methuselahs'. Hitler sneered at 'old Germanic heroism, from time immemorial [with] stone axes etc.' as portrayed by bearded '*Völkisch* comedians'. Hitler also rejected the old strategies of Germanization. 'Nationality, or rather race,' he explained, 'doesn't lie in language but in the blood.' He insisted, in a phrase that was to resonate later, that 'Germanization could only be carried on on the soil and not on the individual'.[117]

Instead, Hitler argued, the restoration of German racial coherence required a multi-pronged strategy. Central to it was discipline. This was a reflection not of German strength, but of German weakness. The British, he believed, did not need discipline in the same way; it came to them naturally. 'When the going gets tough,' he argued, 'the British stand there as one race.' 'The minute it gets tough in Germany', by contrast, 'the deep-seated instincts' and 'blood composition' of the German people came to the surface. In *Mein Kampf* he wrote that 'no new race was being distilled in Germany but rather the various racial elements continued to exist beside each other, with the result that the German people [tended] to disperse in all directions' when challenged. This meant that the Germans needed to be drilled into racial coherence. 'Much of what appears so natural to the foreigner,' he continued, 'still needs to be laboriously taught to our people.' 'For us,' Hitler went on, 'discipline' compensates for the lack of 'blood-based instinct'. 'That is the only way of getting men into line.' One of the ways this could be done, he wrote in *Mein Kampf*, was through conscription, and he praised the way in which Prussian universal military service had made good some of the centuries of German 'fragmentation of the blood'.[118] The restoration of conscription, Hitler argued, was therefore essential not merely for the defence of the Reich but for the racial coherence of the *Volk*.

This is the deeper background to Hitler's reorganization and reorientation of the SA after his release. In part, this was a question of ensuring that activists did not endanger the new 'legal' strategy. The main reason, however, was that Hitler saw the SA not as the vehicle for Germany's military revival but as the motor of her moral and racial regeneration. He issued a new 'statute' for the SA in mid September 1926, which laid down that 'any sort of excesses should be avoided', 'should lend our public appearance an impressive and dignified character'. Its technical task was to provide 'stewarding and protection' for 'mass meetings'. Hitler 'strictly forbade' any sort of 'military posturing'. 'The SA,' he explained, 'is not a military formation. The military training of the nation is the task of the army and not that of the NSDAP.' In early November 1926, Hitler established a central SA headquarters in Munich under Franz Pfeffer von Salomon. The task of the SA was not to engage in 'conspiracy' but 'to capture the street' from 'Marxism'. More broadly, Hitler wanted the SA to provide at least some of the missing discipline and coherence in German society. For this reason, Hitler argued, the SA must show 'strict discipline' to allow Germany to recover over the long term.[119]

This was important because, as we have seen, Hitler's time horizon, which had shortened considerably in 1923, lengthened once more after the failure of the Putsch. He was now expecting the revival of Germany to take generations. 'The battle for the National Socialist idea,' he warned one audience, 'could perhaps last decades, perhaps centuries.'[120] The wooing of the German workers, he wrote in Mein Kampf, 'was a process of transformation and convergence which would not be completed in ten or twenty years but by experience will take many generations'.[121] 'Jewish bastardization and Jewish contamination of the blood,' Hitler feared, 'can only be removed from our national body politic in the course of centuries if at all.'[122] In February 1927, he wrote that 'the welding together of a medley of people from such heterogeneous backgrounds required a process that would take decades'.[123] He would need a long timeline for the implementation of both positive and negative eugenics.

Hitler sought no less than to reverse the political effects of the Reformation, and the Thirty Years War, which he regarded as the root of Germany's fragmentation. Hitler criticized 'Ultramontanism' – that is the tendency of Catholics to place allegiance to the Pope over that to the state – and the allegedly anti-nationalist tendencies in the nineteenth-century church. He accused the church of not 'feeling with the German people' and consequently praised the late nineteenth- and early twentieth-century 'Away from Rome movement' as overcoming the 'unfortunate split in the church' in the interests of the 'internal power of the Reich'. He saw it perpetuated in the form of the Catholic Centre Party, one of the key groups in Weimar Germany, and the sister party of the hated Bavarian BVP. Hitler bemoaned the fact that 'religious feelings still run deeper today than all national or political considerations'.[124] He spoke of the 'brazenness with which one attempted to identify the Catholic belief with a political party'. In this sense, Hitler was more comfortable with Protestantism, 'which better represented German concerns'. This was the main stated reason for his antagonism to organized Christianity, and especially to the most organized church, Roman Catholicism, though his private enmity went much deeper than that. His hostility was political rather than metaphysical.

That said, unlike many other right-wing ideologues, Hitler believed that a compromise was possible, especially with Roman Catholicism, by taking the church out of politics. To the disgust of many Völkisch activists, and party members such as Ernst Count Reventlow, he therefore preached that one should continue to attack Catholic political parties and internationalist sympathies, but avoid slighting purely religious sensibilities. The Centre Party was to be opposed not for confessional reasons, but 'solely for national-political reasons'. 'If you consider yourself appointed by destiny to preach the truth,' he wrote, 'then do that, but then also have the courage not to do this under the guise [Hitler's exact word was *Umweg*] of a political party.' In return, Hitler promised to keep the NSDAP out of religion. 'Political parties,' he insisted, 'have no business getting involved with religious issues' so long as these did not undermine the morality of the race. Hitler refused to take sides between religions.[125]

Hitler saw a central role for the arts and the humanities in the racial recovery of Germany. Cultural activity, he believed, helped to distil and refine the best elements in the German people. In some ways, this was an exercise in cultural nationalism, as Hitler insisted on the value of nineteenth-century German painting and music over contemporary aberrations. In other ways, it was a more universalist project, which appealed not to the Gothic or Germanic past, but to the European classical tradition.[126] One should study antiquity for the 'preservation of the nation,' he argued, because it 'remains the first teacher not only for today but for all time'. 'In future,' he continued, 'the Hellenic cultural ideal should remain preserved for us in all its beauty.' He also saw an important role for history. It should be taught not as 'learning off by heart or rattling off of historical dates', but as a teleological quest for 'the forces' which were 'the cause of the effects which we then perceive as historical events'. Its 'main value lies in the recognition of the great lines of development', because one learns history as a teacher for the future and in order to secure the survival of one's people.[127]

The exercise of Führer powers might be charismatic and autocratic, but its basis was popular. Hitler insisted that 'extraordinary geniuses do not need to make allowance for ordinary humanity', because although they might have 'advisers' by their side, 'the decision was made by one man alone'. This was necessary if only to secure the succession. He spoke of the need for a 'true Germanic democracy in the free choice of the leader, who would have to take over full responsibility for all actions and omissions. In this system, Hitler continued, 'there would be no vote on individual questions'. Moreover, perhaps inspired by the Westminster example, he accepted that 'parliaments are necessary' because they provided a mechanism through which those 'heads' who would 'later be given special tasks' could 'slowly be raised up'.[128] Parliament thus had a selective rather than a representative function. This was a sort of democracy, though not as we know it. Hitler laid down the principle of one man, one woman, one vote, once, at least for the lifetime of the Führer. Thereafter, parliament could counsel, but it could not control. He called this 'Germanic Democracy'.

The publication of the second volume of *Mein Kampf* in December

1926 marked the completion of an important phase in Hitler's ideological development. That said, there were some themes which were later to acquire considerable importance which did not feature in *Mein Kampf* at all, or were not explicit there, or were at least not dealt with in great detail. There was plenty of anti-Semitism, but no express call for the murder of all European Jews.[129] There was a demand for the seizure of 'living space' in the east by military means, to be sure, but this was conceived of as an instrument to balance over-mighty Anglo-America rather than necessarily as a blueprint for another world war (provided the western powers allowed him to expand eastwards). The importance of the United States was evident, in his speeches rather more than in *Mein Kampf*, but a sustained engagement with the 'American Union' was yet to come. There was also no statement on the related 'European Question', which was already a matter of keen debate not merely in Germany as a whole but within the party itself. Hitler, in other words, was not yet arrived at his final doctrinal destination. He had another book in him, which – as we shall see – he wrote but never published.

6

Regaining Control of the Party

Hitler elaborated his ideological positions over and over again, in public and in private, in order to re-establish ideological coherence in the party and thereby his own authority. There was, at first, considerable resistance. Hitler's willingness to compromise with Catholicism scandalized many. There was also resistance on the 'left'. To be sure, Hitler was pushing an open door with anti-capitalism. 'We will turn National Socialism into a party of class struggle,' Goebbels wrote in his diary in May 1925, 'that is good. Capitalism must be called by its name.' There was a nagging sense of unease, though, as to where Hitler really stood, particularly when he opposed plans to seize the property of the German princes deposed in 1918, a cause dear to many on the left. 'Will he become a nationalist or socialist?' Goebbels wondered in mid June 1925. 'Just as I wanted,' a reassured Goebbels wrote in July 1925, 'sharply against bourgeoisie and capitalism. I would be prepared to sacrifice everything for that man.' Goebbels was also electrified by the publication of the first volume of *Mein Kampf* in October. 'I am finishing Hitler's book,' he wrote. 'Who is this man? Half plebeian, half God! Is he really Christ or only John [the Baptist].'[1]

Not long after, however, Goebbels was assailed by doubts again. Like many 'northerners', he feared the 'pigsty' in Munich. 'I am not going to put up with this Byzantinism any longer,' he despaired, 'we must get to Hitler.' Observing the antics of Julius Streicher, Goebbels exclaimed, 'Poor Hitler! Poor National Socialism!' Two days later, after he had been offered the role of editor of the *Völkischer Beobachter*, Goebbels was writing 'we have sorted things out with Hitler [who] will also draw me in closer'.[2] This was to be a common pattern among Hitler's followers in the mid to late 1920s, and indeed thereafter. They were frequently assailed by doubts, only to have their faith restored by Hitler's intense entreaties.[3] Their conversion was not so much a single road to Damascus experience, as a stop-start process. In some cases, it made the final submission all the more lasting, while in others doubts kept returning until the very end.

The most contentious area remained foreign policy, where the publication of *Mein Kampf* did not immediately settle matters. Many could not stomach the abandonment of South Tyrol, which Hitler made an absolute test of loyalty, because of the value he placed on Mussolini's favour. In August 1926, for example, Hans Frank, a loyal member, who later became the governor of Nazi-occupied Poland, temporarily left the party over the issue. The really critical issue, however, was Russia. The left and the 'northerners' were wedded to an alliance with a free Russia, and if necessary even with Bolshevik Russia, against Anglo-American Jewish international capitalism. Hitler, of course, wanted to colonize the east, and was determined to stamp out any dissent on the question. He sent Gottfried Feder to a meeting of the Arbeitsgemeinschaft in late January 1926 to enforce the anti-Russian line. This went down very badly with Goebbels, who launched an impassioned attack on 'western capitalism' and a defence of a Russian alliance.[4]

There was also no consensus over the vexed question of internationalism, which Hitler despised, but to which other senior figures remained strongly attached. Gregor Strasser, in particular, was convinced that Germany should make common cause with the 'have-nots' of the world, including colonized peoples of colour. He saw Germany as one of the global underdogs, and envisaged her leading a 'League of Oppressed Peoples' in alliance with Russia, Morocco, Persia, India and the other wretched of the earth. 'The fragmented, martyred, exploited, [and] enslaved Germany,' Strasser argued, 'was the natural protagonist and ally of all national liberation fighters', wherever they were oppressed by 'French tyranny, British imperialism, [and] American financial exploitation,' that is, virtually the entire world. Goebbels, for his part, was impressed by Gandhi, whom he likened to a 'messiah', though he doubted that his non-violent methods could be applied in Germany.[5] Strasser's internationalism also extended to the field of European integration. In late January 1926, he produced a draft of a new party programme in which he called for a 'United States of Europe as a European League of Nations with a single currency and measurement system'.[6]

Matters came to a head on 14 February 1926, when Hitler convened a party congress at Bamberg specifically to settle matters of doctrine, in particular foreign policy. There he insisted on the inviolability of the twenty-five-point programme. Significantly, it was grand strategy, not the debate about socialism or the referendum on the expropriation of princely property, which Hitler concentrated on.[7] The meeting turned into a Valentine's Day massacre of foreign policy dissenters on the 'left' of the party; it was their internationalism, not their socialism which Hitler objected to. Rehearsing the themes that would appear in the second volume of *Mein Kampf* a few months later, Hitler rejected an 'eastern orientation', on either traditional Bismarckian or contemporary ideological lines, and proclaimed the primacy of eastern 'policy', that is the seizure of living space in the east. Goebbels and other critics were aghast at this 'reactionary' turn.[8]

In mid April 1926, Hitler called another meeting in Munich to demand an end to intra-party squabbling and the establishment of conformity over Russia.[9] It was attended by most of the main figures, including Hess, Streicher and Goebbels; the latter's heartfelt outpourings were rewarded by the Führer with a tearful hug. Hitler essentially repeated his stump speech over three hours, but Goebbels was now much more receptive to what he called the 'Bamberg arguments'. This time he recorded in his diary that Hitler's remarks were 'glowing'. 'Italy and Britain are our allies,' he wrote approvingly, 'Russia wants to eat us. All that is in the forthcoming volume of *Mein Kampf*.' With respect to the 'social question', where Goebbels had long mistrusted Hitler's 'reactionary' tendencies, he now saw 'completely new insights. He has thought through everything.' Hitler's 'ideal', Goebbels continued, was 'a blend of collectivism and individualism', in which soil belonged 'to the people' while production, which was 'creative', should be left to private enterprise. 'Corporations and trusts,' he continued, 'will be socialized. One can talk about that.' Goebbels concluded with the words 'I bow to the greater, the political genius.'[10]

Hitler now moved to reorganize the Nazi Party itself and to turn it into an instrument to gain power. He envisaged a vanguardist role for the NSDAP, which would lead society and the electorate, rather than reflect or represent it. 'A little group of fanatics,' he proclaimed, 'carries the mass along with it.' 'Look at Russia and Italy,' Hitler continued, 'you can only push through the fight for the majority when you have a powerful minority behind you.' Here, of course, Hitler was making a virtue out of a vice, but the allusion to the Bolshevik model was revealing. The party was given new statutes. A series of guidelines and circulars followed, some laying down general principles, others deciding individual questions of policy or personnel. Deviators were expelled, either at Hitler's request or on the recommendation of the USCHLA. Members were forbidden to join other parties or groups in order to avoid mixed loyalties. 'It is a false deduction,' Hitler explained to Eitel Leopold von Görtz-Wrisberg, a member of the *Bundesleitung* of the Frontkriegerbund in Thuringia, 'to rely on a man who also belongs to another association because one never knows whose orders he will actually follow'. Hitler also insisted on the payment of membership dues, if only for psychological reasons. 'One only loves that,' he argued, 'for which one makes sacrifices.'[11]

Crucial to the effectiveness of the party was the establishment of a focal point – what Hitler called a 'common apex' and the 'real Führer' – holding the whole organization together. 'The idea must also have a geographical central point,' Hitler continued, citing the respective roles of 'Mecca, Rome, [and] Moscow', because if that was lacking then there was a danger of fragmentation. 'The geopolitical [sic] importance of a central focal point of a movement' should not be underestimated, he elaborated in *Mein Kampf*, 'only the availability of a place with the magic of a Mecca or Rome can in the long run give the movement a force'. The new Rome, Mecca and Moscow was to be Munich, whose party organization was placed directly under that of the Reich leadership. He therefore demanded 'concentration of the entire work initially on one place: Munich'.[12]

The city was not chosen because of its closeness to National Socialism – the sobriquet 'capital of the movement' was still ten years off[13] – but for the opposite reason. Official Munich was now deadly hostile, and Hitler was banned from public speaking in Bavaria for more than two years after his release from Landsberg. Some suggested that the NSDAP should shift base to Thuringia, which would have better reflected its *Schwerpunkt* at the time. Hitler accepted 'that he now had more followers in the former red Saxony and Thuringia than in nationalist Bavaria', and that 'the liberation of Germany might come from the water's edge [that is from the north] and no longer from Bavaria. Hitler countered, however, that Munich was the Golgotha of Nazism, 'hallowed ground', where the 'blood' of 'martyrs' had been shed in 1923. To leave the city for an 'easier' patch would be to break faith with the dead, and indeed would mean 'the end of the movement'. The fight in Munich should not be ducked. 'Precisely because' the NSDAP was being 'fought the hardest' in Munich, he explained at an NSDAP 'leaders conference' in Rosenheim, 'this position must not be abandoned'. In his mind, the Bavarian capital was the theatre of a political war of attrition. For all these reasons, Hitler determined that the movement should stick it out in Munich and announced plans to build a party headquarters in the city.[14]

Munich was also 'geopolitically' significant. Hitler explained that it was 'closer to [our] German brothers in Austria than any other place and provided the best connection to the *Anschluss* movement' there.[15] Perhaps more importantly, the city was also an excellent jumping-off point to conquer Franconia, which was far more promising terrain in the mid to late 1920s. Hitler's first major engagement after the refounding of the NSDAP was a speech to 5,000 people in Nuremberg in early March 1925, at a time when he was still banned from speaking in Munich.[16] There were more party members there than in Munich.[17] He backed Julius Streicher to the hilt, not just against the Weimar authorities but also in the face of bitter criticism within the party. In early December 1925, Hitler went to Nuremberg to testify on Streicher's behalf in a court case spawned by his persecution of Lord Mayor Luppe. Six months later, Hitler celebrated Nuremberg as a 'mighty fortress in our movement'.[18] It was also no accident that Hitler convened the crucial party congress in the Franconian city of Bamberg, which gave the appearance of meeting the northerners halfway but actually gave him a much greater home advantage than he would have enjoyed in the now largely unsympathetic Bavarian capital. Coburg was another focus of activity.[19] Pivoting on Franconia, the party could spread out like an oil slick, especially into Thuringia. Convinced of the effectiveness of the 'southern' strategy, Hitler held his nose, tolerated Streicher and Esser and demanded that the rest of the NSDAP fall in line behind them.

The political centrality of Franconia was underlined by the growth of the Nuremberg annual party rally. In August 1927, Nazis converged on the city from all directions; 10,000–15,000 of them, according to the hostile authorities, more if the NSDAP is to be believed. Despite the rain, which forced the cancellation of several events, and the vast expense, it was generally believed to be a success. In a remarkable physical feat, Hitler kept his arm outstretched in salute for more than ninety minutes as his cohorts filed by.[20] It was the first time he wore an SA uniform in public, a mark of favour towards his party soldiers but also a sign of confidence that it had internalized his message that power could only be achieved through legal means. Afterwards, attendees repaired to the Luitpoldhain, a large park, where Hitler performed a 'dedication' ceremony for twelve NSDAP banners by touching them with another banner, stained with the sacred blood of the hatter Andreas Bauriedl, 'martyred' during the failed Munich Putsch.

There was also the considerable cultural importance of Franconia. Hitler drew on the Wagnerian tradition in Bayreuth for strength and inspiration. He invited Winifred and Siegfried to his first major speech after his release in the Munich Bürgerbräukeller on 27 February 1925. Afterwards, he was chauffeured to Plauen and stayed at Wahnfried. Hitler remained in close contact with the Wagners from now on. Sometimes, they came to his Munich flat in Thierschstrasse 41, but more often Hitler went to Bayreuth, regularly stopping off on his way to Berlin. He would then stay in a nearby hotel, and slip into Wahnfried under the cover of darkness. He attended the festival for the first time in August 1925, though as the guest of an unknown benefactor, not as an official invitee; Hitler signed the Bayreuth 'List of Arrivals' as a writer, reflecting the fact that he was engaged on volume two of *Mein Kampf* at the time. Even in that exacting environment, people were impressed by Hitler's knowledge of music.[21] Winifred joined the party in January 1926. Despite rumours at the time and since, her relationship with Hitler – for all its intensity – was not romantic, at least not on his side. Nor was Wagner the inspiration behind Hitler's anti-Semitism; the composer merited only the briefest of mentions in *Mein Kampf*.[22] Rather, Hitler's interest in Wagner was artistic and metaphysical; he used the relationship with Winifred to recharge his spiritual batteries. After 1933, his annual visit to Bayreuth would become part of the Nazi political calendar.

Hitler's interest in Bayreuth was not just personal. Wagner's operas expressed for him the very profundity of the German soul. Hitler was therefore determined to rescue the Wagnerian tradition from what he classed as foreign contamination, especially the Jews. Here he was somewhat at odds with Winifred and Siegfried, who were desperate to bring Americans to Bayreuth, if only for financial reasons.[23] Many of those attending, and some of those performing in the 1920s, were Jews. Hitler refused to attend in 1927, because the bass-baritone singing Wotan, Friedrich Schorr, was of Jewish origin; in fact, he stayed away for the next four years. Goebbels accused Siegfried of crawling to the Jews. More generally, Hitler saw cultural activity and production as an integral part of the racial elevation of the German people. Bringing them to broader attention and understanding was a major concern for him. In the debate between left and right Wagnerians, Hitler sided with the 'left-winger' Wilhelm Ellenbogen, who argued that Wagner should be brought to the masses.[24]

Central, western and northern Germany was as yet less fertile ground for Hitler, but he was determined to change that. In November 1926, he persuaded a reluctant Goebbels to take charge of the party in the imperial capital.[25] Goebbels now took the fight to the left in the streets and the neighbourhoods of working-class Berlin. His aim in this 'battle for Berlin' was no less than the 'conquest' of the city.[26] On 1 May 1927, Hitler spoke in the capital at a meeting organized by Goebbels, albeit not in public, because he was still banned from speaking in Prussia. Progress in the north and west was held up by the emergence of a new antagonism in the party, this time between Goebbels and the Strasser brothers. Gregor Strasser had been appointed propaganda leader in September 1926, much to the chagrin of Goebbels, who coveted the role for himself.

Slowly but surely, Hitler sorted out the party. One of the leading conservatives, Count Reventlow, abandoned his cronies Wulle and Gräfe, and swore loyalty to Hitler; Gräfe was ostracized. The leading '*Völkisch*' critic Artur Dinter was sacked as *Gauleiter* of Thuringia. 'There is not the slightest doubt,' Hess wrote in late March 1927, 'as to who leads and gives the orders.' 'The Führer principle,' he added, meant that there was 'absolute authority downward and responsibility upward.'[27] Looking back in the summer of 1927, Hitler claimed that he had now cleared up 'the whole jumble of mutually antagonistic, abusive and slandering groups' after his release from prison. 'They had to be disciplined again,' he said. Dissent was not tolerated. 'The number of proposals is so great,' Hitler explained, 'that they cannot be treated at one great meeting', quite apart from the fact that such a way of proceeding resembled despised 'parliamentarism'. These events were intended for mobilization, not consultation or deliberation. 'The party congress,' Hitler explained, 'should fulfil its purpose of giving the movement new impetus through a large assembly of delegates.'[28] Most submissions at Nuremberg in 1927 were summarily dismissed by Hitler: 'Petition pointless', he would say, 'petition cannot be implemented', 'petition impossible' or even 'petition violates our principles'.[29] In this sense, Hitler was already practising 'Germanic Democracy'.

By the end of 1927, things were looking up for Hitler and National Socialism. The speaking bans were progressively lifted: in late January for Saxony, and in early March for Bavaria; he was still not allowed to appear in public in Prussia. Hitler had enforced his ideological line across the board. He had built a capable team. Göring, at least in those days, provided social connections and a sense of élan. Goebbels, who was a genuine intellectual, had a genius for communication. Gregor Strasser brought his considerable organizational skills to the table. Hess, although widely considered to be a crank, was in fact well educated, spoke several languages and wrote extremely well. Many of Hitler's associates were highly intelligent, none were conventionally stupid. They were, to say the least, a diverse group, intellectually and temperamentally, but each of them brought a range of talents to the party. With the exception of Röhm, who had left in a huff, they were all in for the long haul.

Hitler was also finding his niche personally. He was now very much rooted in a section of Munich society, surrounded by well-wishers and a frequent guest at various salons. His emotional life at the time remains a mystery.[30] In March 1925, Hitler felt obliged to deny rumours of an engagement. 'I am so deeply married to politics,' he proclaimed, 'that I cannot allow myself to get engaged.'[31] He was close to the daughters and wives of his associates, especially the photographer Heinrich Hoffmann's daughter Henriette and Hanfstaengl's wife Helene, a statuesque German-American. These 'safe' relationships were completely unphysical. One day in the mid to late 1920s, Hitler reportedly placed his head in Helene's lap and proclaimed himself her slave. 'If only,' he sighed, 'I had someone like you to look after me.' When she asked why he did not marry, he replied, 'I can never marry because my life is dedicated to my country,' his stock response.[32] Hitler's relationship with his niece Geli, by contrast, was intense and may have been intimate. When she announced in November 1927 that she wanted to marry Emil Maurice, the chauffeur and body-guard, Hitler erupted in fury. Maurice was sacked the next day.[33]

Though Hitler had reasserted control over most of the party, the Weimar Republic in turn had stabilized. It was increasingly Americanized, partly in the technological sense that Hitler applauded, but mainly in the finan-cial and cultural sense he so despised. Moreover, the party remained divided both ideologically and in terms of personalities. Few grasped the significance of the United States to Hitler's thinking, and although the Russian issue was now largely resolved, a new gulf was opening up over the question of European integration, on which the left-wingers remained keen. The 'left' had shifted from north Germany to Berlin, and was itself divided between the Strassers and Goebbels. The party was flatlining electorally. Its message seemed oddly out of tune with the parochial con-cerns of the German people.

Hitler, however, remained unconcerned. He pointedly refused to engage in day-to-day politics, which he accused of 'smothering' the idea.[34] 'The life of a people,' Hitler proclaimed, 'is not determined by the so-called issues of the day.' Instead, he argued that 'the issues of the day are just products of [one] great circumstance which is that we signed the peace treaty [of Versailles] some time ago'. This is why Hitler continued to stress the misery of the German people, even during the relatively good times of what were later known as the 'golden years'. 'Even in the field of econom-ics,' he argued in August 1927, 'the so-called consolidation is a fallacy or an intentional lie.' In any case, as we have seen, his timeline for the regen-eration of the German people was at this point a very long one. That said, Hitler was also conscious that his opportunity might come well before that. 'The current period of tranquillity in the world,' he wrote, 'gives one the impression that we are standing on firm ground,' but this was mis-taken. 'The quiet of today,' Hitler warned, 'can also be seen' as merely 'a lull in the fighting which might already be over tomorrow'.[35]

PART THREE

Unification

In his New Year's greetings to Winifred Wagner, Hitler looked forward to 1928 with optimism. 'I must only look to the future,' he wrote, 'and at the end of this year I now once again joyfully believe in it.' 'I now know once more,' Hitler continued, 'that fate will bring me to the point where I had hoped to come four years ago [1923].'[1] It is hard to tell the reasons for his optimism, but Hitler was to be proved right. Within five years of writing these lines, he had taken power in Germany, not through revolutionary violence as he had attempted in 1923, but by quasi-legal means. Throughout this period, Hitler grappled with questions of unification. He engaged in greater detail with the United States as both a model and a challenge. Hitler also took issue with the idea of European unity, which many Germans then saw as the answer to the twin challenges of Soviet communism and American capitalism. Instead of the chimera of a United States of Europe, he promoted the unification of Germany under his leadership, a prospect which seemed realistic after his election successes in 1930 and 1932. Finally, Hitler also sought to reunify the NSDAP, which was in danger of disintegrating even as his chances of assuming the chancellorship grew.

7

The American Challenge

Germany in the late 1920s appeared increasingly stable. Governments and population were becoming more and more reconciled to the power of Anglo-America and international capitalism. Partly, this was for lack of choice. Germany was still subject to a punitive reparations regime, which threatened control of national assets such as the Reichsbahn. Parker Gilbert, the American banker who was agent-general for reparations, insisted on balanced budgets before he would start talks on the remission of reparations payments. Austerity and external subjection seemed to go hand in hand. There was widespread anxiety about the threat of mass emigration, particularly if the economy worsened. Many felt that Germany was too weak to survive as an independent national state and should seek shelter within a United Europe.[1] The idea of 'Pan-Europa', first mooted in 1923 by Count Richard Coudenhove-Kalergi, the son of an Austro-Hungarian diplomat who had married a Japanese woman, was gaining ground; among his early backers was the Hamburg banker Max Warburg, pointed in his direction by the Rothschilds.[2] In 1924 Heinrich Mann published a tract calling for a 'United States of Europe' to prevent the continent from becoming an 'economic colony of America or a military colony of Asia'.[3] The Heidelberg Programme of the SPD in 1925 supported the idea of a 'United States of Europe'. European integration was also very much on the diplomatic agenda with calls for a Franco-German rapprochement finding widespread support in both countries. Others rejected the idea, claiming, as the senior German diplomat Bernhard Wilhelm von Bülow wrote, that 'in Pan-Europa Germany would play the role of Saxony, at best that of Bavaria', and that it was in any case with regard to its notions of an 'international currency' and 'absolute freedom of movement' not 'realizable'.[4]

There was also a more positive embrace of the new order, culturally, economically and politically. The largely benevolent conquest of Europe by the United States continued.[5] American-style capitalism attracted many Germans.[6] The American values of hard work, energy and opportunity were seen as ways of reviving Germany.[7] German businessmen made regular pilgrimages across the Atlantic to observe 'Fordism' in action. German commentators remarked not merely on the wealth of Americans, but on their splendid physique and open countenance, which contrasted unfavourably with the wizened and downcast aspects of their own compatriots.[8] Hollywood took Germany by storm.[9] In 1928, the first transatlantic flight by a Zeppelin airship took place, linking the new continent more closely with the Reich from which so many Americans had emigrated. Meanwhile, the economy improved. Radical parties steadily lost ground. A new Germany appeared in the making. It seemed unpromising territory for Hitler and the NSDAP, which had shot to brief prominence in 1923 on the back of severe economic and political dislocation.

Despite this, Hitler threw himself into the Reichstag elections of 1928 with gusto. He raced from meeting to meeting. On one day, Hitler spoke at no fewer than eleven venues in Munich: the Bürgerbräukeller, Augustinerkeller, Hofbräuhauskeller, Franziskanerkeller, Restaurant 'Zur Blüte', Malthäserbräu, Arzbergerkeller, Thomasbräukeller, Hackerbräukeller, Schwabingerbräu and Altes Hackerbräuhaus.[10] He campaigned on what he regarded as the central issue of the day: Germany's continuing enslavement by her wartime enemies as represented by the forces of western imperialism and international capitalism. 'The situation of Germany is comparable to that of a colony,' he stated. 'Germany no longer has any sovereignty.' Famine and emigration, he charged, stalked the land: 'Ireland's fate looms threatening before Germany's future.' 'Hitler compares Germany with India,' one audience member recalls him saying during the latter stages of the Reichstag campaign, 'which was allowed to keep its princes by Britain, [and] its own representation, [with] the whole parliamentary glamour', in order to distract from the 'real truth, that the Briton is the sole lord and the Indian is the slave'. Whether he was speaking of colonialism, Ireland or India, what was driving Hitler was not solidarity with the wretched of the earth, but Germany's racial relegation. There was, however, also a socialist tinge to his claims. Marxists, Hitler argued, should criticize not German society, but the 'unjust distribution of the world's resources'.[11] Germany, he was effectively arguing, had been proletarianized in geopolitical terms. It was a theme to which Hitler would return at length after he took power.

The main vehicle of Anglo-American enslavement remained Hitler's old bugbear, international capitalism, and its directing mind, world Jewry. 'We know the relationships between these families,' he thundered at the height of the election campaign, 'the Warburgs and Friedländer from Berlin to New York.' 'If these people agree among themselves,' he continued, 'then the end of the German people is at hand.' In Germany itself, the principal instrument of coercion was the reparations regime. Hitler's main target here was Parker Gilbert, whose interventions into the parliamentary budgetary discussions had made him something of a hate figure in German society and politics. When Gilbert criticized the Reichstag for debating an increase in civil service pay, Hitler fumed that 'we are just an international colony, which is exposed to foreign arbitrariness and international exploitation'. He complained that Germany was compelled to hand over 'entire national properties as collateral for international Jewish big capital'. He accused the government of having 'mortgaged the entire socialist republic' just as it had 'already handed over the German Reichsbahn with all its income to international capital'.[12]

The NSDAP therefore sidestepped any discussion of economic specifics by arguing that it all came down to politics in the end, in other words, the lost war. Germany's domestic constitution, the party claimed, was determined by the structures of international governance imposed upon her. 'Do not speak to me of the Weimar constitution,' Hitler demanded, 'our three constitutions are: peace treaty, Dawes Plan and Locarno Pact. Those are the three constitutions according to which Germany is governed.'[13] End Germany's political subjection by the global powers that be, the Nazis argued, and all political, economic or social issues would resolve themselves. When the votes were counted in May 1928, however, it was clear that the Nazis had suffered a catastrophic defeat. The gains made during the 1924 elections were wiped out. It appeared as if the Germans were not looking for a new political movement, a new idea or a new leader after all. To all intents and purposes Nazism seemed extinct as an electoral phenomenon.

To make matters worse, the Nazi Party in 1928 was only slightly less divided than it had been during and immediately after Hitler's incarceration in Landsberg. The main fractures persisted, and others were soon to appear. Foreign policy was still hotly disputed. Some agreed with Rosenberg that Russia was an ideological enemy to be despoiled; others saw the Soviet Union as a potential ally against Anglo-America. The South Tyrol issue continued to give trouble.[14] A new subject of contention was European unity, which found widespread support in the NSDAP.[15] Goebbels had looked forward to a time 'when we have liberated ourselves [and] we can speak of the United States of Europe [as] equal partners'.[16] The most ardent supporters of European unity, however, were the Strasser brothers, Otto and Gregor, who saw it as the key to repelling not so much Bolshevik Russia, as the all-consuming ambition of Anglo-American capitalism.

Hitler was also plagued by turf wars and personal squabbles. The perennial bad penny here was Julius Streicher, whose behaviour in Nuremberg outraged even the local party elite, especially the SA, not to mention the rest of the political spectrum. Hitler tried to avoid being sucked in, and in fact gave the city a wide berth for most of 1928. When one of Streicher's rivals founded a separate Ortsgruppe Nuremberg-Mitte in opposition to Streicher, he merely remarked that 'this would mean the end of all organization',[17] but did not intervene. It was only after Streicher came out on top that Hitler went to the Franconian capital to shake Streicher's hand in public and to put the seal on his victory.[18] That, however, was not the end of the matter. Later in the year, the party's arbitration committee was called upon to investigate an anonymous claim that Streicher was conducting 'champagne parties' at party expense, but also spreading false rumours about Hitler's sexual overtures to women. The initiators appear to have been partisans of Artur Dinter, who had been sacked as *Gauleiter* of neighbouring Thuringia for his attack on the churches. He was now expelled from the party altogether. Streicher had survived again, but he was such a divisive character that it would not be long before his authority was challenged once more.

If Franconia was essentially a sideshow, albeit a particularly lurid one, the disputes between Berlin and Munich, and increasingly within the Berlin party, were more serious. This was partly about policy, with the more 'left-wing' northerners pitched against the more conservative southerners. It was also a question of culture and access, however. 'Munich is governed by a terrible bureaucracy,' Goebbels wrote in disgust, 'and the chief is surrounded by a camarilla.' The main problem, though, was the growing stagfight in Berlin itself between the two 'left' factions, around Goebbels and the Strasser brothers. This was essentially a struggle for control of the party propaganda apparatus. Once again, Hitler was repeatedly called upon to intervene. 'There is no way of dealing with Dr Strasser,' Goebbels complained, 'that skunk is too crafty and too mean. Now Hitler will have to lay down the law.' 'No answer yet from Hitler,' he noted disconsolately. When none came, Goebbels considered resignation.[19] These rows were complicated by deep differences over economic and social affairs, with Goebbels and the Strasser brothers still prominent on the anti-capitalist 'left' of the party. They were all, in different ways, enthusiasts for 'Europe', which they saw as the repository of cultural and racial value not so much against Soviet Russia, with which they continued to feel a sense of affinity, as against the Anglo-American capitalist 'west'.

Hitler did not welcome these and other disputes as an opportunity to divide and rule. On the contrary, he saw them as a waste of his own time and a mortal threat to the unity of the movement. Hitler therefore seized the opportunity of the 1928 Reichstag election campaign to make another attempt to re-establish ideological coherence, to reassert his own authority and to set out a path for German recovery. It was typical of his approach to focus not on the immediate issues of the day but on broad ideological principles.[20] Hitler's text 'Determination of [our] Standpoint after the Reichstag Election', later known to English audiences as the 'Secret' and then the 'Second Book', was begun in the summer of 1928, when Hitler took himself off to the Obersalzberg. 'Wolf [Hitler] is in Berchtesgaden,' Winifred Wagner wrote, 'and is writing a new book, which I am to receive as a birthday present. Hess, who has already had a read, thinks a lot of it.'[21]

Work continued on the manuscript intermittently for about eighteen months. It drew on many themes that he had long rehearsed in his speeches and publications. Like Mein Kampf, the Second Book needs to be seen in the context of his many other pronouncements at the time, some of which found their way into the text. Its composition also reflects Hitler's continuing conception of himself as a 'writer'.[22] He was a man of the spoken word, to be sure, but he was also given to programmatic statements and, in his own way, profound thought about the state of the world and Germany's place in it. The resulting text, when taken together with Hitler's other statements throughout the mid and late 1920s, is absolutely critical to understanding the development of his thinking and the path which Nazism took after 1933.

The main focus of the text was the overwhelming power of Anglo-America, and especially of the United States. This theme had been present in Mein Kampf, and especially in subsequent speeches, but it now completely dominated Hitler's thinking. 'The American Union,' Hitler argued, 'has created a power factor of such dimensions that it threatens to overthrow all previous state power rankings', and had the capacity to challenge even the British Empire. This was partly a question of space. Thanks to the expulsion and extermination of the Native Americans, Hitler argued, land was plentiful. 'The relationship between the population size and territorial extent of the American continent,' he wrote, 'is much more favourable than the analogous relationship of the European peoples to their living spaces.' Moreover, Hitler added, the United States had great potential for further growth. It contained '40 to 50 per cent of all available natural resources', and its industry not only benefited from a huge domestic market, but was also highly competitive on the world stage. 'The American Union', Hitler claimed, was no longer just focused on its 'internal market' but now 'appeared as a world competitor, advantaged by its sources of raw materials, which are as unlimited as they are cheap'.[23]

Anglo-American superiority was also a question of race. As we have seen, Hitler had come to believe, and continued to believe until the end of his life, in the high racial value of the British, the 'Anglo-Saxons', who were one of the world's 'master races'. Throughout the late 1920s, he returned to their economic, military, diplomatic, colonial and political strength again and again. The key to British power, however, was demographic. Hitler spoke admiringly of the 'racial value of Anglo-Saxondom as such', which constantly thirsted for 'space' in order to escape their 'insular location'. The British, he said, had attempted expansion in Europe but had been frustrated by racially 'no less' valuable states; here he may have had the failure of the English medieval empire in France in mind. So instead, London had embarked on a colonial policy whose main aim was to find 'outlets for British human material' while 'maintaining their link to the motherland' – something which Germany, on his reading, had spectacularly failed to do – as well as markets and raw materials for the British economy. The result, Hitler concluded crushingly, was that the ordinary Briton had the edge over his German counterpart. 'The German people as such do not measure up to the average value of, for example, the British.'[24] In Hitler's view they were quite simply superior to the Germans.

The other repository of 'racial value', on Hitler's reckoning, was the United States. It had an Anglo-Saxon settler core, enlarged and preserved over time. 'The American Union,' he wrote, 'has established particular criteria for immigration, thanks to the teachings of its own racial researchers' (here he probably once again meant Madison Grant).[25] Hitler also admired US measures to keep its population racially robust through selection. In part, this was a question of eugenics. Hitler remarked privately that he had studied the laws of several American states concerning prevention of reproduction by people whose progeny would, in his view, probably be of no value or even injurious to the racial stock.[26] For the rest, American superiority rested on selective immigration. 'The fact that the American Union sees itself as a Nordic-Germanic state and in no sense as an international peoples' mush,' Hitler remarked, no doubt rebutting Israel Zangwill's idea of the United States as a 'melting pot', was clear from 'the distribution of the immigrant quotas among the European peoples'.[27] Whereas Scandinavians, Britons and 'finally' (sic) Germans were at the top of the list, Slavs and Latins were not favoured, and then Chinese and Japanese were right at the bottom of the hierarchy.

Perhaps surprisingly, the relationship between whites and the long-established black community did not loom large in Hitler's view of the United States, though Nazi bureaucrats would later study segregation closely when drawing up anti-Semitic legislation. In particular, he did not show much interest in the South, or in the Confederacy's struggle to preserve slavery. Reports of his enthusiasm for the Ku Klux Klan, though superficially plausible, come from unreliable sources.[28] In fact, the only verifiable comment Hitler ever made about slavery was clearly condemnatory. He spoke of the 'transplanting of millions of Negroes to the American continent' as an example of 'barbarian customs' on a par with slavery in the ancient world and the treatment of the Aztecs and Incas.[29] One way or the other, Hitler's enthusiasm for America was based on a concern with whites and Jews, not blacks, and an admiration not for the agrarian south but for the industrial north.

If Hitler had a healthy respect for the demographic, 'racial', economic and thus military might of the United States, he also had a keen sense of what we would today call her 'soft power'. Partly this was a positive sense of what the American way of life had to offer, which he had already documented on earlier occasions. Hitler never actually used the phrase 'American Dream', but his rhetoric showed him to be fully aware of the concept. 'The European of today,' he wrote, 'dreams of a living standard' which might be possible in Europe, but 'actually exists in America'. 'The American,' he noted simply, lived 'on average better than we do.' This was because 'the relationship between population size and territory in America is so close,' he argued, 'that prosperity is spread more generally'.[30] This was epitomized, on Hitler's reading, by the very high level of motorization in the United States.

That said, Hitler was also deeply concerned by aspects of American culture. He contrasted the glories of the ancient world with the 'crassly different' 'parvenu-culture' of America. Hitler and Hess sneered at one American multi-millionaire who was so vulgar as to have erected a faux palace of Versailles with a golden bath, liveried servants and a picture gallery in which the original price tags for the paintings were still visible.[31] Hitler was particularly worried about the influence of American popular culture in Germany, and inveighed against the 'department store vampires' who not only destroyed many smaller shops, but also offered 'all kinds of trinkets, neon lights and tea shops, escalators and palm gardens,' to ensnare the unwary. Hitler thus unfolded a whole vista of moral panic. Perhaps his greatest concern, however, was music, a matter close to his own heart. 'Jazz music,' he argued, 'has achieved the equality of people, but through lowering standards.'[32] This ambivalence about the nature of America, which should never be mistaken for pure contempt, was to remain with him to the end.

Anglo-American strength was contrasted with German weakness. Again, this was partly a matter of space. In the Second Book and on many other occasions in the late 1920s, Hitler elaborated on Germany's geopolitical exposure. 'Everywhere unprotected, open territories,' he lamented, the western parts of which contained important industrial facilities. Germany was surrounded by potential predators, such as France and Russia, not to mention being boxed in navally and commercially by England. To make matters worse, France was linked by alliance to Poland in the east, and Czechoslovakia and Yugoslavia in the southeast. Germany, in short, was encircled: 'surrounded' and 'completely hemmed in'. Moreover, Germany not only was vulnerable, but lacked critical territorial mass. It was impossible to defend in depth, he thought, especially given recent advances in technology. Millions of Germans, Hitler bewailed, were jammed into an area 'which a modern aeroplane can traverse from north to south in about two hours'. More generally, Germany was too small to count in the world. 'Germany is, from the purely geographic point of view,' he claimed, so territorially limited that 'it amounted to a [mere] province in comparison to other states and countries on this earth'.[33]

If all this was broadly in the classic Prusso-German geopolitical tradition, Hitler's emphasis on Germany's other alleged critical weakness was not. This was 'race', where the Second Book elaborated themes which had been sketched only in outline in *Mein Kampf* and his speeches during the mid 1920s. As we have seen, this was particularly true with regard to his relentless focus on the alleged weakness of the German people itself, especially when contrasted with the British. 'Our people in particular,' he wrote, 'sorely lack in their racial fragmentation those characteristics which, for example, distinguish the Briton', namely 'holding together in times of danger'.[34] He attributed this only partly to alleged Jewish corruption and much more to other factors, such as Germany's longstanding religious, political and territorial fragmentation.

The separatist spectre, which had so exercised Hitler in 1921–3, had somewhat receded, but Hitler was still concerned enough to deliver several broadsides against the BVP. In a philippic delivered in Munich in late February 1928, he condemned Bavarian 'monarchists', rejected their claims to 'reserved [state] rights' and decried their 'federalist' mantras as a mere smokescreen for wider ambitions. Hitler's objection to Bavarian, and other, particularist, demands was rooted in his long-held belief that only a 'completely coherent form of state' could cope with the external challenges to the German Reich. He continued to fight a grudge match against the BVP, Bavaria's monarchists, and their clerical backers, with accusations of sexual deviance, religious misbehaviour and philo-Semitism being hurled back and forth,[35] exceeding in intensity and hatefulness any exchanges he had with the Weimar left.[36]

German fragmentation, in Hitler's eyes, was aggravated and epitomized by the Weimar Republic. Democracy, he claimed, undermined authority and made coherence impossible. 'With regard to the army,' he complained, one 'recognized the law of authority, but the nation was subjected to the law of humanity.' And 'what is majority,' Hitler asked, but 'the embodiment of lies, and inadequacy and stupidity'? 'Democracy,' he pronounced, 'contradicts the law of all growth' because 'it cannot tolerate any leaders.' In short, Hitler argued, 'if a people allows western democracy to govern its state constitution, in other words if it introduces western parliamentarism', then it would create a 'system' which would 'inevitably' lead to the 'filtering out of existing talent'. For all these reasons, Hitler regarded the 'democratic principle', which he invariably associated with the west and with Jewry, as 'a principle of destruction of peoples and states'.[37]

The Westminster parliament posed an intellectual and rhetorical difficulty for Hitler, as it seemed to suggest that democracy and national coherence were not incompatible. Reprising a theme he had already ventilated in *Mein Kampf*, he explained the paradox away through the principle of selection. 'British democracy,' he argued, 'was no more than just a small closed elite.' 'Never forget,' he continued, 'that until the 1880s only 470,000 people enjoyed the franchise, in other words a small group of selected people.' Hitler emphasized how political tradition was handed down in England through the great families, and he stressed the stabilizing effect of the monarchy, which was 'the centre of gravity' in England's political system. Finally, Hitler argued that an ancient democracy like Rome had always elected a dictator in times of crisis, and that 'this England elected a dictator in the war', namely Lloyd George, while the German parliament had merely 'blathered'.[38] In other words, whereas in his view democracy had undermined the coherence of the *Volk* in Germany, it had served as an instrument of positive racial selection in Britain.

Hitler also saw war and conflict as a threat to the German people. Here there was a clear contradiction in his thinking. On the one hand, Hitler saw 'struggle' as central to the life and survival of a people. On the other hand, he believed that war killed the best and the bravest, sparing the weakest and most cowardly. 'The nature of war is such,' he wrote, 'that it leads to a racial selection in a people which involves the disproportionate destruction of its best elements.' This could lead 'in 100 years to the gradual bleeding to death of the best [and] most valuable part of a people'. For this reason, Hitler damned unnecessary wars as 'crimes against the body politic, as in against the future of a people'. On the one hand, Hitler would with pathos invoke the memory and sacrifice of the front; on the other hand, he repeatedly stressed the horrors of war and injury, which he had experienced at first hand. Contemptuously dismissing a familiar civilian trope, he candidly described his preference for mutilation over death. 'At home they said [it was] wonderful to die a hero's death,' Hitler remarked, but 'the frontline soldier took a different view.' 'If someone at home said that they would rather be dead than lose a limb,' Hitler continued, the truth was that the men in Flanders would have gladly sacrificed their hand or another limb in order to receive a 'blighty' which would get them out of the fighting and give them a chance of survival. 'For those who have themselves served as soldiers,' he said, war 'was not something beautiful' but something 'terrible'.[39]

The greatest challenge to the coherence of the German people, however, was their shortage of living space in central Europe and resulting lack of food security. Here again Hitler was rehearsing familiar themes from *Mein Kampf*, but in his speeches of the late 1920s and in the Second Book he took the argument a stage further. Bismarck might have united 'the mass of the German people in central Europe', but he had not solved 'the second question of the German people in Europe', which was 'the question of future food supply'. So when British tariffs had 'cut off' the 'economic opportunities' open to the Reich, the 'pot boiled over and [we] had 20 million people too many'. The excess population, Hitler claimed, had been compelled to emigrate, partly to the British Empire and South America but mainly to the United States. 'For three hundred years,' he claimed, 'we have sent out 10,000 people a year, so that virtually the entire continent of North America became [demographically] German.'[40]

The background to Hitler's claims is the fact between 1820 and 1930 about 5.9 million Germans settled in the US.[41] In the period 1860–90 they were the largest group of immigrants. By 1900, around a tenth of the population of the US was of German descent,[42] among them one Friedrich Drumpff, who registered at Ellis Island as 'Frederick Trump', Donald Trump's grandfather, who arrived in 1885. Richard Wagner often spoke of emigrating to America, and even wrote a march to mark the centennial of the Declaration of American Independence in 1876.[43] In Canada, Germany was the third-largest source of emigrants after the United Kingdom and France.[44] Those who left often stayed in close touch with the old country, and a substantial proportion – about 25 per cent – returned, often with tales of success in the New World.[45] North America was thus a huge and largely positive presence in the German imaginary of the 1920s, looming much larger than Soviet Russia.

To make matters worse, Hitler continued, emigration was not only quantitatively but qualitatively a threat to the German people. It was invariably the best and fittest who left. Nor did Hitler hold back with his view of those who remained. 'The coward and weakling would rather die at home,' he said, 'than pluck up the courage' to move and better his lot. In numerous speeches throughout the late 1920s, Hitler hammered this theme home again and again. Germany had 'sent [America] her best selection for centuries'. 'Only those who emigrate,' he claimed, 'who resist deprivation', were of 'value'. 'It is the most resistant, the most energetic,' he lamented, 'who emigrate', with the result that in the event of conflict a people that consists of emigrants will 'triumph over the motherland'. In racial terms, Hitler warned, this amounted to the 'gradual de-Nordification of our people', and to 'the general reduction of our racial value'; it meant that the worst remained.[46] The implication of all this was bleak: the German people of Hitler's time in his view consisted of the dregs left after North America had taken the cream.

Of course, Germany's perceived loss was Anglo-America's gain. Hitler repeated his claim that, after independence, the American Congress had only adopted English as the language of the new union by one vote, ensuring that the United States would remain part of what one might loosely call the Anglosphere. 'A whole continent,' he claimed, 'became British as a result of this decision.' Hitler feared the power of what he called 'Anglicization' on Germans. He lamented that Germans tended to 'Anglicize more and more' in 'Anglo-Saxon countries' and were therefore 'presumably lost' to our people not just in terms of their 'practical capacity for work' but also 'spiritually'. 'For that reason,' Hitler argued, 'the initiative' was passing from the 'mother states to the colonies', because that was where one found a 'concentration of people of the highest value'. 'The motherland's loss,' he lamented, 'was the new country's gain.' The result, Hitler lamented, was that 'Germany is sinking more and more while a new continent is rising across the ocean, settled with German blood.'[47]

All these racial chickens, Hitler continued, had come home to roost in the First World War. Right from the start, Germany had faced the full might of the British, French and Tsarist empires, though it was the first that Hitler really feared. Moreover, he argued in a newspaper article, in 1917 'The American Union was determined to throw its own power into the scales in support of the world coalition threatening Germany.'[48] This was the decisive moment which made German defeat inevitable, and Hitler never forgot it. He personally experienced the meaning of it in the summer of 1918, remembering the date correctly to the day nearly ten years later. 'Germany sent away its best sons for 300 years,' he recalled. 'When the year 1918 came around we suddenly saw south of the Marne on 17 July the descendants of our people, our emigrants. They were powerful sturdy people, who stood opposite us as enemies.' 'They were the representatives of the new continent,' Hitler continued. 'It was our own blood. The blood that we let go.' Moreover, he went on, nobody had yet registered that this encounter had been 'a presentiment of' the 'battle of the peoples' (or racial battle: *Volkskampf*) to come. Here Hitler was once again referring to the final showdown he expected between Germans and Anglo-Saxons.[49]

Hitler rejected some of the common cures on offer. He did not believe that Germany could export its way to a secure food supply. Picking up a remark made by Chancellor Caprivi in the 1890s, Hitler said of Weimar politicians, 'one does not want to export people, rather one says that we export goods'. In reality, Hitler warned, the British had cut off German goods through high tariff walls before 1914, and continued to enslave Germany today through Versailles and the reparations settlement. The nostrums offered on the left were also rejected, especially the plan to seek salvation in instruments of international governance. On the one hand, Hitler shared the widespread view that the League of Nations was a toothless tiger. 'A League of Nations without a League of Nations police force,' he claimed, 'is a state without a legal system and without police authority.' On the other hand, Hitler continued to see the League as a device for the subjection of Germany. 'The League of Nations is dominated by the saturated nations, indeed it is their instrument.' These nations, he claimed, had no interest in addressing international injustice, in particular the 'spatial distribution of the world'. This meant that the world was run in accordance with not international law, but the law of capital: 'not the right of the peoples', as he put it, 'but the rights of the bankers of the peoples'.[50]

The Führer reserved a special scorn for those who thought Germany should seek salvation in 'Europe'. Here his words were directed against high-level attempts to integrate the continent by people like Aristide Briand, and Count Coudenhove-Kalergi's Pan-Europa Union, but also elements of the National Socialist 'left' such as the Strasser brothers and even Goebbels. He trenchantly entitled the ninth chapter of the Second Book 'Neither border policy nor economic policy nor Pan-Europa'.[51] Hitler's objection was not to the idea of containing the United States as such, but to the desirability and practicality of doing so through European integration. He conceded that 'the pan-European movement does really seem to have some at least apparently appealing aspects'. Unsurprisingly, though, Hitler reacted allergically not only to Coudenhove's own mixed racial heritage, but also to his vision for a United Europe as a kind of Habsburg Empire writ large. 'The Pan-Europa envisaged by the global bastard [meaning mixed-race] Coudenhove,' he thundered, 'would eventually play the same role against the American Union as the old Austrian state played against Germany or Russia.'[52]

He rejected the various 'mechanistic' calculations of combined European economic and demographic potential arrayed against the US. 'In the lives of the peoples,' he reminded his readers, 'values not figures are decisive.' Not only was the United States made up of 'millions of people of the highest racial value', some of the best blood from Europe, but the old continent was left with the inferior residue. This, on Hitler's reading, was the result of European susceptibility to 'western democracy', 'cowardly pacifism', Jewish subversion, 'bastardization and niggerification', which not only enabled the Jews slowly to assume 'world dominance', but also weakened the continent fatally in the face of the American challenge. Given that the strength of the United States was primarily a product of its racial value, Hitler argued, 'then this hegemony will not be overcome through a purely formal unification of European peoples'. 'The idea of resisting this Nordic state [the US],' he continued, 'with a Pan-Europa made up of Mongols, Slavs, Germans, Latins, etc.', in other words an entity dominated by 'anyone but Germanic elements', was a 'utopia'. Pan-Europa, in short, could be no more than a 'merger under Jewish protectorate at Jewish instigation', and would 'never create a structure which would be able to stand up to the American Union'.[53]

Hitler claimed there was another way of dealing with the challenge of the United States. 'North America can in future only be resisted by a state,' he argued, 'which has understood how to raise the value of its people and to create the necessary state form' for this task. This required a combination of domestic and diplomatic measures. 'Domestic policy,' Hitler wrote in the Second Book, 'should secure a people the internal power for its foreign-political assertion', while 'foreign policy must secure the life of the people for its internal development'. The two were those 'complementary activities'. If, on the one hand, he insisted that diplomatic successes without internal strengths were pointless, he also argued that a mistaken system of alliances could have harmful domestic effects 'because the order was sent from outside that the people should be educated in a pacifist manner'.[54]

On the domestic front, Hitler aimed at a thoroughgoing racial regeneration of the German people. This was only partly a matter of eliminating the allegedly pernicious influence of the Jews. It was, he asserted, primarily a question of raising the general racial level of the German people to that of their Anglo-American rivals. Education was central to this project. Hitler spoke of establishing a 'boarding school on the British model' to train German youth. 100 million Reichsmarks on universities, he believed, were better spent than the same sum on a battle cruiser. Hitler also wanted to overcome Germany's historic fragmentation. He spoke of his desire to rebuild Berlin as 'a great metropolis of the new German Reich' to provide a counterbalance to 'small statery'. At the same time, Hitler sought to make up what Germans lacked in natural coherence through discipline. It was for this reason, as well as for reasons of party discipline, that he stressed the importance of obedience to the leadership.[55]

The long-term answer to Germany's predicament, however, remained the capture of *Lebensraum* in the east, a theme which Hitler had already elaborated at length in *Mein Kampf*, and which he repeated throughout the Second Book and in many speeches. Colonial expansion was once again roundly rejected.[56] This capture of space was partly in order to eliminate Germany's geopolitical vulnerability, which would remain even if the borders of 1914 were restored. It would improve the food supply situation in the event of war, and give Germany more room to manoeuvre militarily. 'Above all,' Hitler argued, only the acquisition of space in Europe would 'preserve the [necessary] people' from emigration so that they would be 'available as millions of soldiers for the next decisive moment'.[57] Moreover, only more living space would enable the Germans to resist the lure of the American way of life. 'Neither the living space of today, nor the reconstitution of the borders of 1914,' Hitler warned, 'will enable us to lead a life analogous to that of the American people.'[58] This connection between (the lack of) *Lebensraum* and emigration, albeit with regard to overseas colonies rather than eastern lands, was a staple of late nineteenth century and early twentieth century German discourse.[59]

As in *Mein Kampf*, Hitler continued to argue that the necessary living space was to be found in the east in the 'thinly populated' Russian western lands bordering Germany. The key to this *Raumpolitik*, he explained, was that one could only Germanize 'space', not the people living in it, as imperial Germany had mistakenly attempted to do with the Poles they had ruled over before 1914. The National Socialist movement, Hitler continued, was not interested in 'Germanization' but 'only in the expansion of its own people'. 'The existing population', Hitler insisted, should not be assimilated. Instead it was a question of 'either shutting out these alien elements, in order to prevent the further corruption of our own blood' or 'simply removing them and allocating the land which thereby became available to our own people'. As the Bolsheviks consolidated their hold on power, Hitler increasingly regarded the Soviet Union as a vacuum crying out to be filled.[60] Once again, Hitler sought living space in Russia, not because he specifically targeted the Slavs, but because their territories were geographically contiguous and they had been so corrupted by Bolshevism as to render them ripe for hostile takeover.

Hitler knew that Germany would not 'be able to confront fate on her own' and 'would need allies'. He admired the spirit of the soldiers who had scrawled 'We accept declarations of war' on the railway carriages taking them to the front, but he damned such behaviour as 'a mad stupidity' in terms of a 'political creed'. He devoted an entire chapter of the Second Book to that subject. As in *Mein Kampf*, Hitler rejected the alliances secured by the German Reich in 1914, whose low value he had seen during the First World War. Here Hitler primarily had the Habsburgs in his sights. He was less opposed, at least in principle, to a Russian alliance. If Russia achieved an 'internal change', he wrote, 'then it could not be excluded that Russia,' which was 'today in reality Jewish-capitalist', would become 'national-anti-capitalist' and thus a worthy partner for Germany. The danger, Hitler argued – and here he was echoing a widespread strand of contemporary thinking – was that an alliance with Russia would expose Germany to a pre-emptive strike by the west.[61] The long and short of this was that Hitler, his eye firmly on putting the Russophile wing of the NSDAP in its place, firmly rejected alignment with Soviet Russia. It was a subject on which he would brook absolutely no argument.

He was not only clear about the need for allies, but remarkably candid about the kind of concessions necessary to secure them. Reprising a theme from *Mein Kampf*, Hitler derided the idea that Germany should not ally with any of its enemies from the First World War, or those states with whom she had border disputes. If that were so, he pointed out, there could be no alliance with France, because of Alsace-Lorraine and its attempts to grab the Rhineland, none with Belgium, over Eupen-Malmedy, none with Britain, because of the robbed colonies, none with Denmark, because of North Schleswig, none with Poland, over West Prussia and Upper Silesia, none with Czechoslovakia, because it was oppressing 4 million Germans, none with Yugoslavia, because it was sitting on 400,000 Germans, and none with Italy, because of South Tyrol. In other words, Hitler continued, according to the national bourgeois camp there could be no alliance with anybody in Europe, leaving Germany dependent on the 'din of their huzzas' and their 'big mouths' to regain the lost status and territories.[62]

In considerably greater detail than in *Mein Kampf*, Hitler developed the idea of an Italian alliance in the Second Book. This made ideological sense, given the similarities between fascism and National Socialism, but the main object of the connection was geopolitical: to break open the encircling ring of hostile powers. To ram home his argument against internal Nazi critics, the relevant sections were published as a separate pamphlet. Hitler also attempted to reach out to Mussolini directly. A hoped-for meeting in February 1928, however, never came to pass.[63] In an earnest of his good intentions in this matter, and in order to make the party's official position crystal-clear, Hitler met with Ettore Tolomei, the hammer of the Germans in South Tyrol, in the Munich suburb of Nymphenburg, in late 1928. In the following year, he met for the first time with Mussolini's confidant Giuseppe Renzetti, also in Munich.[64] Although most members fell into line eventually, the issue continued to be very divisive within the NSDAP, and it gave other elements of the German right a convenient stick to beat Hitler with.

The main focus of Hitler's alliance policy, as in *Mein Kampf*, remained Britain. Hitler rejected the idea that Britain would never accept German continental hegemony on account of its traditional balance of power policy. He believed that a grand bargain which left Britain supreme overseas and Germany in Europe was possible.[65] It proved to be a fatal misunderstanding of the principles of British foreign policy. Even more pernicious in the long run was Hitler's belief that Anglo-American commercial and political rivalry would ultimately end in war, driving Britain into Germany's arms. The ultimate global balance he envisaged, therefore, was an Aryan triumvirate, in which a rejuvenated Reich and the British Empire faced off against the North American Union.

Restoring Germany's diplomatic position, Hitler argued, depended on eliminating the global power of the Jews. To him, the struggle against world Jewry was an international contest, but it would primarily be waged internally. By Hitler's reckoning, the Jews had prevailed in France, where the 'Jewish stock exchange' reigned supreme, and Russia. They had been defeated in Mussolini's Italy, he believed. 'The most bitter struggle for the victory of Jewry,' he argued, 'is currently taking place in Germany', where the NSDAP was the sole standard-bearer of the resistance. Crucially, Hitler added, 'this battle has not yet been decided in Britain', where the 'Jewish invasion was still resisted by the old British tradition'. 'The instincts of Anglo-Saxondom are still so strong and vibrant,' Hitler continued, 'that one cannot speak of a complete victory of Jewry.' If the Jews prevailed, he thought, then England would be lost, 'but if the British win, then a change of policy by Britain towards Germany could still happen'.[66] In other words, the question of whether Britain would become an ally of the German Reich would be decided not so much by German diplomacy as by the alleged internal battle against Jewry in the United Kingdom itself.

Hitler had set himself an enormous task, and he was not sure that he would, or even could, prevail. He was convinced, however, that he must make the attempt, even if the chances for success were slim. 'If a decision has clearly been found to be necessary,' Hitler wrote, then it must be carried out 'with brutal ruthlessness and all means at one's disposal', even 'if the final result were to be itself unsatisfactory or require improvement' or if the likelihood of success was as low as 'a few per cent'. He compared the situation of Germany with that of a dying cancer patient. Did it make sense to hold off operating just because the chances of success were very small, or there was no chance of a full recovery? Worst of all, Hitler continued, would be for the surgeon to carry out the necessary operation with less than full commitment. By analogy, Hitler argued, Germany needed a 'political operation' to rescue it from 'a mob of greedy enemies at home and abroad'. 'The continuation of this situation is our death,' he went on, so that 'any opportunity' of escaping it should be 'seized'. 'What is lacking in terms of likelihood of success,' Hitler concluded, 'must be made up for through vigour of execution.'[67] This insistence on the need to take risks, to at least attempt the impossible, was a theme to which Hitler would return repeatedly in the years ahead.

Even if he succeeded across the board, Hitler did not expect to crush Anglo-America or achieve German world hegemony. He called for 'a Europe of free and independent national states with separate and clearly limited spheres of influence'. In terms of international governance, Hitler stated that one could imagine 'a new Association of Peoples in the far future, consisting of individual states of national value' which might 'resist the threatened domination of the world through the American Union'. 'Because it seems to me,' he continued, 'that the nations of today are less harmed by the continuation of British world domination than by the rise of an American one.'[68] In short, Hitler argued, the best Germany could hope for was to achieve global parity with the United States through confederation with like-minded European states, especially the British Empire.

Hitler probably planned to publish the Second Book up to the spring and early summer of 1929.[69] Thereafter, he appears to have laid the project to one side, for what reason is not clear. The most probable explanation is that the bleak view of the racial quality of the German people in the book, expressed far more radically than in *Mein Kampf*, risked alienating a core constituency among nationalists and indeed the population at large. That sentiment, which continued to inform his thinking and was to guide his policies after the seizure of power, was now locked away in Hitler's desk. It would only resurface, privately, during the final showdown with the United States.

Instead, from now on, Hitler sought to play down the racial fissures in non-Jewish German society, and indeed to talk up its supposed racial quality. In blatant contradiction to his consistently vowed sentiments in the 1920s, he wrote that 'our government sometimes tries to convince our people that we are not an equal people to, for example, [those of] America and Britain', and to 'inculcate a spirit of second-classness'. 'And yet,' Hitler continued, 'we know that it is not so,' and he asked where one would find a people which 'head for head, man against man, was more energetic, and as capable as the German people'.[70] This was partly racial whistling in the wind, to keep up the spirits of a population battered by present economic woes and past military defeats. In part, Hitler's rhetoric was also designed to paper over the cracks between the various German tribes, of whose differences and varying racial value, in his terms, he was painfully aware.

Slowly, the NSDAP regrouped after the 1928 election fiasco. Hitler urged Goebbels to take one of the few seats the party did win, in order to gain a parliamentary platform for propaganda and the prized legal immunity from prosecution for libel or incitement to violence.[71] The Nazis now made their voice increasingly heard in the Reichstag and Berlin generally. The party also began to reorganize nationally. The failure of the NSDAP at the 1928 election, together with Hitler's protestations of legality, per-suaded the authorities across Germany to start relaxing the restrictions on the party and on him. In the autumn of 1928, the speaking bans were lifted in Anhalt and in Prussia, the largest state. In the face of the failure of a national strategy aimed at winning over patriotic workers, Hitler switched tack. The NSDAP began to put greater focus on rural areas.

The essentially 'socialist' nature of NSDAP economic policy did not change, however. Its small delegation in the Reichstag distinguished itself largely by its ferocious anti-capitalism. In keeping with Hitler's own repeat-edly expressed antipathy to international finance capitalism, members put forward proposals to confiscate 'the fortune of the princes of bank and stock market'. The party was well to the left of the spectrum on taxation and called for more state and social spending. To the charge that they were mere clones of Mussolini, NSDAP Reichstag members responded, 'We are not fascists. We are socialists.' Emil Kirdorf, one of the few big business figures already aligned with the Nazis, was so infuriated by the relentless anti-capitalist barrage that he resigned his membership in August 1928, though he continued to profess loyalty to Hitler personally. Neither the party nor Hitler himself, however, changed course. In August 1928, he authorized the establishment of the 'Greater German Trade Union', a trade union with strong nationalist sentiments. A year later, in August 1929, Hitler approved the creation of the 'National Socialist Factory Cell Organ-ization' (NSBO), effectively a Nazi trade union organization, which was regarded with a very jaundiced eye by employers. That same year he author-ized a strongly anti-capitalist 'catechism' on Nazi economic policy penned by Hans Buchner, the economics editor of the *Völkischer Beobachter*.[72]

The propaganda effort was greatly improved. In late January 1928, Hitler had attended a screening of the first (silent) film of the Nuremberg

Party Congress in the Munich Bürgerbräukeller, accompanied live by Arthur Seidel's arrangement of music from Wagner's *Walküre*.[73] For financial reasons, however, there was no party congress in 1928, so a 'leadership conference' was held in Munich in late August and early September instead. Hitler, who did not go to Bayreuth in 1927 and 1928, began to plan for a conference the next year which would be synchronized with the Festival.[74] At Hitler's request, the new *Reichsorganisationsleiter*, Gregor Strasser, began to reorganize the party bureaucracy. A *Reichsrednerschule* was set up under Fritz Reinhardt to train speakers. Far from hogging the limelight, Hitler sought to develop a cadre of capable orators and sub-leaders capable of deputizing for him. Over time, the school was to train some 6,000 speakers, a massive increase which considerably amplified the reach of the party across the Reich.[75] The NSDAP was developing the capacity to grow into a mass party.

None of this could disguise the fact that Hitler was in something of a rut in early 1929. He was making some electoral inroads in Protestant rural areas, but with a few exceptions he had nowhere advanced beyond ten per cent at the polls, and generally the party scored much lower. That said, support was more evenly distributed than before the failed Putsch, with a higher presence in the north and west, and a lower standing in Bavaria. The situation was transformed by two developments, both of them concerning Hitler's main preoccupation, the United States. The first was a new scheme of reparations payments worked out by the Wall Street banker Owen Young. This was in gestation since January 1929, and its terms were formally announced in early June.[76] Germany was actually required to pay less than under the Dawes Plan, and less up front, but the resulting longer period of obligations – last payments were scheduled for 1988 – was a profound psychological blow.

The Young Plan rejuvenated the Nazi campaign against the attempt to turn Germans into 'slaves of global loan and commercial capitalism' by subjecting them to annual 'Tributes'; anti-capitalist anti-Semitism dominated the discourse.[77] Picking up one of Hitler's most common themes, Fritz Reinhardt predicted that the plan would lead to mass emigration, or 'the export of people', as he put it.[78] Hitler himself claimed that the aim of the plan and its alleged Jewish and other backers from 'international high finance' was 'to turn our people economically and spiritually into white world Negroes'.[79] The main emphasis of his visual propaganda during the election campaign was on the way in which international finance had imposed its 'bondage' on Germany.[80] The battle against the enslavement of Germany by international capitalism thus remained at the heart of the Nazi critique of Weimar foreign policy.[81] The campaign against the

Young Plan not only became Hitler's most important activity over the next two years, it also enabled him to take the stage nationally. In other words, his return to prominence was a reaction to the threat not of world communism but of global capitalism.

For the first time since the ill-fated Munich Putsch, Hitler now joined a broader conservative and right-wing front. In April 1929, he entered into an alliance with the DNVP. 'The chief considers the political situation very positive,' Goebbels noted in late May 1929, 'and that we must learn to wait and avoid a banning [of the party] in all circumstances.'[82] In July 1929, Hitler, the DNVP and various other right-wing organizations came together to launch the campaign against the Young Plan, which they hoped to stop through a referendum. Hitler's main target was nationalist workers, who were to be mobilized through attacks on plutocratic exploitation and patriotic sentiment, both classic Nazi themes. Hitler's decision was partly tactical. 'Tactical considerations have caused us to wage the struggle together with a number of other groups,' he wrote not long afterwards. He stressed the necessity of mobilizing the German people 'beyond the limits of our party against this renewed monstrous attempt at enslavement'.[83] From his point of view, the alliance made eminent political and ideological sense, as it aligned the NSDAP with German national capitalism, which he approved of, against the might of international finance capitalism, his great enemy.[84]

The second development was the Wall Street Crash of October 1929, which eventually triggered the Great Depression, which formed the backdrop to German politics in the early 1930s.[85] As US banks came under pressure, they recalled or refused to renew short-term loans. This resulted in a crisis of liquidity for the heavily indebted business and public sector in Germany. The economy, never as robust as it appeared during the brief period of 'normality', began to slide. Unemployment began to rise, and after a series of bank failures it skyrocketed.

Strikingly, the Wall Street Crash seems to have made no impression on Hitler whatsoever. It did not dent Hitler's belief in the power of the United States, which he attributed to race and space rather than economics alone.[86] In a lecture on 'Politics and Economics' on 10 January 1930, by which time the Depression was raging in the United States, he contrasted Europe with America, 'which has already long been pursuing a conscious policy of eugenics', as her 'immigration measures proved'. 'Germany,' he lamented once again, 'had often lost its best elements and America had shown itself able to integrate these nationally into its state form'; here Hitler was referring to the Anglicization of German immigrants. 'The new lands,' he continued, 'became more powerful as they were able to raise their hands against the motherlands.' 'Europe, hitherto the greatest actor in the world,' Hitler went on, had yielded much in this regard to America. Far from being reassured by the Wall Street Crash that the colossus had feet of clay, Hitler was preaching the same sermon in late January 1930, which he delivered eighteen months earlier in the Second Book. 'The whole of Europe,' he warned, 'is heading for a very unpleasant fate if it does not somehow put an end to America's expansionist economic activity.'[87]

By contrast, Hitler continued to show little interest in the Soviet Union. He puzzled over the antagonism between Stalin and Trotsky, which he was inclined to consider a diversionary manoeuvre. In any case, Hitler did not think much of Stalin, who, even if he was not himself 'circumcised', allegedly largely associated with Jews and was their creature. He defined 'Soviet power' as the 'Jewish dictatorship which currently carries the name of Stalin and tomorrow might be embodied by someone quite different'. He persisted in regarding Soviet communism as an affliction of the Russian people, which threatened Germany in the form of the virus of Bolshevism rather than the might of the Red Army. 'In Stalin Jewry has finally found the man,' Hitler remarked, 'who like Lenin is destroying the last remains of Aryan culture with Asiatic brutality.' Unless it was careful, he warned, Germany would suffer the same 'fate' as Russia, where 30 million had died slowly of hunger. Throughout the early 1930s, in fact, Hitler, in so far as he took any notice of the Soviet Union, simply dismissed Russia as 'a hell of misery and deprivation',[88] which should serve as a warning for Germany.

The Anti-Young Plan coalition succeeded in forcing a plebiscite at the end of the year, but the result was a crushing defeat. Nor did the agitation really bring the Nazis and the Conservative right together, and it certainly did not increase funding for the party from business circles. The real significance of the campaign against the Young Plan lay elsewhere. It showed the continued relevance of Hitler's critique to the current situation, and it provided him with a platform on which to renew his appeal to the electorate. Despite serious financial difficulties, the revived party congress at Nuremberg was a major event: forty special trains brought 23,000 SA and SS troopers and 40,000 ordinary members to the city. They totally dominated the city with three days of assemblies and speeches, a 'dedication' of the 'blood flags' at the Luitpoldhain and finally a parade through Nuremberg during which Hitler took the salute at a marchpast which lasted three full hours.[89] Helped also by the growing world economic crisis, NSDAP fortunes at the polls began to improve, below the radar at first and then, in some places, dramatically. In Saxony, they trebled their previous result in the May 1929 Landtag elections, turning Otto Strasser into a major figure there, and even giving him some national prominence.

In Coburg, Saxony, Baden and Thuringia the NSDAP regained some of the lost ground in Bavaria, especially in Munich, where Gauleiter Wagner – who was close to Hitler – took charge from the autumn of 1929.[90] In Thuringia, they did so well in December 1929 that they held the balance of power. The NSDAP, and Hitler, were back in the game.

Success brought new opportunities. In Thuringia, the Nazis took power as part of a coalition under Wilhelm Frick.[91] In Saxony, with Hitler's express approval, they tolerated an SPD-KPD cabinet. Hitler's motivation was to show that the Nazis were ready for government. 'In the course of the years,' he explained, 'the Jewish press managed to inculcate into the minds of millions of Germans the view that the National Socialists were completely unsuited ever to take over a governmental post, let alone the entire government.'[92] This was why he had authorized Frick to go into government in Thuringia. Privately, Hitler added that he had demanded the Interior Ministry in order to enable Frick to conduct a 'gradual purging' of the administration of 'revolutionary tendencies'.[93] There were also risks, however. Frick's unhappy tenure was not an advertisement for Nazi governance, and the coalition in Thuringia collapsed amidst much recrimination in April 1930. Participation in government, even at the local level, was also very unpopular among the more 'revolutionary' elements of the NSDAP. Hitler had to intervene directly, for example, to veto a demand from the Gau Brandenburg for a blanket ban on coalitions.[94]

Things were also beginning to look up for Hitler personally. Thanks to the generosity of patrons, the sales of his works and a systematic under-reporting of his actual income to the tax authorities, his finances had stabilized.[95] In October 1929, Hitler moved to a large unfurnished flat on the affluent Munich Prinzregentenplatz with a staff of two live-in housekeepers, Ernst and Maria Reichert, his former landlords in the Thierschstrasse.[96] The furnishings were made by the Jewish-owned M. Ballin Royal Bavarian Furniture Factory;[97] the nephew of the celebrated German-Jewish writer Lion Feuchtwanger lived only 100 yards away.[98] Hitler's emotional life, too, appeared to be stabilizing. Geli Raubal was registered as a subtenant with the Reicherts, clearly with the purpose of avoiding awkward questions about why she was sleeping under the same roof as her uncle. Among the Nazi inner circle, though, her close relationship with Hitler was no secret. Geli acted as hostess, or at least was often present, when Hitler received guests.[99] She also accompanied him to numerous events: to a dinner with the Hesses,[100] to Bayreuth (chaperoned by her patron Helene Bechstein),[101] to various performances in Munich, on excursions into the countryside, and even to the famous Passion Play at Oberammergau.[102] Geli , a spirited young woman who does not appear to have had serious political interests of her own, was popular with everybody.

Beneath the surface, however, Hitler's emotional life was complex and even turbulent.[103] Goebbels noted in his diary that he had heard 'incredible things of the chief. He and his niece and Maurice [the chauffeur].'[104] Things were to become even more complicated. In the autumn of 1929, Hitler first encountered Eva Braun, who was working as an assistant in Heinrich Hoffmann's photo atelier. Hitler, then forty years of age, was clearly charmed by the seventeen-year-old girl; he made compliments and brought her presents.[105] Their relationship at this time was almost certainly not physical, but Hitler's attentiveness may well have infuriated Geli. A few months later Goebbels complained that his leader was involved in 'too many affairs'.[106] Moreover, Hitler was a highly controlling presence in Geli's life. Helene Hanfstaengl, who knew Geli well, remembers that 'I always had the feeling he [Hitler] was trying to run her life and tyrannizing her'.[107] Despite her vaunted high spirits, she generally looks glum, aloof and even caged in surviving photographs. The result of all this was a rather overwrought atmosphere in Hitler's apartment on the Prinzregentenplatz.

The picture that emerges of Hitler around this time is of a man lonely, but not withdrawn; sociable, but not gregarious. He spoke openly about himself to men and women; he was not emotionally 'buttoned-up'. Hitler was determined, however, not to commit himself to a woman. Marriage made sense only if one wished to establish a family, he remarked to his confidant Otto Wagener around this time. Though he professed to love children, he claimed that he had to deny himself this happiness, because he had another bride – Germany – and was married: to the German *Volk*, and its destiny.[108] It was an important part of his public persona, as well as his charismatic status within his entourage, that Hitler had a right to deviate from the norm. 'A genius is entitled to be different and to live differently from others,' Goebbels wrote in his diary, adding that 'The myth of Hitler must remain like a rocher de bronze,' a phrase which invoked the Prussian 'soldier king's' famous statement about the sovereignty of the monarch.[109]

At home or in politics, Hitler remained at the centre of things. He made all the major decisions, and his leadership style was distinctive. He had his own way of choosing his associates, he explained privately. Rather than choosing someone on the basis of qualification or favour, he would give him a chance to busy himself in the general area.[110] If the individual succeeded, he would grow into his new role and if not he would be replaced by someone else. This approach resulted in rapid turnover of staff. Moreover, far from being controlling, Hitler was loath to involve himself in matters of detail. He remarked that his memory automatically jettisoned any unnecessary ballast whenever things are going well and there was no needed for him to involve himself.[111] 'The chief,' Goebbels observed in frustration in late November 1928, 'stays out of everything – a convenient tactic – and leaves everything to his officials.'[112]

Hitler could hold his cards very close to his chest. He argued that knowledge of plans, and certainly concrete intentions, should be restricted on a need-to-know basis, and even then the executors should be told only as much as was absolutely necessary. This was probably a necessary precaution in the highly porous environment of the Nazi leadership, in which – as in any other organization – gossip and loose talk were rife.[113] At the same time, Hitler was pathologically reluctant to take decisions. 'Hitler,' his economic adviser Otto Wagener recalls, 'actually never issued instructions. He wanted to refrain from making decisions.' Instead, Hitler would outline his general principles, and then it 'was up to the individual to issue instructions in his area and to work in such a way that the general direction laid out by Hitler, the great goal crystallized from these conversations, was striven for and, in time, attained.'[114] The result was a confusing leadership style, in which the uncontested charisma of the leader was matched by an equal lack of clarity about what he was concretely asking his following to do. Still, Goebbels conceded in late 1929 that for all his faults – 'he is too soft and works too little' – Hitler 'has instinct, can handle people, is a tactician of genius, and has the will to power'.[115]

The improved prospects for the NSDAP caused Hitler to reconsider his timeline, well before his actual electoral breakthrough. Power, though still far off, was no longer a complete impossibility. 'In three years,' he predicted with remarkable accuracy in November 1929, 'we will be the masters of Germany'.[116] At the same time, Hitler was still planning for a long campaign, with the realization of his ultimate aims in the distant future, perhaps even after his death. It is telling that the second of the two ministries he had demanded in Thuringia was that for *Volksbildung*, which was in charge not merely of primary and secondary education, but also of the University of Jena and the theatres. Hitler wanted Frick to use this power to turn the population into 'fanatical National Socialists'.[117] Central to this project was the appointment of the Nazi racial theorist Hans Günther to a newly established 'Chair for Racial Questions' at Jena, another indication that Hitler was thinking of a long-term racial regeneration of the German people, rather than just a quick political fix.[118]

Much the same thinking informed Hitler's conception of the SA. He was at pains to stress, even in private, that they were not expected to prepare for another putsch. The SA had neither the arms nor the training to stage one. Instead, Hitler told Otto Wagener that he wanted the SA to provide a reservoir of trainable German youth as a preparation for military service in a future new German army.[119] Meanwhile, in January 1929, Hitler made Heinrich Himmler head of the SS.[120] It was Hitler who gave the organization its notorious motto 'My Honour Is Loyalty'. In addition to its security functions, Hitler wanted the SS to act as the guardian of the supposed German racial community, beginning with strict racial selection criteria for admission to its own ranks. In other words, Hitler's domestic policy should not be dated from his seizure of power. He was already engaged in the long-term attempted transformation of the German people while in opposition.

8

Breakthrough

In early 1930, the plates of German politics began to shift under the impact of the economic crisis. There were 3.2 million men out of work at the start of the year – about 14 per cent of the labour force – and the number was rising. Agriculture had been in crisis since the late 1920s. The SPD government under Chancellor Hermann Müller buckled under the pressure and finally disintegrated in March 1930. The new chancellor was the Centre Party leader in the Reichstag, Heinrich Brüning, who embarked on a course of austerity measures which deepened, or at least did not end, the economic crisis. He skilfully blamed all cuts on external constraints, particularly French policy.[1] Fresh elections were set for the autumn. From then on, until the end of the Weimar Republic, the NSDAP was in permanent campaign mode, as one election followed another – Reichstag, Landtag and presidential in quick succession. German politics never really settled down again, as contests in even the smallest of territories took on a disproportionate importance in the national context.

The steady advance of the NSDAP was epitomized by the new party headquarters in Munich. Hitler's originally planned skyscraper was dropped on the grounds that National Socialism was 'rooted . . . in not just the historical but also the cultural traditions of our people'. 'Despite the apparent grandiosity of such a high structure,' he went on, 'one cannot overlook the fact that it would be an experiment, whose role models do not lie in us but outside us. What is natural in New York would be artificial in Munich.' In late May 1930, Hitler settled for a large nineteenth-century neo-classical townhouse, the Palais Barlow on the Brienner Strasse. He went about the renovation of the building, which was financed through an extraordinary appeal to the membership, with great care. Hitler envisaged a 'marriage of utility and beauty . . . which we also want to achieve in due course on a large scale'.[2]

As the party fortunes waxed, internal divisions came to the fore again. The main clash was between the Strasser brothers and Hitler. This was partly a question of authority. In April 1930, the Saxon Nazis supported a metalworkers' strike on Gregor Strasser's instructions over Hitler's clearly expressed objections. Moreover, the Strassers and Goebbels were still engaged in a stagfight over propaganda; not for the first or last time, a frustrated Goebbels repeatedly considered resignation.[3] Doctrinal differences were also very important, however, especially as there were many Strasser sympathizers in the SA and among the *Gauleiter*. Here the problem was not so much their 'leftist' stance on economics, which caused Hitler tactical problems with the middle class and business, but with which he did not fundamentally disagree, as their heterodox views on race and foreign policy, to which Hitler took violent exception. Contrary to Strasser's repeated demand that Germany form a 'League of the Oppressed' against imperialism, Hitler refused to put Germans on the same level as the allegedly 'inferior' Egyptian fellahin, Hindus or Siamese. Hitler contrasted the 'racial inferiority of the Indian' with the qualities of the 'Nordic Briton'. He rejected the demands of blacks and Indians as 'an attempt' to reverse the 'natural ranking order of the races'. For this reason, Hitler warned against 'joining the general world wailing and shrieking against Britain'. He dismissed Otto Strasser's admiration for the Indian leader Gandhi as 'a racial perversity'.[4]

Hitler trod carefully, too carefully for some party critics. Goebbels decried the delay in confronting the Strassers. 'I don't believe a word of this any longer,' he wrote in his diary in mid March 1930. 'Hitler is very nervous,' Goebbels noted a few weeks later, 'he obviously feels very insecure.' Hope would alternate with despair as Hitler took action one day – 'Bravo! Hitler is starting to lead' – only to lapse back into hesitation the next. 'He is avoiding taking a decision,' Goebbels lamented in late June 1930, 'that is the old Hitler. The vacillator! The eternal procrastinator!' In part, no doubt, all this was due to his habitual indecisiveness. 'He hasn't got the courage to move against Strasser,' Goebbels lamented, 'how is that meant to work if he later has to act [*sic*] the dictator in Germany?'[5] But there was method in Hitler's tergiversation too. Where his charisma failed, he had no effective instruments to enforce his will. Hitler could not risk an internal party eruption which might set off so many secondary detonations as to consume the whole organization. The forces arrayed against him required a series of controlled explosions, in so far as they could not simply be defused.

In April 1930, Hitler moved to re-establish his authority among the *Gauleiter* and in the SA. Gauleiter Friedrich Hildebrandt in Mecklenburg-Lübeck was sacked for making Strasserite criticisms of Hitler's approaches to industry; he was later reinstated. Hitler also reminded the SA, many of whom were straining to engage in revolutionary action, of its primary function. 'Our weapons are not the dagger or the bomb, machine guns or hand grenades or military formations' but rather 'our weapons are exclusively the stringent truth of our idea, the victorious power of our theses, [and] the indefatigability of our propaganda work.'[6] That said, Hitler encouraged the SA to take on the communist *Rotfront* cadres in the fight for the control of the streets, so that Nazi brawling became a standard feature of Weimar politics.

Otto Strasser, for his part, refused to knuckle under. In early July 1930, he established a 'left-wing' breakaway group of 'Revolutionary National Socialists'. Its founding proclamation announced that 'the socialists are leaving the NSDAP'. The new movement never got off the ground. Gregor Strasser, still under Hitler's spell, broke with his brother. Only 800 party members and some functionaries defected, mainly in the north. Otto's group remained propagandistically active over the next two and a half years, but it never mobilized more than 5,000 people.[7] Despite extensive unhappiness in the SA, neither the organization nor any substantial part of it followed Otto into opposition. The rebellion was not trivial, but it was perfectly containable. Moreover, it allowed the party leadership to blame illegal tendencies on the Strasserite fringe.[8] Hitler had read the situation correctly. In the first of a series of controlled explosions, one of his rivals had blown himself up without bringing the whole edifice down.

Hitler now turned to deal with the crisis in the SA.[9] Here the problem was not so much ideological – although many sympathized with the Strasserite left – as tactical. The north-eastern SA under the leadership of Walter Stennes demanded a much more radical approach to the seizure of power. Hitler insisted on a policy of legality, in rhetoric but also in practice, so as not to give the authorities an excuse to ban the party and its structures. This was an old debate, but it came to a head in the late summer and autumn of 1930. The SA leader, Pfeffer von Salomon, was both disaffected and ineffective. On the very first day of September, a squad of SA men demolished Goebbels's offices in Berlin. The rebellion seemed on the verge of spreading to the countryside. Hitler did not try to confront Stennes directly.[10] He was desperate to avoid a breach before the Reichstag elections of 1930. Instead, Hitler sought to end the controversy by sacking Salomon and taking over as (nominal) supreme commander of the SA himself. Röhm returned from Latin America to take over the actual running of the SA, with the formal title of 'chief of staff' (*Stabschef*). Stennes backed off. An uneasy peace returned. Once again, Hitler's tactics had paid off, as another high-profile defection would surely have seriously damaged the party at the polls and possibly even led to its implosion.

Perhaps mindful of the dangers of too much consultation, the new edition of *Mein Kampf* in 1930 deleted references to 'Germanic Democracy', and to the 'election of the Führer', one of the few major changes to the text over time.[11] The new passage stressed the 'principle of Führer authority, paired with the highest responsibility'. In the same vein, Hitler also ordained that the local party organizations should no longer elect their own leaders – as envisaged in the first editions of *Mein Kampf* – but that these should be appointed from the top down.[12] In other words, Hitler was not simply establishing his own absolute authority, but the primacy of the 'Führer principle' throughout the entire movement. The need for these 'Führers' was justified by necessity. 'The ideal solution,' he remarked later, 'would be for the nation to be gripped by' a single figure, 'without any organizational intermediary bodies', but he conceded that this was 'unfortunately impossible'.[13] Hitler's largely rhetorical experiment with 'Germanic Democracy' was over. The NSDAP would be a party of one leader and many sub-leaders.

As always, ideological concerns rather than everyday issues were at the heart of the Nazi campaigning in advance of the 1930 Reichstag election. Hitler made a serious effort to conciliate Catholics, peppering his speeches with religious language; one appearance in Würzburg was even garnished with an 'amen'.[14] This was not just electoral opportunism, but reflected Hitler's desire to heal the confessional rift in Germany. He also reminded the electorate of the dangers of federalism and supposed racial division in two articles drawn directly from *Mein Kampf*.[15] One of them appeared the same day as Goebbels tidied up his vandalized offices in Berlin. 'The office looked awful,' he noted, with 'two big puddles of blood in my room'. This 'blood of comrades', he continued, was 'a terrible sight'. 'That is how we Germans are,' Goebbels went on, which made him doubt that 'we will ever be able to liberate this people'.[16] Hitler elaborated his concerns about the cohesion of the German people in a more guarded form than he had expressed himself towards Strasser. 'The German people may be made up of different races,' he told an audience of students, but its external appearance was determined through the 'higher-value racial elements', the encouragement and improvement of which was the task of domestic policy. This would have to focus on the need for 'breeding' the German people onto a higher racial plane.[17]

The answer to these challenges, Hitler argued, was not a vote for one of the Weimar parties. 'In elections,' he explained, 'there is never a victory but only the periodic exchange of overseers.' If Germans wanted to do more than simply rotate their overseers, they would have to vote NSDAP and its programme of purported racial regeneration through the conquest of living space. 'Adolf Hitler,' one Saxon paper reported, 'announced that the supreme principle of his party was the creation and securing of sufficient living space'; this – it argued – was what differentiated the NSDAP from both the Marxist and the bourgeois parties. Space was Hitler's answer to everything, from reparations to inflation, unemployment and the crisis of German agriculture. 'The life of the individual,' he observed in mid August 1930, was 'always determined by the space available to society. Whatever living space is available determines the life of the whole and with that the life of the individual.' The Americans, he reminded his listeners, had solved this problem. This need for *Lebensraum* as a panacea for all Germany's ills was hammered home to audiences again and again across Germany.[18]

While anti-Semitism generally receded as a theme in Hitler's speeches in the early 1930s, perhaps for tactical reasons, it was by no means concealed. In late February 1930, Hitler condemned the Jews as a 'world plague whose flags fly from Vladivostok to the heart of the American Union'. In early March 1930, he spoke of the 'real rulers' of 'German parliamentary democracy', namely the 'Jewish world money power'. In late July 1930, Hitler inveighed again against the 'string-pullers of humanity, the Jews'.[19]

When the votes were counted in mid September 1930, it became clear that the Nazis had made a colossal breakthrough. Hitler had been optimistic about the outcome, but the final tally of about 18 per cent of the national vote far exceeded his expectations. It was a massive increase on the pathetic 2.6 per cent secured in the 1928 elections. The NSDAP was now the second-largest party in the Reichstag after the Social Democrats. In Franconia, the result was particularly good, with most areas registering a Nazi vote of well over 30 per cent, and in Coburg as high as 43 per cent.[20] The Nazi vote was preponderantly but by no means exclusively Protestant and middle-class, with the self-employed more represented than workers; the membership tended to be young and male. That said, the NSDAP won votes from across the entire spectrum, and the range of its supporters was growing.[21] What these results signified about the appeal of Hitler's programme to the various sections of the electorate is impossible to say for certain. There is no evidence, for example, that the unemployed voted for him in disproportionate numbers, in either this contest or the subsequent elections; instead, they seem to have trended towards the communists.[22] Nor do we know for sure whether those who did cast their ballot for the NSDAP did so in support of Hitler's *Lebensraum* vision or his anti-Semitism, or for some other reason.[23]

One way or the other, the political implications of the vote were enormous. Hitler's strategy had been vindicated. Otto Strasser was left completely isolated. The legal path to power now seemed realistic on a shorter timeframe than anybody had dared hope. Success also bred success. 'You have no idea,' Rudolf Hess wrote to his parents, 'how the situation of the movement and especially of Hitler himself has really changed overnight', so that 'we have suddenly become presentable'. 'People who previously gave Hitler a wide berth,' he continued, 'now suddenly "must" speak to him.'[24] The Nazis became attractive for a new type of man. It was around this time that Albert Speer, a talented young architect, first encountered Hitler and was mesmerized by him.[25] In early January, Hitler met former Reichsbank president Hjalmar Schacht at Göring's flat; Mussolini's liaison man Giuseppe Renzetti was also present.[26]

Electoral success did not change the content of Hitler's speeches, which remained more or less unchanged until the takeover of power, but were continually elaborated and refined. Hitler still refused to engage with day-to-day politics, and claimed this as a virtue. '[Our] fate will not be decided by the issues of the day,' he announced in mid November 1930. This was because in his view day-to-day politics were a distraction from the issues that really mattered. 'The politician,' he told the Nationalklub in Hamburg at the start of December 1930, 'must not limit himself to the issues of the day but must devote himself to matters of principle.'[27] With some exceptions, there was no sign of any ideological softening or repositioning, even for tactical purposes.

Hitler's hostility to the world of finance, especially in its international form, remained undimmed; it was also closely connected to his anti-Semitism. 'If a people dissipates its strength,' he warned in mid November 1930, it would be dominated by another force, that of 'supra-state finance'.[28] The economic programme of the NSDAP remained ferociously anti-capitalist with its demand to nationalize major banks, to ban trading in stocks and bonds, to limit interest rates, and to confiscate 'illicit' gains from speculating on the stock market, war, revolution and inflation.[29] It supported the metalworkers' strike in the autumn of 1930, during which Hitler claimed that 'behind these forces supporting our enslavement [lay] the inexplicable narrow-mindedness of German business, or at least part of that business'.[30] In the budget debate in the following year, the party chose as its spokesman none other than Gottfried Feder, the scourge of capitalism, interest payments and 'debt-slavery'. If the NSDAP was generally on the extreme left of the extreme right, it was economically on the extreme right of the extreme left.

Occasionally, Hitler played down the role of the Jews in all this, for example in that speech to the Nationalklub in Hamburg, which contains no anti-Semitic outbursts.[31] Privately, though, Hitler was much exercised about the alleged power of the Jews in the US. He believed them to have seized almost all the key positions in American society, giving them total control. Their headquarters, Hitler argued, lay in New York, where, on his reckoning, about 3 million Jews sat like tapeworms at the source.[32] In an interview with a Jewish Associated Press journalist, moreover, Hitler went out of his way to tell his American audience that 'Germany's situation was the fault of Jewish capital'.[33] This was clearly a shot across the bows of Wall Street. More generally, Hitler saw himself as a victim of the 'Jewish press', and anti-Semitism simply as a form of German 'self-defence'.[34]

On Hitler's reading, the German people remained enslaved: by international capital, the Jews and the victor powers. The United States remained the dominant force in the world. 'Excessively rich America,' he pronounced in early December 1930, as the country reeled under the impact of the Depression, 'is conquering the whole with its unlimited opportunities.' The hated Young Plan, which remained at the heart of Hitler's critique of the status quo, epitomized the master–slave relationship. German hunger was blamed on the Young Plan. He even portrayed the 300 dead of a mining accident in the North-Rhine Westphalian town of Alsdorf as 'the victims of the Young system of robbery'. In his speech to the Hamburg Nationalklub he spoke of the 'tribute' payments to international masters. This slavery, he claimed, also had a devastating psychological effect on the nation, by inhibiting creativity in music and art. Hitler thus feared that the 'German people would slowly die out [and] perish for lack of importance'. He argued that Germany was simply the 'plaything of the nations' and was at best condemned to the indignity of being simply 'a second Holland, a second Switzerland'.[35]

Even after the 1930 election, Hitler did not depart from his view that Germany was racially fragmented, and the German people themselves of decidedly mixed quality. He seemed at this point to include Germans, Romans, Celts and even Slavs among the Aryans. They were subdivided into families of nations. The Italians, Spaniards and southern Frenchmen were part of the Romance family; the Danes, Swedes, Germans and Anglo-Saxons formed the Germanic family; and the Ukrainians, White Russians, Bulgarians and Yugoslavs were part of the Slavic family. Far from believing in existing racial purity, it seems, Hitler was clear that patterns of migrations over the past millennium had led to displacements and admixtures, rather than pure races, generally speaking.[36] The only people, Hitler claimed, who had managed to maintain their blood completely pure and unadulterated, thanks to their marriage laws and other factors, were the

Jews. Everybody else, and particularly the fragmented Germans, were racially a melange.

This presented a problem for Hitler. On the one hand, he wanted German racial purity to overcome the divisions of the past; that was a central part of his programme. On the other hand, the public diagnosis of current German racial inferiority could only deepen divisions and damage the NSDAP at the polls. The German *Volk*, he remarked privately, would be only more splintered, set against one another, and atomized by stirring up the racial problems. This would render it insignificant as far as foreign policy goes. Racial theories could be discussed among the inner circle, Hitler explained, but for the public at large they were poison. Such discussion would only rouse superiority and inferiority complexes.[37] For all the candour in *Mein Kampf* and his various speeches, Hitler could not level with the German people on this matter. The Second Book remained safely locked in a drawer.

For this reason, Hitler was careful to avoid public rhetoric which would divide Germans racially. References on his part to blond hair and blue eyes were relatively rare, not just because Hitler possessed neither. The only known remark he made at this time was with reference to his American prisoners of July 1918, supposedly descended from German emigrants. He remarked in private conversation that one should not harbour the narrow belief that every teacher must be a blond Germanic type. This he considered complete nonsense. For this reason, Hitler expressly and repeatedly forbade any talk of dividing the German people into two racial halves: the Germanic and the non-Germanic people, even though this was very much his own view. Instead, Hitler laid down that the Germans in particular must avoid anything that tended to create even more divisiveness in the religious, political and ideological spheres. If people were told that they were racially different, then the result would be not the unification of all Germans, but the bringing about of the final separation and dissolution of the concept of Germany.[38]

Instead, Hitler planned a more gradual and comprehensive racial reformation of the Germans over the longer term. One should accept the mixing of blood as it was, Hitler argued privately, and not call one [German] blood worse than the other, one mixture better than another. Rather, one should employ other means to breed a higher form from what he rather unflatteringly described as the existing grey mass. Here Hitler had not so much medical eugenics in mind as a much broader range of social and cultural instruments. One must try to bring to the surface the valuable traits of the people living in Germany, Hitler argued, in order to cultivate and to develop them. This required ways and means to prevent the propagation of all the

bad, inferior, criminal, decadent tendencies and congenital diseases likely
to damage the people. Central to this project, Hitler explained, would be
educating young people in the beauty of movement, the beauty of the body
and the beauty of the spirit, through athletics, personal grooming, physical
training, public performances of competitive games and contests and the
revival of the performing arts along the old Greek models. This selective
breeding would be furthered by the encounter of Germans of all backgrounds in kindergarten, primary school, the Hitler Youth and the League
of German Girls. Then, when these children grew up, they would be able
to leave all party considerations behind and elect the man, the only one,
who represented them and went to the Reichstag on their behalf. Only
then, Hitler claimed, would they see true democracy in Germany.[39]

Once again, Hitler was reviewing his timetable. Even as he celebrated
the party's advance at the polls, he foresaw the road ahead to be a long
and hard one. He expected the takeover of power after a final election
victory to be preceded, rather than be followed, by the racial regeneration
of Germany. He confided that he sometimes had the feeling that it would
not be granted to him to experience the great future which lay ahead, and
that only a coming generation would be mature enough to translate his
ideas and plans into action. He therefore saw it as his mission to bring
about the basis for such a community of the *Volk*, especially to guide the
young people of Germany along the paths that lead to this goal.[40]

The way forward, Hitler continued to argue, lay in a domestic regeneration, which would enable a radical new foreign policy. Ending
Germany's internal divisions remained his priority.[41] Again and again,
Hitler returned to the theme of the Thirty Years War and the deep rift it
had created in the life of the nation, ultimately leading to the catastrophe
of 1918–19.[42] He also lamented the split caused by class conflict, which
had weakened the Reich in the face of its internal and external enemies.
Far from trying to spare bourgeois sensibilities for electoral purposes,
Hitler continued to lambast 'prejudice', and 'class madness'. 'The smallest
title,' he complained, tried to 'elevate itself over the even smaller title.' The
NSDAP, Hitler proclaimed, was against 'class antagonism and class
prejudice'.[43] Central to this integrative and modernizing project was the
motorization of Germany, which Hitler regarded as essential to reaching
social and racial parity with the United States. In 1930, picking up on the
widespread contemporary discussions about the development of a 'people's
car', he remarked that Germany would need a version of the Model T. Ford
within the budget of an ordinary family.[44]

In strategic terms, Hitler stuck to *Lebensraum* as the universal panacea
throughout 1930–31, in public and in private. Because of Germany's past

internal divisions, especially the religious ones, she had been 'left out' of the first partition of the world. 'We had to watch,' he complained, 'how nations [such as] the Portuguese and the Dutch divided up the world with the British.'[45] 'If a people is starving,' he argued, 'then it has the right to seize territory for itself.'[46] *Lebensraum* also drove his understanding of international economics. 'In the final analysis,' he remarked of the economic crisis in early December 1930, 'the question of participation in world trade is not a matter of the raising of production but exclusively a question of the conquest of markets. Sales is the greatest problem, not production.'[47] Returning to old themes from *Mein Kampf* and the Second Book, he argued that there were only two ways of feeding the German people. 'Either one pursues export, which means competing with the world,' Hitler suggested, 'or we create ourselves a new market through the expansion of our living space.'[48]

For this reason Hitler continued to reject solutions based on 'world economy and world trade';[49] only living space in the east would do. Significantly, Hitler did not seek present-day world domination for Germany; that ship had already sailed. He spoke conditionally of a claim which would have existed in the past, had Germany not been so divided. 'No people would have had a better right to the concept of world domination,' he lamented, 'than the German people', but that moment had passed.[50] All that Hitler was seeking in the here and now was simple parity with Anglo-America.

Nazism might have made an electoral breakthrough, but there were still huge barriers between Hitler and the takeover of power. The principal pillars of power within the state remained largely sceptical towards Hitler and the NSDAP. President Hindenburg, for example, stayed aloof. The chancellor, Heinrich Brüning, met with Hitler but no agreement was secured. To the fury of the government, Hitler leaked the content of their conversation. The Reichswehr was not only profoundly sceptical about the party's commitment to legality, but also violently hostile to its 'socialist' domestic politics. These, the record of a conference in the Defence Ministry in late October 1930 claimed with reference to the nationalization measures set out in the Nazi economic programme, were 'pure communism'.[51] Hitler also hit the buffers in Nuremberg, which he acclaimed as 'the most German city ever',[52] and where he planned to hold another party rally in 1931, in a central place easily accessible from Austria and Czechoslovakia. His appeal to Mayor Luppe fell on deaf ears, and the city council refused to authorize the annual party congress for the second year running.

Nor did the 1930 elections, despite claims to the contrary by the Nazis themselves and their enemies, reconcile big business to Hitler. A few bosses now began to 'hedge' against the eventuality of a Nazi victory by seeking a rapprochement. Hitler also made some headway with individual business figures. In late September 1930, he met with the shipping magnate Wilhelm Cuno in Hamburg,[53] who arranged for him to address the Nationalklub in Hamburg two months later. The vast majority of business leaders, however, were still repelled by Hitler's anti-capitalist rhetoric. His economics adviser Wagener was far to the left of any entrepreneur. Moreover, Nazi Party journals, especially that of the 'Factory Cell Organization' continued to lambast the 'liberal-capitalist system',[54] to criticize bosses and to call for the nationalization of key industries. Throughout 1931, donations from business remained few and far between.

This meant that the party remained dependent on alternative sources of financing, especially donations and subscriptions by the membership or sympathizers. The NSDAP also made money selling newspapers, books, tickets to meetings and in many other ways.[55] All SA members had to take out a party-organized insurance. Costs were generally low, as there were few salaried staff; most officers worked for free. Here the NSDAP much more closely resembled the SPD than the parties of the centre and right, who were generally in receipt of monies from big business or other vested interests. This model of financing was a response to weakness, but it became a source of strength. It gave the NSDAP a certain resilience and independence, and enabled Hitler to deal with potential donors more confidently; he could not simply be 'bought'. Moreover, the fact that the party charged for entry to meetings also deterred hecklers and timewasters, as well as ensuring that those who attended were highly motivated.

Hitler's political strategy after the election was three-pronged. First, Hitler sought to tighten his grip on the party organization. In early November 1930, Hitler issued an instruction to regulate relations between the SA and SS; the latter was beginning to grow in importance as the provider of a 'police service inside the party'.[56] Generally speaking, both organizations were forbidden to attempt to poach members from each other, although a request to transfer was not to be unreasonably refused, and neither was entitled to give orders to the other, unless the task specifically required it. Secondly, smarting after his rebuff by Brüning, and sensitive to the *froideur* coming from President Hindenburg, Hitler reached out to the mainstream right. In September 1930, he made Göring a special envoy to forge alliances with conservatives.[57] Hitler tried to patch up relations with the nationalist paramilitary organization the Stahlhelm, meeting on several occasions with the leadership.[58] He told the NSDAP 'leaders' conference' in Cologne that while the election victory enabled the party to speak 'in a different tone' with the Stahlhelm, it was 'wise', given the size of that organization, 'not to antagonize the Stahlhelm'. He left the question of tactical collaboration to the discretion of local leaders but in general he hoped that one would work more closely. 'The brown and grey soldiers,' he demanded, 'must stand together in the battle against the current system.'[59]

Likewise, Hitler attempted to appease the agrarian conservatives, no easy task given his own well-documented hostility and that of his agricultural adviser Walther Darré. The latter's demand for 'new aristocracy of blood and soil' had put a big question-mark over the supposed racial value of the German nobility.[60] At a meeting with the prominent East Elbian landowner Prince Eulenburg-Hertefeld in January 1931, Hitler reassured him that he did not plan to expropriate anybody within Germany (except, implicitly, the Jews), not least because the land available was not sufficient for his purposes. Referring Eulenburg to the relevant passages in *Mein Kampf*, he explained that the necessary land would be secured further east.[61] In effect, Hitler was proposing to bypass awkward distributional questions by enlarging the cake.

Thirdly, Hitler began not merely to outline but to conduct an active foreign policy. He was now a power in the land, a fact which brought with it both dangers and opportunities. Hitler was very concerned that Brüning's aggressive push for German rearmament, partly designed to deflect attention from internal woes, would provoke pre-emptive strikes from France and Poland. The Poles were prepared to meet him halfway. In the autumn of 1930, an emissary from Marshal Piłsudski came to Munich. He proposed a ten-year peace and friendship treaty after a Nazi takeover of power, based on close economic ties, the resolution of outstanding border issues and some form of central European federation directed against the Soviet Union. Hitler, who was a keen admirer of the marshal, needed no persuading. He remarked privately that he was determined to follow Piłsudski's advice and conclude a ten-year pact with Poland immediately after taking over the government. Hitler saw a treaty with Poland as the first step towards the consolidation of central Europe.[62] Unlike some in his entourage, he was optimistic that Britain would not oppose these schemes.

Even more important than keeping the Poles at arm's length, in Hitler's mind, was wooing Anglo-America. After all, London and Washington would have to agree not only to Hitler's plans for a new European order, but to his assumption of power in the first place. This now seemed possible. The election changed the international standing of the Nazis, which had been generally low after the failed Munich Putsch.[63] The Anglo-American press, especially *The Times* and the newspapers owned by William Randolph Hearst, now besieged Hitler with requests for interviews. 'The domestic and foreign press is beating down the doors,' Hess exulted; they were wiring from America, telephoning from London and were 'plunged into despair when Hitler coolly declared that he was not available'.[64] Hitler gave a series of international interviews immediately after the election, principally to the British and American press, including the *Daily Mail*, the *Sunday Express* and *The Times*. He told his economic adviser Otto Wagener that he needed to win over England.[65]

In public and in private, Hitler was convinced that a deal with the British – whom he regarded as a 'fraternal people'[66] – could be done on the basis of the territorial status quo in the west, the renunciation of colonies and common enmity against the Soviet Union.[67] In his charm offensive in the British media in the autumn of 1930, Hitler therefore emphasized the threat of Bolshevism. He stressed the commonality of interest between the two countries and showed himself knowledgeable about British history.[68] Hitler hoped that agreement would be reached without recourse to war, hoping that an 1866-style conflict like that between Austria and Prussia could be avoided.[69] The allusion to the Austro-Prussian War of 1866 was significant, partly because it suggested that he regarded the differences between Germans and Britons as no greater than those between Reich Germans and those in Austria, but also for the way in which he conceived a future war with Britain. It should be avoided if possible, and if waged should be conducted swiftly and followed by a generous compromise peace similar to the one that Bismarck concluded with the Austrians after their defeat at Sadowa, enabling the rapid conclusion of the Austro-German Dual Alliance at the end of the subsequent decade. The contours of the 1940 constellation are already visible here.

Immediately after the election, Putzi Hanfstaengl was recalled and instructed to mount a proper foreign press effort.[70] It became his job to manage relationships with the large numbers of journalists in Berlin, most of them British and American. This was not an easy task. Although Hitler was intrinsically 'good copy', he was also erratic in his behaviour, missed deadlines and never really understood the concept of an 'exclusive'. To Hanfstaengl's frustration, he often made policy announcements prematurely and in obscure places. There could be no doubting the content of Hitler's message to the Americans, however. In an interview with Hearst's *New York American*, Hitler railed against 'war debt slavery' and the fact that the reparations settlement had turned German workers into 'convict labour for an entire generation and, in addition, bequeathed to its children and children's children the Versailles Treaty and Young Plan, endless slavery, and the sentences of unforgettable tribute paying'. As with Britain, what Hitler wanted was an accommodation with the United States, in this case on the basis of a hemispheric partition of the world. 'Our whole movement,' he announced in mid October 1930, 'aims at a German Monroe Doctrine. This demands Germany for the Germans just as America demands America for the Americans'.[71] Here Hitler was reprising a concept which he had first ventilated before the 1923 putsch, and to which he would return repeatedly in 1940–41.

Mussolini, so long aloof, began to come off the fence. As late as May 1930, he had told a German journalist that fascism was not 'an article for export', mainly in order to reassure the German government. Now he began to view the rise of Nazism as an opportunity for Italy. A year later, in May 1931, Mussolini received Hermann Göring, the first high-ranking Nazi to be so honoured.[72] His confidant Giuseppe Renzetti met with Hitler on no fewer than ten occasions in 1930–31, and another sixteen times after that before the takeover of power.[73] In an interview with the *Gazzetta del Popolo* two weeks after the election, Hitler repeated his views on South Tyrol. The purpose here was not primarily to establish common ground between Nazism and fascism; in fact he insisted upon the differences between the two movements. Hitler's main motive was strategic: to break open the ring of encircling alliances around Germany, and to dissuade the great powers from stopping a Nazi victory at the polls. In short, whether with Poland, Anglo-America or Italy, Hitler was already beginning to conduct an active foreign policy long before his takeover of power.

More mundane matters soon intruded. Hitler was to spend much of 1931 not so much selling the movement abroad as trying to deal with its liabilities at home. One of these was Göring, whose high-level connections, both to German high society and internationally, were indispensable to the party. His growing importance, and the drugs he took to ease the pain from his injuries, unbalanced him not merely politically but mentally, and caused Hitler considerable anxiety. Worse still was the problem of the new SA leader, Ernst Röhm, whose obvious homosexuality, and that of his entourage, not only repelled other party leaders but was also a gift to the enemy press. 'Disgusting!' Goebbels wrote in late February 1931. 'Hitler doesn't pay enough attention here,' with the result that the party risked becoming an 'El Dorado for queers'.[74] Hitler, though vehemently opposed to homosexuality in theory, was in fact remarkably tolerant of Röhm's activities in practice. 'The SA,' he pronounced, 'is not a moral institution for the education of upper-class girls but an association of raw fighters.' Their 'private life', Hitler continued, 'can only be taken into consideration if it violates important principles of the National Socialist world view'.[75]

More worryingly, the SA was also continuing to challenge Hitler's authority. Behind the scenes, Röhm not only was developing his own foreign policy positions, but engaged in private diplomatic contacts with foreign powers.[76] Just how much of this Hitler knew by the spring and summer of 1931 is unclear. It was no secret, though, that many SA leaders, especially Walter Stennes, remained committed to a strategy of revolutionary upheaval. They were egged on by their men, who had been comprehensively 'mobilized' for the electoral battles and now struggled to get down from their 'highs'. In March 1931, Hitler endorsed Röhm by name but only ambivalently. 'I am the SA,' he announced, 'and you belong to the SA,' warning that 'if I am ever in the situation where I have to give up the SA, I would do it with a bleeding heart to rescue the [rest of] the movement'. This was a clear shot across the bows. In April 1931, Stennes finally broke away from the NSDAP, attacking 'bigwigification' (*Verbonzung*) within the party and the unnecessary expenditure on 'bronze and marble' in the new party headquarters. He also played on the divisions between Munich and the northern Nazis. But when Stennes loyalists occupied the party headquarters, Hitler acted. Stennes was replaced with Göring.[77] Not long afterwards, he joined forces with Otto Strasser, but even together they failed to gain much traction. Once again, Hitler conducted a controlled explosion within the party, which was smaller than it would have been if Stennes and Otto Strasser had left together.

The behaviour of the SA put a lot of strain on Hitler's 'legality strategy'. This was always something of a euphemism. It did not mean that the Nazis never broke the law; they did this all the time through attacks on political rivals.[78] Rather, it signified that Hitler was committed not to stage another 1923-style insurrection, or confront the state directly with violence. This strategy was critical not only to denying the Weimar authorities a pretext to shut down the NSDAP, but also to reassuring bourgeois opinion about the respectability of the movement. In the spring and summer of 1931, these concerns came to the fore during the Eden Dance Trial. When four SA men were put on trial for assault and attempted murder, the prosecutor, a young Jewish lawyer called Hans Litten, called Hitler as a witness. Though Hitler was no stranger to court appearances, he had generally got the better of his interlocutors. This time, however, he was deeply embarrassed under a forensic cross-examination which showed his complicity in Nazi street violence. Litten's probing put salt in Hitler's wounds, because he could not openly disavow the SA without widening the gulf left by the Stennes revolt nor embrace them without abandoning the legality strategy.[79]

For Hitler, the SA rebellion was partly about the maintenance of his authority. 'I am not the attorney of the National Socialist movement,' he insisted, 'but its founder and leader.' He therefore laid down the new structure of the SA. Hitler's emphasis on the importance of 'leadership' also stemmed from his concern for the long-term regeneration of German society. Somewhat in violation of his own call not to speak of supposed German racial divisions, he explained in early May 1931 that 'Germany is not racially pure' but was 'composed of purely Nordic, eastern elements and of mixtures of all these parts'. 'That is why,' he continued, 'in every question which requires a blood-based position there will be different answers,' which in a democracy will fall on the 'racially inferior side'. 'For this reason,' Hitler concluded, 'there is no other form of organization conceivable for us than one based on the recognition of the Führer and his authority.'[80] The Germans, he seemed to be suggesting once again, were not yet ready for democracy; they were not racially coherent enough. Later that month, Hitler established the Reichsführerschule in Munich to train a new generation of leaders. Far from believing the Germans to be naturally disciplined, therefore, Hitler believed that they needed strong leadership to knock them into racial shape.

The crushing of the Stennes revolt did not end the divisions within the NSDAP. Göring continued to feud with Goebbels. 'Göring continues to agitate uninterruptedly against me,' Goebbels complained in early June 1931, 'because of a pathological jealousy', adding that his rival was trying 'literally [to] crawl into Hitler's arse' and that 'he would manage to do so if he were not so fat'.[81] Röhm remained a liability. Moreover, Hitler and he had still not sorted out Gregor Strasser, together with Röhm the last grandee on the 'left' of the party, who remained loyal after his brother Gregor and Stennes had left. To the frustration of many, Hitler continued to prevaricate. This was a matter partly of temperament and partly of calculation. He could not afford to lose a confrontation and even to win one, if the result was to split the party. Doing nothing, Hitler told Wagener, generally worked in politics. Politics was always a struggle, he continued, a pressure one side tries to exert. If one pushed back, the attack might be reinforced, but if one evaded and offered no resistance whatsoever, then the push stopped being a push and became mere a gust of wind which dissipated itself. But, as such, it could not pull down anything.[82]

Even as he battled his enemies within the party throughout the spring and early summer of 1931, Hitler kept a watchful eye on the international scene. In early May 1931, he established the 'Foreign Section' in Hamburg, a symbolic move in a city which regarded itself as 'the gateway to the world'. Around the same time Hitler assured the *Daily Express* correspondent Sefton Delmer in a Berlin restaurant: 'From now on, you just watch! My men will be quiet and disciplined and orderly. My job is to prevent the millions of Germans unemployed from coming under communist influence, as they easily might. I want to turn them instead into an orderly citizen force for the defence of Germany against the internal and external Bolshevik enemy.' Not long after he told Delmer that he had two main foreign policy aims, the cancellation of reparations and 'a free hand in the east' to enable 'the surplus millions of Germans to expand into the Soviet Union'. When challenged how he could attack Russia without crossing Polish land, Hitler replied, 'A way can be found for everything.'[83] Hitler repeated these remarks in an interview with the London *Times* in early June 1931. 'Germany,' he told them, 'must export men . . . particularly towards the east. Herr Hitler does not specify this conception precisely, but his mind seems to take the Polish Corridor in its stride and to contemplate German colonisation of an unlimited eastern area.'[84] If *Mein Kampf* had not been clear enough, Hitler was now openly signalling his strategic intent to the west.[85]

Hitler also remained preoccupied with the power of the United States, and still showed no sign of taking on board the shattering economic impact of the depression there. Reviewing the list of Germany's rivals, he stated in early February 1931 that the United States had become a 'competitor on the world market', especially 'since the war' because it was 'a giant state with unimaginable productive capacities'.[86] The US was not merely an economic but also a cultural threat, most dramatically expressed through the ubiquitous American popular music. 'If we believe,' he warned, 'that we must make American jazz music like American half-Negroes, then our own achievements must be lamentable'. Hitler also worried about Hollywood, and in particular its film version of Erich Maria Remarque's *All Quiet on the Western Front*. He did not object to its portrayal of the horrors of war, on the contrary. The 'frontline soldier', Hitler wrote in a remarkably candid autobiographical passage, 'knows that behind the term "glorious victory" there lies a huge amount of dirt, struggle, pain, misery and deprivation', as well as 'weakness', meaning 'the overcoming of one's own weaknesses' through 'self-mastery'. 'We are no warmongers,' he claimed, 'because we know war.' Hitler objected to the *Schandfilm* because it claimed to show the futility of war, and thus undermined German capacity for future struggle.[87]

If Hitler did not pay much attention to the parlous economic situation of the United States, he was certainly aware of the collapse of the German economy. Output was declining steadily, be it because of a shortage of capital or of purchasing power. It was the crisis of the Austrian and German financial sector precipitated by the collapse of the Viennese

Kreditanstalt bank in May 1931, however, which finally drove the economy off the cliff. Bankruptcies multiplied, share prices plummeted, and unemployment soared.[88] The Brüning government responded by doubling down on its policy of austerity, which in turn doused demand and aggravated the depression. By the end of 1931, industrial production was only one-third of what it had been in 1928.

Hitler blamed all this not on economics but on politics. In February 1931, he saw the 'coming famine in Germany' as the product of Versailles and the Young Plan. Two months later, Hitler traced the rise in unemployment back to geopolitical causes. In early May, he attributed the 'great German deprivation' to the 'atomization' of German political life in 1918–19. Two months after that, when the Kreditanstalt crisis was in full swing, he once again reminded his listeners that the real immediate cause of all their 'economic worries, immiseration, unemployment, collapse, poverty, suicide, emigration and so on' was the Young Plan. More fundamentally, Hitler continued to argue that the crisis was all the result of the Versailles Treaty. He continued to attack the reparations scheme to the end of the year and indeed beyond not only in speeches, but in interviews with the foreign press.[89] It goes without saying, of course, that Hitler saw the pernicious power of the Jews behind Germany's economic misery and indeed behind the workings of the financial system as a whole.[90]

Crucial for Germany's international position, Hitler argued, was her relative not absolute economic deprivation. He described the 'poverty' of the German people as being relative to an advanced 'living standard' rather than an 'absolute' one.[91] Here again, he was picking up on the appeal of the American way of life, which had preoccupied him since the mid 1920s. This is why he so feared American competition.[92] In particular, Hitler feared that Germany would not be able to maintain the living standard differential with non-whites. 'The white race,' he explained in early September 1931, 'was able on the basis of its greater strength to dominate other peoples of inferior worth',[93] but the increasing poverty of the Germans put a question-mark over their whiteness. If the depression caused many individuals to worry about slipping down the socio-economic ladder, what Hitler feared was the resulting racial relegation of the entire German people.

Hitler was also beginning to think more creatively about how to revive the economy. He believed in the 'multiplier effect', by which a sum of money invested could generate a much larger figure through salaries and consumption. Hitler therefore claimed that an annual reparations bill of 2 billion RM actually deprived the German economy of about 10 to 12 billion marks.[94] Though now routine, the multiplier effect was a new-fangled and disputed concept at the time and contemporary experts laughed Hitler out of court.[95] Hitler also believed in deficit-financing by the state to stimulate the economy, what we today call 'priming the pump'. He lampooned German economists for standing before a stopped clock without considering that all that was needed was to rewind it.[96] Hitler may well have been influenced here by John Maynard Keynes, or at least by Keynesian thinking.

Thanks to the collapsing economy, Nazism began to surge forward again at the polls. In mid May 1931, the NSDAP gained 37 per cent of the vote in the regional elections in Oldenburg and became the largest party in the Landtag there. The Republic was now subjected to mass battery fire by the party propaganda machine. The recently disciplined SA was part of this strategy, which Hitler conceived of in political rather than military terms, but expressed in the language of the battlefield. 'The SA man,' he stated, 'is a political fighter' whose job it was 'to enable the leadership of the movement to protect the movement.' 'For National Socialism,' Hitler continued, 'propaganda is and remains the attack artillery.' The SA, he explained, were 'the infantry'. 'The SA and SS,' Hitler elaborated, served to 'cover' the propaganda barrage, while 'the organization [meaning the Party] occupies and fortifies the captured positions'. The growing success of the Nazis increased the number of those switching from other parties. Hitler gave orders that those who were likely to do so should not be criticized in the party press.[97]

The Nazi advance and the failure of the Brüning government to get to grips with the escalating political and economic crisis led some of the established elites to take a greater interest in Hitler. It was around this time that Emil Georg von Stauss, a director of the Deutsche Bank, met him in Berlin at Göring's instigation.[98] Hitler also made the acquaintance of Walther Funk, the economics editor of the conservative *Berliner Börsen-Zeitung*. He was the first voice in Nazi policy which was not fundamentally anti-capitalist. Hitler signalled to him that the Nazi economic programme was flexible. For all that, despite high hopes and Hitler's repeated claims to his associates that the world of finance had seen the light,[99] the NSDAP made no breakthrough with big business in the summer of 1931. Looking back on those events, his press secretary Otto Dietrich recalled that 'The authoritative men of [the economy] and the associational officials of industry displayed a cool political reserve and awaited developments'. The result, he wrote, was that Hitler had to continue 'to rely in his propagandistic endeavors on the financial sacrifices of his party comrades, on membership dues and entrance fees for rallies'.[100]

In terms of high politics, though, Hitler began to make serious progress. In early July 1931, Hitler had his first meeting with the head of the mainstream conservative DNVP, Alfred Hugenberg. There followed encounters with the two leaders of the Stahlhelm, Seldte and Duesterberg. He also met with the chairman of the DVP, Eduard Dingeldey, and privately signalled his respect for Brüning's foreign and domestic policy, which he was traducing in public. Göring conveyed as much directly to the chancellor.[101] Hitler's strategy here was to undermine the government through '100 conferences'.[102] Likewise, his dealings with big business, which picked up again in the autumn, were not so much intended to win over its leaders as to 'neutralize them'.[103] Central to this strategy was shattering their confidence in the Weimar system. 'Hitler,' Hess remarked in early September 1931, 'is now more in Berlin than Munich' because 'he has set himself the task of causing the remaining pillars of the current government in industry and banking to totter'.[104] He was, as yet, a great deal further from achieving this than he claimed, but a lot of progress had been made.

In mid September, however, there was a shattering event, which nearly ended Hitler's career. His somewhat irregular personal life was the subject of much concern within the party. 'Hitler chats about marriage', Goebbels noted earlier in the year, 'he feels very lonely and yearns for [the right] woman, which he cannot find.' In the autumn of 1931, matters came to a head. Relations between Geli and Hitler deteriorated, partly because of his desire to 'protect' her, and partly because he opposed her plans to become an opera singer. What triggered the final tragic climax is unclear. It may have been Hitler's controlling nature, his growing interest in Eva Braun or his ill-concealed infatuation with Goebbels's girlfriend Magda Quandt, which peaked in September 1931. 'Hitler is in seventh heaven,' Goebbels noted in his diary on 26 August, 'beautiful women, that is his taste,' adding that Magda had rather overstepped the mark with 'the chief', which caused him considerable anguish. A fortnight later, Goebbels and Magda told Hitler of their intention of getting married. He was visibly 'crushed', 'resigned' and 'lonely'. Hitler 'is unlucky with women,' Goebbels opined, 'because he is too soft on them', which 'women don't like' because 'they must [have] a master over them'. 'He loves Magda,' Goebbels recorded, 'and he too seeks a suitable girlfriend whom he can later marry'.[105] All this this may have aggravated the tensions between Hitler and Geli. Whatever the reason, after a row with Hitler two days later, on 18 September 1931, Geli locked herself in her room and shot herself with his pistol. Hitler, who was in Nuremberg at the time, rushed back to Munich.

Geli's death was a massive emotional blow.[106] For a long time afterwards, Hitler was inconsolable. At first, he seems to have said little. A few days afterwards, he sat 'completely quietly and cowed' in Goebbels's flat, saying 'not a word of Geli'. In late November he poured his heart out. 'The chief speaks of women, whom he loves very much,' Goebbels wrote, 'of the [right] one, whom he cannot find', of 'the hysterical women who pursue him', and 'of Geli, whom he has lost and whom he mourns with all his heart'. At Goebbels and Magda's wedding in mid December 1931, where he was best man, Hitler broke down in tears. 'Then he speaks of Geli,' Goebbels reports. 'He loved her very much' and she was 'his "good comrade" '.[107] That Christmas, he wrote his personal greetings on a black-framed postcard. 'I am having very sad days,' he told Winifred Wagner, adding that 'the great loneliness first has to be overcome'. Hitler explained that he had recently passed through Bayreuth, but had not stopped off at Wahnfried because he 'could not bring himself' to seek her out, because – candidly acknowledging his morose state – 'what is the point of depriving people of joy just because one is unhappy oneself'.[108]

Hitler also had to deal with the huge political fallout. Geli's death, the manner of her passing and the rumours surrounding it were a public rela-tions disaster. Thanks to the SA, the Nazis already had a grim reputation for violence and sodomy. Now the enemy press went to town on Hitler himself. They had a field day with the fact that he seemed to be in an intense and controlling relationship with his much younger niece, who had then shot herself with his pistol. It did not look good. Hitler responded with a two-pronged strategy. The first step was damage limitation. He did not go to the funeral in Vienna in order to avoid turning the event into a media spectacle at his expense, though he slipped into Austria quietly immediately after in order to pay his respects at her grave. A few days later, Hitler published a 'Declaration', denying any breach with Geli or intent to stop her from getting engaged.[109] He did not retreat from the public eye, and continued his punishing schedule of speeches, though observers noted that he 'looks very worn out'.[110] With some difficulty, the crisis was contained, though Hitler remained the target of innuendo and sensationalism until he took power.

It soon became clear, however, that a much broader response was neces-sary. For political reasons, the general whiff of sexual depravity, incest and hysteria emanating from Hitler's entourage would have to be replaced by a more wholesome odour of domesticity. Heinrich Hoffmann was put to work to produce a photographic celebration of Hitler, which appeared in March 1932, six months after Geli's suicide. This album, entitled 'The Hitler Nobody Knows', invited Germans to rethink their conception of Hitler the man. Instead of the single-minded political warrior, surrounded by homoerotic thugs and hysterical women, they were presented with a much more domesticated 'Führer', who communed with nature and, though childless himself, loved children. Images and text stressed his sobriety and clean-living: no alcohol, no smoking and no meat.[111] There was no sign of Eva Braun, or indeed of any other woman. Germany had Hitler entirely to herself.

In late September 1931, Hitler predicted to Goebbels twice that they would soon take power.[112] In order to prepare for that event, Hitler had already begun to establish new party structures. In June, he had set up the Imperial Leaders' School in Munich. 'What we expect from the future', Hitler told them in late September 1931, 'must already be visible in us today' so that 'our current organization must already embody that which is to come in the Third Reich,' one of his few uses of that term to describe a Nazi regime.[113] He appointed Otto Dietrich as his press chief on 1 August 1931. Right at the end of October, Hitler made Baldur von Schirach 'youth leader'. A few days later, he established the 'Economic Council', under the chairmanship of Gottfried Feder, which was charged with advising on 'preparations for economic legislation' and 'for all fundamentally important matters of economic policy'.[114] On New Year's Eve, he set up the 'Race and Settlement Office' under Walther Darré. The contours of the coming Third Reich were increasingly visible.

The problem was how to crack open the Brüning government, which produced more emergency legislation in early October 1931, and looked set to rule by presidential decree for the foreseeable future. The key was President Hindenburg himself, the clique of conservatives around him and the broader network of established right-wing power brokers in the Stahlhelm, among estate owners and in industry.[115] Once again, Hitler's aim here was not so much to win over as to neutralize these actors, by reducing their instinctive dislike for, and distrust of, the NSDAP. A meeting with the Empress Hermine, the second wife of Wilhelm II, went reasonably well. Moving beyond the piecemeal contacts of the past, in December 1931 he tasked the North Badenese entrepreneur Wilhelm Keppler, who had already been serving as his personal economic adviser for seven months, to reach out to businessmen beyond the usual NSDAP circles.[116] Hitler indicated to him that he was not wedded to any part of the Nazi economic programme, and expressed the fear that Otto Wagener, Strasser and Gottfried Feder would repel business with their socialist talk.[117] He met with Hindenburg for the first time on 10 October 1931, and though Hitler managed to improve the atmosphere between them a little, the president made no secret of his determination to prevent Hitler from seizing power outright. It was the start of a clash of two charismas, and for now Hitler was outshone by the older man.[118]

In the course of the next day, the limits to Hitler's charm offensive became evident at a joint rally with the mainstream right in Bad Harzburg.[119] This was a complete failure, as each party sought to dominate and marginalize the other. Hitler first let the nationalists wait, and then left before they had completed their parades. There were even brawls between Stahlhelm and SA. 'Hitler is furious,' Goebbels noted, 'because one is trying to push us against the wall.'[120] The feeling was mutual. It was clear that, just as with the Bavarian conservatives, the common ground between the mainstream nationalist right and Hitler was not large enough to permit a stable alliance. There would not be room for both of them in the new Germany.

Central to Hitler's strategy remained the maintenance of a strict façade of 'legality', partly to reassure established elites, middle-class voters and foreign opinion, especially in Anglo-America, but also to deny the authorities an excuse to ban the party or its organizations. In mid November 1931, for example, Hitler once again stressed the need for the 'complete legality of the party' and his opposition to 'any illegal possession and use of weapons'. He was therefore deeply embarrassed when shortly afterwards a disaffected party official leaked documents, drafted in the Boxheimer Hof in Hessen without Hitler's knowledge by some local party figures, which suggested that the NSDAP was planning a coup, or at least to take over power in the aftermath of a communist one. His subsequent *Tagesbefehl* to the SA and SS sought to calm matters. 'Do not allow yourselves to be provoked,' he wrote, 'do not allow yourselves to be seduced.' This was all the more important, as the paramilitary formations were expanding at a considerable rate – twenty-eight new regimental-sized units were established in the autumn of 1931 alone[121] – and they were getting restless again. Hitler was always treading a fine line, seeking to impress and intimidate audiences by mass rallies, and to keep his men in fighting trim, but at the same time avoiding a premature eruption of revolutionary violence.

Meanwhile, Hitler never lost sight of the broader international context. In November 1931, he took time out to read Julian Corbett's book on British seapower.[122] Hitler also made direct overtures to the Duce via Renzetti.[123] In December 1931, Hans Nieland, the head of the newly founded 'Foreign Section', was sent to Rome in search of support from Mussolini. Hitler's main audience, though, was Anglo-America. Alfred Rosenberg was dispatched to London.[124] In the meantime, Hitler reached out to the American ambassador, Frederic M. Sackett, through the intercession of Emil Georg von Stauss. The encounter was unorthodox, as meetings with the opposition were even more frowned upon among diplomats then than they are now, and it was not a success. Hitler harangued Sackett at length. The ambassador was unpersuaded by his arguments, and dismissed his qualifications for office, but he was impressed by Hitler's 'forcefulness and intensity', which had communicated itself even via the translator.[125]

These moves were accompanied by a barrage of media initiatives towards Anglo-America. In late September, Hitler bemoaned the west's 'unholy war psychosis' to Sefton Delmer of the British *Daily Express* and expressed his hopes for the 'start of a really warm relationship between the British and German peoples'. He claimed that the editors of some of the great papers in Britain and America supported the revision of the Versailles Treaty. During November he gave interviews to the *New York Times* and the *New York Evening Post*. In early December, Hitler convened the foreign press correspondents in the Berlin Kaiserhof. The following day he gave interviews to the *Sunday Graphic* and the *Sunday News*.[126] He even had a radio address to the American people scheduled for 11 December 1931,[127] though it was blocked by the Weimar authorities. Ten years later to the day, he would send them a very different message, when he declared war on the United States in the Reichstag.

Hitler's intensive cultivation of Anglo-American opinion – Goebbels spoke of 'a veritable barrage'[128] – was intended to set out the basis of collaboration, or at least co-existence after a Nazi takeover of power. He did so partly by stressing past injustices, invoking 'Professor Maynard Keynes of Cambridge University' and his critique of the Versailles Treaty, and partly by promising to be a firm hand on the tiller. 'The world must not expect fireworks from me,' he averred, 'the contrary is the case.' 'The National Socialist Movement,' Hitler assured the *New York Times*, 'will win power in Germany by methods permitted by the present constitution in a purely legal way.' This careful formulation, which made no mention of elections or democracy, suggests that Hitler was already thinking of gaining power through the presidency, rather than the ballot box alone. He also promised that a National Socialist Germany would acknowledge its 'private debts', a gesture clearly aimed at placating US opinion. The same points were made in person to the US ambassador. Hitler defended the Weimar state against accusations that it had used American loans 'wastefully' to build 'stadia and swimming pools'[129] on the grounds that this expenditure was necessary to alleviate unemployment; this was a sign of his intent to address joblessness through a programme of public works after he gained power.

Ideologically, Hitler undertook to combat the threat of global Bolshevism, and he also made an open bid for American racial solidarity. Pointing to the alleged vast reserves of French colonial manpower in Africa, he claimed that 'every American schoolchild can realize [that] Europe under French domination will cease to be European and will be in danger of becoming African'. Hitler went on to restate his belief that the United States should serve as a model for Germany. 'It was America,' he told the *New York Times*, 'in spite of its enormous territory, that was the first country to teach us by the immigration law that a nation should [not] open its doors equally to all races. Let China be for the Chinese, America for the Americans, and Germany for the Germans.' In other words, Hitler said, 'we want nothing but a Monroe Doctrine for German men, women and children',[130] a hemispheric division of the world with the great Anglo-American powers based if not on cooperation then at least on non-interference in each other's affairs. Behind closed doors, even as the drama of Weimar domestic politics swirled around him, Hitler also continued to stress the need for 'space'. One activist recalls him gesticulating at the big map of Europe in his office and proclaiming that 'we will in due course control immense territories which we will have to secure'.[131]

Hitler's longstanding ambivalence about the United States remained unchanged in the early 1930s. He saw Germany as engaged in a cultural struggle for mastery, which brought out the worst and the best in both sides. On the one hand, Hitler feared American popular culture. He inveighed against German performances of 'Negro music', composed by 'pretty unmusical Americans'. Germany, Hitler argued, should not compete in this supposed cultural race to the bottom, but rather draw on the spiritual nourishment provided by Wagner and Mozart.[132] On the other hand, he embraced a friendly rivalry on the architectural plane. This was demonstrated by the start of his interest in the reconstruction of Hamburg, the port city through which the import, export and transit trade from Germany and its central and eastern European hinterland passed, and for which Hitler had grander plans. What New York represented on one side of the Atlantic, he told Otto Wagener, Hamburg must become on the other. But instead of the skyscrapers, bustling functionality and impersonality of the American metropolis, in Hamburg incoming liners would gradually be embraced by the green riverbanks of the enchanting Elbe landscape, with its half-timbered houses along the shore and with blossoming gardens.[133] It was a vivid example of how Hitler envisaged a future peaceful relationship between the new Reich and the United States, based on a common set of so-called racial values.

By contrast, Hitler did not engage much with the Soviet Union, and he did not regard it as a world power in the military sense. To be sure, he emphasized the dangers of Bolshevism with his Anglo-American interlocutors, and towards German business audiences. His speeches and public letters posited a stark choice between 'National Socialism' and 'Bolshevism'. Germany was portrayed as a bulwark against 'Asia'. 'Bolshevism' would 'either secure its world victory in the Reich' or it would be 'broken' there.[134] The danger, he told an audience of German entrepreneurs, was that communism 'had occupied a state' and was using this base gradually 'to take over the entire world'.[135] There was something tactical and synthetic about these statements, however, and in private Hitler stated that he did not fear war with Russia so much as the threat of communist revolution in Germany, a theme which he had been elaborating for more than ten years.[136] Besides, Hitler had not changed his view that Bolshevism was allied with and subordinated to the forces of international capitalism. He claimed that while the Marxist parties condemned the capitalist economy in the strongest terms, they worked hand in hand with 'the forces of international high finance, and supra-state world capital'.[137]

9
Making the Fewest Mistakes

In early 1932, it was clear that things were moving Hitler's way. The question was whether they were moving quickly enough. The onset of stomach cramps, sweating and other afflictions briefly convinced him that he was suffering from cancer.[1] Hitler was, in fact, not seriously ill, but he was clearly worn out. Faced with an increasing sense of his own mortality – something which was to become a constant theme in his rhetoric and thinking – the forty-two-year-old Hitler began to think seriously about the question of his successor. It was in this context that he reflected once again on the idea of a party senate, which had languished since the room envisaged for it in the new headquarters, the Braunes Haus in Munich, had been refurbished at great expense. This would help to incubate and select the new leader. 'Without such a party senate,' Hitler remarked, 'should I depart this life prematurely, there would be a struggle for the leadership succession.'[2] His timeline had narrowed again. To the increased prospect of power after the 1930s elections was added the imperative to seize it before time ran out on Hitler himself.

On 6–7 January 1932, Hitler was called to a meeting with the Reichswehrminister Wilhelm Groener, Hindenburg's close associate Kurt von Schleicher and Brüning.[3] They hoped to gain Nazi support in the Reichstag, but were offering little in return. Discussions continued for a few days.[4] Hitler held out for power, and soon broke off negotiations. He bitterly resented their treatment of him as someone who would merely rally a horde of voters behind their betters. Hitler fulminated that he was not merely a 'drummer' for 'reaction'.[5] He henceforth adopted a remarkably stiff tone with Hindenburg, rejecting attempts to bring 'foreign' powers into play as critics of Nazi violence, and accusing him of using article 48 to suppress democracy, making the president himself guilty of tolerating serious 'constitutional violations'.[6] Worse still, Hitler began to worry that the conservative right might stage a coup which would destroy all hopes of a Nazi takeover on the back of their growing popularity.[7]

Hitler sought to break the deadlock, and to head off an authoritarian regime, with a two-pronged strategy. First, he stepped up his campaign to win over the key conservative constituencies. In early January 1932, the former diplomat Prince Victor von Wied arranged for him to meet Konstantin von Neurath, ambassador to London and a stalwart of the conservative right. We do not know what passed between them on that occasion except that Hitler asked Neurath whether he would be willing to serve as foreign minister in any future cabinet headed by him.[8] In late January, Hitler seized the opportunity to speak to the renowned 'Industrial Club' in Düsseldorf, the capital of German heavy industry.[9] His speech was widely reported and often taken as an endorsement by his hosts. In fact, the audience was less weighty than one might imagine – most of the key figures in armaments, steel and coal production did not attend themselves – but the rapturous welcome he received did indicate the extent to which Hitler was gaining traction. At the very least, big business, which continued to support other parties more extensively, was beginning to take out 'insurance policies' with the NSDAP as well.[10] There were no direct references to the Jews, though plenty of coded ones.[11] The standard anti-capitalist language was muted, a little, over the next few months. There was no let-up, however, in Hitler's assault on international capitalism. 'National Socialism,' he reiterated in mid February 1932, privileged the life of the people over 'the interests of international finance capital, which had led to the destruction of all natural bases of the German people and the German economy'.[12]

The other way of breaking the logjam was for Hitler to capture the presidency himself, or at least to use his candidature to drive a wedge between Hindenburg and Brüning.[13] In late January 1932, he discussed the issue with Goebbels. 'He is still undecided,' Goebbels noted, adding that 'I argue for his candidature' because 'he alone will drive Hindenburg off the field'.[14] There was one immediate problem to be sorted out. The president had to be a German citizen and Hitler was stateless, with no chance of naturalization by one of the bigger Länder. His only hope was to secure appointment to public office in one of the smaller ones, which would give him local citizenship and, on the strength of it, that of the Reich as a whole. Luckily for Hitler, the Nazis had gained power in Brunswick, and the little cameo that followed was an illustration of the fragmented nature of the German polity that Hitler so deplored. Attempts to appoint him as an extraordinary professor for 'the organic study of society and politics' at the Technical University there miscarried, but he was made a state councillor instead.[15] Hitler was now finally a German citizen, nearly twenty years since he had taken up arms for the Reich.

Nazi strategy in the presidential campaign was carefully thought out. First, Hitler declared, one should wait for the SPD to support Hindenburg, which would paint him into a left-wing corner. Only then would Hitler himself declare. That was 'Machiavellian', Goebbels commented, 'but right'.[16] The hope was that Hitler would beat Hindenburg into first place, and then prevail in the run-off. He skilfully tried to frame his venerable rival – who enjoyed iconic status as supreme commander during the war – as old and out of touch, and also tainted by his politicization by the Weimar Republic. 'We regret,' he announced in mid February 1932, 'that Field Marshal von Hindenburg allowed himself to be prevailed upon to use up his name in this struggle.' The choice of words was significant: the old man was not merely being used, but 'used up'.[17] Hitler had to tread carefully, however, as any sign of overt disrespect might boomerang.[18] For this reason he gave strict instructions that there should no 'personal' attacks on Hindenburg.[19]

The Nazis were confident of success. A few days before the first round of voting, Hitler predicted to foreign journalists that he would secure 12 million votes. He actually secured 11.3 million, Hindenburg more than 18 million. It was a significant improvement on the 1930 Reichstag election, but nowhere near enough to capture the presidency. Hitler, as Goebbels noted, was 'totally surprised by the result'.[20] There was no question, however, of backing down now. Hitler threw himself into the second round of the campaign. He doubled down on his message of 'change' and his attacks on reaction. 'National Socialism,' he announced in late March 1932, aimed to 'proclaim a new political ideal' on 'the ruins of the bourgeois and proletarian ideology'. A future 'Nazi regime', he added, just in case his meaning had been unclear, 'will not represent a return to the past'. Hitler underlined the vigour and modernity of his message by attempting – unsuccessfully, because the authorities forbade it – to address the German people through radio broadcasts[21] and embarking on a whirlwind tour of the Reich by aeroplane. At Hanfstaengl's suggestion, he included a journalist on each flight, often a Briton or an American, a measure borrowed from FDR's campaign strategy.[22]

Hitler also tried to split the conservative coalition behind Hindenburg. In late March 1932, he met with representatives of the Christlich-Soziale Volksdienst (CSVD), one of the more moderate smaller right-wing parties sustaining Brüning in the Reichstag. He hoped to dissuade them from supporting an authoritarian solution to the continuing crisis and to back him in the second round of the presidential elections. The meeting was not a success. The CSVD announced its intention to endorse Hindenburg. 'One cannot discuss with Hitler,' his interlocutors remarked, because

' "the other" is always in the wrong if he represents a different opinion to Hitler'. One of them predicted that 'if Hitler comes to power, then that can only end in a catastrophe'. 'God protect our Fatherland,' he continued, 'that this man will not control our fate.'[23]

The continuing controversy surrounding the SA chief of staff, Ernst Röhm, did not help matters, especially given Hindenburg's known aversion to homosexuality.[24] In early March 1932, at the height of the first round of the presidential election campaign, a Social Democrat weekly paper published extracts from letters proving his homosexuality beyond all doubt. The row rumbled on for more than a month, damaging the party and Hitler personally, but despite his own personal distaste, he refused to throw Röhm to the wolves. 'Hitler does not want to drop Röhm,' Goebbels noted in his diary, 'but he is strongly opposed to the queers.'[25] In early April, Hitler felt obliged to make a public statement backing Röhm and condemning the 'dirtiest and most revolting agitation' against him.[26]

Throughout the two rounds of the presidential election campaign, Hitler did not vary his core message. Foreign policy remained at the centre of his concerns: it featured prominently in his public and private utterances.[27] Hitler continued to blame Germany's internal woes on her international inferiority as epitomized by the Versailles Treaty and the reparations regime. 'The German people,' he lamented, had 'suffered since November 1918 from a hardly bearable spiritual, political and material deprivation'; the defeat had 'stamped them as second-class citizens of the world'. He slammed the Young Plan, his old bugbear, for being responsible for the 'complete destruction of the German economy'. Above all, Germany suffered from the 'limitation of [her] living space'. The 'political deprivation', in short, had been 'converted into economic deprivation'. Wherever he went to canvass support for his presidential bid, to Hamburg, Stettin or Leipzig, Hitler hammered home the same familiar theme.[28]

During the campaign, Hitler's attitude to women was challenged. It was not a subject on which he had said or written much hitherto. Now, he was forced to rebut claims that he 'wanted to deprive German woman of her rights and drive her from her job'. Hitler responded that 'there is no battle for the man which is not also a battle for the woman'. He envisaged a largely reproductive role for women, to produce and raise as many healthy children for Germany as possible. Hitler defined the woman as 'the smallest, but most valuable unit in the structure of the entire state' by virtue of motherhood.[29] Privately, Hitler was even prepared to set aside conventional morality so long as it led to an increase in the number of 'racially valuable' births. For example, when Magda Goebbels fearfully reported her discovery that her parents had not been married when she was born, Hitler laughed off this embarrassing fact, which could have been exploited by hostile press elements.[30]

On 3 April 1932, Hitler took to the air for the first of several 'flights over Germany', which ended on 9 April. The following day, Germany went to the polls again. Hitler won 13.4 million votes, or 36.8 per cent of the total. It is doubtful that many of these ballots were cast primarily in the hope of gaining living space in the east, or sorting out the 'Jewish Problem', yet unless they were either deaf or illiterate voters cannot have been entirely ignorant of his diagnosis either. One way or the other, whether it constituted a mandate for aggression and genocide or not, the result was very respectable, but nowhere near enough to dislodge Hindenburg from the presidency, where he remained. Hitler did not know it, but the Nazi vote had effectively peaked. He was aware, though, that he had a problem on his hands. 'You had a head of state who was not against you', Hitler reflected in an interview with an Italian paper, in fact 'the king in the end summoned Mussolini, whereas I still have President Hindenburg against me,' a man 'who still enjoys undisputed personal respect'.[31]

There was no time for a prolonged inquest, however, as the NSDAP was almost immediately plunged into a fresh round of campaigning. In late April 1932, there were Landtag elections scheduled in Prussia, Bavaria, Württemberg, Anhalt and Hamburg, areas which totalled about 80 per cent of the population of the Reich. He took to the skies once again between 16 and 22 April for another week-long 'flight over Germany'. Hitler was hampered by various constraints, especially the banning of the SA.[32] The results of these contests, which took place on 24 April, showed no change from the second round of the presidential contest earlier that month. The punishing cycle of elections continued, with polls in Oldenburg and Mecklenburg-Schwerin, when the NSDAP gained absolute majorities. This was the first major breakthrough of the party at regional level,[33] after its false start in Thuringia.

At the end of May, Brüning resigned the chancellorship. Reichstag elections were scheduled for July. Hindenburg appointed the conservative Catholic aristocrat Franz von Papen chancellor. Hitler still hoped to take the electoral route to power. The day after Brüning resigned, he told a meeting in Wismar that he hoped the party would grow 'until the last German has been won over', a sentiment he repeated on numerous occasions throughout the rest of the year.[34] Hitler was not deterred by a setback at the Landtag elections in Hesse in late June, where the NSDAP fell short of an absolute majority. His third 'flight over Germany' was his longest, lasting two weeks in the second half of July. During the campaign, Hitler spoke in more than fifty towns and cities. In terms of intensity, technological innovation and sheer razzmatazz, the Nazi campaigns of 1932 were like nothing Germany had ever witnessed before. Otto Dietrich, who accompanied Hitler on most trips as press secretary, later calculated that by the end of the year he had covered 50,000 kilometres by air, and 25,000 by road. 'It was political propaganda,' he wrote, 'which even put American efforts [Roosevelt was at this time conducting his own victorious election campaign] in the shade.'[35]

Hitler's campaign themes were the usual ones: the need to drill Germans into national unity by reconciling socialism and nationalism, and banishing 'class madness and class prejudice'.[36] Capitalism and the Jews were given the customary battering and the nationalist right was slammed not only as 'pro-Jewish' but also as the instrument of 'money-grubbing capitalism'.[37] As usual, he had little to say about the Soviet Union itself, but he did inveigh against the 'murderous scum of the communist criminal fraternity' and the 'lying slogans of the Marxists'. Though the communists were the main target of SA street violence, they were not Hitler's primary concern. Instead, Hitler once more stressed the need to secure *Lebensraum*, which he defined once again as the 'determining and driving force', which trumped considerations of 'export and import and the world economy'. *Lebensraum*, in short, was his economic programme. To those who demanded concrete answers to the specific political and economic problems of the day, Hitler responded as always with the healing power of ideology. 'Imagined futures,' he explained, were 'the most powerful realities which exist in the lives of peoples.'[38]

One of those swept up by Hitler's message and rhetoric was the twenty-nine-year-old film director Leni Riefenstahl. Earlier in the year, she had attended one of Hitler's speeches in the Berlin Sportpalast. 'It seemed to me,' she later recalled, 'as if the ground opened in front of me like a hemisphere which suddenly split in the middle [and] out of which an incredible jet of water was flung,' so mighty, she claimed, 'that it touched the heavens and caused the earth to quake'. 'There is no doubt,' Riefenstahl added, 'I was infected.' After reading *Mein Kampf* carefully, she wrote to Hitler in mid May 1932 and secured a meeting with him towards the end of the month. Hitler, who was deeply conscious of the need for the party to master the medium of film, immediately recognized Riefenstahl's talent. 'If we ever get to power,' he allegedly told her, 'then you must make my films.'[39]

Hitler sought to distance himself from Papen's 'cabinet of the barons' or 'gentlemen's club', and portrayed himself as the defender of average Germans against a distant and, in Hindenburg's case, aged elite. He was open, however, to collaboration with conservatives on his own terms. When approached by two emissaries from the giant chemical combine IG Farben in June 1932, Hitler gave them an enthusiastic welcome, despite earlier Nazi attacks on the firm as a nest of 'money-grubbing Jews' and an instrument of alleged Jewish international capitalism.[40] Their plan to produce synthetic fuel fitted his conception of autarchy perfectly, and he also told them of the projected system of motorways for Germany. Hitler also signalled some flexibility on restoring the Hohenzollerns. Despite his longstanding hostility to the various princely houses, and the former imperial family, he feared a direct confrontation. 'Hitler is for a purified monarchy,' Goebbels noted on the very first day of June 1932, and seems genuinely if briefly to have toyed with making Prince August Wilhelm ('Auwi') regent, and ultimately his son Alexander emperor. 'Hitler,' Goebbels believed, 'exaggerates the [pro-] Hohenzollern instincts among the people.'[41]

Given the fraught relationship between Papen's centralizing cabinet, which could draw only on Hindenburg's authority, and the democratically elected regional governments, it is no surprise that the thorny old issue of German federalism came to the fore again. Hitler portrayed the NSDAP as the 'guardian of the unity of the Reich' against 'certain cliques belonging to the Bavarian People's Party', and, tilting at a very old windmill, 'Rhenish separatists'.[42] The BVP, in fact, remained in Hitler's sights at least as much as the communists.[43] His anti-Semitism, by contrast, was somewhat muzzled throughout the campaign, both at home and abroad. In July 1932, he published an interview with the American magazine *Liberty*, which was in most respects a carbon copy of one given to the same journalist, George Sylvester Viereck, in 1923, including frank references to the need for *Lebensraum* in the east, but without the diatribes against 'the Jews'.[44]

When the ballots were counted at the end of July 1932, the NSDAP had secured 13.7 million votes, about 300,000 more than in the presidential election but the same percentage (37 per cent) as then. To those who looked closely at the party's performance since April, the message was clear: Hitler had peaked. He would now have to try again to use his substantial electoral mandate to persuade Papen, and ultimately Hindenburg, to appoint him chancellor and rule by presidential decree. Given that they badly needed parliamentary backing for their emergency decrees, a deal might be possible. On 5 August, Hitler met with General Kurt von Schleicher, now minister of defence. Eight days later the two of them were joined by Papen and Hindenburg. They were unwilling to offer Hitler more than the vice-chancellorship, in return for the which the NSDAP would have become part of the governing coalition, a poisoned chalice for him. He refused 'to join a government which we do not lead'.[45] No agreement was reached. Hindenburg was adamant: he could not, 'before God, before his conscience and the Fatherland' hand over the entire power of government to a party like the NSDAP, which was 'so biased in its attitude to those who thought differently'.[46] He later made these sentiments public, much to the fury and embarrassment of the NSDAP. Hitler was still on the outside looking in, and later that day he withdrew to the Obersalzberg to reflect on his options.

Within the NSDAP itself, Hitler's first priority was the management of expectations. The most critical moment for any movement, to adapt Tocqueville, is when it is on the verge of success or appears to be. That is the time when discipline frays, and pent-up emotions rise to the surface. Just before the July vote, perhaps sensing that the electoral tide would not yet carry him as far forward as he wished, Hitler stressed the need for patience. What did 'three or four or ten years' matter in the 'grand sweep of German history', Hitler asked. 'If a great project was being accomplished,' he continued, 'then it is better it arrives at its goal in five or ten years' time' rather than 'prematurely compromising a good cause'. To settle for the mere trappings of power, Hitler argued, would be a betrayal of the party mission. He was fighting, he averred, 'not for ministerial posts or [parliamentary] seats', but 'for the political power in Germany'. 'I do not know whether we will reach our goal today,' he had said then, but if not, 'then in ten or twenty years', because 'the youth belongs to us and therefore also the future'.[47] This kind of theorizing in distant time frames was typical for Hitler.

By early August 1932, however, words were no longer enough for many party faithful, especially the SA. They wanted rewards for their years of sacrifice, and were frustrated both by the failure to win an overall majority in July and by the collapse of the subsequent negotiations with Papen.[48] Some now demanded immediate revolutionary action to seize power. Hitler was well aware of their grievances because he asked Röhm to distribute a questionnaire among the SA rank and file.[49] Others, such as Gregor Strasser, called for compromises to enter into a coalition government. Both tendencies were a major threat to Hitler's strategy and authority. He was seriously embarrassed by a brutal murder in Potempa in August 1932, when the SA stamped an unemployed communist to death in front of his family.[50] The SA were also increasingly brawling with the Stahlhelm and other right-wing groups, complicating Hitler's relations with the mainstream right. The July election result had shown that the SA were a liability among voters. Hitler told the SA to disperse for a fortnight on 13 August, the same day as his failed meeting with Papen and Hindenburg.

At around this time, Hitler suffered another personal blow. Since the suicide of Geli Raubal, he had brooded over his loss. When Ferdinand Liebermann made a bust of her, he was so moved that his eyes filled with tears.[51] Later in the year, Hitler made a brief visit to Geli's grave in Vienna. This did not stop Hitler from 'pining' for a new woman.[52] Two of those he showed most interest in, Helene Hanfstaengl and Magda Goebbels, were married. It may be that he cultivated the connection precisely because they were spoken for. Hitler enthused openly to Goebbels about his wife, 'whom he admires very much and considers to be a most beautiful, kind and intelligent woman'.[53] He may also have had a dalliance with the daughter of the *Gauleiter* of Kurhessen, Karl Weinrich.[54] The only permanent relationship he established, however, was with Eva Braun. Hitler was deeply shocked when she tried to commit suicide in the autumn of 1932.[55] He rushed to the hospital with flowers. She recovered quickly and, unlike with Geli Raubal, there was no public scandal. In public, Hitler continued to describe himself as a 'bachelor'.[56]

It was clear that Hitler's main enemy lay on the right. In order to destabilize Papen, and head off the prospect of a conservative coup, Hitler now turned up the rhetoric against the conservative 'cabinet of the barons'. He also lambasted the 'bourgeois' – a term of abuse in his lexicon – parties, organizations and newspapers. Three days after his catastrophic meeting with Hindenburg, Hitler attacked the 'bourgeois reactionaries' who were pursuing narrowly 'class and corporate' interests.[57] Hitler reiterated the revolutionary and anti-capitalist credentials of Nazism and denied being a mere 'drummer' for the conservative establishment. When Papen announced new emergency decrees in Münster at the end of August, which were welcomed by business for offering tax relief but little direct work creation, he was battered by the Nazi press. Hitler needed to demonstrate the illegitimacy and unsustainability of the Papen government by showing its complete lack of popular and parliamentary support. 'One can perhaps govern without the Reichstag,' he remarked pointedly in late August 1932, 'but one cannot govern without the people'; no government, in fact, could survive, he said, without a 'living connection to the people'.[58] Hitler had also come to the view that he would have to unbolt Hindenburg himself from the presidency. To do this, Hitler approached some of the other Weimar parties, who were equally concerned about Papen's intentions. Right at the end of August, just after Hindenburg had finally refused Nazi demands, he met with Göring, Röhm and Goebbels in secret conclave.[59]

Contact was established with the Catholic Centre Party, who were hostile to the Nazis ideologically but conceded Hitler's electoral mandate and feared Papen's 'dictatorship of the master class'.[60] A black-brown coalition in the Reichstag, however improbable for other reasons, was mathematically possible. Negotiations were begun on 30 August 1932. Hitler's aim was to undermine Papen further and to prevent the Centre Party from backing or tolerating a coup designed to keep the Nazis out of power. The Centre Party agreed in principle to support Hitler as chancellor, subject to

Hindenburg's approval. On economic policy, they both rejected Papen's decrees. Hitler was determined to force new elections, and at a meeting of Nazi leaders on 8 September he prevailed over Gregor Strasser, who wanted to join or at least tolerate a Schleicher cabinet.[61] 'Hitler is now going for broke,' Goebbels noted. 'Hindenburg must be deposed by the Reichstag. An audacious plan.'[62] Hitler now seized the opportunity to bring Papen down. When the communists proposed a vote of no confidence in the government two days later, he instructed his deputies to support it. The Centre Party and the Social Democrats joined in. The government suffered a disastrous defeat by 512 votes to 42. Fatally damaged, Papen had no choice but to set a date for fresh elections in early November. Hitler would get another chance at an overall majority.

Meanwhile, Hitler sought to keep the party, and especially the SA, on a leash. Morale was low. 'SA in depression,' Goebbels noted.[63] He and others yearned for an open struggle against 'the system'. For now, however, Hitler was telling them to wait it out. In the place of revolutionary action, he preached attentism. Throughout the autumn and the rest of the year, he invoked the rhetoric not only of endurance but of inevitability. 'I will not sell out the party for some sort of title,' he averred, 'I will fight on! One year, two years, [or even] three years.' His great 'rival', Hitler pointed out, was eighty-five, whereas he was forty-three, and healthy. Convinced that 'destiny' was on his side, Hitler was confident that 'it will eventually be our turn', adding, 'I will not give in.' Hitler was now engaged in a war of attrition, in which he banked on an electoral breakthrough, a change of heart by Hindenburg and his entourage, or simply outlasting his opponents. This was a very different Hitler from the panicked adventurer of 1923. In late 1932, he showed himself to have nerves of steel. 'Today we need only one thing,' he told the NSDAP Gautag, 'and that is nerves. We must keep our nerve and not yield.'[64]

In the meantime, Hitler began to prepare the movement for power. Goebbels was promised control of propaganda and education. 'We discussed problems of the seizure of power,' Goebbels reported of one long nocturnal session. 'We talked through the whole question of the education of the people,' he wrote. 'I will get schools, universities, film, radio, theatre, [and] propaganda.' This was an enormous brief. 'The national education of the German people,' Goebbels wrote, 'will be placed in my hands.'[65] In early September 1932, Hitler established the 'Military Political Office' (Wehrpolitisches Amt) of the NSDAP. Noting that Germany would need to regain its 'external' military security and re-establish its 'internal' capacity for defence, Hitler claimed that the German people expected 'a corresponding participation in the building up of territorial defence' by the party. To this end, Franz Ritter von Epp, a Bavarian war veteran and Nazi Party Reichstag member, was charged with laying down 'the principles . . . which should be decisive for the integration of the armed forces into the state'.[66] When the time came, Hitler and the movement would be able to hit the ground running.

In the autumn of 1932, Hitler threw himself into the new Reichstag election campaign.[67] He fought on multiple fronts, against his enemies: the 'Berlin Jewry, gentlemen's club, [and] bourgeois parties'.[68] The source of Germany's economic woes, he continued to argue, was political, the external subjection of the Reich due to its internal weakness. 'Germany is sick,' Hitler claimed, 'Germany's economy is collapsing', but 'only because her political power is collapsing.' Defeat, he argued, had led to reparations and debt-slavery which caused the misery confronting Germany on a daily basis. Indeed, Hitler took credit for having predicted all this even during the economically prosperous years of the Weimar Republic. 'This is the economic disintegration of the German nation which I predicted,' he said, 'but only because I did not allow myself to be distracted by so-called booms from the fact that when politics collapses, the economy must collapse with it.'[69]

Since politics was the problem, politics was also the solution. 'First you must banish German divisions,' he claimed, 'and then you can banish German deprivation.' For this reason Hitler called a few days before the vote for a 'People's Community' which would 'slowly' reconcile Germans 'across all professions, classes [and] all confessional divides'. Central to the whole project, finally, was tackling the Jewish question. Compared to the first nine months of the year, there was a perceptible increase in Hitler's anti-Semitic rhetoric, reflecting the widening gulf with the old elites. Some of this was directed against 'Jewish-international Bolshevism', but most of it was targeted at the capitalist clique supposedly supporting Papen. Thus Hitler repeatedly denounced the government's economic programme as written 'in its essential parts by the Jew Jakob Goldschmidt [the former director of the Darmstadt Bank]'. 'Either the German people escapes the clutches of the Jews,' he warned, 'or it will decay.'[70]

In a remarkable 'open letter' to Chancellor Papen, Hitler rejected short-term domestic 'reforms'. The 'supreme duty of a true statesman,' he argued, was 'the improvement of the blood of the people's body politic'. The problem, Hitler said, was that Germany's 'blood values' had been 'spoiled within short periods of time', but could only be 'improved over longer periods'. This was why the lack of living space was so fatal. Hitler now reprised the link between space and race, between *Lebensraum* and standard of living which had informed his thinking since the mid 1920s. He spoke again of the desperate need to address the tension between the living space currently 'allotted' to the German people and what it needed on the strength of its 'numbers', 'blood-based capabilities' and the 'resulting cultural requirements and [expectation] of a general living standard'.[71] The two possible internal solutions, namely exports ('the sending-out of German work capacity as goods') or emigration ('the deportation of the German workforce as emigrants') either did not work, in the case of exports, or was unacceptable, in the latter case. Once again, Hitler was offering the German people a way out of their domestic travails through external territorial expansion, in effect through a war of aggression.

Throughout the campaign, Hitler confronted the establishment, rejecting the notion that he was a mere 'drummer' for the old elites. He cast himself as the defender of the Weimar constitution against the reactionary and putschist tendencies of Papen and his cronies. 'According to the imperial constitution,' he insisted, 'I am legally entitled to be entrusted with the government.' He noted pointedly that while the NSDAP had been persecuted for more than a decade on account of its alleged illegality, it was now Papen who had abandoned the constitution. In an allusion to the Bourbons, he lampooned Papen and his men as 'restoration politicians, who have learned and forgotten nothing'; he spoke of the 'Hugenberg-Papen Reaction'. Playing to the populist gallery, Hitler professed himself 'against the Junker domination and chimney barons' and 'for the Lower Saxon farmer and worker'. Hitler also attacked the 'bourgeois parties', which he lumped in together with 'Berlin Jewry'. He made fun not only of 'bourgeois politicians' and 'bourgeois flags', but the whole 'bourgeois mentality'. In case anybody had not got the message, Hitler concluded that the German people 'must logically be led out of bourgeois concepts as much as out of the Marxist world of ideas'.[72] As if to underline his determination to break the bourgeois mould, the NSDAP and KPD engaged in a symbolically important joint transport strike on 2 November 1932, just days before the vote.

Finally, Hitler rounded on his internal critics. In mid October 1932, he announced that he refused to be a 'beautification minister' for another presidential cabinet, which would be intended 'not to allow him work but to shut him up'. Three days later, Hitler announced that he had no intention of taking on the post of interior minister, as that would have given political cover to the government's plan to suppress 'the masses'. He said that he had 'not got on the train' on 13 August at the failed meeting with Hindenburg 'because I had no intention of getting out again a few months later'. 'I will not on principle get into any train,' he continued, 'which is heading in a completely different direction from my own, or which I know will be derailed.' 'When we take power,' Hitler vowed, 'then we will keep it.' 'Whoever marches into the capital,' he laid down, 'must stay there.'[73] Hitler could not have been clearer: once in power, he had no intention of ever giving it up.

So Hitler tore around the country once again, cajoling, motivating and upbraiding in a punishing schedule of speeches. Between 11 October and 5 November he undertook his fourth 'flight over Germany'. There was, however, no triumphant progression towards an inevitable takeover of power. 'On [our] journeys through the Reich,' his press secretary Otto Dietrich recalled not long after, 'we sensed despite all sympathy and affection the inner reservations of dismissive or agitated national comrades', and 'we saw next to greeting hands, clenched fists and faces contorted with hatred'.[74] By mid October 1932, in fact, there were unmistakable signs of popular fatigue and disillusionment with the Nazis. When Hitler spoke at the great Congress Hall at Nuremberg, he failed to fill it: the 10,000 listeners who turned up were substantially fewer than on previous visits earlier in the year.[75]

When the results came in on 6/7 November 1932, they were a huge disappointment but not a complete surprise. The NSDAP had lost some 2 million votes and 34 seats; the communists had made substantial gains. On 8 November, the same day that FDR swept to victory in the US presidential election, Hitler called a meeting of Nazi leaders in Munich to discuss next steps. Strasser repeated his demand that the NSDAP join a presidential cabinet. Hitler remained firm. He was convinced that the other side would crack first. Relations between him and Strasser, already very strained, deteriorated further. A day later, Hitler rejected Papen's renewed offer of the vice-chancellorship. The negotiations dragged on. Towards the end of the month Hindenburg met Hitler again, and indicated that he would accept him as chancellor if he secured a parliamentary majority, which was no concession at all, as he was unlikely to secure one, and did not need Hindenburg if he did. At every turn Strasser urged compromise, and on a number of occasions it seemed as if Hitler might do so. Right at the end of the month, however, he announced to a meeting of the Nazi leadership in Weimar, over Strasser's strenuous objections, that he would hold out for the chancellorship itself.[76]

There was a perceptible shift in Hitler's strategy after the November vote. He now effectively gave up hope of a purely electoral path to power. An internal NSDAP analysis of the election results suggested that the party had maximized its vote, that 'it must not come to another election', and that there was 'nothing more . . . to be done with words, placards and leaflets. Now we must act!'[77] There were many who saw this as an argument for revolutionary measures, but not Hitler, who dismissed such talk as suicidal, He concentrated instead on a narrower front, that is, persuading or browbeating Hindenburg to let him govern by emergency decree.[78] 'I was with Hitler late into the night,' Goebbels noted, and he spoke of 'a rejection of the parliamentary solution' and 'demanded a presidential solution for us as well'.[79] He was no longer objecting to the use of emergency powers as such, but argued that they should be based on the 'sustainable part of the people', in other words the NSDAP. This demand was rejected by Hindenburg and his chief secretary Meissner on the grounds that it would lead to a dictatorship by Hitler. 'The old man' had not budged since the summer. Hitler was stymied again.

Despite his pressing domestic preoccupations in the second half of 1932, Hitler never ceased to think about the crucial international context to events in Germany. He sought to break up the circling coalition by developing an alternative global vision for Germany and Anglo-America. In an interview with the *New York American* conducted by Karl von Wiegand he called on 'the big powers of the Western World to combine under a "world economic dictatorship" to stave off the growing power of Russia, China, India and the east'. Hitler wanted the western powers – of which he named America, England, Germany, France, and Italy – to agree to deny their competitors the 'machinery' and 'technical experts' they needed to develop their economies. 'Once these countries with their low wages and low standard of living become industrialized,' he warned, 'then the Western industrial nations will be economically destroyed.' Hitler ruled out visiting America himself for now – 'takes too long'[80] – at least until there was a regular passenger airline connection.

On 2 December, Hindenburg appointed Schleicher chancellor.[81] He planned to rely on the army, if necessary, to keep order internally, to stimulate employment through work-creation schemes, and to secure the prestige victory of German equality in armaments on the international stage. He also hoped to broaden the slender parliamentary base of his administration by winning over the Nazis through the wavering Gregor Strasser. Hitler was alarmed on several counts. Firstly, the threat of a conservative coup which would shut him out of power indefinitely was now greater than ever. Secondly, he feared that an active foreign policy would provoke a pre-emptive strike by France and Poland. Two days after Schleicher came to power, Hitler wrote to the Reichswehr commander in exposed East Prussia, Walther von Reichenau, that he thought that Germany was already 'in the middle of a new encirclement policy, if not at its completion', in which France and Poland had the Reich in a vice grip. In this context, 'the theoretical acceleration of the German rearmament' was the 'worst' possible thing one could do. The most dangerous period after winning the right to rearm would be the immediately 'following period, because theoretical equality had to be followed by practical, technical and organizational rearmament'. 'If there were ever grounds for a preventive war,' he continued, 'then in this case', 'an attack by France on Germany' was to be expected. Besides, a military-backed putsch, perhaps involving some element of a Hohenzollern restoration, might itself precipitate an intervention by outside powers.[82]

The most immediate threat posed by Schleicher, however, was to the unity of the NSDAP. Strasser was on the verge of open revolt unless Hitler settled for the general's terms. A day after Schleicher's appointment, the two met in Berlin. There is no evidence that Schleicher planned to divide the party, which would have been pointless, as the breakaway faction could only provide him with limited parliamentary cover. Instead he wanted to use Strasser as a lever to shift the NSDAP as a whole.[83] Sharp words were exchanged at a meeting in the Berlin Kaiserhof on 6 December.[84] Hitler was now under the greatest pressure he had been under since the party struggles of the mid to late 1920s. Money was short. There was a large turnover of membership in the party and SA, but a growing net outflow. Hitler also seemed to be losing his charismatic touch. Attendances at speeches were down and on one occasion during the Thuringian election campaign in early December 1932, when he spoke more briefly than usual, people began to leave early,[85] something previously unheard of. That campaign went badly for the NSDAP. To add to his woes, a disaffected functionary from the Franconian Party, Hans Sauer, published a devastating critique of Gauleiter Julius Streicher in December 1932.[86] Then on 8 December, there was a bombshell: Strasser resigned, together with Gottfried Feder. Morale plummeted. 'Trouble and money worries,' Goebbels noted the following day, 'it is always the same.'[87] The NSDAP seemed as far from power as they had been at the start of the year.

Once again, Hitler held his ground. He immediately assembled his senior officials and Reichstag deputies in Berlin to ensure their loyalty. Strasser was condemned as a traitor who had stabbed the party in the back. His bureaucratic empire was broken up: Robert Ley received the leadership of the party organization, Goebbels was assigned 'the education of the people', and agrarian matters were hived off as well. In this way, Hitler implicated other party stakeholders in the purging of the Strasser faction.[88] 'Strasser is isolated,' Goebbels noted with satisfaction, adding that he was 'a dead man'.[89] Hitler remained adamant that he would only accept the chancellorship.[90] For the rest, Hitler tried to avoid being sucked into confrontation. In Franconia, he neither opposed nor supported Streicher, who managed to cling to power there. It was typical Hitler:

decisive, radical action in some quarters, tergiversation in others. Once again, the crisis had been contained. Like his brother, Gregor Strasser had ultimately succeeded only in blowing himself up, and not Hitler along with the entire party. Within the NSDAP, the last barrier to Hitler's absolute power had now fallen.

The party crisis prompted Hitler to reflect on the structure of the movement and issue new guidelines. Hitler was well aware of the dangers of over-governing.[91] Some sort of bureaucracy was needed. The danger, he warned, was that the Germans would indulge in their propensity to over-administrate. 'The German is too inclined to succumb to the error,' he noted, 'to see in [the party] organization a field for pedantic and mechanical work.' Instead, he demanded that 'one should not organize mechanically what one *can*, but only that which one *must* organize'. The main point was that one should avoid 'building a top-down schematic organization', but rather 'build up gradually' a 'leadership apparatus' from 'below'. This would enable the party to weed out unqualified 'careerists' and promote the tested and talented. Here Hitler articulated a governing style which was to characterize the Reich as a whole after the assumption of power.

Hitler did not use the opportunity to establish total control, only his absolute authority. To be sure, the opening sentence of his first of two memoranda on the reform of the movement stated unambiguously that the 'basis of the political organization is loyalty'. From this he deduced the need for 'obedience'. Yet Hitler also knew that the movement depended on the goodwill and creativity, rather than just the blind conformity, of its members. 'Constant supervision,' he argued, 'gradually destroys the authority of every agency' by insulting the 'honour' of officers and sapping their 'initiative'. For this reason, Hitler called for leaders to be given 'greater room for manoeuvre'. The *Gauleiter*, in particular, were expected 'to make independent judgements' in 'hundreds and thousands of questions'.[92] At the end of the document there was a brief concession to participatory structures, when Hitler referred to a future 'little senate of the party' whose task it would be 'to discuss important party issues' in committees or 'plenary' session. Nothing more was heard of this idea, however.

Despite the failure of his overtures to Strasser, Schleicher continued to pursue an understanding with Hitler. Hindenburg, however, still refused point-blank to countenance Hitler as chancellor, who in turn would not accept a lesser office. Hitler moved to end the dispute in Franconia. Holding his nose, he backed Streicher over the SA, whose leader backed down but revolted again at the end of the month. Moreover, although Strasser had been ousted, and founded no breakaway organization, he still retained a strong and sullen following in the larger cities. Money was so short that

Göring sent an emissary to the chargé d'affaires in the American Embassy to explore whether the party might raise a loan in the United States.[93] Frustration mounted further.

As the month drew to a close, Hitler steadied Goebbels. 'We must remain stubborn,' the latter wrote in his diary after their meeting, and 'study Roman, Prussian and British history to see how something like this is done'.[94] Hitler had gone into 1932 with great hopes, but he now spent a miserable Christmas and New Year. Wherever he looked there was ill-feeling, disappointment and reproach. Unlike many, Hitler had no family to fall back on. He missed Geli in ways that Eva Braun could not compensate for. 'The Christmas celebration,' Hitler wrote to Winifred Wagner, 'has been only a feast of mourning for me for two years', and 'I cannot bring myself to be as I was before.' 'Unfortunately,' he continued, 'there are always new mountains to be overcome.'[95]

Hitler and the NSDAP appeared to have hit a wall. Hitler's New Year Proclamation struck a defiant but also forlorn note. 'The suggestion of the clever ones', he remarked sarcastically, that we might 'gradually prevail' from 'inside' the system and 'through the back door' was rejected.[96] To most observers this sounded like whistling in the wind. On 1 January 1933, the liberal *Frankfurter Zeitung* spoke for many when it announced confidently that 'The mighty Nazi assault on the democratic state has been repulsed.'[97]

Suddenly, Hitler's luck turned, partly because he made his good fortune by standing fast, and partly because his opponents woefully miscalculated. He threw himself into the election campaign in the tiny state of Lippe in order to regain lost momentum. Hitler was still running on empty: Otto Dietrich had to advance his own money to book a hall for electioneering purposes.[98] Lippe was classic Nazi territory: rural and Protestant, and as the British ambassador observed, Nazi efforts there had 'the magnetic attraction of a jazz band'.[99] The excellent result – a huge increase on the previous election, which had taken place in 1929 before the great gains of the following years – in no way reflected any broader surge in support for the NSDAP, but gave the impression of renewed dynamism. In mid January 1933, Hitler assembled his senior leaders and officials in Weimar, crushing all residual support for Strasser.

Meanwhile, the reactionary front around Hindenburg had begun to crack. On 4 January, Papen began a fresh round of negotiations with Hitler at the house of the Cologne banker von Schröder.[100] He hoped to use the Nazis to unbolt Schleicher from the chancellorship. Six days later, they met at the residence of Joachim von Ribbentrop, a wine salesman and Nazi sympathizer who had offered himself as an intermediary.[101] A few days after the Lippe result, Hindenburg was engulfed by the 'Osthilfe' scandal, in which several of his aristocratic associates were exposed as having embezzled funds intended to help struggling agrarians in East Elbia. The DNVP leader, Alfred Hugenberg, met with Hitler on 17 January; his confidant Reinhold Quaatz remarked that 'he seemed to have come to terms with Hitler without the understanding being perfect'.[102] Likewise, there was movement on Hindenburg's side. He still rejected 'Hitler as the chancellor of a presidential cabinet, because he demanded [control of] the Reichswehr, wanted [to introduce a] dictatorship and was a fantasist', but on 21 January, Meissner thought that the president 'would perhaps be won over to a chancellorship of Hitler if he secured a majority to pass an enabling law'.

In a fulminating speech at the Berlin Sportpalast on 22 January 1933, Hitler's new confidence was palpable. Victory, he predicted, would go not to the infallible, but to those 'who make the fewest mistakes'.[103] Two days later, he met yet again with Papen, Frick and Göring at Ribbentrop's house and it was agreed that Hitler would be recommended to Hindenburg at the head of a right-wing cabinet. Three days after that, Hitler conferred with Hugenberg, who eventually came aboard. So did Franz Seldte, the head of the Stahlhelm. He, Papen and the rest of the plotters believed that they could control Hitler, continuing to govern in the old fashion while hiding behind the electoral mandate of the NSDAP. At a meeting with Hitler Hugenberg resisted giving Nazis control of the Interior Ministry, but Papen overruled him.[104] Göring assured Meissner that Hitler would respect not only the constitutional rights of the president, but also his supreme command of the armed forces.[105] Schleicher tried to head off the danger by dissolving the Reichstag and calling fresh elections, or at least threatening to do so, but there was no appetite for that in Hindenburg's circle. His position hopeless, Schleicher resigned on 28 January 1933. That same day, Hindenburg, Meissner and Papen reluctantly agreed to a Nazi-led government, with the strongest possible balancing conservative participation within and outside the cabinet.

The democratic parties were still more worried about an authoritarian dictatorship under Papen or Schleicher than they were about Hitler's imminent appointment as chancellor. The head of the Bavarian People's Party, Fritz Schäffer, seems to have offered Hitler his backing, and that of his fellow Catholic Centre Party, for a cabinet led by him. If so, he apparently declined on the grounds that he did not want to be dependent on them.[106] On Sunday, 29 January Hitler and Göring met Papen in the Wilhelmstrasse. The outlines of a deal were now clear. Hitler would become chancellor, Papen vice-chancellor and commissar for Prussia, while Göring would get the Prussian Ministry of the Interior. Hitler also demanded a new election so that he could secure a majority for an enabling act. Separately, Hitler reassured Schleicher via an intermediary that he had no objection to having him as defence minister. A day later, Hitler and Papen met at the latter's apartment in Berlin. He persuaded Duesterberg to let Seldte join the cabinet, thus securing Stahlhelm support. He gave his word of honour that there would be no changes to the cabinet even after fresh elections; there was also an expectation that he would try to bring the Centre Party into the government, or at least secure their acquiescence. Hitler feared to the last that Papen would back out, or that the president would maintain his veto.

On 30 January 1933, Hindenburg appointed Hitler chancellor.[107] Göring's securing of the post of Prussian interior minister crucially gave him control over the all-important Prussian police. Werner von Blomberg, the adviser to the Geneva disarmament conference, became Reichswehr minister; Schleicher was sidelined. Over Hugenberg's objections, Hitler achieved his demand for another and final election to gain Reichstag backing for an enabling law. His enemies had blinked first, having convinced themselves that, as Hugenberg put it, 'we are containing Hitler'.[108] Papen, the ultimate author of this strategy, was particularly bullish. 'You are mistaken,' he told one critic, 'we have hired him for our act.'[109] 'What is your problem,' he asked another critic. 'I have the confidence of Hindenburg' so that within two months 'we will have pressed Hitler so hard into the corner that he squeaks'.[110] Thanks to their weakness and miscalculation, the conservatives let Hitler in through the back door when his waning electoral appeal was bolting the front entrance ever more firmly against him. There were no more mistakes to make. Some regretted their actions almost immediately. 'I've just committed the greatest stupidity of my life,' Hugenberg supposedly remarked the day after Hitler's appointment, 'I have allied myself with the greatest demagogue in world history.'[111]

It was an astonishing and fateful achievement. Against all the odds, Hitler had hung on until all others, including some in his own party, had given up or given way. He called Schleicher's bluff over Strasser, the threatened dissolution of the Reichstag and new elections. Hitler rejected all compromise, but he did not, in the end, overdo it. Hitler was not infallible, but he indeed made the fewest mistakes. He settled for just enough, securing not so much power itself as the power to achieve power.

PART FOUR

Mobilization

The first four years of the Third Reich were characterized by Hitler's frenetic mobilization of German society. This involved the progressive removal of restraints on his authority and the 'coordination' of all sectors of German society and politics. It led to a 'battle of production', that is, the economic and agricultural mobilization of the country in support of re-armament and autarchy. It also involved a 'battle of consumption', in which the regime sought to match the cultural and economic appeal of western modernity. In parallel with all this, Hitler embarked on a long-term project of racial regeneration, designed – as he saw it – to eliminate the negative and accentuate the positive in the German *Volk*. Its ultimate aim was to 'lift' the Germans onto a higher racial plane where they could co-exist – and if necessary compete – with Anglo-America. Throughout this period, there was a fundamental tension in Hitler's timeline. On the one hand, he believed that the racial regeneration of Germany would take decades if not centuries, and could only be completed long after his own death. On the other hand, Hitler expected that the Reich would need to be ready for conflict within eight to ten years. By the end of this period, this tension between the racial and the diplomatic clocks was becoming ever more apparent.

10
The 'Fairy Tale'

For Hitler and the NSDAP, his appointment as chancellor was a moment of pure euphoria. In the late morning of 30 January 1933, Hitler was received by Hindenburg. Shortly after, he held a victory party in the Kaiser-hof Hotel. In the course of the day, Hitler issued a proclamation calling upon the party to stand by him as he tackled the 'massive' task ahead.[1] In the late afternoon, he convened his first cabinet meeting. The day concluded with a torchlight parade by the SA through Berlin, watched by Hitler and Hindenburg from separate windows in the Chancellery. These celebrations were broadcast by all German radio stations, with one significant exception; of this, more presently. 'Am I dreaming or am I awake?' Hess wrote to his wife the next day, describing how he was sitting in the office of the new chancellor in the Imperial Chancellery on the Wilhelmsplatz, while ministerial bureaucrats approached silently on plush carpets to bring documents to Hitler. Outside, the crowd sang the national anthem and shouted '*heil*'. Hess could hardly believe that 'what [he] had not thought possible to the last moment' was now 'reality'.[2] The *Gauleiter* of Swabia, Karl Wahl, recalled how he was overcome by tears of emotion.[3] 'Hitler is chancellor,' Goebbels wrote in his diary, 'it is like a fairy tale.'[4]

Over the coming years, this sense of enchantment spread to what was probably the majority of the German population.[5] The process of electoral seduction, which had never claimed more than 37 per cent of the votes in free and fair contests, now continued with all the resources of the state at Hitler's disposal. In an incessant round of speeches, parades, congresses and other events, he relentlessly wooed the German people, and they – by and large – submitted to his advances. The regime's claim that Germany had united solidly behind the 'Führer' was exaggerated, but essentially true.[6]

For many others, 30 January 1933 was the beginning of a nightmare. They wept tears of a different sort at Hitler's victory. Within hours, SA squads fanned out across the country to arrest and beat leftists, Jews and, to a lesser extent, Catholics and conservatives as well. Over the next weeks and months, a brutal, and increasingly efficient, terror apparatus sprang into action. Thousands were incarcerated in basements and warehouses and often subject to severe mistreatment. There were many murders. Organized labour was crushed; the trade unions soon abolished. Much of the repression was conducted through the politicized regular court system rather than the extrajudicial security apparatus.[7] Violence was thus at the heart of the Nazi regime from the very beginning.[8] To be sure, there was widespread complicity and cooperation with the regime, with denunciations as important as surveillance.[9] Despite all the consensus, however, the Third Reich would not have functioned without coercion. Hitler had taken office legally enough, but he was to consolidate and retain power illegally.

The challenge facing Hitler at the start of his rule was massive, both at home and abroad. The chancellorship did not give him absolute power, only the power to achieve that power. For now, he was still 'boxed in' by the old elites. The old civil service was still fundamentally sceptical.[10] His 'seizure of power' could only take place in stages.[11] In the short term, Hitler feared a military-backed conservative coup.[12] He also worried about the threat of a communist revolt, or at least of a general strike.[13] If he got through the first few weeks, Hitler would need to assert his control within the government, and to co-opt, sideline or eliminate both the Centre Party and his conservative coalition partners. More generally, Hitler would have to win over and mobilize major institutions and sectors such as the army and industry. He also needed to dismantle German federalism, especially in Bavaria, whose state radio had refused to broadcast the celebrations on 30 January 1933. Abroad, his immediate worry was to keep 'international Jewry' at bay and to fend off the threat of a preventive war waged by France and Poland before Germany was ready.

In the medium term, Hitler wanted to prepare the Reich for armed conflict, both physically and mentally.[14] On Hitler's reckoning, this required the elimination of the Jews from German national life, the removal of all other supposedly harmful elements, the encouragement of allegedly positive racial strands within the German people, and the 'gathering' of as many racially sound Germans into the new Reich as possible. Hitler wanted to begin by restoring Germany's position in Europe and establish strong alliances, not only with sympathetic powers such as the Italy of Mussolini – his envoy Renzetti was summoned to the Chancellery on 30 January to witness the torchlight parade at Hitler's side – but especially with Britain. He also had his eye on the capture of *Lebensraum* in the east – that is, Russian lands beyond Poland – necessary in his view to enable Germany to survive any future blockade and to feed its surplus population.

The realization of these short- and medium-term aims required Hitler to lull his adversaries, at home and abroad, into a false sense of security. Often this took the form of deliberate deception. Hitler's first speech to the Reichsrat immediately after taking power suggested quite disingenuously that he intended to maintain the federal structure and spirit in Germany. He also frequently made speeches proclaiming his pacifist intent, or reassured foreign diplomats and visitors in private conversation. Sometimes, Hitler 'hid in plain sight', revealing his ultimate plans without provoking a storm of concern. On other occasions, however, Hitler was entirely frank, as he needed to be if he hoped to win western support for, or at least acquiescence in, his plans for territorial expansion in the east. Besides, the undisciplined behaviour of the Nazi rank and file, as well as some leaders, was such that the fundamental nature of the regime, the true extent of its hostility to Jews and its aggressive foreign policy were constantly on view or even being blurted out. The overall result was to lend to Hitler's intentions all the secrecy of a stage whisper, audible to everybody but the entirely or wilfully deaf (of which there proved to be many).

There was, in fact, nothing mysterious about Hitler's long-term aim, which had been public knowledge since the 1920s. This was to make the Reich one of the great world powers, not necessarily the sole or dominant one. Here his point of reference was the British Empire and, especially, the United States. The capture of *Lebensraum* in the east was not conceived of as a final showdown with the Jews or Slavs, but rather as a necessary measure to gain the critical territorial mass and resources to balance Anglo-America. It would also provide the necessary space for the racial elevation of the Germans into a position of parity with the Anglo-Saxons. In short, after taking power, Hitler sought to implement the programme which he had set out in general terms in numerous writings and speeches over the previous fourteen years.

If the content and sequencing of these aims were clear in 1933, at least to Hitler himself, his timetable was not. He was clearly in a hurry to achieve his short-term objectives, but the schedule for his medium- to long-term plans varied considerably. Sometimes, Hitler seems to have envisaged that Germany would be ready for a major war within a decade. On other occasions, he seems to have had a much longer timeframe in mind. What is clear is that Hitler expected the complete racial transformation of the German people to take generations, with a completion date well after his own death. For that reason, he seems to have wanted to avoid a confrontation with the British Empire and the United States if at all possible, or at least until the homogeneity and mental strength of the

German people were on a par with those of Anglo-America. In the end, of course, events took a different turn.

To the surprise of many, Hitler rose quickly to the challenge of government. Those who dealt with him during the first years of his chancellorship were impressed by his command of the issues. Hitler gripped the cabinet – which was full of experienced and hard-bitten rivals – from the start.[15] He made no attempt to monopolize proceedings and with a few exceptions refrained from launching into the kind of lengthy tirades which he famously indulged in later. Likewise, the military were astonished by the speed with which this ex-soldier from the ranks asserted his superiority over them at their first encounter only days after the takeover of power.[16] Photographs and footage from the time show a dapper man who appeared physically fit, trim and very much in charge. 'The chief is performing here with unbelievable authority,' Hess wrote to his wife the day after the appointment, 'and [his new] punctuality' was such that 'I have even decided to buy myself a watch', before adding: 'A new time period and a new division of time has begun.'[17]

In office, Hitler kept formal hours, at least to begin with, and even when he began to revert to earlier patterns, his overall level of commitment did not change. The total amount of time that Hitler 'worked', organizing repression and mobilization at home and the planning of aggressive war abroad, was considerable. His legislative programme was massive, and ran to thirty-three volumes before the outbreak of war.[18] Moreover, as we shall see, Hitler never really let go, even when he was supposedly relaxing on the Obersalzberg, watching films in his private cinema or being uplifted at Bayreuth. He worked so to speak 'from home',[19] but he was still working. Hitler was therefore in no sense a 'lazy' chancellor.[20]

Hitler's first moves were devoted to consolidating his grip on power in Germany. A few days after he was appointed chancellor, the 'Decree for the Protection of the German People' gave the government draconian powers to suppress the right to free assembly and political expression, at first used primarily against communists. The feared conservative coup and communist uprising never materialized; the only serious public protest was in the little Swabian town of Mössingen. Hitler increasingly wriggled out of the corset put in place by Papen. He could count on the collaboration of key figures in the army, especially the new Reichswehr minister, Werner von Blomberg, who supported his plans for total mobilization, and his head of the ministerial office, Walther von Reichenau,[21] with whom he had already been in contact before the takeover of power. The new foreign minister, Konstantin von Neurath, was less pliable, but he too had met Hitler before 1933, and the two men saw eye to eye if not on the ultimate goal then at least on the first steps. President Hindenburg himself, widely expected to act as a powerful restraint on Hitler, became his greatest supporter. They differed on some important issues, but their relationship grew more and more cordial.[22]

The Führer's next aim was to gain a working majority in the Reichstag. One method, which Hindenburg favoured, was to bring in the Centre Party. Hitler's negotiations with their leader, Monsignor Kaas, did not win the Catholics over, but he did manage to pin the blame for the failure of the discussions, and thus for the dissolution of the Reichstag, on them.[23] The other path was to win the Reichstag elections called on 1 February after the collapse of negotiations with the Centre Party; these were scheduled for early March. Hitler rallied the conservatives in the cabinet against the left by fighting the forthcoming election under the slogan 'Attack against Marxism'.[24] All this reassured President Hindenburg, from whom Hitler's authority still derived.

Throughout February and early March 1933, Hitler's principal domestic focus was on the Reichstag election. He now had the entire apparatus of central government at his disposal, including most public radio stations. The south German states of Bavaria and Württemberg were important exceptions. To Hitler's fury, the broadcast of one of his speeches was interrupted in Stuttgart by saboteurs; a war of words with the Land government of Dr Bolz followed.[25] In the rest of Germany, however, Hitler's dominance of the airwaves was pretty much complete. His radio broadcast of 2 February 1933, approved by the cabinet, was entitled 'Fourteen years of Marxism have ruined Germany'.[26] Hitler's fear of communism was real enough, but he hammed it up for electoral purposes. He did not want to ban the KPD immediately.[27] Hitler even suggested deferring repressive legislation so as to avoid thereby 'reducing' the 'communist threat' in the 'election campaign'.[28] The subordinate relationship of communism to capitalism was emphasized again during the Reichstag election campaign. 'Marxism,' one Nazi poster headlined, 'is the guardian angel of capitalism.'[29]

During the first weeks of his chancellorship Hitler evaluated every move in the light of its electoral implications and its potential impact on his political standing more generally. At a meeting of the 'Committee on Economic Policy' of the government, Hitler stressed that 'decisions' must be taken 'with regard' to their impact on the 'coming election campaign'.[30] For example, he supported a 'raising of the tax on department stores' as the 'most popular form of taxation', but suggested avoiding 'all detail' on the government's economic programme 'in electoral propaganda'. Hitler reminded the cabinet that the government needed 18 or 19 million votes.

'An economic programme that will meet the approval of such a large group of voters,' he remarked pointedly, 'does not exist in the whole world.'[31] Hitler was not always successful: his attempt to remove the charge for medications provoked such conservative hostility that he only managed to get it halved.[32] Otherwise, Hitler took the view that there should be no major initiatives before the elections. 'Reforms need time,' he explained, and could only be 'tackled once the people had decided for or against the government.'[33] The six weeks following the takeover of power were thus characterized by the signalling of intent rather than concrete measures.

On 3 February, Hitler set out his strategic vision to the Reichswehr leadership at their request.[34] He promised to crush 'pacifism', to strengthen the 'will to resist' and the 'extermination of Marxism root and branch'. More importantly, he promised that he would make no attempt to amalgamate the army and the SA. Hitler also argued that unemployment could only be tackled and the German peasant could only be 'saved' through an active 'settlement policy', which required an expansion of Germany's *Lebensraum*, which was 'too small'. He considered an economic solution – 'the attainment of new export possibilities' – but favoured 'the capture of new living space in the east and its ruthless Germanization'. One could only 'Germanize' territory, he insisted over and over, not the people living in it. These remarks were made in secret, but their principal content differed little from the thoughts Hitler had already elaborated in *Mein Kampf* and countless speeches before he took power. The timeline he had in mind was 'six to eight years in order to completely exterminate Marxism', after which 'the army would be ready to pursue an active foreign policy', namely 'the expansion of the living space of the German people', probably in the east. Significantly, Hitler expected that the following stage, the establishment of a 'completely healthy state', would take 'a period of 50–60 years',[35] by which time he himself would be long dead.

In public, Hitler sought to conceal his intentions in foreign policy, at least until he was ready to throw off the mask. His main fear was a Franco-Polish preventive war, and perhaps also a Franco-Russian alliance. 'The most dangerous time,' he told the Reichswehr chiefs only a few days after the takeover of power, 'is the period of the building-up of the Wehrmacht.' 'Then it will be clear,' he continued, 'whether France has statesmen.' If she did, Hitler went on, then she 'would not leave us time but fall on us, presumably with [her] eastern satellites'.[36] Hitler sought to head off the danger through a series of interviews with British, American and Italian journalists. In them, he emphasized the threat from Bolshevism and Soviet Russia. Hitler denied giving inflammatory speeches, and on the same day he addressed the military leaders about his expansionist plans he told a group of Anglo-American journalists that 'everyone who, like me, knows war, [also] knows what a cost it represents in resources'. Towards the end of February 1933, Hitler gave an interview to Louis Lochner of Associated Press in which he reassured the world that his proposed labour service was not a paramilitary force in disguise.[37]

Hitler's domestic policy was primarily designed to provide the means to implement his foreign policy programme. He told the cabinet a few days after the Reichswehr meeting that 'every publicly supported work-creation measure must be judged under the aspect of whether it is necessary' in order to give the German people back the capacity to defend themselves. For the benefit of those who had not got this message, which Hitler was to repeat ad nauseam over the next weeks, months and years, 'the chancellor underlined once again that the supreme principle over the next 4–5 years must be everything for the Wehrmacht'.[38] On 20 February, Hitler told a group of specially selected businessmen, some of them leaders of German industry, that he planned to use the mandate he expected from the March election to end parliamentary democracy in Germany for good, and crush the left.[39]

The burning of the Reichstag building on the evening of 27 February came as a serious shock to Hitler, and to many ordinary Germans. A Dutch communist drifter, Marinus van der Lubbe, was arrested that same night. What exactly happened is still unclear, but there can be no doubt that, whatever the role of individual Nazis, Hitler himself neither ordered nor knew of the deed in advance.[40] He was completely taken by surprise and seems genuinely to have believed the communists to be responsible.[41] Hitler responded with the draconian decree for the 'protection of the people and state'. This abolished the rights of assembly, freedom of the press, and of expression as well as increasing police powers of surveillance. Significantly, the legislation also suspended the autonomy of the federated states if they failed to guarantee public order, and conferred upon Hitler, rather than on the president, the right to impose imperial commissars on them. The main target may have been the Communist Party, which was now subjected to even greater repression, but the secondary objective was clearly to facilitate an attack on German federalism. Hitler now had an instrument to tackle the *Länder* and an argument – their failure to deal with the Marxist threat – for doing so.

In Bavaria, however, the federal authorities still held out. The Bavarian minister of the interior, Karl Stützel, refused to bow to demands to curb the anti-Nazi press.[42] In late February 1933, several weeks into Hitler's tenure, the acting chief minister, Dr Heinrich Held, vowed in an interview

with the *New York Times* that 'in keeping with the letter of the constitution, I shall defend Bavarian independence at all costs, even in the face of
force with which we may be confronted'.[43] The BVP leader Fritz Schäffer
even threatened to arrest any imperial commissar sent by the Nazis at the
Bavarian border.[44] With Held's connivance, Schäffer met with Crown
Prince Rupprecht to discuss the possibility of a Wittelsbach restoration to
forestall a Nazi takeover in Munich. Held was summoned to Berlin. There
was a heated discussion. Now the roles were reversed from their last
meeting in 1924. Hitler held all the cards. He warned Held that any
step towards a restoration of the monarchy would result in a 'serious
catastrophe'.[45] The plan collapsed when Hindenburg refused to
support it, vindicating Hitler's strategy of embracing the president.[46]

The Reichstag election of March 1933 took place in an atmosphere of
extreme intimidation, in which the instruments of government and the
Nazi Party organizations were deployed to telling effect. Thousands of SA
men were deputized as police officers in Prussia by Göring. Moreover,
Hitler now had the endorsement of Hindenburg. Hitler himself was elected
for the constituency of Oberbayern-Schwaben, his first and only Reichstag
seat, and the Nazi vote in Bavaria rose to its highest level yet. Even so, the
NSDAP fell short of the desired overall majority, securing nearly 44 per
cent of the vote. This meant that Hitler would continue to base his authority not on a popular mandate, but on the presidential powers conferred
by Hindenburg.

Once the votes were in, Hitler moved against his old enemy, German
particularism. 'What is required,' he told the cabinet, was 'an audacious
approach' to the relations between the Reich and the federal states, especially Bavaria.[47] He began with the smaller and weaker states, installing
an imperial commissar in Hamburg, followed by Bremen, Lübeck and
Hessen. Then he crushed Württemberg, the weaker of the two southern
German states. On 8 March, a Nazi *Reichsstatthalter* was installed in
Stuttgart, as well as in Baden, Saxony and Schaumburg-Lippe. That same
evening, Hitler finally decided to bite the bullet in Munich. 'This evening
we were all at the Führer's,' Goebbels noted in his diary. 'There it was
decided that it is now Bavaria's turn.'[48] This was not an easy decision, as
there were some within the party who feared considerable resistance in
Munich, no doubt recalling the fiasco of 1923.

Hitler, however, kept his nerve. He took personal charge of the negotiations with the BVP in Berlin, tellingly them bluntly that the election had
seen a repudiation of separatism and particularism.[49] Hitler also sent
Röhm to Munich to deliver an ultimatum. The BVP did not attempt a
Wittelsbach restoration, though Held initially resisted demands – backed

up by the threat of force from the SA – to appoint Ritter von Epp as *Reichsstaathalter* in Munich. He even gave instructions for the Bavarian police to be put in state of readiness. Heavily armed units took up positions in front of the Bavarian Landtag, the Foreign Ministry and the Ministry of the Interior, with instructions to open fire on the Nazis if necessary. Civil war seemed possible.[50] Ten years earlier, the Bavarian police had not hesitated to shoot; this time they were overawed by the SA and SS. On 9 March, Bavarian autonomy was extinguished; control of the police went over to Heinrich Himmler and Reinhard Heydrich. The French envoy to Munich was sent packing. Foreign representation in individual German federal states – and thus any potential interference – ceased. In due course, the flying of the traditional blue and white Bavarian colours was forbidden, even at the traditional *Oktoberfest*.[51] German federalism was dead.

It was a big moment for Hitler. He had imposed his will on an enemy which had defied him for more than a decade. It was also a watershed in German history. Hitler claimed that 'what had been desired and attempted' in vain 'over centuries' was 'now reality', namely 'the coordination of the political will of the federal states with the will of the nation'. He promised that he 'did not want to rape the federal states' but to give them 'the rank and the place' to which 'they were entitled by virtue of history and tradition'.[52] That same day, the old red, white and black imperial flag and the Nazi swastika replaced the Weimar colours of black, red and gold (or 'mustard', as its enemies called it contemptuously) as the state flag. Significantly, Hitler did not revert to the old flag of the Second Reich, which could soon only be shown on special occasions such as the funerals of soldiers from the former imperial army.

The first phase of the seizure of power was complete. Hitler's government controlled Germany not only from east to west, but also from north to south. On 13 March 1933, Goebbels was made Reich minister for people's enlightenment and propaganda. Shortly afterwards, Hitler appointed Schacht president of the Reichsbank. The second phase was about to begin.

Central to the next stage was the passage of an enabling law, which would grant Hitler the power to legislate without recourse to the Reichstag. He also expected this measure to strengthen Germany against the outside world. The key to this was winning over the Centre Party, which would give Hitler valuable political cover.[53] 'The acceptance of the enabling law by the Centre Party,' he told the cabinet, 'would lead to an increase of prestige abroad.'[54] Hitler, who was now domestically in a significantly stronger position, held out the prospect of a concordat between the new regime and the Catholic Church.[55] Fearing the left, under severe political and often physical pressure from the Nazis, the Centre Party buckled. Through a mixture of political skill and brute force, Hitler was now on the verge of what had eluded Brüning, Papen and Schleicher before him, which was to turn a presidential cabinet into a broadly based authoritarian regime with the backing of a parliamentary majority.

Hitler consecrated this burgeoning German unity with an opening ceremony for the new Reichstag in the garrison church of Potsdam. This event, which has gone down in history as 'The Day of Potsdam', was intended to suggest a synthesis between the old Prussian traditions and the young National Socialist movement. Hitler and Hindenburg's joint appearance was framed by old Prussian battle flags against the background of Frederick the Great's bronze sarcophagus. Seats were reserved for the Hohenzollerns. One contained the crown prince, a Nazi sympathizer, in the uniform of a colonel of the Death's Head Hussars; the place reserved for Wilhelm II was symbolically left empty, to suggest an emperor if not over the sea then at least beyond the Rhine in Holland. Catholic dignitaries rubbed shoulders with Protestants. The president delivered a speech invoking the glories of the Prussian past, especially its unification of the 'German tribes', and expressed the hope that it would serve as an example for the regeneration of Germany in present times. Hitler looked on in reverence, careful not to be seen to upstage the national treasure that was Hindenburg. With or without the consent of the older man, though, his charisma was already beginning to pass to the younger chancellor.[56] The rift between German conservatism and the Nazis was symbolically healed by the public handshake between Hitler and Hindenburg – immortalized by a photograph – immediately after the ceremony. It was Hitler's first major act of state choreography, which he had rehearsed incognito in the garrison church on the previous day.[57]

Once these opening ceremonies were over, the Reichstag returned to its temporary home in the Kroll Opera House to pass Hitler's enabling law.[58] This measure gave him the power to legislate without Reichstag approval. Hitler explained that he needed the powers in order to 'rebuild people and Reich' as well as 'win over the German worker for the national state'. Hitler's enduring concerns about German federalism, even after the co-ordination of Bavaria, came to the fore again when he warned that he would regard any attempt at a 'monarchic restoration' as an 'attack on the unity of the Reich' and 'would respond accordingly'. Turning to the most pressing issue of the day for most Germans, the economy, Hitler defined his two main economic tasks as the 'saving of the German farmer' and the 'integration of the army of unemployed into the production process'.

In order to achieve all this, Hitler argued, it was necessary to bring the interminable cycle of voting which had characterized the last years of the Weimar Republic to an end. Anxious to reassure critics worried that the proposed law would give Hitler unprecedented power, he stressed its limited and temporary character. There had, in fact, been many enabling laws in the course of the Weimar Republic,[59] but it should have been obvious, not least because Hitler had made no secret of his intentions in the past, that the Nazis would never voluntarily relinquish any power they were given.

Hitler was speaking to a largely captive audience. Together with the Centre Party, the Nazis and their conservative allies made up a majority of the Reichstag. The communists had been banned. The only voice of opposition came from the SPD deputies. Otto Wels, their chairman, gave an impassioned speech against the enabling law. Referring to the already intense wave of repression directed against his party, he announced in words that have since passed into legend that the Nazis could take their freedom but not their 'honour'. When Wels had finished, Hitler leaped up to deliver a withering response. He lambasted the SPD for not having launched a communard-style revolt against the Versailles settlement in 1919. 'It would have been equally possible,' he said, to have given their revolution 'the same elan and direction which France gave its rising in 1870.' It was, as ever, the international connections of the SPD and not their socialism which affronted Hitler. He attacked them for spreading 'untruths' about the situation in Germany, and the fact that they – allegedly – 'constantly tried to run down Germany abroad'. This mattered to Hitler, because he wanted to avoid giving neighbouring powers an excuse to intervene.

There was a widespread expectation on the left that Nazism would simply be a repeat of the Bismarckian anti-socialist repression, which the movement had weathered successfully. Hitler told Wels that this was not the case. 'Do not confuse us with the bourgeois world,' he warned, and he also counselled the SPD against the hope 'that their star might rise again'. In fact, Hitler warned, he was a very different proposition; there were no half measures for him. 'I do not want to make the mistake,' Hitler remarked menacingly, 'of just provoking enemies rather than destroying or reconciling them.' To the SPD rank and file he held out an olive branch. 'I will shake hands with anyone who is committed to Germany,' Hitler promised. But for the SPD leadership, the message was clear. 'You gentlemen,' Hitler hurled at Wels and his fellow deputies, 'are no longer needed.' Shortly afterwards, the enabling act passed with 441 votes in favour and 94 against, including that of Otto Wels. That same day it went through the completely Nazi-controlled Reichsrat unopposed and became law.

German democracy was not simply done to death by a small clique of men in smoke-filled rooms. It committed suicide under duress in public.

Over the next fortnight, Hitler legalized the destruction of German federalism with two 'laws for the coordination of the federal states with the Reich'. State legislatures were reconstituted on the basis of the proportion of each party (in so far as it still existed) had gained in the March Reichstag election. Their legislative powers were taken away and conferred upon the state governments, which in turn were to be appointed by the imperial commissars nominated by Hitler.[60] In Prussia, the largest state, Hitler took on the role of imperial commissar himself, and conferred the powers back to Göring, underlining where the source of authority lay. 'All power lies with the federal authority,' he told the assembled *Statthälter*, adding that 'it must be prevented that the centre of gravity of German life is ever again transferred to individual areas or even organizations', another swipe at the BVP.[61] All the switches, as the title of the laws suggested, were to be turned in the same direction. The Reichsrat was now defunct and was eventually abolished early in the following year. 'Coordination' was in a sense symbolic, since the state governments were by now all under Nazi control anyway, but it underlined Hitler's determination to create a unified polity from which all regional political diversity had been eliminated.

Pulling down hundreds of years of German tradition was one thing, putting something else in its place was quite another. It soon became clear that there was no clarity over what was to come next. Some, such as the minister of the interior, Wilhelm Frick, wanted to turn the Third Reich into a unitary state and rationalize the territorial asymmetry of the Reich into supposedly more sensible administrative units. Hitler was not so sure. He felt that some of the damage done by the traditional 'fragmentation' had been compensated by the NSDAP, which had 'never known regional associations', but was instead based on the '*Gau-system*', something which France had implemented.[62] In other words, the National Socialist *Gau* – whatever its medieval German etymological origin – was in Hitler's mind the new German equivalent to the French department. It was intended to represent a totally new principle of regional administration.

At the same time, Hitler was ambivalent about Frick's vision, in which there was, as he put it, 'a new current [which] wishes to clear away everything, to standardize everything, and to centralize everything across the Reich'. He urged caution. One would have to start from the facts of nature, and avoid behaving like a 'bear who batters the hermit to death in order to kill a fly'. He therefore laid down that 'the objective is to retain the existing construction so long as it is useful', and to change it so that 'in future the good is preserved and the useless is eliminated'. Here Hitler expounded a kind of National Socialist subsidiarity principle, which paralleled a very similar rule he had enunciated a year earlier for the NSDAP itself. 'One must not ask "what can be removed",' he explained, 'but what must be removed.' The key thing, Hitler remarked presciently, was that 'the particularism of the princes must not be replaced by the particularism of an ideology'. [63]

Hitler's real concern here was for the future, when the old guard had passed away, and there was a danger of falling back into bad old habits. 'After our departure', he predicted, there would be a 'shift' in the quality of leadership, which might lead to the 'separation' of parts of the Reich. Hitler clearly wanted to head off the danger that his new Reich would disintegrate, like that of Alexander or Charlemagne, into feuding successor states, thus refederalizing Germany. Avoiding such an outcome was a central part of his long-term programme. 'Posterity,' he reminded the *Reichsstatthalter*, 'will judge us by the final result' and not by 'the revolution' itself. Hitler did not quite put it this way himself, but he seems to have envisaged a Weberian shift from the largely charismatic rule of Führer and first-generation *Gauleiter* to a more legal and bureaucratic structure after his death. In the second generation, he suggested, the 'authority' of the party leadership would no longer be so 'firm', and a great deal would depend on the 'general tendencies' within the bureaucracy. This was why, Hitler argued, 'the construction [of the state]' would have to be sound so that the coherence of the unified national state could not be subverted. Hitler was thus under no illusion that the German tendency towards fragmentation had been banished by 'coordination'; transcending particularism would be a project of many generations.

By the spring of 1933, the German left had been largely eliminated. Next in line were Hitler's conservative allies. They shared many of his immediate internal and external aims, but in terms of style, background and world view the two were far apart. [64] The NSDAP presented itself as not only an anti-capitalist but also an anti-bourgeois party. Picking up Hitler's rhetoric before 1933, it lambasted the conservatives for their 'reactionary' nature and their 'class snobbery', [65] which stood in the way of the creation of a true 'People's Community'. The violence meted out to conservatives, though never quantitatively as significant as that experienced by the communists and Social Democrats, escalated from isolated incidents in early 1933 to a systematic campaign. On 7 May, the leader of the DNVP party caucus, Ernst Oberfohren – who had opposed Hugenberg's policy of cooperation with Hitler – was found shot dead in his apartment. The official verdict spoke of suicide, but it was probably murder. Senior DNVP members had their houses searched by the police, or were accused of corruption. Party meetings were broken up by the SA. All this reflected Hitler's growing view that the main internal challenge to his rule now came not from the German left more generally, but from the left inside the Nazi Party, and the German right in its many forms: federal, monarchic, aristocratic, clerical and conservative nationalist.

A network of camps was erected across the Reich. In late March 1933, the first prisoners were sent to Dachau outside Munich.[66] Most were leftists of one sort or another, but there were also some conservatives and Catholic Bavarian federalists. The two sons of Hitler's old adversary Heinrich Held were deemed 'no better than Jews' and placed in a punishment detail.[67] The purpose of these early ventures was to persecute the political rather than the (perceived) racial enemies of the regime. While Hitler was aware of the existence of British concentration camps in South Africa during the Boer War, and alluded to them on a number of other occasions, there is no evidence that these influenced the decision to set up Dachau and other places. There was no central coordination of the camp system at this stage,[68] and Hitler does not seem to have played a direct role in either the establishment or the running of the camps.

In the summer of 1933, Hitler moved against the remnants of the Weimar system. He proclaimed 1 May a national holiday, fulfilling a longstanding left-wing demand. The day after, he abolished the trade unions. Over time, the NSBO were amalgamated into the new German Labour Front, under Robert Ley, which was given the job of organizing German workers. On 22 June 1933, the SPD was banned. Two days later, under pressure, the DNVP disbanded itself. A day later, the Staatspartei, the former DDP, followed suit. The two Catholic parties, the Centre Party and the BVP, were the last to wind themselves up, under severe pressure, in early July. On 14 July a law specifically banned the establishment of new political parties.

That same month, after long negotiations, Hitler finally agreed a concordat with the Roman Catholic Church. This guaranteed the church freedom of worship and the right to levy church taxes and to run its own affairs. Catholic schools and theological faculties remained open. The secrecy of the confessional was not challenged. In return, new bishops were required to pledge an oath of allegiance to the Reich on taking office. Most importantly, the Vatican agreed to forbid clerics not just from involvement in political parties – an academic issue by now – but from any kind of political activity. Hitler's intention here was not just to tame the German Catholic milieu but to find a modus vivendi with the papacy as an international actor. It was as much an instrument of foreign as of domestic policy.[69]

If the last vestiges of German democracy had now been eliminated, this did not mean that Hitler's authority was absolute. The rule of law was by no means completely extinguished.[70] Some judges continued to hand down impartial sentences, such as the acquittal of a number of the defendants in the Reichstag Fire trial. This event, designed to showcase the new Germany and impale the communists, turned into a public relations disaster for Hitler. Moreover, Hindenburg opposed (in the end, unsuccessfully) some of Hitler's more extreme demands, such as the execution of Marinus van der Lubbe for what he considered treason but the president regarded as no more than an aggravated crime against property. Germany was, in effect, still a duumvirate headed by Hitler and Hindenburg and would remain so for another year.

Thanks to the enabling law, however, Hitler now had more than enough power to press ahead with his programme at home and abroad, so long as he retained Hindenburg's support. The main focus of his domestic programme was the closely connected questions of rearmament and reducing unemployment, which ran at 6 million people, some 34 per cent of the entire labour force.[71] In early April 1933, Hitler appointed the Nazi stalwart Fritz Reinhardt, who had written so passionately about the dangers of German emigration in the early 1930s, as state secretary in the Finance Ministry. Over the next few years, Reinhardt rolled out several programmes which bore his name designed to tackle the problem of unemployment and to provide labour for rearmament.[72] These aimed to generate employment through public works, especially major infrastructural projects, such as the long-planned construction of motorways, and direct support for housing repairs and renovations. The best way of getting the German people back to work, Hitler announced to an audience of motorway workers, was by 'setting the German economy in motion again' through 'monumental works'.[73] These programmes, and Hitler's vast expenditure on armaments, were largely paid for by Schacht's dubious 'MEFO bills', in effect a system of deferred payments, drawn on a front (state) company. The actual number of jobs thereby created seems to have been extremely modest; nor did they much boost business confidence, at least at first, but they did enable Hitler to change the broader narrative.[74]

No doubt in order to showcase the new mood, Hitler made a big fuss of the return of the List Regiment veteran Ignaz Westenkirchner from the United States in the autumn of 1933.[75] He had emigrated in 1928, the same year as Hitler's Second Book had warned about the exodus of Germans across the Atlantic, but had failed to make his way in Reading, Pennsylvania. Westenkirchner thus epitomized one of the problems Hitler was most concerned about. On being approached by his old comrade, the Führer paid for his passage home. Westenkirchner was given a job with the *Völkischer Beobachter* and pictures of him joshing with Hitler and Amann were published in various magazines and books.[76] The prodigal son had returned home. Not long afterwards, Hitler repeated the exercise when he covered the fare of the dressmaker Anton Karthausen and his family, which had failed to make its way in Brownsville, Texas.[77] These were, of course, primarily symbolic moves, widely reported not only in the German but also in the American press, designed to damage the narrative of the American dream.[78] Hitler was not yet ready to promote the large-scale return of recent German emigrants, still less of German-Americans, to the Reich. In fact, despite his well-documented concern with German-Americans in the 1920s, he now showed little interest in the activities of his sympathizers in the United States,[79] almost certainly in order to avoid provoking Washington.

Both public works and rearmament required massive deficit financing, in effect the printing of money to pay workers and stimulate demand. Although fundamentally 'socialist' in outlook and politics when it came to the economy, however, Hitler did not nationalize industry. In fact there were large-scale privatizations during the first five years or so of his regime, not for ideological reasons, but to raise cash quickly by flogging off distressed enterprises.[80] What Hitler did very effectively was to nation-alize German industrialists, by making them instruments of his political will. Control, not ownership was the key. The major German economic institutions, especially industry, business and the banks, were completely sidelined from decision-making.[81] Unlike the Reichswehr, they were not let into any secrets about *Lebensraum*, at least at the beginning. They were simply told what to do, and if they jibbed were threatened with imprisonment, expropriation or irrelevance.

Hitler's initial focus on work creation followed, rather than contra-dicted, his axiomatic primacy of foreign policy. He had long regarded the raising of the German standard of living as a central front in the struggle for the survival of the Reich on the international stage. Here you needed butter, not guns; of this, more presently. The Autobahns – ostensibly 'civil-ian' – had a clear military purpose as well. Besides, rearmament required a steady flow of raw materials. Some of these, such as coal, were available at home, or in the case of oil and rubber could be produced synthetically, albeit at considerable cost; Hitler encouraged IG Farben, for example, to press ahead with the mass production of oil derived from the hydrogenation of coal.[82] Until then, however, much of what was needed had to be pur-chased abroad with hard currency, which in turn had to be paid for through exports, or exchanged for German goods.[83] 'We know', Hitler conceded, that the lack of raw materials 'does not permit complete autarchy for our Reich'. He therefore emphasized 'over again' that the government was not hostile to exports, not least because these 'fed' so many Germans, by paying for the import of foodstuffs.[84] Moreover, Hitler was well aware that the Reichswehr was initially unable to absorb more than a fraction of the financial resources available to it from January 1933.[85] Investing more money in rearmament before the ground was ready would have been akin to pouring a bucket of water on parched soil.

Now reasonably secure at home, Hitler turned his attention to the world around him. He was still preoccupied by the danger of a Franco-Polish preventive war, and there were also intelligence reports of a possible Russo-Polish rapprochement.[86] Some sort of intervention to enforce the terms of the Versailles Treaty was indeed discussed in Warsaw, though it found no favour among the French.[87] Hitler sought to prevent the diplomatic isolation of Germany which a Franco-Polish attack would require. Central to this endeavour was improving relations with the western powers, France, Britain and the United States. In February 1933, the Führer told Ribbentrop – who headed a special office on foreign policy – of his desire for better relations with London.[88] Over the next three years, Hitler also paid greater attention to Paris than before or after.[89] With the exception of a brief interlude during the Ruhr Crisis of 1923, and a few unflattering comments in *Mein Kampf*, he had largely ignored France, but for the first three years after the takeover of power she posed the most immediate military threat. For this reason, Hitler went out of his way to stress, more or less truthfully, his lack of interest in the return of Alsace-Lorraine.

Hitler also protested, this time entirely disingenuously, his pacifist intentions more generally. 'The German people,' he claimed during his speech on the enabling law, 'wants to live in peace with the world.'[90] In this context, the war veteran card proved particularly effective. When the British conservative opponent of Nazism Duff Cooper claimed that the Third Reich was preparing for war, Hitler countered by saying that 'we leaders of the National Socialist movement are almost without exception former frontline soldiers', adding that he did not think that anybody who had experienced the war would be 'enthusiastically preparing' for a new conflict.[91] He also trod carefully on rearmament. Hitler reminded the cabinet 'that we need to show restraint with rearmament'.[92] His success here owed much to the fact that the Reichswehr had been engaged in such deception more or less since its founding and to the existence of ready-formulated plans for rearmament and conscription among its leadership.[93] The Führer rebuked the DNVP leader Alfred Hugenberg for speaking openly of the return of colonies and the acquisition of *Lebensraum*; Hugenberg flounced out of the cabinet in a huff. The purpose of Hitler's strategy was simple: to gain time so that he could throw off the mask later when he was ready. 'I am pursuing a policy of understanding,' Hitler explained to the *Reichsstatthalter*, 'in order to enable a later policy of strength.'[94]

An important part of Hitler's charm offensive towards the rest of the world, especially the west, was his championship of the Olympic Games. These were scheduled to take place in Berlin in 1936, a location chosen some-time before Hitler's rise to power. Hitler made clear that the Third Reich would not only host the event, but lay on the most spectacular Olympic Games in history. Hitler evidently hoped to showcase his achievements in front of a global audience whose very presence would legitimize his regime. In order to head off a threatened boycott, however, he had to promise that he would respect the inclusivity of the Olympic charter and welcome 'competitors of all races' to Berlin. While insisting that they reserved the right to determine the composition of the German team themselves, the Nazis even conceded that Jews could compete for the Third Reich.[95]

At the same time, and without any sense of contradiction, Hitler sought to bluff the west into thinking that rearmament, in reality a slow and complicated process, was much further advanced than it actually was.[96] This was designed to deter any preventive strike. Central to this strategy was bigging-up the German air force. The parallels with the Kaiser's plan to use the German high seas fleet as a deterrent against Britain were so obvious that the Luftwaffe became known as a 'risk air force',[97] not yet big enough to devastate Europe perhaps, but sufficiently powerful to raise the costs of outside intervention. In this endeavour, Hitler was extremely successful. He was able to tap into widespread elite and popular hysteria about the likelihood of mass civilian casualties from air raids. Serious expansion of the Luftwaffe began only in 1934, and it became a formidable tactical fighting force only from 1938, but the German air force exerted a hold over the British and French imaginations almost from the very beginning.

The same caution characterized Hitler's early policy towards the Soviet Union. To be sure, he broke off the military cooperation which the Reichs-wehr had pursued since the early 1920s,[98] and he resisted all suggestions from the conservative right, including elements within the Foreign Office, that Germany should ally with Russia against Poland and the west. The Soviet Union, in fact, was generally not a high priority at this time, and Hitler regarded it as an ideological but not a military danger.[99] That said, Hitler wanted to keep the lines to Moscow open. This was partly in order to maintain the supply of raw materials from the Soviet Union; partly because he hoped Moscow might help restrain Warsaw from launching a pre-emptive attack on Germany; and partly in order to lull the Soviets into a false sense of security. In more or less the same breath Hitler continued to attack 'Marxism as an ideology of decomposition' and its 'international apostles',[100] while at the same time signalling publicly that he was ready for 'friendly' relations with the Soviet Union; the battle against German communism, Hitler added, was simply a 'domestic affair'.[101] It is a measure not merely of the Soviet capacity for self-deception, but also of Hitler's ability to dissimulate, that he built up over the next eight years the level of rapport necessary to achieve both tactical and strategic surprise over Stalin.

Hitler sought to avoid provoking Germany's neighbours unnecessarily. One of the potential areas of contention was the millions of Germans living beyond the borders of the Reich, but within Europe. Hitler regarded them with considerable ambivalence. As we have seen, he had always been much more interested in Germans who had headed west, especially those emigrating to the United States. Despite what happened from 1938, Hitler did not primarily regard ethnic Germans in Europe as a fifth column for the Third Reich. In some cases, in particular the Germans of South Tyrol, they were actually a barrier to his planned alliances. He also feared that they might be taken 'hostage' by hostile powers. For this reason, Hitler told representatives of Germans abroad, he would use a 'hammer' at home, but 'pincers' in foreign policy. *Volkstumspolitik* was delegated to Hess, a clear signal that he did not consider it *Chefsache*. Hess, explicitly quoting Hitler, laid down that German minorities should 'maintain the best possible relations with their respective host people'.[102] Many ethnic Germans outside the Reich, who had expected a more robust policy right away, were bitterly disappointed with this attitude.

There were only two exceptions. One was Austria, where the population was mainly German, there were many supporters of unification – *Anschluss* – with Germany and a strong Nazi party. They were under severe pressure, not so much from the left as from the locally dominant conservative clerical elites led by Chancellor Engelbert Dollfuss. Hitler planned to settle the Austrian question sooner rather than later. He feared the influence of 'Viennese Half-Jewry' and the (Habsburg) 'legitimists'; his concerns about Habsburg restorationist tendencies extended well beyond Vienna to Hungary and some other successor states of the old Dual Monarchy. Hitler therefore recommended to the cabinet that 'the same method be applied against Austria' which had led to 'immediate success' in Bavaria.[103] Vienna got its retaliation in first, however, and banned the Austrian NSDAP in June 1933. The number of Austrian Nazi exiles – already substantial – increased. Some of them were corralled into the 'Austrian Legion', a paramilitary force based in a camp at Lechfeld close to the Austrian border. It was tasked, as Hitler told the head of the Austria SA, Obergruppenführer Reschny in the summer of 1933, with supporting the local party 'in the event of a rising'. No date was set, however, and no further action taken.[104]

The other neighbouring state to which the Nazis were hostile from the start, and in which they took a keen interest in the very significant German minority from a very early stage, was Czechoslovakia. When relations with Poland improved, there was no attempt to extend the thaw to the Czechs. Hitler's attitude to the Czech people at this point is unclear but he made no secret of his contempt for the Czechoslovak state, which he regarded as nothing more than a Franco-Russian thorn in the side of the Reich. In a meeting with the Hungarian foreign minister Gömbös in the summer of 1933, Hitler signalled his intention to 'liquidate' Czechoslovakia.[105] That said, for the first four years or so of his rule the Führer took relatively little interest in what was happening in Czechoslovakia.[106]

Instead, Hitler began to explore the possibility of a rapprochement with Poland. In the short term, this would enable him to break the ring of encirclement around Germany and forestall a preventive war. Strategically, a Polish alliance would provide him with a partner or at least staging ground for the pursuit of *Lebensraum* further east. Such a policy ran contrary to established opinion in the army and the Foreign Office, where conservatives preferred the Russian Bolsheviks to the Polish upstarts. Neurath, for example, insisted that an improvement of relations with Poland was neither possible nor desirable, and he repeatedly argued that Warsaw could only be restrained by maintaining the connection to Moscow. Hitler, by contrast, signalled a change of course on Poland very early on. This became evident when the matter of subsidies for the loss-making Gruben und Hüttenwerke IG Kattowitz, which now lay in Poland, but had formerly been part of German Upper Silesia, came up for discussion in cabinet. These had long been paid in order to maintain the German interest in the area. Hitler, departing from his usual mantra of the primacy of politics over economics, laid down clearly that 'the whole matter should be viewed purely from the perspective of its financial benefits, irrespective of 'military considerations'.[107] It was eventually sold off to a Polish consortium.

More generally, Hitler wanted not just to forestall outside intervention, but also to secure at least the benevolent neutrality of Anglo-America, and alliances with Italy and other like-minded powers. Hitler, and the Nazis generally, seem at first to have been hopeful that they could appeal to the 'better' – that is racist – nature of the United States. They saw in Roosevelt's America a cognate polity, not merely because of its policies of racial exclusion – in which immigration legislation weighed much more heavily than segregation – but because the 'New Deal' seemed to chime with what Hitler was trying to achieve in Germany.[108]

There was some American sympathy for the new Germany, but from the start Hitler struggled to get his message across in the United States.[109] He was irritated by the widespread and unexpected criticism of his racial policies in the American press. In remarks to the Imperial Commission for the associations of leading German medics, Hitler argued that the Americans had 'the least excuse' to protest because they had been 'the first to draw practical and political conclusions from . . . the different value of different races'. He claimed, alluding to the 1924 immigration legislation, that these laws had already prevented the entry of 'so-called Jewish refugees from Germany'.[110] The gulf became evident in the spring of 1933, when two Americans involved in the Geneva Disarmament Conference, Allen Dulles and its chairman, Roosevelt's close associate Norman Davis, met Hitler in the Chancellery. Ominously for him, the encounter took place in the context of rising US concerns over anti-Semitic agitation. The meeting got off to a bad start when Hitler asked how the post-bellum American South would have felt if it had been confronted like Germany with a treaty designed to keep it in permanent subjection. Davis responded that the South had been treated much worse than Germany because it had even been forced to accept black judges. He showed no sympathy at all with Hitler's longstanding fear of Germans being enslaved by other whites, or indeed the Jews. Davis then went on to express profound concern about German rearmament. It was a complete non-meeting of minds between American and Nazi racism.[111]

Hitler's hopes for a rapid understanding with Britain were also quickly dashed. To be sure, there were some – such as the press baron Lord Rothermere – who welcomed Hitler as a bulwark against communism.[112] 'There has been a sudden expansion of their national spirit,' he wrote in the *Daily Mail*, 'like that which took place in England under Queen Elizabeth.' Rothermere hailed the 'plain blunt patriotism of Hitler', who had rescued Germany from 'its alien elements', the Jews. 'The world's greatest need today is realism,' he concluded. 'Hitler is a realist.' The overwhelming view in the press, parliament and Foreign Office, though, was negative. Hitler's treatment of the Jews, in particular, caused widespread consternation. The only real disagreement was over the extent to which outside intervention was legitimate or effective.[113]

Before he made serious diplomatic moves, Hitler needed to win over, or at least neutralize, public opinion in Britain and the United States. This required the regime to tone down its domestic violence, at least in so far as it affected the outside world and could be monitored by the international press, especially the British and American papers, which Hitler assumed to be controlled by the Jews. It was for this reason also that he instructed the SA, SS and the NSDAP generally in early March to avoid attacks on foreign cars and individuals.[114] This made little difference, partly because SA discipline left a lot to be desired, partly because Hitler himself continued to encourage violence with very public nudges and winks, but primarily because the fundamental nature of the Nazi regime outraged world opinion, especially in Britain and America. Almost from the start, therefore, Hitler and the Third Reich were subjected to a barrage of negative publicity in the Anglo-American press.[115]

At the heart of this critique were the British and American foreign correspondents in Berlin. Their dean, the Associated Press representative Louis Lochner, was a constant thorn in the side of the Nazi authorities.[116] Dealing with them was the task of Hitler's foreign press chief, Putzi Hanfstaengl. He set up an office opposite the Chancellery headed by the Quaker Agnethe von Hausberger, who had grown up in the United States.[117] His monopoly of foreign press contacts was constantly being challenged by Goebbels and by the return of Kurt Lüdecke, who was aligned with Alfred Rosenberg, from the United States. Over the next four years or so, Hanfstaengl sought to maximize favourable press coverage. He gossiped and joshed with foreign correspondents at his favourite cafés; the early Third Reich was an open and leaky system, light years away from the totalitarianism of Soviet Russia.[118] That said, foreign journalists were also subjected to a systematic policy of intimidation by the Nazi authorities. Göring warned them that their telephone conversations were being monitored. Goebbels frequently protested against bad coverage, and sometimes managed to have journalists arrested, disciplined or recalled.[119] There was nothing, however, that the Nazis could do about poor press coverage from across the Channel or the Atlantic.

Hitler was extremely sensitive to his negative image in the outside world. In early March 1933, he warned the cabinet that he 'considered the global press agitation against the German government very dangerous'.[120] A week later, he complained to Papen that alleged outrages perpetrated by the SA against foreign diplomats were being used as a pretext to launch a 'systematic barrage' with the aim of 'stopping the national revival' of Germany.[121] Hitler was deeply concerned about this, because he firmly believed that Germany's isolation and defeat in the war had been the result of an Anglo-American press campaign against the Reich. He was also worried about the way in which he was being portrayed personally. In a candid admission of his concern with his global image, Hitler sponsored the compilation of an entire volume of caricatures by Hanfstaengl – *Hitler in der Karikatur der Welt* – which appeared in the autumn of 1933 together with detailed rebuttals.[122] It was for this reason that Hitler was anxious to establish an effective apparatus for engaging with world opinion, and 'escaping world political isolation'. Hitler told the cabinet that they would have to establish 'a new organization' to 'influence public opinion abroad'. This necessitated a clear demarcation of competencies between the Foreign Office and the Propaganda Ministry of Goebbels. Hitler added that whereas Germany was pursuing a traditional 'cabinet policy', that of other countries was being 'driven by quite different forces', a clear reference to the supposed power of the Jewish press.[123]

One way of getting the Führer's message across was through the dissemination of *Mein Kampf* abroad. Here Hitler was conflicted. On the one hand, he went to considerable lengths to restrict the publication of some foreign-language editions, even going to court in France. On the other hand, he endorsed or at least tolerated other versions. An Italian edition was honoured with a new preface by Hitler.[124] An abridged English version was published in the autumn of 1933 by Hurst and Blackett in London and Houghton Mifflin in New York. Despite subsequent claims, for example by the Zionist leader Chaim Weizmann, that these editions tended to play down Hitler's racism and territorial ambitions, they were in fact not bowdlerized in any meaningful sense of the word.[125] The emphasis on *Lebensraum* and the alleged malevolent power of world Jewry was as strong in these editions as it was in the original.[126] The Führer also openly signalled his plans in an interview with the *Daily Telegraph* in May 1933, when he stated that he did not want naval or colonial competition with Britain, but eastern enlargement.[127] None of this is surprising, because although Hitler always sought to conceal his immediate diplomatic and military moves, it was very much in his strategic long-term interest to win over Anglo-American audiences to his way or thinking on race and space.

Significantly, while Hitler devoted considerable effort to converting Anglo-America, he was reluctant to pursue a more broadly-based international coalition against world Jewry and the other pillars of the global order. His interpretation of the institutions of global governance and the workings of the world economy was likely to appeal to those have-nots of the international system, and that was a very large proportion of the literate non-Anglo-world population, who felt short-changed by the power of Anglo-America and 'the Jews', and who did not think that history had ended with the advent of liberalism.[128] There were many senior Nazis, Rosenberg and Goebbels among them, who wished to pick up where Strasser had left off and forge global alliances, if not with the wretched of the earth on the Indian continent, then at least with the many others who had got the rough end of the stick from global capitalism or British imperialism, or believed themselves to have done so. They created a lively fascist and anti-Semitic 'international' in the 1930s.[129] Hitler himself had no interest in any of these transnational entanglements, at least for the moment. He planned to export Nazis to the east in large numbers when the time was right, but – with the exception two small nearby markets in Austria and Czechoslovakia – he had no intention of exporting Nazism itself to the world at large.

At the heart of the negative foreign press campaign, Hitler believed, lay a Jewish conspiracy. The need for 'defensive measures' against the 'atrocity propaganda' preoccupied him throughout the second half of March 1933.[130] He decided to launch a time-limited boycott of Jewish businesses.[131] Julius Streicher, a fanatical anti-Semite and editor of *Der Stürmer*, was put in charge of the 'Central Committee for Defence against Jewish Atrocity and Boycott Agitation'.[132] Its main addressee was Anglo-America. Hitler told the cabinet that he would be prepared 'to delay the start of the boycott, if the governments of Britain and the United States immediately made satisfactory declarations against the atrocity propaganda'.[133] 'What would America do,' he asked, 'if the Germans in America behaved as badly towards America' as the German Jews did against Germany? This was a particularly bitter issue for Hitler, because of his beliefs about the role of German emigrants fighting against their Fatherland in the American army in the World War. Moreover, Hitler argued, alluding to the immigration of *Ostjuden* from the late nineteenth century, Germany had 'let in every foreigner for hundreds of years' without restriction, so that she had a huge population density. In America, he continued, the figure was much lower, and yet 'America had introduced quotas and simply excluded certain peoples' from immigrating.[134] There it was again, the old preoccupation with Jewish interference from America, coupled with the spatial superiority and racial exclusivity of the United States. It had changed very little since Hitler's first articulations in the 1920s.

In these early days, the Third Reich encouraged Jewish emigration, especially to Palestine. This was the policy of the Foreign Office, the Economics Ministry and particularly of the SS, subject to confiscating most of the Jews' property.[135] They looked for help to German and World Zionism, which was interested in increasing the number of immigrants to the *Yeshuv*. The apotheosis of this cooperation was the Haavara Agreement between the German Zionist Federation, the Jewish Agency and the Nazi Ministry of Finance in August 1933 to facilitate the passage of German Jews to Palestine. This was a Zionist rather than a Nazi initiative, designed to enable Jews who wished to flee the discriminatory policies of the Third

Reich to move at least some of their assets to Palestine. With the benefit of hindsight, the Haavara Agreement saved many lives, as it permitted the departure of Jews who would otherwise almost certainly have been killed later. There is no evidence that it was encouraged or sanctioned by the 'Führer', though he made no attempt to reverse it either.[136]

Hitler, in fact, was at best ambivalent about the emigration of German Jews. He used the reluctance of other powers to accept Jewish refugees, and that of Britain to admit them to Palestine, in order to lambast them for hypocrisy,[137] but he did not favour their large-scale systematic removal there or anywhere else. This was partly because Hitler remained completely hostile to the idea of a Jewish state as such, which would on his reading simply serve as the headquarters of an international conspiracy. The main reason, however, was that he sought to hold German Jews to ransom for the good behaviour of world Jewry. This became clear when a leading New York Jewish lawyer, Maxie Steuer, visited Berlin in the spring or early summer of 1933 bringing an offer from major figures of the American Jewish community, including Warburgs, Speyers and Guggenheims, to finance the departure of all German Jews, not excepting those who had recently immigrated from eastern Europe. Both Neurath and Schacht were enthusiastic. To Hanfstaengl's astonishment, Hitler rejected the proposal, reminding him that he wanted to keep the Jews as hostages.[138]

From the start, therefore, there was a tension running through Hitler's policy towards the Jews after 1933. On the one hand, he wanted to make life as difficult for them as possible so that they would leave and enable an evolutionary solution to the 'problem'. On the other hand, he wanted to keep at least some of them in the country as hostages for the good behaviour of the Anglo-American Jews in the western 'plutocracies'. This tension partly reflected differing pressures within the regime, but mainly one in Hitler's own mind, which was to resolve itself over time.

The confrontation between Hitler and what he regarded as world Jewry in the spring of 1933 nearly derailed his grandiose plans for the Olympic Games. In late May of that year, the American Jewish Congress under its president, Bernard S. Deutsch, spoke out against holding the games in Germany. There were also deep divisions within the American Olympic establishment. The US representative on the International Olympic Committee was the Louisiana Republican Ernest Lee Jahncke, who had just finished a term as secretary of the navy. Jahncke was a non-Jewish German-American, whose father had been born in Hamburg, who hated Hitler and who was strongly against the Nazi 'sordid exploitation of the Games'. It was thanks largely to the enthusiastic support of the president of the US Olympic Committee, and strong anti-Semite, Avery Brundage, that the threat of an American-led international boycott of the Berlin Olympic Games never materialized.

Another minefield that Hitler had to negotiate with the United States was the role of German-Americans, who constituted by far the largest group of *Auslandsdeutschen*. As we have seen, this group lay at the heart of his whole world view, and he had milked the two high-profile returns for all they were worth. That said, Hitler was anxious not to alienate Washington by interfering in its internal affairs. For this reason, the American NSDAP-Ortsgruppen were disbanded in spring 1933, not long after Hitler came to power. Their place was taken by a new organization, 'League of the Friends of the New Germany', generally known as the Bund. The Bund was a very two-edged weapon, however. To be sure, it garnered support on the racist and isolationist right, but it was fundamentally anathema to the American mainstream. The Bund was subjected to severe criticism from the very beginning not only by Jewish groups but by many other Americans, including the majority of German-Americans, for whom any form of external interference was unacceptable. The Third Reich reacted by banning German citizens from involvement in the Bund, and towards the end of the year Hitler assured an interviewer from Hearst Press, the German-American Karl von Wiegand, that he had 'forbidden party members abroad from making National Socialist propaganda in order not to endanger the diplomatic relations with those countries'.[139]

Here, Hitler was no doubt reacting to the activities of the Jewish Representative Samuel Dickstein of New York, who began to hold informal hearings in 1933 in the House of Representatives on Nazi activities in the United States. This eventually led, a year later (March 1934), to the establishment of 'The Special Committee on Un-American Activities Authorized to Investigate Nazi Propaganda and Certain other Propaganda Activities'. It was chaired for optical reasons by the non-Jewish Congressman John W. McCormack from Massachusetts, though the German press invariably referred to the 'Dickstein Committee'. Two months later, President Roosevelt ordered FBI Director Hoover to begin a 'very careful and searching investigation' of American fascism, with a particular focus on 'any possible connection with official representatives of the German government'.[140] In fact, the very notion of 'Un-American' behaviour was first given institutionalized political expression in the confrontation between the United States and Nazism. Clearly, Hitler was losing the battle for America. The 'othering' of US fascists, of German America, of Nazism and of the Führer himself, was well underway.

Meanwhile, Hitler sought to come to a financial arrangement with Washington. The Third Reich desperately needed to reduce the debt interest payments on loans. At the same time, despite his long-term ambition to achieve autarchy, Hitler's plans for rearmament required the import of raw materials, which could only be paid for with foreign currency derived from exports. Hitler also wanted to explore the possibilities for deeper forms of economic cooperation in Europe. Picking up a theme he had already ventilated before 1933, Hitler feared the rise of non-European economic actors – here he seems to have been thinking not just of the US but also Japan and possibly China – as these imported western machinery and competed with the established industrial powers.[141] He hoped that the old world could be persuaded at the World Economic Conference in Washington to join a boycott of the export of machinery to these rising powers. Failure to do so, he lamented, would destroy European industry. If that were not possible, however, Hitler wanted – as he put it to a delegation from eastern Germany in late April 1933 – to compensate for losses in 'world trade' through the 'development of its domestic market'.[142]

In May 1933, Schacht was sent to Washington to discuss the interlinked questions of the international economy, Germany's debts and armaments. He met no fewer than four times privately with President Roosevelt, besides having countless other conversations with his advisers, various senators, ministers, bankers and prominent American Jews. They even issued a joint declaration, which stressed the need for the abolition of international trade constraints and for stable currencies. They also agreed that tackling unemployment was an urgent priority both through domestic credit expansion and, remarkably, the establishment of an international programme to mobilize public and private credit for productive purposes. What was being signalled here, on the face of it, was nothing less than a possible global Keynesian alliance for global prosperity. Roosevelt's New Deal, it seemed, was internationally aligned with Hitler's new order in Germany.[143]

In June, Hitler's first major move in foreign policy was the announcement of an effective debt moratorium. German firms would pay for imports with Reichsmarks which would not be converted until the trade balance had improved. In the meantime, creditors could use their frozen balances to pay for German goods. There was no concerted world reaction, not even from the United States. Hitler had got away with it.

Otherwise, Hitler continued to go out of his way to avoid difficulties with the United States. He expressly forbade attacks on Roosevelt and his government.[144] Hitler also sought to dampen the fire he himself had started with 'world Jewry'. The time for a direct confrontation was not yet ripe, in his view, and for this reason spontaneous acts of violence from below were strongly discouraged. 'The front we must watch today,' he warned the *Reichsstaathalter* in early July 1933, lay 'outside of Germany'. 'This front is dangerous,' Hitler continued, and 'we must not provoke it un-necessarily.' 'To reopen the Jewish question again today,' he concluded, 'means stirring up the entire world again.'[145] What Hitler did not yet know was that President Roosevelt was already implacably opposed both to him and to Nazism. In January 1933, between his election and inauguration, Roosevelt remarked privately that Hitler's rise was 'a portent of evil' not merely for Europe but also for the United States. Hitler, he predicted, 'would in the end challenge us because his black sorcery appealed to the worst in men; it supported their hates and ridiculed their tolerances; and it could not exist permanently in the world with a system whose reliance on reason and justice was fundamental'.[146]

The 'Elevation' of the German People

On the domestic front, Hitler's position grew ever more secure. Germany was now a one-party state. 'We are in the middle of the slow completion of the total state,' Hitler told his *Reichsstatthalter* in early July 1933. The task ahead, he announced, was to create a 'legal basis' for this 'total National Socialist state'.[1] A week later, the NSDAP was declared to be the only political party in the Reich. A series of measures designed to ensure the penetration of the state by the party followed in the second half of the year; these were largely unsuccessful, leaving unfinished business to the very end of the Reich. In late September 1933, Hitler announced his intention 'to bring the National Socialist party gradually into the federal authority'.[2] Rudolf Hess, the deputy Führer of the NSDAP, began to play an ever greater role in the meetings of the Reich cabinet and in government more generally.[3] In December 1933, this tendency found expression in the 'Law to Secure the Unity of Party and State', whose very name seemed to embody the symbiosis between the two.

Despite these steps, Hitler believed that the Nazification of the state was not the solution. He wanted to maintain the effectiveness of the administration and economy, and to prevent interference by party-appointed incompetents. He therefore spent much of the summer and autumn of 1933 telling the party leadership to ease off on the enforcement of Nazism at the local level if this cut across economic productivity and the smooth functioning of the state. When asked by Hess whether the entire 'state apparatus' should be staffed exclusively by party members, he replied simply 'that that was not necessary'.[4] Underlying Hitler's scepticism about the value of Nazification by party-book was a much broader crisis of identity in the movement throughout the spring and summer of 1933.[5] Until then the NSDAP, though large, had been smaller than the SPD. It was in Hitler's mind an elite group, tested through adversity, and therefore entitled to a leadership role in the Third Reich.

With the takeover of power, however, and especially after the March

1933 Reichstag elections, the NSDAP was flooded with membership applications by careerists, sarcastically known as 'March victims', although the
largest number of entrants were actually registered in May.[6] Hitler feared
the 'embourgeoisement' of the party and its dilution by 'opportunists'. He
had, in fact, anticipated this problem in *Mein Kampf*, where he distinguished between revolutionary 'members' and more passive 'supporters';
he had even envisaged an immediate ban on new members after the seizure
of power.[7] There was also the question of what the future role of the general
party organization should be now that power had been attained. Surely
not governance, as this was now in the hands of the Nazis running the
state, or individual Nazi executive institutions. Surely not propaganda, as
this was the domain of Goebbels and his Propaganda Ministry. On 1 May
1933, the party announced that it would accept no further applications
until 1937. The contradiction, though, was plain. How could one demand
the penetration of the party into all walks of life and government while
at the same time closing the lists to new members?

Hitler resolved this tension through a deep programme of domestic
transformation in Germany. There was no point in 'coordinating' everything, he explained, somewhat tactlessly given that he was speaking to the
imperial commissars, if one did not have the 'right man' to execute it.[8] At
one level, Hitler was merely stressing the importance of finding the most
qualified candidate for a post, rather than simply appointing a Nazi time-
server. At another level, however, Hitler was making a much broader point
about the supposed need to transform German society in a more fundamental way. He wanted not simply outward conformity, but inner
acceptance and reproduction of the new order, and for that greater 'racial'
coherence was necessary. This is what Hitler meant when he told an audience of SA men in Kiel in the early summer of 1933 that 'we must continue
the struggle for the soul of the German person'.[9] Germans, he was suggesting, would need to learn what the Anglo-Americans had long since
mastered, which was the achievement of national cohesion not through
threats or bribes, but through instinct.

Here, Hitler believed that he had a mountain to climb. The sense of German fragility and racial weakness, which had stalked his writings and
speeches throughout the 1920s, continued to haunt him after 1933. Hitler's
view of the German people as it actually existed was deeply unflattering.
He was deeply conscious of their poverty and ignorance. Hitler despaired
of the low civilizational level of the average 'unwashed' recruit in his remarks
to the Reichswehr leadership. 'It is a fact that racially lower-ranking people
have to be forced into culture,' he remarked, and the filth of many German
recruits reflected the fact that they were more likely to sympathize with

equally degraded foreigners than with their own fellow countrymen.[10] Moreover, far from being racially pure, Hitler told an audience of major industrialists in the autumn of 1933, the German people were 'a combined nation, which is made up of many different groups and parts' and contained 'many people' who were completely 'unsuited' for a higher culture.[11] Hitler's attitude towards the Germans was affectionate to be sure, but also highly condescending. Racially fragmented, liable to be easily manipulated by the Jews and foreign propaganda, and vulnerable to the blandishments of American popular culture, his German *Volk* left a lot to be desired.

One way of creating the desired 'racial state'[12] was to eliminate the negative. Here, Hitler's main target was German Jewry, agents in his mind of foreign subversion and internal racial decomposition. Their systematic exclusion began with the 'Law for the Restoration of the Professional Civil Service' in early April 1933, and other measures followed. There were many agencies and individuals at work here, of course, but Hitler was in control at all times, either driving the process forward or refusing to be bounced into 'premature' action by over-zealous bureaucrats or party leaders.[13] The war on the Jews proceeded slowly, partly because, as we have seen, Hitler did not want to alienate the outside world unnecessarily, and partly because of the intricate definitional issues involved. Removing 'full' Jews was one thing, but what about the so-called half and quarter Jews? Hitler was reluctant to condemn the hundreds of thousands of people involved out of hand, because by his reckoning so much 'valuable' blood was mixed in with what he thought of as the dross. Even on his own terms, of course, Hitler's laws were riddled with contradictions, because while he would come to define a 'Jew' as someone with two 'Jewish' grandparents, this 'scientific' assessment was based on the religious affiliation of the ancestors concerned and not their supposed 'racial' category, which would have been impossible to establish anyway.

Interestingly, there was at this point little sense of enmity towards Slavs, as such. They had not featured much in his thinking during the 1920s, and Slavophobia played no role in Hitler's policies in the first years after 1933.[14] Partly, no doubt, this was due to diplomatic sensitivities with regard to Poland, but the main reasons were ideological. Hitler had targeted Russia for expansion, not because the Slavs were inferior but because Jewry and Bolshevism had in his view rendered the state defenceless, an alleged fate which he feared would also befall Germany. Moreover, Hitler was well aware that the German *Volk* included many people of Polish or Czech origin. In both domestic politics and foreign policy, in fact, Hitler was much less anti-Polish than the German conservative mainstream.

The other important front in the campaign to eliminate 'unworthy'

strands in the German national body politic was the attack on the disabled
and those suffering from hereditary illnesses.[15] Unlike the Jews, Hitler did
not see them as foreign agents, but just as a drain on state resources and a
threat to the physical and mental health of the German people. In mid July
1933, Hitler rushed through a 'Law for the Prevention of Hereditarily Dis-
eased Offspring'.[16] This permitted the compulsory medical sterilization of
those suffering from 'hereditary' physical or mental disabilities which might
be passed on to their progeny, including blindness, deafness, schizophrenia,
manic depression and physical deformities. Its purpose, he explained to the
cabinet, was to ensure that 'hereditarily ill people' did not 'reproduce in
large numbers' while 'millions of healthy children remained unborn'.[17] Hitler took a close interest in the execution of these measures. When told of
the number of deaths during sterilization operations, he suggested radio-
therapy instead.[18] Hitler's motivation in all this was not just antipathy
towards the disabled, but a concern to preserve the able-bodied. The purpose of his war on the 'weak' was to make Germany fit for war against the
'strong'.

In all this, Hitler drew on many traditions within existing German
eugenics, but he was particularly impressed by the American model. His
inspiration was not so much the American South, but the 'miscegenation'
and eugenics laws across the entire Union.[19] The US *Eugenic News*
remarked that 'to one versed in the history of eugenic sterilization in
America, the text of the German statute reads almost like the American
model sterilization law'.[20] One of Hitler's authorities was Leon Whitney,
whose book *The Case for Sterilization* he specifically requested. His main
inspiration, however, remained Madison Grant, author of *The Passing of
the Great Race*, who was unpopular among Nazis generally because of
his sceptical view of Germans, but to whom Hitler wrote that he considered that work 'his Bible'.[21] One area where Hitler did not seek to emulate
the United States was smoking, which formed such an important part of
the American Dream. He refused to allow it in his presence, not even by
his closest political associates, or by Eva Braun. In time, Nazi scientists
conducted research into the harmful effects of tobacco, banned smoking
in offices and waiting rooms (though with little success) and introduced
non-smoking carriages on trains.[22]

The removal of supposedly harmful elements, however, was not enough
for Hitler. If Germany was to have any chance of prevailing against the
racially superior Angloworld, Hitler would have to accentuate the allegedly positive in German society. There would have to be a general
civilizational and racial 'elevation' (*Hebung*) of the Germans in order
to distil their better elements into what he regarded as 'racial' purity.

Reversing centuries of demographic drain overseas, and confronting the cultural and socio-economic lure of the New World, the Reich would have to articulate an attractive and viable vision for German racial renewal.

Central to Hitler's project of racial distillation and elevation were 'standards of living'. This was partly because he feared, as he warned the Reichswehr leadership, that a 'low standard of living' would render Germans vulnerable to 'Bolshevism',[23] but the main reason was that he was explicitly competing with the west, and the 'American way of life' in particular. The battle for the soul of the German working class was primarily fought not against the Soviet Union, but against the United States. Hitler did not share the widespread German cultural snobbery about civilization, consumption and technology. In his mind, prosperity and technological progress both reflected and increased 'racial' value, just as a low standard of living both accelerated racial degeneration and was the product of it. The domestic focus of the regime, therefore, was not propaganda, but consumption.[24]

For this reason, Hitler threw his personal prestige behind increasing German car ownership. Early on in his chancellorship, he introduced tax relief for new vehicles.[25] In the spring of 1934 he instructed the bureaucracy to look into the production of an affordable 'people's car'.[26] In a series of speeches to representatives of the German automobile industry, he praised the 'psychological liberation' which came with car ownership, and looked forward to a time when what had been 'a luxury' became 'common property'. He lamented the fact that 'whereas there were about 23 million cars in circulation in America, with another 3 to 4 million being produced every year, Weimar Germany had managed to put only about 450,000 on the roads and had produced about a tenth of that number in recent years. This was despite the fact that Germany had just over half the population of the United States. 'The Ford car', he continued, was the vehicle through which 'millions' or at least 'hundreds of thousands' could achieve the 'elevation of their standard of living'. He therefore called upon German industry to bring 'purchasing price and maintenance costs' of this car into 'a sustainable relationship to the income of the broad mass of the people', as was already the case in the United States.[27] Interestingly, Hitler did not show the same enthusiasm for lorries as a means of moving goods, putting more faith in the railways.[28] The automobile was primarily an object of consumption rather than propulsion.

Next to the automobile, the aeroplane was central to the Nazi project of modernity. Here, too, Germany had to play catch-up. The British and Americans were well ahead not merely in military and naval but also in civil aviation. Hitler pushed strongly for the increased use of air travel, expressing the view that 'in a few years nobody would even consider undertaking travel of more than 500 kilometres in anything other than an aeroplane'. He put the construction of a huge airport at the centre of his plans for the reconstruction of Berlin, arguing that it was the modern equivalent to the King of Prussia's creation of the Unter den Linden. 'The airport of Tempelhof', Hitler insisted, must become 'the largest and most beautiful civilian airport of the world'. 'Nothing,' Hitler admonished the planners, 'could ever make the same impression as when a foreigner arrived at the still-to-be-built southern railway station or at the airport Tempelhof' and saw facilities which 'silenced any criticism' through their 'beauty and size'.[29] In other words, don't tell, show. Positively or negatively, the United States remained a major point of reference in Hitler's plans.

Another area in which Hitler sought to compete with Anglo-America was in the provision of wireless sets. In 1933, Germany had only 4.3 million licensed radio receivers out of a population of 66 million inhabitants,[30] a much lower proportion than either the United States or Britain. In order to redress this imbalance, Goebbels corralled some twenty-eight different companies to mass-produce an affordable radio. The resulting 'people's receiver' was presented to the German 'Radio Fair' in Berlin in August 1933; 100,000 sets were placed on the market for 76 Reichsmark each. The associated poster proclaimed that 'all Germany hears the Führer', but that was a wild exaggeration. In fact, no more about 25 per cent of Germans would have the necessary radio set to do so (assuming they wanted to). The 'people's receiver' was not part of some closed totalitarian information circle. It had not one but many channels – that was the whole point – and foreign broadcasts could be heard without interference, at least until the outbreak of war.[31] It was thus an instrument primarily not of propaganda, but of consumption.[32] Of course, consumption was also propaganda, a much better advertisement for the Third Reich than speeches or declarations.

Nor did Hitler overlook the importance of leisure, the enjoyment of which he regarded as central to his 'standard of living project' and thus to Germany's supposed 'racial' wellbeing. In the 1920s, he had praised the way in which North Americans communed with nature, driving out from the cities into the countryside. The Nazi 'Strength through Joy' movement was given the task of organizing leisure activities for the masses, and opening the mountains, lakes and beaches of Germany to a much broader range of social groups than previously; Jews, of course, were excluded. Here again, the United States was at least the implicit model.[33] Hitler had himself photographed with three young children, of suitably 'Nordic' appearance, against a mountain holiday backdrop. Within a few years, the regime was offering package tours, mostly to enormous purpose-built resorts on the Baltic Sea, but also, for the lucky few, beyond the Reich to Norway and the Mediterranean. One of the purposes of the 'Strength through Joy' movement was specifically to offer an alternative to 'American' models of leisure.[34]

The role envisaged for women in this modernization programme was decidedly limited.[35] 'The words women's emancipation,' he told a meeting of the NS-Frauenschaft, were 'only words invented by the Jewish intellect.' Hitler contrasted the 'world of the man', which was characterized by 'the state', 'struggle' and 'commitment to the community', with the 'smaller world' of the woman, made up of 'husband, family, her children and her house'.[36] Generally speaking, Hitler was opposed to working women, unless they were secretaries or domestics. He had a particular horror of women in politics, and paid little attention to the Reichsfrauenführerin Gertrud Scholz-Klink. He was not keen on women in the professions either.[37] He made an exception for 'creatives', however. Gerdy Troost, the wife of the architect Paul Troost, was given numerous contracts to remodel Hitler's personal spaces. He also sponsored the work of Leni Riefenstahl. Likewise Hitler accepted the role of women in the performing arts, be it the managerial role of Winifred Wagner at Bayreuth, or the actresses in the cinema or on stage.[38] He was also an admirer of the Czech film star Anny Ondra, wife of the boxer Max Schmeling.

In Hitler's world, the cooperation of women was essential for the running of the larger whole. His concern was mainly demographic. 'Every child [the German woman] brings into the world,' he announced, 'is a battle which she endures' for the survival of her people.[39] Natalist policies were thus at the centre of Hitler's 'positive' eugenics after 1933. Germans were encouraged to found families.[40] The Reinhardt programmes offered loans to freshly married couples to pay for furniture and other household items. A quarter of the principal would be remitted at the birth of each child. These loans were only available to previously working women.[41] The Nazis also considerably upgraded the importance of 'Mother's Day' and introduced a decoration which was punched with Hitler's signature and awarded to mothers at different levels depending on the number of children of 'German blood' they had borne.[42] These policies were accompanied by coercive measures to promote more 'healthy' births.[43] Abortion was banned. Divorce was made easier in order to encourage remarriage and more births. Homosexuality was already illegal, but the Nazis discouraged it still further by tightening the legal definition of homosexual acts. Tens of thousands of transgressors were sent to state prisons. Taken together, these measures had some effect. Within six years, the number of births had jumped back to the level of 1924, the vast majority of them in wedlock. This increase reflected not greater fecundity, but the younger age of marriage; few couples actually took advantage of the financial inducements to establish larger families.[44]

The German people were not merely to be improved socio-economically, they were also to be physically and spiritually uplifted through education, sport and art. In late March 1933, Hitler called for the 'political detoxification' and 'moral renovation of the body politic of the people'. 'The entire education system, theatre, film, literature, press, [and] radio,' he continued, 'are all means to this end' and were designed to 'preserve the eternal values' of the German people.[45] For this reason, Hitler put particular emphasis on education. He sponsored a variety of elite schools, such as the 'National Political Institutes of Education' (NAPOLAs), and the *Adolf-Hitler Schulen*. His model here was the British public schools, whose mix of physical and mental toughening he hoped to surpass. 'On the one side, Eton College,' he wrote later, 'and on our side the Adolf-Hitler Schools or the NAPOLAs.' There were 'two worlds', Hitler continued, 'in the one case children of the people, in the other case only the sons of this money aristocracy, these financial magnates'.[46] Throughout the Third Reich, in fact, the British public school system served as an inspiration for Nazi education policy. Exchanges were encouraged and a delegation from Eton was invited to visit.[47]

Though he had a horror of physical exercise himself, Hitler was keen that German youth should spend much of its leisure time on sporting activities. His enthusiasm for sport was driven by two factors. First, he saw an opportunity for the Third Reich to shine internationally in the light of its sporting achievements. When Max Schmeling knocked out the American Steve Hamas in a widely publicized bout in Hamburg, and celebrated by giving the Hitler-salute to the audience, the Führer was ecstatic. Nowadays, we are accustomed to see leaders identifying with major sporting figures, but at that time Hitler, like Mussolini, was something of a pioneer. More importantly, Hitler saw sport as part of the general racial toughening of German youth, necessitated by the supposedly lamentable current condition of the *Volk*. In contrast to the 'beer philistines' of the past, 'the German boy of the future must be slim and lissom, as fast as a greyhound, as tough as leather, and as hard as Krupp steel'. To be 'tough' was the highest accolade Hitler could award, and it was often used in connection with British tenacity. 'We must,' Hitler continued, 'raise a new person so that our people does not decay.'[48]

If Hitler saw German youth as 'Sparta's children', he did not neglect Athens.[49] To be sure, he had very little interest in literature. Hitler read no novels or poems, and the Goethe Museum in Weimar tried in vain to get him to visit; when in the city he went to Nietzsche's house instead.[50] Just the same, he gave a subsidy which made the museum possible. Hitler defended humanistic education against demands for a more technical training. This was not least because he wished to associate present-day Germans with the cultural achievements of antiquity, rather than the primitive Germanic tribes of the same period.[51] Hitler had no time for Himmler's enthusiasm in this connection. Instead, he insisted on connecting his *Kampf* with that linking 'Greekness and Germanness' across the millennia.[52]

Hitler's interest in art and artists was not mere surface glamour, or personal indulgence; it was a central plank in his project of 'racial' elevation. In September 1933, he established the Reichskulturkammer to coordinate and superintend artistic production. In his first keynote speech on culture, given that year – which he repeated over and over on subsequent occasions – Hitler stressed that the artistic 'disposition' was part of the supposed racial 'inheritance'.[53] Discerning and enjoying 'true art', Hitler believed, assisted the programme of racial 'sifting' or filtering. 'It is the task of art,' Hitler remarked during the debate on the enabling law, 'to express a particular spirit of the age', so that 'blood and race will once more become the inspiration of artistic intuition'. Art should turn away from 'cosmopolitan contemplativeness' towards celebrating 'heroism'.[54] One of the main vehicles of racial improvement here was the appreciation of architecture, which he believed expressed the 'racial core' of the 'body politic of the people'.[55]

The other medium Hitler relied on most here was music, especially the works of Richard Wagner, whose idea of an artistic *Gesamtkunstwerk* – embracing the aural, the spiritual and the intellectual – had particular appeal. Hitler appeared as guest of honour at the commemoration at the Leipzig Gewandhaus to mark the fiftieth anniversary of the composer's death. By August 1933, he had seen *Die Meistersinger von Nürnberg* no fewer than 135 times. Contrary to widespread belief, and despite the various ways in which his works might be interpreted, Hitler did not use Wagner to promote anti-Semitism,[56] but rather as a source of inspiration and edification for the German people.[57] Fourteen months or so after the seizure of power, Hitler used the occasion of the laying of the foundation of the Richard Wagner monument in Leipzig to praise the composer as a man who 'embodied the best of our people', and called for 'coming generations of our people to be drawn into the magic world of this powerful sound poet'.[58]

Hitler sought to bring Wagner to the masses and thereby to uplift them.[59] He took his time, however, about reaching out to the obvious partner, the Wagner Festival at Bayreuth, run by his friend Winifred. This was a potential minefield at many levels. An international event attended by many foreign Jews and at which German Jews performed as a matter of course, the festival could not be Aryanized overnight without throwing the organization into confusion and creating a public *éclat*. Besides, Hitler wanted to bring Wagner to the people, not entomb him in a purpose-built shrine. He pointedly refused, for example, to give Bayreuth a monopoly on Wagner or to suppress the rival performances at the Munich Prinz-regententheater. Despite many hints, he never acceded to Winifred's demand that *Parsifal* only be performed at Bayreuth. Prominent foreigners were already beginning to boycott the festival. Arturo Toscanini, perhaps the most eminent of all living conductors, who had performed to general acclaim at the 1930 and 1931 festivals, refused Winifred's invitation for 1933, citing political reasons; his was the first name on a New York petition expressing solidarity with German Jews. In early April 1933, Winifred and her daughter Friedelind were invited for lunch at the Chancellery. She asked Hitler to appeal to Toscanini, which he did, but – embarrassingly – without success. Hitler was furious. To rub it in, the Italian went to the rival festival at Salzburg instead.

Then Hitler went to ground as far as Bayreuth was concerned. He ignored Winifred's birthday present of tickets in late April. The festival spent most of the spring and summer of 1933 in crisis, as international interest, especially in the United States, slumped, and with it ticket sales. Hitler stepped in only at the last moment, in late June 1933 to guarantee tickets and thus the continuation of the festival. Hitler allowed Winifred to keep Jewish performers for the 1933 festival, and kept on some Jews at the Berlin Staatsoper because they would be needed at Bayreuth; the rest were sacked. At almost the last minute, Hitler announced his intention to attend in person, and was welcomed with great fanfare. The character of the whole festival now changed radically. Instead of being an exclusive international gathering of Wagner connoisseurs, Bayreuth increasingly became a socially more accessible and ideologically more conformist instrument of the Nazi regime. It also became a signature event in Hitler's own political calendar, conveniently timed before the annual party congress in nearby Nuremberg. For now, however, Hitler was still anxious not to give more offence to foreign guests than absolutely necessary. He forbade, for example, the singing of the 'Horst Wessel Lied' and even of the national anthem within the festival building, though the ubiquitous swastikas surrounding the precincts must have told their own story.[60]

The Führer also hoped that art would help to overcome the persisting regional divisions in Germany. Though administratively rigorously centralized through the establishment of various imperial 'chambers',[61] it was rhetorically regionalized. In his speech announcing the creation of a *Haus der Kunst*, Hitler distinguished between the legitimate 'distinctiveness of the German lands', the 'variety of our inner life' and the allegedly pernicious 'spirit of division' which threatened 'the unity of the nation'. 'If Berlin is the capital of the Reich,' he continued, 'Hamburg and Bremen the capitals of German shipping, Leipzig and Cologne the capitals of German commerce, Essen and Chemnitz the capitals of German industry, then Munich should once again become the capital of German art.' 'May this city,' he continued, 'reflect back on its real mission', which was to be 'the site of the elevated and the beautiful'.[62] This, then, was the role which Hitler envisaged for Munich, not just political 'capital of the movement', an accolade granted at the city's own request some way into the Third Reich,[63] but the artistic capital of Germany. 'The capital of art and of our movement is Munich and will stay Munich,'[64] Hitler announced at the laying of the foundations of the Haus der Deutschen Kunst in mid October 1933.

Hitler's artistic tastes were conservative, but not in any meaningful sense of the word kitschy. Some senior Nazi figures, in particular Goebbels, admired modernists such as Emil Nolde, Edvard Munch and Ernst Barlach, all of whom were initially considered part of new 'Germanic' art. Hitler had no interest in them. He preferred Böcklin, Makart, Feuerbach and Spitzweg, all painters still highly regarded today. His artistic sensibility was recognized even by connoisseurs.[65]

If Hitler laid particular stress on high culture, he did not neglect popular entertainment. He was quick to recognize both the opportunities and the threat of cinema and popular music.[66] Hitler did not ban Hollywood or foreign productions as such,[67] and western films formed a major part, sometimes the largest part, of the cinematic offering in the first years of the Third Reich.[68] Many Hollywood studio bosses – some of them Jewish – tried to protect their profits by avoiding offending Hitler.[69] The Führer himself was an avid consumer of American films, including a few banned by the regime, such as *Mickey Mouse*, not least because there were not enough German productions to satisfy his demand.[70] The new German cinema thus did not replace Hollywood, but coexisted and competed with it. Most home-grown productions were pure entertainment, but in so far as they contained a political message, this was primarily directed not against Bolshevism, but against the idea of a better future for Germans across the Atlantic. *Der Kaiser von Kalifornien* (1936), for example, portrayed the career of the German-born pioneer John Sutter as an example of extreme cultural and economic alienation; unlike most contemporary American westerns, it also portrayed the Red Indians in a favourable light. As for jazz, where Hitler's objections to 'Negro music' were well known,

it was widely played and indeed – in the shape of 'Charlie and his Orchestra' – later even offered to international audiences by the regime itself.[71]

That said, Hitler intervened repeatedly in the cinematic field. Sometimes, his motivations were ostensibly aesthetic. On other occasions, the
concern was political. When the International Film Congress met in Berlin
in 1935, Hitler sent a welcoming message, and gave a private audience to
the leaders of the various international delegations. He hoped that the
'high cultural mission of film' would help to 'deepen mutual understanding
among nations'. This was code for a demand to avoid the production of
any films – such as those supposedly sponsored by Jewry – which tended
to complicate Nazi Germany's relations with the outside world.[72]

The final and, as it would turn out, most important way in which Hitler
sought to raise what he regarded as the racial value of the German people
was through agrarian policy. In the short term, he wanted to revive the
agricultural sector in Germany, improve rural living standards, and
increase the production of foodstuffs for the purposes of national self-
sufficiency. This was a critical battlefront for the new government, because,
in comparison with Britain and the United States, Germany was still a
very rural country; it fact it was distinctly 'backward'. When Hitler came
to power, more than 9 million people, just under 30 per cent of the total
workforce, were employed in agriculture. In June 1933, Hitler appointed
Walther Darré minister for agriculture and food supply. That autumn of
1933, he and Herbert Backe set up the 'Imperial Nourishing Estate', whose
immediate task was to set agricultural prices; this meant the end of the
free market in that sector.[73] Hitler did not, however, want to return Germany to some sort of pre-modern rural arcadia. Rather, he saw agriculture
as the key to incubating a new German elite, a 'new aristocracy from blood
and soil', as Darré put it in his seminal text on the subject. Nazi agrarian
policy was specifically intended to supplant the 'old' Junker aristocracy,
which had supposedly failed Prussia and Germany, and it was designed
to be open to every 'real German'.[74] It also sought to rationalize German
farming, whether noble or not.

In the autumn of 1933, Hitler introduced the *Reichserbhofgesetz* (State
Hereditary Farm Law). He wanted to prevent, as he told the cabinet, the
reduction of the German population to 30–35 million within thirty-five
years. Hitler's reasoning here was that the weakness of the farming sector,
which he attributed to the workings of the capitalist system, endangered
the food supply and thus the substance of the nation. It was for this reason,
he argued, that 'the whole power of the people lay in the maintenance of
a healthy farming class'. One way or the other, Hitler argued, 'the farmer
would have to be lifted out of the free economy'.[75] The demographic,

THE 'ELEVATION' OF THE GERMAN PEOPLE 227

political, military and racial purpose of the new law was made clear in the preamble, which committed the Reich to maintain the peasantry as the 'blood source of the German people' by preserving the inherited holding through the prevention of fragmentation by inheritance.[76]

Unlike the previous late nineteenth- and early twentieth-century Prussian agrarian legislation, which had been designed to protect Germans against Slavic subversion, mainly by Poles, the criteria of the *Reichserbhofgesetz* were racial, rather than national. Those specifically excluded from 'the capacity to become farmers' were Jews and Africans. By contrast, the law placed peoples of 'tribally related blood' on the same level as non-Jewish 'Germans'. The Ministry of the Interior defined these as peoples who 'had lived in coherent national settlements in Europe some time back in historical time'. Gypsies were explicitly excluded, even if they were sedentary, but the list of acceptable farmers included not only all supposed 'Aryans', but also many other 'races' such as the Hungarians, Estonians, Finns, Slavs, Danes and Lithuanians.[77] If they had German citizenship, they could become or remain farmers. In other words, the potential racial pool comprised virtually the entire European continent. Some of these exemptions may have been driven by diplomatic considerations, but Hitler's relatively relaxed view of the Slavs, and perhaps also a sense that he would have to make do with the demographic material he had, probably also played a role. This was to have important long-term consequences.

At home, the historical inspiration for the *Reichserbhofgesetz* was the seventeenth- and eighteenth-century Prussian *Bauernschutz*, which was designed to protect not so much the peasant as a pool of recruits for the army. Abroad, it was clearly the law of primogeniture as practised by the British aristocracy, according to which the entire estate passed to the eldest surviving son by entail, while his younger brothers were forced to seek productive employment in the army, the law, the church and even commerce. So long as the supply of land remained the same, the effect of the *Reichserbhofgesetz*, and also its intent, was to reduce the rural population, and to increase agricultural productivity.

In the longer term, of course, Hitler planned to expand the supply of land. He envisaged putting Germany's food supply on a secure basis beyond the threat of war and blockade. Hitler also looked to the capture of new territories to sustain a vibrant class of racially sound soldier farmers and colonists which would gradually elevate the rest of the German people from the current trough. Like the modern United States, which had moved from a (perhaps mythical) Jeffersonian system of rural smallholders to large-scale farming with machinery, Hitler wanted to transition from an economically unsustainable, and in his view racially pernicious, system of intensive cultivation of smaller holdings to more extensive farming on a large scale. Like the United States, he sought to increase his population through the encouragement of valuable elements and the elevation of those not completely beyond the pale. The difference, in geopolitical terms, was that while generations of Americans were urged to 'go west', Hitler told the Germans – as he had done ever since the mid 1920s – to 'look east'.

This was what we might call Hitler's 'German Dream', a vision competing with, but also in some ways inspired by, the 'American Dream'. Here 'living standards' not only mattered as much as 'living space', but were interdependent in ways pioneered by the United States. In Hitler's view, Germany needed space to realize its full racial potential, but it also needed racial strength to secure space. Given that Germany was short of space to start with, this placed a particular premium on increased racial cohesion at home. This deadly dialectic of space and race was to drive policy and politics throughout the Third Reich.

In economic terms, Nazism 'worked', or perhaps Hitler was simply lucky. His programme drew substantially on existing plans and budgets from the late Weimar period. He also seems to have benefited from a 'natural' cyclical upturn. Whether the work-creation schemes actually made any difference is unclear.[78] Most of the money set aside for them had not been spent by the end of 1933. One way or the other, it seemed as if Hitler's insistence that the key to prosperity was politics rather than economics had been vindicated. Business confidence eventually recovered. Within a year, German unemployment had fallen by more than a third; six months later it was 60 per cent lower than at the start of Hitler's chancellorship. Even allowing for statistical sleights of hand, it was an impressive achievement, and, as Hitler himself was quick to point out, a better performance than FDR had managed in the United States.[79] Whether or not the Führer deserved the credit, he reaped the political benefits.

Luckily for Hitler, the spectre of German emigration receded after 1933. To be sure, there was a dramatic outflow of Germans opposed to Nazism, about 360,000 people by the end of the decade (not counting Austrians), but these were elements the Führer was glad to be rid of, even if he maintained a watchful eye on the activities of émigré circles. Unlike the nineteenth and early twentieth centuries, however, there were few purely economic emigrants, probably because the United States was still in the throes of a Depression from which Nazi Germany was beginning to emerge.

In the autumn of 1933, about nine months into his chancellorship, Hitler made a 'State of the Reich' speech to the Imperial Commission behind closed doors. It was revealing both of what Hitler thought he had accomplished, and of his sense of what remained to do. On 20 September 1933, Hitler summoned the 'General Council of the Economy', which included figures from leading German business such as Siemens, Thyssen and Krupp. He began by emphasizing the importance of 'will' and 'will-power' in restoring hope and life where previous governments had given up. Hitler admitted that there had been 'mistakes' but made the Tolstoyan observation that 'the greatest and most successful war, which appears to world history as a single grandiose event, was actually 'the sum of all decisions taken, a mixture of right and wrong ones'. 'Usually,' Hitler continued, picking up an argument he had made during January 1933, victory went to those 'who had merely made the fewest mistakes'. If this period would 'certainly later appear as a period of storm and stress',[80] Hitler concluded, its results had still been overwhelmingly positive. Here Hitler was historicizing his first months, indicating that the domestic tur-bulences of the seizure of power were not only inevitable and excusable, but now a thing of the past.

It was the future, however, with which Hitler was primarily concerned. He repeated his old dictum that 'the political deed' was anterior to economic activity.[81] He now called upon industry to maintain the momentum, to create employment and encourage consumption and investment. The key to this was confidence, which is why Hitler, either consciously or uncon-sciously, resorted to FDR's rhetoric in his first inaugural speech that the 'only thing' Americans had to fear 'was fear itself'. Germans, he explained, were in a perpetual state of 'fear': the fear that the 'neighbours' would consider expenditure profligate, fear of political instability and fear of taxation. Hitler wanted to 'exterminate' this 'complex of fears'. 'Only when people regain a certain joy of living,' he argued, 'will they gradually ensure that money circulates again.' The key, he explained, was to ensure 'that everybody did not want to limit themselves, but that everybody wanted to better themselves'. 'One must construct a ladder,' he continued, 'which everybody can somehow climb up.'

The role of the state in all this, according to Hitler, was to give the 'patient' enough 'injections' to revive him. 'One must,' he explained, 'wind up the economy so far that there is a general undertow which then carries along others as well.' Hitler put his faith in two stimuli. The first was, as we have seen, public works, especially 'giant road construction projects'. The second was in the field of 'house repairs', with the purpose of 'tempt-ing a much larger sum out of hiding through the investment of a comparatively small amount and thus making it productive'. This was what we would today call the 'multiplier effect'.[82] 'Somebody must begin with [repairing] the first window pane,' Hitler demanded, 'the rest would follow. He was articulating, so to speak, a 'broken windows' theory of economic recovery.

Behind the Führer's bravura, however, lay ill-concealed anxiety. He worried about the return of mass unemployment, especially in the winter. 'We naturally have only one concern this winter,' he announced, which was to ensure that 'the number of unemployed must not rise under any circumstances'.[83] Hitler was also anxious about the relationship between the army, which was his preferred vehicle for German rearmament, and the SA, which hoped to play that role itself. He worried about the interference of the party in the state and economy. Above all, Hitler feared the hostility of the outside world, which had been put on its guard, as he saw it, by Germany's domestic resurgence and rearmament. He warned that 'the whole world currently stands together against us'. This was dangerous, Hitler explained, because it would take another three to four years before the Reich could offer any effective defence. There was thus a 'perilous interval' before Germany was ready to bestride the European stage again. Finally Hitler worried about the Jews, because they were 'often very influential abroad'.[84]

On the domestic front, Hitler responded with the 'Winter Relief Project', which was designed to create a sense of national solidarity to get Germans through the physically and psychologically difficult winter months. He also called upon party leaders 'to completely reduce the revolutionary manifestations'. 'There is no more National Socialist goal in Germany,' Hitler declared, and stressed that 'gradual evolution was the precondition for the economic revival which Germany desperately needs'. In case anybody hadn't got the message, Hitler laid down that 'direct interventions by the imperial commissars into the administration must cease', especially 'in judicial matters'. (They didn't, of course.) On military questions, he signalled that 'the Wehrmacht was the sole bearer of arms in Germany', and that 'he did not at all intend to establish a second army in Germany beside it'.[85] For now, Hitler could not go much further, partly because he wanted to avoid confrontation with Röhm and partly because, despite public denials, he was dependent on cooperation between the SA and the Reichswehr to defend Saxony, Silesia and East Prussia against Czech or Polish attack, and the Rhineland and Palatinate against the French.[86]

In this context, Hitler stressed the importance of 'camouflaging' rearmament by disciplining the home front. 'All agencies in the Reich,' Hitler ordained, should exercise 'the greatest care' and 'press reports on German rearmaments should be avoided on principle'. The press should also stop 'constantly publishing pictures of the SA', as their paramilitary bearing tended to excite suspicion.[87] Hitler even opposed a relaxation of domestic gun law, on the grounds that it was 'currently undesirable for foreign-political reasons', because it would give ammunition to the claims of outside powers that Germany was secretly rearming. As for the Jews, he claimed that he would have preferred a 'gradual intensification' of measures but had been forced by the 'Jewish-inspired boycott' to undertake immedi-ate harsh reprisals. That said, Hitler did not want his enemies to be 'given any sort of propaganda material against Germany'. He gave an example of an incident in Nuremberg in which a non-Jewish German girl had had her pigtails cut off because of a relationship with a Jew. 'This event,' Hitler lamented, 'found its way into the entire foreign press.'[88] In short, Germany would have to tread softly on the 'Jewish' front for the moment.

Despite these concerns, Hitler now made another dramatic move. In October 1933, he took Germany out of both the Geneva Disarmament Conference and the League of Nations itself. In the preceding cabinet meeting, he dismissed the danger of 'sanctions' by saying that it was just a question of 'holding one's nerve'.[89] The move was flanked by gestures to the other malcontents of the international system. Hitler expressed will-ingness to receive the Soviet ambassador.[90] The following month, he sent Göring to Italy in order to secure a first personal meeting between himself and the *Duce*. To be on the safe side, Hitler warned party leaders to avoid provoking the French, especially in the Rhineland, so as not to give them a pretext for military intervention.[91] As Hitler predicted, the League and the western powers responded only with bluster. A few days after the announcement, a relieved Hitler noted that 'the critical moment has passed'.[92] Not for the first or the last time, Hitler had called the bluff of the international community.

Rather than push his luck further, the Führer drew back from the brink and tried to prevent the powers from combining against him. He signalled his desire for an understanding with Britain through the colonial issue. He knew well, of course, how central the Empire was to British power and he was also conscious of how the French had brought their subject races to bear on European battlefields in the past, both subjects which he had rehearsed many times before, and reprised from to time after he took power. 'According to remarks of the French minister for war,' he reminded his listeners in March 1933, 'a large part of the coloured French forces can immediately be used on the French mainland.'[93] For this reason, the Führer continued, one should include them among the forces to be discussed at the Geneva rearmament conference. In his various interviews with the British press in 1933, he laid claim to colonies himself, but left open where these were to be found, denied that he would ever go to war for them and generally emphasized his desire not to antagonize Britain on this account.[94] In truth, Hitler remained focused on the east.

Nearer to home, Hitler sought to prise open the Franco-Polish ring of encirclement. In November–December 1933, in the face of considerable resistance from the German Foreign Office, Hitler instructed his diplomats to reach agreement with Warsaw.[95] On 26 January 1934, the German-Polish Declaration was signed. It was a major achievement.[96] This rapprochement was not merely a temporary, insincere expedient. It formed part of Hitler's long-term plan to co-opt the Poles for a junior partnership against the Soviet Union. 'The German-Polish policy,' he told Rosenberg shortly afterwards, 'should not end after ten years, but should continue.'[97] Over the next four years or so, relations with Warsaw were generally excellent. Senior Nazis such as Göring and Goebbels visited. Hitler repeatedly expressed his admiration for General Piłsudski, and deeply regretted his death; in private conversation, he spoke of the Poles as the best soldiers in the world, next to the British and Germans.[98] Hitler not only provided money for a German-Polish Institute in Berlin but specifically laid down that the Battle of the Annaberg, an iconic event when German Freikorps had worsted Polish 'bandits' in 1921, should not be commemorated.[99] So close was the relationship, that Nazis in the German minority in Poland, such as Gauleiter Forster of Danzig, complained that they were being marginalized.[100]

Hitler was by no means out of the woods, either at home or abroad. The French remained hostile. Louis Barthou, who was appointed foreign minister in early February 1934, was well aware of Hitler's plans. He had read *Mein Kampf* in German. Barthou was the driving force behind a Franco-British-Italian warning to Hitler in mid February 1934 not to interfere in Austria. He also sought a rapprochement with Russia, as well as trying to breathe new life into the 'Little Entente' of Czechoslovakia, Romania and Yugoslavia. Hitler now feared an understanding between Austria, France and perhaps Italy at his expense. 'The Führer asked me,' Rosenberg noted in his diary in mid May 1934, 'how I imagined that the French could be held in check throughout the autumn.'[101] Most importantly, Barthou had the support of the British, who were increasingly on their guard against Hitler. His decision to leave the League of Nations precipitated the first serious thinking in London about a new continental military commitment. The permanent under-secretary in the Foreign Office, Vansittart, was already speaking of 'Germany as the eventual enemy'.[102] The ring of encirclement Hitler had broken up through his Polish gambit was being restored in different form. A fresh effort would be required to escape international isolation.

Throughout the first half of 1934, therefore, Hitler made renewed attempts to win over the Angloworld. In early April, he gave an interview to Louis Lochner designed, as the *Völkischer Beobachter* put it, 'to make the personality of Adolf Hitler more accessible to the American people'.[103] There, Hitler announced that he was a fan of personal diplomacy and wanted to conduct face-to-face negotiations with all the main world leaders, including President Roosevelt. On 2 May 1934, he met with James D. Mooney, head of General Motors, which was the owner of the major German car manufacturer Opel. His agenda was partly to promote the production of automobiles, and partly to impress his visitor with the political dynamism of the Third Reich.[104] Perhaps more significant was Hitler's meeting with the press baron William Randolph Hearst, which took place at the Führer's request in the summer of 1934. When Hitler challenged him as to why he was so 'misrepresented, so misunderstood' in North America, Hearst not only responded that his compatriots 'believe in democracy and are averse to dictatorship', but also referred pointedly to the 'very large and influential and respected element in the United States who are very resentful of the treatment of their fellows in Germany'.[105] This, of course, could only reinforce the fateful connection in Hitler's mind, between American power and world 'Jewry'.

In diplomatic terms, the key was London, in what Rosenberg, after one of his many consultations with Hitler on this matter, called 'the struggle for Britain'. Hitler told Rosenberg in early May 1934 that next to the 'implementation of our ideology', his most important concern was 'the struggle for Britain'. Adding to Hitler's frustration were his terrible relations with the British ambassador in Berlin, Phipps, and his unhappiness with the German ambassador to London, Hösch, whom he – rightly – suspected of being hostile to the Third Reich. He now began to ruminate about a suitable replacement. Despite many other preoccupations, Hitler obsessed about the British, who remained a 'dangerous enemy' in the light of his own experiences in the First World War. 'The "battle for Britain",' Rosenberg noted later that summer, 'continues constantly.'[106]

12

Guns and Butter

Despite all his successes, Hitler was still not completely in the clear domestically. Germany had survived the winter of 1933–4 without too much hardship, but although unemployment continued to fall, the economy was in dire straits. The huge rearmament and infrastructural contracts kept industry so busy that it was failing to export, thus reducing the vital flow of foreign currency necessary to purchase scarce raw materials. Hitler warned in late March 1934 that it was now a matter of 'preventing a catastrophe'.[1] 'Every shell needs a copper ring,' Hitler pointed out, adding that 'we have no copper in Germany'. Everybody, he declared, should understand what that meant. Hitler also feared a 'bank catastrophe' sparked off by defaulting loans to department store owners. The finance minister, Kurt Schmitt, pleaded that military expenditure be reduced. The Reichsbank president, Hjalmar Schacht, told Hitler at a meeting on the Obersalzberg that rearmament trumped all other considerations, and declared the increased army budget viable on that basis.[2] By the summer of 1934, however, the distortions caused by massive armaments spending and the raw materials crisis showed no signs of abating. Hitler demanded that the German economy develop locally sourced or produced alternatives, be they synthetic oil and rubber, artificial fibres for clothing or soy beans. 'If necessary,' he said, the Reich should support these endeavours 'financially'.[3]

There was also a tension in Nazi economics between spending, which was needed to fuel the recovery, and saving, which was required to fund rearmament; the maintenance of 'living standards' in the here and now clashed with the capture of 'living space' in the future. Hitler encouraged Germans to save, as an antidote to 'liberal finance capital', as a patriotic duty, and in order to fund houses, travel and cars.[4] Most of the money thus 'lent' to the Reich was invested in weaponry. Hitler, to borrow the language of the time, gave Germans 'guns not butter'; not jam today, but war tomorrow. There was no contradiction in Hitler's mind, though, because he believed the American example showed that the seizure of 'living space' was vital to the provision of 'living standards'.

In the sphere of high politics, Hitler faced two challenges. First, the antagonism between the SA and the Reichswehr remained unresolved and was rapidly turning into a battle of wills between Hitler and Röhm. In late February 1934, Hitler issued his 'Guidelines for Cooperation with the SA'. These gave Blomberg 'sole responsibility' for the 'defence of the Reich', and thus control of 'mobilization' and the conduct of operations in wartime. The SA was given the task of 'pre-military training' after the 'toughening-up' of German youth, and 'the training of all those who have not been drafted to serve in the Wehrmacht'. Hitler justified these functions with reference to strategic necessity and military reality. He expected 'economic turbulence' in about eight years. This, he explained, could only be avoided 'if one found living space' for Germany's 'excess population'. This might require 'short decisive blows towards the west and then the east', for which the SA was not suitable.[5] The dispute with Röhm was also symptomatic of a much broader divide. Whereas the brownshirts wanted to take Germany further to the 'left' and spoke openly of the need for a 'Second Revolution', Hitler sought a period of domestic calm in order to grow the economy and rearm.

Secondly, there was a growing threat on the 'right', from 'reactionary' elements around Vice-Chancellor Papen and his associates, who aimed to win Hindenburg back to their side and restore the shackles on Hitler in the cabinet. They were suspected of enjoying covert support in Dollfuss's Austria and even Mussolini's Italy. In June 1934, the SA absorbed the Stahlhelm, increasing its numbers and equipment. That same month, Papen gave a much-discussed speech at Marburg University critical of Nazi terror measures, which also hinted at the restoration of the monarchy in Germany. Some of his collaborators, such as Edgar Jung, even had Habsburgist sympathies. Hitler was aware of these conservative conspiracies in broad outline.[6] Tensions mounted still further as the Führer became convinced, or affected to be, that Röhm was plotting not only with retired General von Schleicher,[7] but also with foreign powers,[8] to effect his removal. One way or the other, the challenges from right and left, at home and abroad, were becoming increasingly fused in Hitler's mind.

To make matters worse for him, Hitler's plans for a *Reichsreform* were beginning to run into trouble.[9] In late January 1934, he promulgated the 'Law on the Reconstruction of the Reich'. Hitler defined its aim as 'a unified Reich with a unified administration', which was to establish a 'structure' which would enable the German people to deploy its immense strength. Its 'clarity' would compensate for the 'inadequacy of the individual'.[10] The 'prerogatives' of the *Länder* were transferred to the Reich, and the state governments were directly subordinated to that of the Reich. The old Weimar Reichsrat, long defunct, was finally abolished on 14 February 1933. In practice, however, the Nazis were replicating many of the old features of German particularism, just as Hitler had feared. This was most pronounced, as one might expect, in Bavaria, where the local Nazi leadership began conspiring to subvert the authority of the Reich not long after the abolition of federalism. Throughout the Third Reich, German particularism remained alive and kicking in the form of the regional party structures.[11]

In the summer of 1934, Hitler struck at home and abroad. He travelled to Venice in mid June for his first meeting with Mussolini.[12] This was a big moment for Hitler, long awaited since 1922, and he had tears in his eyes when they shook hands. The meeting began badly, because the Führer's unprepossessing dark suit, black shoes, soft hat and lightly coloured coat contrasted with the *Duce*'s bombastic uniform. They soon got down to business, however, especially when the two dictators went for a two-hour walk in the park on their own, without a translator. Nobody knows exactly what was said on that occasion, or whether the *Duce*, whose German was enthusiastic but far from perfect, and the Führer might have misunderstood each other. Hitler, at any rate, emerged from the meeting genuinely under the impression that Mussolini had agreed to the removal of Dollfuss, the installation of a new chancellor and NSDAP participation in a new Austrian government.[13] On the strength of these apparent commitments, Hitler decided to move against Austria. Whether he conceived the putsch or approved one that was already in preparation is not clear. Either way, the two moves, against Röhm and Dollfuss, were, one must assume, part of an integrated strategy.

Hitler first dealt with his domestic enemies. On 27 June 1934, Blomberg and Reichenau persuaded him that the SA was planning a coup against the army, and probably also against the regime.[14] They promised to hold the ring while the SS moved against Röhm.[15] Hitler was also told by Röhm's deputy, Viktor Lutze, that there was something afoot.[16] When Göring's 'Research Institute' (*Forschungsamt*) – which conducted surveillance of domestic and foreign targets – reported that intercepts suggested Röhm was about to move, Hitler suddenly jumped from his chair. 'I have enough,' he announced. 'I am going to make an example.'[17] Hitler flew to Munich and then motored down to Bad Wiessee to confront Röhm. Pistol in hand, he supervised the arrest of the SA chief in person, running back up several flights of stairs when it appeared that their quarries might offer resistance. It was by any standards an extraordinary scene, in which Hitler behaved in ways more typical of a pre-1914 Balkan conspirator or Al Capone of Chicago than the leader of a major European power. Shortly after, Röhm was done to death in custody, protesting his innocence to the end. Elsewhere in Germany, the SS, the Gestapo, the police, and in places even the army, disarmed the brownshirts and incarcerated many of their leaders. Several dozen other SA leaders were also gunned down or summarily executed, as was Gregor Strasser.

Simultaneously, Hitler also decapitated the 'right'. Even before moving against Röhm, Hitler had ordered the arrest of Papen's associate Dr Edgar Jung, the author of the Marburg speech, who was subsequently murdered.[18] The former Generalstaatskommissar, Gustav von Kahr, Hitler's betrayer in 1923, was killed along with a number of other Bavarian conservatives, including Hitler's *bête noire*, Otto Ballerstedt.[19] The motive here was partly revenge, but partly also to crush any remaining separatist tendencies. Two of Hitler's military opponents, retired General von Schleicher and his associate Ferdinand von Bredow, were murdered. So were several other figures close to Vice-Chancellor Papen, including his main strategist, Herbert von Bose, and the Catholic politician Erich Klausener, who had contributed to the Marburg speech. Papen himself escaped elimination, but his future was now very uncertain. What stayed Hitler's hand was the desire not to cloud his relationship with the ailing Hindenburg. 'The Führer does not want to undertake anything yet against the reactionaries,' Rosenberg wrote in his diary, 'his consideration for Hindenburg is almost touching.'[20] The events of the Röhm putsch were typical of Hitler. He had put off the showdown with Röhm as long as possible, and prepared the ground carefully. He then acted ruthlessly, crushing two serious challenges to his authority in one stroke.

Despite the presentational difficulties involved, the regime made no attempt to hide Hitler's central role in the death of his former comrades. 'The Führer personally led the action,' one official report announced, 'and did not hesitate for a moment to confront the mutineers in person and to call them to account.' 'The behaviour of the Führer during this nocturnal flight into the unknown was one of the utmost determination,' it continued, adding that 'Röhm was personally arrested in his bedroom by the Führer'.[21] In his justificatory speech to the Reichstag a fortnight after the events, the Führer did not mince his words. Not only had he 'given the order to shoot dead those principally guilty of treason', but he also instructed his men to crush any further resistance with violence.[22] Hitler stressed that he had pre-empted an SA 'night of the long knives',[23] a phrase which has since lived on in the literature, albeit as a description of his own actions and not those of Röhm.

On the other hand, Hitler was under no illusions about how badly the murders had gone down at home and abroad; US Ambassador Dodd, a Southerner whose relations with Hitler were steadily deteriorating, boycotted his apologia to the Reichstag.[24] Hitler therefore made considerable efforts in press communiqués and declarations and in the privacy of the cabinet to blacken the reputation of Röhm and his circle, by emphasizing their well-known homosexual tendencies and their – greatly exaggerated – connections to foreign powers.[25] He stressed that he had acted in order to 'cauterize the festering sores of our domestic poisoned wells and the poisoning by outside powers'.[26] The Führer also made a hysterical speech to a closed session of party leaders shortly after the murders at which he threatened to shoot himself if the various pillars of the Reich could not act in a unified manner.[27] He then reached out to the foreign press, especially in America, to push his version of events. A week after Röhm's killing, Hitler gave an interview to the New York Herald which began with a robust defence of his actions.[28]

The cornerstone of Hitler's apologia, however, was his contention that the elimination of the SA restored domestic stability to the Reich after a period of cleansing but turbulent upheaval. 'Revolution,' he told the Reichstag in mid July 1934, 'is not a permanent condition for us.' Slow, evolutionary change was now the order of the day. Later that autumn, Hitler promised that 'there will not be another revolution in Germany for a thousand years'. 'The National Socialist revolution is completed,' he announced, adding that 'it has achieved what could be expected of it as a revolution'.[29] Whether Hitler was consciously echoing Napoleon's similar pronouncement when he came to power is not known, but it is clear that Hitler was seeking to reassure the German people that he had completed the Nazi revolution and in doing so ended it.

The Führer now turned to deal with the nearest external enemy, namely Dollfuss. He spent much of early July 1934 preoccupied with Austria and seems to have superintended the planned operation in some detail.[30] It seems that a group of Austrian SS members managed to convince Hitler that they could stage a putsch with the assistance of parts of the military and the police. In the middle of the month, Hitler met with Theodor Habicht and the other conspirators in Munich, presumably to concert the final measures. As in 1923, the plan was to seize and impose one's will on the political leadership. Hitler then headed for Bayreuth. It was the first festival that he had fundamentally shaped and he marked its importance by staying a full week. Jews were now banned from performing, and those associated with Bayreuth emigrated to the United States. That did not prevent Hitler from consorting openly with individual Jews, such as Alice Strauss, the Jewish daughter-in-law of the composer Richard Strauss. Artistically, the central focus of the festival was a new production of *Parsifal*, with sets designed by Alfred Roller, which the Führer funded. To show his reverence, the Führer attended in full evening dress, not just in dinner jacket. The production was condemned by traditionalists as 'the de-Christianization of the most Christian of all dramatic works',[31] which was exactly what Hitler had intended. Not for him the preservation of a masterpiece in aspic; to Hitler art was a living, breathing organism, subject to constant change.

In the late afternoon of 25 July 1934, Hitler was called to the phone. The news from Vienna was catastrophic. The cabinet meeting, during which the conspirators had hoped to capture the whole government, had been postponed by a day, and when the Nazis took over the Chancellery, most ministers had managed to escape. Showing a characteristic mixture of brutality and incompetence, the conspirators had so badly wounded Dollfuss during his arrest, probably unintentionally, that the chancellor had bled to death in custody. Hitler still ordered the Austrian SA to stage an uprising in the countryside. They made little headway in the capital, rather more in parts of the countryside, especially Styria. Most police and army units resisted fiercely. Soon, the surviving putschists were pinned against the Yugoslav border. There was no chance of securing even the minimal aims of a Nazi role in government. To make matters worse, Mussolini responded by sending troops to the Brenner Pass, warning Berlin not to intervene. Powerless to affect the outcome, and fearful of giving France the excuse to launch a preventive war, Hitler backed down. Even at the height of his humiliation, however, Hitler exerted control, vowing to avoid 'a second Sarajevo',[32] meaning a general conflagration sparked by a minor event. He would make war on his terms, and not be bounced into it.

Mussolini's reaction baffled Hitler, as he believed that the move against Dollfuss had been agreed at Venice. 'I don't understand that,' he remarked to Fritz Wiedemann. 'I filled him in on all the details of our Austrian policy in Venice.'[33] It also infuriated him, and sent German-Italian relations into a long decline. There was now no question of a return visit by Mussolini to Germany in the autumn. Instead, Hitler looked to the Balkans. 'I debated for a long time with the Führer,' Goebbels recorded in late July 1934. 'He has finally broken with Rome' and 'will seek closer relations with Yugoslavia'.[34] The economic relationship, which was already close thanks to the 1 May 1934 German-Yugoslav trade treaty, deepened further, though Hitler took little political interest in the region.[35]

The failure of the coup left Hitler with a dim view of the local Nazis, and perhaps of the Austrians in general, whom he regarded with a mixture of affection and exasperation. He no longer relied on the Austrian party, which was in any case banned. 'Habicht is finally finished with Hitler,' Goebbels noted. Hitler told Reichenau that he intended 'to liquidate the National Socialist policy towards Austria', and 'to disband the Austrian Legion' which would be turned into a 'purely humanitarian organization' to look after Austrian refugees.[36] At least nominally, the Legion became the 'Hilfswerk Nordwest' and was employed for public works. To ease the financial burden of maintaining a paramilitary force almost 10,000 strong, its members were increasingly integrated into the growing German economy. Hitler sent Papen to Vienna, partly to get him out of Berlin and partly in order to mend fences with the Austrian regime, at least for the time being.[37] Still, German pressure on Austria, which had started in 1933 with the '1,000 mark prohibition', a levy on Germans travelling to Austria in order to hit Austria's tourism, and similar measures, continued for a while. It was only in July 1936 that Papen managed to negotiate a gentlemen's agreement in which Hitler recognized the 'complete sovereignty of the federal state of Austria', promised better cultural relations and left Vienna free to deal with the Austrian Nazis as an internal matter, all in return for an amnesty for party members not accused of the most serious crimes. That said, Austria continued to be a concern after the failed putsch, not least because of continued rumours of a Habsburg restoration.[38]

If Hitler had suffered a severe diplomatic setback, he continued to tighten his grip on Germany itself. First, after the events of 30 June 1934, the SS increasingly replaced the SA as the most important military party institution. On 20 July 1934, specifically citing the 'great achievements of the SS especially in connection with the events of 30 June 1934', Hitler elevated the Reichsführer SS to a position comparable to that of the chief of staff of the SA, that is, immediately responsible to Hitler.[39] In theory, this put Himmler on the same level as Röhm's replacement, Viktor Lutze. In practice, the events of 30 June, and Himmler's own relentless empire-building, meant that the SS took on a far more dominant role in the Third Reich.

Secondly, the elimination of the Papen wing of the conservative opposition left Hitler free to capitalize on the illness of Hindenburg, who finally died in early August 1934. There was now nobody else left to claim his legacy, or to take up his suggestion in a last posthumously sent letter to Hitler that he should restore the monarchy. Even before the field marshal had breathed his last, Hitler presented the cabinet with the draft of a 'Law on the Head of State of the German Reich', which simply amalgamated the office and powers of the presidency with those Hitler already possessed as 'Führer and chancellor' after Hindenburg's death.[40] He then organized a referendum to demonstrate, as he put it, the 'unshakeable unity' of the

German people to the outside world and especially to 'a particular international conspiracy [the Jews]'.[41] Having long acted on the basis of presidential power, Hitler had now finally captured the presidency itself. The officials of the Imperial Chancellery swore an oath to Hitler.[42] Seeing the writing on the wall, the Reichswehr leadership, at the initiative of Blomberg and Reichenau, suggested that the army swear its own personal oath of allegiance to the Führer.[43]

All this was accompanied by the consolidation of Hitler's authority within German society. Central to this was the 'Führer' myth, the charismatic hold which Hitler had long enjoyed over his followers, and now extended over much of the population.[44] It was expressed every day in the form of the greeting 'Heil Hitler' in conversation or written communications. Hitler gave careful thought to the management of this cult of personality. He let it be known that 'the German greeting "Heil Hitler" should become the credal greeting of the Germans among themselves'. Hitler also suggested that 'in social written communications "Heil Hitler" should in principle by used in closing, without, however, completely excluding an alternative valediction'.[45] He left it 'to the tactfulness of the individual' to decide when the use of his name at the end of his letter was appropriate or not, and stressed that there should be 'no reproach' against those who abstained from doing so for good reason. Hitler's sense here of what was appropriate and enforceable is palpable. He was also determined to avoid the kind of exaggerated cult of the personality, bordering on deification, which might expose him to ridicule. When Hitler got wind of the fact that the non-Christian faith group 'German Faith Movement' was propagating the idea of a 'divinely gifted' and 'divinely sent' Führer, he insisted that this article of their creed be deleted.[46]

Not everything went Hitler's way. Many Germans remained immune to his appeal, even if very few resisted actively. In the plebiscite called on 19 August 1934 to approve his absorption of the presidency, which was hardly a free and fair vote, just over 10 per cent of those who turned out refused to do so. This was twice as many as had voted 'no' in the November 1933 referendum on leaving the League, and together with the greatly increased number of non-voters and spoiled ballots suggested unease either with the events of 30 June or perhaps with Nazi rule generally. There was no disguising the setback. The photograph of a consternated Hitler, Goebbels and other Nazis leaders receiving the results tells its own story.[47] Towards the end of the month, the Führer vented his frustration in a speech at the Ehrenbreitstein fortress near Koblenz, vowing that he was 'convinced' that he would convert the 'tenth man', that is, the 10 per cent who had voted against him in the plebiscite.[48] Clearly, he had some way to go before German national unity was complete.

In terms of high politics, though, the Führer's authority was now more or less absolute. 'Now the Führer is the *sole* master in Germany,' Rosenberg recorded in his diary, so that 'all preconditions for a National Socialist state are finally in place'.[49] The Reichstag was completely compliant,[50] serving primarily as an acclamatory forum at which Hitler announced major policies or – later – issued declarations of war. Government departments did Hitler's bidding,[51] and were increasingly imbued with National Socialist spirit by Hess in the Party Chancellery, which had secured the right to be consulted on all government legislation by July 1934, and eventually also control over the appointment of senior officials.[52]

Where the state administration failed to deliver, Hitler ordered or encouraged the establishment of alternative structures. 'Wherever the formal bureaucracy of the state proves itself unfitted to solve a problem,' Hitler vowed, 'there the German nation will bring into play its own more living organisation in order to clear the way for the realisation of its vital necessities . . . Whatever can be solved by the state will be solved through the state, but any problem which the state through its essential character is unable to solve will be solved by means of the movement.'[53] Contrary to his recent announcement that the revolution was over, Hitler repeatedly urged party leaders in private not to rest on their laurels but to show greater activism.[54] 'The conquest of power,' he remarked, 'is a process that will never ever be finished.'[55]

The political consequences of all this were twofold. First, there was the emergence of a 'court' around Hitler.[56] This was partly a social phenomenon, and the Führer proved adept at managing it,[57] but its most important manifestation lay in the exercise of authority. Every political system, even western democracies, generates some sort of antechamber of power, but the greater the authority vested in the leader, the more important that space will be. Access to Hitler brought power, or at least the appearance of it. Like Charlemagne, who progressed from one imperial palace to another, when Hitler moved between the Chancellery in Berlin, his Munich flat, the Bayreuth Festival, his retreat at Berchtesgaden and later between military headquarters, the seat of power and much of his entourage went with him. On the Obersalzberg, in particular, Hitler held court as a monarch would at his summer residence. A whole ersatz Imperial Chancellery was established in a neighbouring village so that government could continue to function.

The most striking sign of the new politics was Hitler's preoccupation with his mortality, and thus with the question of the succession. In the absence of democratic procedures this would have to be regulated in advance in order to avoid chaos. Hitler therefore decreed in early December 1934 that Hermann Göring should succeed him as 'Führer und Reichskanzler'. The government, the Wehrmacht, the SA and the SS were all instructed to swear an oath of allegiance to his successor personally. Hitler also laid down that in the event of his absence or incapacity, his functions should be exercised by a triumvirate, with Göring taking on the leadership of the state, Blomberg of military matters, and Hess those pertaining to the party.[58] The distinction between the two arrangements seems to reflect a reserve on Hitler's part about empowering any one potential rival while he was still alive.

There were still important restraints on Hitler's power. Some of these were voluntary. Unlike Stalin's Russia, the Third Reich was not, or at least not yet, a totalitarian state. Hitler was convinced that mere outward conformity without inner conviction was worthless, because it would crumble under challenge. For that reason, Hitler never tired of exhorting and persuading Germans, and – in his own way – consulting them at various levels. Rather than abandoning referenda after the fiasco of August 1934, he continued holding them until the late 1930s. The cabinet functioned normally for another few years, despite the removal of Papen and the weakening of the conservative faction there. Most importantly of all, Hitler did not avoid collective meetings with his *Gauleiter* and *Reichsstatthalter*. On the contrary, these remained an important forum for the discussion and announcement of policy – and not merely its acclamation – throughout the Third Reich.[59]

The other limits to Hitler's authority were structural. For all the partial identity of aims, important constituencies within key institutions, such as the Foreign Office and the army, remained profoundly hostile – to him personally, and to National Socialism generally. The same was true of the churches. Some resistance from the 'Confessing Church' aside, the Protestant confessions posed relatively few problems. Though born a Catholic, Hitler was politically more comfortable with Lutheranism and Calvinism, because they were largely national in structure and focus. German Protestants were also generally more at ease with him, though the overtly Nazi Deutsche Christen were still a minority. Relations with the Catholic Church were much more fraught, despite the Concordat. Hitler remained deeply suspicious of the hold which the Catholicism maintained over millions of Germans and he profoundly feared its international reach. 'The Catholic Church,' he warned a meeting of *Reichsstatthalter* in early November 1934, had 'always been an enemy of a strong state power'.[60] From the mid 1930s onwards, in fact, this 'black' threat loomed much larger in his imagination than the 'red' menace from Social Democracy and German communists. Hitler was determined to take on the church at some future point, but for now he bided his time. He gave the order that there should be 'no creation of unnecessary new areas of conflict with the churches'.⁶¹

In early February 1934, Hitler introduced a highly symbolic new pan-German citizenship law, which removed the need for a qualifying state citizenship, which was abolished; Hitler had experienced the rigours of the old system at first hand in the 1920s. Seven months later he merged the interior ministries of the Reich and its largest state, Prussia. His much heralded 'imperial reform', however, made little headway. In late 1934 and early 1935, Frick announced his intention to divide Germany into some twenty *Reichsgaue*, with about a million inhabitants each, whose bound-aries were to be determined by economic and strategic factors.⁶² Hitler's attempt to introduce some demographic and geographic rationality into the historically developed hodge-podge of German *Länder* foundered in the face of the determination of local actors, most of them Nazis, to pre-serve their power and identity. Hitler managed only to achieve the amalgamation of the two Mecklenburgs, a meagre outcome for all the effort invested. In the face of this controversy, Hitler twice forbade public discussion of changes and eventually backed off.⁶³

In day-to-day matters, Hitler's *bêtes noires*, the bureaucrats, continued to drag their feet on everything, not only because they wanted to, but because they couldn't help it. 'The Führer is now very angry with the min-isterial bureaucracy,' Rosenberg noted in mid July 1934, and had announced that 'I will teach these gentlemen the right pace'.⁶⁴ Five months later, he erupted at a meeting of *Reichsstatthalter*, expressing the view that 'even today the state has tens of thousands of bureaucrats', some of whom were 'secret' and others of whom were 'lethargic' enemies of the movement. 'Years will pass,' he continued, 'until these enemies are removed.'⁶⁵ Such explosions were to remain routine until the end of the Third Reich. Hitler's frustration was not confined to the state administration but also extended to the many party bureaucracies set up after 1933. For example, when Hitler passed on a petition from four Hamburg workers to Hess's office, which in turn entrusted the matter to a local agency, the matter seems to have been lost in the system for four months.⁶⁶ 'It is an outrageous waste of the authority of the Führer,' Wiedemann thundered after repeated failed attempts to gain clarity, 'if assignments issued in his name are ignored.'⁶⁷ The result of all this was an impenetrable administrative thicket.

These problems were greatly aggravated by endemic personal rivalries and high political manoeuvring. Throughout the twelve years of the Third Reich, *Gauleiter*, ministers, *Reichsstatthalter*, the SA and the SS faced off against each other in a series of arguments without end, just as the Nazi leaders had battled each other incessantly before 1933. Göring continued to fight Goebbels; Feder battled Schacht over the economy; the *Reichsstatthalter* of Braunschweig und Anhalt, Wilhelm Loeper, tangled with the Anhaltine *Staatsminister* Alfred Freyberg; and the interior minister, Wilhelm Frick, the *Reichsstatthalter* of Bavaria, Franz Xaver Ritter von Epp, and the Bavarian chief minister, Ludwig Siebert, fought a three-way battle in the best traditions of German particularism. All these, and many other, differences landed on Hitler's desk for adjudication,[68] with each side claiming that the other was subverting 'the will of the Führer'. In a particularly heated exchange, Walther Darré 'literally' told Hitler's personal adjutant over the phone that his letters were 'an arse-wipe' and that he 'should kiss my arse'.[69] Sometimes, the rows took place in the Führer's presence such as that between the Nuremberg chief of police, Freiherr von Malsen-Ponickau, and Gauleiter Julius Streicher of Franconia, which exploded in front of Hitler just before the 1933 party congress.[70] In short, far from pulling together to transform the Third Reich and prepare for the next war, authorities and personalities competed for everything: for Hitler's favour, his attention, for status, power and, as rearmament took off, resources.

There is little evidence that Hitler encouraged these rivalries as a way of enhancing his own position. It is true that Meissner, who served as head of Hitler's Presidential Chancellery after Hindenburg's death, recalls his 'tendency to assign several associates the same task simultaneously', which he partly attributed to his 'keen mistrust and the principle of "divide and rule"'. While this may have been the result of his actions and his personality, Hitler himself never articulated any such theory. Instead, as Meissner also records, Hitler 'often expressed the view' that 'such a parallel entrustment of many with the same task' helped to forestall 'passivity' among individuals, and to 'motivate' them to greater achievement. Besides, the resulting 'competition' led him to be 'better informed about what was going on'.[71] In other words, the Führer sought the 'survival of the fittest' in a kind of bureaucratic Darwinism, rather than paralysis through perpetual strife. Hitler wanted to shake up the system, not to seize it up through the creation of a 'polycratic chaos'.

In fact, the interminable personal struggles which plagued the Nazi system even more than they do most polities wearied and infuriated Hitler. 'In the National Socialist state,' Hitler decreed, 'only one person is ever responsible for something.'[72] He also preferred party leaders to resolve their own disputes wherever possible instead of constantly seeking his mediation. His main concern, as he put it on one occasion, was 'to avoid that everyone came running to him when there were differences of opinion'.[73] This is evident from his handling of a clash between Rosenberg and Rust. 'When the Führer heard that we were in agreement,' Rosenberg recorded, 'he laughed happily,' adding that 'he did not want to hear any more' and would bless anything they agreed.[74] The squabbles in Munich – 'the confused governing situation of the Bavarian government', as he put it to Lammers[75] – reduced the Führer to despair. To be sure, Hitler wanted to be consulted about and to pronounce on major matters of policy, but he had no desire to superintend everything. He was not what one would today call a 'control freak'.

That said, Hitler had only himself to blame for the way in which matters great and small landed at his door. It was a product not merely of the fact that he was the font of all authority, but also of his tendency to make decisions on the hoof. Hitler would promise one thing on one occasion, and the contrary on another occasion, either changing his mind or forgetting what he had said in the first place. In some cases, Hitler may have been misunderstood, or have expressed himself so Delphically as to invite misunderstanding. For example, when Christian Weber appealed to him in his struggle with Hermann Göring over the establishment of a hunting museum in Munich, Hitler responded that he had '*not* [emphasis in the original]' agreed to Weber's request. Such denials were routine throughout the Third Reich, whether it was his supposed commitment when visiting a coal mine to achieve a 'just distribution of wages', his promise to make Julius Lippert mayor of Berlin, or his offer to fund construction work in Breslau in advance of the 'Festival of the League of German Singers' and the 'German Gymnastics Festival' in that city.[76]

The nature of the resulting high political culture defies easy characterization. Hitler was beyond doubt its primary motor and focus, but Nazi initiatives did not necessarily originate with him. Where Hitler gave a direct steer, the bureaucracy responded with alacrity, filling out the detail, and providing options for the Führer to choose from. On other occasions, the execution of policy was left to the various institutions. This modus operandi was, in some ways, the Nazi equivalent of the old 'mission tactics' in the Prussian army. Hitler set out the ideological parameters within which politics and policy unfolded. Ministers and bureaucrats thus sought to anticipate his will, even before it had been expressed. This tendency was vividly described by Werner Willikens, the state secretary for food, in February 1934, when the Third Reich was just over a year old. 'Everyone who has the opportunity to observe it,' he wrote, 'knows that the Führer can hardly dictate from above everything which he intends to realise sooner or later. On the contrary, up till now everyone with a post in the new Germany has worked best when he has, so to speak, worked towards the Führer.' Willikens condemned those who 'simply waited for orders and instructions'. 'Anyone who makes mistakes,' he continued, 'will notice it soon enough.' 'But anyone who really works towards the Führer along his lines and towards his goal,' Willikens concluded, 'will certainly both now and in the future one day have the finest reward in the form of the sudden legal confirmation of his work.'[77]

Perhaps the best analogy for Hitler's style of governance comes from the world of music. If he conceived of his programme as a Wagnerian *Gesamtkunstwerk*, the execution of it resembled more closely a giant jamming session than a formal symphony. There was no score or individual parts, and no rehearsals, but only an agreed ideological chord progression following the Führer's lead, characterized by multiple improvisations by party leaders, ministers and bureaucrats. Much of the time no conductor was needed, so that the music did not stop when Hitler was out of the room. Intentionally or not, Hitler had turned the supposed weaknesses of the German people – a *Volk* (and thus a party) noted for its divisions, divas and primadonnas[78] – into strength; he harnessed their creative destructiveness and destructive creativity. This partly explains the 'cumulative radicalization' of the regime, as institutions and individuals vied for the Führer's favour,[79] though, of course, Hitler's radicalism had been there from the start, and at the latest from *Mein Kampf*, and he did not always choose the most radical option presented to him. It certainly accounts for the stupendous range and quantity of legislation which Hitler managed to produce during his tenure as chancellor, and for the extreme murderousness of the regime during the war.

The regime sought to obscure the many fractures in the German polity through carefully choreographed displays of national unity, in parades and rallies. These took place on many occasions, for example on Hitler's birthday, but easily the most important was the autumn annual party congress at Nuremberg. In September 1934, no doubt in an attempt to show that the ghosts of the Röhm putsch had been laid to rest, the proceedings involved hundreds of thousands of brownshirts, and Hitler himself appeared in SA uniform. The Reichswehr participated for the first time, partly in order to demonstrate its commitment to the new state and partly to impress outside observers with the military vitality of the new state. Hitler was ubiquitous throughout, or at least appeared to be.[80] Leni Riefenstahl filmed the whole event, and Hitler willingly put up with the disruption caused by her 170-odd collaborators, and their accompanying plethora of wires, cranes and cameras. The end product – entitled *The Triumph of the Will* at Hitler's suggestion – has entered cinematic legend; a good third of its two hours were devoted solely to the Führer.[81]

The party congress took place against a background of anxiety about the performance of the economy. This was partly a geographical concern.

Some areas had not benefited much from the upswing since 1933. One of these was Hamburg, a city Hitler had always been intensely concerned about; he visited no fewer than twenty-seven times. This was partly because he saw it as the sea gate into the Reich from abroad, especially Anglo-America, and partly because it was the port through which emigrants had left for the United States. In April 1934, in a highly symbolic move, the legendary Ballinstadt – where huge numbers of mainly eastern European, but also German, emigrants, had waited for their passage – was closed. Stopping the export of people was one thing, the reduced exports of goods as a result of the focus on rearmament and the domestic market was another. Hamburg, which had never really recovered from the 1929 slump, languished economically, and this may explain the fact that nearly one-quarter of the city's electorate voted against Hitler in the August referendum after Hindenburg's death. This was twice the national average, and by far and away the worst result of any region. Hitler responded with alacrity. He proclaimed the city an 'emergency area' in early November 1934, effectively putting it under special measures, banning further inward migration and pushing industrial contracts in its direction.[82]

The economic position in the Third Reich was aggravated by the fact that while there had been considerable spending on civilian work creation throughout 1933 and much of 1934, the military budget surged ahead by the end of that year. The economy struggled to export enough to maintain the balance of payments for raw material imports, so that military experts warned of dire consequences for rearmament. This led to a raw materials shortage and credit 'squeeze'.[83] In the autumn of 1934, Schacht reacted by announcing his 'New Plan', whose very name suggested an affinity with Roosevelt's 'New Deal'. Unlike its American counterpart, however, the plan was driven by the need to speed up rearmament by replacing trade with world markets on a purely economic basis with bilateral relationships underpinned by political connections. Some of these were with South American countries, but the closest links were forged in the Balkans. It was to prove a valuable source of raw materials and agricultural products, and a captive market for German manufactured goods.[84] These were traded using special 'clearing' arrangements that amounted to mass barter on credit. Economic, or rather resource, considerations rather than political influence remained the driving force here.

Hitler also remained anxious about Germany's strategic position. He was rattled by Stanley Baldwin's parliamentary speech supporting increased RAF expenditure in the late summer and his remark that Britain's frontier was 'on the Rhine'. Hitler told the *Reichsstatthalter* in early November 1934 that this might not be 'as critical' as in May 1933, with the threatened Polish preventive strike, or in the summer of 1934, during the Röhm crisis, but it was still 'not completely without risk'. It would take about another two years or so to exit the danger zone. 'From 1936 onwards,' he opined, 'it is unlikely that any state will risk an attack on Germany on its own.' Even then, Germany should concentrate on its domestic transformation. 'The Reich government has no interest in any kind of armed conflict,' Hitler stated, because if he were granted 'another 10–12 years of peace' then the construction of National Socialism could be completed. A month later, he claimed with satisfaction that 'the French had now finally missed the opportunity to wage a preventive war'.[85] There was, however, still no cause for complacency.

For this reason, Hitler continued to engage with the world outside. In November 1934, Hitler told two visiting French parliamentarians, Robert Monnier and Jean Goy, that *Mein Kampf* was now obsolete, that he had no territorial claims against France itself, and certainly not to Alsace-Lorraine. On his return, Goy reassured the French press that Hitler gave 'the impression of being a balanced person', both 'intellectually' and 'morally'; he pleaded for understanding of the new Germany and the avoidance of a 'ring of steel' around it which would perpetuate traditional blocs.[86] In December 1934, Hitler agreed to see Lord Allen of Hurtwood, a close associate of the Labour prime minister, Ramsay MacDonald, and Henri Pichot, the head of the French war veterans association.[87] The latter – to whom Hitler appeared like a 'volcano' and a 'hurricane' – was promised that the return of the Saar from League of Nations administration already expected for 1935 would end all territorial disputes with Germany.[88] Early the following year, Hitler met with the French automobile producer Louis Renault and promised him too that all territorial disputes had now been laid aside.[89] All of these moves were designed to improve the Third Reich's global image until she was ready to take the fight to the world outside.

In the meantime, Hitler pressed ahead with revising the Versailles settlement bit by bit. His next target was the Saar region. This low-hanging fruit was due to be returned to the Reich in any case, subject to a plebiscite, fifteen years after it was removed in 1920. In early June 1934, the Council of the League of Nations announced that the vote would be held in mid January of the following year. The Saar's importance was primarily symbolic, but its industrial capacity was also important for rearmament. Hitler saw the vote as a referendum on his regime, not least because German exiles exhorted the electorate of the Saarland to give him a bloody nose with the slogan 'Beat Hitler on the Saar'. He appointed the local *Gauleiter*, Josef Bürckel, as 'general plenipotentiary of the Reich Government for the Saar'. He also reined in the pro-Nazi Protestant Deutsche Christen, whose antics were likely to damage 'opinion abroad and especially the German chances in the plebiscite on the Saar'.[90] In January 1935, the Saar, under the eyes of an international peace force, voted overwhelmingly to return to Germany, an outcome which Nazi propaganda hailed as a thumping endorsement of Hitler and his regime.

Keen to consolidate his hold on the returned province, and anxious to appease Paris, Hitler immediately announced – again – that Germany 'no longer had any territorial demands against France', a phrase which referred to French lands such as Alsace-Lorraine. The following day, he repeated the sentiment to an American journalist from the Hearst organization in an interview given on the Obersalzberg. Hitler begged his interlocutor not to be taken in by the contrary assertions of the Jews, to whom he referred using a standard code. 'I have only one request to make of the American people,' he said, which was that they should in future 'not believe a word of the professional international well-poisoners and agitators' who had emigrated from Germany. The next few weeks and months were thus dominated by the usual eyewash about Hitler's peaceful intentions. He had already told the Berlin Diplomatic Corps that 'Germany will always be a guarantor of peace'. 'If I speak of peace,' he averred, 'I am only expressing the deepest wish of the German people.'[91]

In March 1935, Hitler announced the reintroduction of conscription, in defiance of the provisions of the Versailles Treaty. This was another gamble, because the French and British would have been within their rights to enforce the disarmament clauses. The public reaction was anxious, and many leading Nazis expressed concern behind the scenes. 'If the French have any élan,' Rosenberg told Hitler, 'the bombers should now be zooming off in Paris.' The Führer replied simply: 'I think we will get through.'[92] Partly, he sought to reduce the risk through bluff: the announcement on conscription was accompanied by the unveiling of the new Luftwaffe, whose actual power lagged far behind the propagandistic presentation. Partly, he relied on the usual spreading of chaff to disorientate the international community. Towards the end of the month, he finally received the British foreign secretary, Sir John Simon, and the lord privy seal, Anthony Eden, with much fanfare. He had delayed their visit until after the reintroduction of conscription had been announced.[93] Winifred Wagner was pressed into service to dine with her two countrymen after the negotiations; she spoke so animatedly to Simon that he was unable to eat his meal.[94] Hitler also gave conciliatory interviews to the foreign, including the American, press.[95] Despite his pledge to brazen things out, Hitler was in fact extremely anxious about the negative reaction to his announcement.[96]

This time, there was a hefty diplomatic price. Alarmed by Hitler's latest infringement, Britain, France and Italy combined at Stresa in April 1935 to condemn Nazi Germany. The resulting 'Stresa Front' was a major threat to Hitler's plans. There was also the Franco-Soviet 'Treaty of Assistance', which was signed in May 1935, and was entirely directed against Nazi Germany. Hitler welcomed the propagandistic benefits of the antagonism with communism, but the echoes of the pre-1914 Franco-Russian alliance surrounding Germany were worrying. One way or the other, the ring of encirclement which Hitler had so laboriously prised open in 1933–4 was now in danger of closing around Germany again.

All these concerns took a severe toll on Hitler's private life, especially his relationship with Eva Braun. His interest in her was entirely unpolitical, and, leaving aside her role in the dynamics of Nazi court politics, in which favour and access played an important part, there is no suggestion that she affected his thinking or influenced any particular policy. At first, he saw her regularly in Munich, where she had a flat, and at the Berghof, where she was officially described as Hitler's private secretary. In the absence of any formal status, Eva was overshadowed by Magda Goebbels, who enjoyed the status of an unofficial 'First Lady'. To make matters worse, Eva was rejected not only by the Berghof wives, but also by Angela Raubal, Hitler's housekeeper, and Geli's mother. As if all this were not bad enough, Eva was upset by the interest Hitler showed in other women, especially unmarried ones like Sigrid von Laffert, a young blonde aristocrat, who was frequently seen at his side in Berlin. To cap it all, the Führer was increasingly absent as he dealt with domestic crises, or sought to find a way out of his international isolation. Eva did not see him at all for the first three months of 1935, as he sought an understanding with Britain. In late April, she lamented to her diary that 'love does not at the moment seem to be part of his programme'.[97] At the end of May 1935, she made another suicide attempt, this time taking an overdose of sleeping tablets.[98] Hitler responded by increasing his attentions and banishing Angela Raubal early the next year. Eva was now, at least in her own mind, 'the lady of the house' at the Berghof.[99]

The strain also seems to have affected Hitler's health. Since the start of 1935, he had been suffering from nightly tinnitus and hoarseness. Hitler, who was inclined to hypochondria, feared the onset of throat cancer. In late May, he was operated on and had a benign vocal chord polyp removed. He slept nearly fourteen hours under anaesthetic, and took a three-month break from public speaking to allow his voice to recover.[100]

Hitler now sought to break up the Stresa Front. His opening came when Mussolini embarked on a confrontation with Abyssinia, from the neighbouring Italian colony of Eritrea, which finally erupted in full-scale war later in the autumn.[101] This pitted Rome against Paris and London. Hitler seized the opportunity not to mend fences with Italy, which was still in bad odour over the Austrian fiasco, but to seek a rapprochement with Britain, his favoured alliance partner and in his mind a kindred power in so many ways. In June 1935, he pulled off a major coup with the Anglo-German Naval Agreement. Operating with an exaggerated sense of German ship construction since 1933, London conceded that Germany could build up to 35 per cent of the British tonnage. This move split the Stresa powers, and tore another brick out of the wall which the Versailles Treaty had built around Germany.[102] Its real significance, however, lay in Hitler's belief that the agreement signalled a partition of spheres between the British Empire, whose continued dominance at sea was now officially recognized by the Reich, and Germany, which would be supreme on the continent.[103] Hitler was exultant. 'The Führer is in good form,' Goebbels noted, and gave 'an outline of his foreign political plans' which involved 'eternal alliance with Britain', but 'expansion towards the east'.[104]

The Führer also hoped that Winifred Wagner and the Mitford family would serve as a conduit to Britain. Unity owed her middle name – 'Valkyrie' – to her grandfather Bertie Redesdale, who had adored Wagner's music, and known his son Siegfried. Diana Mitford was later married to the British fascist leader, and Hitler enthusiast, Sir Oswald Mosley. The Führer met with Leo Amery, the future British arch anti-appeaser. 'We got on well together I think,' Amery recorded in his diary, 'owing to the fundamental similarity of many of our ideas.'[105] Even if the Briton was referring to the economic sphere, it was a tribute to the Führer's capacity to win over a sceptical interlocutor. Sometime after, Hitler received the press baron Lord Rothermere on the Obersalzberg as if he were 'a prince'.[106]

In the summer of 1935, American protestors against Nazi anti-Semitism boarded a German ship in New York and tore down its flag, much to Hitler's outrage. In late August, Schacht warned – not for the first time – of the economic costs of Hitler's anti-Semitism. He demanded that the legal position of Jews be regulated once and for all, in order to avoid disruptive popular anti-Semitic excesses. Hitler reacted by issuing a strict instruction that 'individual actions' by party members and organizations against the Jews should cease. Violations should be reported to him instantly; transgressors would be treated as 'provocateurs, rebels and enemies of the state'.[107] This ordinance was, however, only a temporary measure until the systematic legal clarification demanded by Schacht had been put in place. Under pressure, Hitler suddenly decided to announce this at the forthcoming annual party rally. At very short notice, the Interior Ministry and its experts were convened in Nuremberg to thrash out a new discriminatory programme against the Jews.[108] Hitler reviewed all proposals himself. Then the Reichstag was hastily convened and presented with the resulting 'Law for the Protection of German Blood and Honour'.

The resulting 'Nuremberg Laws', as they became collectively known, represented a substantial radicalization of Jewish policy.[109] Marriages between Jews and citizens of 'German or racially related blood' were declared illegal. Extramarital sexual relations between the two groups were also banned. Under the Reich Flag Law, Jews were forbidden from raising the imperial and the (black, white and red) national flag and from showing the national colours, and thus effectively extruded from the national community. Infringements were to be punished with heavy prison sentences. The Reich Citizenship Law determined that citizenship was restricted to those 'of German or racially related blood' who had 'shown through their behaviour that they were willing and suited loyally to serve the German people and Reich'. All others were classed as merely 'belonging to the state', and thus as second-class citizens. The purpose of these measures, as the preamble laid out, was to restore 'the purity of blood [as] the precondition for the continued existence of the German people' and the safeguarding of 'the German nation for all times'.

Central to the whole project was the definition of who was 'a Jew' and who was 'a German', and how to categorize the people who were neither clearly one nor the other. The legislation introduced to purge the civil service of Jews in 1933, the 'Aryan paragraph', had defined very restrictively all those as 'non-Aryan' who had a Jewish parent or grandparent. The Nuremberg Laws, on the face of it, actually eased the situation, by introducing greater latitude and greater precision. They no longer distinguished between so-called Aryans and non-Aryans, but between Germans and 'related' people on the one side and various supposed types of Jews on the other. Those with three or more Jewish grandparents were categorized as Jews, pure and simple. Those with two Jewish grandparents were classed as 'half caste of the first degree'. They were stamped as 'identifying' or 'counting' as Jews, and treated as full Jews, only if they were or became religiously observant Jews; were married to or subsequently married a Jew; were the product of a marriage with a full Jew contracted after the laws had been announced; or were the product of an extramarital liaison with a Jew.[110]

Brutal and comprehensive though the legislation was, it did not represent the most radical options on the table at the time.[111] Hitler, in fact, did not always opt for the broadest definition of what constituted a Jew, and by introducing an element of voluntarism incentivized behavioural change in what would otherwise have been a supposedly biologically determined hierarchy. So far as the author is aware, Hitler never knowingly compromised on 'full' Jews,[112] but he showed flexibility on 'half castes' and 'counted Jews'.

Moreover, he subsequently approved many exceptions from the application of the rules, something which he alone could do.[113] This represented, to be sure, a further arbitrary element in what was already a very arbitrary system. Hitler's purpose here, though, was not simply the exercise of the Führer's will for the sake of it, or to make tactical exceptions for personal reasons, though these also took place, especially where artists, or the relatives of 'high-ups', were concerned. Rather, whatever his later dismissive comments about 'half castes', it seems he was as genuinely concerned to preserve the 'valuable' racial elements as he was to eliminate 'harmful' ones.

The Führer also adopted a relatively open position on what constituted a German, explicitly placing peoples of 'racially related blood' on an equal basis. These were defined as 'peoples living in defined areas within Europe' and 'those of their descendants in non-European parts of the world which had kept themselves racially pure'.[114] The reference to overseas populations probably reflected Hitler's preoccupation with German emigration to the United States and the British Empire, and his respect for supposed American racial value generally. What is striking, though, is the relatively inclusive definition of 'racially related', which mirrored that of the State Hereditary Farm Law. It embraced not only the Dutch, Scandinavians and French, but also Poles, Czechs and Russians; there is no trace, as yet, of any anti-Slavic hauteur. The reasons for this flexibility are not hard to divine, as they reflect Hitler's longstanding anxiety about the quality of the German people. Given the limited racial material available to him, the Führer could not afford to be too choosy. If one tugged too strongly on the various supposed racial skeins in the German *Volk*, too quickly, its whole fabric would probably unravel.

Hitler showed very little interest in people of colour, because he did not regard them as autonomous agents in the international conspiracy against Germany. To be sure, the American anti-miscegenation laws provided stimulus to Nazi racists. German bureaucrats specifically drew on the United States, rather than their own colonial experience, when putting forward their proposals to discriminate against Jews and people of colour. The American example proved of limited use, however, because Jews were far better integrated into pre-1933 Germany than blacks were in the United States.[115] The rigorous application of the American 'one drop' rule would have torn German society apart. An 'Octoroon' might be beyond the pale on the far side of the Atlantic, but Hitler was not yet ready to write off everybody with seven-eighths of 'Aryan' blood. Besides, Hitler had little interest in blacks in general, and none in African-Americans. His admiration for US racism rested on the restrictive immigration laws, which had primarily been directed against eastern European Jews. While blacks and others were often caught in the crossfire, Hitler's first racial laws were directed only against Jews.[116]

In October 1935, therefore, Bormann let it be known that 'the Führer does not wish' that black people from the former German colonies living in the Reich, 'most of whom had fought for Germany', should be hindered in their attempts 'to find work and bread', or indeed 'harassed in any other way'.[117] For all the hardship blacks suffered under National Socialism, the contrast with the treatment of the Jews is striking.[118] There was never any systematic internment of blacks in Nazi Germany.[119] The antithesis to the 'Aryan' or 'German' body was not the black body, but the 'Jewish' body.[120] Everyday racism was not the same as a genocidal world view. Hitler seems to have rated Arabs, Persians and Indians more highly, but he also did not take them very seriously, at least for now. His entourage responded to periodic visits from Middle Eastern nationalists with neither sympathy nor hostility, but hilarity.[121] One way or the other, for Hitler the great struggle was between Jew and German, and ultimately between Teuton and Anglo-Saxon.

Taken together, therefore, the Nuremberg Laws were both a radicalization and a regularization of Hitler's racial policy. They were not necessarily conceived as the first step towards an imminent, or even a distant, physical extermination of the Jews through murderous means. Rather, Hitler explicitly stated in his address to an extraordinary meeting of the Reichstag in Nuremberg that the laws were intended to be a final resolution ('a unique secular solution') of the racial question.[122] This was a gradualist vision, in keeping with the thrust of steps taken since the takeover of power. Towards the end of the year, Hitler explained his position to Justice Minister Gürtner in a meeting to discuss the future of Jews in the professions. When Gürtner offered him a choice between immediately rescinding all licences, doing so piecemeal on a discretionary basis and a 'solution of the problem through natural means, that is through letting them die out', the Führer's response was instructive. When he was informed that the 'natural' route would take at most a few decades, he instructed that there should for now be no further measures against Jews working in the free professions.[123] Given time, the existing measures would take their course, gradually extruding Jews from national life, while the supposedly positive measures of racial elevation slowly lifted the German people to a higher racial plane.

The new laws not only increased the pressure on Germany's already hard-pressed Jews, but also created a diplomatic and bureaucratic nightmare as individuals and countries scrambled to establish their racial classification. Egyptians were told that they would be treated 'not according to their citizenship but according to their race', and that marriages between non-Jewish Egyptians and Germans would be permitted on the same basis as those between other Europeans and non-Jewish Germans.[124] When the Turkish embassy and other interested Turkish parties enquired as to their status, they were reassured that 'the Turkish people were regarded as a European people in Germany', and that they would be treated accordingly under the racial laws.[125] With respect to Turks, therefore, the Third Reich was somewhat to the left of the German far right today.

More serious was the reaction in Britain and the United States, where the Nuremberg Laws were widely condemned in press and parliament. Hitler's immediate worry here was that the laws would lead to a boycott of the Olympic Games in Berlin, scheduled for the following year, with the winter games due to start within a few months. Shortly before they were proclaimed, he was told by the visiting former American ambassador Charles H. Sherrill that the anti-Semitism of the regime was seriously damaging its image in the United States. Sherrill obligingly spoke in some detail about the power of American Jews, who numbered some 5 million in total, about half of them in New York, where they made up about a third of the population. Despite being boycotted by many clubs and in society, he continued, their power in the press was considerable. As for politics, Sherrill stressed that there were two Jews in the cabinet: Frances Perkins, minister for labour, and Henry Morgenthau, at the Treasury, and that New York was run by Fiorello La Guardia, described as 'a Jew' with a Jewish wife. As a result, Sherrill warned, there was a real danger that Jewish groups would achieve an international boycott of the forthcoming games.[126] All this, of course, was grist to Hitler's mill. It confirmed his longstanding belief of the power of international Jewry in the United States and its malicious intent towards Germany.

On the eve of the start of the Winter Olympics in Garmisch-Partenkirchen in February 1936, Hitler was shocked to hear of the murder of Wilhelm Gustloff, the head of the Swiss branch of the Foreign Section of the NSDAP. He was gunned down in Davos by the Croatian Jewish student David Frankfurter; the event was very widely reported on and discussed in the world media.[127] Gustloff had been a tireless promoter of anti-Semitism and Nazi ideology in Switzerland. Hitler saw his assassination as part of a wider Jewish conspiracy against the Reich. His response was superficially 'measured' – so as not to overshadow the Olympics – but the message was unmistakable. In his funeral oration at Schwerin, Hitler claimed that world Jewry had now thrown off the mask. He identified the 'directing hand, which has organized this crime' and would organize future crimes. 'This time,' he continued, 'the carrier of these deeds has appeared in person for the first time.' He vowed to pick up the gauntlet. 'We understand the challenge,' he said, 'and we accept it.'[128]

Things were looking up with regard to Britain. King George V of England died in late January 1936, an event which Hitler registered with interest.[129] His successor, Edward VIII, was not only politically engaged but an admirer of Nazi Germany and a fervent anti-Semite. Hitler was well aware of this, and noted with interest reports that the new king disapproved of French attempts to revive the Entente Cordiale against Germany, that he had considerable sympathy for Germany's situation, and – perhaps most importantly of all – that he disagreed with his father's view that the monarch should unquestionably accept the decisions of the cabinet.[130] Hitler's hopes of persuading Britain surged once more. In early February 1936, he received the former minister for air, Lord Londonderry.[131] 'How often,' Hitler remarked to him, 'did I tell myself as a simple soldier during the world war, when I was deployed opposite the British forces, that it was absolutely insane to fight against these people, who could have been members of our own nation.' 'This sort of thing', he added, 'must never repeat itself.'[132]

On mainland Europe, however, the strategic situation of the Reich was deteriorating. Hitler had by now largely accepted that the hoped-for British alliance was beyond his grasp and was coming around to the view that he would have to achieve his aims if not against the British, then without them.[133] The Russo-French alliance concluded the previous year was wending its way towards inevitable ratification by the parliament in Paris. Taken together with the Russo-Czech military relationship, this threatened Germany on two sides, causing Hitler to worry, for the first time, about Soviet military power rather than just the generic threat of 'Bolshevism'. 'The Führer is seriously wrestling with himself,' Goebbels noted in his diary, on the very last day of February, because 'the Russian treaty has been accepted in the chamber [of Deputies] in Paris' and 'only' needed to pass the 'senate'.[134] Hitler wanted to remilitarize the Rhineland in response so as to create a larger buffer against France, and to consolidate his grip on a vital sector of the German rearmament effort.

In the first days of March Hitler steeled himself to act. Once he had taken the decision, Hitler affected resolution. 'His face radiates calm and determination,' Goebbels noted, 'another critical moment has come, but now action must be taken.' 'The world belongs to the courageous,' he continued, 'those who do not dare anything, do not win anything either'. The following day, Hitler met with Göring, Ribbentrop and the Reichswehr leadership in the Imperial Chancellery. He announced his intention to remilitarize the Rhineland, executing all necessary preparations in complete secrecy. To throw Paris off the scent, Hitler gave a conciliatory interview to the French press. He disregarded all voices counselling caution, especially those from the military.[135] On 7 March, the bloodless remilitarization of the Rhineland went ahead, accompanied by a memorandum to the Locarno powers justifying the move as a response to their alleged violations of the pact, a summoning of the Reichstag and the announcement of a general election – in effect a plebiscite – 'which would give the German people an opportunity to approve his policy and measures'.[136] This was coupled to an offer to negotiate a mutually demilitarized zone with France and Belgium, a non-aggression pact with those states, and various other meaningless gambits designed to simulate goodwill.[137]

The world held its breath and waited to see how the great powers would react to a flagrant breach not only of the Versailles Treaty but also of the Locarno agreements. It soon became clear that Hitler had once again read the position correctly. The Americans were largely unconcerned; the French and British did not move. The British foreign secretary, Anthony Eden, announced that 'it is the appeasement of Europe as a whole that we have constantly before us' and therefore called for 'a calmer and quieter atmosphere' in which to explore new relationships with Germany. King Edward VIII made no secret of his view that no action should be taken against Germany. Winston Churchill was one of the few to lament the loss of a 'bulwark' and warned that Hitler was 'proceeding night and day and is steadily converting nearly seventy millions of the most efficient race in Europe into one gigantic, hungry war-machine'. Without Britain, France could or would do nothing. 'Dans le domaine du bluff,' Gamelin later remarked ruefully, Hitler 'était plus fort que nous.'[138]

More broadly, Hitler wanted to improve the image of the Third Reich worldwide, and particularly in Anglo-America.[139] In the short term, he hoped to do this through the Berlin Olympics. Over the longer term, he wanted to remodel Hamburg, the first glimpse most overseas visitors – the vast majority of whom arrived by ship – would get of the Third Reich. Hitler pushed an ambitious programme of construction designed to turn Hamburg into a port metropolis to rival New York. In June 1936, he announced that the creation of the new 'Führer City Hamburg' would involve a shift in the centre of gravity from its existing focus around the Binnenalster to the Elbe waterfront at Altona. It was to be dominated by one of Hitler's pet projects, the largest suspension bridge in the world, with one level for cars and another for trains, gigantic skyscrapers, including a 250-metre high *Gauhochhaus*, inspired by the Chrysler Building in New York and the Field Building in Chicago, and a *Volkshalle* which could accommodate 150,000 people.[140]

If Hitler was conscious of the need to deploy 'soft power', he did not neglect the more traditional coercive instruments available to him. In mid June 1936, he issued a 'Decree on the Establishment of a Chief of the German Police', designed to effect the 'unified concentration of all police tasks in the Reich'.[141] This combined all the main German security agencies, the Gestapo, the Sicherheitspolizei, and the Sicherheitsdienst, under the control of Heinrich Himmler, and his deputy, Reinhard Heydrich. Nominally, Himmler was subject to the authority of the minister of the interior, Wilhelm Frick, but in practice he now held the absolute police power in Germany, responsible only to Hitler himself.

In the late summer of 1936, the Führer was all set to put on a show for the German people and the world at large, beginning with the first half of the Bayreuth Festival in late July, followed by two weeks of the Olympic Games in early August, before returning to the second half of the Bayreuth Festival. Hitler agreed to this cumbersome arrangement in order to facilitate the many visitors expected for the Olympics, some of whom he hoped to attract to Bayreuth. This would be followed by the party rally in the first fortnight of September, the first since the remilitarization of the Rhineland. An integrated programme of culture, sport and rhetoric would demonstrate the distance travelled in the four years between the seizure of power in 1933 and the *Parteitag der Ehre* at which the Führer would celebrate the restoration of German 'honour both at home and abroad'. It would also provide him with an opportunity to influence visiting foreign dignitaries, especially from Anglo-America.

Hitler's enjoyment of the Bayreuth Festival was overshadowed, for the second time in two years, by external events. Earlier that summer, the Spanish nationalist General Francisco Franco had risen in revolt against the Republican government in Madrid, plunging Spain into civil war. By the end of July, the nationalists were in severe difficulties, with much of their force cut off in Morocco by the Republican navy. Increasingly alarmed, members of the NSDAP's Foreign Section – with the blessing of their chief, Wilhelm Bohle, who probably wanted to raise his profile against the Foreign Office – sought out Hitler in Bayreuth and handed him a personal letter from Franco asking for military aid.[142] The Führer, who astonished his interlocutors with his detailed knowledge of Spanish politics and history, as well as the actual state of play on the ground, reacted swiftly, ordering the dispatch of German transport planes to airlift the Spanish Foreign Legion from Morocco to the Iberian Peninsula. Göring was not best pleased by this first mission for the Luftwaffe, and nor were either Ribbentrop, or the Foreign Office, which would have preferred to remain completely on the sidelines,[143] but Hitler insisted.

The reason why Hitler intervened in Spain was not economic, although the resources of the Iberian Peninsula were important to German rearmament,[144] but geo-ideological. He told Ribbentrop 'that Germany could not tolerate a communist Spain under any circumstances'. Given the internal state of France, he continued, articulating a kind of Nazi 'domino-theory', it would only be a matter of time before the conflagration spread to and consumed France. In that event, Hitler feared, Germany would be 'encircled' between the French communists and the Soviet Union.[145] What was striking about the episode was Hitler's ability to take important decisions quickly, and to either persuade or override doubters. It also precipitated – or reflected – an increased sense of the Soviet threat in particular and that of communism more generally. For the first time ever, Hitler seems genuinely to have feared a Soviet attack. In mid August, he even asked Rosenberg to make some propagandistic preparations in the event of a Russian surprise attack.[146]

Hitler did not place much faith in Rosenberg's schemes. Instead, he advanced on two other fronts. In mid August 1936, Hitler appointed Ribbentrop ambassador to London in the hope that his business connections would help in establishing a rapport there.[147] He also stepped up the pace of rearmament. In the summer of 1936, the army presented plans for a massive expansion of the Wehrmacht by 1940 to field a striking force larger than that which had taken the field against France in 1914. A substantial proportion of funds were earmarked for fortifications and for horse-transport rather than motor vehicles. The High Command, and probably Hitler himself, envisaged a long, conventional war, rather than a *Blitzkrieg*.[148] This meant that an even greater proportion of German industry would have to be devoted to military purposes. The problem was that the economy was already struggling with the demands of rearmament, especially the question of how to pay for the necessary raw material imports, and indeed the whole programme. In the late summer and autumn of 1936, both Schacht and the commissioner for price stability, the Leipzig mayor Carl Goerdeler, increased their warnings that the existing fiscal and monetary imbalances were unsustainable.

Hitler responded with a memorandum on the 'Four Year Plan' for Germany, setting out both his economic vision and his grand strategy.[149] The problem, he argued, was that Germany was 'overpopulated' and could not 'feed itself'. This situation was aggravated by rising 'living standards' which were leading to an 'increased and understandable run on the food market'. Simply reducing that standard, however, was not an option because the resulting 'malnutrition' would exclude a substantial and 'valuable' portion of the population from the 'body politic of the nation'; it would reverse his gradual policy of racial elevation. Indeed, Hitler continued, 'the precondition for normal consumption' was the 'integration of all Germans into the economy'. Here Hitler was merely restating his view that the establishment of a consumer society was necessary to the improvement of Germany's racial stock. The difficulty, he claimed, was that while the supply of consumer goods could be substantially increased, that of foodstuffs and raw materials could not. 'A lasting solution,' he argued, and here Hitler was once again merely repeating what he had been saying for a decade, lay in the 'expansion of the living space', that is of the 'raw material and sustenance basis of our people'. 'It is the task of the political leadership,' Hitler went on, 'to solve this question one day.'

In the meantime, Germany would have to find 'temporary relief within the framework of today's economy'. 'Because the sustenance of the German people will be increasingly dependent on imports,' he argued, and they were also dependent on foreign raw materials, such imports must be encouraged 'with all means'. The obvious solution, increasing German exports, Hitler rejected as 'theoretically possible, but unlikely in practical terms' because 'Germany does not export into a political or economic void, but into extremely contested areas'. He also refused to use valuable foreign exchange to pay for food imports, because it was needed to buy raw materials for the armaments programme. He therefore expressed his intention to ride roughshod over 'the interests of individual gentlemen', signalling that henceforth the 'self-preservation' of the German people trumped that of private enterprise. Strikingly, Hitler made the Jews 'answerable' for any damage they might inflict on the German economy, another instance of his determination to treat them as 'hostages'.[150] No doubt invoking the spirit of Stalin's Five Year Plans, Hitler called for a 'multi-year plan' which would 'make our national economy independent of the outside world'. He concluded with the demand that both the German army and the German economy must be ready for war in 'four years' time'.

The casualty of all this, in terms of high politics, was Schacht.[151] Hitler only informed him of the Four Year Plan on the eve of its public announcement at the party congress in early September 1936.[152] From Hitler's point of view, Schacht had served his purpose and was now largely redundant. He had provided stability at the start of the regime, settled the foreign debt question, decoupled Germany from the world economy and dependence on the United States, and reoriented German trade towards more pliable partners within Europe, especially the Balkans. Schacht's departure was now simply a matter of time, his continuance in office a mere sop to world opinion. 'The Führer is very sceptical about Schacht,' Goebbels noted later in the year, 'but he will not release him from responsibility for reasons of foreign policy.'[153]

Six weeks after penning his memorandum, Hitler appointed Göring the general plenipotentiary for the implementation of the Four Year Plan with a mandate to effect 'the unified direction of all the strength of the German people and the tight concentration of all relevant agencies in party and state'. [154] Göring became, at least in name, the economics and mobilization tsar of the Reich. In a fit of energy he convened meetings, issued decrees and generally sought to convey an increased dynamism to the civil administration, the military leadership and the captains of German industry. Across the board, investment in plant, raw materials and labour was stepped up.[155] All residual economic rationality was abandoned.[156] The message was clear: Hitler wanted Germany to be ready, if not for war, then at least for confrontation by the early 1940s.

In this context, the Olympic Games in Berlin, which opened amid much fanfare in August 1936, were even more important to the international position of the Third Reich. They began with the Olympic relay, an invention of the Nazis. On 20 July 1936 Greek maidens in skimpy serge frocks handed over the flame as it began its journey towards Berlin.[157] The whole ceremony, which was filmed by Leni Riefenstahl, was designed to emphasize the links between Nazi Germany and Ancient Greece. The entire proceedings were broadcast by radio through the massive Olympia-Weltsender Berlin, a station capable of reaching forty countries. The American team, which included blacks and Jews, was given a particularly rousing (calculated) official and (spontaneous) popular reception. The press were under strict instructions from Goebbels not to offend the sensitivities of the visitors, especially people of colour. There were some awkward moments, for example when the black athlete Jesse Owens won the 100 and 200 metre races, the relay race and the long jump. Leni Riefenstahl celebrated his achievements on camera, though she did not film the Germans formed in long queues in pursuit of an autograph. Contrary to myth, Hitler did not refuse to congratulate Owens. Having been upbraided by Olympic officials for shaking hands with some victors early in the games, he had decided not to meet anyone. Moreover, Owens, despite his reservations about the regime, offered a salute during the conferral of his medal. During the US presidential election campaign later that year, when Owens backed the Republican candidate against Roosevelt, he even praised Hitler as 'a man of civility'.[158]

The Berlin Olympics were by any standards a triumph for Hitler.[159] In his speeches and welcoming words he had addressed not merely a German but a world audience. The presence of so many foreign athletes and visitors legitimated the regime and by extension its many acts since 1933, especially the recent remilitarization of the Rhineland. 'The foreign press [reporting] on the Olympic Games is fantastic', Goebbels claimed, 'everything is going like clockwork. A big success.'[160] There was no attempt on his life. The only serious security breach was the 'kiss ambush' when a Californian woman managed to kiss the Führer.[161] There were no serious racial incidents. To cap it all, the German team won the most medals, although outclassed by the Americans, especially blacks, in the athletics events.

In Bayreuth, Hitler continued his diplomatic efforts during the second half of the festival, which resumed after the Olympic Games. There, Unity and Diana Mitford were constantly in Hitler's presence, partly because he enjoyed their company but mainly in order to facilitate communication with the British establishment as the Führer conceived it. Eager to consolidate relations with the new pro-German monarch, Hitler even offered a bespoke production of his *Lohengrin* in Covent Garden to Edward VIII as a coronation present. Crushingly, the king – who appears to have been no fan of Wagner – accepted only on condition that he would not have to attend himself, and the space available at Covent Garden for the production was much too small anyway. Undeterred, Hitler suggested a *Gastspiel* of the Berliner Staatsoper in the British capital, followed by one of the London Philharmonic Orchestra in Germany, conducted by Sir Thomas Beecham, the head of Covent Garden and a man believed to be close to Edward VIII.[162] Despite some preparatory visits and correspondence, nothing came of these plans, but they illustrated not only Hitler's determination to use what he took to be the inside track in British politics and society to secure an alliance, but also the high value he attached to cultural diplomacy. If the Kaiser had dreamed of joint Anglo-German fleet reviews held in an atmosphere of friendly rivalry, the Führer seems to have envisaged *Tannhäuser*-style singing contests in a similar spirit.

In late August and early September, Hitler's pursuit of Britain reached a climax. Lord Lloyd, whom Ribbentrop identified as a member of the 'diehard Churchill Group', was invited to the party rally in order to create 'a breach' in the 'ranks of the hostile front of [British] right-wing conservatives'.[163] So were a number of other 'important Britons' who were entrusted to the care of Rosenberg.[164] David Lloyd George, Germany's nemesis in the First World War, was received by Hitler at Berchtesgaden in early September. It was an amicable meeting, at which the former prime minister expressed support for the Third Reich and admiration for its programme of motorway construction. Lloyd George also presented the Führer with a signed photograph of himself bearing the inscription 'To Chancellor Hitler, in admiration of his courage, his determination and his leadership'. He subsequently wrote that Hitler was a 'born leader of men' and 'a magnetic, dynamic personality with a single-minded purpose, a resolute will and a dauntless heart'. He did not believe Hitler had any aggressive intent and thought that 'the establishment of a German hegemony in Europe which was the aim and dream of the old pre-war militarism, is not even on the horizon of Nazism'.[165]

At a reception in Nuremberg a few days later, Hitler signalled that he was prepared to settle his colonial demands 'on the basis of mutual cooperation' and 'a closer understanding with Great Britain'. Hitler's real concern, it was clear to his interlocutors, was not the colonies but Germany's shortage of foodstuffs and raw materials and – so they thought – 'securing Europe against the Bolshevik assault'. Noting that the British themselves needed colonies in order to 'feed their population', he asked whether they had found 'some other way' of doing so despite 'the lack of raw materials'. If so, Hitler continued, they should 'please send him the formula'. All this, he averred, was 'no imperialism, but a question of survival for Germany', and was motivated not by the desire 'to disturb the strategic lines of communication of the British Empire', but, 'on the contrary', driven by a desire to 'avoid' any such clash 'at all costs'.[166] Hitler did not spell out his proposed bargain in detail, but its general outlines were clear: Germany would respect the global position of the British Empire in return for the freedom to secure territory in Europe.

The autumn of 1936, with its triad of the Bayreuth Festival, the Berlin Olympics and the Nuremberg rally, was in many ways the apotheosis of the Third Reich. It had excelled itself in music, sport and political choreography. The culmination of those heady eight weeks came on the evening of 11 September, when Albert Speer's 'Lichtdom', using ideas developed by others, threw a huge arc of light over the rally by means of 151 anti-aircraft searchlights, and took everybody's breath away.[167] Against this dramatic backdrop, the main speakers, Goebbels, Rosenberg and Hitler himself, their remarks closely coordinated,[168] relentlessly hammered home both Germany's rebirth and the Bolshevik threat.[169] The Spanish Civil War, Hitler warned, was evidence of the activities of the 'Jewish Revolution headquarters in Moscow'.[170] 'The party congress was the most unified so far,' Rosenberg wrote in his diary, adding that 'the Führer [was] happy and reinvigorated'. [171]

It is easy to see why Hitler looked back in the autumn of 1936 in satisfaction at the achievements of his first four years in office. There is no doubt that Hitler's will moved mountains domestically. Prices were controlled in ways that defied conventional economics. Alternative sources of energy were found. The multiplier effect he had predicted before taking power initially created a virtuous circle during the first few years in which everything seemed possible. The Germany economy had been completely revived; unemployment was close to zero. There was no significant resistance to Hitler's authority. His domestic enemies were either dead, in prison, in exile, cowed or converted. Germany's standing abroad and her territorial integrity had been triumphantly restored.

None of this had been as easy as it looks in retrospect. Hitler had taken great risks and shown iron nerves. He had seen off the threat of preventive war by France and Poland. Relations with Warsaw remained good even after the death of Piłsudski, whose Berlin memorial service Hitler attended with what appears to have been genuine reverence.[172] He had bounced back from a failed putsch in Austria. Unsurprisingly, therefore, Hitler saw these events as a vindication of his view that politics was primarily a matter of 'will'. 'Nobody,' he told the Annual Congress of the German Labour Front in September 1936, 'should counter me with the phrase "That will not work"!' 'Nobody can and should say that to me,' he continued, 'I am not one of those men to whom one can say "That will not work".' 'It must work,' Hitler vowed, 'because Germany must live.' 'The word impossible,' he told a meeting of leading German industrialists convened in mid December 1936 to facilitate the implementation of the Four Year Plan, 'does not exist here'.[173]

By the end of 1936, however, Hitler was reaching the limits of what could be achieved by determination alone. He could not simply will the Germans a standard of living comparable to the British and the Americans. The paramount symbol of that aspiration, the Volkswagen project, was already in trouble by the summer of 1936, because the car industry did not think it viable. Most importantly of all, the Führer could not indefinitely increase both domestic consumption and armaments production. No amount of will would secure raw materials on the world market as the Reich's foreign currency reserves dwindled. The structure of the rest of the world's economies failed to reconfigure to German needs. Although he believed that both guns and butter were central to his racial project, Hitler would soon have to choose between them, at least temporarily.

In the last four months of the year, moreover, the skies darkened not merely physically, but strategically. Hitler was watching events in Austria with mounting concern. Since the failed coup two years earlier, the Führer had gone out of his way to avoid trouble there. When he heard that the Austrian SA were trying to re-establish 'terrorist groups', his adjutant Fritz Wiedemann let their commander, SA-Obergruppenführer Reschny, know that 'the Führer sharply forbade any such action'.[174] In the summer of 1936, he approved a 'gentlemen's agreement' with the Austrian chancellor Schuschnigg, drawn up by Papen with a view to improving relations through the lifting of travel and other restrictions. The problem was that Austria appeared to be drifting further out of the German orbit, with talk of her joining a 'Danubian Pact'. Hitler regarded this scheme as a stalking horse for the thing he feared most, which was a Habsburg restoration. If this now seems implausible, one must remember that it was less than two decades after the end of the Habsburg Empire, and the dynasty still retained many supporters. Hitler's worst fears were confirmed in the late summer, when he was told of the request of Prince Starhemberg, the leader of the conservative Austrian 'Home Defence' (Heimwehr) militia, to see him and to try to persuade him to support plans for a 'restoration in Austria' carried out with the combined support of the Heimwehr and the German nationalists.[175]

Meanwhile, the confrontation with world communism loomed ever larger, as the Soviet Union shifted in Hitler's view from largely passive victim to mortal threat. 'The confrontation with Bolshevism is coming [and] we need to be prepared,' Hitler told Goebbels in mid November 1936, adding, presciently, that 'we will be completely ready by 1941'. For now, the main communist challenge lay in Spain, where the Republican government was strongly supported by Stalin. 'Moscow seems to be committing itself very strongly in Spain,' Goebbels reported after a meeting with Hitler in mid November, 'but it will encounter us', because 'Spain must not and will not turn red'.[176] 'It was his sole objective,' Hitler remarked shortly afterwards, 'that Spanish foreign policy after the end of the war would be determined by neither Paris, nor London, nor Moscow', and that therefore Spain would not be 'in the enemy camp', but if possible a 'friend of Germany', in the 'inevitable' confrontation over the reordering of Europe.[177]

To make matters worse, the hope of a British alliance was dwindling.[178] Ribbentrop sent regular warnings from London that opinion was turning against the Third Reich. 'He talks of London,' Goebbels noted, where there was 'a lot of Jewish agitation [but] the king is on our side.' A gruesome performance by Sir Thomas Beecham's visiting London Philharmonic Orchestra, after which Hitler felt compelled to applaud 'politely', did not help. Hitler persisted, however, and continued to try to influence British opinion through the Mitfords, to whom he authorized payments through Goebbels. The Führer attended Oswald Mosley's wedding to Diana Mitford in Berlin, with the dinner held at Hitler's request at Goebbels's house at Schwanenwerder. A month later, it was probably out of deference to Britain that he gave Epp short shrift when he broached the colonial question again.[179]

Then in early December 1936, Hitler received the catastrophic news that

King Edward VIII, the pro-German monarch of whom he had expected so much, was likely to abdicate. The Führer, Goebbels reported, was 'very upset about it'.[180] He ensured that the German press was gagged for the duration of the crisis as the Reich government observed events. In the course of the next month, Hitler repeatedly erupted against the 'hypocritical' Baldwin government and the 'cowardice and mendacity' of the British public.[181] 'The Führer speaks of England,' Goebbels reported; he considered its population 'a satiated people without ideals'. 'The king,' Hitler continued, 'deserved sympathy' because British men lacked 'spunk'.[182] On 10 December, Edward finally abdicated. Some two weeks later, Ribbentrop returned to Berlin to report. His account confirmed Hitler's view. 'Edward was toppled by Baldwin and the clerics,' Goebbels wrote after discussing the matter with Hitler, 'because he was too independent and pro-German.' 'Mrs Simpson,' the two men agreed, 'was only the pretext'; the real cause was the fact that public opinion in 'London was completely in the hands of the Jews'.[183] It was during the abdication crisis, in fact, that Hitler seems to have come to the view that Britain was beyond redemption.

Relations with the United States were also deteriorating, though a breach was not imminent. The prevailing expectation, as expressed by a dispatch from the ambassador in Washington, Hans Luther, was that despite his rhetorical philippics against treaty-breakers and race-haters, Roosevelt would observe a policy of strict neutrality with regard to Europe. Europeans might find it ironic, Luther remarked, to hear such strictures from 'the head of a state which had gained possession of a huge continent through wars and the breach of numerous treaties',[184] and, he might have added, had a long and continuing record of racial discrimination to boot. One way or the other, there was no getting around the fact that, as Luther warned in early October 1936, 'our National Socialist state form is decisively rejected on principle by every American government'.[185]

Meanwhile, Hitler stepped up his efforts to turn Berlin into a truly global capital. He pressed ahead with the construction of Tempelhof airport. In mid October 1936, Hitler told Albert Speer that he planned to appoint him *Generalbauinspekteur* with a wide-ranging remit to remodel the city as the capital of a world power on a par – implicitly – with London and Washington. Speer was allowed to draft his own job specification which gave him more or less unlimited powers to transform Berlin according to his, and the Führer's, vision.[186]

Hitler also reacted to the changing global environment by consolidating his alliances. In October 1936, he concluded an agreement with Italy which was ostensibly directed towards collaboration over the League of Nations, the Soviet threat, the Spanish Civil War, Austria, colonial matters and the Balkans. Its real target, however, was Britain. Shortly afterwards, Mussolini referred to the alliance publicly as an 'axis' between Berlin and Rome.[187] The Führer also sought a connection with Japan. This was an important step, for hitherto it had been an open question whether the Third Reich would 'opt' for Tokyo or for China, though Hitler's own sympathies had lain with Japan for some time. In early June 1936, he met with the Japanese ambassador Count Mushakoji in Berlin, and a month later at Bayreuth with the man who was to succeed him, General Hiroshi Oshima.[188] They agreed the need for a common front against the Soviet Union and world communism; neither man mentioned London or Washington. Hitler expected a new Russo-Japanese War imminently, and planned to use the opportunity to seize land from the Soviet Union.[189] In early November 1936, the Third Reich and Japan signed what became known as the 'Anti-Comintern Pact'. Over time, Hitler was to refer repeatedly to this new 'world-political triangle' as evidence for the fact that 'the isolation of Germany was over'.[190]

The 'axis' was ostensibly directed against the Soviet Union and world communism, but in truth Japan's main enemies were the British Empire and the United States. It was in this spirit that the Führer confided to the Italian foreign minister, Count Ciano, that anti-communism was the lowest common denominator against the western powers, and also that the pact was designed to change British behaviour. A common front against the Soviet Union was thus not merely compatible with, but very much part of, the joint struggle against the western powers. 'The Führer thinks,' Goebbels records, that 'the fruits of this agreement will only ripen in five years' time. He really pursues policy in the long term.'[191] This turned out to be an uncannily precise prediction, as both the German Reich and the Japan went to war together five years and one week later in 1941, not with the Soviet Union, but against the United States.

During his first three and a half years in power, Hitler's timeline did not shift much. 'I know,' he remarked in September 1933, 'that this great process of the internal welding together of our people cannot be achieved from one day to the next.' 'What gradually disintegrated over 30, 40, 50 [or] 100 years,' Hitler continued, could not be put together again 'in a few months'.[192] Ten months later, he was still speaking in terms of a secular project of transformation. 'The National Socialist state,' he told the Reichstag, 'will internally exterminate, if necessary in a hundred year war, the last remnants' of 'the "Jewish-international" poison'.[193] In cabinet, in January 1935, he spoke of the reform of local government as taking twenty to thirty years.[194] 'None of our technical projects will be finished in fewer than ten or twenty years,' he warned in May 1935, while 'none of the spiritual tasks would be completed within fifty or even a hundred years.'[195] He clearly envisaged a long-term process of transformation, in which conflict with the western powers was to be avoided as long as possible.

That said, there was – as we have seen – a change of tone in late 1936. He seems to have sensed that the days of easy victories were almost over. He continued, all the same, to take enormous risks, because he believed that there was no other way of saving Germany. Hitler did not have the luxury of certainty, as he explained with astonishing frankness on the anniversary of the 1923 putsch, a time when his gamble had failed catastrophically. 'I have had to take some very difficult decisions over the past three and half years,' he announced, 'on which sometimes the future of the entire nation depended.' 'I unfortunately never had 51 per cent certainty [of success]', but rather there was 'often 95 per cent likelihood of failure and only 5 per cent of success'.[196] Hitler could not have been clearer. He was planning to roll the dice again and again in the coming years until his luck ran out.

PART FIVE

Confrontation

At the start of 1937, the Third Reich appeared secure. Hitler had created a new age, with its own values and calendar. Time seemed to stretch to the horizon. In the course of the year, however, Hitler became convinced that he was running out of time, and that Anglo-America – suffering in his view from Jewish-induced false consciousness – had turned against him. He had also lost the standard of living battle with the west. The next phase of the Third Reich was therefore to be one of confrontation. This was a diplomatic battle, in which Hitler accepted that he had 'lost' Britain and the United States, and sought to consolidate his alliances with Italy and Japan. It was a military contest, in which the Führer went from bloodless victories over Austria and Czechoslovakia to more costly but still remarkable triumphs over Poland, much of Scandinavia and then – most spectacularly of all – over the British and French field armies in the west. It was, finally, a racial contest in which Hitler speeded up the elimination of the 'negative' strands in German society, and brought forward the acquisition of 'living space' in the east required for his planned 'elevation' of the German people in order to prepare them for the likely clash with the 'Anglo-Saxons'.

13

'Living Standards' and 'Living Space'

In Germany, 1937 was a year when time seemed to stand still. There were no major headline-grabbing domestic or foreign initiatives. Hitler promised the Reichstag in late January that the 'era of surprises was over [and that] peace was now our most prized possession'.[1] He had gathered all the low-hanging fruit at home and abroad. His rule was not yet absolute, but there were no major challenges to his authority, either within the party or in the country at large. National Socialism, the Führer principle and the Hitler-myth were the new normal.[2] The chancellor's portrait adorned thousands of public buildings and spaces; countless schools and streets were named after him. In March 1937, he overcame his almost atavistic resistance to being depicted on postage stamps, so that his image – adapted from one of Heinrich Hoffmann's photographs – became even more ubiquitous.[3] The Führer was omnipresent, sometimes even featuring in the dreams (or nightmares) of ordinary people.[4] Germany enjoyed more or less full employment.[5] Life as a Jew, gypsy, homosexual, leftist or Bavarian monarchist was harsh, but, by contrast with the first years of the regime, appeared increasingly predictable. There were fewer arrests, and the camp population actually fell during the first part of the year. Beyond Germany, the world had got used to Hitler. There was, in short, a general sense of a lull, which later felt like the quiet before the storm.[6] 'It is very quiet on the political front,' Goebbels remarked in the late summer of 1937.

'Give us four years time,' Hitler had promised in his first radio address at the start of his chancellorship, 'and then judge us,' a phrase which he repeated in various formulations and which was ultimately rendered by the Nazi propaganda machine as the ubiquitous 'Give me four years and you will not recognize Germany again!'[7] As the fifth year of the Third Reich dawned in 1937, the Führer and the movement now looked back on their 'achievements', in what was widely understood to be an 'accountability moment'. In a series of speeches to mark special days in the Nazi calendar, for example the anniversaries of the seizure of power and the launching of the NSDAP programme, Hitler celebrated and wildly exaggerated the economic, political and military progress made since 1933 over and over. Goebbels reinforced this message in a travelling exhibition entitled 'Give Me Four Years', which Hitler opened in person in Berlin, and in a similarly named newsreel.

Hitler pressed ahead with his programme of domestic transformation undisturbed. The removal of the Jews from German national life continued. That said, there was a recognizable pause in anti-Jewish measures in the spring and summer of 1937. For now, because of the alleged power of international Jewry, Hitler still had to tread carefully. A third decree of the 'State Citizenship Law', planned by Hitler for February 1937, involving special status for non-Jewish businesses, was put on hold in June on the grounds that it would antagonize foreign owners of such enterprises. The measure was finally enacted a year later. In May 1937, Hitler also ordered that plans for a special citizenship document be dropped.[8] He explained his strategy in a private speech to party leaders. His 'final objective' of removing the Jews, Hitler explained, had not changed. He wanted to avoid, however, having to take any steps that he might have to 'reverse', or which might 'harm' the Third Reich. 'I always go to the limit,' he continued, 'but not beyond'; he claimed to have a 'nose' for what was possible and what not. Rather than provoking his enemies to all-out resistance, Hitler argued, he was trying to manoeuvre them into a 'corner' before delivering the mortal blow.[9] For this reason, Hitler did not undertake any major new initiative on the Jewish front throughout 1937.

In one area, however, the regime did radicalize racial policy. Hitler had long hung back on the issue of the 'Rhineland bastards', the offspring of black French colonial soldiers during the Rhineland occupation of the 1920s, for fear of offending France, but on 18 April 1937, he ordered the discreet 'sterilization' of these offspring. He dismissed the suggestion of the Foreign Office, which was worried about the French reaction, that the victims should simply be confined to barracks or deported.[10] The task was given to the Gestapo and completed in the course of the year.[11] These measures did not apply to 'full-blooded' black Africans, about whom Hitler and the regime were considerably more relaxed.[12] To be sure, their situation worsened as the Third Reich progressed and they often found themselves subject to the Nuremberg Laws, but not apparently at Hitler's direct request. Clearly identifiable as 'alien', blacks posed a much reduced risk of racial 'contamination'. They found employment as waiters, as minstrels, in circuses or as extras on films designed to show the inequities of British imperial rule. They were also in demand for the 'German African Revue', which was designed to celebrate German colonialism and remind the *Volk* of its global mission. An audience in Lower Austria was startled to hear the performers announce that 'We believe in Germany, Heil Hitler.'[13] Though the black residents suffered great hardship during the Third Reich, the contrast with the treatment of Hitler's principal racial enemy, the Jews, is striking.

The other strand of Hitler's policy was to accentuate the positive, by continuing the racial 'elevation' begun in 1933. Central to this project was the German woman. Hitler managed to keep the formidable 'imperial women's leader', Gertrud Scholtz-Klink, at arm's length; she failed in her quest for a face-to-face discussion.[14] As his personal adjutant, Fritz Wiedemann, remarked, Hitler took a dim view of women in politics generally, though he was prepared to make exceptions.[15] He also sought to drive women out of the workplace, or at least the professions, and back into the home. In the summer of 1937, Hitler announced that appointments to the higher reaches of the civil service should be reserved 'in principle' to men. 'He would make only a few exceptions', mainly in the 'area of welfare, education and health'.[16] Female lawyers, by contrast, were to be phased out.

Hitler saw women primarily as agents of racial reproduction and regeneration. If this was socially 'regressive', especially with regard to women in the workforce, it also had some surprisingly 'progressive' implications. Hitler was determined to remove traditional barriers to increased fertility among the racially 'superior' elements of the German people. In January 1937, Hitler erupted in cabinet against attempts to force unmarried mothers to name the fathers of their children, outraged by a recent Hanoverian case in which a woman had been given a prison sentence for refusing to cooperate with the authorities in that regard. 'That sort of absurdity,' he thundered, 'must end at once.' Hitler supported the right of a woman to remain silent, even if the intention was to establish the father's 'Aryan' credentials. He 'considered it barbarism', he added, 'to apply pressure in order to force a statement'. Towards the end of the year Hitler laid down that the Hanoverian woman should not be forced to serve her sentence. In the same spirit, the new 'midwives' law removed at his request the old clause excluding midwives from practice for 'moral transgressions', such as extramarital sexual relations.[17] Above all, Hitler was concerned to revise marriage law, to reduce the stigma of infidelity, to remove that attached to sex outside marriage and illegitimacy and generally increase the emphasis on reproduction.[18]

Despite his emphasis on 'blood', Hitler's programme of racial elevation was not confined to biology and reproduction. Intellectual and cultural instruments remained extremely important to him. One critical front was education, understood in the broadest terms to encompass not merely schooling but also law and military service. On the negative side, Hitler demanded that 'the *Volk* should be educated to believe that treason was the greatest possible crime, which would ordinarily receive the death penalty'.[19] On the positive side, Hitler wanted German youth to be exposed to the classical tradition, which he saw as an instrument of character formation, and an aesthetic ideal, rather than as part of a humanistic education. Here the British public school system, or least his understanding of it as a nursery of imperial rulers, served as an inspiration. Hitler understood the resulting 'natural selection process' in meritocratic terms, as necessary to sustain the new *Führerstaat*. It was intended to combat not so much Jewry or other 'harmful' elements, whose removal was simply assumed, as the innate tendency towards fragmentation within the German *Volk* itself. Hitler conceived this not merely as a struggle which divided classes, regions, confessions and even individuals, but as a contest playing out within every German breast. This is why he urged that opposition should be 'internal to the person'. Germans must resolve the dialectic or thesis and antithesis within themselves, not against each other.[20] Every man was to be his own synthesis.

Another front was the arts, in which Hitler maintained a keen interest, not just for his own amusement but for the edification and improvement of the *Volk*. In his view, the appreciation of true art both reflected and increased racial value. It was part of what he called the regime's 'incredible endeavours to elevate the *Volk* in countless areas of life'. Hitler showcased what he regarded as sublime art in the 'Grosse Deutsche Kunstausstellung' in the new Munich Haus der Deutschen Kunst. He opened the exhibition in mid July 1937 with a speech spelling out the role of art in the political and racial regeneration of Germany. He explicitly related the Reich's cultural collapse to the lost war, the growth of socialism and communism, the spread of 'liberal economic concepts', and the evils of internationalism. The resulting 'ideological and political fragmentation' had led to the 'gradual dissolution of a sense of common purpose in the *Volk*' and the 'weakening of the German body politic'. Central to this misery, Hitler argued, was the way in which Jewry 'exploited its position in the press with the help of so-called art critics', in order to 'destroy' all 'healthy instincts' in the population at large. He tried to expose that influence in a parallel exhibition on 'Degenerate Art', and in the speech he fired off broadsides against 'Cubism, Dadaism, Futurism, Impressionism and so on'.[21]

Eliminating Jewish and other alien influences was only half the racial battle. Hitler believed that the real problem was that the German *Volk* was made up, as he put it, of 'a number of more or less separate races', which had over time developed into 'that mixture which we see in our *Volk* today'. The originally 'constitutive' element in the *Volk* had been the same 'Aryan manhood' which had characterized the 'ancient civilizations', but had subsequently been diluted through admixture with 'other' – here he meant primarily 'non-Jewish', but also 'non-Aryan' – racial elements. The purpose of art, Hitler claimed, was to combat this adulteration by contributing to the 'unification' or 'standardization' of the 'racial body politic'. The close link between artistic appreciation and racial 'elevation' in his mind was made clear towards the end of Hitler's speech, when he praised antiquity, which 'in appearance and sensibility' was closer to the present day than ever before. He objected to modern art because of its alleged celebration of ugliness and disfigurement in the form of 'deformed cripples and cretins, women, who can only provoke disgust, [and] men who are closer to animals than humans'. Instead, the Führer wanted art which would make 'our men, boys and youths, girls and women, healthier and thus stronger'. He was developing a 'glowingly beautiful type of person', which he had paraded on the catwalk of the Olympic Games, displaying 'radiant, proud, bodily strength and health before the whole world'.[22] Hitler's hope was that if Germans contemplated statues of Roman and Greek youths long and appreciatively enough they would begin to resemble them, at least inwardly. Hitler laid so much stress on the 'rebirth of the nation' through its 'cultural cleansing' that he spoke of it as being 'in the first instance' a cultural question. This, he claimed, was more important 'for the future' than mere political and economic revival. It is clear from these remarks that Hitler was thinking in terms of generations rather than a quick fix.

Hitler intervened repeatedly to ensure that the works displayed at the Haus der Deutschen Kunst enjoyed his imprimatur, overturning a more liberal selection shortly before the opening.[23] Unlike Goebbels, he never flirted with modernism.[24] Hitler called for art to be 'clear' and 'true', though he was always clearer on what he considered degenerate than on what constituted true German art.[25] In painting, Hitler favoured the Italian Renaissance and German masters from the nineteenth century, who might broadly be characterized as Romantic. He rigorously policed what was exhibited in the Haus der Deutschen Kunst, boasting that he would always ruthlessly remove anything which was not artistically perfect.[26] With regard to architecture and spectacle, Hitler was firmly classical in his sympathies. For example, the Munich pageant accompanying the 'Grosse Deutsche Kunstausstellung' was dominated by themes from antiquity rather than the Middle Ages.

The genre in which Hitler's aesthetics and political ambitions combined most strikingly was architecture, especially his plans for the remodelling of Berlin. On 30 January 1937, the fourth anniversary of his appointment as chancellor, he signed a 'Decree for a General Building Inspector for the Imperial Capital'. Albert Speer was formally appointed to the post, the first step in what was intended to be the transformation of Berlin into a truly global capital representing the might of the Third Reich.[27] Over the next few years, he and his team produced ever more precise and grandiose plans, which Hitler pored over and commented on in detail. Speer and Hitler settled on two great thoroughfares, the 'North–South' and 'East–West' axes, at the heart of which would lie the Great Hall of the People. As we shall see, the architectural inspiration for the new Berlin – or *Germania* – came from many sources: the ancient world, of course, but also Paris, London and, especially, Washington.

All these measures suggested that Hitler's tempo had lessened somewhat. Rome had not been built in a day and nor would the Third Reich be. Whatever the outward signs of conformity in the Reich, Hitler himself was under no illusion of the distance he still had to travel. In early March 1937, he rejected the first sentence of the proposed new Criminal Code, which appeared to him to exaggerate the extent to which German society had already been Nazified. He stressed that 'the National Socialist Weltanschauung had not yet been completely implemented', and that 'every law' should be 'adapted to the stage in which *Volk* and state found itself at that particular moment'.[28] In other words, the Führer believed that a truly Nazi society was still some way off; in 1937, it was an aspiration rather than a reality. Hitler seems at this point to have envisaged a gradual process by which the German people would rid itself of harmful elements over time and acquire positive characteristics in their stead. In his speeches he was still referring to a timeframe of about a hundred years, that is a completion date long after his death.[29]

Here the relevant model was not so much antiquity as the British Empire, which in the Führer's eyes had so long served as the nursery of British racial superiority. It is perhaps no accident that Hans Günther's *Rassenkunde* ('Racial Science'), a text Hitler was familiar with, used a Victorian portrait of a Guards officer in order to illustrate the Nordic ideal type.[30] Nor is it surprising that Hitler's two favourite Englishwomen, Diana and Unity Mitford, were listed as model Aryans ('Botticelli-Typus') in Paul Schultze-Naumburg's book of 'Nordic beauties' (*Nordische Schönheiten*).[31] His 'high estimation of the English character' on account of his war experiences was still a commonplace among the Führer's entourage,[32] and – as we have seen – formed a staple of his speeches. In almost every respect, the British symbolized what was still Hitler's preferred mode of racial elevation by evolution rather than revolution.

By 1937, the ferocious pace at which Hitler had initially tackled federalism, the multi-party system and democratic structures had perceptibly slackened. He was beginning to run out of steam, especially when confronted with his old enemy of German particularism, which responded to his plans for imperial reform with a mixture of obstruction, special pleading and guile. In late January 1937, Hitler pushed through the 'Greater Hamburg Law', which was necessary to facilitate his monumental building plans in the city state. Shortly afterwards, worn down by local resistance, and with his mind on other things, he decided in April 1937 that the whole issue of *Reichsreform* was to be put on hold.[33] The chief of the Imperial Chancellery, Hans-Heinrich Lammers, Hitler's principal gatekeeper at the time, announced wearily that the Führer believed that 'the moment for a reform of the Reich had not yet come'. Time, in this case, seemed to stretch far into the distance. Hitler's reflections on the succession also suggested a longer timeline, as well as providing an insight into his constitutional thinking. Looking to the future, he ruminated in cabinet that it would not be wise completely to sideline the Reichstag in favour of the Führer. Rather Hitler envisaged that a new 'State Basic Law', which would regulate his succession, should be hammered out by an 'extraordinary constitutional Reichstag' appointed by himself.[34] His main concern was to prevent the return of the 'hereditary monarchy', and to ensure the emergence of a competent new Führer to complete the secular task of the racial regeneration of Germany.

All this said, Hitler's personal grip on government continued to tighten in key areas. He asserted his authority over the German bureaucracy. A new law proclaimed towards the end of January 1937 gave him the authority, in consultation with the minister of the interior, to remove any civil servant whose commitment to the 'National Socialist state' was in doubt.[35] Even if this power was to be exercised in conjunction with the justice minister and on the basis of sworn testimony and expert witnesses, and in fact he seems to have made little use of this new authority, the message was clear. Hitler also tried to shake up the bureaucracy by bringing in outside talent. For this reason he wanted a more flexible remuneration system, which would make it possible to 'recruit and retain' people of 'real ability' for the 'state sector'. Otherwise, Hitler feared, there was a great risk that the state sector would simply experience 'negative selection', in which the best minds left for the business economy from whence they would control the state, rather than vice versa, as Hitler wished.[36]

Hitler's increased role was most obvious in the field of criminal justice. In March 1937, he demanded greater latitude for judges to increase or reduce punishments, and, if necessary, impose the death penalty retrospectively.[37] Throughout the year, Hitler also began to intervene directly in the judicial process, reversing court decisions, changing sentences and in some cases even sacking officials, one of whom Hitler ordered out within twenty-four hours.[38] Such interventions now became routine in the

Third Reich. Over the next few years, Hitler repeatedly sought to undermine the independence of the judiciary, to simplify the removal of judges,
and to transfer competency in political cases from the civil courts to other
authorities.[39]

The growing role of Hitler in government was matched by the declining
importance of the cabinet. If it met nineteen times in 1934, this number
had dropped to six by 1937. Hitler himself attended less and less, though
when he did so he was not always voluble or dominant.[40] There was an
increased use of circulation to discuss and agree legislation;[41] most business was now being done elsewhere. The cabinet met for the last time in
February 1938, and, while further meetings were planned over the next
two years, they never happened[42] – all pretence at formal collective deliberation had been abandoned. From now on, laws were made either by
circulation or completely on the hoof.[43] Responsible government was overtaken by autocracy, informality and adhocery. This had two serious
consequences for German politics.

It deepened the polycratic chaos in Germany's administration. The key
to power lay in access to Hitler, and in denying that access to others. Some,
such as Goebbels, were exceptionally successful in this regard.[44] Once Hitler's attention had been secured, a decision had to be extracted, or the
parameters of independent action explored. For example, an area where
Hitler had expressly reserved the right of final judgement, namely the application of the Nuremberg Laws, rapidly became a minefield as various
organizations and institutions sought to engage in special pleading. Eventually, Lammers was forced to try to establish some sort of 'consistency' in a
circular to the main departmental chiefs and other parties. This expressed
Hitler's wish that all requests for exemptions from the racial laws should
be channelled through the Imperial Chancellery and not, as hitherto, reach
him in an ad hoc and random manner through various avenues.[45]

Despite these efforts, Hitler still found himself mediating more and more
disputes between ministries, and individuals, some of them quite junior.[46]
Perhaps the most involved battle which Hitler was dragged into was the
long-running saga of the *Gauleiter* of Franconia, Julius Streicher.[47] This
had begun shortly after the takeover of power, when Streicher fell out with
the senior SS commander in the city, Freiherr von Malsen-Ponickau.
Despite Streicher's well-known sexual and financial scandals, and
Himmler's support for his man, the *Gauleiter*'s standing with Hitler as an
Alter Kämpfer was so strong that Malsen backed off for the time being.
Not even Lammers could make any headway in Nuremberg, and when he
told Streicher that the instructions to curb the excesses of his violently
anti-Semitic newspaper *Der Stürmer* came directly from Hitler, he merely

received a rude reply. Goebbels had no luck either. The new SS commander and police president, Dr Benno Martin, was made of sterner stuff, however. He soon teamed up with the Nuremberg mayor, Liebel. Rather than face Streicher head on, they built up a case against him through careful police work, including wire taps. Hitler agreed to a commission of inquiry and restricted the hitherto easy access which the *Gauleiter* had enjoyed. Eventually, Streicher was sacked with Hitler's approval.

The Führer did not encourage this bureaucratic free-for-all, or requests to mediate, even if these placed him at the centre of the web. For one thing, they exposed him to misinterpretation and hasty judgement, as he was constantly doorstepped by people in search of '*Führer-Entscheidungen*', which often contradicted earlier pronouncements. For example, when he was 'reminded' that he had committed public funds for replacement housing during the remodelling of Berlin, Hitler insisted to Lammers that he 'had not made any such decision'.[48] As for arbitrating disputes, Hitler told party leaders not to write to him with their grievances but to sleep on them instead. Most problems, he suggested, would solve themselves, and the rest should be settled in conversation rather than through an exchange of peppery letters or memoranda, which only aggravated things. Thus, when confronted with two squabbling Bavarian ministers, Hitler tasked Hess with bringing about a 'personal exchange between the antagonists' in order to achieve 'a compromise'.[49] Nor did Hitler want people to be reporting to him all the time. 'I am not the chairman of a supervisory board!' he exclaimed. Rather, he wanted party administrators to take the initiative and show a sense of responsibility.[50]

Six months after his last attempt, Lammers issued a fresh directive to try to curb the flood of petitions and requests directed towards the Führer.[51] Hitler's immediate concern here was to prevent the machinery of government from seizing up, but these measures were also part of the broader long-term selection process by which he sought to improve the German people and its leadership caste. Cohesion, Hitler told party leaders, would come from 'schooling', not superintendence or control, which would only stifle initiative and creativity.[52] He therefore enunciated a kind of National Socialist subsidiarity principle, by which the Third Reich should only regulate those areas which it absolutely had to. For the rest, he wanted Germans to develop the 'confidence' to make (the right) decisions for themselves.

All this made for an informal and often chaotic governing style, which was complicated by the fact that Hitler kept ever more irregular hours. Until 1936 he had followed a reasonably conventional routine. Thereafter, the Führer increasingly reverted to his earlier Bohemian lifestyle, rising late and going late, often very late, to bed, often after visiting the opera or watching a film, sometimes two in a row.[53] That said, Hitler was not simply lazy. The overall number of hours he put in remained unchanged and because his view of politics was all-encompassing, none of his cultural activities can just be classified as entertainment, just as his numerous meetings with Unity Mitford, and her family,[54] were part of his plan to engage Britain. Whether attending the Bayreuth Opera Festival, watching films late into the night or going to exhibitions, Hitler was, in effect, always working.

The exception here was his relationship with Eva Braun, which had stabilized. He admired Unity's beauty – the Führer preferred blondes – and he saw her as a conduit to Britain, but he had no romantic or sexual interest in her. 'She's a very attractive girl,' he allegedly told Leni Riefenstahl, 'but I could never have an intimate relationship with a foreigner, no matter how beautiful she might be.'[55] This may have been, as Riefenstahl claimed, out of 'patriotic' love for German women, but the main motivation was probably security. It is no accident that around this time Hitler issued instructions that party leaders should not marry foreigners, even if, like Englishwomen, they were considered racially unproblematic. His relationship with Eva remained clandestine, because public knowledge of it would have undermined the claim that Hitler was married to Germany, and more particularly to German womanhood. 'I cannot afford to marry,' he said, 'otherwise I will lose half of my most loyal [female] followers.'[56] One way or the other, Hitler's personal life had settled into a pattern. He would see Eva either secretly in her Munich flat, or on the Obersalzberg, in whose confines she ruled acknowledged and supreme.

The Berghof now began to change its character. Originally more or less accessible to all, the Obersalzberg increasingly became a gated community, what Hitler's press secretary later called a 'golden cage'.[57] The mountain turned into a gigantic building site, as the various institutions and grandees sought to expand their presence. Huge areas were cordoned off and the mountain air was thick with dust and fumes. Martin Bormann, the head of the Party Chancellery, used the opportunity to strengthen his position in the Nazi firmament, largely at the expense of the Imperial Chancellery, and to control access to Hitler. He sought to ingratiate himself with the Führer through the construction of the 'Kehlsteinhaus' in 1937–8, a tea room perched on top of a summit overlooking Austria, which could be reached only by a lift-tunnel blasted through the rock. What Hitler made of these changes is unknown, but it is clear that whatever the reasons he had for going to the Obersalzberg, the unfettered appreciation of nature was no longer one of them.

*

Abroad, Hitler remained preoccupied with Germany's position in the world and his own international reputation. He monitored international responses to his speeches closely, for example, when he promised in January 1937 that the era of surprises was over.[58] His principal international focus continued to be Anglo-America. Despite the failure to get through to London or Washington, Hitler was not yet seriously alarmed. Though fearful of the Jewish lobby in America, and the power of the United States more generally, Hitler still regarded Roosevelt and his New Deal with some respect. In April 1937, the Führer welcomed Roosevelt's idea of a global conference to resolve all outstanding issues. When the German ambassador complained shortly afterwards that the embassy building in Washington was too small and in any case located in the middle of an undesirable 'Negro Quarter', Hitler immediately supported the construction of a more 'dignified' representation, if necessary at the cost of a million dollars.[59] When, in the summer of 1937, the former head of the Hamburg trade office of the Foreign Office, Baron von Rechenberg, penned an inflammatory pamphlet 'exposing' Roosevelt as a pawn of the Jews and an inveterate enemy of the Reich, which he sent to both the Foreign Office and Hitler, he did not at first gain any traction.[60] There was no suggestion, for now, that the Führer was expecting a breach with the United States any time soon.

It was the same with regard to Britain. The general drift of Ribbentrop's dispatches from London was that while there was profound concern in Britain about Hitler's 'ultimate intentions', there was also a sincere desire for peace, if necessary bought with colonial concessions.[61] For this reason, Hitler continued to use various 'go-betweens' in search of that elusive understanding.[62] One of them was the Jewish Princess Hohenlohe – born plain Stephanie Richter in Vienna – who was invited 'on the instruction of the Führer' to the party rally at Nuremberg so that she could bring 'a further important personality from England'.[63] Another was the former King Edward VIII, now Duke of Windsor, for whom Hitler confessed 'a certain weakness', who visited Germany in September 1937 with the full cooperation of the authorities.[64] The duke's visit included a stopover at a coalmine in the Ruhr (where he gave the Hitler salute)[65] and culminated with his much-publicized reception by Hitler at the Berghof. It was widely regarded as a propaganda coup for the Third Reich, and as a violation of the duke's pledge to keep a low profile after his abdication, and it infuriated the king and the British government. Hitler's private meeting with him produced nothing of consequence.[66]

Some of the Führer's other favoured 'go-betweens', the British fascist leader Oswald Mosley, his wife Diana and her sister Unity, were also proving to be more of a liability than an asset. Mosley visited Germany a month after the duke, and he too was received by Hitler on the Obersalzberg.[67] There were also meetings with Hess, Göring, Goebbels and Ribbentrop. The British Embassy ignored Mosley, but kept a close eye on his movements. Once again, little came of the talks. Hitler rejected Diana and Mosley's plan to set up a radio station – 'Air Time Limited' – on the German North Sea island of Heligoland, as this had fallen foul of the military authorities.[68] Unity, for her part, was now under surveillance by the British Secret Service. There were demands to have her passport confiscated.[69] Her value as a 'go-between', which Hitler had in any case wildly exaggerated from the start, was rapidly diminishing.

Hitler's need for mediators with the outside world heavily influenced his view of the German aristocracy. It was connected across Europe, and had a pan-European, generally conservative orientation.[70] Philipp von Hessen-Kassel, for example, was the son-in-law of King Victor Emmanuel III of Italy, and played an important role in connecting Hitler to Mussolini.[71] He enjoyed an excellent rapport with Hitler on the basis of shared artistic interests. But there was already a strong element of ambivalence in Hitler's attitude. For all his enthusiasm to connect with the British aristocracy, the head of the Gestapo, Heinrich Müller, was put to work checking whether any of them had Jewish blood,[72] a suspicion which Hitler entertained about the cosmopolitan nobility in general.

Around this time, Hitler broke with his principal interpreter of US affairs, Putzi Hanfstaengl, in one of the Third Reich's more bizarre episodes. For reasons that remain obscure, but are to be located in the ups and downs of Nazi court politics, Hanfstaengl had fallen out of favour by 1937. His enemies, Göring, Goebbels and Unity Mitford prominent among them, decided that he should be taught a lesson. Hitler himself knew in advance that a 'prank' was about to be played,[73] though he may not have been aware of all the details. In early February 1937, Hanstaengl was urgently summoned to Berlin.[74] On arrival, he was told he was needed in Spain immediately, and shortly after take-off he was given the impression that he was about to be thrown out of the aeroplane. This was probably, as those involved later claimed, an elaborate hoax rather than an assassination attempt, but Hanfstaengl was badly shaken. Soon after, he fled to Britain, eventually ending up in America.

In the meantime, Hitler was being warned with ever-increasing frequency and intensity about the hostility of the American public and elites. The air attaché in Washington, Boetticher, stressed both the immense military potential of the United States and the strength of the 'forces of capital', and the 'dark influences dependent on American Jewry in America itself'.[75] This sense of a fundamental antagonism between the United

States and Nazi Germany grew during the spring and summer of 1937, despite the appointment of a new, and initially more optimistic, German ambassador, Dieckhoff.[76] In March 1937, the half-Jewish New York Mayor Fiorello La Guardia heavily criticized Hitler at a rally in the city, provoking furious diplomatic protests, and an exchange of insults between the German and the American press.[77] If it was no surprise that the Third Reich was resisted by Jews and liberals, Hitler also struggled to gain traction in the American South, where the Third Reich enjoyed a terrible reputation, and where pro-British and anti-dictatorial sympathies were strong. It was not that Southerners opposed racism, it was just that they didn't much like Nazis.[78] Hitler was finding the Americans hard to please.

Worse still, the Third Reich was not merely losing America, it was losing German America.[79] The president of the Deutschen Ausland-Instituts, Dr Strolin, reported on his return from a lengthy trip to the United States that the vast majority of German-Americans, even including those who attended cultural events, were no friends of the new Germany. This was the result partly of the 'dominating influence of the Jews' in places like New York, he claimed, but also of the more or less universal US antipathy to 'militarism', the suppression of press freedoms and the generally 'different world view' of Americans, including German-Americans.[80] In May 1937, the Third Reich was reminded of this breach when Cardinal Mundelein of Chicago, whose father was of German descent, took time out from attacking Hollywood filth and extramarital sex to lambast Hitler, particularly his treatment of the Catholic Church there; German diplomatic protests proved to be of no avail.

The Führer's relations with most other powers remained reasonably good throughout most of 1937. This was partly due to the fact that Hitler continued to tread carefully in the matter of German minority rights, and the role of German citizens abroad. He distinguished carefully between *Volksdeutsche*, whom he defined as those of German descent, but citizens of another state, and *Auslandsdeutsche*, citizens of the Reich residing in foreign parts who were under the umbrella of the Auslandsorganization.[81] Relations with Poland remained particularly warm, at least at the diplomatic level. When a special four-volume edition of the late Marshal Piłsudski's orders and speeches appeared in early 1937, the list of subscribers was headed by the Polish president, the marshal's widow and Hitler.[82] In May 1937, he instructed Ribbentrop 'that the overall Polish-German relationship should not be exposed to serious strain on account of minority questions'.[83] To be sure, Hitler was critical of Poland in private. 'With Poland [there is] no love-match,' he had told Goebbels, 'but a relationship based on reason [which] has enabled our rearmament'.[84] Even so, there is no evidence that Hitler was planning an attack on Poland either at the time or in the future.

Hitler sought to rally Europe, or at least the authoritarian states, behind him by casting himself as a bulwark against the Soviet Union. He repeatedly played the Bolshevik card in his discussions with Hungary, Romania and other powers, urging them to patch up their differences, a strategy which continued until 1945.[85] Despite this rhetoric, there is no evidence that after a brief moment of anxiety in 1936 Hitler privately considered the Soviet Union an imminent military threat at this point. Outside of Spain, therefore, the struggle was waged on the ideological and propagandistic plane. This is why Hitler emphasized the importance of the Paris International Exhibition in the summer of 1937, which he saw as an opportunity to showcase the attractions of National Socialism to a world audience, especially Europeans.[86] He took a keen interest in the German pavilion, which was co-designed by Speer. Hitler's aesthetic priorities became clear when he rejected the request of the Economics Ministry to send representatives to those discussions.[87] Speer was aware of the Soviet designs when he was drawing up his own, and the intensity of the competition was surely heightened by the fact that his rival was a Jew from Odessa.[88] In the end, the Soviet and the Nazi pavilions directly faced off against each other on the majestic Trocadéro Esplanade in what was widely seen as a dramatic clash of the two systems.[89]

For all the surface stability, Hitler faced increasing domestic and international challenges throughout 1937. Economically, the most serious was the crisis of his standard of living project, which had been designed not merely to strengthen the regime at home, but to inoculate the German people against the appeal of Anglo-American consumerism, and to provide the basis for German racial improvement. These efforts were epitomized by an exhibition in Düsseldorf in the summer of 1937, held simultaneously with the Paris fair, entitled 'A Nation of Workers and Creators'.[90] This was intended to highlight the economic growth since Hitler took power, the merits of self-sufficiency and the range of products now available to German consumers, including the Coca-Cola dispensed from a reconstructed bottling plant. Among the local talent showcased was the German company Henkel; Hitler himself visited their pavilion and was photographed amid a display of washing powder and washing machines.[91] One wonders whether he remembered his remarks to Hess about the need to bring modern conveniences to the German people back in the 1920s. Likewise, Hitler maintained a keen interest in the Volkswagen project, choosing the site of the planned factory at Fallersleben (christened Wolfsburg).[92]

In truth, however, Hitler was losing the standard of living battle.[93] The Führer might, as he never tired of claiming, have dealt with the unemployment problem better than FDR, but he was nowhere near matching the American Dream. The figures spoke for themselves. After six years of Hitler, about half of all Germans owned a radio set, as opposed to 68 per cent of Britons and 84 per cent of Americans.[94] The Volkswagen was in difficulty, as German industry struggled to come up with a car which was also profitable;[95] the task was passed on to the German Labour Front. For all the sound and fury about motorization, in fact, no civilian Volkswagen ever made it to the Volk. Despite all the increased industrial activity, wages did not rise much.[96] Overall, the German standard of living, even after Hitler's economic 'miracles', was a third lower than that of Britain, partly due to inferior productivity.[97] Hitler effectively conceded defeat in a speech in May 1937. He began to emphasize sufficiency in basic goods and developed a theory of excess.[98] Hitler warned against inflation, and – no doubt aware of the Anglo-American advantage in productivity – linked wage increases to increased productivity. He urged German workers to travel abroad as tourists to see how well off they were themselves, but the comparisons he made were with Soviet poverty, which he could easily outperform, rather than Anglo-American prosperity, which he had no hope of matching.

These trends were aggravated by the economic bottlenecks produced by rearmament, which competed for resources not only with consumption but also with culture. All three fronts mattered to Hitler, as they were all theatres in the one struggle against Anglo-American capitalism. What distinguished them was the question of timing. Consumption and culture were part of a long-term racial vision; rearmament was geared to a much shorter-term strategy. Ideally, Hitler wanted to advance in all three theatres simultaneously, but that was increasingly difficult as the demand for raw materials grew. He found himself arbitrating so many requests to balance the allocation of steel for armaments with that for the construction or renovation of theatres, opera houses and other buildings that in May 1937 he requested a list of all urgent building plans which required the use of steel.[99] Two months later, Hitler was told that if he authorized the expansion of the Schiller Theater in Berlin, he would have to reduce the steel allocation to others, including the Wehrmacht.[100] Hitler's reaction then was to approve the plans for the theatre with 'immediate effect' and demand more steel overall, threatening to take the matter out of the remit of the Four Year Plan and into his own hands. For now, consumption and culture retained their importance alongside rearmament, and in some cases trumped narrowly military priorities, but soon one or more of them would have to give way.

The immediate consequence of all this was further to undermine the position of Schacht, who felt that he was being asked to do the impossible, and who was simply regarded as a failure by Hitler. His presidency of the Reichsbank was renewed in mid March 1937, but the Führer reduced the extension of his term from the four years envisaged in the draft of the announcement to a mere twelve months. Schacht was on notice. Hitler's main motivation in keeping him on was to reassure the outside world. When Schacht tried to extract a promise not to issue any more inflationary MEFO bills, which would have endangered Hitler's rearmament plans, the Führer bridled. There was a furious exchange, and when Schacht stood his ground, Hitler gave way in part.[101] Throughout the summer Schacht protested, obstructed and generally dragged his heels. In a letter copied to Hitler he warned that 'one cannot either bake bread or cast cannon with paper'.[102] A visibly unnerved Hitler summoned him at once to the Obersalzberg. The interview was unproductive. Schacht once again offered to resign, but Hitler still needed him to cover his rearmament programme abroad.

Worrying though the economic situation was, Hitler perceived the main threat to his authority in 1937 to come from another quarter, namely organized religion. He was horrified to be told by his intelligence services in late March 1937 that Pope Pius XI was about to issue a blistering encyclical. It had been in gestation for several months, during which the ailing pontiff consulted with the German church about the growing menace of Nazism.[103] Entitled 'With Burning Concern', the encyclical was signed on 14 March 1937, and read from German pulpits on Palm Sunday, 21 March 1937. It condemned the regime's 'open and covert' attacks on the Church, and the 'illegal and inhumane' pressure exerted against believers. It also struck at the very root of Hitler's ideology, attacking 'race and blood' as 'false coins' which 'do not deserve Christian currency', and rejected repressive 'human laws' which were so 'in contradiction with the natural law' as to be 'vitiated with a taint which no force, no power can mend'. For Hitler, there was no doubt about it. He was under attack from Roman Catholicism, a threat which might be domestic in manifestation but international in origin.

Retaliation was swift. Distribution of the encyclical was banned.[104] A stiff note was sent to the Vatican.[105] Relations cooled dramatically.[106] When German academics were invited to the opening of the Papal Academy of Sciences in Rome, Hitler banned them from attending in light of 'the current attitude of the Holy See towards the German Reich'.[107] It was the German Catholic Church, however, which bore the brunt of the Führer's wrath. 'We will never accept,' Hitler warned in a speech in late April 1937, 'that anything should place itself above the authority of [the state] not even a church.'[108] In 1937, the Gestapo, especially Reinhard Heydrich, spent much more time investigating the 'black', that is clerical, threat than the 'red' menace of social democracy and communism, which had by then been largely crushed.[109] Likewise, the Propaganda Ministry considered the struggle against the Catholic Church the 'most important domestic political confrontation'.[110]

The regime's main strategy was to discredit the church as an institution. Hitler urgently instructed the Justice Ministry to resume legal proceedings against alleged clerical child abusers, which had been largely suspended in the interests of good relations.[111] He authorized the use of material gathered during the court cases for political purposes by local *Gauleiter*.[112] Goebbels – at Hitler's direct instigation – exploited the propaganda opportunities mercilessly, dragging the church through the mud at every opportunity, in newspaper articles and radio broadcasts. Almost daily, Germans were treated to lurid accounts of clerical sexual abuse, not all of them invented. The Führer himself was more restrained in his remarks, but made unmistakable references to the trials in his own speeches.[113] The regime also pressurized the Catholic milieu in general. Sometimes tensions spilled over into violence, for example in July 1937, when participants in a Corpus Christi procession in the strongly Catholic Ermland region of East Prussia resisted police trying to confiscate the flag of a Catholic youth association.[114] Hitler was on the verge of plunging Germany into a new *Kulturkampf*.

For all his sound and fury, Hitler was anxious to avoid a complete breach with the Catholic Church for as long as possible. This was partly because he feared the international influence of the Vatican, and partly because he did not want to alienate German Catholics from the *Volksgemeinschaft* and drive them into the hands of the external enemy. 'According to confidential sources,' the Italian ambassador to the Vatican reported in June 1937, 'Hitler has affirmed the need to avoid confessional wars and his determination that the German people not be divided into two separate religious parties.'[115] Towards the end of July 1937, Hitler ordered a sudden end to the prosecution of alleged clerical child abusers.[116] In the autumn, he considered a plan to abolish all religious holidays, but thought better of it, on the grounds that it was 'not appropriate at present'. By the end of the year, Hitler had re-established an uneasy truce with the Roman Catholic Church.

One of the reasons why Hitler was so anxious about the power of the Catholic Church was because he saw the Vatican as allied to the Habsburg cause in Austria. The Führer was unsettled by the increased activity of the restorationist movement there. In mid January 1937, he was confronted with a warning from Papen in Vienna about the growth of the legitimist cause, which was focused on the young Otto von Habsburg, son of the last emperor,

Karl, and a serious political figure in his own right.[117] Not long afterwards, Göring met with Mussolini in Rome and told him that Germany would never tolerate a 'Habsburg Restoration' in Austria in any form.[118]

What Hitler was worried about here was not Habsburg armies, but the power of the legitimist idea, which he regarded as a direct challenge to his own imperial authority. He knew that insignia of the old Holy Roman Empire were in Vienna and could be used to underpin claims in the Reich. Hitler saw himself as the culmination of all the strands of German history. He contained and resolved a multitude of contradictions. The great picture window on the Berghof looked out on the Untersberg in which – as Hitler liked to tell guests[119] – the court of the emperor Charlemagne, or as in some accounts of Barbarossa, was asleep and waiting for the last epic battle to establish a new Reich. German political history, on his reading, had ended in 1933, now Otto von Habsburg threatened to drag Germans back into the past. Quite apart from being a representative of a loathsome dynasty, Otto was a menace to Hitler's entire imaginative project. The effect of all this was to enhance Hitler's fears of an international Catholic conspiracy against him, to increase his desire to reach an understanding with Italy, Hungary and other powers affected by the Habsburg threat, and to strengthen his determination to settle the Austrian question as soon as possible. The skeletal military contingency plan against Austria drawn up in late June 1937 was thus logically given the code name 'Otto'.[120]

Amidst all this, Hitler had not given up his plans to secure *Lebensraum* for the German people. It was central to his entire economic theory. Once again, his main point of reference remained the global powers, especially the United States. The Americans not only had plenty of space, it was also very fertile. In the Mississippi Delta, he argued in May 1937, 'a people could live there in plenty', provided there was no flooding, a reference to the catastrophic floods there that decade, and another sign that the Führer was well aware of events across the Atlantic. The Germans, by contrast, had no space. Reprising themes familiar from earlier speeches, Hitler claimed that they lived jammed together in a tiny area, while the Russians, the British and especially the North Americans lived in 'superfluity'.[121] 'Our living space is too small,' he reiterated a few months later, and needed to be supplemented by 'colonies'.[122] This meant lifting the Germans out of their current position as 'a people which did not belong to the exclusive ranks of the global propertied elite'.[123] Germany, Hitler effectively argued, picking up a theme from his 1920s rhetoric, was still part of the global proletariat.

The purpose of food, Flann O'Brien once said, is to 'keep people alive and in their own country'. With this in mind, the Third Reich had sought self-sufficiency from the very beginning, but the limits of greater agricultural productivity were clear by 1937. Yearly 'battles of production' had increased output substantially, perhaps as much as by a third. Now the law of diminishing returns applied. It was against this background that in February 1937 Hitler instructed the Ministry of Agriculture to start planning the settlement of lands beyond the current borders of the Reich.[124] He announced that 'the final non-negotiable aim for us is a Great Reich', which would 'establish and secure the future food supply of Germany'.[125] The area under consideration was Czechoslovakia and, especially, Ukraine. It emphatically did not include, at this point, Poland, whose diplomatic and military cooperation was vital to any campaign against the Soviet Union.

There was as yet no timetable, no sense of immediate urgency about these plans. 'The Zugspitze [Germany's highest mountain] cannot be climbed in one step,' he warned, 'one takes one step at a time, but we are pretty much halfway up.' 'Only a short time has passed,' Hitler continued, 'but I have planned the work of this movement over a longer timescale, and the final implementation of the programme will take as long as it takes until we have raised a generation in Germany which has completed our schooling.'[126] These were generic exhortations, designed to prevent the German people from settling down, setting them ever newer tasks to rejuvenate the race. 'So long as you carry out ambitious projects,' he proclaimed, 'you will remain young.' A few months later, Hitler conceded that his plans were a 'project for the future'. There was no sense at all of when the second half, or the last third, of the programme would be completed, when the 'final objective' would be reached, but the general sense conveyed was that of a generational struggle which would last many decades and perhaps centuries.

In the course of 1937, the new National Socialist year unfolded one last time as Hitler worked through the calendar of invented traditions. The press followed his progress as he switched between the Imperial Chancellery, his Munich flat and the Obersalzberg. It culminated that autumn in a long Indian summer of festivals, rallies and visits. Spurning an invitation to the 700th anniversary of the founding of Berlin, Hitler set off for Bayreuth. He then went on to the party rally at Nuremberg, where he delivered a series of keynote speeches. Germany was now much more secure, the Führer claimed, partly because it had allies such as Italy and Japan, but mainly because of its 'systematic racial policy'. This, Hitler averred, was 'creating the new human being', a perhaps deliberate echo of the Soviet ambition to create 'the new man'. These new people were not merely more numerous – he emphasized the 'growing number of births' – but also better-looking. 'How beautiful our girls and boys are,' Hitler continued, 'how glowing is their glance, how healthy and fresh is their posture, how splendid are the bodies of the hundreds of thousands and millions, which are schooled and nurtured by our organizations'. In short, Hitler celebrated 'the rebirth of a nation through the conscious breeding of a new type of human being'.[127]

The atmosphere at the 1937 rally was electric. One eyewitness described a 'mass hysteria' and 'delirium' with constant shouting and exclamations of 'Heil'. When Hitler passed through in triumph, even the foreign guests were overwhelmed, with many being moved to tears, or joining in the salutes. The Führer welcomed selected outside dignitaries at the castle over breakfast – it is clear that much of the spectacle was designed to impress them. The Corps Diplomatique attended *en gros* for the first time, another triumph.[128] All seemed well.

No sooner had the Nuremberg rally ended than Hitler looked forward to the next pageant, which was the return visit by Mussolini to Germany.[129] It took the *Duce* from Munich to Berlin, to military manoeuvres in the Baltic. Every stage of his progress was carefully choreographed, right down to the moment when the Hitler's train, which had run on parallel tracks with Mussolini's for the final stretch, pulled ahead, allowing the German dictator to greet his visitor in the imperial capital; perhaps there was also a suggestion that Nazi Germany had overtaken fascist Italy.[130] Nothing was left to chance. The acclamation and enthusiasm on display were carefully staged; workers were given the day off to cheer.[131] Very little of substance appears to have been discussed during these days, but that was not really the point. The purpose of the whole exercise was primarily performative: an opportunity for Hitler to showcase his achievements, to assert his dominance over the more 'senior' dictator and to present a common front to the world through a 'face-to-face' diplomacy which challenged the prevailing culture of liberal internationalism in Europe.[132] In early November, the *Duce* joined the Anti-Comintern Pact, but a full-scale military alliance with Rome had to wait another eighteen months.

If Hitler had hoped to use the visit to push his claims to Austria, he was disappointed. Mussolini's train stopped symbolically at the Brenner on the Austro-Italian border. At Innsbruck, the *Duce* alighted to greet the Austrian foreign minister. It was reported that Mussolini had been handed a letter from the widow of Engelbert Dollfuss, Italy's dead ally, murdered by Nazis during their abortive coup in 1934.[133] For Berlin, the symbolism of these moves was clear. Hitler had already promised Mussolini not to undertake any further moves in Austria without consulting him. Now the Führer let it be known to the Foreign Office and Göring, who he felt was pursuing an 'overly aggressive policy', that there was no intention on his side to 'precipitate a crisis'. Instead, Hitler wanted to 'continue to pursue an evolutionary solution'.[134]

Time, it seemed, was still on Hitler's side. More time was needed for rearmament, and for Austria to fall into his lap. The racial elevation of Germany required even more time. Hitler had not yet completely given up hope of securing his objectives if not with, then at least not against, Britain. He might threaten war, as a bluff, but he did not really want it yet. 'You know,' he reassured his party audience in late April 1937, 'I always go to the limit, but not beyond.'[135] The time was not yet ripe to precipitate a confrontation. He did not want the 'threatened world catastrophe' to burst upon him 'too early'. Rather, Hitler stressed, Germany needed peace, a 'period of tranquillity', which was 'necessary in order to let people and state mature politically, psychologically and militarily'. There was, in other words, no rush.

In the autumn of 1937, unbeknown to the vast majority of Germans, and indeed the world at large, Hitler suddenly increased the tempo.[136] He decided not merely to begin, but to effect secular change.[137] Hitler would be present at the future. Time speeded up. Exactly when or why this happened cannot be determined with absolute certainty. Part of the explanation lies in Hitler's increased sense of mortality, a fear on his part that illness or assassination might end his life prematurely.[138] Contemporaries noted that he would now frequently use the expression 'so long as I live'.[139] The principal reason, though, seems to have been Hitler's realization that the conflict with the United States, and perhaps with Anglo-America generally, which he had hoped to avoid, or at least to delay as long as possible, was now much closer than he had previously thought. One way or the other, time was no longer on Hitler's side. What needed to be done had to be done quickly, with the instruments he had, rather than those he would have liked to have had.

The breach seems to date from the first week of October, when Roosevelt launched a fierce attack on the dictatorships.[140] On 5 October 1937, FDR gave a speech at Chicago targeting 'the epidemic of world lawlessness', leaving his audience in no doubt that he meant Japan, Nazi Germany and fascist Italy. 'When an epidemic of physical disease starts to spread,' he continued, 'the community . . . joins in a quarantine of the patients in order to protect the health of the community against the spread of the disease.' If this was not done, Roosevelt warned, 'let no one imagine that America will escape . . . that this Western Hemisphere will not be attacked and that it will continue tranquilly and peacefully to carry on the ethics and the arts of civilization'. When pressed by reporters to clarify his remarks, the president admitted that they indicated 'an attitude' rather than outlining a programme, but the general drift was clear.[141] He had defined the dictatorships as the 'other' of the United States, and the language of disease and quarantine, which immediately gave the speech its name, suggested a 'medicalization' of American rhetoric against the Third Reich. Roosevelt was systematically preparing American public opinion for war with Germany.[142] The Quarantine Speech started a duel between FDR and the Führer which culminated in a full-scale exchange of broadsides eighteen months later, before the Second World War started, and long before the United States itself became a belligerent.

The Quarantine Speech made a deep impression on Hitler.[143] He was particularly upset by the fact that Roosevelt seemed to include the Soviet Union among his democratic friends against the Axis. Hitler attributed the president's belligerence to his alleged need to disguise economic failures through foreign political adventures, a theme to which he would return repeatedly over the next six years. He did not respond publicly, and indeed instructed that the temperature be lowered by the German press, but the Führer did react behind the scenes. On 6 October 1937, the day after Roosevelt's speech, he wrote to Baron von Rechenberg, a former diplomat, to ask for further copies of his incendiary pamphlet – entitled *Roosevelt–Amerika–eine Gefahr* – denouncing Roosevelt as a puppet of the Jews.[144] Nine days later, Hitler instructed that Ribbentrop and Goebbels be supplied with copies.[145] Rechenberg's diatribe, which contrasted the 'real Americans' of white origin with the malevolent Jewish lobby controlling Roosevelt, matched and substantiated Hitler's own repeatedly stated views more or less exactly.[146] At around the same time, Hitler gave the go-ahead for a massive propaganda campaign against Czechoslovakia. It began on 8 October, three days after the Quarantine Speech.[147] The pace now quickened across the board.

The looming confrontation with the United States did not make it any less of a model for Hitler. On the contrary, in the late summer and autumn of 1937, Speer's collaborator and confidant Rudolf Wolters was sent to the other side of the Atlantic to study urban layouts there.[148] The sketches and photos he sent to Hitler were revealing of the Third Reich's preoccupation with the New World, and showed the extent to which the plans for Berlin were influenced by the Washington model. Wolters was in charge of the planning for the new 'North–South axis' in Hitler's monumental Germania project. He was unimpressed by American cities – 'wild and lacking in order' – with one exception. This was Washington, especially the area south of the White House, which Wolters deemed remarkable.[149] The sketch of the Lincoln Memorial and reflecting pool he sent to the Führer was revealingly entitled 'East–West Axis', surely an echo of Hitler's planned 'North–South Axis'. Many of the proportions of governmental architecture which he studied in the United States were to be found, several orders of magnitude larger, in the plans for the North–South axis.[150] Hitler also read independently about American buildings. When Wiedemann visited the US in late 1937, he brought back architectural books for the Führer, whose ambition was to counter the German 'inferiority complex'. The gigantism of Hitler's vision for Germany was primarily driven by his preoccupation with the size of the United States and its monuments.[151] The new Berlin, in other words, was being designed to equal and surpass not just its European rivals but Washington, D.C.

A similar dynamic was at play in the Führer's plans to transform Hamburg, which he believed already had 'something American' about it.[152] If Washington was the model for Berlin, New York was the inspiration for Hamburg. Earlier that year, Hitler had met the representatives of the city in the Imperial Chancellery, where models of the planned bridge across the Elbe and the new shoreline development as well as detailed plans were on display in the hall. 'From the bridge over the Elbe upwards,' he said, 'the World City of Hamburg begins.' What Hitler wanted was something of 'monumental character', which when lit at night would create 'an overwhelming sight'.[153] His main audience here was Anglo-America, as visitors from overseas usually entered Germany via Hamburg. Hitler later told the visiting Austrian chancellor, Schuschnigg, that he wanted to impress Americans on arrival with the building prowess of the Third Reich.[154] The plans were announced publicly in the summer, and in the autumn of 1937 Konstanty Gutschow, the architect tasked with designing the party headquarters skyscraper, went to the United States to study structures such as the Empire State Building in New York.[155]

Hitler's ambivalence about the United States was epitomized by his uncertainty over whether Germany should be represented at the next International Exhibition, which was slated for New York in 1939. It made sense to follow up the Reich's success at Paris with a barnstorming performance on the other side of the Atlantic. Wiedemann, Speer and many others were very keen, but Hitler hesitated.[156] The problem was that the fair made little economic sense, as German trade with the United States had slumped since the trade treaty between the two states had expired two years earlier. Moreover, in the Nazi imaginary New York was the belly of the capitalist and Jewish beast. The Propaganda Ministry and the Foreign Office both argued against participation on the grounds that it would simply allow local critics like Mayor La Guardia to grandstand against the regime. Towards the end of the year, Hitler finally decided to veto the German participation.[157] He would not take his message to the New World, but engage with it on his own terms on the near side of the Atlantic. Hitler's world was beginning to contract.

Returning to Berlin at the end of October 1937, Hitler held two hugely important meetings. The first, on 29 October, was with the NSDAP *Propagandaleiter*. He told them that he did 'not have long to live by human calculation'. He explained this not with reference to any illness, which might have alarmed his audience, but with reference to the fact that members of his family tended not to live very long. Both his parents, he added, had died early. For this reason, Hitler continued, it was 'necessary to solve the problems which needed to be solved as soon as possible', that is, 'within his lifetime'. 'Only' he, the Führer stressed, was in the position to ensure this.[158] Hitler was putting his audience on notice that time was about to speed up. A watershed had been reached.

The second meeting was held in the Imperial Chancellery on 5 November and resulted in the famous 'Hossbach Memorandum'.[159] It should not be understood as inaugurating a new phase in Hitler's policy, but as reflecting a recent shift. The immediate purpose of the meeting, which took place at Blomberg's request, was to discuss the allocation of raw materials to the Wehrmacht, a key question which could only be resolved on the basis of the Führer's overall strategy. This Hitler set out in considerable detail, making clear that his remarks were intended as a guide to 'long-term German policy' and as his 'legacy for the event of his death'. The tension between Hitler's long-time horizon and the possibility of his death was evident. Nothing in the following grand strategic vision was new, indeed it had been rehearsed by Hitler ad nauseam since the 1920s. The main aim of German policy, he said, was 'securing and increasing' the numbers of the *Volk*, which was a 'question of space'. The German people, Hitler argued, were crammed together in central Europe and needed more space. The alternative of autarchy or international trade was rejected, as it was very difficult to achieve with regard to raw materials and simply impossible in terms of food security. Hitler's conclusion was that 'The future of Germany could only be determined by the solution of the question of space,' which must be sought for 'a period of one to three generations'.

The main powers to be taken into account 'today', Hitler continued, were England, France, Russia [*sic*] and the smaller neighbouring states. What was striking about this assessment was not so much the much greater attention given to Britain than any other power, as the fact that the United States does not appear to feature in his calculations. There could be many reasons for this, but the most obvious is that the crucial word was 'today'. As we shall see, Hitler remained preoccupied with the sheer size of the

United States at this time, but it was not the point at issue in the meeting, which was concerned with the near future, and the immediate neighbourhood. Hitler would deal with Europe 'today' and with the world – that is, the United States – tomorrow. The meeting was not called to unveil Hitler's well-known long-term ambition, which was to confront or at least balance the United States, but to set out the short-term steps required to make the medium-term conquest of *Lebensraum* in Russia possible. Hitler had moved from contemplating a more distant global future, to the immediate solution of a pressing problem on the continent. This could only be done through 'force' and that path, he warned, was 'never without risk'. Frederick the Great and Bismarck, Hitler explained, had also acted in 'an unbelievably risky manner'. That being so, he claimed, the only questions that remained to be addressed were the 'when' and the 'how'.

Hitler envisaged three scenarios. Under the first, the latest date for action would be 1943–5, because 'thereafter one could only expect things to develop to [Germany's] disadvantage'. The Wehrmacht, he claimed, was as ready as it would ever be. Within a few years the qualitative edge in equipment and the quantitative advantage in mobilization would be lost. The Reich would be vulnerable to a 'food crisis', because there were insufficient reserves of food and of foreign exchange to buy it. Herein, Hitler admitted, lay a potential 'moment of weakness for the regime'. He also warned of the 'prospect of declining living standards and birth rates'. This was a striking admission that his project of racial elevation and multiplication through a higher standard of living had stalled. Moreover, the outside world had woken up to the danger – a reference to western rearmament but also Roosevelt's rhetoric – and was beginning to prepare itself for the conflict ahead. Developmental time and military time were now running against Germany. For all these reasons, Hitler said that if he were 'still alive' then, it would be his 'final decision to solve the German problem of space by 1943–5 at the latest'.

There were two other scenarios, in which decisive action either could or would have to be taken earlier. One was a domestic French collapse, or France's distraction by a war with another state, which would leave Germany free to act. In that event, his first priority would be 'to crush Czechoslovakia and simultaneously Austria in order to secure the flanks of any move against the west'. The aim here was not the acquisition of *Lebensraum*. In a prefiguring of his wartime plans, Hitler argued that the capture of the densely settled – his exact words were 'not thinly' – Czechoslovakia and Austria would only be a net gain if 2 million people could be expelled from the former and a million from the latter. Rather, the move was a shaping operation designed to pre-empt a French- or British-inspired Czech attack on Germany's southern flank. Hitler was also concerned to deter Poland, which he did not entirely trust, from taking advantage of Germany's difficulty. There was no sense at all, however, that he was planning an attack on Poland himself, quite the opposite. Hitler's third and final scenario concerned the possibility of a war arising out of a confrontation in the Mediterranean.

To his immense frustration, Hitler was strongly contradicted by the military men and the Foreign Office. It was not that they objected to the *Lebensraum* conception – with which they had been familiar at the very latest since Hitler's secret speech to the generals in February 1933. They were highly sceptical, however, that Britain and France would allow Austria or Czechoslovakia to be occupied unopposed. Blomberg and Fritsch both stressed that the Wehrmacht was not yet in a position to fight any resulting war with the western powers.

After the meeting in the Imperial Chancellery, Hitler began to put his new strategy into effect. That very same day, he met with representatives of the Polish minority within the Reich and with the Polish ambassador Lipski.[160] The Polish alliance remained central to his vision. Over the next year or so, Hitler continued to emphasize the mutual respect between Poland and Germany, and to praise the memory of Marshal Piłsudski as a 'towering personality' who had recognized the necessity of a rapprochement.[161] On the day following the meeting, Mussolini finally joined the Anti-Comintern Pact. Shortly after, Hitler met the Hungarian prime minister as part of his plan to isolate Austria and the Czechs. The Hungarians were told to concentrate their demands on the Czechs and leave the Yugoslavs alone. In late December, the army issued a new instruction for a war in the south-east, entitled *Fall Grün*. At around the same time, the expansion of the Luftwaffe and the navy was put on hold, and expenditure on the army was increased.[162] All of this was consistent with a plan to crush Austria and Czechoslovakia quickly, when the opportunity presented itself, and to launch a land war of conquest against the Soviet Union, within eight years.

Central to Hitler's plans was the attitude of Britain. Despite the warning signs, he had still not given up on London. A British alliance would be critical to balance the power of the United States, and British acquiescence was essential to his plans in central Europe, and for his projected war of conquest in the east. In late January 1938, Hitler met with the foreign secretary, Lord Halifax, at the Berghof and presented him with his demands concerning Austria, Czechoslovakia and Danzig; control over the latter was sought not as an anti-Polish gesture but in order to secure the port for the planned war on Russia. He was frank about his concern that, unlike Russia and the United States, Germany did not have enough space. The foreign secretary, who had mistaken Hitler for the footman on arrival, indulged the Führer by replying that all requests could be considered, but that any changes would have to be agreed peacefully.[163] When Halifax praised Hitler for 'preventing the entry of communism into his own country', the translator, Dr Paul Schmidt, added – at any rate in the German protocol – 'that Germany could therefore with justice be regarded as the bulwark of the west against Bolshevism', a much more comprehensive notion with far-reaching implications for the latitude he might enjoy on that basis. Hitler was notorious for hearing what he wanted to hear, and he seems to have come away with a greatly exaggerated sense of British understanding for his position.[164]

The Führer flanked these diplomatic efforts with a concerted domestic campaign. Repression, which had eased off for the first nine months of the year, now resumed in earnest. The main target was the Jews. Considerations of foreign policy, which had previously served to mitigate Hitler's ferocity for fear of antagonizing the United States, now drove an escalation.[165] On 5 November, the same day as the Hossbach meeting, all Soviet Jews were ordered to leave Germany within ten days; these he did not seem to view as potential hostages. Three days later, Goebbels opened the – long-planned – exhibition 'The Eternal Jew', the main thrust of which was directed against capitalism rather than Bolshevism. Right at the end of that month, Hitler told Goebbels that the Jews would have to be expelled from Germany altogether.[166]

14
'England is the motor
of opposition to us'

The Führer spent Christmas and New Year on the Obersalzberg. Returning to Berlin, Hitler threw himself back into work. On 12 January 1938,
Hitler met the Polish foreign minister, Beck. Five days later, he spoke to
the Yugoslav foreign minister, Stojadinović. Both men agreed that a Habsburg restoration was to be averted at all costs. Hitler turned up the heat
against the Czechs in a speech on 20 February 1938 in which he demanded
the right to protect German minorities in Europe, a marked change from
his earlier policy. 'Self-determination' and even – in as many words –
humanitarian intervention became frequent slogans.[1] Despite Ribbentrop's
dispatch, Hitler also kept trying with Anglo-America. In early March
1938, he met the British ambassador, Henderson, who held out the prospect of a return of some of Germany's colonies, either outright or under
some form of joint management. Hitler showed little interest, proclaiming
the colonial question as not yet 'ripe for a solution'.[2] The Führer also
warned Henderson that that he would not tolerate British interference in
the relationship between Germany and 'tribally related countries or countries with a high proportion of ethnic Germans', any more than London
would accept his interference in Irish affairs. If Britain did meddle, Hitler
added, 'then the time had come at which we would have to fight'.[3]

The new tone was unmistakable. Britain was now the main obstacle.
The Soviet Union, which had loomed relatively large for about a year in
1936–7, now receded in Hitler's consciousness once more. As his remarks
to Henderson indicated, he saw London's nationality and imperial problems as an instrument which could be used to deter or contain British
intervention in central Europe. Hitler's speeches began to adopt the language of anti-imperialism. More importantly, in a sign that he had taken
on board Ribbentrop's demand for a global coalition against Britain, the
Führer sought to deepen the relationship with Japan. On 20 February 1938,
he finally announced that he intended to recognize the Japanese puppet-
state of Manchukuo.[4] This had been long delayed so as not to offend China,

but now the common front against the British Empire had priority.[5] When Hermann Kriebel, an old Nazi who had served as general consul in Shanghai came to warn Hitler against putting all his eggs in the Japanese basket, the Führer refused to receive him, remarking: 'I don't need him. He was over there and misjudges the situation. I wasn't there, but my assessment is correct.'[6]

The declining relationship with Anglo-America made Hitler all the more determined to make Berlin a city to put Washington, and the capitals of other rival powers, in the shade.[7] On 11 January 1938, Hitler instructed Speer to build a new Imperial Chancellery in the Vossstrasse to reflect the grandeur of the Third Reich. 'Whoever enters the Imperial Chancellery,' he remarked during a trip to the building site, 'must have the sense of approaching the lord of the world.'[8] That same month, Hitler issued his 'Decree on the Reorganization of Berlin'. Shortly after that, on 28 January 1938, the plans for the new city of Germania were presented to the public. They involved a huge north–south axis, bookended with two massive railway stations. The Great Hall of the People was intended to be the largest indoor auditorium in the world, with space for 180,000 people and a dome sixteen times bigger than that of St Peter's in Rome. It was clearly designed to dwarf the US Capitol. The artificial lake was surely a nod to the Washington reflecting pool as represented in the sketches by Speer's close collaborator Rudolf Wolters. The massive triumphal arch, which Hitler intended to carry the names of the 1.7 million German First World War dead, was doubtless intended to overshadow the much smaller Arc de Triomphe in Paris. The regime press were suitably awe-struck, but the real audience was abroad. The New York Times, for example, wrote that Hitler's project was 'perhaps the most ambitious planning scheme' of the age.[9]

Hitler's interest in the remodelling of German cities went well beyond the imperial capital, to include Nuremberg, Augsburg, Weimar, Goslar, Bayreuth and especially Munich and Hamburg.[10] In late February, he gave a speech on the remodelling of Germany's cities. In late May 1938 he issued a decree on the planned monumental bridge across the harbour at Hamburg, which was intended to rival the San Francisco Golden Gate Bridge. Critics saw all these plans, especially the remodelling of Berlin, as evidence of hubris, even of insanity. Speer's father, also an architect, famously remarked on seeing the plans for Germania that 'you have gone completely crazy'. There was a lot in this. That said, Hitler's main motivation was not megalomania, but insecurity, a desire to bolster shaky German self-esteem in order to prepare the nation for the struggle ahead. He planned such structures, Hitler told an audience of senior military men, not out of 'megalomania', but rather 'because of the cold calculation that such mighty works were the only way of giving the [German] people self-confidence'.[11]

Nor had Hitler completely given up hope of winning the battle of consumption with Anglo-America. On his birthday, Ferdinand Porsche presented Hitler with a model of the planned new Volkswagen; the resulting photograph shows his face to be a picture of delight. Not long after, the Führer laid the foundation stone of the first Volkswagen factory.[12] Its design consciously imitated that of the large American automobile works Porsche had visited during a fact-finding visit to the United States. But Wolfsburg was intended to be much more than just the 'greatest German car factory'. It was to be, as Hitler explained in his accompanying speech, 'a model German workers' city', with exemplary 'social housing' which would serve as a template for similar ventures elsewhere in the Reich. The huge residential apartment blocks housing the car workers and their families – a city of 90,000 inhabitants was planned – were laid out in a distinctly modern, even progressive style. The individual flats were large, being geared towards families with four children, and well appointed. There was central heating, warm water and various modern conveniences, including washing machines in the central laundries.[13] This was the German dream-modernity Nazi style much as Hitler had envisaged in the 1920s.

In late January 1938, Hitler was suddenly engulfed by a crisis not of his own making.[14] The Reichswehr minister, Werner von Blomberg, had recently remarried a much younger and socially lower-ranking woman.[15] Concerned that this new union would be rejected by his brother officers, Blomberg turned to Hitler for support, telling him that his betrothed was a 'typist', and an 'ordinary girl' who had 'a past'.[16] The Führer, ever keen to break down class barriers in Germany, probably assumed that her 'past' simply referred to previous relationships, and spontaneously offered to act as witness at the wedding, which took place in some haste in mid January 1938. Soon after the nuptials, however, it transpired that Blomberg's bride had a police record as a prostitute and as a model of pornographic photos. Göring presented the evidence, including the pictures, to Hitler later that month. It was entirely conclusive. The Führer's outrage knew no bounds. He paced up and down the room, utterly shocked, muttering to himself and shaking his head. 'If a German field marshal marries a whore,' Hitler expostulated, 'then anything is possible.'[17] The Führer felt personally betrayed and misled by Blomberg. While he was happy to endorse marriage across traditional class lines, and was unworried by pre-marital sex, Hitler would never have allowed himself to be associated with pornography and prostitution. He feared becoming a laughing stock, especially abroad. There was no doubt in his, or anyone else's mind, that Blomberg had to go.

This single dislodged stone triggered a landslide. Hitler wanted to replace Blomberg swiftly and discreetly. His eye inevitably fell on the army chief, Fritsch, a plausible candidate who would be acceptable to the army. But the Führer was now on guard. He feared that Blomberg was only the tip of the iceberg, that the lid had been lifted on a senior officer corps where depravity was rife. Recalling earlier accusations of homosexuality against Fritsch, which he had discounted, Hitler immediately demanded that the file be reconstituted and the case reopened, before he would consider him for Blomberg's succession. He questioned Fritsch personally. The meeting did not go well, primarily because Fritsch – in the interests of full disclosure – mentioned his friendly connections to some Hitler Youths, one of which had ended badly. Hitler was immediately suspicious, sensing a much larger and uncontainable scandal involving ever more boys. He was not willing to take chances, not least because homosexual activity was illegal and exposed culprits to the risk of blackmail. Hitler's confidence in the army had been shattered. Fritsch, too, would have to go. In neither case was Hitler motivated by the desire to rid himself of opponents of the strategic vision he had laid out, or restated, in the Chancellery in November 1937. He could, after all, have sacked either man with a minimum of fuss at any point since then.

The Führer was now faced with a major headache. Firstly, he needed to find replacements for both Blomberg and Fritsch. The very fact that Hitler had to cast around for nominations, and consult more widely than he usually did, shows that he had not plotted the changes in advance. Secondly, the Führer had to think of a way of presenting the changes without the embarrassing truth becoming known. Hitler began with the succession to Fritsch. The army wanted General Gerd von Rundstedt, whom Hitler rejected as too old. His own preference was for Walther von Reichenau, the man with whom he had been in contact even before the takeover of power and who had been instrumental in getting the army to swear an oath to Hitler personally after Hindenburg's death. The army, in turn, refused to wear a man widely regarded as a lazy and politicized careerist. In the end, Hitler settled on Walther von Brauchitsch, who committed himself 'to bringing the army closer to the state and its ideas'.[18]

Replacing Blomberg was no less problematic. It was not just a question of finding a name, but also of defining the future of the role itself. There had long been voices calling for a reorganization of the structure of the German High Command. This was a good opportunity to effect a change. The initiative here did not come from Hitler, but from within the army, from Keitel and indeed from the retiring Blomberg, who urged the Führer to take over the supreme command of the army himself.[19] Hitler abolished the position of Reichswehr minister and established in its place a 'supreme commander of the Wehrmacht' – himself – and a High Command of the Wehrmacht (OKW), which would discharge the former ministerial functions of the Wehrmacht Office.[20] Direct formal control of the armed services had now fallen into Hitler's lap.

All that remained now was to communicate these changes to the country and the world at large. Astonishingly, word of the crisis had not leaked. Hitler decided to frame the new appointments as part of a general reshuffle which would change the narrative and give the world something else to talk about.[21] So on 4 February 1938, Hitler announced the new military arrangements together with a raft of other measures. Most important among these was the replacement of Neurath at the Foreign Office by Ribbentrop. The effect of these changes was less dramatic than one might imagine, because Hitler was already in more or less complete control of the German military and foreign policy, and – leaving Fritsch aside – it would have been hard to imagine a more enthusiastic supporter of both National Socialism and Hitler's strategy than the sacked Blomberg. What the whole episode did show however was the considerable skill with which the Führer could retrieve a very difficult situation and even turn it to his advantage.

Hitler now pressed ahead with his plans for Austria. Despite the increased urgency, his aim was not immediate occupation. That would simply have been too risky, and it was unnecessary. Hitler's aim was to neutralize Austria as a threat to his southern flank and to cook the Austrian government slowly in a pot, rather than causing the whole vessel to boil over. This was consistent with the 'evolutionary' approach Hitler and Schuschnigg had agreed on in July 1936. Following the discovery of another putsch plan by some radical Austrian Nazis, the Austrian chancellor, Schuschnigg, came to Berchtesgaden on 12 February, trying to reaffirm Hitler's support for the more moderate Austrian Nazis. The German dictator, however, could prepare for this encounter, through information provided by Austrian Nazis, having received in advance a detailed briefing on how far Schuschnigg was prepared to go. It was a tense meeting, at which Hitler browbeat his interlocutor into granting an amnesty for Austrian Nazis and appointing some prominent Nazis to key positions in the government.[22]

Hitler still favoured an evolutionary solution in Austria, though, and told Austrian Nazis that a violent confrontation should be avoided if at all possible. The Führer, in short, was at pains to prevent a repetition of the events of 1934. The Austrian Nazis, however, continued their demonstrations, seeing the appointment of a Nazi sympathizer, Seyss-Inquart as interior minister, as a clear go-ahead. In response, Schuschnigg suddenly announced on 9 March 1938 that he would hold a referendum on the future status of Austria within four days. The wording of the question and the modalities surrounding the organization of the vote, especially the plan to exclude voters under the age of twenty-four, many of whom were Nazis, made clear that it was directed against any Anschluss.

Hitler was caught completely off-balance. His strategy had caused the pot to boil over after all. The choice was stark. On the one hand, if he allowed the referendum to go ahead, and if – as seemed likely – it resulted in a victory for Schuschnigg, then the subsequent absorption of Austria would be much more difficult. On the other hand, if he attempted another coup, or even invaded outright, Hitler risked another catastrophic failure and perhaps Italian or other great power intervention. The Führer reacted quickly. A day after Schuschnigg's announcement, he instructed the Wehrmacht to prepare for the occupation of Austria within forty-eight hours. He stressed that this was not to be a 'war against a fraternal people', and should therefore be given the appearance of 'a peaceful invasion which has been welcomed by the people'. That said, resistance was to 'be ruthlessly broken through force of arms'.[23] The operation had to be improvised as there had been no detailed prior planning.

Mussolini's attitude would be critical. Rome had previously signalled that it might accept an internal Nazi solution, but Hitler had no mandate for a full-scale invasion and there was no time to get one, nor could he risk being refused. On balance, he told Goebbels, he thought that Italy and Britain would 'do nothing'.[24] So the Führer simply informed Mussolini on 11 March in a letter that was delivered in person by his go-between Philipp of Hesse that it was his 'irrevocable decision' to 'restore peace and order in my native land'; one of the concerns cited was fear of a Habsburg restoration.[25] He did not wait for the reply. Nor did the Austrian Nazis, who staged demonstrations throughout the country on 11 March. There was also increasing pressure from Berlin on Schuschnigg to call off the referendum and resign, which he did later that day. The Austrian Army was ordered not to resist a German entry, and at midnight, Seyss-Inquart was appointed as the new chancellor. Despite these developments, Hitler gave the order to invade.

In the early hours of 12 March 1938, the first Wehrmacht and German police units crossed the Austrian border. Later that afternoon, Hitler followed suit, via his birthplace Braunau am Inn, pressing on without stopping to Linz. While in the city, he asked Hofrat Adolf Eigl about Dr Bloch, of whom he retained a good memory. Hitler also visited the graves of his parents at Leonding. He signed the Anschluss into law, adding 6.7 million inhabitants to the Reich at a stroke. The next day, Hitler entered Vienna to a tumultuous welcome. On the following day, with Unity Mitford at his side, he proclaimed the Anschluss from the balcony of the Hofburg. The confirmation of the Anschluss law by plebiscite (in Austria as well as the old Reich) on 10 April was just a formality.

South of the Brenner nothing stirred. Mussolini gave the Führer a finger, and he took the whole hand. Hitler had read the *Duce* correctly. His relief was palpable. ''I will never never forget this,' he assured Mussolini, a message conveyed by Prince Philipp of Hesse over the phone. The great powers did not retaliate either, even though the Anschluss was another direct violation of the Treaty of Versailles; Great Britain and France merely lodged lukewarm protests against German pressure on Austria on 11 March. 'They said England would be there to stop me,' Hitler later remarked, 'but the only English person I saw there [Unity Mitford] was on my side.'[26] The Führer had got away with it again. Whatever the input of other Nazi leaders, and Göring seems to have been particularly hawkish, the decision to risk the Anschluss was Hitler's alone to take.[27] Fewer than six weeks after the Blomberg-Fritsch crisis, he had once again gripped a dangerous situation, and turned it to his own advantage. Hitler had not intentionally made, but had seized, exactly the sort of 'opportunity' he had envisaged five months earlier in the Imperial Chancellery.

If the west had not reacted to the Anschluss, it had not gone unnoticed. Relations with London and Washington declined sharply. The treatment of the Austrian Jews, in particular, caused renewed horror. The first outrages had already started on 11 March, before the arrival of German troops, and by far surpassed anything the Jews had had to endure in Germany thus far. Roosevelt became active in the cause of Jewish refugees from Nazi Germany, combining the immigration quotas for Germany and Austria, to help those escaping from the latter.[28] He also tried to explore the possibility of getting 'all the democracies to share the burden' of distributing Jewish migrants. Four months later, this led to the international refugee conference at Evian. The German ambassador, Dieckhoff, warned that the United States would not remain neutral in the event of a world war, but would come in on Britain's side.[29] Roosevelt's Naval Expansion Bill of the month following the Anschluss was a clear sign of how the wind was blowing. Hitler made some efforts to reach out to the US. He granted an audience to the former US president Herbert Hoover during his European tour. At around this time, the Führer also met with the founder of the American telecommunications giant ITT, Sosthenes Behn.[30] Behn, whose paternal ancestry was German, had served in the US army in France in the war and was thus the epitome of the kind of emigrant Hitler was so sorry to lose.

The Führer refused, however, to meet Fritz Kuhn, the *Bundesführer* of the Amerika-Deutschen Volksbund, who visited Germany in April

1938.[31] This was because he wished to avoid antagonizing the US government and public opinion, which were already strongly suspicious of Nazi machinations in the western hemisphere, the extent of which they greatly exaggerated. The US security services kept a close watch on German-American organizations, especially the Bund, as did Samuel Dickstein and Martin Dies's committee in the House of Representatives, which had recently been renamed the House Committee to Investigate Un-American Activities, or HUAC.[32] In fact, Hitler's main interest in America was not to establish a fifth column on the far side of the Atlantic but quietly to encourage German citizens resident in the United States to return to the Reich.

It was in this context that the regime made a pitch to lure back German emigrants to the Reich. The Four Year Plan and the demands of rearmament revealed a severe shortage of qualified engineers and other skilled workers. Efforts to find these among German nationals in the United States found an echo among those who had failed to find work, who were suffering from increasing levels of anti-German sentiment on the far side of the Atlantic, who still felt the emotional pull of the Fatherland or who sympathized with the Third Reich. The target audience here, in the first instance, was Reich citizens, not German-Americans, but the plan was to extend the scheme to include *Volksdeutsche* (ethnic Germans) in due course. The exercise failed to bring back more than a small number of people, largely because most of those who wished to avail themselves of the opportunity could not afford the transatlantic passage, even after a fire-sale of their assets, and the regime lacked the foreign currency (*Devisen*) to pay for their passages en masse. Inevitably, some emigrants hoping to leave the United States suggested that they exchange their property with German Jews trying to get to America.[33]

To this effect, the Kameradschaft USA was established in 1938 under the general auspices of the Auslandsorganisation; US citizens were supposed to be strictly off-limits, although in practice the rule was not always observed. There were no fewer than eight offices across the country to welcome back the 'USA returnees', as they were known. Part of the plan was to use their skills to make up shortfalls in German industry, but there was also the hope that they could be used to colonize new living space beyond the existing borders of the Reich. The scheme was a failure, with fewer than a thousand returning to the Reich before the outbreak of war. Many of them were discontented, and some quickly made their way back across the Atlantic.[34] All this merely confirmed Hitler's view that while the Germans who settled in the east remained German, the young men and women who went west were lost to the Reich for ever.

After the Anschluss, Hitler moved quickly to consolidate his authority in Austria, and to exploit his triumph in the Reich itself.[35] Among the first 'transport of prominent people' to Dachau were the two sons of the murdered Archduke Franz Ferdinand; both were very badly treated there. The Anschluss, which brought another 6 million or so Catholics into the Reich, made a rapprochement with the church hierarchy more urgent. One of the very first things Hitler did on entering Vienna in triumph was to meet with Cardinal Innitzer, at the latter's request. In a piece of pure theatre, he approached the cardinal, bowed deeply and offered to kiss his hand. Innitzer raised the cross and chain around his neck and symbolically made the sign of the cross. After the cardinal had left, Hitler expressed his strong satisfaction with the meeting, and expressed his confidence that, by contrast with the Reich, 'he would be able to get on well with the church in Austria'. There, Hitler explained, Catholicism was 'a state church and had a very different relationship with the state'. He had no objection to that. 'Churches should only get involved in politics,' Hitler elaborated, 'if they were also ideologically instruments' of the state authorities. But if anyone tried to make 'the cross the cloak of opposition', he continued, then they would be 'annihilated'. In return for Innitzer's profession of loyalty (he signed off a letter to the Führer with 'Heil Hitler'), Hitler promised that Catholics would be allowed to practise their religion freely.[36]

Control of Austria enabled Hitler to lay exclusive claim to the German imperial tradition, whose 'imperial regalia and imperial insignia' had been moved from Nuremberg during the French Revolutionary Wars and stored in Vienna since the collapse of the Holy Roman Empire.[37] In mid June 1938, the mayor of Nuremberg, referring to Hitler's own numerous past statements on the matter, requested their return to 'the city of the Reich party rallies'. Hitler readily agreed, and when the *Reichsstatthalter* in Austria, Seyss-Inquart, demanded that they remain in Vienna, the Führer gave him short shrift.[38] The return of the insignia to Nuremberg, with its strong party affiliations, symbolized the continuity which Hitler wished to suggest between his Third Reich and the First Reich of Charlemagne. It was also intended, as he explained in mid September, to show 'the whole world' that a 'mighty' German Reich had existed 'a half millennium before the discovery of the New World',[39] evidence, if more was needed, of Hitler's continuing preoccupation with the United States.

Despite this, Hitler remained anxious about the Habsburgist threat. When in the summer of 1938 the members of the 'German Association of Nobles' protested against an article in Julius Streicher's *Der Stürmer* which suggested that the Habsburgs had Jewish blood, Hitler was furious. The Führer was angry with his *Gauleiter* for precipitating the row, but he was also aghast at the way in which the association had sprung to the defence of the Habsburgs at a time when 'a decisive and coherent front of the entire German people against the House of Habsburg' was required. Hitler decreed that there should be no discussion of the incident in the press or in public. He also declared that he wanted the members of the House of Habsburg to be expelled from Austria, and all compensation payments for the sequestration of their property to be stopped. The matter was still being discussed towards the end of the summer, and the question was ultimately left for Hitler to decide.[40] Early in the following year, the necessary laws came into force, and all Habsburg property was seized by the Third Reich. The whole episode testified to the importance which Hitler attached to the Habsburg question and control of the German imperial tradition.

The occupation of Austria was not intended to provide Hitler with a staging ground for further expansion to the south or the south-east. The new name of the province – Ostmark – made clear that he saw it as a 'bulwark' on the southern flank of the Reich,[41] not a sally-port. Hitler's view of south-eastern Europe, at least at this point, was largely uncoloured by pan-German sympathies. He continued to tread carefully with regard to the German minorities across Europe. When Hess protested that a circular by Imperial Organization leader Ley, implying ambitions on South Tyrol, Switzerland, Alsace-Lorraine and western Poland, might cause diplomatic complications Hitler agreed that it should be withdrawn.[42] Relations with Yugoslavia and other Balkan countries were intensified, not so as to render them ripe for annexation but in order to support the economic needs of rearmament. Germany did not run up a large imbalance of payments in the expectation of escaping it through conquest, but rather because there was lower demand for her products than she had hoped.[43]

Hitler also moved to reassure Mussolini, who had been presented with a fait accompli during the Anschluss. Hitler's letter of 11 March 1938 had promised to respect the Brenner border, and was instantly published by the Italian press, but there had been an uptick in South Tyrolean agitation after the annexation of Austria just the same.[44] Luckily for the Führer, his return visit to Italy was scheduled for early May 1938, giving him the opportunity to settle the issue once and for all. Local Nazis protested vigorously, and the huge German delegation heading south by train was struck by the grimness with which they were received when traversing South Tyrol, which contrasted with the adulation in the Reich and the rest of Italy.[45] Hitler remained unmoved. Thanks to the 'experience of two millennia', the Führer publicly told the Duce at the Palazzo Venezia in Rome, both parties now wanted to 'recognize that natural border which providence and history had evidently drawn for our two peoples'. This, he explained, would establish a 'clear demarcation of the *Lebensraum* of both nations'.[46]

Mussolini sought to impress Hitler with a triumphant welcoming display which would exceed that put on by the German dictator for him the previous autumn.[47] The Christian heritage of Rome was largely left out of the fascist itinerary for him, while the Vatican demonstratively ignored Hitler's presence on account of the tensions produced by the papal encyclical a year before. Pius XI condemned the swastika plastered all over the city as 'a cross inimical to the cross of Christ'. The Vatican museums were shut as a sign of disrespect and the darkness of the papal city contrasted markedly with the fireworks and illuminations put on by the regime.[48] Hitler does not seem to have minded. He enthused about the artistic heritage: the Pantheon, the Borghese Museum, the Museo delle Terme and much else. He explored these with the help of an Italian guide, Ranuccio Bandinelli. Hitler was confirmed in his view that the country was a major cultural power, which he hoped to rival with an artistic collection to match that of the Uffizi or the Louvre. This was the genesis of his idea for a *Führermuseum* at Linz. Even in Italy, though, Hitler was plagued by anxiety about the hostility of the United States. He remarked in the Villa Borghese that he had been asked to support an exhibition of German art in America, but had declined on the grounds that 'there was a danger that the paintings would be defaced by the Bolsheviks, and in any case why should one be polite to a people [the Americans] which constantly subjected us to vicious attacks'.[49]

Hitler's next target was Czechoslovakia, which was in his sights not for demographic or territorial, but for strategic reasons. It was a bone in the throat of the Reich, a potential launchpad for an invasion of Germany by another great power. Neutralizing the Czechs was vital if the Reich was to strike out eastwards to secure *Lebensraum*. Hitler opposed the simplest solution, which was a 'strategic assault without any provocation or justification'. Instead, Hitler envisaged either 'action after a time of diplomatic confrontation which gradually escalates into war' or 'lightning action in response to an incident', for example the 'murder of the German envoy after an anti-German demonstration'. Here the Führer may have been thinking back to the murder of Wilhelm Gustloff, but it is also possible that he planned to provoke an incident. If the Czechs were not beaten quickly, he warned, 'then a European crisis would certainly result'. This meant that other powers must be persuaded of the 'futility' of military intervention through a fait accompli. Politically, this would involve the acquisition of allies – 'division of the spoils' – and the 'demoralization' and 'intimidation' of the victim.[50]

The playbook was clear, but Hitler did not plan immediate action. 'The Führer remarked after the incorporation of Austria,' Jodl recorded, 'that he is in no hurry to sort out the Czech question. One first wants to digest Austria.'[51] 'It is not my intention,' Hitler himself explained privately to his generals, 'to crush Czechoslovakia without provocation in the immediate future' unless required to do so by a major shift in Czech internal politics or political developments in Europe provided a particularly favourable and perhaps unique opportunity. Instead, Hitler planned to boil Czechoslovakia in the pot, and to achieve a 'chemical dissolution' of that country through disinformation and intimidation. To this end, Goebbels unleashed a ferocious propaganda assault on the country. The Führer instrumentalized the concept of 'self-determination'.[52] This, he argued, was being denied to the 3 million or so Sudeten Germans who lived around the periphery of Bohemia and Moravia; this was of course the same principle that he had himself surrendered with regard to the Germans of South Tyrol.

On 28 March 1938, Hitler held his first meeting with the Sudeten German leader Konrad Henlein. He let it be known that he 'intended to solve the Czech problem in the not-too-distant future'. The Führer instructed him to raise tensions with Prague, by making 'demands which were unacceptable for the Czech government'.[53] He gave no more detailed indication of his timeline for action. On 2 April, Hitler offered Hungary the return of her former lands (including the Slovak capital Bratislava) in the event of a partition of Czechoslovakia. Three weeks later Henlein set out his stiff and intentionally unacceptable demands to Prague. By early May 1938, the temperature had risen substantially, but there was still no sign that the Führer intended to attack in the near future. In fact, Ribbentrop and Weizäcker told Henlein to avoid escalating the situation too far because 'we want to make the final decision ourselves'.[54]

Despite this, the Czech situation did get out of hand in late May and nearly completely escaped Hitler's control. What exactly happened is still shrouded in mystery, but the rough outlines are known. An anti-appeasement faction in the British Foreign Office and in MI6, aided by the Czechs and German social democrat exiles, probably unwittingly, triggered a crisis in order to torpedo Chamberlain's policy of conciliation towards Germany, and to mobilize resistance to Hitler. It was claimed – plausibly but falsely – that the Führer had mobilized and was planning an imminent attack on Czechoslovakia. No such German military activity actually took place or was even planned at that moment. Prague, however, did mobilize, and Britain warned Hitler off. Europe appeared on the verge of a major war. For the second time in two months, the Führer was caught unawares, but this time there was no way of taking advantage of the crisis without risking a major conflict for which he was totally unprepared. Hitler was forced to back down in a humiliation not experienced since the failure in Austria four years earlier. When two Sudeten German dispatch riders were killed in controversial circumstances, and the pressure for intervention grew, Hitler merely sent his military attaché in Prague to place a wreath on their graves.[55]

London had, in effect, framed a guilty man before he committed his (next) crime. The Führer's personal adjutant Wiedemann, who observed the crisis first in London and then in Berlin, later remarked that 'Hitler adopted the pose of a man who has committed many transgressions, but who is always particularly outraged if he is ever unjustly accused of something.'[56] Instead of deterring Hitler, however, as it was believed then and since, the British intervention electrified him. The events of May 1938 vindicated Hitler's narrative that the Czechs were the pawns of the great powers.[57] Now his aim was not merely to neutralize but to smash Czechoslovakia. 'It is my irrevocable will,' he proclaimed, 'that Czechoslovakia must disappear from the map.'[58]

Military and diplomatic opinion was convinced that this would lead to war with the western powers. While most confined themselves to private complaints, or secret plans to depose Hitler, the chief of the general staff, General Ludwig Beck, penned a lengthy memorandum setting out his objections in early June 1938.[59] He rejected all of the assumptions underlying Hitler's strategy, beginning with the alleged weakness of Czech defences, and culminating in a warning against assuming the passivity of Britain and France. Beck, however, over-egged the pudding. Even sceptical officers thought that Czechoslovakia could be beaten easily, and doubted whether the west would in fact intervene. The Führer, in any case, was unmoved. He issued new instructions to crush the Czechs. This was the paradox of the May crisis. It was not Britain's subsequent abandonment which sealed the fate of the Czechs, but the previous expression of British support.

The consequences of the May crisis reverberated throughout 1938, and in many ways until the outbreak of war the following year. What Hitler had for some time suspected now seemed irrefutable. It was the difference between sensing British hostility during the November 1937 meeting in the Reich Chancellery and knowing it after May 1938. London had thrown off the mask. Britain was prepared to go to war to stop Hitler's planned continental expansion before it had even begun. Moreover, British rearmament was now well underway and, taken together with military expenditure in the Dominions, the Empire already had the largest defence budget in the world.[60] Together with that of France, its potential would soon dwarf that of the German Reich in its current borders. To make matters worse, the enmity of the United States at some point in the future was not only certain, as his ambassador in Washington constantly warned, but would be preceded by the gradual increase in her military power. The American plans 'are clear on one thing', Hitler's usually optimistic military attaché in the United States reported in late May 1938 in the context of the May crisis, 'that the winning of time in an industrial mobilization is a basic factor'.[61] The question was always 'time', not whether but when the German Reich would again confront the United States.[62]

For Hitler, too, time was the crucial variable. If it had speeded up markedly since the autumn of 1937, late May 1938 saw another step change. This was reflected in his rhetoric throughout the summer: 'there must be no problem', he announced on 22 May 1938, 'that we do not solve ourselves'.[63] 'It is not the National Socialist way,' Hitler remarked three weeks later, 'to leave to posterity the execution of tasks which are already foreseeable.'[64] Where Hitler had once said that he was merely starting a long process, he was now unmistakably indicating his determination to finish it.

The Führer no longer believed in an understanding with Britain. He became increasingly sceptical about the value of 'go-betweens' and tried personally to regulate the political interaction of Germans with the outside world more generally. He decreed that he did not want German bureaucrats to make 'official visits' to 'the missions of foreign states' in the Reich, because this would give them a 'source of information' independent of the Foreign Office. Hitler also wanted closer superintendence of 'personal relations' between German officials and foreigners, the content of which should be reported in writing. Two months later, he laid down that the 'invitations of important foreign personalities by state and party authorities' required his permission in 'every case'. As the year drew to a close, Hitler would go several steps further. He told Lammers that he wanted laws to ensure that 'marriages between German citizens and those who did not possess German citizenship' were to be 'forbidden in principle'.[65] Exceptions could only be made by the Führer himself in special cases. This was not a racially motivated measure, because the necessary legislation already existed, but a security-driven one. Across the board, Hitler was pulling down the shutters on the Third Reich.

The Führer now began to prepare Germany for a showdown with Britain. He shifted his rhetoric from admiration of the British to condemnation of their decadence. The Nazi press increasingly portrayed the British as degenerate, effeminate, technologically backward, superannuated and susceptible to Jewish manipulation. Hitler echoed these sentiments.[66] 'Don't talk to me about the English [sic],' he told Wiedemann, 'that is a decadent nation, which won't fight any more.'[67] Such statements have often been misunderstood, confusing cause and effect. Hitler's growing antipathy to Britain was genuine, as was his anxiety about Jewish influence there, but it was driven not by his belief in her weakness and pliability, but rather by his fear of British power and intentions. Hitler was whistling in the wind, to keep up the spirits of his collaborators and perhaps his own as well. The more frightened he was, the louder he whistled.

A clear sign of Hitler's concern about the western powers was his decision to strengthen the western defences of the Reich so that he would have his flanks free to strike south-east and then east. The Führer had long planned some sort of barrier, but the May crisis injected a completely new sense of urgency. At the meeting with the military leadership on 28 May 1938, he gave verbal instructions that the German border from Aachen to Basel should be fortified with the help of the Labour Service and Todt's men by October in time for the planned assault on Czechoslovakia. Further details followed three weeks later.[68] Not long after, on the first day of July 1938, Hitler penned a long memorandum on the state of Germany's fortifications, east and west. His fascination with detail, much of it drawn from his First World War experience, was a portent of his behaviour in the coming conflict. So was concern with psychological factors, especially his fear that fortifications might serve as 'protection' for those who 'did not [want] to fight' and his belief that victory could never be won through the 'purely passive means of protection', but only through the 'offensive use of weapons'. Finally, it was clear that the main threat now came from the west. 'If four or five years ago the political situation made it advisable to concentrate the then available defensive capacity primarily against Poland,' Hitler wrote, 'the current political considerations and necessities require the strongest concentration of all defensive capacity towards the west.'[69]

The May crisis also led Hitler to reconsider his armaments policy.[70] He now wanted more of everything, and he wanted it even faster than before. The army was to be ready for action by April 1939, a full year earlier than the original target date. It was to store ammunition for three months of fighting. More than half of the workforce devoted to aircraft was allocated to the construction of the Junkers 88, a medium-range bomber, whose main intended function was operations against the Western Allies.[71] Hitler instructed his naval adjutant, Captain von Puttkamer, to tell Raeder to speed up the enlargement of the Kriegsmarine. He wanted the navy to bring forward the construction of two battleships to spring 1940; to speed up that of another two; to prepare more dry docks for capital ships; to build all the submarines allowed under the London agreement as soon as the order was given; to build a large number of smaller craft; and to sort out the resulting labour requirements with Göring. The reason for these measures, as Raeder told a hastily convened meeting in the Oberkommando der Kriegsmarine on 25 May 1938, was the foreign political situation, according to which the Führer had to reckon on France and Britain being on the side of the enemies.[72] The following month, the navy operations staff was tasked with working out a strategy against Britain. One way or the other, Hitler now thought that war with Britain was not only possible, but likely and perhaps close.

This meant that Hitler urgently needed to strengthen his global alliances, with a view to raising the costs for Anglo-America around the world. In particular, the Führer wanted to end the Russo-Japanese antagonism, which had already exploded into open warfare, and was to escalate still further. He met with the German ambassador to Tokyo, Eugen Ott, in early June 1938. 'Hitler expanded on the possibility of a war with England,' Ott recalls. 'In spite of his conciliation in the question of naval restriction the British would oppose stubbornly the necessary expansion of the German *Lebensraum* to the east.' The Führer therefore looked to Rome and Tokyo for help. 'Then he asked,' the ambassador continues, 'whether I thought it possible that Japan could be induced to slacken her tense relations with Russia and to turn against the British Empire.'[73] For the first time, Hitler also began to give serious consideration to encouraging anti-colonial movements within the British Empire, something which the left of the party, and many others within the Nazi hierarchy, had been advocating for some time. Criticism of Nazi repression was countered with attacks on British imperial crimes, past and present. German and international audiences were reminded of the incarceration of Boer civilians in concentration camps, an old chestnut of Hitler's from the 1920s.[74] It is striking that the Nazis justified their own measures not with reference to the Soviet Union – the Gulag was not much on their radar – but to the British Empire.

Another priority was sorting out the widening gulf with the armed forces since the start of the year. Here Hitler had two main concerns and they were closely connected in his mind. First, as a result of the Blomberg–Fritsch crisis, he believed that the army leadership was politically at odds with Nazism, defeatist, socially and culturally detached from social realities, and in some cases morally depraved. Hitler frequently described them as a 'caste of particularly snotty Junker blockheads ... full of sterile unfruitfulness, bereft of ideas and cowardly'.[75] Secondly, the events of the May crisis, especially military resistance to the planned attack on Czechoslovakia, which many expected would lead to war with the west, made Hitler doubt the robustness of his generals. This impression was confirmed by Beck's continued criticism of the decision to attack Czechoslovakia. In mid July 1938, he demanded the collective resignation of the generals to force Hitler to change course. When this did not happen, Beck himself resigned a month later. Hitler – who was kept informed of Beck's opposition[76] – increasingly saw the Wehrmacht leadership as cowardly and obstructive, and looked around for alternative military providers. SS units had already participated in the Austrian operation in March, and in August 1938 Hitler decreed that the SS-Verfügungstruppe was 'a standing armed force', separate from both the army and the police, and to be used as part of the Wehrmacht in times of war. Later (in April 1940) the various SS military formations became the 'Waffen-SS'.[77]

The shift to confrontation also had a profound effect on Hitler's racial policy. Eliminating the supposedly negative and accentuating the allegedly positive became more urgent, but there was less time to achieve it. Racial cohesion would be needed to fight the war, but the war would kill the 'best', and spare the worst. So racial time had to be speeded up, and corners cut. The task facing Hitler was now the racial equivalent of Stalin's forced industrialization. Unlike Britain, which had industrialized over many decades, the Soviet Union sought to do so in the space of a few years. Likewise, unlike the British Empire, National Socialism could not afford the luxury of the evolutionary racial development and toughening over the centuries.[78] Over the next five years, therefore, slow extrusion gave way to rapid extermination. This had paradoxical effects. On the one hand, negative eugenics could be pursued quickly and brutally through exclusion and ultimately annihilation. On the other hand, because the slow 'elevation' of racial quality over time was no longer possible, positive eugenics became more inclusive as Hitler had to make do with what he had.

In the summer of 1938, therefore, Hitler escalated the war against the Jews still further. This was primarily a reaction to his sense of external threat, which had been further heightened by the May crisis. Right at the end of that month, Goebbels revived his idea of an 'anti-Jewish' operation for Berlin, originally slated to begin after the Führer's return from Italy. Hitler agreed, and the police chief, Count Helldorf, was instructed to turn up the pressure on the Jewish community.[79] He specifically requested, and here the connection to the Czech crisis was evident, that 'anti-social and criminal Jews' should be conscripted for 'important movements of earth', that is, the construction of the Westwall. [80] Two weeks later, with Hitler's express approval, the police launched a series of raids on the Jewish community in Berlin, provoking widespread protests from foreign embassies and consulates, especially the American and British ones, as their nationals were caught up in the arrests. After four days, they suddenly stopped. 'The decision to end the operation,' Franz Alfred Six of the 'Security Service' wrote in his final report on the operation, 'is said to have been taken on the personal intervention of the Führer.' Hitler appears to have done so for foreign political reasons.[81] He had made his point. The outside world, especially Anglo-America, should be in no doubt of his determination to retaliate against German Jewry.

To Hitler, Anglo-American humanitarian outrage about his treatment of the Jews was simply further evidence of their power in Britain and the United States. There were plenty of people who reinforced him in this view. In the summer of 1938, the SS officer Rolf Mühlinghaus was permitted to report in person to the Führer on his experiences at Oxford (Exeter College). The drift of his remarks was that the complete 'Jewification' of the British establishment prevented an objective view of developments in Germany.[82] In the autumn of 1938, the German military attaché in Washington, Boetticher, who was passing through Berlin, briefed Hitler on the way in which Nazi policies towards the Jews were antagonizing US opinion, even among those who would otherwise be sympathetic. The Führer professed to agree, and promised to show restraint.[83] On the one hand, he wanted to signal to the United States that he would hold the Jews hostage for American behaviour. On the other hand, he wanted to avoid precipitating a showdown with the US, at least until he was ready. Tragically, Roosevelt's hostility to Hitler and his defence of the Jews, however limited the help he gave in practice, endangered them even more than they already were at that stage.

At the same time, Hitler inferred from the unwillingness of other countries to take in the Jews an endorsement of his own position. This each way bet was epitomized by Hitler's attitude to the Evian conference in July 1938, which Roosevelt called in order to discuss how the democracies might distribute the burden of Jewish refugees more fairly.[84] Hitler refused to participate, and when the conference broke up without any British, American or western European offers to take in more Jewish immigrants (only a few Latin American countries opened their doors), his derision knew no bounds. 'They expect,' Hitler remarked, 'that Germany with 140 people per square kilometre should retain its Jews without further ado', but that 'the democratic world empires with only a few inhabitants per square kilometre cannot take such a burden on themselves under any circumstances. So no help, but moral [lectures]!'[85] There was another, more sinister implication of Evian: there was now a question-mark over large-scale emigration as a solution to the 'Jewish Problem'.

In this context, Hitler sought to prevent German Jews from acting as a fifth column for the enemy, and to make them hostages for the – supposed – behaviour of international Jewry. In late July 1938, he told Goebbels that he wanted the Jews out, but would keep back a few rich ones as a bargaining counter.[86] He now regarded the Nuremberg laws as 'actually still far too humane'. Jews, he remarked in mid August 1938, might have been removed 'from the life of the state', but they remained strong 'in the economy'. Historically, Hitler argued – repeating a longstanding theme – the Jews had been 'agents of trade and finance'. On a recent trip through Munich he had asked to see the remaining Jewish shops, and had been horrified to notice that 'they were all practically still there'. The gradual extrusion of the Jews, in other words, had not worked, or at least was not working quickly enough. Hitler announced privately that he would consider actions 'to worsen the conditions of Jewish life through additional legislation to such an extent that the bulk of the Jewish population of Germany simply no longer wanted to stay. That was the best way of getting rid of them.'[87]

Meanwhile, Hitler kept up the pressure to cleanse German art of 'noisy Dadaists, Cubist plaster-moulders and Futurist canvas-colourers', and at the opening of the Second Great German Art Exhibition in mid July 1938 praised the nineteenth century as a model instead. This posed a problem for Nazi art, because, unlike Italian fascism, it never really developed a 'modernistic' style of its own. Hitler managed to generate a lively market in contemporary art, keeping prices up through his own purchases and making his preferences known.[88] Few of its products, with the exception perhaps of the sculptures of Arno Breker, were later judged to be of much lasting value. Hitler seems to have sensed this, but he thought contemporary mediocrity a price worth paying to eliminate the excrescences of modernism and ensure the pre-eminence of 'timeless' artistic worth. That said, Hitler was clear that in the field of culture the 'warm-up time always had to be greater'.[89] It was the old problem: eliminating the negative could be done relatively quickly, but accentuating the positive took time.

Sometimes, the two could be done simultaneously. In August 1938, for example, Hitler swopped 'degenerate art' for Italian old masters via the international art market. This strategy was of a piece with his broader vision. Demographically, Hitler wanted to reverse what he regarded as the disadvantageous trend of the past century, when Germany had sent high-value emigrants to the United States and received supposedly inferior immigrants from eastern Europe. In the same way, Hitler wanted to cleanse German Art of degenerate elements which could be exchanged for pieces of genuinely high artistic merit. His concern, in short, was political as much as aesthetic. 'Painting and sculpture,' Hitler explained, 'often reflected political circumstances.' Roman and Greek art, he continued, had long reflected the grandeur of these civilizations, while even the better pieces produced during their decline had been transparently homosexual. Hitler averred that he would never tolerate such degeneracy in Germany.[90]

The international comparison was also to the fore in Hitler's insistence on the rapid completion of the new Imperial Chancellery. He wanted a grand building which would represent the might of the Third Reich in time for the New Year's reception of foreign diplomats. At the topping-out ceremony in early August 1938, Hitler looked back at the speed with which the work was progressing and remarked that 'this is no longer an American tempo, this is already the German tempo. This is the first time we have shown the world how to do it and that is good.' Once again, the American tempo was the one to beat, and Hitler meant this more generally as well. His very next sentence referred to the crucial *Lebensraum* question. 'We are an overpopulated state,' he explained, 'our viability requires greater efforts.' This meant, Hitler concluded, 'that we must also increase the pace politically'.[91]

Time and space, in short, remained at the centre of Hitler's thinking. While time was running out, there was still a window of opportunity. 'In politics,' he told an audience of generals at the Artillery School in Jüterborg in mid August 1938, 'one must believe in the Goddess of Fortune who only passes once and one must grasp her then! She will never return'.[92] Hitler was about to roll the dice again.

Throughout the late summer and early autumn of 1938, Hitler psychologically and militarily prepared Germany for action against Czechoslovakia.[93] On 2 September 1938, Hitler met with Henlein, and instructed him to subvert any attempt at a negotiated solution. Goebbels, encouraged by the Führer,[94] turned the propagandistic heat back up again. Tension rose across Europe. Hitler warned Unity Mitford to go home for her own safety.[95] War was already in the air when the party faithful gathered for the annual rally at Nuremberg.[96] There Hitler was handed a memorandum by General Thomas, the head of the War Economics Office, the body which oversaw the economic side of German rearmament. It stated that while Germany would begin any contest with an economic advantage over Britain, this would soon be eroded, and in any case the conflict would soon widen into an unwinnable war with the United States, whose resources were inexhaustible.[97] Hitler was furious, and gave Thomas a dressing-down; Dieckhoff, who made similar points about America in a brief private encounter at Nuremberg, received equally short shrift.[98] But both his rhetoric and his policies showed that Hitler had got the message. For those

worried about conflict with the west, the Führer had reassuring words at
the Nuremberg rally about Germany's ability 'already now' to survive a
blockade, adding somewhat contradictorily that true security could only
be achieved 'on the basis of our own living space',[99] which by implication
had not yet been achieved. In the meantime, Hitler put on a massive military display designed to maintain German morale, to deter the Western
Allies and intimidate the Czechs.

These efforts were flanked by a carefully coordinated series of moves.
On 20 September 1938, Hitler met with the Hungarians, and suggested
that they demand a plebiscite in the Magyar districts of Czechoslovakia.[100]
That same day, he met with the Polish ambassador and agreed that Warsaw could demand the district of Teschen. Propagandistically, Hitler
redoubled his attacks on the Jews. In early September 1938, he once again
attacked 'the greatest enemy which threatened to destroy our people, the
international Jewish world enemy',[101] warning them – and their putative
creatures in Washington and London – off intervening in support of
Prague. But when all was said and done, Hitler was pursuing a high-risk
strategy, in which war with the Czechs was virtually certain, and conflict
with the west perfectly possible. The strain was visible even to outsiders.
The American journalist William Shirer, who observed Hitler during this
period, wrote that 'he seemed to have a peculiar tic. Every few steps he
cocked his right shoulder nervously, his left leg snapping up as he did so.
He had ugly black patches under his eyes. He seemed to be . . . on the edge
of a nervous breakdown'.

Throughout late September, the tension mounted yet further. In a series
of meetings with the British prime minister, Neville Chamberlain, at Berchtesgaden, Bad Godesberg and finally in Munich, Hitler threatened war
unless his demands were met. There were times when it appeared that
Britain and France would intervene. On 26 September, President Roosevelt
sent Hitler, and the other main protagonists, a telegram calling for a negotiated solution and hinting, albeit very obliquely, that the United States
would otherwise intervene by 'recognizing' its 'responsibilities as a part of
a world of neighbors'. This démarche was obviously directed against Nazi
Germany, the first such open move, albeit a circumspect one, by the US
administration.[102] Brauchitsch warned that the army was still not ready.[103]
Hitler, who was well informed by Göring's surveillance teams about the
negotiating positions of the other side,[104] and tensions between Prague and
London, held firm. He paraded an infantry division through Berlin en route
to its deployment on the Czech border to show that he meant business. At
the very end of September 1938, Chamberlain buckled at Munich. He
eventually agreed to the more or less instantaneous German occupation of

the Sudetenland. Not long after, Poland seized Teschen and the Hungarians helped themselves to a large slice of southern Slovakia.

War had been averted. The collective sigh of relief was audible across Europe, and in Germany it was palpable. Hitler had been vindicated once again, just as Goebbels and Ribbentrop had said he would be. He had forced a militarily superior coalition to back down.[105] The naysayers in the army and Foreign Office had been confounded. The Führer, General von Reichenau marvelled, had played for 'high stakes'. 'If he had been a poker player,' Reichenau continued, 'he could win hundreds of thousands of marks every night.'[106] The German public, which had dreaded the prospect of war, rejoiced.

Hitler himself felt no sense of relief or satisfaction. On the contrary, he was frustrated and dispirited. Time was running out. He had hoped to overrun the whole of Czechoslovakia before the end of the year. Now he would have to sort out the rump Czech state in the spring. Hitler was also unsettled by Roosevelt's intervention, as evidenced by his detailed reply to the president, which was more than twice the length of the original, in the midst of the crisis. In it, he rehearsed his outrage at the way in which Wilson had turned Germany into a 'pariah' after the war, lamented the plight of the Sudeten Germans and voiced various other grievances.[107] Most worryingly of all for someone who placed such importance on intangibles such as will and national coherence, Hitler was shocked by the evident reluctance of the German people to embark on another conflict. He watched in appalled silence from a window of the Imperial Chancellery as the infantry division parading through Berlin was greeted with fear and averted faces. Goebbels warned Hitler that the people were not ready for war.[108] Hitler was a victim of his own rhetoric here. The German people, like so much of Europe, had believed his constant promises of peace.[109] For all these reasons, Hitler never reckoned the Munich settlement a famous victory but rather a massive concession on his part.[110]

No sooner had he prevailed at Munich, therefore, than Hitler was planning the next move. He told his generals that he was 'determined to solve the question of [the rest of] Czechoslovakia'.[111] This, however, was only to be the first step. The real objective was to gain a launchpad to attack the Soviet Union and, as Halder told the American chargé d'affaires in Berlin, Raymond H. Geist, at some length, to seize the Ukraine.[112] On 21 October, Hitler ordered the OKW to prepare for the destruction of the rump Czech state and the occupation of the Memelland, a small Lithuanian-held former Prussian territory. Two days later, he asked Fritz Todt to investigate the possibility of an extra-territorial railway across the Polish Corridor. Ideally, he wanted to ally with Poland against Russia, or to use eastern Poland as a staging ground. If that was not possible, Hitler hoped to secure 'runways' from which to launch his attack against the Soviet Union.[113] The *Lebensraum* he sought in late 1938 was emphatically not in Poland, but much further east.[114] In late October 1938, Hitler set out his demands of Poland to Ribbentrop: Danzig, an extra-territorial railway, the emigration of Jews from Poland, her accession to the Anti-Comintern Pact and a common policy towards the Soviet Union (which was code for a joint war of aggression). To be sure, granting these requests would have put Poland firmly in the German orbit, but unlike those presented to the Czechs they were not designed to be unacceptable. On the contrary, Hitler fervently hoped for Polish cooperation.

As he prepared his next moves abroad, Hitler was haunted by his continuing sense of German weakness at home. In early November 1938, he once again attacked the 'fragmentation of the national community into classes'. Hitler blamed both the *Bürgertum* and the 'international-Jewish parasites who had penetrated into the German people' for the resulting 'false selection' in the German people. A 'leadership selection' was needed.[115] This, however, would take time. Meanwhile, the home front needed to be secured, and the popular enthusiasm for confrontation so obviously lacking during the Czech crisis needed to be rekindled. Hitler also wanted to take action against the alleged 'parasites' at home and their puppetmasters abroad. He sought to encourage Jews to emigrate more quickly, and the outside world to accept them. The Juni-Aktion had plainly not sufficed. Another shot across the bows of international Jewry was required. In late October 1938, the SS expelled about 17,000 Polish Jews, many of whom ended up in the no man's land between the borders of Poland and the Reich.

On 7 November 1938, the Pole Herschel Grynszpan shot and mortally wounded the German diplomat Ernst vom Rath in the Paris embassy. His motivation is not entirely clear, but it seems likely that he was protesting against the deportation of his Jewish parents from Germany back to Poland. One way or the other, his deed was interpreted by the Nazis as another blow by international Jewry against the Third Reich.[116] Hitler, who was kept informed of Rath's condition, seized the opportunity to retaliate. On receipt of the news of the diplomat's death, the Führer – perhaps at Goebbels's suggestion – ordered a demonstration of 'spontaneous' popular fury against the Jews. The resulting orgy of vandalism, broken glass, harassment, incarceration and murder directed at Jews and Jewish property such as synagogues and shops on 9 November 1938 has gone down in history as the *Reichskristallnacht*.[117]

Normally, Hitler strongly disapproved of pogroms, which he regarded as inefficient, unscientific and unconducive to public order, but on this occasion – perhaps impressed by their recent effectiveness in Austria – he made an exception. His aim was to whip the German people into a frenzy against their supposed enemies at home and abroad, to send the strongest possible signal to international Jewry that any further interference in German affairs would not be tolerated, to speed up Jewish emigration, and to ensure that – if war with the west could not be averted – German Jews would be removed before the outbreak of hostilities.[118] Unlike after the Night of the Long Knives, Hitler made no public speech justifying these measures. *Kristallnacht* was still primarily his work, launched by the Führer for strategic purposes defined by him.[119] His intent seems to have been well understood by some of the wider public. 'The Jews are the enemies of the new Germany [and] last night they had a taste of what this means,' wrote Melitta Maschmann, who worked for the Bund Deutscher Mädel, the day after *Kristallnacht*. 'Let us hope that western Jewry, which has resolved to hinder Germany's "new steps to greatness", will take the events of last night as a warning. If the Jews sow hatred against us all over the world, they must learn that we have hostages for them in our hands.'[120]

The weeks following the violence of 9 November saw an escalation of the legal restrictions against Jews. They were now to be completely shut out of the German economy. Three days later, his 'Decree for the elimination of Jews from the economic life of Germany' laid down that no Jews should be employed in trade or retail by the end of the year.[121] *Kristallnacht* did not yet resolve the tension at the heart of the war on the Jews between the desire to force out the Jews and the desire to keep them as hostages. Emigration was still a priority for the regime. The same day as the Decree was issued, Hitler told Göring that he planned to launch a diplomatic initiative to shame other states into accepting the Jews.[122] A month later, he suggested that the outside world should pay for this solution; Schacht was instructed to investigate the raising of the necessary international loan.[123] Hitler's hope at this stage was that he would cooperate with the Polish government, and perhaps other European authorities, in assisting the departure of as many Jews as possible. The Jewish question, Hitler told the visiting South African defence minister, Oswald Pirow, the child of German immigrants, was 'not only a German but a European problem'. 'The problem,' he reassured his interlocutor, 'would be solved in the near future.' Hitler even went so far as to predict that 'the Jews would one day disappear from Europe'.[124]

These events, and the general sense that Hitler was repressive at home and heading towards war abroad, damaged his previously substantial international appeal. *Kristallnacht* caused particular outrage in Anglo-America, especially in the United States. The press was almost uniformly critical, confirming Hitler in his view that they were agents of international Jewry.[125]

The US ambassador, Hugh Wilson, was recalled for 'consultations'. From now until the end of the Third Reich, all matters were handled by more junior staff. Hitler retaliated by recalling his own ambassador. Britain's diplomatic response was more muted, but the general sense that Hitler was heading for war was palpable in press and politics. Global opinion more generally was shocked. 1938 saw 'peak Hitler' in what was then regarded as the civilized world. By then 1333 street and squares outside Germany were named for him.[126] Hitler was named 'man of the Year', by *Time Magazine*, admittedly a two-edged compliment. Thereafter, approval of Hitler began to slide, at least in western democracies.

To the Führer, therefore, the battle lines were clear by November 1938. Anglo-America and world Jewry had 'thrown off the mask' and were arrayed against him. This was a political, diplomatic, economic and racial struggle. It pitted the Germans against not only the Jews, but British and Americans as well. Increasingly, Hitler's rhetoric spoke of the 'Anglo-Saxons' as a group.[127] Hitler saw all these fronts as interconnected. If war broke out over the 'Jewish question', he claimed, then 'that would prove that England was governed by a mentality which wanted no peace with Germany'. Indeed, Hitler said that he had formed the impression that Chamberlain and Halifax were merely 'dancing on a rope, behind them stood the real string-pullers, the press and the opposition', that is the Jews.[128] The man the Führer really feared, next to Roosevelt, was Winston Churchill, whose fire-breathing speeches against the Third Reich he had been following closely, and whom he accused of wanting to 'destroy' not merely the regime but Germany itself.[129] Hitler pointed out with astonishing prescience that as a result of the British political system 'tomorrow or the day after tomorrow Mr Churchill could well become prime minister'.[130] The duel between Hitler and Churchill, which was to explode onto the world stage eighteen months later, had already begun.

Hitler's concern was not just the supposed power of the Jewish lobby in London, Washington and New York, but the sheer size and quality of the Nordic element in Anglo-America. He knew that anxiety about the power of the British Empire and the United States, which had vanquished the Reich in the Great War, was widely shared in Germany. For this reason, Hitler decided to take the press into his confidence, to brief them on the struggle which lay ahead, and to reassure them that the contest was winnable. Circumstances, he explained at a private meeting of senior press figures, 'have forced me to speak for decades almost only of peace'. Only by constantly emphasizing the German 'desire for peace', Hitler continued, had it been possible to 'win back the freedom of the German people bit by bit and to give it the armaments which were always necessary for the next step'. The problem was, he said, no doubt referring to the lack of martial spirit during the Czech crisis, that 'many people' had therefore come to the erroneous conclusion that the 'regime' (sic) 'wanted to maintain peace under all circumstances'. The result of this, Hitler warned, would be 'defeatism' at the very moment when the Reich needed to steel itself for the next challenge.

For this reason, the Führer explained, it was 'now necessary to reorient the German people psychologically' and to show it that there were aims which could only be secured by force. The purpose of this careful work was to ensure that the Volk was ready 'to stand up even when it starts to thunder and lightning'. The key to this was 'self-confidence'. The task of propaganda was to instil the German people with 'the self-confident conviction that, first of all, the Volk itself represented an asset in Germany, and, secondly, that the leadership of the Volk was sound'. Germans would 'have to learn to believe so fanatically in final victory that even if there were defeats, the Nation would persevere, just as Blücher had done in the face of multiple setbacks'. It is clear from these passages that the great transformation of the German people begun in 1933 was by no means complete. Many Germans, Hitler feared, were mere fair-weather friends of Nazism, who would desert when the going got tough.

Right at the end of his remarks, Hitler turned to the elephant in the room: the might of Anglo-America, Germany's likely enemy in the coming contest. He sought to persuade his audience that all Germans needed to fear was fear itself, that the imbalance was nowhere as great as they thought. Concealing his well-established reservations about the German people, reiterated only minutes earlier, Hitler now sought to boost national self-confidence, and to persuade the listening journalists to do so. 'The value of the German people,' he said, 'is incomparable.' 'I will never allow anybody to tell me,' Hitler continued in blatant contradiction of his previous adverse comparisons with Anglo-America, 'that any other people can have greater value.' He insisted that 'our people, particularly today, represents in its gradual racial improvement [sic!] the highest value which exists on earth today'. This was still a very aspirational superiority. From what we know about the Führer's impatience with the progress of this 'gradual improvement' and his general sense of Anglo-Saxon superiority, this huffing and puffing was just more racial whistling in the wind.

Hitler now did some very elementary and idiosyncratic maths. The United States, he averred, might have '126 or 127 million inhabitants', but if you stripped out the 'Germans, Irish, Italians, blacks, Jews' and so on, that would leave 'not even 60 million Anglo-Saxons'. Likewise, 'the British Empire had hardly 46 million Englishmen and women in the motherland'.

By contrast, Germany would have about '80 million people of one race by 1940'.[131] 'Whoever does not believe in the future of this great bloc,' he concluded, 'is himself a weakling.' What was striking about this peroration was not merely its innumeracy – even according to Hitler's own best-case scenario Anglo-America would have 106 million Anglo-Saxons to pit against 80 million Germans – but also the fact that it subtracted German America from the US total. It was, after all, the spectre of millions of German emigrants fighting on the American side which had driven Hitler to seek land in the east.

In this context, Hitler made a last attempt to reverse the tide of demography. His calculation was simple. He wanted German Jews to emigrate and to confiscate their property, but few states were prepared to take penniless immigrants. Hitler also wanted German emigrants, and ultimately German-Americans, to return to the Reich, but lacked the funds to pay for their passage and resettlement, even if they wanted to return.[132] The 'logical' solution was to exchange German Jews and their property for Germans in America and their assets. For Hitler this was the ultimate 'win-win', where 'negative' met 'positive' eugenics. On 16 December 1938, Göring rang Weizäcker, the state secretary in the Foreign Office. He wanted 'a large-scale operation . . . to bring back those of German origin from America (including those who were already American citizens)' to provide workers for the Four Year Plan. Hitler not only approved the plan, but he seems to have been the inspiration behind the idea that 'one could perhaps even organize an exchange of returning Americans of German origin and Jews to be sent there'.[133] The Foreign Office was deeply sceptical about the practicality of the scheme, and warned that any attempt to lure American citizens back would infuriate Washington.[134] In the end, the outbreak of war put an end to these plans.

As the breach with Anglo-America loomed, Hitler globalized his policy and rhetoric. The Japanese alliance became ever more important. Whereas he had previously welcomed the prospect of a Russo-Japanese war, which would give him the opportunity to seize *Lebensraum* in the east, he now sought to prevent one. His entire policy was henceforth geared to enlisting Tokyo against London and Washington. Part of this strategy was reducing the German footprint in China. In the autumn of 1938, General Falkenhausen's military mission was withdrawn in order to please the Japanese. Some generals resisted this strongly, much to Hitler's fury.[135] Another important plank was reducing Russo-Japanese tensions, which had resulted in a stinging defeat for Tokyo at Changkufeng on the Soviet border with China and Korea in July–August 1938; German propaganda was instructed to discredit any resulting suggestion that the Japanese were not valuable allies.[136] These moves were accompanied by a number of peppery assertions about the quality of the Japanese army, and the degeneracy of the Americans: 'a comprehensively weakened and decadent people'.[137] Hitler genuinely admired Japan, and its ambassador in Berlin, Oshima, but such statements should be primarily read as yet more racial whistling in the wind to keep up German spirits.

Hitler's confrontation with the British Empire also caused him to rethink his attitude towards anti-imperialist movements in Asia and the Middle East. This was partly a question of propaganda as British imperial policies were traduced in order to illustrate the 'hypocrisy' of London's concern for human rights within Germany. 'Enquiries from British politicians about the fate of Germans or members of the Reich inside the borders of the Reich,' he said, 'are misplaced. After all, we don't concern ourselves with similar matters in England, for example events in Palestine,' a reference to the British suppression of the 'Arab Revolt'. The main purpose of Hitler's new global rhetoric, however, was to show Germans the dangers of being colonized themselves, and to caution the west that they would refuse to be so subjected again. 'I am by no means inclined,' Hitler warned at the height of the Sudeten crisis, 'to allow the establishment of a second Palestine here in the centre of Germany. The poor Arabs may be defenceless and abandoned but the Germans in Czechoslovakia are neither defenceless nor abandoned. That needs to be realized.' Hitler of course equated the Arabs with the oppressed Germans, not the Czechs; he in fact received thirty Iraqi nationalists at the Nuremberg rally.[138] Before 1933, Hitler had criticized those who saw Germans as the wretched of the earth, but he was now closer to that argument than he cared to admit.

In the autumn of 1938, the Third Reich began to prepare a propaganda offensive against the British Empire, which was specifically designed as retaliation against the German-language broadcasts of the BBC. The driving force here was Goebbels, in concert with the Führer.[139] The first programmes in English and Arabic were broadcast in the following spring and disseminated anti-colonialism, anti-Semitism and anti-Zionism.[140] How much of this message was actually heard and accepted by the target audience is not clear. Some of it, of course, was redundant. Exporting anti-Semitism to the Middle East was like transporting oranges to Jaffa. It is clear, though, that German propaganda struck a chord with many Third World nationalists. For example, Joseph Said Abu Durra, the leader of the resistance in northern Palestine, wrote to Hitler in late December 1938. He praised 'the great Führer of Germany who has secured his nation undying honour and fame'. He excoriated the 'crimes' committed by 'England, that state which claims to be just, civilized and humane'. The author then went on to attack the Jews, and to suggest that the Arab struggle in Palestine was worthy of German support.[141]

The rapid deterioration of relations with Anglo-America had a profound impact on Hitler's military thinking and armaments policy. He was clearly not planning a large-scale land war in the west, at least not if he could help it. Nor was he planning to attack Poland. He was hoping to despoil the Soviet Union, but he had such a low opinion of the chaos and violence of Stalin's rule that he did not expect to need his entire force or a long time to do that. Hitler's priorities were to produce a naval and aerial capability sufficient to deter or contain the west with one hand, while he secured *Lebensraum* in the east with the other. In December 1938, Hitler authorized a vast naval construction programme to build no fewer than six battleships, various cruisers and nearly 250 U-boats.[142] That same month, he launched the aircraft carrier *Graf Zeppelin*, and the Germania-werft at Kiel was commissioned to build another.[143]

Hitler was particularly anxious about western air power, especially the ability of French and British bombers to strike the Ruhr. He specifically highlighted the threats of Westminster parliamentarians to do just that. Unlike the Americans, who had panicked at the radio broadcast of H. G. Wells' *War of the Worlds*, which featured an invasion from outer space, Hitler claimed he was not 'in fear of bombs from Mars or the Moon'.[144] He was, however, worried by the terrestrial variety. In the late autumn of 1938, Hitler demanded a fivefold increase in the Luftwaffe – 'a gigantic programme compared to which previous achievements are insignificant' – involving a fleet of heavy bombers, long-range fighter escorts, and interceptor aircraft designed to protect the Reich. Hitler also invested a huge proportion of his industrial capacity in anti-aircraft artillery.[145] Fear of Franco-British air attacks was one reason why he was so determined to crush what remained of Czechoslovakia, which he continued to describe as a giant 'aircraft carrier' for the Western Allies. The aggregate cost of these measures was huge, and coming on top of the vast amounts already spent on, or committed to, rearmament completely unrealizable under peacetime conditions. Civilian construction all but ceased. Only Hitler's personal monumental projects were to continue.

By the end of 1938, in short, the contours of the coming struggle were becoming clearer. Unsurprisingly and necessarily, from Hitler's point of view, it would pit the Germans against world Jewry, in its communist and capitalist incarnations, primarily the latter. Unfortunately from Hitler's point of view, it would also range the Reich against the British Empire and the United States. Hitler would have greatly preferred to remain at peace with both, and had had high hopes of allying with at least one of them. The somewhat surprising consequence of the new situation was not just a formal alliance with Japan, long regarded as the rising star in the east, but also a growing rapprochement with the anti-imperialist forces in the British Empire. This was not the place that Hitler wanted to be in, or ever anticipated being in, and by his own lights he had done his best to avoid such an outcome, but it was where he was.

In the New Year, relations with Anglo-America, already very poor, deteriorated still further.

In his annual message to Congress on 4 January 1939, Roosevelt announced that he would use all means 'short of war' to contain the aggressors. 'God-fearing democracies of the world', he explained, 'cannot safely be indifferent to international lawlessness anywhere.' This came a day after a huge leap in US defence expenditure to by far the highest level ever seen in peacetime. A week later, the German military attaché in Washington warned against the 'president and his Jewish friends [and] their boundless armament plans and their attempts to paint a German spectre on the wall'; even if the immediate capacity of the United States to wage war was limited, its potential was massive. Hitler was acutely aware of all this. He told Boetticher that he would destroy Roosevelt by proving to the world that the president was of Jewish descent. Hitler now asked the Washington embassy and other experts to establish the date by which the United States could practically intervene if war broke out in Europe in 1939.[146] It was no longer a question of whether war with America would come, but of when.

Hitler's determination to match the United States was reflected in his architectural visions. In January 1939, he met with Todt and Speer in the Imperial Chancellery for further discussions about the planned remodelling of Hamburg and its huge San-Francisco-style bridge over the Elbe. He noted with satisfaction that the architect, Konstanty Gutschow, 'has also made studies in America'.[147] Hitler explained his thinking to the German High Command. Such monumental construction projects were part of his plan to show the German people 'that it is not second-rate, but the equal of any other people on earth, even America'. 'This,' Hitler continued, 'is why I have ordered this great bridge to be built in Hamburg'. Its purpose was to ensure 'that any German coming from abroad or going abroad or who has had the opportunity to compare Germany with other countries must say to himself: "What is so extraordinary about America and its bridges? We can do the same."' This, Hitler concluded, 'is why I am having skyscrapers built [in Hamburg] which will be just as "impressive" as the American ones'.[148] Here, Hitler was trying to implement in stone and concrete what he was telling the German newspapers to do in print.

Hitler had also still not completely given up on the consumption front. In mid February 1939, he opened the International Car and Motorcycle Exhibition in Berlin. The car industry, he claimed, was important not only in Germany but in 'in large parts of the world'. Hitler stressed that 'The motor car is not a luxury item but an article of consumption', thus reaffirming his commitment to raise German standards of living. This required, he continued, an appropriate pricing structure 'for all classes of potential buyers'. The extent to which Hitler saw all this in the context of international competition was demonstrated by his emphasis on the need to increase the 'confidence of the German people in their own motor cars' and to secure 'a raw materials base independent of the rest of the world'.[149] The 'Motorisierung' of Germany was to be achieved not as part of a general western process but independently and in parallel; separate, but equal, as it were. An advance model of the Volkswagen was displayed at the exhibition with the announcement that mass production would begin as soon as possible. The challenge resonated across the Atlantic loud and clear. 'Hitler declares Auto War,' the Pittsburgh Press headlined, '$400 car actually on view'.[150]

Diplomatically, the rising enmity with Anglo-America drove Hitler to deepen his ties to Japan. The main function of Japan in his strategic concept was to pin down the United States in the Pacific, rather than to distract the Soviet Union in the Far East. Ribbentrop explained this, with Hitler's agreement, to a group of senior military figures towards the end of January 1939.[151] In February 1939, he attended the Japanese Art Exhibition in Berlin as a token of his respect. Despite Hitler's urgings, however, Tokyo was slow to commit itself.[152]

Militarily, Hitler reacted by giving the navy priority in arms procurement and resource allocation.[153] In January 1939, he secretly authorized the 'Z-Plan', a massive programme of construction designed to culminate in the mid 1940s, the moment by which Hitler expected the confrontation with the United States to be unavoidable. It involved the building of 10 battleships, 10 battle cruisers, 4 aircraft carriers, 5 heavy cruisers, 18 light cruisers, 20 smaller cruisers, 64 destroyers, 78 torpedo boats and 249 submarines of various sizes.[154] The total tonnage proposed came to 2 million, and some 200,000 sailors would be required to man these ships. Some 20,000 new machines to make tools would be required to support the effort. All this, of course, was incompatible with the 1935 Naval Agreement with Britain. It was also potentially disastrous for the army and especially for the Luftwaffe, at whose expense the new production was to take place; Göring complained bitterly.[155]

The cumulative strain of past and planned military expenditure on the German economy was now too great to ignore, or to trump with declarations of political 'will'. On 7 January 1939, the Reichsbank directorate warned Hitler that the sums simply did not add up. There was no foreign exchange left to buy vital raw materials. Schacht finally put his foot down.[156] He was promptly sacked as Reichsbank president.

Hitler's mounting anxieties found expression in his landmark speech on 30 January 1939, the sixth anniversary of the takeover of power.[157] The Führer's continuing lack of confidence in German unity, however, especially in the face of external threats, was evident throughout the speech. It was, in fact, his main reason for giving it. The principal challenge came from the west, in particular the United States, and it was words as much as weapons that Hitler feared. He inveighed against 'certain newspapers and politicians in the rest of the world' – meaning Roosevelt and the American press – who claimed that Germany was threatening European peace. Explicitly referring to the president's intervention over Munich, and implicitly to his new year's address to Congress, Hitler vowed that Germany would 'not accept that western states interfered in certain matters' which were the Reich's business and hers alone.[158]

Worst of all the western threats was the idea of democracy, whose political and social divisiveness Hitler blamed for Germany's weakness in times past. Democracy was the enemy, not just internally but externally as well. 'In certain democracies,' Hitler claimed, 'it is apparently a particular privilege artificially to cultivate hatred against the so-called totalitarian states.' Hitler attacked his main enemies in the democratic world, namely the 'war apostles such as Mr Duff Cooper, Mr Eden, Churchill or Mr Ickes'.[159] Hitler's bracketing of Roosevelt's confidant and long-serving secretary of the interior, Harold Ickes, with the British anti-appeasers reflected the Führer's belief that Anglo-America was leaguing against him. He said that while one might be inclined to laugh off the claim 'that Germany planned to attack America', one had to remember that 'one is dealing in these democracies with states whose political construction makes it possible that within a few months these terrible war-hawks might take over the leadership of the government'. Hitler thus once again anticipated Churchill's premiership, something, of course, which he would do more than anybody else to bring about.

The main target of the speech now came into view, 'world Jewry' and its supposed instrument, the administration of Franklin D. Roosevelt. Just as the president had warned Hitler in his New Year's speech to Congress, so Hitler replied in his parliament, the Reichstag. Hitler's intention here was twofold. On the one hand, he wanted to prepare the German people for this contest because otherwise the outbreak of a war provoked by these enemies would put the Germans in a situation for which they were 'psychologically completely unprepared', which would seem 'inexplicable' to them. 'The German people,' he continued, 'must know who the men are who are trying to provoke a war at all costs' and for this reason all propaganda should be focused on the 'Jewish world enemy'. On the other hand, Hitler wanted not merely to expose, but to warn off the enemy, by threatening retaliation so dire that they would desist from plunging the peoples of Europe back into war.

He then issued a coded, but clear warning to Roosevelt and 'world Jewry'. 'If Jewish international finance in and outside Europe should succeed in plunging the peoples into another war,' Hitler announced, 'then the result will not be the Bolshevization of the earth and thus the victory of Jewry, but the destruction of the Jewish race in Europe.' Hitler could not have been more explicit: European Jewry would be held responsible for the behaviour of 'international finance Jewry' not just in Europe, by which London and Paris, rather than Moscow, was meant, but also outside Europe, that is in New York and in Roosevelt's America generally.[160]

Hitler's speech heralded a further intensification of anti-Jewish measures. In late February 1939, Jews were banished from the sleeping and dining cars of the Reichsbahn at Hitler's request.[161] Over the next few months Jews were also deprived of tenancy protection in order to force them to live together in separate accommodation.[162] They also found their access to public swimming pools and other establishments limited.[163] The aim was still to force Jews to leave Germany, and in late January 1939 Reinhard Heydrich was made head of the Reich Centre for Jewish Emigration. There was disagreement among the SS leaders in charge of the policy about where they should be sent. Some saw Palestine as the obvious destination; others warned that this would simply create a 'Vatican of World Jewry', which would in any case not be large enough to accommodate all the Jews to be deported. Truly, as Heydrich put it, Palestine had become a 'World Question'. Emil Schumburg, the official in the Foreign Office charged with coordinating policy with the SS, suggested that Jews be sent to as many different countries as possible, at least initially, in order to increase anti-Semitism to a sufficient degree to make an agreed international solution possible.[164] All this reflected Hitler's continued view that the 'Jewish question' was to be resolved through international action.

The suppression of world Jewry was one way of protecting the Reich in Hitler's eyes, but it was not enough. He would also have to implement his programme of territorial expansion in order to give the German people the living space required for its racial elevation. 'What is the root of all our economic difficulties', he asked during his 30 January speech, before answering that it lay in the 'overpopulation of our *Lebensraum*'. He rehearsed once again the advantage which the 'Gentlemen critics' in Europe (meaning Britain) and 'outside Europe' (meaning the United States) enjoyed through their copious living space, while the Germans were jammed together in central Europe.[165] Unlike the Anglo-Americans, he continued, the Germans were not born with bananas growing into their mouths but had to struggle for every crust. Hitler's plans to attack the Soviet Union in 1939 were therefore mainly driven by positive eugenics, to provide the economic and territorial basis for the gradual elevation of the German people, rather than the desire to eliminate the Jews in Russia. The Wehrmacht was told to prepare for an assault on the Soviet Union, if possible with Polish cooperation, but if not then using Danzig and Memel as jumping-off points to enter Russia through the Baltic states.[166] He also seems to have envisaged a southern front erupting from Slovakia. Hitler's plans were so ambitious, and had been so extensively heralded in *Mein Kampf* and elsewhere, that they were impossible to keep secret. Talk of invading the Ukraine was so ubiquitous in the Anglo-American press that the *Völkischer Beobachter* was constrained to issue a rebuttal in mid February 1939 against the 'Anglo-Saxon warmongers'.[167]

Hitler now took two concrete steps to prepare for the attack on the Soviet Union. First, he made one last attempt to win over Poland.[168] In the first week of January 1939, Hitler met with the Polish foreign minister, Beck, at the Berghof. His request for help against the Soviet Union was rejected, but Hitler did not give up yet. Ribbentrop was dispatched to the Polish capital with a plan for a 'global solution' by which Poland would be compensated for any losses with territory further east. Though this overture achieved nothing, Hitler's 30 January speech contained some flattering references to the Poles and his idol Piłsudski.[169] In mid February Himmler, who enjoyed a good working relationship with his Polish counterparts, was sent to Warsaw with Hitler's offer to guarantee all of Poland's territory minus Danzig, which was under League of Nations administration; he too, drew a blank. A month later, Hitler was still hopeful of wooing Warsaw. 'The Führer is brooding over the solution of the Danzig question,' Goebbels wrote in his diary. 'He wants to apply some pressure to the Poles and hopes that they will respond to it, but we must bite the bullet and guarantee Poland's borders.'[170]

Secondly, Hitler moved to settle what he had been forced to leave unresolved at Munich: the fate of the 'rump Czechoslovakia'. This was a strategic bone in Germany's throat. On 21 January 1939, he met with the Czech foreign minister, František Chvalkovský, to stress his need for closer economic cooperation. Hitler's tactic was brutally simple. He had already deprived Prague of its powerful border fortresses through the annexation of the Sudetenland. Now he intended to browbeat and intimidate the

Czechs, to destroy their 'nerves', until their entire state 'dissolved'. Hitler was able to monitor the effectiveness of his measures through the detailed intelligence reports on Czech intercepts he received from Göring's *Forschungsamt*. This approach was what we would today call 'hybrid warfare'. Hitler received Professor Vojtech Tuka, a Slovak separatist from the Slovak People's Party, and Franz Karmasin, leader of the German minority in Slovakia. The Führer told Tuka that he was resolved to sort out the Czechs and urged him to declare a separate Slovak state, which Tuka agreed to do.

Prague fell into the trap Hitler had set. When the Slovaks, emboldened by Berlin, brought their separatist agitation to the boil, the government declared martial law on 10 March 1939. Hitler now dispatched his two 'annexation specialists', Gauleiter Bürckel and Wilhelm Keppler, to the Slovaks to ensure that they declared independence. He also received the deposed Slovak leader Monsignor Tiso in Berlin.[171] The Führer offered them the choice between an independent state and annexation by Hungary. Tiso eventually agreed to a text prepared by Ribbentrop. Hitler summoned the Czech president, Emil Hácha, and his foreign minister to Berlin. Both men were kept waiting for hours in order to increase the pressure on them. Finally, Hitler appeared at 1 a.m. in the morning and browbeat his visitors, threatening to bomb Prague immediately unless his demands were met. Hácha fainted under the strain. He was revived with injections from Hitler's personal doctor, Theodor Morell. After three hours of pummelling, Hácha signed a prepared statement that he 'confidently placed the fate of the Czech people in the hands of the Führer'. Czechoslovakia had ceased to exist. Shortly after, German troops moved in. That night, Hitler slept in the castle overlooking Prague. Slovakia became a notionally independent state, but in reality a satellite of the Third Reich. France and Britain made no move, as Göring's surveillance teams had correctly predicted. Hitler had done it again.

The Führer had no plans at this stage to remove the local population to make way for Germans. On the contrary, he cast himself as the guarantor of Czech national rights in a German-dominated Europe. The appellation 'Protectorate of Bohemia and Moravia' stemmed from the language of Hitler's proclamation on 15 March 1939 of the 'assumption of the protection of the Czech people through the Reich'. It mimicked that of the British 'protectorates' throughout the world. Six weeks after the annexation, he let it be known that there was no serious historical enmity between Germans and Czechs and that he thought that the latter were adjusting well to their new role within the Reich.[172] The intervening period had seen the start neither of a massive Germanization process, nor of a colonization programme, and that was the way Hitler wanted it.

Hitler's preoccupation with *Lebensraum*, always intense, became an increasing obsession in the spring of 1939. In late March he ruminated that history was really a story of 'migration of the people' and that the same principles which had set the peoples in motion during pre-history and antiquity applied today. A 'technologically highly developed society or a purely industrial state,' Hitler argued, could not survive without its own 'dedicated space'. If this space was not already available, he explained, it would have to be 'fought for . . . that was a natural law'. Failure to realize this would make one 'the booty of those who did not exercise restraint'. The most 'brutal' practitioners here, Hitler argued, were the Americans. Unlike them, or the British, however, Hitler did not favour overseas settlement. He returned to his old trauma, the loss of generations of Germans to emigration. 'Every German who emigrated to America,' Hitler lamented, 'would be lost to the motherland.' This was because 'he would become an American, lose his connection to the homeland and, from our perspective [sic] he would degenerate, because he would put down roots in alien soil'. Hitler readily conceded that the colonization of the US, Canada and Australia had created states of 'material importance and power', but he regarded them as lacking in culture. Hitler expressed himself surprised, and perhaps also pained, that Germans had taken so readily to these new structures. 'It is strange,' Hitler mused, 'that it was those of German origin who were the first to put down roots in new soil and sought to identify with it more strongly than others.'[173]

Shortly after the dismemberment of Czechoslovakia, Hitler suffered three blows which were to change the course of events. Warsaw dug in its heels. On 26 March 1939, Ribbentrop reported to Hitler that the Polish foreign minister, Beck, had announced that he would consider the seizure of Danzig a *casus belli*. Five days later, on the very last day of the month, Hitler learned that Britain and France had guaranteed Poland and Romania. Six days after that, the British-Polish treaty was signed. Stunned by Hitler's bad faith over Czechoslovakia, London had finally decided to make a stand. The European balance of power would be defended. Roosevelt responded to the destruction of Czechoslovakia by immediately imposing punitive tariffs on German goods. A fortnight later, he sent a personal message to Hitler demanding that he undertake not to infringe the sovereignty of a long list of European states, Poland among them. It was, in effect, a complement to the British guarantee of Poland. Anglo-America was drawing the line. The path to *Lebensraum* no longer ran just through Warsaw, but also through London. The day after the Franco-British guarantee to Poland he launched a ferocious attack on British encirclement plans at the launch of the new battleship *Tirpitz*. 'We know from historical documents today,' he claimed,

referring to studies of the origins of the First World War, 'how the encirclement policy of those times was systematically pursued by Britain.' 'England,'
he stated simply in late May 1939, 'is the motor of opposition to us.'[174]

The breach with Britain represented a massive blow to Hitler's grand
strategy, and was also a matter of deep personal distress for him. On
Hitler's side, the relationship had been characterized by respect for British
racial quality, admiration for the Empire and fear of British military capabilities, which he had himself experienced during four long years in
France and Flanders. 'To imagine,' he fulminated in mid April 1939, 'that
I of all people am forced to contemplate such a conflict, I who am accused
in Germany of being an incorrigible admirer of the British Empire, I who
have so often tried to effect a lasting understanding between the Reich and
England, an understanding which even today I consider as necessary for
the preservation of European culture.' 'The sole blame for this,' he concluded, 'lies with the tenacious blindness of Britain's leaders.'[175]

The prospect of war with Britain compelled Hitler to change his racial
rhetoric in public as in private. 'The Briton is proud, brave, tough, resilient
and organizationally gifted,' he conceded, 'he has the adventurousness
and courage of the Nordic race.' That was no reason to despair, however.
As the British were 'diffused' across the world, he continued, 'the quality
[of the Briton] drops. The German average is better.' This was a new line
for Hitler, and he probably did not really believe it himself, but the Führer
now needed to give the German people the confidence in themselves they –
and he – so badly lacked, much in the same way as had been demanded
of the press back in November 1938. Sensitive to the (completely justified)
charge that he had an inferiority complex towards Britain, Hitler pushed
back vigorously. 'I don't suffer in the least from a sense of inferiority,' he
protested two weeks later.[176] Anybody familiar with Hitler's writings and
speeches over the previous twenty years, however, would have known that
the Führer was protesting too much.

Likewise, Hitler now played down the power of the United States, even in
private. When told of US technological superiority, which he had freely admitted in the past, the Führer now liked to contrast American 'quantity' with
German 'quality'. Doubters were told that everything else was 'typical American exaggeration and bluff'. It was clear, however, that Hitler knew better.
When a film of New York shot from the air was shown in the Imperial
Chancellery in the late summer of 1939, the Führer was obviously shaken.
He was 'visibly impressed,' his foreign press chief Otto Dietrich wrote, 'by
the enormous vitality and the powerful progressive impulses radiating
from this, for European sensibilities, immense spatial entity of human
coexistence.'[177]

Hitler was preparing for conflict not just with Britain, but with the United States as well. Anglo-America, always closely linked in his mind, was fusing into one. The Führer's original hopes of separating London and Washington had been dashed. On 28 April 1939, a full fortnight after Roosevelt's letter, Hitler responded with a coruscating speech in the Reichstag which not merely rebutted the president's charges and attacked the United States more generally, but also lambasted Britain, as well as signalling his hostility towards Poland.[178] In the Führer's mind, all of these questions were closely related. The culmination of the speech was Hitler's denial that he planned to attack any of the twenty-odd states whose integrity Roosevelt had demanded he guarantee. As the Führer read out this list its length and apparent absurdity caused a moment of levity in the Reichstag as the assembled deputies roared with laughter. Hitler, in fact, genuinely did not at this point intend to attack most of the states on that list, but he was to do so almost without exception within two years.

The real issue, as always, was space. Anglo-America had it; Germany wanted it. There was, Hitler argued, more than enough to go around. What was required was that the United States and the British Empire should not intrude on German spheres just as the Third Reich respected theirs. Hitler demanded that the United States should recognize his sphere of influence in Europe while he would recognize Washington's in the Americas. If Roosevelt, the president of a geographically remote country, required guarantees of German behaviour in Europe, then surely the Reich 'would have the same right' to ask the same question about US policy in Central and Latin America. If Roosevelt appealed to the Monroe Doctrine, and rejected any German demands as 'an intervention in the internal affairs of the American continent', then surely Germany could make the same argument. 'We espouse exactly the same doctrine,' the Führer went on, 'for Europe, and in all events for the area and interest of the Greater German Reich.' Hitler's idea of a German Monroe Doctrine – which he had first mentioned more than a decade earlier – was picked up by the lawyer Carl Schmitt, who elaborated it into an entire theory of 'large spaces'.[179]

The consequence of the looming conflict with Britain, and ultimately the United States, was twofold. First, in Hitler's mind Poland had replaced Czechoslovakia as the cat's paw of the western powers and was to be crushed. 'I will brew them a devil's potion,' he exclaimed on hearing the news of the Franco-British guarantee.[180] Secondly, the acquisition of the territory necessary to match Anglo-America would have to be speeded up. 'Securing living space,' he told an audience of German workers, using a phrase he repeated over and over that summer, 'is our highest commandment.'[181] If Poland could not be co-opted to this project, she would have to be brushed aside or even eliminated. The demand for Danzig and an extra-territorial railway was not driven by traditional Versailles revisionism but by the logistics of war against the Soviet Union.

On 11 April 1939, five days after the conclusion of the Polish-British treaty, Hitler issued his instructions for *Fall Weiss*, the attack on Poland. The instruction specified not Warsaw, but the 'western democracies' as the main enemy. Six weeks later, Hitler explained that 'The problem of Poland cannot be separated from the confrontation with the west.' Poland would see a German victory in the west as a threat and act to prevent one. His conclusion was that it was therefore pointless 'to spare Poland' and that he was left with the 'decision to attack Poland at the next available opportunity'.[182] In short, Hitler would go to war with Poland as part of his conflict with the western powers, not vice versa. The British guarantee, designed to protect the country, in fact precipitated her destruction.

Throughout the summer of 1939, Hitler hoped for the best. He tried to cajole or bully the Poles, failing which he would have preferred to fight a limited war to secure Danzig and the Corridor. Hitler also held the door open for London. He remained theoretically open to a 'permanent friendship between the German and the Anglo-Saxon people', but stated that this could only be achieved if the 'other side also recognized that there were not only British but German interests' to be defended.[183] Hitler also prepared for the worst case. What really worried him was that the Royal Air Force would use bases in the Low Countries to attack the heart of German industry in the Ruhr. He was already planning to attack in the west, not so much to occupy France, though the French field army would have to be beaten, but to establish bases from which to continue the war against England. 'The army is to seize positions,' he decreed to the generals, 'which are important for the navy and the Luftwaffe.' 'If we succeed in occupying and securing Holland and Belgium, and defeating France,' Hitler continued, 'then we can create the basis for a successful war against Britain. The Luftwaffe can then maintain the inner blockade of Britain from western France, and the navy's submarines can take over the broader blockade.'[184]

The prospect of war with Anglo-America drove Hitler to seek closer relations with his allies. On 22 May 1939, he concluded the 'Pact of Steel' with Italy.[185] Its immediate value was somewhat unclear. A week later, Mussolini warned Hitler that he could not fight before the end of 1942 at the earliest. The Führer, for his part, sought to bind the *Duce* closer to him. In June 1939, he instructed Himmler to organize the resettlement of the South Tyroleans. Agreement was reached towards the end of the month. South Tyroleans were given the 'option' of emigration to the Reich, and staying in Italy but subjecting themselves to Italianization. Only a minority decided to stay: about 80 per cent 'opted' for the Reich, though only about a third of them actually moved. It was the start of a much broader strategy to 'bring home' somewhere between 700,000 and 900,000 Germans from Italy, the Soviet Union, the Baltic States, Hungary, Romania, Bulgaria and Yugoslavia.[186]

If Hitler expected war with Poland, Britain, France, the United States and the Soviet Union, the sequencing of these conflicts depended on the reactions of Warsaw, London, Paris, Moscow and Washington. He did not know, and could not know, in the summer of 1939, whether a major war would begin with the invasion of Poland, or at some later date; he could not even be sure that he would not start with an attack on the western powers, or on all three simultaneously. All he knew was that there would be war; that it would soon involve the major powers, including eventually America; and that it would not be short. The Führer was confident that Poland could be beaten quickly, but beyond that he had no expectation of a *Blitzkrieg*; indeed the concept had yet to be invented. 'A rapid victory in the west,' he admitted privately, 'is doubtful.' As a veteran of the Great War, and admirer of Britain, the Führer could hardly believe otherwise. Hitler had therefore rearmed in depth as well as breadth, just as the number and quality of the opposition warranted.[187] 'Every army or state leadership,' he warned the generals, 'must aim for a short war.' That said, Hitler stressed that one should 'also prepare for a war lasting ten to fifteen years'. He would try to prevail through a 'surprise attack', but it would be 'criminal' to rely on surprise alone.[188]

The Führer's expectation of a long war was reflected in two interrelated anxieties. Firstly, he was acutely conscious of the dire state of the German economy, which slowed rearmament and raised domestic tensions. This drove him to war, not because he wished to head off domestic unrest, but because he could see that he was losing the battle of production with the western powers.[189] Secondly, Hitler feared that the vulnerability of Germany's food supply would bring down the home front as it had done in the First World War. He fretted about the effects of a new British wartime blockade,[190] and even about Roosevelt's peacetime economic sanctions. Hitler lamented the propensity of 'so-called democratic statesmen' to cut off a people from its markets 'for example through boycotts', though he obviously also had wartime blockades in mind, in order to 'starve' it.[191] Clearly, Hitler believed that the economic war with the United States had already begun.

By the summer of 1939, in short, the enemy which Hitler had identified at the start of his political career twenty years earlier, was in full view

again: the western capitalist powers, democracy, plutocracy and the supposed world Jewish conspiracy. Strikingly, Hitler had dropped all reference
to the communist threat. In early June 1939, he declined an invitation to
publish a collection of his previous pronouncements on 'Jewry and Bolshevism', either out of regard for the Soviet Union, or to avoid diluting his
anti-capitalist message, or (as he claimed) because he did not like his
thoughts being 'chopped up'.[192] Even his Spanish intervention was redefined
from a rescue of Europe from Bolshevism to a blow against plutocracy. He
now spoke of 'Spain's struggle against the internationally organized
destruction of its country', by which he meant the depredations of the
'international plutocracy' of the west, and their 'encirclement politicians,
war hawks and war profiteers'.[193]

   In mid June 1939, the machinery of the Third Reich swung into action
against Poland. Operational orders for *Fall Weiss* were issued to the
troops. Only now was an intense propaganda campaign unleashed against
Warsaw.[194] Hitler was using the same modus operandi which he had deployed
to such devastating effect against Czechoslovakia: demoralizing and
isolating the victim, while deterring Britain and France from intervening.
This time it did not work. It was clear that, whatever happened, Poland
would fight, and that it was likely that the west would deliver on its guarantee, however reluctantly.

   The imminence of war drove Hitler to try to weld German society closer
together, to stiffen it for the fight and to forestall the kind of fragmentation which he believed had so bedevilled it in the past. Depending on the
context and the likelihood of success, this sometimes meant taking radical
action or attacking established structures. The approach of conflict affected
Hitler's sense of racial time. The gradual elevation of the German *Volk*
would not be completed before the outbreak of hostilities. This accentuated
Hitler's ambivalence about war. On the one hand, he saw it as a purifying
phenomenon, which toughened the fittest and weeded out the unfit; on the
other hand he feared that, paradoxically, it would kill the best and spare
the weak or cowardly by a process of negative selection. Hitler therefore
stepped up the attack on those 'unworthy of life', immediately before and
during war. In late July 1939, his doctor Karl Brandt killed a deformed
child in a Leipzig hospital, at the request of the parents and as ordered by
Hitler himself. The Führer also sought to prepare the German people for
a euthanasia programme. In early August 1939, his entourage screened
Unworthy Life, a film about the life of the incurably mentally ill.[195]

   Hitler also continued his campaign against the conservatism of the
officer corps. In mid July 1939, he was once again caught up in a sex scandal. His naval liaison officer, Captain Alvin Albrecht, married a woman

who had previously enjoyed the favours of several men. When Admiral Raeder, who had acted as witness at the wedding, tried to have Albrecht disciplined for entering into a 'socially inappropriate' union, citing the Blomberg affair, a shouting-match with Hitler ensued. The Führer condemned the 'typical officer-style intrigue', expressed his contempt for the gossip of officers wives, and demanded to meet the woman himself so that he could form a judgement. They spoke for about ninety minutes on the following day. Afterwards, the new Mrs Albrecht announced in a state of some emotion that the Führer had shown 'complete understanding for her as a woman'. Hitler himself expressed indifference to 'private matters between man and woman', which 'were no business of anyone else so long as they did not affect the public'.[196] It transpired that while the new Mrs Albrecht was extremely affectionate and highly sexed, she was in no sense promiscuous. There the matter rested, though to spare Raeder's feelings her husband was discharged from the service and made the Führer's personal adjutant. What was remarkable here was that Hitler did not run for cover, even after the Blomberg crisis, but stood his ground against what he regarded as the outdated norms of the armed services.

Underlying Hitler's attitude over the Albrecht affair was his contempt for the 'lying nature of the officer corps, for [their] hypocritical moralizing', in judging others on matters which had nothing to do with behaviour, attitude and performance. In his opinion, the real threat to the armed services came from 'cowards and defeatists', a swipe at military opposition to his plans.[197] A month later, Hitler erupted again, this time against the army, which he claimed had privileged traditional military flags over those of the Nazi movement on parade. His own preference was very much for a single national flag with a small corner or a ribbon to indicate the formation in question. The French, he claimed, had done this since the Revolution. 'Unfortunately,' he concluded, 'his army was anything but a revolutionary army.'[198] Hitler's quarrel with the Wehrmacht thus already encompassed a whole range of issues: its alleged cowardice, its partiality to the traditions which had divided Germans for so long and its obsession with the sexual lives of its members at the expense of professionalism.

Meanwhile, Hitler continued the cultural mobilization and elevation of the German people. He pronounced 'the first objective for a new German artistic production' as 'achieved'.[199] German 'architecture' and 'the perhaps even more devastated fields of sculpture and painting' had been 'healed'. At around the same time, Hitler gave Hans Posse, the director of the gallery at Dresden, the task of putting together a collection of pictures for a special 'Führer Museum' at Linz. He followed the progress of the 'Sonderauftrag Linz' and the various purchases associated with it very closely. The Führer

Museum was to be embedded in a larger remodelling of the city, including eventually a planned Führerpfalz, a Gauforum with a massive tower in the shape of the Lighthouse of Alexandria, and a bridge over the Danube. The city was also gifted thousands of new residential buildings to house the workers in the mammoth 'Hermann-Göring Werke'.[200] These were known as *Hitlerbauten*, and, unlike most of the planned monumental structures, many of them were actually erected (by slave labour) in his lifetime.

In late July 1939 Hitler headed to Bayreuth for what would turn out to be the last peacetime festival. He spent a week there, taking a day off to inspect the Westwall, evidence that the approaching war was much on his mind. Hitler spoke with the Mitford sisters, who were also attending the festival, about the deteriorating international situation. He told Diana that he believed that Britain wanted war, which was therefore inevitable. On 27 July, Hitler met with the British press baron Lord Kemsley at Wahnfried and reiterated his view that Germany must have 'colonies', by which he meant space in the east.[201] A day later, Hitler sought solace in the assurances of Diana Mosley, who claimed that 'anti-Semitism in England was steadily increasing', and of her sister Unity Mitford, who dismissed Britain's military readiness.[202]

In the first week of August 1939, Hitler repaired to the Berghof to make the last preparations for war. Three related forces were driving Hitler forward. Firstly, he feared that he was nearly out of time. Much better, Hitler told Ciano, to go to war with the west while he and the *Duce* were still young.[203] Later in the month, the Führer warned his generals that the current favourable constellation would not last more than two or three years. 'Nobody knows,' he added, 'how long I will live.' 'An assassination attempt on Mussolini or myself,' Hitler explained, 'can change the situation to our disadvantage.' For this reason, he continued, the sooner war broke out the better. Secondly, the Führer was conscious that the existing very high level of economic, military and psychological mobilization could not be sustained for long. 'One cannot confront one another with cocked rifles for ever,' he explained.[204] Soon, Germany would either have to strike at Britain's eastern ally Poland, and perhaps take on the western powers, or back down. Thirdly, Hitler was determined to resolve the *Lebensraum* question in the near future, an issue to which he returned repeatedly in the course of the month. But while the Führer was acutely aware of the bottlenecks in the German economy, and the threat to standards of living, there is no evidence at all that his decision for war was driven by immediate considerations of domestic politics.[205]

Frustrated by the attitude of Poland and the west, Hitler summoned Carl Jakob Burckhardt, the Swiss League of Nations high commissioner for

Danzig, to the Obersalzberg. 'There is something in the Anglo-Saxons (and the Americans) which profoundly divides them and us. What is it?' he asked Burckhardt.[206] Hitler swore that he wanted nothing from the west. 'I don't need anything from the most densely inhabited regions of the world,' he explained. Rather, he demanded 'a free hand in the east'. 'Everything I do,' Hitler continued, 'is directed against Russia.' If the west was 'too stupid and too blind to understand that,' the Führer went on, then he would be 'forced to come to terms with the Russians, to attack the west and then after its defeat turn back with all his forces against the Soviet Union'.[207] A fortnight later, he returned to the space argument in an exchange with the British ambassador, Henderson. 'The claim that Germany wishes to conquer the world,' Hitler argued, 'is ridiculous. The British Empire comprises 40 million square kilometres, Russia 19 million, America 9.5 million, whereas Germany does not even stretch to 600,000 square kilometres.'[208]

The key variable throughout August 1939 was Britain. Hitler was under no illusion about her power, nor about her hostility. His only hope was that Britain could be persuaded or bullied into remaining neutral, at least for now. For this reason he huffed and puffed about Germany's ability, unlike in 1914–18, to outlast the enemy, rhetoric which was less a sign of hubris than of his continuing acute sense of vulnerability. 'If there is no more butter,' he assured the Swedish mediator Birger Dahlerus, 'then I will be the first to stop eating butter. My German people will happily and loyally do the same.'[209] Contrary to his confident predictions to some German interlocutors, which were designed to keep spirits up at home, Hitler did not believe that he could call Britain's bluff again, as he had done at Munich. The Führer let it be known to Chamberlain that he knew 'that if war should break out between Germany and Poland Great Britain will be in it'. Hitler threatened London with a 'fight to the finish' if it intervened, but offered a partnership if it was prepared to cooperate.[210] London, however, left Berlin in no doubt that it would defend Poland, and to Hitler's distress, was engaged in military discussion with Stalin on how best to deal with the Nazi threat. He attributed British false consciousness to the machinations of the Jews and their allies. 'The attitude towards Germany was not the will of British people,' he complained to Henderson with reference to the Jewishness of the minister of war, Leslie Hore-Belisha, but 'should be traced back to Jews and anti-Nazis'.[211]

Faced with a united Polish and Franco-British front, Hitler had no option but to turn to Moscow, as he had indicated to Burckhardt.[212] His motivation was partly tactical, in that he wanted to isolate Poland and to derail the Anglo-Russian negotiations. It was also strategic, in that he needed to mitigate the effect of a blockade in the event of a prolonged war with the west.[213] Fear of Soviet military power, which he estimated to be low, played no part in the Führer's calculations.[214] Like most anti-communist observers in the west, Hitler thought of the USSR as a country of shoddy goods, low morale and chaotic violence and purges. On 19 August, he concluded an economic agreement by which the Soviet Union would supply Germany with vital raw materials. The day after, the Führer sent a telegram to Stalin offering him an immediate non-aggression pact. Stalin replied positively on 21 August, and two days later, Molotov and Ribbentrop signed a ten-year non-aggression treaty in the Kremlin.[215] A secret annex delineated the respective spheres of influence: Hitler was granted Lithuania and the western part of Poland, Stalin received Finland, Estonia and Latvia, as well as Poland east of the Rivers Narew, Vistula and San. Hitler received the news on the Obersalzberg and reacted by jumping up from his meal and shouting '[I have] won!'[216] Some Nazis felt a revolutionary affinity with the Soviet Union – Ribbentrop remarked that he had felt as if among old comrades in Moscow – but at this stage Hitler's interest in the pact was purely strategic. His antagonism with the west had made a temporary accommodation with Stalin necessary.[217]

On 22 August 1939, as the pact was being negotiated, Hitler convened his generals on the Obersalzberg for a carefully choreographed meeting.[218] The fifty-odd senior military men were ordered to appear in civilian clothes, probably in order not to attract attention on the journey, while Hitler wore the brown uniform of the party. Göring was resplendent in 'fantastic hunting gear, baggy trousers, blouse-style white shirt and an open green waistcoat'.[219] The meeting was held in Hitler's study, whose enormous picture window provided impressive views over the mountains. The venue was intended to make an impression, and the Führer himself had told an earlier meeting that he had called them here so that they could see 'in what surroundings I like to make my decisions'.[220] That morning, news had broken of the imminent conclusion of a non-aggression pact between Russia and Germany. Hitler used the resulting relief among the military to reassure them about the planned attack on Poland. The Führer told them that he did not expect Britain or France to intervene. Hitherto, he claimed, the two powers had been relying on the Soviet Union, 'but I have now knocked that card out of their hands'. As we have seen, Hitler was expressing more of a hope than an expectation here, but what is striking is that he continued to conceive of the Soviet Union largely in terms of his relationship with the west.

The whole event was as much a performance as a briefing, and Hitler was far from feeling the confidence he simulated. His reference to 1918 and the lack of the 'psychological basis' to fight on showed the continuing concern with German weakness.[221] He was deeply anxious about how his audience would respond. The Führer asked his adjutant, Rudolf Schmundt, 'to find out what the reaction' to his words had been. Hitler fancied himself as something of a 'really good popular psychologist', who could read the mood of any crowd, but he freely admitted that senior military were something of a closed book to him. 'They put on a stiff mask-like demeanour,' he complained, 'from which one could deduce nothing.'[222] Hitler was right to be worried. There were profound reservations among the military, who expected Britain and France to intervene in some way, but there was no doubt that they would do as they were told.

It was Hitler who wobbled, albeit briefly. On 22 August 1939, with a Russo-German pact obviously imminent, Chamberlain wrote to emphasize that the British guarantee to Poland still stood; Henderson delivered it a day later. On the 24th, President Roosevelt sent Hitler a telegram warning that the 'catastrophe' of a general war was 'very near at hand indeed'. He made clear that 'the people of the United States are as one in their opposition to policies of military conquest and domination'. The import of these words was clear. Washington would not stand idly by for long. Meissner, the head of the Führer's Chancellery, recalls the impact of Roosevelt's intervention. 'In verbal remarks during those days,' he writes, 'Hitler called this sudden interest of America in central European matters a superfluous interference which he would have to reject sharply.'[223] The following morning brought more bad news. Mussolini announced his intention to stay neutral, at least for now. Italy, he said, was simply not ready for a war which had come much earlier than envisaged.[224] Hitler was visibly 'very cast down', and one observer recalled that he seemed 'stumped'.[225] The attack on Poland, which had been scheduled for 26 August, was postponed. The next few days were unbearably tense, as tempers frayed in Berlin, especially Hitler's, as he lashed out against the army, the Foreign Office, Italy and anyone else who crossed his path.

Over the next seventy-two hours the Führer struggled to regain his nerve. He sought to persuade his entourage, and himself, that the western powers would not intervene and that even if they did, the outcome would be very different than in 1918. There were frantic last-minute overtures to Britain, reviving the idea of a grand bargain between Berlin and London, but only after the Polish question had been resolved.[226] These went nowhere. In the end, Hitler turned almost helplessly to Göring's confidant Birger Dahlerus, who had been acting as an intermediary. 'You know Britain so well,' he said to the Swede, 'can you explain the origin of my constant failure to come to an agreement with her?'[227] It was the same question he had asked Burckhardt, and which was to haunt him for the rest of his life. On 28 August, Hitler set a new date for the attack on Poland: 1 September 1939.[228]

Hitler was under no illusions about the struggle ahead. He told the senior military on 28 August 1939, before the war had even started, that it would be 'difficult and perhaps hopeless'. Halder remarked that the Führer looked in very bad shape: 'bleary-eyed, frail, his voice breaking, [and] muddled'. 'Hitler,' another witness recorded 'made a nervous, tired impression', with 'distracted glances and movements'. When he explained the situation to the Reichstag, he received only weak 'dutiful applause'. The more Britain seemed likely to intervene, the shriller Hitler became. 'So long as I live,' he vowed, 'there will be no talk of capitulation.' 'If push comes to shove,' he told Brauchitsch, 'I will wage a two-front war.'[229] On 30 August, he received Gauleiter Förster of Danzig to give him the last instructions for the capture of the city. Tension with Warsaw was whipped up in a final crescendo. An incident was manufactured by the SS on the border with Poland, in which an attack on the German radio station at Gleiwitz was faked.[230] Hitler was going to roll the dice again.

15
The 'Haves' and the 'Have-Nots'

On 1 September 1939, the Wehrmacht invaded Poland. That same day, Hitler spoke in the Reichstag in a carefully choreographed appearance. He was addressing two audiences. One was the German people. To them, the Führer sought to justify the decision for war, and to shore up morale. For this reason, Hitler promised 'no privations for Germans which I will not immediately share'. He underlined his new role as 'the first soldier of the German Reich'[1] by donning a simple grey jacket. The other addressee was the western powers, whose intervention he was anxious to avert. To them, Hitler signalled that he had 'no claims in the west' and that 'our Westwall' was 'the border of the Reich for all times'. He also stressed that there would be no 'capitulation'. 'I would like to reassure the world at large,' he averred, that 'there will never be another November 1918 in German history.'[2] It was the first of several wartime speeches, which Hitler used carefully for messaging purposes over the next six years. 'In wartime I must weigh every word as if it were gold,' he said, 'because the world is attentive and sensitive.' Hitler now rationed his appearances. 'It was dangerous,' he remarked, 'to make speeches without having a plausible reason for doing so.'[3]

The Polish campaign was a resounding success.[4] Danzig was captured in a *coup de main*. German tanks quickly overran the border defences, and advanced rapidly into the heart of the country. The plan of attack had been drawn up by the military leadership, but with considerable input from Hitler.[5] He had disguised the offensive preparations as defensive measures. Hitler himself planned the commando operation against the bridge at Dirschau down to the smallest detail. More importantly, he had also insisted the pincer movement from East Prussia would not merely be a limited push to secure the Corridor but a much larger 'great pincer' designed to trap as many Polish forces as possible.[6] Hitler did not, however, interfere in the operational conduct of the campaign, though he insisted on being briefed twice daily by telephone. Instead, shortly after the start of hostilities, Hitler set off on the first of several much-heralded 'frontline travels' to underline his commitment to his men. These journeys were not entirely without risk, as they exposed the Führer to air attack and even friendly fire, but they were essentially propaganda stunts.[7] Hitler popped up at bridges and fords, or in field hospitals, with each photo opportunity calculated to give an impression of dynamism and ubiquity. The Poles proved no push-over, inflicting nearly 50,000 casualties, about a quarter of them dead, and they even launched a serious counter-attack on the Bzura against the forces advancing on Warsaw from the south-west.[8] A fortnight into the campaign Hitler was sufficiently worried to urge the Soviet Union to hasten its intervention. On 17 September, Stalin invaded Poland from the east, taking a lot of pressure off the Wehrmacht. Nazi and Soviet forces met at Brest-Litovsk. Soon Polish resistance collapsed. Ribbentrop set off to Moscow to sort out the final details of the respective zones of occupation. The Führer returned to Berlin in triumph.

Hitler had been vindicated yet again, crowning two years of masterly manoeuvring in central and eastern Europe. Throughout the 1930s he prevented the Sudeten Germans from rebelling prematurely. Hitler had not responded to the Anglo-Czech 'provocation' in May 1938. Then he turned the Poles and the Hungarians against Prague in September of that year. Subsequently Hitler let loose the Slovaks on the Czechs, facilitating the seizure of Bohemia and Moravia in March 1939. During all this time, he had also kept the great powers at arm's length. In September 1939, he isolated Warsaw, securing the collaboration of Slovakia and the Soviet Union for his attack. Each of these moves had been a gamble and required strong nerves, and each time Hitler's audacity had paid off.

His hope that the war could be localized, however, was quickly dashed. On 3 September 1939, Britain and France declared war. Hitler was not surprised, but he was deeply shaken. That same day, Unity Mitford attempted suicide in the Englischer Garten in Munich. It is not clear whether the outbreak of war was the immediate motivation, but the date and symbolism of her act makes it highly likely. Despite his many other commitments, Hitler arranged and paid for the necessary medical care.[9] Unity's despair epitomized the failure of Hitler's British policy, with its assumption of common racial ground and reliance on go-betweens. As for the United States she remained neutral for now, but her fundamental antipathy to the Third Reich was not in doubt. Roosevelt's public strictures were on record; in private he was beginning to talk about concrete ways in which he could prevent Hitler from breaking through to the Atlantic.[10] The United States was already waging a cold war against largely imaginary Nazi subversion in Latin America, and indeed against the generally blameless German population there.[11]

If Hitler had succeeded militarily by late September 1939, the position was more ambivalent politically. He had frequently predicted, despite knowing better, that the western powers would not intervene, and he had promised that there would be no 'two-front war'. Now he had one. The conflict was not popular at home.[12] Most Germans wanted the Poles to be taught a lesson, and to see the return of territories lost to Poland at Versailles, but they had no appetite whatsoever for another war against Britain and France. They greeted the attack on Poland with reserve and the Allied declaration of war with alarm. There was no trace of the enthusiasm which greeted mobilization in 1914. The streets were dark and empty. Hitler was well aware of these sentiments, which he had first noted during the Sudeten crisis, had inveighed against on many occasions since, and which were being monitored in detail by the surveillance apparatus of the Sicherheitsdienst.[13] Victory over Poland brought some relief, but popular anxiety about the threat from Britain and France persisted.

Hitler was therefore determined to take ownership of the Polish victory, which he used to buttress his domestic position and to inspire confidence in his future direction of the conflict against the western powers. His proprietorial feelings were exposed when Fritsch was killed on the front line near Warsaw. Hitler was infuriated by Jodl's remark that 'the Wehrmacht [had] lost its best soldier', which he seems to have read as a challenge to his own status as 'the first soldier' of the Reich. Brauchitsch made matters worse by referring to Fritsch as the 'creator of the new army', another accolade that Hitler felt were rightfully his. The Führer's insecurity and jealousy in these matters was revealed by his decision to keep the news of Fritsch's death under wraps for some time, to deny him the trappings of martyrdom, and then by his absence at the memorial service. Throughout the next seven months, in fact, Hitler carefully curated his image as the victor in Poland, personally selecting photographs for publication and suppressing rival narratives from the army propaganda machine and other sources.[14]

The Führer was in no doubt who the main enemy was: Britain and the Jews. His speech to the Reichstag responding to the declaration of war by the western powers hardly mentioned France or the Poles. Instead, Hitler emphasized the continuity of Britain's policy of a 'balance of power' in Europe in order to make the continent 'defenceless' in the face of the 'ideology of British world domination'. After Spain, the Dutch and France, he continued, it was now Germany's turn to suffer 'the encirclement strategy pursued by Britain', of which Warsaw had merely been an instrument. In his second proclamation to the eastern army serving in Poland, issued the same day that Chamberlain declared war, he listed Britain's alleged pre-First World War 'encirclement strategy', well ahead of Polish treatment of the German minority as the *casus belli*.[15]

Hitler also stressed the ideological dimension of the war, which pitted Germany against the 'Jewish-democratic world enemy', and the 'capitalist war mongers of England and her satellites'.[16] The Jews, Hitler claimed, had manipulated the 'British people' into war with Germany in order to maintain the international capitalist order – run by a 'plutocratic and democratic ruling class' – against the social aspirations of the Third Reich.[17] Hitler would have been confirmed in this view by the fact that Chaim Weizmann, the president of the World Jewish Congress and head of the Jewish Agency for Palestine, had written to Chamberlain on the eve of war – 29 August 1939 – to tell him that 'the Jews stand by Great Britain and will fight on the side of the democracies', and 'place ourselves, in matters big and small, under the co-ordinating direction of his Majesty's Government'; this letter was published in *The Times* three days after Britain declared war. Of course, Weizmann was only responding to Hitler's own repeated declarations of war on the Jews and in any case did not represent all Jews.[18]

For all these reasons, Hitler waged war against the Jews from the very start of hostilities. This was partly because the outbreak of war meant that, from his point of view, the removal of the remaining 300,000 Jews in the Reich had to be accelerated; partly because the defeat of Poland brought several million additional Jews under his control; but mainly because he saw international Jewry as the directing mind behind the enemy coalition. Such was Hitler's fear that Jews constituted a fifth column in Germany that he ordered the confiscation of all Jewish telephones. In late September 1939, he instructed Heydrich that any territories taken from Poland were to be cleared of Jews, all of whom were to be concentrated in a reservation near Lublin. A week later, Hitler said that German Jews should be resettled 'between Bug and Vistula',[19] and during the following month some were indeed transported there. Hitler did not necessarily watch over every stage of the implementation of anti-Jewish policy, but he was certainly responsible for its broad outlines. Towards the end of the year, Bormann stated clearly that all such measures undertaken by Himmler's SS were to be agreed with the Führer.[20]

Equally important to Hitler as the armed campaign against Britain and the Jews was the international propaganda struggle to discredit enemy narratives and to promote those of the Third Reich. The Führer was determined here not to repeat the failures of the First World War. On 8 September, he issued a decree giving Ribbentrop control of external propaganda.[21] It was an important victory for the Foreign Office over Goebbels and it reflected Hitler's desire for coordination between the foreign messaging of the regime and its foreign policy, especially with regard to neutrals.

'Propaganda,' Hitler stated, 'is an important instrument with which the leadership can promote and strengthen one's own will to win and to destroy the will to win and morale of the enemy.' He attached so much importance to this work that he compared the possible destruction of the propaganda machine to the loss of 'certain parts of the Wehrmacht'.[22] Central to this endeavour was the 'enlightenment' of the outside world about the nefarious nature of international Jewry, to which end the anti-Semitic 'World Service' was translated into eight languages.[23] At the same time, at Hitler's express request, Nazi broadcasts in Arabic targeted alleged British imperial atrocities in Palestine in September 1939.[24]

Even at this early stage, therefore, the nature of the war was becoming clear. It was Hitler's response to the German predicament at the heart of Europe, an attempt to escape what he saw as her historic encirclement and subjugation. Now that he had given up all hopes of a British alliance, and of accommodation with Anglo-America, his language shifted from that of Nordic solidarity to that of a global class conflict in which he substituted nations for the classic Marxist social categories. The United States and the British Empire, on this reading, were the 'haves', the lords of all they surveyed. The Germans, by contrast, were firmly among the 'have-nots', ground down by the forces of 'plutocracy', which were determined to extirpate the contagious social model of the Nazi *Volksstaat*. They would have to redress the unjust global distribution of living space by force. The Führer also emphasized the ideological conflict between democracy and dictatorship. Finally, Hitler saw the struggle as a cosmic racial conflict, not just – most obviously – between Germans and Jews, but also an inter-Aryan civil war, between Teutons and Anglo-Saxons.

Allied strategy against the Third Reich in 1939 rested on blockading Germany and bringing the full weight of the combined British, French and (in effect) American economies to bear on the Reich. There was no immediate ground offensive, and instead of massive air-raids on German cities and factories, British and French aircraft dropped leaflets in what was still a largely political and 'phoney' war. The war at sea, by contrast, was waged with vigour from the start as the Allies sought to strangle Germany, and Hitler tried to keep their fingers off his throat. Considerable thought was given to the task of choking off German supplies of oil and iron ore.[25] Time was to expose the British and French strategy as complacent, but at the time it appeared compelling. The figures seemed to tell a clear story. Taken together, the economies of the British and French empires were easily twice the size of that of Germany, even before the United States was taken into account.[26] Their demographic potential, particularly if colonial possessions were taken into account, was also considerably larger.[27] It was only a matter of time before this huge potential was converted into raw military power and hurled against the Reich. On the face of it, the war with the west – even without the blockade – was a contest Germany simply could not win.

Hitler was painfully aware of all this, as his constant rhetoric about the ability of the Reich to outlast another blockade showed. Moreover, for all his public bluster about the decadence of the British, he retained a healthy respect for their spirit and racial quality. The Führer's sense of Germany's weakness was widely shared not only by the population at large but also by the military leadership. It was particularly marked in the Kriegsmarine, whose inferiority was so crushing that Admiral Raeder reacted to the outbreak of war by suggesting that it could only hope 'to die with decency' so as 'to provide the basis for a later rebuilding' of German naval power.[28] Later that month, he warned Hitler that he did not yet have enough submarines to starve out Britain. The army was in better shape, but its superiority over the combined French and British forces, once fully mobilized and deployed, was by no means clear. Likewise, the Luftwaffe enjoyed only a slight and eroding advantage over the RAF in quantity and quality of pilots and aircraft. Indeed, Hitler remained obsessed with the threat of allied air attack on German cities and especially on his exposed western industrial heartlands in the Ruhr. The Luftwaffe, by contrast, did not yet have the range to strike at England; it was still a purely tactical air force.[29]

The Führer's options in 1939 were limited. German society was already very highly mobilized.[30] The Allies would soon catch up as the outbreak of war ended the comparative advantage of dictatorship, namely the higher level of peacetime military and psychological mobilization. Besides, the blockade not merely restricted Germany's access to raw materials and foodstuffs, but also unplugged her from the world economy, which now became an instrument of the Allied war effort. One way or the other, as Keitel told the head of the War Economics Office, General Thomas, 'The Führer himself has recognized that we cannot last out a war of long duration. The war must be finished rapidly.'[31]

Faced with these realities, Hitler took some radical decisions with respect to the economy. All pretence of competing with the west in terms of consumption was abandoned. 'One cannot win the war against England with cookers and washing machines,' he told General Karl Becker, the head of army procurement in early November 1939.[32] Plans for social housing were largely deferred until the end of the war. Plan Z, the attempt to challenge the 'big ships' of the Royal Navy and the United States, was shelved at the start of the war. Hitler decided to concentrate on submarines instead. In late September, Hitler queried the need to continue construction of Germany's first aircraft carrier, the *Graf Zeppelin*, though he was dissuaded from halting it by Raeder.[33] With the army, the emphasis was not so much on tanks as on artillery and ammunition production, which suggests that Hitler was not expecting a *Blitzkrieg* but a long hard slog in the west.

Strategically, Hitler's was concerned to mitigate the effects of encirclement and the blockade. He stepped up efforts to bring Italy into the war as soon as possible. Hitler also pursued closer relations with Japan, principally with a view to keeping the US fleet tied up in the Pacific.[34] In late September 1939, as the Polish campaign was drawing to a close, Hitler received a delegation of visiting Japanese military. He told them that their two countries were the only two great powers in the world which had no clashing interests. The primary basis of German-Japanese collaboration, in other words, was not their mutual antagonism to the Soviet Union and communism, but their shared hostility to the Anglo-American world order.

Hitler's most useful partner, in fact, proved to be Stalin.[35] The Molotov–Ribbentrop Pact provided the Third Reich with the strategic depth and access to grain and oil with which to defy the blockade. Raeder even wanted to ask the Russians for bases from which to harass British shipping, and Hitler agreed to send the request to Moscow via Ribbentrop.[36] That said, Hitler did not regard the agreement as more than an expedient. He never denied his ideological differences with the Soviet Union, or took back anything that he had said, but he did stress the geopolitical common ground against London.[37] The confrontation with the west left him with little choice.

In this emerging global conflict Hitler's alignment with the Soviet Union chimed with the anti-plutocratic thrust of his global rhetoric. He appears to have been half-convinced that Moscow had turned away from Jewish Bolshevism towards a more authentically national Russian orientation, a development he had predicted during the early 1920s. 'At the moment [Soviet] internationalism seems to have receded,' he told the OKW privately later in the year, adding that this probably meant that she would go over to 'Panslavism'. 'It is hard to look into the future [on Russia],' Hitler concluded.[38] For this reason, the Nazi propaganda machine ceased all criticism of the Soviet Union and carefully began to extol the virtues of cooperation. The *Wochenschau* newsreels particularly praised the Russian supplies of foodstuffs and raw materials.[39]

The other way in which Hitler sought to escape the Allied chokehold was by avoiding direct military engagement with the western powers, especially Britain. On the eve of the invasion of Poland, he decreed that while vigorous action was to be undertaken in the east, in the west it was necessary 'to leave the responsibility for the start of hostilities clearly to Britain and France'. Likewise, the Luftwaffe was instructed, 'for now', to restrict operations to the 'repulsion of enemy air attacks across the borders of the Reich'. Hitler was particularly concerned not to provoke the Royal Navy at sea, where the danger of an unexpected clash was much greater. He had decreed at the start of the war that the main thrust of the war at sea should be against British commerce, but it was not until the end of September that Hitler actually authorized the Kriegsmarine ships at large in the Atlantic – in particular the *Graf Spee* and the *Deutschland* – to commence operations. This was followed shortly after by an instruction telling captains to avoid risky engagements as far as possible in order to deny the British cheap propaganda victories. The Führer's sense of naval inferiority was thus palpable. Towards the close of the year, his concerns were vindicated by the fate of the pocket battleship *Graf Spee*. It enjoyed a short career attacking British shipping but was eventually cornered by the Royal Navy off Montevideo and forced to scuttle, to Hitler's great embarrassment.[40] Within weeks, therefore, it was clear that Germany was in practice primarily a regional actor in a world of global powers.

The Führer was also determined to keep the United States out of the war for as long as possible; he wanted to capture Warsaw quickly in order to present the American Congress with a fait accompli when it met after the summer recess.[41] Hitler was well aware, and his diplomats and intelligence services reminded him on many occasions, that much of the New World's immense potential would soon be at the service of the Allies. These fears were realized when the Roosevelt administration put in place a 'cash and carry' system which in practice meant that only the Western Allies could buy American arms. The American embassy in Berlin was formally correct in its behaviour towards the Reich, but largely hostile in practice.[42] Hitler was equally aware, however, that it would take some time for the Americans to be militarily and psychologically ready for war with the Reich.[43] One way or the other, propagandistic bluster aside, there was hardly anyone in the leadership of the Third Reich, least of all Hitler, who seriously believed that a war with Britain and the United States would be easy or even winnable.

For all these reasons, Hitler's diplomacy after September 1939 was dominated by the desire to maintain American neutrality and a genuine wish to reach a negotiated solution with Britain, albeit on his own terms.[44] The Führer was, as he told Halder four days into the war with the west, 'ready to negotiate',[45] hoping at the very least to drive a wedge between Britain and France. Over the next eighteen months or so, Hitler made repeated diplomatic, rhetorical and back-channel overtures to London. On 19 September he used his first wartime radio speech to inaugurate a veritable peace offensive. Hitler spoke in Danzig, no doubt to emphasize his military success, blamed Poland's predicament on the western powers and held out an olive branch.[46] A week later, as the Polish campaign was drawing to a close, he received the intermediary Birger Dahlerus with a view to restarting talks.

Hitler's hope for a peaceful solution with Britain drove his policy towards Poland. To be sure, his attitude towards that country had hardened considerably since the spring of 1939 and it deteriorated further in the course of the campaign. His visits to the front had left him with a highly unfavourable impression. The Poles had only a 'thin Germanic layer' below which the 'material' was 'terrible', he told Rosenberg in late September 1939, adding that the 'Jews' were the 'most awful thing one could image' and that the 'cities were bristling with dirt'.[47] This was not just rhetoric. Shortly after the fighting started, Hitler instructed the army not to interfere with the murderous activities of the SS. So while the Wehrmacht fought the Poles largely according to the rules of war, the treatment meted out to them by the SS and other formations was extraordinarily brutal from the start.[48] When all is said and done, however, it is possible that it was the approach of war, and the conflict itself, which irrevocably turned Hitler into an extreme anti-Polish racist rather than the other way around.[49] In his mind, the Poles had forced him to treat them badly, and he never forgave them for it.

That said, Hitler kept his options open in Poland for at least six weeks after the invasion began, partly in the residual hope of securing its assistance against the Soviet Union, but mainly in order to facilitate an agreement with London. In his remarks to Halder shortly after the British declaration of war, he held out the possibility that 'rump Poland' would be 'recognized', adding that while Germany would control the Narew and the Warsaw industrial area, 'Krakau, Polen' and 'Ukraine' [sic] would be 'independent'.[50] A month into the invasion, Hitler was still considering options for Poland, one of which was a 'rump state'.[51] This suggests that Hitler had not given up his idea of a modus vivendi with Poland based on joint expansion eastwards. A certain residual respect for Poland, even after the invasion, was evident in the fact that Hitler praised Marshal Piłsudski as 'a man of indisputable realist understanding and energy' in his Danzig speech of 19 September, blaming his death for the renewed hostility between Germany and Poland.[52] The Führer also ordered an honour guard to be placed outside Marshal Piłsudski's final resting place in Cracow, where it remained throughout the entire German occupation.[53]

These moves culminated in a dramatic Reichstag address on 6 October 1939, in which Hitler announced victory in Poland and offered Britain a peace settlement which would include an ill-defined rump Polish state-hood.[54] This offer was not merely tactically motivated but – by his own lights – sincerely meant.[55] Failure to accept the proffered hand, he warned, would lead to the destruction of the British Empire. 'This annihilatory struggle,' Hitler proclaimed, 'will not be limited to the mainland [of Europe]. No. It will spread far across the sea. There are no more islands today.'[56]

The war increasingly absorbed most of Hitler's attention after September 1939, but that does not mean that he completely neglected domestic politics. On the contrary, the conflict drove a renewed engagement with internal affairs. Hitler was determined to avoid the repetition of the events of 1918, and therefore stressed the need to build the national solidarity he felt had been missing during the world war.[57] He paid close attention to the summaries of the surveillance services on the state of popular opinion. Following some particularly critical reports in the autumn of 1939, for example, Hitler authorized an increased fat ration for children.[58] To keep up morale at home, the Führer tried to maintain the – albeit restricted – supply of consumer goods. He symbolically insisted on sharing the privations of the home front, for instance by supposedly running his household on ration coupons.[59] The 'Winter Relief Organization', which supplied coal and clothing to poorer Germans, also helped spread the burdens of war, at least psychologically, and to convince Britain of Germany's will to resist. The Führer's speech introducing the initiative stressed that he was looking for the 'self-help of the people' through the 'willing-ness to sacrifice' rather than ordaining it through an 'appeal to the tax-payer'.[60]

Hitler also recognized the need to maintain cultural life even during wartime, partly to keep up the spirits of the population and partly to continue the process of gradual racial elevation of the German people through the appreciation of true art. For his own part, he largely ceased to watch films or to attend concerts and the opera, but he was concerned that the German people would not want for either entertainment or improve-ment, even and especially during the war. The plans for a huge art museum in Linz, for which Hans Posse presented detailed ideas in October 1939, continued to command Hitler's attention,[61] as did his various other projects, despite the demands of conflict.

On the negative side, Hitler further stepped up the suppression of inter-nal dissent and the establishment of ideological coherence, especially in the Wehrmacht. In late September 1939, he set up the Reich Security Main Office (RSHA), which brought all the main German police and security agencies under the direct control of Heinrich Himmler. At around the same time, Hitler agreed 'in principle' to Rosenberg's plan for the 'securing of the National Socialist ideology' in the army.[62] He was determined to prevent a repetition of the protests by some commanders, such as General Blaskowitz, against the behaviour of the SS in Poland, and to steel the army for the long war ahead. A visible sign of Hitler's displeasure with the Wehrmacht and the rising importance of the SS was the creation of new SS military formations. On 18 September 1939, he instructed that the SS Death's Head units, who were tasked with guarding the concentration camps, should detach the younger cohorts for military service in SS regiments and if possible divisions. For now, these formations were to remain under the operational control of the army.[63] The trend, though, was already clear.

The war also accelerated Hitler's plans for the racial transformation of Germany. He expected heavy casualties among the 'best' elements fighting at the front, and decreasing conceptions due to long separations of husbands and wives. One way of compensating for this was through a positive eugenics of increasing the numbers of 'higher-value' births. Some of this could be achieved through traditional methods, such as celebrating Mother's Day or awarding particularly fecund women the *Mutterkreuz*. More controversially, the concept of illegitimacy came under increasing attack, as men – especially those in the SS – were urged to defy convention and produce as many children as possible.[64] Hitler does not at this point seem to have taken much interest in this idea. The problem with supposed positive eugenics, in any case, was that it was a slow process of improvement, bringing change over the longer term. It was a viable strategy in a country at peace but the advent of war meant that this approach had run out of time.

Several factors conspired to drive a radicalization of Hitler's already extreme racial policies from September 1939. War put a new premium on negative eugenics, which could be implemented quickly, albeit at a high domestic and diplomatic price. In October 1939, Hitler ordered Brandt and Bouhler to go ahead secretly with the euthanasia programme, in defiance of the known objections of the Catholic Church and other groupings.[65] The measure was retrospectively dated to the start of the war on 1 September, showing the link Hitler made between the two.[66] Finally, the conquest of Poland had brought with it the unplanned and unwanted acquisition of millions of Polish Jews. According to Hitler's logic, these would have to be deported or otherwise dealt with, partly because they represented 'useless' mouths to be fed, and partly because they constituted a threat behind

German lines.[67] In all of these cases, the war did not so much provide cover for long-planned measures, though this was a consideration, as necessitate in Hitler's mind the speeding-up of what had originally been envisaged as a longer-term and thus more evolutionary process.

The outbreak of war did not fundamentally change Hitler's role in the German political system.[68] Despite this, the polycratic nature of the Third Reich was aggravated by the proliferation of new institutions related to the running of the war economy and military operations. The supreme command typified this phenomenon, as well as reflecting the primacy of the struggle against the west. It was divided between the High Command of the Army (OKH), the army leadership, which later ran the war in the east, and the High Command of the Wehrmacht (OKW), which co-ordinated the three services, ran all other theatres and had general superintendence over the conflict as a whole. There was also no fundamental shift in the character of Nazi high politics. Bitter feuding persisted at all levels, despite the fact that Hitler gave it no encouragement whatsoever.[69] He gave strict instructions that ministers should try to resolve their differences without involving him first.[70] Politics continued to revolve around Hitler himself, the only difference being that the Führer's Headquarters was added to the list of existing centres of power. Perhaps surprisingly, he had not prepared a large central bunker complex from which to direct the war, but rather operated from a series of bespoke regional ones.[71] The Führer's Headquarters was thus an institution, not a place; it was where the Führer was at any given time.

What changed after the outbreak of war was not the extent of Hitler's authority, which was never directly challenged, but its focus. He began to withdraw from day-to-day domestic politics and became inaccessible. Face-to-face meetings with members of the civilian administration, which had been quite common in the 1930s, were increasingly replaced by the dispatch of documents for approval. Likewise, the Führer basically no longer attended the meetings of the *Gauleiter*, but received them afterwards.[72] That said, Hitler remained the ultimate arbiter, and in full control of those areas which mattered most to him, namely ideology, foreign policy and the overall conduct of the war. His immediate supervision of domestic policy was more and more reduced over time, to be sure, but he remained engaged there to the end. As we shall see, he retained tight control over matters affecting popular morale such as rations, prices and the conscription of women. The Führer determined the main lines of development and it was not possible to achieve anything against his will or to change a course he had embarked upon without his express permission. The men around him, including the increasingly ubiquitous Martin Bormann, were executive organs, not controlling ones.[73] Hitler was still in charge, the uncontested master in the Third Reich.

On 12 October 1939, Chamberlain finally rejected German overtures for a negotiated settlement. Despite the fact that this had been on the cards for some time, Hitler was disappointed and furious.[74] London's refusal to compromise had two far-reaching consequences. First, it settled Poland's fate; Stalin's relentless hostility to any form of independent existence for the Poles also influenced the Führer's position.[75] Hitler dropped the idea of a rump Polish state and all restraint towards the population. The treatment of Poles, already very grim, became even harsher. On 17 October 1939, he reprimanded German officers who were conducting discussions with Polish grandees about a possible collaborationist regime.[76] Parts of pre-war Poland were directly annexed to Germany. Towards the end of October, Hitler corralled the remaining Poles under his control into the 'General Government' under the direction of Hans Frank.[77] He had already begun in early October to deport Jews from Germany into reservations there. Concrete instructions were now issued to suppress the entire Polish intelligentsia.[78] All this was done 'on the hoof', not in accordance with any longstanding plan.[79] Hitler's original hope and expectation had been that he would conduct the attack on Russia with the cooperation, or at least the toleration, of Poland. Instead, he now found himself in alliance with the Soviet Union and in occupation of large swathes of Polish territory with millions of Poles, many of them Jews.

The short- to medium-term future of this space, and those who lived in it, was unclear. Hitler still planned to use it as a staging ground for an invasion of the Soviet Union,[80] but the continuing war with Britain complicated this. Time, so short in August 1939, now seemed to expand again. *Lebensraum* in the east remained very much on Hitler's mind, but it would have to wait until the western flank was secure. In the meantime, Hitler announced a joint 'redevelopment project' with the Soviet Union to remove at least part of the European 'causes of conflict'. This involved extensive 'resettlements', not just of Poles but also of Germans.[81] It was driven by a very simple and unexpected fact. From the start, Hitler's policy had been to secure, for the cooped-up German people, the necessary living space in the east to counter-balance Anglo-America. Now he found himself in control of a large territory with nobody to put in it. Hitler faced the same problem in Bohemia and Moravia, albeit in a less extreme form. With full employment in Germany, and little economic migration to the United States or elsewhere, there was no incentive for Reich Germans to settle in Poland or for that matter in the Protectorate. Hitler had no actual demographic surplus to distribute. Instead of a 'people without space', it was now a case of a 'space without people'.

Hitler responded to this problem in three ways. First, he cast around for alternative sources of Germans. Some of these were to come from South Tyrol, where the transfer of the those who had 'opted' for Germany was finalized in October 1939,[82] but most of them were sourced in the Baltic States and the Soviet Union. German populations there were to be repatriated in a huge 'Home to the Reich' operation. Hitler seems to have hit on this solution, which featured in none of his earlier writings or pre-war plans, largely by accident. Originally, he had only intended to absorb those Germans who had shown strong Nazi or nationalist inclinations, but he was prevailed upon by the leader of the German minority in Latvia to save all Baltic Germans from Stalin's clutches. One way or the other, the German-Soviet 'Border and Friendship Treaty' of 28 September created facts on the ground by formalizing the new territorial arrangements.[83]

The new policy was laid out in Hitler's 'Decree for the Strengthening of the German *Volk*' of 7 October 1939. Good racial fences, he suggested, made good neighbours. With this in mind, Hitler undertook to retrieve 'German people who have previously been compelled to live abroad', to achieve 'better demarcations' with the other groups in 'its' – that is Germany's – 'space'.[84] Himmler was tasked with job of 'bringing back' to the Reich the relevant Germans from abroad to facilitate the 'establishment of a new German farmer class', especially through the cultivation of 'new German areas of settlement' by returnees. Over the next fifteen months or so, a series of treaties was concluded with Estonia, Latvia, Romania, Hungary and the Soviet Union in order to facilitate the 'return' of their German populations.[85] Their extent suggests that Hitler had pushed plans for an immediate attack on Russia to a more distant date, because it made no sense to withdraw Germans from thence only to return them a year later (unless he feared they might be used as hostages, but that concern was never mentioned, or even alluded to).[86]

Hitler's remarks to Rosenberg around this time show that his timeframe had indeed expanded again. Immediate war with Russia was not on the agenda; the main concern was wrapping up the Polish campaign and dealing with Britain and France. More to the point, Hitler's vision for Poland itself suggests that he did not necessarily expect to move east again in the near future. For a short period, the locus of *Lebensraum*, which had been firmly in Russia since the 1920s, moved west to Poland. The Führer announced his intention to build 'an impregnable Ostwall on the Vistula, even stronger than in the west'. He also wanted to establish a 'broad belt of Germanization and colonization' at that border. This would be 'an enormous task', namely to create 'a German granary' with 'a strong German farming class' drawn from 'good Germans from across the world'. The phrasing hints that Hitler may even have hoped to lure Germans back from overseas, including the United States. He concluded by remarking that only 'the future' would show whether it would be possible 'to advance the settlement belt after several decades had passed'.[87] In other words, Hitler was now thinking of a war with the Soviet Union only at some future moment, perhaps decades away.

The Führer's second method of filling the space suddenly available to him was to take a closer look at the racial composition of the Polish people. Having lurched from friendship towards extreme hostility within a few months, he swung back a little in the other direction. Hitler had long rejected traditional Germanization programmes with their emphasis on language, and claimed that one could only 'Germanize' the land and not the people. Now, however, he spoke of assimilating as many Poles as possible.[88] 'Those elements which are considered racially valuable,' Hitler stated, could be 'Germanized'; this placed him closer to the more 'moderate' Gauleiter Förster of Danzig than to Gauleiter Greiser of the Wartheland, who relied on killings and deportations.[89] 'The basis' on which the selection was made, he continued, must be 'racial appearance and heredity.' Hitler argued that the tribes originally inhabiting these areas had 'in any case been half shot-through with Slavic and German blood', because the German farmers who settled there hundreds of years ago had been short of women and therefore mated with 'hot-blooded Slavic women'. The solution, Hitler proclaimed, lay in 'language', demanding that 'children must forget Polish and only learn German'. Children thus became a particular focus of the occupation policy. Much could be made of a Pole, the Führer believed, if he were caught young.[90]

It was the start of the greatest assimilation project in modern German history, paradoxically carried out by the man who had condemned similar efforts by the Second Reich.[91] This was less of a volte face than it appeared, however, because Hitler viewed the process of assimilation not as the cultural and linguistic Germanization of racial Slavs, but as the discovery and filtering-out of Germanic elements within the Polish and Czech peoples. In practice, though, the result was the same. Hitler had originally wanted to retrieve and retain the racial cream that had been skimmed off for generations by the Anglo-Americans. Now he found himself picking over what many in his entourage thought of as the central and eastern European dregs. He had little choice. In the absence of high-value colonists from the Reich, or better still returnees from Anglo-America, Hitler had to make do with what was available. These measures pointed to a trend which was to become ever more apparent as the war dragged on. While conflict initially put an end to positive eugenics, and privileged the instant gratification of negative eugenics through deportation, sterilization or murder, the longer it lasted, the lower Hitler's own racial 'standards' fell.

Finally, the Führer sought to remedy the shortage of colonists by reforming German agriculture, especially in the west. This had long been characterized by subdivision and inefficiency. Hitler let it be known that he wanted families whose small holdings in western Germany had been rationalized and the younger sons of farmers to be settled in the east.[92] The slogan for the east would be 'settlement' and in the west it would be 'reallocation', meaning rationalization; the two were closely connected in Hitler's mind. Here the Führer ruled against Walther Darré, who wanted large numbers of smaller holdings, and in favour of Himmler, who desired larger 'defensive farms'. In effect, he was attempting to replicate the primogeniture of the large British estates, the extensive farming of the United States, and perhaps also ancient Rome's land grants to former legionaries. This was not an agrarian utopia, but an American-style vision. To Hitler, therefore, the modernization of German agriculture and the colonization of the east went hand in hand.

The second consequence of Chamberlain's rejection of Hitler's peace overtures, which he feared long before the final response became known, was that the Führer took off the gloves against Britain. 'If the British don't want peace,' the Führer told Rosenberg in late September 1939, he 'would fall upon them with every means at his disposal and destroy them.'[93] He now wanted to do so without further delay. Despite the fact that Germany's preparations were incomplete, Hitler believed that the 'relative balance' would 'not shift to our advantage', but rather that the 'defensive power of the enemy' would 'gradually increase'. If the west was badly equipped with tanks, then this would probably 'no longer be the case' in '6–8 months' time'.[94] Besides, the Führer warned, as the war dragged on the British would be more likely to browbeat the Dutch, Belgians and other neutrals into taking their side. While Germany's social and national cohesion waned as Allied propaganda took effect, Allied aircraft would attack the industry of the Ruhr, enabling Britain to bring the weight of the international economy on the Reich. 'In this sense,' the Führer concluded, 'every further month's delay' in attacking the Anglo-French armies would make the Wehrmacht's job more difficult. If Hitler could now wait in the east, time was running out in the west.[95]

Whatever Hitler may have said about British decadence before the outbreak of war, most of which was designed to disarm objections to his confrontational course, he continued to entertain a strong sense of Britain's innate strength and racial value. The real danger, he told the senior military, was that increasing British mobilization would provide France with 'additional military capacity of high psychological and material value'. Unlike much of the High Command, which was worried about the French army, the Führer saw the upcoming campaign primarily as a contest with Britain. Hitler therefore earnestly warned against the 'under-estimation of British units', particularly in a defensive role, because the 'internal constitution of the Briton' made him a tenacious fighter. This was an allusion to his experience of British toughness during the First World War. Six weeks later, Hitler returned to this theme. 'I am worried by the ever greater presence of the British,' he told the generals. 'The Briton is a tough enemy, especially in defence,' he warned.[96]

The only sphere in which Hitler felt superior to Britain was culture. 'The cultural creativity of Britain,' he remarked, 'is a chapter in itself.' 'We Germans,' he continued, 'certainly do not need any lectures from the British in the field of culture.' 'Our music, our poetry, our architecture, our painting, our sculpture,' he claimed in an enumeration reminiscent of the second verse of the 'Deutschlandlied', did not need to fear comparison with those of Britain. 'I believe that a single German, let us say Beethoven,' Hitler went on, 'has achieved more musically than all Englishmen past and present put together.' This was, of course, a familiar trope from German nationalist rhetoric of the nineteenth century, when patriots had sought to compensate for their manifest political weakness through claims of cultural supremacy.[97] Ironically, Hitler was reprising these themes at a time when he had long since driven many of Germany's most important cultural figures into exile in Anglo-America.

Politically, Hitler's aim was the reversal of the Treaty of Westphalia, in his view the root of all evil in modern German history. The very first line of his memorandum on the forthcoming campaign in the west claimed that 'the dissolution of the first Reich caused by the peace of Münster in 1648' had led to the system of the European 'balance of power'. This had enabled the emergence of the French but 'especially' of the British Empire. The 'decisive characteristic' of this settlement, which had also been desired by Britain, had been the 'fragmentation of the German people'. Hitler thus transferred the primary responsibility for the maintenance of the Westphalian system from its originator, France, to its supposed principal current protagonist, Britain. This was a theme to which Hitler returned again and again over the next eight months or so.[98] Hitler's objection to Westphalia was partly territorial, in that he grieved over the loss of western lands to other countries, but his main concern was conceptual. To him, the treaties epitomized the internal fragmentation and external subordination of the Reich.[99]

The Führer was determined to attack in the west at the earliest possible opportunity. Despite the fact that the vast majority of enemy ground forces there were French, his main target was Britain.[100] Failure to attack, he warned a fortnight later, would allow Britain to box in the German U-boats in the North Sea. To this end, Hitler repeated his demand for the 'destruction of the Franco-British army', which was 'the precondition' for a 'brutal operation against the heart of the British will to resist' in due course.[101] The purpose of the offensive in the west was thus not so much the delivery of military force against the Allied field armies, as the delivery of political effect in London.

Hitler put his stamp on the planned western offensive from the start, both strategically and operationally. He was adamant that one would not simply repeat the 'hackneyed' Schlieffen Plan of 1914. He was already confident that tanks could be sent through the Ardennes, and planned to separate British and French forces.[102] Hitler gave instructions for the capture of the bridges over the Meuse through a *coup de main* and for the use of airborne forces.[103] He ordered that the operation should have no 'established centre of gravity' to begin with, but that it should acquire one in accordance with the 'early successes' to exploit any breakthroughs.[104] Hitler also had a clear vision of the nature of the conflict to come. He demanded that the advancing German armoured spearheads should avoid being caught up in the 'warren of endless terraces of Belgian towns'. The key thing was for them to maintain their 'mobility' and to prevent the enemy front from stabilizing. Hitler called for 'improvisations' and the 'massing' of tanks and guns. He predicted that the 'effect of such a mass deployment, especially of the 8.8 mm [guns]' would be 'devastating' for the enemy. Bombing was to be used not only to destroy enemy positions but also to 'demoralize' them.[105] This was in fact almost exactly how the campaign unfolded.

The planning was accompanied by a renewed propagandistic bombardment of Britain, which was singled out for particular treatment; the French were criticized, if at all, more in sorrow than in anger. Hitler attacked the British Empire on two fronts. On the one hand, he argued that Germany was simply behaving in Europe as Britain had always done across the world, only with greater justification and effectiveness. He contrasted the mayhem in the British mandates over the Arabs of the Middle East with the order the Third Reich had swiftly established among the Slavs of central Europe.[106] A month later, he elaborated on this theme. 'If an

Englishman argues today that he is responsible for the fate of peoples of central and eastern Europe,' he argued, 'then I can only answer that we are equally responsible for the fate of the peoples in Palestine, in Arabia, in Egypt, and even in India.' The symmetry here was clear: if there were to be British mandates in the rest of the world, then why not German protectorates in Europe?

If Hitler wanted to hunt with the imperialist hounds, he was also increasingly running with the colonized hares. The idea that Germany had been enslaved by the British Empire and international high finance, which had been so prominent in his rhetoric throughout the 1920s, and had always been close to the surface after 1933, now returned with a vengeance. Even the simple pleasures of life, he complained, were at the mercy of the empire. Why should the British decide, Hitler asked, whether the Germans drank coffee? He condemned the British for 'oppressing' 350 million Indians, in 'exactly the same way' as millions of Germans were trodden underfoot.[107] Hitler's empathy extended to the other wretched of the earth. He lampooned British claims to be fighting for 'the right to self-determination of the peoples', for where were these rights more denied than in the British Empire, where the principle apparently did not apply? Remarkably, Hitler also rebutted British claims to defend 'civilization', given conditions in 'British mining areas, slums in Whitechapel and in other areas of mass poverty and social degeneration'. For Hitler, the battle against the British Empire was an international class struggle, in which nations took the place of classes. The conflict was framed not just as a German war of national liberation against British domination of the continent, but as a global insurrection against Anglo-American capitalism and imperialism.

The Jews were central to this rhetoric, though they were by no means the Führer's only target. He inveighed against the 'money magnates', the 'Jewish and non-Jewish international bank barons' who were trying to destroy the Germany of the 'welfare laws for workers' which had 'removed class distinctions' in the Reich and eliminated unemployment.[108] So fearful were Germany's enemies of this model of 'welfare and social compromise', he claimed, that they feared 'that their own people might be infected by it'. In this respect, apparently, Nazism was for export after all. The regime attached such importance to this passage in Hitler's speech that it was reprinted in the official journal of the Reich Labour Ministry shortly afterwards.[109] Hitler was still trying to 'internationalize' the Jewish question. It was in this spirit that he described his 'peace' speech to the Reichstag as 'an attempt to order and regulate the Jewish problem'.[110]

Hitler saw this campaign as an exercise in self-defence, retaliation against the fearsome British propaganda machine and its supposed Jewish allies in the world, especially the American press. He repeatedly referred throughout the conflict, as he had throughout his career, to 'Jewish-international [capitalism and] journalism' and 'certain international press organs'.[111] Hitler kept a close eye on what British and American magazines were saying from the start of the war, requesting to see the original copies.[112] There were representatives of the Deutscher Nachrichtendienstbüro (DNB) stationed in the Führer's Headquarters to supply the Führermaterialdienst with foreign news, military communiqués and press announcements at Dietrich's request. One way or the other, Hitler's enmity towards Britain had become all-embracing by late 1939. 'I want to beat Britain, whatever it costs,' he told Goebbels, 'and all my thoughts and actions are geared towards that end.'[113]

British enmity was also the framework within which Hitler interpreted the attempt on his life by Georg Elser. The would-be assassin had concealed a bomb in a pillar of the Munich Bürgerbräukeller, timed to explode as Hitler gave the traditional annual address to commemorate the failed putsch of 1923. That evening, however, the Führer left early in order to visit Unity Mitford in hospital. The change of plan saved his life, because the bomb went off as planned, causing extensive damage and loss of life. Despite the fact that Elser was a communist sympathizer, who was carrying an emblem of the Rotfrontkämpferbund when he was arrested, Hitler was convinced that British Intelligence was behind the plot. Goebbels claimed in the Völkischer Beobachter of 15 November 1939 that 'the assassin is called Britain'. Later Hitler thought it might have been Bavarian monar-chists, and for a while Goebbels even privately blamed Otto Strasser.[114] In truth, there is no evidence of a link between British Intelligence and Elser, who appears to have acted completely alone.

Hitler was still relatively unconcerned by the Soviet Union. Elser's manifest communist connections do not seem to have weighed heavily with him. Nor did he fear an immediate Russian attack. 'Russia,' he told the generals in late November 1939, 'is currently no threat', on account of its internal divisions and the weakness of the Red Army. Besides, Hitler added, 'there was the treaty'. This might well change in the future, but he was not expecting any trouble at least for 'the next one or two years'. Hitler was also unworried by Stalin's ambitions in Scandinavia, which the Molotov–Ribbentrop Pact greatly facilitated. As conflict between Finland and the Soviet Union loomed, the visiting Swedish explorer Sven Hedin found him obsessed with Britain.[115] Hitler even described Stalin's demands as 'moderate'. He certainly showed no sense of racial solidarity with the 'Nordic' peoples or any interest in Scan-dinavia outside of his struggle with Britain.[116] No significance should be attached to his very occasional loose use of the phrase 'Greater German

Reich', which almost certainly referred to the Greater Germany of the nineteenth century rather than any ambitions in Northern Europe.[117] Unlike Himmler, in fact, the Führer did not take Scandinavians – whom he considered harmless and dozy fishermen[118] – very seriously.

This did not change after Russia invaded Finland on 30 November 1939. True to the spirit of the pact with Stalin, Hitler imposed an arms embargo on the Finns. His only concern was that trouble in Scandinavia might give Britain a pretext to intervene there and cut Germany off from her source of Swedish raw materials.[119] The Kriegsmarine, which wanted bases in Norway to attack Britain, brought Hitler to a meeting with the former Norwegian defence minister and extreme right-wing politician Vidkun Quisling on 12 December in Berlin. Soon after, Hitler gave orders to plan the invasion of Norway. The operation was conceived not as an extension of German *Lebensraum* or the recovery of a Nordic 'fraternal people', but rather as a pre-emptive strike against any British attempt to interfere with his supplies of iron ore.

Hitler was much more concerned about the United States, at least in the medium and long term. The naval leadership warned him not long after Chamberlain finally rejected the peace overtures that the American position would be decisive. They also argued, and Hitler agreed, that it was vital to pursue the 'siege of Britain' with all possible vigour even at the risk of bringing the United States into the war. The sooner radical measures were taken at sea, the argument went, the shorter the war.[120] It was clear to both the navy and Hitler that American belligerency was not merely possible but likely; it was not a question of whether, but of when. He let it be known that he believed that the war would be over before the Americans were ready to enter it.[121] In late 1939, Hitler was mildly reassured by the reports from his Washington military attaché, Boetticher, that the United States needed another year or so for its military preparations to be complete.[122] Time, however, was not Germany's friend, and the Führer knew it. 'Thanks to her neutrality laws,' Hitler told his generals, America was 'not yet a threat. The strengthening of the enemy through America was not yet substantial.'[123] There was a lot in that double 'not yet'.

The Führer's anxiety about the United States went beyond just military considerations. He continued to be exercised about the American cultural challenge. Hitler knew that the Germans still hankered after Hollywood, even or especially after the outbreak of war. 'I understand you didn't like the movie last night,' he teased Eva Braun on the terrace of the Berghof, 'I know what you want. You want *Gone with the Wind*.'[124] This reference to a film released in December 1939 shows Hitler's consciousness of the enduring power of American popular culture. Yet his preoccupation with the United States went deeper still. In mid December 1939, despite all the pressures of war, Hitler received the American racial theorist Lothrop Stoddard in the Imperial Chancellery. Stoddard's book *The Rising Tide of Color Against White World-Supremacy* had been published in 1920 with a preface by none other than Madison Grant; the German translation appeared five years later. By prior agreement, the content of their discussion was kept completely confidential, but Stoddard spoke freely of his other exchanges. He registered with astonishment that many German racial theorists, like Hitler, did not consider the German people as 'Nordic' but as a mixture of races.[125] The task of creating an actual Nordic race in Germany, therefore, still lay ahead.

Hitler's preoccupation with Anglo-America dominated his *Lebensraum* rhetoric during this period, no less than it had in the past. 'I am stepping for the first time on soil,' he announced in his speech on 19 September 1939 in Danzig, 'which German settlers took possession of half a millennium before the first whites settled in today's state of New York.'[126] Two months later, Hitler lamented to his generals that German history was characterized by 'the adjustment of the number of inhabitants to the lack of space through emigration'. The trauma of losing so many millions of Germans to Anglo-America clearly persisted. Failure to address the lack of space, Hitler argued, would lead to 'national death' through further 'haemorrhaging'. 'I have decided to take a different path,' he concluded, which was 'the adjustment of living space to the number of inhabitants.' This, he averred, could only be done 'by the sword'. Unlike earlier contests this would be a 'racial struggle' for 'oilfields, rubber, minerals, etc.' The ultimate enemy here – 'Britain has been against us since 1870' – was not Jewry or Slavdom, but the rival Nordics who controlled these resources. The racial struggle he was referring to, in other words, was an inter-Nordic civil war, the second titanic clash of the Aryans in two decades.

Hitler's planned western offensive was hugely controversial among the Wehrmacht High Command. Most of them had experienced the British and French during the First World War. They had doubts about the quality of the new army and also about the resilience of the home front. An all-or-nothing attack would be a huge gamble. Despite the authoritarian nature of the Third Reich, Hitler's growing authority, and their ingrained sense of obedience, many generals protested vocally. Not long after Hitler's intentions became known, Brauchitsch was given the task of 'talking the Führer out of his plans'.[127] Several generals wrote to express their reservations. Halder, Oster and Stülpnagel even began to plot Hitler's removal, at least if he ordered a disastrous attack in the west. Mutiny was in the air.[128]

The Führer was incensed. He inveighed against the 'spirit of Zossen', an allusion to the supreme headquarters of the army, and accused the generals, especially Brauchitsch, of cowardice.[129] Nevertheless, he showed willingness to compromise on some important issues. The operational plan remained a subject of furious debate throughout the winter, with constant interference from the Führer, and was by no means finalized.[130] Hitler was also prepared to yield on the date. He had originally wanted to attack by 12 November 1939, which would have given the Wehrmacht only three weeks to prepare. Brauchitsch succeeded in persuading him to delay. Early in the following month, Hitler decreed a further postponement of a week, finally agreeing to wait until the following year. In the end, the date of the attack was to be postponed twenty-nine times.

On the main issue, however, Hitler was absolutely unyielding. He would launch a decisive attack in the west, come what may. The Führer concluded his speech to the generals in late November with a vow. 'I will stand or fall in this battle,' he proclaimed. 'I will not survive the defeat of my people. No capitulation towards the outside and no revolution from within.'[131] The generals had their answer. Hitler would grapple with Britain, which he defined a few days later as 'bearer of the fighting spirit and the leading enemy power'. 'Beating Britain,' he insisted, 'is the precondition for final victory.'[132] The question was no longer whether Hitler would attack in the west, but how and when.

In his 1940 New Year's Day address Hitler asserted that the aim of the 'Jewish-capitalist world enemy' was to 'destroy Germany' and 'the German people'. This was because the Third Reich represented a youthful, dynamic and popular challenge to the international ruling elite, which he understood in national and generational rather than in class terms. The Germans, Hitler claimed in late January 1940, were one of the 'young peoples' of the world. They were challenging the 'so-called propertied classes among the people' who had 'robbed' Germany and were simply sitting on their ill-gotten gains. On this reading, the Germans were, so to speak, at best the poor whites of the international system. In this spirit, Hitler professed sympathy with the other wretched of the earth who groaned under the weight of imperialism and capitalism, particularly that of the British Empire. His empathy extended to not merely the Nordic Boers, but also the decidedly non-Aryan Arabs. Hitler reminded his listeners again that it was the British who 'invented the concentration camp',[133] and argued that the blockade of Germany was simply the latest version of age-old method of waging war against women and children. Once again, Hitler was far more exercised about the earlier British than the current Soviet camps.

The Führer was also worried by Allied propaganda. The Allies hit back, trying to fragment Germans. Instead of bombing the Ruhr as Hitler had feared, British and French aircraft dropped millions of leaflets on Germany, calling on the population to rise up against the Nazis. This strategy has been much derided since, but it struck fear into Hitler's heart. He had seen the colossal effect of Allied propaganda on German morale during the First World War. Hitler claimed that the success of National Socialism over the previous six years had inoculated German society against the Franco-British poison. Never again, he vowed, would Germans be gulled by Allied disinformation into launching an internal revolution like in 1918.[134] Hitler was in fact very far from believing German unity to be beyond question, which explains the frequency and vehemence with which he asserted the opposite.

If the war seemed becalmed on the surface, there was frenetic activity behind the scenes in Berlin. By now, the generals had accepted the need to attack in the west, and internalized the Führer's view that the main thrust should be against Britain.[135] On 10 January 1940, Hitler set an attack date for a week later. That same day, however, a German aircraft with the plans for *Fall Gelb* on board crash-landed near Mechelen on the Belgian side of the border. The weather was in any case too inclement to permit an attack. On 16 January, Hitler postponed the attack to the spring and went back to the drawing board. A month later, Erich von Manstein presented an audacious plan to send German armour through the rugged Ardennes to divide the British and French armies and force them back to the sea. Hitler was enthusiastic. On 24 February 1940, what has become known to history as the *Sichelschnitt* plan was formally adopted.

More or less the entire Wehrmacht was deployed to the west; only small screening units remained in the east. Hitler took a keen interest in details, such as the airborne operation against the Belgian fort Eben-Emael, which covered the approaches to Liège, and in the passage of the panzers through the difficult terrain of the Ardennes.[136] He generally favoured the most audacious solution. His confidence in the plan was absolute, promising the architect Hermann Giesler that he would soon be able to show him Paris.[137] All the same, neither Hitler nor the German High Command was envisaging a quick end to the war, but at best a devastating blow against the Allies in Belgium, followed by an aerial campaign against Britain, and a war of attrition against the remaining French forces either somewhere around the Somme or further south.

The expectation of a longer war and concern about the growing British presence in France were reflected in the renewed stress on greater armaments production; Hitler was in no sense expecting a 'lightning victory'.[138] 'The increasing strength of the enemy forces, especially of the British

Army,' Hitler proclaimed in a directive on 17 January 1940, 'requires that the German Wehrmacht, especially the army and Luftwaffe, be strengthened both numerically and in terms of the quality of its equipment.'[139] His priorities were also revealing. Hitler's emphasis was on artillery, ammunition, barbed wire and machine tools rather than tank production, which consumed only 5 per cent of the steel allocation. This put a premium on the increased mobilization of the German economy, which was already seriously overstretched. In mid March 1940, Hitler appointed Fritz Todt as the new munitions minister. He oversaw the biggest increase in German armaments production yet: it doubled between January and July 1940.[140] The demands of the war economy had important consequences for domestic, occupation and foreign policy. At home, the retreat from consumption continued. Instead of civilian Volkswagen for the *Volksgenossen*, the factory at Fallersleben began from 1940 to mass-produce vehicles for the Wehrmacht. The promise of universal motorization was delayed until after the war.[141]

The need of the German war economy for raw materials and foodstuffs greatly increased Hitler's reliance on the Soviet Union. On 11 February 1940, he concluded a comprehensive economic agreement with Moscow.[142] Stalin supplied him with grain, animal feed and metals, such as phosphates, asbestos, chrome and nickel.[143] Many of the bullets later fired at the British at Dunkirk were coated with Russian-mined cupro-nickel. Hitler bragged that he was safe from the British blockade. To that extent, the Hitler–Stalin Pact gave him the defence in depth and the fruits of *Lebensraum* without actually having to fight for it.[144] His view of the pact remained largely instrumental, but there was genuine strategic and ideological common ground between the Third Reich and Stalin's Soviet Union. The Kremlin cleaved to the pact not merely out of false consciousness or as a desperate expedient in the absence of a common front against Nazism but because it regarded the British Empire as its main enemy.[145] So did Hitler. Stalin saw global capitalism as a mortal threat. So did Hitler.

The other strategic consequence of the needs of the German war economy was Hitler's increased determination to pre-empt any British strike against his supply of Swedish iron ore through Norway.[146] On 27 January, moving beyond hypothetical ruminations about Scandinavia, he requested that the OKW draw up a detailed plan for the occupation of Norway and Denmark. In late February 1940, Hitler appointed General von Falkenhorst to command the operation. This was followed on 1 March 1940 by a directive under the codename *Weserübung*. As with *Fall Gelb*, the planned Norwegian operation was hugely controversial both strategically and tactically. Raeder warned that it 'violated all laws of naval warfare', because the operation was theoretically only feasible with control of the sea.[147] Hitler sought to mitigate the risk through surprise, speed and audacity. He told the assembled commanders that the operation would be 'one of the "cheeki-est" enterprises in modern military history'.[148] There were also furious dis-agreements about individual ship deployments, in particular with regard to that of the destroyers, which he insisted should stay in the exposed waters off Narvik in order to maintain the morale of the landing parties.[149] A week later, Hitler set the date for the attack on Norway as 9 April 1940.

As the showdown with the Western Allies approached, Hitler was anx-ious to avoid both confrontation with the United States and any American diplomatic intervention. When Roosevelt made another speech critical of the Third Reich on 3 January 1940, the Führer instructed that it should be given only brief mention in the German press.[150] Towards the end of March, the head of the War Economics Office, General Thomas, recorded that 'the Führer has again emphasized energetically that everything is to be done so that the war can be ended in 1940 with a great military victory. From 1941 onwards, time works against us (USA-Potential).'[151] It was surely with this in mind, that the Propaganda Ministry – at Hitler's request – was shortly afterwards given explicit instructions not to attack either Roosevelt or the US government directly.[152]

The most pressing issue for Hitler with regard to America, however, was the question of how to respond to the visit of the US undersecretary of state, Sumner Welles. Though contemporaries and subsequent historians have often referred to a 'peace mission', there is no doubt that it was effectively an intervention on the Allied side driven by the president's hostility to the Axis, designed to divide the Führer and the *Duce* and even to promote regime change in Germany.[153] While Hitler may not have known the detail of Roosevelt's intentions he certainly intuited them.[154] Hitler instructed German diplomats to tell Welles that just as the United States rejected European interference in the western hemisphere in accordance with the Monroe Doctrine, so did 'Germany regard the eastern European space as its sphere of interest'. His own encounter with Welles was not a success. He unleashed a torrent of complaints against the Franco-British intention to 'destroy' Germany, the American boycott of German goods and the Monroe Doctrine.[155] The only good thing about the visit, the Führer subsequently remarked, was that Roosevelt 'would certainly hear from his emissary that America would have to pay dearly for any entry into the war'.[156]

On 9 April 1940, Hitler struck at Denmark and Norway.[157] The Danes folded as quickly as expected. Norway, by contrast, was no walkover. The Norwegians put up a much stronger fight than Hitler had foreseen. Oslo and most of the main ports in the south of the country were occupied quickly, but then the fight started in earnest. Over the next three weeks or so, a confused and often desperate battle raged across central and northern Norway. Its outcome was long in the balance. The Allies drove the Germans out of Narvik, the port whose capture had been the main purpose of the operation. Hitler briefly lost his nerve and drafted a radio order instructing the local commander, Dietl, to withdraw, and he also seems to have considered telling him to retreat to Sweden, preferring internment to capture. After a short flap, Jodl succeeded in having the order changed. Dietl was to stand fast, which he did. Hitler let out a sigh of relief; 'the Führer has calmed down again,' Jodl recorded.[158] It took until the middle of the following month before the Wehrmacht had the situation completely under control. Hitler's gamble had paid off. He had defied the principles of naval warfare, against the Royal Navy of all enemies. He coordinated not just the political but all the military moving parts as a combined operation through the OKW. Norway, in short, was Hitler's first military *Gesamtkunstwerk*.

The Führer had prevailed in his first serious encounter with the dreaded *Engländer*, whisking an invasion fleet across the North Sea beneath their very noses. He had waged a brutal campaign against the British, demanding the complete destruction of villages and towns occupied by them. Britain, as the new propaganda magazine *Signal* proclaimed in April 1940, was 'the main enemy of the Reich in this war'.[159] It had extracted a high price, however. The army's losses had been relatively small and those of the Luftwaffe, though not trivial, had been manageable.[160] The Kriegsmarine, by contrast, had been crucified. It had lost one heavy and two light cruisers, ten destroyers, a torpedo boat, six submarines and fifteen smaller vessels. Many other ships were damaged, some very seriously. This was close to a third of the entire fighting strength of the German navy. Raeder's warnings had been vindicated, because nearly all of these vessels were lost not en route on the high seas, but immediately off the Norwegian coast or in the fjords. To be sure, the Royal Navy had also suffered heavily, about the same number of ships, but it was much larger and therefore better able to absorb losses. The Kriegsmarine could not afford another such victory. Its missing destroyers, in particular, were seriously to hamper Hitler's prospects later in the summer.

Well before the campaign in Norway was finished, Hitler turned his attention back to the west. On 1 May 1940, he set the date for the attack as 5 May. On 2 May, he held last-minute discussions on the airborne operations. The date of the attack was delayed yet again, so that on 7 May, Hitler announced 9 May as the new date, followed shortly after by 10 May. On that day, the Führer set off for his field headquarters at the Felsennest in the Eifel region of western Germany. Now the real war would begin, a contest which Hitler did not expect to be either quick or easy. The main target of the offensive remained Britain. In his 'Proclamation' to the attacking Wehrmacht units, the Führer singled out the 'British rulers of the world' in particular for their alleged determination to 'prevent Germany at all costs from achieving unity', and to deny the Reich 'the necessities of life which are necessary to ensure the survival of an 80-million strong people'.[161]

The attack in the west unfolded pretty much as Hitler had envisaged. Key fortresses and bridges were secured by *coup de main* or airborne assault. The German army advanced into Belgium and Holland, sweeping aside local resistance. French and British forces advanced to meet them.[162] The German armour punched through lightly held Allied defences in the Ardennes. Attempts to establish a defensible line were disrupted by incessant attacks from the air, and flanking movements by the panzers; a mixture of adrenaline and narcotics kept the German columns moving. The whole phenomenon became known as '*Blitzkrieg*' – 'lightning war'. Within a fortnight, Belgium and Holland had been completely overrun, and the British and French were falling back to the Channel ports.

Once again, Hitler's hand was visible not merely in the planning of the campaign,[163] but in its execution. The Führer spent most of the first three weeks of the campaign in his Felsennest headquarters, closely watching and intervening in operations.[164] He was also, however, prone to even greater panic and hesitation than during the fighting in Norway. After seven days of advancing at breakneck speed, Hitler suddenly became worried about Allied counter-attacks, especially from the south.[165] That afternoon, Hitler went to the army group commander, Rundstedt, to warn of the 'importance which the southern flank had not only for the operations of the entire army' but 'politically' and psychologically. He feared that any 'setback' would boost not merely the military but also the 'political leadership of our enemies'. For this reason, Hitler concluded, the requirement was not for a 'rapid advance to the Channel coast but rather for the quickest establishment of a dependable defence' along the rivers to the south.[166] 'The Führer is incredibly nervous,' Halder added that evening, 'he is afraid of his own success, wants to risk nothing and would therefore ideally like to halt' the advance; again, his fear was for his 'left' (southern) flank.[167] Hitler wanted to wait until the infantry divisions had come up before authorizing further thrusts by the armoured and motorized formations.

On the same day as Hitler launched his western offensive, the Chamberlain government fell over its mismanagement of the Norway campaign.

Winston Churchill became prime minister of an all-party government. This was extremely bad news for the Führer, as the new British leader represented everything that he hated and feared. Three days after his appointment, Churchill delivered his first address to parliament as prime minister. He vowed to pursue 'victory, victory at all costs, victory in spite of all terror, victory, however long and hard the road may be'. He promised the British people only 'blood, toil, tears and sweat'. Like Roosevelt, and his rival Hitler, Churchill proved to be master of the set-piece oration. The US president had long been in the Führer's sights, but now the prime minister moved centre stage. The rhetorical duel between the Führer and the British leader had begun.

The stunning victories over Britain and France in Norway and Flanders took Mussolini by surprise. He now scrambled to enter the war before Germany had completed her triumph. Hitler's response was revealing of his strategic priorities. He had little interest in seeing the Italians pile in against France, but very much welcomed anything Mussolini might undertake against the British in the western and central Mediterranean, particularly Malta and Gibraltar, or the eastern end, especially the Suez Canal.[168] On the very last day of May, Mussolini sent a letter announcing that Italy would declare war on 5 June; she actually did so five days later. The Italian scavenging operation in southern France was quickly bogged down, and to Hitler's fury not much was done in the Mediterranean either.[169]

Meanwhile, some 300,000 British soldiers were encircled on the Channel coast in a rapidly shrinking pocket. London began to organize their hasty evacuation, but there was no chance of taking more than a fraction of them out if the panzers overran the perimeter defences. For several crucial days, no such attack came.[170] Hitler hesitated, not for political but for military reasons. The original decision to halt the panzers on 24 May was taken by the army group commander, Rundstedt, against the wishes of the High Command; the Führer merely upheld it.[171] This may have been partly motivated by the desire to assert his authority over the OKW, but it is more likely that Hitler was simply showing the same caution he had manifested on several occasions throughout the previous three weeks. His tanks had outrun their supply lines, and, like the rest of the Wehrmacht, he had a healthy – and at this point probably exaggerated – respect for British abilities. The order to halt the attack on Dunkirk was accompanied by an instruction not to move beyond a line to the north and east of the pocket.[172]

Hitler had good reason to be careful. The retreat to Dunkirk is rightly remembered as a British disaster, and there were certainly scenes of panic and cowardice. In general, however, the advancing Germans did not believe they were witnessing a rout. The bulk of the BEF fell back in reasonable order, fighting all the way. German sources all attest to the resistance they encountered: 'the encircled enemy has defended himself tenaciously'; 'the enemy is fighting tenaciously and bravely to gain time for the embarkation of his troops'; 'the battle is hard, the British are as tough as leather'; despite the fact that the cordon around Dunkirk is getting ever smaller, the enemy is defending himself with the courage of despair'.[173] These statements mirror Hitler's own long-established rhetoric about British 'tenacity' and 'toughness'. They somewhat contradict the equally frequent claims by German generals at the time and since that Hitler should have ordered the Wehrmacht to crush the British forces in Dunkirk without mercy. Even if Dunkirk lacked any sort of perimeter line when the tanks were ordered to stop, taking the town might not have been as easy as it looks today.

The Führer did not think that a full-scale ground attack on Dunkirk was either feasible or necessary. He claimed that the 'terrain in Flanders' – which he knew well from the First World War – 'was unsuitable for tanks on account of being waterlogged',[174] obviously fearing that his armoured units would get bogged down among the canals and waterways. He also told Army Group A that it was 'necessary to spare the armoured forces for coming operations', and that 'a further narrowing of the pocket would only result in an undesirable reduction in the activity of the Luftwaffe'.[175] Besides, the day before the tanks were halted, Göring told an enthusiastic Hitler that the Luftwaffe could complete the destruction of the BEF. Shortly afterwards, the Führer remarked on the 'ideological reliability of the Luftwaffe compared to the army', and this may have been an additional reason to deny the *coup de grâce* to the army and grant it to the airforce.[176]

On 24 May 1940, the same day as he confirmed Rundstedt's halt order, Hitler issued a new directive to the Wehrmacht. It fell into three parts. First, he defined the 'next aim of the operation' as the 'destruction of the encircled Anglo-French-Belgian forces through a concentric attack of our northern wing as well as the rapid capture and securing of the Channel coast there'. The Luftwaffe was tasked with 'breaking all enemy resistance' in the pocket, and 'preventing the escape of British forces across the English Channel', and securing the southern flank of Army Group A (Hitler's perpetual concern). Only once this had been done, Hitler decreed, should the Wehrmacht 'proceed to the destruction of [the remaining] enemy forces in France'. The Luftwaffe, for its part, was instructed to begin 'large-scale operations against the British homeland', right away once sufficient aircraft were available. Significantly, the Führer ordered that this be done 'independently' of the operations at Dunkirk and should be continued 'even after' the subsequent push south against the rest of the French army had begun.[177]

Hitler's thinking at Dunkirk is thus clear enough. He halted the tanks for military reasons within an overall political-strategic concept. His main focus was on the delivery of political and psychological effect against Britain. This was to be done, first, through the destruction of the BEF's will to resist at Dunkirk, not its physical annihilation. Secondly, he was already thinking of the next stage of his campaign, which was a devastating aerial and naval assault on the home islands from his new bases. There is no evidence whatsoever that Hitler offered the BEF a 'golden bridge' to retreat across in order to facilitate a negotiated settlement.[178]

Göring's aircraft duly pummelled Dunkirk, but they did not stop the evacuation. Senior Wehrmacht figures, who could see that the British were getting away, demanded an immediate attack. The Führer effectively left the decision to Rundstedt.[179] The offensive was eventually resumed, but the British and French troops holding the perimeter put up a ferocious fight, making good use of the canals and waterways to delay the advance, just as the Führer had feared they would do. On 1–2 June 1940 Hitler went to Brussels to be close to the final showdown in Artois and Flanders. But it was too late. Most of the BEF were long gone. The British rearguard was evacuated on the night of 2–3 June.

Hitler now turned south to finish off the French. On 6 June 1940, he moved his headquarters to Brûly-de-Pesche near Charleville close to the Franco-Belgian frontier. It was christened 'The Wolf's Gorge', an appellation which probably alluded to Hitler's codename – 'Wolf' – during the 1920s, but which may also have been a nod to the gorge of the same name in Carl Maria von Weber's popular opera Der Freischütz. If Hitler had set ambitious goals for the offensive, he had still not lost his innate operational caution, rejecting some of the Army High Command's more ambitious suggestions as 'too risky'.[180] Be that as it may, the German advance was relentless. On 14 June, Paris was abandoned to the Germans. Three days later, France sued for peace. Hitler's triumph was complete.

The scale of the German victory was totally unexpected. France and Britain were both highly developed western societies. The French deployed millions of men, and between them the Allies could command as many or more aircraft, tanks, and artillery, of roughly similar quality, than the Germans. In terms of transport, the British and French were well ahead. Most of the German army marched on foot and much of its artillery and supplies was moved by horse-drawn wagons. The divide was epitomized by the reaction of the commander of Army Group B, Fedor von Bock, to the sight of the British equipment left behind at Dunkirk: 'immeasurable amounts of vehicles, guns, tanks and army equipment', which suggested a 'plenitude of kit which we poor devils admired with envy'.[181] The only slight advantage Hitler had enjoyed was in fighter aircraft; everything else was down to superior German tactics and élan. Hitler's triumph was thus, in the grand scheme of things, a monumental fluke.[182] It was a strange defeat for France and Britain; for Hitler, an even stranger victory.[183]

Like many Germans, Hitler was deeply conscious that the Wehrmacht had beaten an enemy which had bested them twenty years earlier, and that towns and villages which they had fought over for years had fallen within days and sometimes even hours. Following in the wake of his advancing armies, the Führer took several trips down memory lane. At the height of the Dunkirk crisis on 29 May 1940, he went to Ypres immediately after it was captured. The Führer went through the Menin Gate, whose lion represented both Flanders and Britannia. In June, Hitler undertook further trips. On one of them he encountered the already legendary Erwin Rommel of the 7th Panzer Division, who demonstratively signalled his loyalty by rushing towards the Führer with his right arm in salute.[184] Hitler sought to make these journeys more than just a triumphal progress. By visiting not merely the German memorial at Langemarck but also the Canadian one at Vimy Ridge and the French one at Loretto in Artois, he tried to suggest a common fate now transcended. Hitler had refought the Great War and in so doing had finally ended it, or so he believed. In retrospect, though, these trips can also be read as a tacit admission that the war of movement was over, and that the war of attrition was about to begin. Just as the German armies' sweep into Belgium in 1914 was followed by four years of hard slog, Hitler's victory of 1940 was simply the prelude to a much longer struggle.

The interplay between past and present was most evident in Hitler's handling of the armistice discussions with the French.[185] He insisted these take place at Compiègne, in the same heavily symbolic railway carriage in which the Germans had accepted the Allied terms in 1918. In the month between the first time he mentioned the notion to Jodl on 20 May 1940[186] and his arrival at Compiègne on 20 June 1940, Hitler thought carefully about the choreography of the event. 'He even held a dry run beforehand', as witnessed by an astonished German diplomat. Observing the solitary Führer saluting and greeting a void, Erich Kordt remarked, 'He is rehearsing his piece.'[187] When the French arrived, Hitler put on a well-prepared performance. He simply dictated his terms, sitting in the same seat that Foch had spoken from when setting out his conditions in 1918. Hitler did not wait for the details, but left hurriedly while the French plenipotentiaries communicated with the government in Bordeaux. There were no negotiations, as such. It was all for show, for the benefit of the huge array of global media and the *Wochenschau* cameras capturing the whole event. A few days after Compiègne, Hitler visited Paris.[188] He stole into the city in the early hours of 24 June 1940 more as an architectural tourist than as a conqueror. Hitler brought with him Hermann Giesler, delivering on the boast he had made towards the end of the previous year, Speer, the sculptor Arno Breker and the increasingly ubiquitous Bormann.[189] His first destination was the Paris Opera, where he astonished the usher with his detailed knowledge of the original ground plan. Then he was driven via the Madeleine, the Place de la Concorde, the Louvre and down the Champs-Elysées. He paused for longer at the Arc de Triomphe to study the inscriptions, all of which he already knew off by heart. The high point of the visit, however, was Hitler's homage at Les Invalides, where he stood silently beside Napoleon's sarcophagus with lowered head. This was a conscious echo of the famous scene in Potsdam in 1806, when Bonaparte had made a similar pilgrimage to the tomb of Frederick the Great. On leaving the building he told Bormann that he wanted the remains of the Duke of Reichstadt, Napoleon's son by the Austrian princess Marie Louise, transferred from Vienna to Paris.[190] The symbolism could not have been clearer: Hitler saw himself as continuing the Frederician and Napoleonic traditions, resolving in his person the Franco-German antagonism.

In early July 1940, Hitler returned in triumph to Berlin, standing upright in his chauffeured car as he moved through the multitudes. His entrance, which the Führer planned in detail, has been compared to that of a conquering Roman emperor.[191] The city was a sea of flowers and chanting crowds. Hitler was at the zenith of his power. Führer and 'people', the vast majority of whom exulted in the conquests, were closer than ever before; Hitler was dictator by 'approbation', at least for now.[192] The dominance of most of continental Europe had fallen into his lap. Germany now held the seaboard from the Arctic to the Bay of Biscay. Hitler dominated a ring of allied and satellite states to the south and east. No trouble was to be expected from neutral Portugal or Switzerland, a country he despised.[193] Spain and Finland very much leaned to his side. The relationship with the Soviet Union, it seemed, was stable. Hitler now not only directly controlled most of the mainland European economy – with a pre-war GDP larger than that of either the United States or the British Empire and a substantially greater population[194] – he also had access to raw materials and foodstuffs well beyond its borders. Europe had been unified under Nazi leadership.[195]

Hitler wasted no time in ordering the integration of western Europe into the German war economy. On 16 June 1940, even before France had sued for peace, he called for 'coordinated planning for the occupied Belgian, French and Luxembourgeois territories' within the framework of the Four Year Plan.[196] A new order was in the offing.

Hitler hoped to rule this space with as light a touch as possible. In his decree on the administration of the occupied territories in the west, he laid down that 'conduct of the military administration' should be such as to avoid the impression of 'an intended annexation of the occupied territories'. The Hague Convention was to be observed. 'The population is to be spared,' Hitler added, 'economic life is to be kept going.' Hostile action by the population, on the other hand, would be 'suppressed harshly'. In Norway, the Führer promised to release all Norwegian conscripts, holding on to the professionals only so long as the exiled government continued the war, or until they individually swore an oath not to take part in any further hostilities against Germany. In France, he gave members of the Wehrmacht strict instructions to show 'restraint' in their relations with the population, 'as is appropriate for a German soldier'.[197] The Führer also held back with annexations, which were for now limited to the small German-speaking province of Eupen-Malmedy.[198] The purpose of all these moves was the same: to impress on non-Jewish Europeans that the war was over and that the benevolent rule of the Führer was the new normal. He had some success in this regard, at least initially.[199]

In Germany itself, too, Hitler hoped for a return to normality. The hundreds of thousands of Germans who had been temporarily evacuated from western territories after the Allied declaration of war were permitted to reclaim their homes. 'Now the moment of return has come,' he proclaimed with much fanfare in late June 1940.[200] Hitler also used the victory to bind the Wehrmacht leadership more closely to himself, by lavishing honours and gifts – in cash or kind – on them as a reward for service.[201] The Führer was particularly forthcoming towards commanders who were not yet enthusiastic National Socialists.[202] His aim seems to have been to create a military aristocracy, similar to the imperial nobility established by Napoleon: a meritocracy personally loyal to and complicit with the Führer. These men could be trusted to support him in his next adventure. The rewards scheme also militated against the Hohenzollern threat – which resurfaced after the fall of France when the former Kaiser Wilhelm II requested to return home. Hitler refused angrily, exclaiming 'that might just suit reactionary circles'.[203] Wilhelm remained in his Dutch exile at Doorn, where he died a year later. The generals showed little interest in his case. They now had a new more successful and more generous monarch.

If the summer of 1940 saw widespread rejoicing in Germany, there was one man not celebrating, and that was Hitler himself. During his imperial procession through Berlin there was no slave whispering warnings about the passing nature of glory in his ear, but none was needed. Hitler knew better than anyone else, not only his own mortality – which had long obsessed him – but also the enduring strength of Anglo-American power, which had dominated his political thinking from the start. What was striking about his rhetoric and demeanour during this period, surface bluster notwithstanding, was its caution and hesitation. In early June 1940, with victory in the west clear, the Italian ambassador had expected to find Hitler 'light-hearted, contented, exhilarated'; instead, he was 'tired and abstracted' with a 'confused expression' and a 'careworn, anxious, preoccupied look'.[204] Far from devoting his attention to domestic matters now that peace was imminent, the Führer decreed that all domestic initiatives which were 'not connected to the defence of the Reich' should be paused.[205] Much as he would have liked to have distributed one, there was to be no peace dividend. Hitler's mood did not lift in the course of the month. When he came back to Berlin so triumphantly in early July 1940 he insisted that there be no suggestion that he had returned for good.[206]

The reason for Hitler's concern was threefold. Firstly, despite her drubbing in northern France, Britain showed no signs of coming to terms. Churchill rallied the population in a series of dramatic speeches. Like Hitler, the prime minister was a word warrior; the American reporter Ed Murrow said that he 'mobilized the English language and sent it into battle'. In June 1940, Churchill famously vowed not just to 'go on to the end', not merely to fight on the beaches, in the cities and the hills, but also to carry on the fight overseas if the home island fell to invasion.[207] All this was very much not what Hitler, who was paying close attention, wanted to hear. 'He read Churchill's passionate wartime speeches against Germany,' his press chief Otto Dietrich recalled, 'which I supplied him with not merely in extracts but verbatim.' Dietrich opined that, 'measured by his outwardly irrational reaction . . . he secretly admired them'.[208] On 3 July, the British determination to fight on was underlined by its ruthless destruction of the French squadron at Oran in Northern Africa, reluctantly carried out to ensure that these ships did not fall into Nazi hands.

Secondly, Hitler feared the 'racial' cost of continued war. 'It is always the best, the bravest and those most willing to sacrifice themselves who fall,' he lamented to Giesler during their trip to Paris, costing the Reich men 'whose job it would be to embody and to lead the nation'.[209] While Britain posed no immediate challenge on the ground, Hitler was profoundly anxious about the threat from the air. It had been one of the main considerations behind the entire French campaign. Now, if the Führer was to pursue that strategy to its logical conclusion, the British refusal to negotiate would have to be followed by a massive air campaign against the home islands. Hitler hesitated, because he feared Britain's capacity to retaliate. 'My tactics,' he told the Italian ambassador, 'have always been to throw the responsibility on the shoulders of my enemies'. The problem was, Hitler went on, that '[t]otal air warfare is an extremely bloody business, and for that reason it is necessary to make the civilian population believe that everything possible has been done to avoid it'. In other words, Hitler wanted to spare the German population any British retaliatory action. Besides, he concluded, the Luftwaffe had suffered considerable 'wear and tear' in France. It would take time to refit units and to bring the reinforcements necessary to attack Britain.[210] An immediate assault on Britain after Dunkirk, in short, would not have been possible anyway.

Hitler's worry about British air attacks was fuelled by Royal Air Force activity in the summer of 1940.[211] Western German towns and cities were beginning to hear the sirens more and more frequently. Even if many of these were false alarms, there were some fatalities, and the cost to civilian nerves was considerable. In mid June 1940, for example, Fritz Weitzel, the Höherer SS- und Polizeiführer West, was killed in a British raid on Düsseldorf; a week later, Hitler himself issued an order that the SS unit in that town be renamed in the dead man's honour.[212] Hamm in Westphalia, a vital railway junction and marshalling yards, was hit particularly badly. Children were breaking down crying and shouting or were convulsed by epileptic fits for days afterwards. Men suffered heart failure due to shock. Hysterical women who had hitherto been silenced by fear of sterilization relapsed, or so it was reported.[213] These attacks were of very little military importance, but their psychological impact was significant.[214] They subverted Hitler's domestic narrative that the war was under control and victory or a negotiated peace with Britain was imminent.

Thirdly, Hitler was anxious about American intentions.[215] The French defeat had struck the Roosevelt administration like a thunderbolt. Public opinion polls suggested a widespread expectation that if Hitler defeated Britain he would strike next across the Atlantic. The same month as Hitler entered Paris, Roosevelt both appointed the pro-Allied Republican Henry Stimson as secretary of war and introduced a bill for the first peacetime draft in American history to Congress. US spending on the air force and navy, already substantial, surged even higher. To make matters worse, the Nazi advance fundamentally changed Republican Party politics. At its dramatic convention in Philadelphia in late June 1940, the strongly pro-British Wendell Willkie prevailed over the (then) isolationists Tom Dewey, Robert Taft and Arthur Vandenberg. Willkie had the backing not only of *Time* publisher Henry Luce, but also of Wall Street, especially Thomas Lamont of J. P. Morgan. It did not greatly matter to Hitler, therefore, who prevailed in the November 1940 presidential election. Both options across the water were bad.

If the Führer saw London and Washington as increasingly aligned, this was because in his eyes malevolent Jewish and other German-hating forces had manipulated the elites and public opinion in that direction. Hitler's plan since the 1920s had been to divide Britain and the United States and triangulate between them. In the early 1930s, he had looked forward to an 1866 moment in which a defeated Britain entered into an alliance with Germany just as Austria had done after the Battle of Sadowa. The fall of France was potentially such a moment, when Britain could accept her extrusion from Europe, in the same way as Austria had yielded to Prussia in Germany, with Britain then becoming a junior partner in a new dual alliance directed against the United States, and possibly the Soviet Union as well. When Britain continued to resist, Hitler was faced with a dilemma. 'If I crush Britain militarily,' he told Halder, 'the British Empire will collapse – that will be of no benefit to Germany.' 'We would achieve something with German blood,' he continued, 'which would profit only America and others.'[216] Hitler was again thinking ahead to the new multi-polar world he had conceived some twenty years earlier.

On 19 July, Hitler finally gave his much-heralded and frequently postponed 'peace' speech to the German Reichstag. This was framed as a riposte to Churchill and a 'last appeal to general reason'. 'I see no cause,' Hitler said, which required 'the continuation of the struggle.' He warned that it would lead to the 'destruction' of the British Empire, something he had never intended. Hitler also expressed the desire to spare not only Britain but also Germany the resulting casualties, and the pain it would cause 'many women and mothers at home'.[217] Hitler flanked these overtures with other confidence-building measures. The British monarchy was exempted from the vitriolic attacks on other members of the British elite. In the Channel Islands, occupied on 30 June 1940, prayers were said for the Royal Family, 'God save the King' could be sung by prior permission and the unchanged local administration issued German instructions in the name of His Majesty George VI.[218] The islands were thus a laboratory of Anglo-German cooperation under the new order.

Hitler also made serious attempts to head off American intervention. His hope, albeit a dwindling one, was that the United States would recognize its true interest in accepting German domination of Europe in return for the unchallenged American hegemony in the western hemisphere. In an interview with the prominent German-American journalist Karl von Wiegand, Hitler returned to his old notion of a Monroe

Doctrine-style division of spheres. He repeated his lack of interest not only in North America but also in South America. In return he asked only that 'America would not interfere in European matters', appealing to none other than George Washington's remarks (in his 1796 'Farewell Address') on the subject. 'America for the Americans,' he demanded, 'Europe for the Europeans.'[219]

The fall of France gave Hitler an opportunity to 'solve' the Jewish question and deter the United States at the same time. In the summer of 1940, he seriously considered deporting the Jews under his control to the French colony of Madagascar off the East African coast. This plan, which Himmler first suggested to Hitler in late May 1940,[220] was discussed by the Führer with Ciano on 17–18 June, and two days later with Admiral Raeder, whose cooperation would obviously be essential. In the middle of July, Hitler ordered that Jews should no longer be deported eastwards, as they would now be sent to Africa. There they would not only be quarantined in Madagascar and pose no threat to Nazi Germany, but serve as hostages for the good behaviour of the United States. After the war, they could then be sent to the United States.[221] Britain's decision to fight on, which closed the sea lanes to Madagascar, made the whole plan impracticable and it was eventually dropped later in the year.[222]

However chimerical the scheme may seem in retrospect, Hitler does not seem to have conceived the Madagascar Plan as a cover for extermination.[223] On the contrary, when Himmler first suggested it, he did so as an alternative to 'physical extirpation', which the Reichsführer-SS rejected 'out of an inner conviction' as 'un-German and impossible'. Hitler regarded this view as 'very good and correct'.[224] Besides, if Jews were to serve as hostages against Roosevelt, then it was necessary to keep them alive. For this reason, Hitler stuck with the spirit of the plan, if not the letter, for the moment. In early August 1940, he told Otto Abetz that there would be an evacuation of 'all Jews from Europe' but only 'after the war'.[225] This was because there was no prospect of transporting anyone anywhere without the permission of the Royal Navy. At this point, therefore, 'deportation' was not just code for murder, and 'destruction' was still largely a metaphor which denoted something short of physical extermination. Soon, however, the reverse would be true as a more anodyne rhetoric became the cloak for a much darker reality.

Hitler's obsession with Jewry is thrown into stark relief by the relatively mild treatment of the approximately 120,000 black French soldiers captured in May and June 1940; it was an issue in which he showed virtually no interest. To be sure a large number were massacred out of hand during and immediately after the French campaign, but not at the Führer's behest.[226]

Thereafter, treatment was better not least because the Germans hoped to use some of them as auxiliary forces in their future colonial empire. African prisoners were held in POW, not concentration, camps. The only recorded intervention by Hitler in this question was an OKW directive requiring the transfer of non-white French captives to the unoccupied zone.[227] His concern, which dated from the occupation of the Rhineland in the 1920s, was to prevent any 'contamination' of the German population.[228] The general trend was that while conditions for blacks in the camps generally improved over time, those of Jews radically worsened. Hitler's racial war was not primarily one of white against black, but of Aryan against Jew.

In the light of Britain's continuing belligerence and escalating American hostility, Hitler revisited the question of an attack on the Soviet Union. This was driven not by the expectation of a rapid peace or victory over Britain, but rather by its absence. On 21 July 1940, Hitler told Brauchitsch to begin planning for the invasion of Russia, or authorized him to continue doing so; it is unclear from whom the initiative stemmed. Most likely, the plans from 1939 were dusted off.[229] Hitler was motivated here by the demands of the war with Britain, still very much the immediate enemy. Britain's 'hope', he told the generals, was 'Russia' and 'America.' For this reason, the Führer concluded, 'Russia must be dealt with,' and 'intellectual preparations' to do so must begin.[230] One way or the other, two things are clear. Firstly, the decision to attack Russia was driven primarily by the dictates of the confrontation with Anglo-America; ideological antipathy to the Soviet regime played no role at this stage. Secondly, there was as yet no firm date for the operation or even a formal directive. War on Russia was no done deal, at least not in the immediate future.[231]

In the course of July 1940, Hitler increasingly realized that Britain would not come to terms, and would have to be coerced militarily.[232] He had always hoped that this could be done by the Luftwaffe and the Kriegsmarine, but he was also realistic about the limitations of air power.[233] No doubt, with this in mind, Hitler issued Directive 16 for the invasion of Britain, which was to be a combined army and navy operation. Its language was entirely conditional. There was none of the usual bombast, or talk of an 'irrevocable decision'.[234]

On 22 July, the British rejected Hitler's 'appeal'. There was nothing for it. The Luftwaffe would have to be unleashed on Britain, and if that did not work, a landing would be attempted or at least threatened. On 1 August 1940, Hitler issued a directive for a full-scale air assault on Britain.[235] The Luftwaffe was given the task of crushing the RAF, which was to involve the destruction of not merely British planes in the air and on the ground, but also their airfields and supply systems, as well as the aviation and anti-aircraft artillery industries. Once a 'temporary or local air superiority' had been achieved, attention should shift to attacks on Britain's ports to cut off the supply of foodstuffs. 'Retaliatory terror attacks,' Hitler stressed, 'can only be authorized by me.' A week later he agreed with Raeder that a landing could only be 'a last resort' if Britain could not be forced to make peace 'through other means', for example through air attacks. He added that a 'failure' would mean a 'large prestige victory' for Britain.[236] In late August, Hitler declared 'Sealion' the priority for equipment, but only for a 'limited period of time'.[237] A motley invasion fleet of ships and modified barges was assembled in the Channel ports.[238] Infantry and tanks practised opposed landings.

Hitler was under no illusion about the magnitude of the task ahead. Unlike in Poland or western Europe, he now faced an enemy which was by his own reckoning racially superior, and economically more advanced. British war production was growing by the day. Britain had the immense resources not only of the Empire, but also of the United States at its back. The Royal Navy had easily absorbed its losses in Norway, and was many multiples stronger than the Kriegsmarine. By contrast, the Wehrmacht, whose infantry casualties had been relatively low so far, had lost many ships and aircraft in Norway and France, precisely the assets needed to combat Britain. Above all, Britain's will to resist was completely unbroken. The Luftwaffe's prospects against the Royal Air Force were doubtful, but if even air superiority could be attained, translating that into dominance over the vastly superior Royal Navy in the Narrow Sea, engaged on the most important mission in its history, would not be straightforward. The Luftwaffe and Kriegsmarine planners doubted that it could be done.[239] Even if somehow a force could be got across the Channel, it was not clear that it would be able to do so in sufficient strength to defeat the much larger and increasingly well-equipped British field army.

As it turned out, Hitler fell at the first hurdle. The Luftwaffe pounded RAF bases in the south and east of the country. Honours were at first even, and for a moment it seemed as if the Germans might be gaining the upper hand. On the very last day of August, the Luftwaffe succeeded in inflicting heavy losses on the RAF, but suffered grievously itself in turn. Soon, however, technology and the metrics began to tell. Britain could replace aircraft, and – with more difficulty – pilots, more quickly than Göring. Valuable momentum was lost when the Luftwaffe was instructed to attack London in retaliation for RAF raids on Berlin. Throughout all this the British, military and civilian, were probably less united than they claimed at the time or fondly imagined afterwards. Be that as it may, Hitler was deeply impressed and depressed by their unbroken spirit. His original plan to destroy Britain's will to resist had failed. Tempers frayed in the Führer's Headquarters. Hitler exploded at the failure of the Luftwaffe. Witnesses recorded 'heavy diatribes' and 'temper-tantrums'.[240]

On 3 September, Hitler postponed the date of the invasion until 21 September. A fortnight later, he delayed the invasion again, and on 12 October it was put off until spring of the following year. Hitler ordered that preparations continue as a bluff and distraction, but it was clear that the operation was off. This was almost certainly the right decision. A high-level war game conducted at the Army Staff College at Sandhurst in 1974, involving former senior figures from both sides and based on the then known British and Germans plans, concluded that any invasion would have been a complete disaster.[241] The Führer, one of the greatest risk-takers in history, decided not to roll the dice on 'Sealion'. It was too chancy even for such an inveterate gambler as Hitler.

The British would have to be coerced another way. Hitler now experimented with two strategies simultaneously. The first was to put pressure on Britain's position in the Mediterranean, in particular, and to invite other powers to join in the partition of the British Empire more generally. Hitler was also determined to keep the United States out of the area, so as to deny Roosevelt a launchpad against the Reich in any future conflict. In this context, Hitler took a brief interest in Africa and toyed, though not very seriously, with the idea of a German sub-Saharan empire.[242] He preferred, however, to co-opt regional powers to do the job for him: Italy, of course, but also Spain, Vichy France and even Portugal. Throughout the autumn and early winter of 1940, he courted all three powers, especially Franco. This fitted with Raeder's preference for a 'Mediterranean strategy', its sights firmly on British bases in Gibraltar, Malta and (ultimately) Egypt and the Suez Canal.[243]

In October 1940, Hitler redoubled his efforts. The aim of this strategy was, as the Führer put it, 'to bring France and Spain to agree a common line and in this way to establish a continental coalition against Britain'.[244] He hoped that Vichy could be persuaded to surrender some territory to Franco and Mussolini, compensating herself elsewhere in Africa at Britain's expense. This was a delicate question, and the Führer knew that it had to be handled sensitively in order to avoid outraged French colonial administrations declaring for de Gaulle. On 4 October, he met with Mussolini at the Brenner Pass. Three weeks after, the Führer received Pierre Laval, the acting head of the collaborationist French Vichy government. A day later he met Franco at Hendaye and the day after that he met the Vichy leader, Marshal Pétain. Towards the end of the month there was another encounter with Mussolini in Florence, who was worried that

France would steal a march on him.[245] Hitler accompanied these moves with some fraternalist mood music about the value of allies. When the Spanish foreign minister Serrano Süner visited, he personally requested that crowds be mobilized to welcome him.[246] The Führer also ordered the distribution of German decorations 'in order to demonstrate the comradeship of the German people and its Wehrmacht with allied nations' supporting her struggle for freedom.[247]

The second of Hitler's anti-British, and ultimately anti-American, strategies was to turn Moscow and Tokyo against London. This was very much the brainchild of his foreign minister, Ribbentrop. In the Far East, Hitler's concern was to prevent a renewed Russo-Japanese war and to ensure that Tokyo remained focused on the British, and especially the American, threat. On 27 September 1940, he concluded the Tripartite Pact with Italy and Japan.[248] Unlike its predecessor, the Anti-Comintern Pact, this treaty was not even nominally directed against the Soviet Union. In fact this possibility was explicitly excluded in the text. Its target was clearly the western powers. On 13 October 1940, the Führer invited the Soviet foreign minister, Molotov, to come to Berlin in November. There he tried to persuade the Soviet Union to join in the partition of the British Empire, which he characterized as a 'giant bankrupt's estate' of 40 million square kilometres.[249] Hitler urged the Soviet Union to take advantage of this opportunity and to strike towards 'ice-free ports' and the oceans, by which he probably meant the creation of Russian bases in Baluchistan, an old Tsarist fantasy. Hitler's pitch here was well calculated, because Stalin's main concern at this time was still the British Empire, which he perceived as a threat in the Balkans and Central Asia.

If the Führer's most immediate concern was Britain, his continental bloc was also very much directed against the United States. American hostility only increased throughout the summer and autumn of 1940 as the population instinctively identified with 'the few' battling it out in the skies, and the many sheltering in the basements and tube stations during the 'Blitz'. Journalists extolled the defence of democracy, American volunteer pilots served in the RAF, and American war material poured across the Atlantic. The administration, too, ratcheted up the pressure. On 19 July, the same day that Hitler gave his 'peace speech', Roosevelt signed the 'two-ocean navy' bill into law. On 2 September 1940 he exchanged fifty old destroyers for leases on British bases, a move more important for its symbolism than for its military implications. German diplomats in the United States differed in their assessment of US capabilities, and on the timing of its likely belligerency, but they were all agreed on its hostile intent and collusion with, or manipulation by, the forces of international Jewry.[250]

Hitler watched all this closely. He worried not only about US supplies to Britain, but also America's potential help to the Soviet Union.[251] Hitler was uncertain how to respond. On the one hand, Goebbels was pressing him to prepare the German people for the inevitable showdown with the United States. On the other hand he did not want to alarm them, and his allies, prematurely. Hitler hesitated. 'The decision of the Führer on how to handle the British-American agreement,' he let it be known in early September 1940, 'is still awaited.'[252] Hitler also resisted the temptation to interfere in American domestic politics, which Roosevelt would have exploited, and forbade the press from intervening in the election campaign.[253] The Führer was also anxious not to repeat the mistake of the First World War, which was accidentally to provoke the United States into declaring war, or to provide it with a pretext for doing so, through the prosecution of unrestricted submarine warfare. Hitler limited himself to pre-emptive measures, in particular securing his western flank. On 26 September 1940, he decreed that 'England-USA must be thrown out of North-West Africa' and that the 'Canaries, possibly also Azores and Cape Verdes, must be secured previously through the air force'.[254]

In his meeting with Molotov in mid November 1940, Hitler openly confessed not just that he feared that the United States would help itself to the 'bankrupt' British Empire, but also that he wanted greater Russian involvement in Europe to keep out the Americans. This was Hitler restating his belief in a Monroe Doctrine for Germany, which sought to banish the United States to the western hemisphere. He was calling on his old Bolshevik foe to redress the imbalance created by the New World. His aim was to create a global coalition against Anglo-America spanning Eurasia from Spain to Vladivostok and Yokohama. 'Germany wants to create a world coalition of interested parties,' he told Molotov, stretching from 'North Africa as far as East Asia', and consisting of 'Spain, France, Italy, Germany the Soviet Union, and Japan', which would divide up the 'bankrupt' British Empire.[255] Hitler was also anxious to reassure the German population that they were part of a global coalition against an increasingly isolated British Empire. 'Germany and its allies are certainly strong enough,' he told the party faithful in his annual oration on 8 November 1940, 'to counter any combination in this world.' The period September to November 1940 thus marks the high point of Hitler's diplomacy. It was a time of frenetic activity, when all options were still on the table and the future – what he called 'worldwide perspectives'[256] – appeared open.

Nazi moves to create a 'continental bloc' were flanked with another dose of anti-Anglo-American, anti-capitalist, anti-Semitic and anti-imperialist rhetoric. If the British Empire and the United States were the 'haves' of the world order, Hitler argued, the German Reich was the leader of the 'have-nots'. It is not clear whether Hitler lifted this resonant phrase from Ernest Hemingway's eponymous novel, which was published in 1937, but he certainly used it repeatedly long before the appearance of the famous film version with Humphrey Bogart in 1944. 'I have been a have-not all my life,' he claimed, 'I consider myself a have-not and have always fought for them.' For this reason, Hitler announced, he 'acted in the world as a representative of the "have-nots"'.[257] The Führer, in short, was claiming to express not just a German but a global resentment at the unjust distribution of the earth's resources.

In Hitler's reading, inequality was manifested at both the national and the class level, and the two were connected. Germany as a whole was subject to an international ruling class, which had divided Germans from each other. In late 1940, Hitler reprised his old critique of the Westphalian treaties which had led to the fragmentation of the Reich. This meant that Germany had been left behind in the global distribution of territory, being left with less space per head of population than any other major European state. Here the Führer once again rehearsed the facts of *Lebensraum* with the usual statistics.[258] The Reich's main rival, as ever, was Britain, which had walked off with the lion's share. Given that Hitler made no suggestion that the lands occupied in Scandinavia and western Europe were destined for settlement or that gains in central Europe and Poland represented a solution to the perennial German problem of space, the implication was clear. Germany might 'own' large tracts of Europe, but in global terms she was still poor. She did not yet 'have' enough.

The breaking-down of class barriers within Germany, divisions the Führer believed to have been carefully cultivated by the external enemy, was part and parcel of national liberation. Hitler wanted to transcend, as he said in early September 1940, the 'legacies of the past, of origin, of estate, and of profession'. For obvious reasons, the Führer argued, this grand social project was a threat to the established order, especially the British, who would stop at nothing to frustrate it. This, Hitler told an audience of German armament workers in mid November 1940, was why 'plutocratic-capitalist Britain' had gone to war against the German 'welfare state'.[259] The British, Hitler repeated right at the end of the year, 'hate us for our social convictions and our plans and actions [in the social field] seem dangerous to them'.[260]

This was why Hitler was determined to maintain as much as possible of his transformative socio-economic programme and to promise the German people a better life, at least after the war. In early 1940, even before the western campaign, he gave Robert Ley the task of looking into the idea of 'a comprehensive and generous old-age provision for the German people'. Later in the year, after much deliberation, he issued his 'Decree for the Preparation of German Residential Construction after the War'. Victory, he explained, would confront the Reich with tasks 'which it could only fulfil through an increase in population'. The purpose of the decree, therefore, was to promote the 'healthy life of child-rich families' and thereby bring about a larger birth rate.[261]

In Hitler's rhetoric, the Reich was the vanguard of a global war of liberation to free Germany, the European continent and ultimately the entire world from the clutches of international capitalist plutocracy.[262] This message was directed not only at Germans, Europeans and Americans but also to the colonized peoples. The Nazi Arab language broadcasting service, for example, announced that Hitler's speeches heralded 'the day upon which the world will be freed of Churchill, Eden, [and] the Jews'.[263] Towards the end of the year, Hitler even looked forward privately to a black 'awakening' as part of his anti-imperialist turn.[264] To be sure, this trend in Hitler's thinking was part opportunism and part rationalization of the final breach with Britain, but it also reflected his sense of wider historical processes sweeping the world. Anti-Semitism was integral to this vision, as reflected not only in Hitler's reflexive coupling of capitalism with the Jews, but also in the regime's broader narrative. For example, the iconic anti-Semitic propaganda film Der ewige Jude, which was screened in German cinemas from late 1940, made great play of the Rothschilds.[265] Anti-communism, by contrast, played little role, at least for now. Significantly, the Propaganda Ministry ordered the press to identify each and every 'Jew' they mentioned except in the case of those working for Hitler's ally the Soviet Union.[266]

The Führer never managed to weld together a coherent 'continental bloc'. In the Mediterranean, there were just too many moving parts. Coordination with Italy was poor, on both the political and the military fronts.[267] The two powers effectively conducted separate wars, not only failing to assist each other, but actually cutting across one another. What began as an advance on parallel lines soon became diverging axes.[268] Mussolini not only made a complete hash of the campaign against Britain in western Egypt, but also launched a catastrophic invasion of Greece in October 1940, giving the Führer virtually no warning. This antagonized Athens, with whom Hitler had no quarrel. In fact he rather admired the Greeks, and expected them to resist successfully. Italian bungling also gave Churchill a pretext to do what Hitler feared most, which was to intervene in the Balkans and set up air bases there.[269] In early November the first British troops duly appeared in Salonica to cover the deployment of the

RAF there. The Führer was livid, probably unsettled by memories of the First World War, when the British and French armies in Salonica had suddenly surged forwards in 1918 and rolled up the entire south-eastern flank of the Central Powers. Hitler had not driven the British out of Scandinavia just in order for them to reappear on his southern flank. This was to become a major worry for him over the next nine months or so.

Hitler had no more luck in the western Mediterranean. There was no lack of appetite to despoil Britain, but the pre-emptive destruction of the Vichy French squadron at Oran, the Luftwaffe's failure over England, Italy's fiasco in the Cyrenaica, and the Fleet Air Arm's destruction of much of the Italian fleet at Taranto in mid November 1940 showed that the lion still had the capacity to maul any scavengers. If various jackals had popped their heads over the parapet from Lisbon to Kabul after the fall of France in June 1940, they were beginning to scurry back behind cover in the autumn.[270] Another problem was that the demands of Spain, France and Italy in North Africa were mutually contradictory, and Hitler was simply not strong enough to force his view on them in the way he had adjudicated the claims of Hungary and Romania. What really did for the Führer's strategy, however, was Franco's territorial greed in demanding large swathes of (Vichy) French north-west Africa, where Hitler wanted bases to deter the United States.[271] The meeting between the two at Hendaye was so fraught that Hitler later said that he would rather have all his teeth pulled than consent to another encounter with the Spaniard.[272] If Hitler was going to deprive Britain of Gibraltar, Malta and the Suez Canal, he would have to do so himself.

Worse still, Hitler made no headway with the Soviet Union. There was little meeting of minds with Molotov during his two-day visit.[273] The Soviet delegation listened politely to the Führer's monologue on the world situation, and his claim that Britain was already defeated and on the verge of annihilation from the air. Instead of engaging with his invitation to partition the British Empire, however, they asked some pointed questions about German intentions in the Balkans and the Baltic. What, they wanted to know, were the German military missions doing in Romania and Finland, and why had the Soviet Union not been consulted about them as required by the treaty? These questions struck Hitler like a 'cold shower', and he appeared to shrink into himself.[274] The Soviet visitors showed no interest in the Führer's attempts to restart discussion of the division of the British Empire. Hitler did not appear at the subsequent reception, perhaps because he was unhappy with how the talks had gone. No sooner had the first toasts been made than the air-raid sirens announced the approach of RAF bombers. The global reach of the British Empire could not have been more graphically illustrated.

One way or the other, Hitler's attempt to set off another feeding frenzy among the powers of the south and east failed. They were greedy enough, to be sure, but an obstinate sense of fear restrained them. 1940 was not 1938 or 1939. The British Empire was not the Czechoslovak Republic, which was occupied without firing a shot, or Poland, whose territory could be partitioned over toasts in the Kremlin. Whoever wanted a share would have to fight for it.

It is therefore unsurprising that Hitler remained more obsessed with British power than ever. His most immediate anxiety was the threat from the air. The first RAF raid on Berlin took place on 25 August 1940, followed by another seven alarms over the next fortnight. These raids – which the regime dubbed 'terror-bombing' – did little material damage in the big scheme of things but their psychological impact was substantial.[275] Hitler was profoundly concerned about their effects. He took a personal interest in precautionary measures in the capital, such as the construction of shelters and air-raid warnings. He gave strict instructions that the population must go to the shelters when the sirens sounded.[276] In Berlin, Speer was given the necessary building materials and workers, including slave labour, as well as the authority to confiscate all public and private property as necessary.[277] That said, Hitler believed that the best defence lay in deterrence and retaliation. If the British threatened to drop two, three or four thousand kilogrammes of bombs on Germany in one night, he announced in early September 1940, then he would drop hundreds of thousands, perhaps even a million kilogrammes of bombs. He vowed to 'rub out' Britain's cities and to stop the activities of their 'night-pirates'.[278]

As the year drew to a close, the skies were darkening for Hitler. His attempts to rally Europe against Anglo-America had failed. Relations with Russia were deteriorating; he left a letter from Stalin unanswered. The British were getting stronger by the day. On 5 November 1940, Roosevelt won re-election to a third term as president. Time seemed to contract again. Hitler therefore redoubled his efforts against Britain. He committed German forces to the Balkans and the Mediterranean to bail out Mussolini.[279] On 12 November 1940, he issued Directive no. 18, the planned attack on Gibraltar and the Suez Canal.[280] If his immediate target in the western Mediterranean was Britain, its ultimate purpose was to prepare for the confrontation with the United States.[281] Relations between Washington and Vichy were good, and Hitler did not trust Pétain to hold the line against the Americans in northern or western Africa. The military plans for Gibraltar saw the rock not as the final destination, but a stepping stone across the Straits.[282] Nothing came of the plan because when Serrano

Süner arrived in Berchtesgaden to discuss it in mid November, he brought with him unacceptably extensive Spanish demands for French colonies, in particular Morocco. Hitler refused, fearing that this would precipitate a defection to de Gaulle. On 7 December 1940, Franco rejected any idea that he would join the war. Operation Felix was put on hold. For now, the Führer's plan to pre-empt the United States in the western Mediterranean and North Africa had failed.

It was in the context of the failure to mobilize Europe against Anglo-America that Hitler finally turned east.[283] His July directive on Russia had not been followed by concrete preparations, but the idea of attacking the Soviet Union resurfaced with a vengeance immediately after the disastrous Molotov visit in mid November. On 15 November 1940, Hitler demanded the construction of an eastern headquarters, the subsequent Wolf's Lair.[284] On 27 November 1940, Raeder failed to dissuade Hitler from attacking Russia before Britain had been beaten. During the first week of December, Hitler admitted that the attempts to bring Franco into the war had failed, and that Sealion was on the back burner. It would be left to the navy and the Luftwaffe to subdue Britain. He announced that he had intelligence of secret agreements in the making between Britain, America and the Soviet Union. For this reason, Hitler argued, it was necessary to deal with Russia first, which would deprive Britain of all hope. He expected that US intervention would be 'made more difficult' by Japan, which 'had Germany's back'.[285] On 17 December Roosevelt announced a plan for a 'Lend-Lease' programme to supply Britain with more war material. That same day, Hitler told the OKW that the United States would have to be sorted out during 1941, because it would be capable of intervening in Europe from 1942. The day after, on 18 December 1940, Hitler issued his fateful directive for Operation Barbarossa, the attack on the Soviet Union.[286] On 28 December, Hitler headed to the Berghof for Christmas. He had made his decision. He would roll the dice again in the year to come.

PART SIX

Annihilation

In 1941, Hitler embarked on two wars of annihilation. The first, in June 1941, was against the Soviet Union, and was primarily intended to secure the resources and living space Germany 'needed' to balance the power of Anglo-America. The second was the conflict with the United States and 'world Jewry', which had begun much earlier but erupted into open warfare with the Americans at the end of the year. In Russia, Hitler began with plans for the wholescale murder of tens of millions of Slavs, from which he soon retreated. By contrast, Hitler's initially limited and calibrated campaign against 'the Jews' escalated into full-scale genocide, beginning with the mass killings at the start of the invasion of the Soviet Union and culminating in the 'final solution' across Nazi-occupied Europe. Hitler understood both wars as pre-emptive acts of self-defence forced upon him by a circling coalition. The result is well known. Hitler famously failed to overrun the Soviet Union, and he was vastly outproduced by the United States. The 'annihilation' he had planned for his enemies was visited – albeit in a milder but still extremely painful form – on German cities, the German economy, the Wehrmacht, the refugees from the eastern territories, and ultimately on the Third Reich itself.

16
Facing West, Striking East

In early 1941, Hitler appeared to be at the zenith of his power. He dominated the European mainland. Most of the pre-war European economy was now at his disposal, at least in theory. The two neutral powers of the Iberian Peninsula leaned to his side, even if they showed little inclination to become belligerents themselves. Above all, by virtue of the Hitler–Stalin Pact, the Third Reich enjoyed economic defence in depth, enabling her to mitigate the effects of the British blockade. This crucial reliance on the immense resources of Russia masked the essential weakness of the economy of German-occupied Europe. Relations with Moscow were consolidated by the signing of a big economic treaty on 10 January 1941, which increased the supply of Soviet grain, oil, cotton and other raw materials to Germany.[1] Whatever Stalin's actual intentions,[2] and German worries about his ambitions in the Balkans, Hitler did not fear an imminent Russian attack. Even though Moscow was deeply unhappy with the great German successes, the Führer told the Seekriegsleitung, 'it does not itself desire to enter into the war against Germany'.[3]

At home, Hitler's standing was high. His bombastic set-piece speeches on 30 January 1941, the anniversary of the takeover of power, and 24 February, the anniversary of the original party programme, were generally well received.[4] Though the demands of the war meant that Hitler was less ubiquitous than before, he still cut a very dynamic figure, who looked younger than his fifty-one years. The *Wochenschau* newsreels at the start of 1941 show a man completely in control, with no visible signs of wear and tear compared to the 1930s.[5] To be sure, he suffered from some persistent ailments, especially toothache and flatulence, and his doctor, Theo Morell, was already treating him with a large number of questionable substances.[6] But to the world at large, the German public and even his entourage, Hitler's health was reasonably robust and would remain so until the middle of the year.

Despite all this, Hitler remained an anxious man. His most immediate concern in early 1941 was still the British Empire. 'Britain,' he remarked to his generals, 'continues to remain intractable'; all talk of a landing there had ceased.[7] Politically, with the total ascendancy of Churchill, hopes of a compromise peace were fading. Militarily, the Reich was locked in a desperate struggle with the British Empire, at sea and in the air. In the Atlantic, the U-boats sought with some success in the first months of the year to cut the home islands off from the foodstuffs and raw materials they needed to continue the war. Casualty rates there varied throughout the conflict, but the German submariners would lose about 75 per cent of their number by its end, the highest rate of any force on any side.[8] Likewise, the war in the air was already perceived as an existential struggle; by its close the highest level of casualties of any British service had been suffered by Bomber Command. On 1 January 1941, a good year before it actually became British policy, Hitler claimed that Churchill was a promoter of an 'unlimited air war'.[9] At the end of the following month, he was so worried about this that he ordered state and party dignitaries to visit the affected areas after major attacks in order to reassure the population.[10] The Führer refused to undertake this task himself, perhaps in order to avoid angry scenes. Throughout the first four months of the year, in any case, he observed the attacks of Bomber Command with increasing anxiety, issuing instructions for air defence and damage limitation.[11]

The British also posed a direct military threat to Hitler's position in Europe. In early 1941, he observed the advance of the 8th Army in North Africa with alarm. The fall of the Libyan port of Bardia on 5 January forced him to concede that 'the whole of North Africa will be lost without German help'.[12] The Italians were also being clobbered in Greece, where British forces had already landed on Crete and Lemnos and whose large-scale deployment on the mainland was only a matter of time. Hitler feared that a total collapse would bring down Mussolini and open a new front to the south. The Führer was afraid that the British would use their new bases in Greece to attack the Romanian oil fields, whose production was vital for the German war economy, and that the British would link up with the Vichy French in North Africa.[13] Hitler was also worried about his northern flanks. In early March 1941, Royal Navy commandos raided the Lofoten Islands off Norway, exposing the weakness of German defences there. Hitler ordered the dispatch of coastal artillery and reinforcements, the start of a debilitating obsession with the British threat to Norway which lasted until the end of the war.[14]

Meanwhile, the American challenge loomed ever larger. On 3 January 1941, President Roosevelt spoke of a 'world at war', and eight weeks later he referred to 'the Second World War' beginning 'a year and a half ago'.[15]

On 11 March 1941, Roosevelt finally signed the Lend-Lease Act into law. There were also more and more signs of a forthcoming direct American intervention. Towards the end of the month the British and Americans secretly agreed that in the event of a world war involving Japan they would nonetheless pursue a 'Germany first' strategy. If Hitler was unaware of this meeting, he could not mistake the meaning of the seizure of all German and Italian ships in US harbours ordered by Roosevelt three days later.

Worse still, London and Washington were articulating more and more openly the idea of a joint management of the world, based on their Anglo-Saxon kinship and commitment to democratic values. 'Tyrannies may require a large amount of living space,' Henry Luce, the legendary publisher of *Life* magazine, wrote in a much-discussed February 1941 article, '[b]ut Freedom requires and will require far greater living space than Tyranny.' 'Peace cannot endure,' he continued, 'unless it prevails over a very large part of the world.'[16] A clash of two ordering concepts, Nazi *Lebensraum* and Anglo-American liberty, the one even more limitless than the other, was inevitable. The message from Roosevelt and his supporters in the American public sphere could not have been clearer. There was no room in their universe for the Third Reich, and Hitler knew it. If the Americans were securing the western hemisphere today, tomorrow it would be the world.[17]

Hitler was under no illusions about the magnitude of the danger. In early 1941, the German war economy was already geared towards the expected confrontation with Anglo-America. Hitler saw himself in a battle of production not only with the formidable British Empire, but also with the United States. It was a war that he expected to fight, in the first instance, at sea and in the air. The main emphasis in early 1941 was thus not on immediate output for the planned attack on Russia, but greater investment to enable subsequent increases in aerial and naval production to fight Britain and America.[18] There would be temporary priorities awarded to armoured fighting vehicles in the two years ahead, but the general emphasis on the navy, air force and anti-aircraft artillery was to remain unchanged until the end of the war.[19] Given the immense potential of the United States, despite her nominal non-belligerence, Hitler was at pains to stress, as he told a public audience in the first half of 1941, that he was 'in a position today to deploy more than half of the European labour force in this struggle'.[20]

In fact, the combined economies of the British Empire and America – now mobilized against Hitler through Lend-Lease – considerably exceeded that of the German area of control. Besides, pre-war figures were inflated, because the British blockade unplugged the continental economies not merely from many of their traditional markets but also from their supply of raw materials. Worse still, Hitler's victories in 1940 had brought him no substantial new sources of energy or foodstuffs, just millions of new mouths to feed. He was also desperately short of energy supplies, as stocks were running dangerously low.[21] The Reich of 1940–41 was full of people, but desperately short of resources. Starvation was not the answer here, as the workers employed in factories producing for Germany, and their families, would have to be nourished. Hitler had broken Europe. Now he owned it.

Despite the fact that the continent was still generally quiescent, Hitler was already anxious about the first signs of organized resistance to his rule.[22] Hitler saw these acts as the work of British Intelligence and world Jewry. He was unhappy about the Wehrmacht's response, and demanded sterner action. More generally, Hitler attributed the continued hostility of Britain to Jewish manipulation. On the very first day of 1941, his 'Order of the Day' to the Wehrmacht stated that the war was being carried on at the behest of the 'democratic warmongers and their Jewish-capitalist backers'.[23] Four weeks later, he inveighed once more against 'a certain Jewish-capitalist clique'.[24] Towards the end of the following month, Hitler claimed 'that in Britain a certain clique, led by Jewry', was always acting like a 'bellows' supporting war.[25]

The external challenges to the Reich were aggravated by the persistence of domestic weakness and division. Despite the best efforts of the regime, the racial profile of the German people left considerable room for improvement. Hitler's own misgivings, which had been ventilated more or less openly over the previous two decades, were reflected in an official racial primer for distribution to schools in 1941. By means of a comparison with a bottle of milk, this categorized only 20 per cent of the German people as 'particularly valuable', that is, the 'cream' and 'leadership' layer. 56.4 per cent were classified as 'average', that is, 'skimmed' or ordinary milk. The bottom quarter was made up of 20 per cent 'anti-socials' and 3.6 per cent 'hereditary ill', that is, 'the dregs' and 'inferior'.[26] This rather bleak view of the German *Volk* can be explained partly by the supposed failure to filter out the supposed dregs of society, but mostly by the success of Anglo-America in 'creaming off' the best of the German people through hundreds of years of emigration. Colin Ross, one of Hitler's advisers on America, elaborated on this theme, which formed such a staple of the Führer's own rhetoric, at length in his book *Our America: The German Role in the Creation of the United States*, which was also published in 1941.[27]

As if all this were not bad enough, the natural propensity of German bureaucrats to fight each other rather than the common enemy remained unchanged eighteen months into the war. To his frustration, Hitler was still repeatedly called upon to arbitrate turf wars between the various parts of the Nazi hierarchy. As so often, far from encouraging these divides in order to reinforce his authority, the Führer urged the parties to resolve their differences through compromise and then present him with an agreed solution.[28] He may have welcomed the emergence of a gatekeeper who could keep these problems at arm's length. The man who exercised this function throughout the 1930s and the early war years was the chief of the Imperial Chancellery, Hans-Heinrich Lammers, but Hess's deputy Martin Bormann was already beginning to dominate the antechamber of power around Hitler and thus access to the man himself. One of the first to notice this, several months before Hess's abrupt departure, was Arthur Rosenberg, who remarked, looking back on the previous year, that Bormann had 'gradually become the central point person' through whom everything passed.[29]

Taken together, all these challenges meant that Hitler was feeling not triumphant but increasingly embattled, and besieged, even at what appeared to be the height of his power.[30] Strategically, he believed himself to be on the defensive. He sought not world domination, but world power status, that is parity, or at least a recognized sphere of influence. The Führer did not really expect to defeat Anglo-America, only to outlast it: militarily, economically and mentally. In early 1941, Hitler therefore sought to do two things. Firstly, to deliver sufficient military, diplomatic and psychological effect in order to persuade London to fold its hand before the arrival of the Americans. Secondly, to prepare militarily, diplomatically, economically and emotionally for a long war against Anglo-America in case that strategy failed.

Hitler began with sorting out the mess created by Mussolini, and convened a meeting of military leaders at the Berghof in early January 1941. Treating the Italians as equals was ruled out by the Führer because he did not trust them not to leak confidential information to the British. That said, Hitler was anxious to spare Mussolini's feelings and urged that military assistance be presented in such a way as to avoid doing anything which would 'hurt the Duce's feelings' and damage the relationship between the two dictators.[31] German forces, he stressed, should avoid 'all hurtful displays of arrogance'.[32] Hitler put considerable effort and subtlety into the management of the Italian alliance, far more than his generals and admirals.[33] This was primarily a political decision in support of Mussolini and the fascist regime rather than a judgement based on the military value of the Italians, a subject on which he was under no illusions. On 11 January, he issued Directive 22, covering the deployment of forces to the

Mediterranean, which – contrary to Wehrmacht wishes – were to be under at least nominal Italian command.[34] Hitler wanted them to shore up Italy's position, and to prevent the establishment of a British springboard on the far side of the Mediterranean and in Greece. There was no mention of Yugoslavia at this point. Hitler was delighted when Rommel's Afrika Korps, ignoring strict instructions to stay on the defensive, promptly went over to the offensive and drove the British back in disorder.

Next, Hitler took aim at the British war economy in Directive 23 on 6 February 1941.[35] The submarine warfare against the British supply lines in the Atlantic was to be intensified. Just over two weeks later, in a speech to mark the anniversary of the founding of the party, he announced a new phase in the U-boat war, partly to boost morale at home and partly to depress the British.[36] At this point sinkings were running at about 260,000 tons a month, a respectable figure but not enough to starve out the home islands. The problem was that there were far too few U-boats operational, and while construction had grown to thirteen per month (from a mere two a year earlier), the training of crews took time. The productive capacity devoted to the task was considerable: the Reich could have built about thirty medium tanks for every submarine launched.[37] Hitler also stipulated that attacks should be concentrated on ports handling imports. The general purpose of all these operations was to wear down Britain and to prevent her from launching offensives in North Africa and ultimately mainland Europe.

The Führer had no inhibitions, however, about exploring closer cooperation with Japan, which could put pressure on the British Empire in the Far East and prevent the United States from bringing its full force to bear on Europe.[38] In early March 1941, he issued Directive 24.[39] 'The aim of the collaboration under the Tripartite Pact,' Hitler announced, 'must be to persuade Japan to act in the Far East as quickly as possible.' 'This would tie down substantial British forces,' he continued, 'and divert the attention of the United States of America to the Pacific.' The 'common aim of [Axis] strategy,' Hitler elaborated, was 'to subdue Britain quickly and thereby keep the United States out of the war.' Attacks on America should be undertaken only if war with that power 'cannot be avoided'. To this end, he instructed that Japan should be strengthened in every way, for example through the exchange of information, even if the benefits were one-sided. Hitler made no mention of any Japanese action against the Soviet Union; the pact was primarily conceived as an instrument against Britain and a deterrent against the United States.[40]

The other major plank of Hitler's containment strategy against Anglo-America was the persecution of the Jews. Privately, he let it be known in

January 1941 that it was his 'will' that there should be a 'final solution' of the Jewish question in Germany and German-dominated Europe;[41] at this point, this did not necessarily mean mass murder. Publicly, Hitler announced that he regarded the Jews under German occupation as hostages for the good behaviour of the supposedly Jewish-controlled United States. On the anniversary of the seizure of power in late January 1941, Hitler reminded his listeners of the remarks 'which I already gave once before on 1 September 1939 in the German Reichstag', that is, the prediction that 'if the other world [sic] was plunged into a general war by Jewry', then 'all Jewry' would have 'played out its role in Europe'. 'They may still be laughing about this [prediction] today,' he continued, 'just as they previously laughed about my domestic prophecies,' but he promised that 'the coming months and years' would vindicate his remarks.[42] There is no evidence that this shot across the bows of Anglo-America, or any other such 'warning', was understood in its enormity by its addressees in London, Washington and New York.

The open struggle against Britain and the cold war against America were flanked by a massive propaganda campaign. At home, the regime sought complete domination of the media in order to put out a carefully controlled message. Before the war, Hitler had taken a keen interest in film censorship, but after September 1939 he left that task largely to his propaganda minister. In the course of 1941, as relations with Washington plummeted, Goebbels banned the import of American films.[43] Hitler took an increased interest, by contrast, in the official newsreels. Goebbels closely supervised the production of the weekly *Wochenschau* before showing it to Hitler in the Imperial Chancellery or Führer's Headquarters for final approval.[44] He would often demand changes – sometimes fairly minor ones to subject, text, tone and music, and he was particularly concerned with any programmes which featured him.[45] Newspapers, magazines and other media were also subject to close supervision.

Abroad, the Third Reich sought to engage world opinion through a variety of media. In mid January 1941, the Führer ordered a gradual shift from the cumbersome Gothic font, which he considered archaic and which tended to deter foreign readers, to typefaces which would make it easier for German-speaking foreigners to read regime texts; another motivation was to save time in schools.[46] Front and centre in the whole campaign, was the attempt to 'educate' the world about the Jewish threat. In late January, Hitler approved Rosenberg's plan to establish an 'institute to research the Jewish question', to which foreign experts were to be invited.[47] The Führer was thus still hopeful that Anglo-America would see the light. Six weeks later, the 'World Service' announced that

Rosenberg had assembled 'the greatest library on the Jewish question' ever in Frankfurt.[48]

In order to mobilize the German people for the challenge ahead, Hitler continued his programme of domestic transformation. On the social front, he sought to open careers to talent. His main target here was the officer corps. In the spring of 1941, Hitler made a fresh attempt to push through promotion on merit alone, primarily on the basis of combat performance, without any social restrictions or privileging of the general staff, which he described as 'an order, which closes itself off and lives according to its own laws'. He let it be known that 'only thus could the principle of performance, which the Führer supported in the most emphatic manner, be implemented and thus the rejuvenation of the officer corps at all levels for which he was striving be achieved'.[49] For now, however, he made little headway against the entrenched conservatism or, depending on one's viewpoint, professionalism of the officer corps.

In his bid to increase production, Hitler was prepared to countenance increased participation of women in the workforce. In his speech on the occasion of Memorial Day on 16 March 1941, he announced that it was 'not only the man who had shown the capacity to resist but especially also the woman'. Six weeks later, Hitler explained that while 'millions' of German women were in the fields and the factories releasing men for service at the front, many more were required. In the autumn of that year, he returned to this theme, praising 'the German woman, [and] the German girl', for 'replacing millions of men who are at the front today'. 'We can truly say,' Hitler exulted, 'that for the first time in history the entire people is engaged in the struggle, partly at the front, and partly at home.'[50]

On the 'racial' front, Hitler continued his twin-track approach. Efforts to purify the body politic through the murder – 'euthanasia' – of the disabled or those with hereditary illnesses were speeded up in the course of early 1941, despite mounting concern in some sectors of the population. At the same time, the regime redoubled its efforts to encourage the 'racially valuable' elements. The SS *Lebensborn* project began to comb Nazi-controlled Europe for children of 'Nordic' origin, either the offspring of liaisons between German security forces and non-German 'Nordic' women, particularly in Scandinavia, or the supposed descendants of German settlers, especially in eastern Europe.[51] These measures went hand in hand with ambitious settlement plans, initially in Poland. The problem was that Germany – ironically from the point of view of Hitler's *Lebensraum* ideology – suffered from a shortage of people to 'settle' in the new lands; there was now full employment at home, indeed a labour shortage. Most of the effort here was directed at 'resettling' ethnic Germans from the Soviet Union and areas under Soviet occupation. Further treaties were concluded with Moscow in January 1941 to facilitate the 'repatriation' of Germans from the three Baltic States.[52]

The regime had still not given up hope of bringing back German emigrants from overseas. A report to the German Institute for the Outside World in February 1941 from Alexander Dolezalek, an official in the Planning Sections of the Settlement Staff for Litzmannstadt and Posen in Poland, showed just how much Hitler's thinking on this subject informed the settlements plans for the east. The author pointed out that the inflow from ethnic Germans in other parts of eastern Europe was insufficient to colonize the new lands, and because they were mostly farmers, they in any case lacked the industrial and managerial skills necessary to build up the new society. If more were not found then the regime might have to fall back on Polish settlers. 'It appears to me,' the report argued, 'that the only hope is a resettlement from the United States proper. There one finds skilled German workers of all kinds who, in one generation, can develop a united people.' They would be critical to welding the disparate newcomers together. Dolezalek was under no illusions about the difficulty of such an undertaking. Most Germans were too integrated into the United States, with its high standard of living and wide-open spaces. He was therefore resigned to the fact that the best hope of luring Germans 'back' would be after a victorious war which would make them proud to identify with the Third Reich.[53]

The answer to these problems, Hitler believed, lay in invading the Soviet Union, Operation Barbarossa. Its immediate purpose was to strike at Britain, and to deter the United States, psychologically, diplomatically, militarily and economically. Hitler remained convinced that one of the reasons the British were holding out, was the prospect of Russian intervention. This was the main reason given in the directive to launch Barbarossa, and Hitler repeated it on several occasions during the first half of 1941. It was 'the hope that Russia [and the] USA' would intervene 'that keeps Britain going', Hitler told the assembled Wehrmacht leadership at the Berghof on 8 January 1941.[54] For this reason it was necessary to 'smash' the 'last continental hope' of the British, namely 'Russia'. This would also, Hitler added, 'permit Japan to turn with all her strength against the United States' and thus 'prevent [her] from entering the war'.[55] The immediate purpose of the invasion of Russia in 1941, in short, was the delivery of effect against Anglo-America.

Hitler also saw Barbarossa as the solution to the Reich's chronic shortage of foodstuffs and raw materials. The seizure of the Ukraine and the Caucasus would prevent Germany from being strangled by the British blockade or held to ransom by Stalin. His plan was to carry off the grain harvest to the Reich, and to ship oil from the Caucasus by tanker across the Black Sea and up the Danube.[56] The experts were sceptical about the entire strategy. The War Economics Office pointed out that the Reich already enjoyed access to the resources of the Soviet Union by virtue of the Pact, and that an invasion would end that arrangement, cutting Germany off from the supply of vital metals such as manganese.[57] With regard to energy, Hitler was told that even if the oil-fields of the Caucasus were captured more or less intact, Germany simply did not yet have the capacity to transport it back to the Reich, or indeed the steel to build a huge new tanker fleet. As for foodstuffs, there were two equally impractical options: taking the grain crop before it was harvested, in which case the task of gathering it would fall to the administration, or attacking at a later date with the risk that it would be much easier for the enemy to destroy it. The list of objections was almost endless. Hitler thought the risk of inaction was greater. Fortified with the immense natural resources of the Soviet Union, he hoped, Germany might deter the US from entering the war, or at least contain Anglo-America if she did.

Finally, Barbarossa would enable Hitler to achieve his medium- to long-term objective of securing the *Lebensraum* for the German people, in his view, so desperately needed. He had articulated this aim at length for almost twenty years. The looming conflict with the United States made it more urgent. Only by 'solving the questions of land thoroughly and finally', Hitler argued, 'will we be in a position in terms of material and personnel to master the problems we will face within two years', by which he meant the belligerency of the United States.[58] Barbarossa, in short, was the panacea for each and every one of Hitler's major ills. It would solve all of his problems in one fell liberating blow.

In all of this, anti-Bolshevism and fear of the Soviet Union itself, though important, were second-order considerations.[59] Barbarossa was predicated on the assumption that the Soviet Union was not a major threat, but rather a largely helpless victim (though, as we shall see below, there were also times when he talked up Soviet capabilities). 'I will fight,' he told the generals in early February 1941, and professed himself 'convinced that our attack will pass over them like a hailstorm'.[60] In so far as he was worried about Soviet military power it was as a threat against the oil needed to contain Anglo-America. 'Now, in the era of air power,' he told his generals in late January 1941, 'Russia can turn the Rumanian oil-fields into an expanse of smoking debris . . . and the very life of the Axis depends on those fields.'[61] Hitler's relative insouciance about the Soviet communist threat was reflected in the fact that his aims, though grandiose and ultimately delusional, were limited. It is obvious with hindsight that Hitler greatly underestimated the military task ahead, and catastrophically mis-judged the capacity of the Soviet war economy, but that does not mean that he was completely insouciant about the challenge posed by the Red Army. To be sure, he repeatedly ran down the Soviet Union in order to justify his expectation of a swift campaign, but when it came to detailed discussion the Führer showed some awareness of what lay on the other side of the hill. Hitler judged the Russian tank force 'respectable', being very large with some good models, but that 'the majority were obsolete'. Similarly, he rated the Soviet Air Force as 'very large numerically but with very many obsolete types'. Even so, Hitler did not believe that the Luft-waffe could 'knock it out' on account of their own 'losses in the west' and the sheer immensity of the Russian 'space'. Overall, despite various weak-nesses, he judged the Russians a 'tough enemy'.[62] In short, Hitler seems to have believed that the invasion of the Soviet Union would be no cake-walk, but a gamble, justified only by the even greater risk of standing still and awaiting strangulation at the hands of Anglo-America. Hitler's evi-dent anxiety about Soviet power and the natural obstacles was also reflected in his concern to refute the comparison with Napoleon Bona-parte's disastrous invasion of Russia in 1812.[63]

The planned invasion of Russia required Hitler to seek allies. On 14 January, he received Romania's Marshal Antonescu at Berchtesgaden, who offered to join the war on the German side if Stalin intervened against Hitler's planned measures in the Balkans.[64] Hitler therefore put consider-able effort into mediating disputes between Hungary and Romania, who would otherwise have fought each other with even greater gusto than they would Stalin.[65] Hitler needed Finland, Romania and Hungary for largely strategic reasons, to give Germany additional attack frontage. The north-ern and southern thrusts, in particular, depended on their cooperation.[66] Hitler also tried to win over, or at least to reassure, the Turks, whose neutrality was vital for the security of the southern flank.[67] With the exception of Romania's Marshal Antonescu, he did not really trust or value any of his allies; some, such as the Hungarians, he actively despised. There was no real coordination.[68] Hitler feared that involving other pow-ers would lead them to make awkward territorial demands, but the main concern was reliability. 'Be under no illusions about the allies,' he warned the generals at the end of March 1941. 'You can't do much with Romani-ans,' Hitler continued crushingly, 'perhaps they will be able to secure an area which is not under attack with the help of a very large barrier (like a river)'. The conclusion Hitler drew with odd prescience was that 'the fate of large German units should not be made dependent on the steadfastness of a Romanian unit'.[69]

In the course of the first half of 1941, the character of the impending war against the Soviet Union was contested in the Reich leadership. Some German planners, especially Alfred Rosenberg, regarded Operation Barbarossa essentially as a European war of liberation against Bolshevism. They expected a brutal reckoning with Soviet Jewry and the Bolshevik apparatus, to be sure, but for the rest they envisaged recasting the region into a system of friendly and subservient nation states. At first, Hitler seemed to go along with this vision, not least because it fitted his idea of the endgame in Russia. In his instructions for occupation policy in the east of 3 March 1941, he explained that in order to 'end the war' it was 'by no means enough to defeat the enemy army'. Rather, Hitler continued, 'the whole area must be divided up into states with governments with whom we can make peace'. Intriguingly, but entirely consistently with his previous rhetoric and policy, Hitler had no plans entirely to reverse the transformations of the past twenty-five years of Soviet rule. 'Every great revolution,' he stated, 'creates facts which cannot simply be swept away.' The 'socialist idea', Hitler continued, 'can no longer be wished away from today's Russia'. It would have to form the basis of a new state once the 'Jewish-Bolshevik tendency' had been 'eliminated'. What Hitler wanted to 'avoid under all circumstances' was the emergence of a new 'national Russia'. For this reason, Hitler concluded, the solution was to create 'socialist state entities which depend on us'.[70]

The general trend of the debate and the planning, however, was moving in the opposite direction. Barbarossa was to be a campaign of conquest and annihilation, for reasons more to do with Anglo-America than the Soviet Union itself. The planners of the German war economy began to think about how to manage the food question. Their conclusion was bleak. While the Ukraine produced a surplus of grain, most other regions of the Soviet Union which would fall under German control did not.[71] Victory alone would bring no relief, but rather additional useless mouths to feed. In order to ensure that the Reich could survive the British blockade, they argued, about 30 million inhabitants of European Russia would have to be starved to death. Hitler accepted this assessment in January–February 1941.[72] According to this conception, the Germans would have to immediately starve the Russians, so that they would not themselves eventually be starved by the British, as they had been in the First World War.

The 'Hunger Plan' also fitted into Hitler's long-term strategic concept, which was the capture of *Lebensraum* to balance Anglo-America. By clearing the original population off the land, it would make way for German settlers to hold and develop it. This in turn would give the Reich the spatial heft necessary to survive in the world of huge global powers such as the British Empire, and the United States. It would also enable him to provide Germans with the living standard which he had promised but not delivered in the 1930s. If the twentieth-century American dream involved the distribution of plenty, his dystopia required the control of scarcity.[73] Here the history of the United States was not merely in some respects similar,[74] but an inspiration, as was that of the British Empire. The question now was whether German-occupied Russia would be based on the colonial British 'Raj' model of client states, or the annihilatory American model. Would the fate of the Slavs resemble (in Hitler's mind) that of the Indians of the subcontinent or of the 'Red' Indians? The answer was not yet clear, but it was becoming clearer.

All this shows that the Soviet Union was primarily attacked not because it was communist, but because Hitler believed that it could be (relatively) easily despoiled to support the short- and long-term struggle against Anglo-America. Once the invasion was decided, however, the ideological antagonism to the Soviet Union gained greater prominence. Front and centre here, of course, was Hitler's preoccupation with the Jews, whom he saw as the directing mind behind both the Soviet Union and the emerging Anglo-American coalition. Soviet Jews, he believed, would drive resistance to the invasion and constitute a fifth column behind German lines. Hitler resolved to eliminate them in the course of, or immediately after, the invasion. At this point, he seems to have targeted only adult male Jews, whom he regarded as enemy combatants. There was, as yet, no expectation that all Soviet Jews would be murdered, regardless of age or sex, still less any operational plan to achieve this.[75] There was also no direct spatial connection in Hitler's mind between the planned murder of the Jews and the clearing of *Lebensraum* in the east, which was to be at the expense of the Slav population.

In mid March 1941, the broad outline of Hitler's plans for the murder of adult male Soviet Jews was clear. He instructed Himmler to establish four *Einsatzgruppen* of the Sicherheitspolizei and SD, totalling about 3,000 men, to carry out 'special tasks' behind the front lines.[76] Over the next three months, these 'tasks' were more closely defined, and the co-operation of the Wehrmacht and other organizations was secured. Hitler was not merely the initiator of the planned mass executions, but was kept abreast of the preparations, not least because he had to arbitrate any resulting competency disputes.[77] These killings were not the purpose of Operation Barbarossa, but consequent upon it. Hitler did not need to invade the Soviet Union to murder Jews, or to take them hostage; he already had millions of central and western European Jews under his control.

The campaign against the Soviet Jews was not just a front in the struggle against Anglo-America, of course. It was also part of a much broader ideological war against Bolshevism. In late March 1941, Hitler pronounced the conflict to come not merely a war for resources, such as land and raw materials, but also a 'contest between two world views'. He damned 'Bolshevism' as 'synonymous with anti-social criminality'. For this reason, the Führer demanded, German soldiers should abandon the customary rules of war. 'The communist is no comrade,' he claimed, especially the 'commissars' and secret policemen deployed with the Red Army.[78] On 12 May, he issued the notorious 'Commissar Order', according to which these 'political leaders' were to be 'eliminated' by the Wehrmacht immediately after capture. This measure was accompanied by a much more far-reaching directive the following day, which laid down the framework for military justice during Barbarossa. Partisans, he decreed, were 'to be dispatched without mercy', all other opposition was to be 'crushed', and where German units were attacked behind the lines 'measures of collective violence' were to be undertaken against the local population. Beyond that, Hitler determined, with reference to the 'specificity of the enemy' and the fact that Germany's collapse in 1918 and subsequent travails were attributable to 'Bolshevik influence', that actions by Wehrmacht and rear-area forces against civilians should not be prosecuted, even if they would normally be considered military crimes.[79]

Hitler, to sum up, planned two massive murder programmes in the course of or immediately after Barbarossa. Firstly, the killing of hundreds of thousands of communist cadres and millions of male Jews, in order to decapitate the Soviet leadership and to secure the rear areas. Secondly, the death by starvation of about 30 million Soviet citizens in order to use the grain saved to feed the Reich and – though this was implicit rather than explicit at this stage – to clear the land for later settlement by Germans.

In late March 1941, Hitler was suddenly distracted by a crisis in the Balkans. In order to keep the British out and stabilize the Italian position in the Balkans he had long planned to bring Yugoslavia into the Axis orbit. On 14 February, Hitler received the Yugoslav prime minister, Dragiša Cvetković, at the Berghof, followed by a visit from Prince Paul of Yugoslavia on 4 March 1941. Hitler made both men the same offer, which was protection and possible territorial gains, such as Salonica, in return for a general alignment with the Third Reich; both prevaricated, with Paul warning Hitler that such an agreement would cost him his regency. On 25 March, Yugoslavia finally caved in under huge pressure. The pact was extremely unpopular, at least in Serbia, where pro-British feeling ran high. Hitler joked at the signing ceremony that the Yugoslavs looked as if they were at a funeral.[80] An invasion of their country was, at this point, very far from Hitler's mind.

Two days later, the Führer was stunned by news of a coup by Serbian officers in Belgrade.[81] He had long been deeply concerned about British penetration of the country, and must have been further unsettled by the signature of a treaty of friendship and non-aggression between the new regime and the Soviet Union a week later, and the news that Roosevelt was planning to offer Belgrade assistance under the Lend-Lease programme.[82] Hitler issued Directive 25, which authorized the invasion of Yugoslavia and its destruction as an independent state.[83] All Yugoslav professions of friendship were to be ignored. The attack was also conceived as a shaping operation in advance of the long-planned attack on Greece. Hitler now scrambled to make contact with Yugoslavia's internal enemies; Rosenberg was instructed to find Croatian collaborators.[84]

The driving force behind the invasion of Yugoslavia and Greece was not an interest in either country per se, or an established enmity towards the local population, still less the quest for *Lebensraum*.[85] In the directive setting out his plans for the region after the invasion, Hitler envisaged German gains to be relatively modest – some former Habsburg parts of Slovenia adjoining Carinthia and Styria were to be annexed to the Reich.[86] There was no mention of any plans to settle Germans south of those areas. Hitler had shown no previous interest in any of the Yugoslav peoples, and the codename he gave the operation against their state – 'Punishment' – expressed a purely spontaneous rage. He was actually sympathetic to the Greeks, not least because of their classical heritage, and regretted that he 'had' to attack them. 'The Führer says,' Rosenberg noted in his diary, 'that he is very sorry that he has to fight with the Greeks.'[87] Hitler's principal purpose in both operations was to prop up Italy, to exclude Britain from the Balkans, and secure his flanks for the attack on the Soviet Union. The Führer's 'Proclamation' to the German people at the start of the Balkan campaign duly framed the attack as part of the struggle against 'British imperialism' and 'Jewish high finance'. 'We have swept [our] northern flank clear of the British,' he continued, and 'we are determined not to tolerate such a threat in the south either.'[88]

On 6 April 1941, Hitler struck at Yugoslavia, beginning with a massive air attack on Belgrade. That same day, German forces poured into Greece from Bulgaria; other units raced through the Vardar Valley in Yugoslav Macedonia to outflank the Greek defences on the Metaxas Line with Bulgaria from the west. Yugoslavia surrendered in mid April 1941. By then Hitler had already turned his attention south. On 13 April 1941, he issued Directive 27 to complete the destruction of Greece and to drive Britain completely out of the Balkans.[89] The Greeks and the British offered furious resistance but were soon overcome. German aircraft were careful to spare the major sites of classical significance. 'There are to be no bombs on Athens,'[90] Hitler ordained. Within three weeks, mainland Greece had been completely overrun. Most of the British expeditionary force escaped south across the Mediterranean.

By late April and early May 1941, Hitler's position appeared to have improved, but the overall situation had not changed much. In Latin America, for example, particularly in Argentina, the British secret service and propaganda spread misinformation about Hitler's alleged plans to subvert the continent.[91] This was addressed not merely to local governments and populations but also to the American president, who duly recycled these stories in his own speeches against Nazi Germany. In mid April 1941, Roosevelt extended the US defence perimeter to include the Azores. The Romanian oil-fields at Ploesti remained within range of RAF bombers on Crete. Hitler also fretted about British invasion plans against the Iberian Peninsula.[92] In Iraq, British troops landed at Basra in defiance of the new nationalist and pro-Nazi Baghdad government, which turned to Hitler for help.

On 11 April 1941, Hitler let it be known that he had read of the 'national struggle of the Arabs with great interest and sympathy'. The Führer stressed that the Arabs, as an 'old people of culture', had shown themselves eminently capable of ruling themselves. For this reason, Hitler announced that he would recognize 'the complete independence of the Arab states' where it existed or was desired, a clear tilt at the British Empire.[93] Privately, though, he was as scathing of the Arabs as he had been in the 1920s. 'Unfortunately,' Hitler remarked, 'Arabs [are] unreliable and can be bribed,' something which the British and French 'understood' very well.[94] Later that month, Hitler authorized Ribbentrop to receive the Indian nationalist leader Subhas Chandra Bose: the Führer refused a meeting with him himself, at least for now.[95] Bose explained that although British and communist propaganda suggested that Nazism supported the subjugation of other races, the Hitler–Stalin Pact had revealed Hitler's true 'social' and 'anti-imperialist' instincts to many Indians. These exchanges showed the hopes which some of the 'global south' invested in Nazism, but Hitler remained hesitant. Bose and Husseini were much more interested in him than he in them.

Hitler had greater hopes of Japan. In late March and early April he had two meetings with the Japanese foreign minister, Matsuoka, who reached Germany by an adventurous and circuitous route via the Soviet Union. Hitler explained that his aim was to 'break' the 'British hegemony' in Europe and to exclude any 'American intervention in Europe'. In this context the Tripartite Pact had the great merit that it deterred the US from 'entering into the war officially'. Hitler concluded that while there would always be a 'certain risk', now was the best chance Japan would ever have of attacking the British Empire. Hitler promised to intervene 'immediately in the event of conflict between Japan and America' if the latter intervened to protect the British Empire against a Japanese attack.[96] He did not encourage the Japanese to fight the Soviet Union, no doubt partly because he thought he did not need their help and partly because he wanted them to remain focused on Anglo-America. For this reason, Hitler was entirely unperturbed by the Japanese-Russian Non-Aggression Pact of 13 April 1941.

Even now, Hitler had not yet completely given up hope of conciliating Britain. Informal contacts were maintained throughout early 1941, though it is not clear whether the Führer personally encouraged them or was even aware that they were taking place.[97] The most important of these lines of communication, which may have been opened with Hitler's approval, ran from Britain directly to the office of the deputy Führer, Rudolf Hess. He had been planning a mission to England, undertaking various dry runs, and drawing up documents, since the end of the previous year. British Intelligence indulged the dialogue, perhaps in order to find out more about Hitler's intentions, especially towards the Soviet Union.

Hess met with Hitler on 5 May 1941. There is no evidence that he discussed his plans with the Führer on that occasion, but nor did anything that was said then deter him from taking a truly momentous step. On 10 May 1941, Hess, a skilled pilot, took off from Haunstetten airfield near Augsburg and flew more than 1,700 kilometres, some of it over territory closely patrolled by the RAF, to the east coast of Scotland. There he parachuted safely. Hess requested to see the Duke of Hamilton, whom he believed to be sympathetic to a negotiated solution, and presented him with his personal plan for a peace between Germany and Britain.[98] It was one of the war's most dramatic stories, a Shakespearean excursion into the enemy camp. Though it is unlikely that Hitler knew of his deputy's general intention, still less the precise date of the mission, there can be no doubt that Hess believed he was acting in accordance with his wishes.[99] The timing of the mission, immediately after the British humiliation in Greece and before the start of Barbarossa, was certainly propitious, and the use of an aristocratic 'go-between' was something of which Hitler – who greatly overestimated the power of the court and the nobility in Britain – would probably have approved. The drift of Hess's statements to his British interlocutors – that talks would depend on the resignation of the Churchill government, that the U-boats would soon starve out Britain, that Germany had no aggressive intent towards the United States and that

British hopes of American support were illusory – was very much the sort of message that the Führer wanted to convey.

The next morning, Hess's adjutant handed Hitler a long letter, which Hess had written before his departure. No copy of the original exists. The gist of it was that Hess had tried to reach Britain in order to promote a compromise peace; it was clear, by inference, since the Führer had not heard directly from him, that the mission had failed. Hitler was deeply shocked and alarmed – 'crushed' in Rosenberg's phrase.[100] Witnesses said that he had not been so upset since the death of Geli Raubal.[101] All the same, the Führer seems to have decided to give the British some more time to respond; he appears to have made no attempt to issue an immediate pre-emptive statement. Hitler waited nearly two days for news of his deputy, not knowing whether he was dead or alive. In Britain, Hess tried hard to convince his interlocutors, and his final (unsent) letter to Hitler, written in captivity, was full of regret for the failure of his mission, but in no sense apologetic for having tried.[102] By then, however, it was long clear that the British would not negotiate.

Now the risks of the Hess mission could no longer be ignored. Firstly, there was the danger that he would reveal the plan to attack Russia, of which Hess was aware in general terms. Secondly, there was the irritation of the Axis allies Japan and Italy, both of which stood to lose from a German rapprochement with Britain.[103] Thirdly, there was the general embarrassment of the deputy Führer, the third-highest-ranking figure in the Third Reich, suddenly going absent without leave. On the evening of 12 May, German radio announced that Hess, who had been suffering for years from a 'worsening illness', had gone missing with his aircraft and was the victim of 'delusions', and blamed his flight on his adjutants.[104] It was not a moment too soon, because the BBC broadcast Hess's arrival in Britain very shortly afterwards. Hitler continued his damage-limitation exercise the following day. On 13 May 1941, he summoned the *Gauleiter* for an emergency meeting at the Berghof; the Führer tended to gather his old guard around him in times of crisis.[105] Hitler's task was not easy: to discredit Hess, whom everybody there knew very well, without further damaging himself. His remarks made clear that Hess had some peculiar notions, which most of his audience would have been familiar with in any case, but there was no suggestion that the deputy Führer was insane. Hitler did not excoriate Hess's motives, which he described as well-meant and idealistic, but rather his refusal to submit to discipline.[106]

The regime moved quickly to close ranks. On the same day as the radio broadcast disavowing Hess, Hitler abolished the office of the deputy

Führer and replaced it with the Party Chancellery under the leadership of Martin Bormann. There was also an immediate Gestapo investigation into Hess's connections,[107] the main purpose of which was not so much to prove traitorous intent on his part or that of his collaborators, but to establish the extent of his knowledge about Barbarossa, and thus what he might divulge to the British. Hess's removal from the line of succession moved at a rather more leisurely pace. The matter was put on the agenda in early June 1941,[108] but it was only settled right at the end of the month, a week after the start of Barbarossa.[109]

On 17 May 1941, just a week after his deputy had parachuted into Britain, Hitler issued Directive 29, giving the go-ahead for a sea and airborne assault on Crete, codenamed 'Operation Mercury'.[110] This was intended to complete the expulsion of the British from the Balkans, to secure the southern flank for Barbarossa and deprive the RAF of the last base from which it could attack the Romanian oil-fields.[111] Despite the fact that Rommel was simultaneously surging eastwards across North Africa, Hitler was not planning a new Mediterranean strategy to drive Britain from Egypt and the Middle East. He complained to his military leaders that 'one cannot be and help everywhere'. 'In and of itself,' the Führer continued, 'the Orient would not be a problem, were it not for the fact that other plans [Barbarossa] were irrevocable.' 'Once those had succeeded,' he went on, 'then the gate to the Orient could be opened from there.'[112] In other words, Hitler was expecting to break into the Middle East not through the heavily defended front door in Egypt, but by the (allegedly) more lightly guarded back door of the Soviet Caucasus.

These measures were flanked by a political offensive in the Middle East. On 23 May, Hitler issued Directive 30.[113] This proclaimed the 'Arab freedom movement in the Middle East our natural ally against Britain'. In particular, Hitler stressed the importance of developments in Iraq, which threatened Britain's position in the Middle East, and tied down forces there at the expense of other theatres. He ordered that 'everything possible' be done to support the rising by military means.[114] Weapons, a military mission and about twenty aircraft were hurriedly sent to Iraq to help the government there. Hitler classified the personnel deployed as 'volunteers' according to the 'model' of the Condor Legion. They were to wear Iraqi uniforms, while Luftwaffe planes were to sport Iraqi insignia. Hitler also laid down the 'basic principle' of the accompanying propaganda, which was to be conducted by the Foreign Office in consultation with the OKW. 'The victory of the Axis,' he wanted the Arabs to be told, 'will bring the countries of the Middle East freedom from the British yoke and thus self-determination.'[115]

Around the same time, Hitler authorized two of Germany's most power-ful ships, the heavy cruiser *Prinz Eugen* and the battleship *Bismarck*, to set sail from the Norwegian port of Bergen to strike at Allied shipping in the Atlantic. The initiative here had come from the Kriegsmarine; Hitler, who was well aware of their vulnerability to air attack and feared the propaganda effect of the loss of these vessels, only agreed with reluctance. He and the commander of the task force, Admiral Lütjens, were both of the opinion that the greatest threat came from the torpedo-bombers of the British Fleet Air Arm. Hitler was also anxious about the increased likeli-hood of a confrontation with the United States. Relations were already bad enough on account of the U-boat war, but the appearance of German surface ships in the Atlantic might precipitate a crisis. For all these reasons, Hitler asked whether the *Bismarck* could be recalled even after the mission had begun, though he did not press the point.[116] As ever, anxiety and au-dacity coexisted in Hitler's mind.

On 20 May, Hitler launched the attack on Crete. General Student's airborne force ran into heavy resistance from the garrison, which included a large Australian and New Zealand contingent. The British theatre com-mander, General Bernard Freyberg, was (as his name suggested) of partial German-Austrian descent. His divisional commander, Howard Karl [*sic*] Kippenberger, was descended from a German couple who emigrated to New Zealand in 1862. The Royal Navy intercepted and largely scattered the seaborne force, but within a few days Student's men prevailed and the British withdrew. Despite the uncertainty of the opening phase, Hitler hardly interfered in the direction of operations. He was aghast, however, at the cost of the victory, which claimed nearly 20 per cent of the force and nearly 50 per cent of the transport fleet, including irreplaceable pilot instructors. Hitler resolved never again to undertake a large-scale airborne landing. The enemy, he explained, were now on their guard. If Hitler's willingness to gamble had once more paid off, the British had again extracted a high price for their defeat.[117]

In retrospect, we can see that Crete marked the German imperial merid-ian, the last 'easy' success. Britain had once again been humiliated. The Nazi *Wochenschau*, perhaps using music suggested by Hitler, choreo-graphed the arrival of the airborne forces over the water to the strains of Wagner's 'Ride of the Valkyries'. German public opinion exulted in yet another spectacular victory. That said, neither Hitler nor the Nazi leader-ship shared this euphoria, which they regarded as not merely premature but potentially dangerous. The Wehrmacht, too, was under no illusions. On 26 May, Goebbels passed on complaints from frontline soldiers about stories suggesting British cowardice. 'The British,' he reported them as saying, were 'fighting very bravely.'[118]

There was every reason for caution. Hitler's other initiatives ended in abject failure. Britain crushed the Iraqi government and swept aside the German military mission. The Luftwaffe planes there were destroyed. A British occupation of Vichy Syria was only a matter of time. Negotiations with Vichy over the use of the Tunisian port of Bizerta to supply the Afrika Korps collapsed. Hitler feared that if he put too much pressure on Pétain, French North Africa would defect to de Gaulle (French central Africa had already done so the previous summer),[119] blowing his southern flank wide open. German diplomacy also made little headway in Iran. Despite the Shah's personal admiration for Hitler, close trading connections and hope that the Third Reich would provide a third way between Anglo-American capitalist imperialism and Soviet communism, he refused, for example, to support the pro-German putschists in Iraq.[120] Too much of the world was now too far away. The Middle East, as Hitler had always said, would have to wait for Barbarossa. Things were no better at sea. Towards the end of May, the *Bismarck*, the pride of the German surface fleet, was crippled by Fleet Air Arm torpedo-bombers and eventually sunk by the Royal Navy after a dramatic pursuit.

Above all, the fundamental imbalance between the Reich and Anglo-America and the malevolence of the Roosevelt administration had not changed. Right at the start of June 1941, the US navy established a 'South Greenland Patrol' to protect convoys, thus virtually ensuring clashes with German submarines. At his meeting with Mussolini and Ciano at the Brenner Pass on 2 June, Hitler discussed whether to respond and thought better of it for fear of escalating matters. Roosevelt, the Führer remarked, was just jealous: he 'hated' the two dictators because they had 'solved problems which had defeated him'. Despite all the deficits run up, and Roosevelt's vaunted 'brain trust', Hitler claimed, there were still 11–12 million unemployed and mass poverty in cities like New York. American claims about their productive power and capacity to aid Britain were not so easily ignored and absorbed much of Hitler's attention during the encounter. He affected to disbelieve the statistics, but thanks to Bötticher's reports from Washington, the Führer was aware that the British were already receiving an extraordinary 300–400 planes a month from the United States.[121] He may also have known of the Empire Air Training Scheme, his ultimate nightmare of large numbers of 'high-value' whites being trained in the invulnerable spaces of Canada, Australasia and South Africa, in order to carry the war to the Reich.

Hitler's reaction to the growing American threat continued to follow the long-established pattern. Nazi propaganda pushed back vigorously throughout the spring and early summer of 1941. The magazine *Signal*, which was directed at an international audience, accused Roosevelt in April of preparing to attack the Reich by sending arms to Britain under Lend-Lease.[122] Nazi media tried to divide Anglo-America. In late May 1941 the Propaganda Ministry announced at one of its press conferences 'that the warmongers were not the Anglo-Saxons [sic] but the government of the United States and the Jews which stood behind it'.[123] Behind the scenes, Hitler reinforced this message in his meetings with Americans. He told John Cudahy, a strong isolationist and former ambassador to Belgium, that the US drift to war was driven by a false 'business interest' and mendacious claims of German hostile intent. 'To declare that Europe wanted to conquer America,' Hitler explained, 'was tantamount to asserting that America wanted to conquer the moon.'[124]

The other tactic Hitler used was to avoid direct confrontation for as long as possible. As the US navy stepped up its activities in the North Atlantic this became ever more difficult. Clashes between the U-boats and American escorts were inevitable; the key was to prevent these from escalating out of control and give Roosevelt the pretext he needed to enter the war. With Barbarossa imminent, Hitler gave strict orders to avoid US warships and to disengage when attacked by the Americans. On 20 June 1941, for example, a U-boat came close to launching its torpedoes at the battleship USS *Texas*, but was stood down. The next day, which was the eve of the invasion of Russia, Hitler repeated his instructions to the Kriegsmarine. 'The Führer absolutely wishes to avoid any incidents with the United States,' Raeder noted, 'at least until the effects of Barbarossa have become clear,' that is, 'for several weeks'.[125] The message was clear: the confrontation with America would have to wait until Russia had been sorted out.

The extent to which Hitler was already thinking ahead, to the confrontation with Anglo-America, was demonstrated by his Draft Directive 32, entitled 'Preparations for the Time after Barbarossa', issued eleven days before the attack.[126] Following the defeat of the Soviet Union, he claimed, the Axis would dominate all of mainland Europe outside of the Iberian Peninsula. It could then shift the focus of armaments production from the army to the air force and navy (which were already absorbing the preponderance of the German war economy),[127] that is, against Britain and the United States. There would have to be closer cooperation with France. Iran, Turkey and Spain would have to be brought into the Axis orbit, again with a view to intimidating Britain. There would be an intensive economic exploitation of the new territories in the east, watched over by a large holding force of about sixty divisions. The next military steps would be the capture of Gibraltar, Tobruk and Malta, and an attack on the Suez Canal. Meanwhile Iraq would be approached from the Caucasus. The Arab freedom movement would be exploited 'at the right moment'. Then the siege of the British islands would be resumed and an invasion planned.

A few days after the Yugoslav capitulation, Hitler appointed Rosenberg his 'envoy for the central treatment of questions concerning the eastern European space'.[128] The latter, who had already been briefed in detail on the Führer's vision for the east,[129] could now get to work in earnest. In late May 1941, Himmler was formally charged with ensuring security behind the front.[130] Preparations for the next stage of the war against the Jews also proceeded apace. They were flanked with the usual public anti-Semitic rhetoric. Hitler spoke of western opposition to the Axis as the product of the 'purely capitalist-oriented brains of our Jewish democracies'.[131] On 7 June 1941, responding to suggestions for new regulations concerning the status of Jews, he let it be known 'that there would be no more Jews in Germany after the war'.[132] A week or so later, Hitler told a visitor 'that all Jews would have to leave Europe completely after the war', including the 'eastern territories'.[133] The male Soviet Jews would – in practice – be killed on the spot by the *Einsatzgruppen*.[134] Hitler's decision to do so was primarily driven not by his hostility to Bolshevism, important though this was, but by his fear of Britain and the United States.[135]

On 17 June 1941, Hitler issued the final instruction to launch Barbarossa. Millions of men, and thousands of aircraft and vehicles, had been assembled in secrecy, though fewer aircraft than he had fielded against the Western Allies a year earlier due to losses.[136] He had corralled a fractious and leaky coalition of the willing into supporting the attack and holding its tongue. Above all, Hitler had gulled Stalin, the most paranoid man in the world,[137] despite having advertised his intentions for twenty years, and despite the fact that the German mobilization was known to the Russians in broad outline from their aerial reconnaissance and other intelligence sources, and despite specific and credible warnings from his master spy Richard Sorge in Tokyo. Stalin had studied Hitler's modus operandi, and believed that he would have ample warning of an attack because it would be preceded by the usual barrage of press obloquy. But Hitler was constantly changing his modus. He had begun with sudden 'weekend coups' such as the announcement of German rearmament in 1935, the occupation of the Rhineland in 1936 and the annexation of Austria in 1938. Then he had moved on to choreographed crises, as over the Sudetenland in 1938, Poland in 1939 and in the Balkans in early 1941. The lightning strikes against Scandinavia in 1940, and Yugoslavia and Greece in 1941, which had come completely out of the blue, had been outliers. It was one of those which was about to hit Stalin. 'The procedure will be as follows,' Hitler explained, 'we will take a completely different path from before' by 'putting a new barrel in the organ'. 'We will not polemicize in the press,' he continued, but rather 'stay completely quiet and then simply attack' when the time was right.[138]

A few days before the start of the invasion, Goebbels slipped into the Imperial Chancellery through the back door to avoid the foreign journalists loitering at the front.[139] Hitler told him that he hoped to seize the Ukrainian harvest largely intact, that the elimination of Russia would free Japan to take on the United States, and that he would then turn to settle accounts with Britain. He professed optimism, and predicted that the campaign would take about four months. That said, Hitler's insistence that the example of Napoleon would not be repeated – a theme which featured regularly in his discourse – suggested a certain anxiety. Hitler was genuinely confident, much more so than he had been about the projected Operation Sealion, but he also knew that what he was attempting was still a huge gamble based on imperfect intelligence, with an uncertain outcome. 'I feel,' the Führer is said to have remarked at 3 a.m. on the morning of 22 June, hours before the attack, 'as if I am about to push open a door to a dark, unfamiliar room – without knowing what is to be found behind the door.'[140]

On 22 June 1941, the Wehrmacht kicked in the front entrance to the Soviet Union in the most ferocious act of breaking and entering the world has ever seen.[141] The victim was completely dumbstruck; consignments of Soviet oil and grain were still heading west by rail as the Germans invaded. 'We did not deserve this,' Molotov remarked to the German ambassador when he took his leave immediately after the attack had begun.[142] After some bitter border battles, the Soviet front quickly buckled. In the northern and central sectors, German spearheads drove deep into the Baltic lands and White Russia. Much of the Soviet air force was destroyed on the ground. Sometimes, as at the citadel of Brest-Litovsk, the Red Army put up an effective if futile resistance. More often, it was encircled in large numbers. Hundreds of thousands and then millions of Soviet prisoners of war were herded westwards.

Throughout the first weeks of the campaign, Hitler followed events on the ground closely.[143] Three days after the attack started, he became worried that the pockets were too large, with the consequent difficulty of sealing off the enemy, crushing him or forcing him to surrender. Much to his annoyance, the commander of Army Group Centre, Bock, was told to close the pincers earlier than he had intended.[144] This set a pattern, with Hitler generally taking a more cautious view than the hawkish generals.

The Führer also tended towards scepticism at reports of victories. 'Where are the prisoners?' he asked three weeks into the campaign.[145] Hitler's anxiety reflected the limited instruments available to him. He invaded Russia with two armies: one a relatively small modern motorized and armoured force, the other a much larger traditional infantry force, which had to cover vast distances on foot and was supplied from horse-drawn wagons.[146] No matter how far the former advanced, it still had to wait for the latter to come up to consolidate the ground seized and guard the haul of prisoners and materiel.

As instructed by Hitler, the struggle in the east was waged as a war of annihilation from the very beginning.[147] Thousands of commissars were shot on capture or immediately after. So were tens of thousands of other Red Army troops. Millions of Soviet POWs were starved or worked to death.[148] Behind the lines, the *Einsatzgruppen* moved in to murder all male Jews of military age they could find. Women and children were mostly spared, for now.[149] They also executed all Comintern functionaries, all Communist Party functionaries, Jews in party and state posts and various other categories such as 'agitators', 'saboteurs' and 'assassins'.[150] The Wehrmacht was often complicit in these killings. Hitler sought to head off protests from the army through thinly concealed bribes in the form of bonuses and endowments of land for senior officers.[151]

Barbarossa was conceived as both an anti-colonial and a colonizing enterprise.[152] Hitler claimed he was liberating Germany and the world from Anglo-American capitalist imperialism and Jewish manipulation, be it in the guise of plutocracy or of Bolshevism. The resources of the world, so unjustly hoarded by the 'haves', would now be redistributed to the 'have-nots'. Hitler therefore began his proclamation at the start of Barbarossa not by speaking of the Soviet Union, or even the Jews, but by attacking Britain and the balance of power with which it had oppressed Germany and continental Europe for generations. When London had entered the war, he argued, it marked a repeat of the British attempt to 'prevent' the 'consolidation of Europe' by the strongest European power of the time.[153] Hitler inveighed once again against the 'new, hate-filled encirclement policy' of the 'well-known conspiracy between Jews, democracies, Bolsheviks and reactionaries'. It took him ten paragraphs before he actually began to speak about the Soviet Union, listing his gravamina, before circling back to lambast Britain once again.

Barbarossa was clearly a colonial enterprise, because it involved the despoliation and expropriation of the native population. Following close behind the frontline forces, the German administration implemented the long-planned seizure of foodstuffs; this proved to be a far more complicated operation than expected.[154] As the Wehrmacht drove ever deeper into Russia, Hitler moved forward on the settlement of the new *Lebensraum*. Three weeks into the campaign, he summoned Rosenberg to discuss the 'partition of the eastern European space'. Hitler demanded that Crimea and its northern hinterland should be 'cleared of all aliens and settled by Germans'; he also laid down that all of the Baltic lands should become 'German'. The area around Baku, with its vital oil-fields, should become a German 'concession'. 'We must make a Garden of Eden out of our new eastern territories,' Hitler said, 'they are essential to us.' The key thing, he concluded, was to 'divide up the enormous cake' in such a way that we can 'dominate it, administer it, and exploit it'.[155] During this discussion, in which the major stakeholders in the east from the party, economy and Wehrmacht – Bormann, Göring and Keitel – participated, Hitler stressed that 'the task in the east was not a matter for a generation but one for centuries'.[156] Time, which had contracted so quickly over the previous few years, seemed briefly to expand again.

The Führer increasingly argued that he was acting not only for Germany but also on behalf of Europe as a whole. Just as Napoleon had attacked Russia in 1812 with a multinational army of French, Dutch, Italians and Germans from the Confederation of the Rhine, flanked by his uneasy allies Austria and Prussia, so did Hitler invade at the head of a large coalition, which by the end of the year included Finland, Slovakia, Hungary, Romania and Italy, as well volunteer contingents from Spain and many parts of occupied Europe.[157] He went to considerable trouble to manage these allies, many of whom hated each other far more than they did Stalin.[158] When a newsreel reference to Italian troops as 'fast' provoked widespread merriment on account of the implied cowardice, he immediately ordered the offending passages to be cut so as not to jeopardize relations within the Axis.[159] The Führer was particularly solicitous of Antonescu, of whom he spoke with genuine respect.[160] When Odessa was about to fall, Hitler disregarded the heavy weather his allies had made of the siege and instructed that the Romanians be allowed to claim the credit.[161]

Beneath the surface, however, Hitler remained deeply ambivalent about the value of his alliances. The only coalition troops for whom he had untrammelled regard were the Finns and Spaniards. 'These are the bravest of men,' Hitler remarked privately, and 'he did not see them as mere hangers-on but as real allies'.[162] The Spaniards of the 'Blue Division', who arrived later in the autumn, also gained his admiration during the subsequent winter battles.[163] Hitler had a low regard for the Slovak, Italian, Hungarian and (most of) the Romanian forces. He did not think much of his various political allies either. Hitler was particularly scathing about the White Russian émigrés whom he had known well in the 1920s and who were now queuing up to return. He considered them lazy, feckless and generally far inferior to their womenfolk.[164] The Führer's main worry, however, was that he might be forced to share some of his plunder with the rest of Europe. He was infuriated by the suggestion of a 'cheeky' Vichy newspaper[165] that the war against the Soviet Union was a European war from which not only Germany but the whole of the continent should benefit. This made Hitler more determined to ensure that the Reich, which had paid the largest blood price, should also be the primary beneficiary of the campaign.

The tension between the emancipationist and exploitative character of Barbarossa was particularly evident in the discussion over settlement plans. Hitler began his remarks on the future of the east with the claim that 'final decisions', especially on states and borders, should not be proclaimed in advance, but that it would be enough to 'appear as liberators from Bolshevism'. In this sense, Hitler argued, echoing his public statements, 'Germany's struggle was also in Europe's interest'.[166] Somewhat in contradiction to the general tenor of his plans, Hitler agreed with Rosenberg that national sentiment should be encouraged among Ukrainians by giving them a university at Kiev. This shows that in July 1941 Hitler's mind was still open on the future relationship with the planned successor states. He appears to have envisaged a combination of the American and the British forms of colonialism. In some areas, such as the Crimea and other parts of the Ukraine, the local population would be simply replaced by German settlers in the style of the settlement of the American West. In others, such as the remaining areas of the Ukraine, Hitler planned to set up disarmed semi-independent statelets in the style of the Raj. 'Here too,' he remarked, 'the behaviour of the British in India towards the Indian princes is a model.'[167]

That said, Hitler left no doubt that the relationship between the Germans and the Slav population would be a profoundly unequal one, nor did he disguise the fact that his 'European' rhetoric was largely designed to gull world opinion while he created facts on the ground. 'Our steps,' Hitler explained, 'must be driven by tactical considerations,' just as had been done with regard to the occupations in the west. Germany, he continued, should stress that it had been 'forced' to occupy and order a territory and was now obliged to care for its population. 'We should simply pretend,' he said, 'that we are carrying out a [League of Nations-style] mandate,' so that it was 'not clear' that a final settlement was intended. Hitler's caution was driven by the need, as he put it, 'not to make enemies of certain people unnecessarily and prematurely'. Whatever 'needed' to be done – 'shooting, deporting, etc.' – should continue to be done, of course. The recent Soviet call for partisan warfare was a boon in this regard, Hitler argued, because it provided a pretext to 'exterminate everything opposing us'. The key point was 'we will never leave these territories'.[168] The Germans were in the east to stay.

Despite his investment of time and effort in running the Russian campaign and planning for its aftermath in the summer of 1941, Hitler never lost sight of the broader struggle against Anglo-America. The structure of military decision-making reflected these priorities. Hitler headed the High Command of the Wehrmacht (OKW), which was responsible for the war as a whole and all the individual theatres, with the exception of the Russian front, which was run by the High Command of the Army (OKH). The main enemy for the Kriegsmarine, the Luftwaffe and the Wehrmacht as a whole remained Britain, and ultimately America; the concentration on Russia was regarded as purely temporary.

If things were still going well against the Soviet Union, the same could not be said of the hot war against the British Empire and the cold war with the United States. Both London and Washington announced their intention to supply Stalin with war material. Two days after the start of the invasion, Roosevelt unfroze Soviet accounts in the US and a few months later extended Lend-Lease to Stalin. His confidant, Harry Hopkins, was sent to Moscow. Two weeks after the start of Barbarossa, on 7 July 1941, the United States took over the occupations of Iceland and Greenland, not only releasing British troops for service elsewhere but also taking the Americans much closer to the fighting in Europe; the Führer registered this with profound alarm.[169] On 12 July, Britain signed a formal pact with the Soviet Union. Hitler had himself brought about the encirclement he so feared.

Moreover, despite the early successes, Russian resistance was stiffer than Hitler had expected. German infantry and tank losses in the first weeks of the invasion were much heavier than in any previous campaign. Ralph Ross, the Chicago-raised son of Hitler's 'America adviser' Colin Ross, was killed in the Ukraine in early July 1941, six days short of his eighteenth birthday.[170] Not long after, the Führer conceded that while the Soviet officer corps was weak, the commissars were 'hard' and 'the Russian was individually as fanatic as he had been in the [First] World War', that is, 'obstinate and determined'.[171] Hitler admitted privately to Rosenberg that 'the Soviets had many more and better tanks than had been assumed'.[172] A week after that, he remarked with exasperation that the Russians always seemed to have men left over. By mid July 1941, however, Hitler was reasonably confident that the collapse of the Soviet Union was only a matter of time. He did not think, he remarked privately, 'that the resistance in European Russia will last longer than six weeks'.[173]

*

The Führer now turned back to face the main enemy, Anglo-America. On 13 July 1941, Hitler decreed that strong tank forces would be left to secure Russia, but new formations – such as 'tropical armoured divisions' – were to be established for use against Britain.[174] A day later, he issued Directive 32b, his first after the start of the invasion.[175] Its title referred back to the original Directive 32 concerning the time after Barbarossa. That moment, Hitler believed, had now come. 'The military domination of the European space after the defeat of Russia,' he predicted, 'will soon allow us to reduce the size of the army'; only the armoured forces were to be increased. Naval armaments were to be limited to the level necessary for the immediate prosecution of the war 'against Britain, and, in the event, against America'. 'The centre of gravity of armaments,' Hitler decreed, 'will be transferred to the Luftwaffe,' which was to be 'greatly enlarged'. There was no sign of euphoria, or sense of imminent victory. On the contrary, he decreed that all construction 'which did not serve the immediate needs of the Wehrmacht and the war economy' was to cease. As Barbarossa appeared to draw to a close, Hitler's war was not over; it had hardly begun.

That same day Hitler met with Oshima in order to maintain Japanese pressure on the US, to guard against his nightmare scenario, which was the possibility of a rapprochement between Tokyo and Washington, and to assure his interlocutor that he was in no sense intimidated by American industrial potential. 'Europe,' he claimed, was a 'much greater armoury than the USA,' citing the superiority of Krupp, Rheinmetall, Skoda and even Schneider-Creusot. 'As far as soldiers were concerned,' Hitler continued, 'he was not worried at all,' because 'what was the American soldier anyway – he had got to know him in the [First] World War'. The Führer was, of course, protesting too much, especially if one recalls his earlier respectful remarks about the quality of the US troops he had encountered in July 1918, and his bluster revealed the extent of his anxiety about the looming struggle with the overwhelming might of the United States.[176] One way or the other, it was clear that the confrontation could not be ducked. 'If one had to fight against the United States,' he concluded, 'then that should happen on his watch,' because he 'considered the idea of delaying that sort of thing cowardly'. Hitler would not shy away from his 'generational' task. In this respect, time which was lengthening in the east, was shortening again in the west.

Hitler's next two directives, issued on 19 and 23 July 1941, entitled 'Continuation of the War in the East', essentially envisaged a mopping-up operation within the framework of the original plan for Barbarossa.[177] Hitler demanded that Soviet forces be prevented from withdrawing into the depths of Russia, followed by advances to the Dnieper, Leningrad and

towards Moscow. The Romanians were to cover the southern flanks. No
new forces would be sent to fight partisans, who should be dealt with
through terror rather than legal means. In late July, over protests from
commanders such as Bock, he ordered the sealing of smaller and tighter
pockets to prevent the Red Army from escaping eastwards.[178] Around this
time, however, Hitler's optimism in Russia was dented by stiffening Soviet
resistance on the central front. He remarked to Halder on 26 July 1941
that 'the Russians could not be beaten operationally'.[179] A quick decision
there now seemed unlikely.

In response to this, Hitler abandoned the original Barbarossa conception. This had involved both military-political and economic objectives,
with the main thrust being made in the north and centre against the Red
Army and the principal loci of Soviet power, to be followed by the occupation of the Ukraine. Now Hitler had to make a choice; he had neither the
resources nor the time to achieve both objectives. He confessed to his
adjutant on 28 July 1941 that he was having difficulty sleeping because he
was struggling with the two 'souls in his breast'. In political-ideological
terms, Hitler believed that the main task was to eliminate the 'main abscesses'
of Leningrad and Moscow, but the economic objectives all lay to the south,
a land where milk and honey flowed, and where he would find 'oil, grain
and everything that was necessary to secure the Lebensraum'.[180] That
same day, Hitler let it be known to the generals that his main aim was the
elimination of Soviet forces around Leningrad and the capture of the raw
materials of the Donets basin in the south; he was less interested in Moscow.[181] Two days later, Hitler instructed that Army Group Centre should
go over to the defensive.[182] He would strike south, partly to encircle large
bodies of Soviet troops, partly to deprive the Soviet regime of the industrial and agrarian resources of the Ukraine, but mainly in order to secure
these for the Reich to support the struggle against Anglo-America.

Over the next fortnight, there was a perceptible grinding and clashing
of gears as the Wehrmacht regrouped. On 12 August 1941, Hitler issued
a fresh directive in which the primacy of economic objectives was spelled
out.[183] The Wehrmacht was ordered to capture not only the Donets but
also the 'industrial area of Kharkov'. Crimea was to be taken and future
operations against Baku prepared. Army Group Centre would remain on
the defensive until the time had come to renew the offensive on Moscow.

Late July and early August 1941 also marked a discernible shift in
policy towards Soviet Jewry.[184] The timing and motivation of this change,
and whether it originated in a specific order from Hitler, are not clear.
What is certain, however, is that at Hitler's behest Göring issued an order
to Heydrich on 31 July 1941 to present in the near future 'an overall plan

for the organizational, technical and material preparations necessary for the implementation of the desired final solution of the Jewish question'.[185] Subsequently, the *Einsatzgruppen* gradually moved from murdering 'only' or principally male Jews to slaughtering whole communities, including women and children. The Wehrmacht was often complicit in these killings, especially when they overlapped with the campaign against Soviet partisans.[186] Whether or not he actually ordered them in writing, Hitler was the ultimate driving force behind these actions. In late July, he explained to a visiting foreign dignitary that 'if just one state tolerates a single Jewish family', then this would become the 'germ-centre' for a new 'wave of decomposition'. 'If there were no more Jews in Europe', Hitler continued, 'then the unity of European states would no longer be disturbed'.[187]

The Führer does not seem to have followed the activities of the *Einsatzgruppen* in detail. There is no evidence that he was sent or read their reports. It is true that on 1 August 1941, Gestapo Chief Müller asked the *Einsatzgruppen* commanders to provide him with material with which he could brief Hitler. The order referred explicitly only to 'particularly interesting visual material, such as photographs, posters, leaflets, and other documents', in other words objects which could be used for propagandistic purposes; the Führer does not seem to have been sent or studied detailed lists of executions.[188] One way or the other, the escalation of late July and early August 1941 affected primarily Soviet and Baltic Jews under German occupation, most of whom were killed by the end of the year.[189] The vast majority of Polish, Balkan, German and western European Jews were still alive, though their deportation east was already being planned. Deportation was not (yet) a euphemism for murder; the decision to kill *all* European Jews under Nazi control had not yet been taken.

In early August 1941, the cumulative stresses of the Russian campaign and other worries were beginning to take their toll on Hitler's health. On 8 August, he was confined to bed with shivering and diarrhoea. His personal doctor, Dr Morell, tried to revive him, but failed to do so in time for the military briefing that day. It was the first meeting that Hitler had missed. He took out his frustration on Morell; 'Führer very irritable,' the latter wrote in his diary, 'have never experienced such hostility towards myself.' In order to prevent a recurrence, Morell stepped up his treatment. Hitler was daily pumped full of stimulants and other drugs; the list exceeded eighty medicines, more than a dozen of them consciousness altering. Though nominally a vegetarian, Hitler had more and more animal substances coursing in his blood from the autumn of 1941, including derivatives of bulls' testicles and *Homoseran*, which is a by-product of uterine blood.[190] There was no disguising, however, that Hitler's health was in decline. He began to

complain of dizziness, tinnitus and headaches; there were also the first
signs of a tremor.[191]

Hitler's sense of anxiety, especially with regard to Anglo-America, was
greatly increased by news of the signing of the Atlantic Charter on 14 August
1941. Churchill and Roosevelt had met on board a British battle cruiser in
Placentia Bay off Newfoundland and issued a joint declaration. It set out a
sunny vision for a new global order based on international cooperation, social
justice, free trade and equal access to the world's resources.[192] The Charter
also committed the United States and the United Kingdom to 'certain common principles', such as a rejection of territorial change without the 'freely
expressed wishes of the peoples concerned' and support for 'self-government',
which were plainly directed against the Axis. If this was not bad enough,
article six of the Charter explicitly looked forward to 'the final destruction
of the Nazi tyranny'. The preamble signalled that the United States would
investigate further measures to support 'those countries actively engaged in
resisting aggression', including the Soviet Union, by 'the Hitlerite Government
of Germany'. For Churchill, the Charter was something of a disappointment,
because it did not bring an immediate American entry into the war,[193] but for
Hitler it was still a considerable shock. He was particularly infuriated by its
reference to the 'final destruction of the Nazi tyranny'.[194] Roosevelt was much
closer now to finally throwing off the mask. The impact of the Charter on
Hitler is attested by the fact that he continued to engage with it on many
occasions over the next three years.[195]

In mid and late August 1941, the Führer pondered his response. The
Charter was partly a propaganda challenge, with its eight points echoing
the Fourteen Points of President Wilson. Hitler was torn between wanting
to ignore it and the urgent need to refute it. He and Goebbels feared that
Germans and Europe as a whole might be led astray by the siren voices
of Roosevelt and Churchill, just as Germans had believed Wilson only to
be betrayed at Versailles. The 'dynamite contained in the eight-point declaration' would have to be defused.[196] Just as Churchill had issued a joint
statement with Roosevelt, Hitler wanted to respond after consulting with
Mussolini, his main ally, which he did on 25 August 1941. Their joint
communiqué was published towards the end of the month. Mimicking the
language of their Anglo-Saxon rivals, it stressed that the two men had
discussed all political and military matters which affected the development
and length of the war in great detail and in the spirit of close comradeship
and a sense of common destiny. Then followed the substantive reply. 'The
new European order which will emerge from this war,' Hitler and Mussolini announced, 'must remove the causes of past European wars'; here the
Jews were meant. 'The elimination of the Bolshevik threat and of plutocratic

exploitation,' they continued, 'will enable a peaceful, harmonious and fruitful cooperation of all peoples of the European continent both on political as well as on the economic and cultural levels'.[197]

The Charter accelerated rather than caused the shift in Hitler's strategy.[198] He was now even more determined to finish the war in the east and refocus his efforts against the west. Significantly, Hitler's first talk of a separate peace with Russia came on 18 August 1941,[199] shortly after news of the Charter reached him. On that day Hitler once again spoke of completing the aircraft carrier *Graf Zeppelin*, further evidence of his plans to take on Britain and the United States. Two days later he was briefed by scientists from the experimental station at Peenemünde on their work, and the possibility of bombarding America, or at least US forces on Iceland, with rockets. Hitler was excited by their potential, and remarked 'that this development was of revolutionary importance for the conduct of war in the whole world'.[200]

The approach of war with the United States, and the continued grip of the British blockade, much aggravated by the invasion of Russia, injected new urgency into operations in Russia, and vindicated the existing shift from military and ideological objectives towards the pursuit of economic aims. Hitler inveighed in one of his nightly monologues against the British stranglehold over the life of the continent, and looked forward to the time when Europe could be supplied from the granaries and mines of the Ukraine and Volga basin.[201] Two days later, Hitler explained the strategic and economic motivations for these measures at some length in a separate memorandum for the OKW. His very first line reminded the military leadership why they were in the Soviet Union in the first place. 'The aim of this campaign,' he explained, 'is to eliminate Russia as a continental ally of Britain' (it was of course only an ally of Britain because of Hitler's invasion) and thus 'deprive [her] of any hope of escaping [her] fate with the help of the remaining great power'.[202] Hitler then went on to stress the importance of securing the resources of Russia for the German war economy.

Over the next fortnight, Hitler intervened repeatedly to ensure that his instructions were being followed.[203] There was heavy opposition from the generals, some of whom were loath to release units under their command, and others of whom objected that the main enemy force in the central front was still unbroken,[204] but the Führer would brook no argument. The doubters were soon silenced by a string of spectacular victories, when the Wehrmacht encircled Soviet armies at Uman and west of Kiev, taking hundreds of thousands of prisoners.[205] The city of Kiev itself fell towards the end of the following month, to Hitler's immense delight.[206] Once again, the Führer had been vindicated.

In the meantime, Hitler was preparing his next move against the Jews, whom he held responsible not merely for the Atlantic Charter but for the whole thrust of American policy. On 19 August 1941, the Führer reminded Goebbels of his 'prophecy in the Reichstag, that if Jewry succeeded in provoking another world war', the conflict would 'end with the destruction of Jewry'. Hitler noted that his prediction was now 'coming true in these weeks and months with an almost eerie certainty'. Here he distinguished between what was happening 'in the east' where 'the Jews must foot the bill', and what had taken in place in Germany, where they 'had already paid it in part and would have to pay even more in future'. 'Their last refuge,' Hitler concluded, 'remains North America, and there they will sooner or later have to pay as well.'[207] There was a marked increase in the number of Jews murdered around this time, but although some *Einsatzgruppen* commanders recalled after the war that there had been 'an order for the comprehensive liquidation of the Jews from the Führer himself' in mid August,[208] no documentary evidence survives, nor can we be sure what might have triggered such an order. Part of the intensification may have been down to the self-radicalization of the SS apparatus. One way or the other, from 15 August at least one of the *Einsatzgruppen* began to shoot women and children as well as men.[209] The first documented annihilation of an entire Jewish community took place early the following month.[210] On 1 September 1941, all Jews in Germany and Nazi-occupied Europe were ordered to wear a yellow star. This was intended partly to make their identification as a potential enemy agent easier,[211] and partly to signal to the outside world that the Reich had millions of hostages under its control.

Throughout the autumn following the Atlantic Charter, Anglo-America steadily increased the pressure on Hitler. The RAF struck repeatedly at German cities, culminating in a series of raids on Berlin, Cologne and Mannheim in early November. British bombers hammered the *Scharnhorst* and *Prinz Eugen* almost nightly in harbour at Brest.[212] In the Atlantic, there were only twenty-two submarines operational by mid November, which was far too few to make an impact. Sinkings dropped still further. In North Africa, the supply situation was dire, and in late September 1941 Raeder warned Hitler in the strongest terms that the Afrika Korps could not be maintained unless there was an additional large-scale deployment of Luftwaffe units to the theatre. Throughout October, German and Italian ships were attacked so successfully by units based on Malta that supplies to Rommel all but ceased. On 8 November 1941, a vital convoy was completely destroyed; the Italians were too short of fuel oil to intervene. Ten days later, the British went on the offensive in North Africa.

Despite the demands of the Russian campaign, Hitler followed all these developments with alarm. They made clear that the destruction of the British will to resist, which had been a key objective of Barbarossa, was some way off. He also fretted that the British might launch a desperate relief offensive somewhere on behalf of Stalin, catching the Axis unawares. One area of vulnerability was Norway, where the Führer never ceased to fear commando operations, and even a full-scale landing, which would endanger his access to Swedish iron ore. Another worry was the Channel Islands. Hitler's main concern, however, was the Mediterranean, where there was the danger of a British return to the continent via North Africa, Sicily, Sardinia, the Aegean and the Balkans. His fear was that a collapse in the Mediterranean would be followed by the disintegration of the fascist regime in Italy, which is of course exactly what happened in the summer and autumn of 1943. 'The domestic political situation in Italy,' he told the SKL, 'has been put under severe strain by the food shortages and the British bombing attacks.' Hitler went on to warn that the fascist regime was by no means 'as secure as the German government' and that its replacement by another would put Italy 'inevitably into the camp of our enemies'.[213] The Führer blamed Britain's continued refusal to compromise on the manipulation of Churchill by the Jews.[214]

These anxieties were aggravated by signs of restiveness within Hitler's European empire. He worried about the loyalty of the subject peoples, especially the apparently passive Czechs, whose armaments production he deemed insufficient, and the Ukrainians, who he feared might become 'the rallying point of a pan-Russian resistance'.[215] Hitler's main concern, though, was sabotage and guerrilla warfare. The invasion of the Soviet Union ranged communists across the continent against the Third Reich. Resistance movements in western Europe stirred. In Russia the partisan movement slowly gathered momentum and in the autumn of 1941 a nationalist rising broke out in Serbia. On 16 September 1941, Hitler ordered a series of military and diplomatic measures to pacify the Balkans.[216] He was convinced that London (and 'the Jews') were behind all these endeavours, and that they were designed to link up with British landing forces.

Meanwhile, the American threat loomed ever larger. On 11 September 1941, Roosevelt gave a dramatic 'Fireside Chat' to the nation, in which he announced that 'when you see a rattlesnake poised to strike, you do not wait until he has struck before you crush him'. At around the same time, he gave instructions to the US navy to shoot at German raiders on sight (this followed an encounter between USS *Green* and a German submarine).[217] Towards the end of the month, Roosevelt spoke in a crowded ballroom at the symbolically named Mayflower Hotel in Washington, DC. In his short remarks, he mentioned Hitler no fewer than twenty-one times. Roosevelt claimed that the 'shooting' with Germany had already started, that 'history has recorded who fired the first shot', and that 'all that will matter is who fired the last shot'. He also produced a map forged, or at least distorted beyond recognition, by British Intelligence to allege Nazi designs not merely on Latin America 'but against the United States as well'.[218] Much more so than the Atlantic Charter, the president's speeches in September and October 1941 were effectively declarations of war. All this was accompanied by frequent condemnations of Hitler's anti-Semitism, despotism and plans to suppress Christianity.

Hitler registered the growing enmity of the United States with alarm. The German embassy there kept him well informed, and warned him that American diplomats around the world were sharing intelligence with the British.[219] Hitler was particularly preoccupied by the size of the American armaments industry, and well aware that Roosevelt was supplying Stalin with war material and (from 6 November) with billions of dollars' worth of loans. He therefore repeatedly sought to reassure his interlocutors that American capacity was much exaggerated.[220] Publicly, Hitler responded to taunts about American 'numbers' with claims that the number of Europeans working for him far exceeded the number of Americans making weapons for Roosevelt.[221] The threat was not perceived merely as military and economic, however, but also as racial. In a meeting with Italy's Ciano in late October 1941, Hitler acknowledged the challenge of the 'Anglo-Saxons' to the Axis, but added with characteristic bluster that there were not only 500 million Europeans facing 230 million Americans, but that 'only 60 million Anglo-Saxons lived in America, while the rest was made up of Italians, Germans and other races'.[222] This was ironic, given his repeatedly stated scepticism since the 1920s about the alliance-value of most Europeans.

To make matters worse, the state of the German war economy as it faced the combined might of Anglo-America, which had so exercised Hitler at the start of 1941, had not improved by the autumn. On the contrary, in mid September 1941, the Führer was forced to admit that the armaments industry was already 'running at more than full capacity'.[223] Nor was the supply of raw materials or foodstuffs any more secure. The British blockade still stood. Germany's principal source of oil at Ploesti was threatened by Soviet aircraft based in the Crimea. 'The Führer,' it was reported in early September 1941, was 'very anxious to end the threat from there to the oil-producing areas of Ploesti.'[224] The message was clear: unless Hitler could secure additional raw materials and radically increase production, Germany would lose the war of attrition with Anglo-America.

As if all this were not bad enough, Hitler was plunged into a serious domestic crisis in the autumn of 1941. There was considerable popular disquiet about the euthanasia programme and open opposition from the Roman Catholic Church. In August 1941, the Bishop of Münster, Clemens von Galen, denounced the killings from the pulpit.[225] Whatever Galen's motivation, he had mounted a direct challenge to the regime, because the Führer's ignorance of the unpopular killings could no longer be pleaded or assumed. Hitler's outrage was increased by the fact that the BBC broadcast the text of the sermon and the RAF dropped it in pamphlet form over Germany and the front lines.[226] This spat reflected a much broader tension between the Third Reich and Christianity, which the Führer expatiated on privately at length throughout the autumn. He inveighed against 'Jewish Christianity'[227] and celebrated the fact that the obscurantist church was no longer strong enough 'to counter the insights of science with burnings at the stake'. All the same, Hitler lamented that it was still possible for a child to be told the true scientific story about the creation of the earth in one lesson, and then to be subjected to the 'creation story of the Bible' in religion class.[228]

These conflicts aggravated the already poor relations between the regime and the Catholic Church, not least because of the continuing attempts by some local leaders to remove religious imagery from the classroom, known loosely as the 'crucifix decrees'. Worse still, a related high political crisis was brewing in the party around the figure of Josef Wagner, the *Gauleiter* of Westphalia South (which adjoined Münster) and imperial commissar for price control. A strict Catholic, he was already under suspicion, but the pot boiled over when his pregnant daughter announced her intention to marry her lover, an SS man who had broken with the church. Wagner's wife denounced and cursed her daughter in a letter which eventually found its way to Hitler, who was outraged.[229]

The growing number of air attacks also sapped confidence in the regime. They were justified by Allied propaganda as retaliation for German actions in Russia,[230] and were understood by many in the population as a western front established by the Anglo-Americans and the Jews to punish them.[231] Westphalian Catholics, for example, saw a connection between the sin of the euthanasia programme and the particularly heavy RAF raids on Münster and environs. The Führer himself took a keen interest in the resulting evacuation of the civilians from urban areas into the countryside.

Hitler responded to all these challenges with a mixture of evasion and confrontation, both at home and abroad. He rejected calls that Galen be executed, as Bormann argued, or sent to a concentration camp, as the Justice Ministry desired. Instead, Hitler compromised.[232] He would defer the punishment of Galen and the confrontation with the church as a whole until after the war. 'After the war,' he remarked, 'I will also tackle this problem decisively.'[233] In the meantime, Hitler ordered an end to attacks on monasteries on 31 July. He ordered the end to adult and child euthanasia on 24 August 1941, again on the assumption that it would be resumed after the conflict was over; 'wild' (unofficial) euthanasia continued, however, and killed perhaps another 100,000 people. Four days later, the crucifix decree was rescinded. In early September, Hitler demanded an end to any actions 'which might adversely affect the feeling of unity among the populace'.[234] Josef Wagner, by contrast, was crushed. At a carefully choreographed meeting of the *Gauleiter* in Munich on 9 November 1941, he was publicly excoriated and expelled from the room and the party.[235]

With regard to America, Hitler continued to tread very warily. He refused to let the Kriegsmarine off the leash in the Atlantic. Instead, Hitler continued the long rhetorical duel with the United States, culminating in a climactic set-piece attack on Roosevelt on 8 November 1941, to mark the anniversary of the beer hall putsch. Despite the battle raging in Russia, its main emphasis was the struggle with Anglo-America, especially the looming contest with the United States. Despite the battle against Bolshevism raging in the east, Hitler spent far more time attacking western capitalism, and the supposed connection between the stock market and the armaments industry and the belligerent policies of the western democracies.[236] Both Stalin and Churchill were mentioned, but the principal addressee of Hitler's remarks was Roosevelt. The Führer was anxious to discredit the faked map that the president had referred to at the Mayflower Hotel. 'I am not a secondary schoolboy who draws maps in a school atlas,' he averred, pointing out that 'South America [was] as far away as the moon' for him. Surprisingly, Hitler did not make an issue of Roosevelt's disability, though he was well aware of it. In early November 1941, the Führer remarked privately that the otherwise unrestrained American press never mentioned the fact that the president was in a wheelchair, and that his condition was 'very cleverly' concealed at events and in photographs.[237]

Hitler could not, of course, escape the conflict with Britain, which was still his most immediate adversary in the autumn of 1941. Firstly, he sought to shore up his defences in Europe, especially in the west, where he believed a British diversionary attack to be imminent. In late October 1941, during the height of the fighting on the eastern front, he ordered that the Channel Islands be turned into an 'impregnable fortress', which was done with great effort and pointless expense over the next two years.[238] Secondly, Hitler bolstered the Italian position in the Mediterranean, partly by diverting resources from the already faltering effort in the Atlantic, but especially at the expense of the eastern front. In mid September 1941, six submarines and a *Fliegerkorps* were sent to help cover convoy operations; more submarines followed.[239] Towards the end of October, Hitler ordered preparations to be made for the dispatch of a whole air fleet under Albert Kesselring to the Mediterranean. Another *Fliegerkorps* was to be detached from Army Group Centre in support, over the objections of the OKH. Though the purpose of these deployments was to make good Italian deficiencies, Hitler made clear that whatever leading role the Germans might take in practice in that theatre, Italian sensitivities were to be respected.[240]

The purpose of all these measures was political as well as military. Unlike the naval leadership, which believed that the defence of the 'new order' in Europe required the 'defeat' of Britain, Hitler himself stated privately in late October 1941 'that he was even now prepared to make peace with Britain at any time', because the 'European space' already secured was 'sufficient' to guarantee 'the future of the German people'. Germany had its *Lebensraum*, if it could keep it.[241] That said, Hitler did not believe peace was possible so long as the current, allegedly Jewish-dominated, administration was in power in Britain, which is why he increased the military and diplomatic pressure to unseat Churchill.

On 17 September 1941, Hitler met with Ribbentrop to discuss the role of the German Foreign Office in the deportation of Jews in central, southern and western Europe, where the diplomatic ramifications were potentially large.[242] These measures were generally justified as retaliation for resistance activities.[243] A day later, on 18 September 1941, Himmler informed Arthur Greiser, the *Gauleiter* of the Wartheland, that 'the Führer wishes that the old [that is pre-war] Reich and the Protectorate [of Bohemia and Moravia] should be emptied [of Jews] from west to east as soon as possible', and be sent to the ghetto at Lodz.[244] On 7 October, Hitler instructed that 'all Jews must be removed from the Protectorate', sending them not to the General Government in the first instance, but 'further east right away'. These deportations were delayed by the 'large need of the military for transport capacity';[245] the priorities suggest that the struggle against the Jews was perceived as only one front in the overall war, albeit a very important one. The deportations of Jews from Bohemia and Moravia and the German Reich began a week later, on 15 October 1941. On 23 October, Himmler banned all Jewish emigration; now there was no escape.

These measures were not just designed to eliminate the supposed danger of Jewish subversion within, but also to deter the United States. It was for this reason that the Jews of central and western Europe were to be deported, but not as yet systematically murdered. They were explicitly conceived of as hostages held against the eventuality of an American entry into the war.[246] When Rosenberg demanded retaliation against German

Jews for Stalin's deportation of the Volga Germans,[247] Hitler refused. The Foreign Office informed him that the Führer was 'holding back this measure for the event of an American entry into the war'.[248] Hitler made the alleged connection between the war, and especially the possibility of open conflict with the United States, and the Jews on several occasions. On 24 October 1941, he privately repeated the 'prophecy' he had made in January 1939.[249] Three weeks later, Goebbels made the same connection publicly, in a leading article in the journal *Das Reich* under the headline of 'the Jews are to blame'. He added that '[w]e are now experiencing the fulfilment of this prophecy and Jewry is experiencing a fate that, although hard, is still more than deserved', namely a 'gradual process of extermination'.[250] Two days after that Rosenberg rehearsed the same argument at a press conference. The message could not have been clearer.

Meanwhile, Hitler did not neglect his long-term strategy against Anglo-America. With the advance into Russia, the establishment of a vast autarchic German empire in the Ukraine and Caucasus, settled by soldier-farmers in the first instance, seemed to him on the verge of realization.[251] Hitler now had the space to further his longstanding settlement plans, designed to create a US-style settler colony which would absorb Germany's demographic surplus, rather than allowing it to emigrate, as had been the case in the past. Indeed, he hoped over time to bring back some of those emigrants as well as attract high-value colonists from across Europe. 'In ten years,' Hitler predicted in mid October 1941, 4 million Germans would settle there and in twenty years it would be 'at least 10 million', coming 'not just from the Reich, but especially from America, but also from Scandinavia, Holland and Flanders'. 'Here in the east,' he explained, 'there will be a repeat of the process of the conquest of America.'[252]

What Hitler was planning here was by no means a reactionary agrarian utopia. He looked forward to a modern American-style German east, not back to a traditional rural idyll. Hitler specifically ruled out settling German city-dwellers in the Ukrainian countryside. To be sure, a sturdy grain-producing German peasantry was central to his vision for *Lebensraum*, but so were roads and railways linking the new lands with the metropolitan centres of industry. Henceforth, railways would be used only to move goods; most other travel would be by car. Hitler envisaged the Reich as being criss-crossed by two huge motorway arteries, one leading to the new Germanized city of Trondheim in Norway, the other to the Crimea. After the war, the German *Volksgenosse* would be able to use his Volkswagen to see the conquered territories, which might better dispose him to defend them. Hitler saw motorways as an instrument not merely of transportation but also of integration. Just as the original *Autobahnen* had been the 'best surmounter of the smaller German states', so 'the new motor-ways' would bind the 'smaller states of Europe to the German Reich'.[253] 'The railways bypass a space,' he pronounced, 'but roads open it up.'

Hitler's thinking on the fate of the native population fluctuated between the softer British and the more brutal American solutions. On the one hand, he was rapidly moving away from the idea of any sort of statehood for the Ukrainians and other peoples. In a revealing phrase, Hitler spoke of the Slav population privately as Indians, by which he meant a compari-son with those 'Indians' of America rather than the subcontinent.[254] Rosenberg's man at the Führer's Headquarters realized and resented this, warning that there was a danger that the Ostministerium would be left to encourage 'the Slavs crowded into reservations [sic] to emigrate or to die out as soon as possible'. Those who were in the way of German settlement plans, such as the Crimean Tartars, Hitler explained in early October 1941, were to be expelled. The rest should be left to vegetate in their cities, without the benefit of education or any other services.[255] For them, the Führer explained, 'British rule in India' was 'the desired aim of our administration in the east'.[256]

In late September 1941, Hitler approved guidelines for policy towards Ukraine, which were largely driven by the desire to ensure that sowing and reaping for the next harvest proceeded smoothly.[257] So long as the non-Jewish Ukrainians collaborated in agricultural matters the German administration would maintain 'a benevolent attitude'. The 'long-term economic goal' was the 'natural development of the Ukraine into the granary of Europe', while 'the entire eastern space' should become 'the principal market for west European industry', to be paid for by the sale of foodstuffs and raw materials. What Hitler ultimately envisaged, in other words, was not simply a system of violent extraction, but rather an unequal system of exchange in which he set the terms of trade. While Nazi planners drew on many inspirations from European colonialism when conceiving the new 'east',[258] Hitler himself remained resolutely focused on the Anglo-American example. His treatment of the Slav population was inspired not by the German, or any other European, colonial experi-ence in Africa, but by British India, the mandate system and the Anglo-American extermination of the Indians in North America. Even in autumn 1941, therefore, the British 'Indian' solution for the post-Soviet space remained in tension with the 'American' one.

'Operation Typhoon', the attack on the central front preparatory to a drive on Moscow, began on 2 October 1941. Hitler's accompanying proclama-tion reminded the Wehrmacht of the nature and purpose of the campaign.

They were fighting a horde of 'beasts' who were defending a Soviet regime which had turned the riches of Russia into poverty and hunger.[259] 'This is the result,' he claimed, 'of a now twenty-five-year Jewish rule, which as Bolshevism is really just the general form of capitalism.' 'The bearers of this system,' Hitler continued, were in fact 'the same in both cases', namely 'Jews and only Jews'.[260] It was not so much communism that Hitler was fighting in Russia, in other words, as the bestial puppets of capitalism and world Jewry. Above all, the Führer continued, the offensive was a 'decisive battle' designed 'to strike a fatal blow against the instigator of the war, Britain itself'. 'Because in smashing this enemy,' he explained to the troops, 'we will eliminate Britain's last ally on the continent.'[261] Here Hitler was simply rehearsing the original rationale of Barbarossa, which was primarily directed not against the Soviet Union, but against the British Empire.

At first, all went well. German units smashed through the Soviet defences on the central front.[262] Hundreds of thousands of prisoners were taken in great battles of encirclement at Briansk and Vyasma. In the south, the Wehrmacht surged forward once more. All of the Crimea was overrun, with the exception of Sebastopol; SS units soon reached Mariupol on the Sea of Azov. German troops crossed the Mius river, and towards the end of the following month, they took Rostov, the gateway to the Caucasus. A week into the offensive, Hitler moved to claim victory. The Führer hoped, as he remarked privately, to capitalize on the 'effect of this news on world public opinion'.[263] On 8 October 1941, he summoned his press secretary, Otto Dietrich, and told him to announce the following day to the world press that the Soviet Union had been beaten.[264] Hitler's move did not reflect any delusions on his part, but rather a determination to depress Britain, deter the United States[265] and encourage Japan.[266] This message was intended not for domestic but for external consumption, which is why it was communicated via Dietrich rather than Josef Goebbels. Its success depended not so much on the actual conduct of military operations as on the achievement – however temporary – of narratival ascendancy.

For a few weeks in October and early November it seemed as if Hitler's strategy might succeed. The Wehrmacht advanced closer to Moscow in apparent vindication of Dietrich's announcement. There was consternation in London and Washington, which was widely registered by Germany. In mid October, Hitler predicted that 'the rapid collapse of Russia will have a devastating effect on Britain'.[267]

But in the course of November, it became clear that things were not going to plan. Churchill showed no sign of giving way. In early November, the RAF attacked Cologne, Mannheim and Berlin in strength, while the British 8th Army surged forward in North Africa. The Italian position looked more rickety than ever. Far from being intimidated by the German successes in Russia, Roosevelt used them to warn Americans that they would be next. Meanwhile, Soviet resistance stiffened. Hitler remarked that the Red Army was fighting with 'animalistic fanatical madness'.[268] Snow and rain turned the primitive Russian roads into swamps; then the cold and ice immobilized armoured and mechanized units. Resupply became increasingly difficult. The advance slowed. In late November, the Red Army recaptured Rostov and shut the gate to the Caucasus. The day after, there was more bad news. Hitler met with his armaments minister Fritz Todt and Walter Rohland, the head of tank production. The latter told him that the war could not be won; Todt agreed that military victory was now impossible and that the war needed to be ended 'politically'.[269] On 5 December 1941, the Russians launched a large-scale counter-attack before the gates of Moscow. Army Group Centre began to fall back, although it was to be about a week until Hitler became fully aware of the severity of the situation.[270]

Hitler was already convinced that he was stalemated, not just in Russia but globally. With his mechanized forces largely bogged down, the Führer began to lose faith in armoured warfare. 'I have never used the word Blitz-krieg,' he insisted on 8 November 1941, 'because it is a completely stupid word.'[271] In the headquarters at Rastenburg, the recriminations flew fast and thick. On 16 November, Hitler vented his frustration at the dire supply situation and railway bottlenecks with a tirade against the quartermaster general, Eduard Wagner, whom he dubbed a 'ridiculous theoretician'. As the attack stalled, he also accused the generals, especially Bock, of talking him into an assault on Moscow that he had never wanted.[272] On 19 November 1941, two days after the start of the British offensive in North Africa, and against the background of the increasingly deadlocked situation in Russia, Hitler had conceded that Britain and the Reich could not defeat each other.[273] A week later, Hitler went a big step further when he remarked to a visitor that 'if the German people should ever be no longer strong and sacrificial enough to commit its own blood for its existence, then it should pass away and be destroyed by a stronger power'.[274] For the first time in the war, a good week before the great Russian counter-offensive in front of Moscow, and at least a fortnight before the US entry into the war, Hitler was contemplating Germany's defeat and annihilation.

Hitler responded to the worsening situation with a combination of military, economic, racial and diplomatic measures. In Russia, Hitler was depressed about the sluggish progress towards Moscow but he reacted violently only to the stagnation of the southern offensive, which was tasked with breaking into the Caucasus. His agitation contrasted with the attitude of the – as yet – relatively relaxed Wehrmacht leadership.[275] On 2 December the Führer flew to Army Group South to see the situation for himself. When Rundstedt ordered a retreat in the face of the Soviet counter-attack at Rostov, he was summarily sacked by Hitler. It was the first major crisis in the east, and the first ever to result in a public removal from command. For a few days Hitler maintained the illusion that the advance could be resumed quickly,[276] but in fact there would be no further southern offensive that year. The strategic implications of this for Hitler were colossal, much greater than the failure to take Moscow, because all hopes of sweeping down to the very northern oil-fields of the Caucasus had to be abandoned. There would be no energy security for the Reich before Christmas. Barbarossa had failed all along the line: it had not forced the British to sue for peace, it was not deterring Roosevelt, and it had not secured all the resources necessary to face the expected entry of the United States into the war the following year.

The renewed salience of economic considerations, briefly overlain by the military and political priorities of the attack on Moscow, became increasingly obvious from late November 1941. On 22 November, Hitler remarked that 'all wars' were initially driven not by 'racial' factors but by 'economic' ones. They were decided by the 'production of guns, tanks and ammunition'. For this reason, he would have to boost German 'armaments' in such a way as to 'take away the breath' of the enemy.[277] This is what prompted Hitler's decree of 3 December 1941 for the 'Simplification and Increased Output of our Armaments Production',[278] a direct response to the perceived global deadlock. It placed greater emphasis on 'mass production', and 'rationalization' at the expense of the 'technically and aesthetically more accomplished equipment of best artisanal quality'. A more direct repudiation of the German *Mittelstand* and the values of German apprenticeship across the ages, and a more wholehearted embrace of the Fordist model, is hard to imagine. Hitler had finally realized that the war would be won not by German quality but through American quantity.

At around this time, Hitler also escalated his racial policies, though it is not clear whether he did so in response to immediate events or as part of a long-term plan. On 28 November 1941, Hitler received the grand mufti of Jerusalem, a major step directed both against the British Empire and the common enemy of world Jewry.[279] The mufti thanked the Führer for his 'Sympathy for the Arab and especially the Palestinian cause', and commiserated with him on the sufferings they had both experienced at the hands of 'Britons and Jews'. Hitler promised not only to pursue an 'uncompromising battle against the Jews' but also not to tolerate their presence in Palestine, where they constituted a 'state central point for the destructive influence of Jewish interests' in the world more generally. In due course, the mufti would become an enthusiastic supporter of murdering Jews in Palestine and Europe, wherever they were to be found.[280] A day later, in a move unrelated to the mufti's visit, the Reich Security Main Office sent a summons for a conference of state secretaries to sort out the bureaucratic detail of the 'comprehensive solution of the Jewish question'.

Diplomatically Hitler responded to the stalemate by trying to bind Japan more closely to him; he was terrified that Tokyo would leave him in the lurch.[281] Hitler did not know that the Japanese carrier strike force had already left to attack Pearl Harbor on 26 November 1941. Tokyo asked that German support in the event of hostilities with the United States, which had already been promised, should be formalized in a treaty. Determined not to allow Japan to face America alone, and convinced that Roosevelt was on the verge of entering the war anyway, the Führer agreed. A treaty was hastily drafted in which Hitler promised that 'in the case of war between Japan and the United States' he would himself 'immediately' consider himself at war with America; the same would apply for Japan if Germany or Italy found themselves at war with the US.[282] The wording of the text made clear that this was not just a defensive but also primarily an offensive treaty.

On 7 December 1941, the Japanese launched a devastating surprise attack on the American Pacific fleet at Pearl Harbor.[283] Hitler reacted to the news with surprise, but also relief.[284] Despite the steadily mounting tension with the United States, no serious German operational military measures had been prepared in advance. U-boats were concentrated not on the east coast of America, but in the Mediterranean; the rest were spread across the Atlantic. This reflected partly the exigencies of the war against Britain, and partly the desire not to give Roosevelt a pretext to enter the war before Hitler was ready. That said, Hitler was relieved that Japan would tie down substantial British and American resources in the Far East, and he accepted not merely that he would have to deliver on his treaty commitments to Tokyo, but that it was in his vital interest to prevent his ally from going down to defeat on its own. In any case, the Führer was convinced that he was effectively already at war with America.[285] One way or the other, Hitler was determined to anticipate Roosevelt. This time, unlike 1917, the Reich would not wait until attacked by the United States, but would be the first to strike openly. The Führer now scrambled to get from his headquarters in East Prussia to Berlin, to complete the negotiations over the treaty with Japan, to prepare his own declaration of war and to work out an overall strategy to deal with the new situation.

Militarily, Hitler's response was swift. On 8 December, the day after

Pearl Harbor, he issued Directive 39, which ordered the 'immediate end to all major offensive operations' in the east and instructed the Wehrmacht to 'go over to the defensive'.[286] He justified this with reference to the 'unexpectedly early and harsh onset of winter' and the resulting 'supply problems', but that was only part of the story. The directive was primarily a reaction not to the Soviet counter-offensive before Moscow, but to the general sense of stalemate building in the course of the previous month and the new global context created by Japan's entry into the war. It was Hitler's free decision, not one forced upon him by Stalin. The winter crisis before Moscow – which was already raging on the front line – had still not registered with him. Hitler was looking west, even before Pearl Harbor, not east.[287]

On 11 December 1941, Hitler presented the Reichstag with his declaration of war on the United States.[288] The mood was sombre, and his speech was prefaced by a remarkably downbeat introduction by Göring. Hitler's tone was measured and grim, even funereal. He stressed the losses of the Russian campaign, which – he told the Reichstag – had so far cost the Wehrmacht 162,314 dead, 571,767 wounded and 33,334 missing. Hitler cast the new war as a generational struggle which had been forced upon him by the perfidy of Roosevelt and the manipulation of the Jews. Hitler then moved to attack his main target, Roosevelt. On the basis of the reports of the Polish ambassador to Washington, Count Potocki, he accused the American president of having encouraged Warsaw to resist justified German demands in 1939. The Führer explained this perfidy with reference to the workings of US capitalism, which, he claimed, the Nye Commission had blamed for the American entry into the First World War. All this, according to Hitler, was happening at the behest of 'the eternal Jew', the 'power' behind Roosevelt, which sought to reduce Germany to the same chaos and subjection as the Soviet Union. Reprising themes which had formed part of his stock rhetoric over the past couple of years, the Führer framed the struggle as a 'liberation struggle' of Japan and the German Reich against Roosevelt's ambition to establish an 'unlimited economic dictatorship' across the world in conjunction with Britain. It was the revolt of the 'have-nots' against the 'American president and his plutocratic clique'.

Hitler also framed the war as a racial struggle between two 'slivers' of the 'Germanic people'. 'Britain did not cultivate the continent,', he asserted, 'but rather slivers of the Germanic peoples of our continent moved as Anglo-Saxons [sic] and Normans to that Island and enabled a development there which is certainly unique.' This was yet another instance of the Führer's admiration for British exceptionalism. 'In the same way,' Hitler continued, 'America did not discover Europe, but the other way around,' and whatever value it possessed it had drawn from the old continent, even if the United States had since been corrupted by 'Jewish' and 'black African' influences. Indeed, the Führer stressed, Germany had 'helped to defend the United States with the blood of many of its sons'. In that sense, though Hitler did not quite put it that way, the new conflict was also a Germanic civil war. Summarizing towards the end of his speech, therefore, Hitler spoke of the clash between the Reich and an 'Anglo-Saxon-Jewish-capitalist world' which was trying to 'exterminate' Germany. These were the same themes that had driven Hitler since the 1920s. Now they were leading him to their logical conclusion: a war of annihilation against Anglo-Saxons, the Jews and their Bolshevik puppets.

The declaration of war on the United States was the moment to which Hitler's entire career had been building up and also the one which, as we have seen, he had by his own lights tried so hard to avoid or delay.[289] Neither ignorance nor insouciance led him into war with the most powerful state on earth, but rather the conviction that a confrontation was inevitable sooner or later. It was the only formal declaration of war which Hitler made. The speech marked a caesura in Hitler's long rhetorical duel with Roosevelt. The long cold war had turned hot. From now on, the Reich would not merely talk back but shoot back.

Over the next weeks and months, the consequences of Hitler's shift to global war became clear. The first casualties were the Jews, the hostages who were now held responsible of the behaviour of the United States. On 12 December, the day after the declaration of war on the United States, Hitler met with the *Gauleiter* in a hastily convened conference.[290] He reminded them of his threat in 1939 to retaliate against Jewry in the event of their 'plunging' Europe into war. 'The world war is here,' Hitler continued, '[and] the extermination of the Jews must be the necessary consequence.'[291] Likewise, he instructed Rosenberg, whose major speech on world Jewry had been delayed by the American entry into the war, to delete references to 'the New York Jews'. These had evidently been intended as a threat, which was now redundant. Rosenberg suggested that he should now not speak of 'the extermination of the Jews'. 'The Führer,' he records, 'approved this approach and said that they had burdened us with the war' with all its 'destruction', so that 'it was no wonder if the consequences should strike them first'.[292] In Russia, Jews of both sexes and all ages, in or out of uniform, had long been treated as illegal combatants and killed out of hand.[293] Now the Jews of Germany, central and western Europe were to be murdered as well. Whether the entry of the United States into the war was the decisive factor here, or merely an accelerant,[294] one thing is clear: the principal motivation for and context to Hitler's war of annihilation against European Jewry was his relationship with the United States, which was now entering a new and more deadly phase. The murder of the Jews was now a settled matter; what remained open were questions of definition and implementation.

Hitler's global war also required a global strategy. With the Japanese attack on Britain's position in East Asia, the breach with the British Empire – another confrontation which Hitler had tried so hard to avoid – was complete. On 9 December 1941, the secret meeting with the mufti was publicized. Hitler was now irrevocably aligned with anti-colonial forces in the Middle East. For all his private ambivalence about the fate of the white race in the Far East, he exulted in Japanese victories.[295] On 13 December, Hitler met with Oshima to discuss the new situation.[296] In the New Year, he said, major operations in Russia would be resumed. Hitler stated that his 'principal aim' was 'first the destruction of Russia', then an 'advance across the Caucasus towards the south', and the 'torpedoing of the Anglo-Saxon [sic] navies and merchant marine'. His first blow in Russia would be in the south, partly 'because of the oil', to be followed by the strike into Iraq and Iran against the British Empire. Only then would he turn his attention back to the central sector. Capturing Moscow was of 'less importance for him'. On several occasions, Oshima suggested that Japan and the Reich coordinate their operations, but Hitler showed little interest in that. The only thing he specifically asked of the Japanese was that they cut off the supply of American war material to the Soviet Union via Vladivostok, which they never did.

The new military situation also drove Hitler to consolidate his authority within the Wehrmacht. In mid December 1941,he became aware of the magnitude of the crisis on the central front.[297] Many commanders, whose troops were exhausted, outnumbered and often threatened with encirclement, wanted to retreat. Hitler gave permission for some withdrawals, but in general he demanded that the army stand fast. He argued that it was as dangerous to fall back, thus abandoning fixed positions, as it was to hold the line. It would also, the Führer argued, require 'leaving behind artillery and materiel'. The commander of Army Group Centre, Bock, agreed with this assessment, saying that the decision whether or not to fall back was a matter of very fine judgement, and could sometimes only be made by tossing a coin.[298] Over the course of the next few days he was bombarded by telephone calls and orders from Hitler demanding that he 'not retreat a single step' and 'stick it out at all costs'.[299] On 17 December, Bock – who had already offered to step down on health grounds – was invited to submit his resignation and was relieved of his command of Army Group Centre. Two days later, on 19 December 1941, Hitler sacked Brauchitsch and took over supreme command of the army himself.

Hitler saw the new conflict as one of attrition. The key to victory lay in production and destruction. One front was shipping. Hitler saw the 'tonnage problem' as 'the decisive question of the current conduct of the war'. Whoever solved it would 'probably win the war'.[300] Either the U-boats would destroy enough shipping to cut Britain off from its 'lifelines' or they themselves would be destroyed in sufficient number to render the destruction of the Reich inevitable. The same logic applied on the air and on the ground, and to all theatres. The fronts were closely connected in Hitler's mind, not least because of the vast quantities of materiel now being supplied to the Russians by Anglo-America, which he was well aware of.[301] Right at the end of December 1941, the Führer remarked to Raeder that he would rather see the sinking in the Arctic of 'four ships bringing tanks to the Russian front' than the destruction of a much larger tonnage in the South Atlantic.[302] If in the 1930s, Hitler had been engaged in a battle for consumption against the American dream, he was now embarked on a battle of production against the Soviet Union and – especially – Anglo-America.

For this, the Reich needed millions more workers. 'We are not short of soldiers,' Hitler lamented in early December 1941, 'but of workers.'[303] He proposed to make up the shortfall by drafting Russian prisoners. On Christmas Eve, he issued a formal decree determining that the 'decisive' issue for the German war economy was now the question of how to integrate the Soviet prisoners of war into the system of production. This required, he continued, 'the provision of adequate rations and banishing the danger of a typhus epidemic'.[304] The racial hierarchy at the start of Barbarossa had thus been reversed. Then, Hitler had planned to starve the Slavs to death, but keep the Jews of central and western Europe alive as hostages. Now the Slavs would live, if only to work, and the Jews would die.

17

The Struggle against the 'Anglo-Saxons' and 'Plutocracy'

As the new year unfolded, Hitler perceived himself as fighting a global war of annihilation. Germany would either completely destroy her enemies or be completely destroyed by them. 'If the German people has lost its faith,' Hitler told Himmler over a private luncheon on 27 January, 'if the German people was no longer inclined to give itself body and soul in order to survive – then the German people would have nothing to do but disappear.'[1] In Russia, he was locked in a desperate struggle with the Red Army along the entire central front. Globally, Hitler believed he faced a Jewish plutocratic plot to crush the Reich, and subject it to enslavement by the forces of international capitalism. Indeed, the war with the Jews was about to escalate into the greatest crime in European history, which he regarded as an act of pre-emptive destruction.

The most important military and political contest, however, remained the confrontation with Anglo-America, or – as Hitler almost invariably called them, using the common German parlance – the 'Anglo-Saxons' (*Angelsachsen*). The American entry into the war brought this 'racial' struggle even more into the open. Until the end, whether privately or in formal documents, Hitler spoke of 'Anglo-Saxon powers',[2] 'Anglo-Saxon statesmen',[3] 'Anglo-Saxon units' or simply 'the Anglo-Saxons'.[4] They were words which expressed hatred, fear – and respect. When Kesselring praised the abilities of British soldiers, Hitler looked at him sharply and replied 'Yes, they too are Germanic';[5] in fact he considered them, and Americans of Anglo-Saxon descent, the better Germans. The Führer's notion of racial kinship and nagging sense of inferiority resurfaced again when he remarked in a speech that 'in reality we colonized the Britons and not the Britons us'.[6] He continued to enthuse privately about the British.[7] Conscious of the dangers of this particular discourse, Goebbels instructed the Propaganda Ministry on 13 January 1942 that the word 'Anglo-Saxon', which suggested a tribal kinship, should be replaced with the phrase 'Anglo-American plutocracy'.[8] It was no use, almost everybody, from the Führer down, continued to refer to them as 'Anglo-Saxons'. To the outside world, this might have seemed the Nazism of small difference, but for Hitler the distinction was crucial. The war pitted Teutons – *Germanen* – against Anglo-Saxons. It had become a clash of the Aryans.

Worse still, from Hitler's point of view, like Britain, the new enemy had been built up by Germans. In the Führer's mind, it was the best and brightest of Germans who had made their way there in the eighteenth and nineteenth centuries, and had consequently been lost to the Fatherland. The racially valuable part of the United States was not just Germany's alter ego, but its better self. Returning to the theme which had driven the whole *Lebensraum* conception, he told an audience of officer cadets in mid February 1942 that there were 'continents' – by which he principally meant North America – which had been 'elevated to their height by the infusion of German blood'. This, Hitler continued, was the result of the historic mismatch between German population growth and the space available to feed it. The steady decline in German 'living standards' had forced them 'to emigrate to other territories and thus become disloyal to their own homeland and people'. Hitler spelled out the terrifying meaning of this for the cadets, who would soon find themselves fighting their own kin. 'We supplied the cultural fertilizer for all the states who stand against us today,' he lamented. If someone admired 'America and its technology' today, Hitler continued, then he could only point out that 'the engineers of America today' were 'mostly second- or third-generation German emigrants'. 'We supplied them with this material,' Hitler went on, adding that 'all the good soldier material they have came from our German homeland'.[9] In Hitler's conception, the war with the United States was thus also a Germanic civil war.

Nothing epitomizes the ambivalence of the relationship between Nazi Germany, the United States and the British Empire better than the continuing, now clandestine, exchange of photographs between the two sides even after the outbreak of war. There was a daily flight between Lisbon and Berlin from the spring of 1942 until the end of the war, bringing photos to and from the Western Allies (about 40,000 in all).[10] Hitler was on the distribution list, receiving his daily copies in person from Ribbentrop's envoy Walter Hewel, though what use he made of the photographs is not known. The purpose was not simply to gain military or political intelligence, but to engage in a form of covert messaging. Nazi propagandists used pictures supplied by Associated Press to make anti-Semitic and anti-capitalist propaganda points against the USA.[11] Carefully selected pictures of the Führer were sent in the other direction to shape Hitler's image across the Atlantic; they were published in hundreds of American outlets. Even in war, the two sides remained entangled with each other.

The need to counteract Allied narratives increased with the 'United Nations Declaration' of 1 January 1942, which amounted to a declaration of war by most of the world against the German Reich. Recalling the Atlantic Charter, each signatory committed itself to 'employ its full resources, military or economic' against those members of the Axis with which it was already at war, to cooperate with the other Allied powers and not to make a separate peace. The contractants were, to list them in the order in which they appeared in the 'Declaration', the United States, the United Kingdom, the Soviet Union, China, Australia, Belgium, Canada, Costa Rica, Cuba, Czechoslovakia, Dominican Republic, El Salvador, Greece, Guatemala, Haiti, Honduras, India, Luxembourg, Netherlands, New Zealand, Nicaragua, Norway, Panama, Poland, South Africa and Yugoslavia. Others, such as the Free French, signed up subsequently. They all expressed their hope that their declaration 'may be adhered to by other nations which are, or which may be, rendering material assistance and contributions in the struggle for victory over Hitlerism'.[12] The Führer may not have been aware of the Allied 'Germany first' policy,[13] but from the specific reference to his defeat – the German leader was the only one singled out by name – he could work it out for himself.

For all the kinship and ambivalence, therefore, the deadliness of the antagonism between the Third Reich and Anglo-America was not in doubt. This was most clearly demonstrated by the bombing war, which entered into a new phase in early 1942. Churchill had spoken on earlier occasions of the need to attack civilian targets. 'There is one thing that will bring [Hitler] down,' he said, 'and that is an absolutely devastating exterminating attack by heavy bombers from this country upon the Nazi homeland.' It was only now, however, that 'area bombing' became the official strategy. On 14 February 1942, the Air Staff issued a directive that bombing should concentrate on the 'morale of the enemy civilian population and in particular the industrial workers'.[14] The purpose of the exercise was not military, in the narrow sense, but political: to punish and to coerce. Shortly after, Air Marshal Arthur Harris was appointed head of Bomber Command to carry it out. The reason for striking the urban working class was that their densely populated inner city or inner suburban residential areas were much more easily hit from the air than industrial or military installations, which required 'precision-bombing'.[15]

In the spring of 1942, the new strategy was first put into effect with devastating raids on Lübeck in late March, and on Rostock in late April. Four weeks later, the first of a number of '1,000 bomber' raids struck Cologne.[16] Hitherto, the impact of RAF operations had not been trivial, but these attacks were of a completely different order of magnitude. The number of civilian dead was still relatively small, usually in the hundreds, but the physical damage and psychological impact were immense; the total number of at least temporary refugees and homeless ran into the hundreds of thousands. The nights of fire had begun, starting a conflagration which would spread until it consumed the entire Reich.[17] Allied bombing claimed both the innocent and the guilty. German cities were changed for ever. Life would never be the same again. In the course of this campaign some 2.5 million tons of bombs were dropped on continental Europe, most of them on Germany. The R A F lost 22,000 aircraft and nearly 80,000 aircrew, mainly to German fighters and flak; the Americans about 18,000 planes and about the same number of men as the RAF. These were figures comparable to French military losses at Verdun. There were 500,000 German civilian casualties. A second front, the western front, was taking shape not in France but in the skies above the Reich.[18] The war had finally come to Germany.

Hitler was deeply affected by the attacks on German cities, and was under no illusion about what they meant for their inhabitants, his own credibility and his ability to prosecute the war. Though he himself was not directly endangered by the raids, which went nowhere near any of his military headquarters, and from which he was protected by a system of bunkers in Berlin, the Führer was personally affected by the threat to his loved ones, especially Eva Braun. She lived in Munich, which was not only home to crucial industrial plants, including BMW, Krauss-Maffei and Dornier, but was also the 'capital of the movement', and Germany's third-largest residential centre. The city had already been struck in September and December 1941; it was attacked twice in 1942 and at increasingly regular intervals until the end of the war.[19] 'After every air-raid on Munich,' Karl von Eberstein, the SS commander responsible for the city recalls, 'Hitler called her [Eva] in person to see if she was safe.'[20] He wanted Eva to move to the Berghof, but she refused on the grounds that life there was too boring. It was the big attacks on Lübeck, Rostock, Cologne and Bremen which worried Hitler most, however.[21] These not only caused considerable economic damage and dislocation, but also undermined the standing of the regime. The Luftwaffe was failing to defend the Reich; Göring's star, already falling after the failure over England, fell further. The NSDAP, which was tasked with the civilian response, was clearly not up to the job either. Hitler was so appalled by the destruction, and his own impotence, that in April 1942, he refused to allow newsreel footage of the aftermath of the raid on Rostock to be shown.[22]

In the face of the circling coalition, now led by the most powerful state in the world, Hitler was ever more conscious of Germany's weakness in terms of industrial capacity and mineral resources. America and Britain, he explained in a speech on 30 January 1942, 'have the world at their disposal', with everything needed for their war effort.[23] This plenitude, he lamented, was ranged against the 'three great have-nots', that is, Italy, Japan and the Reich. Hitler knew that Germany's chances of prevailing in this war of global redistribution were slim, unless he acted quickly. The Allies were already outproducing Germany in every major armaments category – aircraft, tanks and shipping – and they were increasingly able through bombing and the blockade to prevent Germany and German-occupied Europe from realizing their own economic potential.[24] Sooner or later, the Reich would simply be overwhelmed.

In view of all this, it is hardly surprising that Hitler struggled to develop a coherent strategy in early 1942. As Walter Warlimont, the deputy head of the OKW from December 1941, recalls, no thought had been given to the likely American strategy either.[25] Hitler did not even issue a fresh directive addressing the new situation. Unlike the Anglo-Americans, the Third Reich never developed a worked-out strategy with its Axis partners. No summits, no hymn-singing, hardly any statements, no staff talks worth the name, none of the whole panoply of 'grand alliance'. The Japanese, via Oshima, constantly pressed for closer coordination, but Hitler showed little interest. The reasons for this were simple. Hitler hesitated to support Oshima's demand for an all-out attack on British India, even politically, because he still hoped for a negotiated settlement with London;[26] the Führer dragged his feet about meeting the Indian nationalist leader Subhas Chandra Bose, who was kicking his heels in Berlin. He did not want, he later told Mussolini, any such declaration to complicate a German-British separate peace in the same way as Berlin's Polish policy had scuppered a rapprochement with the Tsarist Empire during the First World War.[27] These exchanges illustrate how much Hitler was still preoccupied with British power, even at this stage of the war. For the rest, Hitler had no strategy for defeating the United States, because there obviously wasn't one. The Führer knew that Germany, like Japan, had no technology, even at a realistic research stage, which could threaten the American mainland. He was quite simply stumped. 'I am not yet sure,' Hitler admitted to Oshima with disarming honesty on 3 January 1942, 'how to defeat the United States.'[28]

To be sure, Hitler concluded a military agreement with Italy and Japan on 18 January 1942, but it was largely for show.[29] There was a rough division of the spheres of operation, with the Germans and Italians keeping west and the Japanese east of 70 degrees longitude east, but that was about it.[30] In mid February 1942, the Führer did not respond to the demands of the Japanese military attachés, Vice Admiral Nomura and Lieutenant General Ichiro Banzai, and indeed of his own naval leadership, to link up the two strategies.[31] Hitler never intended to join hands with the Japanese in the Indian Ocean,[32] primarily because he didn't think he had the capacity to do so in the near future. He also believed that he didn't know enough about Japanese capabilities to make useful suggestions to their High Command.[33] This may well have been the right decision, because, unlike Britain and the United States, who had in many respects a shared strategic culture, Germany and Japan had no experience of military cooperation or joint values to fall back on.

Hitler now had to put out various fires across the continent. Right at the top of his list was the crisis on the central front in Russia, which raged throughout the first three months of 1942. From the beginning, Hitler insisted that withdrawals should only be undertaken in exceptional cases, and only with his express permission.[34] Hitler was convinced that retreats would simply leave the troops facing the same threats in more exposed positions, and, by exposing the flanks, risk a precipitate collapse along the whole front. He attributed the crisis to military, physical and ideological weaknesses in the Wehrmacht. He did not hide his view that the army suffered from poor leadership, that the troops had gone soft, and that the Wehrmacht as a whole lacked the National Socialist spirit which would have enabled them to master the crisis more comfortably. On 8 January 1942, Hitler issued an order which claimed that the attacking Russians were not 'first-class formations', but 'for the most part badly trained forces', which were – 'contrary to frequent initial reports' from the German troops – 'also often numerically inferior'.[35] It was, Hitler stated, a question of 'strength of nerves', 'especially of the leadership'; 'the Russian,' he added cruelly, 'has demonstrated this strength of nerves.' In other words, the Führer suggested, the whole Wehrmacht, especially its leadership, was in a funk and needed to get a grip.

Hitler took a number of steps to help his embattled troops. Some, such as the call to the civilian population to donate items of winter clothing to reinforcements departing for the eastern front, were as much propagandistic as practical, as reflected in the fact that Goebbels was put in charge of the effort.[36] Others, such as his emphasis on the use of air power, had an important effect on operations. When large numbers of German troops found themselves cut off in early 1942, such as at Demyansk, he ordered that they be resupplied by the Luftwaffe. This was done with success, though at considerable cost. Hitler also demanded that tactical air power be used to compensate for the local weakness of the ground forces. If the Luftwaffe was not ready, or prevented from flying by weather conditions, the Führer recommended that counter-attacks be called off. This order caused serious

difficulties on the ground, partly because of the problem of synchronizing
operations between the air force and the army units, and partly because,
as Bock complained, 'apprehensive and hesitant leaders' could hide behind
the Führer's will.[37] In this case, at any rate, Hitler was on the more cautious side of the argument.

The winter crisis also posed a major narratival challenge to the Führer.
He was sensitive to the charge that his invasion, which had begun on the
same June day as Napoleon's about 130 years earlier, might end in the same
way. Hitler desperately wanted to avoid scenes of chaotic retreat, with frozen
German corpses strewn across the newspapers of the world.[38] When issuing
his order to withdraw, for example, Hitler stressed that it was 'the first time
that I have given orders for the retreat of a large section of the front', and
that he expected that this 'withdrawal will take place in a manner worthy
of the German army'.[39] In the middle of January, Hitler announced that the
'operational danger' in the south had been 'dealt with',[40] but elsewhere the
danger persisted another two months. By late March 1942, the last Soviet
attacks had been seen off. It had been a harrowing experience, as Hitler
freely admitted both privately and publicly.[41]

Meanwhile, Hitler moved to tighten his grip on occupied Europe. He
issued a ferocious decree against Soviet partisans which determined that
they should 'in principle' be subject to the 'death penalty'.[42] Six weeks
later, in late January 1942, he appointed a higher SS and police commander in Serbia in order to deal with the guerrilla movement there, which
at that point was largely made up of royalist Chetniks.[43] Hitler was also
grappling with communist partisans under Tito, who were for the most
part based in Croatia and Bosnia. In Bohemia and Moravia, Reinhard
Heydrich governed with a mixture of carrot and (a very big) stick. Despite
his constant recourse to the language of annihilation, Hitler decided not
to use poison gas against partisans, at least for now, probably because
Churchill threatened in a radio broadcast that if it were deployed on the
eastern front, Britain would retaliate with gas against German cities.[44]
This shows that although all of Hitler's attempts to signal to the Anglo-
Americans were unsuccessful, messages going in the other direction were
received by Berlin and acted upon. A result of this was that the Führer
was conscious of the connection between the war against Anglo-America,
the eastern front and the battle in the skies of Germany.

The Führer, no doubt aware of calls for a 'Second Front',[45] was also
profoundly concerned about the threat of a British invasion, or at least of
raids. In late January 1942, naval intelligence highlighted the threat of an
Allied landing in Norway, one of many in the course of the war.[46] This
worried Hitler, not just because of the threat to the supply of iron ore, but

also because of the danger that the Allies would use Scandinavia as a springboard from which to attack northern Germany. The following month, Hitler sent two battleships, sometimes also described as battle cruisers, the *Scharnhorst* and the *Gneisenau*, and the heavy cruiser *Prinz Eugen* from Brest in an audacious 'Channel dash' through the Straits of Dover to new berths in Norway.[47] The main purpose of the mission was to deter any British landing in Scandinavia in the first instance, not to attack British convoys to Russia. In addition, Hitler invested huge resources in the construction of fortifications in Norway. These included pillboxes, gun emplacements, winter-proof highways, airfields, rail connections, U-boat bases and various industrial facilities.[48]

Within Germany itself, Hitler moved to improve the aerial defences of the Reich. He was appalled by the fact that when the RAF had struck Lübeck over a weekend in late March 1942, there was nobody in the relevant Berlin offices to respond. 'The Führer,' Lammers reported a few days later, 'has strongly condemned this situation' and instructed that all supreme Reich authorities and agencies of the Wehrmacht should be contactable 'on all days, including Sundays and holidays'.[49] Hitler removed control of the relief effort for Lübeck, which had hitherto been chaotic, from the Ministry of the Interior, and entrusted it to Goebbels.[50] This reflected a recognition on the Führer's part that combating Allied 'terror-bombing' was as much a matter of propaganda as practicality. It was the start of an ever-growing involvement of the propaganda minister not only in civil defence but in the Nazi war effort more generally.[51] Goebbels became a ubiquitous presence after bombing raids, whereas the Führer refused point blank to visit the shattered cities as Churchill had done, or – with one exception – to allow himself to be photographed among the ruins.

Hitler also explored ways of striking back at the Western Allies. He authorized a series of retaliatory raids on British towns in mid April 1942, though not on London.[52] This resulted in the 'Baedeker raids' – called after the famous guidebook because they targeted sites of cultural importance – in Exeter, Bristol, Bath, Norwich and York.[53] They were so ineffective and the losses were so great that the attacks had to be called off by the summer. Hitler now sought alternative methods of delivering terror to Britain, and to build new weapons of mass destruction. In early June 1942, Wilhelm Ohnesorge, the minister for posts and telegraphs, who was also responsible for one strand of the German atomic research programme, tried to interest Hitler in the possibility of building an atomic bomb. The Führer refused to listen, remarking to the military men in attendance that 'of all people', his 'minister of post' was the one to 'offer him the wonder-weapon which we need'.[54] If Germany was to strike back at her enemies in the near future, other methods would have to be used. Right at the end of June, he instructed his scientists to prepare for the deployment of chemical weapons by the spring of 1943.[55] Time, clearly, was of the essence. It would appear that Hitler disregarded the atomic option, not because of any ethical or scientific reservations, but because it seemed unlikely that it would be available in time to make any difference to the course of the war.

Hitler also struck against Anglo-American economic and military targets. On the high seas, he redoubled his efforts against Allied shipping. The U-boats caught the Americans unawares in the Caribbean and off the east coast, sinking a large number of oil tankers.[56] In the North Atlantic, the 'wolf packs' gathered to attack the convoys feeding the home islands and the entire war machine. In the course of the spring and early summer sinkings steadily mounted to the horror of the Churchill government. The main theatre, however, in which Hitler sought to deliver a decisive blow against Britain was the Mediterranean. In early 1942, the Führer took a personal interest in the fate of every individual Axis ship bringing supplies to Rommel, for example following the progress of a convoy which left Naples for Libya on 5 January 1942 and advising Mussolini on how individual vessels were to be loaded. A fortnight later, Rommel counter-attacked on his own initiative. He pushed the British before him, halting just west of Gazala in early February due to a shortage of supplies. An exultant Hitler told General Nehring, who was on the way from the eastern front to take up the position of chief of staff to the Afrika Korps, that he hoped that the threat to Egypt, combined with their immense and humiliating losses in the Far East, would make Britain more amenable to peace talks.[57]

Hitler now concentrated on the reduction of Malta, which remained a bone in the Axis throat and whose fall would seriously damage Churchill's standing at home. In February 1942, the Luftwaffe began a massive assault on the island, which was intensified from 20 March 1942. By April 1942 Rommel's supply position was greatly eased, while the situation on the island was desperate. In this context, the German and Italian High Commands discussed whether to mount a *coup de main* against the island. In mid April 1942, Hitler agreed to the operation and to a new offensive by Rommel, but failed to send more than a fraction of the reinforcements requested. Soon the Italians got cold feet and demanded not only a huge allocation of fuel oil to enable a landing, but also much greater German military participation. At first, it seemed as if Hitler would concur. His meeting with Mussolini in late April 1942 went very well, and the Führer agreed to deploy a large number of paratroops and other assets against the island. The planned sequencing, though, was crucial, as Hitler did not have the resources to begin with Malta or to carry out the Egypt and Malta operations simultaneously. In the end, it was decided that Rommel's offensive in Libya would come first, in late May or early June, followed by the landing on Malta, 'Operation Hercules', in mid July or at the latest by mid August.[58]

The struggle against the Western Allies was accompanied by an escalation in the war against the Jews. In Hitler's conception, 'they' were responsible for leading the Anglo-Saxons astray. In January 1942, he repeated his prophecy of three years earlier 'that the war will not take the course that the Jews imagine, which is that the European-Aryan peoples will be exterminated', but rather that 'the result of this war will be the destruction of Jewry'.[59] On 20 January 1942, Heydrich finally managed to hold his long-planned conference in a villa at Wannsee. The assembled bureaucrats discussed definitions of who was a Jew – something that continued to concern Hitler throughout the year[60] – and the modalities of 'deportation', which by this stage was coming to mean mass murder. The lists included numbers of Jews in the areas under German control and countries presumably still to be conquered or coerced, such as Sweden. Hitler was determined to banish the Jewish presence in Europe – the whole of Europe – for ever. A Rubicon had clearly been crossed. Despite the slaughter of Soviet and Serbian Jewry in 1941, most European Jews were still alive at the start of 1942; by the end of the year, most of them were dead.[61] Hitler may not have followed every detail of what even Goebbels described as a 'pretty barbaric procedure', but he was certainly, as the propaganda minister went on to say, 'the constant protagonist and advocate of a radical solution'.[62]

Meanwhile, Hitler escalated his foreign propaganda, which was largely directed against Bolshevism, international capitalism and the Jews within Europe, and against the British Empire, the United States, international capitalism and the Jews in the rest of the world. As the Germans prepared to attack the Middle East, the Caucasus and Persia, and even Afghanistan seemed in contention, much of the focus was on the area east of Libya and west of India. Now that the United States had entered the war, Nazi propagandists bombarded Arab audiences throughout the summer of 1942 with stories about the 'Jewish' White House of President Roosevelt.[63] There was also a 'Muslim Moment' in Hitler's strategy.[64] German propagandists cast the Führer as a Koranic figure, a new 'mahdi' or – for the Iranian Shiites – the twelfth Imam.' Hitler regarded these efforts with amusement, but also with approval. Though Hitler believed the Arabs to be racially inferior, of course, he was much more positive about Islam, which he considered a martial religion far superior to Christianity.[65]

It is hard to say exactly how successful Hitler's efforts in the Middle

East were. By no means everybody who heard, or may have heard, the Nazi broadcasts to the Middle East was sympathetic. The later Ayatollah Khomeini, for example, published an anti-Hitler tract in 1942.[66] The Arabs employed by the propaganda apparatus in Berlin were instruments rather than equal allies of the regime.[67] Where Nazi propaganda went beyond local traditions was in its international focus, and in providing a conspiratorial view not merely of the Middle East but of the entire world system. The 'General Standard Guidelines for Foreign Propaganda' of the Foreign Ministry targeted 'Jews, Bolsheviks and plutocrats' as well as that 'exponent of Jewry', Roosevelt.[68] One way or the other, the political programme of radical pan-Arabism, especially its anti-Semitism, chimed with Hitler's.

At home, Hitler threw himself into the production battle in earnest. Despite the nasty shock he had received in 1941 regarding the quantity and quality of Russian equipment, his main focus was on matching not Soviet output, but that of Anglo-America, especially the United States. On 10 January 1942, as the winter crisis raged in the east, Hitler set out his long-term priorities. These had not shifted since 1940–41. 'The long-term aim,' he decreed, 'remains the expansion of the Luftwaffe and the navy to fight the Anglo-Saxon powers'.[69] What had changed was merely the timing. Now, in a concession to the unexpectedly strong resistance put up by the Red Army, and the need to capture the Soviet resources necessary to outlast Anglo-America, Hitler ordered that production should concentrate 'initially' on the 'increased needs' of the army; the other two services were to take a step back, for now.[70] Particular attention was paid to the production of ammunition, which was deemed more urgent than tanks.[71] Naval construction was to focus on submarines, escort vessels and the defence of Norway. Despite the temporary salience of the Russian front, the decree stressed the continued importance of coastal defence (against the British).[72]

In early February 1942, Hitler summoned his armaments minister, Fritz Todt, to discuss how to increase production. He was killed when the plane taking him back from Rastenburg crashed. Hitler now appointed Albert Speer armaments minister. He was in no doubt that despite the short-term emphasis on weapons to defeat the Soviet Union, the main production battle was against Anglo-America. 'The Führer,' the OKW reported in late March 1942, 'has ordered Speer to run up ammunition production on a really big scale, so that two-front trench war can be fought for years.'[73] Hitler was preparing not for one last *Blitzkrieg* against the Soviet Union, but for a long war of attrition against the global coalition. The Führer now issued a spate of orders emphasizing the centrality of production.

'Every additional weapon and bullet,' he announced in April 1942, 'spares German blood.'[74] He also demanded that the Reich follow the US example in production, avoiding artisanal refinements and the endless proliferation of models in favour of mass output.[75] This was a subject to which he would return on many occasions as Germany was more and more crushingly outproduced by the American colossus.

Hitler backed his new minister to the hilt. Speer gradually imposed his authority on the many institutions and individuals running, or claiming to run, the German war economy. The new watchword was 'rationalization'. Hitler issued decrees restricting the use of vehicles for all but the most essential tasks.[76] In late March 1942, he appointed Fritz Sauckel general plenipotentiary for the supply of labour. The slave workers Hitler demanded were brought to the Reich in ever-larger numbers; they were accompanied by 'voluntary' labourers lured by the promise of high wages or driven by conditions at home. German output increased, and Speer's self-promoting propaganda made sure everyone was aware of the fact. The extent to which the surge was a product of the minister's initiatives or reflected decisions that had been taken much earlier is disputed. Large sections of the German armaments industry, such as aircraft and naval production, which made up the bulk of output even in 1942, were not yet under Speer's control.[77] What was clear even at the time, in any case, was that whoever was in charge in Berlin, the chances of matching the production of the enemy coalition, especially that of the United States, were slim. The problem was not the level of mobilization, which was already very high, but the imbalance in resources and industrial capacity.[78]

Nobody was more aware of this than Hitler himself. As we have seen, the immense American industrial potential had been a staple of his thinking in the 1920s, and had dominated his strategy since the late 1930s. He did not know the extent of Allied deliveries to the Soviet Union, which were substantial,[79] but he was well aware they were taking place. The basic problem, which Hitler identified quite clearly, was that whereas Germany controlled most of Europe, it was at war with most of (the rest of) the world, or at least with its resources. The enemy coalition controlled the global commons: the sea lanes and the financial system. The mines, factories and farms of the world were mobilized by Anglo-American capital, transported in Allied shipping and directed against the Reich. By contrast, the Third Reich was confined to a European reservation, whose economies were cut off from the world markets and raw materials they had depended on. Hitler's New European Order was – economically – much less than the sum of its pre-war parts. It was no match for the Anglo-American global cartel.[80] Hitler admitted as much privately to the *Gauleiter* at a meeting in late May 1942.[81]

The Führer also struggled to counter the Anglo-American narrative, of whose negative and positive power he had no doubt. He continued to stress the mortal ideological challenge posed by 'democratic capitalism'.[82] Hitler's critique was embodied by the German propaganda film *Around the Statue of Liberty. A Stroll through the USA*, which was made in 1941 but shown to him in early 1942. Its main purpose was to contrast the glitter of the American Dream with the brutal reality of life in the United States. There was footage of National Guard and police attacking strikers and demonstrators with tear gas. Workers, viewers were informed, had to slave for 'gigantic capital trusts'. The important role played by Jews, such as the Rothschilds, Warburgs and others, was stressed. There were pictures of famous gangsters such as John Dillinger, of blacks dancing to swing music, of women wrestlers, and to crown the grotesquery a man jumping out of the seventh floor of a building in front of a crowd.[83] Decadence, degeneracy and capitalist exploitation – this was the image of the United States which the Führer promoted in order to quell German concerns about fighting their much more prosperous cousins across the Atlantic. 'The Führer has seen the film we made on American cultural life and expressed himself very positively about it,' Goebbels noted on 15 February 1942, adding that Hitler had 'given instructions to show this film to as much of the German public as possible'.[84]

The stress of total war took its toll on Hitler. He became more irritable and withdrawn.[85] His zest was gone. Hitler remained in close contact with events, and was soon to move his headquarters close to the front line in the Ukraine, but the kind of propagandistic expeditions he had undertaken in Poland and France were a thing of the past.[86] Above all, Hitler's physical condition was deteriorating rapidly. This was visible even in the carefully edited newsreels.[87] To those who saw him close up the decline was unmistakable. Goebbels noted after his visit on 20 March that Hitler had 'already gone very grey' and that he 'looked much older' when speaking of the winter crisis. The Führer struck him as 'sick and frail'. Ciano, who saw him a few days later,[88] also thought he had aged considerably.

In early April 1942, Hitler was finally able to turn his attention towards preparing the summer offensive against the Soviet Union. Like Barbarossa, this was ultimately directed against the Western Allies. Unlike Barbarossa, which had both political and economic objectives at the outset, the purpose of 'Operation Blue', as it was codenamed, was primarily economic and military; political considerations played hardly any role in its original conception. Hitler aimed to complete the unfinished business of 1941, which was the capture of the resources necessary to continue the struggle against Anglo-America, and the denial of these resources to the enemy. He set out his objectives in Directive 41 on 5 April 1942.[89] The Wehrmacht was to crush the Soviet Union and cut her off from her principal industrial centres. Sebastopol, which had been under siege since late October 1941, was finally to be taken. Then, Russian forces were to be destroyed west of the Don. After that, the main motorized and armoured forces would wheel south to break into the Caucasus and seize the passes and the oil-fields there; their flanks were to be secured through the capture of Voronezh and Stalingrad to the north and east. Only once this had been done should the Wehrmacht proceed to the next objective, which was the final strangulation of Leningrad and a link-up with the Finns nearby.

The centrality of the economic objectives was emphasized by Hitler on many occasions. 'If I don't get the oil of Maykop and Grozny,' he warned the commander of the 6th Army, Friedrich Paulus, 'then I must end this war.'[90] Contrary to later legend, Operation Blue did not envisage three diverging axes of advance towards Voronezh, Stalingrad and the Caucasus. The two cities were merely to be secured in order to defend the northern flank of the operation. Hitler did not even insist on the capture of Stalingrad, saying only that it should 'at least be subjected to heavy artillery fire in order to knock it out as an armaments and communications centre'; no mention was made of any symbolic or political importance attached to the city. The main thrust was to be directed south, towards the oil-fields.[91] It was a war for oil.[92]

Conscious that he was asking ever more of his soldiers and the German people, the Führer reminded them of what they were fighting for, and why young men were being sent thousands of miles away from their homes. In February 1942, he already let slip that they might have to fight their way to the Caucasus.[93] Now, as the final touches were being put to the plan, he returned to his primary war aims in two speeches in April and May 1942. The Germans, Hitler argued, were a 'subjugated' people who had been put in 'chains' by 'democracy', the 'Jewish brain trusts' and 'stock exchanges and banks', supported by Bolshevism. In order to secure their 'daily bread in order to live' as 'have-nots', they would have to confront the international 'propertied' class. This was a global enemy, but Hitler announced that it would be beaten in Russia. 'The east is the battlefield,' he explained, 'in which the outcome will be decided.'[94] It was there, Hitler told another audience of officer cadets in late May 1942, that Germany would find the resources and the living space to prevent itself from disappearing off the face of the earth.[95] The exploiters might be mainly in the west, but the redistribution would take place primarily in the east.

It was in this spirit that the Nazi regime stepped up plans for the colonization of Russia. Hitler had plenty of space, with more in prospect; what he lacked was the right sort of people to settle it. On 23 April 1942, the Reichsführer-SS, Himmler, penned a memorandum in Hitler's headquarters on 'The retrieval of *Volksdeutsche* from America and Africa after the war'. 'It is our task,' the Reichsführer announced, 'to bring back every person of German blood who has any value at all, in order to settle the captured acres.' This could not be done by the Nazi Party because the main target group of albeit 'politically unquestionably contaminated *Volksdeutsche*' lay in 'America', beyond the political control of the Reich. Instead, Himmler called for 'personal recruitment' through family ties. Himmler was acknowledging the deep entanglement of Germany with America in one breath and demanding their disentanglement in the next.[96]

The fluidity of the American-German racial relationship, which had so preoccupied Hitler since the 1920s, was personified by the case of Hitler's former close associate Ernst Hanfstaengl, a man who had crossed and recrossed the Atlantic. Since fleeing Germany in 1937, he had been resident in Britain. On 30 June 1942, following President Roosevelt's direct request, he arrived in the United States to pursue psychological warfare against the Third Reich. He advised the president on the Führer's mindset. Hanfstaengl was thus the only man who worked directly for both Hitler and Roosevelt; he personified the two degrees of separation between the German Reich and the United States.[97] His son, Egon, whose godfather was Hitler, joined the US army. The Hanfstaengls were thus an example of the very thing that Hitler feared most: Germans in American uniform fighting other Germans.

Perhaps surprisingly, Hitler did not pay much attention to the Dutch or the Scandinavians, about whom Himmler and his SS leaders enthused at length.[98] The discourse around the 'Greater Germanic Reich' was largely generated by them, not the Führer himself. He remained focused on extracting troops from these areas. Hitler's ambivalence was reflected in his jaundiced view of marriages between locals and the German occupiers. He suggested that these relationships were based largely on 'sexual urges which could not be satisfied elsewhere', and hoped that the sight of German women would bring returning soldiers 'to their senses', not least because many of them had effectively lost their chances of finding a man through war deaths. After Himmler remonstrated, Hitler relented a little, but added that 'in his experience' – which was based on looking at marriage applications – German men tended in 90 per cent of cases to 'marry the most unworthy [Scandinavian or Dutch] women and girls' one could possibly imagine.[99]

Perhaps even more surprisingly, Hitler began to take a more positive view of the Slavs. Rosenberg, who had been given such short shrift by his leader in 1941, saw his chance in early May 1942. He showed Hitler pictures of male and female Ukrainian workers in the Heinkel Werke. 'The Führer,' he noted, 'expressed his astonishment about [their] extraordinary good looks' and even their 'beauty'.[100] The Nazi regime now began to look with more favour on the Ukrainians, Czechs and Poles, among whom Hitler assumed there to be about a million of those capable of being 're-Germanized'. Through the instrument of the *Deutsche Volkslisten*, Nazi bureaucrats commenced the laborious process of 'retrieving' the 'high-value' Germans from the Slavic 'mass', which in practice meant the Germanization of large numbers of people Hitler had previously wanted to eliminate. It was a huge exercise in racial hydrogenation, the derivation of an *ersatz Volk* from an 'inferior' base. The man who had started his career criticizing the notion of 'Germanization' of peoples, rather than territory, now superintended the greatest attempted assimilation project in German history.[101]

By contrast, the fate of the Jews was fixed. Nothing could stop the machinery of destruction, which was in full throttle by the middle of the year.[102] The rate of deportation was slowed briefly and slightly in mid June 1942 by the preparations for Operation Blue. These were given priority over what were classified as 'non-essential' transports to the camps, which only involved a tiny proportion of the available rolling stock.[103] Hitler himself seems to have taken relatively little interest in the details of the killings he had ordered,[104] but he was deeply concerned with the intellectual battle against Jewry. He declared the 'systematic intellectual struggle' against 'Jews, freemasons' and their allies to be a vital task. To this end, he wanted all libraries and archives to be examined for material which might be used for the 'ideological tasks of the NSDAP' and 'later scholarly research in institutions of higher education'.[105]

Hitler thought carefully about the execution of Operation Blue.[106] He instructed the Wehrmacht to conduct tighter envelopment operations than in the previous year, to prevent the Red Army from slipping through the net.[107] Hitler envisaged extensive use of the Luftwaffe to deal with the challenges posed by the numerical superiority of the enemy and the vastness of the space. He devoted a great deal of attention to the complex logistics of the whole operation. The Führer also put a lot of effort into coordinating the allied contribution, which was much more important this time around because the Wehrmacht lacked the manpower to complete the tasks on its own.[108] Hitler supplied his partners with precious raw materials and military equipment, often at the expense of German needs. He also embarked on a diplomatic charm offensive. The Führer went to see the future Finnish president, Marshal Mannerheim, in person.

The tape of part of that exchange – the only recording we have of Hitler speaking in private – has survived. It shows him to have been calm and measured in discussion, very far from the ranter of myth.[109] More important than the Finns were the Hungarians and Romanians, especially the latter, to whom much of the protection of the flanks was entrusted.[110]

The attack in Russia was to be accompanied by an offensive in the Mediterranean. Originally, Hitler had hoped to begin with the conquest of Malta, which would have helped Rommel's subsequent operations in North Africa. The Führer soon got cold feet, however. It was during the delayed meeting with Mussolini at Schloss Klessheim and Berchtesgaden on 29/30 April 1942 that it was agreed to delay the assault on the island until after Rommel's attack. Three weeks later, following a sceptical briefing by General Student on plans for the landing, Hitler erupted against the Italians. He did not trust them to keep the operation a secret; he was sceptical of their ability to carry it out; and he feared that in the case of disaster the Luftwaffe would have to bail the Italians out.[111] The Führer said that 'intellectual' preparations should continue, but in practical terms Operation Hercules was off the table. Hitler had flunked another landing operation against the British. The failure to eliminate Malta – Britain's unsinkable aircraft carrier in the Mediterranean – was to become one of the main reasons for the Axis defeat in North Africa.

These moves were part of a broader Axis strategy of loosely coordinated blows against the Soviet Union and the British Empire. The Germans would undertake a giant pincer movement against the Middle East by Rommel's Afrika Korps and the armies pushing down through the Caucasus. In late March and early April 1942, a Japanese strike force had already thrust deep into the Indian Ocean, launching a devastating raid on British bases on Ceylon, and sinking an aircraft carrier. By late May and early June 1942, Japan had taken Burma. With a bit of imagination, India itself was in play. In this spirit, Hitler finally met with the Indian nationalist leader Subhas Chandra Bose in Berlin on 27 May 1942.[112] The encounter, which was the only one the two men ever had, did not go well. Hitler refused to repudiate his wounding comments about Indian nationalism in *Mein Kampf*. The Führer, who was still pining for the British Empire, also told his visitor that it would take 150 years before the Indians were ready for self-government. Hitler therefore refused to issue any declaration on Indian independence. Not being able to find a use for the man himself, he suggested that Bose head for Japan, from whence he could attack British India from the east.

Hitler's strategy for the summer of 1942 was a huge gamble. He assumed that the Russians would stand and fight to defend the vital Donbas industrial region, and therefore allow themselves to be encircled and destroyed. Hitler, like the general staff, was also under the impression that the Soviet Union had been fatally weakened by the losses of 1941 and the winter battles.[113] The biggest problem of all, however, was that both operations depended very heavily on the performance of allies. The Mediterranean strategy required full Italian cooperation. Operation Blue hinged on the ability of the Hungarians and Romanians to secure the northern flank of the Wehrmacht while the mobile units raced south into the Caucasus. Given that Hitler had been warning against reliance on allies since the 1920s, and more recently on the eve of Barbarossa and of Rommel's forthcoming offensive, this was exactly the position that he did not want to be in.

On 26 May 1942, Rommel opened his offensive in North Africa. The Panzerarmee Afrika punched through the British lines and raced towards the Egyptian border. By 11 June, Rommel had taken Bir Hakim, followed by Tobruk on 21 June 1942. That same day, he sent his adjutant, Oberleutnant Brandt, to Hitler to report and to sound him out about future moves. The logistical situation was dire, because once the pressure on Malta had been relaxed, the British were able to resume attacks on German and Italian shipping from the island. In June 1942, only about 50 per cent of Axis cargoes got through. Hitler responded by making Rommel a field marshal, but he sent no new forces and did nothing to address the problem of Malta by deploying Luftwaffe units against the island. Priority was given to the eastern front. The Führer's hope was that the Panzerarmee Afrika could be resupplied via Crete and Tobruk. For now, this did not matter, because Hitler was confident that the fall of Tobruk, after its earlier stout defence, signalled the imminent demise of the British Empire, which would be followed by a negotiated peace.[114]

A few days later, on 28 June, Hitler launched Operation Blue. The Wehrmacht achieved total surprise and made rapid progress. Germany's allies marched behind and sometimes beside the German advance. On 3 July 1942, Hitler flew to the region of Voronezh to see for himself. He did not share the general optimism, agreeing with Bock that the Red Army was not beaten but engaging in flexible defence.[115] He insisted that the encirclement rings not be drawn too wide, so that the Russians would not have the chance to escape.[116] The Luftwaffe was deployed extensively to make up for the shortage of ground forces, and to overcome the challenges of operating over huge spaces.[117] For now, this approach worked well. On 4 July, Sebastopol finally surrendered, clearing the way for a push into the Caucasus across the Straits of Kertsch. Voronezh was captured on 11 July 1942, amidst heavy Soviet losses. Rostov on Don was taken on 23 July.

HITLER

In order to be closer to the action, Hitler moved his headquarters to Vinnytsia in the Ukraine.[118] Victory in the east, or at least the attainment of the objectives set for Operation Blue, seemed within his grasp.

Determined to burnish his credentials as a military genius, Hitler sought to shape the history of the campaign as it unfolded. During the planning stages, he issued a decree containing the 'basic instructions for the military-historical treatment of the Greater German liberation struggle'. Three weeks before the offensive began, he put Colonel Scherff in charge of the 'military-historical section of the army', which would have the task of recording the army's contribution.[119] Hitler also prepared to secure the economic resources so vital to the German war effort. On the very first day of the offensive, he issued a decree stressing that 'the rapid restoration of coal extraction in the Donets area is one of the most important preconditions for the continuation of the operations in the east and the exploitation of the Russian space by the German war economy'.[120] Army Group South was instructed to support this endeavour, which was one of the principal objectives of the offensive, with all the means at its disposal. After the capture of Sebastopol, a new directive, number 43, called for the dropping of paratroops on the oil installations at Maykop, now only a few hundred miles away.[121]

In mid July 1942, Hitler speeded up the murder of the Jews still further, whether in response to the early successes of Operation Blue, or simply because rolling stock had now become available again for the deportations or for some other reason.[122] What is beyond doubt is that both Hitler and Himmler had become impatient with the rate of killing, and that after a meeting on 16 July at the Führer's Headquarters it was resolved to break the various transportation deadlocks. The following day, Himmler went to Auschwitz to witness the gassing of a transport of Jews. He then ordered the camp commandant to accelerate the expansion of the killing facilities. This was done either at Hitler's direct behest, or in response to some more general instruction from the Führer. 'The occupied eastern territories will be free of Jews,' Himmler wrote a fortnight later. 'The carrying-out of this very difficult order has been laid on my shoulders by the Führer.' The escalation was so dramatic that it was noticed on the ground and relayed to the World Jewish Congress and thus to the Allies through intermediaries.[123]

As the Wehrmacht sped through southern Russia, Hitler's settlement plans moved further up the agenda. On 12 July 1942, immediately after the fall of Sebastopol, Hitler ordered that the Crimea be emptied of all 'Russians and Ukrainians living there'.[124] In late July 1942, Himmler presented Hitler with the revised version of the *Generalplan Ost*, with detailed maps and plans for the construction of settler villages. An important part of these plans was the resettlement of German-American returnees, who were deemed to have the right qualities of hardiness and initiative to colonize the steppes as their forefathers had once settled the plains. Some of the planned settlements were thus to be called 'USA-Colonies'.[125] 'The Führer not only listened to me,' Himmler said shortly afterwards, 'he even refrained from constant interruptions, as is his usual habit.'[126] Hitler approved the plan. This vision was by no means purely agrarian. On the contrary, Hitler envisaged not merely the Germanization of some existing cities, but also the construction of a whole new set of urban centres.[127] The modernity of Hitler's vision was also demonstrated by his plans for a huge broad-gauge railway which would connect the population centres of the new territories with the Reich.[128]

At around the same time, the Führer set out how he envisaged the treatment of the native population (or at least of the Slavic residue, once the 'Nordic' elements had been filtered out). Abortions in the occupied eastern territories were to be encouraged, indeed it would be desirable to have a 'vigorous trade in contraception there' to prevent 'the non-German population from multiplying'. The non-German population was not to have any access to the 'German medical welfare system'; they should not, for example, be inoculated or offered any form of preventative medicine. The non-German population should not be taught more than how to read or write. They should certainly not be given any 'higher education', for fear of encouraging 'future resistance'. The German settler population, he stressed, should be kept strictly apart, if necessary at first in temporary barracks. The Slav cities were to be kept run down, so that the native population would not have a 'higher standard of living' than the German settlers would achieve in their planned separate 'newly built cities and villages'.[129] It was a bleak prospect for the Slavs, but still a more promising one than the future Hitler had originally had in store for them under the 'Hunger Plan'. He would not strive to keep them alive, but nor would he now actively set out to kill them. The Slav 'problem' would be solved by evolutionary neglect, rather than radical violence.

The most important part of Hitler's programme, at least in the immediate term, was the war against Anglo-America. As Operation Blue waxed, Hitler turned his attention back to the British Empire and the United States. Rather than attacking Malta, as Kesselring wanted, Hitler backed Rommel's plan to continue the offensive in Libya. This was partly because he was seduced by Rommel's razzmatazz,[130] but his main thinking was strategic and political. He was worried, as he told Mussolini, that if Britain were not ejected soon from North Africa then 'American long-range bombers' would appear there 'within weeks' and begin the bombardment of southern Italy. For this reason, the fall of Tobruk should be taken as an opportunity to finish off the 8th Army. 'It is possible that on this occasion Egypt can be seized from the British,' Hitler remarked cautiously. It might even be possible to combine that offensive with the thrust through the Caucasus in order to 'collapse' Britain's whole position in the 'Orient'.[131] That same day, Rommel attacked again, once more driving the British back, this time across the Egyptian border. On 27 June 1942, he took Marsa Matruh. The instruments used were military, but Hitler's real strategy remained political, namely the destruction of the Churchill government, followed by a negotiated peace.

Hitler now ramped up the military, diplomatic and psychological pressure. Right at the start of July, he issued a joint declaration with Mussolini on Egypt. A day later, he authorized a huge allocation of resources and workers to speed up naval repairs and construction, including the building and conversion of no fewer than five aircraft carriers.[132] Shortly after, the Luftwaffe and Kriegsmarine completed the evisceration of PQ 17, one of the British Arctic convoys carrying supplies to the Soviet Union via Murmansk. The Battle of the Atlantic was also going well, with steadily increasing sinkings of Allied merchantmen. Hitler was delighted with these successes. 'The Führer was deeply moved by the successes in the Arctic and about the activities of our U-boats,' Rosenberg noted, 'he kept on coming back to this event.'[133] In the middle of the month, Hitler received the ousted Iraqi prime minister, Rashid Ali. 'The conversation was conducted in the spirit of trusting friendship,' the subsequent communiqué announced, 'which the German people feel towards the Arab peoples.'[134] The strangulation of Britain and the collapse of her empire, assaulted by the Germans in the west and the Japanese in the east, now seemed a realistic possibility.

On 23 July 1942, Hitler issued Directive 45 on the continuation of the offensive in southern Russia.[135] He declared the Russian forces west of the Don defeated, though he did note the 'assembly of further enemy forces in the area around Stalingrad which the enemy will probably defend with vigour'. Hitler decreed that Russian forces south of the Don were to be eliminated. Thereafter, the advance would divide, and the sub-divisions of Army Group South reflected this. The main thrust, by Army Group A, with most of the armoured and mobile forces, was to push south to secure the Black Sea coast and the oil-fields. Meanwhile, Army Group B was to 'build up a defensive line on the Don' and to advance against the 'enemy forces' at Stalingrad, to 'occupy the city itself' (a new objective), and to 'block' the land bridge between Don and Volga; there was no talk yet of any symbolic or political significance attached to its capture. Once this had been done, 'fast units' were to be sent to Astrakhan to cut the 'main tributary of the Volga'. The Luftwaffe was to support the move on Stalingrad, and to destroy the city, but the 'main centre of gravity of the air war' was to be the capture of the Black Sea ports. His plan here was to resupply the Army Group in the Caucasus by sea.[136]

Given that the region, with its majority Muslim population, now appeared on the verge of falling into his lap, Hitler gave its future some serious thought.[137] This was part of a broader 'Muslim Moment' in the summer of 1942, in which the Third Reich sought, and often found, allies among the Muslims of the Balkans, the Soviet Union and the Middle East.[138] 'The Führer confirmed to me,' one German diplomat wrote in mid August 1942, 'that Germany follows with great interest the fight of the Islamic world against its oppressors and does not intend to enslave or suppress any Islamic country'.[139] In early September 1942, the Führer even got as far as drafting a directive on occupation policy in the Caucasus which held out the prospect of subsequent independence for the peoples of the area. Hitler's motivation here was strategic.[140] Managing the Caucasian oil-fields would be difficult without the support or at least the quiescence of the population. In the Führer's view, this required close supervision to prevent them from indulging in their traditional blood feuds.[141] Hitler wanted to extract oil, and for that he needed order.

In late July 1942, the Wehrmacht surged forward again. The Soviet forces south of the Don were quickly overcome. Army Group B dug in to secure the flanks; the 6th Army pressed on to Stalingrad. Army Group A – the main thrust – advanced towards the Caucasus. Krasnodar was taken on 3 August with its oil refineries, and Maykop, with the first oil-fields, was captured on 9/10 August. Nearly all the facilities, however, had been wrecked by the retreating Red Army. Not long after, the mountains of the Caucasus were reached and German mountain troops scaled Mount Elbrus to plant the swastika to great media acclaim back home and internationally. Hot on the heels of the advance came specialist units – the Mineralölbrigade – tasked with securing the oil-fields and making them operational again. Hitler was given an immediate report on the situation and was briefed on progress at regular intervals.[142] The capture of the Donets mines and some of the first Caucasian oil-fields came at an opportune moment, because the shortage of energy was becoming acute back in the Reich. Very shortly after the capture of Maykop, Hitler attended an emergency meeting with Speer, Sauckel, Kehrl and various industrial magnates on the 'coal crisis'. 'If due to the shortage of coking coal the output of the steel industry cannot be raised as planned,' he warned his stunned interlocutors, 'then the war is lost.'[143]

Despite these concerns, Hitler's spirits rose as the advance continued in mid August 1942. The *Lebensraum* and resource objectives of the Russian campaign appeared on the verge of realization. Africa and much of Asia appeared within his grasp; the world seemed to open up before him.[144] He was thinking hard about ways to strike at the United States itself. Hitler had not originally planned to expand this far, but the global nature of the hostile coalition meant that for a brief moment in the midsummer of 1942, only the world was enough to give him the security he craved. Yet even at this pinnacle of his power, as autumn loomed, and the decisive blow eluded him, the Führer was beginning to draw back. His strategy, he explained to Raeder on 26 August 1942, was to crush Russia and thereby secure a 'blockade-proof and defensible *Lebensraum* from which the war could be waged [against the Anglo-Americans] for many more years'. This would enable the Führer to determine the 'outcome and length' of the broader war, which he defined as the 'battle against the Anglo-Saxon seapowers', in order to make them 'ready for peace'.[145] In other words, victory in Russia would pave the way not for world domination but for a negotiated peace with Anglo-America.

Even at the height of his power, Hitler remained an anxious man, and with good reason. The Japanese advance in the Pacific crashed to a halt after their shattering defeat at Midway in early June. On 16 August 1942, the USAAF launched its first raid on Europe, against the marshalling yards at Rouen. Three days after that, a substantial raiding force of Canadians landed at Dieppe, and although it suffered heavy casualties, the operation shook Hitler.[146] Soon after, Rommel's offensive in North Africa ran out of steam at El Alamein, about 100 kilometres west of Alexandria. The sea routes were now dominated by the British, who had by now sunk a large percentage of the Italian merchant fleet. Hitler simply did not have the supplies, forces or ability to get these across the Mediterranean to help him. The Führer was also unhappy with the recent progress in Russia. He had noticed that most Russian troops had escaped the encirclement south of the Don and melted away south or east to fight another day. Hitler was particularly concerned about the situation in the Caucasus, where the spearhead was too far to the east. He ordered that priority for fuel and resources be given to the right flank attacking the Black Sea ports. This is why he was so infuriated by the scaling of Mount Elbrus by his mountain troops, which he considered a colossal distraction. It was the low-lying coastal strip, not the high ground, which interested him.[147] If necessary, the Luftwaffe could temporarily supply the attacking forces. One way or the other, the Wehrmacht would have to secure the Black Sea ports, or else the offensive towards Baku would grind to a halt.

In early September 1942, Hitler's unease turned to alarm.[148] On 7 September, he sent Jodl to meet the commanders in the Caucasus. They agreed that the forces in the mountains should not swing towards the sea, as Hitler wanted, but hold the passes and release troops for the force advancing from the north down the coast towards the Black Sea port of Tuapse. The Führer's attempts to get his way proved fruitless. Hitler's reaction was stark. He went into a prolonged 'sulk', refusing to take meals with the army leadership for about a month; he also insisted that all future discussion be recorded in full to prevent a recurrence.[149] The commander of Army Group A was summarily sacked on 10 September.

Hitler took over direct command, temporarily, the only time Hitler exercised formal direct operational command during the war. In practice, he intervened little in the day-to-day operations of the Army Group, or at least no more than he would have done anyway;[150] his main aim was to ensure the strategic compliance of the Wehrmacht. The same day as Hitler deprived List of his command, he issued a formal order to Army Group A. Firstly, 17 Army was instructed 'to press on immediately to Tuapse in order to capture the Black Sea coast' and to pave the way for a further attack as far south as Suchumi. Secondly, Hitler announced his intention – 'depending on developments at Stalingrad' – to switch 'fast units' from there at the end of the month to support 1st Panzer Army in its push on Grozny.[151] The advance continued, but at a steadily diminishing speed. On 18 September, Hitler erupted in a long diatribe at Vinnytsia.[152] He considered sacking Jodl, but then changed his mind. Not long after, on 24 September 1942, the chief of the general staff, Franz Halder, was given his marching orders. 'He told me when I took my leave,' Halder later recalled, 'that my constant know-all attitude had used up half of his nerves.'[153] He was replaced by Kurt Zeitzler. One way or the other, whoever was to blame, it was clear that the oil-fields at Baku would not be reached that year.

In consequence, sometime between the beginning of September and mid October, Hitler decided to go over to the strategic defensive in Russia. On 8 September 1942, Army Groups Centre and North were told to hold their positions at all costs, partly to avoid the loss of 'irreplaceable equipment' and partly to avoid jeopardizing 'neighbouring sectors'.[154] Explicitly making a comparison with the 'great defensive battles of the [First] World War', which he deemed much tougher than those of the eastern front, Hitler issued his 'slogan', which was 'dig and dig again, especially while the soil is still soft'. On 14 October, Hitler also in effect called time on Operation Blue in the south. He declared the current campaign to be largely 'completed'. Hitler promised to resume operations in the following year. In the meantime, he demanded that there should be no 'retreats or operational withdrawals' in the face of enemy attacks. Detailed instructions were provided on the construction of trenches and fortifications.[155] The language was unmistakable. The war in the east would no longer be one of manoeuvre but of attrition.

The September crisis was the operational turning point of the war, and also Hitler's final breach with the military leadership. He accused the commanders of not merely misunderstanding the operational plan from the beginning – 'failure to recognize the centre of gravity'[156] – but defying his direct orders. Hitler was also convinced that elements within the headquarters were betraying secrets to the enemy.[157] There was in fact an MI6 agent in or close to the OKW, codenamed 'Knopf', originally recruited by the Poles, who was providing London with detailed accounts of Hitler's thinking.[158] Hitler's main concern, though, was that the failure to take the ports in time had wrecked the strategic purpose of the operation, which was to supply the spearheads across the Black Sea, and to extract the oil – at least that of Maykop – in tankers from Tuapse to Romania and from there up the Danube to Germany.[159] 'Whoever loses the oil,' Hitler lamented, 'loses the war.'[160] In effect, he had conceded that if the war was not lost, it certainly could no longer be won.

Hitler now tried to mitigate the damage. He gave orders for the extraction of oil from Maykop, stressing the 'decisive importance' of rebuilding the installations there.[161] Only a dribble ever reached the Reich. Hitler also instructed the Luftwaffe to destroy the Soviet oil-fields beyond his grasp. On 7 October orders were given to attack the installations at Grozny, which the Luftwaffe executed three days later, and a fortnight afterwards he demanded a raid on faraway Baku.[162] Göring simply did not have the resources for that. Hitler's main response, though, was to switch focus to Stalingrad. Formerly a secondary target, its importance had been steadily growing in Hitler's mind in the course of the campaign, even before the crisis in the Caucasus. If the city could be captured and the Soviet line of communication north–south could be cut, then Hitler could realize at least some of the campaign's strategic objectives. The Führer was optimistic. His faith in the commander of the attacking force was such that he had considered him the only replacement for Jodl. Paulus, he remarked, was 'the only man' whom 'he trusted personally', the first man whom he had 'noticed' among senior Wehrmacht officers, someone who was 'fanatical' about 'motorization' and a man of 'balanced personality' who was able to 'hold his nerve'.[163]

So from October to mid November 1942, the 6th Army battered its way into Stalingrad.[164] The Luftwaffe, at Hitler's direct request, pounded the city into rubble. Paulus advanced slowly through the ruins; the

Russians clung on grimly with their backs to the Volga. Losses were heavy on both sides. Stalingrad's landmarks – the grain elevator, the factories, the tennis racket railway sidings – acquired global significance; its very name seemed to epitomize the stakes. By early October, many Germans, and indeed world opinion, had come to see the struggle as a battle of wills between Stalin and the Führer.[165] Hitler became more and more obsessed with the capture of the city, urging Paulus on. 'The difficulties of the battle for Stalingrad,' he told the men of the 6th Army a month later, 'and the reduced combat strengths are known to me.' Despite this, Hitler demanded that they should attack once more with the same energy 'they had so often shown before' and the 'élan they had so often demonstrated' in order to break through at least at the artillery factory and the metal factory, reaching the Volga and capturing these areas of the city.[166]

That said, Hitler, who intensely personalized his rivalry with Churchill and Roosevelt, was not pursuing a personal vendetta with Stalin, whom he hardly ever mentioned in public. The name of the city was an irrelevance to him. Hitler's immediate target was the Soviet economy and communications system. 'I wanted to get to the Volga at a particular place, at a particular city,' he said, adding that it 'coincidentally carried the same name as Stalin himself'. 'But don't think for a moment,' he continued, 'that I marched there for that reason', but rather because it was 'a very important place'. No fewer than 30 million tonnes of goods, including 9 million tonnes of oil, large quantities of manganese and the entire grain harvest of the Kuban, Hitler claimed, passed through the city every year.[167] His strategic objective was to deliver political effect, not in Moscow but in London. In early October 1942, Hitler brusquely rejected Jodl's suggestion that troops be withdrawn from Stalingrad 'and emphasized for the first time that the capture of Stalingrad was important not only for operational reasons, but also urgently necessary for psychological reasons', that is to impress 'world opinion' and to cheer 'the allies'.[168] If the city fell, Hitler remarked to his entourage, then Churchill might fall or at least become more amenable to making peace.[169] In short, the push on Stalingrad, like the entire war, was primarily driven by the contest against Anglo-America.

This explains why, in early November 1942, Hitler announced the fall of the city. 'There was a major transhipment point there,' he told an audience in the Munich Bürgerbräukeller in his annual address to commemorate the failed putsch, 'which I wanted to take, and you – we are being modest – we actually have it'.[170] The military leadership, who knew better, were aghast at Hitler's optimism. Senior commanders called from Russia to say that Stalingrad was very far from having been taken.[171] In fact, Hitler – who was already resigned to another winter in Russia – was not deluded. He claimed victory prematurely not primarily to cheer the anxious German public, or to depress the Russians, who knew that it was untrue, but rather to influence world opinion, particularly in Britain. A year before, in October 1941, Hitler had for the same reason instructed Dietrich to tell the world press that the Soviet Union was beaten. Now he was doing it again.

In the autumn of 1942, Hitler was engulfed by multiple crises. In the west, the Anglo-Americans launched a series of devastating attacks. On 23 October 1942, Montgomery began his offensive at El Alamein.[172] In the face of crushing Allied material superiority, especially in the air, Rommel was forced to retreat by 3 November. Five days later, the Anglo-Americans mounted Operation Torch, a huge landing in French North Africa. This not merely threatened Rommel's flank, but blew the entire Axis position in the Mediterranean completely open. Not only had the U-boats been unable to stop the invasion, but their sinkings of Allied merchant shipping in the North Atlantic had peaked. Hitler now put his faith in the planned new generation of U-boat, but it would take time to build and deploy these.[173] Then the Russians counter-attacked at Stalingrad in Operation Uranus. They broke through the German lines north of the city on 19 November, and a day later to the south. Some of the allied forces guarding the flanks – Romanian, Hungarian and Italian – fought bravely; many bolted.[174] On 23 November the two pincers met at Kalach on the Don, well to the west of the city. The 6th Army, more than a quarter of a million men and a colossal quantity of equipment, was in the pocket.

Hitler struggled to respond to this succession of blows. On 22 November, he ordered Paulus to stand fast while he worked out a plan.[175] Two days later, immediately after the 6th Army was cut off, Hitler proclaimed Stalingrad a 'fortress'. He forbade any talk of a break-out, and refused to give Paulus freedom of action.[176] Hitler feared that the 6th Army would be caught out on the steppe in the open and annihilated. Much better, he thought, to dig in within the relative shelter of the city, especially in winter, and wait for relief. Perhaps it was with this in mind that Hitler announced the creation of a new decoration, the 'Hand to Hand Fighting Clasp', as 'a visible sign of recognition of soldiers who fought man to man with cold steel and [other] weapons of close combat, but also as an encouragement towards the highest fulfilment of duty'.[177] In the meantime, having been given assurances by Göring, Hitler planned to supply Paulus by air, just as he had done at Demyansk and Cholm the previous winter. From the start to the bitter end of the crisis, the Führer took all the main decisions on Stalingrad himself.[178]

Hitler cast the struggle in Stalingrad as a clash of wills and endurance.

In the end, he told the generals, it was a matter of 'nerves'. The situation of the 6th Army became increasing desperate. Red Army attacks constantly shrank the perimeter. Men froze; equipment seized up. Supplies ran low, as the Luftwaffe could fly in only a small part of the army's requirements. Hitler was fully aware of this. When told in mid December of the daily total achieved in munitions, fuel and supplies, which was a fraction of what was needed, he remarked simply 'that is terrible'.[179] A relief offensive petered out well short of the city. Still, so long as Paulus held on to the three airfields at Stalingrad, and the 6th Army maintained cohesion, there was a chance of holding out until the spring.

Two considerations were uppermost in Hitler's mind over Stalingrad. Firstly, any withdrawal of the 6th Army not only would be risky but would inevitably involve the loss of a huge quantity of equipment, which he could not replace. 'I am afraid,' he confessed, 'that if one now retreats, all the materiel will be lost.'[180] He was particularly worried about the loss of the heavy artillery pieces, but also of the thousands of horses, many of which were on their last legs. Secondly, Hitler was under no illusion that the ground lost could be regained. 'We will not recapture it,' he warned the generals, adding that they should 'not imagine that they will regain the ground after retreating and leaving all that equipment behind'. The Nazi tide was ebbing, leaving a scum of corpses and wrecked equipment, and it would not rise again.

Though the drama at Stalingrad dominated the German public, and has since gained an ascendancy in the historical memory, the main contest in Hitler's mind remained the struggle with Anglo-America. The country and name he singled out with particular ferocity in his rhetoric were not the Soviet Union and Stalin, but the United States and Roosevelt.[181] In strategic terms, the Allied invasion of North Africa presented a much greater threat, which overshadowed the eastern crisis. The entire Mediterranean front, including Mussolini's own position, and the future of the Axis itself were suddenly in contention. By late 1942, the brief aerial concentration on the east for Operation Blue was over. Despite the dire situation at Stalingrad, some 70 per cent of the Luftwaffe was deployed in the west, in the Mediterranean or in the Reich itself.[182]

All this brought home the huge attritional challenge now posed by the Western Allies. Germany was manifestly outmatched in the air. In early September, Hitler lamented with respect to the Dieppe raid that while 'we have 200 fighters' the enemy 'has 2,000'. 'If the battle lasts for three days,' he continued, 'and I lose 37 or 40 machines a day', then we 'have had it,' because the other side might have lost the same numbers of aircraft, but still had plenty to spare.[183] The British now were beginning not only to claim strategic mastery of the skies, but to enjoy the tactical air superiority that had once been the hallmark of the Luftwaffe. Henceforth until the end of the war, Wehrmacht operations against the 'Anglo-Saxon' powers would be seriously constrained by the RAF and – increasingly – the USAAF. Hitler was shocked at the amount of shipping the Allies had been able to assemble for Operation Torch, which showed that his own calculations of the available levels of tonnage were completely awry.[184] Hitler was also furious with the Luftwaffe – one observer reports 'vicious attacks' – for failing to produce a viable long-range bomber with which he could have attacked the bridgehead.[185]

If Hitler was to keep his allies in and the enemy coalition out, he would have to prevent the Anglo-Americans from gaining a foothold in Europe and even on its doorstep. Three days after Torch, he launched Operation Attila, the occupation of Vichy France, designed to pre-empt an Allied landing there. The seizure of the Vichy fleet failed when it was scuttled by the French before German tanks reached Toulon. The last major naval assets potentially available to the Third Reich had slipped from its grasp. The Führer was also determined to hold the line in North Africa. When Rommel descended uninvited on his headquarters in late November 1942 to demand the evacuation of Tunisia, Hitler refused. 'For foreign political reasons,' he explained, 'a larger bridgehead in Africa simply must be held.'[186] Despite the needs of the eastern front, and especially the agony at Stalingrad, Hitler dispatched a huge and well-equipped army to Tunisia, much of it by air, using precious transport capacity, in order to prop up Mussolini and to ensure that the area would not be used as a staging post for air-raids or invasions against his southern flank. The airlift was larger than the one staged at Stalingrad. When in early December 1942 the first Tiger tanks appeared, Hitler decided that they were not to be used piecemeal in Russia but in concentrated form in Africa against the British and Americans.[187]

Hitler was in no doubt about the annihilatory nature of his struggle with the western powers. For him, this was epitomized not merely by the bombing war, but also by the conduct of military operations. The Führer was incensed by the alleged Canadian treatment of German prisoners during the Dieppe raid, after which some were found executed with their hands tied behind their backs. In September 1942, fearing another landing, he ordered the deportation of the Channel Islanders. Two thousand of them were sent to Biberach in Württemberg.[188] On 18 October 1942, Hitler instructed that British 'so-called commandos', irrespective of how they had been deployed or whether or not they were in uniform, should be 'killed down to the last man in battle or on the run'.[189] In order to explain why he was demanding such drastic action, Hitler referred to the production crisis. 'I do not know,' he said, 'whether every officer is aware that the destruction of a single electricity station can cost the Luftwaffe many thousands of tons of aluminium.' The many unbuilt aircraft would then be missing at the front or in the defence of the Reich. 'In the east,' Hitler explained, 'the war is a battle of extermination,' adding that 'Britain and America' had 'joined' this form of warfare through practices which 'in essence' did not differ 'in any way' from those of Russian partisans. The general intention behind the instruction, which was the western equivalent of the commissar-order, was to radicalize the war in the west so that it harmonized with practices in the east.[190]

The annihilatory tendency in Hitler's thinking about Anglo-America was also evident in his pursuit of weapons of mass retaliation. He was convinced that only a cataclysmic blow against Britain would force the RAF to end the attacks on German cities and Churchill to seek peace. Despairing of the Luftwaffe, the most promising avenue seemed to be rockets. In late June 1942, Speer briefed him about the progress of the experiments at Peenemünde. Hitler was initially sceptical.[191] In early October 1942, however, there was the first successful rocket flight. By the middle of the month, Hitler was demanding the 'mass deployment' of rockets, at least 5,000 on the first occasion,[192] so that 'one can make a powerful impression with this weapon'.[193] This was to involve a huge commitment of fuel, steel and other resources. By the end of the war Hitler had invested the equivalent of 39,000 aircraft in a rocket programme which ultimately proved irrelevant to the course of the war.[194] The intended target of these weapons, it is worth repeating, was not the Soviet Union but Britain.

The end of the wars of manoeuvre in Russia and North Africa accentuated the attritional character of the conflict for Hitler. Victory would go to those who could outproduce and outbleed the other side. On 1 October 1942, well before the Soviet counter-offensive at Stalingrad, Hitler told the *Gauleiter* that there would be no early end to the struggle and that the clash of production was now the main battle front. Increased mobilization would be necessary. A key factor, Hitler knew, was labour and he urged Sauckel to remedy the shortage caused by the increasing demands of the war and the absence of so many men at the front.[195] He pushed for greater use of foreign workers, both forced and voluntary. While determined to remove Jews from the armaments factories of the Reich, Hitler agreed to Sauckel's suggestion that Jewish 'skilled workers' be allowed to remain 'initially' in the General government; production took precedence over annihilation, at least for the moment.[196] The demands of the production war drove Hitler to moderate his policy at least towards the non-Jewish population. He instructed that the Serbian prisoners sent to build fortifications in Norway should be 'properly fed' because thereby increasing their productivity was the only way 'the numbers required could be reduced', thus easing the pressure on accommodation, clothing and other supplies.[197] Likewise, in the autumn of 1942, he ordered that the 'native labourers and their families deployed to work in the oil industry should be fed in such a way as to safeguard their willingness and ability to work'.[198] This was a sentiment which Hitler repeated on many occasions until the end of the war. That said, what actually happened was another matter. In the case of the Serbian prisoners, for example, a large number died on the way to Norway, and well over half of them did not survive the war.[199]

Hitler also sought to mobilize the home front further. Towards the end of the following month, as the Soviet pincers were snapping shut at Kalach, he appointed a special envoy to investigate how best 'underemployed or badly employed' manpower could be released for service at the front or other duties.[200] Hitler gave equal attention to the psychological mobilization of the German people, which was becoming increasingly dismayed by the evident stagnation on the battle fronts and the escalating bombing war. The question of how to respond to RAF attacks was not just a practical matter but also one of domestic politics. Hitler expressed his horror at the tendency of the Luftwaffe to play it down. 'People can bear everything,' Hitler continued, but they needed to be told 'the brutal truth',[201] not lies that they knew to be untrue from personal observation. There was also the issue of how to reduce the danger to civilians not required for war production. Baldur von Schirach, who was keen to get children away from their families and indoctrinate them, favoured their mass evacuation in 'whole school classes' to safe areas. Fearful of the effects on morale, Hitler agreed to the plan, but only on condition that 'all compulsion was strictly avoided', adding that it was 'the parents alone who should decide whether their children were evacuated'.[202]

The Führer also tackled the officer corps, whose want of ideological coherence he blamed for the failures in Russia; here the 'September crisis' in the Caucasus weighed much more heavily than the situation at Stalingrad. More broadly, Hitler wanted to break the aristocratic and upper-middle-class stranglehold on the military profession, in order – following the more progressive Prussian tradition – to make it a career open to talent.[203] On 1 October 1942, very shortly after Hitler's speech, Rudolf Schmundt was appointed head of the Heerespersonalamt. This marked a big shift in the Führer's relations with the officer corps, whose social transformation he now pursued with vigour. A flurry of measures followed. The social opening of the officer corps happened not just because of the pressures of war, but because Hitler made it happen.[204]

These modernizing steps were accompanied by some more feudal stratagems to bind the generals closer to their Führer. He was already in the
habit of rewarding them with substantial cash payments. Towards the end
of September 1942, almost immediately after his eruption over the Caucasus, he gave Keitel a particularly fat birthday cheque with his 'sincerest
thanks . . . for the loyalty and devotion with which you have made yourself
available to me . . . [during] a serious crisis'. In October 1942, he made
the first land grant to a general, a confiscated Jewish estate in Silesia to
Ewald von Kleist, whom he shortly afterwards made commander of Army
Group A in the Caucasus. Hitler also made substantial gifts to members
of the government, the party and the SS, including Wilhelm Frick, Alfred
Rosenberg, Konstantin von Neurath, Robert Ley, Joachim von Ribbentrop, Fritz Sauckel, Chief of Police SS-Obergruppenführer Kurt Daluege
and SA-Chief of Staff Wilhelm Schepmann.[205]

Hitler's efforts to rally Germans behind the common cause were complicated by the continuing internecine warfare within the regime. He was
still spending a lot of time mediating disputes between his paladins:
between Goebbels and Rosenberg over how eastern 'colonial policy' was
to be presented;[206] between Rosenberg and Ribbentrop over control of
the entire 'Eastern Question';[207] between Rosenberg and the military commanders over the administration of the captured eastern territories;[208]
between Baldur von Schirach and the various state authorities over the
evacuations of children from the big cities to the countryside;[209] between
Himmler and Ribbentrop over reporting to Hitler.[210] There was also a
low-intensity struggle over controlling access to Hitler between Lammers
and Bormann, in which the latter was gradually gaining the upper hand.[211]
None of these disputes enhanced Hitler's authority in the slightest. On the
contrary they were a waste of everyone's time and energy. Nor did Hitler
encourage the party to establish a parallel state. On 2 December 1942, he
issued a (futile) instruction forbidding the NSDAP from intervening formally in 'private legal matters', which should be left to the courts; at the
most, the party might offer its informal mediation for an 'amicable resolution'.[212] With regard to forms of government, Hitler believed, there was no
contest; whatever was administered least was best.

One way or the other, Hitler was still determined to outlast the enemy
coalition, or at least to give that impression. He told the visiting Dutch fascist
leader Anton Mussert on 10 December 1942 that he 'would not capitulate
but fight', even if he had to recruit fourteen- to sixteen-year-olds.[213] In a
public speech, he claimed that whereas the Kaiser's Germany had given up
at fifteen minutes to twelve, he 'only stopped on principle at five minutes past
twelve'. Besides, he claimed, his position was much better than that of

Frederick the Great, 'who faced a coalition of 54 million with only 3.9 million [population]'. Today, he continued, Germany still held 'bastions far
from its own borders'. It had space to trade. That said, Hitler was under no
illusions. 'I know very well,' he said, 'that the fight is a very difficult one.'[214]

As the year drew to an end there was no disguising the military predicament of the Reich. More than 100,000 men remained besieged in
Stalingrad, with dwindling hopes of resupply or relief. Many more were
being rushed to Tunisia in order to bolster the Axis position. The RAF
battered the Reich nightly, with increasing effectiveness. More than twice
as many U-boats were sunk in 1942 than during the previous twelve
months, most of them in the second part of the year. Allied counter-
measures, which Hitler had expected, were taking their toll.[215] Sinkings
of merchant ships, which had peaked in November 1942, dropped markedly in December. To complete this tale of woe, on the very last days of
the year the Kriegsmarine spectacularly failed to close with and destroy
a poorly defended British Arctic convoy in the Barents Sea. The cause of
this fiasco was not the timidity of the commanding admiral, but Hitler's
well-known reluctance to risk the loss of capital ships, which he now
described as 'dead iron' and a 'miserable copy of the Royal Navy'. 'It was
now his irrevocable decision,' he announced to Raeder's representative at
headquarters, 'to get rid of these useless ships' and deploy the 'good crews
[and] these good weapons' more usefully. Hitler was also worried that
'lying around' in port with the resulting reduction of 'fighting keenness'
would turn the navy into a 'nursery of revolution', as had happened in
1918.[216] He was determined that history should not repeat itself.

In his New Year's Proclamation for 1943 Hitler lost no time in identifying
the cause of the Reich's present travails, namely its own fragmentation
and its nemesis in the shape of the United States of America. Reprising
old themes from the 1920s, he reminded his listeners that thanks to the
'centuries-long decay of the first German Reich', the German people had
become 'mere cultural fertilizer for the other world'. The 'other' world
was Anglo-America, especially the United States, which to Hitler represented first and foremost a massive demographic threat to the Reich.
'Countless millions of Germans,' he told his audience, 'were forced to
leave their homeland.' 'It was they, in particular,' Hitler went on, 'who
helped to build up that continent [America] which is now trying to plunge
Europe into war for a second time.'[217]

In January 1943, the contest escalated further. Meeting at Casablanca in
the middle of the month, Churchill and Roosevelt announced that they
would accept nothing less than the 'unconditional surrender' of Hitler.

Towards the end of January, the USAAF launched its first raid on the Reich, against the port of Wilhelmshaven; Hitler paid close attention to American press claims about the effectiveness of the bombing campaign.[218] In North Africa, the first American ground troops were already in action against the Wehrmacht. The greatest threat, however, came from the productive power of the United States, soon to be epitomized by the iconic image of Norman Rockwell's statuesque 'Rosie the Riveter' bestriding a slain copy of *Mein Kampf*. Hitler conceded as much in his proclamation. 'What America intends to achieve in the way of production,' he said, 'has been communicated to us often enough by the babblings of the principal warmonger Roosevelt,' adding that 'what it can really do and has already achieved is not unknown to us'.[219] The civil war, which in Hitler's mind pitted German engineers and soldiers from both sides of the Atlantic against each other, was now in full swing.

With the plan of bringing back German-Americans to settle the new lands in east now on hold, the Third Reich hoped at least to retrieve some of the lost racial value among the US prisoners of war, whose numbers increased as the ground war in Tunisia intensified. The Coordination Centre for Ethnic Germans of the SS, which was given the task of trawling the camps for 'American and British prisoners of war of German descent',[220] turned up many captives of German origin, but ultimately despaired of converting them. Later, Obersturmbannführer Rimann informed Himmler that 'the continuing interrogation of American POWs of German descent has shown us the problems associated with our plan'. Most were second or third generation, and were 'completely Americanized in attitude and behaviour'. [221] It was no different in the case of the Canadian *Volksdeutsche* captured at Dieppe, who all turned out – depressingly – to be volunteers.[222]

Hitler linked his continuing preoccupation with the fate of German emigrants with his policy towards the Jews. He had often been reproached, the Führer complained to Admiral Horthy, for his rough treatment of the Jews, but what about the '250,000 Germans' who had had to 'emigrate' every year from the Reich? They had had to do so under such terrible conditions, Hitler alleged, that 30 per cent of them died en route to Australia.[223]

Meanwhile, the Reich was being battered by the British Empire. Hitler's fury at the ascendancy of the Royal Navy on the high seas exploded in a confrontation with Admiral Raeder on 6 January 1943. He was sacked and replaced by Dönitz at the end of the month. The RAF continued to pound German cities, and – with increasing effect – German industry as well. In his New Year's proclamation, Hitler acknowledged that the 'homeland' was facing 'heavy bombing attacks'.[224] The first attack on Berlin for more than a year took place on 16 January.[225] This was merely a portent of what was to come. At Casablanca, Churchill and Roosevelt issued a directive for a combined bomber offensive aimed at 'the progressive destruction of the German military, industrial and economic system, and the undermining of the morale of the German people to a point where their armed resistance is fatally weakened'.[226] On 23 January, the 8th Army took Tripoli and advanced on Tunisia, threatening the remaining Axis position in North Africa, and perhaps the fascist regime in Italy with total collapse. Hitler also feared British raids and even full-scale invasions on the Channel Islands, in the Balkans and in Scandinavia, his anxiety stoked by a barrage of false information generated by British Intelligence.

This was the context within which Hitler regarded the crisis in Russia. What was being defended there, he told the soldiers of the eastern front, was the living space and the living standard required to defend Germany against Bolshevism and the 'Jewish-capitalist hyenas', by securing the space necessary for 'a secure food supply' and 'those raw materials without which human cultures are no longer imaginable today'.[227] His main concern here was not Stalingrad, whose real predicament had still not been revealed to the German people, but the situation on the Don, where the Red Army had broken through in January 1943.[228] The whole Donetsk industrial district was in danger, and with it Hitler's entire industrial strategy for waging the war as a whole. When the generals recommended a retreat to save men, he refused. 'Without materiel,' Hitler said, 'I cannot do it.' Men without equipment, he added, were no use. The Donetsk region was already a cornerstone of Speer's plans to raise production. If it were lost, Hitler warned, 'the entire armaments programme will be redundant', including 'the entire tank programme' as well as the 'artillery programme' and the 'great ammunition programme'.[229]

The garrison at Stalingrad, left to its fate as resources were diverted to North Africa and the Don, was slowly ground down. On 21 January, Hitler rejected a direct appeal from Manstein to allow the 6th Army to surrender in order to prevent further bloodshed. Once the Red Army had overrun the last airfield and split the pocket in two, the end was only a matter of time. On 30 January 1943, the anniversary of the seizure of power, Hitler sent his last radio message to stiffen the garrison. He appointed Paulus field marshal, observing that no commander of that rank had ever been taken prisoner in German history. The inference was clear: Paulus should commit suicide rather than go into captivity. On 31 January 1943, the southern pocket surrendered. Two days later, the northern garrison also threw in the towel. Paulus was captured along with his entire staff. 110,000 men became prisoners of war; 60,000 had been killed or had starved to death during the siege. Only 5,000 were ever to return from the Soviet camps. It was the greatest defeat of the Wehrmacht so far.

Hitler was devastated by the fall of Stalingrad, not just by the loss of the men and materiel, but by the way in which Paulus had disobeyed orders. He feared that Stalin would make political capital out of his high-ranking captives. 'You have to imagine it,' he said: '[Paulus] comes to Moscow and [sees] the rat's cage [in the notorious Lubyanka prison].' 'He will sign everything,' Hitler predicted.[230] In fact, it was to take a year and a half, but in the end Hitler was absolutely right: the field marshal did speak against the Nazi regime on a Moscow radio station. Hitler also worried that Paulus's surrender complicated the narrative within which Hitler wanted to embed the disaster at Stalingrad. His plan had been to transfigure the suffering of the garrison into a European epic, which would stand alongside the winter battles of 1941–2 in the regime's story-telling. As the news of the surrender came in, Hitler clutched at straws. Perhaps, he suggested, one could argue that even the staffs fought to the last man, and that they 'only succumbed to overwhelming force when injured and overpowered'.[231] His final communiqué on Stalingrad, issued on 3 February 1943 after the pocket had fallen, stated that the 6th Army had fought 'until the last breath'. 'They died,' Hitler claimed, 'so that Germany should live.'[232]

Stalingrad severely damaged the regime and Hitler's own standing. It came at a time when he was under pressure at home for other reasons. In mid February 1943, the racial policy of the regime ran into unexpectedly fierce opposition. So far, Jews in mixed marriages had been exempt from deportation. When the Gestapo locked up about 2,000 of them in the Berlin Jewish Community Office in the Rosenstrasse, prior to sending them east, their wives staged a noisy protest. Hitler supported Goebbels's decision to back down, but insisted that the Jews had to be removed from the capital one way or the other.[233] During the first half of 1943, Hitler was also anxious about the effect of 'shortages' and rationing on civilian morale.[234] The Third Reich was in the grip of a full-scale political and military crisis.

Hitler scrambled to stabilize the front and shield the economically vital Donetsk basin. Pressure from the generals to withdraw further west mounted.[235] Five days after the fall of Stalingrad, Manstein, the commander of the reformed Army Group South, cornered Hitler, demanding not only a more flexible defence but also a chief of staff for all fronts to ensure a more 'joined-up' strategy.[236] On another visit by Hitler to Army Group at Zaporosje, Manstein was brutally frank. 'It can't go on like this, my Führer,' he exclaimed. Towards the end of the month, Kluge came to Führer Headquarters and berated him about the state of affairs.[237] All this took its toll on Hitler. 'He had suddenly become very old,' his valet Heinz

Linge recalled, 'his left arm and his left leg have been shaking since the loss of Stalingrad.' Guderian, who saw him shortly after the disaster on the Volga, had the same impression. Eva Braun, who hadn't seen Hitler for some time, was shocked by his appearance when they met again in February 1943. Goebbels, whose contact was more regular, was similarly aghast and Hitler himself remarked on the deterioration. The contemporary newsreel footage certainly shows a physical decline in the Führer.[238]

In early March 1943, the British launched the 'Battle of the Ruhr', a four-month sustained aerial assault on the centres of German war production in the west.[239] Night after night, the RAF struck at the major industrial towns: no fewer than six raids on Essen, four on Duisburg and Cologne, two on Bochum, Düsseldorf, Gelsenkirchen and Dortmund, and one on Krefeld, Mülheim, Barmen-Wuppertal, Elberfeld-Wuppertal. Midway through the campaign the RAF destroyed the Möhne and Eder dams, causing severe flooding, huge destruction and thousands of civilian deaths. Not only were many factories repeatedly hit, but there was massive disruption to the transportation network, the supply of component parts and the sleep patterns of the labour force. Hitler was forced to order the evacuation of as many industries, workers and their families as possible, fully aware of the resulting short-term loss of output.[240] The campaign cost him about six weeks of production in all, a huge figure;[241] aircraft output lagged for nine months. Civilian morale, already febrile after the raids in 1942 and the disaster at Stalingrad, plummeted. When Goebbels raised the bombing war with Hitler three days after the start of the offensive, he was cut short. 'The Führer hardly lets me finish,' he wrote, 'and declares immediately that [the bombing] was a worry which preoccupied him deep into the night.'[242]

Despite all these woes, Hitler staged a remarkable military comeback. In late February, the Afrika Korps badly mauled the Americans at the Kasserine Pass in Tunisia. On the eastern front, Manstein counter-attacked vigorously and recaptured Kharkov.[243] The vital Donetsk basin was retained for now. Meanwhile, the German armies in the Caucasus had been withdrawn without further disaster, and a bridgehead at Kerch and the Kuban retained. This not only shielded the Crimea from the Red Army, but gave Hitler a staging post for a fresh offensive in the summer. Where there were no critical strategic or economic interests at stake, Hitler traded space for time in the east. 'Space,' he explained in early March, 'is one of the most important military factors,' because 'one can only operate if one has space.' Had the crisis taken place on the old border of the Reich, Hitler argued, the war would have been lost. 'Here in the east,' he reiterated, 'one can absorb this.' In this spirit, Hitler ordered the evacuation of the

Rzhev salient and other exposed areas in March 1943 in order to free up forces for deployment elsewhere.[244]

Buoyed by the victory at Kasserine, Hitler mused once more about the nature of his racial struggle with the 'Anglo-Saxons'. Somewhat contrary to his usual rhetoric, he attributed the poor American performance on the battlefield to the decline of their agriculture as observed in photographs. This he contrasted with the robustness of the British. 'There is no doubt,' Hitler opined, 'that the Briton is the best of the Anglo-Saxons'. He then proceeded to contrast once again the small size of Germany, which could be traversed by an aircraft in an hour and a quarter, with 'entire continents' such as 'America, East Asia, Russia [and] Australia'. From there it was just a small step to speculating on what might have happened had Germans colonized Northern Australia, as the Duke of Windsor had allegedly suggested. Probably, he concluded, the British would simply have rounded them up at the outbreak of war.[245] These reflections were embedded in a broader rumination about the importance of the 'size of the state's space', which had enabled China to carry on fighting despite the loss of so much of its territory to the Japanese. The implication was plain: if Germany was to prevail in the clash of the continents, she would have to retain a comparable space to her rivals in Russia, contiguous to the Reich. The logic of *Mein Kampf*, the Second Book and Barbarossa still applied.

This is the reason why Hitler refused to countenance a separate peace in early 1943, except possibly with Britain, despite the critical military position. A compromise with Roosevelt was never considered, because the Führer regarded him as the guiding spirit of the enemy coalition, but nor did he try to come to terms with the Soviet Union. The main issue here was not Hitler's antipathy to Bolshevism. He had begun to develop a grudging respect for Stalin.[246] Immediately after the defeat at Stalingrad, Hitler told Ribbentrop of his great admiration for the Soviet dictator and the way in which he had revived the Red Army and inspired his people. But when the foreign minister suggested putting out peace feelers to Moscow, the Führer demurred. Six weeks or so later, Hitler also rejected Mussolini and Bormann's request for negotiations with Stalin.[247] In part, this was because he feared that the overture would be interpreted as a sign of weakness; any approach would have to be preceded by a decisive military victory.[248] The main problem was that in order to balance the Anglo-Americans – once a long-term programme and now an urgent necessity – Hitler still needed the resources of the Ukraine and the Caucasus. Stalin was unlikely to give him the latter or to allow him to retain the former. The war with Russia, he told Mussolini, was his 'life's work'. It was fear of the west which drove his intransigence in the east.

It was this determination to hold on to his territorial spoils which caused Hitler to eschew any serious attempts to seek new allies in Russia. He issued oral guidelines which seemed to discourage Wehrmacht plans to establish a Russian committee and even a 'Russian Liberation Army'.[249] Operational considerations played an important role here. Hitler doubted the reliability and effectiveness of Russian auxiliaries. The main reason for Hitler's reserve, however, was that he did not want to tie his hands politically. He showed no interest in the 'Europe Committee' set up by Ribbentrop in early April 1943 to think about the 'overall structure of the future Europe'.[250] By contrast, Hitler, who had earlier supported some sort of post-war system of friendly and allied states, now expressed his contempt for the 'small-state clutter which still exists in Europe today', which should be 'liquidated as soon as possible'.[251]

In the spring of 1943, Hitler still had a coherent strategy to win the war, or at least to force a satisfactory draw. He would hold North Africa, to deny the Anglo-Americans a launchpad against southern Europe. He would secure the Balkans, Scandinavia and the west coast of France against an Allied landing. He would retaliate against the bombing of German cities by attacking those of Britain with weapons nearing readiness, and perhaps even those of the United States. He would continue his war against the Jews. He would shore up his many European and global alliances. He would cut Britain off from its overseas lifelines through an intensified submarine campaign. Finally, he would launch a fresh offensive in Russia in order to secure some of the remaining objectives of Barbarossa, to safeguard those already gained, possibly to knock Stalin out of the war, and at the very least to demonstrate that he still held the military initiative.

Throughout the first few months of the year, Hitler prepared his next move in the east.[252] In March 1943, he announced plans for an offensive south-east of Kharkov, designed to eliminate a relatively small Soviet bulge there. It was the military leaders, especially Manstein and Zeitzler, who eventually persuaded him to launch a much bigger operation at Kursk.[253] Despite this, even complete success merely promised to deliver Stalin a very bloody nose; the purpose of the attack was primarily political rather than military. It was intended, as Hitler said, to act as 'a clarion call to the world',[254] to show that the Third Reich was still a force to be reckoned with.

It was in this context that Hitler stepped up the production battle. He gave more powers to Fritz Sauckel in order to increase the available labour force.[255] In late January 1943, the 'Adolf Hitler Panzer Programme' was announced with great fanfare. It determined that, in the first three months of the year, priority should be given to tank production for the eastern front. Hitler told Speer that there should be 'the highest possible output of tanks' even if 'other important war production was temporarily affected thereby'.[256] This message was reinforced a few months later, when Hitler demanded detailed figures on tank production and let it be known that 'because the battles of this summer entirely depend on numerical superiority in tanks', he expected that 'everything would be done to maintain these figures and if possible to increase them'.[257] Despite this, tanks amounted to no more than 7 per cent of production in this period; the proportion of industrial capacity devoted to aircraft construction was more than five times larger.[258]

The military and economic mobilization was to be accompanied by a 'total' mobilization of the home front. In early January 1943, even before Stalingrad fell, Hitler issued a decree demanding the release of more men to serve at the front.[259] Towards the middle of the month he spoke (apparently for the first time) of a 'total war', and once again stressed the need to free up more manpower.[260] Further decrees demanding the weeding-out of shirkers followed.[261] It was also in January 1943 that Hitler introduced compulsory 'war-related' labour service for women below the age of forty-five. This measure was intended to bring another 5.5 million women into the workforce. In practice, there were so many exemptions – for example, for mothers with a child under five or two children under eight years of age – and so little enforcement that nobody who did not actually want to work was forced to do so against her will.[262]

Hitler wanted the mobilization to be not just material, but also emotional and psychological. The military defeat at Stalingrad was to be transformed into a propaganda myth of endurance and renewal.[263] Taking his cue from the Führer's phrase, Goebbels publicly announced 'total war' in a thunderous speech at the Berlin Sportpalast in February 1943, shortly after the fall of Stalingrad. In the summer, Hitler ordered work started on a major new war film – *Kolberg* – about the heroic defence of a fortress during the Napoleonic Wars which was designed not merely to stiffen the spirit of resistance in Germany but to cultivate appreciation for Hitler's idol Bonaparte – who was to be portrayed as an 'admirable figure'. Goebbels and the Führer gave instructions that the director – Veit Harlan – should be given access to whatever Wehrmacht extras he needed to create a 'large canvas'. No expense was to be spared in order to make a film which would put Hollywood in the shade.[264] Speer's armament efforts also came into their own, for whatever the actual increase in production, there is no doubt that he could tell a powerful story about the economy,[265] which reassured not merely Hitler but the German people. For example, when discussing the construction of the Atlantic Wall, Hitler demanded 'an appropriate propaganda' under the slogan 'further strengthening of the Atlantic Wall since Dieppe'.[266] Here production and propaganda were two sides of the same coin.

The Führer was acutely conscious of fractures within his vaunted *Volksgemeinschaft*, but his room for manoeuvre was limited. On the one hand, he was reluctant to force middle-class women into menial work, especially if they were of childbearing age. This was not just an ideological issue. Hitler was aware that discontented female munitions workers had been a major source of unrest during the First World War. He was also anxious to preserve the illusion of normality as much as possible in order to keep civilian spirits up. On the other hand, the spectacle of bourgeois women being spared the rigours routinely expected of their proletarian counterparts sat ill with the regime's ideology. Especially problematic were the privileges claimed by the wives and families of senior party members, which were bad for morale. Hitler repeatedly demanded that these were not to be abused, and that party members and their relations must behave in a way that was 'exemplary' for the rest of the population.[267] As a token of his determination to break with convention, Hitler awarded the first war medals to women. The British air-attacks, which ground men and women into the dust equally, proved a great leveller.[268]

Hitler's answer to the problem of shortages was more immediate. These were to be remedied by pillaging the occupied territories. 'The Führer urgently points out,' Speer recorded, 'that shortages in the Reich should be dealt with in the first instance at the expense of the occupied territories.'[269] For example, if there was a dearth of bicycles for armaments workers then those in Holland, Belgium, Denmark and so on should be confiscated. The same applied to trams. In due course, two decrees to that effect followed.[270] This was the implicit bargain Hitler now struck with the German people: their European empire would not bring them the plenty that had been promised, but at least it helped to alleviate the want.[271]

Hitler was clear about the basic problem, which was not only a matter of production but also of transportation and mobility. In mid January 1943, he stressed the need to release more vehicles for the army in the east.[272] In early February 1943, he lamented the loss of locomotives and the large casualties among train crew, which he hoped to reduce by the deployment of anti-aircraft weapons.[273] A month later, the dire shortage of transport led him to appoint a 'plenipotentiary for the registration of motor vehicles'.[274] 'The war,' he remarked, 'was in its essence a question of transport.' The Germans' failure to 'master' the 'problem of mobility', Hitler went on, had cost them

Stalingrad, and was at the root of the crisis in North Africa. The main advantage enjoyed by Germany, he claimed, was that of 'interior lines', which reduced the amount of transport needed, but he warned that whoever solved the problem of mobility first would win the war.[275]

In May 1943, two central planks of Hitler's strategy collapsed. The Axis forces in Tunisia capitulated. In military terms, it was a much greater disaster than Stalingrad, with well in excess of 130,000 Wehrmacht personnel taken prisoner, many more than had entered captivity with Paulus.[276] Characteristically, Hitler intervened in person to demand (unsuccessfully) that the last planes out evacuated not the wounded but vital heavy equipment.[277] This move reflected not the Führer's heartlessness per se, but his prioritizing of materiel over men. Strategically, the end in Africa was even more catastrophic than the disaster on the Don. 'Tunisgrad'[278] – as it became known – blew the Axis position in the Mediterranean wide open, undermined Mussolini's standing in Italy and provided the Allied air forces with bases to attack fortress Europe from the south.

The Führer's problem was that he could not be sure where the Anglo-Americans would strike next. British Intelligence mounted an ingenious deception campaign, Operation Mincemeat, to persuade him that the blow would fall in Sardinia and Greece, rather than their next target, Sicily.[279] The anxiety about the Balkans remained with Hitler, tying down considerable resources, until he evacuated the region just over a year later.[280] Part of the motivation here was economic, to protect the mineral resources of the Balkans. Hitler also felt politically vulnerable. On 20 May 1943, he expressed his fears about the British family connections and sympathies of the Italian High Command. Hitler said that he expected everything he sent to the *Duce* would be passed on to London. Hitler's expectation was that the Italians would soon abandon the Axis.[281]

It was in this context that Hitler issued a decree in May 1943 forbidding leading state, party and military men from maintaining 'international' contacts. 'The experiences of the war,' he stated with obvious reference to the situation in Italy, 'have shown me beyond doubt that family relationships between German men and foreign circles can very easily have damaging effects on the common good.' 'This applies particularly,' Hitler continued, 'for the international family connections of governing and formerly governing princely houses.' For this reason, he forbade senior figures from being married to women from countries 'which are at war or in a state of political hostility with us'. The same applied if they had familial, social or business relationships to enemy countries and were thus to be regarded as 'internationally bound'.[282] The Third Reich was turning still further in on itself. In Hitler's mind, the 'go-betweens', once a valuable part of his engagement with the west, were no longer a sally-port, but a weak spot in his own defences.

Hitler also suffered a catastrophic setback at sea. The intensified submarine campaign against the British supply lines across the Atlantic culminated in March, with nearly 630,000 tons of shipping sunk, at the cost of fifteen U-boats lost. If that rate had been maintained, Britain would probably have been starved out, and the Allied war machine on the near side of the Atlantic would have ground to a halt. Allied counter-measures, especially the increased use of radar, soon turned the tide. After an inconclusive April, sinkings dropped to 264,000 tons in May 1943; forty-one submarines were lost. Devastated by this battering, Dönitz temporarily withdrew his U-boats from the Atlantic. Hitler accepted the defeat with resignation and without recrimination. He had long foreseen the development of Allied countermeasures, and had been surprised at the run of good luck enjoyed by the U-boats.[283] Right at the end of the month, Hitler ordered a 'rapid increase in the production of U-boats'. He demanded the production of 'at least' forty submarines per month. Speer was put in charge of this effort.[284] U-boats were redeployed to the Mediterranean and the Arctic. It was clear, though, that the Kriegsmarine would not be bringing Britain to its knees anytime soon.

Everything now depended on the planned summer offensive in the east. Throughout the late spring and early summer of 1943, a huge strike force was assembled. In late June 1943, Hitler received word of a possible Russian willingness to make a separate peace.[285] He did not immediately reject the overture, but nor did he seize on it. That same month, Hitler rejected once again the idea of deploying anti-Soviet prisoners of war under General Vlasov.[286] He also refused to countenance Hans Frank's suggestion that the Third Reich capitalize on the revulsion against Stalin associated with the discovery of the murdered Polish officers at Katyn (April 1943) to pursue a more conciliatory course in Poland, and to recruit Poles into the Wehrmacht.[287] The reason for Hitler's hard line was not primarily racial, but political. He feared that it would complicate any compromise peace with Stalin, supposedly repeating the mistakes of Bethmann-Hollweg's pro-Polish policy, which had stood in the way of an arrangement with Tsarist Russia.[288] Hitler also doubted the military value of such formations, Polish or Russian, and he feared that they would just become the vehicle for Slavic political ambitions. Besides, it would risk repeating the error the German High Command had made of sending Lenin to revolutionize Russia in 1917.[289] This was an extraordinary remark for Hitler to make, for it showed that he was perfectly aware that the Bolshevik revolution was not the result of a Jewish-plutocratic plot, but the product of a bold gambit by the German High Command.

On 5 July 1943, Hitler finally launched his attack at Kursk, Operation Zitadelle.[290] The contrast with the offensives of the previous four years was striking. Hitler knew that he was no longer capable of a war of large-scale manoeuvre. For all the firepower and armour he concentrated at Kursk, the offensive was a limited and primarily attritional operation designed to eliminate a large Soviet salient. In those terms, it seemed set to succeed. The Wehrmacht lacked the element of surprise, but it managed to batter its way through the first lines of the Red Army defences. Soviet manpower and equipment losses were substantial.[291] Those of the Germans were far lower. The legendary tank battle at Prokhorovka on 12 July was particularly costly for the Red Army.[292] There was no question of any strategic breakthrough, but a major tactical victory over the Soviet Union, which could be exploited politically and propagandistically, appeared possible.

In fact, Hitler by then had already decided to call off the operation. On 10 July, the Allies landed in Sicily. The Italian defence collapsed within days. On 12 July, the Red Army launched a major offensive against Army Group Centre near Orel, north of Kursk. It is not clear which of these two challenges caused Hitler to halt the attack at Kursk;[293] he did not immediately divert forces from the east, and given that Kursk was primarily a political operation designed, among other things, to reassure allies, it would have been counter-productive to do so. There is no doubt, however, that from now on the Anglo-American threat to his southern flank absorbed the greater part of his attention. The Kriegsmarine was instructed to move the bones of the Hohenstaufen emperor Frederick II, one of Hitler's idols, from Sicily to the mainland.[294] The battle for the island dragged on until the middle of the following month, but by then Hitler was already in the middle of the crisis he had long feared. Perhaps bowed down by the stalemate at Kursk, the Allied invasion of Sicily, and the imminent defection of Italy, Hitler suffered a major physical collapse on 18 July. He required substantial medication from Dr Morell before he was able to see the *Duce* at their meeting the following day.[295]

On 25 July 1943, Mussolini was deposed in a coup. The new Badoglio government pledged continued allegiance to the Axis, but Hitler was not deceived. He was well aware that the Marshal was his 'bitterest enemy'. The defection of Italy was now imminent. Hitler's reaction was swift. Sicily would have to be evacuated – fast. Unusually, Hitler gave priority to saving men rather than equipment. 'Materiel here, materiel there,' he remarked, 'that doesn't matter, the people are more important.' The reason for this soon became clear. The Führer assumed that the Hermann Göring Division would be able to overawe the Italians without the use of heavy equipment. 'We will be able to sort out the Italians with small arms alone,' he remarked.[296] A day later, Hitler ordered the transfer of substantial forces from the east to Italy, and the consequent surrender of the Orel salient to the Red Army. He laid down that these were to be 'politically sound units, which are above all politically close to fascism', and nominated the 3rd SS Panzer Division ('Death's Head'); it was partly recruited from concentration camp guards.[297] Their mission was thus as much political as it was military. These reinforcements were unable to stop the Allies landing at Salerno south of Naples. Determined German counterattacks were seen off. The Anglo-Americans now had a foothold on the European mainland.

To make matters worse, the collapse of the Mussolini regime was accompanied by the worst Allied bombing raids yet. For three days and three nights between 25 and 27 July 1943, the Americans pounded the port of Hamburg by day, and the RAF bombarded the residential areas by night. The resulting firestorm cost the lives of about 30,000 civilians. Industrial and harbour facilities were wrecked. The emergency services were overwhelmed. Hitler was devastated. Dönitz, who witnessed his reaction, recalled that he was 'then just a human being full of, and bowed down by, pain'.[298] Studying the photographs of incinerated women and children, he attributed a 'brutal annihilatory will' to the Anglo-Americans, and vowed that he would show no 'mercy' in future.[299] His motivation here was also political. The Allied bombing campaign was putting the German home front under unbearable pressure. It would have to be stopped, Hitler warned, 'otherwise people will eventually go mad'. The Führer was convinced that retaliation alone would force the Allies to back off. 'The Briton will only stop,' Hitler insisted, 'when his cities are destroyed, otherwise not.' 'I can only win this war,' he concluded, 'by destroying more of the enemy than he can destroy on our side,' or 'at least' by 'teaching him the horrors of war'.[300] In Hitler's mind, the air war had thus become an attritional war of annihilation with the Anglo-Americans.

The Italian collapse and the cataclysmic turn in the bombing war triggered a severe crisis of the regime in the autumn of 1943. At a popular level, the air-raids were interpreted by many as the retaliation of Jewish plutocrats against Nazi policies. This hardened opinion against the Allies and 'the Jews' among segments of the population, but it also damaged the standing of the regime, particularly as the general military situation declined. NSDAP officials were abused and jostled in the street after raids.[301] In Nuremberg, the local leadership reported in September 1943 that party members were concealing their badges when out on the street, that the greeting 'Heil Hitler' was becoming less common, and that the leadership was not enforcing conformity for fear of a backlash.[302] Despite the severity of the attacks, opposition to mass evacuations did not abate. On the contrary, city dwellers were increasingly defying the party. When the *Gauleiter* of Westphalia South, Albert Hoffmann, tried to withdraw ration cards from people who had returned to the area without permission, there was a mass demonstration by hundreds of women on the Adolf Hitler Platz in the city of Witten. The police refused to intervene.[303]

These events placed Hitler in a quandary. If he did not respond, there was a risk that the authority of the Nazi regime as a whole would be undermined. If he clamped down too vigorously, there was the danger that unrest would grow, and that it would be exploited by the BBC. As we have seen, the deteriorating situation abroad and at home also took its toll on Hitler's health. This may be the reason why Hitler was increasingly unwilling to show himself in public. Not only did he refuse to visit the bombed-out cities, but he also made fewer and fewer public speeches. There were only three in the whole of 1943, and just two the following year.[304] The charisma of the Führer was waning fast.

The multiple challenges also provoked a high-political crisis in the Third Reich. Rosenberg lamented that there was actually 'no [proper] government' in the Third Reich. Its relentless focus on the overworked Führer meant that important matters were not decided or even discussed. The lack of direction was leading to the emergence of 'warlord-style groups' in the Nazi elite. This, Rosenberg acknowledged, was a structural problem to do with access to Hitler, which was often impossible to secure. Meanwhile, the usual polycratic squabbles continued. The Führer-state, which was meant to represent the essence of decision, in fact resulted in perpetual tergiversation. Given Hitler's longstanding critique of the failures of parliamentary democracy to act, this was very ironic, as leading Nazis were well aware. 'Even in authoritarian states,' Rosenberg mused ruefully, 'it is not easy to reach decisions.'[305]

If this was problematic in civil affairs, it was potentially fatal in military matters. Critics felt that Hitler was neglecting the east, that he was the only man with an overview of the war as a whole, and that he was making the wrong resource allocation between the fronts. For this reason, the commanders of Army Groups South and Centre in Russia, Manstein and Kluge, tried in early September 1943 to persuade Hitler to give up the OKW theatres of conflict and turn the running of the entire war over to Zeitzler. If not, he should at least appoint an overall commander on the eastern front.[306] Either way, the request amounted to the removal of Hitler from operational command.

Hitler reacted vigorously to all of these challenges. Within twenty-four hours of hearing of the arrest of Mussolini, he vowed to 'free [him] immediately through an airborne operation' once he had identified where he was being held.[307] Six weeks later, in a daring operation, a commando force rescued Mussolini from a hotel in the central Italian Apennine mountain range and brought him to see Hitler. A fortnight later, the Führer installed the *Duce* at the head of the Republic of Salò, an Italian puppet state, which nominally controlled the entire top half of the country. The Allied forces which landed at Salerno were quickly hemmed in, and the relatively narrow front between the Adriatic and the Mediterranean was fortified. Hitler would make the Allies fight their way every step up the Italian boot. He was absolutely in his element here: he would turn, not just the peninsula, but the entire continent into a 'Fortress Europe'.[308]

Despite the deteriorating situation, Hitler would not believe that a separate peace with the west was possible, because he believed that Churchill's enmity towards him was personal.[309] He was still very hesitant about the establishment of a Russian liberation army.[310] Hitler also rejected the idea of a separate peace with Russia, which was being strongly pushed by Tokyo and Ribbentrop so that Germany could turn its full attention against the Anglo-Americans.[311] His objection was not primarily ideological, but territorial. Hitler warned the Japanese ambassador that he could not accept any terms that would require the return of the Ukraine to Stalin. Its retention, he stressed, was essential for the prosecution of the war against the western powers.[312] In short, Hitler's thinking on these subjects had not changed. He was wary of anything that might tend to encourage Slav nationalism, or to weaken his chances of holding on to a slice of Russian *Lebensraum* large enough to secure the future of the Reich, and to make it a plausible rival to Anglo-America. The war in east was still mainly about the west.

Nor did the decline in his strategic position make the Führer any more inclined to accept the 'European' vision of the Foreign Office. In early September 1943, it proposed the establishment of a European 'confederation' to keep out the 'Anglo-Saxons'.[313] Once again, Hitler showed no interest in any such arrangement, not even with the more 'Nordic' peoples of Europe. Hitler's scepticism about the value of European allies, especially among the supposedly cognate Scandinavian peoples, was demonstrated by his meeting with the famous Norwegian writer Knut Hamsun in late June 1943, which soon degenerated into a shouting match.[314] He told the

Dutch fascist leader Anton Mussert towards the end of the year that he had no intention of 'de-Netherlanding' the Dutch, that he wanted to preserve the Netherlands as they were, with all their 'peculiarities and customs'. Hitler also made clear that he had no 'intention' of pursuing a one-size-fits-all approach to the 'small states'. Instead, Hitler planned to conclude treaties with each of these entities 'individually'.[315] In fact, Hitler rejected the idea of a European 'standard last' or a 'unitary constitution'. 'We must not take from the peoples all the freedom we can,' he argued, but rather leave them 'as much freedom as possible'. One should only try to 'solve in conjunction with the other Germanic peoples' those matters which 'must be solved together'.[316] Hitler, in other words, favoured a form of European subsidiarity.

Hitler's European policy was driven not only by political and military considerations but also by the demands of the German war economy. In mid September 1943, he agreed to Speer's suggestion that there should be overall 'European production planning', and perhaps also the establishment of a European 'production bureau'.[317] This was to include France as an 'equal' member, whatever that meant. At around the same time, Speer was put in charge of Italian industry.[318] Hitler stated that it was 'self-evident' that, as 'the leading power in Europe', Germany would 'retain the absolute leadership of production planning'.[319] The predominance of the Reich in this new European system was axiomatic. For this reason, the Reichsmark, which was intended to become the leading fully convertible currency on the continent after the war, was occasionally referred to as the 'Euro-Mark' in the Third Reich's internal planning documents.[320]

These moves were flanked by measures to maintain morale and increase ideological and racial cohesion. In mid September 1943, Stalin had set up the National Committee for a Free Germany, a group of captured officers opposed to Hitler.[321] The Führer was sensitive to the threat they posed to his legitimacy, and began to give speeches to the military leadership, and to force them to reaffirm their loyalty to him.[322] He also speeded up his efforts to improve the political consciousness of the officer corps more generally. In October 1943, Hitler summoned the commanders of the home military districts and the Reserve Army to the Führer Headquarters. Here he harangued them on the need to transcend pure professionalism in favour of political commitment. He specifically did not want a Soviet-style commissar, however, but someone who could motivate those who 'spiritually cannot keep up'. The slogan should be 'Here officer, there *politruk* [Soviet political officer]'.[323] In late December 1943, Hitler decreed that 'in the fifth year of the war, the political-ideological leadership and education of the armed forces should be intensified'. This was to be done through the establishment of a 'National Socialist Leadership Staff' in the OKW itself, whose head was to coordinate with the NSDAP as 'bearer of the political will'.[324]

Hitler was also concerned to stiffen the political spine of German society more generally. In August 1943, he appointed Himmler minister of the interior. His job was to prevent a repetition of the Italian fiasco in Germany.[325] The racial war was a key theatre, both in the 'negative' and in the 'positive' sense. On 6 October 1943, the Reichsführer gave a secret speech to the *Gauleiter* at Posen in which he explained that the Jews had been killed in order to maintain the coherence of the home front. That was 'negative eugenics'. Four days later, Hitler issued a decree on the treatment of children born to German fathers and local mothers in the occupied eastern territories. 'Children who are born illegitimately to native women in the occupied eastern territories, and whose fathers are Germans,' he announced, were to be 'registered'. 'The Reich,' he continued, 'will take over responsibility for the children if they are racially valuable.'[326] That was 'positive eugenics'.

If Hitler took the most radical measures against the Jews, and the 'unfit', and was willing to take on the officer corps ever more directly, he was still very reluctant to confront some of the other structures of German society. For example, while willing to recruit female 'anti-aircraft crew', he insisted that there be no public advertisement of the effort. Instead he wanted news of the possibilities to serve to be spread by word of mouth among the party's women's organizations. This most likely reflected his fear of resistance in the more conservative parts of the country.[327] Hitler was also wary of taking on the Roman Catholic church, partly because of its power domestically and partly because of the possible international repercussions. In early December 1943, he remarked – echoing Frederick the Great – 'that he was of the opinion that everyone should seek salvation in his own way', and that 'he did not want to exercise any compulsion', and that 'in the area under his control' anybody could be a member of the church'. Hitler went on to emphasize that he was open not only to the main Christian denominations, but also to Deists and even non-Christians. 'We even have Muslims here with us,' Hitler added,[328] and it is perfectly true that he brought more Muslims to Germany than ever before.[329]

In the autumn and winter of 1943, Hitler was still pursuing a clear military-political strategy. He had always seen the Anglo-Americans as the main enemy; now the Führer saw them as the most immediate operational threat as well. On 3 November 1943, Hitler issued a far-reaching Directive 51 on the conduct of the war.[330] Though the 'danger in the east' remained unchanged, he warned of 'a greater one in the west – the Anglo-Saxon landing!' In the east, Hitler continued, the 'greater [availability of] space' allowed 'the loss of even larger amounts of territory without striking a deadly blow against the vital nerve centres' of the Reich. 'Not so in the west!' he exclaimed. If the enemy secured a breakthrough on a broad front there it would quickly be fatal. He expected that the Allies would attack within the next few months 'at the latest in the spring, but perhaps also earlier'. If the enemy did manage to land, Hitler went on, they should be counter-attacked immediately before they had a chance to consolidate their position. In many ways this directive simply ratified a shift in the centre of gravity of the German war effort which had been going on for some time.[331]

On the eastern front, Hitler ordered the Wehrmacht to dig in. Even before the failure of the Kursk offensive, he agreed to the construction of large-scale fortifications.[332] In mid August 1943, he accepted the idea of an *Ostwall* using natural obstacles such as the Dnieper.[333] The reason why Hitler, despite his overall strategy of holding in the west, and trading space for time in the east, was reluctant to retreat much further in Russia was economic and diplomatic. He had long since given up hope of another assault on the oil-fields of the Caucasus, but he clung to the Kuban bridgehead, and to what he still controlled of the industrial and mining areas of eastern Ukraine, for as long as possible.[334] When that was lost in September 1943, his attention shifted to the defence of the Crimea, which was vital for the protection of the Romanian oil-fields and for ensuring the continued loyalty of his Black Sea allies. Besides, its loss might bring Turkey into the war against him.[335]

Hitler also sought to take the war to the enemy. In the autumn of 1943, the U-boats returned to the Atlantic. In September 1943, Dönitz presented plans for a new and much more formidable submarine, the type XXI, which could 'live' underwater for longer periods and move at such speed as to enable it to shake off escort vessels. Three months later, the Führer authorized mass production of these boats.[336] In the air, Hitler's hopes here rested on the ME 262, a pioneering jet aircraft, whose mass production he authorized in December 1943.[337] Contrary to the desire of the Luftwaffe commanders defending the Reich, who wanted the new jet to be deployed as a fighter against Allied bombers, Hitler ordered its use as a bomber to retaliate against British cities. 'I want bombers, bombers, bombers,' he told the Luftwaffe leadership, 'your fighters are completely useless.'[338] As a result, the ME 262 arrived too late and in too few numbers to make any difference, and at a time when it could hardly even be fuelled.

The Führer's main hope of deterring Britain, however, rested with the development of rockets capable of striking at London. These were, he remarked, 'just as important as tank production'.[339] In this spirit, Hitler ordered that the 'Tank Decree' be modified in favour of a decree for the production of rockets; the necessary workers were to be taken from other tasks.[340] He justified the commitment of scarce resources by describing the rocket programme in July 1943 as a 'decisive measure to relieve the homeland' which could be 'carried out with relatively modest means'.[341] Hitler laid down that only German labour was to be used, preferably from areas which had been 'totally destroyed' by Allied bombing.[342] Speer was given the go-ahead for mass production of these weapons with the explicit aim of prosecuting the war against Britain.[343] 'This will be the retaliation against Britain,' he claimed on 20 August 1943, which would 'force her to her knees'.[344] In early December 1943, Hitler issued orders to the military commanders in the west for the 'preparation and conduct of the long-range struggle against Britain with all the relevant special weapons'.[345]

At the heart of Hitler's strategy in late 1943, in the air, at sea and on the ground, was not war but politics. He conceded in mid October 1943 that his ideal solution, by which he presumably meant total victory, might not be attainable, but that he intended to stay on his feet so as to exploit fortuitous developments as they arose. 'So long as one lies in wait like a cat,' he explained, 'and takes advantage of every opportunity to put one over on the other side, then nothing is lost'. The enemy, he promised, would show such 'moments of weakness'; all Germany had to do was to exploit them. The key was to show 'tenacity' in the knowledge that a sudden internal crisis in one of the coalition states ranged against the Reich could bring about the collapse of the entire enemy front. Besides, he noted, there was the American presidential election scheduled for 1944, which might well bring political change in the United States.[346] The defensive measures in the west were thus also intended to impress the Americans, and if necessary to ensure that they suffered a bloody nose when they landed. He reminded the military leadership again in mid December 1943 that Roosevelt was up for re-election and that he might 'lose' if he suffered a military reverse.[347] Repelling the invasion would also enable Hitler to drive a wedge between London and Washington. In short, Hitler decreed, 'when they attack in the west, then this attack will decide the war'.[348]

In the last two months of the year, the onslaught on Hitler's 'Fortress Europe' intensified. In mid November 1943, the RAF and USAAF commenced a six-month air campaign against the Reich capital.[349] Allied bombers also continued to batter other German cities. During the day, the Americans came for the factories and other parts of the German war economy; at night, the British came for the residential areas and for the Germans themselves. 'What the German homeland has to put up with here,' Hitler said, 'is known to all of us, and what I feel personally about the matter, you can imagine.'[350] City after city in which Hitler had spoken, which he had dominated with triumphal processions, collapsed under a hail of incendiaries and high explosive. The centre of Munich was struck by hundreds of RAF bombers on 6 September 1943, and again on 2 October. During the night of 22 and 23 October 1943, Kassel was engulfed by a firestorm. All the Führer could do was spit defiance against the 'aerial terror', which he claimed would only strengthen German resolve. Erhard Milch, the state secretary of the Air Ministry, argued after the autumn raids 'that Germany itself is the real front line'.[351] Likewise, the 'situation reports', Hitler's daily meetings with the High Command, filed the bombing raids under 'west'. The 'Second Front' already existed, not in France to be sure, but in the skies above Germany.

In short, by the end of 1943, even before the first Allied soldier had set foot in France, the western powers were absorbing the greater part not merely of Hitler's attention,[352] but also of his resources. This was the decisive year in the great attritional battle. The war in the air ate up a huge proportion of the German war economy: in 1943, 41 per cent went on aircraft alone. The next-biggest item that year was ammunition, at 29 per cent. Another 8 per cent or so went on naval vessels, especially submarines, most of which were deployed against the west. Only about 6 per cent of the war economy was devoted to tank production, despite the demands of the eastern front. In autumn 1943, more than 2,000 anti-aircraft guns of 88 mm calibre, or above, were deployed in defence of the Reich, along with about 1,600 day and night fighters, far more than were deployed in the east. At the start of the year, just under 40 per cent of the Luftwaffe was based in the east; by its end, that figure had dropped further to about 35 per cent. One way or the other, most of the German war effort was now geared to fighting the Anglo-Americans, and the proportion increased with every passing month.[353]

Worse still, the Reich had conclusively lost the battle of production. This was not for want of trying. German output increased substantially in 1943,[354] but not nearly enough. This was partly because of the bombing. In mid December 1943, Hitler was informed that production of key weapons, such as assault guns, had been substantially reduced by Allied air-raids.[355] He ended the year with fewer machine guns than he had started.[356] Hitler's main problem, though, was that western output grew so much more quickly. The Reich had drawn level with the Soviet Union in 1943, but she was being completely outproduced by the United States and, to a lesser extent, the British Empire. A substantial proportion of that output was going to the Russians, via the Arctic convoys, Iran and

Vladivostok, giving them the edge in battlefield mobility. While most of the Wehrmacht was deployed in the east, and it suffered most of its casualties fighting the Red Army,[357] its weakness there was largely one of equipment rather than manpower.[358] Thanks to the Western Allies, the Soviet Union faced far fewer German tanks in the east (because they were never made) and many fewer fighters (because these were in the west). It was already clear that National Socialist élan and German brain would prove no match for western industrial brawn. Hitler could outproduce Stalin's Five Year Plan, but not Roosevelt's New Deal.

Meanwhile, the Nazi leadership continued its internecine warfare.The winners and losers in these struggles were becoming clear by the end of 1943. Goebbels extended his authority well beyond propaganda into large swathes of the civilian sector. Himmler had consolidated his control over the security apparatus. Speer was the undisputed master of the German war economy. Göring, by contrast, had lost all authority. Rosenberg had been largely sidelined some time earlier, and his eastern European fiefdom was steadily shrinking anyway. In Hitler's immediate vicinity, the main victor was Martin Bormann, whose unstoppable rise was noted. He had almost completely edged out Hans-Heinrich Lammers, the head of the Imperial Chancellery, whose ability to brief Hitler shrank further throughout the year.[359] Bormann effectively controlled not only civilian access to Hitler, but also (it was believed) what came from the Führer. 'Now Bormann was in power,' Rosenberg wrote in the autumn of 1943, 'because nobody who received a communication from him could distinguish whether this constituted a personal order of the Führer's', or merely reflected 'Bormann's own views'.[360] Hitler's authority, in fact, was not challenged, but the net result of all this was to cause the machinery of government to grind, if not to a halt, then ever more slowly.

As the year drew to a close, Hitler remained a man in full command of his faculties and still master if not of his destiny, then of the Third Reich and much of Europe. German forces still stood everywhere on enemy soil: off the North Cape, halfway down the Italian boot, in Greece, at the Pyrenees and deep inside the Soviet Union. Hitler still cut an impressive figure at military briefings, with no signs of any mental breakdown.[361] Physically, though, the deterioration was dramatic. Not many people knew that the Führer had required a hefty dose from Dr Morell to cope with the Italian collapse during the autumn, but most could see that he was a sick man. The symptoms of Parkinson's disease were now manifest.[362] His decline was visible even in the *Wochenschau* newsreels, at least to the Imperial Chancellery doctor Ernst Schenck, who noticed the stoop but attributed it to a spinal problem.[363] Werner Best, who met him in person in December 1943 for the first time in more than a year, was 'shocked'. 'He gave the impression of a tired, broken [and] old man,' he recalls, he walked haltingly and was so stooped that he appeared 'hunched'. 'His face,' Best continued, 'was sunken and lined', and his 'eyes were rigid and appeared reproachful'. Even so, Best notes, Hitler dominated the conversation with a wide-ranging review of various topics.[364]

18
The Fall of 'Fortress Europe'

On New Year's Day 1944, Hitler issued a proclamation to the German people, and an order to the Wehrmacht. Both showed that the Führer's war aims and legitimating ideology remained unchanged after more than four years of war. Germany, he claimed, was a 'socialist people's state' embarked on a 'survival struggle not merely of the German Reich but of the entire European continent' against the 'Bolshevik-plutocratic world conspirators and their Jewish wire-pullers'.[1] If it did not resist, Hitler warned, the Reich and Europe as a whole risked being enslaved and starved by the forces of international plutocracy and imperialism. 'Wherever Britain rules today,' he remarked, alluding to the recent mass famine in Bengal, when the Allies had diverted grain from starving Indians to support the European fronts,[2] or at the very least refused to supply the necessary shipping to feed the victims, 'hunger and misery are a feature of life'.[3] Globally, therefore, Hitler saw himself as resisting Anglo-American imperialism. In Europe, by contrast, he was desperately trying to hold on to his colonial gains, especially in the east. 'After four years of battle,' he pointed out, 'Germany, which began the war with 634,000 square kilometres of German *Lebensraum*,' now occupied '2,650,000 square kilometres of Europe'.[4]

Hitler conceded that 1943 had been an extremely difficult year. The 'disgraceful treason against the *Duce*' had forced Germany to take 'very tough decisions', including large-scale withdrawals of forces not under attack, which had been difficult for individual soldiers to understand. Men had been withdrawn from the east in order to secure 'the rest of the European *Lebensraum*' against the onslaught of the 'Anglo-Saxon forces'. In the Balkans, the 'subterranean agitation' of 'British-paid traitors' was threatening the German position. Hitler also admitted, referring to the Battle of the Atlantic, that 'the scales of technical innovation in the year 1943' had tilted in the direction of the enemy. Most painful of all, though, had been the Allied air attacks on the Reich, which had reduced many

German cities to 'rubble'.[5] The Führer vowed to surmount these challenges. He swore that 'the hour of reprisal' for the bombing would come. He would rebuild German cities. Above all, the Führer vowed to repel the expected Allied invasion. He promised 'the plutocratic western world' a 'worthy reception' wherever they landed.

Over the next five months, Hitler's confidence was tested by the Allied storm on 'Fortress Europe'. In late January 1944, the Americans and British Empire forces landed behind the German lines at Anzio and Nettuno, not far south of Rome, achieving complete surprise. Hitler demanded that the Allied bridgehead be swiftly sealed off, hammered with artillery fire and then overrun. This was partly because he knew that, once established, the enemy would not be easily dislodged, partly in order to discourage further landings, partly because he feared the effects of Allied air superiority, and partly to reduce the political fallout.[6] Despite determined efforts, however, Kesselring was unable to throw the Allies back into the sea, and after months of heavy fighting around Monte Cassino, he was forced to pull back in mid May. Hitler declared Rome an undefended 'open city', and on 5 June 1944 the Italian capital fell to US general Mark Clark. All this before a single Allied soldier had landed in northern France, which was where Hitler was expecting the main Anglo-American effort to take place.

Meanwhile, Stalin had launched three offensives in the east. In the north, he punched through the German lines around Leningrad and lifted the siege of that city, which had lasted nearly two and a half years. The Soviet dictator was now poised to strike at Finland, and break into the Baltic. Stalin also attacked on two fronts in the Ukraine, cutting off the Crimea and pushing westwards towards Romania and central Europe. Soon the Germans were left holding only a small perimeter line around Sebastopol. The Soviet advance was greatly facilitated by the mobility conferred on the Red Army by hundreds of thousands of Lend-Lease trucks, jeeps and other vehicles.[7]

The cumulative effect of the reverses on Hitler's European allies was shattering. They had been wavering since Stalingrad; now they were openly eyeing the exits. After the loss of Odessa in April 1944, the Romanians became increasingly anxious. Hitler confronted Marshal Antonescu with evidence that his foreign minister was in secret contact with the western powers.[8] Hungary, the furthest away from the Red Army, was also the least dependable, and appeared on the verge of collapsing in early 1944. The Führer also knew that the Finns, who were desperate by the start of the summer, were longing to make a separate peace with Stalin. The war at sea was also going badly. In March 1944, Dönitz withdrew his U-boats from the Atlantic and ordered them to switch from 'wolf-pack' tactics to operating individually or perhaps in pairs or groups of three.

In the air the situation, already bad, became steadily worse. On 1 January 1944, the Americans set up the United States Strategic Air Forces in Europe to coordinate the assault on the Reich. That same day saw a heavy RAF raid on the German capital, one of nine in six weeks. On 6 March, the USAAF launched its first daylight raid on Berlin.[9] Shortly afterwards, however, the 'Battle of Berlin' was called off due to heavy losses and the obstinate refusal of the wide-avenued city to burn.[10] The campaign had cost the RAF around 500 bombers, claimed the lives of 10,000 Berliners, left 400,000 of them homeless, and many more without basic services. Other German cities were also hit, some heavily, in particular Augsburg (25/26 February), Essen (26/27 March) and Munich (24/25 April), where a whole suburb was almost entirely obliterated by the RAF. Even when there were no large-scale attacks in progress, Germans were tormented by the incessant buzzing of RAF Mosquitoes, hitting pinpoint targets and those of opportunity. The raids had a substantial impact on domestic morale, which was depressed both by the human and material devastation and by the increasing evidence of Anglo-American daylight air superiority over the Reich. Hitler was well aware of all this, and there is a rare photograph of him inspecting bomb damage in 1944.[11]

The Führer was also in no doubt about the huge damage being inflicted not merely on German industry, but also on the transportation system and energy supply. In late February, the USAAF launched six devastating raids on German aircraft factories, leading Speer to warn Hitler of a crisis in fighter production.[12] In late April 1944, he was briefed on the production losses at Krupp's, following the renewed attacks on Essen; Hitler was also warned about the reduced fighter output after the attacks on the Dornier plant at Friedrichshafen.[13] The Führer was particularly concerned about the damage Allied air attacks inflicted on vehicle production, which was essential to maintain mobility in modern warfare. Hitler fretted about the good Allied intelligence underlying these raids, which he attributed to domestic treason.[14] Perhaps most worrying of all were the USAAF attacks on the Reich's oil production, to which three large-scale raids from bases in Italy were devoted in April–June 1944. In late May 1944, Speer briefed Hitler on the mounting oil supply problems due to systematic American attacks on the Romanian oil refineries; the Führer was also given a list of damaged oil installations in Hungary and the Reich itself, and an assessment of the expected catastrophic reduction in output.[15]

Finally, there was the horrendous attrition of the Luftwaffe, which was flushed out by the raids, and which was losing hundreds of aircraft a month in German airspace alone.[16] This metric considerably understates the extent to which Hitler's war effort was now geared to fighting the bombing war. More than 800,000 men were permanently deployed to defend the Reich, many of them manning the 14,000 heavy and 40,000 light anti-aircraft guns. Another million men were involved in clearing up or restoring essential services. The Russians noted a growing decline in the quantity and ability of German pilots on the eastern front.[17] The production of aircraft, flak artillery and other weaponry for the defence of the Reich absorbed a huge and growing proportion of Nazi industrial capacity. In short, the American entry into the war was already proving decisive, long before a single man set foot in Normandy.

Hitler's racial anxieties interacted with these politico-military threats. If most European Jews were now dead, he was still worried about the danger posed by the remaining pockets, and of course world Jewry in the Soviet Union and, especially, Anglo-America. Throughout the first few months of 1944, Hitler reiterated his view that the Jews had contaminated Britain[18] and the United States, inducing false consciousness there which pitched them against the German Reich. He fretted over the supposed role of Hungarian Jews in turning that country against him. The Führer also continued to take a close interest in the persecution of the remaining elements of German Jewry. In the first months of the year, he issued no fewer than three new decrees on the status of 'half-castes' in order to ensure that 'German blood' was 'kept pure'.[19]

It is therefore ironic that by early 1944 Hitler's policies had created the very racial dystopia he had wanted to avoid. To be sure, Hitler was well on the way to 'ridding' Europe of Jews, but there were more foreigners, especially Slavs, in Germany than ever before, working in the war economy.[20] The risk of domestic racial 'contamination', reflected in the countless ordinances designed to stop it, was acute. Externally, Hitler was also in exactly the situation he had wanted to avoid. Allied to a coalition of Slavs and Latins, and other global 'have-nots', such as imperial Japan, the Germans manned a shrinking perimeter line against the (principally) 'Anglo-Saxon' onslaught, on land, at sea and in the air. Moreover, many of those now arrayed against the Reich were the descendants of the best elements of the German people who had left over the previous two centuries. Hitler presided over the greatest single wave of immigration into Germany at the very moment when he was under attack by her own emigrants.

The commander of the US Strategic Air Forces in Europe, the man who was directing the American air campaign against the Reich, was General Spaatz. He was born Carl Spatz of German ancestry in Pennsylvania; he

added an 'a' to his name in 1937 to suggest Dutch rather than German origin.[21] The names of some of the USAAF pilots shot down during the massive
raid on Berlin on 6 March 1944 told their own story: Naushalter, Kolb,
Griesel, Frantz, Radtke, Handorf, Lautenschlager, Wagner, Schimmel and
Stauss.[22] The first post-raid reconnaissance pictures were taken by Major
Walter Weitner in a Spitfire of the US 7th Photo Group. This struggle should
be understood not as a gentlemanly joust in the clouds like the 'dogfights' of
the First World War, but as a desperate scramble with atrocities on both
sides.[23] Even so, some of those shot down reported being approached by
German civilians for news of their relatives in America.[24] The long entanglement with the United States continued even in adversity.

Worse still, on the other side of the English Channel, a whole army of
Anglo-Saxons, as both Hitler and the Wehrmacht almost invariably called
them, many of them German in origin, waited to mount their invasion. The
Führer was aware that the supreme command of the Allied Expeditionary
Force had been given to Dwight Eisenhower, though it is not known what
he made of the fact that his adversary descended from the Eisenhauers,
pacifist Mennonites who left the Saarland for Pennsylvania in the eighteenth
century.[25] Among the men who would soon take the fight beyond the Rhine
were General Clarence Huebner (V Corps), whose Stuttgart-born grand-
father Gottfried Hübner had left for America in the early nineteenth century;
General William Schmidt (76th Division), whose father was Austrian; General
Walter Lauer (99th Division), both of whose parents were German; Emil
Reinhardt (69th Division), whose grandfather Heinrich Christian Christoph
Reinhardt was born in Brunswick in 1825; Herman Kramer, born to two
German immigrants; General Donald Stroh (106th Division), whose great
great grandfather was born in Rimsdorf/Saarland, before emigrating to
fight in the American revolution; General Paul Baade (35th Division), whose
grandfather Wilhelm Baade hailed from Windheim, Prussia in 1830; General
Bertram Hoffmeister (Canadian 5th Armoured Division), whose paternal
grandfather emigrated from Hamburg as a teenager.

In late January 1944, Himmler sent out a circular to the head of the
Security Service, the head of the Coordination Centre for Ethnic Germans,
and the head of the SS Main Office. He demanded that those American
prisoners who had German parents or grandparents should be separated
from their comrades and brought to a 'special camp'. Himmler's plan was
'to influence' this 'lost Germany' in a clever way in order 'to gradually
win it back again'.[26] He was not, of course, interested in German Jews
like Henry Kissinger of the US army, who were also preparing to return
to the European mainland, but in the Eisenhowers.[27] In both cases, the
stones the Fatherland had rejected would become capstones in the

coalition facing the Reich. In the Eisenhauers, Germany had exported peace, but it re-imported war.

In this context, it is unsurprising that Hitler should have returned to one of his central preoccupations, which was the supposed inherent racial weakness of the German people. In late January 1944, he summoned the senior military leadership to the Wolf's Lair.[28] He told them that in Germany the racial core had been undermined by domestic divisions since the Reformation, unlike in England, which at this time had begun its ascent to 'later world domination'. 'Already in those days,' he claimed, 'the sun did not go down on the German Reich.' Instead of world power, however, Germany lost importance and her people so that her population numbered only 85 million rather than the 300 million she would otherwise have had, a clear reference to the demographic losses through war and emigration. Without the Thirty Years War, Hitler continued, the New World would certainly have been German. Even so, and here Hitler echoed an enduring myth in early twentieth-century Germany, the United States nearly became German. The decision to make English the official language of America, he averred, was only taken 'with a one-vote majority, and this vote was sadly given by a German'. The Führer's anxiety about the lost Germans and their propensity to turn their back on the Fatherland could not have been more clearly expressed.

This is why Hitler was so exercised about the composition of the German 'people' (Volk), which he distinguished from the Nordic race. 'We know today,' Hitler explained in his briefing to the military, 'that the Volk does not really represent a [single] racial unit but a racial conglomerate', and that the 'values' didn't lie in the conglomerate as a whole but in the 'racial kernels'. 'A people,' he elaborated, 'is a community of people of the same language [and] history', which might endow them with 'similar sentiments' but this did not mean that they were of the 'same racial belonging'. 'We are one people,' Hitler continued, 'but we are not one race.' It was, so to speak, a case of one Volk, and one Führer, but many races. 'Our people,' he explained, 'is composed of a whole series of racial kernels,' but 'the decisive racial kernel, which has formed the German people in the purely organizational sense, is the Nordic one'. This 'Nordic-Germanic' core had imposed itself out of a 'subconscious instinct for domination' and absorbed the others.

Hitler was more ambivalent about this racial mixing than one might imagine. On the one hand, he was determined to distil the Nordic racial core. On the other hand, Hitler saw positive sides to the 'marriage of the races' in the German Volk. 'There is a Slavic race,' he said, 'which is musical', and 'a Germanic race, whose nature is wholly unmusical'. 'Both combined,' Hitler claimed, 'suddenly produce great composers,' such as 'Beethoven

Wagner and Bruckner'. The 'key thing' was to 'gradually bring [each] racial kernel to bear on that part of our community where it is most suited to do the necessary work'. In music, that might be a Slavic-Nordic blend, but, for military purposes, the Reich would need the pure Nordic strain. In other words, in Hitler's vision each racial core would have its function within the German *Volk*.

The Führer blamed the stunted development of Germany's Nordic core on capitalism. 'The process of pure capital formation,' he claimed, and the growth of a 'general education' which had nothing to do with the development of 'true racial value' had led to the creation of a wealthy class which took over politics despite lacking the ability to do so. Capitalism and racism, in Hitler's book, were not compatible. Once again, Hitler illustrated this point with reference to the British. 'We see here the difference between Germany and Britain,' he continued, where '[we] still [find] a very distinctive pure master race which still controls politics and thus ensures a completely unified leadership over the decades'. More than four years into the war, far from dismissing the British as racially corrupted by the Jews, Hitler still saw them as a racial model. In fact, he coined the very term 'master race' to describe their ruling class.

The solution to the racial weakness of the German people, Hitler claimed, lay in the 'mobilization of racial value'. In so far as this involved giving the Germans the discipline they naturally lacked, this required 'drill', by which he meant both 'square-bashing' and 'indoctrination'. Hitler laid more stress, though, on 'understanding', the kind of internal confidence and strength which came naturally to the Nordic core (and, one might add, to Anglo-Saxons). 'That is why discipline and breeding can under no circumstances replace inner conviction,' he explained, but at best complement it. There were many ways of achieving this. One was through culture, especially music, the appreciation of which would help to establish racial value. 'When I strike a chord,' Hitler explained, 'then the strings which are tuned to that chord react,' whereas the others did not, or did so only belatedly. This theory explains why Hitler could not accept that Jews understood great German composers such as Wagner. Another method of racial improvement was the creation of ideological coherence, and here the Führer acknowledged the Bolshevik achievement in effecting 'an immense ideological re-education' in Russia after 1917. Germans would need 'uniformity of world view', 'nerves and power' and 'fanaticism' to prevail. Most importantly of all, Hitler wanted to establish what he considered racial unity in Germany by overcoming the capitalist order and working for the 'construction of a new classless society'.

*

On the military and political front, Hitler continued the strategy he had developed the previous year.[29] He increasingly believed that the only way of dealing with the threat from the air was through 'relocation', and given the ever-increasing range of the Anglo-American bomber fleets that meant going underground. Hitler demanded that these measures should not just be temporary but part of a 'large-scale and final relocation of the entire German industrial capacity below the surface'.[30] While the Anglo-Saxons ruled the skies above, in other words, the Germans and their slave-dwarves burrowed further and further underground, causing the mountains to resonate with the Wagnerian tinkling of hammers on metal.

Meanwhile, Hitler prepared to repel the imminent Allied invasion; this was his main priority.[31] He believed that the best chance he had of doing so was to prevent the Anglo-Americans from getting ashore, or by overrunning the bridgehead before the enemy had time to consolidate. This involved building extensive fortifications, about which Hitler enthused at length. 'I am the greatest fortress-builder of all time,' he remarked without obvious irony in January 1944, 'I built the Westwall [and] I have erected the Atlantic Wall.'[32] Most of the Wehrmacht leadership, who favoured manoeuvre over static warfare, frowned on the Führer's continuing obsession with steel and concrete. In the first few months of the year, a bitter argument raged between Rommel and the commander of the tank forces in the west, the redoubtable Geyr von Schweppenburg, about the deployment of the panzer divisions. Geyr, who still hankered for the great panzer manoeuvres of the early years, wanted to maintain a large operational reserve well behind the coast to strike once the enemy's main 'centre of gravity' had become clear. Rommel, who had extensive experience of Anglo-American air power, knew that his tanks would never reach the beaches unless they were close by.[33] Hitler – who was also under no illusions about the mobility of German formations under conditions of Allied air superiority – tended to agree with Rommel. He warned that, once established, the bridgehead would be 'systematically' expanded 'with the massed deployment of the air force and heavy weapons of all types'.[34] Hitler compromised to keep the peace, and also to hedge his bets. Some of the panzers were kept close to the coast, the rest were held back.

The thinking behind Hitler's strategy remained political rather than military. He still wanted to inflict such a bloody defeat on the Allied landing forces in France that Churchill would be confronted with another Gallipoli, and Roosevelt would lose the presidential election in November. 'A failed landing,' Hitler predicted to his generals in late March 1944, 'will prevent the re-election of Roosevelt in America.' He would probably end up in prison. 'In Britain too,' a defeat would increase 'war-weariness'

and undermine Churchill.[35] 'The British know very well,' he told the
Slovak leader Monsignor Tiso in mid May 1944, 'that if they launch an
invasion today and it failed, they would then have had it.'[36] One way or
the other, the Führer stressed, reprising the theme of Directive 51, the
'western front' was the 'decisive front' upon which 'alone' the 'outcome
of the war and thus the fate of the Reich depended'.[37]

In the east, Hitler continued to stand on the defensive, holding positions
for as long as possible, and then trading space for time. His strategic
objectives there were threefold, all driven by the primacy of the western
front. Firstly, Hitler wanted to retain as much Russian *Lebensraum* and
resources as he could in order to support the German war economy against
Anglo-America. Secondly, at Dönitz's request, the Führer was determined
to keep the Russians out of the Baltic, because he needed it to train crews
for the new generation of U-boats out of range of Allied bombers.[38]
Thirdly, Hitler wanted to keep Stalin at bay until he had seen off the
Anglo-Americans, after which he would settle accounts in the east. His
main focus was on the northern and southern sectors.[39] Reinforcements
were sent to Estonia. General Lindemann, the new commander of Army
Group North, was summoned to the Berghof in early April 1944 and
lectured by Hitler on the importance of defending the Baltic.[40] In the
south, Hitler hung on in the Crimea until 5 May 1944, when he finally
ordered the evacuation of Sebastopol.

Of all the allies, it was Hungary which gave the most cause for concern.
It still lay some way away from the Red Army, but Hitler was convinced
that the Kállay administration had been suborned by the Jews and the
British. 'I have known for some time,' Hitler declared on 12 March 1944,
'that the Hungarian government has been preparing [to] betray the allied
European nations.' He explained this conduct with reference to the allegedly all-powerful role of 'Jewry' in Hungary and the activities of 'individual
reactionaries' and 'corrupt elements of the Hungarian aristocracy'. Hitler
therefore decided to occupy Hungary and pave the way for a 'national'
government there.[41] He summoned its ruler, Admiral Horthy, to the palace
of Klessheim near Salzburg on 18 March 1944 for a meeting which proved
particularly stormy. On 19 March 1944, the Wehrmacht and SS occupied
Hungary.

This was the context to the next stage in Hitler's war against the Jews.
Thousands were seized within days of the invasion, and more than 800,000
were at risk.[42] Under pressure from the recently established War Refugee
Board and his Treasury secretary Henry Morgenthau, Roosevelt issued a
stern warning to Hitler about their fate and that of European Jewry as a
whole. 'In one of the blackest crimes of all history,' the president declared in

a radio broadcast on 24 March 1944, 'the wholesale systematic murder of the Jews of Europe goes on unabated every hour.' It was therefore obvious, he continued, 'that we should again proclaim our determination that none who participate in these acts of savagery shall go unpunished'. The *New York Times* reported on this speech under the headline 'Roosevelt warns Germans on Jews; says all guilty must pay for atrocities'.[43] If Hitler received the message, which is likely, he was certainly not swayed by it. In mid May 1944, the mass deportation of Hungarian Jews began, with 430,000 taken to Auschwitz within two months, three-quarters of whom were immediately murdered.[44] Hitler personally ordered 10,000 Wehrmacht soldiers returning from the Crimea to help the SS to guard the transports.[45]

Hitler's priorities in early 1944 were reflected in his deployment of forces. The vast majority of the Kriegsmarine and the Luftwaffe, and thus a huge proportion of the war economy, were geared towards fighting the Anglo-Americans. It is true that most of the army was still stationed in the east in June 1944, with 164 divisions and 1,900 tanks there, and 111 divisions and 1,900 tanks in France, the Balkans and Italy, but these figures are deceptive. The proper metric here is not 'man-months',[46] but what one might call 'machine-months', that is the amount of time and capacity devoted to production. Taken together, a clear preponderance of the German effort was being directed to fight the war with the western powers, even before the first Allied soldier set foot in Normandy. Moreover, the higher quality and ideological commitment of the forces deployed in the west told their own story. Far from using his feared and trusted SS armoured formations and parachute divisions primarily against the Bolsheviks, Hitler sent most of them to France and Italy,[47] to confront the Third Reich's most dangerous military and ideological enemies.

This was reflected in Hitler's public and private rhetoric. To be sure, he was anxious about Stalin and his ability to 'turn' captured German officers through 'Bolshevik secret police methods'.[48] But whereas he considered the Soviet danger to be a matter of compulsion, Hitler regarded the west as a more insidious and much greater threat. Firstly, he remained anxious that the Anglo-Americans might be seen as more plausible saviours from the perils of Bolshevism. He warned Germans – and Europeans – not to believe in the 'British promises of help'. Only Germany, Hitler claimed, could 'save Europe' from the Soviet Union.[49] Secondly, Hitler continued to see the west as a mortal ideological threat. In early 1944, the Heerespersonalamt published, at Hitler's request, a book entitled *What We Are Fighting For*. The four enemies of the Third Reich were listed as world Jewry, Bolshevism, Britain and the United States. Neither the Soviet Union nor Slavdom was specifically included in this classification (though the USSR was implicit

in the term 'Bolshevism'). Instead, Hitler particularly stressed the importance of propaganda in the west.[50]

Amidst all this, Hitler did not neglect the German home front. He
continued to try to reduce the effect of the relentless bombing on the civilian population. From early 1944 almost all major urban centres were
included in the mass evacuations of children to safer areas, but Hitler
remained adamant that this should not involve any compulsion against
hesitant parents. Nor did he try to take advantage of the programme to
lure these young people away from their families and communities for
purposes of political indoctrination.[51] Likewise, Hitler remained extremely
reluctant to use the ration card system to prevent evacuees – most of them
women – from returning to their endangered cities. He preferred them to
be educated about the dangers of bombing instead. 'The [Führer] believes,'
Goebbels recorded in mid January 1944, 'that the goal we aim for can be
reached particularly through propaganda activities that once again bring
before parents' eyes quite graphically the dangers their children face.'[52]

Worried about the huge losses of young men at the front, and its long-
term demographic consequences, Hitler let it be known that the traditional
concept of marriage needed to be rethought. After the war, he pointed out,
there would be between 3 and 4 million women without husbands and no
hope of getting one. They could not, Hitler continued, get their children
'from the Holy Ghost', but only from the remaining German men. For this
reason, it might be necessary to deploy some of the most valuable surviving
men to impregnate these women. Hitler was perfectly aware, of course, that
many German women would resist this innovation for emotional reasons,
and out of stubbornness, while serving soldiers might be disconcerted to
learn that their womenfolk would be redistributed in this way after their
violent deaths. For this reason, Hitler decided to tread carefully.[53]

Hitler was concerned not only with women and reproduction, but also
with women and production. The issues this raised were ventilated at
length during a meeting at the Berghof in late April 1944, when the question of women's pay came up.[54] Robert Ley, the leader of the German
Labour Front, stated that he had been fighting for years for 'equal pay for
equal work for women'. Hitler was not so sure. He explained that pay was
determined by two considerations, not only 'performance' but also
'according to the responsibilities which an individual had in the framework of the national community and the state'. One could not pay simply
according to performance because in that case one would have to pay
twenty-four-year-olds more than fifty-year-olds. 'The [working] woman,'
he said, 'only has to look after herself,' whereas the man had to care for
his family. 'If a woman has children,' Hitler continued, 'she must – that

is always our ideal – stay at home and not work.' This was because 'the work of supporting a family' had 'traditionally' been rated more highly than work done by women, 'even if women performed the same'. Hitler was also worried that more pay for women without increased production of consumer goods for them to buy would lead to inflation.

Hitler was aware, of course, that many women had to work to feed their families. 'Only if a woman has children to be fed,' he said, 'would one be able to pay her children's allowances.' Once again, Hitler was determining pay not by performance, but by social function. 'In principle,' he explained, 'our state must part company with the idea that pay is just compensation for work done.' 'We must do everything,' he exhorted, 'to preserve our people!' 'The one,' Hitler went on, 'only works for himself in the framework of the national community' while another 'maintains the *Volk* with family and sustains the future'. Hitler ended the discussion by saying that certain occupations were 'not jobs for men', such as teaching, waiter service and hairdressing, and these should be reserved for women. 'So,' he said in conclusion, there should be 'equal pay for women only in exceptional circumstances in order to avoid trouble'.

In June–July 1944, Hitler's position was rocked by three existential challenges. On 6 June, the Anglo-Americans landed in Normandy, achieving complete surprise. At first, Hitler was unsure whether the landing was the main Allied effort or a diversion to be followed by a descent on the Pas-de-Calais or some other area.[55] He constantly spurred his commanders on to greater efforts, to prevent Eisenhower from consolidating his position ashore, and to crush the bridgehead the Allies had established between the Orne and Vire rivers, if necessary through the use of heavy artillery.[56] About a week after the landing, Hitler loosed a barrage of V1 missiles against southern England, especially London,[57] but the effect was much more modest than he had hoped. That same day, Hitler barred all leave for the Wehrmacht and Waffen-SS.[58] On 17 June 1944, he made a rare trip to Soissons to meet Rommel and Rundstedt, and to thank those involved in the rocket deployment. That same day, Hitler rejected calls to evacuate the Channel Islands. Not long after, Hitler ordered the 9th and 10th SS panzer divisions transferred from the east to Normandy.

Hitler's strategy was clear. He told the military leaders gathered at the Berghof in late June, that due to the 'crushing aerial superiority of the enemy' and their ship-borne heavy guns, the chances of a successful counter-attack were low. That said, Hitler warned that they should 'under no circumstances allow the development of a war of movement in France', because 'the enemy enjoys a far greater mobility than we do thanks to his mastery of the air and superior number of motor vehicles'. For this reason, Hitler stressed, 'everything depends on pinning down the enemy by establishing a ring of containment around the bridgehead, and then wearing him down through the deployment of all means at close quarters'.[59] A long stalemate ensued in the woods and hedges of the Normandy *bocage*. It was a brutal encounter, in which both sides – particularly the Hitler Youth SS Panzer Division and the dreaded Canadians – committed atrocities, although those on the German side were much worse. Operationally, the Wehrmacht may have performed better than the Allies,[60] but thanks to the massive application of long-range firepower,[61] the Anglo-Americans were winning the battle of attrition. It was only a matter of time before they blasted through the German lines and broke out into the open country beyond.

Then, on 22 June 1944, three years to the day after the start of Barbarossa, Stalin launched 'Operation Bagration', a massive offensive directed against Army Group Centre.[62] Hitler, who had expected the blow to fall in the Ukraine or the Baltic, was taken completely by surprise. Within a week the German front had given way; more than 350,000 men were lost before the offensive had run its course. On 27 June, Lindemann, the commander of Army Group North, warned that his force was in danger of being cut off.[63] Hitler replaced him with General Friesner, the first of a series of rapid command changes in that strategically vital area. For the Army High Command, the Russian offensive quickly became the most pressing problem.[64] The Führer was also profoundly worried by the Soviet advance, but his main concern in the east was not the central sector, where he could continue to trade space for time, but Romania and, especially, the Baltic. At a crisis meeting a fortnight after the start of the offensive, Dönitz – 'at the Führer's request' – pointed out the importance of holding on to the area in order to safeguard the import of Swedish iron ore and preserve the training grounds for submarine crews.[65]

While all this was going on, the Anglo-American air fleets pummelled the Third Reich's transportation system, communications networks and energy supply. These attacks had begun before the invasion, and escalated thereafter into an unprecedented aerial battering. In the four months from June 1944, more bombs were dropped on the Reich than during the entire war until that point.[66] Allied bombing was also growing more accurate, not least because of the collapse of the Luftwaffe, which allowed Anglo-American fighter-bombers to roam at will. Railways were blown up; canals mined. On 2 June, Hitler lamented the shortages of oil.[67] In late June, he was presented by Speer with a list of the systematic Allied attacks on refineries and hydrogenation plants, and warned of the inevitable 'catastrophic consequences'.[68] Shortly after that, his armaments minister handed over a detailed memorandum on the effects of the Anglo-American bombing on the fuel situation. On 2 June 1944, on the eve of the invasion, Hitler was forced to cut the number of motor vehicles available to the Wehrmacht and SS by 'on average 30 per cent' to save fuel.[69] At the very moment when he most needed mobility and energy, it was being sapped by enemy action.

In late June 1944, Hitler reflected on the challenges facing the Third Reich in two secret landmark speeches at Berchtesgaden. His starting point was Germany's central location. The Reich, he warned, was encircled, just as it had been before 1918. 'We are built into this Europe,' Hitler argued, and therefore have 'enemies in all corners' of the map, the 'same ones' as in the World War. This meant that Germany either would have to be 'a state of Spartan toughness with an outlook held by the entire nation and an army which was always ready to strike' or else 'we shall always be the cultural fertilizer or the butt of others'. The German people, he reiterated, risked extinction if it failed to prevail in war, which ensured 'the natural selection of the strong' and 'the elimination of the weak'. To ensure this, Hitler continued, he would have to do two things. First, to achieve his original aim of 'liberating the German people from international capitalist influences', that is the Jews. This he had achieved. 'The Jew,' Hitler said simply, 'is gone.'[70]

Secondly, Hitler would also have to strengthen the German people racially. He began this section of his speech by reminding his audience that 'race is something different from *Volk*' and that the German people was 'made up of a whole series of racial kernels'. His usual biological determinism was tempered by a sense of uncertainty, when he referred to the 'Mendelian laws of selection' by which a child could supposedly inherit the characteristic of either the father or the mother. The conception of race he now expounded was in many ways voluntarist and inclusive. Hitler stressed that for him external appearance was less decisive than internal character. It was quite possible, he claimed, that there might be 'a person who looked absolutely un-Nordic, but who was in their inner core [and] in their behaviour completely Nordic'. The Führer also stressed that the Germans needed discipline – he used the word *Drill*, which means the same in English as in German – to make up for their lack of inherent and instinctive racial coherence. 'Thanks to our racial fragmentation as a result of the lack of a herd-instinct', he argued, a 'barbaric education' was required to 'make good what nature has unfortunately denied us' by 'overcoming' the 'different racial kernels' in the German people.[71] It was his old theme: the Germans required discipline to provide the coherence which came naturally to the British.

The Führer's second speech, to the leaders of the German war economy,[72] was very different. It addressed the problem of production, and was given in the shadow not only of the Allied bombing but also of the 'Morgenthau Plan'. Speer seems to have seen, or got wind of, an early version of the plan of US Treasury Secretary Henry Morgenthau to de-industrialize Germany after her defeat. 'Should the war be lost,' Speer wrote in his notes for Hitler, the result would be 'merciless extirpation of German industry, to eliminate competition in world markets. The enemy has concrete economic plans, which confirm this.'[73] The Führer's speech also emphasized the dangers of defeat, though he warned the industrialists that the only choice they would have then would be whether to commit suicide or to allow them themselves to be 'strung up' or be sent to work in Siberia by the Soviet security forces.[74] Typically, Hitler had geared his speech to his audience, who were in practice far more worried about the terrors of Bolshevism than Anglo-American capitalism.

Just the same, the Führer's main focus in his remarks to these leading industrialists was on the contest with the western powers, both as a battle of production and as an ideological struggle. He contrasted the 'liberal state' of capitalism, in which 'the economy' was 'in the end a servant of capital', and the Volk was 'the servant of the economy', with the National Socialist state, in which the Volk was 'dominant', 'the economy' was 'an instrument to preserve the Volk' and 'capital' was merely 'a means to lead the economy'. These remarks were intended to put his audience in their places, and to remind them of the Nazi primacy of politics over the economy. The basis of national survival, Hitler continued, was the availability of 'living space' with all the precious natural resources to feed the population and supply the factories with raw materials. That was what the war was about, the Führer reiterated, and everything had to be geared to winning it. 'War is the mobilization of all the forces of the people,' he said, 'and everything has to be subordinated to that.'

Hitler spelled out what this meant for German industry. 'This is not just a war of soldiers,' he explained, 'but especially of engineers'. By this Hitler meant not only inventors, but also the machine tool engineers needed for mass production. He expressed some admiration for the quality and quantity of Soviet output, particularly with regard to the legendary T-34 tank, but his principal concern was the Anglo-Americans. Their technological advances in the field of detection had basically neutralized the U-boat arm. They had also achieved a 'mass production of aircraft', which threatened to 'crush' the Reich. He now called upon German industry to support the mass production of new weapons, such as the Panther tank, the upgraded Tiger tanks and especially the new U-boats. For this reason, Hitler wanted a move away from 'quality work' – what he also

called 'German workmanship' – towards 'mass production' for war purposes. This was another explicit rejection of Germany's artisanal past,
and any sense of a *Mittelstand* future.

What both speeches had in common was an underlying anxiety about
the challenge of Anglo-America, both racially and economically. By referring to the danger of Germans becoming mere 'cultural fertilizer' for other
peoples, his first set of remarks hinted at one of his enduring preoccupations, namely the way in which German emigration had invigorated the
United States. This obsession was made explicit in his second speech, when
he came to the question of engineers. 'The engineers of the Americans,'
he claimed, 'are for the most part of German origin,' especially of 'Swabian-
Alemannic blood'. Astonishingly, Hitler sought to counter this threat by
insisting that he had German engineers as well. 'And I have the same group
of Alemannic,' he continued, 'they are working for us today.' 'Superiority
of the enemy,' Hitler scoffed, 'there you can see how little they are superior.'[75] As so often, the Führer was protesting too much. One was once
again left with the overwhelming impression that in Hitler's mind the best
Germans were fighting and producing for the other side.

These were the last major speeches Hitler made at Berchtesgaden. He
had not had much joy there of late. For years it had been a building site;
lately much of the complex had been draped in camouflage netting and
shrouded in artificial fog to confuse potential Allied bombers. The mag-
nificent views onto the Untersberg were often obscured. On 14 July Hitler
left the Berghof for Rastenburg, never to return.

Though there was considerable war weariness in Germany by mid 1944,
there was neither elite nor popular appetite for a revolution against their
Führer. Active resistance was confined to a relatively small number of
people, driven by a variety of motives including fear of losing the war,
patriotism, fear of a Soviet victory, opportunism and genuine revulsion at
the crimes being perpetrated in Germany's name. In the course of 1943,
they had become increasingly organized, working out a rough plan for the
post-war order, and – in a stroke of genius – had subverted the existing
regime contingency plans for civil unrest – code-named 'Valkyrie' – into
their own blueprint for a coup. Such was the centrality of Hitler, rather
than the regime as a whole, that the conspirators were agreed that any
action must begin with his removal, and preferably death. Various attempts
to kill Hitler in the course of 1943 were unsuccessful, and the leader of the
conspiracy, Count Stauffenberg, had already brought explosives into Hitler's
presence on three occasions in July without going through with the attempt,
but later in the month, the conspirators were ready to move again.

On 20 July 1944, Stauffenberg arrived at Führer Headquarters in Rastenburg with two bombs in his briefcase.[76] Almost immediately things began to go wrong. Hitler's schedule was changed at short notice. Stauffenberg only had time to prime one of the charges. The meeting was moved from the usual bunker to another location. Despite this, the plot nearly worked. Stauffenberg succeeded in placing his briefcase close to Hitler under a stout oak table. He then left the barracks. The bomb went off as planned, but Hitler was shielded from the worst of the blast by the table. Fortunately for him, the explosion took place in a wooden barracks, so that much of the force was dissipated outwards, and not in the bunker, where everybody inside would have been cremated. Though his injuries were far from trivial, Hitler got away with perforated ear-drums and some heavy bruising. He had been very lucky: the blast was large and four of the people in the building were so seriously injured that they soon died of their wounds.

Stauffenberg, who had observed the detonation from a safe distance, assumed that Hitler had been killed. Now a central flaw in the conspiracy became apparent. Stauffenberg had to return to Berlin to tell the conspirators that Hitler was dead, and lead the coup. Valuable time was lost, and although Valkyrie did unfold in many places, especially in Paris, a major nerve-centre of the conspiracy, where the army placed more than 1,000 SS and SD men under arrest, the regime soon regained the initiative. Symbolically, the turning point came when the commander of the Grossdeutschland Wachbatallion, Major Otto Ernst Remer, sent to apprehend Goebbels, who believed that Hitler was dead and that he was suppressing a coup, was put on a direct telephone to Hitler in Rastenburg. The sound of the Führer's voice was enough to persuade Remer. Goebbels was released and began to direct counter-measures. In the evening a radio broadcast announced that the Führer was alive and would soon address the German people. Stauffenberg and several of his co-conspirators were shot out of hand by the commander of the Reserve Army, General Fromm, who was trying to cover up his own involvement in the failed plot. The coup was over.

The 20 July plot and its background epitomized the weakness and strength of Hitler's governing style. Far from being paranoid, at least until this point, Hitler had thrived on giving his military and administrative elites sufficient room to explore their lethal creativity. This made him extraordinarily vulnerable to enemies within the walls. Until this point, more than eleven years into the regime, and four years into the war, those attending the daily briefings were neither searched nor disarmed. Stauffenberg was able to bring explosives into Hitler's presence on at least four separate occasions. It took the Führer six weeks after the coup to get around to forbidding the bearing of arms in his presence, and to ordering the guard detail to search all strangers for concealed weapons.[77] Here we must not mistake the Führer's trust for mere laziness or gullibility. For it was this very flexibility which also made Hitler's power so resilient. What blunted the coup was the decision of the communications centre in Berlin to pass on the messages from the Wolf's Lair, rather than those from Olbricht's office in the Reserve Army Headquarters. What killed it was the quick-wittedness of the commander of the standby battalion, the ardent National Socialist Otto Ernst Remer, who disobeyed the order to arrest Goebbels once he had spoken to Hitler in person. The regime was saved not because the troops followed orders – thanks to the thoroughness of the plotters these remained ambiguous – but because key personnel acted on their own initiative.

Though Hitler's injuries were not life threatening, and he was active again the same day, the explosion inflicted much more damage than it first appeared. Visitors to the headquarters remarked on how stooped and worn out Hitler looked.[78] His ears bled for several weeks afterwards, and he was unable to travel by air. The only upside, Hitler noted, was that the blast seemed to have cured the severe shaking in his left leg, although he 'wouldn't recommend such a cure'.[79]

Hitler was shocked by the attempt on his life, but not surprised. He had long suspected elements of the officer corps of treachery. Now Hitler felt vindicated. His radio speech the day after the explosion painted the conspirators as a 'small clique', of reactionary nobles, who had been trying to repeat the 'stab in the back' of 1918.[80] In his subsequent address to the *Gauleiter*, the Führer claimed that 'these traitors' had been engaged in 'sabotage' not just since '1941', but since the 'seizure of power'.[81] Hitler also saw his survival as a sign of 'providence', of his triumph in adversity. In the immediate aftermath of the explosion, he told the visiting Mussolini that he had experienced a 'miraculous deliverance, especially because it is not the first time that I have escaped death in this way'. This made him 'more than ever convinced' that he was destined to 'bring our great cause', that is the war, to 'a happy conclusion'.[82] Physically, therefore, Hitler was seriously affected by the plot. Politically, he was re-energized. Now he would press ahead with the implementation of National Socialist principles, especially in the army.

Despite his desire for vengeance, and determination to stamp out 'treachery', Hitler moved cautiously. The extent of it, which became increasingly clear as the Gestapo unmasked more and more high-ranking military men and civil servants, was sobering. Dealing with the plot was thus both an opportunity and a threat. He could make an example of the conspirators and showcase the resilience of his regime, but there was also a risk that he would showcase the resistance and turn them into martyrs, just as he had been after the beer hall putsch. For this reason, Hitler was anxious to avoid long show trials.[83] About a fortnight after the attempted coup, he established an *Ehrenhof* – supposedly at the request of the army itself – to investigate military complicity in the events. Hitler promised a 'ruthless purge'.[84] Those who made it to trial were sentenced by Roland Freisler, the brutal head of the Volksgerichtshof, who took his instructions from Hitler. It was at the Führer's express request that death sentences were to be carried out through ignominious hanging, and not by the more honourable method of a firing-squad. He also insisted that the executions be filmed, though there is no hard evidence that he actually watched the recordings.[85]

Hitler did not have much time to dwell on the events of 20 July, in any case. The military situation, already precarious, deteriorated dramatically. After an unsuccessful attempt on 18 July – Operation Goodwood – the Western Allies launched Operation Cobra on 25 July. On 31 July, the Anglo-Americans broke through at Avranches. Hitler's counter-attack at Mortain never got off the ground, and all his attempts to stabilize the front failed.[86] What Hitler had feared was now reality. The Allies were in open country and with their mobility and command of the air, there was nothing to stop them. Most of the German troops trapped in the pocket at St Lo-Falaise escaped, but the human and especially the material cost was horrendous. The 120–140, 000 killed and wounded could perhaps be replaced, albeit with great difficulty and with inferior recruits,[87] but the 1,300 tanks, 500 assault guns, and 5,500 artillery pieces, not to mention all the lorries and jeeps, could not possibly be.

Throughout August–September the Allies surged eastwards across France. On 15 August, they landed in southern France. Hitler was powerless. His attempts to establish a front along the Seine quickly collapsed. Paris was liberated on 19 August; the Führer's order for the destruction of the city was disobeyed by the German commander. On 11 September, the Americans crossed the Reich border west of Bitburg. On 17 September, the British and Americans launched an airborne operation to capture the Rhine bridges at Nijmegen and Arnhem. They hoped to punch through the German lines and push for Berlin. Around the same time, the Americans thrust in the direction of Cologne. They were the first Allies to capture a major Germany city, Aachen, on 21 October 1944.[88] It was an immensely symbolic moment, because the Holy Roman Emperors had traditionally been crowned there and the cathedral still contained the bones of Charlemagne. The garrison there surrendered to men of the US 1st Infantry

Division, commanded by General Clarence Huebner, whose grandfather had been born in Stuttgart.

In the east, first the central and then the southern fronts gave way, the lines massively weakened by the transfer of powerful units to the west. Army Group North temporarily lost contact with Army Group Centre when Soviet forces reached Tukums on the Baltic on 30 July. Communication was re-established after a vigorous counter-attack. During August 1944, the Red Army surged through White Russia, crossing a few kilometres into East Prussia in the middle of the month. The Polish Home Army rose in revolt, taking control of Warsaw from the German occupiers. On 14 September, Stalin launched an offensive against Riga. A fortnight later, Soviet forces reached the Baltic Sea just north of Memel, cutting off Army Group North once again, this time for good. In the south, Stalin launched an offensive against Romania on 20 August, capturing Bucharest by the end of the month. Army Group Ukraine was shattered, with the loss of about 400,000 men, though the materiel losses were less grievous than in the west. On 29 August, a major revolt broke out in Slovakia. The entire German eastern front hung in the balance.

The immediate result of the disasters was the collapse of Hitler's remaining alliance system. In Romania, Marshal Antonescu was sacked on 22 August 1944 and King Michael took his country first out of the war and then over to the other side. On 7 September 1944, Marshal Mannerheim's Finland signed an armistice with the Soviet Union. A day later, Bulgaria jumped ship. On 15 October, Admiral Horthy announced that Hungary was leaving the war. Hitler immediately launched a special forces operation which took his son hostage. Horthy abdicated, and a puppet Hungarian fascist grouping took power, but all pretence of a coalition of European states fighting the United Nations had now collapsed. Hitler's allied admirals, marshals and kings had all departed. Only Japan remained true. Once again, Germany stood almost alone against a world of enemies.

As if all this were not bad enough, the Allied breakout from Normandy enabled an escalation of the strategic air campaign, which targeted German industry, energy supply and communication system with renewed ferocity. Speer gave Hitler detailed accounts of the effects of Allied raids with the help of photographs and diagrams.[89] He warned his Führer of the resulting loss of steel, tank engine and motor vehicle production.[90] Even where raw materials were being mined, or goods produced, they often could not be completed or moved due to damage to road, rail and canal networks.[91] Krupp's Gusstahlfabrik in Essen was not completely destroyed physically, despite repeated attacks, but from October 1944 it ceased production after the bombers ended its source of electrical power.

By the middle of November, Speer was warning Hitler that the vital Ruhr industrial area was effectively cut off from the rest of the Reich.[92]

Worse still, these attacks were accompanied by devastating raids against civilian targets: Darmstadt, Freiburg and Heilbronn, as well as familiar targets such as Munich and Berlin. The Führer was deeply shaken by the bombing, not least because he feared for Eva Braun's safety in Munich.[93] Allied raids took a steady toll on his health and nerves.[94] Hitler saw these attacks as evidence of the annihilatory intent of the Western Allies. 'The will of the enemy,' he warned in mid September 1944, 'is clearly directed towards the destruction of the German people.' In order to achieve this, Hitler continued, the enemy 'considers every means legitimate' including 'bloody terror through bombing attacks against women and children'.[95] 'He is mobilizing his strength in order to smash our Reich,' he claimed a month later, and to destroy 'the German people and its social order.' 'His final aim,' Hitler reiterated, 'is the extermination of the German person.'[96] The (in his mind) pre-emptive war of annihilation which Hitler had himself launched on the world enemy was now coming home to Germany.

Unsurprisingly, the disasters of the late summer and autumn of 1944 led to renewed calls for a separate peace within the military and civil leadership of the Third Reich, and offers from Japan to mediate with the Russians.[97] Hitler refused, on the grounds that any overtures would be understood as a sign of weakness, and would be rejected in any case.[98] He refused point-blank to approach the west, telling Papen, who had offered himself as a conduit, that 'this war must be fought through to the end without compromise'.[99] As for trying to find out what the Russians thought, he remarked, that would be as pointless as 'touching a red-hot oven simply in order to establish whether it was hot'.[100] Significantly, Hitler laid down that he would only agree to a settlement which guaranteed the survival of future generations. This was code for his determination to hold on to as much 'living space' as he possibly could in any final settlement. 'The world knows no empty spaces,' he reminded a party audience, adding that 'peoples which are numerically or biologically too weak and cannot fill their Lebensraum will at best receive a reservation [sic]'.[101] The language was chosen with care. If the Germans did not act like Americans, Hitler warned, they would end up as Red Indians.

In the face of all these challenges, Hitler mounted an astonishing rally in the late autumn of 1944. Despite all the rhetoric, his strategy was not simply a strategy of perseverance, of clinging grimly to each and every part of his shrinking empire. On the contrary, Hitler set clear priorities in accordance with an overall strategy which was largely unchanged since the end of 1943. He would hold not simply where he could, but where he needed to.

He would withdraw where he had to, and where he could give way without fatal results. The purpose of this strategy was to retain as much of the economic potential of Europe as possible, and thus a credible military capability. This would allow him, he hoped, to outlast the enemy, and to exploit any splits that might have emerged in the coalition. 'We must carry on the fight until this moment arrives,' he remarked, adding that 'it may be closer than anybody imagines'.[102] He repeated these sentiments on the very last day of August 1944. 'There will be moments,' Hitler predicted, in which the tensions between the Allies become so great that there is a breach.' In the meantime, his job was to 'keep his nerve under all circumstances'.[103]

Hitler was clear about the resulting strategic priorities. The most pressing issue, he explained to the generals, might appear to be 'the stabilization of the eastern front', but because the Wehrmacht enjoyed the advantage of interior lines, that should be perfectly doable. The western front, by contrast, was much more problematic and was in fact the 'decisive' theatre, because defeat there risked losing the 'points of departure for the U-boat war'. Unlike most of the Wehrmacht leadership, especially the army chief of staff, Guderian, who were exercised by the Soviet onslaught on the Reich,[104] therefore, Hitler's strategy remained firmly western-centric.

In accordance with this approach, Hitler withdrew from southern and western France to more defensible positions.[105] He managed to get most of his men, though not their equipment, out by September 1944.[106] Hitler also ordered the Wehrmacht to pull out of the Balkans, taking with it all the equipment, raw materials and foodstuffs it could manage.[107] The main reason for the withdrawal was fear of being cut off by the Red Army offensive into Hungary, but Hitler also calculated that the resulting vacuum would cause tensions between the west and Stalin; the fighting between British forces and Greek leftists later that year vindicated his hopes. In a policy of 'scorched earth', Hitler ordered the destruction of anything – east, west and in the Reich itself – that could not be moved and might be of use to the advancing enemy.[108] At the same time, the Führer held his ground in key areas. He insisted that as many of the French ports be retained as possible, partly to deny the Anglo-Americans the facilities to land more men and equipment, partly to tie down Allied forces, and partly to support a resumption of the U-boat campaign once the new submarines went into mass production. In the south of France, the key cities of Toulon and Marseille were soon lost, much to Hitler's chagrin, but the Wehrmacht continued to hold Brest, Lorient, St Nazaire for some time, and in a few cases until the end of the war, long after the Allies had overrun the surrounding hinterland.[109] He also held on to Holland, and thus the bases from which to maintain the missile offensive against Britain.

Hitler then turned his attention to stabilizing the fronts. In the late summer and autumn of 1944, he issued a flurry of decrees demanding the fortification of 'Germany's western emplacement', a line from the German north coast, along the Dutch coast and back across France and Germany to Belfort. Hitler also called for defensive positions in Italy and along the Adriatic.[110] Once safely out of France, the Wehrmacht resisted stubbornly. The British airborne forces at Arnhem were crushed, and while the Germans were unable to hold on to Aachen, they managed to get the Americans bogged down in bloody fighting in the Hürtgen Forest amid scenes comparable to the First World War. By November 1944, the western front had been stabilized, at least for the time being.

In the east, Hitler gave priority to holding Kurland, in order to protect the U-boat training areas and the Estonian shale oil reserves, and Hungary, on account of the oil and bauxite reserves there.[111] He ordered the suppression of the Warsaw Rising, which was completed with great bloodshed in early October 1944.[112] The Slovak rebellion was also crushed, and the Jews of that country were deported and murdered. For the rest, Hitler relied on the *Ostwall*, a defensive system which was more psychological than military, whose main purpose was to reassure the civilian population and prevent large refugee flows. It was far inferior in fortifications and firepower to anything that Hitler had created, or was still planning, to keep out the Anglo-Americans. In late November 1944, Hitler left the 'Wolf's Lair' for good. Thereafter the defence of East Prussia, and – until early 1945 – the whole of eastern Germany, was a low priority for Hitler.[113]

Instead, Hitler's main aim in the autumn and winter of 1944 was the delivery of a crushing blow against the Western Allies. His motivation for doing so was unchanged: to undermine Churchill and Roosevelt, and if possible to split the Allied coalition. He increasingly cited the case of Frederick the Great as an example of how a great leader could survive an encircling coalition through 'steadfastness', which eventually enabled him to exploit divisions among his foes.[114] One method of delivering such a blow was the missile offensive. The V1 barrage had caused extensive damage and disquiet in southern England, but had not made much impact on the political leadership in London. Hitler had higher hopes for the more sophisticated V2 rocket, for which reason he was determined to hold on to bases to continue the 'long-range struggle' against Britain. Another weapon deployed against the west was new, more advanced aircraft. The development of the Me 262 was speeded up, and in September 1944, the Führer tasked the designer and manufacturer Ernst Heinkel with building a smaller and more easily mass-produceable jet fighter.[115] Hitler also looked to the new U-boats, and was given optimistic briefings about the success of the 'snorkel' submarines.[116]

The Führer's best hope of changing the dynamic, however, was a devastating counter-attack against the Anglo-American field armies. It was for this reason that he decided in late August 1944 to launch a major offensive in the west at the earliest possible opportunity.[117] 'It was his intention,' he told Oshima shortly afterwards, 'to take the offensive in the west on a large scale.' Hitler hoped to take advantage of the rainy weather in September and October to conceal his preparations, negating Allied air superiority, and launching his attack 'after the beginning of November'.[118] His objective, he explained on 16 September 1944, was to thrust through the Ardennes, capture Antwerp and thus force the Allies to withdraw to Britain. Hitler expected that the Luftwaffe would provide about 1,500 fighter aircraft in support. The projected start date was now late November, and it was to be delayed still further.[119] Throughout the autumn there was a furious debate in the OKW. Few shared Hitler's belief that the spearheads would ever reach Antwerp, and most would have been more than satisfied with getting to the Meuse. On 11 November, Hitler issued his guidelines for the operations plan, which stressed the importance of tactical and strategic surprise, as well as exploiting the adverse weather conditions. He alone would decide the timing of the attack.[120]

Over the course of ten weeks, Hitler quietly assembled a huge force in the west, including a whole new panzer army. His plan, as he told Oshima, was to deploy more than 'one million' men, 'to combine them with units to be withdrawn from the front in every area', and to wait for 'the replenishment of the air forces'.[121] Hitler ordered the systematic starving of other theatres of forces, and the avoiding of defensive battles which might suck in and consume reserves needed for the offensive.[122] This applied to the eastern front in general, where the Red Army continued to mount attacks. One of these thrusts, towards Gumbinnen in late October 1944, led to a massacre among the civilian population in the East Prussian village of Nemmersdorf.[123] Hitler remained insistent that spare forces were not to be sent there, but preserved for the planned offensive in the west. He was more interested in what was happening in Kurland, where the Wehrmacht was hit with three separate offensives between late October and December 1944. For the sake of clarity, Hitler laid down his priorities in detail in late November 1944. 'Unperturbed by even the greatest crises and loss of territory,' the OKW war diarist records, the Führer determined 'that the west[ern] and east [ern fronts] should have priority over the other theatres of war', but that the west should have 'priority' over the east, and 'within the west[ern front]', priority should be given to the army groups involved in the forthcoming offensive.[124] Hitler completed his preparations at the new Führer Headquarters – Adlerhorst – in the Taunus mountains just north of Frankfurt, not far from Germany's western border.

In order to support his strategy, Hitler launched one last great mobilization effort in the second half of 1944. His first task was psychological, to restore public confidence in the regime after the military defeats of the summer and the attempt on his life. The latter had shaken the German public, and the Führer himself saw it as evidence of an 'internal circulatory disruption', something that Germans of all ages and all times have taken very seriously.[125] On 25 July 1944, five days after the attempt on his life, Hitler appointed Goebbels 'imperial plenipotentiary for total war'. This was a largely symbolic move,[126] in which the propaganda minister was empowered to mobilize energies and lift the spirits of the population; the actual running of the war economy remained in Speer's hands. Hitler also sought to maintain morale by holding out the prospect of relief from the relentless Allied bombing. In early July 1944, he gave Speer permission to show colour footage of the rocket programme and, if possible, of the new jet fighter, to the *Gauleiter* in closed session, taking care not to reveal any technical secrets.[127] A little later, Hitler also authorized the release of films of the V2 rocket for the *Wochenschau* and thus for public viewing, although these were not actually shown until much later.[128] These were supposed to reassure the public that the hour of 'reprisal' against the Anglo-American attacks – which the Führer was constantly announcing – was soon at hand.

In the racial theatre, Hitler continued his relentless campaign against 'world Jewry' and other elements. By the winter of 1944, the deportation and murder of most of the Hungarian and Slovak Jews had been completed. In the field of 'positive' eugenics, Hitler remained preoccupied with the racial qualities of the British and the lost Germans on the other side of the Atlantic. A few days before the start of his great offensive in the west, he expressed his respect for the 'toughness and tenacity' of the British, and lamented once again to the generals that the 'American continent' had 'become British rather than German'.[129]

One of the most pressing tasks facing Hitler was the recruitment of more manpower to replace the huge losses of the summer and autumn of 1944. By September 1944, it was clear that the traditional methods were not enough to meet the shortfall. The Wehrmacht proposed to fill the gaps through the establishment of regional militias based on the old Prussian *Landsturm* model. Hitler was extremely reluctant to countenance such a step, partly because he feared the establishment of regional – and perhaps separatist – armies behind the lines.[130] The fear of another 'stab in the back' loomed large. On 16 August Bormann sent a copy of the original *Landsturm* Ordinance of April 1813 to the Nazi Party leadership with Hitler's request that they read it. Not long after, the Führer gave various *Gauleiter* permission to run the local defence efforts. Over the next few weeks Bormann then persuaded him to establish a new militia on a national basis.[131] This *Volkssturm* would be made up of 'all men fit to bear arms' between the ages of sixteen and sixty to defend the 'soil of the homeland'. It was to be under the control of the NSDAP, rather than the Wehrmacht, and it was to be deployed according to the orders of Himmler as the commander of the Reserve Army. The very name of the new organization – a *Volkssturm*, rather than a regional *Landsturm* – reflected Hitler's continuing preoccupation with the threat of regionalism.

The main mobilization front, though, remained production. Hitler was desperate to replace the equipment lost in Normandy and – to a lesser extent – in Belorussia and south-eastern Europe during the summer. The Wehrmacht was also extremely short of fuel.[132] Hitler was determined to equip the armies in the west for the forthcoming offensive. His main competitor had always been Anglo-America, and the proportion of the war effort – between 70 and 80 per cent by late 1944[133] – devoted to fighting the Western Allies increased with every passing month. In mid October Hitler conferred with Speer about British (including Canadian and Australian) and American aircraft production. The armaments minister could report steep increases on the German side, but though his statistics on the comparative picture were hopelessly optimistic, even Speer had to concede that Germany was playing catch-up, since with the exception of the automobile industry it had possessed, unlike the United States, 'no mass production' before the war.[134]

There were still shortages of every kind of weapon in the Wehrmacht itself, making the equipment of the new *Volkssturm* formations highly problematic. Hitler stressed that the militia would be useless without weapons, and ordered that they be equipped with the redundant defensive weapons of obsolete and grounded Luftwaffe bombers. The unwitting symbolism of this move was exceeded only by the bathos of the *Volkssturm* initiation ceremony on 19 November 1944 when the borrowed small arms carried by the new levies had to be returned after the parade. Hitler was entirely clear that the Waffen-SS and regular army should receive priority for deliveries. His general view of the military quality of the *Volkssturm* units was low, and he intervened on a number of occasions to remove weapons from them in order to equip Wehrmacht troops. He also insisted that armaments production took priority over recruitment, and approved Speer's exemptions for *Volkssturm* draftees doing important factory work.[135] For Hitler, National Socialist élan was good, but fire-power was better.

All these measures meant that Hitler acquired a whole slew of new disputes to adjudicate. Bormann battled Himmler for control of the *Volkssturm*, Speer over the recruitment of armament workers and Ley over the construction of fortifications.[136] Rosenberg continued his steady descent.[137] In each case, Hitler – be it the *Volkssturm* or the establishment of a *Generalkommissar* for the west[138] – took the main decisions, even if he sometimes admitted that the logically right choice could not be made for reasons of personnel. The apparent winner of these battles was Bormann, who continued his yeast-like ascent in the antechamber of power around Hitler. In political terms, however, the real rising star was Karl Dönitz, to whose advice Hitler increasingly deferred, and whose standing had increased exponentially in the course of the year.[139] This partly resulted from the fact that after the missile offensive had fizzled out, the expected new U-boats represented Hitler's only credible hope of delivering a powerful blow against the Anglo-Americans. It also reflected Hitler's sense that Dönitz was a sincere National Socialist, whose Kriegsmarine – unlike the imperial fleet during the First World War – was imbued with a fanatical fighting spirit.

Moreover, despite all the stress of military leadership and government, Hitler was still in full command of his senses and physically robust enough to rule decisively. To be sure, he frequently bewailed his poor health in front of the generals and spoke of his desire for release, even through death.[140] On the very last day of August 1944, Hitler complained that he had he not been to the theatre, or a concert or a film, for five years on account of the war, and said that his death would be 'for [him] personally a liberation from worries', sleepless nights and 'severe nervous problems'. In December 1944, he told his personal doctor, Theo Morell, of pains brought on by the military and political situation; interestingly, it was the July plot, the air war over the Reich and the forthcoming offensive in the west which most exercised him, rather than the eastern front.[141] It is also true that Hitler was forced to issue an order forbidding participants at discussions from carrying out 'individual discussions',[142] which he found deeply distracting. We should not read into this measure any implication that he was losing control over his audience. It was simply an overdue response to the age-old German habit of conducting loud and lengthy parallel private conversations during meetings in full view and hearing of the principal speaker.

One way or the other, by early December 1944, Hitler had pulled off an astonishing rally. Unlike the autumn of 1943, there was no sustained internal crisis of the regime. Hitler's standing was largely unchallenged, among both the elite and the population as a whole, despite his virtual public absence. The Führer's charisma had become routinized, and the basis of his legitimacy almost traditional. Some of those who had engaged in treasonable activities, such as Field Marshal von Kluge, found themselves unable, even in the face of death, entirely to let go of their faith. Militarily, all the fronts had been stabilized, at least for now, partly because of increased German resistance, and partly because the Allied advance in the autumn had been so rapid that it had outrun their supply lines.[143]

On 16 December 1944, Hitler launched his major offensive in the Ardennes, the same wooded and rugged terrain in which he had achieved his great breakthrough over four years earlier. He achieved complete strategic and tactical surprise. Thanks to the bad weather, on which the German planners relied, the Allied aircraft were initially unable to react effectively. German tanks pushed deep into the American lines, creating a huge 'bulge', creating consternation in Washington and London. Hitler followed progress closely, frequently intervening in the course of operations.[144] Thousands of Americans were taken prisoner. There was never much likelihood, though, of Hitler reaching his objective of Antwerp, or of splitting the US from the British forces. Even had he got there, the German spearheads would have been dependent on a long and vulnerable supply line. The lunge for Antwerp was a poorly thought-out parody of the original race to the sea in 1940. As it was, Hitler's armoured formations were plagued from the start by a shortage of fuel, and while his men captured many American vehicles, too few were able to drive them, a poignant reflection of the continuing relative backwardness of the Third Reich. The lack of trucks forced Hitler to rely on some 50,000 horses for his mobility, yet another example of the technological gulf that separated him from the Anglo-Americans.[145]

Soon, the offensive became bogged down. The Americans put up a fierce resistance at Bastogne. When the skies cleared, Allied aircraft soon devastated the German columns. Hitler's soldiers, who had been told to salute each other with the 'German greeting', wagged that they were more likely to use the 'German glance', looking out for enemy aeroplanes. Short of fuel, the panzer spearheads were reduced to scavenging for petrol in the desolate landscape. The Germans never even reached the Meuse, let alone Antwerp. In late December 1944, Hitler switched focus to northern Alsace in Operation *Nordwind*.[146] The Führer spoke of his determination to 'smash [the Americans] piece for piece, to exterminate them division by division'.[147] Once again, his motive was primarily political. Hitler told the generals that he hoped to show 'Aryan' Americans the futility of continuing the war. 'The criticism [of the war] at home,' he claimed, 'is huge.'[148] It was no use. The Alsatian offensive too ran aground. Early in the New Year, it was clear that Hitler's entire western strategy had failed.[149]

The Führer was in no doubt as to the cause of his defeat in the Ardennes. It was the same crushing Allied material superiority which was costing him the war as a whole. This was why, he explained to the generals, Germany could not stand on the defensive. With every passing day, Hitler continued, especially as they made the French and Belgian ports operational, the 'deployment of material' by the Western Allies would increase. They would bring to bear their superiority in 'ammunition and equipment', enabling them to implement a 'tactic which we got to know at Aachen'. This involved the tanks 'shooting individual bunkers to bits' and then the occupation of a completely devastated terrain by relatively small infantry forces. 'The human losses,' he continued, 'will not be as large for him as they will be over time for us.' Meanwhile, Hitler went on, the Anglo-Americans 'will demolish slowly but surely all of our rail connections' and deprive the Wehrmacht of more and more 'transport capacity'. The 'effects on the front,' he predicted, would be seen in 'a reduction in the supply of ammunition, fuel, weapons, equipment, motor vehicles and so on.' [150] It was a playbook he, and the Wehrmacht, now knew only too well.

In mid January 1945, Hitler left Adlerhorst and returned to Berlin. He did not install himself, as originally planned, in the army headquarters at Zossen. Hitler feared that the barrack complex there was too vulnerable to Allied air attack. Instead, Hitler took up residence again in the Wilhelmstrasse at the heart of Berlin, where he spent most of the rest of the war. His position was much worse than it had been at the end of the previous summer. Militarily, much of the conflict was already being waged on German territory. Economically, Allied bombing and the loss of raw materials and factories in the former Nazi empire had created a dire situation. In early January 1945, Speer gave Hitler a detailed briefing with graphs and tables on the disastrous state of the transport system, which was running at about 50 per cent of capacity with severe consequences for the armaments industry. Not long after, he warned Hitler that munitions production had fallen so catastrophically that he could not promise to keep the many fronts supplied.[151] Politically, the Führer was completely isolated. More and more countries were joining the United Nations coalition against him. Hitler's allies – as he claimed once again in his New Year address[152] – had all left the Reich in the lurch. For this reason, he did not see his translator, Paul Schmidt, again.[153] There was nobody left to lie to except the Germans themselves, and for them no translation was needed.

Despite these setbacks, the main outlines of Hitler's strategy remained unchanged. He still hoped to turn the tide militarily, or at least force a negotiated peace through a tenacious defence. He insisted on the construction of extensive fortifications, at least in the west;[154] the *Ostwall* remained largely on paper and the christening of more than a dozen towns there as 'fortresses' was largely symbolic. In both cases, Hitler generally refused to allow withdrawals. This was not because he lacked imagination for a flexible defence, but because he was under no illusions about the superiority of Allied equipment. Once they left the relative security of their bunkers, Hitler feared, German troops risked being caught in the open and would soon lose heart.[155] Hitler also retained his belief in the 'new weapons' which would enable him to deliver devastating effect against the Western Allies. In early January 1945, he reiterated his belief that the ME 262 should be used as a bomber, alongside its deployment as a fighter against the Anglo-American air fleets. These moves were accompanied by the usual measures, which were now more like exhortations, for increased human mobilization.[156] So far, so familiar.

There was, however, a new note in Hitler's rhetoric which reflected a fundamental change in strategy. He still had a concrete plan for victory, but he realized that defeat was now more likely.[157] In fact, Hitler had often believed that success was doubtful, but that without the attempt, failure was certain. He had also long been convinced that defeat could be the spur to national renewal. Hitler frequently quoted Clausewitz's remarks on the subject. In order to live on, however, a nation would have to go down fighting in a struggle which through heroism and sacrifice bore within it the seeds of its rebirth. A disgraced people, by contrast, would never rise again. Hitler was therefore determined to 'choreograph' his own defeat.[158] This also marked a decisive moment in his temporal vision. He had begun as a mere drummer, convinced that he was paving the way for the messiah. Then he became the Führer, increasingly convinced that he could not merely seize power in Germany, but also roll out his programme within his own lifetime. Now he reverted to his earlier timeframe, in which the exemplary end of the Third Reich, and his own death, would serve as the inspiration for the renewal of the German people. As Hitler's time on earth ran out, racial time expanded once more.

Hitler's defiance in the last months of the Third Reich should therefore not be understood as mere nihilism or a narcissistic desire to build his funeral pyre ever higher for some kind of Wagnerian *Götterdämmerung*. Hitler despised macho posturing and he never endorsed a death wish, or pointless bravado in the face of danger. This emerged quite clearly in a somewhat comic exchange with his military leadership in January 1945. When Hermann Fegelein praised SS General Paul Hausser as a man who said that 'the highest service that I can deliver is to die in the front line before the enemy', Hitler was brusque. 'I don't want that at all,' he responded, 'that is no kind of wisdom.' Fegelein retorted that Hausser was in the habit of walking tall through artillery fire and upbraiding his adjutants for taking cover and 'being so sensitive'. Hitler wasn't having this either. 'I would also take cover [in that situation],' he replied. 'I only ever knew one general [in the First World War] who did not take cover,' Hitler added, 'but he couldn't hear [the artillery fire].'[159] Hitler, in other words, was not interested in gallant deaths per se, but in the delivery of military or political effect.

In the course of January 1945, the storm on Germany itself began in earnest. There was a brief lull in the west after the Americans had cleared the Wehrmacht and SS out of the Ardennes by the middle of the month. There was no let-up, though, in the air. New Year's Day was marked by massive bombing raids on German industry, airfields and the transport network.[160] The following night brought huge RAF attacks on Ludwigshafen and Nuremberg, with nearly 1,800 people killed there. A day after that, USAAF hit installations at Aschaffenburg in western Germany. Then the RAF struck at Hanover in strength, and again at Munich. The USAAF raided Rastatt and Hamm, where some of the largest marshalling yards in the Reich were located. The Luftwaffe was increasingly unable to intervene, despite a huge paper strength in personnel and machines. Hitler was outraged by what was now an Allied aerial safari. 'He has no losses at all,' he stormed to his generals on 10 January, 'it is as if he were just on parade, in bright sunshine!' Soon, Hitler continued bitterly, the enemy 'won't need any fighters any more'. Luftwaffe interceptors were being swarmed by Allied escorts before they had a chance to reach the bombers. 'This a rabbit [hare] shoot,' he lamented.[161]

On 12 January, the Red Army attacked at Baranow, a day later in East Prussia, and the following day it launched a huge offensive on the Vistula.[162] Within twenty-four hours a bridgehead was established on the river north of Warsaw; the OKW reported a deep 'breach'.[163] Shortly after, the Wehrmacht evacuated Warsaw, and a day later Cracow, the seat of Hans Frank's General Government. Hitler sought to shore up the line by putting Himmler in charge of a new Heeresgruppe Weichsel. He defined this task as 'organizing national defence behind the entire eastern front'.[164] The main purpose behind this exercise was probably motivational and narratival: to stiffen the ranks ideologically, and to place the SS at the heart of the final resistance effort for the sake of posterity. Militarily, the decision made no difference. The Red Army was now breaking through all along the front. On 22 January, it reached the Oder to the north and south of Breslau. Bromberg fell on 23 January, and Posen was encircled on 27 January. That same day, Soviet troops liberated Auschwitz; most of the extermination camps had now been abandoned. By late January the Russians had captured the ruins of the Wolf's Lair, Hitler's longtime headquarters at Rastenburg. Hitler, who had denuded the eastern front to support the offensive in the Ardennes, was powerless to stop the rout.

The Russian surge was not just a military disaster, but also a political nightmare. The evacuation of the civilian population, which Hitler had been avoiding since the autumn of the previous year, could no longer be put off. On 23 January 1945, mass evacuations from East Prussia began, apparently without a direct order from the Führer. Hitler, in fact, insisted on priority still being given to the prosecution of the war and the needs of the war economy. He told Dönitz, who was organizing the shipping to embark refugees from East Prussia, that 'the remaining coal reserves must be kept back for military purposes and may not be used for the evacuation of refugees'. When Memel was abandoned, Hitler's main concern was the removal of the 'heavy equipment' and the destruction of the harbour facilities, rather than rescue of the civilian population.[165] A week later, Hitler gave instruction that refugees should be decanted to Denmark in order to ease the situation in the Reich, but stressed again that this should only happen 'without affecting the current troop and supply transports'.[166]

Instead, Hitler put the Russian advance – and the associated stories of murder and rape, many of them true – to propagandistic use. In his last radio speech, given on the occasion of the twelfth anniversary of the take-over of power on 30 January 1933, Hitler promised to master the 'terrible fate which is currently taking place in the east', which was 'exterminating people in their tens and hundreds of thousands' in the cities and the countryside.[167] The spectre of annihilation, long threatened from the air, was now visible on the ground as well. He implored Germans to rely on their own strength to repel the Bolshevik hordes, and not to depend on the west to save them, because it would itself fall victim to the Judaeo-communist virus. In a passage which revealed his enduring belief in the manipulative relationship between western plutocracy and the Soviet regime, Hitler claimed that the west was now 'unable to banish the demons they have called from the steppes of Asia'. That said, there was a palpable sense that the Russian threat was now, for the first time in almost two years, moving to the top of Hitler's agenda. From now on, Hitler paid more attention to the eastern front. 'The Führer ordered,' the war diary of the OKW recorded on 29 January 1945, 'in view of the situation in the east, to go over to the defensive in the west.'[168] Armoured forces were transferred to the east.[169]

In late January 1945 and early February, faced with overwhelming odds on all fronts, Hitler was forced to recognize the failure of his mobilization project. Despite the pressures of war, he was unable to overcome the deep-seated resistance within German society to the prosecution of total war. This became clear during an interminable and increasingly bizarre exchange with some generals on 27 January, when Hitler attempted to persuade them that officers of a certain age, who were no longer capable of discharging the duties associated with their existing or former rank, be recruited to serve in a more junior capacity. This idea met with furious resistance from the generals, who insisted that no man should be required to serve below a man who held a rank inferior to that at which he had retired. It violated their sense of professional honour. The Führer pointed out the absurdity of the situation. 'At the same moment in which I am summoning the *Volkssturm* and recruit God knows what kind of people into the Wehrmacht by disregarding the question of age,' he said, 'I am sending completely fit people, who are actually soldiers, home to man redundant posts in the bureaucracy.'[170] Hitler's logic was impeccable, but he was unable to make any headway. Twelve years into the Third Reich, which had so transformed Germany and Europe, the whole episode showed how little Hitler had changed the Germans themselves.

The real problem, though, was not men but materiel. In early 1945, Germany was awash with adult males, foreign and local. The Luftwaffe, for example, comprised 2 million men, hundreds of thousands of whom no longer had meaningful functions.[171] Hitler did not have enough weapons to give them. The war economy, already in a parlous state, was further battered by the capture of the Upper Silesian industrial area by the Red Army. Hitler also lamented the lack of nickel, and worried about the effect of the 'decline of material' on jet aircraft production. 'The worst thing that can happen to us,' though, was 'the destruction of the German transport system.' 'We have enough coal,' he explained, 'there is so much being produced in the mines that we can cannot carry it all off.' In fact, Hitler continued, 'we have more than 80,000 wagons [of coal] more, but we cannot transport them'. On 30 January 1945, the normally optimistic Speer sent the Führer a memorandum warning him that without Upper Silesia production would collapse.

Hitler reacted the next day with the demand for an 'Emergency Programme' to produce more weapons. This was proclaimed a 'currently more important task' than 'recruitment [of those workers] into the Wehrmacht, the *Volkssturm* or other purposes'.[172] It was no use. The deteriorating levels of equipment provision amounted to a steady 'de-motorization' of the Wehr-macht. The OKH conceded in early February 1945 that 'the active conduct of operations is no longer possible'.[173] Even where vehicles were available, there was often not enough petrol to drive them, because Hitler issued strict instructions that fuel should only be provided for the artillery and pan-zers.[174] In what can only be described as desperation, Hitler demanded the established of cyclist units led by lieutenants with 'tank-busting weapons' (probably bazookas) which would take on enemy armoured formations.[175] All this was the result of the systematic destruction of the Nazi war economy and transportation system by Anglo-American air fleets, which were now steadily bombing the Reich back into the early nineteenth century. There was really no need for Morgenthau to de-industrialize Germany; those Swabian-American engineers were doing that already.

Despite the shift in military gravity towards the eastern front, Hitler's overall strategy had not changed. He still hoped to make the Anglo-Americans sicken of the fight and to split the enemy coalition.[176] In order to profit from any such development, Hitler needed to ensure the survival of the Reich and maintain a capacity to strike at the Anglo-Americans. To that end, his military dispositions were not driven by classic strategic considerations, but by economic ones. 'Modern war,' he told Dönitz on 5 February 1945, 'was principally an economic war whose needs must be given priority.'[177] Hitler laid down as the priorities on the eastern front not the Vistula or East Prussia, where the Soviet military threat was great-est, but first the industrial Vienna basin and the Hungarian oil-fields (which now provided 80 per cent of Germany's requirements), and then the Upper Silesian industrial area and the Bay of Danzig, which was vital for the submarine war.[178] He refused Dönitz's offer to send 1,500 naval ratings from Gdynia to fight in Danzig as infantry because they were irreplaceable specialists.[179] Substantial forces still remained in Kurland – more than 630 tanks in mid February 1945, despite withdrawals – for the same reason.[180] There were also still some 400,000 men in Norway to safeguard the iron-ore supply and support the submarine campaign.

The new element in February 1945 was diplomacy. Despite Hitler's hopes and stratagems, three-power unity between Roosevelt, Churchill and Stalin was reaffirmed at the Yalta conference between 4 and 12 Feb-ruary 1945. Either in reaction to this, or following some other logic, Hitler finally authorized, or at least tolerated, negotiations for a separate peace. On 6 February, he was briefed by the supreme SS commander in Italy, SS-Obergruppenführer Karl Wolff, on apparent Allied overtures in that theatre via Switzerland and the Catholic Church.[181] Hitler apparently received the information without comment. On 19 February Himmler began a dialogue with Count Bernadotte about a possible separate peace with the Western Allies, seemingly without Hitler's knowledge.[182] The Führer did, however, reluctantly bless Ribbentrop's overtures to the western powers at around the same time, which were conducted by the Foreign Office diplomat Fritz Hesse in Stockholm.

Hesse's instructions bore Hitler's imprint, much more than that of Ribbentrop. They stressed the 'biological' strength of some 200 million Russians who were about to be reinforced by another 100 million or so mainly Slav eastern Europeans. In this context, the Western Allies were told, they could ill afford to lose the Germans, who were the 'only biological factor' which could provide a 'counterweight to the immense Bolshevik mass of Slavs in the east'.[183] Persisting with the 'Morgenthau Plan', the argument continued, would simply do Stalin's work in Germany for him. The Soviet dictator would also be able to rely on the '20 million bombed-out', desperate people who were now tending towards communism. The main addressee of the document was Britain. It was in her 'own deepest interest' to establish a front in Germany against the Soviet Union on the first day after the 'possible' defeat of the Third Reich, especially as the United States would probably lapse back into 'isolationism'. London would therefore need to abandon 'the old British idea of a balance inside Europe', and accept that 'every further weakening of Germany through the Anglo-American air force and through the advance of the British and Americans would in the long term be a policy of self-destruction from the British point of view'. The pitch was no different from those which Hitler had been making for a decade, except that he was now threatening London not with German strength but the spectre of a complete German collapse. Hesse's cover was soon exposed, the Allies showed no interest, and Hitler's plan came to nothing.

Instead of negotiating, the Allies surged forward again. The eastern front buckled under repeated Soviet blows. The much-vaunted *Ostwall* gave way within a few days; the Wehrmacht was forced to admit shamefacedly in February 1945 that all the digging had been in vain.[184] On 11 February the last defenders of Buda Hill in Budapest surrendered after a six-week siege. Four days later, Breslau was surrounded; supplies had to be flown in by air. In East Prussia, the Red Army pinned the Wehrmacht ever more against the Baltic coast as the main thrust pushed westward. Hitler rolled with the punch, determined to hold on to as much of the province as possible, and especially Königsberg.[185]

In the west, the Canadians advanced through the Reichswald near Kleve in early February, where there was bitter fighting, closely watched by Hitler, as the town was completely destroyed.[186] Towards the end of the month, their spearheads met with the Americans at Geldern. The Americans also advanced in the Palatinate in western Germany. Hitler told the defenders there to show the same 'fanatical toughness with which the Americans defended Bastogne'.[187] In the air, the Allies kept up a relent-less pressure. On 3 February, the USAAF launched a large-scale attack on Berlin which killed the head of the 'People's Court', Roland Freisler. The bombers also damaged much of the government district, including the new Imperial Chancellery and Hitler's own apartment. On the night of 13/14 February 1945 came the most terrible blow of all. A massive Anglo-American strike on Dresden devastated one of Europe's most beau-tiful cities and killed about 35,000 civilians. Hitler was particularly affected by the destruction. In the immediate aftermath, he seriously considered shooting a British or American prisoner of war for every dead civilian in Dresden.[188] He also discussed repudiating the Geneva Conven-tion with regard to the Anglo-Americans (Stalin was not a signatory).[189] It was only after hearing strenuous objections from Ribbentrop and the Wehrmacht leadership that Hitler desisted. His sense that the Western Allies were fighting a war of annihilation against the German people remained strong.[190]

The strain under which Hitler was operating became apparent on 24 February 1945, when he hastily convened his *Gauleiter* for a meeting. They were shocked by his appearance, especially the fact that not merely his hands but his entire body was trembling. Hitler's message was stark, and reflected his narratival strategy. 'Should the German people give up,' he warned, 'then it would be demonstrated that they had no moral worth, and in that case they would deserve destruction. That would be the right-ful judgement of history and Providence.' Hitler then announced that he would stay on the defensive in the west and counter-attack in the east. He also promised new submarines and jet fighters, but was not specific. Towards the end Hitler 'predicted that, if Germany held firm during the crisis, a day would come' when the Allies were riven by 'serious conflicts'. Hitler's ninety-minute speech was a disappointment to his audience, who had been expecting concrete information about the deployment of new weapons. 'For the first time,' the *Gauleiter* of Swabia, Karl Wahl, recalls, 'the impression upon his listeners was not convincing' because the 'sensa-tional news which all anticipated was not forthcoming'.[191]

That same day, Hermann Esser read out a statement by Hitler in Munich at a meeting to mark the anniversary of the drawing-up of the NSDAP programme. Hitler repeated the message given to the *Gauleiter* about the 'unnatural alliance between exploitative capitalism and human-destroying Bolshevism', though in fact he had spent most of his career claiming that this alliance was anything but unnatural. Hitler then reiterated the perils posed by the Red Army advance to German women and children, but referred to the 'Jewish-Bolshevik destruction of peoples and their west European [he meant British] and American pimps', phrasing which suggests that Hitler still saw the Soviet Union primarily as the instrument of the Anglo-Americans. The Führer also stressed the example of Frederick the Great, though more as the man who had made the second Reich possible than as the great survivor of the Seven Years War. 'When the greatest king of our history, Frederick II, was in danger of being defeated in his seven-year war against a world coalition [sic],' Hitler claimed, 'it was solely down to his heroic soul that the germ cell and core of a future Reich came out victorious in the end.'[192] Once again, the narratival strategy was clear: an exhortation to resist now as the precondition not for victory but for rebirth.

Despite widespread concerns about the military situation, Hitler's authority remained unchallenged, among the Nazi leadership, the Wehrmacht and the population at large. At the meal with his *Gauleiter* after the meeting on 24 February, he once again dominated the room and revived many of them with his visions of splitting the Allied coalition.[193] They all still accepted his mediation of their disputes, as did all other members of the Nazi hierarchy. The Führer sided with Goebbels against Speer on the recruitment of armament workers, with Speer against Bormann on the same issue with regard to the *Volkssturm*.[194] Despite the steady crumbling of the 'Hitler Myth' more generally, as the military situation deteriorated,[195] loyalty to Hitler still inspired a large proportion of the army rank and file.[196] There was thus no prospect of Hitler being toppled, by either a palace revolt or a popular revolution.

In March 1945, Hitler made one last attempt to change the strategic dynamic. He launched two offensives on the eastern front, both of them driven by economic rather than narrowly military considerations. In early March, the Wehrmacht counter-attacked at Lauban in Lower Silesia as part of an operation designed to recover the vital industrial area there. At around the same time, a larger thrust, long in the preparation,[197] was mounted in Hungary with a view to protecting Germany's last remaining oil reserves around Lake Balaton. On the night of 3 March 1945, the Luftwaffe conducted its first bombing raids on Britain for a long time, striking targets in the midlands, the north and the east of England. The firing of V2 rockets against Britain continued, the last one being launched on 27 March 1945. That same day, the now redundant commander of the rocket programme, Hans Kammler, was appointed the 'general plenipotentiary for jet aircraft' with all powers necessary to develop and produce jet aircraft.[198] Above all,

Hitler still put his faith in the new submarines and in the U-boat war more generally, on whose progress he was briefed by the navy throughout the month. According to Dönitz, the two first boats of type XXIII had performed well on operations and mass production could begin soon. The first type XXI, he claimed, would go on patrol within a few days.[199]

Despite the dire military situation, Hitler remained reluctant to draw on another human resource, though for very different reasons. He had long puzzled over how best to use the various potentially pro-Axis flotsam and jetsam which had ended up in Germany either as prisoners of war or as refugees. 'One does not know,' he remarked to his generals in late March 1945, 'what else is ambling around here,' adding that he had 'just heard to my astonishment of the sudden appearance of a Ukrainian SS division'. The Führer reserved particular contempt for Bose's Indians. 'The Indian Legion,' he pronounced, 'is a joke.' 'There are Indians,' he continued, 'who cannot kill a louse, they would rather allow themselves to be eaten.' 'They would not kill any British,' he predicted. Hitler argued that because the Indians deployed by the Japanese in Burma, who were after all fighting to liberate their homeland, had performed badly – 'they ran away like stampeding sheep' – they would be highly unlikely to do better in Europe. It would be more sensible, he concluded, to put them to work on prayer mills.[200]

These discussions were, in any case, somewhat academic. Throughout March 1945, the enemy coalition tightened its grip on Germany still further. The Western Allies, who had moved slowly in January and February, made spectacular gains. On 7 March, the Americans took Cologne; more importantly, they seized the bridge over the Rhine at Remagen intact. Men and tanks poured across. Further north, Hitler vainly hoped to hold on to a bridgehead around Duisburg to enable the transport of coal out of the Ruhr via the Dortmund–Ems canal.[201] The British – again closely watched by Hitler[202] – prepared to mount a massive airborne and amphibious assault across the Rhine. Churchill came to Venlo on 25 March to watch the 'Anglo-Saxons' – the British 2nd Army, the 1 Canadian and the 9 US Army – crossing the last great natural obstacle in western Germany. A day later, the Americans took Darmstadt. Despite all Hitler's exhortations, resistance in the west was crumbling fast. The entire left bank of the Rhine was now in Allied hands, the crossings of the river were secure, and the way to Berlin for eighty-five Allied divisions from the west lay open. March 1945 also saw the heaviest bombing of the entire war against both industrial and civilian targets.[203]

Hitler was powerless to do anything against the succession of Anglo-American blows, both on the ground and in the air. He reshuffled the military leadership in the west, replacing Rundstedt (for 'age reasons') with

Kesselring, who in turn was replaced in Italy by General von Vietinghoff,[204] but these were largely cosmetic moves. Hitler was pleased with the excellent performance of the Me 262 against Allied bombers,[205] but there were too few of them to make much difference. He was aghast at the dismal performance of the rest of the Luftwaffe, which had largely disappeared from the skies over Germany. 'What particularly worries me about the Luftwaffe,' Hitler complained in late March 1945, 'are the so-called missing figures for aircraft.'[206] Clearly, many pilots were treating discretion as the better part of valour. By contrast, Hitler was increasingly impressed with the attitude of Dönitz's Kriegsmarine. In late March 1945, he ordered that command of fortresses in the west should be given in the first instance to naval officers because, though many fortresses had surrendered in the course of the war, no ship had been lost without fighting to the last.[207] This sentiment was strengthened by Hitler's increasing reliance on the navy as the one branch of the Wehrmacht which could still plausibly deliver, if not victory, then at least a painful blow against the Western Allies. The extent of his belief in the new submarines is demonstrated by the fact that he allocated for their production a quantity of steel equivalent to 5,100 tanks, not to mention the man hours and other opportunity costs.[208]

In the east, despite initial losses, the Red Army soon contained the German counter-offensive at Lauban and at Lake Balaton. Within ten days, the Russians were on the advance again. On 25 March 1945, Hitler ordered the withdrawal from the bulge around Sarajevo. Five days later, the German front in Hungary had completely collapsed, though Hitler refused to authorize any retreat.[209] On the central sector, the Red Army thrust deeper and deeper into Germany. Hitler continued to insist that the Baltic coastline – especially Danzig, Pillau and Gdynia – be held, ordering the Kriegsmarine to resupply the Baltic ports by sea. Most of Pomerania and the rest of Silesia were overrun. Danzig fell on 30 March 1945, and with it vital shipyards. Königsberg, though surrounded, still held out. Millions of refugees were now on the move, desperately trying to escape the Red Army.

Despite his blood-curdling warnings of the fate that awaited them at the hands of the hordes in the east, Hitler still gave the war effort priority over evacuation. 'Our strongly reduced transport capacity,' he decreed in mid March 1945, 'must under all circumstances be used efficiently.' 'Given the current crisis, the order of priority for the transports,' Hitler continued, 'must solely be determined by their immediate importance for the conduct of the war.' Hitler therefore laid down that during withdrawals, priority should be given first to the operational forces of the Wehrmacht, then to the transport of coal, then to foodstuffs. 'Even refugee transports can only be authorized after all these needs have been completely satisfied,' he warned, 'if genuinely empty space is available.'[210] Hitler also announced that he expected the military, civil and party authorities to act accordingly, which was also a signal that he did not want them to be the first to take flight.[211] He was well aware of the misery of the refugees, many of whom fled on wagon trains; his decree of 23 March 1945 noted the 'lack of fodder' in the Reich caused by the number of 'trek-horses from the eastern territories'.[212] Towards the end of the month, Hitler relented a little, and gave permission for the priority evacuation of the wounded and refugees from Danzig and Gotenhafen, rather than of the equipment from Pillau.[213]

The net result of the Allied advances and the Anglo-American bombing in March 1945 was the final collapse of the German war economy. With Upper Silesia lost, even Speer threw in the towel. On 15 March 1945, he sent Hitler a memorandum in which he warned that 'the final collapse of the German economy was to be expected with certainty within 4–8 weeks', after which 'the war could no longer be continued militarily'.[214] A few days later, at his last Führerkonferenz, Speer warned Hitler of the effect of Allied attacks on production, especially of steel, which had dropped to two-thirds of previous output.[215] The fall of Danzig knocked out one of three U-boat assembly sites. The Ruhr was about to fall into Allied hands, and it was already effectively cut off from the rest of Germany by the destruction of railways and canals; Hitler was told in late March 1945 that no coal had been received from there for eight days.[216] The Führer was now in the strange situation of having plenty of men, but too few weapons; this was another reason why he baulked at arming the Ukrainians and Indians.[217] He also had more workers than factories to employ them.

Speer's memorandum seems to have induced something close to panic in Hitler. Three days later, he ordered the evacuation of the civilian population of all western territories threatened by the Anglo-American advance, by foot if necessary.[218] This would have involved the flight of millions of people, far more than from East Prussia, Silesia and Pomerania. Here the boot was on the other foot than in the east, where Hitler did his best to discourage people from taking to the road. Most people either welcomed the Anglo-American advance, or simply looked forward to an end to the bombing and shelling. Goebbels, for once, disagreed with Hitler. 'The Führer has now decided,' he recorded in mid March 1945, 'that one should continue to evacuate in the west, despite the extraordinary difficulties that are associated with it.' This was just not practical, Goebbels continued, 'because the population simply refuses to leave their villages and towns'.[219] One would have to use force, and that might backfire. Most people stayed put. After a few days, Speer persuaded Hitler not to proceed with the idea.

A day after ordering the evacuation in the west, Hitler issued his notorious 'Nero Order' (19 March 1945). It demanded that all 'transport, communications, industrial and supply installations' in danger of being overrun by the enemy should be destroyed.[220] One should no longer assume that they could be recaptured intact, because any installations would be wrecked by the Allies before they withdrew. This task was to be carried out by the military authorities. Hitler's decree on industry struck a new and much bleaker tone, because it was effectively an admission that the war was lost. The practical effect was minimal. Speer protested energetically against the measure, which was then qualified by two further decrees. On 30 March 1945, Hitler laid down that 'on no account must the measures taken weaken [our] own fighting capacity'. He also conceded that 'production should be maintained [until the last possible moment]', even at the risk of losing intact plants to 'rapid movements of the enemy'. Factories and other installations were to be destroyed only when they were 'immediately' threatened by the enemy. Wherever possible they were to be 'immobilized' with a view to their later recapture rather than completely destroyed.[221] Clearly, Hitler had overcome his initial panic.

The 'Nero Order' can be interpreted as evidence of Hitler's disenchantment with the German people. According to Speer's account, he believed that, having lost the war, they did not need any economy to sustain them. This view assumes that Hitler moved from an exalted view of the German people to a feeling that they had 'failed' him. In fact, the Führer had always had a very ambivalent attitude towards the German *Volk*. His whole programme, after all, was designed to address its alleged weaknesses. Moreover, we only have Speer's word for it.[222] Neither the Nero Order itself, nor any of Hitler's own correspondence, nor anything he said subsequently suggests that Hitler had given up on the German people. No doubt he became frustrated and even petulant, and he may well have let off steam with Speer, but the intent of his policy was not condemnatory and destructive, but exhortatory and regenerative. The more heroically the German people fell, the Führer believed, the more quickly and completely they would rise again.

Hitler was now preparing for the end. Sometime in the course of March, the air attacks on the Reich capital became so intense that the military briefings were moved underground permanently.[223] On 7 March, despite his request that she remain at Berchtesgaden, Eva Braun joined him in Berlin. The rapid approach of the Allies meant that a siege of the city was imminent. Hitler would now have to decide whether to stay in Berlin or move to some sort of – largely mythical – 'Alpine Redoubt' in the south.[224]

He was still making up his mind. A major consideration in his mind was the threat of Allied air attack. Berchtesgaden was horribly exposed. When he was asked in late March whether it would be permissible to reduce the smokescreen around the Obersalzberg at least in his absence in order to conserve stocks, Hitler reminded his interlocutor that 'that is one of the last bolt-holes we have'. One serious air attack, he predicted, and 'the entire installation will be gone'. For this reason, Hitler seems already to have been tending towards staying in Berlin. A surreal conversation in late March 1945, during which he discussed the question of knocking down the street lights on each side of the 'east–west axis' to enable the creation of a runway to fly in supplies, also suggests that Hitler was disinclined to leave the city.[225]

April 1945 proved to be the last month of Hitler's life. On its first day, the British and Americans surrounded Model's Army Group B in the 'Ruhr Pocket'.[226] Many of his men lacked basic firearms, such was the lack of equipment, or at least of transport to bring it to the front, despite the fact that they were fighting in what had been the industrial heart of the Reich. Hitler rejected a request for aerial resupply out of hand. In northern Germany, the British reached the Elbe. Hitler, who was anxious to prevent the northern half of the Reich being cut off, stressed that the river 'should be seen not as a defensive line but as lifeline for the north German space' which had to be kept open.[227] Just over a week later, the British attacked on the eastern side of the Italian peninsula, and five days after that the Americans began their own offensive on the western side. Five days later again, the Allies secured a breakthrough on the entire Italian front. On 14 April 1945, the Anglo-Americans split the Ruhr Pocket in two. The eastern half surrendered on 16 April 1945, followed by the western half a day later. An entire army group of nineteen divisions – 350,000 men – went into Anglo-American captivity. It was by far the largest single German surrender of the war. Their commander, Field Marshal Model, committed suicide a few days later. The Allied forces now fanned out in all directions. On 19/20 April, the Americans captured Leipzig. Eisenhower held back, however, from a direct attack on Berlin.

In the air, the assault on German infrastructure and cities continued, at a slightly slower pace than the previous month. These were now blows upon bruises. Most of the targets had already been attacked many times before. The attacks were not, however, random or sadistic, but followed a clear military or political rationale.[228] On 9/10 April, the RAF sank the *Admiral Scheer* in Kiel harbour. The following afternoon, Dönitz reported to Hitler that no fewer than twenty-four U-boats had been destroyed in shipyards and harbours since the start of the month, and another twelve damaged.[229] Six days later, the RAF sent the *Lützow* to the bottom at Swinemünde. On 10 April the RAF, which had already launched thirteen raids on Plauen in Saxony, completed the destruction of that unfortunate city. The USAAF hit Dresden again on 17 April. On 18 April 1945, the RAF launched a massive air-raid on the tiny island of Heligoland in the North Sea, mainly in order to destroy the U-boat installations there. That same night, the British launched their last attack on Berlin. Hitler followed these raids closely and wordlessly in his bunker. There was very little he could do about them. In desperation, the Luftwaffe mounted 'Operation Werewolf' over the Steinhuder Meer, which involved the sacrificial deployment of 'ramming fighters' to crash directly into the Allied bombers. That same day, the Japanese *kamikaze* pilots launched themselves against the American fleet off Okinawa.

Meanwhile, the Russians progressively eliminated the German pockets of resistance along the Baltic, which were being resupplied by the Kriegsmarine, and moved ever closer to Berlin. Hitler upbraided the Wehrmacht for being unwilling, by contrast with the 'Anglo-Saxons', to fight with their backs against the sea.[230] On 9 April 1945, Königsberg surrendered. Hitler ordered its commander, General Lasch, to be condemned to death in absentia and gave orders for the arrest of his family. At Hitler's insistence, in keeping with his submarine strategy, the Wehrmacht still clung to Kurland and indeed remained there until the end of the war. These highly trained divisions, some of them armoured, were missing on the central front, where the next Soviet blow was to be expected. By 9 April, the Red Army was advancing into central Vienna and the city surrendered four days later. Hitler followed all these developments closely, frequently intervening in decisions, but there was now an increasing air of unreality as he engaged in pointless command reshuffles, reorganized non-existent units, and brooded for hours over Giesler and Speer's architectural models.

In mid April 1945, Hitler was still hoping against hope that he could split the Allied coalition, either by delivering a devastating blow with the new weaponry, through exploiting the internal contradictions of the Grand Alliance or through some other miracle.[231] He was determined to maintain his military capability, refusing, for example, to guarantee no first use of his substantial remaining stocks of chemical weapons.[232] On 12 April, his spirits soared when he heard of the sudden death of President Roosevelt.[233] Hitler's euphoria reflected the extent to which he had long regarded the American president as the linchpin of a global coalition against him. It proved infectious, at least for a few moments. That evening, Bormann rang his *Gauleiter* to tell them that Roosevelt's death was 'the best news we have had for years' and that they should announce to 'all men that the most dangerous man of this war is dead'.[234] Three days later, Wolff came to report on the progress of negotiations with the Allies in northern Italy, though it is doubtful that he told Hitler the truth about how far they had developed.[235]

The physical and mental pressure on Hitler was now immense. Dönitz speaks of his 'great spiritual strain' and 'extraordinary inner suffering'. Hitler was also increasingly prone to choleric eruptions against all and sundry, principally the Wehrmacht leadership. 'Though generally controlled and stoic,' Dönitz testified, 'he could very easily become agitated to the extent of erupting in powerful rages.' Despite this, most accounts agree that Hitler remained lucid until shortly before the end, and perhaps to the very end. Kesselring, the commander in the west, who last saw him on 12 April 1945, spoke of his continuing 'intellectual vigour', which stood 'in conspicuous contradiction to his bodily feeling'.[236] Dönitz, whose final meeting with Hitler was nine days later, states that 'there can be no question of any kind of reduction in his intellectual powers'. Hitler, he insisted, remained in full control of his senses and retained his astonishing technical knowledge.[237]

Far from closing his eyes to the military realities, Hitler was now preparing for the inevitable moment when the Reich would be split in half, either by the British advance on the Elbe, or a meeting between the American and Soviet forces east of Leipzig.[238] On 15 April, he issued an instruction for a revised command structure for the eventuality of 'interruption of the land connection in central Germany'. Hitler left open which part of the Reich he would choose, stating only that he would retain supreme command there. If he found himself in the southern half of the Reich, then command in the north should pass to Admiral Dönitz. In the event of Hitler ending up in the northern half, the command of the southern part of the Reich would pass to Kesselring. 'For the rest,' he added, there would be 'no change' in the current 'unified conduct of operations by myself', at least so long as the communications situation permitted.[239]

On 16 April, the Red Army launched a massive attack on the Seelow Heights above the Oder.[240] That same day, Hitler issued his last *Tagesbefehl*, addressing the 'soldiers of the eastern front'. It was a blood-curdling warning that the 'Jewish Bolshevik mortal enemy' planned 'to smash Germany and to exterminate our people'. If they did their duty, he promised, then 'this last assault of Asia' would be repulsed, just as the 'breach' made by the 'enemies in the west' would be dealt with.[241] 'In this moment, in which fate has removed the greatest war criminal of all times [Roosevelt] from the face of the earth,' he concluded, 'the turning point of this war will be decided.' He also sent reinforcements, mainly *Volkssturm* and Hitler Youth anti-tank teams.[242] To the north, Rokossovsky's Second

White Russian Front advanced into Mecklenburg, covering Zhukov's drive on Berlin. To the south, Koniev's Ukrainian Front pushed back Schörner's Army Group Centre and swung north towards the capital. Within a few days, the Wehrmacht was forced to fall back to Berlin. Hitler was now relying on Gruppe Steiner, north of Berlin, Busse's 9th Army to the south-east and Walther Wenck's 12th Army to the south-west of the capital to come to his rescue.

In the midst of the confusion, Hitler celebrated his fifty-sixth birthday. On 20 April 1945, virtually the entire Nazi political and military leadership assembled to congratulate their Führer one last time. The mood, unsurprisingly, was subdued, not helped by the final Allied air raid on the city.[243] Many of those present urged Hitler to leave the city for Berchtesgaden before it was too late. Hitler seems to have seriously considered doing so, because on the same day he issued Dönitz with instructions to prepare for the 'immediate' defence of the 'north', which suggest that he himself was intending to head south.[244] That afternoon, Hitler was filmed in the Chancellery garden decorating a delegation of Hitler Youth who had distinguished themselves against the Russians; it is the last known footage of the Führer. His hand was visibly shaking. The next day, Hitler was woken up by Russian gunfire; the first Soviet long-range artillery shells landed in the city. Zhukov was moving much more quickly than expected. Thanks to the huge forces still deployed in Kurland, Scandinavia and elsewhere, Hitler only had about 100,000 men to defend the capital, many fewer than in the Baltic, most of them of doubtful value. On 22 April 1945, Hitler was again woken by the sound of Russian artillery,[245] now closer. That same day, a relief offensive by Steiner, in which the Führer had vested all his hopes, never materialized. Hitler reacted with an eruption in front of a small number of generals which has gone down in legend. Contemporaries speak of him having some kind of 'breakdown'.

That same day, Hitler pulled himself together and announced his decision to stay in Berlin. His motivation for doing so was clear. Hitler had given up all hope of winning the war or securing an acceptable negotiated peace. Flying to Berchtesgaden would only prolong the agony, and he had already said that he would be vulnerable to Allied air attack there. Hitler's main consideration, though, was narratival. Posterity would never forgive him for an ignominious flight from the Reich capital and a chase across the Alps. In his own mind, at least, he had not fled Rastenburg before the advancing Red Army, but had moved his headquarters west to supervise the offensive in the Ardennes. He told Jodl and Keitel that he should not have left the Wolf's Lair after all, but should have fallen at his post there. Now he said that he would stay to motivate the defenders of Berlin.[246] The war diary of the OKW for that day records that Hitler had decided 'as far as his person was concerned not to take evasive action towards the south, but to lead the battle in Berlin in person and remain in the Reich Chancellery'.[247] His aim was to die heroically as an inspiration to the remaining forces of the Third Reich under his successor, but above all to future generations. Hitler had often spoken of the 'ruin value' of buildings,[248] and he now proposed to maximize the *Ruinenwert* of his own body.

On 23 April, Hitler let it be known through Goebbels that he had taken over personal command of the defence of Berlin. 'The Führer,' as the war diary of the OKW put it in accordance with the approved narrative, 'resides in the Reich capital [and] this fact gives the battle for Berlin the character of a battle of European importance.'[249] Privately, in Hitler's presence, Goebbels spelled out the thinking behind the decision to remain in Berlin. 'If things go well,' he said, 'then everything is fine anyway.' 'If it doesn't go well,' Goebbels continued, 'and if the Führer were to find an honourable death in Berlin and Europe were to become Bolshevik,' then 'in five years at latest, the Führer would be a legendary personality'. 'National Socialism', he went on, would become 'a myth' and the Führer would be 'hallowed by his last great action', so that 'everything human that they criticize in him today would be swept away with one blow.'[250]

This strategy shaped Hitler's ambivalent attitude to his entourage in the last week or so of his life. On the one hand, he had made a number of references to making a final stand surrounded by his generals and trusted party comrades. On the other hand, he wanted the struggle to continue, which required at least some of them to escape Berlin and carry on the fight. What Hitler seems to have had in mind was not a move to partisan warfare – the guerilla force *Werwolf* was originally an SS initiative in which he showed little interest[251] – but a longer conventional defence to inspire future generations. The Führer actually ordered Keitel, Jodl and Bormann to head south in order to conduct the 'overall operations' from there.[252] This explains why Hitler was both personally disappointed at the number of party leaders scrambling to leave the city[253] and content to let them depart. He had no intention of taking either them or any of his other followers hostage. On the contrary, Hitler urged those with no useful function – secretaries, cooks and ministers alike – to leave the city.[254] He told Morell to go home, get rid of his uniform and 'act as if you had never known me'.[255] Some needed no encouragement. Speer, who was summoned to say goodbye when Hitler heard that he was in the vicinity, did not even get a handshake in a cool parting.[256] Others, including Eva Braun and some of the secretaries, refused to leave. So did Keitel, Jodl and Bormann.

Despite his blood-curdling rhetoric, it was not the Führer's expectation or desire that the defeat of the Third Reich would result in the annihilation of the German people. He fully expected that negotiations would take place after his death,[257] told his foreign minister to make sure that the embassies abroad remained in good working order, and gave him permission to go to Nauen, where the last remaining communications centre with contact to the outside world was located;[258] he never got there. In his last meeting with Ribbentrop on or shortly after 20 April 1945 Hitler conceded for the first time, at least to him, that the war was lost. He then gave Ribbentrop a list of four points to guide his future discussions with the British. Firstly, that the maintenance of German unity was in Britain's interest in order to balance the Soviet Union. Secondly, to maintain the European national states if necessary under the mutual guarantee of the great powers. Thirdly, the establishment of a close Anglo-German understanding up to and including a union with the British Empire, if necessary with its capital in London. Fourthly, the preservation of the national elements in Germany because it was on these that Britain and the United States would have to depend to preserve the European balance of power.[259] The echoes of Hitler's earlier rhetoric towards Britain, and indeed Hess's recent abortive mission, are unmistakable.

The Führer now prepared to defend not merely Berlin, but the Chancellery to the last. He appointed SS-Brigadeführer Wilhelm Mohnke the *Kampfkommandant*. He gave instructions for his papers to be burned. Walther Wenck's 12th Army was tasked with the relief of Berlin, and immediately began a forlorn attempt to reach the city.[260] Hitler also ordered the entire front against the 'Anglo-Saxons' to turn and face the Russians.[261] For the first time, the whole German war effort was to be directed against the Bolsheviks. Late on 23 April he radioed Dönitz to send all possible help to Berlin; all other fronts, he stressed, were secondary.[262] A day later, he subordinated the OKH under OKW with a view to the 'continuation of the overall operations'.[263] He also gave permission for the backlog of railway wagons to be unloaded where they stood and the equipment distributed to the local army groups.[264] He continued to express his hope that the Bolsheviks and the 'Anglo-Saxons' would fall out among themselves 'within the hour'.[265] Over the next few days, he fired off a string of further orders, such as a demand for a 'concentric relief attack on Berlin', and issued increasingly fantastical instructions for other fronts.[266] By now, as some wags pointed out, it was possible to travel between the eastern and western fronts by S-Bahn; truly Hitler was operating on interior lines. The purpose of all these activities and exhortations, which seem delusional in retrospect, was not military, however, but political.

The military situation continued to deteriorate. 25 April 1945 was particularly bad. Koniev's spearheads met with those of Zhukov. Berlin was surrounded. It was also on that day that the American and Soviet forces met at Torgau, cutting the Reich in half, and that the delegates of the anti-Hitler United Nations coalition assembled at San Francisco to establish a permanent organization. Finally, 25 April 1945 saw the last major RAF operation in Europe when 350 Lancasters – manned by crews from Britain, Australia, Canada, Rhodesia and Poland – appeared over the Obersalzberg. The Berghof itself took three direct hits and was seriously damaged, though not destroyed.[267] The bombers missed the Kehlsteinhaus altogether. Göring, who was in residence, was unhurt. Still, the RAF had made an important political and psychological point. Hitler was not safe anywhere. He had now been 'bombed out' of two homes.

In the last week of April, Hitler's hopes for a carefully choreographed death began to unravel.[268] On 23 April, he received a telegram from Göring stating that if he received no reply by a certain time, he would assume that Hitler was dead and take over the succession as chancellor in accordance with the decree of 1941. This was almost certainly not a coup, but rather an attempt by Göring to jump the gun in starting negotiations. Hitler seems to have ignored the message and reacted only later on that evening when Göring – who had heard nothing and must have assumed that the Führer was dead or incapacitated – sent Ribbentrop a telegram to the same effect. The Führer responded with a radio message to Göring rescinding his right to the succession and declaring his behaviour 'a betrayal of my person and of the National Socialist cause'. 'I enjoy,' he insisted, 'full freedom of action,' adding that he 'forbade' Göring from undertaking any 'further measures'.[269] Hitler ordered that Göring be placed under arrest at Berchtesgaden, which was done immediately, but he did not order him shot out of hand. Two days later, Hermann Fegelein went absent without leave from the bunker, though nobody seems to have noticed at first. Soon after, however, Hitler received news that Himmler had been in unauthorized communication with the Western Allies. This was a serious blow both to the Führer personally and to his heroic narrative of a nation and party fighting to the last. Himmler was sacked.[270] It was in this context that Fegelein, who appears to have been involved in the Reichsführer's activities, was hauled back to the bunker and executed, not for desertion but for treason.

Matters came to a head on 28 April 1945. Hitler heard that Mussolini had not only been captured and executed with his mistress Clara Petacci by Italian partisans, but that his body had been desecrated by a mob. One of his secretaries recalls that the news distressed him deeply.[271] There was a shortlived rising against the Nazis in Munich.[272] The Russians were closing in on the Chancellery. Hitler sent out a series of frantic messages calling for help before it was too late.[273] He was now cut off from the outside world, literally, because the communications team in the bunker had left. A break-out was not feasible, at least not for Hitler, given his physical condition. Nor could he, with his shaking arms and legs, hope to go down fighting with a gun in his hands, as he would ideally liked to have done. There was now a real risk that he would be captured alive below ground, or on the run in the ruins or forests. The Führer might then meet the same fate as the *Duce*, which would have substantially reduced his 'ruin value'.

Hitler resolved to make an end of it.[274] He announced his intention to commit suicide. First he married Eva Braun in a low-key ceremony just before midnight on 28 April, though in the thirty-six hours or so of their marriage he still seems to have referred to her as Fräulein. Then he took his leave of his entourage. Hitler did not insist or even suggest that they follow his example. Instead, Hitler dictated two testaments, a personal and a political one. He was expecting the struggle to continue without him and gave detailed instructions for the fortification of the 'core fortress Alps'.[275] On 29 April, the military position worsened. The British crossed the Elbe at Lauenburg. The Russians inched closer to the Chancellery. Mohnke, the military commander of the Chancellery compound, warned Hitler that he could only hold another day, perhaps two. On 30 April, the US 7th Army occupied Munich. Hitler also received news that Wenck's offensive had finally petered out.[276] There would be no relief force. The Russians were now a few hundred metres from the bunker. That after-noon, between 15.15 and 15.30 Hitler and Mrs Hitler retired to his tiny living room in the bunker. Exactly what happened is not known for sure. It appears that Eva Hitler took poison and that Hitler shot himself imme-diately after. The two bodies were then taken out and burned in the garden of the Chancellery.[277]

Late on 1 May, German radio announced his death. 'The Führer has fallen at the head of the valiant defenders of the imperial capital,' the report went. 'Driven by the will to save his people and Europe from Bol-shevism,' it continued, 'he sacrificed his life.' 'This example of "loyalty unto death",' the report concluded, 'is obligatory for all soldiers.'[278] As far as the circumstances of his demise were concerned, the statement was figuratively if not literally true. Its real distortion lay in the claim that Hitler had died resisting Bolshevism. Not only had his main enemy throughout been western plutocratic international capitalism, not only had Hitler been more responsible than any other person for bringing the communist juggernaut into the heart of Europe, but his entire strategy, right to the end, was predicated on using the spectre of Bolshevism, even encouraging its growth, to deliver political effect in Germany, Europe and above all Anglo-America.

When Hitler's testaments were opened they contained some surprises with regard to his personal life, and choices of personnel.[279] He distributed his worldly goods to various relatives and friends and explained why he had married Eva Braun. Hitler separated the offices of chancellor, which went to Goebbels, and the presidency, which went to Dönitz. Himmler and Göring were expelled from the party. Karl Hanke was made the new Reichsführer-SS. Bormann became party minister. Schörner was made supreme commander of the army. Saur was made armaments minister, a sure sign that Speer had departed in bad odour.

Their policy content, by contrast, was entirely predictable. Hitler bound the new government over to 'the strict observance of the racial laws' and to maintain 'a merciless resistance against the world-poisoners of the peoples, international Jewry'. He claimed that 'the sacrifice of our soldiers and my own connection with them into death' would 'one day' provide the 'seed for the achievement of a true People's Community'. The choice of Dönitz as president reflected not only the admiral's strategic salience in the last six months of the war, and his own fanatical National Socialism, but also Hitler's conviction that he was best placed to inspire the revival of Germany after his own death. This is clear from the praise for which he singled out the navy. 'May it once again be part of the German officer's sense of honour,' he wrote, 'as is already the case with the navy, that the surrender of a city or a territory is impossible and that the leaders, in particular, must lead from the front in this manner in the loyal fulfilment of duty until death.'

The rest of the document would also have been no surprise to anyone who had followed Hitler's rhetoric and policy since 1919. He reiterated his view that the war was 'desired and provoked solely by those international statesmen who were either of Jewish origin or who worked for Jewish interests'. 'I never wanted,' Hitler continued, 'that the first unholy world war' should have been followed by 'a second one against Britain or even America.' He lamented that German cities and cultural treasures had been reduced to 'ruins', that millions of adult males had died at the front, and that hundreds of thousands of women and children had been burned in their cities, but reminded his readers that he had 'left no one in any doubt' that the 'real guilty party' – the Jews – 'would have to pay for their guilt', if 'by more humane means'. This was an oblique, but unmistakable reference to his mass murder of the Jews in the gas chambers, the guillotine of genocide. Strikingly, this Last Will and Testament made no mention of either communism or the Soviet Union, but inveighed instead against the real villains: 'international money and finance conspirators', who treated the 'peoples of Europe' like 'blocks of shares'. He was referring, of course, to the same international capitalists, most of them Jewish, that he had targeted in his first political statements back in 1919. As in the beginning, so at the end.

Conclusion

The life of Adolf Hitler remains perhaps the most extraordinary story in modern history. Coming from a relatively humble background, he rose to dominate much of continental Europe. On the way, Hitler mastered a series of challenges, each of which could have ended his ascent there and then. Periods of disappointment and destitution in Vienna were followed by extremely hazardous service in the First World War. Hitler not only threaded his way through the post-war turbulences, but carved out a niche for the NSDAP in the thicket of competing right-wing nationalist organizations in Munich. He rallied the movement after a disastrous coup attempt, trial and subsequent imprisonment. Hitler then persuaded more and more Germans to vote for him, and manipulated or bullied the coterie around President von Hindenburg into making him chancellor. He revived the German economy, or appeared to do so, eliminated all domestic dissent, and embarked on an unprecedented programme of rearmament. Hitler then greatly enlarged German territory without firing a shot, and in the first two years of war, scored some remarkable military victories. At each stage, things could have gone wrong for him, for example, his personal intervention against Röhm, the remilitarization of the Rhineland, the Munich crisis, the Norway campaign and the audacious attack in the west.

Of course, Hitler benefited from the support, complicity and stupidity of others, and from sheer good luck, at home and abroad. But for the early sponsorship by the Reichswehr, the NSDAP might never have got off the ground. Without the Depression, Hitler might not have gained the electoral traction which brought him to the threshold of power in 1932. If the old elites had not miscalculated, he might never have been made chancellor. Hitler's first years in power depended on the collaboration of many institutional actors, who shared a partial identity of aims with him. On the international scene, most statesmen and publics did not recognize the threat he posed until very late in the day. Some regarded Hitler as the best hope against the spread of Bolshevism, others had a sneaking and often very open regard for the way in which he challenged the established order.

During the early stages of the Second World War, his enemies were weak or incompetent, or both.

That said, it would be wrong to think that Hitler could have been deterred. His Germany was always sooner or later going to seek *Lebensraum*, which for him was not a matter of greed but of necessity, though the precise timing remained open for a long time. He was always going to fight the Jews, though not necessarily to exterminate them. Resistance only infuriated him. The May crisis of 1938 doomed the Czechs, the Franco-British guarantee doomed Poland, and the war, or at least the US entry into it, doomed European Jewry. Hitler could certainly have been pre-empted or stopped, if the western powers had been prepared to go to war with him earlier, before he occupied so much of Europe, but we would then never have known what he was capable of.

Hitler's career was, of course, ultimately a catastrophic failure. None of his objectives were met, and although he appeared to come close to triumph on a number of occasions, in reality the dice were too heavily loaded against him. Hitler knew this very well, but he also believed that even if the chances of success were no more than a few per cent, it was worth the attempt. Refusal even to try to escape the German predicament at the heart of Europe, he argued, would mean guaranteed death without any hope of renewal. A bold strike against the global hegemon, by contrast, might just come off, Hitler hoped, and if it did not, then a glorious choreographed defeat would provide the basis for national regeneration at a later date.

The Anglo-American capitalist world order against which Hitler revolted structured his entire political career. Sometime before he ever began to speak about the Jews, Hitler experienced the might of the British Empire in Flanders, the demographic and industrial power of the United States at the second Battle of the Marne and the economic stranglehold of global capitalism after the imposition of the Versailles Treaty. Shortly after, he became convinced that the Jews – whose relationship with Anglo-America was in his view essentially symbiotic – were the driving force behind international capitalism and the coalition which had brought down the Reich. Among the instruments used to undermine Germany from within, Hitler believed, was the virus of Bolshevism, which he regarded as a much greater threat than the Soviet Union itself. The root of his Jew-hatred, therefore, was primarily to be found in his hostility to global high finance rather than his hatred of the radical left. Those who do not want to speak about Hitler's anti-capitalism should remain silent on his anti-Semitism.

Hitler's solution to the perceived German predicament fell into two parts. First of all, he called for a programme of racial transformation within Germany, which eliminated 'harmful' elements, especially the Jews, and encouraged the 'elevation' of the racial 'high value' strands in the German *Volk*. Secondly, Hitler demanded the acquisition of *Lebensraum* in the east, which would provide the land and resources to offer a comparable living standard to the United States, and thus end the debilitating emigration of the nation's best and brightest, who might return as enemy soldiers at some future date. It would also make Germany 'blockade-proof' in the event of a renewed round of warfare with Anglo-America.

If Hitler's relationship with the British Empire and the United States was ultimately antagonistic, it was also admiring and entangled. He long hoped for a British alliance and he never ceased to exalt the supposed racial qualities of the 'Anglo-Saxons' on both sides of the Atlantic, and to believe that they represented Germany's 'better' racial half. Anglo-America was Hitler's model, much more so than Stalin's Russia or even Mussolini's Italy. The original for the *Lebensraum* project was the British Empire, and especially the American colonization of the west. Hitler and the Third Reich were thus a reaction not to the Russian Revolution but to the dominance of Anglo-America and global capitalism. The Holocaust was not a distorted copy of Stalin's Great Terror, but a pre-emptive strike against Roosevelt's America.

After he came to power, the British Empire and the United States remained the focal point of Hitler's policies. His entire domestic programme was designed to match the 'living standards' offered by the 'American Dream'. His true nemesis was the British Empire and especially the United States, against whom he battled for control of the 'trophy' of the 'world'. It was Roosevelt's hostility which caused Hitler to speed up his programme from late 1937, British resistance during the May crisis of 1938 which led him to bring forward the dismemberment of Czechoslovakia. The struggle against Britain and America eventually 'forced' Hitler to go to war against them both, and then to extend the theatre of operations ever more widely. The quest for *Lebensraum* led to conflict with Britain over Poland, which in turn 'required' him to occupy much of Scandinavia, France, the Low Countries, the Balkans and North Africa. It drove the attack on Russia. Hitler had originally set out to make Germany a world power, not to achieve global domination, but each gain seemed to require another. By 1941–2, when he was directing operations on three continents, and across the seven seas, it seemed as if only the world would be enough for Hitler. But the prize eluded him: the trophy was lifted once more by the Anglo-Americans, with substantial help from their Soviet allies, of course.

Hitler thus proved no more successful against the 'world of enemies' than the Reich had been during the First World War. On this occasion, though, death and destruction were visited on the civilian population long before the front line reached Germany, not through a blockade, but by means of a relentless campaign of aerial terror. For all the Führer's great architectural visions, the face of German cities after 1945 owed much more to Arthur Harris of RAF Bomber Command than Adolf Hitler. In 1938, Hitler joked that the building work at the new Imperial Chancellery made the area look like the forest of Houthulst in Flanders after four years of British bombardment during the last war. Seven years later, three years of bombing by the RAF and USAAF had reduced not only the Chancellery but huge stretches of urban Germany to a similar condition. In the first war, and immediately afterwards, the British Empire and the United States had starved and pauperized the Reich; in the second war, they pulverized it. The mills of the Anglo-Americans ground slowly, but they ground exceeding small.

Hitler made five key judgements throughout his career. Firstly, he was preoccupied by the power of 'the Jews'. This he wildly exaggerated, to the extent that the centrality of anti-Semitism in his world view can only be described as paranoid. Secondly, Hitler largely discounted the Soviet Union, whose strength he massively underestimated. This was a miscalculation which came back to haunt him. Thirdly, Hitler was convinced of the overwhelming power of Anglo-America. This, as we have seen, he got exactly right. Fourthly and relatedly, Hitler believed that the Germans he actually ruled – as opposed to the people he planned to breed – were too weak and fragmented to prevail against the 'Anglo-Saxons', the global 'master race'. This also turned out to be entirely accurate, although of course it is unlikely that he would have secured a better outcome for himself, even if he had had the 'time' to 'elevate' the German people at his leisure. Fifthly and finally, Hitler had predicted that the Reich would be a 'world power' or 'nothing', and here too he was vindicated, even if this was something of a self-fulfilling prophecy.

It is therefore a terrible irony that Hitler made the very same mistakes that he was determined to avoid after his searching inquest into the causes of the German defeat in 1918. He vowed never to fight a two-front war, but he did. He promised to find better allies than the Kaiser had, preferably the British, and dismissed the 'Pan-Europa' project of the 1920s, yet ended up facing much of the world with a rabble of mostly minor European statelets, and global non-state actors. The formidable Japanese aside, this was truly the 'coalition of cripples' he had lampooned in Mein Kampf. He wanted more than anything else to avoid another struggle with the children of German emigrants, or a production battle with the 'German engineers' on the far side of the Atlantic, and yet his Reich faced Carl Spaatz's bombers in the air and Dwight Eisenhower's armies on the ground. Thanks to Hitler's policies, the sons of Germany returned once more to confront the Fatherland. If in 1917–18, they chastised the Reich with whips, in 1941–5 they scourged it with scorpions. Hitler's second war was thus even more catastrophic than his first. History repeated itself, the first time as defeat, the second time as annihilation.

Notes

Prologue

1. Report F. Wiedemann (Brigade Adjutant), 17.7.1918, BayHSTA, no. 10, 'Stab Juli 1918', fo. 37. 2. Speech, 6.8.1927, RSA, II, p. 446. In a similar vein: Speech, 4.8.1929, RSA, III/2, p. 347; and Speech, 18.1.1928, RSA, II/2, p. 633.

Introduction

1. Frank Schirrmacher, 'Wir haben ihn uns engagiert', Frankfurter Allgemeine Zeitung, 6.10.1998. 2. Alan Bullock, Hitler: A Study in Tyranny (London, 1954), pp. 735–6. 3. Joachim C. Fest, Hitler. Eine Biographie (Frankfurt, 1973). For a recent critique see Magnus Brechtken, 'Joachim Fest und der 20 Juli. Geschichtsbilder, Vergangenheitskonstruktionen, Narrative', in Magnus Brechtken, Christoph Cornelissen and Christopher Dowe (eds.), Verräter? Vorbilder? Verbrecher? Kontroverse Deutungen des 20. Juli 1944 seit 1945, Geschichtswissenschaft 25 (Berlin, 2017), pp. 161–82, especially pp. 169–72. The influential German weekly Der Spiegel, 14.1.2008, describes the phrase 'how it could have come to this' as the 'key question' of German history (Königsfrage). 4. Ian Kershaw, Hitler: Hubris, 1889–1936 (London, 1998), and Hitler: Nemesis, 1936–1945 (London, 2000). See also his Hitler (London and New York, 1991). Some idea of the extent of the research on Hitler since Fest can gained from Gerhard Hirschfeld and Lothar Kettewacker (eds.), Der 'Führerstaat', Mythos und Realität. Studien zur Struktur und Politik des Dritten Reiches (Stuttgart, 1981); Gerhard Schreiber, Hitler-Interpretationen, 1923–1983. Ergebnisse, Methoden und Probleme der Forschung (Darmstadt, 1988); Ian Kershaw, The Nazi Dictatorship: Problems and Perspectives of Interpretation (London, 2015); and Elizabeth Harvey and Johannes Hürter, Hitler: New Research (Berlin and Boston, 2018). 5. Thus Hellmuth Auerbach, 'Hitlers politische Lehrjahre und die Münchener Gesellschaft 1919–1923', Vierteljahrshefte für Zeitgeschichte, 25 (1977); and Hermann Graml, 'Probleme einer Hitler-Biographie. Kritische Bemerkungen zu Joachim C. Fest', Vierteljahrshefte für Zeitgeschichte, 22 (1974), pp. 76–92. 6. Kershaw, Hubris, p. xxvi. Richard J. Evans remarked that Kershaw had written 'less a biography of Hitler than a history of Hitler', 'Review article: new perspectives on Hitler', Journal of Contemporary History, 37 (2002), pp. 147–152 (quotation, p. 150). 7. See Neil Gregor, 'Nazism – a political religion? Rethinking the voluntarist turn', in Neil Gregor (ed.), Nazism, War and Genocide: New Perspectives on the History of the Third Reich (Exeter, 2008), pp. 1–21. 8. Ian Kershaw, The 'Hitler Myth': Image and Reality in the Third Reich (Oxford, 1987). 9. Ian Kershaw, ' "Working towards the Führer": reflections on the nature of the Hitler dictatorship', Contemporary European History, 2 (1991), pp. 103–18. 10. E.g. Ralf Georg Reuth, Hitler. Eine politische Biographie (Munich, 2003). 11. Volker Ullrich, Adolf Hitler. Biographie, vol. 1: Die Jahre des Aufstiegs, 1889–1939 (Frankfurt, 2013), vol. 2: Die Jahre des Untergangs (Frankfurt, 2018). 12. Peter Longerich, Hitler. Biographie (Munich, 2015). 13. Wolfram Pyta, Hitler. Der Künstler als Politiker und Feldherr. Eine Herrschaftsanalyse (Munich, 2015). 14. Hans-Ulrich Thamer, Adolf Hitler.

Biographie eines Diktators (Munich, 2018).   **15.** It does not answer most of the questions thrown up by Thomas Kühne, 'Zwischen Akribie und Groteske. Variationen der "Normalisierung" Adolf Hitlers', *Historische Zeitschrift*, 304 (2017), pp. 405–22.   **16.** For a range of contemporary views see Hermann Pölking, *Wer war Hitler. Ansichten und Berichte von Zeitgenossen* (Berlin, 2017), and Philipp Fabry, *Mutmaßungen über Hitler. Urteile von Zeitgenossen* (Düsseldorf, 1969).   **17.** For 'positive' and 'negative' eugenics, see Daniel J. Kevles, 'International eugenics', in *Deadly Medicine: Creating the Master Race* (Washington, DC, 2004), pp. 41–59, especially p. 50.   **18.** For example Sebastian Conrad, *Globalisation and the Nation in Imperial Germany* (Cambridge, 2010), pp. 10–11, 275–333 *et passim*; and Sebastian Conrad and Jürgen Osterhammel (eds.), *Das Kaiserreich International. Deutschland in der Welt, 1871–1914*, 2nd edn (Göttingen, 2006).   **19.** Michael David-Fox, Peter Holquist and Alexander M. Martin (eds.), *Fascination and Enmity: Russia and Germany as Entangled Histories, 1914–1945* (Pittsburgh, 2012). See also Stefan Ihrig, 'Review article: the history of European fascism – origins, foreign relations and (dis-)entangled histories', *European History Quarterly*, 41 (2011), 278–90, which is mainly about the connections to Spain, Turkey, Italy and Russia.   **20.** Thus Thomas L. Friedman, *The World Is Flat. A Brief History of the 21st Century* (New York, 2005), p. 395.   **21.** E.g. Sven Beckert, 'American danger: United States Empire, Eurafrica, and the territorialization of industrial capitalism, 1870–1950', *American Historical Review*, 122 (2017), pp. 1137–70.   **22.** See Tim Snyder, *Black Earth: The Holocaust as History and Warning* (London, 2015).   **23.** Duncan Bell, 'Founding the world state: H. G. Wells on empire and the English-speaking peoples', *International Studies Quarterly*, 62 (2018), pp. 867–79; Madeleine Herren, *Internationale Organisationen seit 1865. Eine Globalgeschichte der internationalen Ordnung* (Darmstadt, 2009), especially pp. 73–84.   **24.** Thus John M. Hobson, 'Re-embedding the global colour line within post-1945 international theory', in Alexander Anievas, Nivi Manchanda and Robbie Shilliam (eds.), *Race and Racism in International Relations: Confronting the Global Colour Line* (London and New York, 2015), pp. 81–97; Duncan Bell, *The Idea of Greater Britain: Empire and the Future of World Order, 1860–1900* (Princeton and Oxford, 2007); Srdjan Vucetic, *The Anglosphere: A Genealogy of Racialized Identity in International Relations* (Stanford, 2011).   **25.** James Belich, *Replenishing the Earth: The Settler Revolution and the Rise of the Anglo-World, 1783–1939* (Oxford, 2009).   **26.** Aimé Césaire, *Discourse on Colonialism* (New York, 2000), p. 36. For an intriguing if eccentric subaltern interpretation of Hitler see Manuel Sarkisyanz, *From Imperialism to Fascism: Why Hitler's 'India' Was to Be Russia* (Delhi, 2003), and *Hitler's English Inspirers* (Belfast, 2003).   **27.** See Geoff Eley, 'Empire, ideology, and the east: thoughts on Nazism's spatial imaginary', in idem, *Nazism as Fascism: Violence, Ideology, and the Ground of Consent in Germany, 1930–1945* (London and New York, 2013), pp. 131–55.   **28.** E.g. Christopher Clark, *Time and Power: Visions of History in German Politics from the Thirty Years' War to the Third Reich* (Princeton, NJ, 2019); and Allegra Fryxell, 'Turning back the clock? The politics of time in Restoration Europe, 1815–1830', in Michael Broers and Ambrogio Caiani (eds.), *Restoration Europe* (New York, 2018).   **29.** A good cross section of this work can be found in Gregor (ed.), *Nazism, War and Genocide*; and Devin O. Pendas, Mark Roseman and Richard Wetzell (eds.), *Beyond the Racial State: Rethinking Nazi Germany* (Cambridge, 2017).   **30.** Mark Mazower, *Hitler's Empire: How the Nazis Ruled Europe* (London, 2008).   **31.** Adam Tooze, *The Wages of Destruction: The Making and Breaking of the Nazi Economy* (London, 2006).   **32.** Mary Nolan, *The Transatlantic Century: Europe and America, 1890–2010* (Cambridge, 2012); Philipp Gassert, *Amerika im Dritten Reich. Ideologie, Propaganda, und Volksmeinung, 1933–1945* (Stuttgart, 1997); Stefan Kühl, *The Nazi Connection: Eugenics, American Racism and German National Socialism* (Oxford, 1994).   **33.** Johann Chapoutot, *The Law of Blood: Thinking and Acting as a Nazi* (Cambridge, Mass., 2018).   **34.** Lars Lüdicke, *Hitlers Weltanschauung. Von 'Mein Kampf' bis zum 'Nero-Befehl'* (Paderborn, 2016), p. 43 *et passim*.   **35.** Dirk Bavendamm, *Der junge Hitler. Korrekturen einer Biographie, 1889–1914* (Graz, 2009); Brigitte Hamann, *Hitlers Wien. Lehrjahre eines Diktators* (Munich 1996).   **36.** Anton Joachimsthaler, *Hitlers Weg begann in München, 1913–1923* (Munich, 2000).   **37.** Thomas Weber, *Wie Adolf Hitler zum Nazi wurde. Vom unpolitischen Soldaten zum Autor von 'Mein Kampf'* (Berlin, 2016); Othmar Plöckinger, *Geschichte eines Buches.*

Adolf Hitlers 'Mein Kampf', 1922–1945, 2nd edn (Munich, 2011). **38.** Despina Stratigakos, *Hitler at Home* (New Haven, 2015). **39.** Anna Maria Sigmund, *Des Führers bester Freund. Adolf Hitler, seine Nichte Geli Raubal und der 'Ehrenarier' Emil Maurice – eine Dreiecksbeziehung* (Munich, 2005). **40.** Heike B. Görtemaker, *Eva Braun. Ein Leben mit Hitler* (Munich, 2010). **41.** Bill Niven, *Hitler and Film: The Führer's Hidden Passion* (New Haven and London, 2018); Timothy W. Ryback, *Hitler's Private Library: The Books that Shaped His Life* (London, 2009). **42.** Fritz Redlich, *Hitler: Diagnosis of a Destructive Prophet* (New York, 1999). **43.** Johannes Hürter, *Hitlers Heerführer. Die Deutschen Oberbefehlshaber in Kriey gegen die Sowjetunion 1941/42* (Munich, 2006). **44.** Stephen G. Fritz, *The First Soldier: Hitler as Military Leader* (New Haven, 2018). **45.** Christian Goeschel, *Mussolini and Hitler: The Forging of the Fascist Alliance* (New Haven and London, 2018). See also MacGregor Knox, *Common Destiny: Dictatorship, Foreign Policy, and War in Fascist Italy and Nazi Germany* (Cambridge, 2000). **46.** Kurt Bauer, *Hitlers zweiter Putsch. Dollfuß, die Nazis und der 25. Juli 1934* (St. Pölten, Salzburg, Vienna, 2014); Kurt Bauer, 'Hitler und der Juliputsch 1934 in Österreich', *Vierteljahrshefte für Zeitgeschichte*, 59 (2011), pp. 193–27. **47.** Andreas Krämer, *Hitlers Kriegskurs. Appeasement und die 'Maikrise' 1938. Entscheidungsstunde im Vorfeld von 'Münchener Abkommen' und Zweitem Weltkrieg* (Berlin, 2014). **48.** Angela Hermann, *Der Weg in den Krieg 1938/39 . Quellenkritische Studien zu den Tagebüchern von Joseph Goebbels* (Munich, 2011), p. 311. **49.** Rolf-Dieter Müller, *Der Feind steht im Osten. Hitlers geheime Pläne für einen Krieg gegen die Sowjetunion im Jahr 1939* (Berlin, 2011). **50.** Ian Kershaw, *Fateful Decisions: Ten Decisions that Changed the World, 1940–1941* (London, 2007). **51.** Edward B. Westermann, *Hitler's Ostkrieg and the Indian Wars: Comparing Genocide and Conquest* (Norman, Oklahoma, 2016), focuses mainly on comparison, though the question of Hitler's inspiration by the American example is treated briefly pp. 3, 14, 36–39; and Carroll P. Kakel, III, *The American West and the Nazi East: A Comparative and Interpretive Perspective* (New York, 2011). **52.** *Das Deutsche Reich und der Zweite Weltkrieg*, 10 vols. (Stuttgart, 1979–2008). **53.** Richard Evans, *Telling Lies about Hitler: The Holocaust, History and the David Irving Trial* (London, 2002); Peter Longerich, *The Unwritten Order: Hitler's Role in the Final Solution* (London 2001). **54.** Magnus Brechtken and Maximilian Becker, 'Die Edition der Reden Adolf Hitlers von 1933 bis 1945. Ein neues Projekt des Instituts für Zeitgeschichte'. **55.** SA. The author did not use any documents which were subsequently found to be forgeries: Eberhard Jäckel and Axel Kuhn, 'Zu einer Edition von Aufzeichnungen Hitler', *Vierteljahrshefte für Zeitgeschichte*, 29 (1981). **56.** Thus Bavendamm, *Der junge Hitler*, pp. 190–91. **57.** MK. **58.** See also Ian Kershaw, 'Ideologe und propagandist. Hitler im Lichte seiner Reden, Schriften und Anordnnungen, 1925–1928', *Vierteljahrshefte für Zeitgeschichte*, 40 (1992), pp. 263–71; Frank-Lothar Kroll, 'Die Edition von Hitlers Reden, Schriften und Anordnungen', in Horst Möller and Udo Wengst (eds.), *50 Jahre Institut für Zeitgeschichte. Eine Bilanz* (Munich, 1999), pp. 237–47; Wolfram Pyta, 'Die Hitler-Edition des Instituts für Zeitgeschichte', *Historische Zeitschrift*, 281 (2005), pp. 381–94. **59.** Max Domarus (ed.), *Hitler Reden und Proklamationen 1932–1945*, 4 vols. (Leonberg, 1988) (hereafter Domarus). **60.** ES. **61.** ADAP; RH. **62.** FE; HW; FK; and LB. There are some new fragments in Helmut Heiber and David M. Glantz (eds.), *Hitler and His Generals: Military Conferences, 1942–1945* (New York, 2002). **63.** Harald Sandner, *Hitler. Das Itinerar. Aufenthaltsorte und Reisen von 1889 bis 1945*, 4 vols. (Berlin, 2016). **64.** Bernd Sösemann, 'Alles nur Goebbels-Propaganda? Untersuchungen zur revidierten Ausgabe der sogenannten Goebbels-Tagebücher des Münchner Instituts für Zeitgeschichte', *Jahrbuch für Kommunikationsgeschichte*, 10 (2008), 52–76. **65.** Magnus Brechtken, *Albert Speer. Eine Deutsche Karriere* (Munich, 2017). **66.** ET; WA. Wagener's lengthy recollections have not been cited as a verbatim record of Hitler's exact words. **67.** Mikael Nilsson, 'Hitler redivivus. Hitlers Tischgespräche und Monologe im Führerhauptquartier – eine kritische Untersuchung', in *Vierteljahrshefte für Zeitgeschichte*, 67 (January 2019), pp. 105–45. **68.** August Kubizek, *Adolf Hitler. Mein Jugendfreund* (Graz, 1995). **69.** See August Priesack, 'Hitlers Handschrift und Maser's Lesefehler', *Vierteljahrshefte für Zeitgeschichte*, 21 (1973), 334–6, which takes to task Werner Maser, *Hitlers Briefe und Notizen. Sein Weltbild in handschriftlichen Dokumenten* (Düsseldorf, 1973). **70.** Wolfgang

Hänel, *Hermann Rauschning's 'Gespräche mit Hitler'. Eine Geschichtsfälschung* (Ingolstadt, 1984). 71. Mikael Nilsson, 'Constructing a pseudo-Hitler? The question of the authenticity of *Hitlers politisches Testament'*, *European Review of History* (2015), pp. 1–21. 72. By contrast Hamann, *Hitlers Wien*, p. 7, explicitly puts the milieu and the city at the centre rather than Hitler himself. 73. Richard J. Evans, 'Introduction' to special edition of *Journal of Modern History*, 39 (2004), 'Understanding Nazi Germany', pp. 163–7 (quotation on p. 163).

Chapter 1: Sketch of the Dictator as a Young Man

1. See Peter Ernst, 'Adolf Hitlers "österreichisches Deutsch". Eine ohrenphonetische Analyse historischer Film-und Tondokumente', *Zeitschrift für Mitteleuropäische Germanistik*, 3 (2013), pp. 30 and 32. I thank Stefan Gaisbauer for a useful discussion of matters of dialect. For Hitler's long and complicated relationship with Upper Austria see Harry Slapnicka, *Hitler und Oberösterreich. Mythos, Propaganda und Wirklichkeit um das 'Heimatgau' des Führers* (Grünbach, 1998). 2. Walter Ziegler, *Hitler und Bayern. Beobachtungen zu ihrem Verhältnis* (Munich, 2005), p. 5 *et passim*. See also Speech, 22.2.1933, Domarus, I, p. 214. 3. Bavendamm, *Der junge Hitler*, pp. 60–61, 101, 116. 4. I have taken biographical details from Bavendamm, *Der junge Hitler*, pp. 92–3, and Hamann, *Hitlers Wien, passim*. 5. For the changes in address see Bavendamm, *Der junge Hitler*, pp. 94–5. 6. On schooling see Bavendamm, *Der junge Hitler*, pp. 109, 135, 143. 7. See Alfred Zerlik, 'Adolf Hitlers Linzer Schuljahre', *Historisches Jahrbuch der Stadt Linz 1975* (Linz, 1975), pp. 335–88, which contains several copies of his original reports. 8. See Bavendamm, *Der junge Hitler*, p. 156. 9. Adolf and Paula Hitler to the Finanzdirektion Linz, 10.2.1906, SA, p. 46. 10. Hitler to August Kubizek, 7.5.1906 and 8.5.1906, SA, pp. 44–5. 11. Brigitte Hamann, *Hitlers Edeljude. Das leben des Armenarzts Eduard Bloch* (Munich and Zurich, 2010), pp. 80–81, 87, 89 and 91. 12. Hamann, *Edeljude*, p. 95. 13. Hamann, *Hitlers Wien*, pp. 51–2. 14. See Hamann, *Hitlers Wien*, pp. 195–6; Bavendamm, *Der junge Hitler*, pp. 177–8. Gerhart Marckhgott, '"... von der Hohlheit des gemächlichen Lebens". Neues Material über die Familie Hitler in Linz', *Jahrbuch des Oberösterreichischen Musealvereines*, 138, 1 (Linz 1993), pp. 267–77, especially pp. 271, 273 and 275. 15. Quoted in Hamann, *Hitlers Wien*, pp. 59–61. 16. Hitler to Kubizek, 18.2.1908, 19.4.1908 and 21.7.1908, Vienna, SA, pp. 47, 49–50. 17. Hitler to Kubizek, 17.8.1908, SA, pp. 50–51. 18. Hitler to Kubizek, 19.8.1908, Vienna, SA, p. 51. 19. Hitler to Linz magistracy, 21.1.1914, SA, pp. 53–5. 20. See Hamann, *Hitlers Wien*, pp. 224–5, 229ff. 21. Hitler's statement to the police, Vienna, 5.8.1910, SA, p. 52. 22. See Hamann, *Hitlers Wien*, p. 250. 23. Thus Werner Graf, *Adolf Hitler begegnet Karl May. Zur Lektürebiographie des 'Führers'* (Baltmannsweiler, 2012), pp. 11–12. 24. I owe this thought to T. C. W. Blanning, 'Hitler, Vienna and Wagner', *German History*, 18 (2000). 25. Thus Hamann, *Hitlers Wien*, pp. 247, 242, 507–11. 26. Joachimsthaler, *Hitlers Weg*, p. 33. 27. See the detailed compilation in Joachimsthaler, *Hitlers Weg*, p. 27. 28. Bavendamm, *Der junge Hitler*, p. 206. See Hitler to the Magistracy of Linz, Munich, 21.1.1914, SA, pp. 53–5. 29. Joachimsthaler, *Hitlers Weg*, p. 78. 30. Hamann, *Hitlers Wien*, pp. 7–8 *et passim*; Bavendamm, *Der junge Hitler*, pp. 19–20 *et passim*.

Chapter 2: Against a 'World of Enemies'

1. See Joachimsthaler, *Hitlers Weg*, p. 100. 2. His military paybook (*Militärpass*) states that Hitler was 'Kriegsfreiwilliger, 16.8.1914'. Copies in Institut für Zeitgeschichte, Munich (hereafter IfZ), F19/6, fols. 3–4. 3. See generally Thomas Weber, *Hitler's First War: Adolf Hitler, the Men of the List Regiment and the First World War* (Oxford, 2010). 4. Hitler to Anna Popp, Graben/Lechfeld, 20.10.1914, SA, p. 59. 5. Hitler to Joseph Popp, [western front], 20.2.1915, SA, p. 71. 6. The general sense of hostility towards England in the List Regiment is described in Weber, *Hitler's First War*, p. 28. See also Matthew Stibbe, *German Anglophobia*

and the *Great War, 1914–1918* (Cambridge, 2001).   7. Quoted in John F. Williams, *Corporal Hitler and the Great War, 1914–1918: The List Regiment* (London and New York, 2005), p. 49. See also Dieter J. Weiss, *Kronprinz Rupprecht von Bayern (1869–1955). Eine politische Biografie* (Regensburg, 2007), pp. 109–10.   8. I follow here Weber, *Hitler's First War*, pp. 28–50.   9. Hitler to Joseph Popp, [western front], 3.12.1914, SA, pp. 60–61.   10. See Weber, *Hitlers First War*, p. 70.   11. Hitler to Ernst Hepp, [western front], 5.2.1915, SA, p. 69.   12. Hitler to Joseph Popp, 12.2.1915, SA, p. 70.   13. Thus Williams, *Corporal Hitler*, p. 135.   14. Quoted in Williams, *Corporal Hitler*, p. 143.   15. Thus Christopher Duffy, *Through German Eyes: The British and the Somme 1916* (London, 2006).   16. See Weber, *Hitler's First War*, pp. 153–5.   17. The devastating impact of the blockade and the rhetoric it generated are described in C. Paul Vincent, *Politics of Hunger: Allied Blockade of Germany, 1915–1919* (Athens, Ohio, 1985), pp. 124–56.   18. Hitler to Balthasar Brandmayer, Munich, 21.12.1916, SA, p. 78. A letter recently come to light also stresses his determination 'to report immediately back to front-line duties': see Sven Felix Kellerhoff, 'Adolf Hitler sehnte sich nach seiner Ersatz-familie', *Die Welt*, 2.5.2012.   19. Hitler to Wiedemann, January 1917, SA, p. 80. The text of this letter is not, strictly speaking, contemporary as it comes from a subsequent file note of his superior officer Captain Wiedemann (Fritz Wiedemann, *Der Mann der Feldherr werden wollte. Erlebnisse und Erfahrungen des Vorgesetzten Hitlers im I. Weltkrieg und seines späteren persönlichen Adjutanten* (Velbert, 1964)).   20. Max Unold to Wiedemann, Munich, 18.8.1938, Bundesarchiv Koblenz, N1720, Wiedemann 8.   21. Thus Weber, *Hitler's First War*, p. 197.   22. Thus Dino E. Buenviaje, *The Yanks Are Coming Over There: Anglo-Saxonism and American Involvement in the First World War* (Jefferson, NC, 2017), pp. 118–70.   23. See Geoffrey Wawro, *Sons of Freedom: The Forgotten American Soldiers Who Defeated Germany in World War I* (New York, 2018).   24. See Frank Trommler, 'The Lusi-tania' effect: America's mobilization against Germany in World War I', *German Studies Review*, 32 (2009), pp. 241–66; Jessica Bennett and Mark Hampton, 'World War I and the Anglo-American imagined community: civilization versus barbarism in British propaganda and American newspapers', in Joel H. Wiener and Mark Hampton (eds.), *Anglo-American Media Interactions, 1850–2000* (London, 2007), pp. 155–75.   25. David Stevenson, *With Our Backs to the Wall: Victory and Defeat in 1918* (London, 2011).   26. According to the Regimental Order of Anton von Tubeuf, 18.4.1918, these were Algerian Tirailleurs of the 45 Division: BayHSTA, no. 19, 'Kriegstagebuch mit Anlagen, 1.4.1918–30.4.1918', fo. 58.   27. See Weber, *Hitler's First War*, p. 211.   28. F. Wiedemann report, 17.7.1918, BayHSTA, no. 10, 'Stab Juli 1918', fo. 37.   29. Report II Battalion to regimental commander, BayHSTA, no. 17, 'Kriegstagebuch mit Anlagen, 1.9.1918–30.9.1918', fo. 361. For the American learning process see Mark Ethan Grotelueschen, *The AEF Way of War: The American Army and Combat in World War I* (Cambridge, 2007).   30. Colin Ross, *Unser Amerika. Der deutsche Anteil an den Vereinigten Staaten* (Leipzig, 1941), pp. 261–2.   31. BayHSTA, no. 17, Kriegstagebuch (hereafter KTB), II, Battalion, 'Kriegstagebuch mit Anlagen', 1.7.1918–31.7.1918, 'July 1918, 'Gefechtsbericht über die Marneschlacht', 19.8.1918; KTB, II, Battal-ion, referring to the events of 2 July (fol. 2) and 28 July (fol. 6).   32. BayHSTA, Offiziersakte Hugo Gutmann, Kriegsarchiv, OP40983. See Weber, *Hitler's First War*, pp. 215–16, and Othmar Plöckinger, *Unter Soldaten und Agitatoren. Hitlers prägende Jahre im Deutschen Militär 1918–1920* (Paderborn, 2013), pp. 16–17.   33. See Stevenson, *With Our Backs to the Wall*; and Jonathan Boff, *Winning and Losing on the Western Front: The British Third Army and the Defeat of Germany in 1918* (Cambridge, 2012).   34. The war diaries record clashes with the French (29 October 1918, fo. 18) and with the British (20 October, fo. 9): BayHSTA, no 17, KTB, II, Battalion, 'Kriegstagebuch mit Anlagen, 1.10.1918–31.10.1918'; BayHSTA, 'Gefechtserfahrungen in der Abwehrschlacht bei Bapaume', 3.9.1918, KTB, II, Battalion; BayHSTA, no. 17, KTB, II, Battalion, 'Kriegstagebuch mit Anlagen, 1.9.1918–30.9.1918, fols. 5–8; BayHSTA, no. 19, KTB III, Battalion: 'Gefechtsbericht für 28 und 29.9.18' by Huber of 2 Company (dated 7.10.1918), p. 14 (no foliation).   35. See Nick Lloyd, *Hundred Days: The Campaign that Ended World War I* (New York, 2014), pp. 2–7, 115–32 *et passim*.   36. Fridolin Solleder, 'Ein ungleicher Kampf: 3 gegen 33, 12 Oktober 1918', in Fridolin Solleder (ed.), *Vier Jahre Westfront. Geschichte des Regiments List* (Munich, 1932),

p. 339.   37. See Alexander Watson, *Enduring the Great War: Combat, Morale and Collapse in the German and British Armies, 1914–1918* (Cambridge, 2008), pp. 184–231; and Scott Stephenson, *The Final Battle: Soldiers of the Western Front and the German Revolution of 1918* (Cambridge, 2009), pp. 17–66.   38. Thus Weber, *Hitler's First War*, pp. 93–4 *et passim*.   39. See Timothy Ryback, *Hitler's Private Library: The Books that Shaped His Life* (London, 2009), pp. 3–27.   40. Weber, *Hitler's First War*, p. 345; and Joachimsthaler, *Hitlers Weg*, p. 151.   41. Joachimsthaler, *Hitlers Weg*, p. 127.   42. Weber, *Hitler's First War*, p. 141.   43. *Pace* Lothar Machtan, *Hitlers Geheimnis. Das Doppelleben eines Diktators* (Berlin, 2001), and 'Was Hitlers Homosexualität bedeutet. Anmerkungen zu einer Tabugeschichte', *Zeitschrift für Geschichtswissenschaft*, 51 (2003), pp. 334–51.   44. Joachimsthaler, *Hitlers Weg*, p. 157.   45. See Klaus Schwabe, 'World War I and the rise of Hitler', *Diplomatic History*, 38 (2014), pp. 864–79; Gerhard Hirschfeld, 'Der Führer spricht vom Krieg. Der Erste Weltkrieg in den Reden Adolf Hitlers', in Gerd Krumeich (ed.), *Nationalsozialismus und Erster Weltkrieg* (Essen, 2010); and Henrik Eberle, *Hitlers Weltkriege. Wie der Gefreite zum Feldherrn wurde* (Hamburg, 2014).   46. Thus Eberhard Jäckel, *Frankreich in Hitlers Europa. Die deutsche Frankreichpolitik im Zweiten Weltkrieg* (Stuttgart, 1966), p. 13, who notes the contrast. See also Weber, *Hitler's First War*, p. 329.   47. Thus Weber, *Hitler's First War*, pp. 176–8.   48. See Henry Grant (Hugo Gutmann) to Joseph Drexel, 6.11.1946, St Louis, Missouri, in BayHSTA, Offiziersakte Hugo Gutmann, OP 40983.   49. Wiedemann to Thomsen (copy), 28.9.1939 (Thomsen was the counsellor at the embassy in Washington), Bundesarchiv Koblenz, Nachlass Wiedemann 6. See also Sven Felix Kellerhoff, 'Wie Hitler seinen jüdischen Kompaniechef schützte', *Die Welt*, 6.7.2012.

Chapter 3: The 'Colonization' of Germany

1. On demobilization in Munich see Adam R. Seipp, *The Ordeal of Peace: Demobilization and the Urban Experience in Britain and Germany, 1917–1921* (Farnham, 2009), especially pp. 91–130.   2. Speech, 14.4.1926, RSA, I, p. 383.   3. See N. P. Howard, 'The social and political consequences of the Allied food blockade of Germany, 1918–19', *German History*, 11 (1993), pp. 161–88, especially pp. 182–7.   4. Joachimsthaler, *Hitlers Weg*, p. 187. For the general context see Robert Gerwarth, *The Vanquished: Why the First World War Failed to End* (New York, 2016).   5. See Weber, *Wie Adolf Hitler zum Nazi wurde*, pp. 13, 71–72, 79, 80.   6. Benjamin Ziemann, 'Wanderer zwischen den Welten. Der Militärkritiker und Gegner des entschiedenen Pazifismus Major a.D. Karl Mayr (1883–1945)', in Wolfram Wette (ed.), *Pazifistische Offiziere in Deutschland, 1871–1933* (Bremen, 1999), pp. 273–85. Mayr's own account is to be treated with caution: A Former Officer of the Reichswehr [Karl Mayr], 'I was Hitler's boss', *Current History*, 1 (November 1941), pp. 193–9.   7. Othmar Plöckinger, 'Adolf Hitler als Hörer an der Universität München im Jahr 1919. Zum Verhältnis zwischen Reichswehr und Universität', in Elisabeth Kraus (ed.), *Die Universität München im Dritten Reich. Aufsätze. Teil II* (Munich, 2008), pp. 13–47.   8. Weber, *Wie Adolf Hitler zum Nazi wurde*, p. 151.   9. Quoted in Weber, *Wie Adolf Hitler zum Nazi wurde*, pp. 171–2.   10. Thus Weber, *Wie Adolf Hitler zum Nazi wurde*, pp. 152–5, 173.   11. Ernst Deuerlein, 'Hitlers Eintritt in die Politik und die Reichswehr', *Vierteljahrshefte für Zeitgeschichte*, 7 (1959), pp. 177–227, at pp. 178–9. See also William Mulligan, 'Restoring trust within the Reichswehr: the case of the Vertrauensleute', *War & Society*, 20, 2 (October 2002), pp. 71–90, especially pp. 72–3, 82–3, 86.   12. See Weber, *Hitler's First War*, p. 266; Ralf Georg Reuth, *Hitlers Judenhass. Klischee und Wirklichkeit* (Munich, 2009), pp. 103–16; Joachim Riecker, *Hitlers 9. November. Wie der Erste Weltkrieg zum Holocaust führte* (Berlin, 2009); and Gerd Krumeich, *Die unbewältigte Niederlage. Das Trauma des Ersten Weltkriegs und die Weimarer Republik* (Freiburg, 2018).   13. Pyta, *Hitler*, pp. 139–40.   14. Some argue that the treaty was quite lenient. Sally Marks, 'The Myths of Reparations', *Central European History*, 11, 3 (September 1978), pp. 231–55.   15. Speech [title only], 23.8.1919, SA, p. 87; Speech [title only], 24.8.1919, SA, p. 87.   16. Speech [fragment only], [25.8.1919], SA, p. 88.   17. See 'Vortragsfolge der Aufklärungskommandos Beyschlag im Lager Lechfeld. Aus dem "Vorläufigen Bericht"

Beyschlags', 20.8.1919, and 'Schlussbericht des Oblt Bendt an das Gruppenkommando 4. Lager Lechfeld', 25.8.1919, in Deuerlein, 'Hitlers Eintritt', p. 198–9.   18. Deuerlein, 'Hitlers Eintritt', pp. 181 and 185.   19. Reuth, *Hitlers Judenhass*, pp. 153–91, provides the first systematic discussion of the anti-capitalist element of Hitler's early anti-Semitism. See also Friedrich Tomberg, *Das Christentum in Hitlers Weltanschuung* (Munich, 2012), pp. 13–14, and Plöckinger, *Unter Soldaten und Agitatoren*, pp. 263–7.   20. Hitler to Gemlich, 16.9.1919, Munich, SA, pp. 88–90. See also Plöckinger, *Unter Soldaten und Agitatoren*, pp. 272, 340, and Wolfram Meyer zu Uptrup, 'Wann wurde Hitler zum Antisemiten? Einige Überlegungen zu einer strittigen Frage', *Zeitschrift für Geschichtswissenschaft*, 43 (1995), pp. 687–97.   21. See Werner Bergmann and Ulrich Wyrwa, *Antisemitismus in Zentraleuropa* (Darmstadt, 2011), pp. 32–61; Heike Hoffmann, 'Völkische Kapitalismus-Kritik. Das Beispiel Warenhaus', in Uwe Puschner, Walter Schmitz and Justus H. Ulbricht (eds.), *Handbuch zur 'Völkischen Bewegung' 1871–1918* (Munich, London and Paris, 1996), especially, pp. 558–60; and Michele Battini, *Socialism of Fools: Capitalism and Modern Anti-Semitism* (New York, 2016), especially pp. 75–110.   22. See Werner Jochmann (ed.), *Nationalsozialismus und Revolution. Ursprung und Geschichte der NSDAP in Hamburg, 1922–1933. Dokumente* (Frankfurt, 1963), pp. 5–9.   23. I base myself on the full account in Weber, *Wie Adolf Hitler zum Nazi wurde*, pp. 191–4. See also Ulrich von Hasselbach, 'Die Entstehung der nationalsozialistischen deutschen Arbeiterpartei, 1919–1923' (PhD dissertation, University of Leipzig, 1931), p. 20.   24. Quoted in Kershaw, *Hubris*, p. 126.   25. Thus Reginald H. Phelps, 'Hitler and the *Deutsche Arbeiterpartei*', *American Historical Review*, 68 (1963), pp. 974–86.   26. Thus Weber, *Wie Adolf Hitler zum Nazi wurde*, pp. 210–11.   27. See also Joachimsthaler, *Hitlers Weg*, pp. 263–4.   28. Speech, 10.12.1919, SA, p. 99.   29. Speech, 10.12.1919, SA, p. 97.   30. Thus Geoffrey Stoakes, *Hitler and the Quest for World Dominion: Nazi Ideology and Foreign Policy in the 1920s* (Leamington Spa and New York, 1986), pp. 82–3.   31. Remarks, 7.1.1920, SA, p. 101. Hitler used the stronger *verhindert* ('prevents') rather than *behindert* ('obstructs').   32. Speech, 10.12.1919, SA, p. 96.   33. Adam Tooze, *The Deluge: The Great War and the Remaking of the Global Order* (London, 2014).   34. Hitler's occasional use of the phrase is charted in Rainer Sammet, '*Dolchstoss*'. *Deutschland und die Auseinandersetzung mit der Niederlage im Ersten Weltkrieg (1918–1933)* (Berlin, 2003), pp. 250–55.   35. Speech, 20.9.1920, SA, p. 229. See also Gerhard L. Weinberg, 'The world through Hitler's eyes', in idem, *Germany, Hitler and World War II: Essays in Modern Germany and World History* (Cambridge, 1995), pp. 30–53 (here, p. 34).   36. Speech, 20.3.1923, SA, p. 846. See also Christian Koller, '*Von Wilden aller Rassen niedergemetzelt*'. *Die Diskussion um die Verwendung von Kolonialtruppen in Europa zwischen Rassismus, Kolonial- und Militärpolitik (1914–1930)* (Stuttgart, 2001), especially pp. 246–9, 313–19, 325–6, 330, 362–75.   37. For Canadian and other Allied atrocities see Niall Ferguson, *The Pity of War* (London, 1998), pp. 376, 379 *et passim*.   38. Mayr to Hitler, Munich, 10.9.1919, in Kriegsarchiv, Reichswehr Gruppenkommando 4, Nr. 314 Propagandakurse, Teilnehmer, G–Z.   39. Weber, *Wie Adolf Hitler zum Nazi wurde*, p. 99. See also Thomas Raithel, ' "Kommt bald nach . . .". Auswanderung aus Bayern nach Amerika, 1683–2003', in Margot Hamm, Michael Henker and Evamaria Brockhoff (eds.), *Good bye Bayern, Grüß Gott Amerika* (Augsburg, 2004), pp. 23–36 (the figures on p. 25 show a spike in the 1920s).   40. See Gerd Koenen, 'Hitlers Russland. Ambivalenzen im deutschen "Drang nach Osten"', *Kommune*, 1 (2003), pp. 65–78, especially pp. 65–8.   41. Ernst Piper, *Alfred Rosenberg: Hitlers Chefideologe* (Munich, 2007).   42. Kai-Uwe Merz, *Das Schreckbild. Deutschland und der Bolschewismus, 1917 bis 1921* (Berlin, 1995).   43. 27.1.1921, SA, p. 301. Later examples are Article, 6.11.1929, RSA, III/2, p. 434 (which speaks of 'disarming the German people and delivering them up to international high finance'), and Article, 7.11.1929, RSA, III/2, p. 445. The materials used by the Reichswehr educational courses portray socialists largely as instruments of the Entente to weaken Germany: Kriegsarchiv Bayern, Reichswehrgruppenkommando 4, no. 314.   44. Speech, 23.1.1920, SA, p. 106; Remarks, 9.8.1920, SA, p. 183; Remarks, 21.6.1920, SA, p. 150; Remarks, 9.8.1920, SA, p. 183.   45. Hitler to Riehl, 1.3.1920, Munich, SA, p. 112.   46. Thus Weber, *Wie Adolf Hitler zum Nazi wurde*, pp. 40, 335. See also Manfred Weissbecker, ' "Wenn hier Deutsche wohnten . . .". Beharrung und

Veränderung im Russlandbild Hitlers und der NSDAP', in Hans-Erich Volkmann (ed.), *Das Russlandbild im Dritten Reich* (Cologne, 1994), pp. 9–54, especially pp. 13–15. See also Koenen, 'Hitlers Russland', pp. 71–2. 47. Article, March 1921, SA, p. 340; Article, 15.3.1921, SA, p. 393. 48. Article, 26.5.1921, SA, p. 415. 49. Speech, 21.10.1921, SA, p. 506. 50. Thus Albert Krebs, *Tendenzen und Gestalten der NSDAP. Erinnerungen an die Frühzeit der Partei von Albert Krebs* (Stuttgart, 1959), p. 121. 51. Weber, *Wie Adolf Hitler zum Nazi wurde*, p. 364. See also Timothy W. Ryback, *Hitlers Bücher. Seine Bibliothek – sein Denken* (Cologne, 2010). 52. See Paul Hoser, 'Thierschstrasse 41. Der Untermieter Hitler, sein jüdischer Hausherr und ein Restitutionsproblem', *Vierteljahrshefte für Zeitgeschichte*, 65 (2017), pp. 131–61, especially pp. 134, 140, 147, 160, 161. 53. See Paul Madden, 'Some social characteristics of early Nazi Party members, 1919–23', in *Central European History*, 15 (1982), pp. 34–56. 54. Speech, 11.6.1920, SA, p. 142. 55. Thus Hellmuth Auerbach, 'Hitlers politische Lehrjahre und die Münchener Gesellschaft 1919–1923', *Vierteljahrshefte für Zeitgeschichte*, 25 (1977), pp. 14, 23–24. 56. J. Noakes and G. Pridham (eds.), *Nazism, 1919–1945: A History in Documents and Eyewitness Accounts*, vol. 1: *The Nazi Party, State and Society, 1919–1939* (New York, 1990), p. 14, ascribes principal authorship to Hitler and Drexler. 57. Thus Jörg Fisch, 'Adolf Hitler und das Selbstbestimmungsrecht der Völker', *Historische Zeitschrift*, 290 (2010), pp. 93–118 (quotation on p. 105). 58. Joachimsthaler, *Hitlers Weg*, p. 274. 59. Speech, 13.8.1920, SA, p. 186; Speech, 5.10.1921, SA, p. 499. 60. Thus Uwe Degreif, 'Woher hatte Hitler das Hakenkreuz? Zur Übernahme eines Symbols', *Zeitschrift für Kulturaustausch*, 41 (1991), pp. 310–16, especially p. 314. 61. Joachimsthaler, *Hitlers Weg*, pp. 280–81. For the fluctuating print run see Charles F. Sidman, 'Die Auflagen-Kurve des Völkischen Beobachters und die Entwicklung des Nationalsozialismus, Dezember 1920–November 1923', *Vierteljahrshefte für Zeitgeschichte*, 13 (1965), pp. 112–18. 62. Thus Roland V. Layton, 'The Völkischer Beobachter, 1920–1933: the Nazi Party newspaper in the Weimar Era', *Central European History*, 3 (1970), pp. 353–82, especially p. 372; and Detlef Mühlberger, *Hitler's Voice: The Völkischer Beobachter, 1920–1933* (Berne, 2004), vol. 1, p. 22. 63. Ludolf Herbst, *Hitlers Charisma. Die Erfindung eines deutschen Messias* (Frankfurt, 2010), p. 14 *et passim*. 64. See Stefan Aust, *Hitlers erster Feind. Der Kampf des Konrad Heiden* (Reinbek, 2016), pp. 78–82, especially p. 81. 65. Speech, 6.2.1921, SA, p. 312; Joachimsthaler, *Hitlers Weg*, pp. 271–2, 282. 66. See Krebs, *Tendenzen und Gestalten*, p. 119. 67. Deuerlein, 'Hitlers Eintritt', pp. 177–8. 68. Order, Munich, December 1919, SA, p. 95. 69. Longerich, *Hitler*, p. 97. 70. See Auerbach, 'Hitlers politische Lehrjahre', p. 16. 71. Michael Kellogg, *The Russian Roots of Nazism: White Émigrés and the Making of National Socialism, 1917–1945* (Cambridge, 2005), pp. 15–17 *et passim*. 72. Speech, 29.1.1923, SA, p. 824. 73. Mike Joseph, 'Max Erwin von Scheubner-Richter: the personal link from genocide to Hitler', in Hans-Lukas Kieser and Elmar Plozza (eds.), *Der Völkermord an den Armeniern, die Türkei und Europa* (Zurich, 2006), pp. 147–65. See also Auerbach, 'Hitlers politische Lehrjahre', p. 16; Weber, *Wie Adolf Hitler zum Nazi wurde*, pp. 324–5. 74. Speech, 17.12.1922, SA, p. 775. 75. Hitler to Anton Drexler, Munich, 9.12.1920, SA, p. 277. 76. Quoted in Reginald H. Phelps, 'Anton Drexler, der Gründer der NSDAP', *Deutsche Rundschau*, 87 (1961), pp. 1,134–43, here p. 1,140. 77. Thus Wolfgang Horn, *Führerideologie und Parteiorganisation in der NSDAP (1919–1933)* (Düsseldorf, 1972), p. 424 *et passim*. 78. See Joachimsthaler, *Hitlers Weg*, p. 285. 79. Thomas Weber, *Becoming Hitler: The Making of a Nazi* (New York, 2017), pp. 111 and 132. 80. Werner Bräuninger, ' "Die Partei ist kein abendländischer Bund!" Die Sommerkrise der NSDAP im Jahre 1921', in Werner Bräuninger, *Hitlers Kontrahenten in der NSDAP, 1921–1945* (Munich, 2004), pp. 28–37. 81. Hilter to Ausschuss der NSDAP, 14.7.1921, Munich, SA, p. 436. 82. See Phelps, 'Drexler', pp. 1,139–41. 83. Albrecht Tyrell, *Vom 'Trommler' zum 'Führer'. Der Wandel von Hitlers Selbstverständnis zwischen 1919 und 1924 und die Entwicklung der NSDAP* (Munich, 1975), pp. 132–3 *et passim*. 84. Joachimsthaler, *Hitlers Weg*, p. 295. 85. Thus Joachimsthaler, *Hitlers Weg*, p. 301. 86. Tyrell, *Vom 'Trommler' zum 'Führer'*, pp. 132, 139–40, 146–7. 87. See Egon Fein, *Hitlers Weg nach Nürnberg. Verführer, Täuscher, Massenmörder. Eine Spurensuche in Franken mit hundert Bilddokumenten* (Nuremberg, 2002), pp. 84–5. 88. Thus Hellmuth Auerbach,

'Regionale Wurzeln und Differenzen der NSDAP, 1919–1923', in Horst Möller, Andreas Wirsching and Walter Ziegler (eds.), *Nationalsozialismus in der Region. Beiträge zur regionalen und lokalen Forschung und zum internationalen Vergleich* (Munich, 1996), pp. 65–85. 89. Herbert Speckner, 'Die Ordnungszelle Bayern. Studien zur Politik des bayerischen Bürgertums, insbesondere der bayerischen Volkspartei von der Revolution bis zum ende des Kabinetts Dr von Kahr' (PhD dissertation, University of Erlangen, 1955). 90. Se Kai Uwe Tapken, *Die Reichswehr in Bayern von 1919 bis 1924* (Hamburg, 2002), pp. 415, 419 *et passim*. 91. See Bruno Thoss, *Der Ludendorff Kreis, 1919–1923. München als Zentrum der mitteleuropäischen Gegenrevolution zwischen Revolution und Hitler-Putsch* (Munich, 1978), especially pp. 453–55. 92. Weber, *Wie Adolf Hitler zum Nazi wurde, passim.* 93. Speckner, 'Ordnungszelle Bayern', p. 27. 94. Speech, 12.4.1922, SA, p. 624. 95. Speech, 17.12.1922, SA, p. 769. See more generally Richard Steigmann-Gall, *The Holy Reich: Nazi Conceptions of Christianity, 1919–1945* (Cambridge, 2003); Samuel Koehne, 'Reassessing *The Holy Reich*: leading Nazis' views on confession, community and "Jewish" materialism', *Journal of Contemporary History*, 48 (2013), pp. 423–45; Thomas Schirrmacher, *Hitler's Kriegsreligion*, 2 vols. (Bonn, 2007); Rainer Bucher, *Hitlers Theologie* (Würzburg, 2008); Claus-Ekkehard Bärsch, *Die politische Religion des Nationalsozialismus. Die religiösen Dimensionen der NS-Ideologie in den Schriften von Dietrich Eckart, Joseph Goebbels, Alfred Rosenberg und Adolf Hitler* (Munich, 1998). 96. Speech, end of December 1922, SA, p. 775. 97. See Derek Hastings, *Catholicism and the Roots of Nazism: Religious Identity and National Socialism* (Oxford and New York, 2010), pp. 12, 14, 78, 107–42 *et passim*. 98. See Joachimsthaler, *Hitlers Weg*, p. 283. 99. E.g. 'Betr. Verbot des Völkischen Beobachters', Munich, 29.4.1920, Staatsarchiv München, Pol. Dir. 6697; Ramer (Polizeidirektion) to *Völkischer Beobachter*, 5.10.1921, Munich, Staatsarchiv München, Pol. Dir. 6697, fols. 119–20. 100. See Joachimsthaler, *Hitlers Weg*, p. 298. 101. Article, 23.1.1922, SA, p. 553. 102. Speech, 28.7.1922, SA, p. 669; Speech, 16.8.1922, SA, p. 680; Speech, 7.8.1922, SA, p. 674. 103. This paragraph is based on Henry Ashby Turner, Jr, *German Big Business and the Rise of Hitler* (Oxford, 1985), pp. 49–55 (quotation on p. 52). 104. Joachimsthaler, *Hitlers Weg*, p. 304; Peter Manstein, *Die Mitglieder und Wähler der NSDAP, 1919–1933. Untersuchungen zu ihrer schichtmässigen Zusammensetzung*, 3rd edn (Frankfurt, 1990), p. 115, gives a lower figure. 105. Joachim Albrecht, *Die Avantgarde des 'Dritten Reiches'. Die Coburger NSDAP während der Weimarer Republik, 1922–1933* (Frankfurt, 2005), pp. 79–81. 106. Peter Bor, *Gespräche mit Halder* (Wiesbaden, 1949), p. 109. 107. NSDAP pamphlet, 11.2.1922, SA, p. 571; Speech, 5.10.1921, SA, p. 499; Speech, 'Before 9.11.1922', SA, p. 726. 108. Speech, 17.6.1920, SA, p. 147; Speech, 6.3.1921, SA, p. 336; Notes for a speech, 6.3.1921, SA, p. 335. 109. Article, 27.1.1923, SA, p. 798; Speech, 17.4.1920, SA, p. 123; Speech, 28.2.1921, SA, p. 328; Speech, 17.6.1920, SA, p. 148; Speech, 24.11.1920, SA, p. 268. 110. Article, 6.3.1921, SA, p. 330; Speech, 25.1.1923, SA, p. 798; Speech, 11.6.1920, SA, p. 145; Notes for a speech, 'July 1920', SA, p. 154. 111. Speech, 22.9.1920, SA, p. 235; Speech, 13.4.1923, SA, p. 890; Speech, 17.4.1920, SA, p. 122; Speech, 13.4.1923, SA, p. 891; Speech , 7.8.1922, SA, p. 677; 'Nach April 1923', SA, pp. 857, 859. 112. Speech, 31.5.1920, SA, p. 137; Speech, 3.1.1923, SA, p. 777; Speech, 21.4.1922, SA, pp. 629–31; Article, 6.3.1921, SA, p. 330; Speech, 28.9.1922, SA, p. 697; Notes for a speech, 1.9.1921, SA, p. 486. 113. Remarks, 20.8.1920, SA, p. 205; Speech, 26.10.1921, SA, p. 509; Speech, 31.8.1920, SA, p. 219; Circular, 19.11.1921, SA, p. 522. See also Rainer Zitelmann, *Hitler. Selbstverständnis eines Revolutionärs* (Stuttgart, 1987), p. 28 *et passim*; Claus-Christian Szejnmann, 'Nazi economic thought and rhetoric during the Weimar Republic: capitalism and its discontents', *Politics, Religion & Ideology*, 14 (2013), pp. 355–76; and Henry A. Turner Jr, 'Hitlers Einstellung zu Wirtschaft und Gesellschaft vor 1933', *Geschichte and Gesellschaft*, 2 (1976) p. 97. 114. Speech, 5.9.1920, SA, p. 222; Speech, November 1920, SA, p. 268; Speech, 19.8.1921, SA, p. 458. 115. Speech, 26.10.1921, p. 509. 116. Speech, 4.3.1920, SA, p. 114. 117. E.g. Speech, 6.7.1920, SA, p. 158. See also: Speech, 24.6.1920, SA, p. 151; Speech, 21.7.1920, SA, p. 163; Notes for a speech, 31.5.1921, SA, pp. 421–2. 118. See Michael Geyer, 'Insurrectionary warfare: the German debate about a *levée en masse* in October 1918', *Journal of Modern History*, 73 (2001), pp. 459–527, especially pp. 512–13 *et passim*. 119. Notes for a speech, [after 29.1.1921], SA, p. 306; Speech,

11.6.1920, SA, p. 144; Speech, 7.8.1920, SA, p. 176; Speech, 12.4.1922, SA, p. 612; Speech, 11.8.1922, SA p. 677. **120.** Speech, 20.9.1920, SA, p. 229; Speech, 17.2.1922, SA, p. 577. **121.** This is how Keith L. Nelson, 'The "Black Horror on the Rhine": race as a factor in post-World War I diplomacy', *Journal of Modern History*, 42 (1970), pp. 606–27, translates Hitler's use of the term, p. 626. **122.** Speech, 30.11.1922, SA, p. 752; Speech, 24.4.1923, SA, p. 913; Notes for a speech, 20.7.1921, SA, pp. 441–2; Speech, 28.6.1922, SA, p. 665; Speech, 11.6.1920, SA, p. 144; Speech, 11.1.1923, SA, p. 783. **123.** Quoted in Gerwin Strobl, *The Germanic Isle: Nazi Perceptions of Britain* (Cambridge, 2000), p. 45. **124.** See Jared Poley, *Decolonization in Germany: Weimar Narratives of Colonial Loss and Foreign Occupation* (Berne, 2005), pp. 215–47. **125.** Iris Wigger, *Die 'schwarze Schmach am Rhein'. Rassistische Diskriminierung zwischen Geschlecht, Klasse, Nation und Rasse* (Münster, 2007), p. 36 *et passim*. **126.** Marcia Klotz, 'The Weimar Republic: a postcolonial state in a still-colonial world', in Eric Ames, Marcia Klotz and Lora Wildenthal (eds.), *Germany's Colonial Pasts* (Lincoln, Nebr. and London, 2005), pp. 135–47, especially pp. 143–5. **127.** In Jonathan Peter Spiro, *Defending the Master Race: Conservation, Eugenics and the Legacy of Madison Grant* (Lebanon, Va., 2009). **128.** See Kris K. Manjapra, 'The illusions of encounter: Muslim "minds" and Hindu revolutionaries in First World War Germany and after', *Journal of Global History*, 1 (2006), pp. 363–82, especially p. 380. **129.** Speech, 19.8.1921, SA, p. 458; Article, 1.1.1921, SA, p. 281; Article, 27.1.1921, SA, p. 301; Speech, 5.5.1922, SA, p. 638; Speech, 24.4.1923, SA, p. 912; Notes for a speech, 'mid 1922', SA, p. 648. **130.** Speech, 11.6.1920, SA, p. 146; Speech, 26.10.1920, SA, p. 252; Speech, [before 6.6.1920], SA, p. 140; Speech, 12.4.1922, SA, p. 617; Speech, 28.7.1922, SA, p. 663. **131.** Speech, 22.6.1922, SA, p. 645; Speech, 28.6.1922, SA, p. 660. **132.** Speech, 8.11.1922, SA, p. 723. **133.** Thus Lorna Waddington, *Hitler's Crusade: Bolshevism, the Jews and the Myth of Conspiracy* (London and New York, 2012), p. 34. **134.** Speech,18.11.1920, SA, p. 732; Conversation, late December 1922, SA, p. 773. **135.** Speech, 17.6.1923, SA, p. 937. **136.** Speech, 7.5.1920, SA, p. 130; Notes for a speech, 6.3.1921, SA, p. 334; Speech, 5.11.1920, SA, p. 257; Speech, 21.11.1922, SA, p. 739; Speech, 11.6.1920, SA, p. 144. **137.** Hitler and Anton Drexler to Walter Riehl, Munich, 1.3.1920, SA, p. 112. **138.** Court statement, 27.1.1921, SA, p. 303. **139.** NSDAP pamphlet, 24.9.1921, SA, pp. 492–3. **140.** Werner Bräuninger, ' "Als Redner war Ballerstedt mein grösster Gegner". Ein bayerischer Separatist gegen Hitler', in Bräuninger, *Hitlers Kontrahenten*, pp. 19–27 (quotations on pp. 19–21). **141.** Speech, 10.4.1923, SA, p. 877; Speech, 28.12.1921, SA, p. 536; Speech, 17.4.1920, SA, p. 124; Notes for a speech, 25.8.1920, SA, p. 208; Speech, 6.3.1921, SA, p. 335; Notes for a speech, 10.4.1923, SA, p. 869. **142.** Speech, 11.6.1920, SA, pp. 142, 145; Proclamation, 23.9.1922, SA, pp. 694–5; Notes for a speech, 10.4.1923, SA, p. 870. **143.** Speech, 17.4.1923, SA, p. 901. In same vein: Speech, 20.9.1920, SA, p. 230. **144.** Notes for a speech, 8.12.1920, SA, p. 272. **145.** See Brendan Simms, 'The return of the primacy of foreign policy', in William Mulligan and Brendan Simms (eds.), *German History*, 21, 3 (2003), special issue on 'The Primacy of Foreign Policy in German History', pp. 275–92. **146.** Speech, 29.1.1923, SA, p. 822. **147.** See Christian Koller, 'Defeat and foreign rule as a narrative of national rebirth – the German memory of the Napoleonic period in the nineteenth and early twentieth centuries', in Jenny Macleod (ed.), *Defeat and Memory: Cultural Histories of Military Defeat in the Modern Era* (Basingstoke, 2008), pp. 30–45, especially pp. 31–2, 36–9. **148.** Thus Geyer, 'Insurrectionary warfare', especially pp. 508, 524–7. **149.** Speech, 13.8.1920, SA, pp. 187–90; Speech, 6.7.1920, SA, p. 159; Notes for a speech, April/May 1923, SA, pp. 854–5; Speech, 28.7.1922, SA, p. 663; Speech, 21.11.1922, SA, p. 737; Speech, 17.5.1923, SA, p. 928. See also Francis R. Nicosia, *The Third Reich and the Palestine Question* (London, 1985), pp. 26–8. **150.** Speech, 17.5.1923, SA, p. 928; Speech, 10.4.1923, SA, p. 877; Speech, 30.9.1923, SA, p. 1,020. **151.** Speech, 17.1.1921, SA, p. 297; Speech, 27.4.1920, SA, p. 127; Speech, 11.11.1921, p. 515; Speech, 28.7.1922, SA, p. 671; Proclamation, 29.9.1923, SA, p. 1,019. **152.** Speech, 25.7.1923, SA, p. 951; Speech, 4.3.1923, SA, p. 843; Speech, 7.8.1920, SA, p. 177; Speech, 3.1.1923, p. 779. **153.** Thus Rainer Sammet, 'Judenmord als Mittel der Kriegführung. Die mörderische "Lehre" aus der Niederlage im Ersten Weltkrieg', *Historische Mitteilungen*, 23 (2010), pp. 114–46. **154.** Hitler to Gemlich, 16.9.1919, SA, pp. 89–90. **155.** Quoted in Pyta, *Hitler*, p. 173. **156.** Article, 26.5.1921, SA, p. 414; Speech, 17.1.1921, SA, p. 297; Speech,

19.11.1920, SA, p. 263.   **157.** Speech, 12.4.1922, SA, p. 621; Notes for a speech, 17.2.1922, SA, p. 572; Interview, [before October 1923], SA, p. 1,023; Speech,19.6.1920, SA, p. 149.   **158.** See Max H. Kele, *Nazis and Workers: National Socialist Appeals to German Labor, 1919–1933* (Chapel Hill, 1972), pp. 80, 109–10 *et passim*; and Joachim Bons, *Nationalsozialismus und Arbeiterfrage. Zu den Motiven, Inhalten und Wirkungsgründen nationalsozialistischer Arbeiterpolitik vor 1933* (Pfaffenweiler, 1995), pp. 42–57.   **159.** Speech, 7.8.1920, SA, p. 178; Speech, 26.2.1923, SA, p. 841.   **160.** Speech, 10.12.1919, SA, p. 97; Speech, 17.4.1920, SA, p. 122; Speech, 30.11.1920, SA, p. 269; Speech, 12.4.1923, SA, p. 877; Speech, 26.5.1920, SA, p. 135.   **161.** Quoted in Weber, *Wie Adolf Hitler zum Nazi wurde*, p. 267.   **162.** Speech, 28.7.1922, SA, p. 658; Conversation, [end December 1922], SA, p. 774.   **163.** Speech, 20.4.1923, SA, p. 908.   **164.** See Arthur L. Smith, Jr, 'Kurt Lüdecke: the man who knew Hitler', *German Studies Review*, 26 (2003), pp. 597–606, especially p. 598.   **165.** See Brigitte Hamann, *Winifred Wagner oder Hitlers Bayreuth* (Frankfurt, 2002), p. 107.   **166.** Detlev Clemens, *Herr Hitler in Germany. Wahrnehmung und Deutungen des Nationalsozialismus in Grosbritannien 1920 bis 1939* (Göttingen and Zurich, 1996), pp. 45–51.   **167.** Truman Smith notes of a conversation with Hitler, 20.11.1922, SA, p. 733.   **168.** Henry G. Gole, *Exposing the Third Reich: Colonel Truman Smith in Hitler's Germany* (Lexington, Kentucky, 2013), pp. 65–7.   **169.** See David G. Marwell, 'Unwonted exile: a biography of Ernst "Putzi" Hanfstaengl' (PhD dissertation, New York State University, 1988), pp. 21–3, 56, 74 *et passim*.   **170.** Thus Marwell, 'Unwonted exile', p. 87.   **171.** [Mayr], 'I was Hitler's boss', p. 196.   **172.** Speech, 28.9.1922, SA, p. 718.   **173.** Speech, 6.7.1920, SA, p. 158; Speech, 12.9.1923, SA, p. 1,007; Notes for a speech, 31.5.1921, SA, p. 421.   **174.** Stefan Ihrig, *Atatürk in the Nazi Imagination* (London and Cambridge, Mass., 2014), pp. 10–67 and p. 87 (for Hitler specifically).   **175.** Speech, 18.9.1922, SA, p. 691; Conversation, [before 3.11.1922], SA, p. 722; Speech, 14.11.1922, SA, p. 728; Interview, 2.10.1923, SA, p. 1,027. See also Wolfgang Schieder, *Adolf Hitler. Politischer Zauberlehrling Mussolinis* (Berlin, 2017), p. 19 *et passim*.   **176.** Speech, 14.11.1922, SA, p. 728.   **177.** Thus Walter Werner Pese, 'Hitler und Italien, 1920–1926', *Vierteljahrshefte für Zeitgeschichte*, 3 (1955), pp. 113–26, especially, pp. 113–14.   **178.** Interview, 19.8.1923, SA, p. 975; Speech, 21.7.1920, SA, p. 163; Speech, 1.8.1920, SA, p. 169.   **179.** Speech, 8.4.1921, SA, p. 362; Speech, 31.5.1920, SA, pp. 137–8; Speech, 10.9.1922, SA, p. 688.   **180.** Speech, 17.6.1920, SA, p. 148; Speech, 26.6.1920, SA, p. 153.   **181.** Speech, 24.6.1920, SA, p. 151; Speech, 6.7.1920, SA, p. 160. See also Klaus Hildebrand, *Vom Reich zum Weltreich. Hitler, NSDAP und koloniale Frage, 1919–1945* (Munich, 1969).   **182.** Speech, 1.8.1920, SA, p. 168; Speech, 31.5.1921, SA, p. 426; Conversation, [end of December 1922], SA, p. 773.   **183.** Speech, 3.1.1923, SA, p. 780; Speech, 26.2.1923, SA, p. 836; Article, [after 10.3.1921], SA, p. 340; Article, 26.5.1921, SA, p. 412; Article, 26.5.1921, SA, p. 415.   **184.** Speech, 28.7.1922, SA, p. 671; Speech, 8.11.1922, SA, p. 724; Conversation, 14.11.1922, SA, p. 729; Speech, 21.11.1922, SA, p. 736.   **185.** Quoted in Hamann, *Hitlers Bayreuth*, p. 77.   **186.** Conversation, [end of December 1922], SA, pp. 772–3.

Chapter 4: The Struggle for Bavaria

1. Martin Schlemmer, '*Los von Berlin*'. *Rheinstaatbestrebungen nach dem Ersten Weltkrieg* (Cologne, 2007), pp. 80–174.   **2.** Matthias Strohn, *The German Army and the Defence of the Reich: Military Doctrine and the Conduct of the Defensive Battle, 1918–1939* (Cambridge, 2011), pp. 63–86.   **3.** For an example of Nazi Party involvement in these preparations at ground level see Alfred Krebs, *Tendenzen und Gestalten der NSDAP. Erinnerungen an die Frühzeit der Partei* (Stuttgart, 1959), pp. 123–5.   **4.** See Bernhard Fulda, 'Adolf Hitler als Medienphänomen', in Klaus Arnold, Christoph Classen, Susanne Kinnebrock, Edgar Lersch and Hans-Ulrich Wagner (eds.), *Von der Politisierung der Medien zur Medialisierung des Politischen? Zum Verhältnis von Medien, Öffentlichkeiten und Politik im 20. Jahrhundert* (Leipzig, 2010), pp. 141–59 (here p. 144).   **5.** Turner, *Big Business*, pp. 54–5.   **6.** Quoted in Joachimsthaler, *Hitlers Weg*, p. 306.   **7.** See the chart in Joachimsthaler, *Hitlers Weg*, p. 277.   **8.** Joachimsthaler, *Hitlers Weg*, p. 305.   **9.** Detlef Mühlberger, *Hitler's Voice:*

The Völkischer Beobachter, 1920–1933 (Bern, 2004), vol. 1, pp. 29–30.   **10.** Thus Weber, *Becoming Hitler, passim.*   **11.** Speech, 27.6.1923, SA, p. 940.   **12.** Quotations in Joachimsthaler, *Hitlers Weg*, p. 304.   **13.** Speech, 6.7.1923, SA, p. 947.   **14.** See Derek Hastings, *Catholicism and the Roots of Nazism: Religious Identity and National Socialism* (Oxford and New York, 2010), pp. 113, 148–9.   **15.** Thus Stephan Malinowski, *Vom König zum Führer. Sozialer Niedergang and politische Radikalisierung im deutschen Adel zwischen Kaiserreich and NS-Staat* (Berlin, 2003), pp. 374–6.   **16.** See Manfred Franke, *Albert Leo Schlageter, Der erste Soldat des 3. Reiches. Die Entmythologisierung eines Helden* (Cologne, 1981), pp. 110–11.   **17.** Speech, 11.1.1923, SA, p. 786; Speech, 27.1.1923, SA, p. 811; Speech, 11.1.1923, SA, p. 782.   **18.** See the recollections of the eyewitness Hans-Harald von Selchow, 15.10.1956, Sigmaringen, in Bayerisches Hauptstaatsarchiv, Abt. IV, Kriegsarchiv, HS 2775.   **19.** Memorandum, 19.4.1923, SA, pp. 902–5 (quotations on pp. 903 and 905).   **20.** Gottfried Feder, *Der Deutsche Staat auf nationaler und sozialer Grundlage* (Munich, 1923), p. 6.   **21.** 'Arbeitsplan des Ausschusses für Volksernährung der nationalsozialistischen Bewegung in vierzehn Thesen', 25.6.1923, Munich, Staatsarchiv München, Pol. Dir. 6697, fols. 48–53. See also Hitler to Sesselmann, 4.7.1923, SA, p. 943.   **22.** See Bruno Thoss, *Der Ludendorff Kreis, 1919–1923. München als Zentrum der mitteleuropäischen Gegend zwischen Revolution und Hitler-Putsch* (Munich, 1978), pp. 460–61. Hitler later reiterated this theme in *Mein Kampf*: MK, I, p. 1,551.   **23.** Speech, 27.4.1923, SA, p. 915.   **24.** Reported in 'Die Lage der Juden in Bayern', *Bayerische Staatszeitung*, 20.11.1923, Staatsarchiv München, Pol. Dir. 6697, fol. 238.   **25.** See the police statement of the arrested SA man Fritz Huber, 6.6.1923, Polizeidirektion VIa/Ia, Munich, Staatsarchiv München, Pol. Dir. 6697, fol. 3,333.   **26.** Christiane Eifert, 'Antisemit und Autokönig. Henry Fords Autobiographie und ihre deutsche Rezeption in den 1920er-Jahren', *Zeithistorische Forschungen/Studies in Contemporary History*, 6, 2 (2009), pp. 209–29, especially pp. 218–20. See also Max Wallace, *The American Axis: Henry Ford, Charles Lindbergh and the Rise of the Third Reich* (New York, 2003), especially pp. 43–5.   **27.** See the report 'Die Geldquellen Hitlers', *Münchener Post*, 21.6.1923, Stadtarchiv München, Zeitungsausschnitte-Personen, Hitler, Adolf.   **28.** Conversation, [before 17.3.1923], SA, p. 845. Robert D. Murphy, *Diplomat among Warriors* (New York, 1964), p. 41.   **29.** *München-Augsburger Abendzeitung*, 4.2.1923, Staatsarchiv München, Pol. Dir. 6697, fo. 30. Quoted in Hamann, *Hitlers Bayreuth*, p. 75. Raffael Scheck, 'Swiss funding for the early Nazi movement: motivation, context and continuities', *Journal of Modern History*, 71, 4 (1999), pp. 793–813.   **31.** Hitler to Karl von Wiegand, [before 22 April 1923], SA, p. 910.   **32.** Pese, 'Hitler und Italien'.   **33.** Interview, 20.8.1923, SA, pp. 974–5.   **34.** Thus Marwell, 'Unwonted exile', pp. 85–7, 90, 96 *et passim.*   **35.** Police Statement, 13.1.1923, SA, pp. 787–9.   **36.** Joachimsthaler, *Hitlers Weg*, p. 305.   **37.** See Lothar Gruchmann , 'Hitlers Denkschrift an die bayerische Justiz vom 16. Mai 1923. Ein verloren geglaubtes Dokument', *Vierteljahrshefte für Zeitgeschichte*, 39 (1991), pp. 305–28, especially pp. 306 and 324.   **38.** See the account by Kriminalkommissar Anton Altmann, 'Versammlung der Nationalsozialisten im Zirkusgebäude am 14.7.1923', in Staatsarchiv München, Pol. Dir. 6697, fol. 7, and following documents.   **39.** Dieter Groh, *Negative Integration und revolutionärer Attentismus. Die deutsche Sozialdemokratie am Vorabend des Ersten Weltkrieges* (Frankfurt, 1973).   **40.** Speech, 27.1.1923, SA, p. 812.   **41.** Quoted in Ihrig, *Atatürk in the Nazi Imagination*, p. 87.   **42.** See Georg Franz-Willing, *Krisenjahr der Hitlerbewegung. 1923* (Preussisch Oldendorf, 1975), pp. 173–6.   **43.** Thus Matthias Damm, *Die Rezeption des italienischen Faschismus in der Weimarer Republik* (Baden-Baden, 2013), pp. 330–32.   **44.** Erwin Bischof, *Rheinischer Separatismus, 1918–1924. Hans Adam Dortens Rheinstaatbestrebungen* (Berne, 1969), pp. 118, 125.   **45.** Quoted in Joachimsthaler, *Hitlers Weg*, p. 317.   **46.** See the testimony in HP, II, p. 566.   **47.** Speech, 16.9.1923, SA, p. 1,014.   **48.** Georg Franz-Willing, *Putsch und Verbotszeit der Hitlerbewegung, November 1923–Februar 1925* (Preussisch Oldendorf, 1977), pp. 15–19. For Hitler's more conciliatory rhetoric in this context see 30.10.1923, SA, p. 1,050.   **49.** Proclamation, 25.9.1923, SA, p. 1,014.   **50.** Memorandum, 27.9.1923, SA, p. 1,015.   **51.** Udo Bermbach, *Houston Stewart Chamberlain. Wagners Schwiegersohn – Hitlers Vordenker* (Stuttgart and Weimar, 2015), pp. 559–61.   **52.** See Weber, *Becoming Hitler*, pp. 281–6.   **53.** Alexander

Klotz, 'Gustav von Kahr (1862–1934). Nicht nur der Verantwortung seines Amtes nicht gewachsen', *Bayernspiegel. Zeitschrift der bayerischen Einigung und bayerischen Volksstiftung*, 6 (1998), pp. 2–9. **54.** See Franz-Willing, *Putsch und Verbotszeit der HitlerHitlerbewegung bewegung*, p. 9 (with quotation). **55.** See the warnings which Krebs sent to Hitler in Krebs, *Tendenzen und Gestalten*, p. 125. **56.** Hitler to Kahr, 27.9.1923, Munich, SA, p. 1,017. **57.** Proclamation, 29.9.1923, SA, p. 1,019. **58.** HP, III, p. 854. For contemporary Nazi concerns about Kahr's relationship to the BVP and separatist tendencies see the documents in Ernst Deuerlein (ed.), *Der Hitler-Putsch. Bayerische Dokumente zu 8./9. November 1923* (Stuttgart, 1962), pp. 183, 214, 218, 238–9 *et passim*. **59.** Speech, 23.10.1923, SA, pp. 1,043 and 1,049. **60.** Interview, [30.9.1923], Bayreuth, SA, p. 1,022. **61.** Interview, [before October 1923], SA, p. 1,023. **62.** Rob Dorman, 'Monroe Doctrine for Germany', *Standard Examiner*, September 1923. I thank Tom Weber for supplying me with this reference. **63.** Interview, 14.10.1923, SA, pp. 1,035–7. **64.** See HP, III, p. 1,025. **65.** Joachimsthaler, *Hitlers Weg*, p. 318. **66.** On this see also John Dornberg, *Der Hitlerputsch. 9 November 1923* (Munich, 1983), pp. 12–13. **67.** HP, II, pp. 567–8. See also the printed declaration: 'Proklamation an das deutsche Volk!', Stadtarchiv München, 282/1. **68.** Proclamation, 8.11.1923, SA, pp. 1,056–7 (quotation on p. 1,057). **69.** Thus Marwell, 'Unwonted exile', pp. 101–2; Peter Conradi, *Hitler's Piano Player* (London, 2004), p. 57. **70.** Werner Bräuninger, ' "Hitler bedroht Kronprinz Rupprecht". Die Auseinandersetzung mit dem Monarchisten Joseph Graf von Soden-Fraunhofen', in Bräuninger, *Hitlers Kontrahenten*, pp. 98–124 (quotation on p. 99). **71.** Thus Hamann, *Hitlers Bayreuth*, p. 87. **72.** HP, II, p. 568. **73.** One-page pamphlet, dated 8–9 November 1923, in Stadtarchiv München, Zeitgeschichtliche Sammlungen, 282/1. **74.** Kahr Proclamation, 'Der Hitler-Putsch', 9.11.1923, Stadtarchiv München, 282/1. **75.** 'Die Wahrheit dringt doch durch', by 'Ein Mitkämpfer der völkischen Freiheitsbewegung', in Stadtarchiv München, 282/1. **76.** The material relating to Hitler's time there is collected in Peter Fleischmann (ed.), *Hitler als Häftling in Landsberg am Lech 1923/24. Der Gefangenen-Personalakt Hitler nebst weiteren Quellen aus der Schutzhaft-, Untersuchungshaft- und Festungshaftanstalt Landsberg am Lech* (Neustadt an der Aisch, 2015). **77.** Hess to Klara and Fritz Hess, 8.11.1923, HB, p. 313. **78.** Othmar Plöckinger, *Geschichte eines Buches. Adolf Hitlers 'Mein Kampf', 1922–1945*, 2nd edn (Munich, 2011), pp. 30–31. **79.** Quoted in Otto Gritschneder, *Bewährungsfrist für den Terroristen Adolf H. Der Hitler-Putsch und die bayerische Justiz* (Munich, 1990), p. 35. **80.** Thus Hamann, *Hitlers Bayreuth*, pp. 97–9. **81.** HP, I, pp. 299–300 and 305–6. **82.** See Volker Dotterweich, 'Vom "Marsch nach Berlin" zum "Marsch nach Landsberg". Hitlers Wege nach Landsberg, 1923–1939', in Volker Dotterweich and Karl Filser (eds.), *Landsberg in der Zeitgeschichte – Zeitgeschichte in Landsberg* (Munich, 2010), pp. 151–93, on which much of this paragraph is based. See also Hermann Kriegl, *Die 'Hitler-Stadt'. Hass auf Juden – NS Dynamik 'Endlösung'* (Landsberg am Lech, 2009), especially pp. 57–60. **83.** Hermann Fobke to Ludolf Haase, 23.6.1924, Landsberg, in Werner Jochmann, *Nationalsozialismus und Revolution. Ursprung und Geschichte der NSDAP in Hamburg 1922–1933. Dokumente* (Frankfurt, 1963), pp. 90–92 (quotation on p. 92). This letter also contains a description of Hitler's daily routine. **84.** Hitler to Vogel, 10.1.1924, Landsberg, SA, p. 1,060. **85.** See generally David Jablonsky, *The Nazi Party in Dissolution: Hitler and the Verbotzeit, 1923–1925* (London, 1989), pp. 26–7, 30, 32. **86.** For example, in Decree, May 1923, RSA, I, p. 85, Hitler described Rosenberg's journal *Der Weltkampf* as belonging to the 'indispensable [intellectual] armoury of every National Socialist leader'. **87.** Jablonsky, *Nazi Party in Dissolution*, pp. 55, 160, 175 (quotation on p. 65). **88.** Thus the *Münchner Neueste Nachrichten* report as quoted in HP, IV, p. 1,597. **89.** Bernd Steger, 'Der Hitlerprozess und Bayerns Verhältnis zum Reich, 1923/24', *Vierteljahrshefte für Zeitgeschichte*, 25, 4 (1977), pp. 441–66, especially pp. 442–8, 455. **90.** E.g. HP, I, pp. 20–22, 40. **91.** HP, I, pp. 32–3. **92.** HP, II, p. 533. **93.** Quoted in Jablonsky, *Nazi Party in Dissolution*, p. 71. **94.** HP, III, pp. 1,014, 1,024 and 1,036. **95.** HP, IV, pp. 1,574–89 (with quotations). **96.** GT, I/1/I, 13.3.1924, p. 107; 15.3.1924, I/1/I, p. 107; 17.3.1924, I/1/I, p. 108. **97.** Proclamation, 1.4.1924, SA, p. 1,228. **98.** His declaration is reported in 'Das Programm Hitlers', *Münchner Neueste Nachrichten*, 16.5.1924, Stadtarchiv München, Zeitungsausschnitte,

Personen, 212/6, Hitler, Adolf, 1924/IV. **99.** See Albrecht Ritschl, *Deutschlands Krise und Konjunktur, 1924–1934. Binnenkonjunktur, Auslandsverschuldung und Reparationsproblem zwischen Dawes-Plan und Transfersperre* (Berlin, 2002). **100.** As reported for May 1924 by Walter Stang, who worked for the *Deutsche Zeitung*, and was a frequent visitor of Hitler's at Landsberg, quoted in MK, I, p. 627. **101.** Thus Angelika Müller, 'Der "jüdische Kapitalist" als Drahtzieher und Hintermann. Zur antisemitischen Bildpolemik in den nationalsozialistischen Wahlplakaten der Weimarer Republik, 1924–1933', in *Jahrbuch für Antisemitismusforschung* 7, ed. Wolfgang Benz for the Zentrum für Antisemitismusforschung der Technischen Universität Berlin (Frankfurt and New York, 1998), pp. 174–97, especially pp. 174–9. **102.** Thus Christopher Clark, 'Weimar politics and George Grosz', in *The Berlin of George Grosz: Drawings, Watercolours and Prints, 1912–1930* (New Haven and London, 1997), pp. 21–7 (here p. 27). **103.** Jablonsky, *Verbotzeit*, p. 85. For the social diversity of the Nazi voter see Thomas Childers, *The Nazi Voter: The Social Foundations of Fascism in Germany, 1919–1933* (Chapel Hill, 1983). **104.** Jablonsky, *Verbotzeit*, p. 93. **105.** See the two documentations (16 November 1923–20 February 1924; 3 April 1924–10 December 1924) in Fleischmann (ed.), *Hitler als Häftling in Landsberg am Lech*, pp. 231–376. **106.** See Hitler to Ludolf Hasse, 16.6.1924, SA, p. 1,238, and Declaration, 7.7.1924, SA, p. 1,241. See also Hermann Fobke to Ludolf Haase, 23.6.1924, Landsberg, in Jochmann, *Nationalsozialismus und Revolution*, pp. 90–92. **107.** Quoted in Plöckinger, *Geschichte eines Buches*, p. 48. **108.** E.g. Declaration, [before 7.7.1924], SA, p. 1,241; Declaration, 29.7.1924, SA, p. 1,243, and Declaration, 4.8.1924, SA, p. 1,243. **109.** Hitler to Stier, 23.6.1924, SA, p. 1,239. **110.** Jablonsky, *Verbotzeit*, pp. 101–2 (with quotations). **111.** Quoted in Plöckinger, *Geschichte eines Buches*, p. 56. **112.** Jablonsky, *Verbotzeit*, p. 91. **113.** Declaration, 16.10.1924, SA, p. 1,247. See in the same vein: Hitler to W. Hollitscher, Landsberg, 20.10.1924, SA, p. 1,247. **114.** Quoted in Plöckinger, *Geschichte eines Buches*, p. 60.

Chapter 5: Anglo-American Power and German Impotence

1. Declaration, 7.7.1924, SA, p. 1,241. See also Declaration 29.7.1924, SA, p. 1,243. **2.** E.g. Walter Stang of the 'Grossdeutschen Ringverlages', in Othmar Plöckinger (ed.), *Quellen und Dokumente zur Geschichte von 'Mein Kampf', 1924–1945* (Stuttgart, 2016), p. 24. **3.** Thus the recollection of Julius Schaub, in Julius Schaub, *In Hitlers Schatten. Erinnerungen und Aufzeichnungen des persönlichen Adjutanten und Vertrauten, 1925–1945*, ed. Olaf Rose (Stegen am Ammersee, 2010), p. 50. **4.** Schaub, *In Hitlers Schatten*, p. 43. Plöckinger, *Geschichte eines Buches*, pp. 50, 66, 152 *et passim* comprehensively refutes the idea that Hess was some sort of co-author. **5.** As reported in Hess to Ilse Pröhl, 23.7.1924, in Plöckinger (ed.), *Quellen und Dokumente*, p. 79. **6.** Thus Sven Felix Kellerhoff, *'Mein Kampf'. Die Karriere eines deutschen Buches* (Stuttgart, 2015), p. 55. **7.** Hitler to Siegfried Wagner, 5.5.1924, SA, pp. 1,232–3. **8.** Hess, 19.5.1924, HB, p. 328. **9.** Hess memorandum, 16.6.1924, HB, p. 339. **10.** Hess memorandum, 9.4.1924, HB, p. 319. **11.** Hess to Klara Hess, HB, p. 324. **12.** Hess memorandum, 9.4.1924, HB, p. 319. **13.** Hess memorandum, 16.6.1924, HB, p. 339. **14.** Hess memorandum, 16.6.1924, HB, p. 339. **15.** See Wolfgang Horn, 'Ein Unbekannter Aufsatz Hitlers aus dem Frühjahr 1924', *Vierteljahrshefte für Zeitgeschichte*, 16 (1968), pp. 280–94. **16.** See MK, I, p. 394. **17.** Thus Hess to Ilse Pröhl, Landsberg, 10.7.1924, HB, p. 345. **18.** See Plöckinger, *Geschichte eines Buches*, p. 23. **19.** See 'Konzeptblätter vom Juni 1924', in Plöckinger (ed.), *Quellen und Dokumente*, pp. 53–5. **20.** Thus Matthias Damm, *Die Rezeption des italienischen Faschismus in der Weimarer Republik* (Baden-Baden, 2013), p. 359. **21.** Hitler to Lüdecke, Munich [sic], 4.1.1924, SA, p. 1,059. See also Arthur L. Smith, Jr, 'Kurt Lüdecke: the man who knew Hitler', *German Studies Review*, 26 (2003), pp. 597–606, especially pp. 599–600. **22.** The visit is described in Hamann, *Hitlers Bayreuth*, pp. 107–10. **23.** See Plöckinger (ed.), *Quellen und Dokumente*, p. 89. **24.** See Sander A. Diamond, 'The years of waiting: National Socialism in the United States, 1922–1933', *American Jewish Historical Quarterly*, 59 (1970), pp. 256–271, especially, p. 264. See also Cornelia Wilhelm, ' "Deutschamerika" zwischen Nationalsozialismus und Amerikanismus', in Horst Möller, Andreas Wirsching and Walter Ziegler (eds.), *Nationalsozialismus in der Region. Beiträge zur regionalen und lokalen Forschung und zum internationalen Vergleich* (Munich, 1996), pp. 287–302.   **25.** Declaration, [before 22.6.1924], SA, p. 1,239.   **26.** Rudolf Hess to Gret Georg, 27.11.1924, HB, p. 356.   **27.** Jeremy Noakes, 'Conflict and development in the NSDAP 1924–1927', *Journal of Contemporary History*, 1 (1966), pp. 3–36.   **28.** Jablonsky, *Verbotzeit*, p. 145.   **29.** See Roger Moorhouse, 'Calling time on Hitler's hoax', *History Today* (December 2014), p. 7.   **30.** Thus Plöckinger, *Geschichte eines Buches*, p. 118.   **31.** See Plöckinger, *Geschichte eines Buches*, p. 74.   **32.** D. C. Watt, 'Die bayerischen Bemühungen um Ausweisung Hitlers 1924', *Vierteljahrshefte für Zeitgeschichte*, 6 (1958), pp. 270–80.   **33.** See Rudolf Hess to Emil Hamm, 11.8.1925, Munich, and Elsa Bruckmann to Hugo Bruckmann, 26.9.1926, Munich, in Plöckinger (ed.), *Quellen und Dokumente*, pp. 105–7.   **34.** GT, 30.12.1924, I/1/I, p. 256; GT, 12.1.1925, I/1/I, p. 260.   **35.** Plöckinger, *Geschichte eines Buches*, pp. 66–7 (with quotations).   **36.** GT, 12.10.1925, I/1/I, p. 364.   **37.** Hitler to Rosenberg, 2.4.1925, RSA, VI, pp. 313–17. See also Piper, *Rosenberg*, p. 126.   **38.** See Donald L. McKale, *The Nazi Party Courts: Hitler's Management of Conflict in His Movement, 1921–1945* (Lawrence, Kan., 1974), pp. 17–52.   **39.** GT, 27.5.1925, I/1/I, p. 308.   **40.** Quoted in MK, II, p. 1,292.   **41.** Wolfgang Horn, *Führerideologie und Parteiorganisation in der NSDAP (1919–1933)* (Düsseldorf, 1972), p. 426.   **42.** See Longerich, *Hitler*, p. 176.   **43.** Miriam Käfer, 'Hitlers frühe Förderer aus dem Münchner Grossbürgertum – das Verlegerehepaar Elsa und Hugo Bruckmann', in Marita Krauss (ed.), *Rechte Karrieren in München. Von der Weimarer Zeit bis in die Nachkriegsjahre* (Munich, 2010), pp. 52–79, especially p. 58.   **44.** GT, 23.11.1925, I/1/I, p. 379.   **45.** Guidelines, 26.2.1925, RSA, I, pp. 7–9.   **46.** Speech, 27.2.1925, RSA, I, pp. 14–28 (quotation, p. 26).   **47.** Article, 26.2.1925, RSA, I, p. 2.   **48.** Speech, 5.3.1925, RSA, I, p. 33.   **49.** Its growth can be charted in the appendices to Albrecht Tyrell (ed.), *Führer befiehl . . . Selbstzeugnisse aus der 'Kampfzeit' der NSDAP. Dokumentation und Analyse* (Düsseldorf, 1969), pp. 352–78.   **50.** Speech, 12.6.1925, RSA, I, p. 91.   **51.** MK, II, p. 985.   **52.** Speech, 5.7.1925, RSA, I, p. 105.   **53.** Decree, 21.3.1925, RSA, I, p. 46.   **54.** Speech, 14.6.1925, RSA, I, p. 101.   **55.** Minutes, NSDAP AGM, Munich, 22.5.1926, RSA, I, p. 431.   **56.** Decree 26.2.1925, RSA, I, p. 9. Hitler reinforced this message in MK, II, p. 1,369.   **57.** See Peter Longerich, *Die Braunen Bataillone. Geschichte der SA* (Augsburg, 1999), pp. 51–2.   **58.** Adrian Weale, *The SS: A New History* (New York, 2010), pp. 29–31.   **59.** See Andreas Gestrich and Michael Schaich (eds.), 'Hitler, *Mein Kampf*: a critical edition. The debate', *German Historical Institute London Bulletin*, 39 (2017). For a literary analysis and critique see Hermann Glaser, *Adolf Hitlers Hetzschrift 'Mein Kampf'. Ein Beitrag zur Mentalitätsgeschichte des Nationalsozialismus* (Munich, 2014).   **60.** Thus Plöckinger, *Geschichte eines Buches*, pp. 7, 13–17, 93–4, 98–9, 117 *et passim*.   **61.** Thus Kellerhoff, *'Mein Kampf'*, p. 9.   **62.** Thus Weber, *Hitler's First War*, p. 269. See also Andreas Wirsching, 'Hitlers Authentizität. Eine funktionalistische Deutung', *Vierteljahrshefte für Zeitgeschichte*, 64 (2016), pp. 387–417.   **63.** See Plöckinger, *Geschichte eines Buches*, pp. 81–3.   **64.** The main changes are highlighted in Bernd Sösemann, 'Hitlers "Mein Kampf" in der Ausgabe des "Instituts für Zeitgeschichte". Eine kritische Würdigung der anspruchsvollen Edition', *Jahrbuch für Kommunkationsgeschichte*, 19 (2017), pp. 121–50, and Kellerhoff, *'Mein Kampf'*, pp. 160–61.   **65.** MK, II, p. 1,453.   **66.** MK, II, pp. 1,239, 1,591, 1,643–5; MK, I, p. 271.   **67.** MK, I, pp. 623, 573.   **68.** Thus Speech, 15.7.1925, RSA, I, p. 125, and MK, I, pp. 423, 531, 533–5, 573.   **69.** E.g. MK, I, pp. 535, 823, 835.   **70.** MK, I, pp. 803–5 and 817; MK, II, p. 1,619.   **71.** Speech, 27.2.1925, RSA, I, pp. 14–28.   **72.** MK, I, p. 351.   **73.** Speech, 28.2.1926, RSA, I, pp. 297–330. See also Werner Jochmann, *Im Kampf an die Macht. Hitlers Rede vor dem Hamburger Nationalclub von 1919* (Frankfurt, 1960), p. 57.   **74.** MK, I, p. 643; MK, I, p. 295; MK, I, p. 837; MK, I, p. 471; Speech, 11.6.1925, RSA, I, p. 88; MK, II, p. 1,523. See also Roman Töppel, '9. November 1923. Der Hitlerputsch, *Mein Kampf* und die Verschärfung von Hitlers Judenhass', *Medaon*, 12 (2018), pp. 23–37.   **75.** Lenin: Speech, 28.10.1925, RSA, I, p. 191. Dawes: Speech, 11.6.1925, RSA, I, p. 87; Speech, 12.7.1925, RSA, I, p. 118; Speech, 13.12.1925, RSA, I, p. 249; Speech, 18.3.1926, RSA, I, p. 353.   **76.** MK,

II, p. 1,427; MK, II, pp. 1,583–5; Speech, 6.3.1927, RSA, II/1, p. 168.   77. E.g. MK, I, p. 611; Speech, 18.5.1927, RSA, II/1, p. 310.   78. MK, I, p. 413; MK, II, p. 1,685; MK, II, p. 1,667.   79. Speech, 28.2.1926, RSA, I, p. 314; Speech, 3.7.1927, RSA, II/1, p. 408; MK, I, pp. 431–3; Speech, 16.5.1927, RSA, II/1, p. 303; Speech, 12.6.1925, RSA, I, p. 94; Speech, 16.12.1925, RSA, I, p. 244; MK, I, p. 411.   80. MK, I, p. 259; MK, I, p. 261; MK, I, p. 259.   81. Thus Gerhard Linkemeyer, *Was hat Hitler mit Karl May zu tun? Versuch einer Klarstellung* (Ubstadt, 1987), pp. 50–51.   82. MK, II, pp. 1,633, 597 and 1,651. For the likely sources of Hitler's thinking on the United States see Roman Töppel, '"Volk und Rasse". Hitlers Quellen auf der Spur', *Vierteljahrshefte für Zeitgeschichte*, 64 (2016), pp. 1–35, especially pp. 13–15, 33.   83. Speech, 12.8.1926, RSA, II/1, p. 41; MK, I, p. 401; MK, II, p. 1,617; Speech, 26.3.1927, RSA, II/1, p. 197.   84. MK, I, p. 791; MK, I, p. 757; Speech, 4.7.1926, RSA, II/1, p. 19; Speech, 9.5.1926, RSA, I, p. 425; Speech, 26.3.1927, RSA, II/1, p. 201; Speech, 18.6.1926, RSA, I, p. 479.   85. Speech, 26.6.1927, RSA, II/1, p. 392; 6.8.1927, RSA, II/2, p. 443.   86. See Alexandra Przyrembel, *'Rassenschande'. Reinheitsmythos und Vernichtungslegitimation im Nationalsozialismus* (Göttingen, 2003), pp. 56–60 (for the debate in the 1920s).   87. MK, I, p. 743; Speech, 6.4.1927, RSA, II/1, p. 236; MK, II, p. 1,117; Speech, 16.5.1927, RSA, II/1, p. 303.   88. Article, 31.3.1926, RSA, I, pp. 362–3.   89. Thomas Welskopp, 'Prohibition in the United States: the German-American experience, 1919–1933', *Bulletin of German Historical Institute Washington*, 53 (Fall 2013), pp. 31–53.   90. MK, II, p. 1,039; Speech, 14.4.1926, RSA, I, pp. 388–9.   91. MK, II, pp. 1,093–95; Speech, 30.3.1926, RSA, I, p. 361; Speech, 1.4.1926, RSA, I, p. 368.   92. MK, I, p. 401; MK, II, p. 1,675; MK, I, p. 473.   93. Speech, 13.4.1927, RSA, II/1, p. 254; Speech, 13.4.1927, RSA, II/1, pp. 260–61; Speech, 6.3.1927, RSA, II/1, p. 168.   94. Speech, 6.8.1927, RSA, II/2, p. 446. In a similar vein: Speech, 6.3.1927, RSA, II/1, p. 168; Speech, 4.8.1929, RSA, III/2, p. 347; and Speech, 18.1.1928, RSA, II/2, p. 633.   95. Speech, 26.3.1927, RSA, II/1, p. 202. So far as the author knows the only historian to make (brief) mention of this strain in Hitler's thinking is Enrico Syring, *Hitler. Seine politische Utopie* (Berlin, 1994), p. 102.   96. Speech, 4.8.1929, RSA, III/2, p. 347. This theme has been noted by Gerhard L. Weinberg, 'Hitler's image of the United States', *American Historical Review*, 69 (1964), pp. 1,006–21, here p. 1,009.   97. MK, II, p. 1,125; MK, II, p. 1,099; MK, II, pp. 1,621–3.   98. MK, I, p. 299; MK, II, p. 1,619; Article, 17.9.1925, RSA, I, p. 154.   99. MK, II, pp. 1,403–9; MK, I, p. 267. For a useful tabular overview of the content of *Mein Kampf* see Plöckinger, *Geschichte eines Buches*, p. 43.   100. Speech, 12.8.1926, RSA, II/1, p. 43; Decree, 1.11.1926, RSA, II/1, p. 83; Article, 23.4.1927, RSA, II/1, p. 281.   101. Article, 28.2.1926, RSA, I, p. 314; MK, II, pp. 1,659–61.   102. MK, II, p. 1,637; MK, II, p. 1,631; MK, II, p. 1,639; MK, II, pp. 1,645–7.   103. MK, I, p. 391. See also Karl Lange, 'Der Terminus "Lebensraum" in Hitlers "Mein Kampf"', *Vierteljahrshefte für Zeitgeschichte*, 13 (1965), pp. 426–37.   104. MK, II, p. 1,657.   105. MK, II, p. 1,657.   106. MK, II, p. 1,657; MK, II, p. 1,631.   107. For a more maximalist view see Günter Moltmann, 'Weltherrschaftsideen Hitlers', in *Europa und Übersee. Festschrift für Egmont Zechlin* (Hamburg, 1961), pp. 197–240; Jochen Thies, *Architekt der Weltherrschaft. Die 'Endziele' Hitlers* (Düsseldorf, 1976). See also Hess to Hewel, 30.3.1927, cited in Gerhard L. Weinberg, 'National Socialist organization and Foreign policy aims in 1927', in Weinberg, *Germany, Hitler and World War II*, pp. 23–9, at p. 28.   108. Speech, 6.4.1927, RSA, II/1, p. 236.   109. Speech, 16.12.1925, RSA, I, p. 241; MK, I, p. 145; MK, I, p. 143; MK, II, p. 1,013.   110. Speech, 6.4.1927, RSA, II/1, pp. 236–7; Speech, 16.12.1925, RSA, I, pp. 242–3.   111. See Ryback, *Hitlers Bücher*, pp. 126, 137–41, and Töppel, '"Volk und Rasse"', pp. 32–3.   112. Speech, 6.4.1927, RSA, II/1, p. 236.   113. MK, II, p. 1,017; MK, II, p. 1,019.   114. For the distinction between 'positive' and 'negative' eugenics see MK, II, p. 670.   115. MK, II, p. 1,741.   116. Thus Eric Kurlander, *Hitler's Monsters: A Supernatural History of the Third Reich* (New Haven and London, 2017), pp. xvii–xviii, and 211 *et passim*. See also Bernard Mees, 'Hitler and *Germanentum*', *Journal of Contemporary History*, 39 (2004), pp. 255–70.   117. MK, I, p. 927; MK, II, p. 997.   118. MK, II, p. 1,013; Speech, 12.6.1925, RSA, I, p. 95; MK, II, pp. 1,013–15; MK, II, p. 1,643.   119. Decree, 17.9.1926, RSA, II/1, pp. 65–8 (quotation on p. 66); Speech, 18.5.1927, RSA, II/1, pp. 309–11 (quotations on p. 310).   120. Speech, 14.6.1925, RSA, I, p. 102.   121.

MK, I, p. 883.   **122.** MK, II, p. 1,427.   **123.** Hitler to Magnus Gött, 4.2.1927, in Paul Hoser, 'Hitler und die katholische Kirche. Zwei Briefe aus dem Jahr 1927', *Vierteljahrshefte für Zeitgeschichte*, 42 (1994), pp. 473–92 (quotation on p. 487).   **124.** MK, II, p. 1,431.   **125.** Speech, 8.7.1925, RSA, IV, p. 114; Declaration, 14.5.1925, RSA, IV, pp. 318–19; Article, 26.2.1925, RSA, IV, p. 3; MK, I, p. 349; MK, I, p. 895.   **126.** Alexander Demandt, 'Klassik als Klischee. Hitler und die Antike', *Historische Zeitschrift*, 274 (2002), pp. 281–314; and Johann Chapoutot, *Der Nationalsozialismus und die Antike* (Frankfurt, 2014), pp. 78–81.   **127.** MK, II, p. 1,075; MK, I, p. 115; MK, II, p. 1.071.   **128.** MK, II, p. 1.139; MK, I, p. 295; MK, II, p. 1,141.   **129.** Thus Longerich, *Hitler*, p. 150.

Chapter 6: Regaining Control of the Party

1. GT, 22.5.1925, I/1/I, p. 305; GT, 15.6.1925, I/1/I, p. 315; GT, 14.7.1925, I/1/I, pp. 326–7; GT, 14.10.1925, I/1/I, p. 365.   **2.** GT, 2.10.1925, I/1/I, p. 360; GT, 19.10.1925, I/1/I, p. 367; GT, 24.10.1925, I/1/I, p. 370; GT, 26.10.1925, I/1/I, p. 371.   **3.** This phenomenon has been documented by Karl-Günter Zelle, *Hitlers zweifelnde Elite. Goebbels – Göring – Himmler – Speer* (Paderborn, 2010), and *Mit Hitler im Gespräch. Blenden – überzeugen – wüten* (Paderborn, 2017).   **4.** GT, 25.1.1926, I/1/II, pp. 48–9.   **5.** GT, 23.12.1924, I/1/I, pp. 254–5.   **6.** Quotations in MK, II, p. 1,654.   **7.** Speech, 14.2.1926, RSA, I, pp. 294–6.   **8.** See the account in GT, 15.2.1926, I/1/II, pp. 55–6.   **9.** Toby Thacker, *Joseph Goebbels: Life and Death* (Basingstoke, 2009), pp. 69–70.   **10.** GT, 13.4.1926, I/1/II, p. 73. See also GT, 16.4.1926, I/1/II, p. 75.   **11.** Speech, 20.10.1926, RSA, II/1, p. 75; Statutes, 22.5.1925, RSA, I, pp. 461–5; Guidelines, 1.7.1926, RSA, II/1, pp. 1–3; Circular, 7.4.1927, RSA, II/1, pp. 241–2; Decree, 9.8.1926, RSA, II/1, p. 39; Decree, 5.2.1927, RSA, II/1, p. 150; Letter, 23.2.1927, RSA, II/1, pp. 159–60; Speech, 30.7.1927, RSA, II/1, p. 426.   **12.** Speech, 14.6.1925, RSA, I, p. 101; Speech, 14.6.1925, RSA, I, pp. 897–9; Decree, 1.7.1926, RSA, II/1, p. 1; MK, I, p. 901; Speech, 12.6.1925, RSA, I, p. 99.   **13.** Thus Andreas Heusler, *Das Braune Haus. Wie München zur 'Hauptstadt der Bewegung' wurde* (Munich, 2008), p. 9.   **14.** Speech, 5.7.1925, RSA, I, p. 105; Speech, 8.7.1925, RSA, I, p. 116; Speech, 14.6.1925, RSA, I, p. 102; Speech, 12.6.1925, RSA, I, p. 99; Speech, 5.7.1925, RSA, I, p. 105.   **15.** Speech, 12.6.1925, RSA, I, p. 99.   **16.** Thus Daniel Roos, *Julius Streicher und 'Der Stürmer', 1923–1945* (Paderborn, 2014), p. 119.   **17.** Fein, *Hitlers Weg nach Nürnberg*, pp. 130–31.   **18.** Speech, 22.5.1926, RSA, I, p. 445.   **19.** See Albrecht, *Die Avantgarde*, p. 172.   **20.** Fein, *Hitlers Weg nach Nürnberg* p. 156.   **21.** Hamann, *Hitlers Bayreuth*, pp. 134–46.   **22.** Thus Hans Rudolf Vaget, 'Hitler's Wagner: musical discourse as cultural space', in Michael H. Kater and Albrecht Riethmüller (eds.), *Music and Nazism: Art under Tyranny, 1933–1945* (Laaber, 2003), pp. 15–31, especially p. 21.   **23.** See Michael Karbaum, *Studien zur Geschichte der Bayreuther Festspiele (1876–1976)* (Regensburg, 1976), pp. 66–7.   **24.** Thus Hamann, *Hitlers Bayreuth*, pp. 160–62.   **25.** Thacker, *Goebbels*, pp. 74–7; Martin Broszat, 'Die Anfänge der Berliner NSDAP 1926/27', *Vierteljahrshefte für Zeitgeschichte*, 8 (1960), pp. 85–118.   **26.** Andreas Wirsching, *Vom Weltkrieg zum Bürgerkrieg? Politischer Extremismus in Deutschland und Frankreich, 1918–1933/39. Berlin und Paris im Vergleich* (Munich, 1999), pp. 440–67 (quotation on p. 444).   **27.** Quoted in Weinberg, 'National Socialist organization and foreign policy aims', pp. 25, 27.   **28.** Speech, 30.7.1927, RSA, II/1, p. 416; Decree, 3.7.1926, RSA, II/1, p. 9.   **29.** Quoted in Fein, *Hitlers Weg nach Nürnberg*, p. 157.   **30.** See Henriette von Schirach, *Frauen um Hitler. Nach Materialien von Henriette von Schirach* (Munich, 1985), pp. 29–55.   **31.** Declaration, 5.3.1925, RSA, I, p. 32.   **32.** Quoted in Conradi, *Hitler's Piano Player*, pp. 71–2.   **33.** See Sigmund, *Des Führers bester Freund*, pp. 97–129.   **34.** Speech 21.1.1927, RSA, II/1, p. 136. Listeners were also struck by the fact that Hitler's speeches did not address day-to-day issues: Krebs, *Tendenzen und Gestalten*, pp. 126–7.   **35.** Speech, 26.6.1927, RSA, II/1, p. 388; Speech, 12.3.1927, RSA, II/1, p. 183; Essay, August 1927, RSA, II/2, p. 501; Speech, 2.4.1927, RSA, II/1, p. 228.

Part Three: Unification

1. Hitler to Winifred Wagner, 30.12.1927, RSA, II/2, p. 587.

Chapter 7: The American Challenge

1. See Vanessa Conze, *Das Europa der Deutschen. Ideen von Europa in Deutschland zwischen Reichstradition und Westorientierung (1920–1970)* (Munich, 2005).   2. Reinhard Frommelt, *Paneuropa oder Mitteleuropa. Einigungsbestrebungen im Kalkül deutscher Wirtschaft und Politik, 1925–1933* (Stuttgart, 1977), p. 15.   3. Originally published 1924, here in Heinrich Mann, *Sieben Jahre. Chronik der Gedanken und Vorgänge. Essays* (Frankfurt, 1994), pp. 174–85.   4. Quoted in Jürgen Elvert, *Mitteleuropa! Deutsche Pläne zur europäischen Neuordnung (1918–1945)* (Stuttgart, 1999), p. 87.   5. Thus Victoria di Grazia, *Irresistible Empire: America's Advance through Twentieth-Century Europe* (Cambridge, Mass., 2006); Mary Nolan, *The Transatlantic Century: Europe and America, 1890–2010* (Cambridge, 2012), pp. 76–103.   6. Alf Lüdtke, Inge Marssolek and Adelheid von Saldern (eds.), *Amerikanisierung. Traum und Alptraum im Deutschland des 20. Jahrhunderts* (Stuttgart, 1996); Mary Nolan, *Visions of Modernity: American Business and the Modernization of Germany* (New York and Oxford, 1994); Anselm Doering-Manteuffel, *Wie westlich sind die Deutschen? Amerikanisierung und Westernisierung im 20. Jahrhundert* (Göttingen, 1999).   7. Philipp Gassert, 'Amerikanismus, Antiamerikanismus, Amerikanisierung', *Archiv für Sozialgeschichte*, 39 (1999), pp. 531–61.   8. See Wolfgang Schivelbusch, *The Culture of Defeat: On National Trauma, Mourning and Recovery* (London, 2003), p. 389.   9. Thomas J. Saunders, *Hollywood in Berlin: American Cinema and Weimar Germany* (Berkeley, 1994), especially pp. 117–44.   10. Speech, 14.5.1928, RSA, II/2, p. 836.   11. Speech, 30.3.1928, RSA, II/2, p. 760; Speech, 19.5.1928, RSA, II/2, p. 844; Speech, 19.5.1928, RSA, II/2, p. 843; Speech, 2.12.1927, RSA, II/2, p. 566.   12. Speech, 17.4.1928, RSA, II/2, p. 789; Speech, 2.12.1927, RSA, II/2, p. 563; Speech, 15.1.1928, RSA, II/2, p. 615.   13. Speech, 19.5.1928, RSA, II/2, p. 843.   14. GT, 29.8.1928, I/1/III, p. 73.   15. For an overview of the Nazi view of Europe see Thomas Sandkühler, 'Europa und der Nationalsozialismus. Ideologie, Währungspolitik, Massengewalt', in special edition of *Zeithistorische Forschungen/Studies in Contemporary History*, 9, 3 (2012), pp. 428–41.   16. GT, 20.3.1924, I/1/I, p. 109.   17. Quoted in Fein, *Hitlers Weg nach Nürnberg*, p. 161.   18. Thus Daniel Roos, *Julius Streicher und 'Der Stürmer', 1923–1945* (Paderborn, 2014), pp. 181–2.   19. GT, 6.12.1929, I/2/I, p. 32; GT, 22.6.1928, I/1/III, p. 42; GT, 30.6.1928, I/1/III, p. 46; GT, 1.7.1928, I/1/III, p. 46.   20. Thus Frank-Lothar Kroll, 'Die Edition von Hitlers Reden, Schriften und Anordnungen', in Horst Möller and Udo Wengst (eds.), *50 Jahre Institut für Zeitgeschichte. Eine Bilanz* (Munich, 1999), pp. 237–47, especially pp. 244–5, and Wolfram Pyta, 'Die Hitler-Edition des Instituts für Zeitgeschichte', *Historische Zeitschrift*, 281 (2005), 381–94, especially p. 386.   21. Quoted in Hamann, *Hitlers Bayreuth*, pp. 165–6.   22. E.g., Speech, 9.4.1932, RSA, V/1, p. 47; Speech, 17.10.1932, RSA, V/2, p. 68; Speech, 27.10.32, RSA, V/2, p. 123.   23. Second Book, RSA, II/A, p. 70 (all subsequent citations from this volume are from the Second Book); Speech, 17.4.1928, RSA, II/2, p. 783; Speech, 6.8.1927, RSA, II/2, p. 443; RSA, II/A, p. 14; RSA, II/A, p. 15; Speech, 3.3.1928, RSA, II/2, p. 735; Speech, 6.8.1927, RSA, II/2, p. 447.   24. Speech, 25.6.1931, RSA, IV/1, p. 418; Speech, 16.10.1927, RSA, II/2, p. 521; Speech, 16.11.1927, RSA, II/2, p. 546; Speech, 10.12.1927, RSA, II/2, pp. 577–8; Speech, 3.3.1928, RSA, II/2, p. 733; Speech, 2.5.1928, RSA, II/2, p. 828; RSA, II/A, pp. 124–5; RSA, II/A, p. 125; RSA, II/A, p. 87.   25. RSA, II/A, p. 86. See also Stefan Kühl, *The Nazi Connection: Eugenics, American Racism, and German National Socialism* (Oxford, 1994), p. 37.   26. WA, pp. 145–6.   27. RSA, II/A, p. 92.   28. See Johnpeter Horst Grill and Robert L. Jenkins, 'The Nazis and the American South in the 1930s: a mirror image?', *Journal of Southern History*, 58 (1992), pp. 667–94, especially pp. 671–2.   29. Hitler to Magnus Gött, 2.3.1927, in Hoser, 'Hitler und die katholische Kirche', p. 489.   30. RSA, II/A, p. 14; Speech,

2.12.1927, RSA, II/2, p. 566; Speech, 15.1.1928, II/2, p. 615.   31. Hess to Klara and Fritz
Hess, Munich, 18.12.1928, HB, p. 395.   32. Article, 29.12.1928, RSA, VI, p. 343; Speech,
26.4.1928, RSA, II/2, p. 796.   33. RSA, II/A, p. 38; RSA, II/A, pp. 105-6; Speech,
26.4.1928, RSA, II/2, p. 795; Speech, 3.3.1928, RSA, II/2, p. 721.   34. RSA, II/A, p.
20.   35. Speech, 29.2.1928, RSA, II/2, pp. 681-7; Speech, 29.2.1928, RSA, II/2, p. 700
(BVP and Jews); and Speech, 21.3.1928, RSA, II/2, p. 751 (BVP closeness to Jewish sexual
deviant).   36. Alfons Beckenbauer, 'Wie Adolf Hitler durch eine niederbayerischen Grafen
zu einem Wutausbruch gebracht wurde. Aus den unveröffentlichten Memoiren des Joseph
Maria Graf von Soden-Fraunhofen – zugleich ein Beitrag zur Geschichte des monarchischen
Gedankens in Bayern während der Weimarer Zeit', in *Verhandlungen des Historischen
Vereins für Niederbayern*, 103 (Landshut, 1977), pp. 5-29.   37. Speech, 21.11.1927, RSA,
II/2, p. 555; Speech, 10.12.1927, RSA, II/2, p. 580; Speech, 11.5.1928, RSA, II/2, p. 835;
Speech, 2.5.1928, RSA, II/2, p. 810; Speech, 12.1.1928, RSA, II/2, p. 599.   38. Speech,
2.5.1928, RSA, II/2, p. 828.   39. RSA, II/A, p. 6; RSA, II/A, p. 7; Speech, 3.3.1928, RSA,
II/2, pp. 722-3; Speech, 17.4.1928, RSA, II/2, p. 788.   40. Speech, 17.4.1928, RSA, II/2,
p. 780; Speech, 3.3.1928, RSA, II/2, p. 732.   41. Figures in Horst Rössler, 'Massenexodus:
die neue Welt des 19. Jahrhunderts', in Klaus J. Bade (ed.), *Deutsche im Ausland – Fremde
in Deutschland. Migration in Geschichte und Gegenwart* (Munich, 1992), pp. 148-50.
See also James Boyd, 'The Rhine exodus of 1816/1817 within the developing German
Atlantic World', *Historical Journal*, 59 (2016), pp. 99-123.   42. Monika Blaschke,
'"Deutsch-Amerika" in Bedrängnis. Krise und Verfall einer "Bindestrichkultur"', in Bade
(ed.), *Deutsche im Ausland*, pp. 171 and 176.   43. Lieselotte Overvold, 'Wagner's American
Centennial March: genesis and reception', *Monatshefte*, 68 (1976), pp. 179-87.   44. Udo
Sautter, 'Deutsche in Kanada', in Bade (ed.), *Deutsche im Ausland*, p. 185.   45. See Karen
Schniedwind, 'Fremde in der Alten Welt. Die transatlantische Rückwanderung', in Bade
(ed.), *Deutsche im Ausland*, pp. 179-85.   46. RSA, II/A, p. 8; Speech, 3.3.1928, RSA,
II/2, p. 730; Speech, 14.4.1928, RSA, II/2, p. 777; Speech, 26.4.1928, RSA, II/2, p. 796;
RSA, II/A, p. 85. See also Günter Moltmann, 'Nordamerikanische "Frontier" und deutsche
Auswanderung – soziale "Sicherheitsventile" im 19. Jahrhundert?', in Dirk Stegmann,
Bernd-Jürgen Wendt and Peter-Christian Witt (eds.), *Industrielle Gesellschaft und
politisches System. Beiträge zur politischen Sozialgeschichte* (Bonn, 1978), pp. 279-96,
especially pp. 293-4.   47. Speech, 18.1.1928, RSA, II/2, pp. 632-3; RSA, II/A, pp. 79, 8,
78; Speech, 15.1.1928, RSA, II/2, pp. 613-14.   48. Article, 3.11.1928, RSA, III/1, p.
202.   49. Speech, 18.1.1928, RSA, II/2, p. 633. The date in the copy of the original document is illegible, but it is clear that 1918 is meant. I thank Dr Klaus Lankheit of the Institut
für Zeitgeschichte, Munich, one of the original editors, for this information.   50. Speech,
6.8.1927, RSA, II/2, p. 445; RSA, II/A, p. 95; Speech, 6.8.1927, RSA, II/2, p. 455.   51.
RSA, II/A, p. 78. For Hitler's attitude to Coudenhove-Kalergi see also Dina Gusejnova,
European Elites and Ideas of Empire, 1917-1957 (Cambridge, 2016), pp. 195-6.   52. RSA,
II/A, p. 91.   53. RSA, II/A, pp. 88-2.   54. RSA, II/A, p. 90; RSA, II/A, p. 27; Speech,
2.5.1928, RSA, II/2, p. 808.   55. Hess to Ilse Pröhl, 8.3.1928, HB, p. 391; Hess to Klara
and Fritz Hess, 18.12.1928, HB, p. 395; Speech, 21.8.1927, RSA, II/2, p. 497; Speech,
29.2.1928, RSA, II/2, p. 691.   56. RSA, II/A, pp. 60, 119, 123, 129, 182 *et passim*.   57.
RSA, II/A, p. 60.   58. RSA, II/A, p. 82.   59. Paul Rohrbach, *Die deutschen Kolonien. Ein
Bilderbuch aller deutscher Kolonien* (Dachau, 1912), p. 3 *et passim*; Friedrich Ratzel, *Wider
die Reichsnörgler* (Munich, 1884), pp. 10-11, 15-16, 23 *et passim*. I thank William O'Reilly
for these references and for his help in understanding the phenomenon of German emigration
to the United States. See also Woodruff D. Smith, '"Weltpolitik" und "Lebensraum"', in
Sebastian Conrad and Jürgen Osterhammel (eds.), *Das Kaiserreich transnational.
Deutschland in der Welt, 1871-1914* (Göttingen, 2006), pp. 29-48, especially pp. 31 and
47.   60. RSA, II/A, pp. 34, 60, 123 (quotations) *et passim*. Manfred Weissbecker, '"Wenn
hier Deutsche wohnten . . ." Beharrung und Veränderung im Russlandbild Hitlers und der
NSDAP', in Hans-Erich Volkmann (ed.), *Das Russlandbild im Dritten Reich* (Cologne,
1994), pp. 9-54.   61. RSA, II/A, pp. 103, 149, 147, 113, 114.   62. RSA, II/A, pp. 149-
50.   63. GT, 19.1.1928, I/1/II, p. 317; GT, 22.1.1928, I/1/II, p. 317.   64. Wolfgang

Schieder, *Faschistische Diktaturen. Studien zu Italien und Deutschland* (Göttingen, 2008), p. 235. 65. RSA, II/A, pp. 126–9. 66. RSA, II/A, pp. 135, 186. 67. RSA, II/A, p. 32. 68. RSA, II/A, p. 181. 69. GT, 5.7.1929, I/1/III, p. 281. 70. Speech, 16.11.1930, RSA, IV/1, p. 111. 71. Thus Thacker, *Goebbels*, pp. 97–9. 72. Turner, *Big Business*, pp. 69, 95 (quotations, pp. 66 and 70). 73. See Fein, *Hitlers Weg nach Nürnberg*, p. 160. 74. Hamann, *Hitlers Bayreuth*, p. 177. 75. See Turlach O Broin, 'Mail-order demagogues: the NSDAP School for Speakers, 1928–34', *Journal of Contemporary History*, 51 (2016), pp. 715–37. 76. Michael Wala, *Weimar und Amerika. Botschafter Friedrich von Prittwitz und Gaffron und die deutsch-amerikanischen Beziehungen von 1927 bis 1933* (Stuttgart, 2001), pp. 122–51. See also Philipp Heyde, *Das Ende der Reparationen. Deutschland, Frankreich und der Youngplan, 1929–1932* (Paderborn, 1998), pp. 35–75. 77. Hannah Ahlheim, *'Deutsche, kauft nicht bei Juden!' Antisemitismus und politischer Boykott in Deutschland 1924 bis 1935* (Göttingen, 2011), pp. 82–90. 78. Fritz Reinhardt, *Deutschland erwache!* (Herrsching am Ammersee, 1930), p. 5 *et passim*; Fritz Reinhardt, *Menschenexport in Sicht* (Herrsching am Ammersee, 1931), especially pp. 2–4. I am very grateful to Darren O'Byrne for drawing these texts to my attention. 79. Hitler to Josef, Count Soden Fraunhofen, 7.11.1929, RSA, III/2, p. 445. 80. See Gerhard Paul, *Aufstand der Bilder. Die NS-Propaganda vor 1933* (Bonn, 1992), pp. 84–9. 81. Thus Hermann Balle, 'Die propagandistische Auseinandersetzung des Nationalsozialismus mit der Weimarer Republik und ihre Bedeutung für den Aufstieg des Nationalsozialismus' (PhD dissertation, University of Erlangen-Nuremberg, 1963), pp. 166–71 (quotations on 167 and 170). 82. GT, 29.5.1929, I/1/III, p. 257. 83. Article, 9.4.1930, RSA, III/3, p. 156. 84. Thus Turner, 'Hitlers Einstellung', pp. 89–117, especially p. 97. See also Peter Krüger, 'Zu Hitlers "nationalsozialistischen Wirtschaftserkenntnissen"', *Geschichte und Gesellschaft*, 6 (1980), pp. 263–82. 85. Barry Eichengreen, *Golden Fetters: The Gold Standard and the Great Depression, 1919–1939* (Oxford, 1992), especially pp. 241–6; Charles P. Kindleberger, *The World in Depression, 1929–1939* (London, 1973), pp. 108–27; Harold James, *The German Slump: Politics and Economics, 1924–1936* (Oxford, 1986). 86. Here I disagree with Gerhard L. Weinberg, 'The world through Hitler's eyes', in Weinberg, *Germany, Hitler and World War II*, p. 50, and Andreas Hillgruber, 'Hitler und die USA, 1933–1945', in Otmar Franz (ed.), *Europas Mitte* (Göttingen and Zurich, 1987), pp. 125–44, especially p. 129, where Hillgruber advances no evidence for his claim that the 1929 crash was a watershed for Hitler's view of the United States. Enrico Syring, *Hitler. Seine politische Utopie* (Berlin, 1994), pp. 103–4, has it right. 87. Speech, 10.1.1930, RSA, III/3, p. 8; Article, 29.1.1930, RSA, III/3, p. 44. 88. GT, 3.4.1929, I/1/III, p. 219; Article, 11.1.1930, RSA, III/3, p. 14; Article, 11.1.1930, RSA, III/3, pp. 12–13; Article, 8.2.1930, RSA, III/3, pp. 81–2; Speech, 7.4.1931, RSA, IV/1, p. 267. On 8.3.1930 (Article, RSA, III/3, p. 122), Hitler did express a fear of Russian armaments. 89. Fein, *Hitlers Weg nach Nürnberg*, pp. 175–6. 90. For Coburg see Albrecht, *Die Avantgarde*, pp. 172–4. For Wagner see Ulrike Haerendel, 'Vom "Hitlerputsch" zur Gleichschaltung. Münchens Weg zur nationalsozialistischen "Hauptstadt der Bewegung" 1923 bis 1935', in Fritz Mayrhofer and Ferdinand Opll (eds.), *Stadt und Nationalsozialismus* (Linz, 2008), pp. 171–2. See also Clemens Vollnhals, 'Der Aufstieg der NSDAP in München 1925 bis 1933. Förderer und Gegner', in Richard Bauer et al. (eds.), *München – "Hauptstadt der Bewegung"* (Munich, 1998), pp. 157–65. 91. Donald R. Tracey, 'The development of the National Socialist Party in Thuringia, 1924–30', *Central European History*, 8 (1975), pp. 23–50, especially pp. 42–3. 92. Article, 1.2.1930, RSA, III/3, p. 58. 93. Hitler to unknown recipient, draft, 2.2.1930, RSA, III/3, p. 61. 94. Thus Karsten Rudolph, 'Nationalsozialisten in Ministersesseln. Die Machterübernahme der NSDAP und die Länder, 1929–1933', in Christian Jansen, Lutz Niethammer and Bernd Weisbrod (eds.), *Von der Aufgabe der Freiheit. Politische Verantwortung und bürgerliche Gesellschaft im 19. und 20. Jahrhundert* (Berlin, 1995), p. 251. 95. Oron James Hale, 'Adolf Hitler: taxpayer', *American Historical Review*, 60 (1955), pp. 830–42, identifies 1929 as the turning point (p. 836). See also Wulf C. Schwärzwäller, *Hitlers Geld. Vom armen Kunstmaler zum millionenschweren Führer* (Wiesbaden, 2001), pp. 112–56. 96. Hoser, 'Thierschstrasse 41', p. 148. 97. Stratigakos, *Hitler at Home*, pp. 18–20. 98. Edgar Feuchtwanger,

Als Hitler unser Nachbar war. Erinnerungen an meine Kindheit im Nationalsozialismus (Munich, 2014). **99**. See Krebs, *Tendenzen und Gestalten*, p. 142. **100**. Thus Hess to Klara and Fritz Hess, Munich, 18.12.1928, HB, p. 395. **101**. See Hamann, *Hitlers Bayreuth*, p. 185. **102**. GT, 20.7.1930, I/2/1, p. 202. **103**. See Sigmund, *Des Führers bester Freund*, *passim*. **104**. GT, 19.10.1928, I/1/III, p. 105. **105**. Heike B. Görtemaker, *Eva Braun. Leben mit Hitler* (Munich, 2010), p. 21. **106**. GT, 6.12.1929, I/2/1, p. 34. **107**. Quoted in Conradi, *Hitler's Piano Player*, pp. 81-2. **108**. WA, p. 33. **109**. GT, 6.12.1929, I/2/1, p. 34. **110**. WA, p. 5. **111**. WA, p. 58. **112**. GT, 25.11.1928, I/1/III, p. 131. **113**. Thus WA, p. 175. **114**. WA, p. 178. **115**. GT, 6.12.1929, I/2/I, p. 33. **116**. GT, *c*.22.11.1929, I/1/III, p. 378. **117**. See Hitler to unknown recipient, 2.2.1930, RSA, III/3, pp. 60-61 (quotation on p. 61). **118**. For long timeline see Syring, *Hitler. Seine politische Utopie*, p. 101. **119**. WA, p. 8. **120**. Weale, *The SS*, pp. 39-46.

Chapter 8: Breakthrough

1. See Paul Köppen, '"Aus der Krankheit konnten wir unsere Waffe machen." Heinrich Brünings Spardiktat und die Ablehnung der französischen Kreditangebote 1930/31', *Vierteljahrshefte für Zeitgeschichte*, 62 (2014), pp. 349-76, especially p. 371. **2**. Article, 21.2.1931, RSA, IV/1, p. 212; Appeal, 26.5.1930, RSA, III/3, pp. 207-9; Article, 21.2.1931, RSA, IV/1, p. 214. **3**. GT, 30.1.1930, I/2/I, p. 75; GT, 22.2.1930, I/2/I, p. 93; GT, 4.3.1930, I/2/I, p. 102. **4**. Article, 24.5.1930, RSA, III/3, pp. 204-6. **5**. GT, 20.3.1930, I/2/I, p. 114; GT, 2.4.1930, I/2/I, p. 123; GT, 8.4.1930, I/2/I, p. 143; GT, 29.6.1930, I/2/I, p. 186; GT, 28.3.1930, I/2/I, p. 119. **6**. GT, 28.4.1930, I/2/I, p. 144. **7**. See Patrick Moreau, *Nationalsozialismus von links. Die 'Kampfgemeinschaft Revolutionärer Nationalsozialisten' und die 'Schwarze Front' Otto Strassers 1930-1935* (Stuttgart, 1985), pp. 41-8. **8**. E.g. Witness Statement, 25.9.1930, RSA, III/3, p. 440. **9**. Daniel Siemens, *Stormtroopers: A New History of Hitler's Brownshirts* (New Haven and London, 2017), pp. 57-8. **10**. Thus GT, 30.8.1930, I/2/I, pp. 228-9. **11**. Plöckinger, *Geschichte eines Buches*, pp. 193-5. **12**. MK, I, footnote 72. **13**. Memorandum, 15.12.1932, RSA, V/2, p. 274. **14**. Speech, 5.8.1930, RSA, III/3, p. 300. **15**. Article, 30.8.1930, RSA, III/3, p. 376; Article, 6.9.1930, RSA, III/3, p. 383. **16**. GT, 3.9.1930, I/2/I, p. 232. **17**. Speech, 2.7.1930, RSA, III/3, p. 259. **18**. Speech, 2.5.1930, RSA, III/3, p. 176; Speech, 11.6.1930, RSA, III/3, p. 223; Speech, 10.8.1930, RSA, III/3, p. 311; Speech, 6.6.1930, RSA, III/3, p. 219. See also: Decree, 6.3.1930, RSA, III/3, p. 118; Speech, 2.5.1930, RSA, III/3, p. 175; Speech, 16.6.1930, RSA, III/3, p. 230; Speech, 18.8.1930, RSA, III/3, p. 351. **19**. Speech, 24.2.1930, RSA, III/3, p. 106; Decree, 6.3.1930, RSA, III/3, p. 116; Speech, 24.7.1930, RSA, III/3, p. 290. **20**. See the figures in Fein, *Hitlers Weg nach Nürnberg*, p. 194. **21**. See Jürgen W. Falter, 'Die Wähler der NSDAP 1928-1933. Sozialstruktur und parteipolitische Herkunft', in Wolfgang Michalka (ed.), *Die nationalsozialistische Machtergreifung* (Paderborn, Munich, Vienna and Zurich, 1984), pp. 47-59; Richard F. Hamilton, *Who Voted for Hitler?* (Princeton, 1982), pp. 3-8 *et passim*; and Childers, *The Nazi Voter*, pp. 119-91. **22**. See Jan-Bernd Lohmöller, Jürgen W. Falter, Johann de Rijke and Andreas Link, 'Der Einfluss der Weltwirtschaftskrise auf den NSDAP-Aufstieg', in Jürgen W. Falter, Christian Fenner and Michael Th. Greven (eds.), *Politische Willensbildung und Interessenvermittlung* (Opladen, 1984), pp. 391-401, especially pp. 400-401. **23**. For some cautious remarks on this see Richard Bessel, 'The Nazi capture of power', *Journal of Contemporary History*, 39 (2004), pp. 169-88, especially p. 170. **24**. Hess to Fritz Hess, Munich, 24.10.1930, HB, p. 405. **25**. Brechtken, *Albert Speer*, pp. 31-4. **26**. GT, 6.1.1931, I/2/I, p. 319. **27**. Speech, 16.11.1930, RSA, IV/1, p. 108; Speech, 1.12.1930, RSA, IV/1, p. 141. **28**. Speech, 16.11.1930, RSA, IV/1, p. 115. **29**. Thus Turner, *Big Business*, p. 127. **30**. Article 1.11.1930, RSA, IV/1, p. 43. **31**. Speech, 1.12.1930, RSA, IV/1, pp. 141-4. **32**. WA, pp. 68-9. **33**. Speech, 18.1.1931, IV/1, p. 174. **34**. Article, 8.4.1931, IV/1, p. 274; Speech, 25.10.1930, RSA, IV/1, p. 30. **35**. Speech, 1.12.1930, RSA, IV/1, p. 142; Speech, 29.1.1931, RSA, IV/1, pp. 180-81; Speech, 23.10.1930, RSA, IV/1, pp. 26-7; Speech, 1.12.1930, IV/1, p. 142; Speech, 13.11.1930, RSA,

IV/1, p. 103; Speech, 13.11.1930, RSA, IV/1, p. 96; Speech, 16.11.1930, RSA, IV/1, p. 110. **36.** WA, pp. 204–6.   **37.** WA, p. 213.   **38.** WA, pp. 276–7.   **39.** WA, p. 214.   **40.** WA, p. 214.   **41.** Thus Speech, 13.11.1930, RSA, IV/1, p. 91.   **42.** E.g. Speech, 6.9.1930, RSA, III/3, p. 384; Speech, 2.11.1930, RSA, IV/1, p. 47; Speech, 5.11.1930, RSA, IV/1, p. 53; Speech, 7.12.1930, IV/1, p. 153.   **43.** Speech, 13.11.1930, RSA, IV/1, p. 104; Speech, 23.11.1930, RSA, IV/1, p. 131.   **44.** See Reiner Flik, *Von Ford lernen? Automobilbau und Motorisierung in Deutschland bis 1933* (Cologne, Weimar and Vienna, 2001), pp. 58–9.   **45.** Speech 8.11.1930, RSA, IV/1, p. 80. In the same vein see Speech, 5.11.1930, RSA, IV/1, p. 53.   **46.** Speech, 29.1.1931, RSA, IV/1, p. 181.   **47.** Speech, 7.12.1930, RSA, IV/1, p. 152.   **48.** Speech, 8.11.1930, RSA, IV/1, p. 79. In the same vein see Speech, 7.12.1930, RSA, IV/1, p. 152; Speech, 24.4.1931, RSA, IV/1, p. 332; Article, 4.7.1931, RSA, IV/2, p. 26; Speech, 9.9.1931, RSA, IV/2, p. 99; Speech, 3.11.1931 RSA, IV/2, p. 180.   **49.** Declaration, 6.2.1931, RSA, IV/1, p. 185.   **50.** Speech, 5.11.1930, RSA, IV/1, p. 53. In same vein see Speech, 13.11.1930, RSA, IV/1, p. 95.   **51.** Thilo Vogelsang, 'Neue Dokumente zur Geschichte der Reichswehr, 1930–1933', *Vierteljahrshefte für Zeitgeschichte*, 2 (1954), pp. 397–436 (quotation on p. 406).   **52.** Fein, *Hitlers Weg nach Nürnberg*, p. 201.   **53.** Turner, *Big Business*, pp. 129–31.   **54.** Quoted in Turner, *Big Business*, p. 218.   **55.** Thus Horst Matzerath and Henry A. Turner, 'Die Selbstfinanzierung der NSDAP, 1930–1932', *Geschichte und Gesellschaft*, 3 (1977), pp. 59–92, especially pp. 69–70. This picture is confirmed by Otto Dietrich, *12 Jahre mit Hitler* (Munich, 1955), pp. 185–8.   **56.** Decree, 7.11.1930, RSA, IV/1, p. 64.   **57.** Albrecht Tyrell, 'Der Wegbereiter – Hermann Göring als politischer Beauftragter Hitlers in Berlin 1930–1932/33', in Manfred Funke, Hans-Adolf Jacobsen, Hans-Helmuth Knütter and Hans-Peter Schwarz (eds.), *Demokratie und Diktatur. Geist und Gestalt politischer Herrschaft in Deutschland und Europa. Festschrift für Karl-Dietrich Bracher* (Düsseldorf, 1987), pp. 178–97.   **58.** See the memoirs of the deputy leader, Theodor Duesterberg, *Der Stahlhelm und Hitler* (Wolfenbüttel and Hanover, 1949), pp. 13–14.   **59.** Speech, 22.11.1930, RSA, IV/1, pp. 122–3.   **60.** Malinowski, *Vom König zum Führer*, especially pp. 445, 478, 508, 516. See also Georg H. Kleine, 'Adelsgenossenschaft und Nationalsozialismus', *Vierteljahrshefte für Zeitgeschichte*, 26 (1978), pp. 100–143, especially p. 113.   **61.** 'Aufzeichnung des Fürsten Eulenburg-Hertefeld über seine Besprechung mit Hitler am 24. Januar 1931', in Kurt Gossweiler and Alfred Schlicht, 'Junker und NSDAP, 1931/32', *Zeitschrift für Geschichtswissenschaft*, 15 (1967), pp. 653–62.   **62.** WA, pp. 49–53.   **63.** Adolf Kimmel, *Der Aufstieg des Nationalsozialismus im Spiegel der französischen Presse, 1930–1933* (Bonn, 1969), pp. 73–81; William F. Sheldon, 'Das Hitler-Bild in der "Time" 1923–1933', in Joachim Hütter, Reinhard Meyers and Dietrich Papenfuss (eds.), *Tradition und Neubeginn. Internationale Forschungen zur deutschen Geschichte im 20. Jahrhundert* (Cologne, 1975), pp. 67–81, especially pp. 75–7; and Frank McDonough, 'The Times, Norman Ebbut and the Nazis, 1927–37', *Journal of Contemporary History*, 27 (1992), pp. 407–24 (for Nazi attempts to influence Ebbutt, p. 40).   **64.** Thus Hess to Fritz Hess, Munich, 24.10.1930, HB, p. 405.   **65.** WA, p. 89.   **66.** WA, p. 90.   **67.** Thus WA, p. 230.   **68.** Interview, 2.10.1930, RSA, IV/1, pp. 3–4.   **69.** WA, p. 90.   **70.** Conradi, *Hanfstaengl*, pp. 80, 83, 85.   **71.** Interview, 4.10.1930, RSA, IV/1, p. 5; Interview, 14.10.1930, RSA, IV/1, p. 21.   **72.** Alfred Kube, *Pour le mérite und Hakenkreuz. Hermann Göring im Dritten Reich* (Munich, 1986), pp. 17–18. See also Hans Woller, 'Machtpolitisches Kalkül oder ideologische Affinität? Zur Frage des Verhältnisses zwischen Hitler und Mussolini vor 1933', in Wolfgang Benz, Hans Buchheim and Hans Mommsen (eds.), *Der Nationalsozialismus. Studien zur Ideologie und Herrschaft* (Frankfurt, 1993), pp. 42–63.   **73.** See Wolfgang Schieder, *Faschistische Diktaturen. Studien zu Italien und Deutschland* (Göttingen, 2008), pp. 236–41.   **74.** GT, 20.2.1931, II/1, pp. 349–50; GT, 27.2.1931 II/1, p. 354.   **75.** Decree, 3.2.1931, RSA, IV/1, p. 183. For Hitler and Röhm's homosexuality see Burkhard Jellonnek, *Homosexuelle unter dem Hakenkreuz. Die Verfolgung von Homosexuellen im Dritten Reich* (Paderborn, 1990), pp. 58–61.   **76.** 'Das aussenpolitische Exposé von Ernst Röhm über die Zukunft Europas' [April 1931], in Hans-Günter Richardi and Klaus Schumann, *Geheimakte Gerlich/Bell. Röhms Pläne für ein Reich ohne Hitler* (Munich, 1993), pp. 206–14.   **77.** Speech, 7.3.1931, RSA, IV/1, p. 229; Speech, 4.4.1931, RSA, IV/1,

p. 260.   **78.** See Richard Bessel, *Political Violence and the Rise of Nazism: The Storm Troopers in Eastern Germany, 1925–1934* (New Haven, 1984); and Conan Fischer, *Stormtroopers: A Social, Economic and Ideological Analysis, 1929–35* (London, 1983).   **79.** Benjamin Carter Hett, *Crossing Hitler: The Man Who Put the Nazis on the Witness Stand* (Oxford, 2008), pp. 83–9, 263–75.   **80.** Speech, 7.4.1931, RSA, IV/1, p. 272; Decree, 27.4.1931, RSA, IV/1, pp. 336–8; Speech, 2.5.1931, RSA, IV/1, p. 352.   **81.** GT, 8.6.1931, I/2/I, p. 34.   **82.** WA, p. 106.   **83.** Milan Hauner, *Hitler: A Chronology of His Life and Time*, 2nd edn (Basingstoke, 2005), p. 73; Interview, 1.5.1931, RSA, IV/1, pp. 347–8.   **84.** Interview, 9.6.1931, RSA, IV/1, p. 407.   **85.** WA, pp. 154–9.   **86.** Speech, 8.2.1931, RSA, IV/1, p. 194. In the same vein Speech, 22.2.1931, IV/1, p. 220; and Speech, 19.4.1931, RSA, IV/1, p. 317.   **87.** Speech, 24.4.1931, RSA, IV/1, p. 334; Speech, 5.11.1930, IV/1, p. 56; Speech, 11.12.1930, IV/1, p. 164.   **88.** Karl Erich Born, *Die deutsche Bankenkrise 1931. Finanzen und Politik* (Munich, 1967), especially pp. 64–109.   **89.** Speech, 8.2.1931, RSA, IV/1, p. 194; Speech, 16.4.1931, RSA, IV/1, pp. 307–8; Speech, 9.5.1931, RSA, IV/1, p. 371; Speech, 3.7.1931, RSA, IV/2, pp. 4–5; Interview, July 1931, RSA, IV/2, p. 46; Interview, 14.7.1931, RSA, IV/2, p. 35; Interview, 22.12.1931, RSA, IV/2, p. 302.   **90.** E.g. WA, p. 185 on Hitler's response to the devalation of Sterling in autumn 1931.   **91.** Speech, 25.6.1931, RSA, IV/1, p. 414.   **92.** Speech, 25.6.1931, RSA, IV/1, p. 417.   **93.** Speech, 4.9.1931, RSA, IV/2, p. 73.   **94.** Article, 1.11.1930, RSA, IV/1, p. 45.   **95.** Turner, *Big Business*, p. 129.   **96.** WA, p. 198.   **97.** Article, 4.4.1931, IV/1, p. 252; Hitler to Rosenberg, 24.8.1931, RSA, VI, pp. 352–3.   **98.** Turner, *Big Business*, p. 143.   **99.** Hess to Klara and Fritz Hess, 3.9.1931, Berlin, HB, p. 413.   **100.** Quoted in Turner, *Big Business*, pp. 171–12.   **101.** Thus at any rate Heinrich Brüning, *Memoiren, 1918–1934* (Stuttgart, 1970), p. 272.   **102.** GT, 24.8.1931, I/2/II, p. 83.   **103.** Thus Turner, *Big Business*, p. 217.   **104.** Hess to Klara and Fritz Hess, 3.9.1931, Berlin, HB, p. 413.   **105.** GT, 20.1.1931, I/2/II, p. 200; GT, 26.8.1931, I/2/II, p. 85; GT, 14–16.9.1931, I/2/II, pp. 97–101.   **106.** Dietrich, *12 Jahre*, p. 197.   **107.** GT, 25.9.1931, I/2/II, p. 107; GT, 22.12.1931, I/2/II, p. 154; GT, 27.10.1931, I/2/II, p. 135.   **108.** Quoted in Hamann, *Hitlers Bayreuth*, p. 210.   **109.** Declaration, 21.9.1931, RSA, IV/2, pp. 109–11.   **110.** Reported in footnote to speech, RSA, IV/2, p. 111.   **111.** Thus Stratigakos, *Hitler at Home*, pp. 20–23, 149–54 *et passim*.   **112.** GT, 25.9.1931, I/2/II, p. 107; GT, 30.9.1931, I/2/II, p. 12.   **113.** Speech, 25.9.1931, RSA, IV/2, p. 116.   **114.** Decree, 2.11.1931, RSA, IV/2, pp. 177–8.   **115.** Volker Hentschel, *Weimars letzte Monate. Hitler und der Untergang der Republik* (Düsseldorf, 1978), pp. 117–19.   **116.** Thus Sven Tode, *Die Gelita Story. 125 Jahre DGF Stoess AG* (Hamburg, 2003), pp. 119–20.   **117.** Turner, *Big Business*, p. 239.   **118.** Thus Wolfram Pyta, *Hindenburg. Herrschaft zwischen Hohenzollern und Hitler* (Munich, 2007), pp. 635–7. For an eyewitness account see Levetzow to Donnersmarck, in Gerhard Granier, *Magnus von Levetzow. Seeoffizier, Monarchist und Wegbereiter Hitlers. Lebensweg und ausgewählte Dokumente* (Boppard am Rhein, 1982), pp. 307–11.   **119.** Larry Eugene Jones, 'Nationalists, Nazis and the assault against Weimar: revisiting the Harzburg Rally of October 1931', *German Studies Review*, 29 (2006), pp. 483–94, especially pp. 486–8.   **120.** GT, 12.10.1931, I/2/II, p. 121.   **121.** Interview, 20.12.1931, RSA, IV/2, p. 297; Hitler to Groener, 14.11.1931, RSA, IV/2, p. 202; Decree, 28.11.1931, RSA, IV/2, pp. 212–15; Order of the Day, 1.12.1931, RSA, IV/2, p. 225; Decree, 12.10.1931, RSA, IV/2, pp. 132–4.   **122.** Granier, *Levetzow*, p. 163.   **123.** Jens Petersen, *Hitler–Mussolini. Die Entstehung der Achse Berlin–Rom 1933–1936:* (Tübingen, 1973), pp. 44–5.   **124.** Waddington, *Hitler's Crusade*, p. 42.   **125.** Quotation from Bernard V. Burke, *Ambassador Frederic Sackett and the Collapse of the Weimar Republic, 1930–1933: The United States and Hitler's Rise to Power* (Cambridge, 1994), p. 8.   **126.** Hitler to Sefton Delmer, 30.9.1931, RSA, IV/2, p. 120; Hitler to Brüning, 14.10.1931, RSA, IV/2, p. 145; Press Conference, 4.12.1931, RSA, IV/2, p. 233; Interview, 5.12.1931, RSA, IV/2, pp. 236–5.   **127.** Thus GT, 11.12.1931, I/2/II, p. 169.   **128.** GT, 5.12.1931, I/2/II, p. 164.   **129.** Article, 7.12.1931, RSA, IV/2, pp. 248–9; Article, 7.12.1931, RSA, IV/2, p. 251; Interview, 20.12.1931, RSA, IV/2, p. 297; Article, 7.12.1931, RSA, IV/2, p. 251; Interview, 20.12.1931, RSA, IV/2, p. 295. See also Burke, *Sackett*, p. 185.   **130.** Article, 7.12.1931, RSA, IV/2, p. 252; Interview, 20.12.1931, RSA, IV/2, pp. 299–300; Broadcast, 11.12.1931, RSA, IV/2,

p. 259. 131. Quoted in Krebs, *Tendenzen und Gestalten*, p. 145. 132. Speech, 3.7.1931, RSA, IV/2, p. 21. 133. WA, p. 248. 134. Hitler to Brüning, 14.10.1931, RSA, IV/2, pp. 148, 158. 135. Speech, 26.1.1932, RSA, IV/3, p. 88. 136. WA, p. 58. 137. Article, 10.9.1930, RSA, III/3, p. 395.

Chapter 9: Making the Fewest Mistakes

1. See Krebs, *Tendenzen und Gestalten*, p. 137. 2. WA, p. 270, which dates these remarks to 'just before Christmas 1931'. 3. Heinrich Brüning, *Memoiren, 1918–1934* (Stuttgart, 1970), pp. 504–6. 4. See GT, I, 2/II, 10/11.1.1932, pp. 192–3. 5. Speech, 26.1.1932, RSA, IV/3, p. 108. 6. Hitler to Hindenburg, 28.2.1932, RSA, IV/3, p. 146. 7. See WA, pp. 368–74, 453–60, 474–7. 8. Lars Lüdicke, *Constantin von Neurath. Eine politische Biographie* (Paderborn, 2014), p. 205. 9. Hitler to Haniel, 25.1.1932, RSA, IV/3, pp. 68–9. Originally, the Industrieklub had invited Gregor Strasser. 10. Turner, *Big Business*, p. 97. See also Volker Hentschel, *Weimars letzte Monate. Hitler und der Untergang der Republik* (Düsseldorf, 1978), pp. 115–16; and Henry Ashby Turner, Jr, 'Fritz Thyssen und "I paid Hitler"', *Vierteljahrshefte für Zeitgeschichte*, 19 (1971), pp. 225–44, especially pp. 231–3. Claims that Hitler received substantial foreign financial help to take power have also been disproved: Hermann Lutz, 'Fälschungen zur Auslandsfinanzierung Hitlers', *Vierteljahrshefte für Zeitgeschichte*, 2 (1954), pp. 386–96. 11. Speech, 26.1.1932, RSA, IV/3, p. 104. See also Turner, *Big Business*, pp. 204–17. 12. Proclamation, 16.2.1932, RSA, IV/3, p. 128. 13. Larry Eugene Jones, 'Adolf Hitler and the 1932 presidential elections: a study in Nazi strategy and tactics', in Markus Raasch and Tobias Hirschmüller (eds.), *Von Freiheit, Solidarität und Subsidiarität – Staat und Gesellschaft der Moderne in Theorie und Praxis* (Berlin, 2013), pp. 549–73, especially pp. 555–6. 14. GT, 20.1.1932, I/2/II, p. 199. 15. Manfred Overesch, 'Die Einbürgerung Hitlers 1930 [sic]', *Vierteljahrshefte für Zeitgeschichte*, 40 (1992), pp. 543–66. 16. GT, 3.2.1932, I/2/II, p. 209. 17. Christoph Raichle, *Hitler als Symbolpolitiker* (Stuttgart, 2014), pp. 29–31 (quotation on p. 30). 18. See Jones, 'Adolf Hitler and the 1932 presidential elections', pp. 563–4, 569. 19. Raichle, *Symbolpolitker*, p. 32. 20. GT, 14.3.1932, I/2/II, p. 242. 21. Article, 22.3.1932, RSA, IV/3, pp. 264–5; Adolf Hitler to Nordische Rundfunk AG, 17.3.1932, RSA, IV/3, pp. 245–6. 22. Thus Conradi, *Hitler's Piano Player*, p. 91. 23. 'Streng vertraulicher Bericht über die Besprechung mit Adolf Hitler am 22. März 1932', in William L. Patch, 'Adolf Hitler und der Christlich-Soziale Volksdienst. Ein Gespräch aus dem Frühjahr 1932', *Vierteljahrshefte für Zeitgeschichte*, 37 (1989), pp. 145–55 (quotations on pp. 151, 152, 153, 155). 24. See Jason Crouthamel, ' "Comradeship" and "friendship": masculinity and militarisation in Germany's homosexual emancipation movement after the First World War', *Gender & History*, 23 (2011), pp. 111–29, especially pp. 121 (re Hindenburg and homosexuals) and 124–5. 25. GT, 28.3.1932, I/2/II, p. 250. 26. Declaration, 6.4.1932, RSA, V/1, p. 32. 27. For Hitler's private preoccupation with foreign policy at this time see GT, 23.2.1932, I/2/II, p. 225. 28. Declaration, 2.4.1932, RSA, V/1, p. 4; Speech, 23.1.1932, RSA, IV/3, pp. 53–4; Speech, 8.1.1932, RSA, IV/3, p. 19; Speech, 1.3.1932, RSA, IV/3, p. 155; 2.3.1932, RSA, IV/3, pp. 165–6; Speech, 4.3.1932, RSA, IV/3, p. 171. 29. Speech, 4.4.1932, RSA, V/1, pp. 20–21; Declaration, 2.4.1932, RSA, V/1, p. 12. 30. GT, 25.10.1931, I/2/II, p. 133. 31. Interview, 29.4.1932, RSA, V/1, p. 101. 32. Thus GT, 12.5.1932, I/2/II, p. 279. See also Longerich, *Braunen Bataillone*, p. 154. 33. Thus Rudolph, 'Nationalsozialisten in Ministersesseln', p. 263. 34. Quoted in Raichle, *Symbolpolitiker*, p. 36, with other citations. 35. Otto Dietrich, *Mit Hitler an die Macht. Persönliche Erlebnisse mit meinem Führer* (Munich, 1934), p. 70. 36. Speech, 2.6.1932, RSA, V/1, p. 150; Speech, 14.6.1932, RSA, V/1, p. 173. 37. Thus Müller, 'Der "jüdische Kapitalist" als Drahtzieher und Hintermann', p. 182 (with quotations). 38. Proclamation, 22.6.1932, RSA, V/1, p. 190; Speech, 3.7.1932, RSA, V/1, p. 205; Preface, 15.7.1932, RSA, V/1, p. 222; Speech, 20.7.1932, RSA, V/1, p. 243; Speech, 12.6.1932, RSA, V/1, p. 164. 39. Lutz Kinkel, *Die Scheinwerferin. Leni Riefenstahl und das 'Dritte Reich'* (Hamburg and Vienna, 2002), pp. 35, 39–41 (quotations on pp. 35 and

41). 40. Turner, *Big Business*, pp. 247–8. 41. GT, 1.6.1932, I/2/II, p. 294. See also GT, 3.6.1932, I/2/II, p. 295. 42. Speech, 28.6.1932, RSA, V/1, p. 201. For the continued strength of Bavarian particularism see Robert S. Garnett, Jr, *Lion, Eagle, and Swastika: Bavarian Monarchism in Weimar Germany, 1918–1933* (New York, 1991), pp. 294–307. 43. Speech, 3.7.1932, RSA, V/1, p. 205. 44. See Ian Kershaw, 'Adolf Hitler. George Sylvester Viereck, 1932', in the *Guardian* series 'Great Interviews of the 20th Century' (2007), pp. 7–9. 45. Meeting protocol, 13.8.1932, RSA, V/1, p. 167. 46. Quoted in Detlef Junker, *Die Deutsche Zentrumspartei und Hitler 1932/33. Ein Beitrag zur Problematik des politischen Katholizismus in Deutschland* (Stuttgart, 1969), p. 59. See also Wolfram Pyta, *Hindenburg. Herrschaft zwischen Hohenzollern und Hitler* (Munich, 2007). 47. Speech, 19.6.1932, RSA, V/1, p. 189; Speech, 14.6.1932, RSA, V/1, p. 176; Speech, 24.6.1932, RSA, V/1, p. 198. 48. See Thomas D. Grant, *Stormtroopers and Crisis in the Nazi Movement: Activism, Ideology and Dissolution* (London and New York, 2004), pp. 137–8 *et passim*. 49. Thus Thomas Childers and Eugene Weiss, 'Voters and violence: political violence and the limits of National Socialist mass mobilization', *German Studies Review*, 13 (1990), pp. 481–98, especially pp. 484, 489, 494. 50. Richard Bessel, 'The Potempa murder', *Central European History*, 10 (1977), pp. 241–54, especially pp. 242, 251; Paul Kluke, 'Der Fall Potempa', *Vierteljahrshefte für Zeitgeschichte*, 5 (1957), pp. 279–97. 51. Thus GT, 5.2.1932, I/2/II, p. 211. 52. Thus GT, 2.5.1932, I/2/II, p. 273. 53. GT, 3.9.1932, I/2/II, p. 356. 54. GT, 7.10.1932, I/2/III, p. 31. 55. Heike B. Görtemaker, *Eva Braun. Leben mit Hitler* (Munich, 2010), pp. 59–63. 56. Speech, 29.10.1932, RSA, V/2, p. 123. 57. Interview, 16.8.1932, RSA, V/1, p. 309. 58. Speech, 29.10.32, RSA, V/2, p. 123; Interview, 16.8.1932, RSA, V/1, p. 309; Speech, 30.8.1932, RSA, V/1, p. 322. 59. GT, 1.9.1932, I/2/II, p. 354. 60. See Junker, *Die Deutsche Zentrumspartei*, pp. 86–96. 61. Kershaw, *Hubris*, p. 385. 62. GT, 11.9.1932, I/2/I, pp. 360–61. 63. GT, 11.9.1932, I/2/I, p. 361. 64. Speech, 7.9.1932, RSA, V/1, p. 349; Speech, 4.9.1932, RSA, V/1, p. 331. 65. GT, 9.8.1932, I/2/II, p. 335. 66. Decree, 8.9.1932, RSA, V/1, p. 351. 67. See Othmar Plöckinger, *Reden um die Macht? Wirkung und Strategie der Reden Adolf Hitlers im Wahlkampf zu den Reichtagswahlen am 6. November 1932* (Vienna, 1999). 68. Hitler to Brüning, 16.10.1932, RSA, V/2, p. 58. 69. Speech, 13.10.1932, RSA, V/2, p. 22; Speech, 30.10.1932, RSA, V/2, p. 129. 70. Speech, 25.10.1932, RSA, V/2, p. 109; Speech, 3.11.1932, RSA, V/2, p. 171; Speech, 17.10.1932, RSA, V/2, p. 75; Speech, 16.10.1932, RSA, V/2, p. 64; Speech, 20.10.1932, RSA, V/2, p. 91; Speech, 29.10.1932, RSA, V/2, p. 122; Speech, 30.10.1932, RSA, V/2, p. 133. 71. Hitler to Papen, 16.10.1932, RSA, V/2, pp. 30–31. 72. Speech, 17.10.1932, RSA, V/2, p. 72; Speech, 2.11.1932, RSA, V/2, p. 151; Interview, 4.10.1932, RSA, V/2, p. 10; Speech, 19.10.1932, RSA, V/2, p. 83; Hitler to Papen, 16.10.1932, RSA, V/2, p. 38; Proclamation, 6.11.1932, RSA, V/2, p. 185; Speech, 28.10.1932, RSA, V/2, p. 120; Hitler to Papen, 16.10.1932, RSA, V/2, p. 58; Speech, 17.10.1932, RSA, V/2, p. 69 and p. 72; Speech, 2.11.1932, RSA, 5/2, p. 164; Speech, 16.10.1932, RSA, V/2, p. 65. 73. Speech, 16.10.1932, RSA, V/2, p. 64; Speech, 17.10.1932, RSA, V/2, p. 69; Speech, 22.10.1932, RSA, V/2, p. 92; Speech, 17.10.1932, RSA, V/2, p. 70; Speech, 18.12.1932, RSA, V/2, p. 288. 74. Dietrich, *Mit Hitler an die Macht*, p. 90. 75. Fein, *Hitlers Weg nach Nürnberg*, p. 215. 76. Udo Kissenkoetter, *Gregor Strasser und die NSDAP* (Stuttgart, 1978), pp. 164–77. 77. Quoted in Henry Ashby Turner, Jr, *Hitler's Thirty Days to Power: January 1933* (London, 1996), p. 74. See also Thomas Childers, 'The limits of National Socialist mobilisation: the elections of 6 November 1932 and the fragmentation of the Nazi constituency', in Thomas Childers (ed.), *The Formation of the Nazi Constituency, 1919–1933* (London, 1986), pp. 232–59 (especially, pp. 232–55). 78. Thus Turner, *Thirty Days*, p. 16 *et passim*. 79. GT, 21.11.1932, I/2/III, p. 64. 80. Interview, 19.8.1932, RSA, V/1, pp. 313–15. 81. Irene Strenge, *Kurt von Schleicher. Politik im Reichswehrministerium am Ende der Weimarer Republik* (Berlin, 2006), pp. 198–9. 82. Hitler to Reichenau, 4.12.1932, RSA, V/2, p. 243. See also Thilo Vogelsang, 'Hitlers Brief an Reichenau vom 4. Dezember 1932', *Vierteljahrshefte für Zeitgeschichte*, 7 (1959), pp. 429–37. 83. Thus Turner, *Thirty Days*, p. 25. 84. GT, 6.12.1932, I/2/III, p. 75. 85. See the notes to 1.12.1932, in RSA, V/2, p. 225. 86. Fein, *Hitlers Weg nach Nürnberg*, pp. 219–23. 87. GT, 9.12.1932, I/2/III, p. 77. 88. See the account in GT, 9.12.1932,

I/2/III, p. 78.   89. GT, 10.12.1932, I/2/III, p. 79.   90. Speech, 18.12.1932, RSA, V/2, p. 288.   91. Memorandum, 15.12.1932, RSA, V/2, pp. 273–8.   92. Memorandum, 15.12.1932, RSA, V/2, pp. 273–8; Memorandum, 20.12.1932, RSA, V/2, pp. 292–6.   93. Turner, *Thirty Days*, pp. 71–2.   94. GT, 29.12.1932, I/2/III, p. 92.   95. Quoted in Hamann, *Hitlers Bayreuth*, p. 230.   96. Proclamation, 31.12.1932, RSA, V/2, p. 310.   97. Quoted in Turner, *Thirty Days*, p. 1.   98. Dietrich, *12 Jahre*, p. 187.   99. Quoted in Turner, *Thirty Days*, p. 56.   100. Heinrich Muth, 'Das Kölner Gespräch am 4. Januar 1933', *Geschichte in Wissenschaft und Unterricht*, 37 (1986), pp. 463–80, 529–41.   101. Michael Bloch, *Ribbentrop* (London, 1992), pp. 28–9.   102. Larry Eugene Jones, 'Die Tage vor Hitlers Machtübernahme. Aufzeichnungen des Deutschnationalen Reinhold Quaatz', *Vierteljahrshefte für Zeitgeschichte*, 37 (1989), pp. 759–74, especially pp. 766 and 768 (quoting Meissner).   103. Quoted in Turner, *Thirty Days*, p. 77.   104. Turner, *Thirty Days*, pp. 138–9.   105. Otto Meissner, *Staatssekretär unter Ebert – Hindenburg – Hitler. Der Schicksalsweg des deutschen Volkes von 1918–1945, wie ich ihn erlebte* (Hamburg, 1950), pp. 263–4.   106. Thus Turner, *Thirty Days*, p. 141. See also Klaus Schönhoven, 'Zwischen Anpassung und Ausschaltung. Die bayerische Volkspartei in der Endphase der Weimarer Republik 1932/33', *Historische Zeitschrift*, 224 (1977), pp. 340–78, especially pp. 362–3, where Schäffer's approach is less clear-cut.   107. Letter of Appointment, 30.1.1933, RSA, V/2, p. 395.   108. quoted Duesterberg, *Der Stahlhelm und Hitler*, p. 39.   109. Lutz Graf Schwerin von Krosigk, *Es geschah in Deutschland. Menschenbilder unseres Jahrhunderts* (Tübingen and Stuttgart, 1951), p. 147.   110. Quoted Ewald von Kleist-Schmenzin, 'Die letzte Möglichkeit. Zur Ernennung Hitlers zum Reichskanzler am 30. Januar 1933', *Politische Studien*, 10 (1959), pp. 89–92 (quotation on p. 92).   111. Larry Eugene Jones, ' "The greatest stupidity of my life": Alfred Hugenberg and the formation of the Hitler cabinet, January 1933', *Journal of Contemporary History*, 27 (1992), pp. 63–87 (quotation on p. 63).

Chapter 10: The 'Fairy Tale'

1. Proclamation, 30.1.1933, RSA,V/2, pp. 396–8.   2. Hess to Ilse Hess, 31.1.1933, HB, pp. 424–5.   3. Karl Wahl, '... es ist das deutsche Herz' (Augsburg, 1954), p. 68.   4. GT, 31.1.1933, I/2/III, p. 120.   5. Michael Burleigh, *The Third Reich: A New History* (London, 2000). See also Hans-Ulrich Thamer, *Verführung und Gewalt. Deutschland 1933–1945* (Berlin 1986).   6. Generally: Hans-Ulrich Wehler, *Deutsche Gesellschaftsgeschichte*, vol. 4: *Vom Beginn des Ersten Weltkrieges bis zur Gründung der beiden deutschen Staaten, 1914–1949* (Munich, 2003), pp. 600–690.   7. Thus Nikolaus Wachsmann, *Hitler's Prisons: Legal Terror in Nazi Germany* (New Haven, 2004). For the centrality of violence and exclusion to the concept of *Volksgemeinschaft* see Michael Wildt, *Volksgemeinschaft als Selbstermächtigung. Gewalt gegen Juden in der deutschen Provinz 1919 bis 1939* (Hamburg, 2007); and Peter Fritzsche, *Life and Death in the Third Reich* (Cambridge, Mass., 2008).   8. See Richard J. Evans, 'Coercion and consent in Nazi Germany', *Proceedings of the British Academy*, 151 (2007), pp. 53–81; Jane Caplan, 'Political detention and the origin of the concentration camps in Nazi Germany, 1933–1935/6', in Neil Gregor (ed.), *Nazism, War and Genocide: New Perspectives on the History of the Third Reich* (Exeter, 2008), pp. 22–41 (which stresses continuities); and Riccardo Bavaj, *Der Nationalsozialismus. Entstehung, Aufstieg und Herrschaft* (Berlin, 2016), pp. 63–74.   9. Robert Gellately, *Backing Hitler: Consent and Coercion in Nazi Germany* (Oxford, 2001).   10. See now Darren O'Byrne, 'Political civil servants and the practice of administration under National Socialism' (PhD dissertation, University of Cambridge, 2018), pp. 182–90.   11. Thus Karl Dietrich Bracher, Wolfgang Sauer and Gerhard Schulz, *Die Nationalsozialistische Machtergreifung. Studien zur Errichtung des totalitären Herrschaftssystems in Deutschland, 1933/34* (Cologne and Opladen, 1960).   12. See Wolfram Pyta, 'Vorbereitungen für den militärischen Ausnahmezustand unter Papen/Schleicher', in *Militärgeschichtliche Mitteilungen*, 51 (1992), pp. 385–428; and Patrick Oliver Heinemann, *Rechtsgeschichte der Reichswehr, 1918–1933* (Paderborn, 2017), pp. 368–9, here p. 378.   13. RH, 30.1.1933, I/1, p. 3; RH, 1.2.1933, I/1,

p. 9. **14.** See Bernhard R. Kroener, *'Der starke Mann im Heimatkriegsgebiet'. Generaloberst Friedrich Fromm. Eine Biographie* (Paderborn, 2005). **15.** Lothar Gruchmann, 'Die "Reichsregierung" im Führerstaat. Stellung und Funktion des Kabinetts im nationalsozialistischen Herrschaftssystem', in Günther Doeker and Winfried Steffani (eds.), *Klassenjustiz und Pluralismus. Festschrift für Ernst Fraenkel zum 75. Geburtstag am 26. Dezember 1973* (Hamburg, 1973). **16.** See Pyta, *Hitler*, pp. 206–7. **17.** Hess to Ilse Hess, 31.1.1933, Berlin, HB, p. 425. **18.** Werner Hoche (ed.), *Die Gesetzgebung des Kabinetts Hitler*, 33 vols. (Berlin, 1933–9). **19.** Thus Stratigakos, *Hitler at Home*. **20.** His schedule can be found in Bundesarchiv Berlin, Lichterfelde R 43 II 1609c; and Bundesarchiv Koblenz, N1720 Wiedemann 4. **21.** Brendan Simms, 'Walther von Reichenau. Der politische General', in Ronald Smelser and Enrico Syring (eds.), *Die Militärgeschichte des dritten Reiches. 27 biographische Skizzen* (Berlin, 1995), pp. 423–45 **22.** Thus Pyta, *Hindenburg, passim*. **23.** See Rudolf Morsey, 'Hitlers Verhandlungen mit der Zentrumsführung am 31. Janur 1933', *Vierteljahrshefte für Zeitgeschichte*, 9 (1961), pp. 182–94. **24.** RH, 1.2.1933, I/1, p. 9. **25.** Andreas Morgenstern, 'Sabotage gegen eine Rundfunkübertragung', in Haus der Geschichte Baden-Württemberg (ed.), *Anständig gehandelt. Widerstand und Volksgemeinschaft 1933–1945* (Stuttgart, 2012), pp. 34–6. **26.** RH, 1.2.1933, I/1, p. 15. **27.** Thus Meissner, *Staatssekretär*, p. 293. **28.** RH, 2.2.1933, I/1, pp. 29–30. **29.** Müller, 'Der "jüdische Kapitalist" als Drahtzieher und Hintermann', p. XXX (with quotation). **30.** RH, 1.2.1933, I/1, p. 14. **31.** RH, 8.2.1933, I/1, p. 55; RH, 2.2.1933, I/1, p. 24. **32.** See O'Byrne, 'Political civil servants', pp. 182–9. **33.** RH, 2.2.1933, I/1, p. 24. **34.** The notes of Lieutenant General Liebmann are printed in Thilo Vogelsang, 'Neue Dokumente zur Geschichte der Reichswehr, 1930–1933', *Vierteljahrshefte für Zeitgeschichte*, 2 (1954), pp. 397–436, at pp. 434–5. There is a longer version in Andreas Wirsching, '"Man kann nur Boden germanisieren". Eine neue Quelle zu Hitlers Rede vor den Spitzen der Reichswehr am 3. Februar 1933', *Vierteljahrshefte für Zeitgeschichte*, 49 (2001), pp. 517–50. For the calling of the meeting see Kirstin A. Schäfer, *Werner von Blomberg. Hitlers erster Feldmarschall. Eine Biographie* (Paderborn and Munich, 2006), p. 104. **35.** Wirsching, '"Man kann nur Boden germaniseren"', pp. 546–7. **36.** Vogelsang, 'Neue Dokumente', p. 456. **37.** Remarks, 3.2.1933, Domarus, I, p. 200; Interview Lochner, 25/26.2.1933, Domarus, I, pp. 212–13. **38.** RH, 8.2.1933, I/1, pp. 50–51; RH, 21.2.1933, I/1, p. 94. **39.** See Tooze, *Wages of Destruction*, pp. 99–101. **40.** Sven Felix Kellerhoff, *Der Reichstagsbrand. Die Karriere eines Kriminalfalls* (Berlin, 2008); and Marcus Giebeler, *Die Kontroverse um den Reichstagsbrand. Quellenprobleme und historiographische Paradigmen* (Munich, 2010), especially pp. 283–8. For a recent challenge to the orthodoxy, see Benjamin Carter Hett, *Burning the Reichstag: An Investigation into the Third Reich's Enduring Mystery* (Oxford, 2014). **41.** GT, 28.2.1933, I/2/III, p. 137. **42.** See Thomas Fürst, *Karl Stützel. Ein Lebensweg in Umbrüchen. Vom königlichen Beamten zum Bayerischen Innenminister der Weimarer Zeit (1924–1933)* (Frankfurt, 2007), pp. 426–30. **43.** Quoted in Geoffrey Pridham, *Hitler's Rise to Power: The Nazi Movement in Bavaria, 1923–1933* (London, 1973), p. 302. **44.** See Schönhoven, 'Zwischen Anpassung und Ausschaltung', pp. 366–7. **45.** For a record of their discussion see Falk Wiesemann, *Die Vorgeschichte der nationalsozialistischen Machtübernahme in Bayern 1932/1933* (Berlin, 1975), pp. 294–303 (quotation on p. 302). **46.** Martina Steber, '"… dass der Partei nicht nur äussere, sondern auch innere Gefahren drohen". Die Bayerische Volkspartei im Jahr 1933', Wirsching (ed.), *Das Jahr 1933. Die nationalsozialistische Machteroberung und die deutsche Gesellschaft* (Göttingen, 2009), pp. 70–91, especially pp. 71–3. **47.** RH, 7.3.1933, I/1, p. 160. **48.** GT, 8.3.1933, I/2/III, p. 389. **49.** See Susanne Wanninger, 'Nationalsozialistische Pläne zur Regierungsbildung in Bayern. Eine Denkschrift von Rudolf Buttmann vom März 1933', in Wirsching (ed.), *Das Jahr 1933*, pp 92–109, especially pp. 92, 95, 97; and Wolfgang Dierker, '"Ich will keine Nullen, sondern Bullen". Hitlers Koalitionsverhandlungen mit der Bayerischen Volkspartei im März 1933', *Vierteljahrshefte für Zeitgeschichte*, 50 (2002), pp. 111–48. **50.** Wiesemann, *Die Vorgeschichte der nationalsozialistischen Machtübernahme*, pp. 277–8. **51.** Hans Günter Hockerts, 'Warum war München die "Hauptstadt der Bewegung"?', in Stefanie Hajak and Jürgen Zarusky (eds.), *München und der Nationalsozialismus. Menschen, Orte, Strukturen* (Berlin,

2008), p. 37; Daniel Rittenauer, 'Bayerische Landessymbole in der Zeit des Nationalsozial-ismus 1933–1945', *Zeitschrift für bayerische Landesgeschichte*, 76 (2013), pp. 185–213, especially pp. 200–203.   52. 12/13.3.1933, Domarus, I, p. 222.   53. Hartmut Jäckel, 'Brauchte Hitler das Zentrum? Zur Abstimmung über das Ermächtigungsgesetz am 23. März 1933', *Die Zeit*, 18.3.1983; Josef Becker, 'Zentrum und Ermächtigungsgesetz, 1933', *Vier-teljahrshefte für Zeitgeschichte*, 9 (1961), pp. 195–210.   54. RH, 20.3.1933, I/1, p. 239.   55. Klaus Scholder, *Die Kirchen und das Dritte Reich*, vol. 1: *Vorgeschichte und Zeit der Illu-sionen, 1918–1934* (Frankfurt, Berlin and Vienna, 1977), pp. 300–321.   56. Wolfram Pyta, 'Geteiltes Charisma. Hindenburg, Hitler und die deutsche Gesellschaft im Jahre 1933', in Wirsching (ed.), *Das Jahr 1933*, pp. 47, 50, 54 *et passim*.   57. Thus Theodor Duesterberg, *Der Stahlhelm und Hitler* (Wolfenbüttel, 1949), pp. 48–9. See also Werner Freitag, 'Martin Luther, Friedrich II und Adolf Hitler – der Tag von Potsdam im neuen Licht', in *Das Land Brandenburg und das Erbe Preussens. Preussen und der Nationalsozialismus* (Potsdam, 1992), pp. 15–31. The performative dimension also struck the eyewitness Andre François-Poncet, *Als Botschafter in Berlin, 1931–1938* (Mainz, 1948), p. 105.   58. Speech, 23.3.1933, Domarus, I, pp. 229–37.   59. Thus Daniel Koerfer, 'Die grosse Vollmacht', *Frankfurter Allgemeine Zeitung*, 22.3.2013, p. 38.   60. As set out in RH, 29.3.1933, I/1, p. 273.   61. Speech, 6.7.1933, Domarus, I, p. 287.   62. RH, 6.7.1933, I/1, p. 634.   63. RH, 6.7.1933, I/1, p. 635. On this phemonenon see O'Byrne, 'Political civil servants', pp. 259–60.   64. See Hermann Beck, 'Konflikte zwischen Deutschnationalen und Nationalsozialisten während der Machtergreifungszeit', *Historische Zeitschrift*, 292 (2011), pp. 645–80.   65. Beck, 'Kon-flikte zwischen Deutschnationalen und Nationalsozialisten', pp. 646, 662, 655, 659.   66. Christopher Dillon, ' "We'll meet again in Dachau": the early Dachau SS and the narrative of civil war', *Journal of Contemporary History*, 45 (2010), pp. 535–54. See also Karin Orth, *Das System der nationalsozialistischen Konzentrationslager. Eine politische Organisation-sgeschichte* (Hamburg, 1999), pp. 23–6.   67. Christopher Dillon, *Dachau and the SS: A Schooling in Violence* (Oxford, 2015), pp. 168–9 (quotation on p. 169).   68. Thus Christian Goeschel and Nikolaus Wachsmann, 'Before Auschwitz: the formation of the Nazi concen-tration camps, 1933–9', *Journal of Contemporary History*, 45 (2010), pp. 515–34, especially pp. 521–2.   69. Thus Longerich, *Hitler*, pp. 351–2, on which this paragraph is based. See also Scholder, *Die Kirchen und das Dritte Reich*, vol. 1, pp. 482–524.   70. Thus Lothar Gruchmann, *Justiz im Dritten Reich, 1933–1940. Anpassung und Unterwerfung in der Ära Gürtner* (Munich, 1988).   71. See Dan P. Silverman, *Hitler's Economy: Nazi Work Creation Programs, 1933–1936* (Cambridge, Mass., 1998).   72. See O'Byrne, 'Political civil servants', p. 160.   73. 23.9.1933, Domarus, I, p. 302.   74. Christoph Buchheim, 'Das NS-Regime und die Überwindung der Weltwirtschaftskrise in Deutschland', *Vierteljahrshefte für Zeit-geschichte*, 56 (2008), pp. 381–414.   75. There is a very small file on the matter in the archive of the Auswärtiges Amt (R80522, USA, Privata 1933). I thank Dr Gerhard Keiper for drawing it to my attention.   76. This paragraph is largely based on Weber, *Hitler's First War*, pp. 291–2.   77. Michael Zalampas, *Adolf Hitler and the Third Reich in American Magazines, 1923–1939* (Bowling Green, Ohio, 1989), pp. 44–5.   78. Thus Klaus P. Fischer, *Hitler & America* (Philadelphia, 2011), p. 50.   79. These are described in Arthur L. Smith, Jr, *The Deutschtum of Nazi Germany and the United States* (The Hague, 1965), especially pp. 59–90.   80. See Germà Bel, 'Against the mainstream: Nazi privatization in 1930s Germany', *Economic History Review*, 63 (2010), pp. 34–55, especially pp. 35, 36, 42, 46–8, 52.   81. Thus Tooze, *Wages of Destruction*, p. 11 *et passim*.   82. Tooze, *Wages of Destruction*, p. 117.   83. Michael Ebi, *Export um jeden Preis. Die Deutsche Exportförderung von 1932–1938* (Stuttgart, 2004), pp. 12–13 *et passim*.   84. Declaration, 23.3.1933, Domarus, I, p. 234.   85. Thus Avraham Barkai, *Nazi Economics* (Oxford, New York and Munich, 1990), p. 159.   86. RH, 29.5.1933, I/1, p. 508; RH, 7.4.1933, I/1, pp. 313–14; RH, 25.4.1933, I/1, p. 381. See also Roland Ray, *Annäherung an Frankreich im Dienste Hitlers? Otto Abetz und die deutsche Frankreichpolitik, 1930–1942* (Munich, 2000), pp. 100–102; and Józef Lipski, *Diplomat in Berlin, 1933–1939* (New York and London, 1968). For the intelligence reports see Zachary Shore, *What Hitler Knew* (Oxford, 2003), pp. 19–20.   87. See Hans Roos, 'Die "Präventivkriegspläne" Pilsudskis von 1933', *Vierteljahrshefte für Zeitgeschichte*,

3 (1955), pp. 344–63, especially p. 362.   88. Alexander Wolz, 'Ribbentrop und die deutsche Aussenpolitik, 1934–1936', *Historische Zeitschrift*, 300 (2015), pp. 374–415, especially p. 381.   89. See Wilhelm von Schramm, … *sprich vom Frieden, wenn du den Krieg willst. Die psychologischen Offensiven Hitlers gegen die Franzosen 1933 bis 1939. Ein Bericht* (Mainz, 1973).   90. Speech, 23.3.1933, Domarus, I, p. 235.   91. Interview, 18.10.1933, Domarus, I, p. 319. See also Bernd Sösemann, 'Mediale Inszenierung von Soldatentum und militärischer Führung in der NS-Volksgemeinschaft', in Christian Th. Müller and Matthias Rogg (eds.), *Das ist Militärgeschichte! Probleme – Projekte – Perspektiven* (Paderborn, Munich, Vienna and Zurich, 2013), pp. 358–79, especially pp. 361–2.   92. RH, 12.5.1933, I/1, p. 448.   93. Thus Carl Dirks and Karl-Heinz Janssen, *Der Krieg der Generäle. Hitler als Werkzeug der Wehrmacht* (Berlin, 1999), pp. 84, 114–26 *et passim*.   94. RH, 6.7.1933, I/1, p. 633.   95. David Clay Large, 'Hitler's Games: race relations in the 1936 Olympics', *German Historical Institute London Bulletin*, 29, 1 (May 2007), pp. 5–27, especially pp. 8–11.   96. Thus Michael Geyer, *Aufrüstung oder Sicherheit. Die Reichswehr in der Krise der Machtpolitik 1924–1936* (Wiesbaden, 1980), pp. 355–8.   97. Thus R. J. Overy, 'German air strength 1933 to 1939: a note', *Historical Journal*, 27 (1984), pp. 465–71, especially pp. 467–9.   98. Sergej Slutsch and Carola Tischler (eds.), *Deutschland und die Sowjetunion, 1933–1941. Dokumente aus russichen und deutschen Archiven*, vol. 1: *30 Januar 1933–31 Dezember 1934*, part I: *Januar 1933–Oktober 1933* (Munich, 2014), pp. 671 and 726.   99. Thus Meissner, *Staatssekretär*, pp. 339–40.   100. Speech, 7.5.1933, Domarus, I, p. 300.   101. Speech, 23.3.1933, Domarus, I, p. 236.   102. Quoted Tammo Luther, *Volkstumspolitik des Deutschen Reiches, 1933–1938. Die Auslanddeutschen im Spannungsfeld zwischen Traditionalisten und Nationalsozialisten* (Stuttgart, 2004), p. 83 (quotations on pp. 65 and 97).   103. RH, 26.5.1933, I/1, pp. 491–4.   104. See Hans Schafranek, *Söldner für den 'Anschluss'. Die Österreichische Legion, 1933–1938* (Vienna, 2011), 32–3, 134, 148 (the Hitler quotation is on p. 33).   105. See P. Pritz, 'Das Hitler–Gömbös Treffen und die deutsche Aussenpolitik im Sommer 1933', *Acta Historica Academiae Scientarum Hungaricae*, 25 (1979), pp. 115–43, here p. 125.   106. Thus Boris Celovsky, *Germanisierung und Genozid. Hitlers Endlösung der tschechischen Frage. Deutsche Dokumente, 1933–1945* (Dresden and Brno, 2005), pp. 19–20.   107. RH, 22.4.1933, I/1, p. 359; RH, 12.7.1933, I/1, p. 65.   108. See Markus Urban, 'Offizielle und halboffizielle Amerikabilder im "Dritten Reich". Deutsche Amerikaliteratur als Spiegel der politischen Entwicklung?', in Jan C. Behrends, Árpád von Klimó and Patrice G. Poutrus (eds.) *Antiamerikanismus in 20. Jahrhundert. Studien zu Ost- and Westeuropa* (Bonn, 2005), pp. 52–71, especially, pp. 60–62; Gassert, *Amerika im Dritten Reich*, pp. 183–5.   109. Herbert Sirois, *Zwischen Illusion und Krieg. Deutschland und die USA, 1933–1941* (Paderborn, 2000); Fischer, *Hitler & America*, pp. 46–69; Michaela Hoenicke Moore, *Know Your Enemy: The American Debate on Nazism, 1933–1945* (New York, 2010). For a contemporary lament see: Friedrich Schönemann, *Amerika und der Nationalsozialismus* (Berlin, 1934), pp. 5, 8 *et passim*.   110. Quoted in Zalampas, *Adolf Hitler and the Third Reich in American Magazines*, p. 31.   111. Memorandum by the chairman of the American Delegation (Davis) of a conversation with the German chancellor (Hitler), 8.4.1933, *Foreign Relations of the United States*, 1933, I, pp. 85–89. I thank Dr Bill Foster, Vice-Principal of Homerton College Cambridge, for drawing this exchange to my attention. See also Peter Grose, *Allen Dulles: Spymaster. The Life and Times of the First Civilian Director of the CIA* (London, 2006), pp. 114–16.   112. E.g. Viscount Rothermere, 'Youth Triumphant', *Daily Mail*, 10.7.1933.   113. Thus Philipp Caspar Mohr, *'Kein Recht zur Einmischung'? Die politische und völkerrechtliche Reaktion Grossbritanniens auf Hitlers 'Machtergreifung' und die einsetzende Judenverfolgung* (Tübingen, 2002), pp. 64, 113, 164, 204 *et passim*.   114. Proclamation, 10.3.1933, Domarus, I, p. 219.   115. Amelie Artmann and Stefan Hoerdler, 'Zur Rezeption der frühen NS-Gewalt in der Presse', in Stefan Hoerdler (ed.), *SA-Terror als Herrschaftssicherung. 'Köpnicker Blutwoche' und öffentliche Gewalt im Nationalsozialismus* (Berlin, 2013), pp. 200–213; Martin Herzer, *Auslandskorrespondenten und auswärtige Pressepolitik im Dritten Reich* (Cologne, Weimar and Vienna, 2012), pp. 34–5 *et passim*.   116. Louis Lochner, *Always the Unexpected: A Book of Reminiscences* (New York, 1956).   117. Conradi, *Hitler's Piano Player*, p. 106.   118. See Andrew

Nagorski, *Hitlerland: American Eyewitnesses to the Nazi Rise to Power* (New York, 2012); and Erik Larson, *In the Garden of Beasts: Love and Terror in Hitler's Berlin* (London, 2011). **119.** Herzer, *Auslandskorrespondenten und auswärtige Pressepolitik*, pp. 73–105. **120.** RH, 2.3.1933, I/1, p. 147. **121.** Hitler to Papen, 11.3.1933, RH, I/1, p. 205. **122.** See Conradi, *Hitler's Piano Player*, pp. 141–2. **123.** RH, 24.5.1933, I/1, pp. 477–9. **124.** Plöckinger, *Geschichte eines Buches*, p. 197 **125.** See James J. Barnes and Patience P. Barnes, *Hitler's Mein Kampf in Britain and America: A Publishing History 1930–39* (Cambridge, 1980), pp. 2, 9, 13, 24–25 (re Weizmann), 33–4 (re excisions); and Dan Stone, 'The "*Mein Kampf* ramp": Emily Overend Lorimer and Hitler translations in Britain', *German History*, 26 (2008), pp. 504–19. **126.** E.g. Adolf Hitler, *My Struggle* (London, 1933), pp. 124–30, 209 *et passim* (re Jews) and 256–8 (re *Lebensraum*). **127.** Interview, 2.5.1933, Domarus, I, p. 265. **128.** Thus Otto Dietrich, *Mit Hitler in die Macht. Persönliche Erlebnisse mit meinem Führer* (Munich, 1934), pp. 201–3. **129.** Madeleine Herren, '"Outwardly . . . an innocuous conference authority": National Socialism and the logistics of international information management', *German History*, 20 (2002), pp. 67–92. See also Michael Arthur Ledeen, *Universal Fascism: The Theory and Practice of the Fascist International, 1928–1936* (New York, 1972), pp. xviii, 163 *et passim.* **130.** RH, 29.3.1933, I/1, p. 270. **131.** Yfaat Weiss, 'Projektionen vom "Weltjudentum". Die Boykottbewegung der 1930er Jahre', *Tel Aviver Jahrbuch für deutsche Geschichte*, 26 (1997), pp. 151–79; Ahlheim, '*Deutsche kauft nicht bei Juden*', pp. 246–9. **132.** Thus Fein, *Hitlers Weg nach Nürnberg*, p. 254. **133.** RH, 31.3.1933, I/1, p. 277. **134.** Proclamation, 28.3.1933, Domarus, I, pp. 248–51. **135.** Thus Francis R. Nicosia, *Zionism and Anti-Semitism in Nazi Germany* (Cambridge, 2008), p. 79 *et passim*. See also Moshe Zimmermann, 'Mohammed als Vorbote der NS-Judenpolitik? Zur wechselseitigen Instrumentalisierung von Antisemitismus und Antizionismus', *Tel Aviver Jahrbuch für deutsche Geschichte*, 33 (2005), pp. 292–305, especially pp. 294–9. **136.** Francis R. Nicosia, *The Third Reich and the Palestine Question* (New Brunswick, NJ, 2000), pp. 41–9. **137.** Nicosia, *Zionism and Anti-Semitism*, p. 78. **138.** Quoted in Ernst Hanfstaengl, *15 Jahre mit Hitler. Zwischen Weissem und Braunem Haus*, 2nd edn (Munich and Zurich, 1980), p. 305. The question of (private) American money to assist Jewish emigration was raised again with Hitler in March 1934: Richard Breitman, Barbara McDonald Stewart and Severin Hochberg (eds.), *Advocate for the Doomed: The Diaries and Papers of James G. McDonald, 1932–1935* (Bloomington, Ind., 2007), pp. 317–18. **139.** Interview, 30.10.1933, Domarus, I, p. 325. **140.** I thank Dermot Trainor for many conversations on this subject. **141.** Stefan Hübner, 'Hitler and Ostasien, 1904 bis 1933. Die Entwicklung von Hitlers Japan- and Chinabild vom Russisch-Japanischen Krieg bis zur "Machtergreifung"', *OAG-Notizen*, 9 (2009), pp. 22–41, especially p. 31. **142.** RH, 26.4.1933, I/1, pp. 376, 375, 389. **143.** Wolfgang Schivelbusch, *Three New Deals: Reflections on Roosevelt's America, Mussolini's Italy and Hitler's Germany, 1933–1939* (New York, 2007). **144.** Anweisung des Propaganda-Ministeriums, 5.7.1933: Gabriele Toepser-Ziegert (ed.), *NS-Presseanweisungen der Vorkriegszeit. Edition und Dokumentation*, vol. 1: *1933* (Munich, New York, London and Paris, 1984), p. 52. **145.** RH, 6.7.1933, I/1, p. 631. **146.** Quoted in Eric Rauchway, *The Money Makers: How Roosevelt and Keynes Ended the Depression, Defeated Fascism and Secured a Prosperous Peace* (New York, 2015), p. xxiv.

Chapter 11: The 'Elevation' of the German People

1. RH, 6.7.1933, I/1, p. 629. **2.** RH 28.9.1933, I/2, p. 869. **3.** Peter Longerich, *Hitlers Stellvertreter. Führung der Partei und Kontrolle des Staatsapparates durch den Stab Hess und die Partei-Kanzlei Bormann* (Munich, 1992). **4.** RH, 1.12.1933, I/2, p. 986. **5.** Thus Jeremy Noakes, 'Leaders of the people? The Nazi Party and German society', *Journal of Contemporary History*, 39 (2004), pp. 189–212 (especially pp. 189–90). **6.** See Jürgen W. Falter, 'Die "Märzgefallenen" von 1933. Neue Forschungsergebnisse zum sozialen Wandel innerhalb der NSDAP-Mitgliedschaft während der Machtergreifungsphase', *Geschichte* *und Gesellschaft*, 24 (1998), pp. 595–616, especially pp. 596 and 600.   7. Thus Zitelmann, *Hitler. Selbstverständnis eines Revolutionärs*, pp. 400–401.   8. RH, 6.7.1933, I/1, p. 630.   9. Speech, 7.5.1933, Domarus, I, p. 266.   10. Wirsching, 'Man kann nur den Boden germanisieren', p. 546.   11. RH, 20.9.1933, I/2, p. 812. The distinction between 'race' and 'people' was a commonplace among Nazi theorists: Christopher M. Hutton, *Race and the Third Reich: Linguistics, Racial Anthropology and Genetics in the Dialectic of Volk* (Cambridge, 2005), p. 110; and Mark Roseman, 'Racial discourse, Nazi violence, and the limits of the racial state model', in Devin O. Pendas, Mark Roseman and Richard F. Wetzell (eds.), *Beyond the Racial State: Rethinking Nazi Germany* (Cambridge, 2017), p. 33 *et passim*.   12. Thus Michael Burleigh and Wolfgang Wippermann, *The Racial State: Germany 1933–1945* (Cambridge, 1992).   13. See David Bankier, 'Hitler and the policy-making process on the Jewish Question', *Holocaust and Genocide Studies*, 3 (1988), pp. 1–20.   14. Thus John Connelly, 'Nazis and Slavs: from racial theory to racist practice', *Central European History*, 32 (1999), pp. 1–33, especially pp. 2–3.   15. Hans-Walter Schmuhl, *Rassenhygiene, Nationalsozialismus, Euthanasie. Von der Verhütung zur Vernichtung 'lebensunwerten Lebens', 1890–1945* (Göttingen, 1987), pp. 151–72 (which uses the term 'negative eugenics'). See also Gisela Bock, *Zwangssterilisation im Nationalsozialismus. Studien zur Rassenpolitik und Frauenpolitik* (Opladen, 1986), pp. 80–94.   16. Jeremy Noakes, 'Nazism and eugenics: the background to the Nazi sterilization law of 14 July 1933', in R. J. Bullen, H. Pogge von Strandmann and A. B. Polonsky (eds.), *Ideas into Politics: Aspects of European History, 1880–1950* (London, 1984), pp. 75–94.   17. RH, 14.7.1933, I/1, pp. 664–5.   18. RH, 16.7.1935, II/2, p. 1,104.   19. See James Q. Whitman, *Hitler's American Model: The United States and the Making of Nazi Race Law* (Princeton, NJ and Oxford, 2017), p. 32.   20. Quoted in Stefan Kühl, *The Nazi Connection: Eugenics, American Racism, and German National Socialism* (Oxford, 1994), p. 39. For a systematic comparison from a legal perspective see Judy Scales-Trent, 'Racial purity laws in the United States and Nazi Germany: the targeting process', *Human Rights Quarterly*, 23 (2001), pp. 259–307.   21. Quoted in Kühl, *The Nazi Connection*, p. 85.   22. See Robert N. Proctor, *The Nazi War on Cancer* (Princeton, NJ, 1999), p. 207 *et passim*.   23. Wirsching, 'Man kann nur Boden germanisieren', p. 546.   24. Thus Wolfgang König, *Volkswagen, Volksempfänger, Volksgemeinschaft. 'Volksprodukte' im Dritten Reich. Vom Scheitern einer nationalsozialistischen Konsumgesellschaft* (Paderborn, Munich, Vienna and Zurich, 2004), pp. 17–19 *et passim*.   25. Dorothee Hochstetter, *Motorisierung und 'Volksgemeinschaft'. Das Nationalsozialistische Kraftfahrkorps (NSKK) 1931–1945* (Munich, 2005), pp. 151–66, especially p. 158.   26. See Paul Kluke, 'Hitler und das Volkswagenprojekt', *Vierteljahrshefte für Zeitgeschichte*, 8 (1960), pp. 341–83, especially p. 366.   27. Speech, 15.2.1936, Domarus, II, pp. 576–9.   28. See Christopher Kopper, 'Modernität oder Scheinmodernität nationalsozialistischer Herrschaft. Das Beispiel der Verkehrspolitik', in Christian Jansen, Lutz Niethammer and Bernd Weisbrod (eds.), *Von der Aufgabe der Freiheit. Politische Verantwortung und bürgerliche Gesellschaft im 19. und 20. Jahrhundert* (Berlin, 1995), pp. 399–411, especially pp. 401 and 403.   29. RH, 29.10.1934, II/1, pp. 129–30.   30. Tooze, *Wages of Destruction*, pp. 147–8.   31. Eva Susanne Bressler, *Von der Experimentierbühne zum Propagandainstrument. Die Geschichte der Funkausstellung 1924 bis 1939* (Cologne and Vienna, 2009), p. 204.   32. Thus König, *Volkswagen, Volksempfänger, Volksgemeinschaft*, p. 258.   33. Thus Rüdiger Hachtmann, 'Tourismus- geschichte – ein Mauerblümchen mit Zukunft! Ein Forschungsüberblick', *H-Soz-Kult*, 6.10.2011, p. 3.   34. Shelley Baranowski, *Strength through Joy: Consumerism and Mass Tourism in the Third Reich* (Cambridge, 2004), pp. 38–9 *et passim*.   35. Dorothee Klinksiek, *Die Frau im NS-Staat* (Stuttgart, 1982).   36. Speech, 8.9.1934, Domarus, I, pp. 450–51. In same vein, 13.9.1935, Domarus, II, p. 531.   37. Matthew Stibbe, *Women in the Third Reich* (London, 2003), p. 85.   38. See Friedemann Beyer, *Frauen für Deutschland. Filmidole des Dritten Reichs* (Munich, 2012), pp. 18–24 *et passim*.   39. Speech, 8.9.1934, Domarus, I, pp. 450–51. In same vein, 13.9.1935, Domarus, II, p. 531.   40. Lisa Pine, *Hitler's 'National Community': Society and Culture in Nazi Germany* (London, 2017), pp. 118–28.   41. Buchheim, 'Das NS-Regime und die Überwindung der Weltwirtschaftskrise', p. 392.   42. Irmgard Weyrather, *Muttertag und Mutterkreuz. Der Kult um die 'deutsche*

Mutter' im Nationalsozialismus (Frankfurt, 1993), pp. 55–84 (quotation on p. 55). See also Claudia Koonz, *Mothers in the Fatherland* (New York, 1988). **43.** Gabriele Czarnowski, *Das kontrollierte Paar. Ehe-und Sexualpolitik im Nationalsozialismus* (Weinheim, 1991). **44.** Thus Ute Frevert, 'Frauen an der "Heimatfront" ', in Christoph Klessmann (ed.), *Nicht nur Hitlers Krieg. Der Zweite Weltkrieg und die Deutschen* (Düsseldorf, 1989), pp. 51–69. **45.** Speech, 23.3.1933, Domarus, I, p. 232. **46.** Quoted in Kiran Klaus Patel, 'Welfare in the warfare state: Nazi social policy on the international stage', *Bulletin of the German Historical Institute*, 37 (2015), pp. 3–38, here p. 20. **47.** See Helen Roche, 'Zwischen Freundschaft und Feindschaft: exploring relationships between pupils at the Napolas (*Nationalpolitische Erziehungsanstalten*) and British public schoolboys', *Angermion: Yearbook for Anglo-German Literary Criticism, Intellectual History and Cultural Transfers/Jahrbuch für britisch-deutsche Kulturbeziehungen*, 6 (2013), pp. 101–26. **48.** Speech, 14.9.1935, Domarus II, pp. 533–4. **49.** Helen Roche, 'Classics and education in the Third Reich: *die alten Sprachen* and the Nazification of Latin- and Greek-teaching in secondary schools', in Helen Roche and Kyriakos Demetriou (eds.), *Brill's Companion to the Classics, Fascist Italy and Nazi Gemany* (London and Boston, 2018), pp. 238–63. See also Helen Roche, *Sparta's German Children: The Ideal of Ancient Sparta in the Royal Prussian Cadet Corps, 1818–1920, and in National Socialist Elite Schools (the Napolas), 1933–1945* (Swansea, 2013). **50.** See Paul Kahl, '"Geschaffen durch die hochherzige Unterstützung des Führers und Reichskanzlers Adolf Hitler". Das Weimarer Goethe-Nationalmuseum in der Zeit des Nationalsozialismus', in Tanja Baensch, Kristina Kratz-Kessemeier and Dorothee Wimmer (eds.), *Museen im Nationalsozialismus. Akteure – Orte – Politik* (Cologne, Weimar and Vienna, 2016), pp. 293–305, especially pp. 293, 297–9. **51.** Thus Helen Roche, ' "In Sparta fühlte ich mich wie in einer deutschen Stadt" (Goebbels): the leaders of the Third Reich and the Spartan nationalist paradigm', in Geraldine Horan, Felicity Rash and Daniel Wildmann (eds.), *English and German Nationalist and Anti-Semitic Discourse, 1871–1945* (Oxford, 2013), pp. 91–115. **52.** Quoted in Helen Roche, '"Anti-Enlightenment": National Socialist educators' troubled relationship with humanism and the Philhellenist tradition', *Publications of the English Goethe Society*, 82, 3 (2013), pp. 193–207 (quotation on p. 196). **53.** See Arne Fryksén, 'Hitlers Reden zur Kultur. Kunstpolitische Taktik oder Ideologie?', in *Probleme Deutscher Zeitgeschichte* (Stockholm, 1971), pp. 235–66, especially p. 258 (quotations on p. 254). **54.** Speech, 23.3.1933, Domarus, I, p. 232. **55.** Thus Winfried Nerdinger, 'Funktion und Bedeutung von Architektur im NS-Staat', in Wolfgang Benz, Peter Eckel and Andreas Nachama (eds.), *Kunst im NS-Staat. Ideologie, Ästhetik, Protagonisten* (Berlin, 2015), pp. 279–300 (quotation on p. 285). **56.** Thus Pyta, *Hitler*, pp. 63, 69, 99. **57.** Hans Rudolf Vaget, 'Hitler's Wagner: musical discourse as cultural space', in Michael H. Kater and Albrecht Riethmüller (eds.), *Music and Nazism: Art under Tyranny, 1933–1945* (Laaber, 2003). I thank Erik Levi of Royal Holloway for supplying me with this reference. **58.** Speech 6.3.1934, Domarus, I, p. 369. Hans Rudolf Vaget, 'Wagner-Kult und nationalsozialistische Herrschaft. Hitler, Wagner, Thomas Mann und die "nationale Erhebung" ', in Saul Friedländer and Jörn Rüsen (eds.), *Richard Wagner im Dritten Reich* (Munich, 2000), pp. 264–81. **59.** Thus Pyta, *Hitler*, p. 95. **60.** Holger R. Stunz, 'Hitler und die "Gleichschaltung" der Bayreuther Festspiele. Ausnahmezustand, Umdeutung und sozialer Wandel einer Kulturinstitution, 1933–1934', *Vierteljahrshefte für Zeitgeschichte*, 55 (2007), pp. 237–68, especially pp. 258–60; and Hamann, *Hitlers Bayreuth*, pp. 238, 240, 241, 242, 245–7, 250–51. **61.** See Wolfgang Ruppert, 'Bildende Kunst im NS-Staat', in Benz, Eckel and Nachama (eds.), *Kunst im NS-Staat*, pp. 29–47, especially p. 32. **62.** Domarus, I, p. 316. **63.** Andreas Heusler, *Das Braune Haus. Wie München zur 'Hauptstadt der Bewegung' wurde* (Munich, 2008), p. 9. **64.** Quoted in Hans Günter Hockerts, 'Warum war München die "Hauptstadt der Bewegung"?', in Stefanie Hajak and Jürgen Zarusky (eds.), *München und der Nationalsozialismus. Menschen, Orte, Strukturen* (Berlin, 2008), p. 35. **65.** Thus Birgit Schwarz, *Geniewahn: Hitler und die Kunst* (Vienna, Cologne and Weimar, 2009), pp. 19, 30 *et passim*. See also Frederic Spotts, *Hitler and the Power of Aesthetics* (London, 2003). **66.** Thus Bill Niven, *Hitler and Film: The Führer's Hidden Passion* (New Haven and London, 2018). **67.** See the figures for bannings in Klaus-Jürgen Maiwald,

Filmzensur im NS-Staat (Dortmund, 1983), p. 137.   68. For some statistics see Markus Spieker, *Hollywood unterm Hakenkreuz. Der amerikanische Spielfilm im Dritten Reich* (Trier, 1999), pp. 348-55.   69. See Ben Urwand, *The Collaboration: Hollywood's Pact with Hitler* (Cambridge, Mass. and London, 2013).   70. Volker Koop, *Warum Hitler King Kong liebte, aber den Deutschen Micky Maus verbot. Die geheimen Lieblingsfilme der Nazi-Elite* (Berlin, 2015), especially pp. 11-58.   71. See generally Michael H. Kater, *Different Drummers: Jazz in the Culture of Nazi Germany* (New York, 1992).   72. Thus Benjamin G. Martin, *The Nazi-Fascist New Order for European Culture* (Cambridge, Mass., 2016), pp. 62-5 (quotations on p. 64).   73. Tooze, *Wages of Destruction*, pp. 167 and 186.   74. R. Walther Darré, *Neuadel aus Blut und Boden* (Munich, 1930), pp. 12-13, 60 (quotations on p. 124) *et passim.*   75. RH, 26.9.1933, I/2, pp. 832-3.   76. Uwe Mai, '*Rasse und Raum*'. *Agrarpolitik, Sozial- und Raumplanung im NS-Staat* (Paderborn, Munich and Vienna, 2002), p. 50.   77. See Mai, '*Rasse und Raum*', p. 55.   78. For a sceptical view see Buchheim, 'Das NS-Regime und die Überwindung der Weltwirtschaftskrise', pp. 381-2, 392 *et passim.*   79. Silverman, *Hitler's Economy*, pp. vii, 231 and 235.   80. RH, 20.9.1933, I/2, pp. 806-7.   81. RH, 20.9.1933, I/2, p. 807.   82. RH, 20.9.1933, I/2, pp. 814 and 816.   83. RH, 20.9.1933, I/2, p. 815.   84. RH, 28.9.1933, I/2, pp. 865-8.   85. RH, 28.9.1933, I/2, p. 868; RH 28.9.1933, I/2, p. 870; RH, 10.1.1934, I/2, p. 1,070.   86. See Immo von Fallois, *Kalkül und Illusion. Der Machtkampf zwischen Reichswehr und SA während der Röhm-Krise 1934* (Berlin, 1994), pp. 40, 89.   87. RH, 28.9.1933, I/2, p. 865.   88. RH 28.9.1933, I/2, p. 870; RH 1.12.1933, I/2, p. 986; RH, 28.9.1933, I/2, p. 866.   89. RH, 13/14.10.1933, I/2, p. 905.   90. RH, 27.9.1933, I/2, p. 838.   91. Speech, 18.10.1933, Domarus, I, p. 317.   92. RH, 17.10.1933, I/2, p. 908.   93. 17.3.1933, Domarus, I, p. 276.   94. RH, 4.12.1933, I/2, p. 999. See also Hildebrand, *Vom Reich zum Weltreich*, pp. 622-3 *et passim.*   95. See Zach Shore, 'Hitler's opening gambit: intelligence, encirclement, and the decision to ally with Poland', *Intelligence and National Security*, 14 (1999), pp. 103-22, especially pp. 117-18.   96. Thus Meissner, *Staatssekretär*, p. 343. See also Hans Roos, *Polen und Europa. Studien zur polnischen Aussenpolitik, 1931-1939* (Tübingen, 1957), pp. 108-28.   97. RT, 2.2.1935, p. 169.   98. See Friedelind Wagner's report of Hitler's remark on 4.8.1936 in Hamann, *Hitlers Bayreuth*, p. 326.   99. RH, 5.5.1936, III, p. 852; RH, 14.5.1936, III, p. 853.   100. RH, 22.10.1935 II/2.   101. RT, 14.5.1934, p. 119.   102. B. J. C. McKercher, 'Deterrence and the European balance of power: the Field Force and British grand strategy, 1934-1938', *English Historical Review*, 123, 500 (2008), pp. 98-131 (quotation on p. 115).   103. Domarus, I, pp. 372-3.   104. Edwin Black, 'Hitler's carmaker: the inside story of how General Motors helped mobilize the Third Reich', *History News Network*, 14.5.2007.   105. This, at any rate, was Hearst's own account, quoted in Conradi, *Hitler's Piano Player*, p. 174.   106. RT, 14.5.1934, p. 119; RT, 28.6.1934, pp. 138-9; RT, 11.7.1934, p. 147. See also RT, 15.5.1934, p. 124 and RT, 28.6.1934, p. 139.

Chapter 12: Guns and Butter

1. RH, 22.3.1934, I/2, pp. 1,197-8.   2. See Tooze, *Wages of Destruction*, pp. 80-81.   3. RH, 7.6.1934, I/2, p. 1,310.   4. See Johannes Bähr, ' "Dein Sparen hilft dem Führer". Sparen in der Zeit des Nationalsozialismus', in Robert Muschalla (ed.), *Sparen. Geschichte einer deutschen Tugend* (Darmstadt, 2018), pp. 91-106.   5. Quoted in Immo von Fallois, *Kalkül und Illusion. Der Machtkampf zwischen Reichswehr und SA während der Röhm-Krise 1934* (Berlin, 1994), p. 118.   6. See Larry Eugene Jones, 'The limits of collaboration: Edgar Jung, Herbert von Bose, and the origins of the conservative resistance to Hitler, 1933-34', in Larry Eugene Jones and James Retallack (eds.), *Between Reform, Reaction and Resistance: Studies in the History of German Conservatism from 1789 to 1945* (Providence, RI and Oxford, 1993), pp. 465-501, especially pp. 486, 494-7.   7. Meissner, *Staatssekretär*, p. 365.   8. RH, 3.7.1934, I/2, p. 1,356,   9. Thus Uwe Bachnick, *Die Verfassungsreform vorstellungen im nationalsozialistischen Deutschen Reich und ihre Verwirklichung* (Berlin, 1995), pp. 48-65.   10. RH, 22.3.1934, I/2, p. 1,199.   11. See Martin Broszat,

'Reichszentralismus und Parteipartikularismus. Bayern nach dem Neuaufbau-Gesetz vom 30. Januar 1934', in Ursula Büttner, Werner Johe and Angelika Voss (eds.), *Das Unrechtsregime. Internationale Forschung über den Nationalsozialismus*, vol. 1: *Ideologie – Herrschaftssystem – Wirkung in Europa* (Hamburg, 1986), pp. 178–202, especially pp. 185–6.   12. Goeschel, *Mussolini and Hitler*, pp. 46–7.   13. For Hitler's account of the meeting see RT, 19.6.1934, p. 136; and GT, 17.6.1934, I/3/I, p. 65.   14. See Heinz Höhne, *Mordsache Röhm. Hitlers Durchbruch zur Alleinherrschaft, 1933–1934* (Reinbek bei Hamburg, 1984), p. 242.   15. Klaus-Jürgen Müller, 'Reichswehr und "Röhm-Affäre". Aus den Akten des Wehrkreiskommandos (Bayer.) VII', *Militärgeschichtliche Mitteilungen*, 3, 1 (1968), pp. 107–44.   16. Described in retrospect in RT, 7.7.1934, p. 141.   17. Quoted in Heinz Höhne, *Die Zeit der Illusionen. Hitler und die Anfänge des Dritten Reiches, 1933–1936* (Düsseldorf, Vienna and New York, 1991), p. 213.   18. See RT, 28.6.1934, p. 139.   19. Wolfram Selig, 'Ermordet im Namen des Führers. Die Opfer des Röhm-Putsches in München', in Winfried Becker and Werner Chrobak (eds.), *Staat, Kultur, Politik. Beiträge zur Geschichte Bayerns und des Katholizismus* (Kallmünz, 1992), pp. 341–56, especially p. 349 (Ballerstedt) and p. 352 (Kahr).   20. RT, 28.6.1934, p. 139. See also RT, 15.5.1934, p. 124.   21. Domarus, I, pp. 399–400.   22. Speech, 13.7.1934, Domarus, I, p. 421.   23. Domarus, I, p. 421.   24. See Robert Dallek, *Democrat and Diplomat: The Life of William E. Dodd* (Oxford, 2013), pp. 178–9.   25. Quoted Domarus, I, p. 398.   26. Speech, 13.7.1934, Domarus I, pp. 420, 422 *et passim*.   27. For a brief description by the eyewitness Werner Best see Siegfried Motlok (ed.), *Dänemark in Hitlers Hand. Der Bericht des Reichsbevollmächtigten Werner Best über seine Besatzungspolitik in Dänemark mit Studien über Hitler, Göring, Himmler, Heydrich, Ribbentrop, Canaris u. a.* (Husum, 1988), pp. 125–6.   28. RH, 11.7.1934, I/2, p. 1,375.   29. Speech, 13.7.1934, Domarus, I, p. 412; Speech, 4.9.1934, Domarus I, pp. 447–8.   30. Thus Bauer, 'Hitler und der Juliputsch 1934'.   31. See Hamann, *Hitlers Bayreuth*, pp. 252–62, 271, 273, 283, 285 (quotation).   32. Bauer, *Hitlers zweiter Putsch*, pp. 136, 141, 159–60, 223 (quotation) *et passim*.   33. Quoted in Bauer, *Hitlers zweiter Putsch*, p. 183.   34. GT, 30.7.1934, I/3/I, p. 86.   35. See Perica Hadži-Jovančić, 'Ergänzungswirtschaft, Grosswirtschaftsraum and Yugoslavia's responses to German economic theories and plans for the Balkans in the 1930s', *Godišnjak za društvenu istoriju/Annual of Social History*, 2 (2017), pp. 31–56; Roland Schönfeld, 'Deutsche Rohstoffsicherungspolitik in Jugoslawien, 1934–1944', *Vierteljahrshefte für Zeitgeschichte*, 24 (1976), pp. 215–58; Stephen G. Gross, *Export Empire: German Soft Power in Southeastern Europe, 1890–1945* (Cambridge, 2015).   36. Quoted in Schafranek, *Söldner für den 'Anschluss'*, pp. 157–8, 315.   37. See Franz Müller, *Ein 'Rechtskatholik' zwischen Kreuz und Hakenkreuz: Franz von Papen als Sonderbevollmächtigter Hitlers in Wien, 1934–1938* (Frankfurt, 1990).   38. Blair R. Holmes, 'Europe and the Habsburg Restoration in Austria, 1930–1938', *East European Quarterly*, 9 (1975), pp. 173–84, especially pp. 179–80.   39. Proclamation, 20.7.1934, Domarus, I, p. 426.   40. RH, 1.8.1934, I/2, p. 1,384.   41. Speech, 17.8.1934, Domarus, I, p. 442.   42. RH, 27.8.1934, I/2, p. 1,391.   43. The text of the oath is printed in Domarus, I, pp. 430–31.   44. Kershaw, '*Hitler Myth*'; and Ian Kershaw, *Hitler: A Profile in Power* (London, 1991). M. Rainer Lepsius, 'The model of Charismatic leadership and its applicability to the rule of Adolf Hitler', *Totalitarian Movements and Political Religions*, 7(2006), pp. 175–90.   45. RH, 3.4.1935, II/1, p. 1,085.   46. RH, 1.11.1934, II/1, p. 1,040.   47. See Domarus, I, p. 445.   48. Speech, 26.8.1934, Domarus, I, p. 445.   49. RT, 2.8.1934, p. 150.   50. Peter Hubert, *Uniformierter Reichstag. Die Geschichte der Pseudo-Volksvertretung, 1933–1945* (Düsseldorf, 1992), pp. 15, 23–45 *et passim*. See also Joachim Lilla, *Statisten in Uniform. Die Mitglieder des Reichstags, 1933–1945. Ein biographisches Handbuch* (Düsseldorf, 2004).   51. Jane Caplan, *Government Without Administration: State and Civil Service in Weimar and Nazi Germany* (Oxford, 1988).   52. Longerich, *Hitlers Stellvertreter*, p. 19 *et passim*.   53. Quoted in Noakes, 'Leaders of the people?', p. 191 (speaking at the Party Congress on 11 September 1935).   54. Peter Diehl-Thiele, *Partei und Staat im Dritten Reich. Untersuchungen zum Verhältnis von NSDAP und allgemeiner innerer Staatsverwaltung* (Munich, 1969), pp. 17–21.   55. Quoted in Noakes, 'Leaders of the people?', p. 192.   56. Heike B. Görtemaker, *Hitlers Hofstaat. Der innere Kreis im*

Dritten Reich und danach (Munich, 2019), especially pp. 97–214. **57.** Thus Fabrice d'Almeida, *High Society in the Third Reich* (Cambridge, 2008), pp. 63–86. **58.** RH, 7.12.1934, II/1, p. 224. **59.** Thus Martin Moll, 'Steuerungsinstrument im "Ämterchaos"? Die Tagungen der Reichs- und Gauleiter der NSDAP', *Vierteljahrshefte für Zeitgeschichte*, 49 (2001), pp. 215–73. **60.** RH, 1.11.1934, II/1, p. 134. **61.** RH, 20.6.1935, II/1, p. 1,094. **62.** See Jeremy Noakes, 'Federalism in the Nazi state', in Maiken Umbach (ed.), *German Federalism: Past, Present, Future* (Basingstoke, 2002), pp. 113–45, especially p. 129. **63.** Noakes, 'Federalism in the Nazi state', p. 130. See also Bachnick, *Die Verfassungsreformvorstellungen im nationalsozialistischen Deutschen Reich*, p. 20 *et passim*. **64.** RT, 11.7.1934, p. 149. **65.** RH, 1.11.1934, cabinet, II/1, p. 135. **66.** Wiedemann to Friedrichs (Stellvertreter des F.), 24.1.1935, ED 9 (Aktenstücke aus der Adjutantur des Führers), IfZ. **67.** Wiedemann to Friedrichs (copy or draft), 7.2.1935, ED 9, IfZ. **68.** See RH, 7.8.1935, RH, II/2, pp. 711–13, in which Hitler comes down on Goebbels's side over control of television; for the struggle in and over Bavaria see RH, 1.2.1936, III, pp. 103–5; and RH, 13.11.1936, III, p. 896. **69.** 'Wiedergabe des zwischen Hauptmann Wiedemann und Reichsminister Darré am 18 mai 1936 um 10.15 geführten Gesprächs', IfZ, ED 9; copy of draft, Wiedemann to Bormann, 8.6.1935. **70.** Fein, *Hitlers Wegnach Nürnberg*, pp. 260–61. **71.** Meissner, *Staatssekretär*, p. 619. **72.** RH, 17.10.1935, II/2, p. 879. **73.** Hitler's remarks as quoted in RT, 30.10.1936, p. 215. **74.** RT, 1.5.1936, p. 183. **75.** RH, 27.10.1936, III, p. 891. **76.** RH, 15.11.1934, II/1, p. 1,043; RH, 15.8.21935, II/1, p. 1,120; RH, 2.7.1936, III, p. 419; RH, 26.3.1936, III, p. 833. **77.** Thus Ian Kershaw, ' "Working towards the Führer": reflections on the nature of the Hitler dictatorship', *Contemporary European History*, 2, 2 (1993), pp. 103–18 (Willikens quotation on p. 116). **78.** See the lament in Hans-Heinrich Wilhelm, 'Hitlers Ansprache vor Generälen und Offizieren am 26. Mai 1944', *Militärgeschichtliche Mitteilungen*, 20, 2 (1976), pp. 123–70, especially p. 151. **79.** Hans Mommsen, 'Cumulative radicalisation and progressive self-destruction as structural determinants of the Nazi dictatorship', in Ian Kershaw and Moshe Lewin (eds.), *Stalinism and Nazism: Dictatorships in Comparison* (Cambridge, 1997), pp. 75–87. **80.** See Markus Urban, *Die Konsensfabrik. Funktion und Wahrnehmung der NS-Reichsparteitage, 1933–1941* (Göttingen, 2007), pp. 43–7. **81.** Thus Fein, *Hitlers Wegnach Nürnberg*, p. 298. **82.** Frank Bajohr, ' "Führerstadt" als Kompensation. Das "Notstandsgebiet Hamburg" in der NS-Zeit', in Fritz Mayrhofer and Ferdinand Opll (eds.), *Stadt und Nationalsozialismus* (Linz, 2008), pp. 267 and 287 (figures on p. 267). **83.** Ebi, *Export um jeden Preis*, pp. 116–17. **84.** William S. Grenzebach, *Germany's Informal Empire in East-Central Europe: German Economic Policy toward Yugoslavia and Rumania, 1933–1939* (Stuttgart, 1988). **85.** RH, 1.11.1934, II/1, pp. 135–6; RH, 4.12.1934, II/1, p. 202. **86.** Roland Ray, *Annäherung an Frankreich im Dienste Hitlers? Otto Abetz und die deutsche Frankreichpolitik, 1930–1942* (Munich, 2000), pp. 128–33 (quotations on p. 133). **87.** RH, 19.12.1934, II/1, p. 1,057. **88.** Ray, *Annäherung*, pp. 137–8 (quotation on p. 138). **89.** RH, 21.2.1935, II/1, p. 375. **90.** RH, 7.8.1934, I/2, p. 1,014; RH, 26.9.1934, II/1, p. 1,023. **91.** Radio Address, 15.1.1935, Domarus, II, p. 472; Interview, 16.1.1935, Domarus, II, p. 474; Speech, 1.1.1935, Domarus, II, p. 467; Interview, 17.1.1935, Domarus, II, p. 476. **92.** RT, 18.3.1935, p. 176. **93.** RH, 7.3.1935, II/1, p. 1,077. **94.** Thus Hamann, *Hitlers Bayreuth*, pp. 302–3. **95.** RH, 4.4.1935, II/1, p. 1,086. **96.** Thus Meissner, *Staatssekretär*, p. 399. **97.** Görtemaker, *Eva Braun*, pp. 63, 78, 91, 109 (quotation), 111. **98.** Hitler told his foreign press secretary about the incident: Dietrich, *12 Jahre*, p. 200. **99.** Görtemaker, *Eva Braun*, pp. 190, 194 (quotation). **100.** Ernst Günther Schenck, *Patient Hitler. Eine medizinische Biographie* (Augsburg, 2000). **101.** Manfred Funke, *Sanktionen und Kanonen. Hitler, Mussolini und der internationale Abessinienkonflikt, 1934–36* (Düsseldorf, 1971). **102.** Jost Dülffer, *Weimar, Hitler und die Marine. Reichspolitik und Flottenbau 1920–1939* (Düsseldorf, 1973), pp. 348–53; and M. L. Alch, 'Germany's Naval Resurgence, British Appeasement, and the Anglo-German Naval Agreement of 1935' (PhD dissertation, University of California, Los Angeles, 1977), pp. 553–667 (for the negative reaction of Britain's allies). **103.** Thus Thomas Hoerber, 'Psychology and reasoning in the Anglo-German Naval Agreement, 1935–1939', *Historical Journal*, 52 (2009), pp. 153–74, especially pp. 171–2.

104. GT, 19.8.1935, I/3/I, p. 67. 105. Quoted in Richard S. Grayson, 'Leo Amery's imperialist alternative to appeasement in the 1930s', *Twentieth Century British History*, 17 (2006), pp. 489–515 (quotation on p. 505). 106. Thus Wiedemann, *Der Mann der Feldherr werden wollte*, p. 213. 107. RH, 20.8.1935, II/2, pp. 743–4. 108. Fein, *Hitlers Wegnach Nürnberg*, pp. 312–13. 109. Cornelia Essner, *Die 'Nürnberger Gesetze', Oder, Die Verwaltung des Rassenwahns, 1933–1945* (Paderborn, 2002). 110. Walter Strauss, 'Das Reichsministerium des Innern und die Judengesetzgebung. Als Rassereferent im Reichsministerium des Innern, verfasst von Bernhard Lösener', *Vierteljahrshefte für Zeitgeschichte*, 9 (1961), pp. 262–313. 111. Kershaw, *Hubris*, pp. 563–9. 112. Though some did slip through the net: Bryan Mark Rigg, *Hitler's Jewish Soldiers. The Untold Story of Nazi Racial Laws and Men of Jewish Descent in the German Military* (Lawrence, Kansas, 2002); Günter Schubert, 'Hitlers "jüdische" Soldaten. Ein Defizit der Holocaustforschung oder nur ein Medienereignis?', *Jahrbuch für Antisemitismusforschung*, 7 (1998), pp. 307–21. Only a small number of the cases discussed there are those of 'full Jews' in the sense of the Nazi racial laws. 113. John M. Steiner and Jobst Freiherr von Cornberg, 'Willkür in der Willkür. Befreiungen von den antisemitischen Nürnberger Gesetzen', *Vierteljahrshefte für Zeitgeschichte*, 46 (1998), pp. 143–87, especially pp. 151–2, 161. 114. Wilhelm Stuckart and Hans Globke, *Kommentare zur deutschen Rassengesetzgebung* (Munich, 1936), I, p. 55. 115. James Q. Whitman, *Hitler's American Model: The United States and the Making of Nazi Race Law* (Princeton, NJ and Oxford, 2017), pp. 55–56, 80, 128, 96 *et passim*. 116. See Robbie Aitken and Eve Rosenhaft, *Black Germany: The Making and Unmaking of a Diaspora Community, 1884–1960* (Cambridge, 2013), p. 266. 117. Quoted in Karsten Linne, *Deutschland jenseits des Äquators? Die NS-Kolonialplanungen für Afrika* (Berlin, 2008), p. 43. See also Susann Lewerenz, *Die Deutsche Afrika-Schau (1935–1940). Rassismus, Kolonialrevisionismus und postkoloniale Auseinandersetzungen im nationalsozialistischen Deutschland* (Frankfurt, 2006); and Peter Martin and Christine Alonzo (eds.), *Zwischen Charleston und Stechschritt. Schwarze im Nationalsozialismus* (Hamburg and Munich, 2004). 118. See Aitken and Rosenhaft, *Black Germany*, pp. 250–57. 119. See Eve Rosenhaft, 'Blacks and gypsies in Nazi Germany: the limits of the "racial state"', *History Workshop Journal*, 72, 1 (2011), pp. 161–70, especially pp. 162–3. 120. Thus Daniel Wildmann, *Begehrte Körper. Konstruktion und Inszenierung des 'arischen' Männerkörpers im 'Dritten Reich'* (Würzburg, 1998), p. 13. 121. See the scene described by Ernst Hanfstaengl, *Zwischen Weissem und Braunem Haus. Memoiren eines politischen Aussenseiters* (Munich, 1970), p. 319. 122. 15.9.1935, Domarus, II, p. 537. 123. RH, 12.12.1935, II/2, p. 986. 124. RH 1.7.1936, III, p. 417. 125. RH, 30.4.1936, III, p. 293. See also Ihrig, *Atatürk in the Nazi Imagination*, pp. 108–46. 126. RH, 24.8.1935, II/2, p. 748. 127. Armin Fuhrer, *Tod in Davos. David Frankfurter und das Attentat auf Wilhelm Gustloff* (Berlin, 2012), pp. 44–52. 128. Speech, 12.2.1936, Domarus, II, p. 575. 129. He discussed it with Goebbels, GT, 23.1.1936, I/3/I, p. 367. 130. Luther to Auswärtige Amt, 21.1.1936, ADAP, Series C, IV, p. 996, which carries the marginal note 'The chancellor is aware.' 131. Ian Kershaw, *Making Friends with Hitler: Lord Londonderry and Britain's Road to War* (London, 2004). 132. 4.2.1936, Domarus, II, p. 572. 133. Thus Josef Henke, *England in Hitlers politischem Kalkül, 1935–1939* (Boppard am Rhein, 1973), p. 36 *et passim*. 134. GT, 29.2.1936, I/3/I, p. 388. 135. GT, 29.2.1936, I/3/I, pp. 388–9; GT, 4.3.1936, I/3/II, p. 31. 136. RH, 6.3.1936, III, pp. 164–5. 137. Speech, 7.3.1936, Domarus, II, p. 595. 138. Philip Towle, 'Taming or demonising an aggressor: the British debate on the end of the Locarno system', in Gaynor Johnson (ed.), *Locarno Revisited: European Diplomacy 1920–1929* (London and New York, 2004), pp. 178–98 (quotations, pp. 181, 185, 189). 139. Arnd Krüger, *Die Olympischen Spiele 1936 und die Weltmeinung. Ihre aussenpolitische Bedeutung unter besonderer Berücksichtigung der USA* (Berlin, Munich and Frankfurt, 1972). 140. See Dirk Schubert, 'Führerstadtplanungen in Hamburg', in Michael Bose, Michael Holtmann, Dittmar Machule, Elke Pahl-Weber and Dirk Schubert, '. . . ein neues Hamburg entsteht . . .'. *Planen und Bauen von 1933–1945* (Hamburg, 1986), pp. 16–45, especially pp. 34–35. 141. Decree, 17.6.1936, Domarus, II, p. 624. 142. Hans-Henning Abendroth, *Mittelsmann zwischen Franco und Hitler. Johannes Bernhardt erinnert 1936*

(Marktheidenfeld, 1978), pp. 28–36; and Hans-Henning Abendroth, *Hitler in der spanischen Arena. Die deutsch-spanischen Beziehungen im Spannungsfeld der europäischen Interessenpolitik vom Ausbruch des Bürgerkrieges bis zum Ausbruch des Weltkrieges, 1936–1939* (Paderborn, 1973), pp. 15–73. **143.** Dieckhoff Memorandum, 25.7.1936, ADAP, Series D, III, pp. 11–12. **144.** See Pierpaolo Barbieri, *Hitler's Shadow Empire: Nazi Economics and the Spanish Civil War* (Cambridge, Mass., 2015). **145.** Hans-Henning Abendroth, 'Die deutsche Intervention im Spanischen Bürgerkrieg. Ein Diskussionsbeitrag', *Vierteljahrshefte für Zeitgeschichte*, 30 (1982), pp. 117–29 (quotation on p. 121). **146.** RT, 12.8.1936, p. 191. **147.** Thus RT, 12.8.1936, p. 190. **148.** Thus Tooze, *Wages of Destruction*, pp. 211–13. **149.** Hitler's memorandum on the Four Year Plan, Obersalzberg, August 1936, ADAP, Series C, V, pp. 793–801. **150.** Thus Herbert A. Strauss, 'Hostages of "world Jewry": on the origin of the idea of genocide in German history', *Holocaust and Genocide Studies*, 3 (1988), pp. 125–36, here p. 135. See also Peter Longerich, *The Unwritten Order: Hitler's Role in the Final Solution* (Stroud, 2001/3), p. 54. **151.** Christopher Kopper, *Hjalmar Schacht. Aufstieg und Fall von Hitlers mächtigstem Bankier* (Munich and Vienna, 2006), pp. 309–11 *et passim*. **152.** GT, 1.9.1936, I/3/II, p. 172. **153.** GT, 15.11.1936, I/3/II, p. 252. **154.** RH, 18.10.1936, III, pp. 556–7. **155.** Dieter Petzina, *Autarkiepolitik im Dritten Reich* (Stuttgart, 1968), p. 83. **156.** Tooze, *Wages of Destruction*, pp. 222–30 *et passim*. **157.** See the description in David Clay Large, *Nazi Games: The Olympics of 1936* (London, 2007), pp. 3–5. **158.** See David Clay Large, 'Hitler's Games: race relations in the 1936 Olympics', *German Historical Institute London Bulletin*, 29, 1 (May 2007), pp. 5–27 (quotation p. 22). **159.** Thus Wiedemann, *Der Mann der Feldherr werden wollte*, pp. 208–9. **160.** GT, 7.8.1936, I/3/II, p. 151. **161.** See Oliver Hilmes, *Berlin 1936. Sechzehn Tage im August* (Munich, 2016). **162.** Hamann, *Hitlers Bayreuth*, pp. 323–5. **163.** Ribbentrop, 'Notiz für den Führer', Wildungen, 28.8.1936, ADAP, Series C, V, 2, p. 868. **164.** RT, 17.9.1936, pp. 205–6. **165.** David Lloyd George, 'I talked to Hitler', *Daily Express*, 17.9.1936. **166.** Memorandum of Major Dutton, c.9.9.1936, ADAP, Series C, V, 2, pp. 906–8. **167.** Fein, *Hitlers Weg nach Nürnberg*, p. 328. **168.** GT, 16.9.1936, I/3/II, p. 184. **169.** Speech, 14.9.1936, Domarus, II, p. 645. **170.** Speech, 9.9.1936, Domarus, II, p. 638. In the same vein: Speech, 13.9.1936, Domarus, II, p. 728. **171.** RT, 17.9.1936, p. 204. **172.** GT, 2.12.1936, I/3/II, p. 273. See also RH, 21.1.1936, III, p. 807; RH, 5.5.1936, III, pp. 852–3; RH, III, 2.11.1936, p. 893. **173.** Speech, 12.9.1936, Domarus, II, p. 643; Speech, 17.12.1936, Domarus, II, p. 658. **174.** Wiedemann to Reschny, Berlin, 25.4.1936, ADAP, Series C, V/1, pp. 441–2. **175.** RH, 15.8.1936, III, p. 876. **176.** GT, 15.11.1936, I/3/II, p. 251; GT, 13.11.1936, I/3/II, p. 249. **177.** Quoted in Abendroth, 'Die deutsche Intervention im Spanischen Bürgerkrieg', p. 122. **178.** See Geoffrey T. Waddington, 'Hitler, Ribbentrop, die NSDAP und der Niedergang des britischen Empire 1935–1938', *Vierteljahrshefte für Zeitgeschichte*, 40 (1992), pp. 273–306, especially pp. 276–85; Hermann Graml, *Hitler und England. Ein Essay zur nationalsozialistischen Aussenpolitik 1920 bis 1940* (Munich, 2010), p. 92; and Wolz, 'Ribbentrop und die deutsch Aussenpolitik', p. 410. **179.** GT, 25.11.1936, I/3/II, p. 264; GT, 14.11.1936, I/3/II, pp. 250–51; GT, 17.9.1936, I/3/II, p. 185. **180.** GT, 4.12.1936, I/3/II, p. 276. **181.** As reported in GT, 5.12.1936, I/3/II, p. 278; GT, 7.12.1936, I/3/II, p. 281. **182.** GT, 8.12.1936, I/3/II, p. 282. **183.** GT, 21.12.1936, I/3/II, p. 300. **184.** Luther to Auswärtiges Amt, Washington, 18.8.1936, ADAP, Series C, V/2, p. 851. **185.** Luther to Ministerialdirektor Ritter (AA), Washington, 2.10.1936, ADAP, Series C, V/2, pp. 949–50. **186.** RH, 19.10.1936, III, pp. 553–4. **187.** Jens Petersen, *Hitler–Mussolini. Die Entstehung der Achse Berlin–Rom, 1933–1936* (Tübingen, 1973), pp. 491–2 (quotation on p. 492). **188.** Carl Boyd, *The Extraordinary Envoy: General Hiroshi Oshima and Diplomacy in the Third Reich, 1934–1939* (Washington, DC, 1980), pp. 41–2. **189.** As described in Goebbels, GT, 9.6.1936, I/3/II, p. 102. **190.** Thus Speech, 8.11.1937 Domarus, II, p. 757, and Speech, 6.9.1938, Domarus, II, p. 893. **191.** GT, 27.11.1936, I/3/II, p. 266. In the same vein see GT, 15.11.1936, I/3/II, pp. 251–2. **192.** Speech, 23.9.1933, Domarus, I, p. 302. **193.** Speech, 13.7.1934, Domarus, I, p. 411. **194.** RH, 24.1.1935, II/1, p. 326. **195.** Speech, 21.5.1935, Domarus, II, p. 506. **196.** Speech, 8.11.1936, Domarus, II, p. 654.

Chapter 13: 'Living Standards' and 'Living Space'

1. Quoted Meissner, *Staatssekretär*, p. 423.   2. A good sense of this is conveyed by Paul Spies and Gernot Schaulinski (eds.), *Berlin 1937. Im Schatten von Morgen* (Berlin, 2017).   3. See the account in Domarus, II, p. 683, based on the editor's own recollection of remarks made by the Reichspostminister, Dr Ohnesorge.   4. See Dietmar Süss, *'Ein Volk, ein Reich, ein Führer'. Die deutsche Gesellschaft im Dritten Reich* (Munich, 2017), pp. 123, 125.   5. Thus Barkai, *Nazi Economics*, p. 106.   6. Thus Gianluca Falanga, *Berlin 1937. Die Ruhe vor dem Sturm* (Berlin, 2007), pp. 11–13 *et passim*.   7. See Sven Felix Kellerhoff, ' "Gebt mir vier Jahre Zeit!" ', Welt/N24, Geschichte Bilanz 1937, 30.1.2017; Proclamation, 1.2.1933, Domarus, I, p. 194. See also Heinz Höhne, *'Gebt mir vier Jahre Zeit'. Hitler und die Anfänge des Dritten Reichs* (Berlin, 1999).   8. See Longerich, *Unwritten Order*, pp. 5–56.   9. ES, 29.4.1937, pp. 147–8.   10. RH, 7.5.1937, IV, p. 749.   11. Reiner Pommerin, *Sterilisierung der Rheinlandbastarde. Das Schicksal einer farbigen deutschen Minderheit 1918–1937* (Düsseldorf, 1979), pp. 64, 77–8.   12. See Aitken and Rosenhaft, *Black Germany*, pp. 232–3, 250–59, for the contrasting treatment of blacks and Jews.   13. Quoted in Aitken and Rosenhaft, *Black Germany*, p. 257.   14. Thus Massimiliano Livi, *Gertrud Scholtz-Klink. Die Reichsfrauenführerin. Politische Handlungsräume und Identitätsprobleme der Frauen im Nationalsozialismus am Beispiel der 'Führerin aller deutschen Frauen'* (Münster, 2005), pp. 114–15 (quotation on p. 115).   15. Wiedemann to Eva von Schröder, 1.7.1938, BAK, N1720 Wiedemann 8.   16. Hitler's remarks are conveyed in RH, 25.7.1937, IV, p. 460.   17. RH, 26.1.1937, IV, p. 71; RH, 9.12.1937, IV, p. 657; RH, 5.1.1938, V, p. 965; RH, 21.12.1938, V, p. 1,067.   18. Elizabeth D. Heineman, *What Difference Does a Husband Make? Women and Marital Status in Nazi and Postwar Germany* (Berkeley, Los Angeles and London, 1999), pp. 17–18.   19. RH, 11.5.1937, IV, p. 276.   20. ES, 29.4.1937, pp. 166–7, 140, 142.   21. 'Hitlers Rede zur Eröffnung der "Grossen Deutschen Kunstausstellung" 1937', in Peter-Klaus Schuster (ed.), *Nationalsozialismus und 'Entartete Kunst'. Die 'Kunststadt' München 1937* (Munich, 1987), pp. 242–52 (quotation on p. 250).   22. See Daniel Wildmann, *Begehrte Körper. Konstruktion und Inszenierung des 'arischen' Männerkörpers im 'Dritten Reich'* (Würzburg, 1998), pp. 23–6, 37–40.   23. Thus Ines Schlenker, *Hitler's Salon: The Grosse Deutsche Kunstausstellung at the Haus der Deutschen Kunst in Munich, 1937–1944* (Berne, 2007), pp. 19–20, 23, 63, 130–39 *et passim*.   24. See Brandon Taylor and Wilfried van der Will (eds.), *The Nazification of Art: Art, Design, Music, Architecture and Film in the Third Reich* (Winchester, 1990), pp. 128–43.   25. Thus Schlenker, *Hitler's Salon*, pp. 65–6.   26. See Sabine Brantl, *Haus der Kunst, München. Ein Ort und seine Geschichte im Nationalsozialismus* (Munich, 2007), p. 99.   27. See Hans J. Reichhardt and Wolfgang Schäche, *Von Berlin nach Germania. Über die Zerstörungen der 'Reichshauptstadt' durch Albert Speers Neugestaltungsplanungen* (Berlin, 2008), pp. 38–9, 50, 87, 95–6, 109–10 *et passim*, and Wolfgang Ribbe, 'Auf dem Weg nach Germania? Die Reichshauptstadt als nationalsozialistisches Ziel und in den Planungen für Hitlers Berlin', in Fritz Mayrhofer and Ferdinand Opll (eds.), *Stadt und Nationalsozialismus* (Linz, 2008), pp. 19–20 *et passim*.   28. RH, 9.3.1937, IV, p. 173.   29. ES, 29.4.1937, p. 143.   30. See Strobl, *Germanic Isle*, p. 57.   31. Thus Michaela Karl, *'Ich blätterte gerade in der Vogue, da sprach mich der Führer an'. Unity Mitford. Eine Biographie* (Hamburg, 2016), p. 252.   32. See the notes made by Fritz Wiedemann during the war in Bundesarchiv Koblenz, N1720 Wiedemann 4.   33. See Walter Baum, 'Die "Reichsreform" im Dritten Reich', *Vierteljahrshefte für Zeitgeschichte*, 3 (1955), pp. 36–56, especially, p. 48.   34. RH, 7.4.1937, IV, pp. 740–41; RH, 26.1.1937, IV, p. 71.   35. Friedrich Hartmannsgruber, 'Die Reichskanzlei im Dritten Reich und das Verfahren zur Zwangspensionierung von Beamten', in Winfried Becker and Werner Chrobak (eds.), *Staat, Kultur, Politik. Beiträge zur Geschichte Bayerns und des Katholizismus. Festschrift. zum 65. Geburtstag von Dieter Albrecht* (Kallmünz, 1992), pp. 397–411 (quotation on p. 398).   36. RH, 9.12.1937, IV, p. 651. For Hitler's troubled relationship with the professional civil service see Caplan, *Government Without Administration*, pp. 102–3 *et passim*, and O'Byrne, 'Political civil servants', pp. 170–80.   37. RH, 9.3.1937, IV, p. 172.   38. RH, 10.12.1937, IV, p. 659; RH, 6.10.1937, IV, p. 789.   39. RH, 27.4.1938, V, pp.

320–21; RH, 6.7.1938, V, p. 1,029; RH, 25.7.1938, V, p. 1,038; RH, 17.8.1938, V, p. 1,044. **40.** E.g. RH, 19.3.1937, IV, p. 200. **41.** For numerous examples of circulation see RH, 7.4.1937, IV, p. 740; RH, 15.4.1937, IV, p. 742; RH, 11.5.1937, IV, pp. 751, 772. See also O'Byrne, 'Political civil servants', p. 235. **42.** See the planned meetings: RH, 23.11.1938, V, p. 1,063 (re December 1938), and p. 1,064 (re January 1939). **43.** Thus Friedrich Hartmannsgruber in his preface to RH, V, p. 963. See also Dieter Rebentisch, *Führerstaat und Verwaltung im Zweiten Weltkrieg. Verfassungsentwicklung und Verwaltungspolitik 1939–1945* (Stuttgart, 1989), p. 41. **44.** Thus Elke Fröhlich, 'Hitler–Goebbels–Strasser: a war of deputies, as seen through the Goebbels diaries, 1926–27', in Anthony McElligott and Tim Kirk (eds.), *Working towards the Führer: Essays in Honour of Sir Ian Kershaw* (Manchester, 2003). **45.** RH, 25.10.1937, IV, p. 548. **46.** RH, 26.1.1937, IV, p. 713; RH, 5.3.1937, IV, p. 728; RH, 29.6.1937, IV, p. 765; RH, 10.8.1937, IV, p. 774. **47.** See Martin Moll, 'Der Sturz alter Kämpfer. Ein neuer Zugang zur Herrschaftsanalyse des NS-Regimes', *Historische Mitteilungen*, 5 (1992), pp. 19–25. **48.** RH, 5.2.1938, V, p. 977. **49.** RH, 9.3.1938, V, p. 992. **50.** ES, 29.4.1937, pp. 153–6, 159–60. **51.** RH, 5.4.1938, V, pp. 251–2. **52.** ES, 29.4.1937, pp. 160–62. **53.** Dietrich, *12 Jahre*, p. 228. **54.** For an account of Deborah Mitford's encounter see her diary entry for 7 June 1937, quoted in Deborah Devonshire, *Wait for Me! Memoirs of the Youngest Mitford Sister* (London, 2010), p. 89. **55.** Mary S. Lovell, *The Mitford Girls: The Biography of an Extraordinary Family* (London, 2013). **56.** Quoted in Dietrich, *12 Jahre*, p. 235. **57.** Dietrich, *12 Jahre*, p. 213. **58.** See, for example, 'Die Auslandspressestimmen zur Rede des Führers von 30 Januar 1937', in LOC Third Reich Collection, DD253.A84.1937. **59.** RH, 10.8.1937, IV, p. 771. **60.** Rechenberg submitted the memorandum on 30 August 1937: RH, 4.10.1937, IV, p. 781. It is not clear whether Hitler saw it then. **61.** See Ribbentrop to Hitler and Neurath, 14.2.1937, London, ADAP, Series C, VI/2, pp. 436–6; Ribbentrop to Hitler and Neurath, 20.2.1937, London, ADAP, Series C, VI/1, pp. 546–8. **62.** The key text here is Karina Urbach, *Go-Betweens for Hitler* (Oxford, 2015). **63.** Wiedemann to Bormann, 2.7.1937, N1720 Wiedemann 5, Bundesarchiv Koblenz. For Hitler's face-to-face meeting with her see Martha Schad, *Stephanie von Hohenlohe. Hitlers jüdische Spionin* (Munich, 2012), pp. 36–7. **64.** As quoted in 'Aufzeichnung des Staatssekretärs des Auswärtigen Amts von Mackensen', 25.8.1937, Berlin, ADAP, Series C, VI/2, p. 1,095. **65.** See Valentine Low, 'For sale: duke's salute pictures', *The Times*, 22.7.2015, p. 7. **66.** Thus, at any rate, Paul Schmidt, *Statist auf diplomatischer Bühne, 1923–45* (Bonn, 1949), p. 383. **67.** Karl, *Unity*, pp. 240–41. **68.** See Lovell, *Mitford Girls*, p. 254. **69.** See Karl, *Unity*. **70.** See Karina Urbach, 'Introduction', in Karina Urbach (ed.), *European Aristocracies and the Radical Right, 1918–1939* (Oxford, 2007), pp. 1–12, and Dina Gusejnova, *European Elites and Ideas of Empire, 1917–1957* (Cambridge, 2016). **71.** Jonathan Petropoulos, *Royals and the Reich: The Princes von Hessen in Nazi Germany* (Oxford, 2006); Ian Kershaw, *Making Friends with Hitler: Lord Londonderry and Britain's Road to War* (London, 2004). **72.** See Karina Urbach, 'Age of no extremes? The British aristocracy torn between the House of Lords and the Mosley movement', in Urbach (ed.), *European Aristocracies*, p. 54. **73.** Thus Karl, *Unity*, p. 235, quoting Unity's diary. **74.** Hanfstaengl, *Zwischen Weissem und Braunem Haus*, pp. 362–3. **75.** Quotations in Alfred M. Beck, *Hitler's Ambivalent Attaché: Lt. Gen. Friedrich Boetticher in America, 1933–1941* (Washington, DC, 2005), pp. 64, 66. **76.** See Warren F. Kimball, 'Dieckhoff and America: a German's view of German-American relations, 1937–1941', *Historian*, 27, 2 (1965), pp. 218–43. **77.** See Memorandum Neurath, 12.3.1937, Berlin, ADAP, Series C, VI/1, pp. 573–4; Borchers to Dieckhoff, 13.3.1937, New York, ADAP, Series C, VI/1, pp. 575–8. **78.** See Grill and Jenkins, 'The Nazis and the American South in the 1930s', pp. 668–9. **79.** See Kimball, 'Dieckhoff and America', p. 235. **80.** 'Bericht des Präsidenten des Deutschen Auslandsinstituts Oberbürgermeister Dr Strolin, Stuttgart, über seine Reise nach den Vereinigten Staaten von Amerika im September–Oktober 1936', 2.12.1936, Stuttgart, ADAP, Series C, VI/1, pp. 142–7. **81.** Hitler's formulation in RH, 25.1.1938, V, 1938, p. 70. **82.** Rolf-Dieter Müller, *Der Feind steht im Osten. Hitlers geheime Pläne für einen Krieg gegen die Sowjetunion im Jahr 1939* (Berlin, 2011), p. 60. **83.** As summarized in a Memorandum of 27.5.1937, Berlin, ADAP, Series C, VI/2 , pp. 844–6 (quotation on p. 845). **84.** GT, 2.12.1936, I/3/II, p. 273. **85.** E.g., Memorandum, 16.11.1936, ADAP, Series

C, VI/1, pp. 68–70; and Memorandum, 15.12.1936, ADAP, Series C, VI/1, pp. 201–4. **86.** ES, 24.2.1937, pp. 99, 101–2. **87.** RH, 22.2.1937, IV, pp. 724–5. **88.** Karen A. Fiss, 'In Hitler's salon: the German pavilion at the 1937 Paris Exposition Internationale', in Richard A. Etlin (ed.), *Art, Culture, and Media under the Third Reich* (Chicago, 2002), pp. 316–42, especially 318–21. **89.** See Danilo Udovički-Selb, 'Facing Hitler's pavilion: the uses of modernity in the Soviet pavilion at the 1937 Paris International Exhibition', *Journal of Contemporary History*, 47 (2012), pp. 13–47. **90.** See Stefanie Schäfers, *Vom Werkbund zum Vierjahresplan. Die Ausstellung 'Schaffendes Volk', Düsseldorf 1937* (Düsseldorf, 2001). **91.** See S. Jonathan Wiesen, *Creating the Nazi Marketplace: Commerce and Consumption in the Third Reich* (Cambridge, 2011), pp. 94–5. **92.** RH, 16.7.1936, III, p. 873. **93.** Thus König, *Volkswagen, Volksempfänger, Volksgemeinschaft*, pp. 258–82. **94.** The figures are taken from Tooze, *Wages of Destruction*, p. 149. **95.** Wolfgang König, 'Adolf Hitler vs. Henry Ford: the *Volkswagen*, the role of America as a model, and the failure of a Nazi consumer society', *German Studies Review*, 27, 2 (2004), pp. 249–68, especially pp. 256–7; Hans Mommsen and Manfred Grieger, *Das Volkswagenwerk und seine Arbeiter im Dritten Reich* (Düsseldorf, 1996). **96.** Thus Buchheim, 'Das NS-Regime und die Überwindung der Weltwirtschaftskrise', pp. 411, 413. **97.** See Tooze, *Wages of Destruction*, p. 138. **98.** ES, 20.5.1937, pp. 194, 199. **99.** RH, 4.5.1937, IV, p. 747. **100.** RH, 1.7.1937, IV, p. 767. **101.** Thus Kopper, *Hjalmar Schacht*, pp. 312–15 (quotation on p. 314). **102.** RH, 19.3.1937, IV, p. 736. **103.** See Emma Fattorini, *Hitler, Mussolini and the Vatican: Pope Pius XI and the Speech that Was Never Made* (Cambridge, 2011), pp. 115–19. **104.** For the ban see RH, 7.4.1937, IV, p. 739. **105.** RH, 4.5.1937, IV, p. 746. **106.** See Fattorini, *Hitler, Mussolini and the Vatican*, pp. 115–19. **107.** Vorträge Lammers bei Hitler, 27.5.1937, RH, IV, p. 753. **108.** Speech, 29.4.1937, in ES, p. 127. **109.** See Robert Gerwarth, *Hitler's Hangman: The Life of Heydrich* (New Haven and London, 2011), pp. 104–5. **110.** Quoted in Hans Günter Hockerts, *Die Sittlichkeitsprozesse gegen katholische Ordensangehörige und Priester, 1936/1937. Eine Studie zur nationalsozialistischen Herrschaftstechnik und zum Kirchenkampf* (Mainz, 1971), p. 218. **111.** See Hockerts, *Die Sittlichkeitsprozesse*, pp. 73–4. **112.** RH, 22.6.1937, IV, p. 762. **113.** E.g. RH, 1.5.1937, IV. **114.** As reported to Hitler in RH, 1937, IV, pp. 775–6. **115.** Quoted in Fattorini, *Hitler, Mussolini and the Vatican*, p. 135. See also the nearly identical phrasing in Speech, 6.6.1937, Domarus, II, p. 699. **116.** Hockerts, *Die Sittlichkeitsprozesse*, pp. 74–5. **117.** RH, 13.1.1937, IV, p. 707. Hitler had already discussed the issue with the Hungarian minister of the interior, von Kozma: Memorandum of meeting with Kozma, 15.12.1936, ADAP, Series C, VI/1, p. 203. **118.** See Geoffrey T. Waddington, 'Hitler, Ribbentrop, die NSDAP und der Niedergang des britischen Empire 1935–1938', *Vierteljahrshefte für Zeitgeschichte*, 40 (1992), pp. 273–306, especially pp. 305–6 (quotation on p. 305). **119.** Thus Stratigakos, *Hitler at Home*. **120.** See Erwin A. Schmidl, 'Die militärischen Aspekte des Anschlusses', in Gerald Stourzh and Birgitta Zaar (eds.), *Österreich, Deutschland und die Mächte. Internationale und österreichische Aspekte des 'Anschlusses' vom März 1938* (Vienna, 1990), pp. 291–302, here p. 293. **121.** ES, 20.5.1937, pp. 190–92. **122.** Speech, 3.10.1937, Domarus, II, p. 740. **123.** Hitler speech, 13.9.1937, in Wolf Gruner (ed.), *Die Verfolgung und Ermordung der europäischen Juden durch das nationalsozialistische Deutschland, 1933–1945*, vol. 1: *Deutsches Reich, 1933–1937* (Munich, 2008), p. 702. **124.** See Uwe Mai, 'Rasse und Raum'. *Agrarpolitik, Sozial- und Raumplanung im NS-Staat* (Paderborn, etc., 2002), pp. 78–80. **125.** Speech, 20.5.1937, Domarus, II, p. 222. **126.** Speech, 24.2.1937, Domarus, II, p. 85. **127.** Proclamation, 10.9.1937, Domarus, II, p. 717. **128.** See the description in Schmidt, *Statist auf diplomatischer Bühne*, pp. 369, 395. **129.** See Christian Goeschel, 'Staging friendship: Mussolini and Hitler in Germany in 1937', *Historical Journal*, 60 (2017), pp. 149–72. See also Wenke Nitz, *Führer und Duce. Politische Machtinszenierungen im nationalsozialistischen Deutschland und im faschistischen Italien* (Cologne, 2013). **130.** Thus Goeschel, 'Staging friendship', pp. 164–5. **131.** Wolfgang Benz, 'Die Inszenierung der Akklamation – Mussolini in Berlin 1937', in Michael Grüttner, Rüdiger Hachtmann and Heinz-Gerhard Haupt (eds.), *Geschichte und Emanzipation. Festschrift für Reinhard Rürup* (Frankfurt, 1999), pp. 401–17, especially pp. 405–9. **132.** Thus Goeschel, 'Staging friendship', pp. 149, 164–5 *et passim*. **133.** Goeschel,

'Staging friendship', p. 159. **134.** 'Aktennotiz über Besprechung beim Reichsminsiter des Auswärtigen von Neurath, 1.10.1937, Berlin', ADAP, Series D, I, pp. 380–81 (quotations on p. 380). See also Georg Christoph Berger Waldenegg, 'Hitler, Göring, Mussolini und der "Anschluss" Österreichs an das Deutsche Reich', *Vierteljahrshefte für Zeitgeschichte*, 51 (2003), pp. 147–82. **135.** ES, 29.4.1937, p. 148. **136.** The idea that 1937–8 marked a step change is, of course, a commonplace in the literature: E.g. Rainer F. Schmidt, *Die Aussenpolitik des Dritten Reiches, 1933–1939* (Stuttgart, 2002), p. 218. **137.** On the general phenomenon see Frank-Lothar Kroll, 'Der Faktor "Zukunft" in Hitlers Geschichtsbild', in Frank-Lothar Kroll (ed.), *Neue Wege der Ideengeschichte. Festschrift für Kurt Kluxen zum 85. Geburtstag* (Paderborn and Munich, 1996), pp. 391–409, especially pp. 394–5; Frank-Lothar Kroll, 'Geschichte und Politik im Weltbild Hitlers', *Vierteljahrshefte für Zeitgeschichte*, 44 (1996), pp. 327–53; and Christopher Clark, 'Time of the Nazis: past and present in the Third Reich', *Geschichte und Gesellschaft*, Special Issue 25, 'Obsession der Gegenwart: Zeit im 20. Jahrhundert' (2015), pp. 156–87. **138.** Fest, *Hitler*, pp. 737–8. **139.** E.g. the eyewitness Werner Best: see Matlok (ed.), *Dänemark in Hitlers Hand*, p. 128. Speech, 11.9.1937, Domarus, II, p. 724, and Speech, 31.10.1937, Domarus, II, p. 745. **140.** Sirois, *Zwischen Illusion und Krieg*, pp. 105–10. See also Detlef Junker, 'Hitler's perception of Franklin D. Roosevelt and the United States of America', *Amerikastudien*, 38 (1993), pp. 25–36. **141.** Quoted in Dorothy Borg, 'Notes on Roosevelt's "Quarantine" speech', *Political Science Quarterly*, 72 (1957), pp. 405–33, (quotation on p. 423). **142.** Steven Casey, *Cautious Crusade: Franklin D. Roosevelt, American Public Opinion, and the War against Nazi Germany* (New York, 2001). **143.** See the (subsequent) eyewitness account of Nicolaus von Below, *Als Hitlers Adjutant, 1937–45* (Mainz, 1980), pp. 47–8. **144.** Lammers to Rechenberg (copy), 6.10.1937, Berlin, AA Pol. Abteilung, Akten betr. politische und kulturelle Propaganda USA, R105012, Pol. Archiv AA. **145.** Staatssekretär and Chef der Reichskanzlei to Ribbentrop and Goebbels, 15.10.1937, Berlin, AA Pol. Abteilung, Akten betr. politische und kulturelle Propaganda USA, R105012, Pol. Archiv AA. **146.** There is a copy of *Hitler – Amerika – eine Gefahr* in Akten betr. Baron von Rechenberg, Anti-kommunistische Propaganda in Amerika, Pol. Archiv AA 99511. **147.** Engelbert Schwarzenbeck, *Nationalsozialistische Pressepolitik und die Sudetenkrise 1938* (Munich, 1979), pp. 421–2. **148.** André Deschan, 'Rudolf Wolters – der Mann hinter Speer', in Wolfgang Benz, Peter Eckel and Andreas Nachama (eds.), *Kunst im NS-Staat. Ideologie, Ästhetik, Protagonisten* (Berlin, 2015), pp. 319–31, especially p. 324. The connection to Washington was also made by Leon Krier, *Albert Speer: Architecture, 1932–1942* (Brussels, 1985), p. 49. **149.** R. Wolters, 'Studienreise nach Nordamerika', LOC Third Reich Collection, E169.5938.1937, fols. 58 and 59 (sketches). **150.** Thus Deschan, 'Wolters', p. 324. **151.** See BAK, N1720, 4 (unfoliated). **152.** Quoted in Schubert, 'Führerstadtplanungen in Hamburg', p. 19. **153.** See the account in 'Vertretung Hamburgs in Berlin an das Hamburgische Staatsamt, 16.3.1937, Berlin', in Werner Johe, *Hitler in Hamburg. Dokumente zu einem besonderen Verhältnis* (Hamburg, 1996), pp. 161–3 (quotations on p. 162). **154.** See Jochen Thies, 'Hitler's European building programme', *Journal of Contemporary History*, 13 (1978), pp. 413–31, here p. 414. **155.** For the centrality of the 'American' dimension see Sylvia Necker, *Konstanty Gutschow 1902–1978. Modernes Denken und volksgemeinschaftliche Utopie eines Architekten* (Hamburg, 2012), pp. 209–43, especially pp. 222, 229. **156.** See Wiedemann, *Der Mann der Feldherr werden wollte*, pp. 222–3. **157.** RH, 2.12.1937, IV, p. 801. See also Lammers to Göring, RH, 8.12.1937, IV, p. 647–8. **158.** Memorandum of Max Domarus, 31.10.1937, on the basis of information provided by the eyewitness *Gaupropagandaleiter* of Würzburg, Domarus, II, p. 745. **159.** Walter Bussmann, 'Zur Entstehung und Überlieferung der "Hossbach-Niederschrift", *Vierteljahrshefte für Zeitgeschichte*, 16 (1968), pp. 373–84; Hermann Gackenholz, 'Reichskanzlei, 5. November 1937', in R. Dietrich and G. Oestreich (eds.), *Forschungen zu Staat und Verfassung. Festgabe für Fritz Hartung* (Berlin, 1958); Peter Graf Kielmansegg, 'Die militärisch-politische Tragweite der Hossbach-Besprechung', *Vierteljahrshefte für Zeitgeschichte*, 8 (1960), pp. 268–75. The text is not an approved verbatim record of what was said, but undoubtedly reflects the content of the meeting. **160.** Sandner, *Hitler*, vol. 3. **161.** Speech, 20.2.1938, Domarus, II, p. 802. **162.** Thus Krämer, '*Maikrise*', pp. 50 and 54. **163.** There is some doubt as to whether

Hitler demanded Danzig at all. Lord Halifax's own account, *Fulness of Days* (London, 1957), pp. 186–7 (quotation on p. 187), suggests that he himself raised the issue, while Hitler 'said nothing about Danzig'. **164.** See Hartmut Lehmann, 'Der Statist als Akteur. Chefdolmetscher Dr. Paul Schmidt zwischen Hitler und Lord Halifax am 19. November 1937', in Volker Dotterweich and Walther L. Bernecker (eds.), *Deutschland in den internationalen Beziehungen des 19. und 20. Jahrhunderts. Festschrift für Josef Becker zum 65. Geburtstag* (Munich, 1996), pp. 221–33, especially pp. 223–4 and 230 (quotation on p. 223). **165.** See Longerich, *Unwritten Order*, p. 60. **166.** GT, 30.11.1937, I/4, p. 429.

Chapter 14: 'England is the motor of opposition to us'

1. Thus Jörg Fisch, 'Adolf Hitler und das Selbstbestimmungsrecht der Völker', *Historische Zeitschrift*, 290 (2010), pp. 93–118, especially pp. 107–10. **2.** Quoted in Linne, *Deutschland jenseits des Äquators?*, p. 48. See also Jost Dülffer, 'Kolonialismus ohne Kolonien. Deutsche Kolonialpläne 1938', in Franz Knipping and Klaus-Jürgen Müller (eds.), *Machtbewusstsein in Deutschland am Vorabend des Zweiten Weltkrieges* (Paderborn, 1984), pp. 247–70 (quotation on p. 250). **3.** Memorandum by Schmidt (translator), 4.3.1938, Berlin, ADAP, Series D, I, pp. 196–203. **4.** RH, 17.2.1938, V, p. 980. See also Gerhard L. Weinberg, 'German recognition of Manchoukuo', *World Affairs Quarterly*, 28 (1957), pp. 149–62. **5.** See Graml, *Hitler und England*, p. 98; and Astrid Freyeisen, *Shanghai und die Politik des Dritten Reiches* (Würzburg, 2000), pp. 199–201. **6.** Quoted in Wiedemann, *Der Mann der Feldherr werden wollte*, p. 174. **7.** See Dietrich, *12 Jahre*, p. 243. **8.** Quoted Sandner, *Hitler*, vol. 3, p. 1,502. **9.** Quoted in Roger Moorhouse, 'Germania: Hitler's dream capital', *History Today*, 62 (March 2012), p. 20. **10.** RH, 20.1.1938, V, pp. 970–71. **11.** 10.2.1939, quoted in Jost Dülffer, Jochen Thies and Josef Henke (eds.), *Hitlers Städte. Baupolitik im Dritten Reich* (Cologne and Vienna, 1978), p. 297. See also Winfried Nerdinger, 'Hitler als Architekt. Bauten als Mittel zur Stärkung der "Volksgemeinschaft"', in Hans-Ulrich Thamer and Simone Erpel (eds.), *Hitler und die Deutschen. Volksgemeinschaft und Verbrechen* (Dresden, 2010), pp. 74–81. **12.** Bernhard Rieger, *The People's Car: A Global History of the Volkswagen Beetle* (Cambridge, Mass., 2013), pp. 71–2. **13.** See Marie-Luise Recker, *Die Grossstadt als Wohn- und Lebensbereich im Nationalsozialismus. Zur Gründung der 'Stadt des KdF-Wagens'* (Frankfurt, 1981), pp. 7 (quotation), 78–81. **14.** Karl-Heinz Janssen and Fritz Tobias, *Der Sturz der Generäle. Hitler und die Blomberg-Fritsch-Krise 1938* (Munich, 1994); Klaus-Jürgen Müller, *Das Heer und Hitler. Armee und nationalsozialistisches Regime, 1933–1940* (Stuttgart, 1969), pp. 262–92. **15.** See Schäfer, *Blomberg*, pp. 11, 173–82. **16.** Quoted in Janssen and Tobias, *Sturz der Generäle*, p. 30. **17.** Quoted in Wiedemann, *Der Mann der Feldherr werden wollte*, p. 112. **18.** Quoted in Müller, *Heer und Hitler*, p. 263. **19.** Schäfer, *Blomberg*, pp. 187–8. **20.** See RH, 4.2.1938, V, p. 108. **21.** Thus Wiedemann, *Der Mann der Feldherr werden wollte*, p. 114. **22.** Martin Moll, 'Die Annexion Österreichs 1938 als erster Schritt zur Entfesselung des Zweiten Weltkrieges? Forschungsstand und offene Fragen', *Bulletin für Faschismus- und Weltkriegsforschung*, 15 (2000), pp. 37–72, which sees Göring as the main driver. See also Schmidl, 'Die militärischen Aspekte des Anschlusses'. **23.** 'Weisung betreffend Unternehmen Otto', 11.3.1938, Berlin', in Herbert Michaelis and Ernst Schraepler (eds.), *Das Dritte Reich. Innere Gleichschaltung. Der Staat und die Kirchen. Antikominternpakt – Achse Rom–Berlin. Der Weg ins Grossdeutsche Reich* (Berlin, 1966), pp. 650–51. **24.** GT, 10.3.1938, I/5, p. 199. **25.** Hitler to Mussolini, 11.3.1938, ADAP, Series D, I, pp. 468–70 (quotation on p. 470). **26.** Quoted in Lovell, *Mitford Girls*, p. 244. **27.** Thus Georg Christoph Berger Waldenegg, 'Hitler, Göring, Mussolini und der "Anschluss" Österreichs an das Deutsche Reich', *Vierteljahrshefte für Zeitgeschichte*, 51 (2003), pp. 147–82, here p. 152 *et passim*. **28.** See Richard Breitman and Allan J. Lichtman, *FDR and the Jews* (Cambridge, Mass., 2013), pp. 100–102. **29.** RH, 23.4.1936, III, p. 1,002. **30.** Anthony Sampson, *The Sovereign State: The Secret History of ITT* (London, 1973), p. 29. **31.** See Wiedemann, *Der Mann der Feldherr werden wollte*, p. 217. **32.** Walter Goodman, *The Committee: The*

Extraordinary Career of the House Committee on Un-American Activities (New York, 1968). **33.** 'Die Rückwanderung aus den Vereinigten Staaten von Amerika. Bd I 1938–1942', R67398, and 'Rückwanderer USA, Einzelfälle', R67435, Archiv Auswärtiges Amt, ADAP, Series D, IV, pp. 571–3. **34.** See Arthur L. Smith, Jr, 'The Kameradschaft USA', *Journal of Modern History*, 34 (1962), pp. 398–408, especially pp. 399, 400, 404. **35.** See Arnold Suppan, 'Hitler und die Österreicher. Zwischen totaler Gleichschaltung und partieller Unterdrückung', *Geistes-, sozial- und kulturwissenschaftlicher Anzeiger. Zeitschrift der philosophisch-historischen Klasse der Österreichischen Akademie der Wissenschaften*, 150 (2015), pp. 31–56, here p. 37. **36.** For an account of the meeting see ET, 14.3.1938, pp. 15–16 (quotations on p. 16); and Viktor Reimann, *Innitzer. Kardinal zwischen Hitler und Rom* (Vienna, 1967), pp. 93–4. **37.** Wilhelm Schwemmer, 'Die Reichskleinodien in Nürnberg, 1938–1945', *Mitteilungen des Vereins für die Geschichte der Stadt Nürnberg*, 65 (1978), pp. 397–413. See also Sidney D. Kirkpatrick, *Hitler's Holy Relics* (London and New York, 2010), p. 127. **38.** RH, 16.6.1938, V, p. 1,022; RH, 13.7.1938, V, p. 1,034. **39.** Speech, 12.9.1938, Domarus, II, p. 905. **40.** RH, 25.7.1938, V, p. 1,039; RH, 17.8.1938, V, p. 1,042; RH, 9.8.1938, V, p. 585. **41.** Speech 3.4.1938, Domarus, II, p. 843. **42.** RH, 31.5.1938, V, p. 1,011. **43.** See William S. Grenzebach, *Germany's Informal Empire in East-Central Europe: German Economic Policy toward Yugoslavia and Rumania, 1933–1939* (Stuttgart, 1988), pp. 218–19, 234, 236–7 *et passim*; and Andreas Hillgruber, *Hitler, König Carol und Marschall Antonescu. Die deutsch-rumänischen Beziehungen, 1938–1944* (Wiesbaden, 1954), pp. 13–23. **44.** Leopold Steurer, *Südtirol zwischen Rom und Berlin, 1919–1939* (Vienna, Munich and Zurich, 1980), pp. 291–3. **45.** Schmidt, *Statist*, p. 391. For Hitler's vehement, and sincere, renunication see *Memoirs of Ernst von Weizäcker*, trans. John Andrews (London, 1951), pp. 129–30. **46.** Speech, 7.5.1938, Domarus, II, p. 861. See also Günther Pallaver and Leopold Steurer (eds.), *Deutsche! Hitler verkauft euch! Das Erbe von Option und Weltkrieg in Südtirol* (Bozen, 2011), p. 19. **47.** Ralph-Miklas Dobler, *Bilder der Achse. Hitlers Empfang in Italien 1938 und die mediale Inszenierung des Staatsbesuches in Fotobüchern* (Berlin, 2015), pp. 176–82, 51–94. See also Paul Baxa, 'Capturing the fascist moment: Hitler's visit to Italy in 1938 and the radicalization of fascist Italy', *Journal of Contemporary History*, 42 (2007), pp. 227–42. **48.** Fattorini, *Hitler, Mussolini and the Vatican*, pp. 144–5 (quotation on p. 144). **49.** Quoted in Ranuccio Bianchi Bandinelli, *Hitler, Mussolini und ich. Aus dem Tagebuch eines Bürgers*, translated and annotated by Elmar Kossel (Berlin, 2016), p. 91. **50.** Draft of new Operation Green, 21.4.1938, ADAP, Series D, II, pp. 237–40. **51.** Quoted in Krämer, *'Maikrise'*, p. 59. **52.** Thus Jost Dülffer, 'Humanitarian intervention as legitimation of violence – the German case 1937–1939', in Fabian Klose (ed.), *The Emergence of Humanitarian Intervention: Ideas and Practice from the Nineteenth Century to the Present* (Cambridge, 2016), pp. 208–28. **53.** 'Bericht Henleins über seine Audienz beim Führer, 28.3.1938', in Celovsky, *Germanisierung und Genozid*, p. 136. **54.** Quoted in Krämer, *'Maikrise'*, p. 145. **55.** Krämer, *'Maikrise'*, pp. 13, 31, 184–7, 197–8, 242, 258, 273, 279 *et passim*. **56.** Wiedemann, *Der Mann der Feldherr werden wollte*, p. 127. **57.** Krämer, *'Maikrise'*, p. 213. **58.** Quoted in Wiedemann, *Der Mann der Feldherr werden wollte*, p. 127. **59.** See Klaus-Jürgen Müller, *Generaloberst Ludwig Beck. Eine Biographie* (Paderborn, etc., 2008), pp. 307–33. **60.** Thus Peter Jackson, 'British power and French security, 1919–1939', in Keith Neilson and Greg Kennedy (eds.), *The British Way in Warfare: Power and the International System, 1856–1956* (Farnham, 2010), p. 131. **61.** Quoted in Beck, *Bötticher*, p. 110. **62.** Thus Beck, *Bötticher*, pp. 108–9. **63.** Speech, 22.5.1938, Domarus, II, p. 864. **64.** Speech, 14.6.1938, Domarus, II, p. 873. **65.** RH, 17.6.1938, V, p. 462; RH, 10.9.1938, V, p. 669; RH, 21.12.1938, V, p. 1,069. **66.** See Strobl, *Germanic Isle*, pp. 96–130. **67.** Quoted in Wiedemann, *Der Mann der Feldherr werden wollte*, p. 151. **68.** See RH, 18.6.1938, V, p. 463. **69.** Adolf Hitler, 'Denkschrift zur Frage unserer Festungsanlagen', 1.7.1938 (http://www.krawa.info/Quellen/DENKSCHRIFT.pdf); John D. Heyl, 'The construction of the *Westwall*, 1938: an exemplar for National Socialist policymaking', *Central European History*, 14 (1981), pp. 63–78. **70.** See Bernhard R. Kroener, 'Die personellen Ressourcen des Dritten Reiches im Spannungsfeld zwischen Wehrmacht, Bürokratie und Kriegswirtschaft, 1939–1944', in Bernhard R. Kroener et al.,

Das Deutsche Reich und der Zweite Weltkrieg, vol. 5: *Organisation und Mobilisierung des deutschen Machtbereichs*, part 1: *Kriegsverwaltung, Wirtschaft und personelle Ressourcen, 1939–1941* (Stuttgart, 1988), pp. 693–1,001. **71.** See Tooze, *Wages of Destruction*, p. 250. **72.** Quoted in Krämer, *Kriegskurs*, p. 394. For the naval turn against Britain see also Jürgen Rohwer, 'Weltmacht als Ziel? Parallelen in Hitlers und Stalins Flottenbau-Programmen', in Ernst Willi Hansen, Gerhard Schreiber and Bernd Wegner (eds.), *Politischer Wandel, organisierte Gewalt und nationale Sicherheit* (Munich, 1995), pp. 175–6. **73.** Quoted in Krämer, *Kriegskurs*, p. 438. **74.** See Paul Moore, ' "And what concentration camps those were!": foreign concentration camps in Nazi propaganda, 1933–9', *Journal of Contemporary History*, 45 (2010), pp. 649–74, especially pp. 663–7. **75.** Quoted in Hans Frank, *Im Angesicht des Galgens. Deutung Hitlers und seiner Zeit auf Grund eigener Erlebnisse und Erkenntnisse* (Munich, 1953), p. 243. There is no reason to doubt Frank's otherwise self-serving account in this case. **76.** Thus Müller, *Beck*, pp. 334–64. **77.** See ET, 25.8.1938, p. 34. **78.** See Strobl, *Germanic Isle*, p. 87. **79.** GT, 31.5.1938, I/5, p. 326. **80.** Quoted in Christian Faludi (ed.), *Die 'Juni-Aktion' 1938. Eine Dokumentation zur Radikalisierung der Judenverfolgung* (Frankfurt and New York, 2013), pp. 42–3. **81.** 'Bericht betr. Judenaktion in Berlin vom 17.6 bis 21.6.1938', in Faludi, *'Juni-Aktion'*, pp. 75, 298–301 (quotation on p. 299). **82.** RH, 25.7.1938, V, p. 1,037. **83.** See Wiedemann, *Der Mann der Feldherr werden wollte*, pp. 189–90. **84.** Jochen Thies, *Evian 1938. Als die Welt die Juden verriet* (Essen, 2017); Fritz Kieffer, *Judenverfolgung in Deutschland – eine innere Angelegenheit? Internationale Reaktionen auf die Flüchtlingsproblematik, 1933–1939* (Stuttgart, 2002), especially pp. 155–77. **85.** Speech 12.9.1938, Domarus, II, p. 899. **86.** GT, 24.7.1938, I/5, p. 393. Longerich, *Unwritten Order*, p. 63, notes the 'hostages' theme in Hitler's argumentation. **87.** ET, 13.8.1938, p. 31. **88.** See Schlenker, *Hitler's Salon*, pp. 25, 204 and 232–57 (with list of his purchases). **89.** Speech, 10.7.1938, Domarus, II, pp. 877–8. **90.** See description of the conversation in ET, 20.8.1938, pp. 33–4. **91.** 'Rede Hitlers zum Richtfest der Neuen Reichskanzlei in der Deutschlandhalle', 2.8.1938, in Angela Schönberger, *Die neue Reichskanzlei von Albert Speer. Zum Zusammenhang von nationalsozialistischer Ideologie und Architektur* (Berlin, 1981), pp. 179–81. **92.** Quoted in Krämer, *'Maikrise'*, p. 384. **93.** See Angela Hermann, 'Verhandlungen und Aktivitäten des nationalsozialistischen regimes im Vorfeld von "München" ', in Jürgen Zarusky and Martin Zückert (eds.), *Das Münchener Abkommen von 1938 in europäischer Perspetive* (Munich, 2013), pp. 145–57. **94.** See Hermann, 'Verhandlungen und Aktivitäten', p. 149. **95.** Karl, *Unity*, p. 277. **96.** RH, 4.9.1938, V, p. 660. **97.** See the description in Wiedemann, *Der Mann der Feldherr werden wollte*, p. 107. For the importance of Thomas's reports throughout 1938 see Manfred Messerschmidt, 'Das strategische Lagebild des OKW (Hitler) im Jahre 1938', in Franz Knipping and Klaus-Jürgen Müller (eds.), *Machtbewusstsein in Deutschland am Vorabend des Zweiten Weltkrieges* (Paderborn, 1984), pp. 145–58. **98.** Sylvia Taschka, *Diplomat ohne Eigenschaften? Die Karriere des Hans Heinrich Dieckhoff (1884–1952)* (Stuttgart, 2006), pp. 178–9. **99.** Speech, 6.9.1938, Domarus, II, p. 891. **100.** Thomas Sakmyster, *Miklós Horthy. Ungarn 1918–1944* (Vienna, 2006), pp. 217–18. **101.** Speech, 6.9.1938, Domarus, II, p. 890. **102.** See Barbara Rearden Farnham, *Roosevelt and the Munich Crisis: A Study of Political Decision-making* (Princeton, NJ, 1997), pp. 108–36. **103.** Wiedemann, *Der Mann der Feldherr werden wollte*, p. 170. **104.** Günther W. Gellermann, *. . . und lauschten für Hitler. Geheime Reichssache. Die Abhörzentralen des Dritten Reiches* (Bonn, 1991), p. 117. See also Hitler's recollections in 20.5.1942, Henry Picker, *Hitlers Tischgespräche im Führerhauptquartier* (Munich, 2009), p. 457. **105.** See Pierre Caquet, 'The balance of forces on the eve of Munich', *International History Review*, 40, 1 (2018), pp. 21–40. **106.** Conversation reported in 'Reiseberichte aus dem Sudetenland, 1938', in Helmuth Groscurth, *Tagebücher eines Abwehroffiziers, 1938–1940. Mit weiteren Dokumenten zur Militäropposition gegen Hitler*, ed. Helmut Krausnick and Harold C. Deutsch (Stuttgart, 1970), p. 133. **107.** Hitler to Roosevelt, 27.9.1938, Berlin, Domarus, II, pp. 935–7. **108.** See the account in Wiedemann, *Der Mann der Feldherr werden wollte*, pp. 175–6. **109.** See Bernd Sösemann, ' "Frieden in Europa" im Konzept der hegemonialen NS-Politik. Zur Eigendynamik aussenpolitischer Propagandakommunikation', in Frank

Bösch and Peter Hoeres (eds.), *Aussenpolitik im Medienzeitalter. Vom späten 19. Jahrhundert bis zur Gegenwart* (Göttingen, 2013), pp. 167–88. **110.** E.g. Wiedemann, *Der Mann der Feldherr werden wollte*, p. 187. **111.** Conversation reported in 'Reiseberichte aus dem Sudetenland, 1938', in Groscurth, *Tagebücher eines Abwehroffiziers*, p. 133. **112.** See Müller, *Feind steht im Osten*, p. 108. **113.** See Müller, *Feind steht im Osten, passim.* **114.** Thus Mai, *'Rasse und Raum'*, p. 292. See also RH, 20.12.1938, V, pp. 928–30. **115.** ES, 8.11.1938, pp. 234, 238–9. **116.** Jonathan Kirsch, *The Short, Strange Life of Herschel Grynszpan: A Boy Avenger, a Nazi Diplomat and a Murder in Paris* (New York and London, 2013), pp. 142–3. **117.** Dieter Obst, *'Reichskristallnacht'. Ursachen und Verlauf des antisemitischen Pogroms vom November 1938* (Frankfurt, 1991), especially, pp. 62–4, 79–83, 101–203. **118.** Hitler's desire to avoid 'another 1918' is emphasized by Alan E. Steinweis, *Kristallnacht 1938. Ein deutscher Pogrom* (Stuttgart, 2011), pp. 48–9. **119.** Thus Angela Hermann, 'Hitler und sein Stosstrupp in der "Reichskristallnacht"', *Vierteljahrshefte für Zeitgeschichte*, 56 (2008), pp. 603–19. See also Stefan Kley, 'Hitler and the pogrom of November 9/10, 1938', *Yad Vashem Studies*, 28 (2000), pp. 87–113. **120.** Quoted in David Cesarani, *Final Solution: The Fate of the Jews 1933–1949* (London, 2016), pp. 198–9. **121.** RH, 18.11.1938, V, p. 813. **122.** Kieffer, *Judenverfolgung in Deutschland*, pp. 320–62. **123.** Longerich, *Unwritten Order*, p. 221. **124.** 'Gespräch zwischen Adolf Hitler und dem Südafrikanischen Minister Pirow am 24. November 1938 über Deutschlands Machtstellung in der Welt und die "Judenfrage"', in Susanne Heim (ed.), *Die Verfolgung und Ermordung der europäischen Juden durch das nationalsozialistische Deutschland 1933–1945*, vol. 2: *Deutsches Reich 1938–August 1939* (Munich, 2009) (quotations on p. 488). **125.** Christoph Kreutzmüller, 'Augen im Sturm. Britische und amerikanische Zeitungsberichte über die Judenverfolgung in Berlin, 1918–1938', *Zeitschrift für Geschichtswissenschaft*, 62 (2014), pp. 41–6. **126.** Thus Guntram Schulze-Wegener, *Deutschland zur See. 150 Jahre Marinegeschichte* (Hamburg, 1998), p. 165. **127.** E.g. Speech, 26.9.1938, Domarus, II, p. 927. See also Speech, 9.10.1938, Domarus, II, pp. 954–6. **128.** 'Gespräch zwischen Hitler und Pirow', pp. 490–91. **129.** Speech, 8.11.1938, Domarus, II, p. 967. See also Speech, 6.11.1938, Domarus, II, p. 964, responding to Churchill's radio speech of 16 October 1938. **130.** ES, 8.11.1938, pp. 234–59 (quotation on p. 253). **131.** ES, 10.11.1938, pp. 268–86. See also Wilhelm Treue, 'Hitlers Rede vor der deutschen Presse (10. November 1938)', *Vierteljahrshefte für Zeitgeschichte*, 6 (1958), pp. 175–91. **132.** Thus Kieffer, *Judenverfolgung in Deutschland*, p. 485 *et passim.* **133.** Weizäcker memorandum, 16.12.1938, ADAP, Series D, IV, pp. 571–2. So far as I am aware this gambit has not been discussed by any previous biographer of Hitler. **134.** Dieckhoff to Ribbentrop, 16.12.1938, Berlin, ADAP, Series D, IV, pp. 572–3. **135.** ET, 16.10.1938, p. 40. **136.** See Stefan Hübner, 'National Socialist foreign policy and press instructions, 1933–9: aims and ways of coverage manipulation based on the example of East Asia', *International History Review*, 34 (2012), pp. 271–91, especially pp. 281–2. **137.** See the account in Wiedemann, *Der Mann der Feldherr werden wollte*, pp. 224–5. **138.** Speech, 9.10.1938, Domarus, II, p. 956; Speech, 12.9.1938, Domarus, II, pp. 904–5. See also Klaus-Michael Mallmann and Martin Cüppers, *Halbmond und Hakenkreuz. Das 'Dritte Reich', die Araber und Palästina* (Darmstadt, 2011), pp. 41–56. **139.** GT, 17.11.1938, I/6, p. 189. **140.** Hans Goldenbaum, 'Nationalsozialismus als Antikolonialismus. Die deutsche Rundfunkpropaganda für die arabische Welt', *Vierteljahrshefte für Zeitgeschichte*, 64 (2016), pp. 449–89, especially pp. 452–3. **141.** Joseph Said Abu Durra to Hitler, 23.12.1938, in Rolf Steininger (ed.), *Der Kampf um Palästina 1924–1939. Berichte der deutschen Generalkonsuln in Jerusalem* (Munich, 2007), pp. 136–7. **142.** Tooze, *Wages of Destruction*, p. 288. **143.** Marcus Faulkner, 'The Kriegsmarine and the aircraft carrier: the design and operational purpose of the *Graf Zeppelin*, 1933–1940', *War in History*, 19, 4 (2012), pp. 492–516, especially p. 510. **144.** Speech 8.11.1938, Domarus, II, p. 968. **145.** R. J. Overy, 'Hitler and air strategy', *Journal of Contemporary History*, 15 (1980), pp. 405–21, at p. 409; Tooze, *Wages of Destruction*, p. 288 (quotation). **146.** Beck, *Bötticher*, pp. 126–30 (quotation on p. 125). **147.** Hartmut Frank, '"Das Tor der Welt". Die Planungen für eine Hängebrücke über die Elbe und für ein Hamburger "Gauforum" 1935–1945', in Ulrich Höhns (ed.), *Das ungebaute Hamburg. Visionen einer anderen Stadt in* *architektonischen Entwürfen der letzten hundertfünfzig Jahre* (Hamburg, 1991), pp. 78–99 (quotation on p. 94).   **148.** Quoted from Thies, 'Hitler's European building programme', p. 414.   **149.** Speech, 17.2.1939, Domarus, II, p. 1,081.   **150.** 'Hitler declares Auto War. $400 car actually on view', *Pittsburgh Press*, 17.2.1939.   **151.** Thus Wolfram Pyta, 'Weltanschauliche und strategische Schicksalsgemeinschaft. Die Bedeutung Japans für das weltpolitische Kalkül Hitlers', in Martin Cüppers, Jürgen Matthäus and Andrej Angrick (eds.), *Naziverbrechen. Täter, Taten, Bewältigungsversuche* (Darmstadt, 2013), p. 30.   **152.** See Boyd, *Extraordinary Envoy*, pp. 99–100.   **153.** Thus Sönke Neitzel, 'Der Bedeutungswandel der Kriegsmarine im Zweiten Weltkrieg. Das militärische und politische Gewicht im Vergleich', in Rolf-Dieter Müller and Hans-Erich Volkmann (eds.), *Die Wehrmacht. Mythos, und Realität* (Munich, 1999), p. 245.   **154.** See the figures in Jürgen Rohwer, 'Weltmacht als Ziel? Parallelen in Hitlers und Stalins Flottenbau-Programmen', in Ernst Willi Hansen, Gerhard Schreiber and Bernd Wegner (eds.), *Politischer Wandel, organisierte Gewalt und nationale Sicherheit* (Munich, 1995), p. 176.   **155.** Lutz Budrass, *Flugzeugindustrie und Luftrüstung in Deutschland 1918–1945* (Düsseldorf, 1998), pp. 584–5.   **156.** See Tooze, *Wages of Destruction*, pp. 297–301.   **157.** Stefan Kley, 'Intention, Verkündigung, Implementierung. Hitlers Reichstagsrede vom 30. Januar 1939', *Zeitschrift für Geschichtswissenschaft*, 48 (2000), pp. 197–213. See also Hans Mommsen, 'Hitler's Reichstag speech of 30 January 1939', *History and Memory*, 9 (1997), pp. 147–61.   **158.** Speech, 30.1.1939, Domarus, III, p. 1,055.   **159.** Speech, 30.1.1939, Domarus, III, p. 1,054.   **160.** See Saul Friedländer, *Das Dritte Reich und die Juden. Die Jahre der Verfolgung, 1933–1939* (Munich, 2007), p. 335; and L. J. Hartog, *Der Befehl zum Judenmord. Hitler, Amerika und die Juden* (Bodenheim, 1997).   **161.** Alfred Gottwaldt and Diana Schulle, '*Juden ist die Benutzung von Speisewagen untersagt*'. Die antijüdische Politik des Reichsverkehrsministeriums zwischen 1933 und 1945 (Teetz, 2007), pp. 51–4.   **162.** Thus Raul Hilberg, *The Destruction of the European Jews*, vol. I (New Haven and London, 2003), pp. 170–71.   **163.** On all this see Longerich, *Unwritten Order*, p. 68.   **164.** See Magnus Brechtken, 'Auswärtiges Amt, Sicherheitsdienst und Reichssicherheitshauptamt 1933 bis 1942. Antisemitismus und Judenpolitik zwischen Machtfrage und Radikalisierungserfahrung', in Johannes Hürter and Michael Mayer (eds.), *Das Auswärtige Amt in der NS-Diktatur* (Munich, 2014), pp. 156–7. For Palestine as 'Weltfrage' see Dieter Schwarz, *Das Weltjudentum. Organisation, Macht und Politik* (Berlin, 1939), p. 9. Schwarz is a pseudonym for Franz A. Six, Herbert Hagen and Reinhard Heydrich. It is striking that the overwhelming focus of this book, which was written sometime before the Hitler–Stalin Pact, is on the western rather than Soviet threat of 'world Jewry'.   **165.** Speech, 30.1.1939, Domarus, III, p. 1,052.   **166.** Müller, *Der Feind steht im Osten*, pp. 117–18 *et passim*.   **167.** See 'Nazis assail Simms' story', *Pittsburgh Press*, 17.2.1939.   **168.** Müller, *Der Feind steht im Osten*, pp. 108–9, 112–13, 120.   **169.** Speech, 30.1.1939, Domarus, III, p. 1,065.   **170.** GT, 25.3.1939, I/6, p. 300.   **171.** See James Mace Ward, *Priest, Politician, Collaborator: Jozef Tiso and the Making of Fascist Slovakia* (Ithaca, NY and London, 2013), pp. 180–82.   **172.** Speech, 28.4.1939, Domarus, III, p. 1,152. See also Tara Zahra, *Kidnapped Souls: National Indifference and the Battle for Children in the Bohemian Lands, 1900–1948* (Ithaca, NY, 2008), pp. 169–251.   **173.** Quoted from the personal recollection of remarks made by Hitler on 22.3.1939 in the Imperial Chancellery, in Hermann Giesler, *Ein anderer Hitler. Bericht seines Architekten Hermann Giesler. Erlebnisse, Gespräche, Reflexionen* (Leoni, 1977), pp. 367–76.   **174.** Speech, 1.4.1939, Domarus, III, p. 1,120; Speech, 23.5.1939, Domarus, III, p. 1,198.   **175.** Speech, 19.4.1939, Domarus, III, p. 1,143.   **176.** Speech, 23.5.1939, Domarus, III, pp. 1,198–9; Speech, 4.6.1939, Domarus, III, p. 1,207.   **177.** Dietrich, *12 Jahre*, pp. 181–2 (quotation on p. 182).   **178.** Speech, 28.4.1939, Domarus, III, pp. 1,148–79 (rebuttal of Roosevelt, pp. 1,167–79).   **179.** See Günter Maschke in Carl Schmitt, *Staat, Grossraum, Nomos. Arbeiten aus den Jahren 1916–1969*, ed. Günter Maschke (Berlin, 1995), pp. 345–348. For a sceptical view of the impact of Schmitt on Nazi strategic thinking see Jürgen Elvert, 'Carl Schmitt. Ein Vordenker nationalsozialistischer Grossraumplanung?', *Historische Mitteilungen*, 19 (2006), pp. 260–76, especially pp. 272–4.   **180.** Quoted Domarus, III, p. 1,015.   **181.** Speech, 1.5.1939, Domarus, III, p. 1,185.   **182.** Speech 23.5.1939, Domarus, III, p. 1,197.   **183.** Speech,

28.4.1939, Domarus, III, p. 1,158.   **184.** 'Bericht über Besprechung am 23.5.1939 im Arbeitszimmer des Führers, neue Reichskanzlei', by Rudolf Schmundt, IMT 37, pp. 546–56.   **185.** Mario Toscano, *The Origins of the Pact of Steel* (Baltimore, 1967), especially pp. 307–95.   **186.** See Günther Pallaver and Leopold Steurer (eds.), *Deutsche! Hitler verkauft euch! Das Erbe von Option und Weltkrieg in Südtirol* (Bozen, 2011), p. 17.   **187.** Thus R. J. Overy, 'Hitler's war and the German economy: a reinterpretation', *Economic History Review*, 35 (1982), pp. 272–91, especially pp. 272 and 289.   **188.** 'Bericht über Besprechung am 23.5.1939 im Arbeitszimmer des Führers', p. 551.   **189.** See the exchange between Tim Mason and Richard Overy in 'Debate: Germany, "domestic crisis" and war in 1939', *Past & Present*, 122 (1989), pp. 200–240.   **190.** See 23.5.1939 remarks re blockade to army, Domarus, III, p. 1,197.   **191.** Speech, 28.4.1939, Domarus, III, p. 1,160.   **192.** Helmut Schaller, *Der Nationalsozialismus und die slawische Welt* (Regensburg, 2002), p. 231.   **193.** Speech, 6.6.1939, Domarus, III, pp. 1,209–10.   **194.** Müller, *Der Feind steht im Osten*, p. 146.   **195.** ET, 8.8.1939, p. 57. For Hitler's use of film to promote euthanasia see Karl Ludwig Rost, *Sterilisation und Euthanasie im Film des 'Dritten Reiches'. Nationalsozialistische Propaganda in ihrer Beziehung zu rassenhygenischen Massnahmen des NS-Staates* (Husum, 1987), pp. 60, 63, 66–7 *et passim*.   **196.** ET, 12.7.1939 and 13.7.1939, pp. 53–4 (with quotations).   **197.** ET, 13.7.1939 and 17.7.1939, p. 54 (with quotations).   **198.** ET, 15.8.1939, p. 57 (with quotation).   **199.** Speech, 16.7.1939, Domarus, III, p. 1218.   **200.** 'Hitlerbauten' in Linz. Wohnsiedlungen zwischen Alltag und Geschichte, Exhibition Catalogue of Nordico Stadtmuseum Linz (Salzburg, 2013), pp. 126–9 *et passim*.   **201.** Wilhelm Lenz and Lothar Kettenacker, Lord Kemsleys Gespräch mit Hitler Ende Juli 1939', *Vierteljahrshefte für Zeitgeschichte*, 19 (1971), pp. 305–21, especially pp. 309–10 and 318–20.   **202.** ET, 28.7.1939, p. 56.   **203.** See Ray Moseley, *Mussolini's Shadow: The Double Life of Count Galeazzo Ciano* (New Haven and London, 1999), p. 76.   **204.** As quoted in Rudolf Schmundt's notes of his speech on 22.8.1939, Domarus, III, p. 1,235.   **205.** See Jost Dülffer, 'Der Beginn des Krieges 1939. Hitler, die innere Krise und das Mächtesystem', *Geschichte und Gesellschaft*, 2 (1976), pp. 443–70.   **206.** Carl J. Burckhardt, *Meine Danziger Mission, 1937–1939* (Munich, 1960), p. 345.   **207.** Burckhardt, *Meine Danziger Mission*, pp. 339–50 (quotations on pp. 342 and 348). For the essential veracity of Burckhardt's account see the rehabilitation by Ulrich Schlie, 'Er verstand es, Hitler aus der Reserve zu locken', *Die Weltwoche*, 8 (29 February 1996), pp. 49–50.   **208.** Meeting, 25.8.1939, Domarus, III, p. 1,256.   **209.** Report, 27.8.1939, Domarus, III, p. 1,271.   **210.** Josef Henke, 'Hitler und England mitte August 1939. Ein Dokument zur Rolle Fritz Hesses in den deutsch-britischen Beziehungen am Vorabend des Zweiten Weltkrieges', *Vierteljahrshefte für Zeitgeschichte*, 21 (1973), pp. 231–42 (quotations on p. 241). For a sceptical view of Hesse see Helmut Krausnick, 'Legenden um Hitlers Aussenpolitik', *Vierteljahrshefte für Zeitgeschichte*, 2 (1954), pp. 217–39. Hermann Graml, 'Hitler und England im August 1939', in Peter Weilemann, Hanns Jürgen Küsters and Günter Buchstab (eds.), *Macht und Zeitkritik. Festschrift für Hans-Peter Schwarz zum 65. Geburtstag* (Paderborn, 1999), pp. 49–60, argues that Hitler had already completely given up on Britain.   **211.** Meeting, 23.8.1939, Domarus, III, p. 1,249.   **212.** For Hitler's central role in negotiating the pact see Ingeborg Fleischhauer, *Der Pakt. Hitler, Stalin und die Initiative der deutschen Diplomatie 1938–1939* (Berlin and Frankfurt, 1990), pp. 408–18 *et passim*.   **213.** See Tooze, *Wages of Destruction*, p. 321.   **214.** See Müller, *Der Feind steht im Osten*, pp. 149, 167 *et passim*.   **215.** Joachim von Ribbentrop, *Zwischen London und Moskau. Erinnerungen und letzte Aufzeichnungen. Aus dem Nachlass herausgegeben von Annelies von Ribbentrop* (Leoni am Starnberger See, 1953), pp. 178–85.   **216.** Quoted in Dietrich, *12 Jahre*, p. 79.   **217.** Roger Moorhouse, *The Devils' Alliance: Hitler's Pact with Stalin, 1939–1941* (New York, 2014).   **218.** There are several accounts of what was said. See Winfried Baumgart, 'Zur Ansprache Hitlers vor den Führern der Wehrmacht am 22. August 1939', *Vierteljahrshefte für Zeitgeschichte*, 16 (1968), pp. 120–49; Hermann Boehm and Winfried Baumgart, 'Zur Ansprache Hitlers vor den Führern der Wehrmacht am 22 August 1939', *Vierteljahrshefte für Zeitgeschichte*, 19 (1971), pp. 294–304. I have chosen quotations from the various descriptions of the meeting.   **219.**

Quoted in Boehm and Baumgart, 'Zur Ansprache Hitlers', p. 295. 220. Baumgart, 'Zur Ansprache Hitlers', p. 145. 221. Speech, 22.8.1939, Domarus, III, p. 1,237. 222. See the account in ET, 22.8.1939 and 24.8.1939, pp. 58–9 (quotations on p. 58). 223. Meissner, *Staatssekretär*, p. 504. 224. Mussolini to Hitler, 25.8.1939, Domarus, III, p. 1,260. See also Goeschel, *Mussolini and Hitler*, pp. 158–63. 225. ET, 25.8.1939, p. 59. See also Rainer A. Blasius, *Für Grossdeutschland – gegen den grossen Krieg. Staatssekretär Ernst Frhr. Von Weizäcker in den Krisen um die Tschechoslowakei und Polen, 1938/39* (Cologne and Vienna, 1981), p. 131. 226. See Graml, *Hitler und England*, pp. 119–21. 227. Quoted Domarus, III, p. 1,271. 228. Gerhard L. Weinberg, 'Hitlers Entschluss zum Krieg', in Klaus Hildebrand, Jürgen Schmädeke and Klaus Zernack (eds.), *1939. An der Schwelle zum Weltkrieg. Die Entfesselung des Zweiten Weltkrieges und das internationale System* (Berlin and New York, 1990), p. 32. 229. Quotations in HT, 28.8.1939, I, pp. 38–40. 230. See Peter Polak-Springer, ' "Jammin' " with Karlik": the German-Polish "radio war" and the Gleiwitz "provocation", 1925–1939', *European History Quarterly*, 43 (2013), pp. 279–300.

Chapter 15: The 'Haves' and the 'Have-Nots'

1. Speech, 1.9.1939, Domarus, III, p. 1,316. 2. Speech, 1.9.1939, Domarus, III, pp. 1,314, 1,316. 3. Quoted in Pyta, *Hitler*, pp. 196–7. 4. For the exceptionally brutal nature of the campaign from the start and Hitler's own role see Alexander B. Rossino, *Hitler Strikes Poland: Blitzkrieg, Ideology and Atrocity* (Lawrence, Kan., 2003), pp. 14, 77, 107 *et passim*; and Jochen Böhler, *Der Überfall. Deutschlands Krieg gegen Polen* (Frankfurt, 2009), especially pp. 94–101. 5. Halder plays down Hitler's role: Peter Bor, *Gespräche mit Halder* (Wiesbaden, 1950), pp. 136–7. 6. Thus, at any rate, the retrospective analysis of Major Deyhle, 18.10.1940, DVW, pp. 28–9 (quotation on p. 29). 7. See Raichle, *Symbolpolitiker*, p. 178; Nikolaus von Vormann, *So begann der Zweite Weltkrieg. Zeitzeuge der Entscheidungen – Als Offizier bei Hitler 22.8.1939–1.10.1939* (Leoni am Starnberger See, 1988), pp. 86–95, 120–23. 8. See Rolf Elble, *Die Schlacht an der Bzura im September 1939 aus deutscher und polnischer Sicht* (Freiburg, 1975), p. 36 *et passim*. 9. Karl, *Unity*, pp. 306–8. 10. See John Lamberton Harper, *American Visions of Europe: Franklin D. Roosevelt, George F. Kennan, and Dean G. Acheson* (Cambridge, 1994), p. 59. 11. Thus Max Paul Friedman, *Nazis and Good Neighbors: The United States Campaign against the Germans of Latin America in World War II* (Cambridge, 2003), p. 239 *et passim*. 12. Ian Kershaw, 'Überfall auf Polen und die öffentliche Meinung in Deutschland', in Ernst Willi Hansen, Gerhard Schreiber and Bernd Wegner (eds.), *Politischer Wandel, organisierte Gewalt und nationale Sicherheit* (Munich, 1995), pp. 237–50, especially pp. 243–4. 13. Groscurth, *Tagebücher eines Abwehroffiziers*, 7.9.1939, p. 200. 14. Thus Raichle, *Symbolpolitiker*, p. 209 with quotation. 15. Proclamation, 3.9.1939, Domarus, III, pp. 1, 339–42. 16. Proclamation, 3.9.1939, Domarus, III, p. 1,342. 17. Proclamation, 3.9.1939, Domarus, III, p. 1,340. 18. Hellmuth Auerbach, *Die angebliche Kriegserklärung der Juden an Deutschland im Jahre 1939* (Munich, 1986), pp. 1–4 (quotation on p. 1). 19. RT, 29.9.1939, p. 290. 20. See Longerich, *Unwritten Order*, p. 75. 21. KP, p. 31. See also Peter Longerich, *Propagandisten im Krieg. Die Presseabteilung des Auswärtigen Amtes unter Ribbentrop* (Munich, 1987), pp. 134–6. 22. FE, 8.9.1939, pp. 91–2 (quotations on p. 92). 23. Hanno Plass, 'Der *Welt-Dienst*. Internationale antisemitische Propaganda 1939 bis 1945', in Michael Nagel and Moshe Zimmermann (eds.), *Judenfeindschaft und Antisemitismus in der deutschen Presse über fünf Jahrhunderte. Erscheinungsformen, Rezeption, Debatte und Gegenwehr* (Bremen, 2013), pp. 821–40, especially p. 825. 24. Goldenbaum, 'Nationalsozialismus als Antikolonialismus', p. 467. 25. Patrick Salmon, 'British plans for economic warfare against Germany 1937–1939: the problem of Swedish iron ore', *Journal of Contemporary History*, 16 (1981), pp. 53–71. 26. See the table in Tooze, *Wages of Destruction*, p. 136. The huge military potential of the British Empire is described by David Edgerton, *Britain's War Machine: Weapons, Resources and Experts in the Second World War* (London, 2011), p. 7 *et passim*. 27. See J. Lee Ready, *Forgotten Allies: The Military Contribution of*

the Colonies, Exiled Governments, and Lesser Powers to the Allied Victory in World War II, vol. I: The European Theatre (Jefferson, NC, and London, 1985). **28.** 'Gedanken des Oberbefehlshabers der Kriegsmarine zum Kriegsausbruch', 3.9.1939, in LV, p. 19. **29.** See Karl-Heinz Völker, Dokumente und Dokumentarfotos zur Geschichte der deutschen Luftwaffe. Aus den Geheimakten des Reichswehrministeriums 1919–1933 und des Reichsluftfahrtministeriums 1933–1939 (Stuttgart, 1968), pp. 460–66. **30.** Tooze, Wages of Destruction, passim. **31.** Quoted in Tooze, Wages of Destruction, p. 337. **32.** Quoted in Tooze, Wages of Destruction, p. 335. **33.** Carl-Axel Gemzell, Raeder, Hitler und Skandinavien. Der Kampf für einen maritimen Operationsplan (Lund, 1965), p. 214. See also Ulrich H.-J. Israel, Graf Zeppelin. Einziger deutscher Flugzeugträger (Herford, 1994), p. 152. **34.** See Beck, Bötticher, p. 149. **35.** Roger Moorhouse, The Devils' Alliance: Hitler's Pact with Stalin, 1939–1941 (New York, 2014), pp. 161–91. **36.** Gemzell, Raeder, Hitler und Skandinavien, pp. 215–16. For Nazi-Soviet naval cooperation more generally see Jürgen Rohwer, 'Weltmacht als Ziel? Parallelen in Hitlers und Stalins Flottenbau-Programmen', in Hansen, Schreiber and Wegner (eds.), Politischer Wandel, pp. 176–7. **37.** Speech, 6.10.1939, Domarus, III, p. 1,382. **38.** Speech, 23.11.1939, Domarus, III, p. 1,423. **39.** Bianka Pietrow-Ennker, 'Das Feindbild im Wandel. Die Sowjetunion in den nationalsozialistischen Wochenschauen, 1935–1941', Geschichte in Wissenschaft und Unterricht, 41 (1990), pp. 337–51, especially pp. 341–4. **40.** Thus Werner Rahn, 'Hitler und die Marineführung im Zweiten Weltkrieg. Aufzeichnungen und Beobachtungen von Zeitzeugen', in Christian Th. Müller and Matthias Rogg (eds.), Das ist Militärgeschichte! Probleme – Projekte – Perspektiven (Paderborn, 2013), pp. 215–16 (quotation on p. 216); Gerhard Hümmelchen, Handelsstörer. Handelskrieg deutscher Überwasserstreitkräfte im Zweiten Weltkrieg (Munich, 1960), pp. 31–2, 38, 69. **41.** Vormann, So begann der Zweite Weltkrieg. **42.** David Mayers, 'Nazi Germany and the future of europe: George Kennan's views, 1939–1945', International History Review, 8, 4 (1986), pp. 550–72. **43.** Thus Beck, Boetticher, pp. 146–7. Hitler studied Bötticher's reports, or at least summaries of them, closely: Andreas Hillgruber, Hitlers Strategie. Politik und Kriegführung 1940–1941, 3rd edn (Bonn, 1994), pp. 195–6, 375. **44.** Ulrich Schlie, Kein Friede mit Deutschland. Die geheimen Gespräche im Zweiten Weltkrieg 1939–1941 (Munich, 1994), passim. **45.** HT, 7.9.1939, I, p. 65. **46.** Bernd Martin, Friedensinitiativen und Machtpolitik im Zweiten Weltkrieg 1939–1942 (Düsseldorf, 1974), pp. 57–60. **47.** RT, 29.9.1939, p. 290. **48.** Helmut Krausnick, 'Hitler und die Morde in Polen. Ein Beitrag zum Konflikt zwischen Heer und SS um die Verwaltung der besetzten Gebiete', Vierteljahrshefte für Zeitgeschichte, 11 (1963), pp. 196–209. **49.** I owe this thought, which the author says 'may be an exaggeration', to Martin Winstone, The Dark Heart of Hitler's Europe: Nazi Rule in Poland under the General Government (London and New York, 2015), pp. 24–5. **50.** HT, 7.9.1939, I, p. 65. **51.** Speech, 6.10.1939, Domarus, III, p. 1,383. Hitler's thinking about a Polish 'Reststaat' is discussed in Martin Broszat, Nationalsozialistische Polenpolitik, 1939–1945 (Stuttgart, 1961), pp. 13–18; and Christoph Klessmann, Die Selbstbehauptung einer Nation. Nationalsozialistische Kulturpolitik und polnische Widerstandsbewegung im Generalgouvernement, 1939–1945 (Düsseldorf, 1971), pp. 27–8. **52.** Speech, 19.9.1939, Domarus, III, p. 1,356. **53.** See Harry Kenneth Rosenthal, German and Pole: National Conflict and Modern Myth (Gainesville, 1976), pp. 103–4, 108. **54.** Speech, 6.10.1939, Domarus, III, p. 1,391. **55.** Thus Schlie, Kein Friede mit Deutschland, passim. **56.** Speech, 6.10.1939, Domarus, III, p. 1,393. **57.** Speech, 9.10.1939, Domarus, III, p. 1,395. **58.** Ministerial Conference, 30.10.1939, KP, p. 215. **59.** See Raichle, Symbolpolitiker, p. 201. **60.** Speech, 9.10.1939, Domarus, III, p. 1,395. **61.** Hanns Christian Löhr, Das braune Haus der Kunst. Kunstbeschaffung im Nationalsozialismus, 2nd edn (Berlin, 2016), p. 149. **62.** Quoted in Volker R. Berghahn, 'NSDAP und "geistige Führung" der Wehrmacht 1939–1943', in Vierteljahrshefte für Zeitgeschichte, 17 (1969), pp. 17–71 (quotation on p. 71). **63.** FE, 18.9.1939, p. 95. See also Bernd Wegner, Hitlers politische Soldaten. Die Waffen-SS 1933–1945 (Paderborn, 1982), p. 122; Jan Erik Schulte, Peter Lieb and Bernd Wegner (eds.), Die Waffen-SS. Neue Forschungen (Paderborn, 2014). **64.** Vandana Joshi, 'Maternalism, class and citizenship: aspects of illegitimate motherhood in Nazi Germany', Journal of Contemporary History, 46 (2011), pp. 832–53,

606   NOTES TO PP. 357–66

especially p. 883; Ute Frevert, 'Frauen an der "Heimatfront" ', in Christoph Klessmann (ed.), *Nicht nur Hitlers Krieg. Der Zweite Weltkrieg und die Deutschen* (Düsseldorf, 1989), p. 58; Elizabeth D. Heineman, *What Difference Does a Husband Make? Women and Marital Status in Nazi and Postwar Germany* (Berkeley, Calif., 1999), pp. 44–74. **65.** Winfried Süss, *Der 'Volkskörper' im Krieg. Gesundheitspolitik, Gesundheitsverhältnisse und Krankenmord im nationalsozialistischen Deutschland, 1939–1945* (Munich, 2003), p. 81. **66.** Hitler's authorization to Bouhler and Brandt, '1.9.1939', Berlin, in Ernst Klee (ed.), *Dokumente zur 'Euthanasie'* (Frankfurt, 1985), p. 39. **67.** Hans Mommsen, *Das NS-Regime und die Auslöschung des Judentums in Europa* (Göttingen, 2014), pp. 114–22 *et passim*. **68.** Rebentisch, *Führerstaat*, pp. 117, 123, 128, 131. **69.** E.g. Dietrich versus Goebbels: K P, p. 32. Ribbentrop versus Goebbels: Longerich, *Propagandisten im Krieg*, pp. 331–2. **70.** FE, 8.9.1939, p. 92. **71.** Franz W. Seidler and Dieter Zeigert, *Die Führerhauptquartiere. Anlagen und Planungen im Zweiten Weltkrieg* (Munich, 2000), p. 25. **72.** Moll, 'Steuerungsinstrument', p. 228. **73.** Thus Rebentisch, *Führerstaat*, pp. 397, 399, 401–4, 412, 416 *et passim*. For a warning against exaggerating Bormann's power see Peter Longerich, *Hitlers Stellvertreter. Führung der Partei und Kontrolle des Staatsapparates durch den Stab Hess und die Partei-Kanzlei Bormann* (Munich, London and New York, 1992). **74.** Martin, *Friedensinitiativen*, pp. 76–77. **75.** Thus Winstone, *Dark Heart*, p. 28. **76.** Broszat, *Polenpolitik*, p. 17. **77.** See Martyn Housden, 'Hans Frank – empire builder in the east, 1939–41', *European History Quarterly*, 24 (1994), pp. 367–93, especially pp. 371–2; Dieter Schenk, *Hans Frank. Hitlers Kronjurist und Generalgouverneur* (Frankfurt, 2006), pp. 146–9. **78.** HT, 18.10.1939, I, p. 107. **79.** Thus Gerhard Wolf, *Ideologie und Herrschaftsrationalität. Nationalsozialistische Germanisierungspolitik in Polen* (Hamburg, 2012), pp. 76–90. **80.** See his remarks to Keitel of 17.10.1939, quoted in Helmut Schaller, *Der Nationalsozialismus und die slawische Welt* (Regensburg, 2002), p. 182. **81.** Speech, 6.10.1939, Domarus, III, p. 1,383. See also Michael Wildt, ' "Eine neue Ordnung der ethnographischen Verhältnisse". Hitlers Reichstagrede vom 6. Oktober 1939', *Zeithistorische Forschungen*, 3 (2006), pp. 129–37. **82.** See Isabel Heinemann, *'Rasse, Siedlung, deutsches Blut'. Das Rasse- und Siedlungshauptamt der SS und die rassenpolitische Neuordnung Europas* (Göttingen, 2003), pp. 144–5. **83.** Wolf, *Ideologie und Herrschaftsrationalität*, pp. 88–9. **84.** FE, 7.10.1939, pp. 101–2 (quotations on p. 101). **85.** See Hellmuth Hecker, *Die Umsiedlungsverträge des Deutschen Reichs während des Zweiten Weltkrieges* (Hamburg, 1971), pp. 15–23, 61–77, 78–101, 102–83. **86.** Thus Broszat, *Polenpolitik*, p. 13. **87.** RT, 29.9.1939, p. 291. **88.** ET, 26.9.1939, pp. 62–3. **89.** Catherine Epstein, *Model Nazi: Arthur Greiser and the Occupation of Western Poland* (Oxford, 2010). **90.** On this more 'inclusive' side to the occupation policy see Maren Röger, 'Besatzungskinder in Polen, Nationalsozialistische Politik und Erfahrungen in der Volksrepublik', *Vierteljahrshefte für Zeitgeschichte*, 65 (2017), pp. 25–50, here p. 28. **91.** The irony is noted by Wolf, *Ideologie und Herrschaftsrationalität*, p. 467. **92.** See Uwe Mai, *'Rasse und Raum'. Agrarpolitik, Sozial- und Raumplanung im NS-Staat* (Paderborn, Munich, Vienna and Zurich, 2002), pp. 117, 142 (quotation). **93.** RT, 29.9.1939, p. 97. **94.** HT, 27.9.1939, I, pp. 86–9. **95.** Hitler memorandum, 9.10.1939, DVW, pp. 4–21. **96.** Speech, 23.11.1939, Domarus, III, p. 1,425. **97.** Speech, 8.11.1939, Domarus, III, p. 1,410. **98.** Speech, 23.11.1939, Domarus, III, pp. 1,422–3. See also Claire Gantet, 'Der Westfälische Frieden', in Etienne François and Hagen Schulze (eds.), *Deutsche Erinnerungsorte*, vol. 1 (Munich, 2001), pp. 86–104, especially pp. 101–2. **99.** Memorandum, 9.10.1938, Domarus, III, p. 1,394. **100.** HT, 27.9.1939, I, p. 89. **101.** Hitler memorandum, DVW, 9.10.1939, p. 19. **102.** As quoted by ET, 6.12.1939, p. 69. See also Deyhle, 'Notizen zum Kriegstagebuch', DVW, p. 29. **103.** Directive 8, 20.11.1939, HW, p. 38. **104.** OKH, 28.12.1939, DW, p. 25. **105.** Hitler memorandum, 9.10.1939, DW, pp. 16–19. **106.** Speech, 6.10.1939, Domarus, III, p. 1,390. **107.** Speech, 8.11.1939, Domarus, III, pp. 1,409–10. **108.** Speech, 8.11.1939, Domarus, III, p. 1,411. **109.** Thus Patel, 'Welfare in the warfare state', pp. 4–5. **110.** Speech, 6.10.1939, Domarus, III, p. 1,391. **111.** Speech, 6.10.1939, Domarus, III, p. 1,389. **112.** KP, p. 45. **113.** GT, 12.12.1939, I/7, p. 228. **114.** Thus Peter Steinbach and Johannes Tuchel, *Georg Elser. Der Hitler-Attentäter* (Berlin, 2010), pp. 95, 133–5. **115.**

For a detailed account of the meeting see Sarah K. Danielsson, *The Explorer's Roadmap to National-Socialism: Sven Hedin, Geography and the Path to Genocide* (Farnham, 2012), pp. 12–173. **116.** See Gerd R. Ueberschär, *Hitler und Finnland, 1939–1941. Die deutsch-finnischen Beziehungen während des Hitler-Stalin-Paktes* (Wiesbaden, 1978), pp. 33–6 *et passim*. **117.** For Hitler's intermittent usage see: Hans-Dietrich Loock, 'Zur "grossgermanischen Politik" des Dritten Reiches', *Vierteljahrshefte für Zeitgeschichte*, 8 (1960), pp. 37–63. **118.** ES, 29.4.1937, p. 124. **119.** See Deyhle, 'Notizen zum Kriegstagebuch', DVW, p. 30. **120.** 'Denkschrift der Seekriegsleitung über den verschärften Seekrieg gegen England', 15.10.1939, in Michael Salewski, *Die deutsche Seekriegsleitung 1935–1945*, vol. 3: *Denkschriften und Lagebetrachtungen* (Frankfurt, 1973), pp. 72–86. **121.** For example to Sven Hedin: Danielsson, *Explorer's Roadmap*, p. 173. **122.** Beck, *Bötticher*, pp. 149–50. **123.** Speech, 23.11.1939, Domarus, III, p. 1,424. **124.** As reconstructed by automated lip reading on *Hitler's Private World Revealed*, Channel 5, November 2006. **125.** See Ryback, *Hitlers Bücher*, pp. 146–8. Lothrop Stoddard, *Into the Darkness: Nazi Germany Today* (London, 1941), pp. 171–80. **126.** Speech, 19.9.1939, Domarus, III, p. 1,354. **127.** As related to Halder, HT, 29.11.1939, I, p. 106. **128.** Thus Harold C. Deutsch, *Verschwörung gegen den Krieg. Der Widerstand in den Jahren 1939–1940* (Munich, 1969). **129.** ET, 10.12.1939, p. 70. **130.** Thus Hans-Adolf Jacobsen, *Fall Gelb. Der Kampf um den deutschen Operationsplan zur Westoffensive 1940* (Wiesbaden, 1957), pp. 27, 37 *et passim*; and Christian Hartmann, *Halder. Generalstabschef Hitlers 1938–1942* (Paderborn, Munich, Vienna and Zurich, 1991), pp. 166–7. **131.** Speech, 23.11.1939, Domarus, III, p. 1,427. **132.** HW, 29.11.1939, p. 40. **133.** Speech, 24.2.1940, Domarus, III, pp. 1,455–6, 1,464–5; Speech, 30.1.1940, Domarus, III, p. 1,459. **134.** Speech, 30.1.1940, Domarus, III, p. 1,460. See also: Speech, 24.2.1940, Domarus, III, p. 1,466. **135.** See Rundstedt order, 12.1.1940, DVW, p. 137. **136.** Thus Bor, *Gespräche mit Halder*, p. 166. **137.** According to Giesler, *Ein anderer Hitler*, p. 387. He dates the conversation to the 'winter of 1939–1940'. **138.** Thus Karl-Heinz Frieser, *Blitzkrieg-Legende. Der Westfeldzug 1940*, 4th edn (Munich, 2012), p. 32. **139.** FE, 17.1.1940, pp. 109–10. **140.** Tooze, *Wages of Destruction*, p. 347. **141.** König, *Volkswagen, Volksempfänger, Volksgemeinschaft*, p. 172. **142.** Müller, *Der Feind steht im Osten*, p. 171. **143.** Thus Moorhouse, *Devils' Alliance*. **144.** For the extent of the cooperation see Heinrich Schwendemann, 'Stalins Fehlkalkül. Die wirtschaftliche Zusammenarbeit zwischen dem Deutschen Reich und der Sowjetunion 1939–1941', in Christoph Koch (ed.), *Gab es einen Stalin-Hitler-Pakt? Charakter, Bedeutung und Deutung des deutsch-sowjetischen Nichtangriffsvertrages vom 23. August 1939* (Frankfurt, 2015), pp. 293–312, especially pp. 294 and 307. **145.** Thus Gabriel Gorodetsky, *Grand Delusion: Stalin and the German Invasion of Russia* (New Haven, 1999); and Albert L. Weeks, *Stalin's Other War: Soviet Grand Strategy, 1939–1941* (Lanham, Boulder, New York and Oxford, 2002), p. vii *et passim*. **146.** See Adam Claasen, 'Blood and iron, and der Geist des Atlantiks: assessing Hitler's decision to invade Norway', *Journal of Strategic Studies*, 20 (1997), pp. 71–96. **147.** Quoted in Walther Hubatsch, '*Weserübung*'. *Die deutsche Besetzung von Dänemark und Norwegen 1940. Nach amtlichen Unterlagen dargestellt, mit einem Anhang. Dokumente zum Norwegenfeldzug 1940* (Göttingen, Berlin and Frankfurt, 1960), p. 396. **148.** Quoted in Hans-Martin Ottmer, '*Weserübung*'. *Der deutsche Angriff auf Dänemark und Norwegen im April 1940* (Munich, 1994), p. 59. **149.** Quoted in Hubatsch, '*Weserübung*', p. 366. **150.** KP, 4.1.1940, p. 257. **151.** Quoted in Tooze, *Wages of Destruction*, p. 337. **152.** KP, 1.4.1940, p. 307. **153.** Stanley E. Hilton, 'The Welles mission to Europe, February–March 1940: illusion or realism?', *Journal of American History*, 58 (1971), pp. 93–120, especially pp. 93, 95–6, 103, 110 *et passim*. **154.** 'Richtlinien des Fuehrers für die Unterhaltung mit Sumner Welles', 29.2.1940, ADAP, Series D, VIII, pp. 644–5. **155.** 'Unterredung zwischen dem Führer und Reichskanzler und dem amerikanischen Unterstaatssekretär Sumner Welles', 2.3.1940, DAP, Series D, VIII, pp. 660–65. **156.** As quoted in ET, 'February 1940', pp. 72–3. (The dating is awry.) **157.** Henrik O. Lunde, *Hitler's Pre-Emptive War: The Battle for Norway, 1940* (Philadelphia and Newbury, 2009). **158.** On the 'Führungskrise at Narvik', see Ottmer, '*Weserübung*', pp. 141–3 (quotation on p. 142). **159.** Quoted in Rainer Rutz, *Signal. Eine deutsche*

Auslandsillustrierte als Propagandainstrument im Zweiten Weltkrieg (Essen, 2007), p. 186. **160.** Adam A. R. Claasen, *Hitler's Northern War: The Luftwaffe's Ill-Fated Campaign, 1940–1945* (Lawrence, Kan., 2001), pp. 139–40. **161.** Proclamation, 9.5.1940, Domarus, III, p. 1,502. **162.** Brian Bond and Michael D. Taylor (eds.), *The Battle of France and Flanders 1940: Sixty Years On* (Barnsley, 2001). **163.** Thus Deyhle, 'Notizen zum Kriegstagebuch', DVW, p. 29. **164.** OKW diary (Jodl), 16.5.1940, DW, p. 35. **165.** Halder diary, 17.5.1940, DW, p. 40. **166.** War diary of Army Group A, 17.5.1940, DW, p. 42. **167.** Halder diary, 17.5.1940, DW, p. 41. **168.** See Gianluca Falanga, *Mussolinis Vorposten in Hitlers Reich. Italiens Politik in Berlin, 1933–1945* (Berlin, 2008), pp. 160–61. **169.** Enno von Rintelen, *Mussolini als Bundesgenosse. Erinnerungen des deutschen Militärattachés in Rom, 1936–1943* (Tübingen, 1951), p. 89. **170.** For a brief recent summary of the debate see Bruno Comer, 'Waarom Hitler treuzelde bij Duinkerke', *De Franse Nederlanden/Les Pays-Bas Français*, 39 (2013) (with a French abstract), pp. 178–87. **171.** Halder, KTB, 24.5.1940, quoted in DW, p. 74. **172.** 'Der "Halt-Befehl"', 24.5.1940, DW, p. 120. **173.** War diary, Army Group A, 24.5.1940, DW, p. 75; War diary, Army Group A, 29.5.1940, DW, p. 93; War diary, Army Group B (Bock), 30.5.1940, DW, p. 97; War diary, Army Group B, 2.6.1940, DW, p. 107. **174.** Halder diary, 25.5.1940, DW, p. 78. **175.** War diary, Army Group A, 24.5.1940, DW, p. 75. **176.** As described in ET, 23/25.5.1940, p. 80. **177.** HW, 24.5.1940, pp. 53–5. **178.** This myth was disproved long ago by Hans Meier-Welcker, 'Der Entschluss zum Anhalten der deutschen Panzertruppen in Flandern 1940', *Vierteljahrshefte für Zeitgeschichte*, 2 (1954), pp. 274–90, especially pp. 285–6. **179.** See the account of the debates in ET, 27.5.1940, p. 81. **180.** HT, 6.6.1940, I, p. 336. **181.** War diary, Army Group B (Bock), 2.6.1940, DW, p. 107. **182.** See Joe Maiolo, 'The Axis could have won the war [wrong]', in 'The great misconceptions of World War Two', *BBC History Magazine*, 14 (May 2013), p. 24. **183.** See Ernest R. May, *Strange Victory: Hitler's Conquest of France* (London, 2009). **184.** Peter Lieb, 'Erwin Rommel. Widerstandskämpfer oder Nationalsozialist?', *Vierteljahrshefte für Zeitgeschichte*, 61, 3 (2013), pp. 303–43. **185.** Hermann Böhme, *Entstehung und Grundlagen des Waffenstillstandes von 1940* (Stuttgart, 1966), especially pp. 48–68. **186.** Jodl diary, 20.5.1940, DW, p. 53. **187.** Quoted in Raichle, *Symbolpolitiker*, p. 299. On the performative dimensions here see also Pyta, *Hitler*, p. 303. **188.** Cédric Gruat, *Hitler in Paris. Juni 1940* (Berlin and Schmalkalden, 2011), especially pp. 36–55. **189.** Giesler, *Ein anderer Hitler*, pp. 386–96. **190.** They were repatriated amid great pomp in mid December 1940: Georges Poisson, *Hitler's Gift to France: The Return of the Ashes of Napoleon II: Crisis at Vichy – December 15, 1940* (New York, 2008). **191.** Raichle, *Symbolpolitiker*, p. 330. **192.** Thus Götz Aly, *Hitlers Volksstaat. Raub, Rassenkrieg und nationaler Sozialismus* (Frankfurt, 2005), p. 333 *et passim*. See also Thomas Kühne, *Belonging and Genocide: Hitler's Community, 1918–1945* (New Haven, 2010). **193.** See Klaus Urner, *'Die Schweiz muss noch geschluckt werden!' Hitlers Aktionspläne gegen die Schweiz* (Zurich and Munich, 1998), pp. 7, 20, 22, 29–30. (The title refers to words used by an SD report, not Hitler himself.) **194.** Tooze, *Wages of Destruction*, p. 383. **195.** See Thomas Sandkühler (ed.), *Europäische Integration. Deutsche Hegemonialpolitik gegenüber Westeuropa, 1920–1960*, Beiträge zur Geschichte des Nationalsozialismus 18 (Göttingen, 2002); Kiran Klaus Patel, 'Der Nationalsozialismus in transnationaler Perspektive', *Blätter für deutsche und internationale Politik*, 49 (2004), pp. 1,123–34; and Jonas Scherner, 'Europas Beitrag zu Hitlers Krieg. Die Verlagerung von Industrieaufträgen der Wehrmacht in die besetzten Gebiete und ihre Bedeutung für die deutsche Rüstung im Zweiten Weltkrieg', in Christoph Buchheim and Marcel Boldorf (eds.), *Europäische Volkswirtschaften unter deutscher Hegemonie, 1938–1945* (Munich, 2012), pp. 69–92; and Eberhard Jäckel, *Frankreich in Hitlers Europa. Die deutsche Frankreichpolitik im Zweiten Weltkrieg* (Stuttgart, 1966). **196.** FE, 16.6.1940, p. 126. See also John R. Gillingham, *Industry and Politics in the Third Reich* (London, 1985), pp. 139–62. **197.** FE, 9.5.1940, p. 118; FE, 7.7.1940, p. 130. **198.** Martin Schärer, *Deutsche Annexionspolitik im Westen. Die Wiedereingliederung Eupen-Malmedys im Zweiten Weltkrieg* (Berne, Frankfurt and Las Vegas, 1978), pp. 57, 276–7 (the decree is on p. 57). **199.** See Mark Mazower, 'Hitler's New Order, 1939–45', *Diplomacy & Statecraft*, 7, 1 (1996), pp. 29–53, especially pp. 29–30. **200.** FE, 25.6.1940,

p. 129.   201. Gerd R. Ueberschär and Winfried Vogel, *Dienen und Verdienen. Hitlers Geschenke an seine Eliten* (Frankfurt, 1999), p. 73 *et passim*.   202. Thus Norman J. W. Goda, 'Black marks: Hitler's bribery of his senior officers during World War II', *Journal of Modern History*, 72 (2000), pp. 413–52, especially p. 433.   203. As quoted in ET, 28.5.1940, p. 81.   204. Dino Alfieri, *Dictators Face to Face* (London and New York, 1954), p. 56.   205. FE, 5.6.1940, p. 123.   206. KP, 6.7.1940, p. 416.   207. Richard Toye, *The Roar of the Lion: The Untold Story of Churchill's World War II Speeches* (Oxford, 2013), especially pp. 12–72.   208. Dietrich, *12 Jahre*, p. 260.   209. Quoted in Giesler, *Ein anderer Hitler*, p. 395.   210. Alfieri, *Dictators Face to Face*, pp. 57–8 (quotation on p. 57).   211. See generally Richard Overy, *The Bombing War: Europe, 1939–1945* (London, 2013), p. 73.   212. FE, 21.6.1940, p. 128.   213. Dr Wilms, 'Einwirkung des Fliegeralarms und der Bombenangriffe auf die Bevölkerung des Luftschutzortes I. Ordnung Hamm (Westf.), 19. Juli 1940', in Ursula von Gersdorff (ed.), *Frauen im Kriegsdienst, 1914–1945* (Stuttgart, 1969), pp. 317–19.   214. Armin Nolzen, ' "Menschenführung" im Bombenkrieg. Die Tätigkeiten der NSDAP nach Luftangriffen', https://www.historicum.net/persistent/old-purl/1805, accessed 22 January 2019.   215. For the centrality of the United States in Hitler's thinking after the fall of France, see Hillgruber, *Hitlers Strategie*.   216. Meeting, 13.7.1940, Domarus, III, p. 1,538.   217. Speech, 19.7.1940, Domarus, III, pp. 1,557–8.   218. Peter Lieb, 'Hitler's Britain. Die Kanalinseln im Zweiten Weltkrieg', *Militärgeschichte* 3 (2016), pp. 4–9, especially p. 5.   219. Interview, 15.6.1940, Domarus, III, p. 1,524. (The correct date is 9 June 1940.) See also Lothar Gruchmann, *Nationalsozialistische Grossraumordnung. Die Konstruktion einer 'deutschen Monroe-Doktrin'* (Stuttgart, 1962), pp. 160–61.   220. Helmut Krausnick (ed.), 'Denkschrift Himmlers über die Behandlung der fremdvölkischen im Osten (Mai 1940)', 5 (1957), *Vierteljahrshefte für Zeitgeschichte*, 5 (1957), pp. 194–8, especially p. 197.   221. Thus Tobias Jersak, 'A matter of foreign policy. "final solution" and "final victory" in Nazi Germany', *German History*, 21 (2003), pp. 369–91, especially p. 377.   222. See Longerich, *Unwritten Order*, p. 96.   223. Magnus Brechtken, *'Madagaskar für die Juden'. Antisemitische Idee und politische Praxis, 1885–1945* (Munich, 1997), pp. 226–36 *et passim*.   224. Quoted in Longerich, *Unwritten Order*, p. 92.   225. Michael Mayer, 'Diplomaten im Krieg. Die Deutsche Botschaft Paris und die NS-Unrechtspolitik im besetzten Frankreich', in Johannes Hürter and Michael Mayer (eds.), *Das Auswärtige Amt in der NS Diktatur* (Munich, 2014), pp. 177–96 (here p. 178).   226. I could find no evidence of a direct order from Hitler to shoot African prisoners in: Peter Martin ' ". . . auf jeden Fall zu erschiessen". Schwarze Kriegsgefangene in den Lagern der Nazis', *Mittelweg*, 36 (1999), pp. 76–91; Raffael Scheck, *Hitler's African Victims: The German Army Massacres of Black French Soldiers in 1940* (New York, 2006).   227. Martin, ' ". . . auf jeden Fall zu erschiessen" ', p. 85.   228. See Raffael Scheck, 'French colonial soldiers in German prisoner-of-war camps (1940–1945)', *French History*, 24 (2010), pp. 420–46, especially pp. 423, 425 and 427–8.   229. Thus Müller, *Der Feind steht im Osten*, pp. 195–6, 202, 208.   230. HT, 22.7.1940, II, pp. 30–32.   231. Thus Müller, *Der Feind steht im Osten*, pp. 216–21. See also Hans-Günther Seraphim and Andreas Hillgruber, 'Hitlers Entschluss zum Angriff auf Russland (Eine Entgegnung)', *Vierteljahrshefte für Zeitgeschichte*, 2 (1954), pp. 240–54, especially pp. 246–51.   232. Walter Ansel, *Hitler Confronts England* (Durham, NC, 1960), pp. 121–89.   233. Adolf Hitler, 'Denkschrift zur Frage unserer Festungsanlagen', 1.7.1938, in Otto-Wilhelm Förster, *Das Befestigungswesen* (Neckargemünd, 1960), pp. 123–48.   234. Directive 16, 16.7.1940, HW, pp. 61–5. See also Karl Klee, *Das Unternehmen 'Seelöwe'. Die geplante deutsche Landung in England 1940* (Göttingen, Berlin and Frankfurt, 1958); and Monika Siedentopf, *Unternehmen Seelöwe* (Munich, 2014). For a strong case in favour of the idea that Hitler was not bluffing, see Robert Forczyk, *We March Against England: Operation Sea Lion, 1940–41* (Oxford, 2016), especially pp. 42–66.   235. Directive 17, 1.8.1940, HW, pp. 65–6.   236. Memorandum by Raeder on meeting with Hitler, 13.8.1940, in Karl Klee (ed.), *Dokumente zum Unternehmen 'Seelöwe'. Die geplante deutsche Landung in England 1940* (Göttingen, 1959), p. 258.   237. FE, 20.8.1940, pp. 135–6 (quotations on p. 135).   238. Egbert Kieser, *Hitler on the Doorstep: Operation 'Sea Lion': The German Plan to Invade Britain, 1940* (London, 1997), pp. 222–34.   239. See Anthony J. Cumming,

'The warship as the ultimate guarantor of Britain's freedom in 1940', *Historical Research*, 83 (2010), pp. 165–88, especially pp. 185–7.   **240.** ET, 17/19.8.1940, pp. 86–7.   **241.** Richard Cox, *Sealion* (London, 1977). See also Andrew Roberts, 'Hitler's England: what if Germany had invaded Britain in May 1940?', in Niall Ferguson (ed.), *Virtual History: Alternatives and Counterfactuals* (London, 1997), pp. 281–320.   **242.** Thus Kum'a N'dumbe III, *Was wollte Hitler in Afrika? NS-Planungen für eine faschistische Neugestaltung Afrikas* (Frankfurt, 1993), p. 9 *et passim*.   **243.** Klaus Schmider, 'The Mediterranean in 1940–1941: crossroads of lost opportunities?', *War & Society*, 15 (1997), pp. 19–41. See also Ian Kershaw, 'Did Hitler miss his chance in 1940?', in Gregor (ed.), *Nazism, War and Genocide*, pp. 110–30.   **244.** Quoted in Matthias Ruiz Holst, *Neutralität oder Kriegsbeteiligung? Die deutsch-spanischen Verhandlungen im Jahre 1940* (Pfaffenweiler, 1986), p. 116.   **245.** See HT, 29.10.1940, II, p. 154.   **246.** KP, 16.9.1940, p. 508.   **247.** FE, 30.10.1940, p. 150.   **248.** Theo Sommer, *Deutschland und Japan zwischen den Mächten 1935–1940. Vom Antikominternpakt zum Dreimächtepakt* (Tübingen, 1962), pp. 426–49.   **249.** Meeting, 13.11.1940, Domarus, III, p. 1,614.   **250.** Kimball, 'Dieckhoff and America', p. 225.   **251.** Meeting, 21.7.1940, Domarus, III, p. 1,562.   **252.** KP, 4.9.1940, p. 488.   **253.** Thus Dietrich, *12 Jahre*, p. 261.   **254.** Quoted in Holger H. Herwig, 'Prelude to *Weltblitzkrieg*: Germany's naval policy toward the United States of America, 1939–41', *Journal of Modern History*, 43 (1971), pp. 649–68, especially pp. 657–8.   **255.** Meetings, 12/13.11.1940, Domarus, III, pp. 1,612, 1,614. Here Hitler's vision matched that of Ribbentrop, see Wolfgang Michalka, *Ribbentrop und die deutsche Weltpolitik, 1933–1940. Aussenpolitische Konzeptionen und Entscheidungsprozesse im Dritten Reich* (Munich, 1980).   **256.** Speech, 8.11.1940, Domarus, III, p. 1,605; Meeting, 13.11.1940, Domarus, III, p. 1,614.   **257.** Speech, 10.12.1940, Domarus, III, p. 1,627.   **258.** Speech, 10.12.1940, Domarus, III, p. 1,627.   **259.** Speech, 4.9.1940, Domarus, III, p. 1,581; Speech, 14.11.1940, Domarus, III, p. 1,617.   **260.** Quoted in Strobl, *Germanic Isle*, p. 141.   **261.** FE, 15.2.1940, p. 111; FE, 15.9.1940, pp. 13–38. See also König, *Volkswagen, Volksempfänger, Volksgemeinschaft*, p. 126.   **262.** Speech, 4.9.1940, Domarus, III, pp. 1,577–81.   **263.** Quoted in Goldenbaum, 'Nationalsozialismus als Antikolonialismus', p. 465.   **264.** ET, 11.12.1940, pp. 91–2.   **265.** Thus Frank Bajohr, ' ". . . die hatten immer das meiste Geld". Funktion und Bedeutung eines antijüdischen Klischees im "Dritten Reich" ', in Fritz Backhaus (ed.), *Juden. Geld. Eine Vorstellung* (Frankfurt, 2013), pp. 343–52 (here p. 345). See also Stefan Mannes, *Antisemitismus im nationalsozialistischen Film. Jud Süss und Der ewig Jude* (Cologne, 1999), pp. 108–9.   **266.** KP, 23.8.1940, p. 475.   **267.** R. L. DiNardo and Daniel J. Hughes, 'Germany and coalition warfare in the world wars: a comparative study', *War in History*, 8 (2001), pp. 166–90; Malte König, *Kooperation als Machtkampf. Das faschistische Achsenbündnis Berlin-Rom im Krieg 1940/41* (Cologne, 2007), pp. 26–49 *et passim*.   **268.** Thus Lothar Gruchmann, 'Die "verpassten strategischen Chancen" der Achsenmächte im Mittelmeerraum 1940/41', *Vierteljahrshefte für Zeitgeschichte*, 18 (1970), pp. 456–75, especially p. 462 *et passim*.   **269.** ET, 28.10.1940, p. 88.   **270.** For Spain see Holst, *Neutralität oder Kriegsbeteiligung*, p. 130.   **271.** See ET, 24.10.1940, p. 88, and Gerhard L. Weinberg, 'Pearl Harbor: the German Perspective', in Weinberg, *Germany, Hitler, and World War II*, pp. 194–204, especially p. 199.   **272.** Paul Preston, 'Franco and Hitler: the myth of Hendaye 1940', *Contemporary European History*, 1 (1992), pp. 1–16 (especially pp. 5–7); Stanley G. Payne, *Franco and Hitler: Spain, Germany, and World War II* (New Haven, 2008).   **273.** Ribbentrop, *Zwischen London und Moskau*, pp. 231–5.   **274.** Thus the account of a Soviet eyewitness, Valentin Bereshkow, *In diplomatischer Mission bei Hitler in Berlin 1940–1941* (Frankfurt, 1967), pp. 26–9 (quotation on p. 25).   **275.** Laurenz Demps (ed.), *Luftangriffe auf Berlin. Die Berichte der Hauptluftschutzstelle 1940–1945* (Berlin, 2012), pp. 33–5.   **276.** KP, 30.9.1940, p. 531.   **277.** FE, 30.9.1940, p. 143; FE, 12.10.1940, p. 146.   **278.** Speech, 4.9.1940, Domarus, III, p. 1,580.   **279.** HT, 4.11.1940, II, p. 166; HT, 6.11.1940, II, pp. 168–9; HT, 8.11.1940, II, p. 172; HT, 11.11.1940, II, p. 175; HT, 5.12.1940, II, pp. 209–10.   **280.** Directive 18, 12.11.1940, HW, pp. 67–71.   **281.** Thus Norman J. W. Goda, 'The riddle of the Rock: a reassessment of German motives for the capture of Gibraltar in the Second World War', *Journal of Contemporary History*, 28 (1993), pp. 297–314.   **282.** See Halder, KTB, 4.11.1940, II, p. 166; KTB,

6.11.1940, II, p. 169; KTB, 8.11.1940, II, p. 172; KTB, 11.11.1940, II, p. 175; *et passim*. 283. Ian Kershaw, *Fateful Choices: Ten Decisions that Changed the World, 1940–1941* (London, 2008), pp. 54–91. 284. ET, 15.11.1940, p. 91. 285. As reported in BT, 3.12.1940, p. 170. 286. Directive 21, 18.12.1940, HW, pp. 84–8.

Chapter 16: Facing West, Striking East

1. See Gustav Hilger, *Wir und der Kreml. Deutsch-sowjetische Beziehungen 1918–1941. Erinnerungen eines deutschen Diplomaten* (Frankfurt, 1955), p. 303; and Heinrich Schwendemann, *Die wirtschaftliche Zusammenarbeit zwischen dem Deutschen Reich und der Sowjetunion von 1939 bis 1941. Alternative zu Hitlers Ostprogramm?* (Berlin, 1993), pp. 276–86. 2. See Evan Mawdsley, 'Crossing the Rubicon: Soviet plans for offensive war in 1940–1941', *International History Review*, 25 (December 2003), pp. 818–65, especially pp. 817–20. 3. Ingeborg Fleischhauer, *Die Chance des Sonderfriedens. Deutsch-sowjetische Geheimgespräche, 1941–1945* (Berlin, 1986), p. 15. 4. 'Meldungen aus dem Reich', VI, 3.2.1941, p. 1,964; 27.2.1941, p. 2,045. 5. Thus Ellen Gibbels, 'Hitlers Nervenkrankheit', *Vierteljahrshefte für Zeitgeschichte*, 42 (1994), pp. 155–220, especially pp. 165–6. 6. Ernst Guenther Schenck, *Patient Hitler. Eine medizinische Biographie* (Augsburg, 2000), *passim*. 7. BT, 1.2.1941, p. 173 (with quotation). 8. Jonathan Dimbleby, *The Battle of the Atlantic: How the Allies Won the War* (London, 2015), p. xix. 9. Proclamation, 1.1.1941, Domarus, IV, pp. 1,650–51 (quotation on p. 1,650). 10. FK, 28.2.1941, p. 629. 11. FE, 25.4.1941, pp. 169–70. 12. For Hitler's preoccupation with the Mediterranean at this time see Ralf Georg Reuth, *Entscheidung im Mittelmeer. Die südliche Peripherie Europas in der deutschen Strategie des Zweiten Weltkrieges, 1940–1942* (Koblenz, 1985), p. 41 (quotation), pp. 70–71 *et passim*. 13. BT, 1.2.1941, p. 173. 14. See Gerd R. Ueberschär, *Hitler und Finnland, 1939–1941. Die deutsch-finnischen Erziehungen während des Hitler-Stalin-Paktes* (Wiesbaden, 1978), p. 283. 15. Quoted in David Reynolds, *From World War to Cold War: Churchill, Roosevelt, and the International History of the 1940s* (Oxford, 2006), p. 19. 16. Henry R. Luce, 'The American Century', *Life*, 17.2.1941, p. 64. 17. Thus Stephen Alexander Wertheim, 'Tomorrow, the world: the birth of U.S. global supremacy in World War II' (PhD dissertation, Columbia University, 2015). 18. Thus Tooze, *Wages of Destruction*, pp. 440–43. 19. See Philips Payson O'Brien, *How the War Was Won: Air–Sea Power and Allied Victory in World War II* (Cambridge, 2015), pp. 67–94. 20. Speech, 4.5.1941, Domarus, IV, p. 1,708. 21. Thus Tooze, *Wages of Destruction*, p. 411. 22. ET, 7.4.1941, p. 400. 23. Order, 1.1.1941, Domarus, IV, p. 1,649. 24. Speech, 30.1.1941, Domarus, IV, p. 1,659. 25. Speech, 24.2.1941, Domarus, IV, p. 1,668. 26. Josef Burgstaller, *Erblehre, Rassenkunde und Bevölkerungspolitik. 400 Zeichenskizzen für den Schulgebrauch* (Vienna, 1941), p. 32. 27. Colin Ross, *Unser Amerika. Der deutsche Anteil an den Vereinigten Staaten* (Leipzig, 1941), especially pp. 14, 222, 262. 28. See Longerich, *Propagandisten im Krieg*, p. 142. 29. RT, 2.2.1941, p. 356. 30. Thus R. H. S. Stolfi, *Hitler's Panzers East: World War II Re-interpreted* (Stroud, 1992), pp. 219–22. 31. See Malte König, *Kooperation als Machtkampf. Das faschistische Achsenbündnis Berlin-Rom im Krieg 1940/41* (Cologne, 2007), pp. 54–5 (quotation on p. 55). 32. Directive 22e, February 1941, HW, p. 99. 33. See Göschel, *Mussolini and Hitler*, *passim*. 34. Directive 23, 11.1.1941, HW, pp. 93–5. 35. Directive 22, 6.2.1941, HW, pp. 100–103. 36. Speech, 24.2.1941, Domarus, IV, pp. 1,667–8. 37. Thus Alan Warren, *World War II: A Military History* (Stroud, 2008), p. 92. 38. Andreas Hillgruber, 'Japan und der Fall "Barbarossa". Japanische Dokumente zu den Gesprächen Hitlers und Ribbentrops mit Botschafter Oshima von Februar bis Juni 1941', in Andreas Hillgruber, *Deutsche Grossmacht- und Weltpolitik im 19. und 20. Jahrhundert* (Düsseldorf, 1977), pp. 223–52. 39. Directive 24, 5.3.1941, HW, pp. 103–5. 40. See Wolfram Pyta, 'Weltanschauliche und strategische Schicksalsgemeinschaft. Die Bedeutung Japans für das weltpolitische Kalkül Hitlers', in Martin Cüppers, Jürgen Matthäus and Andrej Angrick (eds.), *Naziverbrechen. Täter, Taten, Bewältigungsversuche* (Darmstadt, 2013), pp. 21–44, especially pp. 21–2, 31. 41. Longerich, *Unwritten Order*,

pp. 98–9. 42. Speech, 30.1.1941, Domarus, IV, p. 1,663. 43. Felix Moeller, *Der Filmminister*. *Goebbels und der Film im Dritten Reich* (Berlin, 1998), p. 73; Klaus-Jürgen Maiwald, *Filmzensur im NS-Staat* (Dortmund, 1983), p. 137. 44. Maiwald, *Filmzensur im NS-Staat*, p. 188. 45. Moeller, *Filmminister*, pp. 385–86. For Hitler's censorship of the *Wochenschau* see Ulrike Bartels, *Die Wochenschau im Dritten Reich*. *Entwicklung und Funktion eines Massenmediums unter besonderer Berücksichtigung völkisch-nationaler Inhalte* (Frankfurt, 2004), pp. 143–4. 46. See Plöckinger, *Geschichter eines Buches*, p. 185. 47. Thus RT, 2.2.1941, p. 363. 48. Quoted in Hanno Plass, 'Der Welt-Dienst. Internationale antisemitische Propaganda 1939 bis 1945', in Michael Nagel and Moshe Zimmermann (eds.), *Judenfeindschaft und Antisemitismus in der deutschen Presse über fünf Jahrhunderte. Erscheinungsformen, Rezeption, Debatte und Gegenwehr* (Bremen, 2013), p. 835. 49. Quoted in MacGregor Knox, '1 October 1942: Adolf Hitler, Wehrmacht officer policy, and social revolution', *Historical Journal*, 43 (2000), pp. 801–25, at p. 817. 50. Speech, 16.3.1941, Domarus, IV, p. 1,674; Speech, 4.5.1941, Domarus, IV, p. 1,708; Speech, 3.10.1941, Domarus, IV, p. 1,766. 51. Volker Koop, *'Dem Führer ein Kind schenken'. Die SS-Organisation Lebensborn e.V.* (Cologne, Weimar and Vienna 2007), pp. 197–8 *et passim.* 52. Hellmuth Hecker, *Die Umsiedlungsverträge des Deutschen Reichs während des Zweiten Weltkrieges* (Hamburg, 1971), pp. 138–71. 53. Arthur L. Smith, Jr, 'The Kameradschaft USA', *Journal of Modern History*, 34 (1962), pp. 398–408, especially pp. 405–6 (quotation on p. 405). 54. Minutes of meeting, 8.1.1941, in Kurt Assmann, 'Die Seekriegssleitung und die Vorgeschichte des Feldzuges gegen Russland', in *Der Prozess gegen die Hauptkriegsverbrecher vor dem internationalen Militärgerichtshof*, vol. 34 (Nuremberg, 1949), p. 696. In the same vein see BT, 1.2.1941, p. 173, and 30.3.1941, p. 181 55. Assmann, 'Die Seekriegsleitung', p. 696. 56. Thus Joel Hayward, 'Too little, too late: an analysis of Hitler's failure in August 1942 to damage Soviet oil production', *Journal of Military History*, 64, 3 (2000), pp. 769–94, here p. 773. 57. Tooze, *Wages of Destruction*, p. 458. 58. HT, 30.3.1941, II, p. 335. 59. BT, 30.3.1941, pp. 180–81. 60. BT, 1.2.1941, p. 174. 61. Quoted in Hayward, 'Too little, too late', p. 783. 62. See the separate accounts of Hitler's pronouncements to the Wehrmacht leadership on 30 March 1941, HT, 30.3.1941, II, pp. 335–8; and the record made by Hermann Hoth: Bert Hoppe and Hildrun Glass (eds.), *Die Verfolgung und Ermordung der europäischen Juden durch das nationalsozialistische Deutschland, 1933–1945*, vol. 7: *Sowjetunion mit annektierten Gebieten I. Besetzte sowjetische Gebiete unter deutscher Militärverwaltung, Baltikum und Transnistrien* (Munich, 2011), p. 119. 63. For example: Hitler meeting with Kvaternik, 21.7.1941, SD, II, p. 552. 64. Hillgruber, *Hitler, König Carol*, pp. 118–19. 65. Thus Richard L. DiNardo and Daniel J. Hughes, 'Germany and coalition warfare in the world wars: a comparative study', *War in History*, 8 (2001), pp.166–90, especially p. 173. See also István Deák, *Europe on Trial* (Boulder, 2015). 66. See Mario D. Fenyo, *Hitler, Horthy and Hungary: German-Hungarian Relations, 1941–1944* (New Haven and London, 1972), p. 14. 67. See Reiner Möckelmann, *Franz von Papen. Hitlers ewiger Vasall* (Darmstadt, 2016), pp. 94–9. 68. See Peter Gosztony, *Hitlers fremde Heere. Das Schicksal der nichtdeutschen Armeen im Ostfeldzug* (Düsseldorf and Vienna, 1976), pp. 76–8 *et passim.* 69. HT, 30.3.1941, II, p. 336. 70. KTB, 3.3.141, I, p. 340. 71. See Tooze, *Wages of Destruction*, pp. 459, 477. 72. See Christoph Dieckmann, 'Das Scheitern des Hungerplans und die Praxis der selektiven Hungerpolitik im deutschen Krieg gegen die Sowjetunion', in Christoph Dieckmann and Babette Quinkert (eds.), *Kriegführung und Hunger, 1939–1945. Zum Verhältnis von militärischen, wirtschaftlichen und politischen Interessen* (Göttingen, 2015), pp. 88–122, especially pp. 89–90, 94–5. 73. See Timothy Snyder, *Black Earth: The Holocaust as History and Warning* (London, 2016). 74. For the parallels see Edward B. Westermann, *Hitler's Ostkrieg and the Indian Wars: Comparing Genocide and Conquest* (Norman, Okla., 2016), pp. 3, 14, 36–7; and Carroll P. Kakel, III, *The American West and the Nazi East: A Comparative and Interpretive Perspective* (New York, 2011). 75. Thus Christian Streit, 'Ostkrieg, Antibolschewismus und "Endlösung"', *Geschichte und Gesellschaft*, 17 (1991), pp. 242–55, especially pp. 245–9 *et passim.* 76. See Andreas Hillgruber, 'Die "Endlösung" und das deutsche Ostimperium als Kernstück des Rassenideologischen Programms des

Nationalsozialismus', *Vierteljahrshefte für Zeitgeschichte*, 20 (1972), pp. 133–53, especially p. 144; and Helmut Krausnick and Hans-Heinrich Wilhelm, *Die Truppe des Weltanschauungskrieges. Die Einsatzgruppen der Sicherheitspolizei und des SD 1938–1942* (Stuttgart, 1981). **77.** See, for example, the record of a meeting between Göring and Heydrich, 26.3.1941, in Hoppe and Glass (eds.), *Die Verfolgung und Ermordung der europäischen Juden*, vol. 7, pp. 113–17, especially p. 116. **78.** HT, 30.3.1941, II, pp. 336–7. See also Johannes Hürter, *Hitlers Heerführer. Die deutschen Oberbefehlshaber im Krieg gegen die Sowjetunion 1941/42* (Munich, 2006), pp. 1–13. **79.** FE, 13.5.1941, pp. 172–3. **80.** Joachim von Ribbentrop, *Zwischen London und Moskau* (Leoni am Starnberger See, 1954), p. 224. **81.** See Ernst L. Presseisen, 'Prelude to "Barbarossa": Germany and the Balkans, 1940–41', *Journal of Modern History*, 32, 4 (December 1960), pp. 359–70, especially p. 369. **82.** Hilger, *Wir und der Kreml*, p. 304. **83.** Directive 25, 27.3.1941, HW, pp. 106–8. **84.** RT, 28.3.1941, p. 364. **85.** The low salience of the Balkans is stressed in Jörg K. Hoensch, 'Nationalsozialistische Europapläne im Zweiten Weltkrieg', in Richard G. Plaschka, Horst Haselsteiner, Arnold Suppan, Anna M. Drabek and Birgitta Zaar (eds.), *Mitteleuropa-Konzeptionen in der ersten Hälfte des 20. Jahrhunderts* (Vienna, 1995), p. 319; and Hans-Ulrich Wehler, ' "Reichsfestung Belgrad". Nationalsozialistische "Raumordnung" in Südosteuropa', in *Vierteljahrshefte für Zeitgeschichte*, 11 (1963), pp. 72–84, especially p. 80. **86.** 'Memorandum des Wehrmachtsführungsstabes im Oberkommando der Wehrmacht von Anfang April 1941 [6.4.1941]', in Wolfgang Schumann (ed.), *Griff nach Südosteuropa. Neue Dokumente über die Politik des deutschen Imperialismus und Militarismus gegenüber Südosteuropa im zweiten Weltkrieg* (East Berlin, 1973), p. 121. **87.** RT, 9.4.1941, p. 375. **88.** Proclamation, 6.4.1941, Domarus, IV, pp. 1,687–8. **89.** Directive 27, 13.4.1941, HW, pp. 112–15. **90.** RT, 9.4.1941, p. 375. **91.** See Ronald C. Newton, *The 'Nazi Menace' in Argentina, 1931–1947* (Stanford, Calif., 1992), pp. 230–32. **92.** ET, 9.5.1941, p. 102. **93.** Quoted in Volker Koop, *Hitlers Muslime. Die Geschichte einer unheiligen Allianz* (Berlin, 2012), p. 212. **94.** ET, 24.4.1941, p. 102. **95.** Johannes H. Voigt, 'Hitler und Indien', *Vierteljahrshefte für Zeitgeschichte*, 19, 1 (1971), pp. 33–63, especially p. 53. **96.** Hitler meeting with Matsuoka, 27.3.1941, SD, I, pp. 502–14; and Hitler meeting with Matsuoka, 4.4.1941, SD, I, pp. 518–24. **97.** Bernd Martin, *Friedensinitiativen und Machtpolitik im Zweiten Weltkrieg 1939–1942* (Düsseldorf, 1974); and Schlie, *Kein Friede mit Deutschland*. **98.** For this complex relationship see James Douglas Hamilton, *The Truth about Rudolf Hess* (Barnsley, 2016). **99.** Peter Padfield, *Hess: Flight from the Führer* (London, 2001); Rainer F. Schmidt, *Rudolf Hess. 'Botengang eines Toren'? Der Flug nach Grossbritannien vom 10. Mai 1941* (Düsseldorf, 1997). **100.** RT, 14.5.1941, p. 387. **101.** See Schmidt, '*Botengang*', p. 192. **102.** Hess to Hitler, 14.6.1941. An English translation can be found in Peter Padfield, *Hess, Hitler and Churchill: The Real Turning Point of the Second World War – A Secret History* (London, 2013), pp. 257–8. **103.** See Hitler's worries as recorded in RT, 14.5.1941, p. 387. **104.** Quoted in Schmidt, '*Botengang*', p. 185. **105.** Thus Moll, 'Steuerungsinstrument', pp. 234–6. **106.** This is based on the summary in Schmidt, '*Botengang*', pp. 190–91, from which the quotations are taken, and the record of the Gauamtsleiter Wilhelm Knoth of Kassel: Franz Graf-Stuhlhofer, 'Hitler zum Fall Hess vor den Reichs- und Gauleitern am 13. Mai 1941. Dokumentation der Knoth-Nachschrift', *Geschichte und Gegenwart*, 18 (1999), pp. 95–100, which has been paraphrased. For doubts about the authenticity of the Knoth document, which this author considers credible, see Moll, 'Steuerungsinstrument', p. 235, fn. 82. **107.** See Heydrich to Himmler, 15.5.1941, Bundesarchiv Berlin-Lichterfelde, NS 19 3872. **108.** Lammers, Betr. Stellvertretung und Nachfolge des Führers, 4.6.1941, BAK, N1128 Adolf Hitler Nr. 25. **109.** FE, 29.6.1941, p. 180. **110.** Directive 29, 17.5.1941, HW, pp. 117–19. **111.** See Reuth, *Entscheidung*, p. 77. **112.** ET, 24.4.1941, p. 102. **113.** Directive 30, 23.5.1941, HW, pp. 120–22. **114.** Quoted in Mallmann and Cüppers, *Halbmond und Hakenkreuz*, p. 82. **115.** Directive 30, 23.5.1941, HW, p. 121. **116.** See Karl Jesko von Puttkamer, *Die unheimliche See. Hitler und die Kriegsmarine* (Munich, 1952), pp. 47–8. **117.** Heinz A. Richter, *Operation Merkur. Die Eroberung der Insel Kreta im Mai 1941* (Mainz and Ruhpolding, 2011), pp. 201, 242, 277. **118.** KP, 26.5.1941, p. 751. **119.** Hitler meeting with Mussolini, 2.6.1941, SD, I, p. 561. **120.** See Jennifer Jenkins, 'Iran in the Nazi New Order, 1933–1941', *Iranian Studies*, 49 (2016), pp. 727–51, especially pp. 728, 741 and 745. **121.** Hitler meeting with Mussolini, 2.6.1941, SD, I, pp. 565–6. **122.** Rainer Rutz, *Signal. Eine deutsche Auslandsillustrierte als Propagandainstrument im Zweiten Weltkrieg* (Essen, 2007), pp. 197–8. **123.** Quoted in Günter Moltmann, 'Nationalklischees und Demagogie: Die deutsche Amerikapropaganda im Zweiten Weltkrieg', in Ursula Büttner et al. (eds.), *Das Unrechtsregime. Internationale Forschung über den Nationalsozialismus*, vol. 1: *Ideologie – Herrschaftssystem – Wirkung in Europa* (Hamburg, 1986). **124.** Quoted in Detlef Junker, 'Hitler's perception of Franklin D. Roosevelt and the United States of America', in C. A. van Minnen and J. F. Sears (eds.), *FDR and His Contemporaries: Foreign Perceptions of an American President* (London, 1992), p. 153. **125.** LV, 21.6.1941, p. 263. **126.** Directive 32, 11.6.1941, HW, pp. 129–34. See also Karl Klee, 'Der Entwurf zur Führer-Weisung Nr. 32 vom 11. Juni 1941. Eine quellenkritische Untersuchung', *Wehrwissenschaftliche Rundschau*, 6 (1956), pp. 127–41. **127.** O'Brien, *How the War Was Won.* **128.** FE, 20.4.1941, p. 168. **129.** RT, 2.4.1941, p. 372. **130.** See Hans Buchheim, 'Die höheren SS- und Polizeiführer', *Vierteljahrshefte für Zeitgeschichte*, 11 (1963), pp. 362–91, especially pp. 365, 372. **131.** Speech, 4.5.1941, Domarus, IV, p. 1,699. **132.** Thus Lammers to Bormann, 7.6.1941, in Andrea Löw (ed.), *Die Verfolgung und Ermordung der europäischen Juden durch das nationalsozialistische Deutschland 1933–1945*, vol. 3: *Deutsches Reich und Protektorat Böhmen und Mähren, September 1939–September 1941* (Munich, 2012). **133.** Hitler meeting with Mussolini, 12.6.1941, SD, I, p. 573. **134.** Helmut Krausnick, 'Hitler und die Befehle an die Einsatzgruppen im Sommer 1941', in Eberhard Jäckel and Jürgen Rohwer (eds.), *Der Mord an den Juden im Zweiten Weltkrieg. Entschlussbildung und Verwirklichung* (Stuttgart, 1985), pp. 88–106. **135.** Thus Shlomo Aronson, *Hitler, the Allies and the Jews* (Cambridge, 2004), p. 32. **136.** O'Brien, *How the War Was Won.* **137.** Thus Gromyko in Schwendemann, 'Stalins Fehlkalkül', p. 294. **138.** GT, 16.6.1941, I/9, p. 378, summarizing Hitler's instructions. **139.** GT, 16.6.1941, I/9, pp. 376–9. **140.** Dietrich, *12 Jahre*, p. 82. **141.** David Stahel, *Operation Barbarossa and Germany's Defeat in the East* (Cambridge, 2009). **142.** Quoted in Hilger, *Wir und der Kreml*, p. 313. **143.** Stahel, *Operation Barbarossa*, pp. 228–30, 400 *et passim.* **144.** See BT, 26.6.1941, pp. 198–9. **145.** BT, 2.7.1941, p. 207. **146.** Thus David Stahel, 'Rediscovering Operation Barbarossa – the importance of the military campaign', in Christoph Dieckmann and Babette Quinkert (eds.), *Kriegführung und Hunger, 1939–1945. Zum Verhältnis von militärischen, wirtschaftlichen und politischen Interessen* (Göttingen, 2015), p. 64. **147.** Alex J. Kay, Jeff Rutherford and David Stahel (eds.), *Nazi Policy on the Eastern Front, 1941: Total War, Genocide, and Radicalization* (Rochester, NY, 2012); Stephen G. Fritz, *Ostkrieg: Hitler's War of Extermination in the East* (Lexington, 2011); and Johannes Hürter (ed.), *Notizen aus dem Vernichtungskrieg. Die Ostfront 1941/42 in den Aufzeichnungen des Generals Heinrici* (Darmstadt, 2016). **148.** See Christian Streit, *Keine Kameraden. Die Wehrmacht und die sowjetischen Kriegsgefangenen, 1941–1945* (Stuttgart, 1978), pp. 88–9. **149.** Krausnick and Wilhelm, *Die Truppe des Weltanschauungskrieges*. **150.** See Longerich, *Unwritten Order*, p. 110. **151.** Norman J. W. Goda, 'Blackmarks: Hitler's bribery of his senior officers during World War II', *Journal of Modern History*, 72 (June 2000), p. 434. **152.** Thus Snyder, *Black Earth, passim.* **153.** Proclamation, 22.6.1941, Domarus, IV, p. 1,726. **154.** See Dieckmann, 'Das Scheitern des Hungerplans', pp. 99–101. **155.** 'Aufzeichnungen Martin Bormanns über die Besprechung Adolf Hitlers mit seinen Mitarbeitern über die Ziele des Krieges gegen die Sowjetunion', 16.7.1941, Führerhauptquartier (FHQ), in Czesław Madajczyk (ed.), *Vom Generalplan Ost zum Generalsiedlungsplan* (Munich, 1994), pp. 15–18. **156.** RT, 20.7.1941, p. 400. **157.** Sönke Neitzel, 'Hitlers Europaarmee und der "Kreuzzug" gegen die Sowjetunion', in Michael Salewski and Heiner Timmermann (eds.), *Armeen in Europa – Europäische Armeen* (Münster, 2004), pp. 137–50, and Jochen Böhler and Robert Gerwarth (eds.), *The Waffen-SS: A European History* (Oxford, 2017). **158.** See R. L. DiNardo, 'The dysfunctional coalition: the Axis powers and the eastern front in World War II', *Journal of Military History*, 60 (October 1996), pp. 711–30. **159.** See the account in KB, 2.10.1941, p. 46. **160.**

RT, 1.9.1941, p. 403. **161.** KB, 18.10.1941, p. 79. See also RT, 1.9.1941, p. 403. **162.** RT, 20.7.1941, p. 400. **163.** See the summary of his comments on 4/5.1.1942, in Werner Jochmann (ed.), *Adolf Hitler. Monologe im Führerhauptquartier, 1941–1944* (Munich, 2000), p. 178. **164.** See his remarks as summarized in KB, 23.10.1941, p. 97. **165.** 'Aufzeichnungen Martin Bormanns', p. 16. **166.** RT, 20.7.1941, p. 393. **167.** 'Aufzeichnungen Martin Bormanns', p. 17. **168.** 'Aufzeichnungen Martin Bormanns', pp. 16–17. **169.** Hitler meeting with Oshima, 14.7.1941, SD, II, p. 550. **170.** See the facing portrait of Ralph Colin Ross, *Von Chicago nach Chungking. Einem jungen Deutschen erschliesst sich die Welt* (Berlin, 1941). **171.** Hitler meeting with Oshima, 14.7.1941, SD, II, p. 543. **172.** RT, 20.7.1941, reporting a conversation on 16 July, p. 396. **173.** Hitler meeting with Oshima, 14.7.1941, SD, II, p. 543; Hitler meeting with Kvaternik, 21.7.1941, SD, II, p. 552. **174.** FE, 13.7.1941, p. 182. **175.** Directive 32b, 14.7.1941, HW, pp. 136–9. **176.** For German anxieties about Britain and the US at this time, see the memorandum by Raeder which was approved by Hitler: 'Denkschrift zum gegenwärtigen Stand der Seekriegführung gegen England Juli 1941', in Michael Salewski, *Die deutsche Seekriegsleitung 1935–1945*, vol. 3: *Denkschriften und Lagebetrachtungen* (Frankfurt, 1973), pp. 192–210. **177.** Directive 33, 19.7.1941, HW, pp. 140–42; Directive 34, 23.7.1941, HW, pp. 145–7. See also Stahel, 'Rediscovering Operation Barbarossa', p. 74. **178.** BT, 25.7.1941, p. 230. **179.** Halder, KTB, 26.7.1941, III, p. 123. **180.** ET, 28.7.1941, p. 107. **181.** As described in BT, 28.7.1941, p. 233. **182.** Thus Halder, KTB, 30.7.1941, III, p. 133. **183.** Directive 34a, 12.8.1941, HW, pp. 148–50. **184.** Hans Mommsen, *Das NS-Regime und die Auslöschung des Judentums in Europa* (Göttingen, 2014), pp. 131–48. **185.** Quoted in Hillgruber, 'Die "Endlösung"', p. 142. **186.** E.g. Waitman W. Beorn, 'A calculus of complicity: the *Wehrmacht*, the anti-partisan war, and the Final Solution in White Russia, 1941–42', *Central European History*, 44 (2011), pp. 308–37, especially pp. 311–12 re Hitler's instructions; and Omer Bartov, 'The barbarisation of warfare: German officers and men on the eastern front, 1941–1945', *Jahrbuch des Instituts für deutsche Geschichte*, 13 (1984), pp. 305–39. **187.** Hitler meeting with Kvaternik, 21.7.1941, SD, II, p. 557. **188.** Thus Klaus-Michael Mallmann, Andrej Angrick, Jürgen Matthäus and Martin Cüppers (eds.), *Die 'Ereignismeldungen UdSSR' 1941. Dokumente der Einsatzgruppen in der Sowjetunion* (Darmstadt, 2011), p. 17 (with quotations). **189.** Peter Longerich, *Holocaust: The Nazi Persecution and Murder of the Jews* (Oxford, 2010), p. 192. **190.** See Norman Ohler, *Blitzed: Drugs in Nazi Germany* (London, 2016), pp. 137–41 (quotation on p. 138). **191.** See the summary in Gibbels, 'Hitlers Nervenkrankheit', p. 167. **192.** Nicholas J. Cull, 'Selling peace: the origins, promotion and fate of the Anglo-American new order during the Second World War', *Diplomacy & Statecraft*, 7 (1996), pp. 1–28, especially pp. 14–16. **193.** David Reynolds, 'The Atlantic "Flop": British foreign policy and the Churchill–Roosevelt meeting of August 1941', in Douglas Brinkley and David R. Facey-Crowther (eds.), *The Atlantic Charter* (New York, 1994), pp. 129–50. **194.** Thus Below, *Als Hitlers Adjutant*, p. 287; these memoirs were originally written just a few years after the end of the war. See Tobias Jersak, 'Die Interaktion von Kriegsverlauf und Judenvernichtung. Ein Blick auf Hitlers Strategie im Spätsommer 1941', *Historische Zeitschrift*, 268 (1999), pp. 311–74. **195.** E.g. Speech, 30.9.1942, Domarus, IV, p. 1,913; Speech, 21.3.1943, Domarus, IV, p. 2,000. **196.** GT, 19.8.1941. II/1, p. 269. **197.** Communiqué, 29.8.1941, Domarus, IV, pp. 1,749–50. **198.** See Klaus Jochen Arnold, 'Hitlers Wandel im August 1941: ein Kommentar zu den Thesen Tobias Jersaks', *Zeitschrift für Geschichtswissenschaft*, 48 (2000), pp. 239–50. **199.** GT, 18.8.1941, II/1, p. 262. **200.** Historisch-Technisches Museum Peenemünde (ed.), *Wunder mit Kalkül. Die Peenemünder Fernwaffenprojekte als Teil des deutschen Rüstungssystems* (Berlin, 2016), p. 72. **201.** Jochmann (ed.), *Hitler. Monologe*, 19/20.8.1941, pp. 58–9. **202.** Hitler 'Studie', 22.8.1941, KTB, OKW, I/2, pp. 1,063–8 (quotation on p. 1,063). **203.** E.g., BT, 4.9.1941, p. 268. **204.** Thus BT, 15.9.1941, p. 277. **205.** David Stahel, *Kiev 1941: Hitler's Battle for Supremacy in the East* (Cambridge, 2013). **206.** KB, 22.9.1941. **207.** GT, 19.8.1941, II/1, p. 265. See also Tobias Jersak, 'A matter of foreign policy: "final solution" and "final victory" in Nazi Germany', *German History*, 21 (2003), pp. 369–91, especially pp. 378–9. **208.** Thus Ralf Ogorreck, *Die Einsatzgruppen und die*

'Genesis der Endlösung' (Berlin, 1996), p. 179, drawing on the testimony of Einsatzkommandoleiter Bradfisch. **209.** See Streit, 'Ostkrieg, Antibolschewismus und "Endlösung"', p. 248. **210.** Thus Longerich, *Unwritten Order*, pp. 120–21. **211.** Thus GT, 19.8.1941, II/1, p. 265. **212.** Gerhard Bidlingmaier, *Einsatz der schweren Kriegsmarineeinheiten im ozeanischen Zufuhrkrieg* (Neckargemünd, 1963), p. 231. **213.** LV, 27.10.1941, p. 302. **214.** In remarks recorded in K B, 19.10.1941, p. 84. **215.** RT, 1.10.1941, pp. 411–12 (quotation on p. 412). **216.** FE, 16.9.1941, pp. 198–9. See also FE, 7.12.1941, p. 213). **217.** See Thomas A. Bailey and Paul B. Ryan, *Hitler vs. Roosevelt: The Undeclared Naval War* (New York and London, 1979), pp. ix–x *et passim*. **218.** Franklin D. Roosevelt, 'Address for Navy and Total Defense Day', 27.10.1941; John F. Bratzel and Leslie B. Rout, Jr, 'FDR and the "Secret Map"', *Wilson Quarterly*, 9 (1985), pp. 167–73. See also Stanley E. Hilton, *Hitler's Secret War in South America 1939–1945: German Military Espionage and Allied Counterespionage in Brazil* (Baton Rouge and London, 1981). **219.** See Beck, *Bötticher*; and Pyta, 'Weltanschauliche und strategische Schicksalsgemeinschaft', p. 36. **220.** K B, 20.10.1941, p. 109; K B, 25.10.1941, p. 105; K B, 20.9.1941, p. 30; K B, 24.10.1941, p. 99. **221.** Speech, 8.11.1941, Domarus, IV, p. 1,777. **222.** Hitler meeting with Ciano, 25.10.1941, SD, I, pp. 633–4. **223.** FE, 11.9.1941, p. 197. **224.** K B, 6.9.1941, p. 4. **225.** See Ullrich, *Hitler. Die Jahre des Unterganges*, pp. 299–300. **226.** His remarks are reported in RT, 14.12.1941, p. 415. See also Schmuhl, *Rassenhygiene*, p. 352. **227.** K B, 22.10.1941, p. 92. **228.** K B, 25.10.1941, p. 107. **229.** Moll, 'Der Sturz alter Kämpfer', pp. 30–36. **230.** Katja Klee, *Im 'Luftschutzkeller des Reiches'. Evakuierte in Bayern, 1939–1953. Politik, soziale Lage, Erfahrungen* (Munich, 1999), p. 84. **231.** Nicholas Stargardt, *The German War: A Nation under Arms, 1939–1945: Citizens and Soldiers* (New York, 2015), pp. 345–81. **232.** Thus Nathan Stoltzfus, *Hitler's Compromises: Coercion and Consensus in Nazi Germany* (New Haven and London, 2016), pp. 201–3. **233.** As recorded in RT, 14.12.1941, p. 416. **234.** Quoted in Stoltzfus, *Hitler's Compromises*, pp. 202–3. **235.** See Moll, 'Steuerungsinstrument', p. 237. **236.** Speech, 8.11.1941, Domarus, IV, p. 1,772. **237.** As recounted in K B, 7.11.1941, p. 123. **238.** Peter Lieb, 'Hitler's Britain. Die Kanalinseln im Zweiten Weltkrieg', *Militärgeschichte. Zeitschrift für historische Bildung* (2016), pp. 4–9 (quotation on p. 4). **239.** Reuth, *Entscheidung*, p. 101. **240.** For the issues see König, *Kooperation als Machtkampf*, pp. 78–9. **241.** Quoted in Rahn, 'Hitler und die Marineführung', p. 221. **242.** Christopher Browning, *Die Entfesselung der 'Endlösung'. Nationalsozialistische Judenpolitik 1939–1942* (Munich, 2003), pp. 469–70. **243.** See Ben Shepherd, 'The clean Wehrmacht, the war of extermination, and beyond', *Historical Journal*, 52 (2009), pp. 455–73, especially p. 459. **244.** Himmler to Greiser, 18.9.1941, in Löw (ed.), *Die Verfolgung und Ermordung*, vol. 3, p. 542. **245.** K B, 7.10.1941, p. 64. **246.** Thus Longerich, *Unwritten Order*, pp. 130 and 148. **247.** RT, 12.9.1941, p. 408. **248.** Reported in K B, 21.9.1941, p. 35. **249.** Jochmann (ed.), *Hitler. Monologe*, 24.10.1941, p. 106. **250.** Quoted in Longerich, *Unwritten Order*, pp. 148–9. **251.** Rolf-Dieter Müller, *Hitlers Ostkrieg und die deutsche Siedlungspolitik* (Frankfurt, 1991), pp. 25–9 *et passim*. **252.** K B, 17.10.1941, p. 80. **253.** K B, 5.10.1941, p. 56; K B, 20.9.1941, p. 28; K B, 2.10.1941, p. 48. **254.** Jochmann (ed.), *Hitler. Monologe*, 17.10.1941, p. 91. **255.** K B, 18.10.1941, p. 81; K B, 5.10.1941, pp. 53–6; RT, 14.12.1941, p. 581; K B, 17.10.1941, pp. 71–6. **256.** Thus RT, 1.10.1941, pp. 411–12. **257.** 'Richtlinien für die der Ukraine gegenüber zu verfolgende Politik', in K B, 17.10.1941, pp. 75–6. **258.** Thus Patrick Bernhard, 'Hitler's Africa in the East: Italian colonialism as a model for German planning in eastern Europe', *Journal of Contemporary History*, 51 (2016), pp. 61–90. **259.** Proclamation, 1 and 2 October 1941, Domarus, IV, p. 1,756. The 'beasts' theme formed a standard part of his rhetoric: Proclamation, 12.9.1941, Domarus, IV, p. 1,752; Speech, 3.10.1941, Domarus, IV, p. 1,765; Speech, 8.11.1941, Domarus, IV, p. 1,775. **260.** Proclamation, 1 and 2 October 1941, Domarus, IV, p. 1,756. **261.** Proclamation, 1 and 2 October 1941, Domarus, IV, p. 1,758. **262.** David Stahel, *Operation Typhoon: Hitler's March on Moscow, October 1941* (Cambridge, 2013). **263.** K B, 8.10.1941, p. 69. **264.** Karl-Dietrich Abel, *Presselenkung im NS-Staat. Eine Studie zur Geschichte der Publizistik in der nationalsozialistischen Zeit* (Berlin, 1968), p. 19. **265.** Thus Bernd Martin, *Friedensinitiativen und Machtpolitik im Zweiten Weltkrieg*

1939–1942 (Düsseldorf, 1974), pp. 474–5. **266.** Thus Pyta, 'Weltanschauliche und strategische Schicksalsgemeinschaft', p. 39. **267.** KB, 17.10.1941, p. 73. **268.** Speech, 8.11.1941, Domarus, IV, p. 1,775. **269.** Franz W. Seidler, *Fritz Todt. Baumeister des Dritten Reiches* (Frankfurt and Berlin, 1988), p. 356. **270.** He hardly mentioned Army Group Centre in a lengthy 'Führerbesprechung' on 6 December 1941: see HT, 6.12.1941, III, pp. 339–42. **271.** Quoted in Pyta, *Hitler*, p. 361. **272.** Thus ET, 16.11.1941, p. 114 (with quotation). **273.** HT, 19.11.1941, III, p. 295. **274.** Scavenius meeting, 27.11.1941, SD, I, p. 657. **275.** Thus Christian Hartmann, *Halder. Generalstabschef Hitlers 1938–1942* (Paderborn, 1991), p. 297. **276.** 'Notizen aus der Führerbesprechung vom 6. Dezember 1941', HT, III, p. 330. **277.** Quoted in Enrico Syring, 'Hitlers Kriegserklärung an Amerika vom 11. Dezember 1941', in Wolfgang Michalka (ed.), *Der Zweite Weltkrieg. Analysen, Grundzüge, Forschungsbilanz* (Munich and Zurich, 1989), pp. 683–96, here p. 688. **278.** FE, 3.12.1941, pp. 210–12. **279.** See David Motadel, *Islam and Nazi Germany's War* (Cambridge, Mass., and London, 2014), pp. 42–3. **280.** Richard J. Evans, 'The German Foreign Office and the Nazi past', *Neue Politische Literatur*, 56 (2011), pp. 165–83. **281.** Pyta, 'Weltanschauliche und strategische Schicksalsgemeinschaft', p. 42. **282.** Thus Eberhard Jäckel, 'Die deutsche Kriegserklärung an die Vereinigten Staaten von 1941', in Friedrich J. Kroneck and Wilhelm G. Grewe (eds.), *Im Dienste Deutschlands und des Rechtes* (Baden-Baden, 1981), pp. 117–37 (quotations pp. 131–2). **283.** Evan Mawdsley, *December 1941: Twelve Days that Began a World War* (New Haven and London, 2011). **284.** See Gerhard Krebs, 'Deutschland und Pearl Harbor', *Historische Zeitschrift*, 253, 1 (1991), pp. 313–69. See also Puttkamer, *Die unheimliche See*, p. 5 **285.** Meissner, *Staatssekretär*, p. 576. **286.** Directive 39, 8.12.1941, HW, pp. 171–4. **287.** 'Notizen aus der Führerbesprechung vom 6. Dezember 1941', HT, III, p. 330. **288.** Speech, 11.12.1941, Domarus, IV, pp. 1,794–811. See also Syring, 'Hitlers Kriegserklärung'. **289.** Gerhard L. Weinberg, 'Pearl Harbor: the German perspective', in Weinberg, *Germany, Hitler, and World War II*, pp. 194–204, especially p. 195. **290.** Moll, 'Steuerungsinstrument', pp. 238–43. **291.** GT, 13.12.1941, II/2, p. 498. **292.** Alfred Rosenberg, 'Vermerk über Unterredung beim Führer am 14.12.1941', in RT, p. 579. **293.** By contrast, Jews fighting in the Allied armies – including those from Palestine – were treated more or less as normal combatants, whether at Hitler's request or by default is not clear. Thus Yoav Gelber, 'Palestinian POWs in German captivity', *Yad Vashem Studies*, 14 (1981), pp. 89–137. **294.** See the contrasting views of Christian Gerlach, 'The Wannsee Conference, the fate of German Jews, and Hitler's decision in principle to exterminate all European Jews', *Journal of Modern History*, 70 (1998), pp. 759–812; and Hermann Graml, 'Ist Hitlers "Anweisung" zur Ausrottung der europäischen Judenheit endlich gefunden?', *Jahrbuch für Antisemitismusforschung*, 7 (1998), pp. 352–62. **295.** See RT, 14.12.1941, p. 416. **296.** Hitler meeting with Oshima, 13.12.1941, SD, I, pp. 682–8. **297.** Thus Klaus Schmider, 'Hitler, Roosevelt and the Road to Pearl Harbor' (unpublished MS). I thank Dr Schmider for letting me have sight of this extremely important draft. **298.** BT, 16.12.1941, pp. 351–4 (quotations on p. 353). **299.** BT, 17.12 and 18.12.1941, pp. 354–5. **300.** Thus GT, 13.12.1941, II/2, p. 494. **301.** Thus the eyewitness Below, *Als Hitlers Adjutant*, p. 297. **302.** Quoted in Werner Rahn, 'Seestrategisches Denken in der deutschen Marine 1914–1945', in Hansen, Schreiber and Wegner (eds.), *Politischer Wandel*, p. 157. **303.** 'Notizen aus der Führerbesprechung vom 6. Dezember 1941', HT, III, p. 330. **304.** FE, 24.12.1941, pp. 214–15.

Chapter 17: The Struggle against the 'Anglo-Saxons' and 'Plutocracy'

1. Quoted in Nicholas Stargardt, *The German War: A Nation under Arms, 1939–1945: Citizens and Soldiers* (London, 2015), p. 227. **2.** Directive 44, 21.7.1942, HW, p. 195. **3.** Proclamation, 30.1.1943, Domarus, IV, p. 1,977. **4.** Decree, 1.1.1944, Domarus, IV, p. 2,075. For further examples see Directive 45, 23.7.1942, HW, p. 199; Directive 47, 28.12.1942, HW, p. 210; Directive 51, 3.11.1943, HW, p. 233; and FE, 29.3.1943, p. 330. **5.** Quoted in

Albert Kesselring, *Soldat bis zum letzten Tag* (Bonn, 1953), p. 81. **6.** Speech, 15.2.1942, Domarus, IV, p. 1,842. **7.** E.g. Jochmann (ed.), *Hitler. Monologe*, 28.9.1941, p. 73; Picker, *Hitlers Tischgespräche*, 29.5.1942, p. 479. **8.** See Moltmann, 'Nationalklischees und Demagogie', p. 223. **9.** ES, 15.2.1942, pp. 313–15. See also Picker, *Hitlers Tischgespräche*, 7.2.1942, p. 142; and Rüdiger Hachtmann, ' "Die Begründer der amerikanischen Technik sind fast lauter schwäbisch-allemannische Menschen". Nazi-Deutschland, der Blick auf die USA und die "Amerikanisierung" der industriellen Produktionsstrukturen im "Dritten Reich" ', in Alf Lüdtke, Inge Marssolek and Adelheid von Saldern (eds.) *Amerikanisierung. Traum und Alptraum im Deutschland des 20. Jahrhunderts* (Stuttgart, 1996), pp. 37–66. **10.** See Norman Domeier, 'Geheime Fotos. Die Kooperation von Associated Press und NS-Regime (1942–1945)', *Zeithistorische Forschungen/Studies in Contemporary History*, 14 (2017), pp. 199–230. **11.** See Harriet Scharnberg, 'Das A und P der Propaganda. Associated Press und die nationalsozialistische Bildpublizistik', *Zeithistorische Forschungen/Studies in Contemporary History*, 13 (2016), pp. 11–37. **12.** Dan Plesch, *America, Hitler and the UN: How the Allies Won World War II and Forged a Peace* (London and New York, 2011), pp. 33–7 (quotations on p. 34). **13.** See Steven T. Ross, *American War Plans, 1941–1945* (London and Portland, 1997), pp. 9, 17, 21, 47 *et passim.* **14.** Quoted in Alan Warren, *World War II: A Military History* (Stroud, 2009), p. 231. **15.** See Richard Overy, ' "The weak link"? The perception of the German working class by RAF Bomber Command, 1940–1945', *Labour History Review*, 77, 1 (2012), pp. 11–33 (especially p. 24). **16.** Martin Rüther (ed.), *Köln, 31. Mai 1942. Der 1000-Bomber-Angriff* (Cologne, 1992), pp. 46–52. **17.** Jörg Friedrich, *Der Brand. Deutschland im Bombenkrieg, 1940–1945* (Munich, 2002). **18.** Thus Roger Beaumont, 'The bomber offensive as a second front', *Journal of Contemporary History*, 22 (1987), pp. 3–19 (figures pp. 12–13). **19.** Hans-Günter Richardi, *Bomber über München. Der Luftkrieg von 1939 bis 1945 dargestellt am Beispiel der 'Hauptstadt der Bewegung'* (Munich, 1992), pp. 97–102 *et passim*; Irmtraud Permooser, *Der Luftkrieg über München 1942–1945. Bomben auf die Hauptstadt der Bewegung* (Oberhaching, 1996), especially pp. 65–7, 377–87. **20.** See Karl von Eberstein, 'Women around Hitler', in 'Adolf Hitler: a composite picture', IFZ, F135/4 Dokumentation Adolf Hitler. **21.** For Hitler's reaction to the bombing of Cologne see below, *Als Hitlers Adjutant*, p. 311. **22.** See Felix Moeller, *Der Filmminister. Goebbels und der Film im Dritten Reich* (Berlin, 1998), p. 399. **23.** Speech, 30 January 1942, Domarus, IV, p. 1,830. **24.** O'Brien, *How the War Was Won*. **25.** Matthias Rawert, 'Die deutsche Kriegserklärung an die USA 1941', *Militärgeschichte. Zeitschrift für historische Bildung* (2011), p. 19. **26.** Thus Voigt, 'Hitler und Indien', pp. 55–7. **27.** Hitler meeting with Mussolini, 29.4.1942, SD, II, p. 75. **28.** Hitler meeting with Oshima, 3.1.1942, SD, II, p. 41. **29.** Bernd Martin, 'Die "Militärische Vereinbarung zwischen Deutschland, Italien und Japan" vom 18. Januar 1942', in Andreas Hillgruber (ed.), *Probleme des Zweiten Weltkrieges* (Cologne and Berlin, 1967), pp. 134–44; Gerhard L. Weinberg, 'Global conflict: the interaction between the European and Pacific theaters of war in World War II', in Weinberg, *Germany, Hitler, and World War II*, pp. 205–16. **30.** Norman Rich, *Hitler's War Aims*, vol. 1: *Ideology, the Nazi State, and the Course of Expansion* (New York, 1992), p. 235. **31.** See Alan Donohue, 'Hitler as military commander: from Blau to Edelweiss, January–November 1942' (PhD dissertation, Trinity College Dublin, 2015), p. 251. **32.** Thus Milan Hauner, *India in Axis Strategy: Germany, Japan, and Indian Nationalists in the Second World War* (Stuttgart, 1981), pp. 280–84, 404–6. **33.** Thus Puttkamer, *Die unheimliche See*, p. 51. **34.** E.g. 'Führerentscheidungen vom 3.1.1942', KTB, III, p. 373. **35.** 'Führerbefehl vom 8. Januar 1942', FHQ, in KTB, OKW, II/2, p. 1,264. **36.** FE, 30.12.1941, p. 216. **37.** BT, 23.3.1942, p. 406. **38.** For the 1812 theme: Speech, 26.4.1942, Domarus, IV, p. 1,872. **39.** 'Führerbefehl an die Heeresgruppe Mitte vom 15. Januar 1942 zum Rückzug auf die "Winterstellung" ', FHQ, 15.1.1942, p. 1,269. **40.** BT, 18.1.1942, p. 360. **41.** See the graphic description in Speech, 26.4.1942, Domarus, IV, p. 1,872. **42.** FE, 7.12.1941, p. 213. **43.** FE, 22.1.1942, p. 229. **44.** Thus Florian Schmaltz, *Kampfstoff-Forschung im Nationalsozialismus. Zur Kooperation von Kaiser-Wilhelm-Instituten, Militär und Industrie* (Göttingen, 2005), p. 26. **45.** Derek Watson, 'Molotov, the making of the Grand Alliance and the Second Front 1939–1942', *Europe-Asia Studies*, 54

(2002), pp. 51–85.   **46.** Michael Salewski, *Die deutsche Seekriegsleitung 1935–1945*, vol. 2: *1942–1945* (Munich, 1975), pp. 9–10.   **47.** Thus Puttkamer, *Die unheimliche See*, pp. 49–50.   **48.** Hitler to Speer, 13.5.1942, in FE, p. 249. See also Robert Bohn, *Reichskommissariat Norwegen. 'Nationalsozialistische Neuordnung' und Kriegswirtschaft* (Munich, 2000).   **49.** 'Lammers (Reichsminister und Chef der Reichskanzlei) an die obersten Reichsbehörden Betr. Ständige Diesntbereitschaft in den Obersten Reichsbehörden', 31.3.1942, Berlin, in IfZ, ED 9.   **50.** GT, 30.3.1942, II/3, p. 583.   **51.** For the growth of his role see Dietmar Süss, *Tod aus der Luft. Kriegsgesellschaft und Luftkrieg in Deutschland und England* (Munich, 2011), pp. 132–3.   **52.** Heinz Dieter Hölsken, *Die V-Waffen: Entstehung, Propaganda, Kriegseinsatz* (Stuttgart, 1984), p. 83.   **53.** GT, 27.4.1942, II/4, pp. 183–4.   **54.** Rainer Karlsch, *Hitlers Bombe. Die geheime Geschichte der deutschen Kernwaffenversuche* (Munich, 2005), pp. 84–93 (quotation on p. 92).   **55.** Schmaltz, *Kampfstoff-Forschung*, p. 26.   **56.** Gerhard Sandner, 'U-Boot-Krieg in der Karibik. Anmerkungen und Ergänzungen zum gleichnamigen Buch von G. T. M. Kelshall', in Beate M. W. Ratter and Gerhard Sandner (eds.), *Territorialkonflikte im Karibischen Meeresraum. Interessenhintergründe, Stilformen und Lösungsansätze* (Hamburg, 1993), pp. 117–31.   **57.** Reuth, *Entscheidung*, pp. 133 and 148.   **58.** Reuth, *Entscheidung*, pp. 159–62; Junge to Wangenheim, 1.5.1942, in Reuth, *Entscheidung*, p. 236; Keitel, 'Beabsichtigte Operationen im Mittelmeerraum', FHQ, 4.5.1942, summarizing the results of talks between the Führer and Duce, in Reuth, *Entscheidung*, p. 237.   **59.** Speech, 30.1.1942, Domarus, IV, 1,829; GT, 27.3.1942, II/3, p. 561; Speech, 24.2.1942, Domarus, IV, p. 1,844; Speech, 30.9.1942, Domarus, IV, p. 1,920; Speech, 8.11.1942, Domarus, IV, p. 1,937. See also Hitler's private remarks reported in GT, 15.2.19, II/3, p. 320.   **60.** See Steiner and Cornberg, 'Willkür in der Willkür', p. 172.   **61.** Christian Gerlach, *The Extermination of the European Jews* (Cambridge, 2016), pp. 99–100.   **62.** GT, 27.3.1942, II/3, p. 561. See also Czesław Madajczyk, 'Hitler's direct influence on decisions affecting Jews during World War II', *Yad Vashem Studies*, 20 (1990), pp. 53–68; and Martin Broszat, 'Hitler und die Genesis der "Endlösung"', *Vierteljahrshefte für Zeitgeschichte*, 25, 4 (1977), pp. 739–75.   **63.** Jeffrey Herf, 'Hitlers Dschihad. Nationalsozialistische Rundfunkpropaganda für Nordafrika und den Nahen Osten', *Vierteljahrshefte für Zeitgeschichte*, 58 (2010), pp. 259–86, especially pp. 266–74.   **64.** Thus Motadel, *Islam and Nazi Germany's War*, pp. 38–70, 88–90, 104 *et passim*. See also Francis R. Nicosia, *Nazi Germany and the Arab World* (Cambridge, 2014).   **65.** See Motadel, *Islam and Nazi Germany's War*, pp. 63–6; and Volker Koop, *Hitlers Muslime. Die Geschichte einer unheiligen Allianz* (Berlin, 2012), pp. 53–5, 65–8, 72–3, 214.   **66.** Thus Motadel, *Islam and Nazi Germany's War*, p. 109.   **67.** Thus Goldenbaum, 'Nationalsozialismus als Antikolonialismus', p. 460.   **68.** Quoted in Goldenbaum, 'Nationalsozialismus als Antikolonialismus', pp. 466 and 472.   **69.** FE, 10.1.1942, p. 219.   **70.** Guntram Schulze-Wegener, *Die deutsche Kriegsmarine-Rüstung, 1942–1945* (Hamburg, Berlin and Bonn, 1997), p. 19.   **71.** Thus Tooze, *Wages of Destruction*, pp. 568–9.   **72.** FE, 10.1.1942, pp. 219–21.   **73.** Quotes in Tooze, *Wages of Destruction*, p. 568.   **74.** FE, 14.4.1942, p. 245. See also FE, 17.4.1942, p. 246; FE, 30.5.1942, pp. 253–4; FE, 23.6.1942, p. 258.   **75.** Picker, *Hitlers Tischgespräche*, 9.4.1942, p. 292.   **76.** FE, 29.6.1942, p. 260.   **77.** Rolf-Dieter Müller, 'Speers Rüstungspolitik im Totalen Krieg. Zum Beitrag der modernen Militärgeschichte im Diskurs mit der Sozial- und Wirtschaftsgeschichte', *Militärgeschichtliche Zeitschrift*, 59 (2000), pp. 343–85, especially pp. 348, 356. See also Martin Kitchen, *Speer: Hitler's Architect* (New Haven, 2015).   **78.** Thus Tooze, *Wages of Destruction*, *passim*.   **79.** See Hubert P. van Tuyll, *Feeding the Bear: American Aid to the Soviet Union, 1941–1945* (Westport, 1989).   **80.** Mark Harrison (ed.), *The Economics of World War II: Six Great Powers in International Comparison* (Cambridge, 1998), pp. 1–42.   **81.** GT, 24.5.1942, II/4, p. 355.   **82.** Speech, 26.4.1942, Domarus, IV, p. 1,868.   **83.** See the description in Moltmann, 'Nationalklischees und Demagogie', pp. 226–7 (with quotations).   **84.** GT, 15.2.1942, II/3, p. 318.   **85.** Christa Schroeder, *Er war mein Chef* (Munich and Vienna, 1985), p. 67.   **86.** Thus Raichle, *Hitler als Symbolpolitiker*, p. 217.   **87.** See the analysis by Gibbels, 'Hitlers Nervenkrankheit', pp. 167–9.   **88.** *Diary 1937–1943: The Complete Unabridged Diaries of Count Galeazzo Ciano. Italian Minister for Foreign Affairs, 1936–1943*, edited by Malcolm Muggeridge (London, 2002), p. 514.   **89.** Directive 41, 5.4.1942, HW, pp. 183–8.   **90.** Quoted by Bernd Wegner in Horst Boog et al.,

Das Deutsche Reich und der Zweite Weltkrieg, vol. 6: Der globale Krieg. Die Ausweitung zum Weltkrieg und der Wechsel der Initiative 1941–1943 (Stuttgart, 1990), p. 783. 91. Thus Donohue, 'Hitler as military commander', pp. 5–6, 9–10, 11, 31 et passim, contradicting later apologias of the generals. 92. See Joel Hayward, 'Hitler's quest for oil: the impact of economic considerations on military strategy, 1941–1942', Journal of Strategic Studies, 18 (December 1995), pp. 94–135, especially pp. 117, 127. 93. Speech, 15.2.1942, Domarus, IV, p. 1,842. 94. Speech, 26.4.1942, Domarus, IV, p. 1,869. 95. Speech, 30.5.1942, Domarus, IV, pp. 1,887–8. 96. 'Aktenvermerk für Reichsleiter Bormann über die Rückholung der Volksdeutschen aus Amerika und Afrika nach dem Kriege', 23.4.1942, FHQ, Bundesarchiv Berlin-Lichterfelde, NS 19 1467. 97. Thus Steven Casey, 'Franklin D. Roosevelt, Ernst "Putzi" Hanfstaengl and the S-Project, June 1942–June 1944', Journal of Contemporary History, 35 (2000), pp. 339–59 (especially p. 339). 98. Geraldien von Frijtag Drabbe Künzel, Hitler's Brudervolk: The Dutch and the Colonization of Occupied Eastern Europe, 1939–1945 (London, 2016), pp. 36–9; and Steffen Werther, ' "Nordic-Germanic" dreams and national realities: a case study of the Danish region of Sønderjylland, 1933–1945', in Anton Weiss-Wendt and Rory Yeomans (eds.), Racial Science in Hitler's New Europe, 1938–1945 (Lincoln and London, 2013), pp. 129–49. 99. Quoted in Koop, 'Dem Führer ein Kind schenken', pp. 197–8. 100. 'Vermerk betreffend eine Unterredung Rosenbergs mit Hitler am 8. Mai 1942 über Fragen der Ostpolitik', 8.5.1942, IMT, Dokument 1520-PS, p. 289. 101. Thus Gerhard Wolf, Ideologie und Herrschaftsrationalität. Nationalsozialistische Germanisierungspolitik in Polen (Hamburg, 2012), pp. 467–88, especially, pp. 467, 475, 481–2 (quotation on p. 475). 102. For the 'acceleration' during the first six months of 1942 see Gerlach, The Extermination of the European Jews, pp. 87–90. 103. Alexander Brakel, Der Holocaust. Judenverfolgung und Völkermord (Berlin, 2008), p. 89. 104. Of course, absence of evidence is not necessarily evidence of absence, and more documentation may emerge. 105. FE, 1.3.1942, p. 237. 106. My understanding of Operation Blue has benefited immensely from reading Donohue, 'Hitler as military commander', especially p. 30 et passim, which contests the view that he was a military dilettante. 107. Directive 41, 5.4.1942, HW, pp. 183–8. 108. Donohue, 'Hitler as military commander', pp. 155, 69–71, 497–8. 109. Thus Bernd Wegner, 'Hitlers Besuch in Finnland. Das geheime Tonprotokoll seiner Unterredung mit Mannerheim am 4. Juni 1942', Vierteljahrshefte für Zeitgeschichte, 41 (1993), pp. 117–37, especially pp. 125–7. 110. Andreas Hillgruber, Hitler, König Carol und Marschall Antonescu. Die deutsch-rumänischen Beziehungen, 1938–1944 (Wiesbaden, 1954). 111. See Reuth, Entscheidung, p. 239. 112. Romain Hayes, Subhas Chandra Bose in Nazi Germany: Politics, Intelligence and Propaganda, 1941–1943 (London, 2011), pp. 114–16. 113. See Bernd Wegner, 'The tottering giant: German perceptions of Soviet military and economic strength in preparation for "Operation Blau" (1942)', in Christopher Andrew and Jeremy Noakes (eds.), Intelligence and International Relations, 1900–1945 (Exeter, 1987), pp. 293–311. 114. Reuth, Entscheidung, pp. 192–3, 199, 197. 115. HT, 6.7.1942, III, p. 475. 116. BT, 3.7.1942, p. 457. 117. Thus Joel S. A. Hayward, Stopped at Stalingrad: The Luftwaffe and Hitler's Defeat in the East, 1942–1943 (Lawrence, Kan., 1998). 118. Markus Eikel, 'Hitlers Lagezentrum "Wehrwolf" in der Ukraine 1942/43', Militärgeschichte. Zeitschrift für historische Bildung (2009), pp. 8–11. 119. FE, 6.6.1942, p. 255; FE, 17.5.1942, pp. 251–2. 120. FE, 28.6.1942, p. 259. 121. Directive 43, 11.7.1942, HW, pp. 192–4. 122. Longerich, Holocaust, p. 356. 123. Thus Christopher R. Browning, 'A final Hitler decision for the "Final Solution"? The Riegner Telegram reconsidered', Holocaust and Genocide Studies, 10 (Spring 1996), pp. 3–10 (quotation on p. 7). 124. Wilhelm Keitel, 'Betr. Aussiedlung aus der Krim', 12.7.1942, FHQ, Bundesarchiv Berlin-Lichterfelde, NS 19 2508, fol. 2. The document begins with the words 'The Führer has expressed his intention'. 125. See Arthur L. Smith, Jr, 'The Kameradschaft USA', Journal of Modern History, 34 (1962), p. 407. 126. Quoted in Tooze, Wages of Destruction, p. 526. 127. See Speer's contemporary account of Hitler's remarks on the subject: FK, 7–9.9.1942, pp. 182–3. 128. Anton Jochimsthaler, Die Breitspurbahn Hitlers. Eine Dokumentation über die geplante transkontinentale 3-Meter-Breitspureisenbahn der Jahre 1942–1945 (Freiburg, 1981). 129. Bormann to Rosenberg, 23.7.1942, FHQ, printed in its entirety in Helmut Schaller, Der Nationalsozialismus und die slawische Welt (Regensburg, 2002), pp. 239–40. It conveys a

direct instruction from Hitler.   130. Thus Kesselring, *Soldat bis zum letzten Tag*, pp. 168–9.
131. Hitler to Mussolini, 23.6.1942, in Reuth, *Entscheidung*, p. 250.   132. FE, 3.7.1942, p.
261. This document is a retranslation from English. The original has been lost.   133. RT,
14.7.1942, p. 441.   134. Communiqué, 15.7.1942, Domarus, IV, p. 1,897.   135. Directive 45,
23.7.1942, HW, pp. 196–200.   136. Donohue, 'Hitler as military commander', p. 271.   137.
RT, 14.7.1942, p. 447.   138. Thus Motadel, *Islam and Nazi Germany's War*.   139. Quoted
in David Motadel, 'The "Muslim question" in Hitler's Balkans', *Historical Journal*, 56 (2013),
p. 1,018.   140. Thus Manfred Zeidler, 'Das "kaukasische Experiment". Gab es eine Weisung
Hitlers zur deutschen Besatzungspolitik im Kaukasus?', *Vierteljahrshefte für Zeitgeschichte*,
53 (2005), pp. 475–500. The draft directive is printed on pp. 499–500.   141. Picker, *Hitlers
Tischgespräche*, 9.5.1942, p. 389.   142. Thus Hayward, 'Too little, too late', p. 781.   143.
Quoted in Tooze, *Wages of Destruction*, pp. 573–4 (quotation on p. 574).   144. See Stephen
G. Fritz, *The First Soldier: Hitler as Military Leader* (New Haven and London, 2018), pp.
235–56.   145. LV, 26.8.1942, p. 405.   146. Thus Below, *Als Hitlers Adjutant*, p. 318. See also
the recollection of Halder to Geyr, 23.8.1942, Aschau, in IfZ, ED 91 v. Geyr, vol. 10.   147.
Donohue, 'Hitler as military commander', pp. 273, 278.   148. Wegner in Boog et al., *Das
Deutsche Reich und der Zweite Weltkrieg*, vol. 6, pp. 951–61.   149. LB, pp. 11–12.   150.
Donohue, 'Hitler as military commander', pp. 308 and 323.   151. 'Führerbefehl an die Heeres-
gruppe A über die Fortsetzung der Operationen', 10.9.1942, KTB, OKW, II/2, p. 1,297.   152.
'Besprechung des Führers mit Generalfeldmarschall Keitel am 18. September, 1942', in
Johannes Hürter and Matthias Uhl, 'Hitler in Vinnica. Ein neues Dokument zur Krise im
September 1942', *Vierteljahrshefte für Zeitgeschichte*, 63 (2015), pp. 601–38.   153. Halder
to Geyr von Schweppenburg, 9.6.1964, Aschau, in IfZ, ED 91 v. Geyr, vol. 10.   154. 'Führerbefehl über "Grundsätzliche Aufgaben der Verteidigung" ', 8.9.1942, in KTB, OKW, II/2,
pp. 1,292–7.   155. Hitler, 'Operationsbefehl Nr. 1, betr weitere Kampfführung im Osten',
14.10.1942, FHQ, in KTB, OKW, II/2, p. 1,301.   156. Hürter and Uhl, 'Hitler in Vinnica',
p. 623.   157. See the account in Giesler, *Ein anderer Hitler*, p. 404.   158. Ben Macintyre,
'How Hitler's inner circle was penetrated by an MI6 agent', *The Times*, 13.2.2010, pp. 34–
5.   159. Hürter and Uhl, 'Hitler in Vinnica', p. 607.   160. Quoted in Pyta, *Hitler*, p.
404.   161. FE, 12.10.1942, p. 286.   162. Hayward, 'Too little, too late', pp. 790–92.   163.
Hürter and Uhl, 'Hitler in Vinnica, pp. 615, 634–5. See also Torsten Diederich, *Paulus. Das
Trauma von Stalingrad. Eine Biographie* (Paderborn, 2008).   164. Manfred Kehrig, *Stalingrad. Analyse und Dokumentation einer Schlacht* (Stuttgart, 1976), pp. 36–128.   165.
Antony Beevor, *Stalingrad* (London, 1998), p. 187.   166. 'Führerbefehl betr. Fortführung
der Eroberung Stalingrads durch die 6 Armee', 17.11.1942, in KTB, OKW, II/2, p. 1,307.   167.
Speech, 8.11.1942, Domarus, IV, pp. 1,937–8.   168. ET, 2.10.1942, p. 129.   169. Jochmann
(ed.), *Hitler. Monologe*, 2.9.1942, p. 383.   170. Speech, 8.11.1942, Domarus, IV, p.
1,938.   171. See the account in ET, 10.11.1942, p. 134.   172. For a subaltern view see Anwar
Sadat, 'Rommel at El Alamein: an Egyptian view (1942)', in Bernard Lewis (ed.), *A Middle
East Mosaic* (New York, 2000), pp. 314–16.   173. Heinrich Waas, 'Eine Besprechung über
den U-Boot-Krieg bei Hitler in der Reichskanzlei im Herbst 1942 und ihre Bedeutung für
den Kriegsverlauf', *Geschichte in Wissenschaft und Unterricht*, 38 (1987), pp. 684–95.   174.
For the performance of the Italians see Thomas Schlemmer (ed.), *Die Italiener an der Ost-
front 1942/43. Dokumente zu Mussolinis Krieg gegen die Sowjetunion* (Munich, 2005), pp.
58–69 *et passim*.   175. Beevor, *Stalingrad*, pp. 269–70.   176. ET, 26.11.1942, p. 139.   177.
FE, 25.11.1942, p. 301.   178. Thus Geoffrey Jukes, *Hitler's Stalingrad Decisions* (Berkeley,
Calif., 1985).   179. LB, 12.12.1942, p. 118.   180. LB, 12.12.1942, pp. 75, 84.   181. Speech,
8.11.1942, Domarus, IV, p. 1,933.   182. Horst Boog, 'Der anglo-amerikanische strategische
Luftkrieg über Europa und die deutsche Luftverteidigung', in Boog et al., *Das Deutsche
Reich und der Zweite Weltkrieg*, vol. 6, pp. 564–5.   183. Hürter and Uhl, 'Hitler in Vinnica',
p. 637.   184. Thus Joachim von Ribbentrop, *Zwischen London und Moskau. Erinnerungen
und letzte Aufzeichnungen. Aus dem Nachlass herausgegeben von Annelies von Ribbentrop*
(Leoni am Starnberger See, 1953), p. 261.   185. ET, 8.11.1942, p. 134.   186. Quoted in
Pyta, *Hitler*, p. 460.   187. FK, 1/2/3.12.1942, p. 203.   188. Lieb, 'Hitler's Britain', p.
5.   189. Directives 46 and 46a, HW, 18.10.1942, pp. 206–9. See also Manfred

Messerschmidt, 'Kommandobefehl und NS-Völkerrechtsdenken', *Revue de Droit Pénal Militaire et de Droit de la Guerre*, 11 (1972), pp. 110–33, especially pp. 121–9. **190.** Thus Peter Lieb, *Konventioneller Krieg oder NS-Weltanschauungskrieg? Kriegführung and Partisanenbekämpfung in Frankreich 1943/44* (Munich, 2007), p. 143. **191.** FK, 23.6.1942, p. 138. **192.** FK, 13/14.10.1942, p. 194. **193.** Quoted in Historisch-Technisches Museum Peenemünde (ed.), *Wunder mit Kalkül*, pp. 40–41. **194.** Ralf Schabel, *Die Illusion der Wunderwaffen. Die Rolle der Düsenflugzeuge und Flugabwehrraketen in der Rüstungsindustrie des Dritten Reiches* (Munich, 1994), pp. 176–7. **195.** FK, 10/11/12.8.1942, p. 171. **196.** See FK, 20/21/22.9.1942, p. 189. **197.** FK, 13.8.1942, p. 178. **198.** FE, 12.10.1942, pp. 286–7. **199.** LB, 8.6.1943, p. 266. Hitler's demand that foreign labour should be well treated for reasons of productivity is multiply attested: FK, 3/4/5.1.1943, p. 218; FK, 30.5.1943, p. 267; FE, 30.5.1943, p. 340. See also 'Besprechung beim Führer im Berghof am 25.4.1944 mit Lammers, M.B., Ley, Sauckel, Fischböck, Abetz, Leibel, Speer', IfZ, F19/3. I thank Mikael Nilsson for drawing the Serbian deaths to my attention; see Arnt Tole Andersen, *Krigstid og Pangeliv på Ørland 1940–45* (Belgrade, 1997), pp. 65–144. **200.** FE, 22.11.1942, p. 300. **201.** LB, 12.12.1942, pp. 116–17. **202.** Hitler's views are conveyed in 'Schreiben des Chefs der Reichskanzlei an mehrere Reichsminister', 17.12.1942, in Herwart Vorländer, *Die NSV. Darstellung und Dokumentation einer nationalsozialistischen Organisation* (Boppard am Rhein, 1988), p. 421. **203.** ET, 26.9.1942, p. 128. **204.** See MacGregor Knox, '1 October 1942: Adolf Hitler, Wehrmacht officer policy, and social revolution', *Historical Journal*, 43 (2000), pp. 801–25, especially pp. 819–22. **205.** Norman J. W. Goda, 'Black marks: Hitler's bribery of senior officers during World War II', *Journal of Modern History*, 72 (2000), pp. 435–6 (quotation on p. 436). **206.** 'Vermerk über eine Unterredung mit dem Führer im Führer-Hauptquartier', 8.5.1942, IMT Dokument 1520-PS, p. 284. **207.** 'Vermerk über eine Unterredung mit dem Führer', pp. 288–9. **208.** Zeidler, 'Das "kaukasische Experiment" ', p. 484 (re Caucasus). **209.** Lammers's orders of 7 and 11 December 1942, Berlin, in Vorländer, *Die NSV*, p. 420. **210.** Himmler to Schellenberg, 5.12.1942, Bundesarchiv Berlin-Lichterfelde, NS 19 2032. **211.** Lammers was seeing Hitler regularly, but by no means daily during 1942. See the record of his meetings in Bundesarchiv Berlin-Lichterfelde, R43II 1609a; and Lammers's memorandum 'Betr Behandlung der an der Reichskanzlei eingehenden Briefe an den Führer', 27.11.1942, Berlin, IfZ, ED 9. **212.** FE, 2.12.1942, pp. 302–3 (quotation on p. 303). **213.** Andreas Hillgruber and Jürgen Förster, 'Zwei neue Aufzeichnungen über "Führer" Besprechungen aus dem Jahre 1942', in *Militärgeschichtliche Mitteilungen*, 11 (1972), pp. 109–26 (quotation on p. 126). **214.** Speech, 8.11.1942, Domarus, IV, p. 1,935. **215.** Waas, 'U-Boot-Krieg'. **216.** Rahn, 'Hitler und die Marineführung', pp. 226–30 (with quotations). **217.** Proclamation, 1.1.1943, Domarus, IV, p. 1,967. **218.** FK, 3.4.1943, p. 246. **219.** Proclamation, 1.1.1943, Domarus, IV, p. 1,968. **220.** Obersturmbannführer Waldemar Rimann to Brandt, 30.6.1943, Bundesarchiv Berlin-Lichterfelde, NS 19 3097. See also Valdis O. Lumans, *Himmler's Auxiliaries: The Volksdeutsche Mittelstelle and the German National Minorities of Europe, 1833–1945* (Chapel Hill and London, 1993), p. 200. **221.** Obersturmbannführer Waldemar Rimann to Brandt, 30.9.1943, Bundesarchiv Berlin-Lichterfelde, NS 19 3097. **222.** Volksdeutsche Mittelstelle to Himmler, 23.1.1943, Bundesarchiv Berlin-Lichterfelde, NS 19 3097. **223.** Protocol, Hitler meeting with Horthy, 23.4.1943, ADAP, Series E, vol. 5, p. 685. I am very grateful to Wolfram Pyta for drawing this source to my attention. **224.** New Year's Proclamation, 1.1.1943, Domarus, IV, p. 1,968. **225.** Demps (ed.), *Luftangriffe*, p. 37. **226.** Quoted in Beaumont, 'The bomber offensive as a second front', p. 13. **227.** Order of the Day, 1.1.1943, Domarus, IV, p. 1,971. **228.** See David M. Glantz, *Operation Don's Main Attack: The Soviet Southern Front's Advance on Rostov, January–February 1943* (Lawrence, Kan., 2018). **229.** LB, 1.2.1943, p. 122. **230.** LB, 1.2.1943, p. 128. **231.** LB, 1.2.1943, p. 130. **232.** Communiqué, 3.2.1943, Domarus, IV, p. 1,985. **233.** GT, 9.3.1943, II/7, p. 514. See also Nathan Stoltzfus, *Resistance of the Heart: Intermarriage and the Rosenstrasse Protest in Nazi Germany* (New York, 1996). **234.** FK, 1.5.1943, p. 252. **235.** Eberhard Schwarz, *Die Stabilisierung der Ostfront nach Stalingrad. Mansteins Gegenschlag zwischen Donez und Dnjepr im Frühjahr 1943* (Göttingen and Zurich, 1986), pp. 69–70, 142–5. **236.**

See Pyta, *Hitler*, p. 445.   **237.** As reported in ET, 18.2.1943 and 28.2.1943, pp. 144–5.   **238.** On all this see Gibbels, 'Hitlers Nervenkrankheit', pp. 170–71 (with quotations).   **239.** Alan W. Cooper, *The Air Battle of the Ruhr: RAF Offensive March to July 1943* (Shrewsbury, 1992), especially pp. 36–45.   **240.** FE, 28.6.1943, pp. 345–6.   **241.** See the detailed analysis in Tooze, *Wages of Destruction*, pp. 596–601.   **242.** GT, 8.3.1943, II/7, p. 505.   **243.** Schwarz, *Die Stabilisierung der Ostfront nach Stalingrad*, pp. 201–24.   **244.** Bernd Wegner, 'Der Krieg gegen die Sowjetunion, 1942/3', in Boog et al., *Das Deutsche Reich und der Zweite Weltkrieg*, vol. 6, pp. 1,087–9.   **245.** LB, 5.3.1943, pp. 171–2.   **246.** Thus Pyta, *Hitler*, pp. 465–6.   **247.** See Bernd Martin, 'Verhandlungen über separate Friedensschlüsse 1942–1945. Ein Beitrag zur Entstehung des Kalten Krieges', *Militärgeschichtliche Mitteilungen*, 19–20 (1976), pp. 95–113; Schmidt, *Statist*, p. 562; and Friedrich-Karl von Plehwe, *Schicksalsstunden in Rom. Ende eines Bündnisses* (Berlin, 1967), p. 23.   **248.** See the account in Ribbentrop, *Zwischen London und Moskau*, pp. 263–4.   **249.** These are referred to in: Brandt to Bormann, 10.3.1943, in Bundesarchiv Berlin-Lichterfelde, NS 19 3768, fo. 2.   **250.** Jörg K. Hoensch, 'Nationalsozialistische Europapläne im Zweiten Weltkrieg. Versuch einer Synthese', in Richard G. Plaschka et al. (eds.), *Mitteleuropa-Konzeptionen in der ersten Hälfte des 20. Jahrhunderts* (Vienna, 1995), pp. 322–4 (quotations on p. 323).   **251.** GT, 8.5.1943, II/8, p. 236; Speech, 7.5.1943, Domarus, IV, p. 2,011.   **252.** See Karl-Heinz Frieser, 'Die Schlacht im Kursker Bogen', in Karl-Heinz Frieser et al., *Das Deutsche Reich und der Zweite Weltkrieg*, vol. 8: *Die Ostfront 1943/44. Der Krieg im Osten und an den Nebenfronten* (Stuttgart, 2007), pp. 83–103.   **253.** Thus Roman Töppel, 'Kursk – Mythen und Wirklichkeit einer Schlacht', *Vierteljahrshefte für Zeitgeschichte*, 57 (2009), pp. 350–51. See also Marcel Stein, *Der Januskopf. Feldmarschall von Manstein – eine Neubewertung* (Bissendorf, 2004), pp. 189–93.   **254.** Operationsbefehl No. 6, 15.4.1943, FHQ, in Ernst Klink, *Das Gesetz des Handelns. Die Operation 'Zitadelle' 1943* (Stuttgart, 1966), pp. 292–4 (quotation on p. 292).   **255.** FE, 4.3.1943, p. 326.   **256.** FE, 22.1.1943, p. 318.   **257.** FK, 4.5.1943, p. 253.   **258.** Thus Tooze, *Wages of Destruction*, pp. 595–6.   **259.** FE, 8.1.1943, pp. 309–10.   **260.** FE, 13.1.1943, pp. 311–13.   **261.** E.g., FE, 10.5.1943, pp. 335–6.   **262.** Thus Stibbe, *Women in the Third Reich*, p. 95. See also Stoltzfus, *Hitler's Compromises*, p. 241.   **263.** See Pyta, *Hitler*, pp. 429–30.   **264.** Thus the account in Veit Harlan, *Im Schatten meiner Filme. Selbstbiographie, herausgegeben und mit einem Nachwort versehen von H. C. Opfermann* (Gütersloh, 1966), pp. 180–84 (quotations on p. 184).   **265.** For Speer's narrative skills see Tooze, *Wages of Destruction*, pp. 556–7.   **266.** FK, 6/7.2.1943, p. 232.   **267.** FE 21.3.1942, p. 243; FE, 10.5.1943, pp. 336–7.   **268.** Thus Nicole Kramer, *Volksgenossinnen an der Heimatfront. Mobilisierung, Verhalten. Erinnerung* (Göttingen, 2011), p. 167.   **269.** FK, 1.5.1943, p. 252.   **270.** FE, 30.5.1943, p. 339; and FE, 28.6.1943, p. 341.   **271.** See generally Götz Aly, *Hitler's Beneficiaries: How the Nazis Bought the German People* (London, 2007).   **272.** FE, 16.1.1943, pp. 314–15.   **273.** FE, 8.2.1943, p. 319.   **274.** FE, 3.3.1943, p. 323.   **275.** Speech, 7.5.1943, Domarus, IV, p. 2,012.   **276.** For the seriousness of the losses compared to Stalingrad see Gerhard Schreiber, 'Das Ende des nordafrikanischen Feldzugs und der Krieg in Italien 1943 bis 1945', in Frieser et al., *Das Deutsche Reich und der Zweite Weltkrieg*, vol. 8, p. 1,109.   **277.** Thus the account of the radio operator in Alfons Schulz, *Drei Jahre in der Nachrichtenzentrale des Führerhauptquartiers* (Stein am Rhein, 1996), pp. 153–4.   **278.** See Peter Lieb, *Krieg in Nordafrika, 1940–1943* (Ditzingen, 2018), p. 140.   **279.** See Ben Macintyre, *Operation Mincemeat: The True Spy Story that Changed the Course of World War II* (London, 2010).   **280.** Directive 48, 26.7.1943, HW, pp. 218–23.   **281.** LB, 20.5.1943, p. 227.   **282.** FE, 19.5.1943, pp. 337–8.   **283.** Thus Puttkamer, *Die unheimliche See*, p. 58.   **284.** FE, 31.5.1943, p. 341.   **285.** Fleischhauer, *Die Chance des Sonderfriedens*, pp. 108–11, 166–7.   **286.** Catherine Andreyev, *Vlasov and the Russian Liberation Movement* (Cambridge, 1987); Alexander Dallin, *German Rule in Russia 1941–1945: A Study of Occupation Policies* (New York, 1957), pp. 567–600; and George Fischer, 'Vlasov and Hitler', *Journal of Modern History*, 23 (1951), pp. 58–71.   **287.** See Martin Broszat, *Nationalsozialistische Polenpolitik, 1939–1945* (Stuttgart, 1961), pp. 188–90.   **288.** See Helmut Krausnick, 'Zu Hitlers Ostpolitik im Sommer 1943', *Vierteljahrshefte für Zeitgeschichte*, 2

624 NOTES TO PP. 488–95

(1954), pp. 310–11. 289. LB, 8.6.1943, p. 258. 290. David M. Glantz and Jonathan M. House, *The Battle of Kursk* (Lawrence, Kan., 1999), pp. 79–147; and Frieser, 'Die Schlacht im Kursker Bogen', pp. 104–208. 291. See Töppel, 'Kursk', pp. 362, 373, 377. 292. Karl-Heinz Frieser, 'Schlagen aus der Nachhand – Schlagen aus der Vorhand. Die Schlachten von Char'kov und Kursk 1943', in Roland G. Foerster (ed.), *Gezeitenwechsel im Zweiten Weltkrieg? Die Schlachten von Char'kov und Kursk im Frühjahr und Sommer 1943 in operativer Anlage, Verlauf und politischer Bedeutung* (Hamburg, 1996), pp. 101–35, especially pp. 123–8. 293. Töppel's revisionist arguments, 'Kursk', pp. 379–83, on the salience of the Orel operation are well taken. 294. Martin A. Ruehl, ' "In this time without emperors": the politics of Ernst Kantorowicz's *Kaiser Friedrich der Zweite* reconsidered', *Journal of the Warburg and Courtauld Institutes*, 63 (2000), p. 187. (The order was given by Göring, but it seems likely that he was acting on Hitler's instructions.) 295. Ohler, *Blitzed*, pp. 167–8. 296. LB, 25.7.1943, p. 314. 297. LB, 26.7.1943, p. 371. 298. Quoted in Dieter Hartwig, *Grossadmiral Karl Dönitz. Legende und Wirklichkeit* (Paderborn, 2010), p. 432. 299. As quoted in Giesler, *Ein anderer Hitler*, p. 415. Hitler seems to have been sent the photographs more or less immediately: see LB, 25.7.1943, p. 291. 300. LB, 25.7.1943, p. 295. 301. See Nicholas Stargardt, 'Beyond "consent" or "terror": wartime crises in Nazi Germany', *History Workshop Journal*, 72 (2011), pp. 190–204, especially pp. 190 and 197–9. 302. Neil Gregor, 'A *Schicksalsgemeinschaft*? Allied bombing, civilian morale, and social dissolution in Nuremberg, 1942–1945', *Historical Journal*, 43 (2000), pp. 1,051–70, here p. 1,065. 303. Stoltzfus, *Hitler's Compromises*, p. 235. 304. Thus Pyta, *Hitler*, p. 202. 305. RT, 30.7.1943, p. 481; RT, 13.8.1943, p. 488. 306. Erich von Manstein, *Verlorene Siege* (Bonn, 1955), pp. 524–5. See also Geoffrey P. Megargee, 'Triumph of the null: structure and conflict in the command of German land forces, 1939–1945', *War in History*, 4 (1997), p. 77. 307. LB, 26.7.1943, p. 370. Josef Schröder, 'Zur Befreiung Mussolinis im Sommer 1943', in Josef Schröder, *Hitler und Mussolini. Aspekte der deutsch-italienischen Beziehungen 1930–1943*, ed. Carl August Lückerath and Michael Salewski (Gleichen, 2007), pp. 191–217. 308. See Pyta, *Hitler*, pp. 519–43. 309. Thus Below, *Als Hitlers Adjutant*, p. 347. 310. Thus RT, 13.8.1943, p. 489. 311. Gerhard Krebs, 'Japanische Vermittlungsversuche im Deutsch-Sowjetischen Krieg, 1941–1945', in Josef Kreiner and Regine Mathias (eds.), *Deutschland–Japan in der Zwischenkriegszeit* (Bonn, 1990). 312. See Fleischhauer, *Die Chance des Sonderfriedens*, p. 179. 313. Von Renthe-Fink, 'Notiz für den Reichsaussenminister betreffend Europäischen Staatenbund', 9.9.1943, Berlin, in Karl Drechsler, Hans Dress and Gerhart Hass, 'Europapläne des deutschen Imperialismus im zweiten Weltkrieg', *Zeitschrift für Geschichtswissenschaft*, 19 (1971), pp. 916–31, here pp. 927–31. 314. Tore Rem, *Knut Hamsun. Die Reise zu Hitler* (Berlin, 2016). 315. See the account of the meeting in SS-Obergruppenführer Rauter to Himmler, The Hague, 9.12.1943, Bundesarchiv Berlin-Lichterfelde, NS 19 1556, fol. 191. 316. 'Vorläufige Gedächtnisniederschrift vom Empfang Musserts beim Führer', 2.12.1943 (Abschrift), Archiv Berlin-Lichterfelde, NS 19 1556, fol. 192. 317. FK, 12/13.9.1943, p. 294. 318. FE, 13.9.1943, p. 359. 319. FK, 12/13.9.1943, p. 294. 320. Thus Jonas Scherner and Eugene White (eds.), *Paying for Hitler's War: The Consequences of Nazi Hegemony for Europe* (Cambridge, 2016), p. 9. 321. Gerd R. Ueberschär, 'Das NKFD und der BDO im Kampf gegen Hitler 1943–1945', in Gerd R. Ueberschär (ed.), *Das Nationalkomitee 'Freies Deutschland' und der Bund Deutscher Offiziere* (Frankfurt, 1995), pp. 31–51. 322. Pyta, *Hitler*, pp. 507–13. 323. Berghahn, 'NSDAP und "geistige Führung"', p. 51 (with quotation). 324. FE, 22.12.1943, p. 381. 325. Rebentisch, *Führerstaat*, p. 499. 326. FE, 11.10.1943, p. 363. 327. 'The Rundschreiben of Bormann, 24.8.1943', in Gersdorff (ed.), *Frauen im Kriegsdienst*, p. 411, refers to 'Mundpropaganda und Einzelaufklärung' among 'den Reihen der NS-Frauenschaft und des Deutschen Frauenwerks'. 328. See the account of the meeting in SS-Obergruppenführer Rauter to Himmler, The Hague, 9.12.1943, Bundesarchiv Berlin-Lichterfelde, NS 19 1556, fol. 191. 329. Motadel, *Islam and Nazi Germany's War*, p. 319. 330. Directive 51, 3.11.1943, HW, pp. 233–8. 331. Thus Bernd Wegner, 'Die Aporie des Krieges', in Frieser et al., *Das Deutsche Reich und der Zweite Weltkrieg*, vol. 8, pp. 246–74, especially pp. 247 and 250. 332. FK, 8.7.1943, p. 278. 333. John Erickson, *The Road to Berlin* (London, 1983), p. 122. 334. FK,

19–22.8.1943, p. 288. See also FK, 28.6.1943, p. 274.   335. FE, 22.10.1943, p. 365.   336. FK, 6/7.12.1943, p. 314. See also Puttkamer, *Die unheimliche See*, pp. 58–9.   337. FK, 16/17.12.1943, p. 322.   338. Quoted in Hölsken, *V-Waffen*, p. 90.   339. Quoted in Hölsken, *V-Waffen*, p. 90.   340. FK, 17/18.7.1943, p. 280.   341. Quoted in Historisch-Technisches Museum Peenemünde, *Wunder mit Kalkül*, p. 42.   342. FK, 17/18.7.1943, p. 280. See also FK, 19–22.8.1943, p. 291.   343. FE, 25.7.1943, p. 348. This is a retranslation from the English back into German. The original German document has been lost.   344. Quoted in Hölsken, *V-Waffen*, p. 90.   345. FE, 1.12.1943, p. 377.   346. Stenographic notes of observations by Hitler, 13.10.1943, in Hürter and Uhl, 'Hitler in Vinnica', pp. 600–601. The text appears to be made up of direct quotations and paraphrases. I have indicated the direct quotations, and paraphrased the paraphrases.   347. LB, 20.12.1943, p. 450.   348. LB, 20.12.1943, p. 444.   349. Martin Middlebrook, *The Berlin Raids: R A F Bomber Command Winter 1943–1944* (London, 1988).   350. Speech, 8.11.1943, Domarus, IV, p. 2,055. See also Süss, *Tod aus der Luft*, pp. 146, 241.   351. Quoted in Phillips P. O'Brien, 'East versus west in the defeat of Nazi Germany', *Journal of Strategic Studies*, 23 (2000), pp. 89–113 , here p. 98.   352. For Hitler's focus on the western powers at this time see Below, *Als Hitlers Adjutant*, pp. 350 and 352.   353. O'Brien, *How the War Was Won*.   354. See Cristiano Andrea Ristuccia and Adam Tooze, 'Machine tools and mass production in the armaments boom: Germany and the United States, 1929–44', *Economic History Review*, 66 (2013), p. 965.   355. FK, 16/17.12.1943, p. 326.   356. FK, 6/7.12.1943, p. 229.   357. Rüdiger Overmans, *Deutsche militärische Verluste im Zweiten Weltkrieg* (Munich, 1999), pp. 318–19.   358. See O'Brien, 'East versus west'.   359. See the appointments diary in Bundesarchiv Berlin-Lichterfelde, R43II 1609b, fols. 12, 59, 137, 200–202, which shows most of Lammers's meetings with the Führer to have taken place with Bormann (or others) present.   360. RT, 7.8.1943, p. 484. See also Andreas Zellhuber, '*Unsere Verwaltung treibt einer Katastrophe zu . . .*' *Das Reichsministerium für die besetzten Ostgebiete und die deutsche Besatzungsherrschaft in der Sowjetunion, 1941–1945* (Stamsried, 2006), pp. 334–46.   361. To the best of the author's knowledge, the only time Hitler seems to have rambled aimlessly this year was at LB, 25.7.1943, pp. 306–7, when he repeated his faith in Göring over and over in a somewhat disturbed fashion.   362. Gibbels, 'Hitlers Nervenkrankheit', p. 171.   363. Ernst Günther Schenck, *Patient Hitler. Eine medizinische Biographie* (Augsburg, 2000).   364. Matlok (ed.), *Dänemark in Hitlers Hand*, p. 129.

Chapter 18: The Fall of 'Fortress Europe'

1. Proclamation, 1.1.1944, Domarus, IV, p. 2,073.   2. For a critical view see Madrusree Mukerjee, *Churchill's Secret War: The British Empire and the Ravaging of India during World War II* (New York, 2010).   3. Proclamation, 1.1.1944, Domarus, IV, p. 2,071.   4. Order of the Day, 1.1.1944, Domarus, IV, p. 2,075.   5. Proclamation, 1.1.1944, Domarus, IV, p. 2,071; Order of the Day, 1.1.1944, Domarus, IV, p. 2,075; Proclamation, 1.1.1944, Domarus, IV, p. 2,073.   6. Hitler's instructions are summarized in KTB, OKW, IV/2, Nachtrag, pp. 24–7. For his fear of Allied air superiority in Italy in January 1944, KTB, OKW, IV/2, Nachtrag, pp. 20 and 22.   7. Thus Walter S. Dunn, Jr, *Soviet Blitzkrieg: The Battle for White Russia, 1944* (London, 2000), pp. 76–7.   8. Schmidt, *Statist*, p. 589.   9. Jeffrey L. Ethell and Alfred Price, *Target Berlin: Mission 250, 6 March 1944* (London, 1981).   10. See Demps, *Luftangriffe*, pp. 38–9.   11. In A. J. P. Taylor, *The War Lords* (London, 1976), p. 67.   12. FK, 5.3.1944, p. 337.   13. FK, 30.4.1944, p. 355.   14. FK, 30.4.1944, p. 357.   15. FK, 22/23.5.1944, pp. 370, 382.   16. See Klaus Schmider, 'The last of the first: veterans of the *Jagdwaffe* tell their story', *Journal of Military History*, 73 (2009), pp. 231–49, especially pp. 235, 239.   17. Roger Beaumont, 'The bomber offensive as a second front', *Journal of Contemporary History*, 22 (January 1987), p. 15.   18. Speech, 30.1.1944, Domarus, IV, p. 2,083.   19. FE, 20.2.1944, p. 395 (with quotation); FE, 20.2.1944, p. 395; FE, 1.4.1944, p. 407 (with quotation).   20. A point made by Gerhard Schmitt-Rink, *Hitlers Bild der Weltwirtschaft. Ein Rückblick auf seine ökonomischen Denkfehler und Wissenslücken*

(Berlin, 2010), p. 51.   21. Mark M. Boatner, *The Biographical Dictionary of World War II* (Novato, Calif., 1996), pp. 518–19.   22. See appendix in Ethell and Price, *Target Berlin*, pp. 179–93. This is a list of pilots only and does not include other aircrew.   23. See the exchange between Kenneth P. Werrell, Klaus Schmider and Jeremy Black, 'The air war over Germany: claims and counter-claims', *Journal of Military History*, 73 (2009), pp. 925–32.   24. Ethell and Price, *Target Berlin*, pp. 121–2.   25. Stephen E. Ambrose, *Eisenhower*, vol. 1: *Soldier, General of the Army, President-Elect, 1890–1952* (New York, 1983), pp. 13–14; Carlo D'Este, *Eisenhower: A Soldier's Life* (New York, 2002), p. 58; Dwight D. Eisenhower, *At Ease* (Garden City, NY, 1967), p. 306.   26. Himmler to Chef der Sicherheitspolizei und des SD, Chef des Hauptamtes Volksdeutsche Mittelstelle and the Chef des SS-Hauptamtes, 30.1.194, Feldkommandostelle, Bundesarchiv Berlin-Lichterfelde, NS 19 3097.   27. Niall Ferguson, *Kissinger, 1923–1968: The Idealist* (London, 2015).   28. 'Ansprache des Führers an die Feldmarschälle und Generale am 27.1.1944 in der Wolfsschanze', IfZ, F19/3.   29. Gerhard L. Weinberg, 'German plans for victory, 1944–1945', in Weinberg, *Germany, Hitler and World War II*, pp. 274–86.   30. Hitler's remarks are reported in indirect speech in FK, 5.3.1944, p. 338.   31. Thus Wegner, 'Aporie des Krieges', pp. 496–9.   32. Quoted in Pyta, *Hitler*, p. 473.   33. Rommel memorandum for Hitler, 16.3.1944, in 'Erwin Rommel, Private Chefsachen, Frühjahr 1944', IfZ, ED 100, Sammlung Irving, no. 180 (unfoliated). See also Hans Wegmüller, *Die Abwehr der Invasion. Die Konzeption des Oberbefehlshabers West, 1940–1944* (Freiburg, 1979).   34. Rommel, 'Bericht über den Lagevortrag des Führers', 20.3.1944, in IfZ, ED 100, Sammlung Irving, unfoliated.   35. Rommel, 'Bericht über den Lagevortrag des Führers'.   36. Hitler meeting with Tiso, 12.5.1944, SD, II, p. 446.   37. Rommel, 'Bericht über den Lagevortrag des Führers'; Michael Salewski, 'Die Abwehr der Invasion als Schlüssel zum "Endsieg"?', in Rolf-Dieter Müller and Hans-Erich Volkmann (eds.), *Die Wehrmacht. Mythos und Realität* (Munich, 1999), pp. 210–23.   38. Thus Howard D. Grier, *Hitler, Dönitz and the Baltic Sea: The Third Reich's Last Hope, 1944–1945* (Annapolis, 2007), pp. 12–13.   39. Grier, *Hitler, Dönitz*, p. 13.   40. Grier, *Hitler, Dönitz*, p. 19.   41. FE, 12.3.1944, pp. 399–401 (quotations on pp. 399–400).   42. Krisztián Ungváry, 'Hitler, Horthy und die ungarische Holocaust', *Europäische Rundschau*, 42, 1 (2014), pp. 11–19.   43. Quoted in Jay Winik, 'Darkness at noon', *World Affairs* (Winter 2016), http://www.worldaffairsjournal.org/article/darkness-noon-fdr-and-holocaust.   44. Gerlach, *The Extermination of the European Jews*, p. 114.   45. FK, 9.5.1944, p. 359.   46. Here I disagree with the premise of Norman Davies, *No Simple Victory: World War II in Europe, 1939–1945* (London, 2006), pp. 22–5 (the table on 'man-months' is on p. 23).   47. Thus Peter Lieb, *Konventioneller Krieg oder NS-Weltanschauungskrieg? Kriegführung und Partisanenbekämpfung in Frankreich 1943/44* (Munich, 2007), p. 513.   48. Circular by Fritz Darges, Persönlicher Adjutant des Führers, 1.1.1944, FHQ, IFZ ED9   49. Speech, 30.1.1944, Domarus, IV, p. 2,083.   50. Lieb, *Konventioneller Krieg*, pp. 136–7 and 140. For the more general cultural challenge posed by the west see Moltmann, 'Nationalklischees und Demagogie', pp. 231–32.   51. Thus Gerhard Kock, '*Der Führer sorgt für unsere Kinder . . .*' *Die Kinderlandverschickung im Zweiten Weltkrieg* (Paderborn, 1997), p. 218.   52. Quoted in Stoltzfus, *Hitler's Compromises*, p. 240.   53. Hans-Adolf Jacobsen and Werner Jochmann (eds.), *Ausgewählte Dokumente zur Geschichte des Nationalsozialismus*, vol. 2 (Bielefeld, 1964), document H (no pagination).   54. 'Besprechung beim Führer im Berghof am 25.4.1944 mit Lammers, M.B., Ley, Sauckel, Fischböck, Abetz, Leibel, Speer', in IfZ, F19/3. This document was only released in 2011 and is not in FK.   55. KTB, OKW, IV/1, p. 314. See also Carl Boyd, *Hitler's Japanese Confidant: General Ōshima Hiroshi and MAGIC Intelligence, 1941–1945* (Lawrence, Kans., 1993), pp. 127–8, which quotes Ōshima's reports on conversations with Hitler and the German High Command.   56. KTB, OKW, IV/1, pp. 311–35.   57. KTB, OKW, IV/1, p. 315.   58. Keitel Circular, 'Betr. Urlaubssperre', 13.6.1944, in Bundesarchiv Berlin-Lichterfelde, NS 19 3910, fol. 23.   59. 29.6.1944, Berghof, OKW, KTB, IV/2, p. 1,594. These remarks on Allied mobility were repeated at LB, 31.7.1944, pp. 585–6.   60. Thus Max Hastings, *Overlord: D-Day and the Battle for Normandy* (London, 1984).   61. Adam Tooze, 'Blitzkrieg manqué or a new kind of war? Interpreting the Allied victory in the Normandy campaign', adamtooze.com, 27 August 2017; John Buckley (ed.), *The Normandy*

Campaign 1944: Sixty Years On (Abingdon, 2006). 62. Karl-Heinz Frieser, 'Der Zusammenbruch der Heeresgruppe Mitte im Sommer 1944', in Frieser et al., *Das Deutsche Reich und der Zweite Weltkrieg*, vol. 8, pp. 526–603. 63. Grier, *Hitler, Dönitz*, p. 24. 64. Wolfschanze, 9.7.1944, in KTB, OKW, IV/2, p. 1,595. 65. Discussion, 9.7.1944, Wolfschanze, in KTB, OKW, IV/2, p. 1,595. 66. Tooze, *Wages of Destruction*, p. 649. 67. FE, 2.6.1944, p. 416. 68. FK, 19–22.6.1944, p. 382. 69. FE, 2.6.1944, p. 418. 70. 'Ansprache des Führers vor Generälen und Offizieren am 22.6.1944 im Platterhof', in IfZ, F19/3. 71. 'Ansprache des Führers vor Generälen und Offizieren'. The distinction between 'race' and 'people' is also made in ES, early July 1944, p. 339. 72. ES, early July 1944, pp. 335–68. 73. Quoted in Tooze, *Wages of Destruction*, p. 635. 74. ES, early July 1944, p. 351. 75. ES, early July 1944, p. 365. 76. Ulrich Schlie, *Claus Schenk Graf von Stauffenberg Biographie* (Freiburg, Basel and Vienna, 2018), pp. 26–53; Peter Hoffmann, *German Resistance to Hitler* (Cambridge, Mass., and London, 1988). 77. Adjutantur der Wehrmacht beim Führer, Konteradmiral von Puttkamer, 14.9.1944 (copy), IfZ, ED 9. 78. E.g. Otto Lasch, *So fiel Königsberg. Kampf und Untergang von Ostpreussens Hauptsstadt* (Munich, 1958), p. 22. 79. Discussion, 31.7.1944, LB, p. 609. 80. Rundfunkansprache Hitlers vom 21. Juli 1944 anlässlich des 'Stauffenberg-Attentates', http://www.1000dokumente. de/pdf/dok_0083_ahr_de.pdf, accessed 28 January 2019. 81. Speech, 4.8.1944, Domarus, IV, p. 2,138. 82. Quoted by Schmidt, *Statist*, p. 594. 83. Helmut Ortner, *Der Hinrichter. Roland Freisler. Mörder im Dienste Hitlers* (Vienna, 1993), p. 235. 84. FE, 2.8.1944, p. 439. See also Winfried Heinemann, 'Selbstreinigung der Wehrmacht? Der Ehrenhof des Heeres und seine Tätigkeit', in Manuel Becker and Christoph Studt (eds.), *Der Umgang des Dritten Reiches mit den Feinden des Regimes. XXII. Königswinterer Tagung (Februar 2009)* (Berlin, 2010), pp. 117–29. 85. Thus Bernd Sösemann, 'Verräter vor dem Volksgericht – die denkwürdige Geschichte eines Filmprojekts', in Becker and Studt (eds.), *Der Umgang des Dritten Reiches*, pp. 147–63 (especially p. 157), and Magnus Brechtken, 'Joachim Fest und der 20. Juli 1944. Geschichtsbilder, Vergangenheitskonstruktionen, Narrative', in Brechtken et al. (eds.), *Verräter? Vorbilder? Verbrecher?*, pp. 161–82 (especially pp. 172 and 179). 86. KTB, OKW, IV/1, pp. 338–9; Dieter Ose, *Entscheidung im Westen 1944. Der Oberbefehlshaber West und die Abwehr der alliierten Invasion* (Stuttgart, 1982), pp. 207–59. 87. For the colossal German manpower losses that month see Rüdiger Overmans, *Deutsche militärische Verluste im Zweiten Weltkrieg* (Munich, 1998). 88. Christoph Rass, René Rohrkamp and Peter M. Quadflieg, *General Graf von Schwerin und das Kriegsende in Aachen. Ereignis, Mythos, Analyse* (Aachen, 2007). 89. FK, 21–23.9.1944, p. 410. 90. FK, 21–23.9.1944, pp. 412–13. See also FK, 12.10.1944, p. 425. 91. For Speer's briefing to Hitler on the damage to the transport and communications network in the Ruhr see FK, 1–4.11.1944, p. 431; Alfred C. Mierzejewski, *Bomben auf die Reichsbahn. Der Zusammenbruch der deutschen Kriegswirtschaft 1944–1945* (Freiburg, 1993). 92. Tooze, *Wages of Destruction*, pp. 648 and 650–51. 93. For example, when Hermann Esser went to see Hitler at Berchtesgaden on 13 July 1944, he was immediately asked to report on the most recent air raid: Esser Interrogation, IfZ, F135 Dokumentation Adolf Hitler, fol. 490. 94. See doctor's reports, 'Daily treatment of Adolf Hitler [1944]', IfZ, F135/3 Dokumentation Adolf Hitler, fol. 519, 1–9. 95. FE, 20.9.1944, p. 458. 96. 'Erlass des Führers über die Bildung des deutschen Volkssturmes, 18.10.1944', in Gerd R. Ueberschär and Rolf-Dieter Müller, *1945. Das Ende des Krieges* (Darmstadt, 2005), pp. 160–61 (quotations on p. 160). 97. Ribbentrop, *Zwischen London und Moskau*, p. 265; Boyd, *Hitler's Japanese Confidant*, pp. 158–9. 98. LB, 31.8.1944, pp. 611–12. 99. Meeting, 13.8.1944, quoted Domarus, IV, p. 2,141. See also Möckelmann, *Franz von Papen*, p. 100. Quoted in Ribbentrop, *Zwischen London und Moskau*, p. 266. 101. Proclamation, 12.11.1944, Domarus, IV, p. 2,161. 102. Speech, 22.6.1944, in IfZ, F19/3. 103. LB, 31.8.1944, p. 615. 104. Grier, *Hitler, Dönitz*, p. 61. 105. KTB, OKW, IV/1, p. 346. 106. Joachim Ludewig, *Rückzug: The German Retreat from France, 1944* (Lexington, Ky., 2012). 107. See Hitler's remarks quoted in 'Anordnung des Reichsministers für Ernährung und Landwirtschaft', 8.9.1944, in Schumann (ed.), *Griff nach Südosteuropa*, p. 249. 108. Willi A. Boelcke, 'Hitlers Befehle zur Zerstörung oder Lähmung des deutschen

Industriepotentials 1944/45', *Tradition. Zeitschrift für Firmengeschichte und Unternehmerbiographie*, 13, 6 (1968), pp. 301–16. **109.** Lars Hellwinkel, *Hitlers Tor zum Atlantik. Die deutschen Kriegsmarinestützpunkte in Frankreich, 1940–1945* (Berlin, 2012), p. 175. For a contemporary Wehrmacht assessment of the port capacities in France in August 1944 see KTB, OKW, IV/1, p. 374. **110.** FE, 20.8.1944, pp. 442–3. See also KTB, OKW, IV/1, p. 379; and Directives, 27.7.1944, 29.7.1944, 3.8.1944, 24.8.1944, 29.8.1944, 1.9.1944, 3.9.1944, 12.9.1944, HW, pp. 267–92. **111.** See Henrik O. Lunde, *Hitler's Wave-breaker Concept: An Analysis of the German End Game in the Baltic* (Philadelphia and Oxford, 2013). Hitler instructed that the High Command be informed of the economic importance of holding Hungary: FK, 1–4.11.1944, p. 427. **112.** For the stablization of the eastern front see Karl-Heinz Frieser, 'Die erfolgreichen Abwehrkämpfe der Heeresgruppe Mitte im Herbst 1944', in Friesser et al., *Das Deutsche Reich und der Zweite Weltkrieg*, vol. 8, pp. 604–19. **113.** Thus Alastair Noble, 'The phantom barrier: Ostwallbau, 1944–1945', *War in History*, 8 (2001), p. 464 *et passim.* **114.** LB, 12.12.1944, p. 721. **115.** FK, 24.9.1944, p. 411. **116.** Report 3.12.1944, KTB, OKW, IV/2, p. 1,596. **117.** Hermann Jung, *Die Ardennenoffensive 1944/45. Ein Beispiel für die Kriegführung Hitlers* (Göttingen, 1971), p. 101. **118.** Hitler's words as related by Oshima and translated by the US Magic intercepts, in Boyd, *Hitler's Japanese Confidant*, pp. 134–5. **119.** Grier, *Hitler, Dönitz*, p. 148. **120.** 'Die Vorbereitung einer eigenen Offensive zwischen Monschau und Echternach (bis 16. Dezember)', KTB, OKW, IV/1, pp. 430–40. **121.** Hitler's words as related by Oshima and translated by the US Magic intercepts, in Boyd, *Hitler's Japanese Confidant*, p. 134. **122.** KTB, OKW, IV/1, p. 367. **123.** Richard Lakowski, *Ostpreussen 1944/45. Krieg im Nordosten des Deutschen Reiches* (Paderborn, 2016), pp. 69–79. **124.** KTB, OKW, IV/1, p. 441. **125.** LB, 31.7.1944, p. 587. **126.** Thus Rebentisch, *Führerstaat*, p. 518. **127.** FK, 6–8.7.1944, p. 391. **128.** Thus Felix Moeller, *Der Filmminister. Goebbels und der Film im Dritten Reich* (Berlin, 1998), p. 389. For the close attention Hitler paid to the content of the newsreels, even at this stage of the war, see Ulrike Bartels, *Die Wochenschau im Dritten Reich. Entwicklung und Funktion eines Massenmediums unter besonderer Berücksichtigung völkisch-nationaler Inhalte* (Frankfurt, 2004), pp. 147–8. **129.** LB, 12.12.1944, p. 713. **130.** See David K. Yelton, *Hitler's Volkssturm: The Nazi Militia and the Fall of Germany, 1944–1945* (Lawrence, Kan., 2002), pp. 7, 9. **131.** Yelton, *Volkssturm*, pp. 16–17. **132.** For the saliency of the equipment problem and the fuel shortage in the autumn of 1944 see KTB, OKW, IV/1, pp. 385–6. **133.** Thus O'Brien, 'East versus west', p. 108. **134.** FK, 12.10.1944, pp. 416–17, 424–5. **135.** Yelton, *Volkssturm*, pp. 45, 52, 108. **136.** Yelton, *Volkssturm*, pp. 38, 44; Bormann, 'Anordnung betr. Lenkung des Kräfteeinsatzes zum Stellungsbau', FHQ, 7.9.1944, in Bundesarchiv Berlin-Lichterfelde, NS 19 2588, fol. 8. **137.** RT, 26.10.1944, p. 516; RT, 12.11.1944, p. 520. **138.** Thus Yelton, *Volkssturm*, pp. 45, 52, *et passim.* On Speer's desire to have a Generalkommissar für den Westen, which Hitler rejected in order to avoid offending the relevant *Gauleiter*, see FK, 1–4.11.1944, p. 428. **139.** Thus Neitzel, 'Der Bedeutungswandel der Kriegsmarine im Zweiten Weltkrieg', pp. 251–3 *et passim.* **140.** LB, 31.7.1944, p. 608; LB, 31.8.1944, p. 620. **141.** Thus at any rate the surviving record. See '[1944] Daily treatment of Adolf Hitler', translated by Virginia Bishop, 12.6.1945, IfZ, F135/3 Dokumentation Adolf Hitler. **142.** Adjutantur der Wehrmacht beim Führer, Konteradmiral von Puttkamer, circular, FHQ 14.9.1944, IfZ, ED 9. **143.** Phillips Payson O'Brien, 'Logistics by land and air', in John Ferris and Evan Mawdsley (eds.), *The Cambridge History of the Second World War*, vol. 1: *Fighting the War* (Cambridge, 2015), pp. 608–36. **144.** See KTB, OKW, IV/2, pp. 1,342–8; KTB, OKW, IV/1, pp. 447–8. **145.** See Peter Caddick-Adams, *Snow and Steel: The Battle of the Bulge, 1944–45* (New York, 2014), pp. 221, 532 *et passim*; Antony Beevor, *Ardennes 1944: Hitler's Last Gamble* (London, 2015), p. 84; and see generally John Zimmermann, *Pflicht zum Untergang. Die deutsche Kriegführung im Westen des Reiches 1944/45* (Paderborn, 2009), pp. 227–36. **146.** KTB, OKW, IV/2, pp. 1,347–8. **147.** LB, 28.12.1944, p. 744. **148.** LB, 28.12.1944, p. 743. **149.** See KTB, OKW, IV/2, pp. 1,352–3. **150.** LB, 28.12.1944, pp. 743–4. **151.** FK, p. 444; FK, 14.1.1945, p. 460. **152.** Proclamation, 1.1.1945, Domarus, IV, p. 2,186. **153.** Schmidt, *Statist*, p. 585. **154.** Edgar Christoffel, *Krieg am Westwall 1944/45. Das Grenzland im*

Westen zwischen Aachen und Saarbrücken in den letzten Kriegsmonaten (Trier, 1989), pp. 29–30.   **155.** LB, 23.3.1945, pp. 930 and 933.   **156.** FK, 3–6.1.1945, p. 465; FK, 20.1.1945, pp. 475–6.   **157.** Thus Alfred Jodl, 'Der Einfluss Hitlers auf die Kriegführung', in KTB, OKW, IV/2, p. 1,721.   **158.** Thus Bernd Wegner, 'Hitler, der Zweite Weltkrieg und die Choreographie des Untergangs', *Geschichte und Gesellschaft*, 26 (2000), pp. 493–518, especially pp. 513–18 for Hitler and Clausewitz; Ullrich, *Hitler. Die Jahre des Untergangs*, pp. 591–627.   **159.** LB, 27.1.1945, p. 857.   **160.** KTB, OKW, IV/2, p. 976.   **161.** LB, 10.1.1945, pp. 813–14.   **162.** Heinz Magenheimer, *Abwehrschlacht an der Weichsel 1945. Vorbereitung, Ablauf, Erfahrungen* (Freiburg, 1976), pp. 90–119.   **163.** KTB, OKW, IV/2, p. 1,017.   **164.** FE, 21.1.1945, p. 476.   **165.** OBdM, 22.1.1945, in KTB, OKW, IV/2, pp. 1, 600–601 (quotation of the Seekriegsleitung (Naval High Command) record, p. 1,601). For Hitler's lack of concern for the civilian population in East Prussia see also Lakowski, *Ostpreussen*, p. 139.   **166.** FE, 4.2.1945, pp. 479–80 (quotation on p. 479).   **167.** Speech, 30.1.1945, Domarus, IV, p. 2,195.   **168.** 'Zusammenfassung der Ereignisse in der 2. Januarhälfte, gegeben von Oberst G. Meyer-Detring am 29.1.1945', in KTB, OKW, IV/2, p. 1,053.   **169.** See KTB, OKW, IV/2, 25.1.1945, p. 1,357. 'Abgaben an den Osten', KTB, OKW, IV/2, pp. 1,380–81.   **170.** LB, 27.1.1945, pp. 873–83 (quotation on pp. 874–5).   **171.** Ueberschär and Müller, *1945*, p. 59.   **172.** FE, 31.1.1945, p. 479.   **173.** Andreas Kunz, *Wehrmacht und Niederlage. Die bewaffnete Macht in der Endphase der nationalsozialistischen Herrschaft 1944 bis 1945* (Munich, 2005), pp. 198–9 (quotation on p. 198).   **174.** Thus KTB, OKW, IV/2, p. 1,363.   **175.** KTB, OKW, IV/2, p. 1,042.   **176.** LB, 27.1.1945, pp. 860–61. See also KTB, OKW, IV/2, p. 1,066, for the close eye the military leadership kept on possible Allied disagreements.   **177.** OBdM, 5.2.1945, KTB, OKW, IV/2, p. 1,605.   **178.** OBdM, 23.1.1945, KTB, OKW, IV/2, p. 1,601.   **179.** LV, 21.1.1945, p. 637.   **180.** Grier, *Hitler, Dönitz*, p. 85.   **181.** Kerstin von Lingen, *SS und Secret Service. 'Verschwörung des Schweigens'. Die Akte Karl Wolff* (Paderborn, 2010). See also Catherine Schiemann, 'Der Geheimdienst beendet den Krieg. "Operation Sunrise" und die deutsche Kapitulation in Italien', in Jürgen Heideking and Christof Mauch (eds.), *Geheimdienstkrieg gegen Deutschland. Subversion, Propaganda und politische Planungen des amerikanischen Geheimdienstes im Zweiten Weltkrieg* (Göttingen, 1993), pp. 142–65; and Brendan Simms, 'Karl Wolff – Der Schlichter', in Ronald Smelser and Enrico Syring (eds.), *Die SS. Elite unter dem Totenkopf* (Paderborn, Munich, Vienna and Zurich, 2003), pp. 450–52.   **182.** Peter Longerich, *Heinrich Himmler* (Oxford, 2012), p. 724.   **183.** Reimer Hansen, 'Ribbentrops Friedensfühler im Frühjahr 1945', *Geschichte in Wissenschaft und Unterricht*, 18 (1967), pp. 716–30 (the text of the *Sprachregelung* which informed Hesse's mission is on pp. 725–30); Hansjakob Stehle, 'Deutsche Friedensfühler bei den Westmächten im Februar/März 1945', *Vierteljahrshefte für Zeitgeschichte*, 30 (1982), pp. 538–55.   **184.** See Noble, 'Phantom barrier', p. 464.   **185.** See Lakowski, *Ostpreussen*, pp. 143, 153, 183, 188–9, 194.   **186.** KTB, OKW, IV/2, p. 1,368.   **187.** As reported in KTB, OKW, IV/2, p. 1,380.   **188.** See Ribbentrop, *Zwischen London und Moskau*, pp. 266–7.   **189.** KTB, OKW, IVØ2, p. 1,608.   **190.** Thus Ueberschär and Müller, *1945*, p. 40.   **191.** This account of the meeting, with quotations from the original English, is taken from 'Report of 7th Army Interrogation Center Paul Kubala of Karl Wahl, *Gauleiter* of Augsburg [sic], and Max Amann, Nazi Party member no. 3', IfZ, F135/3 Dokumentation Adolf Hitler, fols. 490k–l. See also the eyewitness recollection of Rudolf Jordan, *Erlebt und erlitten. Weg eines Gauleiters von München bis Moskau* (Leoni am Starnberger See, 1971), pp. 251–8.   **192.** Proclamation, 24.2.1945, Domarus, IV, pp. 2,203, 2,204–5.   **193.** Thus Ian Kershaw, *The End: Hitler's Germany, 1944–45* (London, 2011), pp. 244–5.   **194.** See Yelton, *Volkssturm*, p. 82.   **195.** See Kershaw, *'Hitler Myth'*.   **196.** Thus the conclusion of Allied investigators after the war: Edward A. Shils and Morris Janowitz, 'Cohesion and Disintegration in the Wehrmacht in World War II', *Public Opinion Quarterly*, 12, 2 (Summer 1948), pp. 280–315, especially p. 304; Kershaw, *'Hitler Myth'*.   **197.** See KTB, OKW, IV/2, pp. 1,417–26.   **198.** FE, 27.3.1945, p. 488.   **199.** OBdM, 1.3.1945, KTB, OKW, IV/2, pp. 1,611–12; 12.3.1945, KTB, OKW, IV/2, p. 1,616; 16.3.1945, KTB, OKW, IV/2, p. 1,617.   **200.** LB, 23.3.1945, p. 940. For a kinder view see Rudolf Hartog, *Im Zeichen des Tigers. Die Indische Legion auf deutscher*

Seite, 1941–1945 (Herford, 1991), pp. 198–9.   201. Thus OBdM, 3.3.1945, KTB, OKW, IV/2, p. 1,612.   202. See OBdM account of a meeting with Hitler, 20.3.1945, KTB, OKW, IV/2, p. 1,619.   203. Thus Tooze, *Wages of Destruction*, pp. 649–50.   204. See KTB, OKW, IV/2, p. 1,165.   205. FE, 22.3.1945, p. 473.   206. LB, 23.3.1945, p. 930.   207. OBdM, 26.3.1945, KTB, OKW, IV/2, p. 1,621.   208. Thus Grier, *Hitler, Dönitz*, p. 182.   209. See Lagebuch, 29.3.1945, in KTB, OKW, IV/2, p. 1,206.   210. FE, 14.3.1945, p. 485.   211. OBdM, 21.3.1945 and 25.3.1945, KTB, OKW, IV/2, pp. 1,620–21.   212. FE, 23.3.1945, p. 487.   213. OBdM, 26.3.1945, KTB, OKW, IV/2, p. 1,621.   214. Quoted in Brechtken, *Albert Speer*, p. 278.   215. FK, 22.3.1945, p. 472.   216. OBdM, 28.3.1945, KTB, OKW, IV/2, p. 1,622.   217. LB, 23.3.1945, pp. 939–40.   218. Kershaw, *The End*, pp. 289–91.   219. GT, 15.3.1945, II/15, p. 512.   220. FE, 19.3.1945, pp. 486–7 (quotation on p. 486).   221. FE, 30.3.1945, p. 489. For further qualification see FE, 7.4.1945, p. 491.   222. The two sources for Hitler's remarks are both from Speer himself: see Heinrich Schwendemann, ' "Drastic measures to defend the Reich at the Oder and the Rhine . . ."': a forgotten memorandum of Albert Speer of 18 March 1945', *Journal of Contemporary History*, 38 (2003), pp. 597–614, here p. 607. Schwendemann himself is inclined to accept their authenticity.   223. See Sven Felix Kellerhoff, *Mythos Führerbunker. Hitlers letzter Unterschlupf* (Berlin, 2013), p. 72.   224. Stephen G. Fritz, *Endkampf: Soldiers, Civilians and the Death of the Third Reich* (Lexington, Ky., 2004), pp. 21–2.   225. LB, 23.3.1945, pp. 933–4.   226. Derek S. Zumbro, *Battle for the Ruhr: The German Army's Final Defeat in the West* (Lawrence, Kan., 2006), pp. 239–60.   227. Thus the account in OBdM, 12.4.1945, KTB, OKW, IV/2, p. 1,627.   228. Ralf Blank, *'Bitter Ends'. Die letzten Monate des Zweiten Weltkriegs im Ruhrgebiet 1944/45* (Essen, 2015).   229. OBdM, 10.4.1945, KTB, OKW, IV/2, p. 1,626.   230. As reported in OBdM, 4.4.1945, KTB, OKW, IV/2, p. 1,623.   231. See Kesselring account of his meeting with Hitler in Kesselring, *Soldat bis zum letzten Tag*, p. 387.   232. See Schmaltz, *Kampfstoff-Forschung*, p. 30.   233. Kershaw, *Nemesis*, pp. 791–2.   234. Quoted in Kellerhoff, *Führerbunker*, p. 84. The author points out that Bormann's diary entry that evening was much more laconic.   235. See Lingen, *SS und Secret Service*, p. 69.   236. Kesselring, *Soldat bis zum letzten Tag*, p. 386.   237. Quoted in Hartwig, *Dönitz*, p. 432.   238. See Hitler's instructions of 11 April 1945, as summarized in KTB, OKW, IV/2, p. 1,299.   239. FE, 15.4.1945, p. 492.   240. Richard Lakowski, *Seelow 1945. Die Entscheidungsschlacht an der Oder* (Berlin, 1995), especially pp. 75–89.   241. 'Hitlers letzter Tagesbefehl an die Soldaten der Ostfront', 16.4.1945, in Ueberschär and Müller, *1945*, pp. 167–8.   242. Yelton, *Volkssturm*, p. 126.   243. Demps, *Luftangriffe*, p. 41.   244. 'Erlass betr. Beauftragung Dönitz mit den Vobereitungen für die Verteidigung des Nordraumes', FE, 20.4.1945, p. 493. KTB, OKW, IV/2, p. 1,436, states that Hitler intended to leave on 20 April, but changed his mind on 22 April.   245. 22.4.1945, KTB, OKW, IV/2, p. 1,454.   246. Anton Joachimsthaler, *The Last Days of Hitler: The Legends, the Evidence. The Truth* (London, 1996), p. 102.   247. KTB, OKW, IV/2, p. 1,453.   248. See Raichle, *Symbolpolitiker*, p. 434.   249. KTB, OKW, IV/2, p. 1,262.   250. LB, 25.4.1945, in Helmut Heiber and David M. Glantz (eds.), *Hitler and His Generals: Military Conferences 1942–1945. The First Complete Stenographic Record of the Military Situation Conferences, from Stalingrad to Berlin* (London, 2002), p. 725. (This edition contains a number of records from April 1945 not in the original, German edition edited by Helmut Heiber.)   251. Perry Biddiscombe, *Werwolf! The History of the National Socialist Guerrilla Movement, 1944–1946* (Toronto and Buffalo, 1998).   252. Thus 22.4.1945, KTB, OKW, IV/2, p. 1,453.   253. Thus Joachimsthaler, *Last Days of Hitler*, p. 97.   254. Kellerhoff, *Führerbunker*, p. 89.   255. Quoted in Joachimsthaler, *Last Days of Hitler*, p. 101.   256. Thus Brechtken, *Albert Speer*, p. 287, who shows Hitler's supposed tears on this occasion to be pure invention.   257. See Reimer Hansen, *Das Ende des Dritten Reiches. Die deutsche Kapitulation 1945* (Stuttgart, 1966), pp. 48–50.   258. 'Niederschrift Ribbentrops über die letzten Tage in Berlin', in Diether Krywalski, 'Zwei Niederschriften Ribbentrops über die Persönlichkeit Adolf Hitlers und die letzten Tage in Berlin', *Geschichte in Wissenschaft und Unterricht*, 18 (1967), pp. 742–3.   259. The text of these points is quoted in full in Krywalski, 'Zwei Niederschriften', p. 744.   260. Günther W. Gellermann, *Die Armee*

Wenck – Hitler's letzte Hoffnung. Aufstellung, Einsatz und Ende der 12. deutschen Armee im Frühjahr 1945 (Koblenz, 1984). **261.** Thus KTB, OKW, IV/2, p. 1,454. **262.** Joachimsthaler, *Last Days of Hitler*, p. 107. **263.** KTB, OKW, IV/2, 24.4.1945, p. 1,456; 'Erlass betr. Spitzengliederung der Wehrmacht', FHQ, FE, 24.4.1945, pp. 494–6 (quotation on p. 496). **264.** 'Erlass, betr. Rückgestaute Bestände an Ausrüstungen und Waffen auf den Bahnhöfen', FE, 24.4.1945, pp. 496–7. **265.** Thus the recollection of Gerhard Boldt, *Die letzten Tage der Reichskanzlei* (Hamburg and Stuttgart, 1947, 2007), p. 66. **266.** See 'Ein- und ausgehende Befehle, Meldungen usw. des Führungsstabs B (6. April bis 1. Mai [1945])', KTB, OKW, IV/2, pp. 1,440–46; 26.4.1945, KTB, OKW, IV/2, p. 1,458. **267.** Oliver Haller, 'Destroying Hitler's Berghof: the Bomber Command raid of 25 April 1945', *Canadian Military History*, 20 (2011), pp. 5–20. The author points out that most of the damage on the post-war photographs was caused by the reteating SS right at the end of the conflict. **268.** Hugh Trevor-Roper, *The Last Days of Hitler* (London, 1947). The essential accuracy of this account is stressed by Edward D. R. Harrison, 'Hugh Trevor-Roper und "Hitlers letzte Tage"', *Vierteljahrshefte für Zeitgeschichte* 57, 1 (2009), p. 33. See also Henrik Eberle and Matthias Uhl (eds.), *Das Buch Hitler. Geheimdossier des NKWD für Josef W. Stalin, zusammengestellt aufgrund der Verhörprotokolle des Persönlichen Adjutanten Hitlers, Otto Günsche, und des Kammerdieners Heinz Linge, Moskau 1948/49* (Bergisch Gladbach, 2005); Ada Petrova and Peter Watson, *The Death of Hitler: The Full Story with New Evidence from Secret Russian Archives* (New York, 1995). **269.** FE, 23.4.1945, p. 494. **270.** Longerich, *Heinrich Himmler*, p. 729; Ullrich, *Hitler. Die Jahre des Untergangs*, pp. 649–50. **271.** Traudl Junge, *Bis zur letzten Stunde. Hitlers Sekretärin erzählt ihr Leben* (Munich, 2002), p. 195. **272.** Veronika Diem, *Die Freiheitsaktion Bayern. Ein Aufstand in der Endphase des NS-Regimes* (Kallmünz, 2013). **273.** See Hitler's pleas as conveyed by General Krebs, KTB, OKW, IV/2, p. 1,461. **274.** Mario Frank, *Der Tod im Führerbunker. Hitlers letzte Tage* (Munich, 2005). **275.** 28.4.1945, KTB, OKW, IV/2, p. 1,447. **276.** 30.4.1945, KTB, OKW, IV/2, p. 1,467. **277.** The bodies were later conclusively identified as those of the Hitlers: Kellerhoff, *Führerbunker*, p. 94. **278.** Quoted in Kellerhoff, *Führerbunker*, p. 94. **279.** 'Hitlers politisches Testament', 29.4.1945, in KTB, OKW, IV/2, pp. 1,666–9.

Index

Wartime signatories to the United Nations at the time of Hitler's death, 1

Germany

Signatories of UN Declaration

Non-signatories and colonial territories

The map ignores battle lines and territories occupied in April 1945